Hitler

IAN KERSHAW

Hitler

A Biography

W. W. Norton & Company
New York London

Hitler, 1889–1936: Hubris first published in
Great Britain 1998. First American Edition 1999.
Hitler, 1936–1945: Nemesis first published in
Great Britain 2000. First American Edition 2000.
This one-volume abridgement with a new Preface first published in
Great Britain 2008. First American Edition 2008.

For information about permission to reproduce selections from this book,
write to Permissions, W. W. Norton & Company, Inc., 500 Fifth Avenue,
New York, NY 10110

For information about special discounts for bulk purchases, please contact
W. W. Norton Special Sales at specialsales@wwnorton.com or 800-233-4830

Manufacturing by RR Donnelley, Harrisonburg, VA

Library of Congress Cataloging-in-Publication Data

Kershaw, Ian.
Hitler : a biography / Ian Kershaw.—1st American ed.
p. cm.
Includes bibliographical references and index.
ISBN 978-0-393-06757-6 (hardcover)
1. Hitler, Adolf, 1889–1945. 2. Heads of state—Germany—Biography. I. Title.
DD247.H5K47 2008
943.086092—dc22
[B]   2008037294

W. W. Norton & Company, Inc.
500 Fifth Avenue, New York, N.Y. 10110
www.wwnorton.com

W. W. Norton & Company Ltd.
Castle House, 75/76 Wells Street, London W1T 3QT

1 2 3 4 5 6 7 8 9 0

Contents

v

CONTENTS

List of Illustrations

Every effort has been made to contact all copyright holders. The publishers will be glad to make good in future editions any errors or omissions brought to their attention. (Photographic acknowledgements are given in brackets.)

1. Adolf Hitler in his Leonding school photo (Bayerische Staatsbibliothek, Munich)
2. Klara Hitler (Ullstein Bilderdienst, Berlin)
3. Alois Hitler (Ullstein Bilderdienst, Berlin)
4. Karl Lueger (Hulton Getty, London)
5. August Kubizek (The Wiener Library, London)
6. The crowd in Odeonsplatz, Munich, 2 August 1914 (Bayerische Staatsbibliothek, Munich)
7. Hitler with Ernst Schmidt and Anton Bachmann (Bildarchiv Preußischer Kulturbesitz, Berlin)
8. German soldiers on the Western Front (Hulton Getty, London)
9. Armed members of the KPD Sektion Neuhausen (Bayerische Staatsbibliothek, Munich)
10. Counter-revolutionary Freikorps troops entering Munich (Bayerische Staatsbibliothek, Munich)
11. Anton Drexler (Hulton Getty, London)
12. Ernst Röhm (Bayerische Staatsbibliothek, Munich)
13. Hitler's DAP membership card (Bayerische Staatsbibliothek, Munich)
14. Hitler speaking on the Marsfeld (Bayerische Staatsbibliothek, Munich)
15. NSDAP mass meeting, Munich, 1923 (Collection Rudolf Herz, Munich)

Glossary of Abbreviations

BVP   Bayerische Volkspartei (Bavarian People's Party)

DAP   Deutsche Arbeiterpartei (German Workers' Party)

DDP   Deutsche Demokratische Partei (German Democratic Party)

DNVP   Deutschnationale Volkspartei (German National People's Party)

DSP   Deutschsozialistische Partei (German-Socialist Party)

DSVB   Deutschvölkische Freiheitsbewegung (German Folkish Freedom Movement)

DVFP   Deutschvölkische Freiheitspartei (German Folkish Freedom Party)

DVP   Deutsche Volkspartei (German People's Party)

FHQ   Führer Hauptquartier (Führer Headquarters)

KPD   Kommunistische Partei Deutschlands (Communist Party of Germany)

NSDAP   Nationalsozialistische Deutsche Arbeiterpartei (Nazi Party)

NSFB   Nationalsozialistische Freiheitsbewegung (National Socialist Freedom Movement)

NSFP   Nationalsozialistische Freiheitspartei (National Socialist Freedom Party)

NS-Hago Nationalsozialistische Handwerks-, Handels- und Gewerbeorganisation (Nazi Craft, Commerce, and Trade Organization)

OKH   Oberkommando des Heeres (High Command of the Army)

OKW   Oberkommando der Wehrmacht (armed services)

OT   Organisation Todt

RSHA   Reichssicherheitshauptamt (Reich Security Head Office)

SA   Sturmabteilung (Storm Troop)

SD   Sicherheitsdienst (Security Service)

SPD   Sozialdemokratische Partei Deutschlands (Social Democratic Party of Germany)

SS   Schutzstaffel (lit. Protection Squad)

Maps

1. The legacy of the First World War

2. Poland under Nazi occupation

Paratroop landings

Main German thrusts

Maginot Line

Groningen

12 May   10 May

HOLLAND

Amsterdam   10 May

14 May

Rotterdam   Arnhem

10–11 May

Antwerp

Bruges   Cologne

Dunkirk   Ghent Brussels   17 May   10 May

Calais   Aachen   Bonn

BELGIUM   18 May   10 May

Liège

20–25 May   20 May   Charleroi   13 May   Koblenz

Arras   Dinant

Abbeville   14–20 May   13 May

Amiens   Sedan   LUX.

Luxembourg

Rouen   13 May

Rheims   Metz

Paris   FRANCE   Strasbourg

3. The Western offensive: the Sichelschnitt attack

Key

Occupied territory

German satellite state

DENMARK

Schlewig-Holstein

Hamburg
Hamburg

Mecklenburg

Weser - Ems

East Hanover

Magdeburg-Anhalt

NETHERLANDS

North Westphalia

South Hanover-Brunswick

Essen
Köln
Düsseldorf

South Westphalia

Halle-Mersenburg

BELGIUM

Cologne-Aachen

Kurhessen

Thuringia

Koblenz

Hesse-Nassau

Main-Franconia

Moselland

Westmark

Franconia

Bayreuth

FRANCE

Baden

Wurttemburg-Hohenzollern

Swabia

Munich

Munich-Upper Bavaria

SWITZERLAND

Tirol-Voralberg

Salzburg

ITALY

4. The German Reich of 1942: the Nazi Party Gaue

Konigsberg

Danzig-
West Prussia

East Prussia

Pomerania

Berlin

Mark
Brandenburg

Wartheland

Warsaw

Saxony

Lower Silesia

POLAND

Dresden ●
Sudetenland

Upper
Silesia

Sudetenland

**Protectorate of
Bohemia**

Lower Danube

SLOVAKIA

Upper
Danube

Vienna ●

Steirmark

HUNGARY

Karnten

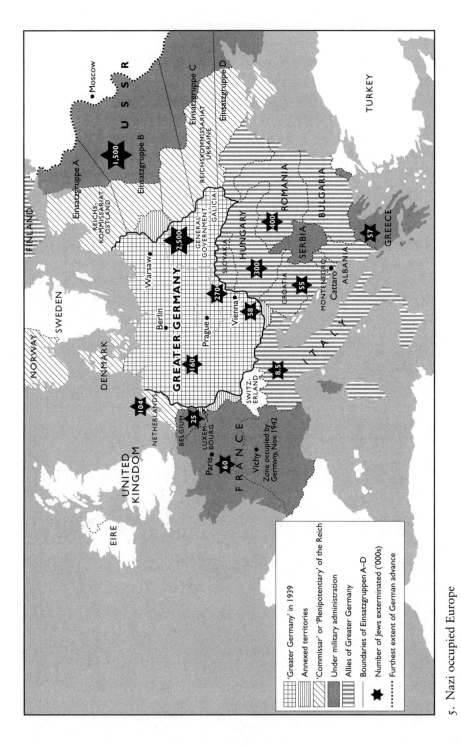

5. Nazi occupied Europe

Legend:
- 'Greater Germany' in 1939
- Annexed territories
- 'Commissar' or 'Plenipotentiary' of the Reich
- Under military administration
- Allies of Greater Germany
- Boundaries of Einsatzgruppen A–D
- Number of Jews exterminated ('000s)
- Furthest extent of German advance

Map labels: FINLAND, NORWAY, SWEDEN, U S S R, Moscow, Einsatzgruppe A, Einsatzgruppe B, Einsatzgruppe C, Einsatzgruppe D, REICHS-KOMMISSARIAT OSTLAND, REICHSKOMMISSARIAT UKRAINE, GALICIA, GENERAL GOVERNMENT, Warsaw, GREATER GERMANY, Berlin, Prague, Vienna, SLOVAKIA, HUNGARY, ROMANIA, BULGARIA, SERBIA, CROATIA, MONTENEGRO, Cattaro, ALBANIA, GREECE, TURKEY, DENMARK, NETHERLANDS, BELGIUM, LUXEM-BOURG, FRANCE, Paris, Vichy, Zone occupied by Germany, Nov. 1942, SWITZ-ERLAND, ITALY, UNITED KINGDOM, EIRE

Numbers on stars: 1,500; 2,500; 400; 57; 300; 270; 58; 55; 160; 8.5; 104; 25; 60

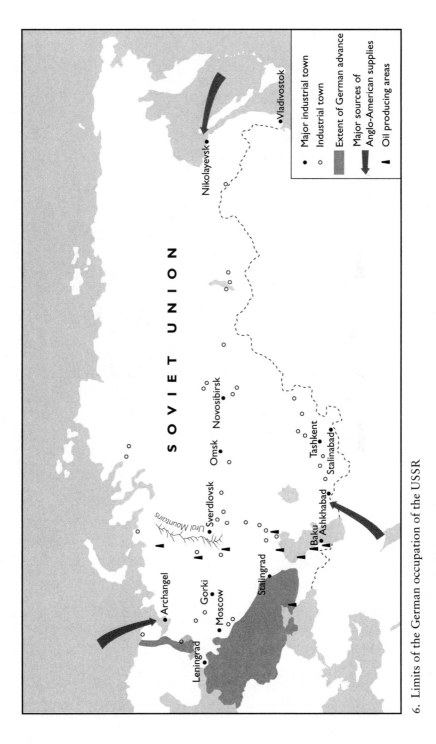

6. Limits of the German occupation of the USSR

7. The Western and Eastern fronts, 1944–5

SWEDEN

Tallinn

Riga

28 July 1944

Danzig

15 December 1944

R. Bug

Minsk

Berlin

R. Oder

Warsaw

SOVIET UNION

Dresden

Breslau

Lublin

Russian forces,
19 April 1945

Kiev

GREATER

Prague

22 June 1944

GERMANY

SLOVAKIA

Vienna

15 December 1944

Budapest

15 September 1944

HUNGARY

Zagreb

Belgrade

ROMANIA

Bucharest

YUGOSLAVIA

R. Danube

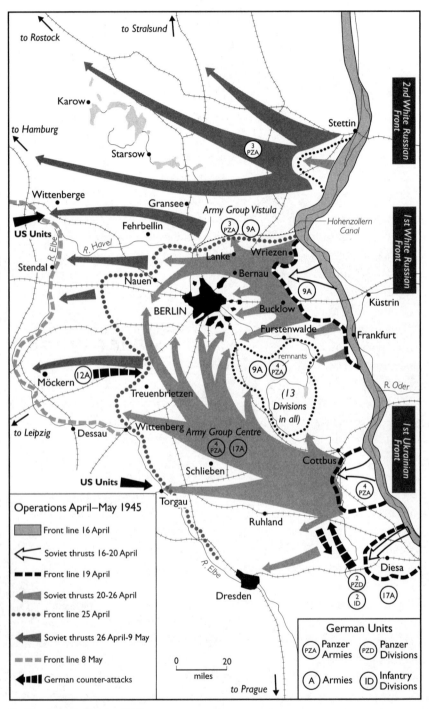

8. The Soviet drive to Berlin

Preface to the New Edition

It has been a source of immense satisfaction to me that the original two-volume biography, *Hitler, 1889–1936: Hubris*, and *Hitler, 1936–1945: Nemesis*, published in 1998 and 2000 respectively, was so well received, as also in the numerous countries where foreign-language editions were published. The warm reception in Germany was particularly gratifying.

My biography was above all intended to be a study of Hitler's power. I set out to answer two questions. The first was how Hitler had been possible. How could such a bizarre misfit ever have been in a position to take power in Germany, a modern, complex, economically developed, culturally advanced country? The second was how, then, Hitler could exercise power. He had great demagogic skills, certainly, and combined this with a sure eye for exploiting ruthlessly the weakness of his opponents. But he was an unsophisticated autodidact lacking all experience of government. From 1933 he had to deal not just with Nazi roughnecks but with a government machine and circles used to ruling. How could he then so swiftly dominate the established political élites, go on to draw Germany into a catastrophic high-risk gamble for European domination with a terrible, unprecedented genocidal programme at its heart, block all possibilities of a negotiated end to the conflict, and finally kill himself only when the arch-enemy was at his very door and his country physically and morally in total ruins?

I found the answer to these questions only partially in the personality of the strange individual who presided over Germany's fate during those twelve long years. Of course, personality counts in historical explanation. It would be foolish to suggest otherwise. And Hitler, as those who admired him or reviled him agreed, was an extraordinary personality (though, however varied and numerous the attempts at explanation are, only speculation is possible on the formative causes of his peculiar psychology). Hitler was not interchangeable. The type of individual that Hitler was unquestionably influenced crucial developments in decisive fashion. A Reich Chancellor Göring, for instance, would not have acted in the same way at numerous key junctures. It can be said with certainty: without Hitler, history would have been different.

But Hitler's disastrous impact cannot be explained through personality alone. Before 1918, there had been no sign of the later extraordinary personal magnetism. He was seen by those around him as an oddity, at times a figure of mild scorn or ridicule, definitively not as a future national leader in waiting. From 1919 onwards, all this changed. He now became the object of increasing, ultimately almost boundless, mass adulation (as well as intense hatred from his political enemies). This in itself suggests that the answer to the riddle of his impact has to be found less in Hitler's personality than in the changed circumstances of a German society traumatized by a lost war, revolutionary upheaval, political instability, economic misery and cultural crisis. At any other time, Hitler would surely have remained a nobody. But in those peculiar circumstances, a symbiotic relationship of dynamic, and ultimately destructive, nature emerged between the individual with a mission to expunge the perceived national humiliation of 1918 and a society ready more and more to see his leadership as vital to its future salvation, to rescue it from the dire straits into which, in the eyes of millions of Germans, defeat, democracy and depression had cast it.

To encapsulate this relationship, as the key to understanding how Hitler could obtain, then exercise, his peculiar form of power, I turned to the concept of 'charismatic authority', as devised by the brilliant German sociologist Max Weber, who died before Hitler had been heard of – at least outside Munich beerhalls. I did not elaborate on this concept, which had figured prominently in my writing on Hitler and the Third Reich over many years. It lay unmistakably, however, at the heart of the inquiry. 'Charismatic authority', as deployed by Weber, did not rest primarily on demonstrable outstanding qualities of an individual. Rather, it derived from the perception of such qualities among a 'following' which, amid crisis conditions, projected on to a chosen leader unique 'heroic' attributes and saw in him personal greatness, the embodiment of a 'mission' of salvation. 'Charismatic authority' is, in Weber's conceptualization, inherently unstable. Continued failure or misfortune will bring its downfall; and it is under threat of becoming 'routinized' into a systematic form of government.

Applying this concept of 'charismatic authority' seemed to me to offer a useful way of tackling both of the central questions I had posed. To my mind, the concept helps in evaluating the relationship between Hitler and the mass following that shaped his rise – though in conditions never, of course, imagined by Max Weber, and where the image of 'heroic' leadership attached to Hitler, exploiting pre-existing pseudo-religious expectations of national salvation, was in good measure a manufactured propaganda product. And I also found it invaluable in examining the way Hitler's highly personalized rule eroded systematic government and administration and was incompatible with it. Of course, by the middle of the war, Hitler's popularity was in steep decline and any 'charismatic' hold over government and society was now waning sharply. By this time, however, Germany had been wedded for a decade or so to Hitler's 'charismatic' domination. Those who owed their own positions of power to Hitler's supreme 'Führer authority' still upheld it, whether from conviction or necessity. They had risen with Hitler. Now they were condemned to fall with him. He had left them no way out. Hitler's authority within the regime started to crumble only as Germany faced imminent and total defeat. And as long as he lived, he posed an insuperable barrier to the only way the war he had brought about could be ended: his country's capitulation.

I linked 'charismatic authority' to another concept as a way of showing how Hitler's highly personalized form of rule functioned. This, as referred to in the text and operating as a kind of leitmotiv throughout the biography, was the notion of 'working towards the Führer', which I tried to use to show how Hitler's presumed aims served to prompt, activate or legitimate initiatives at different levels of the regime, driving on, consciously or unwittingly, the destructive dynamic of Nazi rule. I did not mean, with this notion, to suggest that people at all times asked themselves what Hitler wanted then tried to put it into practice. Some, of course, especially among the party faithful, did more or less just that. But many others – say in boycotting a Jewish shop to protect a rival business, or denouncing a neighbour to the police on account of some personal grievance – were not asking themselves what the Führer's intentions might be, or operating from ideological motivation. They were, nevertheless, in minor ways, helping to sustain and promote ideological goals represented by Hitler and thereby indirectly promoting the process of radicalization by which those goals – in this case, 'racial cleansing' of German society – gradually came more sharply into view as realizable short-term aims rather than distant objectives.

The approach I chose meant the two volumes were necessarily long. But even beyond the text itself there was much to be added. I was keen to provide full reference to the extensive documentary sources – both archival and printed primary sources, and the wealth of secondary literature I had used – first, so that other researchers could follow these up and re-examine them if need be, and second to remove distortions in some accounts or dispose of myths which had attached themselves to Hitler. At times, the notes became in themselves minor excursions on points of detail which could not be expanded in the text, or offered additional commentary upon it. I provided lengthy notes in *Hubris*, for example, elaborating on points of interpretation in historiography, and on differing views of Hitler's psychology; and in *Nemesis* on the authenticity of the text of the final 'table talk' monologues of early 1945 and on the complex (and sometimes conflicting) evidence about the circumstances of Hitler's death and Soviet discovery of his remains. All of this meant that the two finished volumes became massive in size, totalling over 1,450 pages of text and almost 450 pages of notes and bibliography. Of course, not all readers are able to devote sufficient time and energy to a work of such length. And, naturally, not all readers are interested in the scholarly apparatus.

After much consideration, I decided, therefore, to produce this condensed edition. On undertaking it, I was reminded of the passage in the film *Amadeus*, where the Kaiser tells Mozart that he likes his opera – apart from the fact that it contains too many notes. 'Too many notes, Majesty?' an indignant Mozart interjects. 'There are neither too many, nor too few. Just exactly the right number.' That is more or less how I felt about my original two volumes. These took the form and shape that they did because I wanted to write them in exactly that way. So the drastic pruning that has gone into the present edition – losing over 650 pages (more than 300,000 words) of text and the entire scholarly apparatus – was nothing if not painful. And of course, it goes against the grain for a historian to produce a text lacking references and scholarly apparatus. But I console myself that the notes and bibliographical references are all there for consultation by those who want to check them in the full text of the two-volume original version, which will remain in print. And the abridged text, though greatly shortened to create this single, more approachable volume, stays completely true to the original. I have cut out much which provided context, eliminated numerous illustrative examples, shortened or removed many quotations, and deleted some entire sections which described the general social and political climate or the setting in which Hitler operated. In two cases, I have blended chapters together. Otherwise the structure is identical with the originals. The essence of the book remains completely intact. I did not want to, and saw no need to, change the overall interpretation. And, in an exercise devoted to reducing the size of the text, I naturally did not want to add to its length. Apart from insignificant wording adjustments, I have incorporated only one or two minor amendments to what I had written earlier. Since the original notes have been excluded, there seemed no point in including the lengthy bibliographies in the original two volumes of works I had used. I have, however, provided a selection of the most important *printed* primary sources for a biography of Hitler, on all of which (apart from a couple of recent publications) I drew. Most are, of course, in German, though I add where relevant a reference to English translations.

My many debts of gratitude remain unchanged from the lists of acknowledgements in *Hubris* and *Nemesis*. In addition, however, I would like to add my thanks in connection with this edition to Andrew Wylie, and to Simon Winder and the excellent team at Penguin. It is a great pleasure, finally, to add Olivia to the family roster alongside Sophie, Joe and Ella, and to thank, as always, David and Katie, Stephen and Becky, and, of course, Betty, for their love and continuing support.

Ian Kershaw
Manchester/Sheffield, August 2007

Reflecting on Hitler

Hitler's dictatorship has the quality of a paradigm for the twentieth century. In extreme and intense fashion it reflected, among other things, the total claim of the modern state, unforeseen levels of state repression and violence, previously unparalleled manipulation of the media to control and mobilize the masses, unprecedented cynicism in international relations, the acute dangers of ultra-nationalism, and the immensely destructive power of ideologies of racial superiority and ultimate consequences of racism, alongside the perverted usage of modern technology and 'social engineering'. Above all, it lit a warning beacon that still burns brightly: it showed how a modern, advanced, cultured society can so rapidly sink into barbarity, culminating in ideological war, conquest of scarcely imaginable brutality and rapaciousness, and genocide such as the world had never previously witnessed. Hitler's dictatorship amounted to the collapse of modern civilization – a form of nuclear blow-out within modern society. It showed what we are capable of.

The century which, in a sense, his name dominated gained much of its character by war and genocide – Hitler's hallmarks. What happened under Hitler took place – in fact, could only have taken place – in the society of a modern, cultured, technologically advanced, and highly bureaucratic country. Within only a few years of Hitler becoming head of government, this sophisticated country in the heart of Europe was working towards what turned out to be an apocalyptic genocidal war that left Germany and Europe not just riven by an Iron Curtain and physically in ruins, but morally shattered. That still needs explaining. The combination of a leadership committed to an ideological mission of national regeneration and racial purification; a society with sufficient belief in its Leader to work towards the goals he appeared to strive for; and a skilled bureaucratic administration capable of planning and implementing policy, however inhumane, and keen to do so, offers a starting-point. How and why this society could be galvanized by Hitler requires, even so, detailed examination.

It would be convenient to look no further, for the cause of Germany's and Europe's calamity, than the person of Adolf Hitler himself, ruler of Germany from 1933 to 1945, whose philosophies of breathtaking inhumanity had been publicly advertised almost eight years before he became Reich Chancellor. But, for all Hitler's prime moral responsibility for what took place under his authoritarian regime, a personalized explanation would be a gross short-circuiting of the truth. Hitler could be said to provide a classic illustration of Karl Marx's dictum that 'men do make their own history ... but ... under given and imposed conditions'. How far 'given and imposed conditions', impersonal developments beyond the control of any individual, however powerful, shaped Germany's destiny; how much can be put down to contingency, even historical accident; what can be attributed to the actions and motivations of the extraordinary man ruling Germany at the time: all need investigation. All form part of the following inquiry. Simple answers are not possible.

Since he first entered the limelight in the 1920s, Hitler has been viewed in many different and varied fashions, often directly contrasting with each other. He has been seen, for example, as no more than 'an opportunist entirely without principle', 'barren of all ideas save one – the further extension of his own power and that of the nation with which he had identified himself', preoccupied solely with 'domination, dressed up as the doctrine of race', and consisting of nothing but 'vindictive destructiveness'. In complete contrast, he has been portrayed as fanatically driving on a pre-planned and pre-ordained ideological programme. There have been attempts to see him as a type of political con-man, hypnotizing and bewitching the German people, leading them astray and into disaster, or to 'demonize' him – turning him into a mystical, inexplicable figure of Germany's destiny. No less a figure than Albert Speer, Hitler's architect, then Armaments Minister, for much of the Third Reich as close to the Dictator as anyone, described him soon after the end of the war as a 'demonic figure', 'one of those inexplicable historical phenomena which emerge at rare intervals among mankind', whose 'person determined the fate of the nation'. Such a view runs the risk of mystifying what happened in Germany between 1933 and 1945, reducing the cause of Germany's and Europe's catastrophe to the arbitrary whim of a demonic personality. The genesis of the calamity finds no explanation outside the actions of an extraordinary individual. Complex developments become no more than an expression of Hitler's will.

An absolutely contrary view – tenable only so long as it was part of a state ideology and consequently evaporating as soon as the Soviet bloc which had sustained it collapsed – rejected out of hand any significant role of personality, relegating Hitler to no more than the status of an agent of capitalism, a cypher for the interests of big business and its leaders who controlled him and pulled the strings of their marionette.

Some accounts of Hitler have scarcely recognized any problem at all of understanding, or have promptly ruled one out. Ridiculing Hitler has been one approach. Describing him simply as a 'lunatic' or 'raving maniac' obviates the need for an explanation – though it of course leaves open the key question: why a complex society would be prepared to follow someone who was mentally deranged, a 'pathological' case, into the abyss.

Far more sophisticated approaches have clashed on the extent to which Hitler was actually 'master in the Third Reich', or could even be described as 'in some respects a weak dictator'. Did he in fact exercise total, unrestricted, and sole power? Or did his regime rest on a hydra-like 'polycracy' of power-structures, with Hitler, on account of his undeniable popularity and the cult that surrounded him, as its indispensable fulcrum but little else – remaining no more than the propagandist he had in essence always been, exploiting opportunities as they came along, though without programme, plan, or design?

Differing views about Hitler have never been purely a matter of arcane academic debate. They have wider currency than that – and more far-reaching implications. When Hitler was put forward as a sort of reverse copy of Lenin and Stalin, a leader whose paranoid fear of Bolshevik terror, of class genocide, motivated him to perpetrate race genocide, the implications were plain. Hitler was wicked, no doubt, but less wicked than Stalin. His was the copy, Stalin's the original. The underlying cause of Nazi race genocide was Soviet class genocide. It also mattered when the spotlight was turned away from the crimes against humanity for which Hitler bears ultimate responsibility and on to his ruminations on the transformation of German society. This Hitler was interested in social mobility, better housing for workers, modernizing industry, erecting a welfare system, sweeping away the reactionary privileges of the past; in sum, building a better, more up-to-date, less class-ridden, German society, however brutal the methods. This Hitler was, despite his demonization of Jews and gamble for world power against mighty odds, 'a politician whose thinking and actions were far more rational than up to now thought'. From such a perspective, Hitler could be seen as wicked, but with good intentions for German society – or at least intentions which could be viewed in a positive light.

Such revised interpretations were not meant to be apologetic. The comparison of Nazi and Stalinist crimes against humanity was intended, however distorted the approach, to shed light on the terrible ferocity of ideological conflict in inter-war Europe and the motive forces of the German genocide. The depiction of Hitler as a social-revolutionary was attempting to explain, perhaps in somewhat misconceived fashion, why he found such wide appeal in Germany in a time of social crisis. But it is not hard to see that both approaches contain, however unwittingly, the potential for a possible rehabilitation of Hitler which could begin to see him, despite the crimes against humanity associated with his name, as nevertheless a great leader of the twentieth century, one who, had he died before the war, would have had a high place in the pantheon of German heroes.

The question of 'historical greatness' was usually implicit in the writing of conventional biography – particularly so in the German tradition. The figure of Hitler, whose personal attributes – distinguished from his political aura and impact – were scarcely noble, elevating or enriching, posed self-evident problems for such a tradition. A way round it was to imply that Hitler possessed a form of 'negative greatness'; that, while he lacked the nobility of character and other attributes taken to pertain to 'greatness' in historical figures, his impact on history was undeniably immense, even if catastrophic. Yet 'negative greatness' can also be taken to have tragic connotations – mighty endeavour and astounding achievements vitiated; national grandeur turned into national catastrophe.

It seems better to avoid altogether the issue of 'greatness' (other than seeking to understand why so many contemporaries saw 'greatness' in Hitler). It is a red-herring: misconstrued, pointless, irrelevant, and potentially apologetic. Misconstrued because, as 'great men' theories cannot escape doing, it personalizes the historical process in extreme fashion. Pointless because the whole notion of historical greatness is in the last resort futile. Based on a subjective set of moral and even aesthetic judgements, it is a philosophical-ethical concept which leads nowhere. Irrelevant because, whether we were to answer the question of Hitler's alleged 'greatness' in the affirmative or the negative, it would in itself explain nothing whatsoever about the terrible history of the Third Reich. And potentially apologetic, because even to pose the question cannot conceal a certain admiration for Hitler, however grudging and whatever his faults; and because, to look for greatness in Hitler bears the almost automatic corollary of reducing in effect those who directly promoted his rule, those agencies which sustained it, and the German people themselves who gave it so much backing, to the role of mere supernumeraries to the 'great man'.

Rather than the issue of 'historical greatness', we need to turn our attention to another question, one of far greater importance. How do we explain how someone with so few intellectual gifts and social attributes, someone no more than an empty vessel outside his political life, unapproachable and impenetrable even for those in his close company, incapable it seems of genuine friendship, without the background that bred high office, without even any experience of government before becoming Reich Chancellor, could nevertheless have such an immense historical impact, could make the entire world hold its breath?

Perhaps the question is, in part at least, falsely posed. For one thing, Hitler was certainly not unintelligent, and possessed a sharp mind which could draw on his formidably retentive memory. He was able to impress not only, as might be expected, his sycophantic entourage but also cool, critical, seasoned statesmen and diplomats with his rapid grasp of issues. His rhetorical talent was, of course, recognized even by his political enemies. And he is certainly not alone among twentieth-century state leaders in combining what we might see as deficiencies of character and shallowness of intellectual development with notable political skill and effectiveness. It is as well to avoid the trap, which most of his contemporaries fell into, of grossly underestimating his abilities.

Moreover, others beside Hitler have climbed from humble backgrounds to high office. But if his rise from utter anonymity is not entirely unique, the problem posed by Hitler remains. One reason is the emptiness of the private person. He was, as has frequently been said, tantamount to an 'unperson'. There is, perhaps, an element of condescension in this judgement, a readiness to look down on the vulgar, uneducated upstart lacking a rounded personality, the outsider with half-baked opinions on everything under the sun, the uncultured self-appointed adjudicator on culture. Partly, too, the black hole which represents the private individual derives from the fact that Hitler was highly secretive – not least about his personal life, his background, and his family. The secrecy and detachment were features of his character, applying also to his political behaviour; they were also politically important, components of the aura of 'heroic' leadership he had consciously allowed to be built up, intensifying the mystery about himself. Even so, when all qualifications are made, it remains the case that outside politics (and a blinkered passion for cultural grandeur and power in music, art and architecture) Hitler's life was largely a void.

A biography of an 'unperson', one who has as good as no personal life or history outside that of the political events in which he is involved, imposes, naturally, its own limitations. But the drawbacks exist only as long as it is presumed that the private life is decisive for the public life. Such a presumption would be a mistake. There was no 'private life' for Hitler. Of course, he could enjoy his escapist films, his daily walk to the Tea House at the Berghof, his time in his alpine idyll far from government ministries in Berlin. But these were empty routines. There was no retreat to a sphere outside the political, to a deeper existence which conditioned his public reflexes. It was not that his 'private life' became part of his public persona. On the contrary: so secretive did it remain that the German people only learned of the existence of Eva Braun once the Third Reich had crumbled into ashes. Rather, Hitler 'privatized' the public sphere. 'Private' and 'public' merged completely and became inseparable. Hitler's entire being came to be subsumed within the role he played to perfection: the role of 'Führer'.

The task of the biographer at this point becomes clearer. It is a task which has to focus not upon the personality of Hitler, but squarely and directly upon *the character of his power – the power of the Führer*.

That power derived only in part from Hitler himself. In greater measure, it was a social product – a creation of social expectations and motivations invested in Hitler by his followers. This does not mean that Hitler's own actions, in the context of his expanding power, were not of the utmost importance at key moments. But the impact of his power has largely to be seen not in any specific attributes of 'personality', but in his role as Führer – a role made possible only through the underestimation, mistakes, weakness, and collaboration of others. To explain his power, therefore, we must look in the first instance to others, not to Hitler himself.

Hitler's power was of an extraordinary kind. He did not base his claim to power (except in a most formal sense) on his position as a party leader, or on any functional position. He derived it from what he saw as his historic mission to save Germany. His power, in other words, was 'charismatic', not institutional. It depended upon the readiness of others to see 'heroic' qualities in him. And they did see those qualities – perhaps even before he himself came to believe in them.

As one of the most brilliant contemporary analysts of the Nazi phenomenon, Franz Neumann, noted: 'Charismatic rule has long been neglected and ridiculed, but apparently it has deep roots and becomes a powerful stimulus once the proper psychological and social conditions are set. The Leader's charismatic power is not a mere phantasm – none can doubt that millions believe in it.' Hitler's own contribution to the expansion of this power and to its consequences should not be under-rated. A brief counter-factual reflection underlines the point. Is it likely, we might ask, that a terroristic police state such as that which developed under Himmler and the SS would have been erected without Hitler as head of government? Would Germany under a different leader, even an authoritarian one, have been engaged by the end of the 1930s in *general* European war? And would under a different head of state discrimination against Jews (which would almost certainly have taken place) have culminated in out-and-out genocide? The answer to each of these questions would surely be 'no'; or, at the very least, 'highly unlikely'. What-ever the external circumstances and impersonal determinants, Hitler was not interchangeable.

The highly personalized power which Hitler exercised conditioned even shrewd and intelligent individuals – churchmen, intellectuals, foreign diplomats, distinguished visitors – to be impressed by him. They would not for the most part have been captivated by the same sentiments expressed to a raucous crowd in a Munich beerhall. But with the auth-ority of the Reich Chancellorship behind him, backed by adoring crowds, surrounded by the trappings of power, enveloped by the aura of great leadership trumpeted by propaganda, it was scarcely surprising that others beyond the completely naïve and gullible could find him impressive. Power was also the reason why his underlings – subordinate Nazi leaders, his personal retinue, provincial party bosses – hung on his every word, before, when that power was at an end in April 1945, fleeing like the proverbial rats from the sinking ship. The mystique of power surely explains, too, why so many women (especially those much younger than he was) saw him, the Hitler whose person seems to us the antithesis of sexuality, as a sex-symbol, several attempting suicide on his behalf.

A history of Hitler has to be, therefore, a history of his power – how he came to get it, what its character was, how he exercised it, why he was allowed to expand it to break all institutional barriers, why resistance to that power was so feeble. But these are questions to be directed at German society, not just at Hitler.

There is no necessity to play down the contribution to Hitler's gaining and exercise of power that derived from the ingrained features of his character. Single-mindedness, inflexibility, ruthlessness in discarding all hindrances, cynical adroitness, the all-or-nothing gambler's instinct for the highest stakes: each of these helped shape the nature of his power. These features of character came together in one overriding element in Hitler's inner drive: his boundless egomania. Power was Hitler's aphrodisiac. For one as narcissistic as he was, it offered purpose out of purposeless early years, compensation for all the deeply felt setbacks of the first half of his life – rejection as an artist, social bankruptcy taking him to a Viennese doss-house, the falling apart of his world in the defeat and revolution of 1918. Power was all-consuming for him. As one perceptive observer commented in 1940, even before the triumph over France: 'Hitler is the potential suicide *par excellence*. He owns no ties outside his own "ego" . . . He is in the privileged position of one who loves nothing and no one but himself . . . So he can dare all to preserve or magnify his power . . . which alone stands between him and speedy death.' The thirst for personalized power of such magnitude embraced an insatiable appetite for territorial conquest amounting to an almighty gamble – against extremely heavy odds – for a monopoly of power on the European continent and, later, world power. The relentless quest for ever greater expansion of power could contemplate no diminution, no confinement, no restriction. It was, moreover, dependent upon the continuance of what were taken to be 'great achievements'. Lacking any capacity for limitation, the progressive megalomania inevitably contained the seeds of self-destruction for the regime Hitler led. The match with his own inbuilt suicidal tendencies was perfect.

All-consuming though power was for Hitler, it was not a matter of power for its own sake, devoid of content or meaning. Hitler was not just a propagandist, a manipulator, a mobilizer. He was all those. But he was also an ideologue of unshakeable convictions – the most radical of the radicals as exponent of an internally coherent (however repellent to us) 'world-view', acquiring its thrust and potency from its combination of a very few basic ideas – integrated by the notion of human history as the history of racial struggle. His 'world-view' gave him a rounded explanation of the ills of Germany and of the world, and how to remedy them. He held to his 'world-view' unwaveringly from the early 1920s down to his death in the bunker. It amounted to a utopian vision of national redemption, not a set of middle-range policies. But it was not only capable of incorporating within it all the different strands of Nazi philosophy; combined with Hitler's rhetorical skills, it also meant that he soon became practically unchallengeable on any point of party doctrine.

Hitler's ideological goals, his actions, and his personal input into the shaping of events need, then, to be accorded the most serious attention. But they explain far from everything. What Hitler did not do, did not instigate, but which was nevertheless set in train by the initiatives of others is as vital as the actions of the Dictator himself in understanding the fateful 'cumulative radicalization' of the regime.

An approach which looks to the expectations and motivations of German society (in all its complexity) more than to Hitler's personality in explaining the Dictator's immense impact offers the potential to explore the expansion of his power through the internal dynamics of the regime he headed and the forces he unleashed. The approach is encapsulated in the maxim enunciated by a Nazi functionary in 1934 – providing in a sense a leitmotiv for the work as a whole – that it was the duty of each person in the Third Reich 'to work towards the Führer along the lines he would wish' without awaiting instruction from above. This maxim, put into practice, was one of the driving-forces of the Third Reich, translating Hitler's loosely framed ideological goals into reality through initiatives focused on working towards the fulfilment of the Dictator's visionary aims. Hitler's authority was, of course, decisive. But the initiatives which he sanctioned derived more often than not from others.

xl

Hitler was no tyrant imposed on Germany. Though he never attained majority support in free elections, he was legally appointed to power as Reich Chancellor just like his predecessors had been, and became between 1933 and 1940 arguably the most popular head of state in the world. Understanding this demands reconciling the apparently irreconcilable: the personalized method of biography and the contrasting approaches to the history of society (including the structures of political domination). Hitler's impact can only be grasped through the era which created him (and was destroyed by him). An interpretation must not only take full account of Hitler's ideological goals, his actions, and his personal input into the shaping of events; it must at the same time locate these within the social forces and political structures which permitted, shaped, and promoted the growth of a system that came increasingly to hinge on personalized, absolute power – with the disastrous effects that flowed from it.

The Nazi assault on the roots of civilization was a defining feature of the twentieth century. Hitler was the epicentre of that assault. But he was its chief exponent, not its prime cause.

I

Fantasy and Failure

I

The first of many strokes of good fortune for Adolf Hitler took place thirteen years before he was born. In 1876, the man who was to become his father changed his name from Alois Schicklgruber to Alois Hitler. Adolf can be believed when he said that nothing his father had done had pleased him so much as to drop the coarsely rustic name of Schicklgruber. Certainly, 'Heil Schicklgruber' would have sounded an unlikely salutation to a national hero.

The Schicklgrubers had for generations been a peasant family, small-holders in the Waldviertel, a picturesque but poor, hilly and (as the name suggests) woody area in the most north-westerly part of Lower Austria, bordering on Bohemia, whose inhabitants had something of a reputation for being dour, hard-nosed, and unwelcoming. Hitler's father, Alois, had been born there on 7 June 1837, in the village of Strones, as the illegitimate child of Maria Anna Schicklgruber, then forty-one years old and daughter of a poor smallholder, Johann Schicklgruber, and baptized (as Aloys Schicklgruber) in nearby Döllersheim the same day.

Hitler's father was the first social climber in his family. In 1855, by the time he was eighteen, Alois had gained employment at a modest grade with the Austrian ministry of finance. For a young man of his background and limited education, his advancement in the years to come was impressive. After training, and passing the necessary examin-ation, he attained low-ranking supervisory status in 1861 and a position in the customs service in 1864, becoming a customs officer in 1870 before moving the following year to Braunau am Inn, and attaining the post of customs inspector there in 1875.

A year later came the change of name. Alois, the social climber, may have preferred the less rustic form of 'Hitler' (a variant spelling of 'Hiedler', otherwise given as 'Hietler', 'Hüttler', 'Hütler', meaning 'smallholder', the surname of Johann Georg Hiedler, who had later married Alois's mother, apparently acknowledging paternity). At any rate, Alois seemed well satisfied with his new name, and from the final authorization in January 1877 always signed himself 'Alois Hitler'. His son was equally pleased with the more distinctive form 'Hitler'.

Klara Pölzl, who was to become Adolf Hitler's mother, was the eldest of only three surviving children out of eleven – the other two were Johanna and Theresia – from the marriage of Johanna Hüttler, eldest daughter of Johann Nepomuk Hüttler, with Johann Baptist Pölzl, also a smallholder in Spital. Klara herself grew up on the adjacent farm to that of her grandfather Nepomuk. At the death of his brother, Johann Georg Hiedler, Nepomuk had effectively adopted Alois Schicklgruber. Klara's mother, Johanna, and her aunt Walburga had in fact been brought up with Alois in Nepomuk's house. Officially, after the change of name and legitimation in 1876, Alois Hitler and Klara Pölzl were second cousins. In that year, 1876, aged sixteen, Klara Pölzl left the family farm in Spital and moved to Braunau am Inn to join the household of Alois Hitler as a maid.

By this time, Alois was a well-respected customs official in Braunau. His personal affairs were, however, less well regulated than his career. He would eventually marry three times, at first to a woman much older than himself, Anna Glasserl, from whom he separated in 1880, then to women young enough to be his daughters. A premarital liaison and his last two marriages would give him nine children, four of whom were to die in infancy. It was a private life of above average turbulence – at least for a provincial customs officer. When his second wife, Franziska (Fanni) Matzelberger, died of tuberculosis in August 1884 aged only twenty-three, their two children, Alois and Angela, were still tiny. During her illness, Fanni had been moved to the fresh air of the countryside outside Braunau. For someone to look after his two young children, Alois turned straight away to Klara Pölzl, and brought her back to Braunau. With Fanni scarcely in her grave, Klara became pregnant. Since they were officially second cousins, a marriage between Alois and Klara needed the dispensation of the Church. After a wait of four months, in which Klara's condition became all the more evident, the dispensation finally arrived from Rome in late 1884, and the couple were married on

7 January 1885. The wedding ceremony took place at six o'clock in the morning. Soon after a perfunctory celebration, Alois was back at his work at the customs post.

The first of the children of Alois's third marriage, Gustav, was born in May 1885, to be followed in September the following year by a second child, Ida, and, with scarcely a respite, by another son, Otto, who died only days after his birth. Further tragedy for Klara came soon afterwards, as both Gustav and Ida contracted diphtheria and died within weeks of each other in December 1887 and January 1888. By the summer of 1888 Klara was pregnant again. At half-past six in the evening on 20 April 1889, an overcast and chilly Easter Saturday, she gave birth in her home in the 'Gasthof zum Pommer', Vorstadt Nr.219, to her fourth child, the first to survive infancy: this was Adolf.

The historical record of Adolf's early years is very sparse. His own account in *Mein Kampf* is inaccurate in detail and coloured in interpretation. Post-war recollections of family and acquaintances have to be treated with care, and are at times as dubious as the attempts during the Third Reich itself to glorify the childhood of the future Führer. For the formative period so important to psychologists and 'psycho-historians', the fact has to be faced that there is little to go on which is not retrospective guesswork.

By the time of Adolf's birth, Alois was a man of moderate means. His income was a solid one – rather more than that of an elementary school headmaster. In addition to Alois, Klara, the two children of Alois's second marriage, Alois Jr (before he left home in 1896) and Angela, Adolf, and his younger brother Edmund (born in 1894, but died in 1900) and sister Paula (born in 1896), the household also ran to a cook and maid, Rosalia Schichtl. In addition, there was Adolf's aunt Johanna, one of his mother's younger sisters, a bad-tempered, hunchbacked woman who was, however, fond of Adolf and a good help for Klara around the house. In material terms, then, the Hitler family led a comfortable middle-class existence.

Family life was, however, less than harmonious and happy. Alois was an archetypal provincial civil servant – pompous, status-proud, strict, humourless, frugal, pedantically punctual, and devoted to duty. He was regarded with respect by the local community. But he had a bad temper which could flare up quite unpredictably. At home, Alois was an authoritarian, overbearing, domineering husband and a stern, distant, masterful,

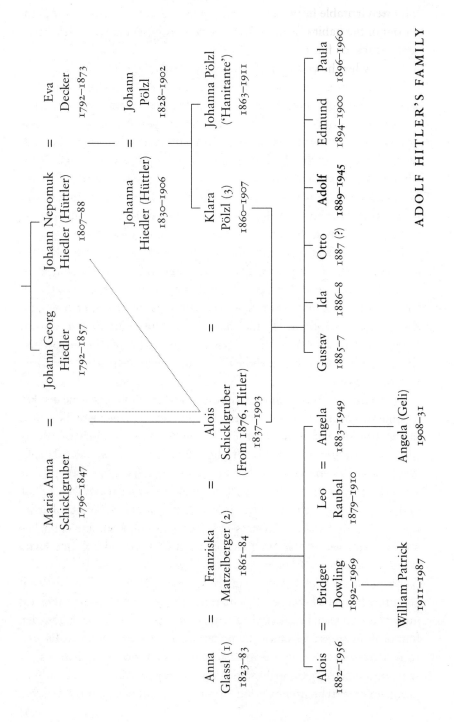

Maria Anna Schicklgruber 1796–1847 = Johann Georg Hiedler 1792–1857 = Eva Decker 1792–1873

Johann Nepomuk Hiedler (Hüttler) 1807–88

Johanna Hiedler (Hüttler) 1830–1906 = Johann Pölzl 1828–1902

Anna Glassl (1) 1823–83 = Alois Schicklgruber (From 1876, Hitler) 1837–1903 = Franziska Matzelberger (2) 1861–84

Klara Pölzl (3) 1860–1907

Johanna Pölzl ('Hanitante') 1863–1911

Gustav 1885–7 · Ida 1886–8 · Otto 1887 (?) · **Adolf 1889–1945** · Edmund 1894–1900 · Paula 1896–1960

Alois 1882–1956 = Bridget Dowling 1892–1969

Leo Raubal 1879–1910 = Angela 1883–1949

William Patrick 1911–1987

Angela (Geli) 1908–31

ADOLF HITLER'S FAMILY

and often irritable father. For long after their marriage, Klara could not get out of the habit of calling him 'Uncle'. And even after his death, she kept a rack of his pipes in the kitchen and would point to them on occasion when he was referred to, as if to invoke his authority.

What affection the young children missed in their father was more than recompensed by their mother. According to the description given much later by her Jewish doctor, Eduard Bloch, after his own forced emigration from Nazi Germany, Klara Hitler was 'a simple, modest, kindly woman. She was tall, had brownish hair which she kept neatly plaited, and a long, oval face with beautifully expressive grey-blue eyes.' In personality, she was submissive, retiring, quiet, a pious churchgoer, taken up in the running of the household, and above all absorbed in the care of her children and stepchildren. The deaths within weeks of each other of her first three children in infancy in 1887–8, and the subsequent death of her fifth child, Edmund, under the age of six in 1900, must have been hammer blows for her. Her sorrows can only have been compounded by living with an irascible, unfeeling, overbearing husband. It is scarcely surprising that she made an impression of a saddened, careworn woman. Nor is it any wonder that she bestowed a smothering, protective love and devotion on her two surviving children, Adolf and Paula. Klara was in turn held in love and affection by her children and stepchildren, by Adolf quite especially. 'Outwardly, his love for his mother was his most striking feature,' Dr Bloch later wrote. 'While he was not a "mother's boy" in the usual sense,' he added, 'I have never witnessed a closer attachment.' In one of the few signs of human affection recorded in *Mein Kampf*, Adolf wrote, 'I had honoured my father, but loved my mother.' He carried her picture with him down to the last days in the bunker. Her portrait stood in his rooms in Munich, Berlin, and at the Obersalzberg (his alpine residence near Berchtesgaden). His mother may well, in fact, have been the only person he genuinely loved in his entire life.

Adolf's early years were spent, then, under the suffocating shield of an over-anxious mother in a household dominated by the threatening presence of a disciplinarian father, against whose wrath the submissive Klara was helpless to protect her offspring. Adolf's younger sister, Paula, spoke after the war of her mother as 'a very soft and tender person, the compensatory element between the almost too harsh father and the very lively children who were perhaps somewhat difficult to train. If there

5

were ever quarrel[s] or differences of opinion between my parents,' she continued, 'it was always on account of the children. It was especially my brother Adolf who challenged my father to extreme harshness and who got his sound thrashing every day . . . How often on the other hand did my mother caress him and try to obtain with her kindness what the father could not succeed [in obtaining] with harshness!' Hitler himself, during his late-night fireside monologues in the 1940s, often recounted that his father had sudden bursts of temper and would then immediately hit out. He did not love his father, he said, but instead feared him all the more. His poor beloved mother, he used to remark, to whom he was so attached, lived in constant concern about the beatings he had to take, sometimes waiting outside the door as he was thrashed.

Quite possibly, Alois's violence was also turned against his wife. A passage in *Mein Kampf,* in which Hitler ostensibly describes the conditions in a workers' family where the children have to witness drunken beatings of their mother by their father, may well have drawn in part on his own childhood experiences. What the legacy of all this was for the way Adolf's character developed must remain a matter for speculation. That its impact was profound is hard to doubt.

Beneath the surface, the later Hitler was unquestionably being formed. Speculation though it must remain, it takes little to imagine that his later patronizing contempt for the submissiveness of women, the thirst for dominance (and imagery of the Leader as stern, authoritarian father-figure), the inability to form deep personal relationships, the corresponding cold brutality towards humankind, and – not least – the capacity for hatred so profound that it must have reflected an immeasurable undercurrent of self-hatred concealed in the extreme narcissism that was its counterpoint must surely have had roots in the subliminal influences of the young Adolf's family circumstances. But assumptions have to remain guesswork. The outer traces of Adolf's early life, so far as they can be reconstructed, bear no hint of what would emerge. Attempts to find in the youngster 'the warped person within the murderous dictator' have proved unpersuasive. If we exclude our knowledge of what was to come, his family circumstances invoke for the most part sympathy for the child exposed to them.

II

Alois Hitler had always been a restless soul. The Hitlers had moved house several times within Braunau, and had subsequently been uprooted on a number of occasions. In November 1898, a final move for Alois took place when he bought a house with a small plot of attached land in Leonding, a village on the outskirts of Linz. From now on, the family settled in the Linz area, and Adolf – down to his days in the bunker in 1945 – looked upon Linz as his home town. Linz reminded him of the happy, carefree days of his youth. It held associations with his mother. And it was the most 'German' town of the Austrian Empire. It evidently symbolized for him the provincial small-town Germanic idyll – the image he would throughout his life set against the city he would soon come to know, and detest: Vienna.

Adolf was now in his third elementary school. He seems to have established himself rapidly with a new set of schoolmates, and became 'a little ringleader' in the games of cops and robbers which the village boys played in the woods and fields around their homes. War games were a particular favourite. Adolf himself was thrilled by an illustrated history of the Franco-Prussian War, which he had come across at home. And once the Boer War broke out, the games revolved around the heroic exploits of the Boers, whom the village boys fervently supported. About this same time, Adolf became gripped by the adventure stories of Karl May, whose popular tales of the Wild West and Indian wars (though May had never been to America) enthralled thousands of youngsters. Most of these youngsters graduated from the Karl May adventures and the childhood fantasies they fostered as they grew up. For Adolf, however, the fascination with Karl May never faded. As Reich Chancellor, he still read the May stories, recommending them, too, to his generals, whom he accused of lacking imagination.

Adolf later referred to 'this happy time', when 'school work was ridiculously easy, leaving me so much free time that the sun saw more of me than my room', when 'meadows and woods were then the battle-ground on which the ever-present "antagonisms"' – the growing conflict with his father – 'came to a head'.

In 1900, however, the carefree days were drawing to a close. And just around the time when important decisions had to be made about Adolf's future, and the secondary education path he should follow, the Hitler family was once more plunged into distress with the death, through measles, of Adolf's little brother Edmund on 2 February 1900. With Alois's elder son, Alois Jr, already spiting his father and living away from home, any careerist ambitions for his offspring now rested upon Adolf. They were to lead to tension between father and son in the remaining years of Alois's life.

Adolf began his secondary schooling on 17 September 1900. His father had opted for the *Realschule* rather than the Gymnasium, that is, for a school which attached less weight to the traditional classical and humanistic studies but was still seen as a preparation for higher education, with an emphasis upon more 'modern' subjects, including science and technical studies. According to Adolf, his father was influenced by the aptitude his son already showed for drawing, together with a disdain for the impracticality of humanistic studies deriving from his own hard way to career advancement. It was not the typical route for a would-be civil servant – the career which Alois had in mind for his son. But, then, Alois himself had made a good career in the service of the Austrian state with hardly any formal education at all to speak of.

The transition to secondary school was a hard one for young Adolf. He had to trek every day from his home in Leonding to school in Linz, a journey of over an hour each way, leaving him little or no time for developing out-of-school friendships. While he was still a big fish in a little pond among the village boys in Leonding, his classmates in his new school took no special notice of him. He had no close friends at school; nor did he seek any. And the attention he had received from his village teacher was now replaced by the more impersonal treatment of a number of teachers responsible for individual subjects. The minimum effort with which Adolf had mastered the demands of the primary school now no longer sufficed. His school work, which had been so good in primary school, suffered from the outset. And his behaviour betrayed clear signs of immaturity. Adolf's school record, down to the time he left in autumn 1905, hovered between poor and mediocre.

In a letter to Hitler's defence counsel on 12 December 1923, following the failed putsch attempt in Munich, his former class teacher, Dr Eduard Huemer, recalled Adolf as a thin, pale youth commuting between Linz and Leonding, a boy not making full use of his talent, lacking in application, and unable to accommodate himself to school discipline.

He characterized him as stubborn, high-handed, dogmatic, and hot-tempered. Strictures from his teachers were received with a scarcely concealed insolence. With his classmates he was domineering, and a leading figure in the sort of immature pranks which Huemer attributed to too great an addiction to Karl May's Indian stories together with a tendency to waste time furthered by the daily trip from Leonding and back.

There can be little doubting that Hitler's attitude towards his school and teachers (with one exception) was scathingly negative. He left school 'with an elemental hatred' towards it, and later mocked and derided his schooling and teachers. Only his history teacher, Dr Leopold Pötsch, was singled out for praise in *Mein Kampf* for firing Hitler's interest through vivid narratives and tales of heroism from the German past, stirring in him the strongly emotional German-nationalist, anti-Habsburg feelings (which were in any case widely prevalent in his school, as in Linz generally).

The problems of adjustment that Adolf encountered in the *Realschule* in Linz were compounded by the deterioration in relations with his father and the running sore of the disputes over the boy's future career. For Alois, the virtues of a civil service career could not be gainsaid. But all his attempts to enthuse his son met with adamant rejection. 'I yawned and grew sick to my stomach at the thought of sitting in an office, deprived of my liberty; ceasing to be master of my own time,' wrote Adolf in *Mein Kampf*.

The more Adolf resisted the idea, the more authoritarian and insistent his father became. Equally stubborn, when asked what he envisaged for his future, Adolf claimed he replied that he wanted to be an artist – a vision which for the dour Austrian civil servant Alois was quite unthinkable. 'Artist, no, never as long as I live!', Hitler has him saying. Whether the young Adolf, allegedly at the age of twelve, so plainly stipulated he wanted to be an artist may be doubted. But that there was a conflict with his father arising from his unwillingness to follow a career in the civil service, and that his father found fault with his son's indolent and purposeless existence, in which drawing appeared to be his main interest, seems certain. Alois had worked his way up through industry, diligence, and effort from humble origins to a position of dignity and respect in the state service. His son, from a more privileged background, saw fit to do no more than dawdle away his time drawing and dreaming, would not apply himself in school, had no career path in view, and scorned the type of career which had meant everything to his father. The dispute amounted, therefore, to more than a rejection of a civil service career. It was a rejection of everything his father had stood for; and with that, a rejection of his father himself.

Adolf's adolescence, as he commented in *Mein Kampf*, was 'very painful'. With the move to the school in Linz, and the start of the rumbling conflict with his father, an important formative phase in his character development had begun. The happy, playful youngster of the primary school days had grown into an idle, resentful, rebellious, sullen, stubborn, and purposeless teenager.

When, on 3 January 1903, his father collapsed and died over his usual morning glass of wine in the Gasthaus Wiesinger, the conflict of will over Adolf's future was over. Alois had left his family in comfortable circumstances. And whatever emotional adjustments were needed for his widow, Klara, it is unlikely that Adolf, now the only 'man about the house', grieved over his father. With his father's death, much of the parental pressure was removed. His mother did her best to persuade Adolf to comply with his father's wishes. But she shied away from conflict and, however concerned she was about his future, was far too ready to give in to Adolf's whims. In any case, his continued poor school performance in itself ruled out any realistic expectation that he would be qualified for a career in the civil service.

His school record in the following two years remained mediocre. In autumn 1905, at the age of sixteen, he used illness – feigned, or most likely genuine but exaggerated – to persuade his mother that he was not fit to continue school and gladly put his schooling behind him for good with no clear future career path mapped out.

The time between leaving school in autumn 1905 and his mother's death at the end of 1907 is passed over almost completely in *Mein Kampf*. In these two years, Adolf lived a life of parasitic idleness – funded, provided for, looked after, and cosseted by a doting mother, with his own room in the comfortable flat in the Humboldtstraße in Linz, which the family had moved into in June 1905. His mother, his aunt Johanna, and his little sister Paula were there to look after all his needs, to wash, clean, and cook for him. His mother even bought him a grand piano, on which he had lessons for four months between October 1906 and January 1907. He spent his time during the days drawing, painting, reading, or writing 'poetry'; the evenings were for going to the theatre or opera; and the whole time he daydreamed and fantasized about his future as a great artist. He stayed up late into the night and slept long into the mornings. He had no clear aim in view. The indolent lifestyle, the grandiosity of fantasy, the lack of discipline for systematic work – all features of the later Hitler – can be seen in these two years in Linz. It was little wonder that Hitler came to refer to this period as 'the happiest days which seemed to me almost like a beautiful dream'.

A description of Adolf's carefree life in Linz between 1905 and 1907 is provided by the one friend he had at that time, August Kubizek, the son of a Linz upholsterer with dreams of his own about becoming a great musician. Kubizek's post-war memoirs need to be treated with care, both in factual detail and in interpretation. They are a lengthened and embellished version of recollections he had originally been commissioned by the Nazi Party to compile. Even retrospectively, the admiration in which Kubizek continued to hold his former friend coloured his judgement. But more than that, Kubizek plainly invented a great deal, built some passages around Hitler's own account in *Mein Kampf*, and deployed some near plagiarism to amplify his own limited memory. However, for all their weaknesses, his recollections have been shown to be a more credible source on Hitler's youth than was once thought, in particular where they touch upon experiences related to Kubizek's own interests in music and theatre. There can be no doubt that, whatever their deficiencies, they do contain important reflections of the young Hitler's personality, showing features in embryo which were to be all too prominent in later years.

August Kubizek – 'Gustl' – was some nine months older than Adolf. They met by chance in autumn 1905 (not 1904, as Kubizek claimed) at the opera in Linz. Adolf had for some years been a fanatical admirer of Wagner, and his love of opera, especially the works of the 'master of Bayreuth', was shared by Kubizek. Gustl was highly impressionable; Adolf out for someone to impress. Gustl was compliant, weak-willed, subordinate; Adolf was superior, determining, dominant. Gustl felt strongly about little or nothing; Adolf had strong feelings about everything. 'He had to speak,' recalled Kubizek, 'and needed someone to listen to him.' For his part, Gustl, from his artisanal background, having attended a lower school than the young Hitler, and feeling himself therefore both socially and educationally inferior, was filled with admiration at Adolf's power of expression. Whether Adolf was haranguing him about the deficiencies of civil servants, school teachers, local taxation, social welfare lotteries, opera performances, or Linz public buildings, Gustl was gripped as never before. Not just what his friend had to say, but how he said it, was what he found attractive. Gustl, in self-depiction a quiet, dreamy youth, had found an ideal foil in the opinionated, cocksure, 'know-all' Hitler. It was a perfect partnership.

In the evenings they would go off, dressed in their fineries, to the theatre or the opera, the pale and weedy young Hitler, sporting the beginnings of a thin moustache, looking distinctly foppish in his black coat and dark hat, the image completed by a black cane with an ivory handle. After the performance, Adolf would invariably hold forth, heatedly critical of the production, or effusively rapturous. Even though Kubizek was musically more gifted and knowledgeable than Hitler, he remained the passive and submissive partner in the 'discussions'.

Hitler's passion for Wagner knew no bounds. A performance could affect him almost like a religious experience, plunging him into deep and mystical fantasies. Wagner amounted for him to the supreme artistic genius, the model to be emulated. Adolf was carried away by Wagner's powerful musical dramas, his evocation of a heroic, distant, and sublimely mystical Germanic past. *Lohengrin*, the saga of the mysterious knight of the grail, epitome of the Teutonic hero, sent from the castle of Monsalvat by his father Parzival to rescue the wrongly condemned pure maiden, Elsa, but ultimately betrayed by her, had been his first Wagner opera, and remained his favourite.

Even more than music, the theme, when Adolf and Gustl were together, was great art and architecture. More precisely, it was Adolf as the future great artistic genius. The young, dandified Hitler scorned the notion of working to earn one's daily bread. He enraptured the impressionable Kubizek with his visions of himself as a great artist, and Kubizek as a foremost musician. While Kubizek toiled in his father's workshop, Adolf filled his time with drawing and dreaming. He would then meet Gustl after work, and, as the friends wandered through Linz in the evenings, would lecture him on the need to tear down, remodel, and replace the central public buildings, showing his friend countless sketches of his rebuilding plans.

The make-believe world also included Adolf's infatuation with a girl who did not even know of his existence. Stefanie, an elegant young lady in Linz to be seen promenading through the town on the arm of her mother, and occasionally greeted by an admirer among the young officers, was for Hitler an ideal to be admired from a distance, not approached in person, a fantasy figure who would be waiting for the great artist when the right moment for their marriage arrived, after which they would live in the magnificent villa that he would design for her.

Another glimpse into the fantasy world is afforded by Adolf's plans for the future when, around 1906, the friends bought a lottery ticket together. Adolf was so certain they would win first prize that he designed an elaborate vision of their future residence. The two young men would live an artistic existence, tended by a middle-aged lady who could meet their artistic requirements – neither Stefanie nor any other woman of their own age figured in this vision – and would go off to Bayreuth and Vienna and make other visits of cultural value. So certain was Adolf that they would win, that his fury at the state lottery knew no bounds when nothing came of their little flutter.

In spring 1906, Adolf persuaded his mother to fund him on a first trip to Vienna, allegedly to study the picture gallery in the Court Museum, more likely to fulfil a growing ambition to visit the cultural sites of the Imperial capital. For two weeks, perhaps longer, he wandered through Vienna as a tourist taking in the city's many attractions. With whom he stayed is unknown. The four postcards he sent his friend Gustl and his comments in *Mein Kampf* show how captivated he was by the grandeur of the buildings and the layout of the Ringstraße. Otherwise, he seems to have spent his time in the theatre and marvelling at the Court Opera, where Gustav Mahler's productions of Wagner's *Tristan* and *The Flying Dutchman* left those of provincial Linz in the shade. Nothing had changed on his return home. But the sojourn in Vienna furthered the idea, probably already growing in his mind, that he would develop his artistic career at the Viennese Academy of Fine Arts.

By the summer of 1907, this idea had taken more concrete shape. Adolf was now aged eighteen but still never having earned a day's income and continuing his drone's life without career prospects. Despite the advice of relatives that it was about time he found a job, he had persuaded his mother to let him return to Vienna, this time with the intention of entering the Academy. Whatever her reservations, the prospect of a systematic study at the Academy in Vienna must have seemed to her an improvement on his aimless existence in Linz. And she did not need to worry about her son's material welfare. Adolf's 'Hanitante' – Aunt Johanna – had come up with a loan of 924 Kronen to fund her nephew's artistic studies. It gave him something like a year's salary for a young lawyer or teacher.

By this stage, his mother was seriously ill with breast cancer. She had already been operated on in January, and in the spring and early summer was frequently treated by the Jewish family doctor, Dr Bloch. Frau Klara – now in the new family home at Urfahr, a suburb of Linz – must have been seriously worried not only about the mounting medical costs, but about her eleven-year-old daughter Paula, still at home and looked after by Aunt Johanna, and about her darling boy Adolf, still without a clear future. Adolf, described by Dr Bloch as a tall, sallow, frail-looking boy who 'lived within himself', was certainly worried about his mother. He settled the bill of 100 Kronen for her twenty-day stay in hospital at the start of the year. He wept when Dr Bloch had to tell him and his sister the bad news that their mother had little chance of surviving her cancer. He tended to her during her illness and was anguished at the intense pain she suffered. He had, it seems, to take responsibility for whatever decisions had to be made about her care. Despite his mother's deteriorating condition, however, Adolf went ahead with his plans to move to Vienna. He left for the capital in early September 1907, in time to take the entrance examination for the Academy of Fine Arts.

Admission to the examination itself was decided on the basis of an entry test resting on assessment of pieces of work presented by the candidates. Adolf had, he later wrote, left home 'armed with a thick pile of drawings'. He was one of 113 candidates and was allowed to proceed to the examination itself. Thirty-three candidates were excluded following this initial test. At the beginning of October, he sat the two tough three-hour examinations in which the candidates had to produce drawings on specified themes. Only twenty-eight candidates succeeded. Hitler was not among them. 'Test drawing unsatisfactory. Few heads,' was the verdict.

It apparently never occurred to the supremely self-confident Adolf that he might fail the entrance examination for the Academy. He had been, he wrote in *Mein Kampf*, 'convinced that it would be child's play to pass the examination . . . I was so convinced that I would be successful that when I received my rejection, it struck me as a bolt from the blue.'

He sought an explanation, and was told by the Rector of the Academy that there was no doubt about his unsuitability for the school of painting, but that his talents plainly lay in architecture. Hitler left the interview, as he put it, 'for the first time in my young life at odds with myself'. After a few days pondering his fate, he concluded, so he wrote, that the Rector's judgement was right, and 'that I should some day become an architect' – not that he then or later did anything to remedy the educational deficiencies which provided a major obstacle to studying for a career in architecture. In reality, Adolf probably did not bounce back anything like so quickly as his own story suggests, and the fact that he reapplied the following year for admission to the painting school casts some doubt on the version of a lightning recognition that his future was as an architect. At any rate, the rejection by the Academy was such a body blow to his pride that he kept it a secret. He avoided telling either his friend Gustl, or his mother, of his failure.

Meanwhile, Klara Hitler lay dying. The sharp deterioration in her condition brought Adolf back from Vienna to be told by Dr Bloch, towards the end of October, that his mother's condition was hopeless. Deeply affected by the news, Adolf was more than dutiful. Both his sister, Paula, and Dr Bloch later testified to his devoted and 'indefatigable' care for his dying mother. But despite Dr Bloch's close medical attention, Klara's health worsened rapidly during the autumn. On 21 December 1907, aged forty-seven, she passed away quietly. Though he had witnessed many deathbed scenes, recalled Dr Bloch, 'I have never seen anyone so prostrate with grief as Adolf Hitler.' His mother's death was 'a dreadful blow', Hitler wrote in *Mein Kampf*, 'particularly for me'. He felt alone and bereft at her passing. He had lost the one person for whom he had ever felt close affection and warmth.

'Poverty and hard reality,' Hitler later claimed, 'now compelled me to take a quick decision. What little my father had left had been largely exhausted by my mother's grave illness; the orphan's pension to which I was entitled was not enough for me even to live on, and so I was faced with the problem of somehow making my own living.' When, he continued, after her death he returned to Vienna for the third time, now to stay for some years, his old defiance and determination had come back to him, and his goal was now clear: 'I wanted to become an architect and obstacles do not exist to be surrendered to, but only to be broken.' He claimed he set out to overcome the obstacles, inspired by the example of his father's rise through his own efforts from poverty to the position of a government official.

In reality, his mother's careful housekeeping – aided by not insignificant contributions from her sister Johanna – had left more than sufficient to pay for the considerable medical costs, as well as a relatively expensive funeral. Nor was Adolf left nearly penniless. There was no question of immediately having to earn his own living. Certainly, the monthly orphans' pension of 25 Kronen which he and his younger sister Paula – now brought up by their half-sister Angela and her husband Leo Raubal – received could scarcely provide for his upkeep in inflation-ridden Austria. And apart from interest, Adolf and Paula could not touch the inheritance from their father until their twenty-fourth year. But what his mother had left – perhaps in the region of 2,000 Kronen once the funeral expenses had been covered – was divided between the two orphaned minors. Adolf's share, together with his orphan's pension, was enough to provide for his upkeep in Vienna for a year without work. And on top of that, he still had the residue of his aunt's generous loan. He scarcely had the financial security which has sometimes been attributed to him. But, all in all, his financial position was, during this time, substantially better than that of most genuine students in Vienna.

Moreover, Adolf was in less of a hurry to leave Linz than he implies in *Mein Kampf*. Though his sister almost forty years later stated that he moved to Vienna within a few days of their mother's death, Adolf was still recorded as in Urfahr in mid-January and mid-February 1908. Unless, as seems unlikely, he made brief visits to Vienna between these dates, it looks as if he stayed in Urfahr for at least seven weeks after the death of his mother. The family household account-book indicates that the break with Linz was not made before May.

When he did return to Vienna, in February 1908, it was not to pursue with all vigour the necessary course of action to become an architect, but to slide back into the life of indolence, idleness, and self-indulgence which he had followed before his mother's death. He even now persuaded Kubizek's parents to let August leave his work in the family upholstery business to join him in Vienna in order to study music.

His failure to enter the Academy and his mother's death, both occurring within less than four months in late 1907, amounted to a crushing double-blow for the young Hitler. He had been abruptly jolted from his dream of an effortless path to the fame of a great artist; and the sole person upon whom he depended emotionally had been lost to him at almost the same time. His artistic fantasy remained. Any alternative – such as settling down to a steady job in Linz – was plainly an abhorrent thought. A neighbour in Urfahr, the widow of the local postmaster, later recalled: 'When the postmaster asked him one day what he wanted to do for a living and whether he wouldn't like to join the post office, he replied that it was his intention to become a great artist. When he was reminded that he lacked the necessary funding and personal connections, he replied tersely: "Makart and Rubens worked themselves up from poor backgrounds." ' How he might emulate them was entirely unclear. His only hope rested upon retaking the entrance examination for the Academy the following year. He must have known his chances were not high. But he did nothing to enhance them. Meanwhile, he had to get by in Vienna.

Despite the drastic alteration in his prospects and circumstances, Adolf's lifestyle – the drifting existence in an egoistic fantasy-world – remained unchanged. But the move from the cosy provincialism of Linz to the political and social melting-pot of Vienna nevertheless marked a crucial transition. The experiences in the Austrian capital were to leave an indelible mark on the young Hitler and to shape decisively the formation of his prejudices and phobias.

2

Drop-out

I

The city where Hitler was to live for the next five years was an extra-ordinary place. More than any other European metropolis, Vienna epitomized tensions – social, cultural, political – that signalled the turn of an era, the death of the nineteenth-century world. They were to mould the young Hitler.

Anticipating that he would be studying at the Academy of Fine Arts, he had in late September or the beginning of October 1907 rented a small room on the second floor of a house in Stumpergasse 31, near the Westbahnhof in Vienna, owned by a Czech woman, Frau Zakreys. This is where he returned, some time between 14 and 17 February 1908, to pick up where he had left off before his mother's death.

He was not long alone. We can recall that he had persuaded August Kubizek's parents to let their son join him in Vienna to carry out his studies to become a musician. Kubizek's father had been most reluctant to let his son go off with someone he regarded as no more than a failure at school and who thought himself above learning a proper trade. But Adolf had prevailed. On 18 February, he sent a postcard to his friend, urging him to come as quickly as possible. 'Dear Friend,' he wrote, 'am anxiously expecting news of your arrival. Write soon so that I can prepare everything for your festive welcome. The whole of Vienna is awaiting you.' A postscript added: 'Beg you again, come soon.' Four days later, Gustl's tearful parents bade him goodbye, and he left to join his friend in Vienna. Adolf met a tired Kubizek at the station that evening, took him back to Stumpergasse to stay the first night, but, typically, insisted on immediately showing him all the sights of Vienna. How could someone come to Vienna and go to bed without first seeing the Court Opera House? So Gustl was dragged off to view the opera building, St Stephen's cathedral (which could scarcely be seen through the mist), and the lovely church of St Maria am Gestade. It was after midnight when they returned to Stumpergasse, and later still when an exhausted Kubizek fell asleep with Hitler still haranguing him about the grandeur of Vienna.

The next few months were to be a repeat, on a grander scale, of the lifestyle of the two youths in Linz. An early search for lodgings for Gustl was rapidly given up, and Frau Zakreys persuaded to swap her larger room and move into the cramped little room that Hitler had occupied. Adolf and his friend now occupied the same room, paying double the rent (10 Kronen each) that Hitler had paid for his earlier room. Within the next few days, Kubizek learnt that he had passed the entrance examination and been accepted for study at the Vienna Conservatoire. He rented a grand piano which took up most of the available space in the room, just allowing Hitler the three paces to do his usual stomping backwards and forwards. Apart from the piano, the room was furnished with simple necessities: two beds, a commode, a wardrobe, a washstand, a table, and two chairs.

Kubizek settled down into a regular pattern of music study. What Hitler was up to was less clear to his friend. He stayed in bed in the mornings, was missing when Kubizek came back from the Conservatoire at lunchtimes, hung around the grounds of Schönbrunn Palace on fine afternoons, pored over books, fantasized over grandiose architectural and writing plans, and spent a good deal of time drawing until late into the night. Gustl's puzzlement about how his friend could combine so much leisure time with studying at the Academy of Fine Arts was ended only after some considerable time. A show of irritation about Kubizek practising his piano scales led to a full-scale row between the two friends about study timetables and ended in Hitler finally admitting in fury that he had been rejected by the Academy. When Gustl asked him what, then, he was going to do, Hitler rounded on him: 'What now, what now? . . . Are you starting too: what now?' The truth was, Hitler had no idea where he was going or what he would do. He was drifting aimlessly.

Kubizek had plainly touched a raw nerve. Adolf had for mercenary reasons not told his family about his failure to enter the Academy. Otherwise, his guardian back in Linz, Josef Mayrhofer, would probably have denied him the 25 Kronen a month he received as his share of the orphans' pension. And he would have come under even more pressure to find a job. But why did he deceive his friend? For a teenager to fail to pass an extremely tough entrance examination is in itself neither unusual nor shameful. But Adolf evidently could not bear to tell his friend, to whom he had always claimed to be so superior in all matters of artistic judgement, and whose own studies at the Conservatoire had started so promisingly, of his rejection. The blow to his self-esteem had been profound. And the bitterness showed. According to Kubizek, he would fly off the handle at the slightest thing. His loss of self-confidence could flare up in an instant into boundless anger and violent denunciation of all who he thought were persecuting him. The tirades of hate directed at everything and everybody were those of an outsized ego desperately wanting acceptance and unable to come to terms with his personal insignificance, with failure and mediocrity.

Adolf had still not given up hope of entering the Academy. But, typically, he took no steps to ensure that his chances would be better a second time round. Systematic preparation and hard work were as foreign to the young Hitler as they would be to the later dictator. Instead, his time was largely spent in dilettante fashion, as it had been in Linz, devising grandiose schemes shared only with the willing Kubizek – fantasy plans that usually arose from sudden whims and bright ideas and were dropped almost as soon as they had begun.

Apart from architecture, Hitler's main passion, as it had been in Linz, was music. Particular favourites, certainly in later years, were Beethoven, Bruckner, Liszt, and Brahms. He greatly enjoyed, too, the operettas of Johann Strauß and Franz Lehár. Wagner was, of course, the *non plus ultra*. Adolf and Gustl were at the opera most nights, paying their 2 Kronen to gain the standing place that they had often queued for hours to obtain. They saw operas by Mozart, Beethoven, and the Italian masters Donizetti, Rossini, and Bellini as well as the main works of Verdi and Puccini. But for Hitler only German music counted. He could not join in the enthusiasm for Verdi or Puccini operas, playing to packed houses in Vienna. Adolf's passion for Wagner, as in Linz, knew no bounds. Now he and his friend were able to see all Wagner's operas performed at one of the best opera houses in Europe. In the short time they were together, Kubizek reckoned they saw *Lohengrin* ten times. 'For him,' remarked Kubizek, 'a second-rate Wagner was a hundred times better than a first-class Verdi.' Kubizek was of a different mind; but to no avail. Adolf would not rest until his friend agreed to forget about going to see Verdi at the Court Opera and accompany him to a Wagner performance at the less highbrow Popular Opera House. 'When it was a matter of a Wagner performance, Adolf would stand no contradiction.'

'When I hear Wagner,' Hitler himself much later recounted, 'it seems to me that I hear rhythms of a bygone world.' It was a world of Germanic myth, of great drama and wondrous spectacle, of gods and heroes, of titanic struggle and redemption, of victory and of death. It was a world where the heroes were outsiders who challenged the old order, like Rienzi, Tannhäuser, Stolzing, and Siegfried; or chaste saviours like Lohengrin and Parsifal. Betrayal, sacrifice, redemption, and heroic death were Wagnerian themes which would also preoccupy Hitler down to the *Götterdämmerung* of his regime in 1945. And it was a world created with grandiose vision by an artist of genius, an outsider and revolutionary, all-or-nothing refuser of compromise, challenger of the existing order, dismissive of the need to bow to the bourgeois ethic of working for a living, surmounting rejection and persecution, overcoming adversity to attain greatness. It was little wonder that the fantasist and drop-out, the rejected and unrecognized artistic genius in the dingy room in the Stumpergasse, could find his idol in the master of Bayreuth. Hitler, the nonentity, the mediocrity, the failure, wanted to live like a Wagnerian hero. He wanted to become himself a new Wagner – the philosopher-king, the genius, the supreme artist. In Hitler's mounting identity crisis following his rejection at the Academy of Arts, Wagner was for Hitler the artistic giant he had dreamed of becoming but knew he could never emulate, the incarnation of the triumph of aesthetics and the supremacy of art.

II

The strange coexistence of the young Hitler and Kubizek continued into midsummer 1908. During those months, almost the only other person apart from his friend with whom Hitler had regular contact was his landlady, Frau Zakreys. Nor did Kubizek and Hitler have any joint acquaintances. Adolf regarded his friendship with Gustl as exclusive, allowing him no other friendships. When Gustl brought a young woman, one of a small number of his music pupils, back to his room, Hitler, thinking she was a girlfriend, was beside himself with rage. Kubizek's explanation that it was simply a matter of coaching a pupil in musical harmony merely provoked a tirade about the pointlessness of women studying. In Kubizek's view, Hitler was outrightly misogynist. He pointed out Hitler's satisfaction that women were not permitted in the stalls of the opera. Apart from his distant admiration for Stefanie in Linz, Kubizek knew of Hitler having no relations with any woman during the years of their acquaintance in both Linz and Vienna. This would not alter during his remaining years in the Austrian capital. None of the accounts of Hitler's time in the Men's Home gives a hint of any women in his life. When his circle of acquaintances got round to discussing women – and, doubtless, their own former girlfriends and sexual experiences – the best Hitler could come up with was a veiled reference to Stefanie, who had been his 'first love', though 'she never knew it, because he never told her'. The impression left with Reinhold Hanisch, an acquaintance from that time, was that 'Hitler had very little respect for the female sex, but very austere ideas about relations between men and women. He often said that, if men only wanted to, they could adopt a strictly moral way of living.' This was entirely in line with the moral code preached by the Austrian pan-German movement associated with Georg Ritter von Schönerer, whose radical brand of German nationalism and racial antisemitism Hitler had admired since his Linz days. Celibacy until the twenty-fifth year, the code advocated, was healthy, advantageous to strength of will, and the basis of physical or mental high achievement. The cultivation of corresponding dietary habits was advised. Eating meat and drinking alcohol – seen as stimulants to sexual activity – were to be avoided. And upholding the strength and purity of the Germanic race meant keeping free of the moral decadence and danger of infection which accompanied consorting with prostitutes, who should be left to clients of 'inferior' races. Here was ideological justification enough for Hitler's chaste lifestyle and prudish morals. But, in any case, certainly in the time in Vienna after he parted company with Kubizek, Hitler was no 'catch' for women.

Probably, he was frightened of women – certainly of their sexuality. Hitler later described his own ideal woman as 'a cute, cuddly, naïve little thing – tender, sweet, and stupid'. His assertion that a woman 'would rather bow to a strong man than dominate a weakling' may well have been a compensatory projection of his own sexual complexes.

Kubizek was adamant that Hitler was sexually normal (though on the basis of his own account it is difficult to see how he was in a position to judge). This was also the view of doctors who at a much later date thoroughly examined him. Biologically, it may well have been so. Claims that sexual deviance arising from the absence of a testicle were the root of Hitler's personality disorder rest on a combination of psychological speculation and dubious evidence provided by a Russian autopsy after the alleged capture of the burnt remains of his body in Berlin. And stories about his Vienna time such as that of his alleged obsession with and attempted rape of a model engaged to a half-Jew, and his resort to prostitutes, derive from a single source – the self-serving supposed recollections of Josef Greiner, who may have known Hitler briefly in Vienna – with no credence and which can be regarded as baseless. However, Kubizek's account, together with the language Hitler himself used in *Mein Kampf*, does point at the least to an acutely disturbed and repressed sexual development.

Hitler's prudishness, shored up by Schönerian principles, was to a degree merely in line with middle-class outward standards of morality in the Vienna of his time. These standards had been challenged by the openly erotic art of Gustav Klimt and literature of Arthur Schnitzler. But the solid bourgeois puritanism prevailed – at least as a thin veneer covering the seamier side of a city teeming with vice and prostitution. Where decency demanded that women were scarcely allowed even to show an ankle, Hitler's embarrassment – and the rapidity with which he fled with his friend – when a prospective landlady during the search for a room for Kubizek let her silk dressing-gown fall open to reveal that she was wearing nothing but a pair of knickers was understandable. But his prudishness went far beyond this. It amounted, according to Kubizek's account, to a deep disgust and repugnance at sexual activity. Hitler avoided contact with women, meeting with cold indifference during visits to the opera alleged attempts by young women, probably seeing him as something of an oddity, to flirt with or tease him. He was repelled by homosexuality. He refrained from masturbation. Prostitution horrified, but fascinated, him. He associated it with venereal disease, which petrified him. Following a visit to the theatre one evening to see Frank Wedekind's play *Frühlings Erwachen* (*Spring Awakening*), which dealt with sexual problems of youth, Hitler suddenly took Kubizek's arm and led him into Spittelberggasse to see at first hand the red-light district, or 'sink of iniquity' as he called it. Adolf took his friend not once, but twice, along the row of lit windows behind which scantily clad women advertised their wares and touted for custom. His voyeurism was then cloaked in middle-class self-righteousness by the lecture he proceeded to give Kubizek on the evils of prostitution. Later, in *Mein Kampf*, he was to link the Jews – echoing a commonplace current among antisemites of his Vienna years – with prostitution. But if this association was present in his mind in 1908, Kubizek did not record it.

Though seemingly repelled by sex, Hitler was at the same time plainly fascinated by it. He discussed sexual matters quite often in lengthy talks late at night with Gustl, regaling him, wrote Kubizek, on the need for sexual purity to protect what he grandly called the 'flame of life'; explaining to his naïve friend, following a brief encounter with a businessman who invited them to a meal, about homosexuality; and ranting about prostitution and moral decadence. Hitler's disturbed sexuality, his recoiling from physical contact, his fear of women, his inability to forge genuine friendship and emptiness in human relations, presumably had their roots in childhood experiences of a troubled family life. Attempts to explain them will inevitably remain speculative. Later rumours of Hitler's sexual perversions are similarly based on dubious evidence. Conjecture – and there has been much of it – that sexual repression later gave way to sordid sado-masochistic practices rests, whatever the suspicions, on little more than a combination of rumour, hearsay, surmise, and innuendo, often spiced up by Hitler's political enemies. And even if the alleged repulsive perversions really were his private proclivities, how exactly they would help explain the rapid descent of the complex and sophisticated German state into gross inhumanity after 1933 is not readily self-evident.

Hitler was to describe his life in Vienna as one of hardship and misery, hunger and poverty. This was notably economical with the truth as regards the months he spent in Stumpergasse in 1908 (though it was accurate enough as a portrayal of his condition in the autumn and winter of 1909–10). Even more misleading was his comment in *Mein Kampf* that 'the orphan's pension to which I was entitled was not enough for me even to live on, and so I was faced with the problem of somehow making my own living'. As we have noted, the loan from his aunt, his share of his mother's legacy, and his monthly orphan's pension certainly gave him sufficient to live comfortably – perhaps even equivalent to that of a young teacher over a year or so at least. And his appearance, when he put on his fineries for an evening at the opera, was anything but that of a down-and-out. When Kubizek first saw him on their reunion at the Westbahnhof in February 1908, young Adolf was wearing a good-quality overcoat, and dark hat. He was carrying the walking-stick with the ivory handle that he had had in Linz, and 'appeared almost elegant'. As for working, in those first months of 1908, as we have noted, Hitler certainly did nothing whatsoever about making his own living, or taking any steps to ensure that he was on the right track to do so.

If he had a reasonable income during his time with Kubizek, Hitler nevertheless scarcely led a life of wild extravagance. His living conditions were unenviable. The sixth district of Vienna, close to the Westbahnhof, where Stumpergasse was situated, was an unattractive part of the city, with its dismal, unlit streets and scruffy tenement blocks overhung with smoke and soot surrounding dark inner courtyards. Kubizek himself was appalled at some of the accommodation on view when he was looking for a room the day after he had arrived in Vienna. And the lodging he and Adolf came to share was a miserable room that stank constantly of paraffin, with crumbling plaster peeling off dank walls, and bug-ridden beds and furniture. The lifestyle was frugal. Little was spent on eating and drinking. Adolf was not a vegetarian at that time, but his main daily fare usually consisted only of bread and butter, sweet flour puddings, and often in the afternoons a piece of poppy- or nut-cake. Sometimes he went without food altogether. When Gustl's mother sent a food parcel every fortnight, it was like a feast. Adolf drank milk as a rule, or sometimes fruit-juice, but no alcohol. Nor did he smoke. The one luxury was the opera. How much he spent on the almost daily visits to an opera or a concert can only be guessed. But at 2 Kronen for a standing place – it infuriated Hitler that young officers more interested in the social occasion than the music had to pay only 10 Heller, a twentieth of the sum – regular attendance over some months would certainly begin to eat away at whatever savings he had. Hitler himself remarked, over three decades later: 'I was so poor, during the Viennese period of my life, that I had to restrict myself to only the very best performances. This explains that already at that time I heard *Tristan* thirty or forty times, and always from the best companies.' By the summer of 1908, he must have made big inroads into the money he had inherited. But he presumably still had some of his savings left, as well as the orphan's pension that Kubizek presumed was his only income, which would allow him to last out for a further year.

Though Kubizek was unaware of it, by summer the time he was spending with his friend in Vienna was drawing to a close. By early July 1908, Gustl had passed his examinations at the Conservatoire and term had ended. He was going back to Linz to stay with his parents until autumn. He arranged to send Frau Zakreys the rent every month to guarantee retention of the room, and Adolf, again saying how little he was looking forward to remaining alone in the room, accompanied him to the Westbahnhof to see him off. They were not to meet again until the Anschluß in 1938. Adolf did send Gustl a number of postcards during the summer, one from the Waldviertel, where he had gone without enthusiasm to spend some time with his family – the last occasion he would see his relatives for many years. Nothing suggested to Kubizek that he would not be rejoining his friend in the autumn. But when he left the train at the Westbahnhof on his return in November, Hitler was nowhere to be seen. Some time in the late summer or autumn, he had moved out of Stumpergasse. Frau Zakreys told Kubizek that he had left his lodgings without giving any forwarding address. By 18 November he was registered with the police as a 'student' living at new lodgings in room 16 of Felberstraße 22, close by the Westbahnhof, and a more airy room – presumably costing more – than that he had occupied in Stumpergasse.

What had caused the sudden and unannounced break with Kubizek? The most likely explanation is Hitler's second rejection – this time he was not even permitted to take the examination – by the Academy of Fine Arts in October 1908. He had probably not told Kubizek he was applying again. Presumably he had spent the entire year in the knowledge that he had a second chance and in the expectation that he would not fail this time. Now his hopes of an artistic career lay totally in ruins. He could not now face his friend again as a confirmed failure.

Kubizek's recollections, for all their flaws, paint a portrait of the young Hitler whose character traits are recognizable with hindsight in the later party leader and dictator. The indolence in lifestyle but accompanied by manic enthusiasm and energy sucked into his fantasies, the dilettantism, the lack of reality and sense of proportion, the opinionated autodidactism, the egocentrism, the quirky intolerance, the sudden rise to anger and the outbursts of rage, the diatribes of venom poured out on everyone and everything blocking the rise of the great artist – all these can be seen in the nineteen-year-old Hitler portrayed by Kubizek. Failure in Vienna had turned Hitler into an angry and frustrated young man increasingly at odds with the world around him. But he was not yet the Hitler who comes fully into view after 1919, and whose political ideas were fully outlined in *Mein Kampf*.

Kubizek had had time to read *Mein Kampf* by the time he wrote his own account of Hitler's political development – something which in any case was of less interest to him than matters cultural and artistic. His passages are in places heavily redolent of Hitler's own tale of his 'political awakening' in Vienna. They are not, therefore, reliable and often not credible – scarcely so when he claims Hitler was a pacifist, an opponent of war at this stage. However, there is no reason to doubt Hitler's growing political awareness. His bitter contempt for the multi-language parliament (which Kubizek visited with him), his strident German nationalism, his intense detestation of the multinational Habsburg state, his revulsion at 'the ethnic babel on the streets of Vienna', and 'the foreign mixture of peoples which had begun to corrode this old site of German culture' – all these were little more than an accentuation, a personalized radicalization, of what he had first imbibed in Linz. Hitler fully described them in *Mein Kampf*. The first months of the Viennese experience doubtless already deepened and sharpened these views. However, even by Hitler's own account it took two years in Vienna for his attitude towards the Jews to crystallize. Kubizek's assertion that Hitler attained his 'world-view' during the time they were together in Vienna is an exaggeration. Hitler's rounded 'world-view' was still not formed. The pathological hatred of the Jews that was its cornerstone had still to emerge.

III

There are no witnesses to Hitler's activity during the nine months that he stayed in Felberstraße. This phase of his life in Vienna remains obscure. It has often been presumed, nevertheless, that it was in precisely these months that he became an obsessive racial antisemite.

Close to where Hitler lived in Felberstraße was a kiosk selling tobacco and newspapers. Whatever newspapers and periodicals he bought beyond those that he devoured so avidly in cafés, it was probably from this kiosk. Which exactly he read of the many cheap and trashy magazines in circulation at the time is uncertain. One of them was very likely a racist periodical called *Ostara*. The magazine, which first appeared in 1905, was the product of the extraordinary and warped imagination of an eccentric former Cistercian monk, who came to be known as Jörg Lanz von Liebenfels (though his real name was plain Adolf Lanz). He later founded his own order, the 'New Templar Order' (replete with a full panoply of mystical signs and symbols, including the swastika), in a ruined castle, Burg Werfenstein, on a romantic stretch of the Danube between Linz and Vienna.

Lanz and his followers were obsessed by homoerotic notions of a manichean struggle between the heroic and creative 'blond' race and a race of predatory dark 'beast-men' who preyed on the 'blond' women with animal lust and bestial instincts that were corrupting and destroying mankind and its culture. Lanz's recipe, laid down in *Ostara*, for overcoming the evils of the modern world and restoring the domination of the 'blond race' was racial purity and racial struggle, involving the slavery and forced sterilization or even extermination of the inferior races, the crushing of socialism, democracy, and feminism which were seen as the vehicles of their corrupting influence, and the complete subordination of aryan women to their husbands. It amounted to a creed of 'blue-eyed blondes of all nations, unite'. There are indeed elements in common between the bizarre fantasies of Lanz and his band of woman-hating, racist crackpots and the programme of racial selection which the SS were to put into practice during the Second World War. Whether Lanz's ideas had direct influence on Himmler's SS is, however, questionable. Unsustainable is Lanz's claim to a unique place in history as the man 'who gave Hitler his ideas'.

The main evidence that Hitler was acquainted with *Ostara* comes from a post-war interview in which Lanz claimed to have remembered Hitler, during the time he lived in Felberstraße in 1909, paying him a visit and asking him for back copies of the magazine. Since Hitler looked so run-down, Lanz went on, he let him have the copies for nothing, and gave him 2 Kronen for his journey home. How Lanz knew that this young man had been Hitler, when it was to be well over ten years before the latter would become a local celebrity even in Munich, he was never asked in the interview more than forty years after the purported meeting. Another witness to Hitler's reading of *Ostara* in post-war interviews was Josef Greiner, the author of some fabricated 'recollections' of Hitler in his Vienna years. Greiner did not mention *Ostara* in his book, but, when later questioned about it in the mid-1950s, 'remembered' that Hitler had a large pile of *Ostara* magazines while he was living in the Men's Home from 1910 to 1913, and had vehemently supported Lanz's racial theories in heated discussions with an ex-Catholic priest called Grill (who does not figure in his book at all). A third witness, a former Nazi functionary called Elsa Schmidt-Falk, could only remember that she had heard Hitler mention Lanz in the context of homosexuality, and *Ostara* in connection with the banning of Lanz's works (though there is in fact no evidence of a ban).

Most likely, Hitler did read *Ostara* along with other racist pulp which was prominent on Vienna newspaper stands. But we cannot be certain. Nor, if he did read it, can we be sure what he believed. His first known statements on antisemitism immediately following the First World War betray no traces of Lanz's obscure racial doctrine. He was later frequently scornful of *völkisch* sects and the extremes of Germanic cultism. As far as can be seen, if we discount Elsa Schmidt-Falk's doubtful testimony, he never mentioned Lanz by name. For the Nazi regime, the bizarre Austrian racist eccentric, far from being held up to praise, was to be accused of 'falsifying racial thought through secret doctrine'.

When Hitler, his savings almost exhausted, was forced to leave Felberstraße in mid-August 1909 to move for a very short time to shabbier accommodation in nearby Sechshauserstraße 58, it was certainly not as a devotee of Lanz von Liebenfels. Nor, anti-Jewish though he undoubtedly already was as a Schönerer supporter, is it likely that he had yet found the key to the ills of the world in a doctrine of racial antisemitism.

Hitler stayed in Sechshauserstraße for less than a month. And when he left, on 16 September 1909, it was without filling in the required police registration form, without leaving a forwarding address, and probably without paying his rent. During the next months, Hitler did learn the meaning of poverty. His later recollection that autumn 1909 had been 'an endlessly bitter time' was not an exaggeration. All his savings had now vanished. He must have left some address with his guardian for his orphan's pension of 25 Kronen to be sent to Vienna each month. But that was not enough to keep body and soul together. During the wet and cold autumn of 1909 he lived rough, sleeping in the open, as long as the weather held, probably in cheap lodgings when conditions forced him indoors.

Hitler had now reached rock-bottom. Some time in the weeks before Christmas 1909, thin and bedraggled, in filthy, lice-ridden clothes, his feet sore from walking around, Hitler joined the human flotsam and jetsam finding their way to the large, recently established doss-house for the homeless in Meidling, not far from Schönbrunn Palace. The social decline of the petty-bourgeois so fearful of joining the proletariat was complete. The twenty-year-old would-be artistic genius had joined the tramps, winos, and down-and-outs in society's basement.

It was at this time that he met Reinhold Hanisch, whose testimony, doubtful though it is in places, is all that casts light on the next phase of Hitler's time in Vienna. Hanisch, living under the assumed name of 'Fritz Walter', came originally from the Sudetenland and had a police record for a number of petty misdemeanours. He was a self-styled draughtsman, but in reality had drifted through various temporary jobs as a domestic servant and casual labourer before tramping his way across Germany from Berlin to Vienna. He encountered a miserable-looking Hitler, down at heel in a shabby blue check suit, tired and hungry, in the hostel dormitory one late autumn night, shared some bread with him and told tales of Berlin to the young enthusiast for all things German. The hostel was a night-shelter offering short-term accommodation only. A bath or shower, disinfection of clothes, soup and bread, and a bed in the dormitory were provided. But during the day the inmates were turned out to fend for themselves. Hitler, looking in a sorry state and in depressed mood, went in the mornings along with other destitutes to a nearby convent in Gumpendorferstraße where the nuns doled out soup. The time was otherwise spent visiting public warming-rooms, or trying to earn a bit of money. Hanisch took him off to shovel snow, but without an overcoat Hitler was in no condition to stick at it for long. He offered to carry bags for passengers at the Westbahnhof, but his appearance probably did not win him many customers. Whether he did any other manual labour during the years he spent in Vienna is doubtful. While his savings had lasted, he had not been prepared to entertain the prospect of working. At the time he was in most need of money, he was physically not up to it. Later, even

Hanisch, his 'business associate', lost his temper over Hitler's idleness while eking out a living by selling paintings. The story he told in *Mein Kampf* about learning about trade unionism and Marxism the hard way through his maltreatment while working on a building site is almost certainly fictional. Hanisch, at any rate, never heard the story at the time from Hitler, and later did not believe it. The 'legend' probably drew on the general anti-socialist propaganda in the Vienna of Hitler's day.

Hanisch had meanwhile thought of a better idea than manual labouring. Hitler had told him of his background, and was persuaded by Hanisch to ask his family for some money, probably under the pretext that he needed it for his studies. Within a short time he received the princely sum of 50 Kronen, almost certainly from his Aunt Johanna. With that he could buy himself an overcoat from the government pawn shop. With this long coat and his greasy trilby, shoes looking like those of a nomad, hair over his collar, and dark fuzz on his chin, Hitler's appearance even provoked his fellow vagrants to remark on it. They nicknamed him 'Ohm Paul Krüger', after the Boer leader. But the gift from his aunt meant that better times were on the way. He was now able to acquire the materials needed to begin the little business venture that Hanisch had dreamed up. On hearing from Hitler that he could paint – Hitler actually told him he had been at the Academy – Hanisch suggested he should paint scenes of Vienna which he would then peddle for him, and they would share the proceeds. Whether this partnership began already in the doss-house, or only after Hitler had moved, on 9 February 1910, to the more salubrious surrounds of the Men's Home in the north of the city is unclear from Hanisch's garbled account. What is certain is that with his aunt's gift, the move to Meldemannstraße, and his new business arrangement with Hanisch, Hitler was now over the worst.

The Men's Home was a big step up from the Meidling hostel. The 500 or so residents were not down-and-out vagrants, but, for the most part, a mixed bunch of individuals – some, clerks and even former academics and pensioned officers, just down on their luck, others simply passing through, looking for work or in temporary employment, all without a family home to go to. Unlike the hostel, the Men's Home, built a few years earlier, offered a modicum of privacy, and for an overnight price of only 50 Heller. Residents had their own cubicles, which had to be vacated during the day but could be retained on a more or less indefinite basis. There was a canteen where meals and alcohol-free drinks could be obtained, and a kitchen where residents could prepare their own food; there were washrooms and lockers for private possessions; in the basement were baths, along with a cobbler's, a tailor's, and a hairdresser's, a laundry, and cleaning facilities; there was a small library on the ground floor, and on the first floor lounges and a reading-room where newpapers were available. Most of the residents were out during the day, but a group of around fifteen to twenty, mainly from lower-middle-class backgrounds and seen as the 'intelligentsia', usually gathered in a smaller room, known as the 'work-room' or 'writing-room', to undertake odd jobs – painting advertisements, writing out addresses and the like. This is where Hanisch and Hitler set up operations.

Hanisch's role was to hawk Hitler's mainly postcard-size paintings around pubs. He also found a market with frame-makers and upholsterers who could make use of cheap illustrations. Most of the dealers with whom he had a good, regular trade were Jewish. Hitler's view, according to Hanisch, was that Jews were better businessmen and more reliable customers than 'Christian' dealers. More remarkably, in the light of later events and his own claims about the importance of the Vienna period for the development of his antisemitism, his closest partner (apart from Hanisch) in his little art-production business, Josef Neumann, was also a Jew – and one with whom Hitler was, it seems, on friendly terms.

Hitler invariably copied his pictures from others, sometimes following visits to museums or galleries to find suitable subjects. He was lazy and had to be chivvied by Hanisch, who could offload the pictures faster than Hitler painted them. The usual rate of production was about one picture a day, and Hanisch reckoned to sell it for around 5 Kronen, split between him and Hitler. In this fashion, they managed to make a modest living.

Politics was a frequent topic of conversation in the reading-room of the Men's Home, and the atmosphere easily became heated, with tempers flaring. Hitler took full part. His violent attacks on the Social Democrats caused trouble with some of the inmates. He was known for his admiration for Schönerer and Karl Hermann Wolf (founder and leader of the German Radical Party, with its main base in the Sudetenland). He also waxed lyrical about the achievements of Karl Lueger, the social reformist but rabble-rousing antisemitic mayor of Vienna.

When he was not holding forth on politics, Hitler was lecturing his comrades – keen to listen or not – on the wonders of Wagner's music and the brilliance of Gottfried Semper's designs of Vienna's monumental buildings.

Whether politics or art, the chance to involve himself in the reading-room 'debates' was more than sufficient to distract Hitler from working. By summer, Hanisch had become more and more irritated with Hitler's failure to keep up with orders. Hitler claimed he could not simply paint to order, but had to be in the right mood. Hanisch accused him of only painting when he needed to keep the wolf from the door. Following a windfall from the sale of one of his paintings, Hitler even disappeared from the Men's Home for a few days in June with Neumann. According to Hanisch, Hitler and Neumann spent their time sight-seeing in Vienna and looking around museums. More likely, they had other 'business' plans, which, then, quickly fell through, possibly including a quick visit to the Waldviertel to try to squeeze a bit more money out of Aunt Johanna. Hitler and his cronies in the Men's Home were at this time prepared to entertain any dotty scheme – a miracle hair-restorer was one such idea – that would bring in a bit of money. Whatever the reason for his temporary absence, after five days, his money spent, Hitler returned to the Men's Home and the partnership with Hanisch. Relations now, however, became increasingly strained and the bad feeling eventually exploded over a picture Hitler had painted, larger than usual in size, of the parliament building. Through an intermediary – another Jewish dealer in his group in the Men's Home by the name of Siegfried Löffner – Hitler accused Hanisch of cheating him by withholding 50 Kronen he allegedly received for the picture, together with a further 9 Kronen for a watercolour. The matter was brought to the attention of the police, and Hanisch was sentenced to a few days in jail – but for using the false name of Fritz Walter. Hitler never received what he felt was owing to him for the picture.

With Hanisch's disappearance, Hitler's life recedes into near obscurity for two years or so. When he next comes into view, in 1912–13, he is still in residence in the Men's Home, now a well-established member of the community, and a central figure among his own group – the 'intelligentsia' who occupied the writing-room. He was by now well over the depths of degradation he experienced in 1909 in the doss-house, even if continuing to drift aimlessly. He could earn a modest income from the sale of his pictures of the Karlskirche and other scenes of 'Old Vienna'. His outgoings were low, since he lived so frugally. His living costs in the Men's Home were extremely modest: he ate cheaply, did not drink, smoked a cigarette only rarely, and had as his only luxury the occasional purchase of a standing-place at the theatre or opera (about which he would then regale the writing-room 'intellectuals' for hours). Descriptions of his appearance at this time are contradictory. A fellow resident in the Men's Home in 1912 later described Hitler as shabbily dressed and unkempt, wearing a long greyish coat, worn at the sleeves, and battered old hat, trousers full of holes, and shoes stuffed with paper. He still had shoulder-length hair and a ragged beard. This is compatible with the description given by Hanisch which, though not precisely dated, appears from the context to refer to 1909–10. On the other hand, according to Jacob Altenberg, one of his Jewish art dealers, in the later phase at least in the Men's Home Hitler was clean-shaven, took care to keep his hair cut, and wore clothes which, though old and worn, were kept neat. Given what Kubizek wrote about Hitler's fussiness about personal hygiene when they were together in 1908, and what was later little short of a cleanliness fetishism, Altenberg's testimony rings truer than that of the anonymous acquaintance for the final period in Meldemannstraße.

But, whatever his appearance, Hitler was scarcely enjoying the lifestyle of a man who had come by a substantial windfall – what would have amounted to a king's ransom for someone living in a men's hostel. Yet this is what was long believed. It was suggested – though based on guesswork, not genuine evidence – that towards the end of 1910 Hitler had become the recipient of a sizeable sum, perhaps as much as 3,800 Kronen, which represented the life-savings of his Aunt Johanna. Post-war inquiries indicated that this was the amount withdrawn from her savings account by Johanna on 1 December 1910, some four months before she died, leaving no will. The suspicion was that the large sum had gone to Adolf. This feeling was enhanced by the fact that his half-sister Angela, still looking after his sister Paula, soon afterwards, in 1911, staked a claim to the whole of the orphan's pension, still at that time divided equally between the two children. Adolf who, 'on account of his training as an artist had received substantial sums from his aunt, Johanna Pölzl', conceded that he was in a position to maintain himself, and was forced to concede the 25 Kronen a month which he had up to then received from his guardian. But, as we have already noted, the household account-book of the Hitler family makes plain that Adolf, alongside smaller gifts from 'Hanitante', received from her a loan – amounting in reality to a gift – of 924 Kronen, probably in 1907 and providing him with the material basis of his first, relatively comfortable, year in Vienna. Whatever became of Aunt Johanna's money in December 1910, there is not the slightest indication that it went to Hitler. And the loss of the 25 Kronen a month orphan's pension would have amounted to a serious dent in his income.

Though his life had stabilized while he had been in the Men's Home, during the time he had been trafficking in paintings, Hitler seems to have remained unsettled. Karl Honisch – keen to distance himself from his near-namesake Hanisch, of whom he had heard nothing good – knew Hitler in 1913. Honisch described him as slight in build, poorly nourished, with hollow cheeks, dark hair flopping in his face, and wearing shabby clothes. Hitler was rarely absent from the Home and sat each day in the same corner of the writing-room near the window, drawing and painting on a long oak-table. This was known as his place, and any newcomer venturing to take it was rapidly reminded by the other inmates that 'this place is taken. Herr Hitler sits there.' Among the writing-room regulars, Hitler was seen as a somewhat unusual, artistic type. He himself wrote later: 'I believe that those who knew me in those days took me for an eccentric.' But, other than his painting skills, no one imagined he had any special talents. Though well regarded, he had a way, noted Honisch, of keeping his distance from the others and 'not letting anyone come too close'. He could be withdrawn, sunk in a book or his own thoughts. But he was known to have a quick temper. This could flare up at any time, particularly in the frequent political debates that took place. Hitler's strong views on politics were plain to all. He would often sit quietly when a discussion started up, putting in the odd word here or there but otherwise carrying on with his drawing. If he took exception to something said, however, he would jump up from his place, hurling his brush or pencil on the table, and heatedly and forcefully make himself felt before, on occasion, breaking off in mid-flow and with a wave of resignation at the incomprehension of his comrades, taking up his drawing again. Two subjects above all roused his aggression: the Jesuits and the 'Reds'. No mention was made of tirades against the Jews.

The criticism of the 'Jesuits' suggests that some embers of his former enthusiasm for Schönerer's vehement anti-Catholicism were still warm, though the Schönerer movement had by this time effectively collapsed. His hatred for the Social Democrats was also long established by this time. His own version in *Mein Kampf* of the emergence of this hatred tells the story – almost certainly fictional – of the victimization and personal threats he allegedly experienced, on account of his rejection of their political views and refusal to join a trades union, at the hands of Social Democrat workers when he was employed for a short time on a building site.

There is, in fact, no need to look beyond the strength of Hitler's pan-German nationalism as an explanation of his detestation of the internationalism of the Social Democrats. The radical nationalist propaganda of Franz Stein's pan-German 'working-class movement', with its repeated shrill attacks on 'social democratic bestialities' and 'red terror', and its boundless agitation against Czech workers, was the type of 'socialism' soaked up by Hitler. A more underlying source of the hatred most likely lay in Hitler's pronounced sense of social and cultural superiority towards the working class that Social Democracy represented. 'I do not know what horrified me most at that time,' he later wrote of his contact with those of the 'lower classes': 'the economic misery of my companions, their moral and ethical coarseness, or the low level of their intellectual development.'

Though Hitler's account of his first encounter with Social Democrats is probably apocryphal, status-consciousness runs through it, not least in his comment that at that time 'my clothing was still more or less in order, my speech cultivated, and my manner reserved'. Given such status-consciousness, the level of degradation he must have felt in 1909–10 when the threat of social decline into the proletariat for a time became dire reality can be readily imagined. But far from eliciting any solidarity with the ideals of the working-class movement, this merely sharpened his antagonism towards it. Not social and political theories, but survival, struggle, and 'every man for himself' marked the philosophy of the doss-house.

Hitler went on in *Mein Kampf* to stress the hard struggle for existence of the 'upstart', who had risen 'by his own efforts from his previous position in life to a higher one', that 'kills all pity' and destroys 'feeling for the misery of those who have remained behind'. This puts into context his professed interest in 'the social question' while he was in Vienna. His ingrained sense of superiority meant that, far from arousing sympathy for the destitute and the disadvantaged, the 'social question' for him amounted to a search for scapegoats to explain his own social decline and degradation. 'By drawing me within its sphere of suffering,' the 'social question', he wrote, 'did not seem to invite me to "study", but to experience it in my own skin.'

By the end of his Vienna period, it is unlikely that Hitler's detestation of Social Democracy, firmly established though it was, had gone much beyond that which had been current in Schönerer's pan-German nationalism – apart from the additional radicality deriving from his own bitter first-hand experiences of the misery and degradation that enhanced his utter rejection of international socialism as a solution. That his hatred of Social Democracy had already by this date, as Hitler claimed in *Mein Kampf*, married with a racial theory of antisemitism to give him a distinctive 'world-view' which remained thereafter unchanged, can be discounted.

IV

Why and when did Hitler become the fixated, pathological antisemite known from the writing of his first political tract in 1919 down to the writing of his testament in the Berlin bunker in 1945? Since his paranoid hatred was to shape policies that culminated in the killing of millions of Jews, this is self-evidently an important question. The answer is, however, less clear than we should like. In truth, we do not know for certain why, or even when, Hitler turned into a manic and obsessive antisemite.

Hitler's own version is laid out in some well-known and striking passages in *Mein Kampf*. According to this, he had not been an antisemite in Linz. On coming to Vienna, he had at first been alienated by the antisemitic press there. But the obsequiousness of the mainstream press in its treatment of the Habsburg court and its vilification of the German Kaiser gradually led him to the 'more decent' and 'more appetizing' line taken in the antisemitic paper the *Deutsches Volksblatt*. Growing admiration for Karl Lueger – 'the greatest German mayor of all times' – helped to change his attitude towards the Jews – 'my greatest transformation of all' – and within two years (or in another account a single year) the transformation was complete. Hitler highlights, however, a single episode which opened his eyes to 'the Jewish Question'.

Once, as I was strolling through the Inner City, I suddenly encountered an apparition in a black caftan and black hair locks. Is this a Jew? was my first thought.

For, to be sure, they had not looked like that in Linz. I observed the man furtively and cautiously, but the longer I stared at this foreign face, scrutinizing feature for feature, the more my first question assumed a new form:

Is this a German?

Following this encounter, Hitler continued, he started to buy antisemitic pamphlets. He was now able to see that Jews 'were not Germans of a special religion, but a people in themselves'. Vienna now appeared in a different light. 'Wherever I went, I began to see Jews, and the more I saw, the more sharply they became distinguished in my eyes from the rest of humanity.'

Now, to stay with his own account, his revulsion rapidly grew. The language Hitler uses in these pages of *Mein Kampf* betrays a morbid fear of uncleanliness, dirt, and disease – all of which he associated with Jews. He also quickly formed his newly-found hatred into a conspiracy theory. He now linked the Jews with every evil he perceived: the liberal press, cultural life, prostitution, and – most significant of all – identified them as the leading force in Social Democracy. At this, 'the scales dropped from my eyes'. Everything connected with Social Democracy – party leaders, Reichsrat deputies, trade union secretaries, and the Marxist press that he devoured with loathing – now seemed to him to be Jewish. But this 'recognition', he wrote, gave him great satisfaction. His already existent hatred of Social Democracy, that party's antinationalism, now fell into place: its leadership was 'almost exclusively in the hands of a foreign people'. 'Only now,' Hitler remarked, 'did I become thoroughly acquainted with the seducer of our people.' He had linked Marxism and antisemitism through what he called 'the Jewish doctrine of Marxism'.

It is a graphic account. But it is not corroborated by the other sources that cast light on Hitler's time in Vienna. Indeed, in some respects it is directly at variance with them. It is generally accepted that, for all the problems with the autobiographical parts of *Mein Kampf*, Hitler was indeed converted to manic racial antisemitism while in Vienna. But the available evidence, beyond Hitler's own words, offers little to confirm that view. Interpretation rests ultimately on the balance of probabilities.

Kubizek claimed Hitler was already an antisemite before leaving Linz. In contrast to Hitler's assertion that his father had 'cosmopolitan views' and would have regarded antisemitism as 'cultural backwardness', Kubizek stated that Alois's regular drinking cronies in Leonding were Schönerer supporters and that he himself was certainly therefore anti-Jewish. He pointed also to the openly antisemitic teachers Hitler encountered in the *Realschule*. He allegedly recalled, too, that Adolf had said to him one day, as they passed the small synagogue: 'That doesn't belong in Linz.' For Kubizek, Vienna had made Hitler's antisemitism more radical. But it had not created it. In his opinion, Hitler had gone to Vienna 'already as a pronounced antisemite'. Kubizek went on to recount one or two episodes of Hitler's aversion to Jews during the time they were together in Vienna. He claimed an encounter with a Galician Jew was the caftan story of *Mein Kampf*. But this, and a purported visit to a synagogue in which Hitler took Kubizek along to witness a Jewish wedding, have the appearance of an outright fabrication. Palpably false is Kubizek's assertion that Hitler joined the Antisemitenbund (Antisemitic League) during the months in 1908 that the friends were together in Vienna. There was no such organization in Austria-Hungary before 1918.

In fact, Kubizek is generally unconvincing in the passages devoted to the early manifestations of Hitler's antisemitism. These are among the least trustworthy sections of his account – partly drawing on *Mein Kampf*, partly inventing episodes which were not present in the original draft version of his recollections, and in places demonstrably incorrect. Kubizek was keen to distance himself in his post-war memoirs from the radical views of his friend on the 'Jewish Question'. It suited him to emphasize that Hitler had from Linz days hated the Jews. His suggestion that Hitler's father (whom he had not known) had been a pronounced antisemite is probably incorrect. Alois Hitler's own more moderate form of pan-Germanism had differed from that of the Schönerer movement in its continued allegiance to the Emperor of Austria and accorded with the line adopted by the dominant party in Upper Austria, the Deutsche Volkspartei (German People's Party), which admitted Jews to membership. The vehemently antisemitic as well as radical German nationalist Schönerer movement certainly had a strong following in and around Linz, and no doubt included some at least of Hitler's teachers among its supporters. But antisemitism seems to have been relatively unimportant in his school compared with the antagonism towards the Czechs. Hitler's own later recollection was probably in this respect not inaccurate, when he told Albert Speer that he had become aware of the 'nationalities problem' – by which he meant vehement hostility towards the Czechs – at school, but the 'danger of Jewry' had only been made plain to him in Vienna.

The young Hitler, himself taken while still in Linz by Schönerer's ideas, could scarcely have missed the emphatic racial antisemitism which was so integral to them. But for the Schönerer supporters in the Linz of Hitler's day, antisemitism appears to have been a subdominant theme in the cacophony of anti-Czech clamour and trumpeted Germanomania. It certainly did not prevent Hitler's warm expressions of gratitude in postcards and the present of one of his watercolours to Dr Bloch, the Jewish physician who had treated his mother in her last illness. The deep, visceral hatred of his later antisemitism was of a different order altogether. That was certainly not present in his Linz years.

There is no evidence that Hitler was distinctively antisemitic by the time he parted company with Kubizek in the summer of 1908. Hitler himself claimed that he became an antisemite within two years of arriving in Vienna. Could, then, the transformation be placed in the year he spent, mainly in Felberstraße, between leaving Kubizek and becoming a vagrant? The testimony of Lanz von Liebenfels would fit this chronology. But we have seen that this is of highly doubtful value. Hitler's descent into abject poverty in autumn 1909 might seem an obvious time to search for a scapegoat and find it in the figure of the Jew. But he had the opportunity less then than at any other time in Vienna to 'read up' on the subject, as he claimed in *Mein Kampf*.

Not only that: Reinhold Hanisch, his close companion over the following months, was adamant that Hitler 'in those days was by no means a Jew hater. He became one afterwards.' Hanisch emphasized Hitler's Jewish friends and contacts in the Men's Home to demonstrate the point. A one-eyed locksmith called Robinsohn spared Hitler some small change to help him out financially from time to time. (The man's name was actually Simon Robinson, traceable in the Men's Home in 1912–13.) Josef Neumann, as we have seen, became, as Hanisch put it, 'a real friend' to Hitler. He was said to have 'liked Hitler very much' and to have been 'of course highly esteemed' by him. A postcard salesman,

Siegfried Löffner (misnamed Loeffler by Hanisch), was also 'one of Hitler's circle of acquaintances', and, as we remarked, took sides with him in the acrimonious conflict with Hanisch in 1910. Hitler preferred, as we observed, to sell his pictures to Jewish dealers, and one of them, Jacob Altenberg, subsequently spoke well of the business relationship they had conducted. Hanisch's testimony finds confirmation in the later comment of the anonymous resident of the Men's Home in the spring of 1912, that 'Hitler got along exceptionally well with Jews, and said at one time that they were a clever people who stick together better than the Germans do'.

The three years that Hitler spent in the Men's Home certainly gave him every opportunity to pore over antisemitic newpapers, pamphlets, and cheap literature. But, leaving aside the fact that the chronology no longer matches Hitler's own assertion of a transformation within two years of arriving in Vienna, Karl Honisch, we saw, makes a point of emphasizing Hitler's strong views on 'Jesuits' and the 'Reds', though makes no mention at all of any hatred of Jews. Hitler certainly joined in talk about the Jews in the Men's Home. But his standpoint was, according to Hanisch's account, by no means negative. Hanisch has Hitler admiring the Jews for their resistance to persecution, praising Heine's poetry and the music of Mendelssohn and Offenbach, expressing the view that the Jews were the first civilized nation in that they had abandoned polytheism for belief in one God, blaming Christians more than Jews for usury, and dismissing the stock-in-trade antisemitic charge of Jewish ritual murder as nonsense. Only Josef Greiner, of those who claimed to have witnessed Hitler at first hand in the Men's Home, speaks of him as a fanatical Jew-hater in that period. But, as we have noted, Greiner's testimony is worthless.

There is, therefore, no reliable contemporary confirmation of Hitler's paranoid antisemitism during the Vienna period. If Hanisch is to be believed, in fact, Hitler was not antisemitic at all at this time. Beyond that, Hitler's close comrades during the First World War also recalled that he voiced no notable antisemitic views. The question arises, then, whether Hitler had not invented his Viennese 'conversion' to antisemitism in *Mein Kampf*; whether, in fact, his pathological hatred of the Jews only emerged in the wake of the lost war, in 1918–19.

Why might Hitler fabricate the claim that he had become an ideological antisemite in Vienna? And, equally, why might a 'conversion' at the end of the war be regarded as something to be concealed by a story of an earlier transformation? The answer lies in the image Hitler was establishing for himself in the early 1920s, and particularly following the failed putsch of 1923 and his trial the following spring. This demanded the self-portrait painted in *Mein Kampf*, of the nobody who struggled from the first against adversity, and, rejected by the academic 'establishment', taught himself through painstaking study, coming – above all through his own bitter experiences – to unique insights about society and politics that enabled him without assistance to formulate at the age of around twenty a rounded 'world-view'. This unchanged 'world-view', he was saying in 1924, provided him with the claim to leadership of the national movement, and indeed with the claim to be Germany's coming 'great leader'. Perhaps by then Hitler had even convinced himself that all the pieces of the ideological jigsaw had indeed fallen into place during his Vienna years. In any case, by the early 1920s no one was in a position to gainsay the story. An admission that he had become an ideological antisemite only at the end of the war, as he lay blinded from mustard gas in a hospital in Pasewalk and heard of Germany's defeat and the revolution, would certainly have sounded less heroic, and would also have smacked of hysteria.

However, it is difficult to believe that Hitler of all people, given the intensity of his hatred for the Jews between 1919 and the end of his life, had remained unaffected by the poisonous antisemitic atmosphere of the Vienna he knew – one of the most virulently anti-Jewish cities in Europe. It was a city where, at the turn of the century, radical antisemites advocated punishing sexual relations between Jews and non-Jews as sodomy, and placing Jews under surveillance around Easter to prevent ritual child-murder. Schönerer, the racial antisemite, had notably helped to stir up the hatred. Lueger was able to exploit the widespread and vicious antisemitism to build up his Christian Social Party and consolidate his hold on power in Vienna. Hitler greatly admired both. Once more, it would have been strange had he of all people admired them but been unaffected by such an essential stock-in-trade of their message as their antisemitism. Certainly, he learnt from Lueger the gains to be made from popularizing hatred against the Jews. The explicitly antisemitic newspaper Hitler read, and singled out for praise, the *Deutsches Volksblatt*, selling around 55,000 copies a day at the time, described Jews as agents of decomposition and corruption, and repeatedly linked them with sexual scandal, perversion, and prostitution. Leaving aside the probably contrived incident of the caftan-Jew, Hitler's description of his gradual exposure through the antisemitic gutter press to deep anti-Jewish prejudice and its impact upon him while in Vienna has an authentic ring about it.

Probably no single encounter produced his loathing for Jews. Given his relations with his parents, there may have been some connection with an unresolved Oedipal complex, though this is no more than guesswork. Hitler's linkage of Jews and prostitution has prompted speculation that sexual fantasies, obsessions, or perversions provide the key. Again, there is no reliable evidence. The sexual connotations were no more than Hitler could have picked up from the *Deutsches Volksblatt*. Another explanation would be a simpler one. At the time that Hitler soaked up Viennese antisemitism, he had recently experienced bereavement, failure, rejection, isolation, and increasing penury. The gulf between his self-image as a frustrated great artist or architect and the reality of his life as a drop-out needed an explanation. The Viennese antisemitic gutter press, it could be surmised, helped him to find that explanation.

But if Hitler's antisemitism was indeed formed in Vienna, why did it remain unnoticed by those around him? The answer might well be banal: in that hotbed of rabid antisemitism, anti-Jewish sentiment was so commonplace that it could go practically unnoticed. The argument from silence is, therefore, not conclusive. However, there is still the evidence from Hanisch and the anonymous acquaintance in the Men's Home about Hitler's friendship with Jews to contend with. This seems to stand in flat contradiction to Hitler's own lurid account of his conversion to antisemitism in Vienna. One remark by Hanisch, however, suggests that Hitler had indeed already developed racist notions about the Jews. When one of their group asked why Jews remained strangers in the nation, 'Hitler answered that it was because they were a different race.' He added, according to Hanisch, that 'Jews had a different smell'. Hitler was said also to have frequently remarked 'that descendants of Jews are very radical and have terroristic inclinations'. And when he and Neumann discussed Zionism, Hitler said that any money of Jews leaving Austria would obviously be confiscated 'as it was not Jewish but Austrian'. If Hanisch is to be believed, then, Hitler was advancing views reflecting racial antisemitism at the same time that he was closely associated with a number of Jews in the Men's Home. Could it have been that this very proximity, the dependence of the would-be great artist on Jews to offload his little street paintings, at precisely the same time that he was reading and digesting the antisemitic bile poured out by Vienna's gutter press, served only to underline and deepen the bitter enmities taking shape in his mind? Would the outsized ego of the unrecognized genius reduced to *this* not have translated his self-disgust into inwardly fermenting race-hatred when the plainly antisemitic Hanisch remarked to him that 'he must be of Jewish blood, since such a large beard rarely grows on a Christian chin' and 'he had big feet, as a desert wanderer must have'? Whether Hitler was on terms of real friendship with the Jews around him in the Men's Home, as Hanisch states, might be doubted. Throughout his life Hitler made remarkably few genuine friendships. And throughout his life, despite the torrents of words that poured from his mouth as a politician, he was adept at camouflaging his true feelings even to those in his immediate company. He was also a clever manipulator of those around him. His relations with the Jews in the Men's Home were clearly, at least in part, self-serving. Robinson helped him out with money. Neumann, too, paid off small debts for him. Löffner was Hitler's go-between with the dealers. Whatever his true feelings, in his contacts with Jewish dealers and traders Hitler was simply being pragmatic: as long as they could sell his paintings for him, he could swallow his abstract dislike of Jews.

Though it has frequently been claimed, largely based on Hanisch's evidence and on the lack of reference to his antisemitic views in the paltry sources available, that Hitler was not a racial antisemite during his stay in Vienna, the balance of probabilities surely suggests a different interpretation? It seems more likely that Hitler, as he later claimed, indeed came to hate Jews during his time in Vienna. But, probably, at this time it was still little more than a rationalization of his personal circumstances rather than a thought-out 'world-view'. It was a personalized hatred – blaming the Jews for all the ills that befell him in a city that he associated with personal misery. But any expression of this hatred that he had internalized did not stand out to those around him where antisemitic vitriol was so normal. And, paradoxically, as long as he *needed* Jews to help him earn what classed as a living, he kept quiet about his true views and perhaps even on occasion, as Hanisch indicates, insincerely made remarks which could be taken, if mistakenly, as complimentary to Jewish culture. Only later, if this line of argument is followed, did he rationalize his visceral hatred into the fully-fledged 'world-view', with antisemitism as its core, that congealed in the early 1920s. The formation of the ideological antisemite had to wait until a further crucial phase in Hitler's development, ranging from the end of the war to his political awakening in Munich in 1919.

V

That was all still in the future. In spring 1913, after three years in the Men's Home, Hitler was still drifting, vegetating – not any longer down and out, it is true, and with responsibility to no one but himself, but without any career prospects. He gave the impression that he had still not given up all hope of studying art, however, and told the writing-room regulars in the Men's Home that he intended to go to Munich to enter the Art Academy. He had long said 'he would go to Munich like a shot', eulogizing about the 'great picture galleries' in the Bavarian capital. He had a good reason for postponing any plans to leave for Munich. His share of his father's inheritance became due only on his twenty-fourth birthday, on 20 April 1913. More than anything else, it might be surmised, the wait for this money was what kept Hitler so long in the city he detested. On 16 May 1913 the District Court in Linz confirmed that he should receive the sizeable sum, with interest added to the original 652 Kronen, of 819 Kronen 98 Heller, and that this would be sent by post to the 'artist' Adolf Hitler in Meldemannstraße, Vienna. With this long-awaited and much-welcome prize in his possession, he need delay his departure for Munich no further.

He had another reason for deciding the time was ripe to leave Vienna. In autumn 1909 he had failed to register for military service, which he would have been due to serve the following spring, after his twenty-first birthday. Even if found unfit, he would still have been eligible in 1911 and 1912 to undertake military service for a state he detested so fervently. Having avoided the authorities for three years, he presumably felt it safe to cross the border to Germany following his twenty-fourth birthday in 1913. He was mistaken. The Austrian authorities had not overlooked him. They were on his trail, and his avoidance of military service was to cause him difficulties and embarrassment the following year. The attempt to put any possible snoopers off the scent in later years is why, once he had become well known, Hitler persistently dated his departure from Vienna to 1912, not 1913.

On 24 May 1913, Hitler, carrying a light, black suitcase containing all his possessions, in a better set of clothes than the shabby suit he had been used to wearing, and accompanied by a young, short-sighted, unemployed shop-assistant, Rudolf Häusler, four years his junior, whom he had known for little over three months in the Men's Home, left the co-residents from the writing-room who had escorted them a short distance, and set off for Munich.

The Vienna years were over. They had indelibly marked Hitler's personality and the 'basic stock of personal views' he held. But these 'personal opinions' had not yet coagulated into a fully-fledged ideology, or 'world-view'. For that to happen, an even harder school than Vienna had to be experienced: war and defeat. And only the unique circum-stances produced by that war and defeat enabled an Austrian drop-out to find appeal in a different land, among the people of his adopted country.

3

Elation and Embitterment

The First World War made Hitler possible. Without the experience of war, the humiliation of defeat, and the upheaval of revolution the failed artist and social drop-out would not have discovered what to do with his life by entering politics and finding his métier as a propagandist and beerhall demagogue. And without the trauma of war, defeat, and revolution, without the political radicalization of German society that this trauma brought about, the demagogue would have been without an audience for his raucous, hate-filled message. The legacy of the lost war provided the conditions in which the paths of Hitler and the German people began to cross. Without the war, a Hitler on the Chancellor's seat that had been occupied by Bismarck would have been unthinkable.

I

Looking back just over a decade later, Hitler spoke of the fifteen months he spent in Munich before the war as 'the happiest and by far the most contented' of his life. The fanatical German nationalist exulted in his arrival in 'a *German* city', which he contrasted with the 'Babylon of races' that, for him, had been Vienna. He gave a number of reasons why he had left Vienna: bitter enmity towards the Habsburg Empire for pro-Slav policies that were disadvantaging the German population; growing hatred for the 'foreign mixture of peoples' who were 'corroding' German culture in Vienna; the conviction that Austria-Hungary was living on borrowed time, and that its end could not come soon enough; and the intensified longing to go to Germany, to where his 'childhood secret desires and secret love' had drawn him. The last sentiments were plainly romanticized. Otherwise, the feelings were genuine enough. And of his determination not to fight for the Habsburg state there can be no doubt. This is what Hitler meant when he said he left Austria 'primarily for political reasons'. But the implication that he had left as a form of political protest was disingenuous and deliberately misleading. As we noted, the prime and immediate reason he crossed the border into Germany was very tangible: the Linz authorities were hot on his trail for evasion of military service.

Hitler wrote that he came to Munich in the hope of some day making a name for himself as an architect. He described himself on arrival as an 'architectural painter'. In the letter he wrote to the Linz authorities in 1914, defending himself against charges of evading military service, he stated that he was forced to earn his living as a self-employed artist in order to fund his training as an architectural painter. In the biographical sketch he wrote in 1921, he stated that he went to Munich as an 'architecture-designer and architecture-painter'. At his trial in February 1924 he implied that he had already completed his training as an 'architecture-designer' by the time he came to Munich, but wanted to train to be a master builder. Many years later he claimed his intention was to undertake practical training in Germany; that on coming to Munich he had hoped to study for three years before joining the major Munich construction firm Heilmann and Littmann as a designer and then showing, by entering the first architectural competition to design an important building, just what he could do. None of these varying and conflicting accounts was true. There is no evidence that Hitler took any practical steps during his time in Munich to improve his poor and dwindling career prospects. He was drifting no less aimlessly than he had done in Vienna.

After arriving in Munich on 25 May 1913, a bright spring Sunday, Hitler followed up an advertisement for a small room rented by the family of the tailor Joseph Popp on the third floor of 34 Schleißheimer-straße, in a poorish district to the north of the city, on the edge of Schwabing, the pulsating centre of Munich's artistic and bohemian life, and not far from the big barracks area. His travelling companion, Rudolf Häusler, shared the cramped room with him until mid-February 1914. Apparently, Hitler's habit of reading late at night by the light of a petroleum lamp prevented Häusler from sleeping, and so irritated him that he eventually moved out, returning after a few days to take the room adjacent to Hitler's, where he stayed until May. According to his landlady, Frau Popp, Hitler quickly set himself up with the equipment to begin painting. As he had done in Vienna, he developed a routine where he could complete a picture every two or three days, usually copied from postcards of well-known tourist scenes in Munich – including the Theatinerkirche, the Asamkirche, the Hofbräuhaus, the Alter Hof, the Münzhof, the Altes Rathaus, the Sendlinger Tor, the Residenz, the Propyläen – then set out to find customers in bars, cafés, and beerhalls. His accurate but uninspired, rather soulless watercolours were, as Hitler himself later admitted when he was German Chancellor and they were selling for massively inflated prices, of very ordinary quality. But they were certainly no worse than similar products touted about the beerhalls, often the work of genuine art students seeking to pay their way. Once he had found his feet, Hitler had no difficulty finding buyers. He was able to make a modest living from his painting and exist about as comfortably as he had done in his last years in Vienna. When the Linz authorities caught up with him in 1914, he acknowledged that his income – though irregular and fluctuating – could be put at around 1,200 Marks a year, and told his court photographer Heinrich Hoffmann at a much later date that he could get by on around 80 Marks a month for living costs at that time.

As in Vienna, Hitler was polite but distant, self-contained, withdrawn, and apparently without friends (other than, in the first months, Häusler). Frau Popp could not recall Hitler having a single visitor in the entire two years of his tenancy. He lived simply and frugally, preparing his paintings during the day and reading at night. According to Hitler's own account, 'the study of the political events of the day', especially foreign policy, preoccupied him during his time in Munich. He also claimed to have immersed himself again in the theoretical literature of Marxism and to have examined thoroughly once more the relation of Marxism to the Jews. There is no obvious reason to doubt his landlady's witness to the books he brought back with him from the Königliche Hof- und Staatsbibliothek (Royal Court and State Library), not far away in Ludwigstraße. In all the millions of recorded words of Hitler, however, there is nothing to indicate that he ever pored over the theoretical writings of Marxism, that he had studied Marx, or Engels, or Lenin (who had been in Munich not long before him), or Trotsky (his contemporary in Vienna). Reading for Hitler, as in Vienna, was not for enlightenment or learning, but to confirm prejudice.

Most of it was probably done in cafés, where Hitler could continue his habit of devouring the newspapers available to customers. This is where he kept abreast of political developments, and where, at the slightest provocation, he could flare up and treat anyone in proximity to his fiercely held views on whatever preoccupied him at the time. Café and beerhall 'discussions' were the nearest Hitler came in his Munich period to political involvement. His statement in *Mein Kampf* that 'in the years 1913 and 1914, I, for the first time in various circles which today in part faithfully support the National Socialist movement, expressed the conviction that the question of the future of the German nation was the question of destroying Marxism' elevates coffee-house confrontation into the philosophy of the political prophet.

Hitler's captive audiences in the cafés and beerhalls were for most part the closest he came to human contact in his months in Munich, and presumably offered some sort of outlet for his pent-up prejudice and emotions. Contrary to his own depiction of the Munich months as a time of further preparation for what fate would eventually bring him, it was in reality an empty, lonely, and futile period for him. He was in love with Munich; but Munich was not in love with him. And as regards his own future, he had no more idea where he was going than he had done during his years in the Vienna Men's Home.

He very nearly ended up in an Austrian prison. Already in August 1913 the Linz police had started inquiries about Hitler's whereabouts because of his failure to register for military service. Evasion of military service was punishable by a hefty fine. And leaving Austria to avoid it was treated as desertion and carried a jail sentence. By way of his relatives in Linz, the Viennese police, and the Men's Home in Melde-mannstraße, the trail eventually led to Munich, where the police were able to inform their Linz counterparts that Hitler had been registered since 26 May 1913 as living with the Popps at 34 Schleißheimerstraße. Hitler was shaken to the core when an officer of the Munich criminal police turned up on Frau Popp's doorstep on the afternoon of Sunday, 18 January 1914 with a summons for him to appear two days later in Linz under pain of fine and imprisonment to register for military service, and promptly took him under arrest prior to handing him over to the Austrian authorities. The Munich police had for some reason delayed delivery of the summons for several days before the Sunday, leaving Hitler as a consequence extremely short notice to comply with its demand to be in Linz by the Tuesday. That, together with Hitler's run-down appearance, lack of ready money, apologetic demeanour, and somewhat pathetic explanation influenced the Austrian consulate in Munich to look with some sympathy on his position. He impressed the consular officials, who thought him 'worthy of consideration', and the Linz magistracy now granted him permission to appear, as he had requested, on 5 February, in Salzburg instead of Linz. No fine or imprisonment was imposed; his travel expenses were paid by the consulate. And, in the event, on duly attending at Salzburg he was found to be too weak to undertake military service.

Hitler returned to his mundane life as a small-time artist; but not for long. The storm-clouds were gathering over Europe. On Sunday, 28 June 1914, the sensational news broke of the assassination in Sarajevo of the heir to the Austrian throne, Archduke Franz Ferdinand, and his wife. Germany, like other countries in Europe, became gripped by war fever. By the beginning of August, the Continent was at war.

II

For Hitler, the war was a godsend. Since his failure in the Art Academy in 1907, he had vegetated, resigned to the fact that he would not become a great artist, now cherishing a pipe-dream that he would somehow become a notable architect – though with no plans for or realistic hope of fulfilling this ambition. Seven years after that failure, the 'nobody of Vienna', now in Munich, remained a drop-out and nonentity, futilely angry at a world which had rejected him. He was still without any career prospects, without qualifications or any expectation of gaining them, without any capacity for forging close and lasting friendships, and without real hope of coming to terms with himself – or with a society he despised for his own failure. The war offered him his way out. At the age of twenty-five, it gave him for the first time in his life a cause, a commitment, comradeship, an external discipline, a sort of regular employment, a sense of well-being, and – more than that – a sense of belonging. His regiment became home for him. When he was wounded in 1916 his first words to his superior officer were: 'It's not so bad, Herr Oberleutnant, eh? I can stay with you, stay with the regiment.' Later in the war, the prospect of leaving the regiment may well have influenced his wish not to be considered for promotion. And at the end of the war, he had good practical reasons for staying in the army as long as possible: the army had by then been his 'career' for four years, and he had no other job to go back to or look forward to. The war and its aftermath made Hitler. After Vienna, it was the second formative period in decisively shaping his personality.

At the beginning of August 1914, Hitler was among the tens of thousands in Munich in the thrall of emotional delirium, passionately enthused by the prospect of war. As for so many others, his elation would later turn to deep embitterment. With Hitler, the emotional pendulum set moving by the onset of war swung more violently than for most. 'Overpowered by stormy enthusiasm,' he wrote, 'I fell down on my knees and thanked Heaven from an overflowing heart for granting me the good fortune of being permitted to live at this time.' That on this occasion his words were true cannot be doubted. Years later, noticing a photograph taken by Heinrich Hoffmann (who was to become his court photographer) of the huge patriotic demonstration in front of the Feldherrnhalle on Munich's Odeonsplatz on 2 August 1914, the day after the German declaration of war on Russia, Hitler pointed out that he had been among the emotional crowd that day, carried away with nationalist fervour, hoarse with singing 'Die Wacht am Rhein' and 'Deutschland, Deutschland über alles'. Hoffmann immediately set to work on enlargements, and discovered the face of the twenty-five-year-old Hitler in the centre of the photograph, gripped and enraptured by the war hysteria. The subsequent mass reproduction of the photograph helped contribute to the establishment of the Führer myth – and to Hoffmann's immense profits.

It was doubtless under the impact of the same elation swaying tens of thousands of young men in Munich and many other cities in Europe during those days to rush to join up that, according to his own account, on 3 August, immediately following the Feldherrnhalle demonstration, Hitler submitted a personal petition to King Ludwig III of Bavaria to serve as an Austrian in the Bavarian army. The granting of his request by the cabinet office, he went on, arrived, to his unbounded joy, the very next day. Though this version has been accepted in most accounts, it is scarcely credible. In the confusion of those days, it would have required truly remarkable bureaucratic efficiency for Hitler's request to have been approved overnight. In any case, not the cabinet office but the war ministry was alone empowered to accept foreigners (including Austrians) as volunteers. In reality, Hitler owed his service in the Bavarian army not to bureaucratic efficiency, but to bureaucratic oversight. Detailed inquiries carried out by the Bavarian authorities in 1924 were unable to clarify precisely how, instead of being returned to Austria in August 1914 as should have happened, he came to serve in the Bavarian army. It was presumed that he was among the flood of volunteers who rushed to their nearest place of recruitment in the first days of August, leading, the report added, to not unnatural inconsistencies and breaches of the strict letter of the law. 'In all probability,' commented the report, 'the question of Hitler's nationality was never even raised.' Hitler, it was concluded, almost certainly entered the Bavarian army by error.

Probably, as Hitler wrote in a brief autobiographical sketch in 1921, he volunteered on 5 August 1914 for service in the First Bavarian Infantry Regiment. Like many others in these first chaotic days, he was initially sent away again since there was no immediate use for him. On 16 August he was summoned to report at Recruiting Depot VI in Munich for kitting out by the Second Reserve Battalion of the Second Infantry Regiment. By the beginning of September he had been assigned to the newly formed Bavarian Reserve Infantry Regiment 16 (known from the name of its first commander as the 'List Regiment'), largely comprising raw recruits. After a few weeks of hurried training, they were ready for the front. In the early hours of 21 October, the troop train carrying Hitler left for the battlefields of Flanders.

On 29 October, within six days of arriving in Lille, Hitler's battalion had its baptism of fire on the Menin Road near Ypres. In letters from the front to Joseph Popp and to a Munich acquaintance, Ernst Hepp, Hitler wrote that after four days of fighting, the List Regiment's fighting force had been reduced from 3,600 to 611 men. The initial losses were indeed a staggering 70 per cent. Hitler's initial idealism, he said later, gave way on seeing the thousands killed and injured, to the realization 'that life is a constant horrible struggle'. From now on, death was a daily companion. It immunized him completely against any sensitivity to human suffering. Even more than in the Viennese doss-house, he closed his eyes to sorrow and pity. Struggle, survival, victory: these were all that counted.

On 3 November 1914 (with effect from 1 November), Hitler was promoted to corporal. It was his last promotion of the war, though he could certainly have been expected to advance further, as least as far as non-commissioned officer (*Unteroffizier*). Later in the war, he was in fact nominated for promotion by Max Amann, then a staff sergeant, subsequently Hitler's press baron, and the regimental staff considered making him *Unteroffizier*. Fritz Wiedemann, the regimental adjutant who in the 1930s became for a time one of the Führer's adjutants, testified after the end of the Third Reich that Hitler's superiors had thought him lacking in leadership qualities. However, both Amann and Wiedemann made clear that Hitler, probably because he would have been then transferred from the regimental staff, actually refused to be considered for promotion.

Hitler had been assigned on 9 November to the regimental staff as an orderly – one of a group of eight to ten dispatch runners, whose task was to carry orders, on foot or sometimes by bicycle, from the regimental command post to the battalion and company leaders at the front, three kilometres away. Strikingly, in his *Mein Kampf* account, Hitler omitted to mention that he was a dispatch runner, implying that he actually spent the war in the trenches. But the attempts of his political enemies in the early 1930s to belittle the dangers involved in the duties of the dispatch runner and decry Hitler's war service, accusing him of shirking and cowardice, were misplaced. When, as was not uncommon, the front was relatively quiet, there were certainly times when the dispatch runners could laze around at staff headquarters, where conditions were greatly better than in the trenches. It was in such conditions at regimental headquarters in Fournes en Weppes, near Fromelles in northern France, where Hitler spent nearly half of his wartime service, that he could find the time to paint pictures and read (if his own account can be believed) the works of Schopenhauer that he claimed he carried around with him. Even so, the dangers faced by the dispatch runners during battles, carrying messages to the front through the firing line, were real enough. The losses among dispatch runners were relatively high. If at all possible, two runners would be sent with a message to ensure that it would get through if one happened to be killed. Three of the eight runners attached to the regimental staff were killed and another one wounded in a confrontation with French troops on 15 November. Hitler himself – not for the only time in his life – had luck on his side two days later when a French shell exploded in the regimental forward command post minutes after he had gone out, leaving almost the entire staff there dead or wounded. Among the seriously wounded was the regimental commander Oberstleutnant Philipp Engelhardt, who had been about to propose Hitler for the Iron Cross for his part, assisted by a colleague, in protecting the commander's life under fire a few days earlier. On 2 December, Hitler was finally presented with the Iron Cross, Second Class, one of four dispatch runners among the sixty men from his regiment to receive the honour. It was, he said, 'the happiest day of my life'.

From all indications, Hitler was a committed, rather than simply conscientious and dutiful, soldier, and did not lack physical courage. His superiors held him in high regard. His immediate comrades, mainly the group of dispatch runners, respected him and, it seems, even quite liked him, though he could also plainly irritate as well as puzzle them. His lack of a sense of fun made him an easy target for good-natured ribbing. 'What about looking around for a Mamsell?' suggested a telephonist one day. 'I'd die of shame looking for sex with a French girl,' interjected Hitler, to a burst of laughter from the others. 'Look at the monk,' one said. Hitler's retort was: 'Have you no German sense of honour left at all?' Though his quirkiness singled him out from the rest of his group, Hitler's relations with his immediate comrades were generally good. Most of them later became members of the NSDAP, and, when, as usually happened, they reminded Reich Chancellor Hitler of the time that they had been his comrades in arms, he made sure they were catered for with cash donations and positions as minor functionaries. For all that they got on well with him, they thought 'Adi', as they called him, was distinctly odd. They referred to him as 'the artist' and were struck by the fact that he received no mail or parcels (even at Christmas) after about mid-1915, never spoke of family or friends, neither smoked nor drank, showed no interest in visits to brothels, and used to sit for hours in a corner of the dug-out, brooding or reading. Photographs of him during the war show a thin, gaunt face dominated by a thick, dark, bushy moustache. He was usually on the edge of his group, expressionless where others were smiling. One of his closest comrades, Balthasar Brandmayer, a stonemason from Bruckmühl in the Bad Aibling district of Upper Bavaria, later described his first impressions of Hitler at the end of May 1915: almost skeletal in appearance, dark eyes hooded in a sallow complexion, untrimmed moustache, sitting in a corner buried in a newspaper, occasionally taking a sip of tea, seldom joining in the banter of the group. He seemed an oddity, shaking his head disapprovingly at silly, light-hearted remarks, not even joining in the usual soldiers' moans, gripes, and jibes. 'Haven't you ever loved a girl?' Brandmayer asked Hitler. 'Look, Brandmoiri,' was the straight-faced reply, 'I've never had time for anything like that, and I'll never get round to it.' His only real affection seems to have been for his dog, Foxl, a white terrier that had strayed across from enemy lines. Hitler taught it tricks, revelling in how attached it was to him and how glad it was to see him when he returned from duty. He was distraught late in the war when his unit had to move on and Foxl could not be found. 'The swine who took him from me doesn't know what he did to me,' was his comment many years later. He felt as strongly about none of the thousands of humans he saw slaughtered about him.

About the war itself, Hitler was utterly fanatical. No humanitarian feelings could be allowed to interfere with the ruthless prosecution of German interests. He vehemently disapproved of the spontaneous gestures of friendship at Christmas 1914, when German and British troops met in no man's land, shaking hands and singing carols together. 'There should be no question of something like that during war,' he protested. His comrades knew that they could always provoke Hitler with defeatist comments, real or contrived. All they had to do was to claim the war would be lost and Hitler would go off at the deep end. 'For us the war can't be lost' were invariably his last words. The lengthy letter he sent on 5 February 1915 to his Munich acquaintance, Assessor Ernst Hepp, concluded with an insight into his view of the war redolent of the prejudices that had been consuming him since his Vienna days:

Each of us has only one wish, that it may soon come to the final reckoning with the gang, to the showdown, cost what it will, and that those of us who have the fortune to see their homeland again will find it purer and cleansed of alien influence (*Fremdländerei*), that through the sacrifices and suffering that so many hundred thousand of us make daily, that through the stream of blood that flows here day for day against an international world of enemies, not only will Germany's external enemies be smashed, but that our inner internationalism will also be broken. That would be worth more to me than all territorial gains.

This was how he saw the colossal slaughter; not in terms of human suffering, but as worthwhile for the making of a better, racially cleansed, Germany. Hitler evidently carried such deep-seated sentiments throughout the war. But this political outburst, tagged on to a long description of military events and wartime conditions, was unusual. He appears to have spoken little to his comrades on political matters. Perhaps the fact that his comrades thought him peculiar hindered him from giving voice to his strong opinions. He appears, too, to have scarcely mentioned the Jews. Several former comrades claimed after 1945 that Hitler had at most made a few off-hand though commonplace comments about the Jews in those years, but that they had no inkling then of the unbounded hatred that was so visible after 1918. Balthasar Brandmayer recalled on the other hand in his reminiscences, first published in 1932, that during the war he had 'often not understood Adolf Hitler when he called the Jew the wire-puller behind all misfortune'. According to Brandmayer, Hitler became more politically involved in the latter years of the war and made no secret of his feelings on what he saw as the Social Democrat instigators of growing unrest in Germany. Such comments, like all sources that postdate Hitler's rise to prominence and, as in this case, glorify the prescience of the future leader, have to be treated with caution. But it is difficult to dismiss them out of hand. It indeed does seem very likely, as his own account in *Mein Kampf* claims, that Hitler's political prejudices sharpened in the latter part of the war, during and after his first period of leave in Germany in 1916.

Between March 1915 and September 1916, the List Regiment fought in the trenches near Fromelles, defending a two-kilometre stretch of the stalemated front. Heavy battles with the British were fought in May 1915 and July 1916, but in one and a half years, the front barely moved a few metres. On 27 September 1916, two months after heavy fighting in the second battle of Fromelles, when a British offensive was staved off with difficulty, the regiment moved southwards and by 2 October was engaged on the Somme. Within days, Hitler was wounded in the left thigh when a shell exploded in the dispatch runners' dug-out, killing and wounding several of them. After treatment in a field hospital, he spent almost two months, from 9 October until 1 December 1916, in the Red Cross hospital at Beelitz, near Berlin. He had not been in Germany for two years. He soon noticed how different the mood was from the heady days of August 1914. He was appalled to hear men in the hospital bragging about their malingering or how they had managed to inflict minor injuries on themselves to make sure they could escape from the front. He encountered much the same low morale and widespread discontent in Berlin during the period of his recuperation. It was his first time in the city, and allowed him to pay a visit to the Nationalgalerie. But Munich shocked him most of all. He scarcely recognized the city: 'Anger, discontent, cursing, wherever you went!' Morale was poor; people were dispirited; conditions were miserable; and, as was traditional in Bavaria, the blame was placed on the Prussians. Hitler himself, according to his own account written about eight years later, saw in all this only the work of the Jews. He was struck too, so he said, by the number of Jews in clerical positions – 'nearly every clerk was a Jew and nearly every Jew was a clerk' – compared with how few of them were serving at the front. (In fact, this was a base calumny: there was as good as no difference between the proportion of Jews and non-Jews in the German army, relative to their numbers in the total population, and many Jews served – some in the List Regiment – with great distinction.) There is no reason to presume, as has sometimes been the case, that this account of his anti-Jewish feelings in 1916 was a backwards projection of feelings that in reality only existed from 1918–19 onwards. Though, as we have noted, Hitler did not stand out for his antisemitism in the recollections of some of his former wartime comrades, two of them did refer to his negative comments about the Jews. And Hitler would have been voicing sentiments that were increasingly to be heard in the streets of Munich as anti-Jewish prejudice became more widespread and more ferocious in the second half of the war.

Hitler wanted to get back to the front as soon as possible, and above all to rejoin his old regiment. He eventually returned to it on 5 March 1917 in its new position a few miles to the north of Vimy. In the summer it was back to the same ground near Ypres that the regiment had fought over almost three years earlier, to counter the major Flanders offensive launched by the British in mid-July 1917. Battered by the heavy fighting, the regiment was relieved at the beginning of August and transported to Alsace. At the end of September, Hitler took normal leave for the first time. He had no wish to go back to Munich, which had dispirited him so much, and went to Berlin instead, to stay with the parents of one of his comrades. His postcards to friends in the regiment spoke of how much he enjoyed his eighteen-day leave, and how thrilled he was by Berlin and its museums. In mid-October, he returned to his regiment, which had just moved from Alsace to Champagne. Bitter fighting in April 1918 brought huge losses, and during the last two weeks of July the regiment was involved in the second battle of the Marne. It was the last major German offensive of the war. By early August, when it collapsed in the face of a tenacious Allied counter-offensive, German losses in the previous four months of savage combat had amounted to around 800,000 men. The failure of the offensive marked the point where, with reserves depleted and morale plummeting, Germany's military leadership was compelled to recognize that the war was lost.

On 4 August 1918, Hitler received the Iron Cross, First Class – a rare achievement for a corporal – from the regimental commander, Major von Tubeuf. By a stroke of irony, he had a Jewish officer, Leutnant Hugo Gutmann, to thank for the nomination. The story was later to be found in all school books that the Führer had received the EK I for single-handedly capturing fifteen French soldiers. The truth, as usual, was somewhat more prosaic. From the available evidence, including the recommendation of the List Regiment's Deputy Commander Freiherr von Godin on 31 July 1918, the award was made – as it was also to a fellow dispatch runner – for bravery shown in delivering an important dispatch, following a breakdown in telephone communications, from command headquarters to the front through heavy fire. Gutmann, from what he subsequently said, had promised both dispatch runners the EK I if they succeeded in delivering the message. But since the action was, though certainly courageous, not strikingly exceptional, it was only after several weeks of his belabouring the divisional commander that permission for the award was granted.

By mid-August 1918, the List Regiment had moved to Cambrai to help combat a British offensive near Bapaume, and a month later was back in action once more in the vicinity of Wytschaete and Messines, where Hitler had received his EK II almost four years earlier. This time Hitler was away from the battlefields. In late August he had been sent for a week to Nuremberg for telephone communications training, and on 10 September he began his second period of eighteen days' leave, again in Berlin. Immediately on his return, at the end of September, his unit was put under pressure from British assaults near Comines. Gas was now in extensive use in offensives, and protection against it was minimal and primitive. The List Regiment, like others, suffered badly. On the night of 13–14 October, Hitler himself fell victim to mustard gas on the heights south of Wervick, part of the southern front near Ypres. He and several comrades, retreating from their dug-out during a gas attack, were partially blinded by the gas and found their way to safety only by clinging on to each other and following a comrade who was slightly less badly afflicted. After initial treatment in Flanders, Hitler was transported on 21 October 1918 to the military hospital in Pasewalk, near Stettin, in Pomerania.

The war was over for him. And, little though he knew it, the Army High Command was already manoeuvring to extricate itself from blame for a war it accepted was lost and a peace which would soon have to be negotiated. It was in Pasewalk, recovering from his temporary blindness, that Hitler was to learn the shattering news of defeat and revolution – what he called 'the greatest villainy of the century'.

III

In reality, of course, there had been no treachery, no stab-in-the-back. This was pure invention of the Right, a legend the Nazis would use as a central element of their propaganda armoury. Unrest at home was a consequence, not a cause, of military failure. Germany had been militarily defeated and was close to the end of its tether – though nothing had prepared people for capitulation. In fact, triumphalist propaganda was still coming from the High Command in late October 1918. The army was by then exhausted, and in the previous four months had suffered heavier losses than at any time during the war. Desertions and 'shirking' – deliberately ducking duty (estimated at close on a million men in the last months of the war) – rose dramatically. At home, the mood was one of mounting protest – embittered, angry, and increasingly rebellious. The revolution was not fabricated by Bolshevik sympathizers and unpatriotic troublemakers, but grew out of the profound disillusionment and rising unrest which had set in even as early as 1915 and from 1916 onwards had flowed into what finally became a torrent of disaffection. The society which had seemingly entered the war in total patriotic unity ended it completely riven – and traumatized by the experience.

Amid the social division, there were certain common targets of aggression. War profiteering – a theme on which Hitler was able to play so effectively in the Munich beerhalls in 1920 – rankled deeply. Closely related was the bitter resentment at those running the black market. Petty officialdom, with its unremitting and intensified bureaucratic intervention into every sphere of daily life, was a further target. But the fury did not confine itself to the interference and incompetence of petty bureaucrats. These were merely the face of a state whose authority was crumbling visibly, a state in terminal disarray and disintegration.

Not least, in the search for scapegoats, Jews increasingly became the focus of intensified hatred and aggression from the middle of the war onwards. The sentiments had all been heard before. What was new was the extent to which radical antisemitism was now being propagated, and the degree to which it was evidently falling on fertile ground. Heinrich Claß, the leader of the arch-nationalist Pan-Germans, could report in October 1917 that antisemitism had 'already reached enormous proportions' and that 'the struggle for survival was now beginning for the Jews'. Events in Russia in 1917 further stirred the pot of simmering hatred, adding the vital ingredient – to become thereafter the keystone of antisemitic agitation – of the Jews portrayed as running secret international organizations directed at fomenting world revolution. As it was realized that the war was lost, antisemitic hysteria, whipped up by the Pan-Germanists, reached fever pitch. Claß used the notorious words of Heinrich von Kleist, aimed at the French in 1813, when a 'Jewish Committee' with the purpose of 'exploiting the situation to sound the clarion call against Judaism and to use the Jews as lightning rods for all injustices' was set up by the Pan-Germans in September 1918: 'Kill them; the world court is not asking you for your reasons!'

IV

The atmosphere of disintegration and collapsing morale, the climate of political and ideological radicalization, in the last two war years could not but make the deepest impression on a Hitler who had welcomed the war so rapturously, had supported German aims so fanatically, and had from the outset condemned all defeatist suggestions so vehemently. He was repelled by many attitudes he encountered at the front. But, as we have seen, it was during the three periods, amounting in total to over three months, that he spent in Germany either on leave or recovering from injury in the last two war years that he experienced a level of disaffection at the running of the war which was new and deeply appalling to him. He had been shocked at the atmosphere in Berlin and, even more so, Munich in 1916. As the war dragged on, he became incensed by the talk of revolution, and incandescent at news of the munitions strike in favour of early peace without annexations which had spread briefly at the end of January 1918 from Berlin to other major industrial cities (though with little actual effect on munitions supplies).

The last two years of the war, between his convalescence in Beelitz in October 1916 and his hospitalization in Pasewalk in October 1918, can probably be seen as a vital staging-post in Hitler's ideological development. The prejudices and phobias carried over from the Vienna years were now plainly evident in his embittered rage about the collapse of the war effort – the first cause in his life to which he had totally bound himself, the summation of all that he had believed in. But they had not yet been fully rationalized into the component parts of a political ideology. That would only emerge fully during Hitler's own 'political training' in the Reichswehr in the course of 1919.

What part the hospitalization in Pasewalk played in the shaping of Hitler's ideology, what significance it had for the shaping of the future party leader and dictator, has been much disputed and, in truth, is not easy to evaluate. In Hitler's own account it has a pivotal place. Recovering from his temporary blindness, but unable to read newspapers, so he wrote, Hitler heard rumours of pending revolution but did not fully comprehend them. The arrival of some mutineering sailors was the first tangible sign of serious disturbance, but Hitler and fellow-patients from Bavaria presumed the unrest would be crushed within a few days. However, it became soon clear – 'the most terrible certainty of my life' – that a general revolution had taken place. On 10 November, a pastor addressed the patients in sorrowful terms about the end of the monarchy and informed them that Germany was now a republic, that the war was lost and that Germans had to place themselves at the mercy of the victors. At this, Hitler later wrote:

I could stand it no longer. It became impossible for me to sit still one minute more. Again everything went black before my eyes; I tottered and groped my way back to the dormitory, threw myself on my bunk, and dug my burning head into my blanket and pillow.

Since the day when I had stood at my mother's grave, I had not wept . . . But now I could not help it . . .

And so it had all been in vain . . . Did all this happen only so that a gang of wretched criminals could lay hands on the fatherland? . . .

The more I tried to achieve clarity on the monstrous event in this hour, the more the shame of indignation and disgrace burned my brow. What was all the pain in my eyes compared to this misery?

There followed terrible days and even worse nights – I knew that all was lost ... In these nights hatred grew in me, hatred for those responsible for this deed.

In the days that followed, my own fate became known to me.

I could not help but laugh at the thought of my own future which only a short time before had given me such bitter concern ...

He drew, according to his own account, the conclusion that: 'There is no making pacts with Jews; there can only be the hard: either-or.' And he made the decision that changed his life: 'I, for my part, decided to go into politics.'

Hitler referred to his Pasewalk experience on a number of occasions in the early 1920s, sometimes even with embellishments. Some have been tempted to read into Hitler's colourful accounts an hallucination which holds the key to his manic ideological obsessions, his 'mission' to save Germany, and his rapport with a German people themselves traumatized by defeat and national humiliation. The balance of probabilities suggests a less dramatic process of ideological development and political awareness.

Without question, Hitler was more than just deeply outraged by the news of the revolution. He felt it to be an absolute and unpardonable betrayal of all that he believed in, and, in pain, discomfort, and bitterness, looked for the culprits who would provide him with an explanation of how his world had collapsed. There is no need to doubt that for Hitler these intensely disturbing few days did amount to no less than a traumatic experience. From the following year onwards, his entire political activity was driven by the trauma of 1918 – aimed at expunging the defeat and revolution which had betrayed all that he had believed in, and eliminating those he held responsible.

But if there is any strength in the suggestion we have put forward that Hitler acquired his deep-seated prejudices, including his antisemitism, in Vienna, and had them revitalized during the last two war years, if without rationalizing them into a composite ideology, then there is no need to mystify the Pasewalk experience through seeing it as a sudden, dramatic conversion to paranoid antisemitism. Rather, Pasewalk might be viewed as the time when, as Hitler lay tormented and seeking an

explanation of how his world had been shattered, his own rationalization started to fall into place. Devastated by the events unfolding in
Munich, Berlin, and other cities, he must have read into them outright
confirmation of the views he had always held from the Vienna days
on Jews and Social Democrats, on Marxism and internationalism, on
pacifism and democracy. Even so, it was still only the *beginning* of the
rationalization. The full fusion of his antisemitism and anti-Marxism
was yet to come. There is no authentic evidence that Hitler, up to and
including this point, had said a word about Bolshevism. Nor would he
do so, even in his early public speeches in Munich, before 1920. The
connection of Bolshevism with his internal hate-figures, its incorporation
into and adoption of a central place in his 'world-view', came only
during his time in the Reichswehr in the summer of 1919. And later
still came the preoccupation with 'living space' – only emerging into a
dominant theme during the composition of *Mein Kampf* between 1924
and 1926. Pasewalk was a crucial step on the way to Hitler's rationalization of his prejudices. But even more important, in all probability, was
the time he spent in the Reichswehr in 1919.

The last implausible point of Hitler's Pasewalk story is that he resolved
there and then to enter politics. In none of his speeches before the putsch
in November 1923 did Hitler say a word about deciding in autumn
1918 to enter politics. In fact, Hitler was in no position in Pasewalk to
'decide' to enter politics – or anything else. The end of the war meant
that, like most other soldiers, he faced demobilization. The army had
been his home for four years. But now once more his future was
uncertain.

When he left Pasewalk on 19 November 1918 to return, via Berlin,
to Munich, he had savings totalling only 15 Marks 30 Pfennige in his
Munich account. No career awaited him. Nor did he make any effort to
enter politics. Indeed, it is not easy to see how he could have done so.
Neither family nor 'connections' were available to gain him some minor
patronage in a political party. A 'decision' to enter politics, should Hitler
have made one in Pasewalk, would have been empty of meaning. Only
staying in the army offered him the hope of avoiding the evil day when
he would once more have to face up to the fact that, four turbulent years
on, he was no nearer his chosen career as an architect than he had been
in 1914, and was without any prospects whatsoever. The future looked
bleak. A return to the lonely existence of the pre-war small-time painter

had no appeal. But little else beckoned. The army gave him his chance. He was able to stave off demobilization longer than almost all his former comrades, and to keep on the payroll, until 31 March 1920.

It was in the army in 1919 that his ideology finally took shape. Above all, the army, in the extraordinary circumstances of 1919, turned Hitler into a propagandist – the most talented demagogue of his day. Not a deliberate choice, but making the most of the conditions in which he found himself, provided Hitler with his entry into politics. Opportunism – and a good slice of luck – were more instrumental than strength of will.

4

The Beerhall Agitator

I

On 21 November 1918, two days after leaving hospital in Pasewalk, Hitler was back in Munich. Approaching thirty years of age, without education, career, or prospects, his only plans were to stay in the army, which had been his home and provided for him since 1914, as long as possible. He came back to a Munich he scarcely recognized. The barracks to which he returned were run by soldiers' councils. The revolutionary Bavarian government, in the shape of a provisional National Council, was in the hands of the Social Democrats and the more radical Independent Social Democrats (the USPD). The Minister President, Kurt Eisner, was a radical; and he was a Jew.

The revolution in Bavaria had preceded that in the Reich itself. It took place in circumstances and developed in ways that were to leave a profound mark on Hitler, and to fit more than the events in Berlin into what became the Nazi caricature of the 1918 revolution. It was more radical, with the leadership in the hands of the Independents; it degenerated into near-anarchy, then into a short-lived attempt to create a Communist-run Soviet-style system; this in turn led to a few days – though a few days which seared the consciousness of Bavarians for many years to come – that amounted to a mini-civil war, ending in bloodshed and brutality; and a number of the revolutionary leaders happened to be Jewish, some of them east European Jews with Bolshevik sympathies and connections. Moreover, the leader of the Bavarian revolution, the Jewish journalist and left-wing socialist Kurt Eisner, a prominent peace-campaigner in the USPD since the split with the Majority Social Democrats in 1917, together with some of his USPD colleagues, had unquestionably tried to stir up industrial unrest during the 'January

Strike' in 1918, and had been arrested for his actions. That was to fit nicely into the Right's 'stab-in-the-back' legend.

The provisional government that was soon constituted under Eisner's leadership was from the outset a highly unstable coalition, mainly composed of the radical but largely idealistic USPD and the 'moderate' SPD (which had not even wanted a revolution). Moreover, it stood no chance of mastering the daunting social and economic problems it faced. The assassination of Eisner by a young, aristocratic former officer, currently a student at Munich University, Graf Anton von Arco-Valley, on 21 February 1919, provided then the signal for a deterioration into chaos and near-anarchy. Members of the USPD and anarchists proclaimed a 'Councils Republic' in Bavaria. The initial failure of attempts at counter-revolution simply strengthened the resolve of the revolutionary hot-heads and ushered in the last phase of the Bavarian revolution: the full Communist takeover in the second, or 'real' Räterepublik – an attempt to introduce a Soviet-style system in Bavaria. It lasted little more than a fortnight. But it ended in violence, bloodshed, and deep recrimination, imposing a baleful legacy on the political climate of Bavaria.

It would be hard to exaggerate the impact on political consciousness in Bavaria of the events between November 1918 and May 1919, and quite especially of the Räterepublik. At its very mildest, it was experienced in Munich itself as a time of curtailed freedom, severe food shortages, press censorship, general strike, sequestration of foodstuffs, coal, and items of clothing, and general disorder and chaos. But, of more lasting significance, it went down in popular memory as a 'rule of horror' imposed by foreign elements in the service of Soviet Communism. The image, constructed and massively shored up by rightist propaganda throughout the Reich as well as in Bavaria itself, was that of alien – Bolshevik and Jewish – forces taking over the state, threatening institutions, traditions, order, and property, presiding over chaos and mayhem, perpetrating terrible acts of violence, and causing anarchy of advantage only to Germany's enemies. The real gainers from the disastrous weeks of the Räterepublik were the radical Right, which had been given the fuel to stoke the fear and hatred of Bolshevism among the Bavarian peasantry and middle classes. Not least, extreme counter-revolutionary violence had come to be accepted as a legitimate response to the perceived Bolshevik threat and now became a regular feature of the political scene.

Its flirt with left-wing socialism over, Bavaria turned in the following years into a bastion of the conservative Right and a magnet for right-wing extremists throughout Germany. These were the conditions in which the 'making of Adolf Hitler' could take place.

The history of the Bavarian revolution was almost tailor-made for Nazi propaganda. Not just the legend of the 'stab-in-the-back', but the notion of an international Jewish conspiracy could be made to sound plausible in the light of the Munich Räterepublik. Though right-wing extremism had no stronger traditions in Bavaria than elsewhere up to this point, the new climate provided it with unique opportunities and the favour of a sympathetic establishment. Many of Hitler's early followers were deeply influenced by the experience of the turbulent months of post-revolutionary Bavaria. For Hitler himself, the significance of the period of revolution and Räterepublik in Munich can hardly be overrated.

II

On his return to Munich, Hitler had been assigned to the 7th Company of the 1st Reserve Battalion of the 2nd Infantry Regiment, where, a few days later, he met up again with several wartime comrades. A fortnight later, he and one of these comrades, Ernst Schmidt, were among the fifteen men from his company (and 140 men in all) assigned to guard duties at the Traunstein prisoner-of-war camp. Probably, as Schmidt later recounted, Hitler suggested they let their names go forward when volunteers were called for to make up the deputation. Hitler, remarked Schmidt, did not have much to say about the revolution, 'but it was plain enough to see how bitter he felt'. Both, according to Schmidt, were repelled by the changed conditions in the Munich barracks, now in the hands of the soldiers' councils, where old standards of authority, discipline, and morale had collapsed. If that was indeed the reason for volunteering, Hitler and Schmidt could have found no improvement on reaching Traunstein. The camp, meant to contain 1,000 prisoners but much overcrowded, was also run by the soldiers' councils which Hitler allegedly so detested. Discipline was poor, and the guards, according to one source, included some of the worst elements among the troops who – like Hitler – saw the army 'as a means of maintaining a carefree existence at the expense of the state'. Hitler and Schmidt had an easy time of things, mainly on gate-duty, at Traunstein. They were there in all for almost two months, during which time the prisoners-of-war, mainly Russians, were transported elsewhere. By the beginning of February the camp was completely cleared and disbanded. Probably in late January, as Schmidt hinted, Hitler returned to Munich. Then, for just over two weeks, beginning on 20 February, he was assigned to guard duty at the Hauptbahnhof, where a unit of his company was responsible for maintaining order, particularly among the many soldiers travelling to and from Munich.

A routine order of the demobilization battalion on 3 April 1919 referred to Hitler by name as the representative (*Vertrauensmann*) of his company. The strong likelihood is, in fact, that he had held this position since 15 February. The duties of the representatives included cooperation with the propaganda department of the socialist government in order to convey 'educational' material to the troops. Hitler's first political duties took place, therefore, in the service of the revolutionary regime run by the SPD and USPD. It is little wonder that in *Mein Kampf* he quickly passed over his own experience of the traumatic revolutionary period in Bavaria.

In fact, he would have had to explain away the even more embarrassing fact of his continued involvement at the very height of Munich's 'red dictatorship'. On 14 April, the day after the communist Räterepublik had been proclaimed, the Munich soldiers' councils approved fresh elections of all barrack representatives to ensure that the Munich garrison stood loyally behind the new regime. In the elections the following day Hitler was chosen as Deputy Battalion Representative. Not only, then, did Hitler do nothing to assist in the crushing of Munich's 'Red Republic'; he was an elected representative of his battalion during the whole period of its existence.

Already in the 1920s, and continuing into the 1930s, there were rumours, never fully countered, that Hitler had initially sympathized with the Majority SPD following the revolution. There were even reported rumours – though without any supportive evidence – that Hitler had spoken of joining the SPD. In a pointed remark when defending Hermann Esser, one of his earliest supporters, in 1921 against attacks from within the party, Hitler commented: 'Everyone was at one time a Social Democrat.'

In itself, Hitler's possible support for the Majority Social Democrats in the revolutionary upheaval is less unlikely than it might at first sight appear. The political situation was extremely confused and uncertain. A number of strange bedfellows, including several who later came to belong to Hitler's entourage, initially found themselves on the Left during the revolution. Esser, who became the first propaganda chief of the NSDAP, had been for a while a journalist on a Social Democratic newspaper. Sepp Dietrich, later a general in the Waffen-SS and head of Hitler's SS-Leibstandarte, was elected chairman of a soldiers' council in November 1918. Hitler's long-time chauffeur Julius Schreck had served in the 'Red Army' at the end of April 1919. Gottfried Feder, whose views on 'interest slavery' so gripped Hitler's imagination in summer 1919, had sent a statement of his position to the socialist government headed by Kurt Eisner the previous November. And Balthasar Brand-mayer, one of Hitler's closest wartime comrades and a later fervent supporter, recounted how he at first welcomed the end of the mon-archies, the establishment of a republic, and the onset of a new era. Ideological muddle-headedness, political confusion, and opportunism, combined frequently to produce fickle and shifting allegiances.

That, as has been implied, Hitler was inwardly sympathetic to Social Democracy and formed his own characteristic racist-nationalist *Weltan-schauung* only following an ideological volte-face under the influence of his 'schooling' in the Reichswehr after the collapse of the Räterepublik is, however, harder to believe. If Hitler felt compelled to lean outwardly towards the Majority Social Democrats during the revolutionary months, it was not prompted by conviction but by sheer opportunism aimed at avoiding for as long as possible demobilization from the army.

Whatever his opportunism and passivity, Hitler's antagonism to the revolutionary Left was probably evident to those around him in the barracks during the months of mounting turmoil in Munich. If indeed, as was later alleged, he voiced support for the Social Democrats in preference to the Communists, it was presumably viewed as a choice of the lesser of two evils, or even, by those in Hitler's unit who knew him of old, as an opportune adjustment betraying none of his real nationalist, pan-German sympathies. Ernst Schmidt, for example, who by then had been discharged but was still in regular touch with him, spoke later of Hitler's 'utter repugnance' at the events in Munich. The nineteen votes cast for 'Hittler' on 16 April, electing him as the second company representative – the winner, Johann Blüml, received 39 votes – on the Battalion Council, may well have been from those who saw him in this light. That there were tensions within the barracks, and between the soldiers' elected representatives, might be read out of the subsequent denunciation by Hitler of two colleagues on the Battalion Council at the Munich tribunal investigating the actions of the soldiers of his regiment during the Räterepublik. Hitler was probably known to those around him, at the latest towards the end of April, for the counter-revolutionary he really was, whose actual sympathies were indistinguishable from those of the 'white' troops preparing to storm the city. Significant, above all, is that within a week of the end of the rule of the councils, Hitler had been nominated – by whom is not known – to serve on a three-man committee to explore whether members of the Reserve Battalion of the 2nd Infantry Regiment had been actively involved in the Räterepublik. This speaks in favour of the recognition within his battalion of his deep antagonism to 'red' rule. At any rate, his new role now prevented Hitler being discharged, along with the rest of the Munich garrison, by the end of May 1919. More importantly, it brought him for the first time into the orbit of counter-revolutionary politics within the Reichswehr. This, rather than any psychological trauma in Pasewalk at the news of the defeat, any dramatic decision to rescue Germany from the 'November criminals', was, within the following months, to open up his path into the maelstrom of extreme right-wing politics in Munich.

III

On 11 May 1919, under the command of Generalmajor von Möhl, the Bayerische Reichswehr Gruppenkommando Nr.4 ('Gruko' for short) was created from the Bavarian units that had been involved in the crushing of the Räterepublik. With the Bavarian government 'exiled' in Bamberg until the end of August, Munich – its centre crammed with barricades, barbed wire, and army control-points – was throughout the spring and summer a city effectively under military rule. Recognizing twin tasks of extensive surveillance of the political scene and combating by means of propaganda and indoctrination 'dangerous' attitudes prevalent in the transitional army, Gruko took over in May 1919 the 'Information Department' (Nachrichtenabteilung, Abt. Ib/P) which had been immediately established in Munich at the suppression of the Räterepublik. The 'education' of the troops in a 'correct' anti-Bolshevik, nationalist fashion was rapidly regarded as a priority, and 'speaker courses' were devised in order to train 'suitable personalities from the troops' who would remain for some considerable time in the army and function as propaganda agents with qualities of persuasion capable of negating subversive ideas. The organization of a series of 'anti-Bolshevik courses', beginning in early June, was placed in the hands of Captain Karl Mayr, who, a short while earlier, on 30 May, had taken over the command of the Information Department. Mayr, one of the 'mid-wives' of Hitler's political 'career', could certainly have claimed prime responsibility for its initial launch.

In 1919, Mayr's influence in the Munich Reichswehr extended beyond his rank as captain, and he was endowed with considerable funds to build up a team of agents or informants, organize the series of 'educational' courses to train selected officers and men in 'correct' political and ideological thinking, and finance 'patriotic' parties, publications, and organizations. Mayr first met Hitler in May 1919, after the crushing of the 'Red Army'. Hitler's involvement in his battalion's investigations into subversive actions during the Räterepublik may have drawn him to Mayr's attention. And we saw that Hitler had already been engaged in propaganda work in his barracks earlier in the spring – though on behalf of the socialist government. He had the right credentials and ideal potential for Mayr's purposes. When he first met Hitler, Mayr wrote much later, 'he was like a tired stray dog looking for a master', and 'ready to throw in his lot with anyone who would show him kindness . . . He was totally unconcerned about the German people and their destinies.'

The name 'Hittler Adolf' appears on one of the early lists of names of informants (*V-Leute* or *V-Männer*) drawn up by the Information Department Ib/P at the end of May or beginning of June 1919. Within days he had been assigned to the first of the anti-Bolshevik 'instruction courses', to take place in Munich University between 5 and 12 June 1919. For the first time, Hitler was to receive here some form of directed political 'education'. This, as he acknowledged, was important to him; as was the fact that he realized for the first time that he could make an impact on those around him. Here he heard lectures from prominent figures in Munich, hand-picked by Mayr, partly through personal acquaintance, on 'German History since the Reformation', 'The Political

History of the War', 'Socialism in Theory and Practice', 'Our Economic Situation and the Peace Conditions', and 'The Connection between Domestic and Foreign Policy'. Among the speakers, too, was Gottfried Feder, who had made a name for himself among the Pan-Germans as an economics expert. His lecture on the 'breaking of interest slavery' (a slogan Hitler recognized as having propaganda potential), on which he had already published a 'manifesto' – highly regarded in nationalist circles – distinguishing between 'productive' capital and 'rapacious' capital (which he associated with the Jews), made a deep impression on Hitler, and eventually led to Feder's role as the economics 'guru' of the early Nazi Party. The history lectures were delivered by the Munich historian Professor Karl Alexander von Müller, who had known Mayr at school. Following his first lecture, he came across a small group in the emptying lecture hall surrounding a man addressing them in a passionate, strikingly guttural, tone. He mentioned to Mayr after his next lecture that one of his trainees had natural rhetorical talent. Von Müller pointed out where he was sitting. Mayr recognized him immediately: it was 'Hitler from the List Regiment'.

Hitler himself thought this incident – he said he had been roused to intervene by one of the participants defending the Jews – had led directly to his deployment as an 'educational officer' (*Bildungsoffizier*). However, he was never a *Bildungsoffizier*, but remained a mere informant, a *V-Mann*. Plainly, the incident helped to focus Mayr's attention on Hitler. But it was certainly Mayr's regular close observation of Hitler's activity for his department rather than a single incident that led to the latter's selection as one of a squad of twenty-six instructors – all drawn from the participants in the Munich 'instruction courses' – to be sent to conduct a five-day course at the Reichswehr camp at Lechfeld, near Augsburg. The course, beginning on 20 August 1919, the day after Hitler's arrival in the camp, was arranged in response to complaints about the political unreliability of men stationed there, many having returned from being held as prisoners-of-war and now awaiting discharge. The task of the squad was to inculcate nationalist and anti-Bolshevik sentiments in the troops, described as 'infected' by Bolshevism and Spartacism. It was in effect the continuation of what the instructors themselves had been exposed to in Munich.

Alongside the commander of the unit, Rudolf Beyschlag, Hitler undertook the lion's share of the work, including helping to stir discussion of

Beyschlag's lectures on, for example, 'Who Bears the Guilt for the World War?' and 'From the Days of the Munich Räterepublik'. He himself gave lectures on 'Peace Conditions and Reconstruction', 'Emigration', and 'Social and Economic Catchwords'. He threw himself with passion into the work. His engagement was total. And he immediately found he could strike a chord with his audience, that the way he spoke roused the soldiers listening to him from their passivity and cynicism. Hitler was in his element. For the first time in his life, he had found something at which he was an unqualified success. Almost by chance, he had stumbled across his greatest talent. As he himself put it, he could 'speak'.

Participants' reports on the course confirm that Hitler was not exaggerating the impact he made in Lechfeld: he was without question the star performer. A central feature of his demagogic armoury was antisemitism. In his ferocious attacks on the Jews, he was, however, doing no more than reflect sentiments which were widespread at the time among the people of Munich, as reports on the popular mood demonstrated. The responses to Hitler's addresses at Lechfeld indicate how accessible the soldiers were to his way of speaking. The commander of the Lechfeld camp, Oberleutnant Bendt, even felt obliged to request Hitler to tone down his antisemitism, in order to prevent possible objections to the lectures as provoking antisemitic agitation. This followed a lecture by Hitler on capitalism, in which he had 'touched on' the 'Jewish Question'. It is the first reference to Hitler speaking publicly about the Jews.

Within the group, and certainly in the eyes of his superior, Captain Mayr, Hitler must have acquired the reputation of an 'expert' on the 'Jewish Question'. When Mayr was asked, in a letter of 4 September 1919 from a former participant on one of the 'instruction courses', Adolf Gemlich from Ulm, for clarification of the 'Jewish Question', particularly in relation to the policies of the Social Democratic government, he passed it to Hitler – whom he evidently regarded highly – for an answer. Hitler's well-known reply to Gemlich, dated 16 September 1919, is his first recorded written statement about the 'Jewish Question'. He wrote that antisemitism should be based not on emotion, but on 'facts', the first of which was that Jewry was a race, not a religion. Emotive antisemitism would produce pogroms, he continued; antisemitism based on 'reason' must, on the other hand, lead to the systematic removal of the rights of Jews. 'Its final aim,' he concluded, 'must unshakeably be the removal of the Jews altogether.'

The Gemlich letter reveals for the first time key basic elements of Hitler's *Weltanschauung* which from then on remained unaltered to the last days in the Berlin bunker: antisemitism resting on race theory; and the creation of a unifying nationalism founded on the need to combat the external and internal power of the Jews.

IV

Following his success at Lechfeld, he was by this time plainly Mayr's favourite and right-hand man. Among the duties of the informants assigned to Mayr was the surveillance of fifty political parties and organizations ranging from the extreme Right to the far Left in Munich. It was as an informant that Hitler was sent, on Friday, 12 September 1919, to report on a meeting of the German Workers' Party in Munich's Sterneckerbräu. He was accompanied by at least two former comrades from Lechfeld. The speaker was to have been the *völkisch* poet and publicist Dietrich Eckart, but he was ill and Gottfried Feder stood in to lecture on the 'breaking of interest slavery'. According to his own account, Hitler had heard the lecture before, so took to observing the party itself, which he held to be a 'boring organization', no different from the many other small parties sprouting in every corner of Munich at that time. He was about to leave when, in the discussion following the lecture, an invited guest, a Professor Baumann, attacked Feder and then spoke in favour of Bavarian separatism. At this Hitler intervened so heatedly that Baumann, totally deflated, took his hat and left even while Hitler was still speaking, looking 'like a wet poodle'. The party chairman, Anton Drexler, was so impressed by Hitler's intervention that at the end of the meeting he pushed a copy of his own pamphlet, *My Political Awakening*, into his hand, inviting him to return in a few days if he were interested in joining the new movement. 'Goodness, he's got a gob. We could use him,' Drexler was reported to have remarked. According to Hitler's own account, he read Drexler's pamphlet in the middle of a sleepless night, and it struck a chord with him, reminding him, he claimed, of his own 'political awakening' twelve years earlier. Within a week of attending the meeting, he then received a postcard informing him that he had been accepted as a member, and should attend a committee meeting of the party a few days later to discuss the matter. Though his immediate reaction, he wrote, was a negative one – he allegedly wanted to found a party of his own – curiosity overcame him and he went along to a dimly-lit meeting of the small leadership group in the Altes Rosenbad, a shabby pub in Herrenstraße. He sympathized with the political aims of those he met. But he was appalled, he later wrote, at the small-minded organization he encountered – 'club life of the worst manner and sort', he dubbed it. After a few days of indecision, he added, he finally made up his mind to join. What determined him was the feeling that such a small organization offered 'the individual an opportunity for real personal activity' – the prospect, that is, of quickly making his mark and dominating it.

Some time during the second half of September, Hitler joined the German Workers' Party, and was given the membership number 555. He was not, as he always claimed, the seventh member. As the first party leader, Anton Drexler, put it in a letter addressed to Hitler in January 1940, but never sent:

No one knows better than you yourself, my Führer, that you were never the seventh member of the party, but at best the seventh member of the committee, which I asked you to join as recruitment director (*Werbeobmann*). And a few years ago I had to complain to a party office that your first proper membership card of the DAP . . . was falsified, with the number 555 being erased and number 7 entered.

Like so much of what Hitler had to say in *Mein Kampf* about his earlier life, his account of entering the party cannot be taken at face value, and was devised, like everything else, to serve the Führer legend that was already being cultivated. And whatever Hitler wrote about wrangling for days about whether or not to join the DAP, the decision might not ultimately have been his to take. In a little noticed piece of evidence, his Reichswehr boss Captain Mayr later claimed that he had *ordered* Hitler to join the German Workers' Party to help foster its growth. For this purpose, Mayr went on, he was provided at first with funds – around the equivalent of 20 gold Marks a week – and, contrary to normal practice about members of the Reichswehr joining political parties, was allowed to stay in the army. He was able to do this, drawing his army pay as well as speaker fees, until his discharge on 31 March 1920. This already enabled him – in contrast to the other DAP leaders who had to fit politics around their normal jobs – to devote all his time to political propaganda. Now, on leaving the army, his confidence boosted by his early successes as a DAP speaker in the Munich beerhalls, he was in a position to do what, since he had made his mark in the anti-Bolshevik course at Munich University and worked with Mayr as a Reichswehr propagandist and informant, had emerged as a ready-made career-opening to replace the fantasies of becoming a great architect and the realities of returning to an existence as a small-time painter of street scenes and tourist attractions. Without Captain Mayr's 'talent-spotting', Hitler might never have been heard of. As it was, if only on the beerhall fringes, he could now become a full-time political agitator and propagandist. He could do for a living the only thing he was good at doing: speaking.

The path from Pasewalk to becoming the main attraction of the DAP had not been determined by any sudden recognition of a 'mission' to save Germany, by strength of personality, or by a 'triumph of the will'. It had been shaped by circumstance, opportunism, good fortune, and, not least, the backing of the army, represented through Mayr's important patronage. Hitler did not come to politics; politics came to him – in the Munich barracks. His contribution, after making his mark through a readiness to denounce his comrades following the Räterepublik, had been confined to an unusual talent for appealing to the gutter instincts of his listeners, in the Lechfeld camp, then in the Munich beerhalls, coupled with a sharp eye to exploiting the main chance of advancement. These 'qualities' would prove invaluable in the coming years.

V

Without the Reichswehr's 'discovery' of his talent for nationalist agitation, Hitler had every prospect of returning to the margins of society – an embittered war veteran with little chance of personal advancement. Without his self-discovery that he could 'speak', Hitler would not have been able to contemplate the possibility of making a living from politics. But without the extraordinary political climate of post-war Germany, and, quite especially, the unique conditions in Bavaria, Hitler would have found himself in any case without an audience, his 'talent' pointless and unrecognized, his tirades of hate without echo, the backing from those close to the avenues of power, on whom he depended, unforthcoming.

When he joined the infant German Workers' Party in September 1919, he was still, as he himself put it, among the 'nameless' – a nobody. Within three years, he was being showered with letters of adulation, spoken of in nationalist circles as Germany's Mussolini, even compared with Napoleon. And little more than four years later, he had attained national, not just regional, notoriety as a leader of an attempt to take over the power of the state by force. He had of course failed miserably in this – and his political 'career' looked to be (and ought to have been) at an end. But he was now a 'somebody'. The first part of Hitler's astonishing rise from anonymity to prominence dates from these years in Munich – the years of his political apprenticeship.

It is natural to presume that such a swift rise even to provincial celebrity status must have been the result of some extraordinary personal qualities. Without doubt, Hitler *did* possess abilities and traits of character that contributed towards making him a political force to be reckoned with. To ignore them or disparage them totally would be to make the same mistakes of underestimation made by his political enemies, who ridiculed him and regarded him as a mere cipher for the interests of others. But Hitler's personality and his talents, such as they were, alone do not explain the adulation already being lavished on him by growing numbers in the *völkisch* camp by 1922. The origins of a leadership cult reflected the mentalities and expectations prevalent in some sectors of German society at the time, more than they did special qualities of Hitler. Nor would his abilities as a mob-orator, which were most of what he had to offer at the time, in themselves have been sufficient to have lifted him to a position where he could, even if for a mere few hours – in retrospect, hours of pure melodrama, even farce – head a challenge to the might of the German state. To come this far, he needed influential patrons.

Without the changed conditions, the product of a lost war, revolution, and a pervasive sense of national humiliation, Hitler would have remained a nobody. His main ability by far, as he came to realize during the course of 1919, was that in the prevailing circumstances he could inspire an audience which shared his basic political feelings, by the way he spoke, by the force of his rhetoric, by the very power of his prejudice, by the conviction he conveyed that there *was* a way out of Germany's plight, and that *only* the way he outlined was the road to national rebirth. Another time, another place, and the message would have been ineffective, absurd even. As it was, indeed, in the early 1920s the great majority of the citizens of Munich, let alone of a wider population to whom Hitler was, if at all, known only as a provincial Bavarian hot-head and rabble-rouser, could not be captivated by it. Nevertheless, at this time and in this place, Hitler's message did capture exactly the uncontainable sense of anger, fear, frustration, resentment, and pent-up aggression of the raucous gatherings in the Munich beerhalls. The compulsive manner of his speaking derived in turn much of its power of persuasion from the strength of conviction that combined with appealingly simple diagnoses of and recipes to Germany's problems.

Above all, what came naturally to Hitler was to stoke up the hatred of others by pouring out to them the hatred that was so deeply embedded in himself. Even so, this had never before had the effect it was to have now, in the changed post-war conditions. What, in the Men's Home in Vienna, in the Munich cafés, and in the regimental field headquarters, had been at best tolerated as an eccentricity now turned out to be Hitler's major asset. This in itself suggests that what had changed above all was the milieu and context in which Hitler operated; that we should look in the first instance less to his own personality than to the motives and actions of those who came to be Hitler's supporters, admirers, and devotees – and not least his powerful backers – to explain his first breakthrough on the political scene. For what becomes clear – without falling into the mistake of presuming that he was no more than the puppet of the 'ruling classes' – is that Hitler would have remained a political nonentity without the patronage and support he obtained from influential circles in Bavaria. During this period, Hitler was seldom, if ever, master of his own destiny. The key decisions – to take over the party leadership in 1921, to engage in the putsch adventure in 1923 – were not carefully conceived actions, but desperate forward moves to save face – behaviour characteristic of Hitler to the end.

It was as a propagandist, not as an ideologue with a unique or special set of political ideas, that Hitler made his mark in these early years. There was nothing new, different, original, or distinctive about the ideas he was peddling in the Munich beerhalls. They were common currency among the various *völkisch* groups and sects and had already been advanced in all their essentials by the pre-war Pan-Germans. What Hitler did was advertise unoriginal ideas in an original way. He gave voice to phobias, prejudice, and resentment as no one else could. Others could say the same thing but make no impact at all. It was less *what* he said, than *how* he said it that counted. As it was to be throughout his 'career', presentation was what mattered. He consciously learnt how to make an impression through his speaking. He learnt how to devise effective propaganda and to maximize the impact of targeting specific scapegoats. He learnt, in other words, that he was able to mobilize the masses. For him this was from the outset *the* route to the attainment of political goals. The ability to convince himself that his way and no other could succeed was the platform for the conviction that he conveyed to others. Conversely, the response of the beerhall crowds – later the mass rallies – gave him the certainty, the self-assurance, the sense of security, which at this time he otherwise lacked. He needed the orgasmic excitement which only the ecstatic masses could give him. The satisfaction gained from the rapturous response and wild applause of cheering crowds must have offered compensation for the emptiness of his personal relations. More than that, it was a sign that he was a success, after three decades in which – apart from the pride he took in his war record – he had no achievements of note to set against his outsized ego.

Simplicity and repetition were two key ingredients in his speaking armoury. These revolved around the unvarying essential driving-points of his message: the nationalization of the masses, the reversal of the great 'betrayal' of 1918, the destruction of Germany's internal enemies (above all the 'removal' of the Jews), and material and psychological rebuilding as the prerequisite for external struggle and the attainment of a position of world power. This conception of the path to Germany's 'salvation' and rebirth was already partially devised, at least in embryo, by the date of his letter to Gemlich in September 1919. Important strands remained, however, to be added. The central notion of the quest for 'living space' in eastern Europe was, for instance, not fully incorporated until the middle of the decade. It was only in the two years or so following the putsch debacle, therefore, that his ideas finally came together to form the characteristic fully-fledged *Weltanschauung* that thereafter remained unaltered.

But all this is to run ahead of the crucial developments which shaped the first passage of Hitler's political 'career' as the beerhall agitator of an insignificant Munich racist party and the circumstances under which he came to lead that party.

VI

The crowds that began to flock in 1919 and 1920 to Hitler's speeches were not motivated by refined theories. For them, simple slogans, kindling the fires of anger, resentment, and hatred, were what worked. But what they were offered in the Munich beerhalls was nevertheless a vulgarized version of ideas which were in far wider circulation. Hitler acknowledged in *Mein Kampf* that there was no essential distinction between the ideas of the *völkisch* movement and those of National Socialism. He had little interest in clarifying or systematizing these ideas. Of course, he had his own obsessions – a few basic notions which never left him after 1919, became formed into a rounded 'world-view' in the mid-1920s, and provided the driving-force of his 'mission' to 'rescue' Germany. But ideas held no interest for Hitler as abstractions. They were important to him only as tools of mobilization. Hitler's achievement as a speaker was, therefore, to become the main popularizer of ideas that were in no way his invention, and that served other interests as well as his own.

When Hitler joined the German Workers' Party, it was one of some seventy-three *völkisch* groups in Germany, most of them founded since the end of the war. In Munich alone there were at least fifteen in 1920. Within the *völkisch* pool of ideas, the notion of a specifically *German* or *national* socialism, tied in with an onslaught on 'Jewish' capitalism, had gained ground in the last phase of the war, and spawned both Drexler's German Workers' Party and what was soon to become its arch-rival, the German-Socialist Party (Deutschsozialistische Partei).

Already during the war, Munich had been a major centre of anti-government nationalist agitation by the Pan-Germans, who found a valuable outlet for their propaganda in the publishing house of Julius F. Lehmann, otherwise renowned for the publication of texts on medicine. Lehmann was a member of the Thule Society, a *völkisch* club of a few hundred well-heeled individuals, run like a masonic lodge, that had been founded in Munich at the turn of the year 1917–18 out of the pre-war Germanen-Orden, set up in Leipzig in 1912 to bring together a variety of minor antisemitic groups and organizations. Its membership list, including alongside Lehmann the 'economics expert' Gottfried Feder, the publicist Dietrich Eckart, the journalist and co-founder of the DAP Karl Harrer, and the young nationalists Hans Frank, Rudolf Heß, and Alfred Rosenberg, reads like a *Who's Who* of early Nazi sympathizers and leading figures in Munich. The colourful and rich head of the Thule Society, Rudolf Freiherr von Sebottendorff – a cosmopolitan adventurer and self-styled aristocrat who was actually the son of a train-driver and had made his fortune through shady deals in Turkey and an opportune marriage to a rich heiress – ensured that meetings could be held in Munich's best hotel, the 'Vier Jahreszeiten', and provided the *völkisch* movement in Munich with its own newspaper, the *Münchener Beobachter* (renamed in August 1919 as the *Völkischer Beobachter*, and eventually bought by the Nazis in December 1920). It was from the Thule Society that the initiative arose towards the end of the war to try to influence the working class in Munich. Karl Harrer was commissioned to attempt this, and made contact with a railway workshop locksmith, Anton Drexler. Having been found unfit for military service, Drexler had in 1917 temporarily found an expression of his nationalist and racist sentiments in the short-lived but huge, rabidly pro-war Fatherland Party. Then, in March 1918, he had founded a 'Workers' Committee for a Good Peace' in an effort to stir enthusiasm for the war effort among Munich's working class. He combined his extreme nationalism with an anti-capitalism demanding draconian action against profiteers and speculators. Harrer, a sports-reporter on the right-wing *Münchner-Augsburger Abendzeitung*, persuaded Drexler and a few others to set up a 'Political Workers' Circle' (Politischer Arbeiterzirkel). The 'Circle', a group of usually three to seven members, met periodically for about a year from November 1918 onwards to discuss nationalist and racist themes – such as the Jews as Germany's enemy, or responsibility for the war and defeat – usually introduced by Harrer. Whereas Harrer preferred the semi-secretive *völkisch* 'club', Drexler thought discussing recipes for Germany's salvation in such a tiny group had scant value, and wanted to found a political party. He proposed in December the setting up of a 'German Workers' Party' which would be 'free of Jews'. The idea was well received, and, on 5 January 1919, at a small gathering – mainly contacts from the railway yards – in the Fürstenfelder Hof in Munich, the German Workers' Party was formed. Drexler was elected chairman of the Munich branch (the only one that existed), while Harrer was given the honorary title of 'Reich Chairman'. Only in the more favourable climate after the crushing of the Räterepublik was the infant party able to stage its first public meetings. Attendance was sparse. Ten members were present on 17 May, thirty-eight when Dietrich Eckart spoke in August, and forty-one on 12 September. This was the occasion on which Hitler attended for the first time.

VII

Hitler's part in the early development of the German Workers' Party (subsequently the NSDAP) is obscured more than it is clarified by his own tendentious account in *Mein Kampf*. And, as throughout his book, Hitler's version of events is aimed, more than all else, at elevating his own role as it denigrates, plays down, or simply ignores that of all others involved. It amounts to the story of a political genius going his way in the face of adversity, a heroic triumph of the will. In his own version, he had joined a tiny body with grandiose ideas but no hope of realizing them, raising it single-handedly to a force of the first magnitude which would come to rescue Germany from its plight. Towering over the weak and vacillating early leaders of the party, certain of himself and of the coming to fruition of his mighty vision, proven successful in his methods, his greatness – so his account was designed to illustrate – was apparent even in these first months after joining the movement. There could be no doubt about his claim to supremacy in the *völkisch* movement against all pretenders.

After dealing with subsequent successes in building up the party's following, Hitler returned to the early party history in a later passage in *Mein Kampf* when, surprisingly briefly and remarkably vaguely, he described his takeover of the party leadership in mid-1921. His terse summary simply indicates that after intrigues against him and 'the attempt of a group of *völkisch* lunatics', supported by the party chairman (Drexler), to obtain the leadership of the party had collapsed, a general membership meeting unanimously gave him leadership over the whole movement. His reorganization of the movement on 1 August 1921 swept away the old, ineffectual quasi-parliamentary way of running party matters by committee and internal democracy, and substituted for it the leadership principle as the organizational basis of the party. His own absolute supremacy was thereby assured.

Here, it seems, embodied in the description in *Mein Kampf*, is the realization of Hitler's ambition for dictatorial power in the movement – subsequently in the German state – which could be witnessed in his early conflicts with Harrer and Drexler, and his rejection of the initial inner-party democratic style. The weakness of lesser mortals, their inability to see the light, the certainty with which he went his own way, and the need to follow a supreme leader who alone could ensure ultimate triumph – these, from the outset, are the dominant themes. The beginning of his claim to leadership can thus be located in the earliest phase of his actitity within the party. In turn, this suggests that the self-awareness of political genius was present from the beginning.

Little wonder that, on the basis of this story, the enigma of Hitler is profound. The 'nobody of Vienna', the corporal who is not even promoted to sergeant, now appears with a full-blown political philosophy, a strategy for success, and a burning will to lead his party and sees himself as Germany's coming great leader. However puzzling and extraordinary, the underlying thrust of Hitler's self-depiction has found a surprising degree of acceptance. But, though not inaccurate in all respects, it requires substantial modification and qualification.

The break with Karl Harrer soon came. It was not, however, an early indicator of Hitler's relentless striving for dictatorial power in the movement. Nor was it simply a matter of whether the party should be a mass movement or a type of closed *völkisch* debating society. A number of *völkisch* organizations at the time faced the same problem, and attempted to combine an appeal to a mass audience with regular meetings of an exclusive 'inner circle'. Harrer tended strongly towards the latter, represented by the 'Workers' Circle', which he himself controlled, in contrast to the party's 'Working Committee', where he was simply an ordinary member. But Harrer found himself increasingly isolated. Drexler was as keen as Hitler to take the party's message to the masses. He later claimed that he, and not Hitler, had proposed announcing the party's programme at a mass meeting in the Hofbräuhausfestsaal, and that Hitler had initially been sceptical about the prospects of filling the hall. As long as Harrer directed the party through his control of the 'Workers' Circle', the question of the more viable propaganda strategy would remain unresolved. It was necessary, therefore, to enhance the role of the Committee, which Drexler and Hitler did in draft regulations that they drew up in December, giving it complete authority and ruling out any 'superior or side government, whether as a circle or lodge'. The draft regulations – bearing Hitler's clear imprint – determined that the Committee's members and its chairman should be elected in an open meeting. Their unity, it went on, would be ensured through strict adherence to the programme of the party (which Hitler and Drexler were already preparing). The new regulations were plainly directed against Harrer. But they were not devised as a stepping-stone on the way to Hitler's supreme power in the party. Evidently, he had no notion of dictatorial party rule at the time. He was ready to accept the corporate leadership of an elected committee. Decisions to stage mass meetings in the next months were, it seems, those of the Committee as a whole, approved by a majority of its members, not Hitler's alone, though, once Harrer had departed and in view of Hitler's increasing success in drawing the crowds to listen to his speeches, it is hard to believe that there was any dissension. Harrer alone, it appears, opposed the staging of an ambitious mass meeting in early 1920, and accepted the consequences of his defeat by resigning. Personal animosity also played a role. Harrer, remarkably, thought little of Hitler as a speaker. Hitler was in turn contemptuous of Harrer.

The party's first mass meeting was initially planned to take place in January 1920, but had to be postponed because of a general ban on public meetings at the time. It was rescheduled for the Hofbräuhaus on 24 February. The main worry was that the attendance would be embarrassingly small. This was why, since Drexler recognized that neither he nor Hitler had any public profile, he approached Dr Johannes Dingfelder, not even a party member but well known in Munich *völkisch* circles, to deliver the main speech. Hitler's name was not even mentioned in any of the publicity. Nor was there any hint that the party's programme would be proclaimed at the meeting.

The twenty-five points of this programme – which would in the course of time be declared 'unalterable' and be in practice largely ignored – had been worked out and drafted over the previous weeks by Drexler and Hitler. Its points – among them, demands for a Greater Germany, land and colonies, discrimination against Jews and denial of citizenship to them, breaking 'interest slavery', confiscation of war profits, land re-form, protection of the middle class, persecution of profiteers, and tight regulation of the press – contained little or nothing that was original or novel on the *völkisch* Right. Religious neutrality was included in the attempt to avoid alienating a large church-going population in Bavaria. 'Common good before individual good' was an unobjectionable banality. The demand for 'a strong central power' in the Reich, and 'the unconditional authority' of a 'central parliament', though clearly implying authoritarian, not pluralistic, government, gives no indication that Hitler envisaged himself at this stage as the head of a personalized regime. There are some striking omissions. Neither Marxism nor Bolshevism is mentioned. The entire question of agriculture is passed over, apart from the brief reference to land reform. The authorship of the programme cannot be fully clarified. Probably, the individual points derived from several sources among the party's leading figures. The attack on 'interest slavery' obviously drew on Gottfried Feder's pet theme. Profit-sharing was a favourite idea of Drexler. The forceful style sounds like Hitler's. As he later asserted, he certainly worked on it. But probably the main author was Drexler himself. Drexler certainly claimed this in the private letter he wrote to Hitler (though did not send) in January 1940. In this letter, he stated that 'following all the basic points already written down by me, Adolf Hitler composed *with* me – and with no one else – the 25 theses of National Socialism, in long nights in the workers' canteen at Burghausenerstraße 6'.

Despite worries about the attendance at the party's first big meeting, some 2,000 people (perhaps a fifth of them socialist opponents) were crammed into the Festsaal of the Hofbräuhaus on 24 February when Hitler, as chairman, opened the meeting. Dingfelder's speech was unremarkable. Certainly, it was un-Hitler-like in style and tone. The word 'Jew' was never mentioned. He blamed Germany's fate on the decline of morality and religion, and the rise of selfish, material values. His recipe for recovery was 'order, work, and dutiful sacrifice for the salvation of the Fatherland'. The speech was well received and uninterrupted. The atmosphere suddenly livened when Hitler came to speak. His tone was harsher, more aggressive, less academic, than Dingfelder's. The language he used was expressive, direct, coarse, earthy – that used and understood by most of his audience – his sentences short and punchy. He heaped insults on target-figures like the leading Centre Party politician and Reich Finance Minister Matthias Erzberger (who had signed the Armistice in 1918 and strongly advocated acceptance of the detested Versailles Treaty the following summer) or the Munich capitalist Isidor Bach, sure of the enthusiastic applause of his audience. Verbal assaults on the Jews brought new cheers from the audience, while shrill attacks on profiteers produced cries of 'Flog them! Hang them!' When he came to read out the party programme, there was much applause for the individual points. But there were interruptions, too, from left-wing opponents, who had already been getting restless, and the police reporter of the meeting spoke of scenes of 'great tumult so that I often thought it would come to brawling at any minute'. Hitler announced, to storms of applause, what would remain the party's slogan: 'Our motto is only struggle. We will go our way unshakeably to our goal.' The end of Hitler's speech, in which he read out a protest at an alleged decision to provide 40,000 hundredweight of flour for the Jewish community, again erupted into uproar following further opposition heckling, with people standing on tables and chairs yelling at each other. In the subsequent 'discussion', four others spoke briefly, two of them opponents. Remarks from the last speaker that a dictatorship from the Right would be met with a dictatorship from the Left were the signal for a further uproar, such that Hitler's words closing the meeting were drowned. Around 100 Independent Socialists and Communists poured out of the Hofbräuhaus on to the streets cheering for the International and the Räterepublik and booing the war-heroes Hindenburg and Ludendorff, and the German Nationalists. The meeting had not exactly produced the 'hall full of people united by a new conviction, a new faith, a new will' that Hitler was later to describe.

Nor would anyone reading Munich newspapers in the days following the meeting have gained the impression that it was a landmark heralding the arrival of a new, dynamic party and a new political hero. The press's reaction was muted, to say the least. The newspapers concentrated in their brief reports on Dingfelder's speech and paid little attention to Hitler. Even the *Völkischer Beobachter*, not yet under party control but sympathetic, was surprisingly low-key. It reported the meeting in a single column in an inside page four days later.

Despite this initial modest impact, it was already apparent that Hitler meetings meant political fireworks. Even in the hothouse of Munich politics, the big meetings of the National Socialist German Workers' Party (NSDAP), as the movement henceforth called itself, were some-thing different. Hitler wanted above all else to make his party noticed.

In this he rapidly succeeded. 'It makes no difference whatever whether they laugh at us or revile us,' he later wrote, 'whether they represent us as clowns or criminals; the main thing is that they mention us, that they concern themselves with us again and again . . .' He observed the dull, lifeless meetings of bourgeois parties, the deadening effect of speeches read out like academic lectures by dignified, elderly gentlemen. Nazi meetings, he recorded with pride, were, by contrast, *not* peaceful. He learnt from the organization of meetings by the Left, how they were orchestrated, the value of intimidation of opponents, techniques of disruption, and how to deal with disturbances. The NSDAP's meetings aimed to attract confrontation, and as a result to make the party noticed. Posters were drafted in vivid red to provoke the Left to attend. In mid-1920 Hitler personally designed the party's banner with the swastika in a white circle on a red background, devised to make as striking a visual impact as possible. The result was that meetings were packed long before the start, and the numbers of opponents present guaranteed that the atmosphere was potentially explosive. To combat trouble, a 'hall protection' squad was fully organized by mid-1920, became the 'Gymnastic and Sports Section' in August 1921, and eventually developed into the 'Storm Section' (Sturmabteilung, or SA).

Only Hitler could bring in the crowds for the NSDAP. In front of a beerhall audience his style was electrifying. While in his Nuremberg cell awaiting the hangman, Hans Frank, the ex-Governor General of Poland, recalled the moment, in January 1920, while he was still only nineteen years old (though already committed to the *völkisch* cause), that he had first heard Hitler speak. The large room was bursting at the seams. Middle-class citizens rubbed shoulders with workers, soldiers, and students. Whether old or young, the state of the nation weighed heavily on people. Germany's plight polarized opinions, but left few unmoved or disinterested. Most political meetings were packed. But, to Frank – young, idealistic, fervently anti-Marxist and nationalistic – speakers were generally disappointing, had little to offer. Hitler, in stark contrast, set him alight.

The man with whom Hans Frank's fate would be bound for the next quarter of a century was dressed in a shabby blue suit, his tie loosely fastened. He spoke clearly, in impassioned but not shrill tones, his blue eyes flashing, occasionally pushing back his hair with his right hand. Frank's most immediate feeling was how sincere Hitler was, how the words came from the heart and were not just a rhetorical device. 'He was at that time simply the grandiose popular speaker without precedent – and, for me, incomparable,' wrote Frank.

I was strongly impressed straight away. It was totally different from what was otherwise to be heard in meetings. His method was completely clear and simple. He took the overwhelmingly dominant topic of the day, the Versailles Diktat, and posed the question of all questions: What now German people? What's the true situation? What alone is now possible? He spoke for over two-and-a-half hours, often interrupted by frenetic torrents of applause – and one could have listened to him for much, much longer. Everything came from the heart, and he struck a chord with all of us . . . When he finished, the applause would not die down . . . From this evening onwards, though not a party member, I was convinced that if one man could do it, Hitler alone would be capable of mastering Germany's fate.

Whatever the pathos of these comments, they testify to Hitler's instinctive ability, singling him out from other speakers relaying a similar message, to speak in the language of his listeners, and to stir them through the passion and – however strange it might now sound to us – the apparent sincerity of his idealism.

Rising attendances marked Hitler's growing success and mounting reputation as the party's star speaker. By the end of 1920 he had addressed over thirty mass meetings – mostly of between 800 and 2,500 persons – and spoken at many smaller internal party gatherings. In early February 1921 he would speak at the biggest meeting so far – over 6,000 people in the Zircus Krone, which could accommodate the largest indoor crowds in Munich. Until mid-1921 he spoke mainly in Munich, where the propaganda and organization of the meetings would ensure a satisfactory turn-out, and where the right atmosphere was guaranteed. But, not counting the speeches made during a fortnight's visit to Austria in early October, he held ten speeches outside the city in 1920, including one in Rosenheim where the first local group of the party outside Munich had just been founded. It was largely owing to Hitler's public profile that the party membership increased sharply from 190 in January 1920 to 2,000 by the end of the year and 3,300 by August 1921. He was rapidly making himself indispensable to the movement.

VIII

Hitler spoke from rough notes – mainly a series of jotted headings with key words underlined. As a rule, a speech would last around two hours or more. In the Festsaal of the Hofbräuhaus he used a beer table on one of the long sides of the hall as his platform in order to be in the middle of the crowd – a novel technique for a speaker which helped create what Hitler regarded as a special mood in that hall. The themes of his speeches varied little: the contrast of Germany's strength in a glorious past with its current weakness and national humiliation – a sick state in the hands of traitors and cowards who had betrayed the Fatherland to its powerful enemies; the reasons for the collapse in a lost war unleashed by these enemies, and behind them, the Jews; betrayal and revolution brought about by criminals and Jews; English and French intentions of destroying Germany, as shown in the Treaty of Versailles – the 'Peace of shame', the instrument of Germany's slavery; the exploitation of ordinary Germans by Jewish racketeers and profiteers; a cheating and corrupt government and party system presiding over economic misery, social division, political conflict, and ethical collapse; the only way to recovery contained in the points of the party's programme – ruthless showdown with internal enemies and build-up of national consciousness and unity, leading to renewed strength and eventual restored greatness. The combination of traditional Bavarian dislike of the Prussians and the experience of the Räterepublik in Munich meant that Hitler's repeated onslaught on the 'Marxist' government in Berlin was certain to meet with an enthusiastic response among the still small minority of the local population drawn to his meetings.

While Hitler basically appealed to negative feelings – anger, resentment, hatred – there was also a 'positive' element in the proposed remedy to the proclaimed ills. However platitudinous, the appeal to restoration of liberty through national unity, the need to collaborate of 'workers of the brain and hand', the social harmony of a 'national community', and the protection of the 'little man' through the crushing of his exploiters, were, to go from the applause they invariably produced, undeniably attractive propositions to Hitler's audiences. And Hitler's own passion and fervour successfully conveyed the message – to those already predisposed to it – that no other way was possible; that Germany's revival would and could be brought about; and that it lay in the power of ordinary Germans to make it happen through their own struggle, sacrifice, and will. The effect was more that of a religious revivalist meeting than a normal political gathering.

Though Hitler was invariably up-to-date in finding easy targets in the daily politics of the crisis-ridden Republic, his main themes were tediously repetitive. Some, in fact, often taken for granted to be part of Hitler's allegedly unchanging ideology, were missing altogether at this stage. There was, for example, not a single mention of the need for 'living space' (*Lebensraum*) in eastern Europe. Britain and France were the foreign-policy targets at this time. Indeed, Hitler jotted among the notes of one of his speeches, in August 1920, 'brotherhood towards the east'. Nor did he clamour for a dictatorship. Such a demand occurs only in one speech in 1920, on 27 April, in which Hitler declared that Germany needed 'a dictator who is a genius' if it were to rise up again. There was no implication that he himself was that person. Surprisingly, too, his first outright public assault on Marxism did not occur before his speech at Rosenheim on 21 July 1920 (though he had spoken on a number of occasions before this of the catastrophic effects of Bolshevism in Russia, for which he blamed the Jews). And, remarkably, even race theory – where Hitler drew heavily for his ideas from well-known antisemitic tracts such as Houston Stewart Chamberlain, Adolf Wahrmund, and, especially, the arch-popularizer Theodor Fritsch (one of whose emphases was the alleged sexual abuse of women by Jews) – was explicitly treated in only one speech by Hitler during 1920.

This scarcely meant, however, that Hitler neglected to attack the Jews. On the contrary: the all-devouring manic obsession with the Jews to which all else is subordinated – not observable before 1919, never absent thereafter – courses through almost every Hitler speech at this time. Behind all evil that had befallen or was threatening Germany stood the figure of the Jew. In speech after speech he lashed the Jews in the most vicious and barbaric language imaginable.

Genuine socialism, declared Hitler, meant to be an antisemite. Germans should be ready to enter into a pact with the devil to eradicate the evil of Jewry. But, as in his letter to Gemlich the previous autumn, he did not see emotional antisemitism as the answer. He demanded internment in concentration camps to prevent 'Jewish undermining of our people', hanging for racketeers, but ultimately, as the only solution – similar to the Gemlich letter – the 'removal of the Jews from our people'. The implication, as in his explicit demands with regard to *Ostjuden* (usually poor refugees from persecution in eastern Europe), was their expulsion from Germany. This was undoubtedly how it was understood. But the language itself was both terrible and implicitly genocidal in its biological similes. 'Don't think that you can combat racial tuberculosis,' he declared in August 1920, 'without seeing to it that the people is freed from the causative organ of racial tuberculosis. The impact of Jewry will never pass away, and the poisoning of the people will not end, as long as the causal agent, the Jew, is not removed from our midst.'

His audiences loved it. More than anything else, these attacks evoked torrents of applause and cheering. His technique – beginning slowly, plenty of sarcasm, personalized attacks on named targets, then a gradual crescendo to a climax – whipped his audiences into a frenzy. His speech in the Festsaal of the Hofbräuhaus on 13 August 1920 on 'Why are we Antisemites?' – his only speech that year *solely* relating to the Jews and probably intended as a basic statement on the topic – was interrupted fifty-eight times during its two hours' duration by ever wilder cheering from the 2,000-strong audience. To go from a report on another Hitler speech a few weeks later, the audience would have been mainly drawn from white-collar workers, the lower-middle class, and better-off workers, with around a quarter women.

At first, Hitler's antisemitic tirades were invariably linked to anti-capitalism and attacks on 'Jewish' war profiteers and racketeers, whom he blamed for exploiting the German people and causing the loss of the war and the German war dead. The influence of Gottfried Feder can be seen in the distinction Hitler drew between essentially healthy 'industrial capital' and the real evil of 'Jewish finance capital'.

There was no link with Marxism or Bolshevism at this stage. Contrary to what is sometimes claimed, Hitler's antisemitism was not prompted by his anti-Bolshevism; it long predated it. There was no mention of Bolshevism in the Gemlich letter of September 1919, where the 'Jewish Question' is related to the rapacious nature of finance capital. Hitler spoke in April and again in June 1920 of Russia being destroyed by the Jews, but it was only in his Rosenheim speech on 21 July that he explicitly married the images of Marxism, Bolshevism, and the Soviet system in Russia to the brutality of Jewish rule, for which he saw Social Democracy preparing the ground in Germany. Hitler admitted in August

1920 that he knew little of the real situation in Russia. But – perhaps influenced above all by Alfred Rosenberg, who came from the Baltic and had experienced the Russian Revolution at first hand, but probably also soaking up images of the horror of the Russian civil war which were filtering through to the German press – he plainly became pre-occupied with Bolshevik Russia in the second half of the year. The dissemination of the *Protocols of the Elders of Zion* – the forgery about Jewish world domination, widely read and believed in antisemitic circles at the time – probably also helped to focus Hitler's attention on Russia. These images appear to have provided the catalyst to the merger of antisemitism and anti-Marxism in his 'world-view' – an identity which, once forged, never disappeared.

IX

Hitler's speeches put him on the political map in Munich. But he was still very much a local taste. And however much noise he made, his party was still insignificant compared with the established socialist and Catholic parties. Moreover, though it is going too far to see him as no more than the tool of powerful vested interests 'behind the scenes', without influential backers and the 'connections' they could provide his talents as a mob-agitator would not have got him very far.

Though Hitler had already signalled his intention of making a living as a political speaker, he was, in fact, until 31 March 1920 still drawing pay from the army. His first patron, Captain Mayr, continued to take a close interest in him and, if his later account can be believed, provided limited funding towards the staging of the mass meetings. At this time, Hitler was still serving both the party and the army. In January and February 1920, Mayr had 'Herr Hittler' lecturing on 'Versailles' and 'Political Parties and their Significance' in the company of distinguished Munich historians Karl Alexander von Müller and Paul Joachimsen to Reichswehr soldiers undertaking 'citizenship education courses'. In March, during the Kapp Putsch, when a short-lived armed coup had attempted to overthrow the government, forcing it to flee from the Reich capital, he sent him with Dietrich Eckart to Berlin to instruct Wolfgang Kapp on the situation in Bavaria. They arrived too late. The Right's first attempt to take over the state had already collapsed. But Mayr was undeterred. He retained both his contact with Kapp and his interest in Hitler. He still had hopes, so he told Kapp six months later, that the NSDAP – which he thought of as his own creation – would become the 'organization of national radicalism', the advance-guard of a future, more successful, putsch. He wrote to Kapp, now exiled in Sweden:

The national workers' party must provide the basis for the strong assault-force that we are hoping for. The programme is still somewhat clumsy and also perhaps incomplete. We'll have to supplement it. Only one thing is certain: that under this banner we've already won a good number of supporters. Since July of last year I've been looking . . . to strengthen the movement . . . I've set up very capable young people. A Herr Hitler, for example, has become a motive force, a popular speaker of the first rank. In the Munich branch we have over 2,000 members, compared with under 100 in summer 1919.

Early in 1920, before Hitler had left the Reichswehr, Mayr had taken him along to meetings of the 'Iron Fist' club for radical nationalist officers, founded by Captain Ernst Röhm. Hitler had been introduced to Röhm by Mayr, probably the previous autumn. Interested in a variety of nationalist parties, particularly with a view to winning the workers to the nationalist cause, Röhm had attended the first meeting of the DAP addressed by Hitler on 16 October 1919 and had joined the party shortly afterwards. Now Hitler came into far closer contact with Röhm, who rapidly came to replace Mayr as the key link with the Reichswehr. Röhm had been responsible for arming the volunteers and 'civil defence' (Einwohnerwehr) units in Bavaria and had in the meantime become an important player in paramilitary politics, with excellent connections in the army, the 'patriotic associations', and throughout the *völkisch* Right. He was, in fact, at this time, along with his fellow officers on the Right, far more interested in the massive Einwohnerwehren, with a membership of over quarter of a million men, than he was in the tiny NSDAP. Even so, he provided the key contact between the NSDAP and the far larger 'patriotic associations' and offered avenues to funding which the constantly hard-up party desperately needed. His connections proved invaluable – increasingly so from 1921 onwards, when his interest in Hitler's party grew.

Another important patron at this time was the *völkisch* poet and publicist Dietrich Eckart. More than twenty years older than Hitler, Eckart, who had initially made his name with a German adaptation of

Peer Gynt, had not been notably successful before the war as a poet and critic. Possibly this stimulated his intense antisemitism. He became politically active in December 1918 with the publication of his anti-semitic weekly *Auf gut Deutsch* (*In Plain German*), which also featured contributions from Gottfried Feder and the young émigré from the Baltic, Alfred Rosenberg. He spoke at DAP meetings in the summer of 1919, before Hitler joined, and evidently came to regard the party's new recruit as his own protégé. Hitler himself was flattered by the attention paid to him by a figure of Eckart's reputation in *völkisch* circles. In the early years, relations between the two were good, even close. But for Hitler, as ever, it was Eckart's usefulness that counted. As Hitler's self-importance grew, his need for Eckart declined and by 1923, the year of Eckart's death, the two had become estranged.

At first, however, there could be no doubt of Eckart's value to Hitler and the NSDAP. Through his well-heeled connections, Eckart afforded the beerhall demagogue an entrée into Munich 'society', opening for him the door to the salons of the wealthy and influential members of the city's bourgeoisie. And through his financial support, and that of his contacts, he was able to offer vital assistance to the financially struggling small party. Since membership fees did not remotely cover outgoings, the party was dependent upon help from outside. It came in part from the owners of Munich firms and businesses. Some aid continued to come from the Reichswehr. But Eckart's role was crucial. He arranged, for example, the funding from his friend, the Augsburg chemist and factory-owner Dr Gottfried Grandel, who also backed the periodical *Auf gut Deutsch*, for the plane that took him and Hitler to Berlin at the time of the Kapp Putsch. Grandel later served as a guarantor for the funds used to purchase the *Völkischer Beobachter* and turn it into the party's own newspaper in December 1920.

To the Munich public, by 1921, Hitler *was* the NSDAP. He was its voice, its representative figure, its embodiment. Asked to name the party's chairman, perhaps even politically informed citizens might have guessed wrongly. But Hitler did not want the chairmanship. Drexler offered it him on a number of occasions. Each time Hitler refused. Drexler wrote to Feder in spring 1921, stating 'that each revolutionary movement must have a dictatorial head, and therefore I also think our Hitler is the most suitable for our movement, without wanting to be pushed into the background myself'. But for Hitler, the party chairmanship meant organizational responsibility. He had – this was to remain the case during the rise to power, and when he headed the German state – neither aptitude nor ability for organizational matters. Organization he could leave to others; propaganda – mobilization of the masses – was what he was good at, and what he wanted to do. For that, and that alone, he would take responsibility. Propaganda, for Hitler, was the highest form of political activity.

In Hitler's own conception, propaganda was the key to the nationaliz-ation of the masses, without which there could be no national salvation. It was not that propaganda and ideology were distinctive entities for him. They were inseparable, and reinforced each other. An idea for Hitler was useless unless it mobilized. The self-confidence he gained from the rapturous reception of his speeches assured him that his diagnosis of Germany's ills and the way to national redemption was right – the only one possible. This in turn gave him the self-conviction that conveyed itself to those in his immediate entourage as well as those listening to his speeches in the beerhalls. To see himself as 'drummer' of the national cause was, therefore, for Hitler a high calling. It was why, before the middle of 1921, he preferred to be free for this role, and not to be bogged down in the organizational work which he associated with the chairmanship of the party.

The outrage felt throughout Germany at the punitive sum of 226 thousand million Gold Marks to be paid in reparations, imposed by the Paris Conference at the end of January 1921, ensured there would be no let-up in agitation. This was the background for the biggest meeting that the NSDAP had until then staged, on 3 February in the Circus Krone. Hitler risked going ahead with the meeting at only one day's notice, and without the usual advance publicity. In a rush, the huge hall was booked and two lorries hired to drive round the city throwing out leaflets. This was another technique borrowed from the 'Marxists', and the first time the Nazis had used it. Despite worries until the last minute that the hall would be half-empty and the meeting would prove a propaganda debacle, more than 6,000 turned up to hear Hitler, speaking on 'Future or Ruin', denounce the 'slavery' imposed on Germans by the Allied reparations, and castigate the weakness of the government for accepting them.

Hitler wrote that after the Zircus Krone success he increased the NSDAP's propaganda activity in Munich still further. And indeed the propaganda output was impressive. Hitler spoke at twenty-eight major meetings in Munich and twelve elsewhere (nearly all still in Bavaria), apart from several contributions to 'discussions', and seven addresses to the newly-formed SA in the latter part of the year. Between January and June he also wrote thirty-nine articles for the *Völkischer Beobachter*, and from September onwards contributed a number of pieces to the party's internal information leaflets. Of course, he had the time in which to devote himself solely to propaganda. Unlike the other members of the party leadership, he had no other occupation or interest.

Politics consumed practically his entire existence. When he was not giving speeches, or preparing them, he spent time reading. As always, much of this was the newspapers – giving him regular ammunition for his scourge of Weimar politicians. He had books – a lot of them popular editions – on history, geography, Germanic myths, and, especially, war (including Clausewitz) on the shelves of his shabby, sparsely-furnished room at 41 Thierschstraße, down by the Isar. But what, exactly, he read is impossible to know. His lifestyle scarcely lent itself to lengthy periods of systematic reading. He claimed, however, to have read up on his hero Frederick the Great, and pounced on the work of his rival in the *völkisch* camp, Otto Dickel, a 320-page treatise on *Die Auferstehung des Abend-landes (The Resurrection of the Western World)* immediately on its appearance in 1921 in order to be able to castigate it.

Otherwise, as it had been since the Vienna days, much of his time was spent lounging around cafés in Munich. He specially liked the Café Heck in Galerienstraße, his favourite. In a quiet corner of the long, narrow room of this coffee-house, frequented by Munich's solid middle class, he could sit at his reserved table, his back to the wall, holding court among the new-found cronies that he had attracted to the NSDAP. Among those coming to form an inner circle of Hitler's associates were the young student Rudolf Heß, the Baltic-Germans Alfred Rosenberg (who had worked on Eckart's periodical since 1919) and Max Erwin von Scheubner-Richter (an engineer with excellent contacts to wealthy Russian émigrés). Certainly by the time Putzi Hanfstaengl, the cultured part-American who became his Foreign Press Chief, came to know him, late in 1922, Hitler had a table booked every Monday evening at the old-fashioned Café Neumaier on the edge of the Viktualienmarkt. His regular accompaniment formed a motley crew – mostly lower-middle class, some unsavoury characters among them. Christian Weber, a former horse-dealer, who, like Hitler, invariably carried a dog-whip and relished the brawls with Communists, was one. Another was Hermann Esser, formerly Mayr's press agent, himself an excellent agitator, and an even better gutter-journalist. Max Amann, another roughneck, Hitler's former sergeant who became overlord of the Nazi press empire, was also usually there, as were Ulrich Graf, Hitler's personal bodyguard, and, frequently, the 'philosophers' of the party, Gottfried Feder and Dietrich Eckart. In the long room, with its rows of benches and tables, often occupied by elderly couples, Hitler's entourage would discuss politics, or listen to his monologues on art and architecture, while eating the snacks they had brought with them and drinking their litres of beer or cups of coffee. At the end of the evening, Weber, Amann, Graf, and Lieutenant Klintzsch, a paramilitary veteran of the Kapp Putsch, would act as a bodyguard, escorting Hitler – wearing the long black overcoat and trilby that 'gave him the appearance of a conspirator' – back to his apartment in Thierschstraße.

Hitler scarcely cut the figure of a mainstream politician. Not surprisingly, the Bavarian establishment regarded him largely with contempt. But they could not ignore him. The old-fashioned monarchist head of the Bavarian government at the time, Minister President Gustav Ritter von Kahr, who had assumed office on 16 March 1920 following the Kapp Putsch and aimed to turn Bavaria into a 'cell of order' representing true national values, thought Hitler was a propagandist and nothing more. This was a not unjustifiable assessment at the time. But Kahr was keen to gather 'national forces' in Bavaria in protest at the 'fulfilment policy' of Reich Chancellor Wirth. And he felt certain that he could make use of Hitler, that he could control the 'impetuous Austrian'. On 14 May 1921 he invited a delegation from the NSDAP, led by Hitler, to discuss the political situation with him. It was the first meeting of the two men whose identical aim of destroying the new Weimar democracy was to link them, if fleetingly, in the ill-fated putsch of November 1923 – a chequered association that would end with Kahr's murder in the 'Night of the Long Knives' at the end of June 1934. Whatever Kahr's disdain for Hitler, his invitation to a meeting in May 1921 amounted to recognition that the latter was now a factor in Bavarian politics, proof that he and his movement had to be taken seriously.

Rudolf Heß, still studying at Munich under the geopolitician Professor Karl Haushofer, introverted and idealistic, and already besotted with

Hitler, was part of the delegation. Three days later, unsolicited and unprompted by Hitler, he wrote a lengthy letter to Kahr, describing Hitler's early life and eulogizing about his political aims, ideals, and skills. Hitler, he wrote, was 'an unusually decent, sincere character, full of kind-heartedness, religious, a good Catholic', with only one aim: 'the welfare of his country'. Heß went on to laud Hitler's self-sacrifice in this cause, how he received not a penny from the movement itself but made his living purely from the fees he received for other speeches he occasionally made.

This was the official line that Hitler himself had put out the previous September in the *Völkischer Beobachter*. It was quite disingenuous. On no more than a handful of occasions, he claimed, did he speak at nationalist meetings other than those of the NSDAP. The fees from these alone would certainly not have been enough to keep body and soul together. Rumours about his income and lifestyle were avidly taken up on the Left. Even on the *völkisch* Right there were remarks about him being chauffeured around Munich in a big car, and his enemies in the party raised questions about his personal financial irregularities and the amount of time the 'king of Munich' spent in an expensive lifestyle cavorting with women – even women smoking cigarettes. In fact, Hitler was distinctly touchy about his financial affairs. He repeated in court in December 1921 in a libel case against the socialist *Münchener Post* that he had sought no fees from the party for sixty-five speeches delivered in Munich. But he accepted that he was 'supported in a modest way' by party members and 'occasionally' provided with meals by them. One of those who looked after him was the first 'Hitler-Mutti', Frau Hermine Hofmann, the elderly widow of a headmaster, who plied Hitler with endless offerings of cakes and turned her house at Solln on the outskirts of Munich for a while into a sort of unofficial party headquarters. A little later the Reichsbahn official Theodor Lauböck – founder of the Rosenheim branch of the NSDAP, but subsequently transferred to Munich – and his wife saw to Hitler's well-being, and could also be called upon to put up important guests of the party. In reality, the miserable accommodation Hitler rented in Thierschstraße, and the shabby clothes he wore, belied the fact that even at this date he was not short of well-to-do party supporters. With the growth of the party and his own expanding reputation in 1922–3, he was able to gain new and wealthy patrons in Munich high society.

X

The party was, however, perpetually short of money. It was on a fund-raising mission in June 1921 to Berlin by Hitler, to try (in the company of the man with the contacts, Dietrich Eckart) to find backing for the ailing *Völkischer Beobachter*, that the crisis which culminated in Hitler's take-over of the party leadership unfolded.

The background was shaped by moves to merge the NSDAP with the rival German-Socialist Party, the DSP. To go from the party programmes, despite some differences of accent, the two *völkisch* parties had more in common than separated them. And the DSP had a following in north Germany, which the Nazi Party, still scarcely more than a small local party, lacked. In itself, therefore, there was certainly an argument for joining forces. Talks about a possible merger had begun the previous August in a gathering in Salzburg, attended by Hitler, of national socialist parties from Germany, Austria, Czechoslovakia, and Poland. A number of overtures followed from the DSP leaders between then and April 1921. At a meeting in Zeitz in Thuringia at the end of March, Drexler – presumably delegated by the NSDAP, but plainly in the teeth of Hitler's disapproval – even agreed to tentative proposals for a merger and – anathema to Hitler – a move of the party headquarters to Berlin. Hitler responded with fury to Drexler's concessions, threatened to resign from the party, and succeeded 'amid unbelievable anger' in reversing the agreement reached at Zeitz. Eventually, at a meeting in Munich in mid-April, amidst great rancour and with Hitler in a towering rage, negotiations with the DSP collapsed. The DSP was in no doubt that Hitler, the 'fanatical would-be big shot', whose successes had gone to his head, was solely responsible for the NSDAP's obstructionism. Hitler, dismissive of notions of a specific political programme to be implemented, interested only in agitation and mobilization, had set his face rigidly from the outset against any possible merger. To Hitler, the similarities in programme were irrelevant. He objected to the way the DSP had rushed to set up numerous branches without solid foundations, so that the party was 'everywhere and nowhere', and to its readiness to resort to parliamentary tactics. But the real reason was a different one. Any merger was bound to threaten his supremacy in the small but tightly-knit NSDAP.

Though the merger with the DSP had been fended off for the time being, an even bigger threat, from Hitler's point of view, arose while he was away in Berlin. Dr Otto Dickel, who had founded in March 1921 in Augsburg another *völkisch* organization, the Deutsche Werkgemein-schaft, had made something of a stir on the *völkisch* scene with his book *Die Auferstehung des Abendlandes* (*The Resurrection of the Western World*). Dickel's mystic *völkisch* philosophizing was not Hitler's style, and, not surprisingly, met with the latter's contempt and angry dismissal. But some of Dickel's ideas – building up a classless community through national renewal, combating 'Jewish domination' through the struggle against 'interest slavery' – bore undeniable similarities to those of both the NSDAP and the DSP. And Dickel, no less than Hitler, had the conviction of a missionary and, moreover, was also a dynamic and popular public speaker. Following the appearance of his book, which was lauded in the *Völkischer Beobachter*, he was invited to Munich, and – with Hitler absent in Berlin – proved a major success before a packed audience in one of Hitler's usual haunts, the Hofbräuhaus. Other speeches were planned for Dickel. The NSDAP's leadership was delighted to find in him a second 'outstanding speaker with a popular touch'.

Hitler, meanwhile, was still in Berlin. He failed to turn up at a meeting with a DSP representative on 1 July for further merger talks, and did not return to Bavaria until ten days later. He had evidently by then got wind of the alarming news that a delegation of the NSDAP's leaders was due to have talks there with Dickel and representatives of the Augsburg and Nuremberg branches of the Deutsche Werkgemeinschaft. He appeared before the NSDAP delegates themselves arrived, beside himself with rage, threatening the Augsburg and Nuremberg representatives that he would see that a merger was stopped. But when his own people eventually turned up, his uncontrolled fury subsided into sulky silence. Three hours of suggestions from Dickel for the formation of a loose confederation of the different groups and recommendations for improvements to the NSDAP's programme prompted numerous out-bursts from Hitler before, being able to stand it no longer, he stormed out of the meeting.

If Hitler hoped his tantrums would convince his colleagues to drop the negotiations, he was mistaken. They were embarrassed by his behaviour and impressed by what Dickel had to offer. Even Dietrich

Eckart thought Hitler had behaved badly. It was accepted that the party programme needed amending, and that Hitler 'as a simple man' was not up to doing this. They agreed to take back Dickel's proposals to Munich and put them to the full party committee.

Hitler resigned from the party in anger and disgust on 11 July. In a letter to the committee three days later, he justified his move on the grounds that the representatives in Augsburg had violated the party statutes and acted against the wishes of the members in handing over the movement to a man whose ideas were incompatible with those of the NSDAP. 'I will and can not be any longer a member of such a movement,' he declared. Hitler had resigned 'for ever' from the party's committee in December 1920. As noted, he threatened resignation yet again following the Zeitz conference in late March 1921. The histrionics of the prima donna were part and parcel of Hitler's make-up – and would remain so. It would always be the same: he only knew all-or-nothing arguments; there was nothing in between, no possibility of reaching a compromise. Always from a maximalist position, with no other way out, he would go for broke. And if he could not get his way he would throw a temper-tantrum and threaten to quit. In power, in years to come, he would sometimes deliberately orchestrate an outburst of rage as a bullying tactic. But usually his tantrums were a sign of frustration, even desperation, not strength. It was to be the case in a number of future crises. And it was so on this occasion. The resignation was not a carefully planned manoeuvre to use his position as the party's star performer to blackmail the committee into submission. It was an expression of fury and frustration at not getting his own way. His threat of resignation had worked before, after the Zeitz conference. Now he was risking his only trump card again. Defeat would have meant the party's amalgamation in Dickel's planned 'Western League' and left Hitler with only the option – which he seems to have contemplated – of setting up a new party and beginning again. There were those who would have been glad, whatever his uses as an agitator, to have been rid of such a troublesome and egocentric entity. And the spread of the party that the merger with Dickel's organization presented offered more than a little compensation.

But the loss of its sole star performer would have been a major, perhaps fatal, blow to the NSDAP. Hitler's departure would have split the party. In the end, this was the decisive consideration. Dietrich Eckart was asked to intervene, and on 13 July Drexler sought the conditions under which Hitler would agree to rejoin the party. It was full capitulation from the party leadership. Hitler's conditions all stemmed from the recent turmoil in the party. His key demands – to be accepted by an extraordinary members' meeting – were 'the post of chairman with dictatorial power'; the party headquarters to be fixed once and for all as Munich; the party programme to be regarded as inviolate; and the end of all merger attempts. All the demands centred upon securing Hitler's position in the party against any future challenges. A day later the party committee expressed its readiness in recognition of his 'immense knowledge', his services for the movement, and his 'unusual talent as a speaker' to give him 'dictatorial powers'. It welcomed his willingness, having turned down Drexler's offers in the past, now to take over the party chairmanship. Hitler rejoined the party, as member no.3680, on 26 July.

Even now the conflict was not fully at an end. While Hitler and Drexler publicly demonstrated their unity at a members' meeting on 26 July, Hitler's opponents in the leadership had his henchman Hermann Esser expelled from the party, prepared placards denouncing Hitler, and printed 3,000 copies of an anonymous pamphlet attacking him in the most denigratory terms as the agent of sinister forces intent on damaging the party. But Hitler, who had shown once more to great effect how irreplaceable he was as a speaker in a meeting, packed to the last seat, in Circus Krone on 20 July, was now in the driving seat. Now there was no hesitancy. This was Hitler triumphant. To tumultuous applause from the 554 paid-up members attending the extraordinary members' meeting in the Festsaal of the Hofbräuhaus on 29 July, he defended himself and Esser and rounded on his opponents. He boasted that he had never sought party office, and had turned down the chairmanship on several occasions. But this time he was prepared to accept. The new party constitution, which Hitler had been forced to draft hurriedly, confirmed on three separate occasions the sole responsibility of the First Chairman for the party's actions (subject only to the membership meeting). There was only one vote against accepting the new dictatorial powers over the party granted to Hitler. His chairmanship was unanimously accepted.

The reform of the party statutes was necessary, stated the *Völkischer Beobachter*, in order to prevent any future attempt to dissipate the energies of the party through majority decisions. It was the first step on transforming the NSDAP into a new-style party, a 'Führer party'. The move had come about not through careful planning, but through Hitler's reaction to events which were running out of his control. Rudolf Heß's subsequent assault on Hitler's opponents in the *Völkischer Beobachter* not only contained the early seeds of the later heroization of Hitler, but also revealed the initial base on which it rested. 'Are you truly blind,' wrote Heß, 'to the fact that this man is the leader personality who alone is able to carry through the struggle? Do you think that without him the masses would pile into the Circus Krone?'

5

The 'Drummer'

I

Hitler was content in the early 1920s to be the 'drummer' – whipping up the masses for the 'national movement'. He saw himself at this time not as portrayed in *Mein Kampf*, as Germany's future leader in waiting, the political messiah whose turn would arise once the nation recognized his unique greatness. Rather, he was paving the way for the great leader whose day might not dawn for many years to come. 'I am nothing more than a drummer and rallier,' he told the neo-conservative writer Arthur Moeller van den Bruck in 1922. Some months earlier, he had reputedly stated, in an interview in May 1921 with the chief editor of the Pan-German newspaper *Deutsche Zeitung*, that he was not the leader and statesman who would 'save the Fatherland that was sinking into chaos', but only 'the agitator who understood how to rally the masses'. Nor, he allegedly went on, was he 'the architect who clearly pictured in his own eyes the plan and design of the new building and with calm sureness and creativity was able to lay one stone on the other. He needed the greater one behind him, on whose command he could lean.'

To be the 'drummer' meant everything to Hitler at this time. It was the 'vocation' that replaced his dreams of becoming a great artist or architect. It was his main task, practically his sole concern. Not only did it allow full expression to his one real talent. It was also in his eyes the greatest and most important role he could play. For politics to Hitler – and so it would in all essence remain – *was* propaganda: ceaseless mass mobilization for a cause to be followed blindly, not the 'art of the possible'.

Hitler owed his rise to at least regional prominence on the nationalist Right in Bavaria not simply to his unparalleled ability as a mob-orator at mass meetings in Munich. As before, this was his chief asset. But linked to this, and of crucial importance, was the fact that he was the head of a movement which, in contrast to the earliest phase of the party's existence, now came to develop its own substantial paramilitary force and to enter the maelstrom of Bavarian paramilitary politics. It was above all in the peculiar conditions of post-revolutionary Bavaria that the private armies, with the toleration and often active support of the Bavarian authorities, could fully flourish.

The vehemently anti-socialist, counter-revolutionary regime of Minister President Gustav Ritter von Kahr turned Bavaria into a haven for right-wing extremists from all over Germany, including many under order of arrest elsewhere in the country. From a new protected base in Munich, for example, Captain Hermann Ehrhardt, a veteran of orchestrated anti-socialist violence in the Freikorps, including the suppression of the Räterepublik, and a leader of the Kapp Putsch, was able to use his Organisation Consul to build up a network of groups throughout the whole of the German Reich and carry out many of the political murders – there were 354 in all perpetrated by the Right between 1919 and 1922 – that stained the early years of the troubled new democracy. It was Ehrhardt, alongside Ernst Röhm, who was to play a leading role in establishing the NSDAP's own paramilitary organization, which was to emerge from 1921 onwards into a significant feature of the Nazi Movement and an important factor in paramilitary politics in Bavaria.

Röhm was, more even than Hitler, typical of the 'front generation'. As a junior officer, he shared the dangers, anxieties, and privations of the troops in the trenches – shared, too, the prejudice and mounting anger levelled at those in staff headquarters behind the lines, at the military bureaucracy, at 'incapable' politicians, and at those seen as shirkers, idlers, and profiteers at home. Against these highly negative images, he heroicized the 'front community', the solidarity of the men in the trenches, leadership resting on deeds rather than status, and the blind obedience that this demanded. What he wanted was a new 'warrior' élite whose actions and achievements had proved their right to rule. Though a monarchist, there was for Röhm to be no return to pre-war bourgeois society. His ideal was the community of fighting men. As for so many who joined the Freikorps and their successor paramilitary organizations, this ideal combined male fantasy with the cult of violence. Like so many, Röhm had gone to war in 1914 in wild enthusiasm, suffered serious facial injury within weeks when shell fragments tore away part of his nose, permanently disfiguring him, had returned to lead his company, but had been forced out of service at the front after being again badly injured at Verdun. His subsequent duties in the Bavarian War Ministry, and as the supply officer of a division, sharpened his political antennae and gave him experience in organizational matters. The trauma of defeat and revolution drove him into counter-revolutionary activity – including service in the Freikorps Epp during its participation in the crushing of the Räterepublik. After brief membership of the German Nationalists, the DNVP, he joined the tiny DAP soon after Hitler, in autumn 1919, and, as he himself claimed, was probably responsible for others from the Reichswehr entering the party. Röhm's interest continued, however, to be dictated by military and paramilitary, rather than party, politics. He showed no exclusive interest in the NSDAP before the SA became a significant element in paramilitary politics.

But Röhm's value to the party in engineering its paramilitary connections is hard to overrate. His access both to leading figures on the paramilitary scene and, especially, to weaponry was crucial. His position in control of weapon supplies for the Brigade Epp (the successor to the Freikorps unit, now integrated into the Reichswehr) gave him responsibility for providing the Einwohnerwehr with weapons. The semi-secrecy involved in concealing the extent of weaponry from Allied control – not difficult since there was no occupying army to carry out inspections – also gave Röhm a great deal of scope to build up a large stockpile of mainly small arms in 1920–21. After the dissolution of the Einwohnerwehr, and the official confiscation of weaponry, various paramilitary organizations entrusted him with their weapon supplies. Presiding over such an arsenal, deciding when and if weapons should be handed out, the 'machine-gun king', as he became known, was thus in a pivotal position with regard to the demands of all paramilitary organizations. And, through the protection he gained from Epp, Kahr, and the Munich political police, he enjoyed influence beyond his rank on the politics of the nationalist Right.

From the beginning, the dual role of paramilitary organization (initially linked to Ehrhardt) and party shock troops under Hitler's leadership contained the seeds of the tension that was to accompany the SA down to 1934. The interest of Röhm and Ehrhardt lay on the paramilitary side. Hitler tried to integrate the SA fully into the party, though organizationally it retained considerable independence before 1924. The build-up of the SA was steady, not spectacular, before the second half of 1922. It was after that date, in conditions of rapidly mounting crisis in Bavaria and in the Reich, that the SA's numbers swelled, making it a force to be reckoned with on the nationalist Right.

Hitler, meanwhile, now undisputed leader of his party, carried on his ceaseless agitation much as before, able to exploit the continued tension between Bavaria and the Reich. The murder of Reich Finance Minister Matthias Erzberger on 26 August 1921 – an indication of the near-anarchism that still prevailed in Germany – and Kahr's refusal to accept the validity for Bavaria of the state of emergency declared by Reich President Friedrich Ebert, kept things on the boil. Material discontent played its own part. Prices were already rising sharply as the currency depreciated. Foodstuffs were almost eight times more expensive in 1921 than they had been at the end of the war. By the next year they would be over 130 times dearer. And that was before the currency lost all its value in the hyperinflation of 1923.

Hitler's provocation of his political enemies and of the authorities to gain publicity was stepped up. After one violent clash between his followers and his opponents, he was sentenced in January 1922 to three months' imprisonment for breach of the peace – two months suspended against future good behaviour (though conveniently forgotten about when the good behaviour did not materialize). Even his powerful friends could not prevent him serving the other month of his sentence. Between 24 June and 27 July 1922 he took up residence in Stadelheim prison in Munich.

Apart from this short interlude, Hitler did not let up with his agitation. Brushes with the police were commonplace. For Hitler, these violent clashes with his opponents were the lifeblood of his movement. They were above all good for publicity. Hitler was still dissatisfied with the coverage – even of a negative kind – he received in the press. Nevertheless, the actions of the NSDAP and its leader ensured that they remained in the public eye. And while his leading supporters hinted darkly at dire consequences if the Bavarian government expelled him from Germany (as he had been warned might happen if the disturbances continued), Hitler made propaganda capital out of the threat of expulsion by pointing to his war record, when he had fought as a German for his country while others had done no more than stay at home and preach politics.

Hitler's most notable propaganda success in 1922 was his party's participation in the so-called 'German Day' (*Deutscher Tag*) in Coburg on 14–15 October. Coburg, on the Thuringian border in the north of Upper Franconia and part of Bavaria for only two years, was virgin territory for the Nazis. He saw the German Day as an opportunity not to be missed. He scraped together what funds the NSDAP had to hire a special train – in itself a novel propaganda stunt – to take 800 stormtroopers to Coburg. The SA men were instructed by Hitler to ignore explicit police orders, banning a formation march with un-furled banners and musical accompaniment, and marched with hoisted swastika flags through the town. Workers lining the streets insulted them and spat at them. Nazis in turn leapt out of the ranks beating their tormentors with sticks and rubber-truncheons. A furious battle with the socialists ensued. After ten minutes of mayhem, in which they had police support, the stormtroopers triumphantly claimed the streets of Coburg as theirs. For Hitler, the propaganda victory was what counted. The German Day in Coburg went down in the party's annals. The NSDAP had made its mark in northern Bavaria.

It was Hitler's second major success in Franconia within a few days. On 8 October, Julius Streicher, head of the Nuremberg branch of the Deutsche Werkgemeinschaft, had written to Hitler offering to take his sizeable following, together with his newspaper the *Deutscher Volks-wille*, into the NSDAP. In the wake of the Coburg triumph, the transfer took place on 20 October. Streicher, a short, squat, shaven-headed bully, born in 1885 in the Augsburg area, for a time a primary school teacher as his father had been, and, like Hitler, a war veteran decorated with the Iron Cross, First Class, was utterly possessed by demonic images of Jews. Shortly after the war he had been an early member of the DSP (German-Socialist Party), as antisemitic as the NSDAP, though he had left it in 1921. His newspaper *Der Stürmer*, established in 1923 and becoming notorious for its obscene caricatures of evil-looking Jews seducing pure German maidens and ritual-murder allegations, would – despite Hitler's personal approving comments, and view that 'the Jew' was far worse than Streicher's 'idealized' picture – for a while be banned even in the Third Reich. Streicher was eventually tried at Nuremberg, and hanged. Now, back in 1922, in a step of vital importance for the development of the NSDAP in Franconia, in the northern regions of Bavaria, he subordinated himself personally to Hitler. The rival *völkisch* movement was fatally weakened in Franconia. The Nazi Party practically doubled its membership. From around 2,000 members about the beginning of 1921 and 6,000 a year later, the party was overnight some 20,000 strong. More than that: the Franconian countryside – piously Protestant, fervently nationalist, and stridently antisemitic – was to provide the NSDAP with a stronghold far greater than was offered by its home city of Munich in the Catholic south of Bavaria, and a symbolic capital in Nuremberg – later designated the 'city of the Reich Party Rallies'. It was little wonder that Hitler was keen to express his gratitude to Streicher publicly in *Mein Kampf*.

Even so, it was striking that, away from his Munich citadel, Hitler's power was still limited. He was the undisputed propaganda champion of the party. But away from his Munich base, his writ still did not always run.

This was in itself ample reason for the interest which his Munich following began to show in building up the leadership cult around Hitler. A significant boost to the aura of a man of destiny attaching itself to Hitler came from outside Germany. Mussolini's so-called 'March on Rome' on 28 October 1922 – fictitious though it was in the Fascist legend of a bold 'seizure of power' – nevertheless deeply stirred the Nazi Party. It suggested the model of a dynamic and heroic nationalist leader marching to the salvation of his strife-torn country. The Duce provided an image to be copied. Less than a week after the *coup d'état* in Italy, on 3 November 1922, Hermann Esser proclaimed to a packed Festsaal in the Hofbräuhaus: 'Germany's Mussolini is called Adolf Hitler.' It marked the symbolic moment when Hitler's followers invented the Führer cult.

The spread of fascist and militaristic ideas in post-war Europe meant that 'heroic leadership' images were 'in the air' and by no means confined to Germany. The emergence of the Duce cult in Italy provides an obvious parallel. But the German images naturally had their own flavour, drawing on particular elements of the political culture of the nationalist Right. And the crisis-ridden nature of the Weimar state, detested by so many powerful groups in society and unable to win the popularity and support of the masses, guaranteed that such ideas, which in a more stable environment might have been regarded with derision and confined to the lunatic fringe of politics, were never short of a hearing. Ideas put into circulation by neo-conservative publicists, writers, and intellectuals were, in more vulgarized form, taken up in paramilitary formations and in the varied groupings of the bourgeois youth movement. The model of Mussolini's triumph in Italy now offered the opening for such ideas to be incorporated into the vision of national revival preached by the National Socialists.

The Führer cult was not yet the pivot of the party's ideology and organization. But the beginnings of a conscious public profiling of Hitler's leadership qualities by his entourage, with strong hints in his own speeches, dates back to the period following Mussolini's 'March on Rome'. Hitler was beginning to attract fawning excesses of adulation – even stretching to grotesque comparisons with Napoleon – from admirers on the nationalist Right. The ground for the later rapid spread of the Führer cult was already well fertilized.

There had been no trace of a leadership cult in the first years of the Nazi Party. The word 'leader' ('Führer') had no special meaning attached to it. Every political party or organization had a leader – or more than one. The NSDAP was no different. Drexler was referred to as the party's 'Führer', as was Hitler; or sometimes both in practically the same breath. Once Hitler had taken over the party leadership in July 1921, the term 'our leader' ('unser Führer') became gradually more common. But its meaning was still interchangeable with the purely functional 'chairman of the NSDAP'. There was nothing 'heroic' about it. Nor had Hitler endeavoured to build up a personality cult around himself. But Mussolini's triumph evidently made a deep impression on him. It gave him a role-model. Referring to Mussolini, less than a month after the 'March on Rome', Hitler reportedly stated: 'So will it be with us. We only have to have the courage to act. Without struggle, no victory!' However, the reshaping of his self-image also reflected how his supporters were beginning to see their leader. His followers portrayed him, in fact, as Germany's 'heroic' leader before he came to see himself in that light. Not that he did anything to discourage the new way he was being portrayed from autumn 1922 onwards. It was in December 1922 that the *Völkischer Beobachter* for the first time appeared to claim that Hitler was a special kind of leader – indeed *the* Leader for whom Germany was waiting. Followers of Hitler leaving a parade in Munich were said 'to have found something which millions are yearning for, a leader'. By

Hitler's thirty-fourth birthday, on 20 April 1923, when the new head of the SA, Hermann Göring – thirty years old, Bavarian born but at the latest from the time of his military training in Berlin a self-styled Prussian, handsome (at this time), wildly egocentric, well-connected and power-hungry, bringing the glamour of the World War decorated flying ace as well as important links to the aristocracy to the Nazi Movement – labelled him the 'beloved leader of the German freedom-movement', the personality cult was unmistakable. Political opponents scorned it. That it was not without its mark on Hitler himself is plain. Eckart told Hanfstaengl, while on holiday with Hitler near Berchtesgaden in the Bavarian alps bordering on Austria in May 1923, that Hitler had 'megalomania halfway between a Messiah complex and Neroism', after he had allegedly compared the way he would deal with Berlin with Christ throwing money-changers out of the temple.

During 1923 there are indications in Hitler's speeches that his self-perception was changing. He was now much more preoccupied than he had been in earlier years with leadership, and the qualities needed in the coming Leader of Germany. At no time before his imprisonment in Landsberg did he unambiguously claim those qualities for himself. But a number of passages in his speeches hint that the edges of what distinguished the 'drummer' from the 'Leader' might be starting to blur.

On 4 May 1923, in a speech castigating the parliamentary system as the 'downfall and end of the German nation', Hitler gave the clearest hint to date of how he saw his own role. With reference to Frederick the Great and Bismarck, 'giants' whose deeds contrasted with those of the Reichstag, 'Germany's grave-digger', he declared: 'What can save Germany is the dictatorship of the national will and national determination. The question arises: is the suitable personality to hand? Our task is not to look for such a person. He is a gift from heaven, or is not there. Our task is to create the sword that this person will need when he is there. Our task is to give the dictator, when he comes, a people ready for him!'

In an interview with the British *Daily Mail* on 2 October 1923, Hitler was reported as saying: 'If a German Mussolini is given to Germany . . . people would fall down on their knees and worship him more than Mussolini has ever been worshipped.' If he was seeing himself – as his followers were seeing him – as the 'German Mussolini', then he was apparently beginning to associate the greatness of national leadership with his own person. He felt by this time, so he said, 'the call to Germany's salvation within him', and others detected 'outright Napoleonic and messianic allures' in what he said.

The lack of clarity in Hitler's comments about the future leadership was, in part, presumably tactical. There was nothing to be gained by alienating possible support through a premature conflict about who would later be supreme leader. As Hitler had stated in October, the leadership question could be left unanswered until 'the weapon is created which the leader must possess'. Only then would the time be ripe to 'pray to our Lord God that he give us the right leader'. But it was predominantly a reflection of Hitler's concept of politics as essentially agitation, propaganda, and 'struggle'. Organizational forms remained of little concern to him as long as his own freedom of action was not constrained by them. The crucial issue was the leadership of the 'political struggle'. But it is hard to imagine that Hitler's self-confidence in this field and his ingrained refusal to compromise would not subsequently have meant his demand for total, unconstrained leadership of the 'national movement'. At any rate, Hitler's comments on leadership in the crisis-ridden year of 1923 seem to indicate that his self-image was in a process of change. He still saw himself as the 'drummer', the highest calling there was in his eyes. But it would not take much, following his triumph in the trial, to convert that self-image into the presumption that he was the 'heroic leader' himself.

II

That was all in the future. Around the beginning of 1923, few, if any, outside the ranks of his most fervent devotees thought seriously of Hitler as Germany's coming 'great leader'. But his rise to star status on Munich's political scene – alongside the Hofbräuhaus, the city's only notable curiosity, as one newspaper put it – meant that individuals from quite outside his normal social circles began to take a keen interest in him.

Two were converts to the party who were able to open up useful new contacts for Hitler. Kurt Lüdecke, a well-connected former gambler, playboy, and commercial adventurer, a widely-travelled 'man of the world', was 'looking for a leader and a cause' when he first heard Hitler speak at the rally of the 'Patriotic Associations' in Munich in August 1922. Lüdecke was enthralled. 'My critical faculty was swept away,' he later wrote. 'He was holding the masses, and me with them, under a hypnotic spell by the sheer force of his conviction ... His appeal to German manhood was like a call to arms, the gospel he preached a sacred truth. He seemed another Luther ... I experienced an exaltation that could be likened only to religious conversion ... I had found myself, my leader, and my cause.' According to his own account, Lüdecke used his connections to promote Hitler's standing with General Ludendorff, a war hero since repulsing the Russian advance into East Prussia in 1914, in effect Germany's dictator during the last two war years, and now the outstanding figure on the radical Right, whose name alone was sufficient to open further doors to Hitler. He also sang Hitler's praises to the former Munich chief of police, already an important Nazi sympathizer and protector, Ernst Pöhner. Abroad Lüdecke was able to establish contacts just before the 'March on Rome' with Mussolini (who at that time had never heard of Hitler), and in 1923 with Gömbös and other leading figures in Hungary. His foreign bank accounts, and sizeable donations he was able to acquire abroad, proved valuable to the party during the hyperinflation of 1923. He also fitted out and accommodated at his own cost an entire stormtrooper company. Even so, many of Lüdecke's well-placed contacts were impatient at his constant proselytizing for the NSDAP, and quietly dropped him. And within the party, he was unable to overcome dislike and distrust. He was even denounced to the police by Max Amann as a French spy and jailed under false pretences for two months. By the end of 1923, Lüdecke had used up almost his entire income on behalf of the party.

An even more useful convert was Ernst 'Putzi' Hanfstaengl, a six-foot-four-inch-tall, cultured part-American – his mother, a Sedgwick-Heine, was a descendant of a colonel who had fought in the Civil War – from an upper middle-class art-dealer family, Harvard graduate, partner in an art-print publishing firm, and extremely well-connected in Munich *salon* society. Like Lüdecke, his first experience of Hitler was hearing him speak. Hanfstaengl was greatly impressed by Hitler's power to sway the masses. 'Far beyond his electrifying rhetoric,' he later wrote, 'this man seemed to possess the uncanny gift of coupling the gnostic yearning of the era for a strong leader-figure with his own missionary claim and to suggest in this merging that every conceivable hope and expectation was capable of fulfilment – an astonishing spectacle of suggestive influence of the mass psyche.' Hanfstaengl was plainly fascinated by the subaltern, petty-bourgeois Hitler in his shabby blue suit, looking partway between an NCO and a clerk, with awkward mannerisms, but possessing such power as a speaker when addressing a mass audience. Hanfstaengl remained in part contemptuous of Hitler – not least of his half-baked, cliché-ridden judgements on art and culture (where Hanfstaengl was truly at home and Hitler merely an opinionated know-all). On Hitler's first visit to the Hanfstaengl home, 'his awkward use of knife and fork betrayed his background', wrote (somewhat snobbishly) his host. At the same time, Putzi was plainly captivated by this 'virtuoso on the keyboard of the mass pysche'. He was appalled at catching Hitler sugaring a vintage wine he had offered him. But, added Hanfstaengl, 'he could have peppered it, for each naïve act increased my belief in his homespun sincerity'.

Soon, Hitler was a regular guest at Hanfstaengl's home, where he gorged himself on cream-cakes, paying court to Hanfstaengl's attractive wife, Helene, in his quaint, Viennese style. She took Hitler's attentions in her stride. 'Believe me, he's an absolute neuter, not a man,' she told her husband. Putzi himself believed, for what it was worth, that Hitler was sexually impotent, gaining substitute gratification from his intercourse with the 'feminine' masses. Hitler was taken by Putzi's skills as a pianist, especially his ability to play Wagner. He would accompany Putzi by whistling the tune, marching up and down swinging his arms like the conductor of an orchestra, relaxing visibly in the process. He plainly liked Hanfstaengl – his wife even more so. But the criterion, as always, was usefulness. And above all Hanfstaengl was useful. He became a type of 'social secretary', providing openings to circles far different from the petty-bourgeois roughnecks in Hitler's entourage who gathered each Monday in the Café Neumaier.

Hanfstaengl introduced Hitler to Frau Elsa Bruckmann, the wife of the publisher Hugo Bruckmann, a Pan-German sympathizer and antisemite who had published the works of Houston Stewart Chamberlain. Hitler's ingratiating manners and social naïvety brought out the mother instinct in her. Whether it was the wish to afford him some protection against his enemies that persuaded her to make him a present of one of the dog-whips he invariably carried around is not clear. (Oddly, his other dog-whip – the first he possessed – had been given to him by a rival patroness, Frau Helene Bechstein, while a third heavy whip, made from hippopotamus hide, which he later carried, was given to him by Frau Büchner, the landlady of the Platterhof, the hotel where he stayed on the Obersalzberg.) Everyone who was someone in Munich would be invited at some stage to the soirées of Frau Bruckmann, by birth a Romanian princess, so that Hitler was brought into contact here with industrialists, members of the army and aristocracy, and academics. In his gangster hat and trenchcoat over his dinner jacket, touting a pistol and carrying as usual his dog-whip, he cut a bizarre figure in the *salons* of Munich's upper-crust. But his very eccentricity of dress and exaggerated mannerisms – the affected excessive politeness of one aware of his social inferiority – saw him lionized by condescending hosts and fellow-guests. His social awkwardness and uncertainty, often covered by either silence or tendency to monologues, but at the same time the consciousness of his public success that one could read in his face, made him an oddity, affording him curiosity value among the patronizing cultured and well-to-do pillars of the establishment.

Hitler was also a guest from time to time of the publisher Lehmann, for long a party sympathizer. And the wife of piano manufacturer Bechstein – to whom he had been introduced by Eckart – was another to 'mother' Hitler, as well as lending the party her jewellery as surety against 60,000 Swiss Francs which Hitler was able to borrow from a Berlin coffee merchant in September 1923. The Bechsteins, who usually wintered in Bavaria, used to invite Hitler to their suite in the 'Bayerischer Hof', or to their country residence near Berchtesgaden. Through the Bechsteins, Hitler was introduced to the Wagner circle at Bayreuth. He was transfixed at the first visit, in October 1923, to the shrine of his ultimate hero at Haus Wahnfried, where he tiptoed around the former possessions of Richard Wagner in the music-room and library 'as though he were viewing relics in a cathedral'. The Wagners had mixed views of their unusual guest, who had turned up looking 'rather common' in his traditional Bavarian outfit of lederhosen, thick woollen socks, red and blue checked shirt, and ill-fitting short blue jacket. Winifred, the English-born wife of Wagner's son Siegfried, thought he was 'destined to be the saviour of Germany'. Siegfried himself saw Hitler as 'a fraud and an upstart'.

The rapid growth in the party during the latter part of 1922 and especially in 1923 that had made it a political force in Munich, its closer connections with the 'patriotic associations', and the wider social contacts which now arose meant that funding flowed more readily to the NSDAP than had been the case in its first years. Now, as later, the party's finances relied heavily upon members' subscriptions together with entrance-fees and collections at meetings. The more came to meetings, the more were recruited as members, the more income came to the party, to permit yet more meetings to be held. Propaganda financed propaganda.

But even now, the party's heavy outgoings were difficult to meet, and funding was not easy to drum up in conditions of rip-roaring inflation. There was a premium on donations made in hard foreign currency. Lüdecke and Hanfstaengl, as already noted, were useful in this regard. Hanfstaengl also financed with an interest-free loan of 1,000 dollars – a fortune in inflation-ridden Germany – the purchase of two rotary presses that enabled the *Völkischer Beobachter* to appear in larger, American-style format. Rumours, some far wide of the mark, about the party's finances were repeatedly aired by opponents in the press. Even so, official inquiries in 1923 revealed considerable sums raised from an increasing array of benefactors.

One important go-between was Max Erwin von Scheubner-Richter, born in Riga, linguistically able, with diplomatic service in Turkey during the war, and later imprisoned for a time by Communists on his return to the Baltic. After the war he had participated in the Kapp Putsch, then, like so many counter-revolutionaries, made his way to Munich, where he joined the NSDAP in autumn 1920. A significant, if shadowy, figure in the early Nazi Party, he used his excellent connections with Russian émigrés, such as Princess Alexandra, wife of the Russian heir to the throne Prince Kyrill, to acquire funds directed at Ludendorff and, through him, deflected in part to the NSDAP. Other members of the aristocracy, including Frau Gertrud von Seidlitz, who used monies from foreign stocks and shares, also contributed to Nazi funds. Hitler was almost certainly a co-beneficiary (though probably in a minor way) of the generous gift of 100,000 Gold Marks made by Fritz Thyssen, heir to the family's Ruhr steelworks, to Ludendorff, but Germany's leading industrialists, apart from Ernst von Borsig, head of the Berlin locomotive and machine-building firm, showed little direct interest in the Nazis at this time. Police inquiries which remained inconclusive suggested that Borsig and car-manufacturers Daimler were among other firms contributing to the party. Some Bavarian industrialists and businessmen, too, were persuaded by Hitler to make donations to the movement.

Valuable funds were also attained abroad. Anti-Marxism and the hopes in a strong Germany as a bulwark against Bolshevism often provided motive enough for such donations. The *Völkischer Beobachter*'s new offices were financed with Czech Kronen. An important link with Swiss funds was Dr Emil Gansser, a Berlin chemist and long-standing Nazi supporter, who engineered a gift of 33,000 Swiss Francs from right-wing Swiss benefactors. Further Swiss donations followed a visit from Hitler himself to Zurich in the summer of 1923. And from right-wing circles in the arch-enemy France, 90,000 Gold Marks were passed to Captain Karl Mayr, Hitler's first patron, and from him to the 'patriotic associations'. It can be presumed that the NSDAP was among the beneficiaries. In addition to monetary donations, Röhm saw to it that the SA, along with other paramilitary organizations, was well provided with equipment and weapons from his secret arsenal. Whatever the financial support, without Röhm's supplies an armed putsch would scarcely have been possible.

In November 1922, rumours were already circulating that Hitler was planning a putsch. By January 1923, in the explosive climate following the French march into the Ruhr, the rumours in Munich of a Hitler putsch were even stronger. The crisis, without which Hitler would have been nothing, was deepening by the day. In its wake, the Nazi movement was expanding rapidly. Some 35,000 were to join between February and November 1923, giving a strength of around 55,000 on the eve of the putsch. Recruits came from all sections of society. Around a third were workers, a tenth or more came from the upper-middle and professional classes, but more than a half belonged to the crafts, commercial, white-collar, and farming lower-middle class. Most had joined the party out of protest, anger, and bitterness as the economic and political crisis mounted. The same was true of the thousands flocking into the SA. Hitler had won their support by promising them action. The sacrifices of the war would be avenged. The revolution would be overturned. He could not hold them at fever-pitch indefinitely without unleashing such action. The tendency to 'go for broke' was not simply a character-trait of Hitler; it was built into the nature of his leadership, his political aims, and the party he led. But Hitler was not in control of events as they unfolded in 1923. Nor was he, before 8 November, the leading player in the drama. Without the readiness of powerful figures and organizations to contemplate a putsch against Berlin, Hitler would have had no stage on which to act so disastrously. His own role, his actions – and reactions – have to be seen in that light.

III

Hitler's incessant barrage of anti-government propaganda was nearly undermined by an event that invoked national unity in January 1923: the French occupation of the Ruhr. On this occasion at least, the Reich government seemed to be acting firmly – and acting with mass popular support – through its campaign of 'passive resistance' against the occupation. Attacks on the Berlin government at this juncture seemed unpromising. Undeterred, Hitler saw advantage to be gained from the French occupation. As usual, he went on a propaganda offensive.

On the very day of the French march into the Ruhr he spoke in a packed Circus Krone. 'Down with the November Criminals' was the title of his speech. It was not the first time he had used the term 'November Criminals' to describe the Social Democrat revolutionaries of 1918. But from now on, the slogan was seldom far from his lips. It showed the line he would take towards the Ruhr occupation. The real enemy was within. Marxism, democracy, parliamentarism, internationalism, and, of course, behind it all the power of the Jews, were held by Hitler to blame for the national defencelessness that allowed the French to treat Germany like a colony.

The propaganda offensive was stepped up with preparations for the NSDAP's first 'Reich Party Rally', scheduled to take place in Munich on 27–29 January. It brought confrontation with the Bavarian government, so frightened about rumours of a putsch that on 26 January it declared a state of emergency in Munich, but so weak that it lacked the power to carry through its intended ban on the rally. At the meetings during the rally, Hitler could once more appear self-confident, certain of success, to the masses of his supporters. The whole rally had been devised in the form of a ritual homage-paying to the 'leader of the German freedom-movement'. The leadership cult, consciously devised to sustain maximum cohesion within the party, was taking off. According to a newspaper report, Hitler was greeted 'like a saviour' when he entered the Festsaal of the Hofbräuhaus during one of his twelve speeches on the evening of 27 January. In the feverish atmosphere in the Löwenbräu-keller the same evening, he was given a similar hero's welcome as he entered the hall, deliberately late, shielded by his bodyguard, arm outstretched in the salute – probably borrowed from the Italian Fascists (and by them from Imperial Rome) – which would become standard in the Movement by 1926.

Hitler's near-exclusive concentration on propaganda was not Röhm's approach, while the latter's emphasis on the paramilitary posed a latent threat to Hitler's authority. At the beginning of February, Röhm founded a 'Working Group of the Patriotic Fighting Associations' (Arbeitsge-meinschaft der Vaterländischen Kampfverbände) comprising, alongside the SA, the Bund Oberland, Reichsflagge, Wikingbund, and Kampfver-band Niederbayern. Direct military control was in the hands of retired Oberstleutnant Hermann Kriebel, previously a chief of staff in the Bavarian Einwohnerwehr. The formations were trained by the Bavarian Reichswehr – not for incorporation in any defence against further inroads by the French and Belgians (the threat of which was by this time plainly receding), but evidently for the eventuality of conflict with Berlin. Once subsumed in this umbrella organization, the SA was far from the biggest paramilitary grouping and there was little to distinguish it from the other bodies. In a purely military organization, it had only a subordi-nate role. The conversion of the SA to a paramilitary organization now not directly or solely under his own control was not to Hitler's liking. But there was nothing he could do about it. However, Hitler was pushed by Röhm into the foreground of the political leadership of the 'Working Community'. He it was who was asked by Röhm to define the political aims of the 'Working Community'. He was now moving in high circles indeed. In early 1923 he was brought into contact by Röhm with no less than the Chief of the Army Command of the Reichswehr, General Hans von Seeckt (who remained, however, distinctly unimpressed by the Munich demagogue, and unprepared to commit himself to the demands for radical action in the Ruhr conflict for which Hitler was pressing). Röhm also insisted to the new Bavarian Commander, General Otto Hermann von Lossow, that Hitler's movement, with its aim of winning over the workers to the national cause, offered the best potential for building a 'patriotic fighting front' to upturn the November Revolution.

Connected with all the strands of nationalist paramilitary politics, if openly directing none, was the figure of General Ludendorff, regarded by most as the symbolic leader of the radical nationalist Right. The former war-hero had returned to Germany from his Swedish exile in February 1919, taking up residence in Munich. His radical *völkisch* nationalism, detestation of the new Republic, and prominent advocacy of the 'stab-in-the-back' legend, had already taken him effortlessly into the slipstream of the Pan-Germans, brought him fringe participation in the Kapp Putsch, and now led to his close involvement with the counter-revolutionary extreme Right, for whom his reputation and standing were a notable asset. The hotbed of Munich's *völkisch* and paramilitary politics provided the setting within which, remarkably, the famous Quartermaster-General, virtual dictator of Germany and chief driving-force of the war effort between 1916 and 1918, could come into close contact and direct collaboration with the former army corporal, Adolf Hitler. Even more remarkable was the rapidity with which, in the new world of rabble-rousing politics to which General Ludendorff was ill-attuned, the ex-corporal would come to eclipse his one-time military commander as the leading spokesman of the radical Right.

The paramilitary politics of spring 1923, in the wake of the French occupation of the Ruhr, were confused and riddled with conflict and intrigue. But, largely through Röhm's manoeuvrings, Hitler, the beerhall agitator, had been brought into the arena of top-level discussions with the highest military as well as paramilitary leadership, not just in Bavaria, but in the Reich. He was now a player for big stakes. But he could not control the moves of other, more powerful, players with their own agendas. His constant agitation could mobilize support for a time. But this could not be held at fever-pitch indefinitely. It demanded action. Hitler's impatience, his 'all-or-nothing' stance, was not simply a matter of temperament.

Activists, as Hitler later acknowledged, could not be kept in a state of tension indefinitely without some release. He proposed a national demonstration on May Day, and an armed attack on the 'Reds'. Increasingly alarmed by the prospect of serious disturbances, the Munich police revoked its permission for the Left's street-parade, and allowed only a limited demonstration on the spacious Theresienwiese near the city centre. Rumours of a putsch from the Left, almost certainly set into circulation by the Right, served as a pretext for a 'defence' by the paramilitary bodies. They demanded 'their' weapons back from safe-keeping under the control of the Reichswehr. But on the afternoon of 30 April, at a meeting with paramilitary leaders, Lossow, concerned about the danger of a putsch from the *Right*, refused to hand over the armaments. Hitler, in a blind rage, accused Lossow of breach of trust. But there was nothing to be done. Hitler had been overconfident. And this time, for once, the state authorities had remained firm. All that could be salvaged was a gathering the following morning of around 2,000 men from the paramilitary formations – about 1,300 from the National Socialists – on the Oberwiesenfeld in the barracks area north of the city, well away from the May Day demonstration and firmly ringed by a cordon of police. Tame exercises carried out with arms distributed from Röhm's arsenal were no substitute for the planned assault on the Left. After standing around for much of the time since dawn holding their rifles and facing the police, the men handed back their arms around two o'clock and dispersed. Many had left already. Most recognized the events of May Day to have been a severe embarrassment for Hitler and his followers.

The May Day affair ought to have shown the government that firm and resolute action could defeat Hitler. But by this time, the Bavarian government had long since ruled out any potential for working together with the democratic forces on the Left. It was permanently at loggerheads with the Reich government. And it had no effective control over its army leaders, who were playing their own game. It was little wonder in this context that it was buffeted in all directions. Incapable of tackling the problem of the radical Right because both will and power were ultimately lacking to do so, it allowed the Hitler Movement the space to recover from the temporary setback of 1 May.

But above all, the lesson of 1 May was that Hitler was powerless without the support of the Reichswehr. In January, when the Party Rally had been initially banned, then allowed to go ahead, Lossow's permission had given Hitler the chance to escape the blow to his prestige. Now, on 1 May, Lossow's refusal had prevented Hitler's planned propaganda triumph. Deprived of his life-blood – regular outlets for his propaganda – the main base of Hitler's effectiveness would have been undermined. But the Bavarian Reichswehr was to remain largely an independent variable in the equation of Bavarian politics in the latter part of 1923. And the part accommodating, part vacillating attitude of the Bavarian authorities to the radical Right, driven by fierce anti-socialism linked to its antagonism towards Berlin, ensured that the momentum of Hitler's movement was not seriously checked by the May Day events. Hitler could, in fact, have been taken out of circulation altogether for up to two years, had charges of breach of the peace, arising from the May Day incidents, been pressed. But the Bavarian Justice Minister Franz Gürtner saw to it that the inquiries never came to formal charges – after Hitler had threatened to reveal details of Reichswehr complicity in the training and arming of the paramilitaries in preparation for a war against France – and the matter was quietly dropped.

For his part, Hitler continued scarcely abated his relentless agitation against the 'November criminals' during the summer of 1923. The fierce animosity towards Berlin, now as before providing a bond between the otherwise competing sections of the Right, ensured that his message of hatred and revenge towards internal as well as external enemies would not be short of an audience. He alone remained able to fill the cavernous Zircus Krone. Between May and the beginning of August he addressed five overfilled meetings there, and also spoke at another ten party meetings elsewhere in Bavaria. But for deeds to follow words, Hitler had to rely on others. He needed most of all the support of the Reichswehr. But he also needed the cooperation of the other paramilitary organizations. And in the realm of paramilitary politics, he was not a free agent. Certainly, new members continued to pour into the SA during the summer. But after the embarrassment of 1 May, Hitler was for some time less prominent, even retreating at the end of May for a while to stay with Dietrich Eckart in a small hotel at Berchtesgaden. Among the members of the various branches of the 'patriotic associations', Ludendorff, not Hitler, was regarded as the symbol of the 'national struggle'. Hitler was in this forum only one of a number of spokesmen. In the case of disagreement, he too had to bow to Ludendorff 's superiority.

The former world-war hero took centre stage at the *Deutscher Tag* (German Day) in Nuremberg on 1–2 September 1923, a massive rally – the police reckoned 100,000 were present – of nationalist paramilitary forces and veterans' associations scheduled to coincide with the anniversary of the German victory over France at the battle of Sedan in 1870. Along with the Reichsflagge, the National Socialists were particularly well represented. The enormous propaganda spectacular enabled Hitler, the most effective of the speakers, to repair the damage his reputation had suffered in May. At the two-hour march-past of the formations, he stood together with General Ludendorff, Prinz Ludwig Ferdinand of Bavaria, and the military head of the 'patriotic associations', Oberstleutnant Kriebel, on the podium.

What came out of the rally was the uniting of the NSDAP, the Bund Oberland, and the Reichsflagge in the newly-formed Deutscher Kampfbund (German Combat League). While Kriebel took over the military leadership, Hitler's man Scheubner-Richter was made business-manager. Three weeks later, thanks to Röhm's machinations, Hitler was given, with the agreement of the heads of the other paramilitary organizations, the 'political leadership' of the Kampfbund.

What this meant in practice was not altogether clear. Hitler was no dictator in the umbrella organization. And so far as there were specific notions about a future dictator in the 'coming Germany', that position was envisaged as Ludendorff's. For Hitler, 'political leadership' seems to have indicated the subordination of paramilitary politics to the building of a revolutionary mass movement through nationalist propaganda and agitation. But for the leaders of the formations, the 'primacy of the soldier' – the professionals like Röhm and Kriebel – was what still counted. Hitler was seen as a type of 'political instructor'. He could whip up the feelings of the masses like no one else. But beyond that he had no clear idea of the mechanics of attaining power. Cooler heads were needed for that. As an 'Action Programme' of the Kampfbund drawn up by Scheubner-Richter on 24 September made plain, the 'national revolution' in Bavaria had to follow, not precede, the winning over of the army and police, the forces that sustained the power of the state. Scheubner-Richter concluded that it was necessary to take over the police in a formally legal fashion by placing Kampfbund leaders in charge of the Bavarian Ministry of the Interior and the Munich police. Hitler, like his partners in the Kampfbund, knew that an attempt at a putsch in the teeth of opposition from the forces of the military and police in Bavaria stood little chance of success. But for the time being his approach, as ever, was to go on a frontal propaganda offensive against the Bavarian government. His position within the Kampfbund now ensured that the pressure to act – even without a clear strategy for the practical steps needed to gain control of the state – would not relent.

IV

Crisis was Hitler's oxygen. He needed it to survive. And the deteriorating conditions in Germany (with their distinctive flavour in Bavaria) as summer turned to autumn, and the currency collapsed totally under the impact of the 'passive resistance' policy, guaranteed an increasing appeal for Hitler's brand of agitation. By the time he took over the political leadership of the Kampfbund, Germany's searing crisis was heading for its denouement.

The country was bankrupt, its currency ruined. Inflation had gone into a dizzy tail-spin. Speculators and profiteers thrived. But the material consequences of the hyper-inflation for ordinary people were devastating, the psychological effects incalculable. Savings of a lifetime were wiped out within hours. Insurance policies were not worth the paper they were written on. Those with pensions and fixed incomes saw their only source of support dissolve into worthlessness. Workers were less badly hit. Employers, eager to prevent social unrest, agreed with trade unions to index wages to living costs. Even so, it was little wonder that the massive discontent brought sharp political radicalization on the Left as well as on the Right.

Bavaria's immediate response to the ending of passive resistance on 26 September was to proclaim a state of emergency and make Gustav Ritter von Kahr General State Commissar with near-dictatorial powers. The Reich responded with the declaration of a general state of emergency and the granting of emergency powers to the Reichswehr. One of Kahr's first acts was to ban – amid renewed putsch rumours – the fourteen meetings which the NSDAP had planned for the evening of 27 September. Hitler was in a frenzy of rage. He felt bypassed by the manoeuvre to bring in Kahr, and certain that the head of the Bavarian state was not the man to lead a national revolution. Alongside attacks on the Reich government for betraying the national resistance – a contrary, though more popular, line to that he had taken earlier in the year towards the policy of passive resistance – Hitler now turned his fire on Kahr.

The weeks following Kahr's appointment were filled with plot, intrigue, and tension which mounted to fever-pitch. The Munich police registered a worsening mood by September, looking for an outlet in some sort of action. Political meetings were, however, not well attended because of the high entry charges and the price of beer. Only the Nazis could continue to fill the beerhalls. As rumours of a forthcoming putsch continued to circulate, there was a feeling that something would have to happen soon.

Hitler was under pressure to act. The leader of the Munich SA regiment, Wilhelm Brückner, told him: 'The day is coming when I can no longer hold my people. If nothing happens now the men will sneak away.' Scheubner-Richter said much the same: 'In order to keep the men together, one must finally undertake something. Otherwise the people will become Left radicals.' Hitler himself used almost the identical argument with head of the Landespolizei Colonel Hans Ritter von Seißer at the beginning of November: 'Economic pressures drive our people so that we must either act or our followers will swing to the Communists.' Hitler's instincts were in any case to force the issue as soon as possible. The favourable circumstances of the comprehensive state crisis could not last indefinitely. He was determined not to be outflanked by von Kahr. And his own prestige would wane if nothing was attempted and enthusiasm dissipated, or if the movement were faced down again as it had been on 1 May.

However, the cards were not in his hands. Kahr and the two other members of the triumvirate which was effectively ruling Bavaria (State Police chief Seißer and Reichswehr commander Lossow) had their own agenda, which differed in significant detail from that of the Kampfbund leadership. In extensive negotiations with north German contacts throughout October, the triumvirate was looking to install a nationalist dictatorship in Berlin based on a directorate, with or without Kahr as a member but certainly without the inclusion of Ludendorff or Hitler, and resting on the support of the Reichswehr. The Kampfbund leadership, on the other hand, wanted a directorate in Munich, centring on Ludendorff and Hitler, certainly without von Kahr, which would take Berlin by force. And while Lossow took it for granted that any move against the Berlin government would be carried out by the military, the Kampfbund presumed that it would be a paramilitary operation with Reichswehr backing. If need be, declared the Kampfbund military leader, Oberstleutnant Kriebel, the Kampfbund would even resist any attempts by the Bavarian government to use armed force against the 'patriotic associations'. Hitler did his best to win over Lossow and Seißer, subjecting the latter on 24 October to a four-hour lecture on his aims.

Neither was persuaded to throw in his lot with the Kampfbund, though the position of Lossow – with chief responsibility for order in Bavaria – was ambiguous and wavering.

At the beginning of November, Seißer was sent to Berlin to conduct negotiations on behalf of the triumvirate with a number of important contacts, most vitally with Seeckt. The Reichswehr chief made plain at the meeting on 3 November that he would not move against the legal government in Berlin. With that, any plans of the triumvirate were effectively scuppered. At a crucial meeting in Munich three days later with the heads of the 'patriotic associations', including Kriebel of the Kampfbund, Kahr warned the 'patriotic associations' – by which he meant the Kampfbund – against independent action. Any attempt to impose a national government in Berlin had to be unified and follow prepared plans. Lossow stated he would go along with a rightist dictatorship if the chances of success were 51 per cent, but would have no truck with an ill-devised putsch. Seißer also underlined his support for Kahr and readiness to put down a putsch by force. It was plain that the triumvirate was not prepared to act against Berlin.

Hitler was now faced with the thread slipping through his fingers. He was not prepared to wait any longer and risk losing the initiative. It was clear, now as before, that a putsch would only be successful with the support of police and army. But he was determined to delay no longer.

At a meeting on the evening of 6 November with Scheubner-Richter, Theodor von der Pfordten (a member of the supreme court in Bavaria and shadowy figure in pre-putsch Nazi circles), and probably other advisers (though this is not certain), he decided to act – in the hope more than the certainty of forcing the triumvirate to support the coup. The decision to strike was confirmed the next day, 7 November, at a meeting of Kampfbund leaders. After a good deal of discussion, Hitler's plan was adopted. It was decided that the strike would be carried out on the following day, 8 November, when all the prominent figures in Munich would be assembled in the Bürgerbräukeller, one of the city's huge beerhalls, to hear an address from Kahr on the fifth anniversary of the November Revolution, fiercely denouncing Marxism. Hitler felt his hand forced by Kahr's meeting. If the Kampfbund were to lead the 'national revolution', there was nothing for it but to act on its own initiative immediately. Much later, Hitler stated: 'Our opponents intended to proclaim a Bavarian revolution around the 12th of November . . . I took the decision to strike four days earlier.'

Kahr had been reading out his prepared speech to the 3,000 or so packed into the Bürgerbräukeller for about half an hour when, around 8.30 p.m., there was a disturbance at the entrance. Kahr broke off his speech. A body of men in steel helmets appeared. Hitler's stormtroopers had arrived. A heavy machine-gun was pushed into the hall. People were standing on their seats trying to see what was happening as Hitler advanced through the hall, accompanied by two armed bodyguards, their pistols pointing at the ceiling. Hitler stood on a chair but, unable to make himself heard in the tumult, took out his Browning pistol and fired a shot through the ceiling. He then announced that the national revolution had broken out, and that the hall was surrounded by 600 armed men. If there was trouble, he said, he would bring a machine-gun into the gallery. The Bavarian government was deposed; a provisional Reich government would be formed. It was by this time around 8.45 p.m. Hitler requested – though it was really an order – Kahr, Lossow, and Seißer to accompany him into the adjoining room. He guaranteed their safety. After some hesitation, they complied. There was bedlam in the hall, but eventually Göring managed to make himself heard. He said the action was directed neither at Kahr nor at the army and police. People should stay calm and remain in their places. 'You've got your beer,' he added. This quietened things somewhat.

In the adjoining room, Hitler announced, waving his pistol about, that no one would leave without his permission. He declared the formation of a new Reich government, headed by himself. Ludendorff was to be in charge of the national army, Lossow would be Reichswehr Minister, Seißer Police Minister, Kahr himself would be head of state as regent (*Landesverweser*), and Pöhner Minister President with dictatorial powers in Bavaria. He apologized for having to force the pace, but it had to be done: he had had to enable the triumvirate to act. If things went wrong, he had four bullets in his pistol – three for his collaborators, the last for himself.

Hitler returned to the hall after about ten minutes amid renewed tumult. He repeated Göring's assurances that the action was not directed at the police and Reichswehr, but 'solely at the Berlin Jew government and the November criminals of 1918'. He put forward his proposals for the new governments in Berlin and Munich, now mentioning Ludendorff as 'leader, and chief with dictatorial power, of the German national army'. He told the crowded hall that matters were taking longer than he had earlier predicted. 'Outside are Kahr, Lossow, and Seißer,' he declared. 'They are struggling hard to reach a decision. May I say to them that you will stand behind them?' As the crowd bellowed back its approval, Hitler, with his pronounced sense of the theatrical, announced in emotional terms: 'I can say this to you: Either the German revolution begins tonight or we will all be dead by dawn!' By the time he had finished his short address the mood in the hall had swung completely in his favour.

About an hour had passed since Hitler's initial entry into the hall before he and Ludendorff (who had meanwhile arrived, dressed in full uniform of the Imperial Army), together with the Bavarian ruling triumvirate, returned to the podium. Kahr, calm, face like a mask, spoke first, announcing to tumultuous applause that he had agreed to serve Bavaria as regent for the monarchy. Hitler, with a euphoric expression resembling childlike delight, declared that he would direct the policy of the new Reich government, and warmly clasped Kahr's hand. Ludendorff, deadly earnest, spoke next, mentioning his surprise at the whole business. Lossow, wearing a somewhat impenetrable expression, and Seißer, the most agitated of the group, were pressed by Hitler into speaking. Pöhner finally promised cooperation with Kahr. Hitler shook hands once more with the whole ensemble. He was the undoubted star of the show. It appeared to be his night.

From this point, however, things went badly wrong. The hurried improvisation of the planning, the hectic rush to prepare at only a day's notice, that had followed Hitler's impatient insistence that the putsch should be advanced to the evening of the Bürgerbräukeller meeting, now took its toll, determining the shambolic course of the night's events. Röhm did manage to occupy the Reichswehr headquarters, though amazingly failed to take over the telephone switchboard, allowing Lossow to order the transport to Munich of loyalist troops in nearby towns and cities. Frick and Pöhner were also initially successful in taking control at police headquarters. Elsewhere, the situation was deteriorating rapidly. In a night of chaos, the putschists failed dismally, largely owing to their own disorganization, to take control of barracks and government buildings. The early and partial successes were for the most part rapidly overturned. Neither the army nor the state police joined forces with the putschists.

Back at the Bürgerbräukeller, Hitler, too, was making his first mistake of the evening. Hearing reports of difficulties the putschists were encountering at the Engineers' Barracks, he decided to go there himself in what proved a vain attempt to intervene. Ludendorff was left in charge at the Bürgerbräukeller and, believing the word of officers and gentlemen, promptly let Kahr, Lossow, and Seißer depart. They were then free to renege on the promises extracted from them under duress by Hitler.

By late evening, Kahr, Lossow, and Seißer were in positions to assure the state authorities that they repudiated the putsch. All German radio stations were informed of this by Lossow at 2.55 a.m. By the early hours, it was becoming clear to the putschists themselves that the triumvirate and – far more importantly – the Reichswehr and state police opposed the coup. At 5 a.m. Hitler was still giving assurances that he was determined to fight and die for the cause – a sign that by this time at the latest he, too, had lost confidence in the success of the putsch.

The putschist leaders were themselves by this time unclear what to do next. They sat around arguing, while the government forces regrouped. There was no fall-back position. Hitler was as clueless as the others. He was far from in control of the situation. As the bitterly cold morning dawned, depressed troops began to drift off from the Bürgerbräukeller. Around 8 a.m. Hitler sent some of his SA men to seize bundles of 50-billion Mark notes direct from the printing press to keep his troops paid. It was more or less the only practical action taken as the putsch started rapidly to crumble.

Only during the course of the morning did Hitler and Ludendorff come up with the idea of a demonstration march through the city. Ludendorff apparently made the initial suggestion. The aim was predictably confused and unclear. 'In Munich, Nuremberg, Bayreuth, an immeasurable jubilation, an enormous enthusiasm would have broken out in the German Reich,' Hitler later remarked. 'And when the first division of the German national army had left the last square metre of Bavarian soil and stepped for the first time on to Thuringian land, we would have experienced the jubilation of the people there. People would have had to recognize that the German misery has an end, that redemption could only come about through a rising.' It amounted to a vague hope that the march would stir popular enthusiasm for the putsch, and that the army, faced with the fervour of the mobilized masses and the prospect of firing on the war-hero Ludendorff, would change its mind.

The gathering acclaim of the masses and the support of the army would then pave the way for a triumphant march on Berlin. Such was the wild illusion – gesture politics born out of pessimism, depression, and despair. Reality did not take long to assert itself.

Around noon, the column of about 2,000 men – many of them, including Hitler, armed – set out from the Bürgerbräukeller. Pistols at the ready, they confronted a small police cordon on the Ludwigsbrücke and under threat swept it aside, headed to Marienplatz, in the centre of the city, and decided then to march to the War Ministry. They gained encouragement from throngs of shouting and waving supporters on the pavements. Some thought they were witnessing the arrival of the new government. The putschists could not help but note, however, that many of the posters proclaiming the national revolution had already been ripped down or papered over with new directions from the ruling triumvirate. The participants on the march knew the cause was lost. One of them remarked that it was like a funeral procession.

At the top of the Residenzstraße, as it approaches Odeonsplatz, the marchers encountered the second, and larger, police cordon. 'Here they come. Heil Hitler!' a bystander cried out. Then shots rang out. When the firing ceased, fourteen putschists and four policemen lay dead.

The dead included one of the putsch architects, Erwin von Scheubner-Richter, who had been in the front line of the putsch leaders, linking arms with Hitler, just behind the standard-bearers. Had the bullet which killed Scheubner-Richter been a foot to the right, history would have taken a different course. As it was, Hitler either took instant evasive action, or was wrenched to the ground by Scheubner-Richter. In any event, he dislocated his left shoulder. Göring was among those injured, shot in the leg. He and a number of other leading putschists were able to escape over the Austrian border. Some, including Streicher, Frick, Pöhner, Amann, and Röhm, were immediately arrested. Ludendorff, who had emerged from the shoot-out totally unscathed, gave himself up and was released on his officer's word.

Hitler himself was attended to by Dr Walter Schultze, chief of the Munich SA medical corps, pushed into his car, stationed nearby, and driven at speed from the scene of the action. He ended up at Hanfstaengl's home in Uffing, near the Staffelsee, south of Munich, where the police, on the evening of 11 November, found and arrested him. While at Hanfstaengl's – Putzi himself had taken flight to Austria –

he composed the first of his 'political testaments', placing the party chairmanship in Rosenberg's hands, with Amann as his deputy. Hitler, according to Hanfstaengl's later account, based on his wife's testimony, was desolate on arrival in Uffing. But later stories that he had to be restrained from suicide have no firm backing. He was depressed but calm, dressed in a white nightgown, his injured left arm in a sling, when the police arrived to escort him to prison in the old fortress at Landsberg am Lech, a picturesque little town some forty miles west of Munich. Thirty-nine guards were on hand to greet him in his new place of residence. Graf Arco, the killer of Kurt Eisner, the Bavarian premier murdered in February 1919, was evicted from his spacious Cell no. 7 to make room for the new, high-ranking prisoner.

In Munich and other parts of Bavaria, the putsch fizzled out as rapidly as it had started. Hitler was finished. At least, he should have been.

V

Like the high-point of a dangerous fever, the crisis had passed, then rapidly subsided. The following months brought currency stabilization with the introduction of the Rentenmark, regulation of the reparations issue through the Dawes Plan (named after the American banker Charles G. Dawes, head of the committee which established in 1924 a provisional framework for the phased payment of reparations, commencing at a low level and linked to foreign loans for Germany), and the beginning of the political stabilization that marked the end of the post-war turbulence and was to last until the new economic shock-waves of the late 1920s. With Hitler in jail, the NSDAP banned, and the *völkisch* movement split into its component factions, the threat from the extreme Right lost its immediate potency.

Sympathies with the radical Right by no means disappeared. With 33 per cent of the votes in Munich, the Völkischer Block (the largest grouping in the now fractured *völkisch* movement) was the strongest party in the city at the Landtag elections on 6 April 1924, gaining more votes than both the Socialists and Communists put together. At the Reichstag election on 4 May, the result was little different. The Völkischer Block won 28.5 per cent of the vote in Munich, 17 per cent overall in the electoral region of Upper Bavaria and Swabia, and 20.8 per cent in

Franconia. But the bubble had burst. As Germany recovered and the Right remained in disarray, voters deserted the *völkisch* movement. By the second Reichstag elections of 1924, a fortnight before Hitler's release from Landsberg, the vote for the Völkischer Block had dwindled to residual limits of 7.5 per cent in Franconia, 4.8 per cent in Upper Bavaria/Swabia, and 3.0 per cent in Lower Bavaria (compared with 10.2 per cent there eight months earlier).

Bavaria, for all its continuing ingrained oddities, was no longer the boiling cauldron of radical Right insurgency it had been between 1920 and 1923. The paramilitary organizations had had their teeth drawn in the confrontation with the legal forces of the state. Without the support of the army, they were shown to be little more than a paper tiger. In the aftermath of the putsch, the Kampfbund organizations were dissolved, and the 'patriotic associations' in general had their weaponry confiscated, a ban imposed on their military exercises, and their activities greatly curtailed. The triumvirate installed by the Bavarian government as a force on the Right to contain the wilder and even more extreme nationalist paramilitaries lost power and credibility through the putsch. Kahr, Lossow, and Seißer were all ousted by early 1924. With the General Commissariat terminated, conventional cabinet government under a new Minister President, Dr Heinrich Held – the leading figure in the Catholic establishment party in Bavaria, the BVP – and with it a degree of calm, returned to Bavarian politics.

Even now, however, the forces which had given Hitler his entrée into politics and enabled him to develop into a key factor on the Bavarian Right contrived to save him when his 'career' ought to have been over. The 'Hitler-Putsch' was, as we have seen, by no means merely Hitler's putsch. The Bavarian Reichswehr had colluded massively in the training and preparation of the forces which had tried to take over the state. And important personages had been implicated in the putsch attempt. Whatever their subsequent defence of their actions, the hands of Kahr, Lossow, and Seißer were dirty, while the war hero General Ludendorff had been the spiritual figurehead of the entire enterprise. There was every reason, therefore, in the trial of the putsch leaders held in Munich between 26 February and 27 March 1924 to let the spotlight fall completely on Hitler. He was only too glad to play the role assigned to him.

Hitler's first reaction to his indictment had been very different from his later triumphalist performance in the Munich court. He had initially refused to say anything, and announced that he was going on hunger-strike. At this time, he plainly saw everything as lost. According to the prison psychologist – though speaking many years after the event – Hitler stated: 'I've had enough. I'm finished. If I had a revolver, I would take it.' Drexler later claimed that he himself had dissuaded Hitler from his intention to commit suicide.

By the time the trial opened, Hitler's stance had changed diametrically. He was allowed to turn the courtroom into a stage for his own propaganda, accepting full responsibility for what had happened, not merely justifying but glorifying his role in attempting to overthrow the Weimar state. This was in no small measure owing to his threats to expose the complicity in treasonable activity of Kahr, Lossow, and Seißer – and in particular the role of the Bavarian Reichswehr.

The ruling forces in Bavaria did what they could to limit potential damage. The first priority was to make sure that the trial was held under Bavarian jurisdiction. In strict legality, the trial ought not to have taken place in Munich at all, but at the Reich Court in Leipzig. However, the Reich government gave way to pressure from the Bavarian government. The trial was set for the People's Court in Munich.

Kahr had hoped to avoid any trial, or at least have no more than a perfunctory one where the indicted would plead guilty but claim mitigating grounds of patriotism. Since some at least of the putschists would not agree, this course of action had to be dropped. But it seems highly probable that the accused were offered leniency for such a proposal even to have been considered. Hitler had, at any rate, become confident about the outcome. He still held a trump card in his hand. When Hanfstaengl visited him in his cell in the courthouse, during the trial, he showed no fear of the verdict. 'What can they do to me?' he asked. 'I only need to come out with a bit more, especially about Lossow, and there's the big scandal. Those in the know are well aware of that.' This, and the attitude of the presiding judge and his fellow judges, explains Hitler's self-confident appearance at the trial.

Among those indicted alongside Hitler were Ludendorff, Pöhner, Frick, Weber (of Bund Oberland), Röhm, and Kriebel. But the indictment itself was emphatic that 'Hitler was the soul of the entire enterprise'. Judge Neithardt, the president of the court, had reputedly stated before the trial that Ludendorff would be acquitted. The judge replaced a damaging record of Ludendorff's first interrogation by one which indicated his ignorance about the putsch preparations. Hitler, meanwhile, was given the freedom of the courtroom. One journalist attending the trial described it as a 'political carnival'. He compared the deference shown to the defendants with the brusque way those arraigned for their actions in the Räterepublik had been handled. He heard one of the judges, after Hitler's first speech, remark: 'What a tremendous chap, this Hitler!' Hitler was allowed to appear in his suit, not prison garb, sporting his Iron Cross, First Class. Ludendorff, not held in prison, arrived in a luxury limousine. Dr Weber, though under arrest, was allowed to take a Sunday afternoon walk round Munich. The extraordinary bias of the presiding judge was later most severely criticized both in Berlin and by the Bavarian government, irritated at the way attacks on the Reichswehr and state police had been allowed without contradiction. Judge Neithardt was informed in no uncertain terms during the trial of the 'embarrassing impression' left by allowing Hitler to speak for four hours. His only response was that it was impossible to interrupt the torrent of words. Hitler was also allowed the freedom to interrogate witnesses – above all Kahr, Lossow, and Seißer – at length, frequently deviating into politically loaded statements.

When the verdicts were read out four days after the trial ended, on 1 April 1924, Ludendorff was duly acquitted – which he took as an insult. Hitler, along with Weber, Kriebel, and Pöhner, was sentenced to a mere five years' imprisonment for high treason (less the four months and two weeks he had already been in custody), and a fine of 200 Gold Marks (or a further twenty days' imprisonment). The others indicted received even milder sentences. The lay judges, as Hitler later acknowledged, had only been prepared to accept a verdict of 'guilty' on condition that he received the mildest sentence, with the prospect of early release. The court explained why it rejected the deportation of Hitler under the terms of the 'Protection of the Republic Act': 'Hitler is a German-Austrian. He considers himself to be a German. In the opinion of the court, the meaning and intention of the terms of section 9, para II of the Law for the Protection of the Republic cannot apply to a man who thinks and feels as German as Hitler, who voluntarily served for four and a half years in the German army at war, who attained high military honours through outstanding bravery in the face of the enemy, was wounded, suffered other damage to his health, and was released from the military into the control of the District Command Munich I.'

Even on the conservative Right in Bavaria, the conduct of the trial and sentences prompted amazement and disgust. In legal terms, the sentence was nothing short of scandalous. No mention was made in the verdict of the four policemen shot by the putschists; the robbery of 14,605 billion paper Marks (the equivalent of around 28,000 Gold Marks) was entirely played down; the destruction of the offices of the SPD newspaper *Münchener Post* and the taking of a number of Social Democratic city councillors as hostages were not blamed on Hitler; and no word was made of the text of a new constitution, found in the pocket of the dead putschist von der Pfordten. Nor did the judge's reasons for the sentence make any reference to the fact that Hitler was still technically within the probationary period for good behaviour imposed on him in the sentence for breach of the peace in January 1922. Legally, he was not eligible for any further probation.

The judge in that first Hitler trial was the same person as the judge presiding over his trial for high treason in 1924: the nationalist sympathizer Georg Neithardt.

Hitler returned to Landsberg to begin his light sentence in conditions more akin to those of a hotel than a penitentiary. The windows of his large, comfortably furnished room on the first floor afforded an expansive view over the attractive countryside. Dressed in lederhosen, he could relax with a newspaper in an easy wicker chair, his back to a laurel wreath provided by admirers, or sit at a large desk sifting through the mounds of correspondence he received. He was treated with great respect by his jailers, some of whom secretly greeted him with 'Heil Hitler', and accorded every possible privilege. Gifts, flowers, letters of support, encomiums of praise, all poured in. He received more visitors than he could cope with – over 500 of them before he eventually felt compelled to restrict access. Around forty fellow-prisoners, some of them volunteer internees, able to enjoy almost all the comforts of normal daily life, fawned on him. He read of the demonstration on 23 April, to celebrate his thirty-fifth birthday three days earlier, of 3,000 National Socialists, former front soldiers, and supporters of the *völkisch* movement in the Bürgerbräukeller 'in honour of the man who had lit the present flame of liberation and *völkisch* consciousness in the German people'. Under the impact of the star-status that the trial had brought him, and the Führer cult that his supporters had begun to form around him, he began to reflect on his political ideas, his 'mission', his 'restart' in politics once his short sentence was over, and pondered the lessons to be learnt from the putsch.

The debacle at the Bürgerbräukeller and its denouement next day at the Feldherrnhalle taught Hitler once and for all that an attempt to seize power in the face of opposition from the armed forces was doomed. He felt justified in his belief that propaganda and mass mobilization, not paramilitary putschism, would open the path to the 'national revolution'. Consequently, he distanced himself from Röhm's attempts to revitalize in new guise the Kampfbund and to build a type of people's militia. Ultimately, the different approaches, as well as power-ambitions, of Hitler and Röhm, would lead to the murderous split in 1934. It would be going too far, however, to presume that Hitler had renounced the idea of a takeover of the state by force in favour of the 'legal path'. Certainly, he subsequently had to profess a commitment to legality in order to involve himself in politics again. And later, electoral success appeared in any case the best strategy to win power. But the putschist approach was never given up. It continued, as the lingering problems with the SA would indicate, to coexist alongside the proclaimed 'legal' way. Hitler was adamant, however, that on any future occasion it could only be with, not against, the Reichswehr.

Hitler's experience was to lead to the last, and not least, of the lessons he would draw from his 'apprenticeship years': that to be the 'drummer' was not enough; and that to be more than that meant he needed not only complete mastery in his own movement but, above all, greater freedom from external dependencies, from competing groupings on the Right, from paramilitary organizations he could not fully control, from the bourgeois politicians and army figures who had smoothed his political rise, used him, then dropped him when it suited them.

The ambivalence about his intended role after the 'national revolution' was still present in his comments during his trial. He insisted that he saw Ludendorff as the 'military leader of the coming Germany' and 'leader of the coming great showdown'. But he claimed that he himself was 'the political leader of this young Germany'. The precise division of labour had, he said, not been determined. In his closing address to the court, Hitler returned to the leadership question – though still in somewhat vague and indeterminate fashion. He referred to Lossow's remarks to the court that during discussions in spring 1923 he had thought Hitler had merely wanted 'as propagandist and awakener to arouse the people'. 'How petty do small men think,' went on Hitler. He did not see the attainment of a ministerial post as worthy of a great man. What he wanted, he said, was to be the destroyer of Marxism. That was his task. 'Not from modesty did I want at that time to be the drummer. That is the highest there is. The rest is unimportant.' When it came to it, he had demanded two things: that he should be given the leadership of the political struggle; and that the organizational leadership should go to 'the hero ... who in the eyes of the entire young Germany is called to it'. Hitler hinted – though did not state explicitly – that this was to have been Ludendorff. On the other hand, in his address to Kampfbund leaders a fortnight before the putsch, he had seemed to envisage Ludendorff as no more than the reorganizer of the future national army. Then again, the proclamation put up during the putsch itself over Hitler's name as Reich Chancellor appeared to indicate that the headship of government was the position he foresaw for himself, sharing dictatorial power with Ludendorff as head of state (*Reichsverweser*, or regent).

Whatever the ambivalence, real or simply tactical, still present in Hitler's remarks at the trial, it soon gave way to clarity about his self-image. For in Landsberg the realization dawned on Hitler: he was not the 'drummer' after all; he was the predestined Leader himself.

6

Emergence of the Leader

I

The year that ought to have seen the spectre of Hitler banished for good brought instead – though this could scarcely be clearly seen at the time – the genesis of his later absolute pre-eminence in the *völkisch* movement and his ascendancy to supreme leadership. In retrospect, the year 1924 can be seen as the time when, like a phoenix arising from the ashes, Hitler could begin his emergence from the ruins of the broken and fragmented *völkisch* movement to become eventually the absolute leader with total mastery over a reformed, organizationally far stronger, and internally more cohesive Nazi Party.

Nothing could have demonstrated more plainly how indispensable Hitler was to the *völkisch* Right than the thirteen months of his imprisonment, the 'leaderless time' of the movement. With Hitler removed from the scene and, from June 1924, withdrawing from all involvement in politics to concentrate on the writing of *Mein Kampf*, the *völkisch* movement descended into squabbling factionalism and internecine strife. By courtesy of Bavarian justice, Hitler had been allowed to use the courtroom to portray himself as the hero of the Right for his role in the putsch. Competing individuals and groups felt compelled to assert Hitler's authority and backing for their actions. But in his absence, this was insufficient in itself to ensure success. Moreover, Hitler was often inconsistent, contradictory, or unclear in his views on developments. His claim to a leadership position could not be ignored, and was not disputed. Any claim to exclusive leadership was, however, upheld only by a minority in the *völkisch* movement. And as long as Hitler was unable directly to influence developments, the narrow core of his fervent devotees was largely marginalized even within the broad *völkisch* Right, often at war with each other, and split on tactics, strategy, and ideology. By the time of his release in December 1924, the Reichstag elections of that month had reflected the catastrophic decline of support for the *völkisch* movement, which had come to form little more than a group of disunited nationalist and racist sects on the extreme fringe of the political spectrum.

Just before his arrest on 11 November 1923, Hitler had placed Alfred Rosenberg, editor of the *Völkischer Beobachter*, in charge of the banned party during his absence, to be supported by Esser, Streicher, and Amann. Like a number of leading Nazis (including Heß, Scheubner-Richter, and Hitler himself), Rosenberg's origins did not lie within the boundaries of the German Reich. Born into a well-off bourgeois family in Reval (now Tallinn), Estonia, the introverted self-styled party 'philosopher', dogmatic but dull, arrogant and cold, one of the least charismatic and least popular of Nazi leaders, united other party bigwigs only in their intense dislike of him. Distinctly lacking in leadership qualities, he was scarcely an obvious choice, and was as surprised as others were by Hitler's nomination. Possibly, as is usually surmised, it was precisely Rosenberg's lack of leadership ability that commended itself to Hitler. Certainly, a less likely rival to Hitler could scarcely be imagined. But this would presume that Hitler, in the traumatic aftermath of the failed putsch, was capable of lucid, machiavellian planning, that he anticipated what would happen and actually wanted and expected his movement to fall apart in his absence. A more likely explanation is that he made a hasty and ill-conceived decision, under pressure and in a depressed frame of mind, to entrust the party's affairs to a member of his Munich coterie whose loyalty was beyond question. Rosenberg was, in fact, one of the few leading figures in the movement still available. Scheubner-Richter was dead. Others had scattered in the post-putsch turmoil, or had been arrested. Even – though Hitler could scarcely have known this – the three trusted lieutenants he had designated to support Rosenberg were temporarily out of action. Esser had fled to Austria, Amann was in jail, and Streicher was preoccupied with matters in Nuremberg. Rosenberg was probably no more than a hastily chosen least bad option.

On 1 January 1924, Rosenberg founded the Großdeutsche Volksgemeinschaft (GVG, 'Greater German National Community'), intended to serve, during the NSDAP's ban, as its successor organization. By the summer, Rosenberg had been ousted, and the GVG had fallen under the control of Hermann Esser (returned in May from his exile in Austria) and Julius Streicher. But the coarse personalities, insulting behaviour, and clumsy methods of Esser and Streicher merely succeeded in alienating many Hitler followers. Far from all Hitler loyalists, in any case, had joined the GVG. Gregor Strasser, for example, a Landshut apothecary who was to emerge in the post-putsch era as the leading figure in the party after Hitler, joined the Deutschvölkische Freiheitspartei (DVFP), a rival *völkisch* organization headed by Albrecht Graefe, formerly a member of the conservative DNVP, with its stronghold in Mecklenburg and its headquarters in Berlin.

Conflict was not long deferred once Hitler was in prison. The DVFP had been less affected by proscription than had the NSDAP. In contrast to the disarray within the Hitler Movement, Graefe and other DVFP leaders were still at liberty to control a party organization left largely in place. And though the DVFP leaders lauded Hitler's actions in the putsch in an attempt to win over his supporters, they were actually keen to take advantage of the situation and to establish their own supremacy. That the DVFP leaders advocated electoral participation by the *völkisch* movement added to the growing conflict. A move towards a parliamentary strategy alienated many Nazis, and was vehemently opposed by NSDAP diehards in northern Germany. Their spokesman, Ludolf Haase, the leader of the Göttingen branch, was increasingly critical of Rosenberg's authority, and above all keen to keep the north German NSDAP from the clutches of Graefe.

Those *völkisch* groups that were prepared, however reluctantly, to enter parliament in order to be in a position one day to destroy it, decided to enter into electoral alliances to allow them to contest the series of regional (Landtag) elections that began in February, and the Reichstag election – the first of two that year – on 4 May 1924. Hitler was opposed to this strategy, but his opposition made no difference. The decision to participate went ahead. It seemed to be borne out by the results. In the February Landtag elections in Mecklenburg-Schwerin, Graefe's stronghold, the DVFP won thirteen out of sixty-four seats. And on 6 April in the Bavarian Landtag elections, the Völkischer Block, as the electoral alliance called itself there, won 17 per cent of the vote.

The Reichstag election results, it seems, helped persuade Hitler that the parliamentary tactic, pragmatically and purposefully deployed, promised to pay dividends. The *völkisch* vote, bolstered by the publicity and outcome of the Hitler trial, had stood up well, with a result of 6.5 per cent and thirty-two seats in the Reichstag. The results in Graefe's territory of Mecklenburg (20.8 per cent) and Bavaria (16 per cent) were particularly good. That only ten of the *völkisch* Reichstag members were from the NSDAP and twenty-two from the DVFP gave some indication, however, of the relative weakness of the remnants of the Hitler Movement at the time.

In the first of two visits he paid to Landsberg in May, Ludendorff, whose contacts in north Germany were extensive despite his continued residence near Munich, seized the moment to try to persuade Hitler to agree to a merger of the NSDAP and DVFP fractions in the Reichstag, and in the second meeting even to full unity of the two parties. Hitler equivocated. He agreed in principle, but stipulated preconditions that needed to be discussed with Graefe. One of these, it transpired, was that the headquarters of the movement would be based in Munich. Hitler was in difficulties because, though he had always insisted on a separate and unique identity for the NSDAP, there was the danger, following the electoral success of the Völkischer Block, that such an uncompromising stance would seem less than compelling to his supporters. Moreover, the DVFP was the stronger of the two parties, as the election had shown, and Ludendorff was now generally regarded as the leading figure in the *völkisch* movement.

Some north German Nazis were, not surprisingly, confused and uncertain about Hitler's position regarding any merger. In a letter of 14 June, Haase, the Nazi leader in Göttingen, sought confirmation that Hitler rejected a merger of the two parties. Replying two days later, Hitler denied that he had fundamentally rejected a merger, though he had stipulated preconditions for such a step. He acknowledged the opposition among many Nazi loyalists to a merger with the DVFP, which, he also pointed out, had made plain its rejection of some of the old guard of the party. Under the circumstances, he went on, he could no longer intervene or accept responsibility. He had decided, therefore, to withdraw from politics until he could properly lead again. He refused henceforth to allow his name to be used in support of any political position, and asked for no further political letters to be sent to him.

Hitler announced his decision to withdraw from politics in the press on 7 July. He requested no further visits to Landsberg by his supporters, a request he felt compelled to repeat a month later. The press announcement gave as his reasons the impossibility of accepting practical responsibility for developments while he was in Landsberg, 'general overwork', and the need to concentrate on the writing of his book (the first volume of *Mein Kampf*). A not insignificant additional factor, as the opposition press emphasized, was Hitler's anxiety to do nothing to jeopardize his chances of parole, which could be granted from 1 October. His withdrawal was not a machiavellian strategy to exacerbate the split that was already taking place, increase confusion, and thereby bolster his image as a symbol of unity. This was the outcome, not the cause. In June 1924, the outcome could not be clearly foreseen. Hitler acted from weakness, not strength. He was being pressed from all sides to take a stance on the growing schism. His equivocation frustrated his supporters. But any clear stance would have alienated one side or the other. His decision not to decide was characteristic.

Hitler's frustration was also increased by his inability, despite his outright disapproval, to curtail Röhm's determination to build up a nationwide paramilitary organization called the Frontbann. Unable to deter Röhm – already freed on 1 April, bound over on probation, his derisory fifteen-month prison sentence for his part in the putsch set aside on condition of good behaviour – Hitler ended their last meeting before he left Landsberg, on 17 June, by telling him that, having laid down the leadership of the National Socialist Movement, he wished to hear no more about the Frontbann. Röhm nevertheless simply ignored Hitler, and pressed on with his plans, looking to Ludendorff for patronage and protection.

A much-vaunted conference in Weimar on 15–17 August, intended to cement the organizational merger of the NSDAP and DVFP, produced only the most superficial unity in a newly-proclaimed National Socialist Freedom Movement (Nationalsozialistische Freiheitsbewegung, NSFB). By the end of the summer, the fragmentation of the NSDAP, and of the *völkisch* movement in general, was, despite all the talk of merger and unity, advancing rather than receding. Only Hitler's position was emerging significantly strengthened by the inner-party warfare.

As summer dragged into autumn, then winter approached, the rifts in the *völkisch* movement widened still further. From the NSFB's point of view, unity without Hitler, and in the face of his continued refusal to commit himself publicly to a unified organization, was impossible. In Bavaria, the *völkisch* feud surrounding the figures of Esser and Streicher widened into open breach. On 26 October, the Völkischer Block decided to join the NSFB to create a united organization to fight the coming elections. With this, it accepted the NSFB's Reich Leadership. Gregor Strasser, the spokesman of the Völkischer Block, hoped that the Großdeutsche Volksgemeinschaft would also soon join the NSFB, but at the same time openly condemned its leaders, Esser and Streicher. Esser's reply in a letter to all GVG affiliations, a bitter attack on the leaders of the Völkischer Block, with a side-swipe at Ludendorff for his support of the Block's position, reaffirmed the Munich loyalist position: 'the only man who has a right to exclude someone who has fought for years for his place in the Movement of National Socialists is solely and singly Adolf Hitler.' But Esser's bravado, and the brash attacks of Streicher, supported by the Thuringian National Socialist, Artur Dinter, could not conceal the sharp decline of the GVG.

The Reichstag elections that took place on 7 December demonstrated just how marginal this perpetual squabbling in the *völkisch* movement was to the overall shaping of German politics. The NSFB won only 3 per cent of the vote. It had lost over a million votes compared with the *völkisch* showing in the May election. Its Reichstag representation fell from thirty-two to fourteen seats, only four of whom were National Socialists. It was a disastrous result. But it pleased Hitler. In his absence, *völkisch* politics had collapsed, but his own claims to leadership had, in the process, been strengthened. The election result also had the advantage of encouraging the Bavarian government to regard the danger from the extreme Right as past. There was now, it seemed, no need for undue concern about Hitler's release from Landsberg, for which his supporters had been clamouring since October.

Only political bias explains the determination of the Bavarian judiciary to insist upon Hitler's early release, despite the well-reasoned opposition of the Munich police and the state prosecutor's office. On 20 December, at 12.15 p.m., he was released. A calculation in the files of the state prosecution office noted that he had three years, 333 days, twenty-one hours, fifty minutes of his short sentence still to serve. History would have taken a different course had he been made to serve it.

The prison staff, all sympathetic to Hitler, gathered to bid their famous prisoner an emotional farewell. He paused for photographs by the gates of the old fortress town, hurrying his photographer, Heinrich Hoffmann, because of the cold, then was gone. Within two hours, he was back at his Munich apartment in Thierschstraße, greeted by friends with garlands of flowers, and nearly knocked over by his dog, Wolf. Hitler said later that he did not know what to do with his first evening of freedom. Politically, he continued at first to remain publicly non-committal. He needed to take stock of the situation in view of the months of internecine warfare in the *völkisch* movement. More important, it was necessary in order to establish with the Bavarian authorities the conditions for his re-entry into politics and to ensure that the ban on the NSDAP was lifted. Now that he was released, serious preparation for his party's new start could begin.

II

'Landsberg', Hitler told Hans Frank, was his 'university paid for by the state'. He read, he said, everything he could get hold of: Nietzsche, Houston Stewart Chamberlain, Ranke, Treitschke, Marx, Bismarck's *Gedanken und Erinnerungen* (*Thoughts and Memories*), and the war memoirs of German and Allied generals and statesmen. Other than dealing with visitors and answering correspondence – neither of which preoccupied him much once he had withdrawn from public involvement in politics in the summer – the long days of enforced idleness in Landsberg were ideal for reading and reflection. But Hitler's reading and reflection were anything but academic. Doubtless he did read much. However, reading, for him, had purely an instrumental purpose. He read not for knowledge or enlightenment, but for confirmation of his own preconceptions. He found what he was looking for. As he remarked to Hans Frank – the party's legal expert who would eventually become Governor General in occupied Poland – through the reading he did in Landsberg, 'I recognized the correctness of my views.'

Sitting in his cell in Nuremberg many years later, Frank adjudged the year 1924 to have been one of the most decisive turning-points in Hitler's life. This was an exaggeration. Landsberg was not so much a turning-point as a period in which Hitler inwardly consolidated and rationalized for himself the 'world-view' he had been developing since 1919 and, in some significant ways, modifying in the year or so before the putsch. As the Nazi Movement fell apart in his absence, and with time on his hands, away from the hurly-burly of active politics, Hitler could scarcely avoid ruminating on past mistakes. And, expecting his release within months, he was even more strongly compelled to look to the way forward for himself and his broken movement. During this time, he revised in certain respects his views on how to attain power. In so doing, his perception of himself changed. He came to think of his own role in a different way. In the wake of the triumph of his trial, he began to see himself, as his followers had started to portray him from the end of 1922 onwards, as Germany's saviour. In the light of the putsch, one might have expected his self-belief to be crushed once and for all. On the contrary: it was elevated beyond measure. His almost mystical faith in himself as walking with destiny, with a 'mission' to rescue Germany, dates from this time.

At the same time, there was an important adjustment to another aspect of his 'world-view'. Ideas which had been taking shape in his mind since late 1922, if not earlier, on the direction of future foreign policy were now elaborated into the notion of a quest for 'living space', to be gained at the expense of Russia. Blended into his obsessive anti-semitism, aimed at the destruction of 'Jewish Bolshevism', the concept of a war for 'living space' – an idea which Hitler would repeatedly emphasize in the following years – rounded off his 'world-view'. Thereafter, there would be tactical adjustments, but no further alteration of substance. Landsberg was no 'Jordan conversion' for Hitler. In the main, it was a matter of adding new emphases to the few basic *idées fixes* already formed, at least in embryo, or clearly taking shape in the years before the putsch.

The modifications in Hitler's 'world-view' that were already forming in the year before the putsch are clearly evident in *Mein Kampf*. Hitler's book offered nothing new. But it was the plainest and most expansive statement of his 'world-view' that he had presented. He acknowledged that without his stay in Landsberg the book which after 1933 (though not before) would sell in its millions would never have been written. No doubt he hoped for financial gain from the book. But his main motivation was the need he felt, as during his trial, to demonstrate his own special calling, and to justify his programme as the only possible way of rescuing Germany from the catastrophe brought about by the 'November Criminals'.

Hitler was already at work on what would become the first volume by May 1924, building upon ideas formed during and immediately after his trial. He called his book at that time by the scarcely catchy title 'Four and a Half Years of Struggle against Lies, Stupidity, and Cowardice', which gave way to the more pithy *Mein Kampf* (*My Struggle*) only in spring 1925. By then, the book had undergone major structural changes. The initial intention of a 'reckoning' with the 'traitors' responsible for his downfall in 1923 never materialized. Instead, the first volume, which appeared on 18 July 1925, was largely autobiographical – though with many distortions and inaccuracies – ending with Hitler's triumph at the announcement of the Party Programme in the Hofbräuhaus on 24 February 1920. The second volume, written after his release and published on 11 December 1926, dealt more extensively with his ideas on the nature of the *völkisch* state, questions of ideology, propaganda, and organization, concluding with chapters on foreign policy.

The presumption, widespread at the time and persisting later, that Hitler at first dictated the indigestible prose to his chauffeur and general dogsbody, Emil Maurice, later to Rudolf Heß (both of whom were also serving sentences for their part in the putsch), is wide of the mark. Hitler typed the drafts of the first volume himself (though some of the second volume was dictated to a secretary). Badly written and rambling as the published version of *Mein Kampf* was, the text had, in fact, been subjected to innumerable stylistic 'improvements' since the original composition. The typescript was read by the culture critic of the *Völkischer Beobachter*, Josef Stolzing-Cerny, and at least parts of it by the future wife of Rudolf Heß, Ilse Pröhl. Both made editorial changes. Others were by Hitler himself. According to Hans Frank, Hitler accepted that the book was badly written, and described it as no more than a collection of leading articles for the *Völkischer Beobachter*.

Before Hitler came to power, *Mein Kampf*, brought out in the party's own publishing house, the Franz Eher-Verlag, run by Max Amann, was scarcely the runaway bestseller he had apparently expected it to be. Its turgid content, dreadful style, and relatively high price of 12 Reich Marks a volume evidently deterred many potential readers. By 1929, the first volume had sold around 23,000 copies, the second only 13,000. Sales increased sharply following the NSDAP's electoral successes after 1930, and reached 80,000 in 1932. From 1933, they rose stratospherically. One and a half million copies were sold that year. Even the blind could read it – should they have wished to do so – once a braille version had been published in 1936. And from that year, a copy of the people's edition of both volumes bound together was given to each happy couple on their wedding day. Some 10 million copies were sold by 1945, not counting the millions sold abroad, where *Mein Kampf* was translated into sixteen languages. How many people actually read it is unknown. For Hitler, it was of little importance. Having from the early 1920s described himself in official documents as a 'writer', he could well afford in 1933 to refuse his Reich Chancellor's salary (in contrast, he pointed out, to his predecessors): *Mein Kampf* had made him a very rich man.

No policy outline was offered in *Mein Kampf*. But the book did provide, however garbled the presentation, an uncompromising statement of Hitler's political principles, his 'world-view', his sense of his own 'mission', his 'vision' of society, and his long-term aims. Not least, it established the basis of the Führer myth. For in *Mein Kampf*, Hitler portrayed himself as uniquely qualified to lead Germany from its existing misery to greatness.

Mein Kampf gives an important insight into his thinking in the mid-1920s. By then, he had developed a philosophy that afforded him a complete interpretation of history, of the ills of the world, and how to overcome them. Tersely summarized, it boiled down to a simplistic, Manichean view of history as racial struggle, in which the highest racial entity, the aryan, was being undermined and destroyed by the lowest, the parasitic Jew. 'The racial question,' he wrote, 'gives the key not only to world history but to all human culture.' The culmination of this process was taken to be the brutal rule of the Jews through Bolshevism in Russia, where the 'blood Jew' had, 'partly amid inhuman torture killed or let starve to death around 30 million people in truly satanic savagery in order to secure the rule over a great people of a bunch of Jewish *literati* and stock-market bandits'. The 'mission' of the Nazi Movement was, therefore, clear: to destroy 'Jewish Bolshevism'. At the same time – a leap of logic that moved conveniently into a justification for outright imperialist conquest – this would provide the German people with the 'living space' needed for the 'master race' to sustain itself. He held rigidly to these basic tenets for the rest of his life. Nothing of substance changed in later years. The very inflexibility and quasi-messianic commitment to an 'idea', a set of beliefs that were unalterable, simple, internally consistent, and comprehensive, gave Hitler the strength of will and sense of knowing his own destiny that left its mark on all those who came into contact with him. Hitler's authority in his entourage derived in no small measure from the certainty in his own convictions that he could so forcefully express. Everything could be couched in terms of black and white, victory or total destruction. There were no alternatives. And, like all ideologues and 'conviction politicians', the self-reinforcing components of his 'world-view' meant that he was always in a position to deride or dismiss out of hand any 'rational' arguments of opponents. Once head of state, Hitler's personalized 'world-view' would serve as 'guidelines for action' for policy-makers in all areas of the Third Reich.

Hitler's book was not a prescriptive programme in the sense of a short-term political manifesto. But many contemporaries made a mistake in treating *Mein Kampf* with ridicule and not taking the ideas Hitler expressed there extremely seriously. However base and repellent they were, they amounted to a set of clearly established and rigidly upheld political principles. Hitler never saw any reason to alter the content of what he had written. Their internal coherence (given the irrational premises) allows them to be described as an ideology (or, in Hitler's own terminology, a 'world-view'). Hitler's 'world-view' in *Mein Kampf* can now be more clearly seen than used to be possible in the context of his ideas as they unfolded between his entry into politics and the writing of his 'Second Book' in 1928.

On Hitler's central, overriding, and all-embracing obsession, the 'removal of the Jews', *Mein Kampf* added nothing to the ideas he had already formulated by 1919–20. Extreme though the language of *Mein Kampf* was, it was no different to that which he had been proclaiming for years. Nor, for that matter, did the inherently genocidal terminology substantially vary from that of other writers and speakers on the *völkisch* Right, extending well back beyond the First World War. His bacterial imagery implied that Jews should be treated in the way germs were dealt with: by extermination. Already in August 1920, Hitler had spoken of combating 'racial tuberculosis' through removal of the 'causal agent, the Jew'. And there could be little doubt whom Hitler had in mind when, four years later in *Mein Kampf*, he wrote: 'The nationalization of our masses will succeed only when, aside from all the positive struggle for the soul of our people, their international poisoners are exterminated.' The notion of poisoning the poisoners ran through another, notorious, passage of *Mein Kampf*, in which Hitler suggested that if 12–15,000 'Hebrew corrupters of the people' had been held under poison gas at the start of the First World War, then 'the sacrifice of millions at the front would not have been in vain'. These terrible passages are not the beginning of a one-way track to the 'Final Solution'. The road there was 'twisted', not straight. But however little he had thought out the practical implications of what he was saying, its inherent genocidal thrust is undeniable. However indistinctly, the connection between destruction of the Jews, war, and national salvation had been forged in Hitler's mind.

As we remarked, the initial anti-capitalist colouring of Hitler's anti-semitism had given way by mid-1920 to the connection in his mind of the Jews with the evils of Soviet Bolshevism. It was not that Hitler substituted the image of the Jews behind Marxism for that of the Jews behind capitalism. Both coexisted in his fixated loathing. It was a hatred so profound that it could only have been based on deep fear. This was of a figure in his mind so powerful that it was the force behind both international finance capital and Soviet Communism. It was the image of a 'Jewish world conspiracy' that was almost unconquerable – even for National Socialism.

Once the link with Bolshevism was made, Hitler had established his central and lasting vision of a titanic battle for supremacy, a racial struggle against a foe of ruthless brutality. What he visualized, he had stated in June 1922, was a fight to the death between two competing ideologies, the idealistic and the materialistic. The mission of the German people was to destroy Bolshevism, and with it 'our mortal enemy: the Jew'. By October the same year he was writing of a life and death struggle of two opposed world-views, incapable of existing alongside one another. Defeat in this great showdown would seal Germany's destruction. The struggle would leave only victors and the annihilated. It meant a war of extermination. 'A victory of the Marxist idea signifies the complete extermination of the opponents,' he remarked. 'The Bolshevization of Germany . . . means the complete annihilation of the entire Christian-western culture.' Correspondingly, the aim of National Socialism could be simply defined: 'Annihilation and extermination of the Marxist *Weltanschauung*.'

By now Marxism and the Jew were synonymous in Hitler's mind. At the end of his trial, on 27 March 1924, he had told the court that what he wanted to be was the breaker of Marxism. The Nazi Movement knew

1. Adolf Hitler (*top row, centre*) in his Leonding school photo, 1899.

2. Klara Hitler, the mother of Adolf.

3. Alois Hitler, Adolf's father.

4. Karl Lueger, Bürgermeister of Vienna, admired by Hitler for his antisemitic agitation.

5. August Kubizek, Hitler's boyhood friend in Linz and Vienna.

6. The crowd in Odeonsplatz, Munich, greeting the proclamation of war, 2 August 1914. Hitler circled.

7. Hitler (*right*) with fellow dispatch messengers Ernst Schmidt and Anton Bachmann and his dog 'Foxl' at Fournes, April 1915.

8. German soldiers in a trench on the Western Front during a lull in the fighting.

9. Armed members of the KPD from the Neuhausen district of Munich during a 'Red Army' parade in the city, 22 April 1919.

10. Counter-revolutionary Freikorps troops entering Munich, beginning of May 1919.

11. Anton Drexler, founder in 1919 of the DAP (German Workers' Party).

12. Ernst Röhm, the 'machine-gun king', whose access to weapons and contacts in the Bavarian army were important to Hitler in the early 1920s.

Deutfche Arbeiter-Partei (D. A. P.)
Ortsgruppe München   Abteilung: ....

Mitgliedskarte

für *Herrn Adolf Hitler* ....

München, den *1. Jan.* 1920.

Nr. *555*   für den Arbeitsausfchuß:

....   *Drexler*
Schriftwart

Diefe Karte gilt als Ausweis bei gefchloffenen Verfammlungen

13. Hitler's DAP membership card, contradicting his claim
to be the seventh member of the party.

14. Hitler speaking on the Marsfeld in Munich at the first Party Rally of
the NSDAP, 28 January 1923.

15. 'Hitler speaks!' NSDAP mass meeting, Zirkus Krone, Munich, 1923.

16. Paramilitary organizations during the church service at the 'German Day' in Nuremberg, 2 September 1923.

17. Alfred Rosenberg, Hitler, and Friedrich Weber (centre, behind Hitler, Christian Weber) during the march-past of the SA and other paramilitary groups to mark the laying of the war memorial foundation stone, Munich, 4 November 1923.

18. The putsch: armed SA men (*centre*, holding the old Reich flag, Heinrich Himmler, right, with fur collar, Ernst Röhm) manning a barricade outside the War Ministry in Ludwigstraße, Munich, 9 November 1923.

19. The putsch: armed putschists from the area around Munich,
9 November 1923.

20. Defendants at the trial of the putschists: *left to right*, Heinz Pernet, Friedrich Weber, Wilhelm Frick, Hermann Kriebel, Erich Ludendorff, Adolf Hitler, Wilhelm Brückner, Ernst Röhm, Robert Wagner.

21. Hitler posing for a photograph, hurriedly taken by Hoffman because of the cold, at the gate to the town of Landsberg am Lech, immediately after his release from imprisonment.

22. Hitler in Landsberg, postcard, 1924.

23. The image: Hitler in Bavarian costume (rejected), 1925/6.
24. The image: Hitler in a raincoat (accepted), 1925/6.

25. The image: Hitler with his alsatian, Wolf, 1925
(rejected, from a broken plate).

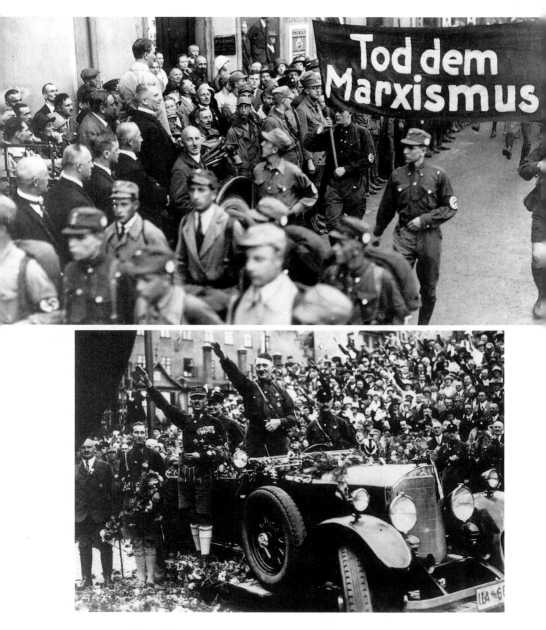

26. The Party Rally, Weimar, 3–4 July 1926: Hitler, standing in a car in
light-coloured raincoat, taking the march-past of the SA, whose banner carries
the slogan: 'Death to Marxism'. Immediately to Hitler's right is Wilhelm Frick
and, beneath him, facing the camera, Julius Streicher.

27. The Party Rally, Nuremberg, 21 August 1927: *left to right*, Julius Streicher,
Georg Hallermann, Franz von Pfeffer, Rudolf Heß, Adolf Hitler, Ulrich Graf.

only *one* enemy, he had emphasized the following month – the mortal enemy of the whole of mankind: Marxism. There was no mention of the Jews. Some newspapers picked up the change of emphasis and claimed Hitler had altered his position on the 'Jewish Question'. There were Nazi followers who were also puzzled. One, visiting him in Landsberg at the end of July, asked Hitler whether he had changed his views about Jewry. He received a characteristic reply. Indeed his position on the struggle against Jewry had altered, Hitler remarked. He had realized while at work on *Mein Kampf* that he had up to then been too mild. In future, only the toughest measures could be deployed if success were to be attained. The 'Jewish Question', he declared, was an existential matter for all peoples, not just the German people, 'for Juda is the world plague'. The logic of the position was that only the complete eradication of the international power of Jewry would suffice.

Hitler's obsession with the 'Jewish Question' was inextricably interwoven with his notions of foreign policy. Once his antisemitism had, by the middle of 1920, fused with anti-Bolshevism into the image of 'Jewish Bolshevism', it was inevitable that his thinking on foreign policy would be affected. However, not only ideological influences, but questions of pure power politics shaped Hitler's changing position. In their concentration on France as the arch-enemy, hostility to Britain, recovery of colonies, and the restoration of Germany's borders of 1914, Hitler's early views on foreign policy were conventionally pan-German. They were no different from those of many nationalist hotheads. In fact, in essence (if not in the extreme way they were advanced) they accorded with a revisionism that enjoyed wide popular backing. Nor, in his emphasis on military might to overthrow Versailles and defeat France, however unrealistic it sounded in the early 1920s, did he differ from many others on the Pan-German and *völkisch* Right. Already in 1920, before he had heard of Fascism, he was contemplating the value of an alliance with Italy. He was determined even then that the question of South Tyrol – the predominantly German-speaking part of the former Austrian province of Tyrol lying beyond the Brenner, ceded to Italy in 1919, and since then subjected to a programme of 'Italianization' – would not stand in the way of such an alliance. By late 1922, an alliance with Britain, whose world empire he admired, was in his mind. This idea had sharpened in 1923 when the disagreements of the British and French over the Ruhr occupation became clear.

The presumed rule of the Jews in Russia stood, on the other hand, as Hitler had pointed out as early as July 1920, firmly in the way of any alliance with Russia. Even so, at this time Hitler shared the view of many on the *völkisch* Right that a distinction could be drawn between 'national' Russians – where the Germanic influence was strong – and the 'bolshevization' of Russia brought about by the Jews. Hitler's approach to Russia was probably in part shaped by Rosenberg, the early NSDAP's leading 'expert' on eastern questions, whose Baltic origins fed a ferocious antipathy towards Bolshevism. It was, most likely, reinforced by Scheubner-Richter, another prolific writer on eastern policy in the infant party, with extremely strong connections to Russian exiles. Dietrich Eckart, too, who was already in early 1919 writing of the identity of Jewry and Bolshevism, probably also exerted some influence.

Russia was coming already before the putsch to loom larger in Hitler's thoughts on foreign policy. He had somewhat vaguely mentioned the 'land question', comparing Germany unfavourably with Russia in its relation of population to the land at its disposal, as early as December 1919. He hinted in a speech on 31 May 1921, through praise of the Brest-Litovsk Treaty of 1918 (which had ended Russian participation in the war) for giving Germany the additional land it needed to sustain its people, at an expansion of German 'living space' at the expense of Russia. On 21 October 1921 he was still speaking, somewhat cryptically, of an expansion with Russia against England opening up 'an unlimited possibility of expansion towards the east'. Such remarks indicated that at this time, Hitler still shared – even if vaguely expressed – the Pan-German view on eastern expansion. This amounted broadly to the notion that eastern expansion could be carried out through collaboration with a non-Bolshevik Russia, whose own territorial demands would be settled also through looking eastwards, towards Asia, leaving the former Russian border areas in the west to Germany. It would have amounted, essentially, to something like a resurrection of the Brest-Litovsk arrangement, while Russia would have been left to find compensation in the lands on its own eastern borders.

By early 1922, these views had shifted. By now, Hitler had abandoned any idea of collaboration with Russia. He saw no prospect of Russia looking only eastwards. Extension of Bolshevism to Germany would prove an irresistible urge. The logic of the changed position was evident. Only through the destruction of Bolshevism could Germany be saved.

And at the same time, this – through expansion into Russia itself – would bring the territory which Germany needed. During the course of 1922 – perhaps reinforced towards the end of the year by contact with the arch-expansionist, Ludendorff – the changed approach to future policy towards Russia was consolidated. By December 1922, Hitler was explaining in private to Eduard Scharrer, co-owner of the *Münchner Neueste Nachrichten* and favourably disposed towards the Nazi Party, the outline of the foreign alliance ideas which he was to elaborate in *Mein Kampf*. He ruled out the colonial rivalry with Britain that had caused conflict before the First World War. He told Scharrer:

Germany would have to adapt herself to a purely continental policy, avoiding harm to English interest. The destruction of Russia with the help of England would have to be attempted. Russia would give Germany sufficient land for German settlers and a wide field of activity for German industry. Then England would not interrupt us in our reckoning with France.

In the light of his comments to Scharrer, it can scarcely be claimed that Hitler developed an entirely new concept of foreign policy while in Landsberg, one based on the idea of war against Russia to acquire *Lebensraum*. And what he wrote in *Mein Kampf* on Germany's need for land being satisfied at the expense of Russia had indeed already been anticipated in an essay he wrote in spring 1924, which was published in April that year. There was no 'transformation' of Hitler's 'vision of the world' in Landsberg. What he came to write in Landsberg was the result of the gradual gestation of his ideas, rather than a flash of intuition, set of new insights, or overnight conversion to a different approach.

The imperialist and geopolitical ideas that went to make up the idea of *Lebensraum* were, in fact, common currency on the imperialist and *völkisch* Right in Weimar Germany. The idea of *Lebensraum* had been a prominent strand of German imperialist ideology since the 1890s. It had been strongly represented in the Pan-German League under Heinrich Claß, supported by the press controlled by founder-member of the League, director of Krupp's, and media tycoon Alfred Hugenberg. For Pan-Germans, *Lebensraum* could both justify territorial conquest by evoking the colonizing of Slav lands by Teutonic knights in the Middle Ages and, emotively, conjure up notions of uniting in the Reich what came to be described as *Volksdeutsche* (ethnic Germans) scattered throughout eastern Europe. For the most part these constituted fairly small minorities, as in the parts of Poland (outside the towns) which Prussia had ruled before 1918. But in a number of areas – Danzig, for example, parts of the Baltic, or the area of Czechoslovakia later known as the Sudetenland – the German-speaking population was sizeable, and often vociferously nationalist. The idea of *Lebensraum* symbolized, then, for Pan-Germans the historic conquest of the East while at the same time, in emphasizing German alleged over-population, cloaking real, modern, power-political imperialist ambitions. It existed alongside, rather than blending with, the mainstream imperialist concentration on overseas trading colonies, encapsulated in the slogan of *Weltpolitik*. In the Weimar era it came to be popularized by Hans Grimm's best-selling novel *Volk ohne Raum* (*People without Space*), published in 1926.

Hitler could scarcely have avoided the imperialist and geopolitical writings in circulation on 'living space'. Among them, whether read at first hand or in bowdlerized form, it seems highly likely that those of Karl Haushofer, the leading exponent of 'geopolitics', were one significant source for his notion of *Lebensraum*. Through Rudolf Heß, Hitler already knew Haushofer by 1922 at the latest. Haushofer's influence was probably greater than the Munich professor was later prepared to acknowledge. If he was not acquainted with them before, Hitler certainly had time on his hands while in prison to read his works, as well as those of Friedrich Ratzel, the other foremost geopolitics theorist. Whether he did so cannot be proved. But it seems at the very least likely that the broad lines of their arguments were made known to him by Haushofer's former pupil, Rudolf Heß.

At any rate, by the time of the Scharrer discussion at the end of 1922, Hitler's thinking on Russia and the 'living space' question was essentially in place. And by spring 1924, his views were effectively fully formed. What Landsberg and the writing of *Mein Kampf* did was to provide elaboration. Beyond that, it showed that Hitler had by then firmly established the link between the destruction of the Jews and a war against Russia to acquire *Lebensraum*.

Already in the first volume of *Mein Kampf*, the choice – which Hitler had still rhetorically left open in his article of April 1924 – of a land-policy directed against Russia, with Britain's support, or a world trading policy upheld by sea-power directed against Britain with Russia's support, was emphatically determined. By the second volume, mainly written in 1925, the enemy in the short term was still seen as France.

But in the baldest language, the long-term goal was now stated to be the attaining of 'living space' at the expense of Russia.

We National Socialists consciously draw a line beneath the foreign policy tendency of our pre-War period. We take up where we broke off six hundred years ago. We stop the endless German movement to the south and west, and turn our gaze towards the land in the east. At long last we break off the colonial and commercial policy of the pre-War period and shift to the soil policy of the future.

  If we speak of soil in Europe today, we can primarily have in mind only Russia and her vassal border states ... For centuries Russia drew nourishment from [the] Germanic nucleus of its upper leading strata. Today it can be regarded as almost totally exterminated and extinguished. It has been replaced by the Jew ... He himself is no element of organization, but a ferment of decomposition. The giant empire in the east is ripe for collapse. And the end of Jewish rule in Russia will also be the end of Russia as a state ...

The mission of the National Socialist Movement was to prepare the German people for this task. 'We have been chosen by Fate,' wrote Hitler, 'as witnesses of a catastrophe which will be the mightiest confirmation of the soundness of the *völkisch* theory.'

  With this passage, the two key components of Hitler's personalized 'world-view' – destruction of the Jews and acquisition of 'living space' – came together. War against Russia would, through its annihilation of 'Jewish Bolshevism', at the same time deliver Germany its salvation by providing new 'living space'. Crude, simplistic, barbaric: but this invocation of the most brutal tenets of late nineteenth-century imperialism, racism, and antisemitism, transposed into eastern Europe in the twentieth century, was a heady brew for those ready to consume it.

  Hitler himself repeatedly returned to the 'living space' notion, which became a dominant theme of his writings and speeches in the following years. His foreign-policy ideas were to be more clearly laid out, but in no significant way altered, in his 'Second Book', written in 1928 (though left unpublished in Hitler's own lifetime). Once established, the quest for *Lebensraum* – and with it the destruction of 'Jewish Bolshevism' – would remain a keystone of Hitler's ideology. One element remained to complete the 'world-view': the leader of genius who would accomplish this quest. In Landsberg, Hitler found the answer.

III

Many years later, Hitler regarded 'the self-confidence, optimism, and belief that simply could not be shaken by anything more' as deriving from his time in Landsberg. His self-perception did indeed alter while he was in prison. Even at his trial, as we have seen, he had been proud to be the 'drummer' of the national cause. Anything else was a triviality, he had declared. In Landsberg this changed – though, as noted, the change had already been under way during the year preceding the putsch.

Hitler was preoccupied from the beginning of his sentence with the question of his own future and that of his party after his release. Since he expected his release within six months, the question was an urgent one. For Hitler, there was no turning back. His political 'career', which had developed into his political 'mission', left him nowhere to go but forwards. He could not return to anonymity, even had he wanted to do so. A conventional 'bourgeois' lifestyle was out of the question. Any retreat, after the acclaim he had won on the nationalist Right at his trial, would have confirmed the impression of his opponents that he was a figure of farce, and would have exposed him to ridicule. And as he pondered over the failed putsch, transforming it in his mind into the martyrs' triumph that would come to have its central place in Nazi mythology, he had no trouble in assigning the blame to the mistakes, weakness, and lack of resolve of all the leading figures to whom he was at the time bound. They had betrayed him, and the national cause: this was his conclusion. More than that: the triumph at his trial; the torrents of adulation ever-present in the *völkisch* press or pouring unabated from letters sent to Landsberg; and not least the collapse of the *völkisch* movement in his absence into derisory sectarian squabbling, and the growing conflict with Ludendorff and the other *völkisch* leaders; all these contributed towards giving him an elevated sense of his own importance and of his unique historic 'mission'. The idea, embryonically forming in 1923, took firm hold in the strange atmosphere of Landsberg. Surrounded by sycophants and devotees, foremost among them the fawning Heß, Hitler now became certain: he himself was Germany's coming 'great leader'.

Such a notion in its full implications was unimaginable before his triumph at the trial and the acclaim that followed. The 'heroic' leadership he now claimed for himself was an invention of his followers before he saw himself in that role. But the role fitted the temperament of one whose personal failures in early life had found an exaggerated wish-fulfilment in unbound admiration for heroic figures, above all the artist-hero Wagner. Whether an extraordinary depth of self-loathing is a necessary precondition for such an abnormal elevation of self-esteem into that of the heroic saviour of the nation is a matter best left to psychologists. But whatever the deep-seated reasons, for such a narcissistic egomaniac as Hitler, the hero-worship which others directed towards him, combined with his own inability to find fault or error in himself, now produced a 'heroic'-leadership self-image of monumental proportions. No one in mainstream German political life, outside the tiny and fractured *völkisch* movement, was aware of or would have taken seriously the change in Hitler's self-perception. At the time it was of no consequence. But for Hitler's demands on the *völkisch* movement, and for his own self-justification, it was a vital development.

In *Mein Kampf*, Hitler pictured himself as a rare genius who combined the qualities of the 'programmatist' and the 'politician'. The 'programmatist' of a movement was the theoretician who did not concern himself with practical realities, but with 'eternal truth', as the great religious leaders had done. The 'greatness' of the 'politician' lay in the successful practical implementation of the 'idea' advanced by the 'programmatist'. 'Over long periods of humanity,' he wrote, 'it can once happen that the politician is wedded to the programmatist.' His work did not concern short-term demands that any petty-bourgeois could grasp, but looked to the future, with 'aims which only the fewest grasp'. Among the 'great men' in history, Hitler singled out at this point Luther, Frederick the Great, and Wagner. Seldom was it the case, in his view, that 'a great theoretician' was also 'a great leader'. The latter was far more frequently 'an agitator': 'For leading means: being able to move masses.' He concluded: 'the combination of theoretician, organizer, and leader in one person is the rarest thing that can be found on this earth; this combination makes the great man.' Unmistakably, Hitler meant himself.

The 'idea' he stood for was not a matter of short-term objectives. It was a 'mission', a 'vision' of long-term future goals, and of his own part in the accomplishment of them. Certainly, these goals – national salvation through 'removal' of the Jews and acquisition of 'living space' in the east – did not amount to short-term practical policy guidelines.

But, incorporated into the notion of the 'heroic' leader, they did amount to a dynamic 'world-view'. This 'world-view' gave Hitler his unremitting drive. He spoke repeatedly of his 'mission'. He saw the hand of 'Providence' in his work. He regarded his fight against the Jew as 'the work of the Lord'. He saw his life's work as a crusade. The invasion of the Soviet Union, when it was launched many years later, was for him – and not just for him – the culmination of this crusade. It would be a serious error to underestimate the ideological driving-force of Hitler's few central ideas. He was no mere propagandist or 'unprincipled opportunist'. He was indeed both a masterly propagandist *and* an ideologue. There was no contradiction between the two.

When he left Landsberg, to try to rebuild a crippled movement, Hitler's leadership claims were, therefore, not only externally enhanced within the *völkisch* movement, but had been inwardly transformed and consolidated into a new perception of himself and awareness of his role. His sense of realism had by no means altogether disappeared beneath his messianic claims. He had no concrete notion of how his aims might be achieved. He still imagined that his goals might be brought to fruition only in the distant future. Since it consisted of only a few basic, but unchangeable tenets, his 'world-view' was compatible with short-term tactical adjustments. And it had the advantage of accommodating and reconciling a variety of otherwise conflicting positions on particular issues and fine points of ideology adopted by subordinate Nazi leaders. Within the framework of his basic 'world-view', Hitler himself was flexible, even indifferent, towards ideological issues which could obsess his followers. Opponents at the time, and many later commentators, frequently underestimated the dynamism of Nazi ideology because of its diffuseness, and because of the cynicism of Nazi propaganda. Ideology was often regarded as no more than a cloak for power-ambitions and tyranny. This was to misinterpret the driving-force of Hitler's own basic ideas, few and crude as they were. And it is to misunderstand the ways those basic ideas came to function within the Nazi Party, then, after 1933, within the Nazi state. What mattered for Hitler was indeed the road to power. He was prepared to sacrifice most principles for that. But some – and those were for him the ones that counted – were not only unchangeable. They formed the essence of what he understood by power itself. Opportunism was always itself ultimately shaped by the core ideas that determined his notion of power.

Following his months in Landsberg, Hitler's self-belief was now such that, unlike the pre-putsch era, he could regard himself as the *exclusive* exponent of the 'idea' of National Socialism and the sole leader of the *völkisch* movement, destined to show Germany the path to its national salvation. The task facing him on release would be to convince others of that.

7

Mastery over the Movement

I

Hitler spent Christmas Eve 1924 at the Hanfstaengls' in their splendid new villa in Munich's Herzogpark. He had put on weight during his time in prison, and looked a little flabby. His blue suit was flecked with dandruff on the collar and shoulders. Four-year-old Egon Hanfstaengl was glad to see his 'Uncle Dolf' again. Within two minutes, Hitler was asking to hear Isolde's 'Liebestod' on Hanfstaengl's elegant Blüthner grand piano. Wagner's music, as Hanfstaengl had often noticed, could transform Hitler's mood. His initial nervousness and tension disappeared. He became relaxed and cheerful. He admired the new house, then suddenly stopped in mid-sentence, glanced over his shoulder, and explained that he had not lost his habit from prison of imagining he was being observed through the peephole. It was, as Hanfstaengl realized, a pathetic piece of play-acting. Putzi had seen Hitler in Landsberg, relaxed and comfortable; and there had been no peephole in his room. He noticed that Hitler had a good appetite during the meal of turkey followed by his favourite Viennese sweet pastries, but that he scarcely touched the wine. Hitler subsequently explained that he had begun on leaving Landsberg to cut out meat and alcohol in order to lose weight. He had convinced himself that meat and alcohol were harmful for him, and, 'in his fanatical way', went on Hanfstaengl, 'finally made a dogma out of it and from then on only took vegetarian meals and alcohol-free drinks'. After the meal, Hitler treated the family to his war-memories, marching up and down the room, imitating the sounds of different sorts of artillery fire at the battle of the Somme. Late in the evening, a well-connected artist, Wilhelm Funk, dropped in at the Hanfstaengls'. He had known Hitler for quite some time, and now ventured his views on how the party could be built up again. Hitler replied in a familiar, and revealing, tone. For one who had 'come up from the bottom', he said, 'without name, special position, or connection', it was less a matter of programmes than hard endeavour until the public was ready to see 'a nameless one' as identical with a political line. Hitler thought he had now reached that position, and that the putsch had been of value to the movement: 'I'm no longer an unknown, and that provides us with the best basis for a new start.'

The new start was Hitler's priority. The immediate aim was to have the ban on the NSDAP lifted. His first political act was to call on his old ally Ernst Pöhner, the former Munich Police President. Through a well-placed intermediary, Theodor Freiherr von Cramer-Klett, a meeting with the Bavarian Minister President Heinrich Held was arranged for 4 January. Pöhner was also influential in persuading Franz Gürtner, the Bavarian Minister of Justice (whom Hitler was to make Reich Minister of Justice in 1933), to have the other Nazis detained in Landsberg released, among them Rudolf Heß.

The meeting with Minister President Held on 4 January, only a fortnight after Hitler's release and the first of three meetings between the two, went well. No one else was present. Hitler was prepared to act humbly. He agreed to respect the authority of the state without condition, and to support it in the struggle against Communism. He distanced himself sharply from Ludendorff's attacks on the Catholic Church, a necessary step since the General's vociferous anti-clericalism – scarcely a winning formula in Bavaria – had recently become notably strident, and linked to an all too public row (involving a court case for libel, which Ludendorff lost) with Rupprecht, the Crown Prince of Bavaria. Behind the public façade of continued reverence for the figurehead of the *völkisch* movement, Hitler's willingness during his meeting with the Bavarian premier to dissociate himself from Ludendorff was not only shrewd, but also a sign of his increasing estrangement from the General, which would rapidly accelerate into complete alienation by 1927.

Not least, Hitler promised Held – an easy promise to make in the circumstances – that he would not again attempt a putsch. Held told Hitler in the most forthright terms that times had changed. He would not tolerate any return to the sort of circumstances that had prevailed before the putsch. Nor would the constitutional government treat the 'revolutionaries of yesterday' as an equal partner. But Hitler got what he wanted. With Gürtner's backing, the way was now paved for the removal of the ban on the NSDAP and the *Völkischer Beobachter* on 16 February. By that time, Hitler's relations with his rivals in the NSFB had been clarified.

By mid-February, events were moving in Hitler's way. On 12 February, Ludendorff dissolved the Reich Leadership of the NSFB. Shortly after-wards, just before the lifting of the ban on the party, Hitler announced his decision to re-found the NSDAP. A flood of declarations of loyalty now poured in.

On 26 February, the *Völkischer Beobachter* appeared for the first time since the putsch. Hitler's leading article 'On the Renewal of Our Movement' placed the emphasis on avoiding recriminations for the divisions in the *völkisch* movement and, learning from past mistakes, on looking towards the future. There was to be no place in the movement for religious disputes – a necessary disclaimer in mainly Catholic Bavaria, and a criticism of the *völkisch* movement which had accused Hitler of making concessions to Catholicism. He refused to accept any external conditions limiting his own leadership, proclaimed the aims of the movement as unchanged, and demanded internal unity. His 'Call to Former Members' in the same edition struck the same tone. Where party members rejoined, said Hitler, he would not ask about the past, and would concern himself only that past disunity should not repeat itself. He demanded unity, loyalty, and obedience. He made no concessions. What was on offer was a 'pax Hitleriana'. The newspaper also carried the new regulations for the reformed NSDAP, based on the statutes of July 1921. Leadership and unity were once more the keynotes. All splits were to be avoided in the struggle against 'the most terrible enemy of the German people . . . Jewry and Marxism'. The SA was to return to the role of party support troop and training ground for young activists that it had occupied before becoming incorporated in the Bavarian paramilitary scene in February 1923. (This was to prove, within weeks, the breaking-point with Ernst Röhm, who, unable to persuade Hitler to agree to retaining the SA as a conventional paramilitary organization, withdrew from political life and departed for Bolivia.) Entry into the refounded party could only come about by taking out new membership. There could be no renewal or continuation of former membership. This both had symbolic value, and also accorded with the stipulation of centralized control of membership from Munich. Retention of his Munich power-base was vital to Hitler. When Lüdecke suggested moving the headquarters to Thuringia – strategically well situated in central Germany, associated with Luther and the cultural traditions of Weimar, in a Protestant area which did not have to reckon with the opposition of the Catholic establishment, as in Bavaria, and, not least, a region with an existing strong base of *völkisch* sympathizers – Hitler conceded that there was something to be said for the idea. 'But I can't leave Munich,' he immediately added. 'I'm at home here; I mean something here; there are many here who are devoted to me, to me alone, and to nobody else. That's important.'

At eight o'clock on the evening of 27 February 1925, Hitler, with his usual sense of theatre, made his re-entry to the Munich political scene where he had left it sixteen months earlier: at the Bürgerbräukeller. Just as before the putsch, red placards advertising the speech had been plastered around Munich for days. People began to take up their seats in the early afternoon. Three hours before the scheduled start, the huge beerhall was packed. Over 3,000 were jammed inside, 2,000 more turned away, and police cordons set up to block off the surrounding area. Some prominent faces were missing. Rosenberg was one. He was irritated at being excluded from Hitler's inner circle in the weeks since his return from Landsberg. He told Lüdecke: 'I won't take part in that comedy . . . I know the sort of brother-kissing Hitler intends to call for.' Ludendorff, Strasser, and Röhm were also absent. Hitler wanted the first party-leader, Drexler, to chair the meeting. But Drexler insisted that Hermann Esser be evicted from the party. Hitler would accept no conditions. And for him, Esser had 'more political sense in his fingertips than the whole bunch of his accusers in their buttocks'. So one of Hitler's most trusted Munich followers, his business-manager Max Amann, opened the meeting.

Hitler spoke for almost two hours. The first three-quarters of his speech offered his standard account of Germany's plight since 1918, the Jews as the cause of it, the weakness of bourgeois parties, and the aims of Marxism (which, he stated, could only be combated by a doctrine of higher truth but 'similar brutality of execution'). Hitler was frank about the need to focus all energy on one goal, on attacking a single enemy to avoid fragmentation and disunity. 'The art of all great popular leaders,' he proclaimed, 'consisted at all times in concentrating the attention of the masses on a single enemy.' From the context, it was plain that he meant the Jews. Only in the last quarter of the speech did Hitler arrive at his real theme of the evening. No one should expect him, he said, to take sides in the bitter dispute still raging in the *völkisch* movement. He saw in each party comrade only the supporter of the common idea, he declared, to lasting applause. His task as leader was not to explore what had happened in the past, but to bring together those pulling apart. At last he came to the climacteric. The dispute was at an end. Those prepared to join should sink their differences. For nine months, others had had time to 'look after' the interests of the party, he pointed out with sarcasm. To great and lasting applause, he added: 'Gentlemen, let the representation of the interests of the movement from now on be my concern!' His leadership had, however, to be accepted unconditionally. 'I am not prepared to allow conditions as long as I carry personally the responsibility,' he concluded. 'And I now carry again the complete responsibility for everything that takes place in this movement.' After a year, he would hold himself to account. There were tumultuous cheers and cries of 'Heil'. Everyone stood for the singing of 'Deutschland, Deutschland über alles'.

Then came the finale. It was a piece of pure theatre. But it had symbolic meaning, not lost on those present. Arch-enemies over the past year and more – Hermann Esser, Julius Streicher, Artur Dinter from the GVG, Rudolf Buttmann, Gottfried Feder, Wilhelm Frick from the 'parliamentary' Völkischer Block – mounted the platform and, among emotional scenes, with many standing on chairs and tables and the crowd pressing forward from the back of the hall, shook hands, forgave each other, and swore undying loyalty to the leader. It was like medieval vassals swearing fealty to their overlord. Others followed. Whatever the hypocrisy, the public show of unity, it was plain, could only have been attained under Hitler as leader. He could with some justice claim to have restored the 'homogeneity' of the party. In the following years, it would become more and more apparent: Hitler, and the 'idea' increasingly embodied in his leadership, constituted the sole, indispensable force of integration in a movement that retained the potential to tear itself apart. Hitler's position as supreme leader standing over the party owed much to the recognition of this fact.

Outside loyalist circles, the immediate response to Hitler's speech on the *völkisch* Right was often one of disappointment. This was mainly because of the way Hitler was plainly distancing himself from Luden-dorff, still seen by many as the leader of the *völkisch* movement. Luden-dorff's standing remained a potential problem. But as so often, luck came to Hitler's aid.

On 28 February 1925, the day after the refoundation of the NSDAP, the first Reich President of the Weimar Republic, the Social Democrat Friedrich Ebert, still vilified by the Right, died at the age of fifty-four from the effects of an appendicitis operation. Against the arguments of some of his advisers, Hitler insisted on putting forward Ludendorff as the National Socialist candidate, and persuaded the General to stand. He regarded the General as no more than a token candidate, without a chance of winning. Why Ludendorff agreed to stand is less easy to understand than why Hitler wanted the candidacy of a rival of whom he was by now in private extremely scathing. It seems that Hitler per-suaded the General that the conservative candidate of the Right, Karl Jarres, had to be stopped, and, flattering Ludendorff's prestige, inveigled him into standing. Probably Ludendorff reckoned with the backing of his *völkisch* friends. But when they decided – in order not to split the right-wing vote – to put their support behind Jarres, the General's fate was sealed. What had seemed to some in Hitler's entourage a risky strategy was, in fact, no great risk at all, and was more or less guaran-teed to damage Ludendorff. That this was the intention was scarcely concealed, even by some leading Nazis.

For Ludendorff, the election on 29 March was a catastrophe. He polled only 286,000 votes, 1.1 per cent of the votes cast. This was 600,000 fewer than the *völkisch* Right had gained at the Reichstag election in December 1924, itself a disastrous result. Hitler was anything but distressed at the outcome. 'That's all right,' he told Hermann Esser, 'now we've finally finished him.' The election winner in the run-off on 26 April was another war-hero, Field-Marshal Hindenburg. Weimar democracy was now in the hands of one of the pillars of the old order. Ludendorff never recovered from his defeat. Hitler's great rival for the leadership of the *völkisch* Right no longer posed a challenge. He was rapidly on his way into the political wilderness. By 1927, Hitler was openly attacking his former ally – and accusing him of freemasonry (an accusation which was never countered).

The *völkisch* movement itself, in 1924 numerically stronger and geographically more widespread than the NSDAP and its successor

organizations, was not only weakened and divided, but had now effectively lost its figurehead. At first, especially in southern Germany, there
were difficulties where local party leaders refused to accede to Hitler's
demand that they break their ties with *völkisch* associations and subordinate themselves totally to his leadership. But increasingly they went over
to Hitler. Most realized the way the wind was blowing. Without Hitler,
they had no future. For his part, Hitler was particularly assiduous during
the coming months in visiting local party branches in Bavaria. The ban
on speaking at public meetings which the Bavarian authorities had
imposed on him on 9 March (followed in subsequent months by a
similar ban in most other states, including Prussia) gave him more time
for speaking in closed party meetings. The handshake with individual
members, invariably a part of such meetings, symbolically cemented the
bonds between himself and the local membership. A sturdy platform of
support for Hitler's leadership was thus laid in Bavaria. In the north,
the path was less even.

II

On 11 March, two days after the speaking ban had been imposed, Hitler
commissioned Gregor Strasser to organize the party in north Germany.
Strasser, a Landshut apothecary, a big, bluff Bavarian, in the pre-putsch
days SA chief in Lower Bavaria, a diabetic who mixed it with the
roughest in beerhall brawls but relaxed by reading Homer in the original,
was probably the most able of the leading Nazis. Above all he was a
superb organizer. It was largely Gregor Strasser's work, building on the
contacts he had established while in the Reich Leadership of the NSFB,
that resulted in the rapid construction of the NSDAP's organization in
north Germany. Most of the local branches in the north had to be
created from scratch. By the end of 1925, these branches numbered 262,
compared with only seventy-one on the eve of the putsch. While Hitler
spent much of the summer of 1925 in the mountains near Berchtesgaden,
working on the second volume of his book, and taking time out to enjoy
the Bayreuth Festival, bothering little about the party outside Bavaria,
Strasser was unceasing in his efforts in the north. His own views on a
'national socialism' had been formed in the trenches. He was more
idealistic, less purely instrumentalist, than Hitler in his aim to win over

the working class. And, though of course strongly antisemitic, he thought little of the obsessive, near-exclusive emphasis on Jew-baiting that characterized Hitler and his entourage in the Munich party. In fact, dating from the period of the rancorous split in 1924, he could barely tolerate the leading lights in the Bavarian NSDAP, Esser and Streicher. Even if he expressed them somewhat differently, however, he shared Hitler's basic aims. And though he never succumbed to Hitler-worship, he recognized Hitler's indispensability to the movement, and remained a Hitler loyalist.

Strasser's views, and his approach, fitted well into the way the party had developed in north Germany, far away from the Bavarian heartlands. A central issue there was the intense detestation, deriving from the deep clashes of the 'leaderless time' of 1924, of the three individuals they saw as dominating affairs in Bavaria – Esser, Streicher, and Amann. The rejection of these figures was to remain a point of tension between the north German NSDAP and the Munich headquarters throughout 1925. This went hand in hand with the refusal to be dictated to by the Munich headquarters, where the party secretary, Philipp Bouhler, was attempting to impose centralized control over party membership, and with it Munich's complete authority over the whole movement. A further integrally related factor was the concern over Hitler's continuing inaction while the crisis in the NSDAP deepened. It was his passivity, in the eyes of the northern party leaders, that allowed the Esser clique its dominance and kept him far too much under the unsavoury influence of the former GVG leaders. His support for them remained a source of intense disappointment and bitterness. Hitler had also disappointed in his neglect of the north, despite his promises, since the refoundation. Beyond this, there were continuing disagreements about electoral participation. The Göttingen party leadership, especially, remained wholly hostile to parliamentary tactics, which, it felt, would result in the 'movement' being turned into a mere 'party', like others. Not least, there were different accents on policy and different emphases on the National Socialist 'idea'. Some of the north German leaders, like Strasser, advocated a more 'socialist' emphasis. This aimed at maximum appeal to workers in the big industrial regions. The different social structure demanded a different type of appeal than that favoured in Bavaria.

But it was not just a matter of cynical propaganda. Some of the leading activists in the north, like the young Joseph Goebbels in the Elberfeld area, close to the Ruhr, were attracted by the ideas of 'national Bolshevism'. Possessed of a sharp mind and biting wit, the future Propaganda Minister, among the most intelligent of the leading figures in the Nazi Movement, had joined the NSDAP at the end of 1924. Brought up in a Catholic family of moderate means, from Rheyd, a small industrial town in the Rhineland, his deformed right foot exposed him from childhood days to jibes, taunts, and lasting feelings of physical inadequacy. That his early pretensions as a writer met with little recognition further fostered his resentment. 'Why does fate deny to me what it gives to others?' he asked himself in an entry in March 1925 in the diary he would keep till nearly the end of his days in the Berlin bunker twenty years later, adding, self-pityingly, Jesus's words on the Cross – 'My God, my God, why hast Thou forsaken me?' His inferiority complex produced driving ambition and the need to demonstrate achievement through mental agility in a movement which derided both physical weakness and 'intellectuals'. Not least, it produced ideological fanaticism.

Goebbels and some other northern leaders thought of themselves as revolutionaries, with more in common with the Communists than with the hated bourgeoisie. There were some sympathies for Russia. And there was talk of a party trade union. Finally, there was the attitude towards Hitler and towards the party's programme. All the north German leaders accepted Hitler's position, and his right to head the party. They recognized him as the 'hero of Munich' for his part in the putsch, and for his stance at the trial. His standing and reputation needed no emphasis. But many of the north German party faithful did not know Hitler personally, had not even met him. Their relationship to him was, therefore, quite different from that of Bavarian party members, especially those in Munich. Hitler was their leader; that was not in question. But Hitler, too, in their eyes, was bound to the 'idea'. Moreover, the 1920 Programme that outlined the 'idea' in terms of the aims of the party was itself in their view deficient and in need of reform.

By late summer 1925, the northern leaders, differing among themselves in matters of interpretation and emphasis on points of the programme, aims, and meaning of National Socialism, were at least agreed that the party was undergoing a crisis. This was reflected in declining membership and stagnation. It was associated by them, above all, with the state of the party in Munich. But all that could be achieved was the establishment, under Strasser's leadership, of a 'Working Community of the North- and West-German Gaue of the NSDAP', a loose organization of northern party districts, mainly for arranging the exchange of speakers.

This was not in any way intended as a challenge to Hitler. Even so, it did come to pose a threat to his authority. The clashes over the Esser clique, and over electoral participation, were not in themselves critical. Of far greater significance was the fact that Gregor Strasser and Goebbels, especially, looked to the Community as an opportunity to reshape the party's programme. Ultimately, Strasser hoped to replace the Programme of 1920. In November, he took the first steps in composing the Community's own draft programme. It advocated a racially integrated German nation at the heart of a central European customs union, the basis of a united states of Europe. Internally, it proposed a corporate state. In the economy, it looked to tying peasants to their landholdings, and public control of the means of production while protecting private property.

Not only was the draft vague, incoherent, and contradictory. It could only be divisive. Hitler plainly recognized the danger signals. He summoned about sixty party leaders to a meeting on 14 February 1926 at Bamberg, in Upper Franconia. There was no agenda. Hitler, it was stated, simply wanted to discuss some 'important questions'.

He spoke for two hours. He addressed in the main the issue of foreign policy and future alliances. His position was wholly opposed to that of the Working Community. Alliances were never ideal, he said, but always 'purely a matter of political business'. Britain and Italy, both distancing themselves from Germany's arch-enemy France, offered the best potential. Any thought of an alliance with Russia could be ruled out. It would mean 'the immediate political bolshevization of Germany', and with it 'national suicide'. Germany's future could be secured solely by acquiring land, by eastern colonization as in the Middle Ages, by a colonial policy not overseas but in Europe. On the question of the expropriation of German princes without compensation (a proposal by the Left, but supported by north German Nazi leaders), Hitler again ruled out the position of the Working Community. 'For us there are today no princes, only Germans,' he declared. 'We stand on the basis of the law, and will not give a Jewish system of exploitation a legal pretext for the complete plundering of our people.' Such a rhetorical slant could not conceal the outright rejection of the views of the northern leaders. Finally, Hitler repeated his insistence that religious problems had no part to play in the National Socialist Movement.

Goebbels was appalled. 'I feel devastated. What sort of Hitler? A reactionary? Amazingly clumsy and uncertain . . . Probably one of the greatest disappointments of my life. I no longer believe fully in Hitler. That's the terrible thing: my inner support has been taken away.'

Hitler had reasserted his authority. The potential threat from the Working Community had evaporated. Despite some initial signs of defiance, the fate of the Community had been sealed at Bamberg. Gregor Strasser promised Hitler to collect all copies of the draft programme he had distributed, and wrote to members of the Community on 5 March asking for them to be returned. The Community now petered out into non-existence. On 1 July 1926, Hitler signed a directive stating that 'since the NSDAP represents a large working community, there is no justification for smaller working communities as a combination of individual *Gaue*'. By that time, Strasser's Working Community of northern and western Gauleiter was finished. With it went the last obstacle to the complete establishment of Hitler's supreme mastery over the party.

Hitler was shrewd enough to be generous after his Bamberg triumph. By September, Strasser himself had been called to the Reich Leadership as Propaganda Leader of the party, while Franz Pfeffer von Salomon (Gauleiter of Westphalia, a former army officer who had subsequently joined the Freikorps, participated in the Kapp Putsch, and been active in opposition to the French in the Ruhr) was appointed head of the SA. Most important of all, the impressionable Goebbels was openly courted by Hitler and completely won over.

To bring about what has often been called Goebbels's 'Damascus' in fact took little doing. Goebbels had idolized Hitler from the beginning. 'Who is this man? Half plebian, half God! Actually Christ, or only John [the Baptist]?' he had written in his diary in October 1925 on finishing reading the first volume of *Mein Kampf*. 'This man has everything to be a king. The born tribune of the people. The coming dictator,' he added a few weeks later. 'How I love him.' Like others in the Working Community, he had wanted only to liberate Hitler from the clutches of the Esser clique. Bamberg was a bitter blow. But his belief in Hitler was dented, not destroyed. It needed only a sign from Hitler to restore it. And the sign was not long in coming.

In mid-March Goebbels made his peace with Streicher after a long talk in Nuremberg. At the end of the month he received a letter from Hitler inviting him to speak in Munich on 8 April. Hitler's car was there to meet him at the station to take him to his hotel. 'What a noble reception,' noted Goebbels in his diary. Hitler's car was again provided the next day to take Goebbels to visit Lake Starnberg, a few miles outside Munich. In the evening, after Goebbels's speech in the Bürgerbräukeller, in which he evidently retreated from his more radical version of socialism, Hitler embraced him, tears in his eyes. Next afternoon Hitler spent three hours going over the same ground he had covered at Bamberg. Then, Goebbels had been sorely disappointed. Now, he thought it was 'brilliant'. 'I love him ... He has thought through everything,' Goebbels continued. 'He's a man, taking it all round. Such a sparkling mind can be my leader. I bow to the greater one, the political genius.' Goebbels's conversion was complete. A few days later, he met Hitler again, this time in Stuttgart. 'I believe he has taken me to his heart like no one else,' he wrote. 'Adolf Hitler, I love you because you are both great and simple at the same time. What one calls a genius.' Towards the end of the year, Hitler appointed Goebbels as Gauleiter of Berlin – a key position if the party were to advance in the capital. Goebbels was Hitler's man. He would remain so, adoring and subservient alike to the man he said he loved 'like a father', down to the last days in the bunker.

The Bamberg meeting had been a milestone in the development of the NSDAP. The Working Community had neither wanted nor attempted a rebellion against Hitler's leadership. But once Strasser had composed his draft programme, a clash was inevitable. Was the party to be subordinated to a programme, or to its leader? The Bamberg meeting decided what National Socialism was to mean. It was not to mean a party torn, as the *völkisch* movement had been in 1924, over points of dogma. The Twenty-Five-Point Programme of 1920 was therefore regarded as sufficient. 'It stays as it is,' Hitler was reported as saying. 'The New Testament is also full of contradictions, but that hasn't prevented the spread of Christianity.' Its symbolic significance, not any practical feasibility was what mattered. Any more precise policy statement would not merely have produced continuing inner dissension. It would have bound Hitler himself to the programme, subordinated him to abstract tenets of doctrine that were open to dispute and alteration. As it was, his position as Leader over the movement was now inviolable.

At Bamberg, too, an important ideological issue – the anti-Russian thrust of foreign policy – had been reaffirmed. The alternative approach of the northern group had been rejected. The 'idea' and the Leader were coming to be inseparable. But the 'idea' amounted to a set of distant goals, a mission for the future. The only way to it was through the attainment of power. For that, maximum flexibility was needed. No ideological or organizational disputes should in future be allowed to divert from the path. Fanatical willpower, converted into organized mass force, was what was required. That demanded freedom of action for the Leader; and total obedience from the following. What emerged in the aftermath of Bamberg was, therefore, the growth of a new type of political organization: one subjected to the will of the Leader, who stood over and above the party, the embodiment in his own person of the 'idea' of National Socialism.

By the time of the General Members' Meeting on 22 May, attended by 657 party members, Hitler's leadership had emerged inordinately strengthened. He frankly admitted that he attributed no value to the meeting, which had been called simply to meet the legal requirements of a public association. The forthcoming Party Rally in Weimar – the opportunity for a visual display of the new-found unity – was what counted in his eyes. Following his 'report' on the party's activities since its refoundation, Hitler was unanimously 're-elected' as party chairman. The party administration remained in the hands of those close to him. A few amendments were made to the party statutes. Altered five times since 1920, these were now couched in their finalized form. They assured Hitler of the control of the party machine. The appointment of his most important subordinates, the Gauleiter, was in his hands. In effect, the statutes reflected the leader party which the NSDAP had become. In the light of the conflict with the Working Community over a new pro-gramme, not least significant was the reaffirmation of the Twenty-Five Points of 24 February 1920. 'This Programme is immutable,' the statutes unambiguously declared.

A few weeks later, the Party Rally held at Weimar – where Hitler was permitted to speak in public – on 3–4 July 1926 provided the intended show of unity behind the leader. An estimated 7–8,000, including 3,600 stormtroopers and 116 SS men, attended. It was the first time that the Schutzstaffel (SS, Protection Squad), founded in April 1925 and arising initially out of Hitler's personal bodyguard, the Stoßtrupp Adolf Hitler

(Adolf Hitler Assault Squad), had been on public display. Also on display for the first time, and handed to the SS as a sign of Hitler's approbation of his new élite organization, was the 'Blood Flag' of 1923, which had led the procession to the Feldherrnhalle. Every stormtrooper present swore a personal oath of loyalty to Hitler. The party leader received a rapturous reception from delegates after his speech. 'Deep and mystical. Almost like a gospel ... I thank fate, that it gave us this man,' wrote Goebbels.

The Nazi Party was still far smaller than it had been at the time of the putsch. In the overall framework of national politics, it was wholly insignificant. To outside observers, its prospects seemed bleak. But internally, the crisis period was over. Though small, the party was better organized as well as geographically more widespread than the pre-putsch party had been. Its image of unity and strength was beginning to persuade other *völkisch* organizations to throw in their lot with the NSDAP. Above all, it was turning into a new type of political organization – a leader party. Hitler had established the basis of his mastery over the movement. In the next years, while still in the political wilderness, that mastery would become complete.

III

Few people saw Hitler on a regular basis in these years. Only his substitute family – the trusted and devotedly loyal group of Munich cronies who formed his coterie of bodyguards, chauffeurs, and secretaries – were in constant touch with him. Some, like Julius Schaub (his general factotum) and Rudolf Heß (his secretary), had served in Landsberg with Hitler for their part in the putsch. This 'houseguard' escorted him, protected him, shielded him from the increasing numbers wanting an audience. Getting to see Hitler was difficult. Those running party business in Munich often had to wait for days before they could sort out some matter with him. For leading figures in the movement, too, he could proved inaccessible for weeks at a time. Even on public occasions he was largely unapproachable. Before a speech, he would remain closeted in his room. Only once the hall was reported as full would he set out. Afterwards, when away from Munich, he would immediately return to his hotel. Journalists might be permitted to see him for a few minutes, if an interview had been prearranged. But scarcely anyone else was allowed an audience.

Hitler's pronounced sense of 'mission', his heroic self-image of 'greatness', the necessity of upholding the aura increasingly attached to him by his supporters, and the Olympian detachment from the intrigues and in-fighting of his subordinates demanded a high degree of isolation. Beyond this, the distance he deliberately placed between himself and even high-ranking members of his movement was calculated to emphasize the sense of awe and admiration in those admitted to his presence, or encountering him at a theatrically staged mass-meeting or rally. At the same time, it enhanced the enigmatic in him. Even those who knew him found it hard to dissect and understand his personality. Hitler was happy to encourage the sense of mystery and fascination.

He was above all a consummate actor. This certainly applied to the stage-managed occasions – the delayed entry to the packed hall, the careful construction of his speeches, the choice of colourful phrases, the gestures and body-language. Here, his natural rhetorical talent was harnessed to well-honed performing skills. A pause at the beginning to allow the tension to mount; a low-key, even hesitant, start; undulations and variations of diction, not melodious certainly, but vivid and highly expressive; almost staccato bursts of sentences, followed by well-timed *rallentando* to expose the emphasis of a key point; theatrical use of the hands as the speech rose in crescendo; sarcastic wit aimed at opponents: all were devices carefully nurtured to maximize effect. As in the meticulous attention to detail in the preparations for the party rallies at Weimar in 1926 and Nuremberg in 1927 and 1929, Hitler was preoccupied with impact and impression. His clothing was also selected to match the occasion: the light-brown uniform with swastika armband, belt, attached diagonal strap crossing over the right shoulder, and knee-high leather boots when among the faithful at big party meetings and rallies; dark suit, white shirt, and tie, when appropriate to conveying a less martial, more 'respectable', appearance to a wider audience.

But the acting was not confined to such occasions. Those who came into contact with Hitler, while retaining a critical distance from him, were convinced that he was acting much of the time. He could play the parts as required. 'He was a kindly conversationalist, kissing the hands of ladies, a friendly uncle giving chocolates to children, a simple man of the people shaking the calloused hands of peasants and workers,' one of his associates later recalled. He could be the model of friendliness in public to someone he was privately castigating and deriding. The play-acting and hypocrisy did not mean that he was solely a cynical manipulator, that he did not believe in the central tenets of his 'world-view'. This fervent belief, coupled with the strength of his domineering personality, carried conviction among those drawn to his message.

The irresistible fascination that many – not a few of them cultured, educated, and intelligent – found in his extraordinary personality-traits doubtless owed much to his ability to play parts. As many attested, he could be charming – particularly to women – and was often witty and amusing. Much of the time it was show, put on for effect. The same could be true of his rages and outbursts of apparently uncontrollable anger, which were in reality often contrived. The firm handshake and 'manly' eye-to-eye contact which Hitler cultivated on occasions when he had to meet ordinary party members was, for the awestruck lowly activist, a moment never to be forgotten. For Hitler, it was merely acting; it meant no more than the reinforcement of the personality cult, the cement of the movement, the bonding force between Leader and fol-lowers. In reality, Hitler showed remarkably little human interest in his followers. His egocentrism was of monumental proportions. The propaganda image of 'fatherliness' concealed inner emptiness. Other individuals were of interest to him only in so far as they were useful.

Hitler's 'coffee-house tirades, his restlessness, his resentments against possible rivals in the party leadership, his distaste for systematic work, his paranoid outbursts of hatred' were seen by Putzi Hanfstaengl as a sign of sexual deficiency. This was no more than guesswork. But Hitler's relations with women were indeed odd in some ways. Why this was so can only be surmised. Yet here, too, he was often acting out a role. On one occasion, he took advantage of Putzi Hanfstaengl's brief absence from the room to fall on his knees in front of Helene Hanfstaengl, describing himself as her slave and bemoaning the fate that had led him to her too late. When Helene told him of the incident, Putzi put it down to Hitler's need to play the role of the languishing troubadour from time to time.

In physical appearance, Hitler was little changed from the time before the putsch. Away from the speaker's podium he looked anything but impressive. His face had hardened. But, as he told Hanfstaengl would be the case, he soon lost the weight he had put on in Landsberg once he started speaking again. Hitler reckoned he lost up to five pounds in weight through perspiration during a big speech. To counter this, his aides insisted on twenty bottles of mineral water being provided at the side of the lectern. His dress sense was anything but stylish. He still often favoured his plain blue suit. His trilby, light-coloured raincoat, leather leggings, and riding-whip gave him – especially when arriving with his bodyguards in the big black six-seater Mercedes convertible he had bought in early 1925 – the appearance of an eccentric gangster. For relaxation, he preferred to wear traditional Bavarian lederhosen. But even when he was in prison, he hated to be seen without a tie. During the heat of the summer, he would never be seen in a bathing costume. Whereas Mussolini revelled in virile images of himself as a sportsman or athlete, Hitler had a deep aversion to being seen other than fully clothed. More than petty-bourgeois proprieties, or prudishness, image was the vital consideration. Anything potentially embarrassing or inviting ridicule was to be avoided at all costs.

As they had done before the putsch, the Bruckmanns helped him to establish useful contacts in 'better' social circles. He had to adjust to a different type of audience from that in the beerhalls – more critical, less amenable to crude sloganizing and emotion. But in essence, little or nothing had changed. Hitler was at ease only when dominating the conversation. His monologues were a cover for his half-baked know-ledge. There was no doubting that he had a quick mind and a biting and destructive wit. He formed instant – often damning – judgements on individuals. And the combination of a domineering presence, resort to factual detail (often distorted), for which he had an exceptional memory, and utter conviction (brooking no alternative argument) based on ideo-logical certitude was impressive to those already half-persuaded of his extraordinary qualities. But those with knowledge and critical distance could often quickly see behind his crude arguments. His arrogance was breathtaking. 'What could I learn that's new?' he asked Hanfstaengl, on being encouraged to learn a foreign language and travel abroad.

Shortly after the Weimar Party Rally, in mid-July 1926, Hitler left Munich with his entourage for a holiday on the Obersalzberg. He stayed in a secluded and beautiful spot situated high in the mountains on the Austrian border above Berchtesgaden, flanked by the Untersberg (where legend had it that the medieval emperor, Frederick Barbarossa, lay sleeping), the Kneifelspitze, and the highest of them, the Watzmann. The scenery was breathtaking. Its monumental grandeur had first captivated Hitler when, under the pseudonym of 'Herr Wolf', he had visited Dietrich Eckart there in the winter of 1922–3. The Büchners, owners of the Pension Moritz where he stayed, were early supporters of the Movement. He liked them, and could enjoy in this mountain retreat a level of seclusion which he could never expect in Munich. He had, he later recalled, gone there in 1925 when he needed peace and quiet to dictate parts of the second volume of *Mein Kampf*. Whenever he could in the next two years, he returned to the Obersalzberg. Then he learnt that an alpine house there, Haus Wachenfeld, belonging to the widow of a north German businessman, was available to let. The widow, whose maiden name had been Wachenfeld, was a party member. He was offered a favourable price of 100 Marks a month. Soon, he was in a position to buy it. That the widow was in financial difficulties at the time helped. Hitler had his summer retreat. He could look down from his 'magic mountain' and see himself bestriding the world. In the Third Reich, at enormous cost to the state, Haus Wachenfeld would be turned into the massive complex known as the Berghof, a palace befitting a modern dictator, and a second seat of government for those ministers who each year had to set up residence nearby if they had a hope of contacting the head of state and expediting government business. Before that, on renting Haus Wachenfeld back in 1928, Hitler had – rather surprisingly since they had never been close – telephoned his half-sister Angela Raubal in Vienna and asked her to keep house for him. She agreed, and soon brought her daughter, a lively and attractive twenty-year-old, also named Angela, though known to all as Geli, to stay with her. Three years later, Geli was to be found dead in Hitler's flat in Munich.

While dictating the last chapters of *Mein Kampf* during his stay on the Obersalzberg in summer 1926, Hitler had, as we saw, consolidated his thinking on foreign policy, especially the acquisition of territory in the east. This idea, especially, was to dominate his speeches and writings of the mid-1920s. However, he was skilful in tailoring his speeches to his audience, as he showed in an important speech he delivered a few months earlier. Hopes of gaining financial support and of winning influential backing for his party had made him keen to accept the invitation of the prestigious Hamburger Nationalklub to address its members in the elegant Hotel Atlantic on 28 February 1926. It was not his usual audience. Here, he faced a socially exclusive club whose 400–450 members were drawn from Hamburg's upper bourgeoisie – many of them high-ranking officers, civil servants, lawyers, and businessmen. His tone was different from that he used in the Munich beerhalls. In his two-hour speech, he made not a single mention of the Jews. He was well aware that the primitive antisemitic rantings that roused the masses in the Zircus Krone would be counter-productive in this audience. Instead, the emphasis was placed entirely on the need to eliminate Marxism as the prerequisite of Germany's recovery. By 'Marxism', Hitler did not merely mean the German Communist Party, which had attained only 9 per cent of the vote at the last Reichstag election, in December 1924. Beyond the KPD, the term served to invoke the bogy of Soviet Communism, brought into power by a Revolution less than a decade earlier, and followed by a civil war whose atrocities had been emblazoned across a myriad of right-wing publications. 'Marxism' had even wider application. Hitler was also subsuming under this rubric all brands of socialism other than the 'national' variety he preached, and using it in particular to attack the SPD and trade unionism. In fact, to the chagrin of some of its followers, the SPD – still Germany's largest political party – had moved in practice far from its theoretical Marxist roots, and was wedded to upholding the liberal democracy it had been instrumental in calling into being in 1918–19. No 'Marxist' apocalypse threatened from that quarter. But Hitler's rhetoric had, of course, long branded those responsible for the Revolution and the Republic which followed it 'the November Criminals'. 'Marxism' was, therefore, also convenient short-hand to denigrate Weimar democracy. And to his well-heeled bourgeois audience in Hamburg, anti-Marxist to the core, his verbal assault on the Left was music to the ears.

Hitler reduced it to a simple formula: if the Marxist 'world-view' was not 'eradicated', Germany would never rise again. The task of the National Socialist Movement was straightforward: 'the smashing and annihilation of the Marxist *Weltanschauung*'. Terror must be met with terror. The bourgeoisie itself was incapable of defeating the threat of Bolshevism. It needed a mass movement as intolerant as that of the Marxists themselves to do it. Winning the masses rested on two premisses. The first was to recognize their social concerns. But in case his audience thought this was back-door Marxism, Hitler was quick to reassure them: social legislation demanded 'the promotion of the welfare of the individual in a framework that guaranteed retention of an independent economy'. 'We are all workers,' he stated. 'The aim is not to get higher and higher wages, but to increase production, because that is to the advantage of each individual.' His audience was unlikely to disagree with such sentiments. The second premiss was to offer the masses 'a programme that is unalterable, a political faith that is unshakeable'. The usual party programmes, manifestos, and philosophies of bourgeois parties would not win them over. Hitler's contempt for the masses was plain. 'The broad mass is feminine,' he stated, 'one-sided in its attitude; it knows only the hard "either-or".' It wanted only a single viewpoint upheld – but then with all available means, and, he added, now mixing his genders and pointing to what is normally taken to be a more masculine characteristic, 'does not shrink from using force'. What the mass had to feel was its own strength. Among a crowd of 200,000 in Berlin's Lustgarten, the individual felt no more than 'a small worm', subject to mass-suggestion, aware only of those around him being prepared to fight for an ideal. 'The broad masses are blind and stupid and don't know what they are doing,' he claimed. They were 'primitive in attitude'. For them, 'understanding' offered only a 'shaky platform'. 'What is stable is emotion: hatred.' The more Hitler preached intolerance, force, and hatred, as the solution to Germany's problems, the more his audience liked it. He was interrupted on numerous occasions during these passages with cheers and shouts of 'bravo'. At the end there was a lengthy ovation, and cries of 'Heil'.

National revival through terroristic anti-Marxism built on the cynical manipulation and indoctrination of the masses: that was the sum total of Hitler's message to the upper-crust of the Hamburg bourgeoisie. Nationalism and anti-Marxism were scarcely peculiarities of the Nazis alone. Nor did they amount in themselves to much of an ideology. What distinguished Hitler's approach to his Hamburg audience was not the ideas themselves, but the impression of fanatical will, utter ruthlessness, and the creation of a nationalist movement resting on the support of the masses. And it was plain from the enthusiastic response that selective terror deployed against 'Marxists' would meet with little or no opposition from the élite of Germany's most liberal city.

Back among his 'own sort', little or nothing had changed. The tone was very different from that adopted in Hamburg. In closed party meetings or, after the speaking ban had been lifted in early 1927, once more in Munich beerhalls and the Circus Krone, the attacks on the Jews were as vicious and unconstrained as ever. In speech after speech, as before the putsch, he launched brutal assaults against the Jews, bizarrely depicted both as the wire-pullers of finance capital and as poisoning the people with subversive Marxist doctrine. Explicit attacks on the Jews occurred more frequently and extensively in 1925 and 1926 than in the subsequent two years. Antisemitism seemed now rather more ritualist or mechanistic. The main stress had moved to anti-Marxism. But only the presentation of his ideas had been modified to some extent; their meaning had not. His pathological hatred of Jews was unchanged. 'The Jew is and remains the world enemy,' he once more asserted in an article in the *Völkischer Beobachter* in February 1927, 'and his weapon, Marxism, a plague of mankind.'

Between 1926 and 1928, Hitler became more preoccupied with the 'question of [living] space' (*Raumfrage*) and 'land policy' (*Bodenpolitik*). Though, as we have seen, the idea of an eastern 'land policy' at the expense of Russia had been present in Hitler's mind at the latest by the end of 1922, he had mentioned it in his public statements – written or spoken – only on a handful of occasions before the end of 1926. He referred in a speech on 16 December 1925 to the 'acquisition of land and soil' as the best solution to Germany's economic problems and alluded to the colonization of the east 'by the sword' in the Middle Ages. He remarked on the need for a colonial policy in eastern Europe at Bamberg in February 1926. And he returned to the theme as a central element of his speech at the Weimar Party Rally on 4 July 1926. The completion of *Mein Kampf*, which ends with the question of eastern colonization, must have further focused his mind on the issue. Once he was allowed to speak in public again in spring 1927, the question of 'living space' became frequently, then from the summer onwards, obsessively emphasized in all his major addresses. Speech after speech highlights in more or less the same language ideas that became embodied in the 'Second Book', dictated during the summer of 1928. Other economic options are mentioned only to be dismissed. The lack of space for Germany's population could be overcome only by attaining power, then by force. The 'eastern colonization' of the Middle Ages was praised. Conquest 'by the sword' was the only method. Russia was seldom explicitly mentioned. But the meaning was unmistakable.

The social-Darwinist, racist reading of history offered the justification. 'Politics is nothing more than the struggle of a people for its existence.'

'It is an iron principle,' he declared: 'the weaker one falls so that the strong one gains life.' Three values determined a people's fate: 'blood-' or 'race-value', the 'value of personality', and the 'spirit of struggle' or 'self-preservation drive'. These values, embodied in the 'aryan race', were threatened by the three 'vices' – democracy, pacifism, and internationalism – that comprised the work of 'Jewish Marxism'.

The theme of personality and leadership, little emphasized before 1923, was a central thread of Hitler's speeches and writings in the mid- and later 1920s. The people, he said, formed a pyramid. At its apex was 'the genius, the great man'. Following the chaos in the *völkisch* movement during the 'leaderless time', it was scarcely surprising that there was heavy emphasis in 1925 and 1926 on the leader as the focus of unity. In his refoundation speech on 27 February 1925, Hitler had stressed his task as Leader as 'bringing together again those who are going different ways'. The art of being Leader lay in assembling the 'stones of the mosaic'. The Leader was the 'central point' or 'preserver' of the 'idea'. This demanded, Hitler repeatedly underlined, blind obedience and loyalty from the followers. The cult of the Leader was thus built up as the integrating mechanism of the movement. With his own supremacy firmly established by mid-1926, Hitler never lost an opportunity to highlight the 'value of personality' and 'individual greatness' as the guiding force in Germany's struggle and coming rebirth. He avoided specific reference to his own claims to 'heroic' status. This was unnecessary. It could be left to the growing number of converts to the Hitler cult, and to the orchestrated outpourings of propaganda. For Hitler himself, the 'Führer myth' was both a propaganda weapon *and* a central tenet of belief. His own 'greatness' could be implicitly but unmistakably underscored by repeated references to Bismarck, Frederick the Great, and Luther, along with allusions to Mussolini. Speaking of Bismarck (if without mentioning his name) in May 1926, he commented: 'It was necessary to transmit the national idea to the mass of the people.' 'A giant had to fulfil this task.' The sustained applause showed that the meaning was not lost on his audience.

Goebbels had been thrilled on more than one occasion in 1926 by Hitler's exposition of the 'social question'. 'Always new and compelling' was how Goebbels described his ideas. In reality, Hitler's 'social idea' was simplistic, diffuse, and manipulative. It amounted to little more than what he had told his bourgeois audience in Hamburg: winning the workers to nationalism, destroying Marxism, and overcoming the division between nationalism and socialism through the creation of a nebulous 'national community' (*Volksgemeinschaft*) based on racial purity and the concept of struggle. The fusion of nationalism and socialism would do away with the class antagonism between a nationalist bourgeoisie and Marxist proletariat (both of which had failed in their political goals). This would be replaced by a 'community of struggle' where nationalism and socialism would be united, where 'brain' and 'fist' were reconciled, and where – denuded of Marxist influence – the building of a new spirit for the great future struggle of the people could be undertaken. Such ideas were neither new, nor original. And, ultimately, they rested not on any modern form of socialism, but on the crudest and most brutal version of nineteenth-century imperialist and social-Darwinistic notions. Social welfare in the trumpeted 'national community' did not exist for its own sake, but to prepare for external struggle, for conquest 'by the sword'.

Hitler repeatedly stated that he was uninterested in day-to-day issues. What he offered, over and over again, was the same vision of a long-term goal, to be striven after with missionary zeal and total commitment. Political struggle, eventual attainment of power, destruction of the enemy, and build-up of the nation's might were stepping-stones to the goal. But how it was to be then attained was left open. Hitler himself had no concrete notion. He just had the certainty of the fanatical 'conviction politician' that it *would* be attained. Clarity was never aimed at. The acquisition of 'living space' through conquest implied at some distant future date aggression against Russia. But it had no more precise meaning than that. Hitler's own firm belief in it need not be doubted. But, even for many of his followers, in the world of the mid-1920s, with Germany engaged diplomatically with the Soviet Union following the Rapallo Treaty of 1922 as well as improving relations with the western powers through the 1925 Treaty of Locarno then membership of the League of Nations, this must have seemed little more than sloganizing or a pipe-dream.

Even on the 'Jewish Question', the wild tirades, vicious as they were, offered no concrete policies. 'Getting rid of the Jews' could only reasonably be taken to mean the expulsion of all Jews from Germany, as when Hitler called for chasing 'that pack of Jews . . . from our Fatherland . . . with an iron broom'. But even this aim seemed less than clear when he stated – to tumultuous applause from the stalwarts of the movement gathered in Munich's Hofbräuhaus on 24 February 1928 to celebrate the eighth anniversary of the launch of the Party Programme – that 'the Jew' would have to be shown 'that we're the bosses here; if he behaves well, he can stay – if not, then out with him'.

In the 'Jewish Question', the 'question of [living] space', and the 'social question', Hitler suggested a vision of a distant utopia. He did not chart the path to it. But no other Nazi leader or *völkisch* politician could match the internal unity, simplicity, and all-encompassing character of this 'vision'. His sense of conviction – he spoke frequently of his 'mission', 'faith', and of the 'idea' – combined with an unrivalled talent for mobilization through reduction to simple 'black–white' choices, was where the ideologue and the propagandist came together.

The interdependence of the various strands of Hitler's pernicious 'world-view' is most plainly evident in his 'Second Book' (an updated statement of his views on foreign policy, left, in the event, unpublished), dictated hurriedly to Max Amann during a stay on the Obersalzberg in the summer of 1928. Hitler felt prompted to produce the book by the heated debates at the time about policy towards South Tyrol. Under Mussolini, Fascist policies of Italianization of the largely German-speaking area had stirred strong anti-Italian feeling in nationalist circles in Austria and Germany, particularly in Bavaria. Hitler's readiness to renounce German claims on South Tyrol in the interest of an alliance with Italy had seen him attacked by German nationalists as well as being accused by socialists of taking bribes from Mussolini. Hitler had dealt with the South Tyrol issue in *Mein Kampf*, and published the relevant sections from the second volume as a separate pamphlet in February 1926. When the issue flared up again in 1928, he was driven to outline his position at length. Probably financial considerations – Amann may well have advised against having the 'Second Book' compete against the second volume of *Mein Kampf*, with its disappointing and diminishing sales – dissuaded Hitler from publishing the book. But in addition, as the South Tyrol question lost its urgency, new issues like the Young Plan arose, and Hitler had neither time nor inclination to revise the text, it may have been felt that its publication would have offered political hostages to fortune.

If occasioned by the South Tyrol question, the 'Second Book' went far beyond it, ranging more expansively than *Mein Kampf* had done over Hitler's broad ideas on foreign policy and 'territorial issues' (*Raum-fragen*), linking them, as always, with his racial interpretation of history and, in the final pages, with the need to destroy what he saw as the threat of 'Jewish domination'. But the 'Second Book' offered nothing new. As we have seen, the essence of Hitler's 'world-view' was fully developed by the time he wrote the second volume of *Mein Kampf* in 1926, existent in embryonic form, in fact, since late 1922. The ideas dominating the 'Second Book' – including the issue of South Tyrol and his interest in the growing economic power of the United States of America – were repeatedly advanced in Hitler's speeches and writings from 1927 onwards. Several passages from these speeches recur almost verbatim at key points in the 'Second Book'.

Long before the dictation of the 'Second Book', then, Hitler was a fixated ideologue. His own inner certainty of the 'truths' about history as racial struggle, and Germany's future mission to obtain 'living space' and, at the same time, eradicate the power of the Jews for ever, were of immense importance as a personal driving-force. Their significance in attracting support for National Socialism can, however, easily be exaggerated. The growth of the NSDAP to a mass party had little directly to do with the arcanum of Hitler's personalized 'world-view'. More complex processes have to be taken into account.

IV

At the end of January 1927, Saxony became the first large German state to lift the speaking ban on Hitler. On 5 March, the Bavarian authorities finally conceded to the pressure to allow Hitler to speak again. His return to the public arena caused little of a stir. Reports from the Bavarian provinces indicated little interest in the NSDAP, for all its vigorous propaganda. Party meetings were often badly attended. Hitler's magic was no longer working, even in Munich. In January 1928, the Munich police reported that 'the advances of the National Socialist Movement repeatedly claimed by Hitler are not true, especially in Bavaria. In reality, interest in the movement both in the countryside and in Munich is strongly in decline. Branch meetings attended by 3–400 people in 1926 now have an attendance of at most 60–80 members.' Even the Party Rally, held for the first time at Nuremberg, on

19–21 August 1927, despite careful orchestration for maximum propaganda effect, failed to raise the expected level of support or interest.

Most other German states followed the examples of Saxony and Bavaria in lifting the ban on Hitler speaking in public. Only Prussia, the largest state, and Anhalt held out until autumn 1928. The authorities, it seemed with justification, could believe that the Nazi menace had passed. Hitler no longer appeared a threat. A confidential report by the Reich Minister of the Interior in 1927 had already judged that the NSDAP was no more than a 'splinter group incapable of exerting any noticeable influence on the great mass of the population and the course of political events'.

Though outwardly making little or no headway in the more settled political climate of the mid-1920s, as Germany's new democracy at last showed signs of stability, significant developments were taking place within the NSDAP. Eventually, these would help to place the party in a stronger position to exploit the new economic crisis that was to hit Germany in autumn 1929.

Most importantly, the NSDAP had become a self-conscious 'leader-movement', focused ideologically and organizationally on the Hitler cult. In retrospect, the 'leaderless time' of 1924, and Hitler's obstinacy – born out of weakness – in refusing to take sides in the internecine strife of the *völkisch* movement, had been enormously advantageous. The defeat at Bamberg of those looking to programmatic changes was, then, at the same time the victory of those loyalists prepared to look no further than Hitler as the embodiment of the 'idea'. For these, the programme detached from the leader had no meaning. And, as 1924 had proven, without Hitler there could be no unity, and hence no movement.

The establishment of the Führer cult was decisive for the development of the Nazi Movement. Without it, as 1924 had shown, it would have been torn apart by factionalism. With it, the still precarious unity could be preserved by calling on loyalty to Hitler as a prime duty. Among the party leadership, feelings had to be subordinated to the overriding need for unity.

Within the movement, the SA had always been the most difficult element to control – and so it would continually prove down to 1934. But here, too, Hitler was successfully able to diffuse trouble by invoking loyalty to his own person. In May 1927, he made an impassioned speech to the Munich stormtroopers, demoralized and rebellious towards the SA leader Franz Pfeffer von Salomon. At the end of his speech, he resorted to his usual ploy. He stepped down from the rostrum, shook hands with each SA man, and gained their renewed pledge of personal loyalty to him.

Clashes over strategy, factional disputes, personal rivalries – all were endemic in the NSDAP. The interminable conflicts and animosities, normally personal or tactical rather than ideological, almost invariably stopped short of any attack on Hitler. He intervened as little as possible. In fact, the rivalry and competition simply showed him, according to his own concept of social-Darwinist struggle, who among his competing underlings was the stronger. Nor did Hitler make any effort to reconcile ideological nuances within the party, unless they threatened to become counter-productive by deviating the single-minded drive for power through mass mobilization into sectarian squabbling. The Führer cult was accepted because it offered all parties the only remedy to this. Personal loyalty to Hitler, whether genuine or forced, was the price of unity. In some cases, Nazi leaders were wholly convinced of Hitler's greatness and 'mission'. In others, their own ambitions could only be upheld by lip-service to the supreme Leader. Either way, the result was that Hitler's mastery over the movement increased to the position where it was well-nigh unchallengeable. And either way, the transmission belt within the party faithful had been manufactured for the subsequent extension of the Führer cult to wider sectors of the German electorate. The Leader cult was indispensable to the party. And the subsummation of the 'idea' in Hitler's own person was necessary, if party energy was not to be dissipated in harmful factional divides. By avoiding doctrinal dispute, as he had done in 1924, and focusing all energies on the one goal of obtaining power, Hitler could – sometimes with difficulty – hold the party together. Along the way, the Führer cult had developed its own momentum.

With the build-up of the Führer cult, Hitler's image was at least as important as his practical contribution to the modest growth of the party in the 'wilderness years'. Of course, a Hitler-speech remained a major event for a local party branch. And Hitler retained the ability in his mass-meetings to win over initially sceptical audiences. But whatever limited success the NSDAP enjoyed before the Depression cannot simply – or even mainly – be attributed to Hitler. As an agitator, Hitler was distinctly less directly prominent than he had been before the putsch. The speaking-ban was, of course, a major hindrance in 1925 and 1926. He spoke at only thirty-one meetings in 1925 and thirty-two in 1926, mainly internal party affairs, a good number of them in Bavaria. In 1927, his speeches increased in number to fifty-six, more than half of them within Bavaria. Most of his sixty-six speeches in 1928 took place in the first five months, up to the Reichstag election. More than two-thirds of them were held in Bavaria. During the whole of 1929, as the NSDAP began to gain ground in regional elections, he held only twenty-nine speeches, all but eight in Bavaria.

One limitation on Hitler's availability as a speaker in these years was posed by his frequent trips to try to establish important contacts and drum up funding for a party with chronic financial problems. Not surprisingly, for a party in the political doldrums, his efforts met with little success. Though (not to the liking of the 'social-revolutionaries' in the NSDAP) he courted Ruhr industrialists and businessmen in a number of speeches in 1926 and 1927, which went down well, they showed little interest in a party that seemed to be going nowhere. The Bechsteins and Bruckmanns, long-standing patrons, continued to give generously. But the aged Emil Kirdorf, whom Frau Bruckmann had brought into personal contact with Hitler, was almost alone among leading Ruhr industrialists in sympathizing with him to the extent of joining the NSDAP, and in making a sizeable donation of 100,000 Marks that went a long way towards overcoming the party's immediate financial plight. As would remain the case, the party was heavily dependent for its income on the contributions of ordinary members. So the stagnation, or at best slow growth, in party membership meant continued headaches for the party treasurer.

As earlier, Hitler paid little attention to administration and organization. Party bosses were resigned to his lengthy absences and inaccessibility on even important concerns. He left financial matters to his trusted business manager Max Amann, and the party treasurer, Franz Xaver Schwarz. Behind the scenes in Munich, Hitler could rely in the party's secretariat upon the indefatigable and subservient Philipp Bouhler, the retiring but inwardly ambitious individual who was later to play a central role in the emergence of the 'euthanasia action'. Above all, it was Gregor Strasser, as Propaganda Leader between September 1926 and the end of 1927 (during which time he streamlined and coordinated propaganda activities throughout the Reich) and especially after he was made Organizational Leader on 2 January 1928, who built up, from the faction-ridden and incoherently structured movement, the nationwide organization that from 1929 onwards was in a position to exploit the new crisis conditions. Hitler's part in this development was minimal, though placing Strasser in charge of organizational matters was one of his more inspired appointments.

Hitler's instinct, as ever, was for propaganda, not organization. His 'feel', when it came to matters of mobilizing the masses, seldom let him down. As director of party propaganda, Gregor Strasser had been given a great deal of scope – Hitler's usual style – to shape the character and pattern of agitation. Following his own leanings, Strasser had made a strong push to win over, especially, the urban proletariat. Even to outside observers, it was plain by autumn 1927 that this strategy was not paying worthwhile dividends, and was at the same time in danger of alienating the lower-middle-class support of the NSDAP. Reports came in from Schleswig-Holstein, Thuringia, Mecklenburg, Pomerania, and other areas indicating that growing unrest in rural areas offered promising terrain for the NSDAP. Hitler was evidently well-informed. And at a meeting of Gau leaders on 27 November 1927 in the 'Hotel Elefant' in Weimar, he announced a change of course. He made plain that significant gains could not be expected at the coming election from 'the Marxists'. Small-shopkeepers, threatened by department stores, and white-collar workers, many of them already antisemites, were singled out as better targets. In December 1927, Hitler addressed for the first time a rally of several thousand peasants from Lower Saxony and Schleswig-Holstein. In the New Year, he himself took over the position of party Propaganda Leader. His deputy, Heinrich Himmler, undertook the routine tasks. The future overlord of the SS empire was at this time still in his twenties, a well-educated and intelligent former agricultural student who had briefly worked for a fertilizer firm and reared chickens. With his short-back-and-sides haircut, small moustache, round glasses, and unathletic build, he resembled a small-town bank clerk or pedantic schoolmaster. Whatever appearances might have suggested, he had, however, few peers in ideological fanaticism and, as time would prove, cold ruthlessness. The young nationalist idealist, already imagining dire conspiracies involving 'the red International', Jews, Jesuits, and freemasons ranged against Germany, had joined the NSDAP in the summer of 1923, influenced by the man whose murder he would orchestrate eleven years later, Ernst Röhm. It was at Röhm's side that, on 8 November that year, the night of the putsch, he had carried the banner at the head of the Reichskriegsflagge unit engaged in attempting to storm the Bavarian War Ministry. From the time of the party's refoundation, he had been active, initially as secretary to Gregor Strasser, then, from 1926, as Deputy Gauleiter of Upper Bavaria-Swabia, and Deputy Reich Propaganda Leader. In the latter capacity in the later 1920s – he was also Deputy Reichsführer-SS from 1927 before being appointed to lead the SS two years later – he proved both efficient and imaginative – apparently coming up with the idea of blanket propaganda coverage of a specific area during a brief period of time, something that became a Nazi hallmark.

But significantly, and in contrast to his normal habits, Hitler intervened directly in drafting texts and in shaping central propaganda. In April 1928, he 'corrected' the interpretation of Point 17 of the party's 'unalterable' 1920 Programme: 'expropriation without compensation' meant, for a party based on the principle of private property, merely the creation of legal means to take over land not administered in the public good; that is, Jewish land-speculation companies.

The shift in propaganda emphasis amounted to a further move away from a 'programmatic' stance directed primarily at winning workers from Marxism to a broader 'catch-all' approach to mobilization. It was a pragmatic readjustment, recognizing the possibility of a widened appeal to a variety of social groups not previously addressed in any systematic way in party propaganda. Unlike some in the party, wedded to a type of 'social-revolutionary' emotive anti-capitalism, which social groups were attracted to Nazism was for Hitler a matter of indifference. The important thing was that they *were* won over. His aim was to gain power. Any weapon to that end was useful. But it did mean that the NSDAP became even more of a loose coalition of competing interest-groups. Only the *absence* of a clear programme and a set of utopian, distant goals built into the image of the Leader could hold them together – for a time.

V

Few Germans had Hitler on their mind in Weimar's 'golden years' of the mid-1920s. The internal developments within his party were of neither interest nor concern to the overwhelming majority of people. Little attention was paid to the former Munich troublemaker who now seemed no more than a fringe irritant on the political scene. Those who did take notice of Hitler were often dismissive or condescending, or both.

The results of the Reichstag election on 20 May 1928 appeared to confirm the correctness of those commentators who for years had been preaching the end of Hitler and his movement. The electorate showed relatively little interest in the campaign – a reflection of the more settled conditions. With its miserable return of 2.6 per cent, the NSDAP won only twelve seats. Electorally, it had lost ground, compared with the Völkischer Block in December 1924. There was at least the consolation that the twelve Nazis who entered the Reichstag now had immunity from legal action for their venomous attacks on opponents and – if anything even more important – daily allowances and free rail passes for first-class travel on the Reichsbahn to ease pressure on party finances. Among the new deputies were Gregor Strasser, Frick, Feder, Goebbels, Ritter von Epp – the former Freikorps leader, a new, much-trumpeted convert from the BVP – and Hermann Göring, recently returned to the fold after his absence since the putsch. 'We are going into the Reichstag ... like the wolf into the sheepflock,' Goebbels told his readers in the *Angriff*, his Berlin newspaper.

There was understandable disappointment and dejection within the party. The need for a readjustment of party propaganda and organiz-ation was plain. Under Strasser's organizational leadership, greater attention was paid to the countyside, and first steps were taken in constructing a panoply of affiliated sub-organizations that became extremely important in tapping the specific interests of middle-class groups.

Meanwhile, the first dark clouds were already gathering over Ger-many's economy. The mounting crisis in agriculture was leading to widespread indebtedness, bankruptcies, forced sales of land, and enor-mous bitterness in the farming community. In the biggest industrial belt,

Ruhr industrialists refused to accept an arbitration award and locked out the whole work-force of the iron and steel industry, leaving 230,000 workers without jobs or wages for weeks. Unemployment was by now sharply on the rise, reaching almost 3 million by January 1929, an increase of a million over the previous year. Politically, too, there were growing difficulties. The 'grand coalition' under the SPD Chancellor Hermann Müller was shaky from the outset. A split, and serious loss of face for the SPD, occurred over the decision to build a battle cruiser (a policy opposed by the Social Democrats before the election). The Ruhr iron dispute further opened the rifts in the government and exposed it to its critics on Left and Right. It was the first shot of the concerted attempt by the conservative Right to roll back the social advances made in the Weimar welfare state. The ensuing conflict over social policy would ultimately lead to the demise of the Müller government. And by the end of the year, the reparations issue began to loom again. It would become acute in 1929.

In the worsening conditions of the winter of 1928–9, the NSDAP began to attract increasing support. By the end of 1928, the number of membership cards distributed had reached 108,717. Social groups that had scarcely been reached before could now be tapped. In November 1928, Hitler received a rapturous reception from 2,500 students at Munich University. Before he spoke, the meeting had been addressed by the recently appointed Reich Leader of the Nazi Students' Federation, the twenty-one-year-old future Hitler Youth leader Baldur von Schirach.

The student union elections gave Hitler an encouraging sign of gathering Nazi strength. But it was above all in the countryside, among the radicalized peasants, that the Nazis began to make particularly rapid advances. In Schleswig-Holstein, bomb attacks on government offices gave the clearest indication of the mood in the farming community. In January 1929, radicalized peasants in the region founded the Landvolk, an inchoate but violent protest movement that rapidly became prey to Nazi inroads. Two months later, following an NSDAP meeting in the village of Wöhrden, a fight between SA men and KPD supporters led to two stormtroopers being killed and a number of others injured. Local reactions showed graphically the potential for Nazi gains in the disaffected countryside. There was an immediate upsurge in Nazi support in the locality. Old peasant women now wore the party badge on their work-smocks. From conversations with them, ran the police report, it was clear that they had no idea of the aims of the party. But they were certain that the government was incapable and the authorities were squandering taxpayers' money. They were convinced 'that only the National Socialists could be the saviours from this alleged misery'. Farmers spoke of a Nazi victory through parliament taking too long. A civil war was what was needed. The mood was 'extraordinarily embittered' and the population were open to all forms of violent action. Using the incident as a propaganda opportunity, Hitler attended the funeral of the dead SA men, and visited those wounded. This made a deep impression on the local inhabitants. He and the other leading Nazis were applauded as 'liberators of the people'.

As the 'crisis before the crisis' – economic and political – deepened, Hitler kept up his propaganda offensive. In the first half of 1929 he wrote ten articles for the party press and held sixteen major speeches before large, rapturous audiences. Four were in Saxony, during the run-up to the state elections there on 12 May. Outright attacks on the Jews did not figure in the speeches. The emphasis was on the bankruptcy at home and abroad of the Weimar system, the exploitation of international finance and the suffering of 'small people', the catastrophic economic consequences of democratic rule, the social divisions that party politics caused and replicated, and above all the need to restore German strength and unity and gain the land to secure its future. 'The key to the world market has the shape of the sword,' he declared. The only salvation from decline was through power: 'The entire system must be altered. Therefore the great task is to restore to people their belief in leadership,' he concluded.

Hitler's speeches were part of a well-organized propaganda campaign, providing saturation coverage of Saxony before the election. It was planned by Himmler, but under Hitler's own supervision. The growing numerical strength of the party, and the improvements made in its organization and structure, now allowed more extensive coverage. This in turn helped to create an image of dynamism, drive, and energy. Local activism, and the winning of influential figures in a community, usually held the key to Nazi progress. Hitler had to be used sparingly – for best effect, as well as to avoid too punishing a schedule. A Hitler speech was a major bonus for any party branch. But in the changing conditions from 1929 onwards, the NSDAP was chalking up successes in places where people had never seen Hitler.

The NSDAP won 5 per cent of the vote in the Saxon election. The following month, the party gained 4 per cent in the Mecklenburg elections – double what it had achieved the previous year in the Reichstag election. Its two elected members held a pivotal position in a Landtag evenly balanced between Left and Right. Towards the end of June, Coburg, in northern Bavaria, became the first town in Germany to elect a Nazi-run town council. By October, the NSDAP's share of the popular vote had reached 7 per cent in the Baden state elections. This was still before the Wall Street Crash ushered in the great Depression.

The revival of the reparations issue provided further grist to the mill of Nazi agitation. The results of the deliberations of the committee of experts, which had been working since January 1929 under the chairmanship of Owen D. Young, an American banker and head of the General Electric Company, to regulate the payment of reparations, were eventually signed on 7 June. Compared with the Dawes Plan, the settlement was relatively favourable to Germany. Repayments were to be kept low for three years, and would overall be some 17 per cent less than under the Dawes Plan. But it would take fifty-nine years before the reparations would finally be paid off. The nationalist Right were outraged. Alfred Hugenberg, former Krupp director, leader of the DNVP and press baron, controlling the nationalist press and with a big stake in the UFA film company, formed in July a 'Reich Committee for the German People's Petition' to organize a campaign to force the government to reject the Young Plan. He persuaded Hitler to join. Franz Seldte and Theodor Duesterberg from the Stahlhelm, Heinrich Claß from the Pan-German League, and the industrial magnate Fritz Thyssen were all members of the committee. Hitler's presence in this company of capitalist tycoons and reactionaries was not to the liking of the national revolutionary wing of the NSDAP, headed by Otto Strasser, Gregor's brother. But, ever the opportunist, Hitler recognized the chances the campaign offered. The draft 'Law against the Enslavement of the German People' drawn up by the committee in September, rejecting the Young Plan and the 'war guilt lie', marginally gained the necessary support to stage a plebiscite. But when the plebiscite eventually took place, on 22 December 1929, only 5.8 millions – 13.8 per cent of the electorate – voted for it. The campaign had proved a failure – but not for Hitler. He and his party had benefited from massive exposure freely afforded him in the Hugenberg press. And he had been recognized as an equal partner by those in high places, with good contacts to sources of funding and influence.

Some of Hitler's new-found bedfellows had been honoured guests at the Party Rally that took place in Nuremberg from 1 to 4 August 1929. The deputy leader of the Stahlhelm, Theodor Duesterberg, and Count von der Goltz, chairman of the Vereinigte Vaterländische Verbände (United Patriotic Associations) graced the rally with their presence. The Ruhr industrialist, and benefactor of the party, Emil Kirdorf had also accepted an invitation. Winifred Wagner, the Lady of Bayreuth, was also an honoured guest. Thirty-five special trains brought 25,000 SA and SS men and 1,300 members of the Hitler Youth to Nuremberg. Police estimated an attendance of around 30–40,000 in all. It was a far bigger and more grandiose spectacle than the previous rally, two years earlier, had been. It reflected a new confidence and optimism in a party whose membership had grown by this time to some 130,000. And compared with two years earlier, Hitler's dominance was even more complete. Working sessions simply rubber-stamped policy determined from above. Hitler showed little interest in them. His only concern, as always, was with the propaganda display of the rally.

He had reason to feel satisfied with the way his movement had developed over the four years since its refoundation. The party was now almost three times as large as it had been at the time of the putsch, and growing fast. It was spread throughout the country, and making head-way in areas which had never been strongholds. It was now far more tightly organized and structured. There was much less room for dissension. Rivals in the *völkisch* movement had been amalgamated or had faded into insignificance. Not least, Hitler's own mastery was complete. His recipe for success was unchanged: hammer home the same message, exploit any opportunity for agitation, and hope for external circumstances to favour the party. But although great strides forward had been made since 1925, and though the party was registering modest electoral gains at state elections and acquiring a good deal of publicity, no realist could have reckoned much to its chances of winning power. For that, Hitler's only hope was a massive and comprehensive crisis of the state.

He had no notion just how quickly events would turn to the party's advantage. But on 3 October, Gustav Stresemann, the only statesman of real standing in Germany, who had done most to sustain the shaky Müller government, died following a stroke. Three weeks later, on

24 October 1929, the largest stock-market in the world, in Wall Street, New York, crashed. The crisis Hitler needed was about to envelop Germany.

8

Breakthrough

I

The Nazi leadership did not immediately recognize the significance of the American stock-market crash in October 1929. The *Völkischer Beobachter* did not even mention Wall Street's 'Black Friday'. But Germany was soon reverberating under its shock-waves. Its dependence upon American short-term loans ensured that the impact would be extraordinarily severe. Industrial output, prices, and wages began the steep drop that would reach its calamitous low-point in 1932. The agricultural crisis that had already been radicalizing Germany's farmers in 1928 and 1929 was sharply intensified. By January 1930, the labour exchanges recorded 3,218,000 unemployed – some 14 per cent of the 'working-age' population. The true figure, taking in those on short-time, has been estimated as over 4½ million.

The protest of ordinary people who took the view that democracy had failed them, that 'the system' should be swept away, became shriller on both Left and Right. Nazi advances in regional elections reflected the growing radicalization of the mood of the electorate. The Young Plan plebiscite had given the party much-needed publicity in the widely-read Hugenberg press. Its value, said Hitler, was that it had provided 'the occasion for a propaganda wave the like of which had never been seen in Germany before'. It had allowed the NSDAP to project itself as the most radical voice of the Right, a protest-movement *par excellence* that had never been tarnished with any involvement in Weimar government. In the Baden state elections on 27 October 1929, the NSDAP won 7 per cent of the vote. In the Lübeck city elections a fortnight or so later, the percentage was 8.1. Even in the Berlin council elections on 17 November, the party almost quadrupled its vote of 1928, though its 5.8 per cent was still marginal, compared with over 50 per cent that went to the two left-wing parties. Most significantly of all, in the Thuringian state elections held on 8 December, the NSDAP trebled its vote of 1928 and broke the 10 per cent barrier for the first time, recording 11.3 per cent of the 90,000 votes cast. Should the Nazi Party exploit the situation by agreeing to enter government for the first time but run the risk of courting unpopularity through its participation in an increasingly discredited system? Hitler decided the NSDAP had to enter government. Had he refused, he said, it would have come to new elections and voters could have turned away from the NSDAP. What happened gives an indication of the way at this time the 'seizure of power' in the Reich itself was envisaged.

Hitler demanded the two posts he saw as most important in the Thuringian government: the Ministry of the Interior, controlling the civil service and police; and the Ministry of Education, overseeing culture as well as policy for school and university. 'He who controls both these ministries and ruthlessly and persistently exploits his power in them can achieve extraordinary things,' wrote Hitler. When his nominee for both ministries, Wilhelm Frick, was rejected – the German People's Party (DVP) claimed it could not work with a man who (for his part in the Beerhall Putsch) had been convicted of high treason – Hitler went himself to Weimar and imposed an ultimatum. If within three days Frick were not accepted, the NSDAP would bring about new elections. Industrialists from the region, lobbied by Hitler, put heavy pressure on the DVP – the party of big business – and Hitler's demands were finally accepted. Frick was given the task of purging the civil service, police, and teachers of revolutionary, Marxist, and democratic tendencies and bringing education in line with National Socialist ideas.

The first Nazi experiment in government was anything but successful. Frick's attempts to reconstruct educational and cultural policy on a basis of ideological racism were not well received, and moves to nazify the police and civil service were blocked by the Reich Ministry of the Interior. After only a year, Frick was removed from office following a vote of no-confidence supported by the NSDAP's coalition partners. The strategy – to prove so fateful in 1933 – of including Nazis in government in the expectation that they would prove incompetent and lose support was, on the basis of the Thuringian experiment, by no means absurd.

In a letter of 2 February 1930 to an overseas party supporter outlining the developments that led to participation in the Thuringian government, Hitler pointed to the rapid advances the party was making in gaining support. By the time he was writing, party membership officially numbered 200,000 (though the actual figures were somewhat lower). The Nazis were starting to make their presence felt in places where they had been scarcely noticed earlier.

Since the Young Campaign the previous autumn, rejecting the plan for long-term repayment of reparations, the NSDAP had been building up to around a hundred propaganda meetings a day. This would reach a crescendo during the Reichstag election campaign later in the summer. Many of the speakers were now of good quality, hand-picked, well-trained, centrally controlled but able to latch on to and exploit local issues as well as putting across the unchanging basic message of Nazi agitation. The National Socialists were increasingly forcing themselves on to the front pages of newspapers. They began to penetrate the network of clubs and associations that were the social framework of so many provincial communities. Where local leaders, enjoying respectability and influence, were won over, further converts often rapidly followed. Other non-Marxist parties seemed, in the gathering crisis, to be increasingly weak, ineffectual, and discredited, or to relate, like the Zentrum (the Catholic party), to only one particular sector of the population. Their disarray could only enhance the appeal of a large, expanding, dynamic and *national* party, seen more and more to offer the best chance of combating the Left, and increasingly regarded as the only party capable of representing the interests of each section of society in a united 'national community'. And as increasing numbers joined the party, paid their entry fees to the growing number of Nazi meetings, or threw their Marks into the collection boxes, so the funds grew that enabled still further propaganda activity to unfold. The tireless activism was, then, already showing signs of success even in the early months of 1930. The extraordinary breakthrough of the September Reichstag election did not come out of thin air.

Even with the deepening Depression and every prospect of increasing National Socialist electoral gains, however, the road to power was blocked. Only crass errors by the country's rulers could open up a path. And only a blatant disregard by Germany's power élites for safeguarding democracy – in fact, the hope that economic crisis could be used as a vehicle to bring about democracy's demise and replace it by a form of authoritarianism – could induce such errors. Precisely this is what happened in March 1930.

The fall of the Social Democrat Chancellor Hermann Müller and his replacement by Heinrich Brüning of the Zentrum was the first unnecessary step on the suicidal road of the Weimar Republic. Without the self-destructiveness of the democratic state, without the wish to undermine democracy of those who were meant to uphold it, Hitler, whatever his talents as an agitator, could not have come close to power.

The Müller administration eventually came to grief, on 27 March 1930, over the question of whether employer contributions to unemployment insurance should be raised, as from 30 June 1930, from 3.5 to 4 per cent of the gross wage. The issue had polarized the ill-matched coalition partners, the SPD and DVP, since the previous autumn. If the will had been there, a compromise would have been found. But by the end of 1929, in the context of the increasing economic difficulties of the Republic, the DVP had – in company with the other 'bourgeois' parties – moved sharply to the right. With no way out of the government crisis, the Chancellor tendered his resignation on 27 March. It marked the beginning of the end for the Weimar Republic.

The fall of Müller had in fact been planned long beforehand. In December, Heinrich Brüning, parliamentary leader of the Zentrum, learnt that Hindenburg was determined to oust Müller as soon as the Young Plan had been accepted. Brüning himself was earmarked to take over as Chancellor, backed where necessary by the President's powers under Article 48 of the Weimar Constitution (enabling him to issue emergency decrees to by-pass the need for Reichstag legislation). The Reich President was anxious not to miss the chance of creating an 'anti-parliamentary and anti-Marxist government' and afraid of being forced to retain a Social Democrat administration.

Brüning was appointed Chancellor on 30 March 1930. His problems soon became apparent. By June, he was running into serious difficulties in his attempts to reduce public spending through emergency decrees. When an SPD motion, supported by the NSDAP, to withdraw his proposed decree to impose swingeing cuts in public expenditure and higher taxes was passed by the Reichstag, Brüning sought and received, on 18 July 1930, the Reich President's dissolution of parliament.

New elections were set for 14 September. For democracy's prospects in Germany, they were a catastrophe. They were to bring the Hitler Movement's electoral breakthrough.

The decision to dissolve the Reichstag was one of breathtaking irresponsibility. Brüning evidently took a sizeable vote for the Nazis on board in his calculations. After all, the NSDAP had won 14.4 per cent of the vote only a few weeks earlier in the Saxon regional election. But in his determination to override parliamentary government by a more authoritarian system run by presidential decree, Brüning had greatly underestimated the extent of anger and frustration in the country, grossly miscalculating the effect of the deep alienation and dangerous levels of popular protest. The Nazis could hardly believe their luck. Under the direction of their newly-appointed propaganda chief, Joseph Goebbels, they prepared feverishly for a summer of unprecedented agitation.

II

In the meantime, internal conflict within the NSDAP only demonstrated the extent to which Hitler now dominated the Movement, how far it had become, over the previous five years, a 'leader party'. The dispute, when it came to a head, crystallized once more around the issue of whether there could be any separation of the 'idea' from the Leader.

Otto Strasser, Gregor's younger brother, had continued to use the publications of the Kampfverlag, the Berlin publishing house which he controlled, as a vehicle for his own version of National Socialism. This was a vague and heady brew of radical mystical nationalism, strident anti-capitalism, social reformism, and anti-Westernism. Rejection of bourgeois society produced admiration for the radical anti-capitalism of the Bolsheviks. Otto shared his doctrinaire national-revolutionary ideas with a group of theorists who used the Kampfverlag as the outlet for their views. As long as such notions neither harmed the party nor impinged on his own position, Hitler took little notice of them. He was even aware, without taking any action, that Otto Strasser had talked of founding a new party. By early 1930, however, the quasi-independent line of Otto Strasser had grown shriller as Hitler had sought since the previous year to exploit closer association with the bourgeois Right. A showdown came closer when the Kampfverlag continued to support striking metal-workers in Saxony in April 1930, despite Hitler's ban, under pressure from industrialists, on any backing of the strike by the party.

On 21 May Hitler invited Otto Strasser to his hotel for lengthy discussions. According to Strasser's published account – the only one that exists, though it rings true and was not denied by Hitler – the key points were leadership and socialism. 'A Leader must serve the Idea. To this alone can we devote ourselves entirely, since it is eternal whereas the Leader passes and can make mistakes,' claimed Strasser. 'What you are saying is outrageous nonsense,' retorted Hitler. 'That's the most revolting democracy that we want nothing more to do with. For us, the Leader is the Idea, and each party member has to obey only the Leader.' Strasser accused Hitler of trying to destroy the Kampfverlag because he wanted 'to strangle' the 'social revolution' through a strategy of legality and collaboration with the bourgeois Right. Hitler angrily denounced Strasser's socialism as 'nothing but Marxism'. The mass of the working class, he went on, wanted only bread and circuses, and would never understand the meaning of an ideal. 'There is only one possible kind of revolution, and it is not economic or political or social, but racial,' he avowed. Pushed on his attitude towards big business, Hitler made plain that there could be no question for him of socialization or worker control. The only priority was for a strong state to ensure that production was carried out in the national interest.

The meeting broke up. Hitler's mood was black. 'An intellectual white Jew, totally incapable of organization, a Marxist of the purest ilk,' was his withering assessment of Otto Strasser. On 4 July, anticipating their expulsion, Strasser and twenty-five supporters publicly announced that 'the socialists are leaving the NSDAP'. The rebels had in effect purged themselves.

The Strasser crisis showed, above all, the strength of Hitler's position. With the elimination of the Strasser clique, any lingering ideological dispute in the party was over. Things had changed drastically since 1925 and the days of the 'Working Community'. Now it was clear: Leader and Idea were one and the same.

III

During the summer of 1930, the election campaign built up to fever pitch. The campaign was centrally organized by Goebbels, under broad guidelines laid down by Hitler. Two years earlier, the press had largely ignored the NSDAP. Now, the Brownshirts forced themselves on to the front pages. It was impossible to ignore them. The high level of agitation – spiced with street violence – put them on the political map in a big way. The energy and drive of the National Socialist agitation were truly astonishing. As many as 34,000 meetings were planned throughout Germany for the last four weeks of the campaign. No other party remotely matched the scale of the NSDAP's effort.

Hitler himself held twenty big speeches in the six weeks running up to polling-day. The attendances were massive. At least 16,000 came to listen to him in the Sportpalast in Berlin on 10 September. Two days later, in Breslau, as many as 20–25,000 thronged into the Jahrhunderthalle, while a further 5–6,000 were forced to listen to the speech on loudspeakers outside. In the early 1920s, Hitler's speeches had been dominated by vicious attacks on the Jews. In the later 1920s, the question of 'living space' became the central theme. In the election campaign of 1930, Hitler seldom spoke explicitly of the Jews. The crude tirades of the early 1920s were missing altogether. 'Living space' figured more prominently, posed against the alternative international competition for markets. But it was not omnipresent as it had been in 1927–8. The key theme now was the collapse of Germany under parliamentary democracy and party government into a divided people with separate and conflicting interests, which only the NSDAP could overcome by creating a new unity of the nation, transcending class, estate, and profession. Where the Weimar parties represented only specific interest groups, asserted Hitler, the National Socialist Movement stood for the nation as a whole. In speech after speech, Hitler hammered this message home. Again and again he pilloried the Weimar system, not now crudely and simply as the regime of the 'November Criminals', but for its failed promises on tax reductions, financial management, and employment. All parties were blamed. They were all part of the same party system that had ruined Germany. All had had their part in the policies that had led from Versailles through the reparations terms agreed under the Dawes Plan to their settlement under the Young Plan. Lack of leadership had led to the misery felt by all sections of society. Democracy, pacifism, and internationalism had produced powerlessness and weakness – a great nation brought to its knees. It was time to clear out the rot.

But his speeches were not simply negative, not just an attack on the existing system. He presented a vision, a utopia, an ideal: national liberation through strength and unity. He did not propose alternative policies, built into specific election promises. He offered 'a programme, a gigantic new programme behind which must stand not the new government, but a new German people that has ceased to be a mixture of classes, professions, estates'. It would be, he declared, with his usual stress on stark alternatives (and, as it turned out, prophetically) 'a community of a people which, beyond all differences, will rescue the common strength of the nation, or will take it to ruin'. Only a 'high ideal' could overcome the social divisions, he stated. In place of the decayed, the old, a new Reich had to be built on racial values, selection of the best on the basis of achievement, strength, will, struggle, freeing the genius of the individual personality, and re-establishing Germany's power and strength as a nation. Only National Socialism could bring this about. It was not a conventional political programme. It was a political crusade. It was not about a change of government. It was a message of national redemption. In a climate of deepening economic gloom and social misery, anxiety, and division, amid perceptions of the failure and ineptitude of seemingly puny parliamentary politicians, the appeal was a powerful one.

The message appealed not least to the idealism of a younger generation, not old enough to have fought in the war, but not too young to have experienced at first hand little but crisis, conflict, and national decline. Many from this generation, born between about 1900 and 1910, coming from middle-class families, no longer rooted in the monarchical tradition of the pre-war years, outrightly rejecting Socialism and Communism, but alienated by the political, economic, social, and ideological strife of the Weimar era, were on the search for something new. Laden with all the emotive baggage that belonged to the German notions of 'Volk' (ethnic people) and 'Gemeinschaft' (community), the aim of a 'national community' which would overcome class divisions seemed a highly positive one. That the notion of 'national community' gained its definition by those it excluded from it, and that social harmony was to be established through racial purity and homogeneity, were taken for granted if not explicitly lauded.

The rhetoric of the 'national community' and the Führer cult stood for a rebirth for Germany in which all the various sectional interests would have a new deal. As the economic and political situation deteriorated, the rationality of voting for a small and weak interest party rather than a massive and strong *national* party – upholding interests but transcending them – was less and less compelling. A vote for the Nazis could easily seem like common sense. In this way, the NSDAP started to penetrate and destroy the support of interest-parties such as the Bayerischer Bauernbund (Bavarian Peasants' League) and seriously to erode the hold of the traditional parties such as the national-conservative DNVP in rural areas. This process was only in its early stages in summer 1930. But it would make rapid advances following the Nazi triumph of 14 September 1930.

IV

What happened on that day was a political earthquake. In the most remarkable result in German parliamentary history, the NSDAP advanced at one stroke from the twelve seats and mere 2.6 per cent of the vote gained in the 1928 Reichstag election, to 107 seats and 18.3 per cent, making it the second largest party in the Reichstag. Almost 6½ million Germans now voted for Hitler's party – eight times as many as two years earlier. The Nazi bandwagon was rolling.

The party leadership had expected big gains. The run of successes in the regional elections, the last of them the 14.4 per cent won in Saxony as recently as June, pointed to that conclusion. Goebbels had reckoned in April with about forty seats when it looked as if there would be a dissolution of the Reichstag at that time. A week before polling-day in September he expected 'a massive success'. Hitler later claimed he had thought 100 were possible. In reality, as Goebbels admitted, the size of the victory took all in the party by surprise. No one had expected 107 seats. Hitler was beside himself with joy.

The political landscape had dramatically changed overnight. Alongside the Nazis, the Communists had increased their support, now to 13.1 per cent of the vote. Though still the largest party, the SPD had lost ground as, marginally, did the Zentrum. But the biggest losers were the bourgeois parties of the centre and Right. The DNVP had dropped in successive elections since 1924 from 20.5 to only 7.0 per cent, the DVP from 10.1 to 4.7 per cent. The Nazis were the main profiteers. One in three former DNVP voters, it has been estimated, now turned to the NSDAP, as did one in four former supporters of the liberal parties. Smaller, but still significant gains, were made from all other parties. These included the SPD, KPD, and Zentrum/BVP, though the working-class milieus dominated by the parties of the Left and, above all, the Catholic sub-culture remained, as they would continue to be, relatively unyielding terrain for the NSDAP. The increased turn-out – up from 75.6 to 82 per cent – also benefited the Nazis, though less so than has often been presumed.

The landslide was greatest in the Protestant countryside of northern and eastern Germany. With the exception of rural parts of Franconia, piously Protestant, the largely Catholic Bavarian electoral districts now for the first time lagged behind the national average. The same was true of most Catholic regions. In big cities and industrial areas – though there were some notable exceptions, such as Breslau and Chemnitz-Zwickau – the Nazi gains, though still spectacular, were also below average. But in Schleswig-Holstein, the NSDAP vote had rocketed from 4 per cent in 1928 to 27 per cent. East Prussia, Pomerania, Hanover, and Mecklenburg were among the other regions where Nazi support was now over 20 per cent. At least three-quarters of Nazi voters were Protestants (or, at any rate, non-Catholics). Significantly more men than women voted Nazi (though this was to alter between 1930 and 1933). At least two-fifths of Nazi support came from the middle classes. But a quarter was drawn from the working class (though the unemployed were more likely to vote for the KPD than for Hitler's party). The middle classes were indeed over-represented among Nazi voters. But the NSDAP was no mere middle-class party, as used to be thought. Though not in equal proportions, the Hitler Movement could reasonably claim to have won support from all sections of society. No other party throughout the Weimar Republic could claim the same.

The social structure of the party's membership points to the same conclusion. A massive influx of members followed the September election. As with voters, they came, if not evenly, from all sections of society. The membership was overwhelmingly male, and only the KPD was as youthful in its membership profile. The Protestant middle classes were over-represented. But there was also a sizeable working-class presence, even more pronounced in the SA and the Hitler Youth than in the party itself. At the same time, the political breakthrough meant that 'respectable' local citizens now felt ready to join the party. Teachers, civil servants, even some Protestant pastors were among the 'respectable' groups altering the party's social standing in the provinces. In Franconia, for example, the NSDAP already had the appearance by 1930 of a 'civil-service party'. The penetration by the party of the social networks of provincial towns and villages now began to intensify notably.

There are times – they mark the danger point for a political system – when politicians can no longer communicate, when they stop understanding the language of the people they are supposed to be representing. The politicians of Weimar's parties were well on the way to reaching that point in 1930. Hitler had the advantage of being undamaged by participation in unpopular government, and of unwavering radicalism in his hostility to the Republic. He could speak in language more and more Germans understood – the language of bitter protest at a discredited system, the language of national renewal and rebirth. Those not firmly anchored in an alternative political ideology, social milieu, or denominational sub-culture found such language increasingly intoxicating.

The Nazis had moved at one fell swoop from the fringe of the political scene, outside the power-equation, to its heart. Brüning could now cope with the Reichstag only through the 'toleration' of the SPD, which saw him as the lesser evil. The Social Democrats entered their policy of 'toleration' with heavy hearts but a deep sense of responsibility. As for Hitler, whether he was seen in a positive or a negative sense – and there was little about him that left people neutral or indifferent – his name was now on everyone's lips. He was a factor to be reckoned with. He could no longer be ignored.

After the September elections, not just Germany but the world outside had to take notice of Hitler. In the immediate aftermath of his electoral triumph, the trial of three young Reichswehr officers from a regiment stationed in Ulm, whose Nazi sympathies saw them accused of 'Preparing to Commit High Treason' through working towards a military putsch with the NSDAP and breaching regulations banning members of the Reichswehr from activities aimed at altering the constitution, gave Hitler the chance, now with the eyes of the world's press on him, of underlining his party's commitment to legality. The trial of the officers, Hanns Ludin, Richard Scheringer, and Hans Friedrich Wendt, began in Leipzig on 23 September. On the first day, Wendt's defence counsel, Hans Frank, was given permission to summon Hitler as a witness. Two days later, huge crowds demonstrated outside the court building in favour of Hitler as the leader of the Reichstag's second largest party went into the witness-box to face the red-robed judges of the highest court in the land.

Once more he was allowed to use a court of law for propaganda purposes. The judge even warned him on one occasion, as he heatedly denied any intention of undermining the Reichswehr, to avoid turning his testimony into a propaganda speech. It was to little avail. Hitler emphasized that his movement would take power by legal means and that the Reichswehr – again becoming 'a great German people's army' – would be 'the basis for the German future'. He declared that he had never wanted to pursue his ideals by illegal measures. He used the exclusion of Otto Strasser to dissociate himself from those in the movement who had been 'revolutionaries'. But he assured the presiding judge: 'If our movement is victorious in its legal struggle, then there will be a German State Court and November 1918 will find its atonement, and heads will roll.' This brought cheers and cries of 'bravo' from onlookers in the courtroom – and an immediate admonishment from the court president, reminding them that they were 'neither in the theatre nor in a political meeting'. Hitler expected, he continued, that the NSDAP would win a majority following two or three further elections. 'Then it must come to a National Socialist rising, and we will shape the state as we want to have it.' When asked how he envisaged the erection of the Third Reich, Hitler replied: 'The National Socialist Movement will seek to attain its aim in this state by constitutional means. The constitution shows us only the methods, not the goal. In this constitutional way, we will try to gain decisive majorities in the legislative bodies in order, in the moment this is successful, to pour the state into the mould that matches our ideas.' He repeated that this would only be done constitutionally. He was finally sworn in on oath to the truth of his testimony. Goebbels told Scheringer, one of the defendants, that Hitler's oath was 'a brilliant move'. 'Now we are strictly legal,' he is said to have exclaimed. The propaganda boss was delighted at the 'fabulous' press reportage. Hitler's newly appointed Foreign Press Chief, Putzi

Hanfstaengl, saw to it that there was wide coverage of the trial abroad. He also placed three articles by Hitler on the aims of the movement in the Hearst press, the powerful American media concern, at a handsome fee of 1,000 Marks for each. Hitler said it was what he needed to be able now to stay at the Kaiserhof Hotel – plush, well situated near the heart of government, and his headquarters in the capital until 1933 – when he went to Berlin.

What Hitler said in the Leipzig Reichswehr trial – which ended on 4 October in eighteen-month custodial sentences on each of the three Reichswehr officers and the cashiering from the army of Ludin and Scheringer – was nothing new. He had been anxious for months to emphasize his 'legal' path to power. But the massive publicity surrounding the trial ensured that his declaration now made maximum impact. The belief that Hitler had broken with his revolutionary past helped to win him further support in 'respectable' circles.

There were those who encouraged Brüning after the election to take the NSDAP into a coalition government, arguing that government responsibility would put the Nazis to the test and limit their agitation. Brüning rejected such a notion out of hand, though he did not rule out cooperation at some future date should the party hold by the principle of legality. After deflecting Hitler's request for an audience immediately after the election, Brüning did arrange to see him – as he did the leaders of the other parties – in early October. Their meeting on 5 October, which took place to avoid publicity in the apartment of Reich Minister Treviranus, established, however, that there was no prospect of cooperation. A chasm separated them. After Brüning's careful statement of the government's foreign policy – a delicate strategy aimed at acquiring a breathing-space leading to the ultimate removal of reparations – Hitler responded with an hour-long monologue. He simply ignored the issues Brüning had raised. He was soon haranguing the four persons present – Frick and Gregor Strasser were there as well as Brüning and Treviranus – as if he were addressing a mass rally. Brüning was struck by the number of times Hitler used the word 'annihilate' ('*vernichten*'). He was going to 'annihilate' the KPD, the SPD, 'the Reaction', France as Germany's arch-enemy, and Russia as the home of Bolshevism. It was plain to the Chancellor, so Brüning later remarked, that Hitler's basic principle would always be: 'First power, then politics.' Brüning clearly saw Hitler as a fanatic – unsophisticated, but dangerous. Though they parted amicably enough, Hitler formed a deep loathing towards Brüning, one taking on manic proportions and permeating the whole party.

Hitler was left to continue his relentless, unbridled opposition to a system whose symbolic hate-figure was now Chancellor Brüning. Continuing the agitation was, in any case, what Hitler, like Goebbels, preferred. That was his instinct. 'Don't write "victory" on your banners any longer,' Hitler had told his supporters immediately after the election. 'Write the word in its place that suits us better: "struggle!"' In any case, it was the only option available. As one contemporary put it, the Nazis followed the maxim: '"After a victory, fasten on the helmet more tightly" ... Following the election victory they arranged 70,000 meetings. Again an "avalanche" passed through the Reich ... Town after town, village after village is stormed.' The election victory made this continued high level of agitation possible. The new interest in the party meant a vast influx of new members bringing new funds that could be used for the organization of still further propaganda and new activists to carry it out. Success bred success. The prospect of victory now presented itself as a real one. Everything had to be subordinated to this single goal. The massive but shallow, organizationally somewhat ramshackle, protest movement – a loose amalgam of different interests bonded by the politics of utopia – could be sustained only by the NSDAP coming to power within a relatively short time, probably something like the space of two or three years. This was to create mounting pressure on Hitler. All he could do for the present was what he had always done best: step up the agitation still further.

V

Behind the public persona, the private individual was difficult to locate. Politics had increasingly consumed Hitler since 1919. There was an extraordinary gulf between his political effectiveness, the magnetism not just felt by ecstatic crowds in mass rallies but by those who were frequently in his company, and the emptiness of what was left of an existence outside politics. Those who knew Hitler personally around this time found him an enigma. 'In my recollection, there is no rounded image of Hitler's personality,' reflected Putzi Hanfstaengl many years later. 'Rather, there are a number of images and shapes, all called Adolf

Hitler and which *were* all Adolf Hitler, that can only with difficulty be brought together in overall relation to each other. He could be charming and then a little later utter opinions that hinted at a horrifying abyss. He could develop grand ideas and be primitive to the point of banality. He could fill millions with the conviction that only his will and strength of character guaranteed victory. And at the same time, even as Chancellor, he could remain a bohemian whose unreliability drove his colleagues to despair.'

For Franz Pfeffer von Salomon, the head of the SA until his dismissal in August 1930, Hitler combined the qualities of common soldier and artist. 'A trooper with gypsy blood' was, given Nazi racial thinking, Pfeffer's reported extraordinary characterization. He thought Hitler had something like a sixth sense in politics, 'a supernatural talent'. But he wondered whether he was at bottom *only* a type of Freikorps leader, a revolutionary who might have difficulty in becoming a statesman after the movement had taken power. Pfeffer took Hitler to be a genius, something the world might experience only once in a thousand years. But the human side of Hitler, in his view, was deficient. Pfeffer, torn between adulation and criticism, saw him as a split personality, full of personal inhibitions in conflict with the 'genius' inside him, arising from his upbringing and education, and consuming him. Gregor Strasser, retaining his own critical distance from the fully-blown Führer cult, was nevertheless also, Otto Wagener recounted, prepared to see 'genius' of a kind in Hitler. 'Whatever there is about him that is unpleasant,' Otto Erbersdobler, Gauleiter of Lower Bavaria, later recalled Gregor Strasser saying, 'the man has a prophetic talent for reading great political problems correctly and doing the right thing at the opportune moment despite apparently insuperable difficulties.' Such unusual talent as Strasser was ready to grant Hitler lay, however, as he saw it, in instinct rather than in any ability to systematize ideas.

Otto Wagener, who had been made SA Chief of Staff in 1929, was among those totally entranced by Hitler. His captivation by this 'rare personality' had still not deserted him many years later when he compiled his memoirs in British captivity. But he, too, was unsure what to make of Hitler. After hearing him one day in such a towering rage – it was a row with Pfeffer about the relations between the SA and SS – that his voice reverberated through the entire party headquarters, Wagener thought there was something in him resembling 'an Asiatic will for destruction' (a term still betraying after the war Wagener's entrenchment in Nazi racial stereotypes). 'Not genius, but hatred; not overriding greatness, but rage born of an inferiority complex; not Germanic heroism, but the Hun's thirst for revenge' was how, many years later, using Nazi-style parlance in describing Hitler's alleged descent from the Huns, he summarized his impressions. In his incomprehension – a mixture of sycophantic admiration and awestruck fear – Wagener was reduced to seeing in Hitler's character something 'foreign' and 'diabolical'. Hitler remained for him altogether a puzzle.

Even for leading figures in the Nazi movement such as Pfeffer and Wagener, Hitler was a remote figure. He had moved in 1929 from his shabby flat in Thierschstraße to a luxury apartment in Prinzregentenplatz in Munich's fashionable Bogenhausen. It matched the change from the beerhall rabble-rouser to politician cavorting with the conservative establishment. He seldom had guests, or entertained. When he did, the atmosphere was always stiff and formal. Obsessives rarely make good or interesting company, except in the eyes of those who share the obsession or those in awe of or dependent upon such an unbalanced personality. Hitler preferred, as he always had done, the usual afternoon round in Café Heck, where cronies and admirers would listen – fawningly, attentively, or with concealed boredom – to his monologues on the party's early history for the umpteenth time, or tales of the war, 'his inexhaustible favourite theme'.

Only with very few people was he on the familiar 'Du' terms. He would address most Nazi leaders by their surname alone. 'Mein Führer' had not yet fully established itself, as it would do after 1933, as their normal mode of address to him. For those in his entourage he was known simply as 'the boss' (*der Chef*). Some, like Hanfstaengl or 'court' photographer Heinrich Hoffmann, insisted on a simple 'Herr Hitler'. The remoteness of his personality was complemented by the need to avoid the familiarity which could have brought with it contempt for his position as supreme Leader. The aura around him dared not be sullied in any way. Along with the remoteness went distrust. Important matters were discussed only with small – and changing – groups or individuals. That way, Hitler remained in full control, never bound by any advice of formal bodies, never needing to adjudicate on disagreements between his paladins. With his fixed views and dominant personality, he was able, as Gregor Strasser pointed out, to overwhelm any individual in his presence, even those initially sceptical. This in turn strengthened his self-confidence, his feeling of infallibility. In contrast, he felt uncomfortable with those who posed awkward questions or counter-arguments. Since his 'intuition' – by which, between the lines, Strasser meant his ideological dogmatism coupled with tactical flexibility and opportunism – could not in itself be combated by logical argument, the party's organizational leader went on, Hitler invariably dismissed any objections as coming from small-minded know-alls. But he registered who the critics were. Sooner or later, they would fall from grace.

Some of the most important matters, he discussed, if at all, only with those in his close circle – the group of adjutants, chauffeurs, and long-standing cronies such as Julius Schaub (his general factotum), Heinrich Hoffmann (his photographer), and Sepp Dietrich (later head of his SS bodyguard). Distrust – and vanity – went hand in hand with his type of leadership, in Gregor Strasser's view. The danger, he pointed out with reference to the dismissal of Pfeffer, was the self-selection of what Hitler wanted to hear and the negative reaction towards the bearer of bad tidings. There was something other-worldly about Hitler, thought Strasser; a lack of knowledge of human beings, and with it a lack of sound judgement of them. Hitler lived without any bonds to another human being, Strasser went on. 'He doesn't smoke, he doesn't drink, he eats almost nothing but greenstuff, he doesn't touch any woman! How are we supposed to grasp him to put him across to other people?'

Hitler contributed as good as nothing to the running and organization of the massively expanded Nazi movement. His 'work-style' (if it could be called such) was unchanged from the days when the NSDAP was a tiny, insignificant *völkisch* sect. He was incapable of systematic work and took no interest in it. He was as chaotic and dilettante as ever. He had found the role where he could fully indulge the unordered, indisciplined, and indolent lifestyle that had never altered since his pampered youth in Linz and drop-out years in Vienna. He had a huge 'work-room' in the new 'Brown House' – a building of tasteless grandiosity that he was singularly proud of. Pictures of Frederick the Great and a heroic scene of the List Regiment's first battle in Flanders in 1914 adorned the walls. A monumental bust of Mussolini stood beside the outsized furniture. Smoking was forbidden. To call it Hitler's 'work-room' was a nice euphemism. Hitler rarely did any work there. Hanfstaengl, who had his own room in the building, had few memories of

Hitler's room since he had seen the party leader there so seldom. Even the big painting of Frederick the Great, noted the former foreign press chief, could not motivate Hitler to follow the example of the Prussian king in diligent attention to duty. He had no regular working hours. Appointments were there to be broken. Hanfstaengl had often to chase through Munich looking for the party leader to make sure he kept appointments with journalists. He could invariably find him at four o'clock in the afternoon, surrounded by his admirers, holding forth in the Café Heck. Party workers at headquarters were no more favoured. They could never find a fixed time to see Hitler, even about extremely important business. If they managed, clutching their files, to catch him when he entered the Brown House, he would as often as not be called to the telephone and then apologize that he had to leave immediately and would be back the next day. Should they manage to have their business attended to, it was normally dispatched with little attention to detail. Hitler would in his usual manner turn the point at issue into a matter on which, pacing up and down the room, he would pontificate for an hour in a lengthy monologue. Often he would completely ignore something brought to his attention, deviating at a tangent into some current whim. 'If Hitler gets a cue to something he is interested in – but that's something different every day,' Pfeffer is reported to have told Wagener in 1930, 'then he takes over the conversation and the point of the discussion is shelved.' On matters he did not understand, or where a decision was awkward, he simply avoided discussion.

This extraordinary way of operating was certainly built into Hitler's personality. Masterful and domineering, but uncertain and hesitant; unwilling to take decisions, yet then prepared to take decisions bolder than anyone else could contemplate; and refusal, once made, to take back any decision: these are part of the puzzle of Hitler's strange personality. If the domineering traits were signs of a deep inner uncertainty, the overbearing features the reflection of an underlying inferiority complex, then the hidden personality disorder must have been one of monumental proportions. To ascribe the problem to such a cause re-describes rather than explains it. In any case, Hitler's peculiar leadership style was more than just a matter of personality, or instinctive social-Darwinist inclination to let the winner emerge after a process of struggle. It reflected too the unceasing necessity to protect his position as Leader. Acting out the Leader's role could never be halted. The famous handshake and steely blue eyes were part of the act. Even leading figures in the party never ceased to be impressed with the apparent sincerity and bond of loyalty and comradeship that they thought accompanied Hitler's unusually long handshake and unblinking stare into their eyes. They were too in awe of Hitler to realize what an elementary theatrical trick it was. The greater became the nimbus of the infallible leader, the less the 'human' Hitler, capable of mistakes and misjudgements, could be allowed on view. The 'person' Hitler was disappearing more and more into the 'role' of the almighty and omniscient Leader.

Very occasionally, the mask slipped. Albert Krebs, the one-time Gauleiter of Hamburg, related a scene from early 1932 that reminded him of a French comedy. From the corridor of the elegant Hotel Atlantik in Hamburg he could hear Hitler plaintively shouting: 'My soup, [I want] my soup.' Krebs found him minutes later hunched over a round table in his room, slurping his vegetable soup, looking anything other than a hero of the people. He appeared tired and depressed. He ignored the copy of his speech the previous night that Krebs had brought him, and to the Gauleiter's astonishment, asked him instead what he thought of a vegetarian diet. Fully in character, Hitler launched, not waiting for an answer, into a lengthy diatribe on vegetarianism. It struck Krebs as a cranky outburst, aimed at overpowering, not persuading, the listener. But what imprinted the scene on Krebs's memory was how Hitler revealed himself as an acute hypochondriac to one to whom he had presented himself up to then 'only as the political leader, never as a human being'. Krebs did not presume that Hitler was suddenly regarding him as a confidant. He took it rather as a sign of the party leader's 'inner instability'. It was an unexpected show of human weakness which, Krebs plausibly speculated, was over-compensated by an unquenchable thirst for power and resort to violence. According to Krebs, Hitler explained that a variety of worrying symptoms – outbreaks of sweating, nervous tension, trembling of muscles, and stomach cramps – had persuaded him to become a vegetarian. He took the stomach cramps to be the beginnings of cancer, leaving him only a few years to complete 'the gigantic tasks' he had set himself. 'I must come to power before long . . . I must, I must,' Krebs has him shouting. But with this, he gained control of himself again. His body-language showed he was over his temporary depression. His attendants were suddenly called, orders were given out, telephone calls booked, meetings arranged. 'The human being Hitler had been transformed back into the "Leader".' The mask was in place again.

Hitler's style of leadership functioned precisely because of the readiness of all his subordinates to accept his unique standing in the party, and their belief that such eccentricities of behaviour had simply to be taken on board in someone they saw as a political genius. 'He always needs people who can translate his ideologies into reality so that they can be implemented,' Pfeffer is reported as stating. Hitler's way was, in fact, not to hand out streams of orders to shape important political decisions. Where possible, he avoided decisions. Rather, he laid out – often in his diffuse and opinionated fashion – his ideas at length and repeatedly. These provided the general guidelines and direction for policy-making. Others had to interpret from his comments how they thought he wanted them to act and 'work towards' his distant objectives. 'If they could all work in this way,' Hitler was reported as stating from time to time, 'if they could all strive with firm, conscious tenacity towards a common, distant goal, then the ultimate goal must one day be achieved. That mistakes will be made is human. It is a pity. But that will be overcome if a common goal is constantly adopted as a guideline.' This instinctive way of operating, embedded in Hitler's social-Darwinist approach, not only unleashed ferocious competition among those in the party – later in the state – trying to reach the 'correct' interpretation of Hitler's intentions. It also meant that Hitler, the unchallenged fount of ideological orthodoxy by this time, could always side with those who had come out on top in the relentless struggle going on below him, with those who had best proven that they were following the 'right guidelines'. And since only Hitler could determine this, his power position was massively enhanced.

Inaccessibility, sporadic and impulsive interventions, unpredictability, lack of a regular working pattern, administrative disinterest, and ready resort to long-winded monologues instead of attention to detail were all hallmarks of Hitler's style as party leader. They were compatible – at least in the short term – with a 'leader party' whose exclusive middle-range goal was getting power. After 1933, the same features would become hallmarks of Hitler's style as dictator with supreme power over the German state. They would be incompatible with the bureaucratic regulation of a sophisticated state apparatus and would become a guarantee of escalating governmental disorder.

VI

At the beginning of 1931, a familiar, scarred face not seen for some time returned to the scene. Ernst Röhm, recalled by Hitler from his self-imposed exile as a military adviser to the Bolivian army, was back. He took up his appointment as new Chief of Staff of the SA on 5 January.

The case of Otto Strasser had not been the only crisis that the party leadership had had to deal with during 1930. More serious, potentially, had been the crisis within the SA. It had been simmering for some time before it exploded in the summer of 1930, during the election campaign. In reality, the crisis merely brought to a head – not for the last time – the structural conflict built into the NSDAP between the party's organization and that of the SA. Impatience at the slow, legal route to power coupled with a sense of being undervalued and financially disadvantaged had prompted a short-lived, but serious, rebellion of the Berlin SA in late August. It had ended with an oath of loyalty to Hitler on behalf of all SA men, together with substantial financial improvements for the SA deriving from increased party dues. Pfeffer, the SA leader, resigned. Hitler himself had taken over the supreme leadership of the SA and SS. The claim within the SA leadership for a high degree of autonomy from the party leadership was, however, undiminished. The scope for continued conflict was still there.

This was the situation awaiting the return of Röhm, not as supreme head but as chief of staff, which was announced by Hitler to assembled SA leaders in Munich on 30 November 1930. Röhm's high standing from the pre-putsch era, together with his lack of involvement in any of the recent intrigues, made his appointment a sensible one. However, his notorious homosexuality was soon used by those SA subordinates who resented his leadership to try to undermine the position of the new chief of staff. Hitler was forced as early as 3 February 1931 to refute attacks on 'things that are purely in the private sphere', and to stress that the SA was not a 'moral establishment' but 'a band of rough fighters'.

Röhm's moral standards were not the real point at issue. Hitler's action the previous summer had defused the immediate crisis. But it was papering over the cracks. The tension remained. Neither the precise role nor degree of autonomy of the SA had been fully clarified. Given the character of the Nazi Movement and the way the SA had emerged within it, the structural problem was insoluble. And the putschist strain, always present in the SA, was resurfacing. The advocacy of taking power by force, advanced in articles in February 1931 in the Berlin party newspaper *Der Angriff* by Walter Stennes, the SA leader in the eastern regions of Germany and the chief instigator of the 1930 SA rebellion, was increasingly alarming to the Nazi leadership. Such noises flatly contradicted, and directly placed in question, the commitment to legality that Hitler had made, most publicly and on oath, following the Reichswehr trial in Leipzig the previous September, and had stressed on numerous occasions since then. The spectre of a ban on the party loomed very much larger with the promulgation of an emergency decree on 28 March, giving the Brüning government wide-ranging powers to combat political 'excesses'. 'The party, above all the SA, seems to be facing a ban,' wrote Goebbels in his diary. Hitler ordered the strictest compliance with the emergency decree by all members of the party, SA, and SS. But Stennes was not prepared to yield. 'It is the most serious crisis the party has had to go through,' commented Goebbels.

When the Berlin SA occupied party headquarters in the city then directly attacked Hitler's leadership, it was high time to take action. Stennes was deposed as SA leader in eastern Germany. Hitler and Goebbels worked hard to ensure declarations of loyalty from all the Gaue. Stennes, increasingly revolutionary in tone, succeeded in winning support from parts of the SA in Berlin, Schleswig-Holstein, Silesia, and Pomerania. But his success was short-lived. A full-scale rebellion did not occur. On 4 April, Hitler published in the *Völkischer Beobachter* a lengthy and cleverly constructed denunciation of Stennes and an emotional appeal to the loyalty of SA men. Even before he wrote, the revolt was crumbling. Support for Stennes evaporated. About 500 SA men in north and eastern Germany were purged. The rest came back into line.

The crisis was over. The SA had been put back on the leash. It would be kept there with difficulty until the 'seizure of power'. Then, the pent-up violence would only be fully released in the first months of 1933. Under Röhm's hand, nevertheless, the SA was returning to its character as a paramilitary formation – and now a much more formidable one than it had been in the early 1920s. Röhm had behaved with exemplary loyalty to Hitler during the Stennes crisis. But his own emphasis on the 'primacy of the soldier', and his ambitions, suppressed as they were in 1931, for the transformation of the SA into a popular militia, bore the seeds of conflict still to come. It prefigured the course of events which would reach their denouement only in June 1934.

VII

Not only political, but personal crisis beset Hitler in 1931. On moving in 1929 into his spacious new apartment in Prinzregentenplatz, his niece, Geli Raubal, who had been living with her mother in Haus Wachenfeld on the Obersalzberg, had come to join him. During the following two years she was frequently seen in public with Hitler. Rumours already abounded about the nature of her relations with 'Uncle Alf', as she called him. On the morning of 19 September 1931, aged twenty-three, she was found dead in Hitler's flat, shot with his pistol.

Hitler's relations with women, as we have already remarked, were in some respects abnormal. He liked the company of women, especially pretty ones, best of all young ones. He flattered them, sometimes flirted with them, called them – in his patronizing Viennese petty-bourgeois manner – 'my little princess', or 'my little countess'. In the mid-1920s, he encouraged the infatuation of a lovestruck young girl, Maria (Mizzi or Mimi) Reiter. But the devotion was entirely one-sided. For Hitler, Mimi was no more than a passing flirtation. Occasionally, if the stories are to be believed, he made a clumsy attempt at some physical contact, as in the case of Helene Hanfstaengl and Henrietta Hoffmann, the daughter of his photographer who was to marry Baldur von Schirach (from 30 October 1931 the Reich Youth Leader of the NSDAP). His name was linked at various times with women from as diverse back-grounds as Jenny Haug, the sister of his chauffeur in the early years, and Winifred Wagner, the Bayreuth maestro's daughter-in-law. But, whatever the basis of the rumours – often malicious, exaggerated, or invented – none of his liaisons, it seems, had been more than superficial. No deep feelings were ever stirred. Women were for Hitler an object, an adornment in a 'men's world'. Whether in the Men's Home in Vienna, the regiment during the war, the Munich barracks until his discharge, and his regular gatherings of party cronies in Café Neumaier or Café Heck in the 1920s, Hitler's environment had always been overwhelm-ingly male. 'Very occasionally a woman would be admitted to our intimate circle,' recalled Heinrich Hoffmann, 'but she never was allowed to become the centre of it, and had to remain seen but not heard . . . She could, occasionally, take a small part in the conversation, but never was she allowed to hold forth or to contradict Hitler.' Beginning with the semi-mythical Stefanie in Linz, Hitler's relations with women had usually been at a distance, a matter of affectation, not emotion. Nor was his long-standing relationship with Eva Braun, one of Hoffmann's employees whom he had first met in autumn 1929, an exception. 'To him,' remarked Hoffmann, 'she was just an attractive little thing, in whom, in spite of her inconsequential and feather-brained outlook – or perhaps just because of it – he found the type of relaxation and repose he sought . . . But never, in voice, look or gesture, did he ever behave in a way that suggested any deeper interest in her.'

It was different with Geli. Whatever the exact nature of the relationship – and all accounts are based heavily upon guesswork and hearsay – it seems certain that Hitler, for the first and only time in his life (if we leave his mother out of consideration), became emotionally dependent on a woman. Whether his involvement with Geli was explicitly sexual cannot be known beyond doubt. Some have hinted darkly at the incestuous relationships in Hitler's ancestry. But lurid stories of alleged deviant sexual practices put about by Otto Strasser ought to be viewed as the fanciful anti-Hitler propaganda of an outright political enemy. Other tales, also to be treated with scepticism, circulated of a compromising letter and of pornographic drawings by Hitler that had to be bought off a blackmailer by the Party Treasurer Schwarz. But whether actively sexual or not, Hitler's behaviour towards Geli has all the traits of a strong, latent at least, sexual dependence. This manifested itself in such extreme shows of jealousy and domineering possessiveness that a crisis in the relationship was inevitable.

Geli, broad-featured, with dark-brown, wavy hair, was no stunning beauty but nonetheless, all accounts agree, a vivacious, extrovert, attractive young woman. She livened up the gatherings in Café Heck. Hitler allowed her, something he permitted no one else, to become the centre of attraction. He took her everywhere with him – to the theatre, concerts, the opera, the cinema, restaurants, for drives in the countryside, picnics, even shopping for clothes. He sang her praises, showed her off. Geli was in Munich ostensibly to study at the university. But little studying was done. Hitler paid for singing lessons for her. But she was clearly never going to make an operatic heroine. She was bored by her lessons. She was more interested in having a good time. Flighty and flirtatious, she had no shortage of male admirers and was not backward in encouraging them. When Hitler found out about Geli's liaison with Emil Maurice, his bodyguard and chauffeur, there was such a scene that Maurice feared Hitler was going to shoot him. He was soon forced out of Hitler's employment. Geli was sent to cool her ardour under the watchful eye of Frau Bruckmann. Hitler's jealous possessiveness took on pathological proportions. If she went out without him, Geli was chaperoned, and had to be home early. Everything she did was monitored and controlled. She was effectively a prisoner. She resented it bitterly. 'My uncle is a monster,' she is reported as saying. 'No one can imagine what he demands of me.'

By mid-September 1931 she had had enough. She planned to return to Vienna. It was later rumoured that she had a new boyfriend there, even that he was a Jewish artist whose child she was expecting. Geli's mother, Angela Raubal, told American interrogators after the war that her daughter had wanted to marry a violinist from Linz, but that she and her half-brother, Adolf, had forbidden her to see the man. At any rate it seems certain that Geli was desperate to get away from her uncle's clutches. Whether he had been physically maltreating her is again impossible to ascertain. It was said that her nose was broken and there were other indications of physical violence, when her body was found. Once more the evidence is too flimsy to be certain, and the story was one put out by Hitler's political enemies. The police doctor who examined the body, and two women who laid out the corpse, found no wounds or bleeding on the face. But that Hitler was at the very least subjecting his niece to intense psychological pressure cannot be doubted. According to the version put out a few days later by the Socialist *Münchener Post* – vehemently denied in a public statement by Hitler – during a heated argument on Friday 18 September he refused to let her go to Vienna. Later that day, Hitler and his entourage departed for Nuremberg. He had already left his hotel the next morning when he was urgently recalled to be told the news that Geli had been found dead in his apartment, shot with his revolver. He immediately raced back to Munich – in such a rush that his car was reported by the police for speeding about halfway between Nuremberg and Munich.

Hitler's political enemies had a field day. There were no holds barred on the newspaper reports. Stories of violent rows and physical mistreatment mingled with sexual innuendo and even the allegation that Hitler had either killed Geli himself or had had her murdered to prevent scandal. Hitler himself was not in Munich when his niece died. And it is not easy to see the reasoning for a commissioned murder to prevent a scandal being carried out in his own flat. As it was, the scandal was enormous. The party's own line that the killing had been an accident, which had occurred when Geli was playing with Hitler's gun, also lacked all conviction. The truth will never be known. But suicide – possibly intended as a *cri de coeur* that went wrong – driven by the need to escape from the vice of her uncle's clammy possessiveness and – perhaps violent – jealousy, seems the most likely explanation.

To go from later, perhaps exaggerated, reports, Hitler appears to have been near-hysterical, then fallen into an intense depression. Those close to him had never seen him in such a state. He seemed to be on the verge of a nervous breakdown. He allegedly spoke of giving up politics and finishing it all. There were fears that he might be suicidal. Hans Frank's account implies, however, that his despair at the scandal and press campaign against him outweighed any personal grief during these days. He took refuge in the house of his publisher, Adolf Müller, on the shores of the Tegernsee. Frank used legal means to block the press attacks.

Whatever the depth of Hitler's grief, politics came first. He did not attend Geli's funeral in Vienna on 24 September. He was speaking that evening before a crowd of thousands in Hamburg, where he received an even more rapturous reception than usual. According to one person who was there, he looked 'very strained' but spoke well. He was back in business. More than ever, the orgiastic frenzy he worked himself up into during his big public addresses, and the response he encountered in what he saw as the 'feminine mass', provided a substitute for the emptiness and lack of emotional bonds in his private life.

Two days later, with permission of the Austrian authorities, he visited Geli's grave in Vienna's sprawling Central Cemetery. Thereafter, he was suddenly able to snap out of his depression. All at once, the crisis was over.

Some who saw Hitler at close quarters were convinced that Geli could have exerted a restraining influence upon him. It is a highly dubious theory. His emotional involvement with Geli, whatever its precise nature, was – everything points to this – more intense than any other human relationship he had before or after. There was something both obsessive and cloyingly sentimental about the way her rooms in the Prinzregentenplatz apartment and in Haus Wachenfeld were turned into shrines. In a personal sense, Geli was indeed irreplaceable (though Hitler soon enough had Eva Braun in tow). But it was a purely selfish dependency on Hitler's part. Geli had been allowed to have no existence of her own. Hitler's own extreme dependency insisted that she should be totally dependent upon him. In human terms, it was a self-destructive relationship. Politically, apart from the short-lived scandal, it was of no significance. It is difficult to imagine Geli turning Hitler away from his deeper, less personal, obsession with power. Nor was his embittered thirst for vengeance and destruction altered by her death. History would have been no different had Geli Raubal survived.

VIII

Little over a week after Geli's death, the city elections in the relatively unresponsive territory of Hamburg gave the Nazis 26.2 per cent of the vote, ahead of the Communists and only fractionally behind the SPD. With as high a vote as 37.2 per cent in rural Oldenburg the previous May, the NSDAP had become for the first time the largest party in a state parliament. The electoral landslide showed no signs of abating. With the Brüning government under siege, ruling by emergency decree and its policies – calculated to demonstrate Germany's inability to pay reparations – sending the economy plummeting to disaster in a catastrophic downward spiral of cascading production levels and soaring levels of unemployment and social misery, more and more voters were cursing the wretched Republic. By the time of the calamitous bank crash in July, when two of Germany's major banks, the Darmstädter and the Dresdner, collapsed, those voters looking to the survival and recovery of democracy were in a dwindling minority. But what sort of authoritarian solution might follow the liquidation of the Weimar Republic was still anything but clear. Germany's power élites were no more united on this issue than were the mass of the population.

With the levels of popular support the Nazis now enjoyed, no potential right-wing solution could afford to leave them out of the equation. In July, Hugenberg, the leader of the DNVP, and Franz Seldte, the head of the huge veterans' organization, the Stahlhelm, had renewed their alliance with Hitler – resurrecting the former grouping to fight the Young Plan – in the 'National Opposition'. Hugenberg assuaged the criticisms of Reich President Hindenburg, who thought the Nazis not only vulgar but dangerous socialists, by assuring him that he was 'politically educating' them towards the national cause to prevent them slipping into Socialism or Communism. Hitler's line was, as ever, pragmatic. The publicity and contacts won through allying with Hugenberg were valuable. But he made sure he kept his distance. At the highly publicized rally of Nationalist Opposition forces at Bad Harzburg on 11 October, resulting in the creation of the 'Harzburg Front' and a manifesto (which he thought worthless) demanding new Reichstag elections and the suspension of emergency legislation, Hitler stood for the march-past of the SA then demonstratively left before the Stahlhelm could begin, having left them waiting for twenty-five minutes. He also refused to attend the joint lunch of the nationalist leaders. He could not suppress his repulsion at such meals, he wrote – deflecting the criticism of his behaviour into a further advertisement for his image as a leader who shared the privations of his followers – 'when thousands of my supporters undertake service only at very great personal sacrifice and in part with hungry stomachs'. A week later, to underline the NSDAP's independent strength, he took the salute at a march-past of 104,000 SA and SS men in Braunschweig, the largest Nazi paramilitary demonstration to date.

Among those taking part at Bad Harzburg, and whose presence there made a stir, was the former President of the Reichsbank Hjalmar Schacht, now turned political adventurer. Some other figures – though not prominent ones – from the world of business were also there. During the 1920s, big business had, not surprisingly, shown little interest in the NSDAP, a fringe party in the doldrums without, it seemed, any prospect of power or influence. The election result of 1930 had compelled the business community to take note of Hitler's party. A series of meetings were arranged at which Hitler explained his aims to prominent businessmen. The reassurances given by Hitler at such meetings, as well as by Göring (who had good links to top businessmen), were, however, not able to dispel the worries of most business leaders that the NSDAP was a socialist party with radical anti-capitalist aims.

Despite growing disillusionment with the Brüning administration, most 'captains of industry' retained their healthy scepticism about the Hitler Movement during 1931. There were exceptions, such as Thyssen, but in general it was the owners of smaller and medium-sized concerns who found the NSDAP an increasingly attractive proposition. The leaders of big business were no friends of democracy. But nor, for the most part, did they want to see the Nazis running the country.

This remained the case throughout most of 1932, a year dominated by election campaigns in which the Weimar state disintegrated into all-embracing crisis. Hitler's much publicized address on 27 January 1932 to a gathering of some 650 members of the Düsseldorf Industry Club in the grand ballroom of Düsseldorf's Park Hotel did nothing, despite the later claims of Nazi propaganda, to alter the sceptical stance of big business. The response to his speech was mixed. But many were disappointed that he had nothing new to say, avoiding all detailed economic issues by taking refuge in his well-trodden political panacea for all ills. And there were indications that workers in the party were not altogether happy at their leader fraternizing with industrial leaders. Intensified anti-capitalist rhetoric, which Hitler was powerless to quell, worried the business community as much as ever. During the presidential campaigns of spring 1932, most business leaders stayed firmly behind Hindenburg, and did not favour Hitler. And during the Reichstag campaigns of summer and autumn, the business community overwhelmingly supported the parties that backed the cabinet of Franz von Papen – a somewhat lightweight, dilettante politician, but one who epitomized the ingrained conservatism, reactionary tendencies, and desire for a return to 'traditional' authoritarianism of the German upper class. He was the establishment figure; Hitler the outsider and, in some respects, unknown quantity. Papen, not Hitler, was, not surprisingly then, the favourite of big business. Only in autumn 1932, when Papen was ousted by Kurt von Schleicher, the general at the heart of most political intrigues, maker and breaker of governments, did the attitude of most leading figures in business, worried by the new Chancellor's approach to the economy and opening to the trades unions, undergo a significant change.

The NSDAP's funding continued before the 'seizure of power' to come overwhelmingly from the dues of its own members and the entrance fees to party meetings. Such financing as came from fellow-travellers in big business accrued more to the benefit of individual Nazi leaders than the party as a whole. Göring, needing a vast income to cater for his outsized appetite for high living and material luxury, quite especially benefited from such largesse. Thyssen in particular gave him generous subsidies, which Göring – given to greeting visitors to his splendrously adorned Berlin apartment dressed in a red toga and pointed slippers, looking like a sultan in a harem – found no difficulty in spending on a lavish lifestyle. Walther Funk, one of Hitler's links to leading industrialists, also used his contacts to line his own pockets. Gregor Strasser, too, was a recipient. Corruption at all levels was endemic.

It would be surprising if none of such donations had reached Hitler. Indeed, Göring is alleged to have said that he passed on to Hitler some of the funding he received from Ruhr industrialists. Hitler had from the earliest years of his 'career', as we have seen, been supported by generous donations from benefactors. But by the early 1930s he was less dependent on financial support from private patrons, even if his celebrity status now unquestionably brought him many unsolicited donations. His sources of income have remained largely in the dark. They were kept highly secret, and totally detached from party finances. Schwarz, the party treasurer, had no insight into Hitler's own funds. But his taxable income alone – and much was doubtless left undeclared – trebled in 1930 to 45,472 Marks as sales of *Mein Kampf* soared following his election triumph. That alone was more than Funk had earned from a year's salary as editor of a Berlin daily. Though for image purposes he repeatedly emphasized that he drew no salary from the party, nor any fee for the speeches he delivered on its behalf, he received hidden fees in the form of lavish 'expenses' calculated on the size of the takings at his meetings. In addition, he was paid handsomely for the articles he contributed to the *Völkischer Beobachter* and, between 1928 and 1931, to the *Illustrierter Beobachter*. And with the foreign press now clamouring for interviews, another door to a lucrative source of income opened. Partly subsidized, if indirectly, by the party, partly drawing substantial royalties from his stated occupation as a 'writer', and partly benefiting from unsolicited donations from admirers, Hitler's sources of income were more than adequate to cover the costs of an affluent lifestyle. His proclaimed modest demands in matters of food and clothes – a constant element of his image as a humble man of the people – fell within a context of chauffeur-driven Mercedes, luxury hotels, grand residences, and a personal livery of bodyguards and attendants.

IX

During 1932, the terminal nature of Weimar's ailing democracy became unmistakable. A prelude to the drama to follow had its setting in the presidential election in the spring.

Reich President Hindenburg's seven-year term of office was due to expire on 5 May 1932. This placed Hitler in a quandary. In the event of presidential elections, he could scarcely refrain from standing. Not to stand would be incomprehensible, and a massive disappointment to his millions of supporters. They might start to turn away from a leader who shied away from the challenge. On the other hand, a personal contest between the corporal and the field-marshal, between the upstart political adventurer and the revered hero of Tannenberg, widely regarded as the symbol of national values above the fray of party politics, could hardly be expected to result in a victory for Hitler. Faced with his dilemma, Hitler dithered for more than a month before deciding to run for president.

A technicality had to be cleared up: Hitler was still not a German citizen. Previous ideas of attaining citizenship for him, in Bavaria in 1929 and Thuringia the following year, had foundered. He remained 'stateless'. Rapid steps were now taken to appoint Hitler to the post of *Regierungsrat* (government councillor) in the Office of State Culture and Measurement in Braunschweig and as a state representative in Berlin. Through his nomination as a civil servant, Hitler acquired German citizenship. On 26 February 1932, he swore his oath as a civil servant to the German state he was determined to destroy.

Just how far the political centre of gravity had shifted to the Right was shown by the perverse alignments in the presidential election campaign. Hindenburg was dependent for support on the Socialists and Catholics, who had formed his main opposition seven years earlier, and made strange and unwelcome bedfellows for the staunchly Protestant and arch-conservative doyen of the military caste. The bourgeois Right, headed by Hugenberg, refused Hindenburg their support. Showing how fragile the professed unity of the Harzburg Front had been, they also denied it to Hitler. But their largely unknown nominee, the deputy leader of the Stahlhelm, Theodor Duesterberg, was hardly a serious candidate. On the Left, the Communists nominated their leader, Ernst Thälmann, sure of support only from his own camp. It was plain from the outset, therefore, that the main contenders were Hindenburg and Hitler. Equally plain was the Nazi message: a vote for Hitler was a vote for change; under Hindenburg, things would stay as they were. 'Old man . . . you must step aside,' proclaimed Hitler at a rally attended by an estimated 25,000 in the Berlin Sportpalast on 27 February.

The Nazi propaganda machine went into top gear. The country was engulfed during the first of five major campaigns that year with a veritable flood of Nazi meetings, parades, and rallies, accompanied by the usual pageantry and razzmatazz. Hitler himself, his indecision resolved, poured all his energies as usual into his speaking tourneys, travelling the length and breadth of Germany, and addressing huge crowds in twelve cities during the eleven-day campaign.

Expectations were built up. But the result was a bitter disappointment. The 30 per cent won by Hitler was lower than the NSDAP's showing in the Oldenburg and Hessen state elections the previous year. With over 49 per cent of almost 38 million votes cast, the Reich President ended up a mere 170,000 votes short of the absolute majority. There had to be a second round.

This time Nazi propaganda had a new gimmick. Hitler took to the skies in a hired plane, American-style, in his first 'Germany Flight' (*Deutschlandflug*), embellished with the slogan of 'the Führer over Germany'. Flying from city to city in a truncated campaign squeezed into less than a week to accommodate an Easter truce in politicking, Hitler was able to hold twenty major speeches in different venues before huge audiences, totalling close to a million persons. It was a remarkable electioneering performance, the like of which had never before been seen in Germany. Hindenburg, with 53 per cent, was re-elected. But while Thälmann had slumped to only 10 per cent, Hitler had increased his support to 37 per cent. He had done much more than merely save face. Well over 13 million, 2 million more than in the first round, had voted for him. The Führer cult, the manufactured commodity of Nazi propaganda and once the property of a tiny collection of fanatics, was now on the way to being sold to a third of the German population.

Quite literally while the votes were being counted, Goebbels was laying the preparations for the next battle: the series of state elections on 24 April in Prussia, Bavaria, Württemberg, Anhalt, and the city elections in Hamburg. All in all, this amounted to about four-fifths of the country. Without a break, the frenetic campaigning continued. In his second 'Germany Flight' between 16 and 24 April, Hitler – this time taking his campaign not just to the cities but deep into the provinces – gave twenty-five big speeches.

The results were closely in line with the votes won by Hitler in the run-off presidential election. Leader and party were largely indistinguishable in the eyes of the voters. In the giant state of Prussia, embracing two-thirds of Reich territory, the NSDAP's vote of 36.3 per cent made it easily the largest party, now far ahead of the SPD which had been the dominant party since 1919. Since the previous election, in 1928, the Nazis had held six seats in the Prussian Landtag. Now they had 162 seats. In Bavaria, with 32.5 per cent, they came to within 0.1 per cent of the ruling BVP. In Württemberg, they rose from 1.8 per cent in 1928, to 26.4 per cent. In Hamburg, they attained 31.2 per cent. And in Anhalt, with 40.9 per cent, they could nominate the first Nazi Minister President of a German state.

'It's a fantastic victory that we've attained,' noted Goebbels, with justification. But he added: 'We must come to power in the foreseeable future. Otherwise we'll win ourselves to death in elections.' Mobilizing the masses was in itself going to be insufficient, Goebbels was recognizing. Despite the immense gains over the previous three years, there were signs that the limits of mobilization were being reached. The way ahead was still anything but clear. But another door was about to open.

X

The state election campaign had been fought in the wake of a ban on the SA and SS. Chancellor Brüning and Interior and Defence Minister Groener, under pressure from the state authorities, had persuaded Hindenburg three days after the President's re-election to dissolve 'all military-like organizations' of the NSDAP. The dissolution was directly occasioned by the Prussian police's discovery, following a tip-off to Reich Minister of the Interior Groener, in raids on Nazi party offices, shortly after the first round of the presidential election, of material indicating the SA's readiness for a takeover of power by force following an electoral victory by Hitler. There had been distinct signs during the presidential election campaigns that the SA – now close to 400,000 strong – was straining at the leash. Talk of a putsch attempt by the Left in the event of a Hitler victory was in the air. The SA had been placed on nationwide alarm. But instead of action, the stormtroopers had sat depressed in their quarters after Hitler's defeat. News of the impending ban leaked to the Nazi leadership two days before it was imposed. Some preparations could therefore be made to retain the SA as distinct units within the party organization by simply reclassing the stormtroopers now as ordinary party members. And since the Left also had its paramilitary organizations which did not fall under the Groener dissolution order, the authorities had delivered the Nazis a further effective propaganda weapon, which Hitler was quick to exploit.

More importantly, the SA ban opened up the machinations that were to undermine the position not only of Groener, but of Brüning too, and to move the Reich government sharply to the Right. The key figure was to be General von Schleicher, head of the Ministerial Office, the army's political bureau, in the Reichswehr Ministry, and seen up to now as Groener's protégé. Schleicher's aim was an authoritarian regime, resting on the Reichswehr, with support from the National Socialists. The idea was to 'tame' Hitler, and incorporate the 'valuable elements' from his Movement into what would have been essentially a military dictatorship with populist backing. Schleicher opposed the ban on the SA, therefore, which he wanted as a feeder organization for an expanded Reichswehr, once the reparations issue was out of the way. In secret talks with Schleicher on 28 April, Hitler had learnt that the Reichswehr leadership no longer supported Brüning. He followed this on 7 May with what Goebbels described as 'a decisive discussion with General Schleicher', attended by some of Hindenburg's immediate entourage. 'Brüning is to go in the next days,' he added. 'The Reich President will withdraw his confidence. The plan is to install a presidential cabinet. The Reichstag will be dissolved; all coercive laws will be dropped. We will be given freedom of action, and will then deliver a masterpiece of propaganda.' Removal of the SA ban and new elections were, then, Hitler's price for supporting a new right-wing cabinet. With the emphasis on elections, it is clear that Hitler thought, as always, essentially of little more than coming to power by winning over the masses.

Brüning was able to survive longer than the conspirators had imagined. But his days were plainly numbered. On 29 May, Hindenburg brusquely sought Brüning's resignation. The following day, in the briefest of audiences, it was submitted.

'The system is collapsing,' wrote Goebbels. Hitler saw the Reich President that afternoon. The meeting went well, he told his propaganda chief in the evening: 'The SA ban will be dropped. Uniforms are to be allowed again. The Reichstag will be dissolved. That's the most important of all. v.Papen is foreseen as Chancellor. But that is not so interesting. Voting, voting! Out to the people. We're all very happy.'

XI

The new Chancellor, Franz von Papen, an urbane and well-connected member of the Catholic nobility, a former diplomat and arch-conservative formerly on the right of the Zentrum, had been sounded out by Schleicher some days before Brüning's fall. Schleicher had not only cleared the ground with Hindenburg for Papen's appointment, but also drawn up a list of cabinet ministers and discussed the matter with some of them even before Papen agreed to serve. With his 'cabinet of barons' independent of parties, Papen made no pretence at parliamentary government. With no prospect of finding a majority in the Reichstag, he was dependent solely upon presidential emergency decrees – and the toleration of the NSDAP.

As prearranged, the Reich President had dissolved the Reichstag, setting new elections for the latest possible date, 31 July 1932. Hitler now had his chance to try to win power by the ballot-box. State elections in Oldenburg at the end of May and in Mecklenburg-Schwerin on 5 June brought the NSDAP respectively 48.4 and 49.0 per cent of the vote. On 19 June in Hessen the Nazis increased their proportion of the vote there to 44 per cent. An absolute majority in the Reichstag election did not seem out of the question.

The second part of Schleicher's deal with Hitler, the lifting of the ban on the SA and SS, eventually took place, after some delay, on 16 June. The ban was already by then being openly flouted. Its lifting ushered in a summer of political violence throughout Germany such as had never been seen before. The latent civil war that had existed throughout the Weimar Republic was threatening to become an actual civil war. Armed clashes and streetfighting between the SA and the Communists were daily occurrences. Nazi violence, it might be thought, ought to have put off the 'respectable' bourgeois following it was increasingly attracting. But since such Nazi supporters saw the threat as lying on the Left, the anti-Communist thuggery purporting to serve the interests of the nation alienated remarkably few voters.

The level of violence was frightening. In the second half of June, after the lifting of the SA ban, there were seventeen politically motivated murders. During July, there were a further eighty-six killings, mainly Nazis and Communists. The numbers of those seriously injured rose into the hundreds.

The Papen government immediately took up plans it had temporarily postponed to depose the Prussian government, still headed by the Social Democrat Otto Braun with another Socialist, Carl Severing, as Interior Minister, and placed the largest state in Germany in the hands of a Reich Commissar. On 20 July, representatives of the Prussian government were told that they were deposed, and that Papen was now acting as Reich Commissar for Prussia. The biggest and most important state, and the vital bulwark of Social Democracy, capitulated without resistance. Papen's destruction of the Prussian bastion without a blow being raised in anger was undertaken by conservatives, not Nazis. But it set the model for the takeover of power in the states more than six months before Hitler became Chancellor.

Meanwhile, Hitler's party had entered upon its fourth election campaign within four months. Goebbels had claimed in mid-April that shortage of money was hindering propaganda. There was little sign of either money or energy being spared, however, as the propaganda machine was cranked up once more. A novel touch was the use of film propaganda and production of 50,000 gramophone records of an 'Appeal to the Nation' by Hitler. There was awareness that boredom with the constant electioneering was setting in. Hitler began a speaking marathon in fifty-three towns and cities during his third 'Germany Flight'. His theme was unchanged: the parties of the November Revolution had presided over the untold ruin of every aspect of German life; his own party was the only one that could rescue the German people from its misery.

When the results were declared on 31 July, the Nazis could record another victory – of sorts. They had increased their share of the vote to 37.4 per cent. This made them, with 230 seats, easily the largest party in the Reichstag. The Socialists had lost votes, compared with 1930; the KPD and Zentrum had made slight gains; the collapse of the bourgeois parties of the centre and right had advanced still further.

The victory for the Nazis was, however, only a pyrrhic one. Compared with the Reichstag election results of 1930, let alone 1928, their advance was indeed astonishing. But from a more short-term perspective the outcome of the July election could even be regarded as disappointing. They had scarcely improved on the support they had won in the second presidential election and in the April state elections.

On 2 August, Hitler was still uncertain what to do. Within two days, while at Berchtesgaden, he had decided how to play his hand. He arranged a meeting with Schleicher in Berlin to put his demands: the Chancellorship for himself, Interior Ministry for Frick, Air Ministry for Göring, Labour Ministry for Strasser, and a Ministry for the People's Education for Goebbels. He was confident that 'the barons would give way'. But he left a question mark over the response of 'the old man', Hindenburg.

The secret negotiations with Reichswehr Minister Schleicher, at Fürstenberg, fifty miles north of Berlin, lasted for several hours on 6 August. When Hitler reported back to other Nazi leaders gathered at Berchtesgaden, he was confident. 'Within a week the matter will burst open,' thought Goebbels. 'Chief will become Reich Chancellor and Prussian Minister President, Strasser Reich and Prussian Interior, Goebbels Prussian and Reich Education, Darré Agriculture in both, Frick state secretary in the Reich Chancellery, Göring Air Ministry. Justice [Ministry] stays with us. Warmbold Economy. Crosigk [i.e. Schwerin von Krosigk] Finance. Schacht Reichsbank. A cabinet of men. If the Reichstag rejects the enabling act, it will be sent packing. Hindenburg wants to die with a national cabinet. We will never give up power again. They'll have to carry us out as corpses . . . I still can't believe it. At the gates of power.'

The deal with Schleicher appeared to offer Hitler all he wanted. It was not total power. But there was little left wanting so far as internal power and control over domestic politics was concerned. From Schleicher's point of view, the concession of a Hitler Chancellorship was a significant one. But the Reichswehr Minister presumably reckoned that as long as the army remained under his own control, Hitler could be kept in check, and would provide the popular basis for an authoritarian regime in which he himself would continue to be the *éminence grise*. The prospect of a civil war, into which the Reichswehr might be drawn, would recede sharply. And the teeth of the Nazis would be drawn by the inevitable compromises they would have to make in the face of the realities of political responsibility. Such was the thinking behind all variants of a 'taming strategy' which would unfold over the following months.

Nazi supporters scented triumph. The whole party expected power, it was reported by telephone from Berlin. 'If things go badly, there'll be a dreadful backlash,' commented Goebbels.

On 11 August, Hitler held a last conference with party leaders at Prien on the Chiemsee, the biggest of the Bavarian lakes, eighty or so miles east of Munich, close to the Austrian border. He was by now aware of the growing opposition in the corridors of power to his Chancellorship. There was still the possibility of threatening a coalition with the Zentrum. But Hitler was adamant that nothing less than the Chancellorship would do. After resting in his flat in Munich, he travelled next day to Berlin by car to avoid all publicity. Röhm had meetings with Schleicher and Papen that day, 12 August, but his soundings about a Hitler Chancellorship were inconclusive. Hitler arrived in darkness at Goebbels's house in Caputh, on the outskirts of Berlin, in the late evening. He was told that matters were still unresolved after Röhm's meetings. It was now 'either-or', he insisted. But if it had been as simple as that, he would not have spent what was left of the evening pacing up and down, pondering how much hinged on the decision of the Reich President. It was clear to Goebbels what was at stake. Unless Hitler were to be given extensive power, meaning the Chancellorship, he would have to refuse office. In that case, 'a mighty depression in the movement and in the electorate would be the consequence'. He added: 'And we have only this one iron in the fire.'

The following morning, 13 August, accompanied by Röhm, Hitler met Schleicher, followed shortly afterwards, this time together with Frick, by a meeting with Chancellor Papen. He was informed by both that Hindenburg was not prepared to appoint him Chancellor. 'I soon realized that I was dealing with a very different man from the one I had met two months earlier,' Papen recalled. 'The modest air of deference had gone, and I was faced by a demanding politician who had just won a resounding electoral success.' Papen suggested Hitler join the government as Vice-Chancellor. The alternative of continued opposition, he argued (convinced that support for the NSDAP had peaked), would surely mean that his party's campaign would start to flag. Whereas, in the event of Hitler's fruitful cooperation and 'once the President had got to know him better', so Papen later wrote, he would be prepared to resign the Chancellorship in the Nazi leader's favour. Hitler rejected point-blank the notion of the head of such a large movement playing second fiddle, and was if anything even more dismissive of the idea that he might consider staying in opposition but allowing one of his associates to take up the post of Vice-Chancellor. Papen advised him at the end of the meeting, at times heated, that the decision was the Reich President's, but he would have to inform Hindenburg that the discussions had led to no positive outcome.

Hitler and his entourage, gathered in Goebbels's house on the Reichs-kanzlerplatz, had by now, not surprisingly, become pessimistic. They could do nothing but wait. When State Secretary Planck rang from the Reich Chancellery around three o'clock, he was asked whether there was any point in Hitler seeing the Reich President, since the decision had evidently been taken. He was told that Hindenburg wanted first to speak to him. Perhaps there was still a chance. Hundreds were gathered in Wilhelmstraße as Hitler arrived at the Presidential Palace for his audience, set for 4.15 p.m. Hindenburg was correct, but cool. According to the notes made by Hindenburg's State Secretary, Otto Meissner, Hitler was asked whether he was prepared to serve in Papen's government. His cooperation would be welcome, the President stated. Hitler declared that, for the reasons he had given to the Chancellor in full that morning, there was no question of his involvement in the existing government. Given the significance of his movement, he must demand the leadership of the government and 'the leadership of the state to its full extent for himself and his party'. The Reich President firmly refused. He could not answer, he said, before God, his conscience and the Fatherland if he handed over the entire power of the government to a single party, and one which was so intolerant towards those with different views. He was also worried about unrest at home and the likely impact abroad. When Hitler repeated that for him every other solution was ruled out, Hinden-burg advised him then to conduct his opposition in a gentlemanly fashion, and that all acts of terror would be treated with utmost severity. In a gesture of pathos more than political reality, he shook Hitler's hand as 'old comrades'. The meeting had lasted a mere twenty minutes. Hitler had controlled himself. But outside, in the corridor, he threatened to explode. Events would inexorably lead to the conclusion he had put forward and to the fall of the President, he declared. The government would be put in an extremely difficult position, the opposition would be fierce, and he would accept no responsibility for the consequences.

Hitler was aware that he had suffered a major political defeat. It was his greatest setback since the failure of the putsch, nine years earlier. The strategy he had followed all those years, that mobilizing the masses – his natural instinct, and what he did best – would suffice to gain power, had proved a failure. He had taken his party into a cul-de-sac. The breakthrough had been made. The NSDAP's rise to the portals of power had been meteoric. He had just won a crushing election victory. But he had been flatly rejected as Reich Chancellor by the one person whose assent, under the Weimar Constitution, was indispensable: Reich President Hindenburg. The 'all-or-nothing' gamble had left Hitler with nothing. With a tired, depressed, desperately disappointed, and fractious party, the prospect of continued opposition was not an enticing one. But it was all that was left. Even given new elections, the chances were that it would prove difficult to hold on to the level of support already mobilized.

The 13th of August 1932 ought to have been a defining moment in Hitler's bid for power. After that, it should never have come to a 30th of January 1933. Without allies in high places, able eventually to persuade the Reich President to change his mind, Hitler would never – even as head of a huge movement, and with over 13 million supporters in the country – have been able to come to power. That the Chancellorship was refused Hitler after he had won a victory, and handed to him after he had suffered a defeat (in the ensuing Reichstag election in November), was not attributable to any 'triumph of the will'.

9

Levered into Power

Hitler took the events of 13 August 'as a personal defeat'. His anger and humiliation was intensified by the government's deliberately brusque communiqué – instigated by Schleicher – on the meeting, which had briefly emphasized Hindenburg's rebuff of Hitler's demand for total power. Hitler's pedantically correct, piqued rejoinder could only claim that he had not demanded 'total' power. At the time, his anger was chiefly directed at Papen. Sent a few days later to intercede with Hitler, by then staying at Obersalzberg, Joachim von Ribbentrop – the vain and humourless future Reich Foreign Minister, on his upward career path not least through his marriage to the heiress of Germany's biggest Sekt manufacturers, Henkel, and a recent recruit to the NSDAP – found him 'full of resentment towards Herr von Papen and the entire cabinet in Berlin'. But if the events of January 1933 were to redeem Papen, Schleicher would emerge as the central target of Nazi aggression for his role in the months between August 1932 and January 1933. His manoeuvrings behind the scenes, particularly his 'betrayal' in August which had led to Hitler's humiliation, were not forgotten. He would pay for them with his life.

As usual, Hitler had the capacity to channel disappointment and depression into outright aggression. Open opposition to the hated Papen government was now proclaimed. The shadow-boxing of the summer was over.

Within days, Hitler had an opportunity to turn attention away from the debacle of his audience with Hindenburg. On 10 August, a group of SA men had murdered an unemployed labourer and Communist sympathizer in the Silesian village of Potempa. The murder was carried

out with extraordinary savagery, and in front of the victim's mother
and brother. As so often, personal and political motives intermingled.
Horrifically brutal though the killing was, it is an indication of how far
public order had collapsed that the event was in itself little more than a
routine act of terror in the awful summer of 1932, symptomatic of the
climate of violence in near-civil war conditions. No one took particular
notice of it at first. Given a list of three dozen acts of political violence
recorded in a single day and night around the time, the Potempa incident
did not stand out. However, the murder had been committed an hour
and a half after the Papen government's emergency decree to combat
terrorism had come into effect. This prescribed the death penalty for
premeditated political murder and set up special courts to provide swift
justice for cases arising under the decree. The trial took place at Beuthen
in a tense atmosphere and amid great publicity between 19 and
22 August, ending with the pronouncement of the death penalty on five
of the accused. To inflame feelings in the Nazi camp still further, two
Reichsbanner men were given relatively light sentences on the very same
day for killing two SA men during disturbances in Ohlau in July. These
murders had not been premeditated, and had taken place before Papen's
emergency decree. But such differences naturally did not weigh among
Hitler's supporters. The Potempa murderers were portrayed as martyrs.
The local SA leader, Heines, threatened an uprising if the death sentences
were to be carried out. His rabble-rousing tirade incited the crowd to
break the windows of Jewish-owned shops in Beuthen and attack the
offices of the local SPD newspaper. In this heated atmosphere, Göring
praised the condemned men and provided money for their families.
Röhm was dispatched to visit them in jail. On 23 August, Hitler himself
sent the telegram that caused a sensation. 'My comrades!' he wrote, 'in
view of this most monstrous verdict in blood, I feel tied to you in
unbounded loyalty. Your freedom is from this moment on a question of
our honour. The struggle against a government under which this was
possible is our duty!' The head of Germany's largest political party was
publicly expressing solidarity with convicted murderers. It was a scandal
Hitler had to take on board. Not to have sympathized with the Potempa
murders would have risked alienating his SA in a particularly sensitive
area, Silesia, and at a time when it was vitally important to keep the
restless stormtroopers on the leash.

The next day, Hitler put out a proclamation castigating the Papen cabinet, and taking the opportunity to turn the events of 13 August on their head by claiming his own refusal to participate in a government capable of such sentences. 'Those of you who possess a feel for the struggle for the honour and freedom of the nation will understand why I refused to enter this bourgeois government,' he declared. 'With this deed, our attitude towards this national cabinet is prescribed once and for all.'

In the event, Papen, acting in his capacity as Reich Commissar in Prussia, backed down and had the death sentences for the Potempa murderers commuted into life imprisonment – a decision which Papen himself acknowledged was political rather than legal. The murderers were freed under a Nazi amnesty as early as March 1933.

The Potempa affair had cast glaring light, at precisely the juncture where the power-brokers were still examining ways and means of incorporating Hitler in government, on Nazi attitudes towards the law. But such unmistakable indications of what a Hitler government would mean for the rule of law in Germany posed no deterrent to those who still thought the only way out of the crisis was somehow to involve the Nazis in the responsibility of public office.

Hitler's rejection of anything less than the office of Chancellor had not only created difficulties for the NSDAP. The problems for the government were now acute. Schleicher had now given up the idea of a Hitler Chancellorship as long as Hindenburg remained Reich President. Papen, himself resolutely opposed, took Hindenburg's continued opposition for granted. Only two possibilities, neither attractive, appeared to remain. The first was a coalition of Zentrum and National Socialists. Feelers were put out from the Zentrum about such a possibility following the events of 13 August. It never stood much chance of emerging as a solution. The Zentrum continued to insist that the NSDAP concede the Chancellorship, but a Hitler Chancellorship had meanwhile become a 'question of honour'. Hitler was unwilling now, as he was to be following the November elections when the possibility was once more raised, of heading a government dependent upon Reichstag majorities for support. In any case, the thought of a reversion to parliamentary government was anathema to Hindenburg and his advisers.

The second alternative was to persevere with a 'cabinet of struggle' without any hope of support in the Reichstag, where the Nazis and Communists together prevailed over a 'negative majority'. This implied going ahead with plans, first advanced by Interior Minister Freiherr

Wilhelm von Gayl earlier in August, for dissolving the Reichstag and postponing new elections in order to provide time to undertake a far-reaching reduction in the powers of the Reichstag through restricted franchise and a two-chamber system with a non-elected first chamber. The intention was to end 'party rule' once and for all. Necessary for such a drastic step were the support of the Reich President and the backing of the army to combat the expected opposition from the Left and possibly also from National Socialists. This solution for a dissolution of the Reichstag and postponement – in breach of the Constitution – of elections beyond the sixty-day limit prescribed, was put to Hindenburg by Papen at a meeting in Neudeck on 30 August. Schleicher and Gayl were also present. Hindenburg gave Papen the dissolution order without ado, and also agreed to the unconstitutional postponement of new elections on the grounds of a national state of emergency. Some leading constitutional lawyers – most prominent among them Carl Schmitt, the renowned constitutional theorist who in 1933 would place himself at the service of the Third Reich – were ready with their legal arguments to back the introduction of an authoritarian state through such a device.

Probably, if he wanted to risk such a solution, Papen should have had the new Reichstag dissolved at its very first sitting on 30 August. By 12 September, when the Reichstag met for its second – and last – sitting, the initiative had been lost. The only item on the agenda that day was a government declaration on the financial situation, announcing details of a programme aimed at economic recovery. A debate was expected to last for several days. However, the Communist Deputy Ernst Torgler proposed an alteration to the order of proceedings. He sought first to put a proposal of his party to repeal the emergency decrees of 4 and 5 September (which had made deep incisions in the system of tariff wage-bargaining), and to couple this with a vote of no-confidence in the government. No one expected much of such a proposal. The amendment to the order of proceedings would have fallen had there been a single objection. The Nazis expected the DNVP deputies to object. Astonishingly, not one did so. In the confusion that followed, Frick obtained an adjournment of half an hour to seek Hitler's decision on how to proceed. Papen, completely taken aback, had to send a messenger to the Reich Chancellery during the adjournment to pick up the dissolution order, signed by Hindenburg on 30 August, which he had not even bothered to bring into the chamber with him.

At a brief meeting with his chief henchmen, Hitler decided that the opportunity to embarrass the government could not be missed: the Nazi deputies should immediately support the Communist vote of no-confidence, thus pre-empting Papen's dissolution order which no one doubted he would now put forward. When the Reichstag reassembled, Papen appeared with the red dispatch box which traditionally contained the orders of dissolution under his arm. Amid chaotic scenes, the Reichstag President Göring announced straight away that he would proceed with the vote on the Communist proposal. At this, Papen tried to speak. Göring ignored him, looking intentionally away from the Chancellor to the left side of the chamber. Papen's State Secretary Planck pointed out to Göring that the Chancellor wished to exercise his right to speak. Göring retorted simply that the vote had begun. After again trying vainly to speak, Papen marched over to the Reichstag President's platform and slapped the dissolution order down on Göring's table. Followed by his cabinet, he then walked out of the chamber to howls of derision. Göring blithely pushed the dissolution order to one side, and read out the result of the division. The government was defeated by 512 votes to 42, with five abstentions and one invalid ballot paper. Only the DNVP and DVP had supported the government. All the major parties, including the Zentrum, had supported the Communist proposal. There had never been a parliamentary defeat like it. It was received with wild cheering in the Reichstag.

Göring now read out Papen's dissolution order, which he declared invalid since the government had already fallen through a vote of no-confidence. This was technically incorrect. Göring was subsequently compelled to concede that the Reichstag had indeed been formally dis-solved by the presentation of Papen's order. The no-confidence motion was, therefore, without legal standing. But this was of purely procedural significance. The government remained, as a consequence, in office. The reality was, however, that it had been rejected by more than four-fifths of the people's representatives. Papen had been shown in the most humiliating way possible to be a Chancellor almost devoid of public support. Hitler was beside himself with joy. The cynical Nazi tactics had meanwhile given a foretaste of how they would behave in power, given the opportunity.

New elections – the fifth of the year – loomed. Papen still had in his possession Hindenburg's approval to postpone the election beyond the sixty days allowed by the constitution. But after the fiasco of 12 September, the cabinet decided two days later that now was not the time to proceed with that experiment. The elections were set for 6 November. The Nazi leadership was aware of the difficulties. The bourgeois press was now completely hostile. The NSDAP could make little use of broadcasting. The public were weary of elections. Even leading party speakers found it difficult to sustain top form. Not least, noted Goebbels, previous campaigns had drained all available funds. The party's coffers were empty.

Electioneering reinvigorated Hitler. And in the fifth long campaign of the year, he set out yet again to do what he did best: make speeches. Once more, his indispensability as the chief propaganda focus of the movement meant he had to embark upon a punishing schedule of speeches and rallies. During his fourth 'Germany Flight' between 11 October and 5 November he gave no fewer than fifty speeches, again sometimes three a day, on one occasion four.

His attack now focused squarely on Papen and 'the Reaction'. The vast support for his own movement was contrasted with the 'small circle of reactionaries' keeping the Papen government, lacking all popular backing, in office. The Nazi press inevitably portrayed Hitler's campaign as a victory march. But grossly inflated figures for attendance at Hitler rallies provided in the party press – in rural areas especially thousands were brought in from outside the area to swell the numbers – hid the plain signs of disillusionment and electoral fatigue. Even Hitler was now unable to fill the halls as he previously had done. For his speech in Nuremberg on 13 October, the Festhalle in Luitpoldhain was only half full. While a Hitler speech might have made a difference to the election result in some places, observers were already predicting in October that his campaign tour would do little to prevent the expected drop in Nazi support. The day before the election, Goebbels, too, was anticipating a defeat.

When the votes were counted, Nazi fears were realized. In the last election before Hitler came to power (and the last fully free election in the Weimar Republic) the NSDAP had lost 2 million voters. In a reduced turn-out – the lowest (at 80.6 per cent) since 1928 – its percentage of the poll had fallen from 37.4 in July to 33.1 per cent, its Reichstag seats reduced from 230 to 196. The SPD and Zentrum had also lost ground slightly. The winners were the Communists, who had increased their vote to 16.9 per cent (now little more than 3 per cent behind the SPD), and the DNVP, which had risen to 8.9 per cent. The DNVP's gains had been largely in winning back former supporters who had drifted to the NSDAP. The lower turn-out was the other main factor that worked to the disadvantage of Hitler's party, as earlier Nazi voters stayed at home. Not only had the party failed, as before, to make serious inroads into the big left-wing and Catholic voting blocks; it had this time lost voters – it seems to all other parties, but predominantly to the DNVP. The middle classes were beginning to desert the Nazis.

II

The November election had changed nothing in the political stalemate – except, perhaps, to make the situation even worse. The parties supporting the government, the DNVP and DVP, had only just over 10 per cent of the population behind them. And with the drop in the vote of both the NSDAP and the Zentrum, a coalition between the two parties, such as had been discussed in August, would in itself not suffice to produce an absolute majority in the Reichstag. The only majority, now as before, was a negative one. Hitler was undeterred by the election setback. He told party leaders in Munich to continue the struggle without any relenting. 'Papen has to go. There are to be no compromises,' was how Goebbels recalled the gist of Hitler's comments.

Now, as before, Hitler had no interest in power at the behest of other parties in a majority government dependent on the Reichstag. By mid-November, Papen's attempts to find any basis of support for his government had failed. On 17 November, mourned by few, his entire cabinet resigned. It was now left to Hindenburg himself to try to negotiate a path out of the state crisis. Meanwhile, the cabinet would continue to conduct the daily business of governmental administration.

On 19 November, the day that Hindenburg received Hitler as part of his meetings with the heads of the political parties, the Reich President was handed a petition carrying twenty signatures from businessmen demanding the appointment of Hitler as Chancellor. It did not mark proof, as was once thought, of big business support for Hitler, and its machinations to get him into power. The idea was, in fact, that of Wilhelm Keppler, emerging as Hitler's link with a group of pro-Nazi businessmen, and put into operation in conjunction with Himmler, who served as the liaison to the Brown House. Keppler and Schacht began with a list of around three dozen possible signatories. But they found it an uphill task. Eight of the 'Keppler Circle', headed by Schacht and the Cologne banker Kurt von Schröder, signed the petition. The results with industrialists were disappointing. A single prominent industrialist, Fritz Thyssen, signed. But he had for long made no secret of his sympathies for the National Socialists. The acting President of the Reichslandbund (Reich Agrarian League), the Nazi-infiltrated lobby of big landowners, was another signatory. The rest were middle-ranking businessmen and landholders. It was misleadingly claimed that leading industrialists Paul Reusch, Fritz Springorum, and Albert Vögler sympathized, but had withheld their names from the actual petition. Big business on the whole still placed its hopes in Papen, though the petition was an indication that the business community did not speak with a single voice. The agricultural lobby, in particular, was the one to watch.

In any case, the petition had no bearing on Hindenburg's negotiations with Hitler. The Reich President remained, as the exchanges of mid-November were to show, utterly distrustful of the Nazi leader. Hitler, for his part, was privately contemptuous of Hindenburg. But he had no way of attaining power without the President's backing.

At his meeting with Hitler on 19 November, Hindenburg repeated, as in August, that he wanted to see him and his movement participating in government. The President expressed the hope that Hitler would take soundings with other parties with a view to forming a government with a parliamentary majority. This was calling Hitler's bluff. Hindenburg knew that it would prove impossible, given the certain opposition of the DNVP. The outcome would have been the exposure of Hitler's failure, and a weakening of his position. Hitler saw through the tactic straight away.

In what Goebbels called a 'chessmatch for power', Hitler replied that he had no intention of involving himself in negotiations with other parties before he had been entrusted by the Reich President, in whose hands the decision lay, with constructing a government. In such an eventuality, he was confident of finding a basis which would provide his government with an enabling act, approved by the Reichstag. He alone was in the position to obtain such a mandate from the Reichstag. The difficulties would be thereby solved.

He repeated to Hindenburg in writing two days later his 'single request', that he be given the authority accorded to those before him. This was precisely what Hindenburg adamantly refused to concede. He remained unwilling to make Hitler the head of a presidential cabinet. He left the door open, however, to the possibility of a cabinet with a working majority, led by Hitler, and stipulated his conditions for accepting such a cabinet: establishment of an economic programme, no return to the dualism of Prussia and the Reich, no limiting of Article 48, and approval of a list of ministers in which he, the President, would nominate the foreign and defence ministers. On 30 November Hitler rejected as pointless a further invitation to discussions with Hindenburg. The deadlock continued.

Schleicher had been gradually distancing himself from Papen. He was imperceptibly shifting his role from *éminence grise* behind the scenes to main part. Meanwhile, he was making sure that lines were kept open to Gregor Strasser, who was thought to be ready 'to step personally into the breach' if nothing came of the discussions with Hitler.

Schleicher threw this possibility into the ring during discussions between himself, Papen, and Hindenburg on the evening of 1 December. Strasser and one or two of his supporters would be offered places in the government. About sixty Nazi Reichstag deputies could be won over. Schleicher was confident of gaining the support of the trade unions, the SPD, and the bourgeois parties for a package of economic reforms and work creation. This, he claimed, would obviate the need for the up-turning of the constitution, which Papen had again proposed. Hindenburg nevertheless sided with Papen, and asked him to form a government and resume office – something which had been his intention all along. Behind the scenes, however, Schleicher had been warning members of Papen's cabinet that if there were to be no change of government, and the proposed breaking of the constitution in a state of emergency were to take place, there would be civil war and the army would not be able to cope. This was reinforced at a cabinet meeting the following morning, 2 December, when Lieutenant-Colonel Ott was brought in to report on a 'war games' exercise which the Reichswehr had conducted, demonstrating that they could not defend the borders and withstand the breakdown of internal order which would follow from strikes and disruption. The army was almost certainly too pessimistic in its judgement. But the message made its mark on the cabinet, and on the President. Hindenburg was afraid of possible civil war. Reluctantly, he let Papen, his favourite, go and appointed Schleicher as Reich Chancellor.

III

In the wake of Schleicher's overtures to Gregor Strasser, Hitler's movement entered upon its greatest crisis since the refoundation of 1925. Strasser was no fringe character. His contribution to the growth of the NSDAP had been second only to that of Hitler himself. The organization of the party, in particular, had been largely his work. His reputation inside the party – though he had made powerful enemies, not least his one-time acolyte Goebbels – was high. He was generally seen as Hitler's right-hand man. Strasser's resignation of all his party offices on 8 December 1932 naturally, therefore, caused a sensation. Moreover, it hit a party already rocked by falling support and shaky morale. If power were not attained soon, the chances that the party might fall apart altogether could not be discounted.

Bombshell though Gregor Strasser's resignation of his party offices was, trouble had been brewing for some considerable time. By the autumn of 1932, as Hitler – once seen by sections of business as a 'moderate' – was viewed as an intransigent obstacle to a conservative-dominated right-wing government, Strasser came to be seen as a more responsible and constructive politician who could bring Nazi mass support behind a conservative cabinet. Strasser's differences with Hitler were not primarily ideological. He was an out-and-out racist; he did not shy away from violence; his 'social ideas' were hardly less vague than Hitler's own; his economic ideas, eclectic and contradictory, were more utopian than, but still compatible with, Hitler's cruder and more brutal notions; his foreign-policy ambitions were no less extensive than Hitler's; and he was ruthless and single-minded in the drive for power. But tactically, there were fundamental differences. And after 13 August, as Hitler's political inflexibility threatened increasingly to block the road to power forever, these differences came more and more to the surface. In contrast to Hitler's 'all-or-nothing' stance, Strasser thought the NSDAP ought to be prepared to join coalitions, explore all possible alliances, and if necessary enter government even without the offer of the Chancellorship.

Schleicher was particularly interested in the possibility that Gregor Strasser could help bring the trade unions behind a 'national' – that is, authoritarian – government. Unlike Hitler, whose dislike of trade unions had never wavered, Strasser was openly conciliatory towards the unions. Given his growing contacts with union leaders interested in a broad coalition to head off the dangers they saw on the far Right and far Left, the prospects of winning their support for a Schleicher cabinet that had Strasser in the government and offered an expansive work-creation programme could not be lightly dismissed.

During the autumn, the rift between Hitler and Strasser widened. After the November election, Strasser lost his place in Hitler's inner circle. In the light of the political sensitivities of the autumn, a public split in the party leadership was scarcely opportune. But by the first week of December, matters could rest no longer.

At a meeting held in secret in Berlin on 3 December, Schleicher offered Strasser the posts of Vice-Chancellor and Minister President in Prussia. Strasser's choices were now to back Hitler, to rebel against him in the hope of winning over some of the party, or to do what by 8 December he had made up his mind to do: resign his offices and withdraw from an active role in politics. Strasser must have realized that the chances of leading a palace revolution against Hitler were minimal. His best support lay among the Nazi Reichstag members. But here, too, he controlled nothing amounting to a firmly organized faction. Pride, as well as his principled objections, prevented him from backing down and accepting Hitler's all-or-bust strategy. He was left, therefore, with only the third possibility. Perhaps disappointed at the lack of open support from his party friends, he withdrew to his room in Berlin's Hotel Exzelsior and wrote out his letter resigning his party offices.

On the morning of 8 December, he summoned those Regional Inspectors of the party – the senior Gauleiter – who happened to be in Berlin to his office in the Reichstag. Six were present besides Reich Inspector Robert Ley when Strasser addressed them. According to the post-war account of one of them, Hinrich Lohse, Strasser told them he had written the Führer a letter, resigning his party offices. He did not criticize Hitler's programme, but rather his lack of any clear policy towards attaining power since the meeting with Hindenburg in August. Hitler was clear, he said, about one thing only: he wanted to become Reich Chancellor. But just wanting the post was not going to overcome the opposition he had encountered. And meanwhile the party was under great strain and exposed to potential disintegration. Strasser said he was prepared to go along with either the legal or the illegal – that is, putschist – way to power. But what he was not prepared to do was simply wait for Hitler to be made Reich Chancellor and see the party fall apart before that happened. Hitler, in his view, should have accepted the Vice-Chancellorship in August, and used that position as a bargaining counter to build up further power. On a personal note, Strasser expressed his pique at being excluded from top-level deliberations, and had no wish to play second fiddle to Göring, Goebbels, Röhm, and others. Now at the end of his tether, he was resigning his offices and leaving to recuperate.

Strasser's letter was delivered to Hitler in the Kaiserhof at midday on 8 December. It amounted to a feeble justification of Strasser's position, couched in terms of wounded pride, and not touching on the fundamentals that separated him from Hitler. It had the ring of defeat in the very way it was formulated. Hitler had been forewarned by Gauleiter Bernhard Rust, who had attended the meeting called by Strasser, to expect the letter. He had immediately summoned the same group of party Inspectors whom Strasser had addressed to the Kaiserhof for a meeting at noon. The group, in dejected mood, were left standing in Hitler's apartment while, in an agitated state, he provided a point-by-point counter to Strasser's reasons for his resignation, as summarized by Robert Ley from the earlier meeting. Entering the Papen cabinet, he said, would have given the initiative to the party's enemies. He would soon have been forced, through fundamental disagreement with Papen's policies, into resignation. The effect on public opinion would have been the apparent demonstration of his incapacity for government – that which his enemies had always claimed. The electorate would have turned their backs on him. The movement would have collapsed. The illegal route was even more dangerous. It would simply have meant – the lessons of 1923 plainly recalled – standing 'the prime of the nation's manhood' in front of the machine-guns of the police and army. As for overlooking Strasser, Hitler disingenuously claimed he entered into discussions with whomsoever was necessary for a particular purpose, distributed tasks according to specific circumstances, and – according to availability – was open to all. He shifted the blame back on Gregor Strasser for avoiding him. His address went on for the best part of two hours. Towards the end, the well-worn tactic was deployed once more: he made a personal appeal to loyalty. According to Lohse's account, he became 'quieter and more human, more friendly and appealing in his comments'. He had found 'that comradely tone which those assembled knew and which completely convinced them . . . Increasingly persuasive to his audience and inexorably drawing them under his spell, he [Hitler] triumphed and proved to his wavering, but upright and indispensable fighters in this toughest test of the movement, that he was the master and Strasser the journeyman . . . The old bond with him was again sealed by those present with a handshake.'

The mood that evening at Goebbels's house, where Hitler returned, was nevertheless still sombre. There was real concern that the movement would fall apart. If that were to happen, announced Hitler, 'I'll finish things in three minutes.' Dramatic gestures soon gave way to concerted moves to counter the possible ramifications of the 'treachery'. Goebbels was summoned the same night at 2 a.m. to a meeting in the Kaiserhof, where he found Röhm and Himmler already with Hitler. Hitler, still stunned by Strasser's action, spent the time pacing the floor of his hotel room. The meeting lasted until dawn. The main outcome was the decision to dismantle the organizational framework that Strasser had erected, and which had given him his power-base in the party. In time-honoured fashion, as he had taken over the SA leadership following the Stennes affair, Hitler himself now formally took over the leadership of the political organization, with Robert Ley as his chief of staff. A new Political Central Commission was set up, under Rudolf Heß, and the two Reich Inspectorates created by Strasser were abolished. A number of known Strasser supporters were removed from their posts. And a major campaign was begun, eliciting countless declarations of loyalty to Hitler from all parts of Germany – also from Strasser sympathizers. Strasser was rapidly turned into the movement's arch-traitor. Hitler began the appeals to loyalty the very next day, 9 December, when he addressed the Gauleiter, Regional Inspectors, and Reichstag deputies. According to the report in the *Völkischer Beobachter*, every single person present felt the need to offer a personal show of loyalty by shaking hands with the Führer. 'Strasser is isolated. Dead man!' noted Goebbels triumphantly. Soon afterwards, Hitler set off on a speaking tour, addressing party members and functionaries at seven meetings in nine days. Again and again the personal appeal was successful. No secession followed Strasser's resignation. The crisis was past.

Strasser now retired fully from all political activity and from public view. He was not excluded from the party. In fact, early in 1934 he applied for, and was granted, the NSDAP's badge of honour, awarded to him as party member No.9, dating from the refoundation of the party on 25 February 1925. Neither this nor a plaintive letter he wrote to Rudolf Heß on 18 June 1934 emphasizing his lengthy service and continuing loyalty to the party could save his skin. Hitler was unforgiving to those he felt had betrayed him. His final reckoning with Gregor Strasser came on 30 June 1934, when the former second man in the party was murdered in what came to be known as 'the Night of the Long Knives'.

Ultimately, the Strasser affair – the most serious of the inner-party crises since 1925 – revealed once again most graphically just how strong Hitler's hold over the party had become, how much the NSDAP had become a 'leader party'.

IV

The events of January 1933 amounted to an extraordinary political drama. It was a drama that unfolded largely out of sight of the German people.

A fortnight after Schleicher had taken over from him as Reich Chancellor, Franz von Papen had been guest of honour at a dinner at the Berlin Herrenklub. Among the 300 or so guests listening to his speech on 16 December, justifying his own record in government, criticizing the Schleicher cabinet, and indicating that he thought the NSDAP should be included in government, was the Cologne banker Baron Kurt von Schröder. A few weeks earlier, Schröder had been a signatory to the petition to Hindenburg to make Hitler Chancellor. For months before that, he had been a Nazi sympathizer, and was a member of the 'Keppler Circle' – the group of economic advisers that Wilhelm Keppler, a one-time small businessman, had set up on Hitler's behalf. Already in November – though nothing came of it at the time – Keppler had told Schröder that Papen might be prepared to intercede with Hindenburg in favour of a Hitler Chancellorship. Now, after Papen's Herrenklub speech, interested by what the former Chancellor had had to say, Schröder met him for a few minutes late in the evening to discuss the political situation. The two had known each other for some time. And since Schröder also knew Hitler, he was the ideal intermediary at a time that relations between the Nazi leader and the former Chancellor were still icy. Out of the discussion came the suggestion of a meeting between Hitler and Papen. The meeting was fixed to take place at Schröder's house in Cologne on 4 January 1933.

Papen arrived around midday. He found Hitler – who had entered through the back door – together with Heß, Himmler, and Keppler, waiting for him. Hitler, Papen, and Schröder adjourned to another room, while the others waited. Schröder took no part in the discussions. Most likely, the question of who was to lead the new government was left open at the meeting. Papen spoke loosely of some sort of duumvirate, and left open the possibility of ministerial posts, even if Hitler himself did not feel ready to take office, for some of his colleagues. After about two hours, discussions ended for lunch with the agreement to deal with further issues at a subsequent meeting, in Berlin or elsewhere. Papen evidently felt progress had been made. In a private audience with the Reich President a few days later, Papen informed Hindenburg that Hitler had lessened his demands and would be prepared to take part in a coalition government with parties of the Right. The unspoken assumption was that Papen would lead such a government. The Reich President told Papen to keep in touch with the Nazi leader.

A second meeting between Hitler and Papen soon followed. It took place this time in the study of Ribbentrop's house in Dahlem, a plush residential suburb of Berlin, on the night of 10–11 January. Nothing came of it, since Papen told Hitler that Hindenburg still opposed his appointment to the Chancellorship. Hitler angrily broke off further talks until after the Lippe election.

Elections in the mini-state of Lippe-Detmold, with its 173,000 inhabitants, would at other times scarcely have been a first priority for Hitler and his party. But now, they were a chance to prove the NSDAP was again on the forward march after its losses the previous November and after the Strasser crisis. Despite the poor state of the party's finances, no effort was spared towards obtaining a good result in Lippe. For close on a fortnight before the election, on 15 January, Lippe was saturated with Nazi propaganda. All the Nazi big guns were fired. Göring, Goebbels and Frick spoke. Hitler himself gave seventeen speeches in eleven days. It paid off. The NSDAP won almost 6,000 more votes compared with the November result, and increased its share of the poll from 34.7 to 39.5 per cent. The bandwagon seemed to be rolling again.

Hitler's position was strengthened, however, less by the Lippe result than by Schleicher's increasing isolation. Not only had his lingering hopes of Gregor Strasser and gaining support from the Nazi ranks practically evaporated by mid-January. The Reichslandbund had by then declared open warfare on his government because of its unwillingness to impose high import levies on agricultural produce. Schleicher was powerless to do anything about such opposition, which had backing not only within the DNVP but also within the NSDAP. Accommodation with the big agrarians would axiomatically have meant opposition from both sides of industry, bosses and unions, as well as consumers. Hugenberg's offers to bring the DNVP behind Schleicher if he were to be given the combined ministries of Economics and Food were therefore bound to fall on deaf ears. Correspondingly, by 21 January, the DNVP had also declared its outright opposition to the Chancellor. Shrill accusations, along with those of the agrarians, of the government's 'Bolshevism' in the countryside because of its schemes to divide up bankrupt eastern estates to make smallholdings for the unemployed were a reminder of the lobbying which had helped bring down Brüning. Schleicher's position was also weakened by the Osthilfe (Eastern Aid) scandal that broke in mid-January. The agrarian lobby was incensed that the government had not hushed up the affair. Since some of Hindenburg's close friends and fellow landowners were implicated, the ire directed at Schleicher could be transmitted directly through the Reich President. And when, in the wake of the scandal, it was revealed that the President's own property at Neudeck, presented to him by German business five years earlier, had been registered in his son's name to avoid death-duties, Schleicher was held responsible by Hindenburg for allowing his name to be dragged through the mud.

Meanwhile, serving as the go-between, Ribbentrop had arranged another meeting between Hitler and Papen on 18 January. Accompanied by Röhm and Himmler, Hitler – encouraged by the Lippe success and by Schleicher's mounting difficulties – now hardened his position from the earlier meetings in the month and expressly demanded the Chancellorship. When Papen demurred, claiming his influence with Hindenburg was not sufficient to bring this about, Hitler, in his usual way, told the former Chancellor he saw no point in further talks. Ribbentrop then suggested that it might be worth talking to Hindenburg's son, Oskar. The following day, Ribbentrop took his suggestion further with Papen. The result was a meeting, arranged for late on the Sunday evening, 22 January, at Ribbentrop's house, at which Oskar von Hindenburg and the Reich President's State Secretary Otto Meissner agreed to be present. Frick accompanied Hitler. Göring joined them later. The main part of the meeting consisted of a two-hour discussion between Hitler and the President's son. Hitler also spoke with Papen, who told him that the President had not changed his mind about making him Chancellor, but recognized that the situation had changed and that it was necessary to incorporate the National Socialists in this or a new government. Hitler was unyielding. He made it plain that Nazi cooperation could only come under his Chancellorship. Apart from the Chancellorship for himself, he insisted only upon the Reich Ministry of the Interior for Frick and a further cabinet post for Göring. These claims were more modest – and were recognized as being such – than those he had put forward to Schleicher the previous August. Papen demanded the post of Vice-Chancellor for himself. On that basis, he now agreed to press for Hitler to become Chancellor – a notable breakthrough – but promised to withdraw if there was any sign that he did not have Hitler's confidence.

The following day, Chancellor Schleicher, by now aware of the threat to his position, informed the Reich President that a vote of no-confidence in the government could be expected at the delayed recall of the Reichstag on 31 January. He requested an order of dissolution and postponement of new elections. Hindenburg agreed to consider a dissolution, but rejected the breach of Article 25 of the Weimar Constitution which an indefinite postponement would have entailed. What he had been prepared to grant Papen five months earlier, he now refused Schleicher.

At the same time, Hindenburg had left himself with little room for manoeuvre. He had once more rejected the idea of a Hitler Chancellorship. That left only the return to a Papen cabinet – Hindenburg's favoured outcome, but scarcely likely to resolve the crisis, and regarded with scepticism even by Papen himself. As rumours hared round Berlin, the prospect of a reversion to Papen's 'cabinet of struggle', with a major role for Hugenberg, and a declaration of a state of emergency was, remarkable though it now seems, seen as more worrying than a cabinet led by Hitler. Fears of such an eventuality were sharply intensified after Schleicher, on 28 January, having been refused the dissolution order by the Reich President, submitted his own resignation and that of his entire cabinet. Within hours, Hindenburg asked Papen to try to work towards a solution within the framework of the Constitution and with the backing of the Reichstag. According to Papen's own account, he was asked by the President to take soundings about the possibilities of a Hitler cabinet. Papen told Ribbentrop that Hitler must be contacted without delay. A turning-point had been reached. After his talk with Hindenburg, he now thought a Hitler Chancellorship a possibility.

By this time, Papen had come round to full acceptance of a government led by Hitler. The only question in his mind was to ensure that Hitler was firmly contained by 'reliable' and 'responsible' conservatives. Following the resignation of the Schleicher cabinet on 28 January, Papen had meetings with Hugenberg and Hitler. Hugenberg agreed that a Hitler cabinet was the only way forward, but stressed the importance of limiting his power. He demanded for himself the Reich and Prussian Ministries of Economics as the price of the DNVP's support. Hitler, unsurprisingly, refused – as he had done since August – to entertain the notion of a government dependent on a parliamentary majority, and held out for the headship of a presidential cabinet with the same rights that had been granted to Papen and Schleicher. He reiterated his readiness to include those from previous cabinets whom the President favoured, as long as he could be Chancellor and Commissioner for Prussia, and could place members of his own party in the Ministries of the Interior in the Reich and Prussia. The demands for extensive powers in Prussia caused problems. Ribbentrop and Göring tried to persuade Hitler to settle for less. Eventually, 'with a bad grace', as Papen put it, he accepted that the powers of Reich Commissar for Prussia would remain with Papen, in his capacity as Vice-Chancellor.

Meanwhile, Papen had taken soundings by telephone from several former cabinet members, conservatives held in esteem by Hindenburg. All replied that they would be prepared to work in a Hitler cabinet, with Papen as Vice-Chancellor, but not in a Papen–Hugenberg 'cabinet of struggle'. This impressed Hindenburg, when Papen reported to him late on the night of 28 January. He was also gratified by the 'moderation' of Hitler's demands. For the first time, the Reich President was now amenable to a Hitler cabinet. The deadlock was broken.

Hindenburg and Papen discussed the composition of the cabinet. The President was glad that the trusted Konstantin Freiherr von Neurath would remain at the Foreign Ministry. He wanted someone equally sound at the Defence Ministry, following Schleicher's departure. His own suggestion was General von Blomberg, the army commander in East Prussia and currently technical adviser of the German delegation to the Disarmament Conference in Geneva. Hindenburg thought him extremely reliable and 'completely apolitical'. The following morning he was ordered back to Berlin.

Papen continued his power-brokerage on the morning of 29 January in discussions with Hitler and Göring. The composition of the cabinet was agreed. All posts but two (other than the Chancellorship) were to be occupied by conservatives, not Nazis. Neurath (Foreign Minister), Schwerin von Krosigk (Finance), and Eltz-Rübenach (Post and Transport Ministry) had been members of the Schleicher cabinet. The occupancy of the Justice Ministry was left open for the time being. Frick was nominated by Hitler as Reich Minister of the Interior. Compensation for the concession made over the position of Reich Commissar of Prussia was the acceptance by Papen that Göring would serve nominally as Papen's deputy in the Prussian Ministry of the Interior. This key appointment effectively gave the Nazis control over the police in the giant state of Prussia, embracing two-thirds of the territory of the Reich. There was no place as yet for Goebbels in a propaganda ministry, part of Nazi expectations the previous summer. But Hitler assured Goebbels that his ministry was waiting for him. It was simply a matter of necessary tactics for a temporary solution. Apart from all else, Hitler needed Goebbels for the election campaign he was insisting must follow his appointment as Chancellor.

Papen had talks the same day with Hugenberg and with the Stahlhelm leaders Seldte and Duesterberg. Hugenberg still objected to the Nazi demands for new elections, from which his own party had nothing to gain. But, tempted by the offer of the powerful Economics Ministry, which he had long coveted, he tentatively offered his cooperation. When, in late January, the deputy Stahlhelm leader Theodor Duesterberg warned him of the consequences of entrusting the Chancellorship to someone as dishonest as Hitler, Hugenberg waved the objections aside. Nothing could happen. Hindenburg would remain Reich President and supreme commander of the armed forces; Papen would be Vice-

Chancellor; he himself would have control of the entire economic sphere, including agriculture; Seldte (the Stahlhelm leader) would be in charge of the Labour Ministry. 'We're boxing Hitler in,' concluded Hugenberg. Duesterberg replied darkly that Hugenberg would find himself one night fleeing through ministerial gardens in his underpants to avoid arrest.

Some of Papen's conservative friends also expressed their deep concern at the prospect of a Hitler cabinet. Papen told them there was no alternative within the framework of the Constitution. To one who warned him that he was placing himself in Hitler's hands, Papen replied: 'You are mistaken. We've hired him.'

A last problem still had to be resolved. Hitler insisted at his meeting with Papen on new elections to be followed by an enabling act. For Hitler, this was crucial. An enabling act was vital to be able to rule without dependency on either the Reichstag or on presidential backing for emergency decrees. But the current composition of the Reichstag offered no hope of passing an enabling act. Papen reported back, via Ribbentrop, that Hindenburg was not in favour of new elections. Hitler told Ribbentrop to inform the President that there would be no further elections after these. By the afternoon of 29 January, Papen was able to tell Göring and Ribbentrop that all was clear. 'Everything perfect,' Göring reported back to the Kaiserhof. Hitler was expected by the Reich President at eleven o'clock the next morning to be sworn in as Chancellor.

Just before the new cabinet entered the Reich President's chambers, it was finally agreed that they would seek the dissolution order that Hitler so badly wanted. At last, shortly after noon, the members of the Hitler cabinet trooped into the Reich President's rooms. Hindenburg gave a brief welcoming address, expressing satisfaction that the nationalist Right had finally come together. Papen then made the formal introductions. Hindenburg nodded his approval as Hitler solemnly swore to carry out his obligations without party interests and for the good of the whole nation. He again approvingly acknowledged the sentiments expressed by the new Reich Chancellor who, unexpectedly, made a short speech emphasizing his efforts to uphold the Constitution, respect the rights of the President, and, after the next election, to return to normal parliamentary rule. Hitler and his ministers awaited a reply from the Reich President. It came, but in only a single sentence: 'And now, gentlemen, forwards with God.'

V

'Hitler is Reich Chancellor. Just like a fairy-tale,' noted Goebbels. Indeed, the extraordinary had happened. What few beyond the ranks of Nazi fanatics had thought possible less than a year earlier had become reality. Against all odds, Hitler's aggressive obstinacy – born out of lack of alternatives – had paid off. What he had been unable to achieve himself, his 'friends' in high places had achieved for him. The 'nobody of Vienna', 'unknown soldier', beerhall demagogue, head of what was for years no more than a party on the lunatic fringe of politics, a man with no credentials for running a sophisticated state-machine, practically his sole qualification the ability to muster the support of the nationalist masses whose base instincts he showed an unusual talent for rousing, had now been placed in charge of government of one of the leading states in Europe. His intentions had scarcely been kept secret over the years. Whatever the avowals of following a legal path to power, heads would roll, he had said. Marxism would be eradicated, he had said. Jews would be 'removed', he had said. Germany would rebuild the strength of its armed forces, destroy the shackles of Versailles, conquer 'by the sword' the land it needed for its 'living space', he had said. A few took him at his word, and thought he was dangerous. But far, far more, from Right to Left of the political spectrum – conservatives, liberals, socialists, communists – underrated his intentions and unscrupulous power instincts at the same time as they scorned his abilities. The Left's underestimation was at least not responsible for getting him into power. Socialists, communists, trade unions were all little more than by-standers, their scope for influencing events emasculated since 1930. It was the blindness of the conservative Right to the dangers which had been so evident, arising from their determination to eliminate democracy and destroy socialism and the consequent governmental stalemate they had allowed to develop, that delivered the power of a nation-state containing all the pent-up aggression of a wounded giant into the hands of the dangerous leader of a political gangster-mob.

There was no inevitability about Hitler's accession to power. Had Hindenburg been prepared to grant to Schleicher the dissolution that he had so readily allowed Papen, and to prorogue the Reichstag for a period beyond the constitutional sixty days, a Hitler Chancellorship might have been avoided. With the corner turning of the economic Depression, and with the Nazi movement facing potential break-up if power were not soon attained, the future – even if under an authoritarian government – would have been very different. Hitler's rise from humble beginnings to 'seize' power by 'triumph of the will' was the stuff of Nazi legend. In fact, political miscalculation by those with regular access to the corridors of power rather than any actions on the part of the Nazi leader played a larger role in placing him in the Chancellor's seat.

His path ought to have been blocked long before the final drama of January 1933. The most glaring opportunity was missed through the failure to impose a hefty jail sentence after the putsch fiasco of 1923 – and to compound this disastrous omission by releasing him on parole within a matter of months and allowing him a fresh start. But those miscalculations, as well as those during the Depression years that opened up the possibility, then the reality, of a Hitler Chancellorship, were not random acts. They were the miscalculations of a political class determined to inflict what injury it could on (or at least make only the faintest attempts to defend) the new, detested, or at best merely tolerated democratic Republic. The anxiety to destroy democracy rather than the keenness to bring the Nazis to power was what triggered the complex developments that led to Hitler's Chancellorship.

Democracy was surrendered without a fight. This was most notably the case in the collapse of the grand coalition in 1930. It was again the case – however vain the opposition might have proved – in the lack of resistance to the Papen coup against Prussia in July 1932. Both events revealed the flimsiness of democracy's base. This was not least because powerful groups had never reconciled themselves to democracy, and were by this time actively seeking to bring it down. During the Depression, democracy was less surrendered than deliberately undermined by élite groups serving their own ends. These were no pre-industrial leftovers, but – however reactionary their political aims – modern lobbies working to further their vested interests in an authoritarian system. In the final drama, the agrarians and the army were more influential than big business in engineering Hitler's takeover. But big business, also, politically myopic and self-serving, had significantly contributed to the undermining of democracy which was the necessary prelude to Hitler's success.

The masses, too, had played their part in democracy's downfall.

Never had circumstances been less propitious for the establishment of successful democracy than they were in Germany after the First World War. Already by 1920, the parties most supportive of democracy held only a minority of the vote. Democracy narrowly survived its early travails, though great swathes of the electorate opposed it root and branch. Who is to say that, had not the great Depression blown it completely off course, democracy might not have settled down and consolidated itself? But democracy was in a far from healthy state when the Depression struck Germany. And in the course of the Depression, the masses deserted democracy in their droves. By 1932, the only supporters of democracy were the weakened Social Democrats (and even many of these were by this time lukewarm), some sections of the Zentrum (which had itself moved sharply to the Right), and a handful of liberals. The Republic was dead. Still open was what sort of authoritarian system would replace it.

The ruling groups did not have the mass support to maximize their ascendancy and destroy once and for all the power of organized labour. Hitler was brought in to do the job for them. That he might do more than this, that he might outlast all predictions and expand his own power immensely and at their own expense, either did not occur to them, or was regarded as an exceedingly unlikely outcome. The underestimation of Hitler and his movement by the power-brokers remains a leitmotiv of the intrigues that placed him in the Chancellor's office.

The mentalities which conditioned the behaviour both of the élites and of the masses, and which made Hitler's rise possible, were products of strands of German political culture that were plainly recognizable in the twenty years or so before the First World War. Even so, Hitler was no inexorable product of a German 'special path', no logical culmination of long-term trends in specifically German culture and ideology.

Nor was he a mere 'accident' in the course of German history. Without the unique conditions in which he came to prominence, Hitler would have been nothing. It is hard to imagine him bestriding the stage of history at any other time. His style, his brand of rhetoric, would, deprived of such conditions, have been without appeal. The impact on the German people of war, revolution, and national humiliation, and the acute fear of Bolshevism in wide sections of the population gave Hitler his platform. He exploited the conditions brilliantly. More than any other politician of his era, he was the spokesman for the unusually intense fears, resentments, and prejudices of ordinary people not attracted by the parties of the Left or anchored in the parties of political Catholicism. And more than any other politician of his era, he offered such people the prospect of a new and better society – though one seeming to rest on 'true' German values with which they could identify. The vision of the future went hand in hand with the denunciation of the past in Hitler's appeal. The total collapse of confidence in a state system resting on discredited party politics and bureaucratic administration had led over a third of the population to place its trust and its hopes in the politics of national redemption. The personality cult carefully nurtured around Hitler turned him into the embodiment of such hopes.

Whatever the future held, for those who could not share the delirium of the SA hordes marching through the Brandenburg Gate in celebration on the evening of 30 January 1933, it was at best uncertain. 'A leap into the dark' was how one Catholic newspaper described Hitler's appointment to the Chancellorship.

Many Jews and political opponents of the Nazis now feared for their well-being – even for their lives. Some made hurried plans to leave the country. There were those, not just on the defeated Left, who foresaw disaster. But others rapidly shook off their initial foreboding, convincing themselves that Hitler and the Nazis had few prospects of ruling for long. Sebastian Haffner, then a young Berlin lawyer, later – after leaving a country whose government he could no longer tolerate – a distinguished journalist and writer, summarized his views at the time: 'No. All things considered, this government was no cause for concern. It was only a matter of what would come after it, and perhaps the fear that it would lead to civil war.' Most of the serious press, he added, took the same line next day.

Few, indeed, predicted that things would turn out so differently.

IO

The Making of the Dictator

I

Hitler is Reich Chancellor! And what a cabinet!!! One such as we did not dare to dream of in July. Hitler, Hugenberg, Seldte, Papen!!! A large part of my German hopes are attached to each. National Socialist drive, German National reason, the non-political Stahlhelm, and – not forgotten by us – Papen. It is so unimaginably wonderful ... What an achievement by Hindenburg!

This was the ecstatic response of Hamburg schoolteacher Louise Solmitz to the dramatic news of Hitler's appointment to the Chancellorship on 30 January 1933. Like so many who had found their way to Hitler from middle-class, national-conservative backgrounds, she had wavered the previous autumn when she thought he was slipping under the influence of radical socialist tendencies in the party. Now that Hitler was in office, but surrounded by her trusted champions of the conservative Right, heading a government of 'national concentration', her joy was unbounded. The national renewal she longed for could now begin. Many, outside the ranks of diehard Nazi followers, their hopes and ideals invested in the Hitler cabinet, felt the same way.

But millions did not. Fear, anxiety, alarm, implacable hostility, illusory optimism at the regime's early demise, and bold defiance intermingled with apathy, scepticism, condescension towards the presumed inability of the new Chancellor and his Nazi colleagues in the cabinet – and indifference.

Reactions varied according to political views and personal disposition. Alongside misplaced hopes on the Left in the strength and unity of the labour movement went the crass misapprehension of Hitler as no more than the stooge of the 'real' wielders of power, the forces of big capital, as represented by their friends in the cabinet. Influenced by years of warnings from their clergy, the Catholic population were apprehensive and uncertain. Among many Protestant churchgoers there was optimism that national renewal would bring with it inner, moral revitalization. Many ordinary people, after what they had gone through in the Depression, were simply apathetic at the news that Hitler was Chancellor. Those in provincial Germany who were not Nazi fanatics or committed opponents often shrugged their shoulders and carried on with life, doubtful that yet another change of government would bring any improvement. Some thought that Hitler would not even be as long in office as Schleicher, and that his popularity would slump as soon as disillusionment set in on account of the emptiness of Nazi promises. But perceptive critics of Hitler were able to see that, now he enjoyed the prestige of the Chancellorship, he could swifly break down much of the scepticism and win great support by successfully tackling mass unemployment – something which none of his successors had come close to achieving.

For the Nazis themselves, of course, 30 January 1933 was the day they had dreamed about, the triumph they had fought for, the opening of the portals to the brave new world – and the start of what many hoped would be opportunities for prosperity, advancement, and power. Wildly cheering crowds accompanied Hitler on his way back to the Kaiserhof after his appointment with Hindenburg. By seven o'clock that evening Goebbels had improvised a torchlight procession of marching SA and SS men through the centre of Berlin that lasted beyond midnight. He wasted no time in exploiting the newly available facilities of state radio to provide a stirring commentary. He claimed a million men had taken part. The Nazi press halved the number. The British Ambassador estimated a maximum figure of some 50,000. His military attaché thought there were around 15,000. Whatever the numbers, the spectacle was an unforgettable one – exhilarating and intoxicating for Nazi followers, menacing for those at home and abroad who feared the consequences of Hitler in power.

Power had not been 'seized', as Nazi mythology claimed. It had been handed to Hitler, who had been appointed Chancellor by the Reich President in the same manner as had his immediate predecessors. Even so, the orchestrated ovations, which put Hitler himself and other party bosses into a state of ecstasy, signalled that this was no ordinary transfer of power. And almost overnight, those who had misunderstood or misinterpreted the momentous nature of the day's events would realize how wrong they had been. After 30 January 1933, Germany would never be the same again.

That historic day was an end and a beginning. It denoted the expiry of the unlamented Weimar Republic and the culminating point of the comprehensive state crisis that had brought its demise. At the same time Hitler's appointment as Chancellor marked the beginning of the process which was to lead into the abyss of war and genocide, and bring about Germany's own destruction as a nation-state. It signified the start of that astonishingly swift jettisoning of constraints on inhumane behaviour whose path ended in Auschwitz, Treblinka, Sobibor, Majdanek, and the other death camps whose names are synonymous with the horror of Nazism.

Remarkable in the seismic upheavals of 1933–4 was not how much, but how little, the new Chancellor needed to do to bring about the extension and consolidation of his power. Hitler's dictatorship was made as much by others as by himself. As the 'representative figure' of the 'national renewal', Hitler could for the most part function as activator and enabler of the forces he had unleashed, authorizing and legitimating actions taken by others now rushing to implement what they took to be his wishes. 'Working towards the Führer' functioned as the underlying maxim of the regime from the outset.

Hitler was, in fact, in no position to act as an outright dictator when he came to office on 30 January 1933. As long as Hindenburg lived, there was a potential rival source of loyalty – not least for the army. But by summer 1934, when he combined the headship of state with the leadership of government, his power had effectively shed formal constraints on its usage. And, by then, the personality cult built around Hitler had reached new levels of idolatry and made millions of new converts as the 'people's chancellor' – as propaganda had styled him – came to be seen as a national, not merely party, leader. Disdain and detestation for a parliamentary system generally perceived to have failed miserably had resulted in willingness to entrust monopoly control over the state to a leader claiming a unique sense of mission and invested by his mass following with heroic, almost messianic, qualities. Conventional forms of government were, as a consequence, increasingly exposed to the arbitrary inroads of personalized power. It was a recipe for disaster.

II

There were few hints of this at the beginning. Aware that his position was by no means secure, and not wanting to alienate his coalition partners in the government of 'national concentration', Hitler was at first cautious in cabinet meetings, open to suggestions, ready to take advice – not least in complex matters of finance and economic policy – and not dismissive of opposing viewpoints. This only started to change in April and May. In the early weeks, Finance Minister Schwerin von Krosigk, who had met Hitler for the first time when the cabinet was sworn in on 30 January, was not alone in finding him 'polite and calm' in the conduct of government business, well-briefed, backed by a good memory, and able to 'grasp the essentials of a problem', concisely sum up lengthy deliberations, and put a new construction on an issue.

Hitler's cabinet met for the first time at five o'clock on 30 January 1933. The Reich Chancellor began by pointing out that millions greeted with joy the cabinet now formed under his leadership, and asked his colleagues for their support. The cabinet then discussed the political situation. Hitler commented that postponing the recall of the Reichstag – due to meet on 31 January after a two-month break – would not be possible without the Zentrum's support. A Reichstag majority could be achieved by banning the KPD, but this would prove impracticable and might provoke a general strike. He was anxious to avoid any involvement of the Reichswehr in suppressing such a strike – a comment favourably received by Defence Minister Blomberg. The best hope, Hitler went on, was to have the Reichstag dissolved and win a majority for the government in new elections. Only Hugenberg – as unwilling as Hitler to have to rely on the Zentrum, but also aware that new elections would be likely to favour the NSDAP – spoke out expressly in favour of banning the KPD in order to pave the way for an Enabling Act. He doubted that a general strike would take place. He was appeased when Hitler vouched for the fact that the cabinet would remain unchanged after the election. Papen favoured proposing an Enabling Act immediately and reconsidering the position once it had been rejected by the Reichstag. Other ministers, anticipating no promises of support from the Zentrum, preferred new elections to the threat of a general strike. The meeting was adjourned without firm decisions. But Hitler had already outflanked Hugenberg, and won support for what he wanted: the earliest possible dissolution of the Reichstag and new elections.

The following evening, Hindenburg was persuaded to grant Hitler that which he had refused Schleicher only four days earlier: the dissolution of the Reichstag. Hitler had argued, backed by Papen and Meissner, that the people must be given the opportunity to confirm its support for the new government. Though it could attain a majority in the Reichstag as it stood, new elections would produce a larger majority, which in turn would allow a general Enabling Act to be passed, giving a platform for measures to bring about a recovery. The dissolution scarcely conformed to the spirit of the Constitution. Elections were turned into a consequence, not a cause, of the formation of a government. The Reichstag had not even been given the opportunity of demonstrating its confidence (or lack of it) in the new government. A decision which was properly parliament's had been placed directly before the people. In its tendency, it was already a step towards acclamation by plebiscite.

Hitler's opening gambit stretched no further than new elections, to be followed by an Enabling Act. His conservative partners, as keen as he was to end parliamentarism and eliminate the Marxist parties, had played into his hands. On the morning of 1 February he told the cabinet of Hindenburg's agreement to dissolve the Reichstag. The elections were set for 5 March. The Reich Chancellor himself provided the government's slogan: 'Attack on Marxism.' That evening, with his cabinet standing behind him in his room in the Reich Chancellery, wearing a dark blue suit with a black and white tie, sweating profusely from nervousness, and speaking – unusually – in a dull monotone, Hitler addressed the German people for the first time on the radio. The 'Appeal of the Reich Government to the German People' that he read out was full of rhetoric but vacuous in content – the first propaganda shot in the election campaign rather than a stated programme of political measures. Full of pathos, Hitler appealed on behalf of the government to the people to overcome class divisions, and to sign alongside the government an act of reconciliation to permit Germany's resurgence. 'The parties of Marxism and those who went along with them had fourteen years to see what they could do. The result is a heap of ruins. Now, German people, give us four years and then judge and sentence us,' he declared. He ended, as he often concluded major speeches, in pseudo-religious terms, with an appeal to the Almighty to bless the work of the government. With that, the election campaign had begun. It was to be a different campaign from the earlier ones, with the government – already enjoying wide backing – clearly separating itself from all that had preceded it in the Weimar Republic.

Towards the end of his proclamation, Hitler had posed for the first time as a man of peace, stating, despite love of the army as the bearer of arms and symbol of Germany's great past, how happy the government would be 'if through a restriction of its armaments the world should make an increase of our own weapons never again necessary'. His tone when invited by Blomberg to address military leaders gathered in the home of the head of the army General Kurt Freiherr von Hammerstein-Equord on the evening of 3 February was entirely different.

The atmosphere was cool, the attitude of many of the officers reserved, when Hitler began his lengthy speech. But what he said could not fail to find appeal. The build-up of the armed forces was the most important premiss to the central aim of regaining political power. General conscription had to be brought back. Before that, the state leadership had to see to it that all traces of pacifism, Marxism, and Bolshevism were eradicated from those eligible for military service. The armed forces – the most important institution in the state – must be kept out of politics and above party. The internal struggle was not its concern, and could be left to the organizations of the Nazi movement. Preparations for the build-up of the armed forces had to take place without delay. This period was the most dangerous, and Hitler held out the possibility of a preventive strike from France, probably together with its allies in the east. 'How should political power, once won, be used?' he asked. It was still too early to say. Perhaps the attainment of new export possibilities should be the goal, he hinted. But since earlier in the speech he had already dismissed the notion of increasing exports as the solution to Germany's problems, this could not be taken by his audience as a favoured suggestion. 'Perhaps – and probably better – conquest of new living space in the east and its ruthless Germanization' was his alternative. The officers present could have been left in no doubt that this was Hitler's preference.

Hitler's sole aim at Hammerstein's had been to woo the officers and ensure army support. He largely succeeded. There was no opposition to what he had said. And many of those present, as Admiral Erich Raeder later commented, found Hitler's speech 'extraordinarily satisfying'. This was hardly surprising. However disdainful they were of the vulgar and loudmouthed social upstart, the prospect he held out of restoring the power of the army as the basis for expansionism and German dominance accorded with aims laid down by the army leadership even in what they had seen as the dark days of 'fulfilment policy' in the mid-1920s.

The strong man in Blomberg's ministry, his Chief of the Ministerial Office, Colonel Walther von Reichenau – bright, ambitious, 'progressive' in his contempt for class-ridden aristocratic and bourgeois conservatism, and long a National Socialist sympathizer – was sure of how the army should react to what Hitler offered. 'It has to be recognized that we are in a revolution,' he remarked. 'What is rotten in the state has to go, and that can only happen through terror. The party will ruthlessly proceed against Marxism. Task of the armed forces: stand at ease. No support if those persecuted seek refuge with the troops.' Though not for the most part as actively sympathetic towards National Socialism as was Reichenau, the leaders of the army which had blocked by force Hitler's attempt to seize power in 1923 had now, within days of his appointment as Chancellor, placed the most powerful institution in the state at his disposal.

Hitler, for his part, lost no time in making plain to the cabinet that military spending was to be given absolute priority. During a discussion in cabinet on 8 February on the financial implications of building a dam in Upper Silesia, he intervened to tell his cabinet colleagues that 'the next five years must be devoted to the restoration of the defence capacity of the German people'. Every state-funded work-creation scheme had to be judged with regard to its necessity for this end. 'This idea must always and everywhere be placed in the foreground.'

These early meetings, within days of Hitler becoming Chancellor, were crucial in determining the primacy of rearmament. They were also typical for the way Hitler operated, and for the way his power was exercised. Keen though Blomberg and the Reichswehr leadership were to profit from the radically different approach of the new Chancellor to armaments spending, there were practical limitations – financial, organizational, and not least those of international restrictions while the disarmament talks continued – preventing the early stages of rearmament being pushed through as rapidly as Hitler wanted. But where Blomberg was content at first to work for expansion within the realms of the possible, Hitler thought in different – initially quite unrealistic – dimensions. He offered no concrete measures. But his dogmatic assertion of absolute primacy for rearmament, opposed or contradicted by not a single minister, set new ground-rules for action. With Hjalmar Schacht succeeding Hans Luther in March as President of the Reichsbank, Hitler found the person he needed to mastermind the secret and unlimited funding of rearmament. Where the Reichswehr budget had on average been 700–800 million RM a year, Schacht, through the device of Mefo-Bills – a disguised discounting of government bills by the Reichsbank – was soon able to guarantee to the Reichswehr the fantastic sum of 35 billion RM over an eight-year period.

Given this backing, after a sluggish start, the rearmament programme took off stratospherically in 1934. The decision to give absolute priority to rearmament was the basis of the pact, resting on mutual benefit, between Hitler and the army which, though frequently troubled, was a key foundation of the Third Reich. Hitler established the parameters in February 1933. But these were no more than the expression of the entente he had entered into with Blomberg on becoming Chancellor. The new policy was possible because Hitler had bound himself to the interests of the most powerful institution in the land. The army leaders, for their part, had their interests served because they had bound themselves, in their eyes, to a political front-man who could nationalize the masses and restore the army to its rightful power-position in the state. What they had not reckoned with was that within five years the traditional power-élite of the officers corps would be transformed into a mere functional élite, serving a political master who was taking it into uncharted territory.

III

In the first weeks of his Chancellorship, Hitler took steps to bring not just the 'big battalions' of the army leadership behind the new regime, but also the major organizations of economic leaders. Landholders needed little persuasion. Their main organization, the Reich Agrarian League (Reichslandbund) – dominated by East Elbian estate-owners – had been strongly pro-Nazi before Hitler became Chancellor. Hitler left agrarian policy in its initial stage to his German National coalition partner Hugenberg. Early measures taken in February to defend indebted farm property against creditors and to protect agricultural produce by imposing higher import duties and provide support for grain prices ensured that the agrarians were not disappointed. With Hugenberg at the Economics Ministry, their interests seemed certain to be well looked after.

The initial scepticism, hesitancy, and misgivings of most business leaders immediately following Hitler's accession to the Chancellorship were not dispelled overnight. There was still considerable disquiet in the business community when Gustav Krupp von Bohlen und Halbach, head of the mighty Krupp's iron and steel concern and chairman of the Reich Association of German Industry, and other leading industrialists received invitations to a meeting at Göring's official residence on 20 February, at which Hitler would outline his economic policy. Krupp, up to then critical of Hitler, went to the meeting prepared, as he had done at meetings with previous Chancellors, to speak up for industry. In particular, he intended to stress the need for export-led growth and to underline the damaging consequences of protectionism in favour of agriculture. In the event, he could make neither point. The businessmen were kept waiting by Göring, and had to wait even longer till Hitler appeared. They were then treated to a classic Hitler monologue. In a speech lasting an hour and a half, he barely touched on economic matters, except in the most general sense. He assuaged his business audience, as he had done on earlier occasions, by upholding private property and individual enterprise, and by denying rumours of planned radical experimentation in the economy. The rest was largely a restatement of his views on the subordination of the economy to politics, the need to eradicate Marxism, restore inner strength and unity, and thus be in a position to face external enemies. The coming election marked a final chance to reject Communism by the ballot-box. If that did not happen, force – he darkly hinted – would be used. It was a fight to the death between the nation and Communism, a struggle that would decide Germany's fate for the next century. When Hitler had finished, Krupp felt in no position to deliver his prepared speech. He merely improvised a few words of thanks and added some general remarks about a strong state serving the well-being of the country. At this point, Hitler left.

The hidden agenda of the meeting became clear once Göring started speaking. He repeated Hitler's assurances that economic experiments need not be feared, and that the balance of power would not be altered by the coming election – to be the last for perhaps a hundred years. But the election, he claimed, was nonetheless crucial. And those not in the forefront of the political battle had a responsibility to make financial sacrifices. Once Göring, too, had left, Schacht bade those present to visit the cash-till. Three million marks were pledged, and within weeks delivered. With this donation, big business was helping consolidate Hitler's rule. But the offering was less one of enthusiastic backing than of political extortion.

Despite their financial support, industrialists continued at first to look with a wary eye at the new regime. But its members were already realizing that their position was also not left untouched by the changes sweeping over Germany. In early April, Krupp capitulated to Nazi pressure to replace the Reich Association by a new, nazified body, for the dismissal of Jewish employees, and the removal of all Jewish businessmen from representative positions in commerce and industry. The following month, the once-mighty Association dissolved itself and was replaced by the nazified Reich Estate of German Industry (Reichsstand der Deutschen Industrie). Alongside such pressure, business recovery, high profits, secure private property (apart from that of Jewish businessmen), the crushing of Marxism, and the subduing of labour saw big business increasingly content to adjust to full collaboration with the new regime, whatever the irksome bureaucratic controls imposed on it.

Hitler's style, as the industrialists experienced on 20 February, was certainly different from that of his predecessors in the Chancellor's office. His views on the economy were also unconventional. He was wholly ignorant of any formal understanding of the principles of economics. For him, as he stated to the industrialists, economics was of secondary importance, entirely subordinated to politics. His crude social-Darwinism dictated his approach to the economy, as it did his entire political 'world-view'. Since struggle among nations would be decisive for future survival, Germany's economy had to be subordinated to the preparation, then carrying out, of this struggle. That meant that liberal ideas of economic competition had to be replaced by the subjection of the economy to the dictates of the national interest. Similarly, any 'socialist' ideas in the Nazi programme had to follow the same dictates. Hitler was never a socialist. But although he upheld private property, individual entrepreneurship, and economic competition, and disapproved of trade unions and workers' interference in the freedom of owners and managers to run their concerns, the state, not the market, would determine the shape of economic development. Capitalism was, therefore, left in place. But in operation it was turned into an adjunct of the state.

Lacking, as he did, a grasp of even the rudiments of economic theory, Hitler can scarcely be regarded as an economic innovator. The extraordinary economic recovery that rapidly formed an essential component of the Führer myth was not of Hitler's making. He showed no initial interest in the work-creation plans eagerly developed by civil servants in the Labour Ministry. With Schacht (at this stage) sceptical, Hugenberg opposed, Seldte taking little initiative, and industry hostile, Hitler did nothing to further the work-creation schemes before the end of May. By then, they had been taken up by the State Secretary in the Finance Ministry, Fritz Reinhardt, and put forward as a programme for action. Even at this stage, Hitler remained hesitant, and had to be convinced that the programme would not lead to renewed inflation. Finally, on 31 May, Hitler summoned ministers and economic experts to the Reich Chancellery, and heard that all but Hugenberg were in favour of the Reinhardt Programme. The following day, the 'Law for Reduction of Unemployment' was announced. Schacht now conjured up the necessary short-term credits. The rest was largely the work of bankers, civil servants, planners, and industrialists. As public works schemes initially, then increasingly rearmament, began to pull Germany out of recession and wipe away mass unemployment more quickly than any forecasters had dared speculate, Hitler garnered the full propaganda benefit.

But indirectly Hitler did make a significant contribution to the economic recovery by reconstituting the political framework for business activity and by the image of national renewal that he represented. The ruthless assault on Marxism and reordering of industrial relations which he presided over, the work-creation programme that he eventually backed, and the total priority for rearmament laid down at the outset, helped to shape a climate in which economic recovery – already starting as he took office as Chancellor – could gather pace. And in one area, at least, he provided a direct stimulus to recovery in a key branch of industry: motor-car manufacturing.

Hitler's propaganda instinct, not his economic know-how, led him towards an initiative that both assisted the recovery of the economy and caught the public imagination. On 11 February, a few days before his meeting with the industrialists, Hitler had sought out the opportunity to deliver the opening address at the International Automobile and Motor-Cycle Exhibition in Berlin. That the German Chancellor should make the speech was itself a novelty: this alone caused a stir. The assembled leaders of the car industry were delighted. They were even more delighted when they heard Hitler elevate car manufacture to the position of the most important industry of the future and promise a programme including gradual tax relief for the industry and the implementation of a 'generous plan for road-building'. If living standards had previously been weighed against kilometres of railway track, they would in future be measured against kilometres of roads; these were 'great tasks which also belong to the construction programme of the German economy', Hitler declared. The speech was later stylized by Nazi propaganda as 'the turning-point in the history of German motorization'. It marked the beginning of the 'Autobahn-builder' part of the Führer myth.

Hitler had, in fact, offered no specific programme for the car industry; merely the prospect of one. Even so, the significance of Hitler's speech on 11 February should not be underrated. It sent positive signals to car manufacturers. They were struck by the new Chancellor, whose long-standing fascination for the motor-car and his memory for detail of construction-types and -figures meant he sounded not only sympathetic but knowledgeable to the car bosses. The *Völkischer Beobachter*, exploiting the propaganda potential of Hitler's speech, immediately opened up to its readers the prospect of car-ownership. Not a social élite with its Rolls-Royces, but the mass of the people with their people's car (*Volksauto*) was the alluring prospect.

In the weeks following his speech, there were already notable signs that the car industry was picking up. The beginnings of recovery for the automobile industry had spin-off effects for factories producing component parts, and for the metal industry. The recovery was not part of a well-conceived programme on Hitler's part. Nor can it be wholly, or even mainly, attributed to his speech. Much of it would have happened anyway, once the slump had begun to give way to cyclical recovery. It remains the case, however, that the car manufacturers were still gloomy about their prospects before Hitler spoke.

Hitler, whatever importance he had attached to the propaganda effect of his speech, had given the right signals to the industry. After the 'gigantic progamme' of road-building he announced on 1 May had met substantial obstacles in the Transport Ministry, Hitler insisted that the

'Reich Motorways Enterprise' be carried through. This was eventually placed at the end of June in the hands of Fritz Todt as General Inspector for German Roadways. In the stimulus to the car trade and the building of the motorways – areas which, inspired by the American model, had great popular appeal and appeared to symbolize both the leap forward into an exciting, technological modern era and the 'new Germany', now standing on its own feet again – Hitler had made a decisive contribution.

IV

By the time Hitler addressed the leaders of the automobile industry on 11 February, the Reichstag election campaign was under way. Hitler had opened it the previous evening with his first speech in the Sportpalast since becoming Chancellor. He promised a government that would not lie to and swindle the people as Weimar governments had done. Parties of class division would be destroyed. 'Never, never will I depart from the task of eradicating from Germany Marxism and its accompaniments,' he declared. National unity, resting on the German peasant and the German worker – restored to the national community – would be the basis of the future society. It was, he declared, 'a programme of national revival in all areas of life, intolerant towards anyone who sins against the nation, brother and friend to anyone willing to fight alongside for the resurrection of his people, of our nation'. Hitler reached the rhetorical climax of his speech. 'German people, give us four years, then judge and sentence us. German people, give us four years, and I swear that as we and I entered into this office, I will then be willing to go.'

It was a powerful piece of rhetoric. But it was little more than that. The 'programme' offered nothing concrete – other than the showdown with Marxism. National 'resurrection' to be brought about through will, strength, and unity was what it amounted to. For all nationalists – not just for Nazis – the sentiments Hitler expressed could not fail to find appeal.

The accompaniment to the campaign was a wave of unparalleled state-sponsored terror and repression against political opponents in states under Nazi control. Above all, this was the case in the huge state of Prussia, which had already come under Reich control in the Papen takeover of 20 July 1932. The orchestrator here was the commissary

Prussian Minister of the Interior Hermann Göring. Under his aegis, heads of the Prussian police and administration were 'cleansed' (following the first purges after the Papen coup) of the remainder of those who might prove obstacles in the new wind of change that was blowing. Göring provided their successors with verbal instructions in unmistakably blunt language of what he expected of police and administration during the election campaign. And in a written decree of 17 February, he ordered the police to work together with the 'national associations' of SA, SS, and Stahlhelm, support 'national propaganda with all their strength', and combat the actions of 'organizations hostile to the state' with all the force at their disposal, 'where necessary making ruthless use of firearms'. He added that policemen using firearms would, whatever the consequences, be backed by him; those failing in their duty out of a 'false sense of consideration' had, on the contrary, to expect disciplinary action. Unsurprisingly in such a climate, the violence unleashed by Nazi terror bands against their opponents and against Jewish victims was uncontrolled. This was especially the case once the SA, SS, and Stahlhelm had been brought in on 22 February as 'auxiliary police' on the pretext of an alleged increase in 'left-radical' violence. Intimidation was massive. Communists were particularly savagely repressed. Individuals were brutally beaten, tortured, seriously wounded, or killed, with total impunity. Communist meetings and demonstrations were banned, in Prussia and in other states under Nazi control, as were their newspapers. Bans, too, on organs of the SPD and restrictions on reporting imposed on other newspapers effectively muzzled the press, even when the bans were successfully challenged in the courts as illegal, and the newspapers reinstated.

During this first orgy of state violence, Hitler played the moderate. His acting ability was undiminished. He gave the cabinet the impression that radical elements in the movement were disobeying his orders but that he would bring them under control, and asked for patience to allow him to discipline the sections of the party that had got out of hand.

Hitler had no need to involve himself in the violence of February 1933. Its deployment could be left safely to Göring, and to leading Nazis in other states. In any case, it needed only the green light to Nazi thugs, sure now of the protection of the state, to unleash their pent-up aggression against those well known to them as long-standing enemies in their neighbourhoods and work-places. The terror-wave in Prussia in

February was the first sign that state-imposed constraints on inhumanity were now suddenly lifted. It was an early indicator of the 'breach of civilization' that would give the Third Reich its historical character.

But it was not that the brutality and violence damaged Hitler's reputation in the population. Many who had been initially sceptical or critical were beginning, during February, to think that Hitler was 'the right man', and should be given a chance. A slight upturn in the economy helped. But the fervent anti-Marxism of much of the population was more important. The long-standing hatred of Socialism and Communism – both bracketed together as 'Marxism' – was played upon by Nazi propaganda and turned into outright anti-Communist paranoia. Pumped up by the Nazis, fear of a Communist rising was in the air. The closer the election came, the shriller grew the hysteria.

The violence and intimidation would probably have continued in much the same vein until the election on 5 March. Nothing suggests the Nazi leadership had anything more spectacular in mind. But on 27 February, Marinus van der Lubbe set fire to the Reichstag.

Marinus van der Lubbe came from a Dutch working-class family, and had formerly belonged to the Communist Party youth organization in Holland. He had eventually broken with the Communist Party in 1931. He arrived in Berlin on 18 February 1933. He was twenty-four years old, intelligent, a solitary individual, unconnected with any political groups, but possessed of a strong sense of injustice at the misery of the working class at the hands of the capitalist system. In particular, he was determined to make a lone and spectacular act of defiant protest at the 'Government of National Concentration' in order to galvanize the working class into struggle against their repression. Three attempts at arson on 25 February in different buildings in Berlin failed. Two days later he succeeded in his protest – though the consequences were scarcely those he had envisaged.

On the evening of 27 February, Putzi Hanfstaengl should have been dining at Goebbels's house, along with Hitler. But, suffering from a heavy cold and high temperature, he had taken to his bed in a room in Göring's official residence, where he was temporarily accommodated, in the immediate vicinity of the Reichstag building. In mid-evening he was awakened by the cries of the housekeeper: the Reichstag was on fire. He shot out of bed, looked out of the window, saw the building in flames, and immediately rushed to ring up Goebbels, saying, breathlessly, that he urgently had to speak to Hitler. When Goebbels asked what it was about, and whether he could pass on a message, Hanfstaengl said: 'Tell him the Reichstag is burning.' 'Is that meant to be a joke?' was Goebbels's reply. Goebbels thought it was 'a mad fantasy report' and refused at first to tell Hitler. But his inquiries revealed that the report was true. At that, Hitler and Goebbels raced through Berlin, to find Göring already on the scene and 'in full flow'. Papen soon joined them. The Nazi leaders were all convinced that the fire was a signal for a Communist uprising – a 'last attempt', as Goebbels put it, 'through fire and terror to sow confusion in order in the general panic to grasp power for themselves'. Fears that the Communists would not remain passive, that they would undertake some major show of force before the election, had been rife among the Nazi leadership – and among non-Nazi members of the national government. A police raid on the KPD's central offices in Karl-Liebknecht House on 24 February had intensified the anxieties. Though they actually found nothing of note, the police claimed to have found vast amounts of treasonable material, including leaflets summoning the population to armed revolt. Göring added to this with a statement to the press. The police discoveries showed that Germany was about to be cast into the chaos of Bolshevism, he alleged. Assassinations of political leaders, attacks on public buildings, and the murder of wives and families of public figures were among the horrors he evoked. No evidence was ever made public.

The first members of the police to interrogate van der Lubbe, who had been immediately apprehended and had straight away confessed, proclaiming his 'protest', had no doubt that he had set fire to the building alone, that no one else was implicated. But Göring took little convincing from officials on the spot that the fire must have been the product of a Communist plot. Hitler, who arrived towards 10.30 p.m., an hour or so after Göring, was rapidly persuaded to draw the same conclusion. He told Papen: 'This is a God-given signal, Herr Vice-Chancellor! If this fire, as I believe, is the work of the Communists, then we must crush out this murderous pest with an iron fist!' The Communist deputies were to be hanged that very night, he raged. Nor was any mercy to be shown to the Social Democrats or Reichsbanner.

Hitler then went to an improvised meeting around 11.15 p.m. in the Prussian Ministry of the Interior, dealing mainly with security implications for Prussia, and from there accompanied Goebbels to the Berlin offices of the *Völkischer Beobachter*, where an inflammatory editorial was rapidly prepared and a new front page of the party newspaper made up.

At the meeting in the Prussian Ministry of the Interior, it was the German National State Secretary Ludwig Grauert, firmly convinced himself that the Communists had set the Reichstag alight, who proposed an emergency decree for the State of Prussia aimed at arson and acts of terror. By the following morning, however, Reich Minister of the Interior Wilhelm Frick had come up with the draft of a decree 'For the Protection of People and State' which extended the emergency measures to the whole of the Reich – something attributed by Blomberg to Hitler's presence of mind – and gave the Reich government powers of intervention in the Länder. The road to dictatorship was now wide open.

The emergency decree 'For the Protection of People and State' was the last item dealt with by the cabinet at its meeting on the morning of 28 February. With one brief paragraph, the personal liberties enshrined in the Weimar Constitution – including freedom of speech, of association, and of the press, and privacy of postal and telephone communications – were suspended indefinitely. With another brief paragraph, the autonomy of the Länder was overridden by the right of the Reich government to intervene to restore order. This right would be made ample use of in the immediate aftermath of the election to ensure Nazi control throughout all the German states. The hastily constructed emergency decree amounted to the charter of the Third Reich.

By the time of the cabinet meeting, Hitler's near-hysterical mood of the previous evening had given way to colder ruthlessness. The 'psychologically correct moment for the showdown' with the KPD had arrived. It was pointless to wait longer, he told the cabinet. The struggle against the Communists should not be dependent on 'juristical considerations'. There was no likelihood that this would be the case. The rounding up of Communist deputies and functionaries had already been set in train by Göring during the night in raids carried out with massive brutality. Communists were the main targets. But Social Democrats, trade unionists, and left-wing intellectuals such as Carl Ossietzky were also among those dragged into improvised prisons, often in the cellars of SA or SS local headquarters, and savagely beaten, tortured, and in some cases murdered. By April, the number taken into 'protective custody' in Prussia alone numbered some 25,000.

The violence and repression were widely popular. The 'emergency decree' that took away all personal liberties and established the platform for dictatorship was warmly welcomed. Louise Solmitz, like her friends and neighbours, was persuaded to cast her vote for Hitler. 'Now it's important to support what he's doing with every means,' an acquaintance who had up to then not supported the NSDAP told her. 'The entire thoughts and feelings of most Germans are dominated by Hitler,' Frau Solmitz commented. 'His fame rises to the stars, he is the saviour of a wicked, sad German world.'

On 4 March, Hitler made a final, impassioned plea to the electorate in a speech broadcast from Königsberg. When the results were declared the next day, the Nazis had won 43.9 per cent of the vote, giving them 288 out of 647 seats in the new Reichstag. Their nationalist coalition partners had gained 8.0 per cent. Despite the draconian terror, the KPD had still managed an astonishing 12.3 per cent, and the SPD 18.3 per cent – together the parties of the Left, even now, gaining almost a third of all votes cast. The Zentrum received only a marginally smaller proportion of the vote (11.2 per cent) than it had done the previous November. Support for the remaining parties had dwindled almost to nothing. Goebbels claimed the result as a 'glorious triumph'. It was rather less than that. Substantial gains had been certain. They had undoubtedly been assisted by a late surge following the Reichstag fire. Hitler had hoped for an absolute majority for the NSDAP. As it was, the absolute majority narrowly attained by the government coalition left him dependent on his conservative allies. He would now not be rid of them at least as long as Hindenburg lived, he was reported as saying on hearing the results. Still, even allowing for the climate of intense repression against the Left, 43.9 per cent of the vote was not easy to attain under the Weimar electoral system. The NSDAP had profited above all from the support of previous non-voters in a record turnout of 88.8 per cent. And though the heaviest support continued to come from Protestant parts of the country, sizeable gains had this time also been made in Catholic areas which the NSDAP had earlier found difficult to penetrate. Not least: leaving aside the Left, not all those who voted for parties other than the NSDAP were opposed to everything that Hitler stood for. Once Hitler, the pluralist system liquidated, was able to transform his public image from party to national leader, a potentially far larger reservoir of support than that given to him in March 1933 would be at his disposal.

V

The election of 5 March was the trigger to the real 'seizure of power' that took place over the following days in those Länder not already under Nazi control. Hitler needed to do little. Party activists needed no encouragement to undertake the 'spontaneous' actions that inordinately strengthened his power as Reich Chancellor.

The pattern was in each case similar: pressure on the non-Nazi state governments to place a National Socialist in charge of the police; threatening demonstrations from marching SA and SS troops in the big cities; the symbolic raising of the swastika banner on town halls; the capitulation with scarcely any resistance of the elected governments; the imposition of a Reich Commissar under the pretext of restoring order. The 'coordination' process began in Hamburg even before the election had taken place. In Bremen, Lübeck, Schaumburg-Lippe, Hesse, Baden, Württemberg, Saxony, and finally Bavaria – the largest state after Prussia – the process was repeated. Between 5 and 9 March these states, too, were brought in line with the Reich government. In Bavaria, in particular, long-standing acolytes of Hitler were appointed as commissary government ministers: Adolf Wagner in charge of the Ministry of the Interior, Hans Frank as Justice Minister, Hans Schemm as Education Minister. Even more significant were the appointments of Ernst Röhm as State Commissar without Portfolio, Heinrich Himmler as commander of the Munich police, and Reinhard Heydrich – the tall, blond head of the party's Security Service (Sicherheitsdienst, SD), a cashiered naval officer, still under thirty, in the early stages of his meteoric rise to command over the security police in the SS empire – as head of the Bavarian Political Police. The weakening of Prussia through the Papen coup and the effective Nazi takeover there in February provided the platform and model for the extension of control to the other Länder. These now passed more or less completely into Nazi hands, with little regard for the German Nationalist partners. Despite the semblance of legality, the usurpation of the powers of the Länder by the Reich was a plain breach of the Constitution. Force and pressure by the Nazi organizations themselves – political blackmail – had been solely responsible for creating the 'unrest' that had prompted the alleged restoration of 'order'. The terms of the emergency decree of 28 February provided

ADOLF HITLER

Mögen Jahrtausende vergehen, so wird man nie von Heldentum reden dürfen, ohne des deutschen Heeres des Weltkrieges zu gedenken.

28. (*previous page*) Hitler in SA uniform (rejected), 1928/9.

29. (*left*) Hitler in rhetorical pose. Postcard from August 1927. The caption reads: 'In the passing of thousands of years, heroism will never be spoken of without remembering the German army of the world war'.

30. Hitler speaking to the NSDAP leadership, Munich, 30 August 1928. *Left to right*: Alfred Rosenberg, Walter Buch, Franz Xaver Schwarz, Hitler, Gregor Strasser, Heinrich Himmler. Sitting by the door, hands clasped, is Julius Streicher: to his left is Robert Ley.

31. Geli Raubal and Hitler, *c.* 1930.

32. Eva Braun in Heinrich Hoffmann's studio, early 1930s.

33. (*facing page*) Reich President Paul von Hindenburg.

34. (*facing page*) Reich Chancellor Heinrich Brüning (*left*) with Benito Mussolini, Rome, August 1931.

35. Reich Chancellor Franz von Papen (*front, right*), with State Secretary Dr Otto Meissner, at the annual celebration of the Reich Constitution, 11 August 1932. Behind von Papen is Reich Minister of the Interior Wilhelm Freiherr von Gayl, who, that very day, put forward proposals to make Weimar's liberal constitution distinctly more authoritarian.

36. Gregor Strasser and Joseph Goebbels watching the SA parade past Hitler, Braunschweig, 18 October 1931.

37. Ernst Thälmann, leader of the KPD, at a rally of the 'Red Front' during the growing crisis of Weimar democracy, *c.* 1930.

38. Nazi election poster, 1932, directed against the SPD and the Jews. The slogan reads: 'Marxism is the Guardian Angel of Capitalism. Vote National Socialist, List 1'.

39. Candidate placards for the presidential election, Berlin, April 1932.

40. Discussion at Neudeck, the home of Reich President Paul von Hindenburg, 1932. *Left to right*: Reich Chancellor Franz von Papen, State Secretary Otto Meissner (back to camera), Reich Minister of the Interior Wilhelm von Gayl, Hindenburg, and Reichswehr Minister Kurt von Schleicher.

41. Reich Chancellor Kurt von Schleicher speaking in the Berlin Sportpalast, 15 January 1933.

42. A photo taken of Hitler in the Kaiserhof Hotel, Berlin, in January 1933, just before his appointment as Chancellor, to test how he looked in evening dress.

43. The 'Day of Potsdam', 21 March 1933: a deferential Hitler bows to Reich President von Hindenburg.

44. SA violence against Communists in Chemnitz, March 1933.

45. The boycott of Jewish doctors, April 1933. The stickers read:
'Take note: Jew. Visiting Forbidden'.

46. An elderly Jew being taken into custody by police in Berlin, 1934.

47. Hindenburg and Hitler on their way to the rally in Berlin's Lustgarten on the 'Day of National Labour', 1 May 1933. The following day, the trades union movement was destroyed.

48. Hitler with Ernst Röhm at a parade of the SA in summer 1933, as problems with the SA began to emerge.

Was
der König eroberte,
der Fürst formte,
der Feldmarschall verteidigte,
rettete und einigte der Soldat.

Hans vom Norden
Nachdruck verboten

DER FÜHRER ALS TIERFREUND

49. The Führer cult: a postcard, designed by Hans von Norden in 1933, showing Hitler in a direct line from Frederick the Great, Otto von Bismarck, and Paul von Hindenburg. The caption reads: 'What the King conquered, the Prince shaped, the Field Marshal defended, the Soldier saved and united'.

50. The Führer cult: 'The Führer as animal-lover', postcard, 1934.

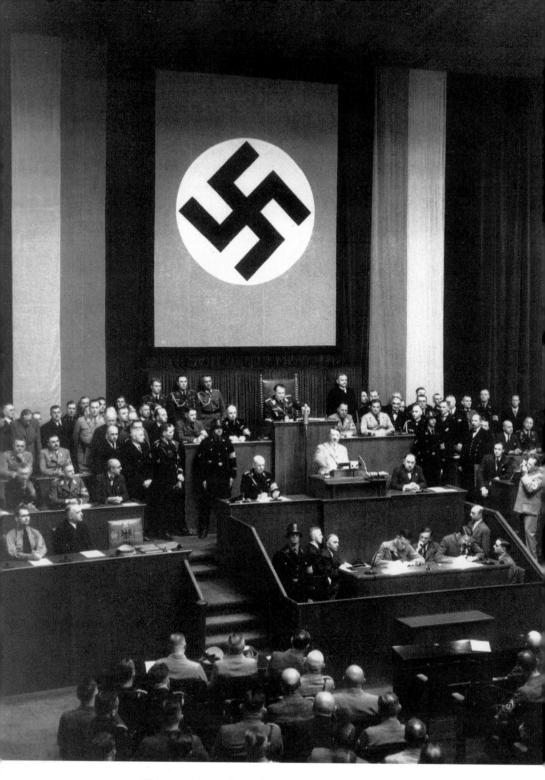

51. Hitler justifying the 'Röhm purge' to the Reichstag, 13 July 1934.

52. Hitler, Professor Leonhard Gall, and architect Albert Speer inspecting the half-built 'House of German Art' in Munich. Undated cigarette-card, *c.* 1935.

53. Hitler with young Bavarians. Behind him (*right*) in Bavarian costume, Hitler-Youth leader Baldur von Schirach. Undated photograph.

54. The Mercedes-Benz showroom at Lenbachplatz, Munich, April 1935.

55. Hitler during a visit to the Ruhr in 1935, accompanied (*left to right*) by his valet, Karl Krause, and the leading industrialists Albert Vögler, Fritz Thyssen (his photo a later insertion?), and Walter Borbet, all important executives of the United Steel Works.

56. 'Hitler in his Mountains': cover of a Heinrich Hoffmann publication of 1935, featuring 88 photographs of the Führer in picturesque settings.

57. The swearing-in of new recruits at the Feldherrnhalle in Odeonsplatz, Munich, on the anniversary of the putsch, 7 November 1935.

58. German troops entering the demilitarized Rhineland across the
Hohenzollern Bridge in Cologne, 7 March 1936.

no justification since there was plainly no need for defence from any 'communist acts of violence endangering the state'. The only such acts were those of the Nazis themselves.

In the triumphalist atmosphere following the election, the open violence of rampant bands of Nazi thugs prompted protests from high quarters to the Reich President as well as to Hitler himself. Hitler responded in characteristic vein with an aggressive defence of his SA men in response to Papen's complaints about affronts to foreign diplomats, prompted by an incident where a mob (including SA and SS men) had behaved threateningly towards the wives of prominent diplomats, beating up one of their chauffeurs, and tearing the flag from the car of the Romanian ambassador. He had the impression, he said, that the bourgeoisie had been rescued too early. Had they experienced six weeks of Bolshevism, then they would have 'learnt the difference between the red revolution and our uprising. I once graphically saw this difference in Bavaria and have never forgotten it. And I will not let myself be taken away by anyone at all from the mission that I repeatedly announced before the election: the annihilation and eradication of Marxism'. Even so, the violence was becoming counter-productive. On 10 March, directly referring to harassment of foreigners but blaming it on Communist provocateurs, Hitler proclaimed that from this day on, the national government controlled executive power in the whole of Germany, and that the future course of the 'national uprising' would be 'directed from above, according to plan'. All molesting of individuals, obstruction of automobiles, and disturbances to business life had to stop as a matter of principle. He repeated the sentiments in a radio address two days later. The exhortations had little effect.

The levels of terror and repression experienced in February in Prussia had by then wracked the rest of the country. Under the aegis of Himmler and Heydrich, the scale of arrests in Bavaria was proportionately even greater than it had been in Prussia. Around 10,000 Communists and Socialists were arrested in March and April. By June, the numbers in 'protective custody' – most of them workers – had doubled. A good number of those arrested were the victims of denunciations by neighbours or workmates. So great was the wave of denunciations following the Malicious Practices Act of 21 March 1933 that even the police criticized it. Just outside the town of Dachau, about twelve miles from Munich, the first concentration camp, intended for Marxist functionaries, was set up in a former powder-mill on 22 March. Its dreaded name soon became a byword for the largely unspoken horrifying events known or presumed to take place within its walls.

A day earlier, the regime had showed its other face. If keen to keep at one remove from the shows of terror, Hitler was again in his element at the centre of another propaganda spectacular. This was the 'Day of Potsdam', a further masterly concoction of the newly appointed Reich Minister of People's Enlightenment and Propaganda, Joseph Goebbels. In complete detachment from the sordid bestialities in the brutal show-down with the Left, National Socialism here put on its best clothes, and proclaimed its union with Prussian conservatism.

The 'Day of Potsdam' was to represent the start of the new Reich building upon the glories of the old. It was also to denote the forging of the links between the new Germany and the traditions of Prussia. The garrison church in Potsdam, where the main ceremony was to take place, had been founded by the Hohenzollern Kings of Prussia in the early eighteenth century. The church symbolized the bonds between the Prussian military monarchy, the power of the state, and the Protestant religion.

On 21 March 1933, Reich President Hindenburg, in the uniform of a Prussian field-marshal and raising his baton to the empty throne of the exiled Kaiser, represented those bonds: throne, altar, and the military tradition in Prussia's glory. He was the link between the past and the present. Hitler marked the present and the future. Dressed not in party uniform but in a dark morning-suit, he played the part of the humble servant, bowing deeply before the revered and elderly Reich President and offering him his hand. National renewal through unity was the theme of Hitler's address. Only with one phrase did he mention those who formed no part of that unity: they were to be rendered 'unharmful'. Hindenburg was elevated to the protector of the 'new uprising of our people'. He it was who had 'entrusted on 30 January the leadership of the Reich to this young Germany'. 'It can't be denied,' wrote one non-Nazi observer, impressed by the 'moderation' of Hitler's speech, 'he has grown. Out of the demagogue and party leader, the fanatic and agitator, the true statesman seems – for his opponents surprisingly enough – to be developing.' The blending of Prussian tradition and the National Socialist regime was underlined at the end of the ceremony by the laying of wreaths on the tombs of the Prussian kings.

Two days later, it was a different Hitler, brown-shirted again and imperious, who entered the Kroll Opera House in Berlin, where Reichstag meetings were now to be held, to the jubilant cheers of serried ranks of uniformed Nazi deputies to propose the Enabling Act that he had wanted since the previous November. The atmosphere for their opponents, particularly the SPD deputies, was menacing. A giant swastika dominated the chamber. Armed men from the SA, SS, and Stahlhelm guarded all exits and surrounded the building. They were giving a hint to opposition deputies of what would be the outcome were the Enabling Act not to find the necessary level of support. In the absence of the eighty-one Communist deputies who had been arrested or taken flight, the Nazis were now in a majority in the Reichstag. But to pass the Enabling Act a two-thirds majority was necessary.

To ensure the two-thirds majority, Frick had worked out that if the Communist deputies were simply deducted from the total membership of the Reichstag, only 378, not 432, votes would be needed. Göring added that, if necessary, some Social Democrats could be ejected from the chamber. That is how little the Nazis' 'legal revolution' had to do with legality. But the conservatives present raised no objections. By 20 March, Hitler could confidently report to the cabinet that, following his discussions, the Zentrum had seen the necessity of the Enabling Act. Their request for a small committee to oversee the measures taken under the Act should be accepted. There would then be no reason to doubt the Zentrum's support. 'The acceptance of the Enabling Act also by the Zentrum would signify a strengthening of prestige with regard to foreign countries,' Hitler commented, aware as always of the propaganda implications. Frick then introduced the draft of the bill, which was eventually accepted by the cabinet. The Reich Minister of the Interior also proposed a blatant manipulation of the Reichstag's procedures to make certain of the two-thirds majority. Deputies absent without excuse should now be counted as present. There would, therefore, be no problem about a quorum. Absenteeism as a form of protest abstention was ruled out. Again the conservatives raised no objections.

The way was clear. On the afternoon of 23 March 1933, Hitler addressed the Reichstag. The programme he outlined in his tactically clever two-and-a-half-hour speech, once he had finished painting the grim picture of the conditions he had inherited, was framed in the broadest of terms. At the end of his speech, Hitler made what appeared to be important concessions. The existence of neither the Reichstag nor the Reichsrat was threatened, he stated. The position and rights of the Reich President remained untouched. The Länder would not be abolished. The rights of the Churches would not be reduced and their relations with the state not altered.

All the promises were soon to be broken. But for the time being they served their purpose. They appeared to give the binding declarations safeguarding the position of the Catholic Church which the Zentrum had demanded in its discussions with Hitler. The SPD leader, Otto Wels, spoke courageously, given the menacing atmosphere, movingly upholding the principles of humanity, justice, freedom, and socialism held dear by Social Democrats. Hitler had made notes as Wels spoke. He now returned to the rostrum, to storms of applause from NSDAP deputies, to make the most savage of replies, every sentence cheered to the rafters. Departing now from the relative moderation of his earlier prepared speech, Hitler showed more of his true colours. A sense of law was alone not enough; possession of power was decisive. There had been no need to put the current bill before the Reichstag: 'we appeal in this hour to the German Reichstag to grant us that which we could have taken anyway'. With 441 votes to the 94 votes of the Social Democrats, the Reichstag, as a democratic body, voted itself out of existence.

Power was now in the hands of the National Socialists. It was the beginning of the end for political parties other than the NSDAP. The Zentrum's role had been particularly ignominious. Fearing open terror and repression, it had given in to Hitler's tactics of pseudo-legality. In so doing, it had helped legitimate the removal of almost all constitutional constraints on his power. He needed in future to rely neither on the Reichstag, nor on the Reich President. Hitler was still far from wielding absolute power. But vital steps towards consolidating his dictatorship now followed in quick succession.

VI

During the spring and summer of 1933, Germany fell into line behind its new rulers. Hardly any spheres of organized activity, political or social, were left untouched by the process of *Gleichschaltung* – the 'coordination' of institutions and organizations now brought under Nazi control. Pressure from below, from Nazi activists, played a major role in forcing the pace of the 'coordination'. But many organizations showed themselves only too willing to anticipate the process and to 'coordinate' themselves in accordance with the expectations of the new era. By the autumn, the Nazi dictatorship – and Hitler's own power at its head – had been enormously strengthened. Beyond indications that his instinct for the realities of power and the manipulative potential of propaganda were as finely tuned as ever, Hitler needed to take remarkably few initiatives to bring this about.

One initiative that did come from Hitler was, however, the creation of Reich Governors (*Reichsstatthalter*) to uphold the 'lines of policy laid down by the Reich Chancellor' in the Länder. With their hastily contrived establishment in the 'Second Law for the Coordination of the Länder with the Reich' of 7 April 1933, the sovereignty of the individual states was decisively undermined. All indications are that Hitler was anxious, with the establishment of the Reich Governors, to have trusted representatives in the Länder who could counter any danger that the grass-roots 'party revolution' might run out of control, ultimately even possibly threatening his own position. The position in Bavaria, where the SA and SS had their headquarters and where radicals had effected an actual 'seizure of power' in the days since the March election, was especially sensitive. The improvised creation of the Reich Governors was brought about with Bavaria, in particular, in mind, to head off the possibility of a party revolution against Berlin. The former Freikorps 'hero' of the crushing of the Räterepublik, Ritter von Epp, was already appointed as Reich Governor on 10 April. A further ten Reich Governors were installed less hurriedly, during May and June, in the remaining Länder, apart from Prussia, and were drawn from the senior and most powerful Gauleiter. Their dependence on Hitler was no less great than his on them. They could be relied upon, therefore, to serve the Reich government in blocking the revolution from below when it was becoming counter-productive.

In Prussia, Hitler reserved the position of Reich Governor for himself. This effectively removed any purpose in retaining Papen as Reich Commissioner for Prussia. Possibly Hitler was contemplating reuniting the position of head of government in Prussia with that of Reich Chancellor, as had been the position under Bismarck. If so, he reckoned without Göring's own power-ambitions. Since Papen's coup the previous July, there had been no Minister President in Prussia. Göring had expected the position to become his following the Prussian Landtag elections on 5 March. But Hitler had not appointed him. Göring therefore engineered the placing on the agenda of the newly-elected Prussian Landtag, meeting on 8 April, the election of the Minister President. Though he had only the previous day taken over the rights of Reich Governor in Prussia himself, Hitler now had to bow to the *fait accompli*. On 11 April, Göring was appointed Prussian Minister President (retaining his powers as Prussian Minister of the Interior), and on 25 April the rights of Reich Governor in Prussia were transferred to him. The 'Second Coordination Law' had indirectly but effectively led to the consolidation of Göring's extensive power-base in Prussia, built initially on his control over the police in the most important of the German states. It was little wonder that Göring responded with publicly effusive statements of loyalty to Hitler, whom he served as his 'most loyal paladin'. The episode reveals the haste and confusion behind the entire improvised 'coordination' of the Länder. But at the price of strengthening the hand of Göring in Prussia, and the most thrusting Gauleiter elsewhere, Hitler's own power had also been notably reinforced across the Länder.

During the spring and summer of 1933, Hitler stood between countervailing forces. The dilemma would not be resolved until the 'Night of the Long Knives'. On the one hand, the pressures, dammed up for so long and with such difficulty before Hitler's takeover of power, had burst loose after the March elections. Hitler not only sympathized with the radical assault from below on opponents, Jews, and anyone else getting in the way of the Nazi revolution; he needed the radicals to push through the upturning of the established political order and to intimidate those obstructing to fall in line. On the other hand, as the creation of the Reich Governors had shown, he was aware of the dangers to his own position if the radical upheaval got out of hand. And he was sensitive to the fact that the traditional national-conservative bastions of power, not least sceptics about National Socialism in the army and important sectors of business, while having no objections to violence as long as it was directed at Communists and Socialists, would look differently upon it as soon as their own vested interests were threatened. Hitler had no choice, therefore, but to steer an uncomfortable course between a party revolution which he could by no means fully control and the support of the army and business which he could by no means do without. Out of these inherently contradictory forces, the showdown with the SA would ultimately emerge. In the meantime, however, there were clear signs of what would become a lasting trait of the Third Reich: pressure from party radicals, encouraged and sanctioned at least in part by Hitler, resulting in the state bureaucracy reflecting the radicalism in legislation and the police channelling it into executive measures. The process of 'cumulative radicalization' was recognizable from the earliest weeks of the regime.

Apart from the all-out assault on the Left in the first weeks of Nazi rule, many outrages had been perpetrated by Nazi radicals against Jews. Since antisemitism had been the 'ideological cement' of the National Socialist Movement from the beginning, offering at one and the same time a vehicle for actionism and substitute for revolutionary leanings threatening the fabric of society, this was scarcely surprising. The takeover of power by the arch-antisemite Hitler had at one fell swoop removed constraints on violence towards Jews. Without any orders from above, and without any coordination, assaults on Jewish businesses and the beating-up of Jews by Nazi thugs became commonplace. Countless atrocities took place in the weeks following Hitler's assumption to power.

Many were carried out by members of the so-called Fighting League of the Commercial Middle Class (Kampfbund des gewerblichen Mittelstandes), in which violent antisemitism went hand in hand with equally violent opposition to department stores (many of them Jewish owned). The extent of the anti-Jewish violence prompted Jewish intellectuals and financiers abroad, especially in the USA, to undertake attempts to mobilize public feeling against Germany and to organize a boycott against German goods – a real threat, given the weakness of the German economy. Beginning in mid-March, the boycott gathered pace and was extended to numerous European countries. The reaction in Germany, led by the Fighting League, was predictably aggressive. A 'counter-boycott' of Jewish shops and department stores throughout Germany was demanded. The call was taken up by leading antisemites in the party, at their forefront and in his element the Franconian Gauleiter and pathological antisemite Julius Streicher. They argued that the Jews could serve as 'hostages' to force a halt to the international boycott.

Hitler's instincts favoured the party radicals. But he was also under pressure to act. On the 'Jewish Question', on which he had preached so loudly and so often, he could scarcely now, once in power, back down in the face of the demands of the activists without serious loss of face within the party. When, on 26 March, it was reported through diplomatic contacts that the American Jewish Congress was planning to call the next day for a world-wide boycott of German goods, Hitler was forced into action. As usual, when pushed into a corner he had no half-measures. Goebbels was summoned to the Obersalzberg. 'In the loneliness of the mountains,' he wrote, the Führer had reached the conclusion that the authors, or at least beneficiaries, of the 'foreign agitation' – Germany's Jews – had to be tackled. 'We must therefore move to a widely framed boycott of all Jewish businesses in Germany.' Streicher was put in charge of a committee of thirteen party functionaries who were to organize the boycott. The party's proclamation of 28 March, prompted by the Reich Chancellor himself and bearing his imprint, called for action committees to carry out a boycott of Jewish businesses, goods, doctors, and lawyers, even in the smallest village of the Reich. The boycott was to be of indefinite duration. Goebbels was left to undertake the propaganda preparations. Behind the entire operation stood pressure from the Fighting League of the Commercial Middle Class.

Led by Schacht and Foreign Minister von Neurath, counter-pressures began to be placed on Hitler to halt an action which was likely to have disastrous effects on the German economy and on its standing abroad. Hitler at first refused to consider any retreat. But by 31 March, Neurath was able to report to the cabinet that the British, French, and American governments had declared their opposition to the boycott of German goods in their country. He hoped the boycott in Germany might be called off. It was asking too much of Hitler to back down completely. The activists were by now fired up. Abandonment of the boycott would have brought not only loss of face for Hitler, but the probability that any order cancelling the 'action' would have been widely ignored. However, Hitler did indicate that he was now ready to postpone the start of the German boycott from 1 to 4 April in the event of satisfactory declarations opposing the boycott of German goods by the British and American governments. Otherwise, the German boycott would commence on 1 April, but would then be halted until 4 April. A flurry of diplomatic activity resulted in the western governments and, placed under pressure, Jewish lobby groups distancing themselves from the boycott of German goods. Hitler's demands had largely been met. But by now he had changed his mind, and was again insisting on the German boycott being carried out. Further pressure from Schacht resulted in the boycott being confined to a single day – but under the propaganda fiction that it would be restarted the following Wednesday, 5 April, if the 'horror agitation' abroad against Germany had not ceased altogether. There was no intention of that. In fact, already on the afternoon of the boycott day, 1 April, Streicher announced that it would not be resumed the following Wednesday.

The boycott itself was less than the success that Nazi propaganda claimed. Many Jewish shops had closed for the day anyway. In some places, the SA men posted outside 'Jewish' department stores holding placards warning against buying in Jewish shops were largely ignored by customers. People behaved in a variety of fashions. There was almost a holiday mood in some busy shopping streets, as crowds gathered to see what was happening. Groups of people discussed the pros and cons of the boycott. Not a few were opposed to it, saying they would again patronize their favourite stores. Others shrugged their shoulders. 'I think the entire thing is mad, but I'm not bothering myself about it,' was one, perhaps not untypical, view heard from a non-Jew on the day. Even the SA men seemed at times rather half-hearted about it in some places. In others, however, the boycott was simply a cover for plundering and violence. For the Jewish victims, the day was traumatic – the clearest indication that this was a Germany in which they could no longer feel 'at home', in which routine discrimination had been replaced by state-sponsored persecution.

Reactions in the foreign press to the boycott were almost universally condemnatory. A damage-limitation exercise had to be carried out by the new Reichsbank President Schacht to assuage foreign bankers of Germany's intentions in economic policy. But within Germany – something which would repeat itself in years to come – the dynamic of anti-Jewish pressure from party activists, sanctioned by Hitler and the Nazi leadership, was now taken up by the state bureaucracy and channelled into discriminatory legislation. The exclusion of Jews from state service and from the professions had been aims of Nazi activists before 1933. Now, the possibility of pressing for the implementation of such aims had opened up. Suggestions for anti-Jewish discriminatory measures came from various quarters. Preparations for overhauling civil service rights were given a new anti-Jewish twist at the end of March, possibly (though this is not certain) on Hitler's intervention. On the basis of the notorious 'Aryan Paragraph' – there was no definition of a Jew – in the hastily drafted 'Law for the Restoration of the Professional Civil Service' of 7 April, Jews as well as political opponents were dismissed from the civil service. An exception was made, on Hindenburg's intervention, only for Jews who had served at the front. The three further pieces of anti-Jewish legislation passed in April – discriminating against the admission of Jews to the legal profession, excluding Jewish doctors from treating patients covered by the national insurance scheme, and limiting the number of Jewish schoolchildren permitted in schools – were all hurriedly improvised to meet not simply pressure from below but *de facto* measures which were already being implemented in various parts of the country. Hitler's role was largely confined to giving his sanction to the legalization of measures already often illegally introduced by party activists with vested interests in the discrimination running alongside whatever ideological motivation they possessed.

The seismic shift in the political scene which had taken place in the month or so following the Reichstag fire had left the Jews fully exposed to Nazi violence, discrimination, and intimidation. It had also totally undermined the position of Hitler's political opponents. There was now little fight left in oppositional parties. The readiness to compromise soon became a readiness to capitulate.

Already in March, Theodor Leipart, the chairman of the trade union confederation, the ADGB, had tried to blow with the wind, distancing the unions from the SPD and offering a declaration of loyalty to the new regime. It was to no avail. The planning of the destruction of the unions was undertaken by the boss of the still relatively insignificant Nazi union, the Nationalsozialistische Betriebszellenorganisation (NSBO, National Socialist Factory Cell Organization), Reinhold Muchow and, increasingly, by Robert Ley, the NSDAP's Organization Leader. Hitler was initially hesitant, until the idea was proposed of coupling it with a propaganda coup. Along the lines of the 'Day of Potsdam', Goebbels prepared another huge spectacular for 1 May, when the National Socialists usurped the traditional celebration of the International and turned it into the 'Day of National Labour'. The ADGB took a full part in the rallies and parades. Over 10 million people altogether turned out – though for many a factory workforce attendance was scarcely voluntary.

The following day, the razzmatazz over, SA and NSBO squads occupied the offices and bank branches of the Social Democratic trade union movement, confiscated its funds, and arrested its functionaries. Within an hour, the 'action' was finished. The largest democratic trade union movement in the world had been destroyed. In a matter of days, its members had been incorporated into the massive German Labour Front (Deutsche Arbeitsfront, DAF), founded on 10 May under Robert Ley's leadership.

The once-mighty Social Democratic Party of Germany, the largest labour movement that Europe had known, was also at an end. It had been forced during the last years of Weimar into one unholy compromise after another in its attempts to uphold its legalistic traditions while at the same time hoping to fend off the worst. When the worst came, it was ill-equipped. The depression years and internal demoralization had taken their toll. Otto Wels's speech on 23 March had shown courage. But it was far too little, and far too late. Support was haemorrhaging away. During March and April, the SPD's paramilitary arm, the huge Reichsbanner, was forced into dissolution. Party branches were closing down. Activists were under arrest, or had fled abroad. Some already began preparations for illegality. Alongside the fear, there was wide disillusionment with Social Democracy. The flight into exile of many party leaders – necessary safety measure that it was – enhanced a sense of desertion. The SPD was by now a rudderless ship. Otto Wels and other party leaders left for Prague, where a party headquarters in exile had already been established. All party activities within the Reich were to be banned, the SPD's parliamentary representation abolished, its assets confiscated.

The remaining parties now rapidly caved in, falling domino-style. The Staatspartei (formerly the DDP, the Deutsche Demokratische Partei) dissolved itself on 28 June, followed a day later by the dissolution of the DVP. The Nazis' conservative coalition partners, the DNVP – renamed in May the German National Front (Deutschnationale Front, DNF) – also capitulated on 27 June. It had been losing members to the NSDAP at an increasing rate; its grass-roots organizations had been subjected to repression and intimidation; the Stahlhelm – many of whose members supported the DNVP – had been placed under Hitler's leadership in late April and was taken into the SA in June; and the party's leader, Hugenberg, had become wholly isolated in cabinet, even from his conservative colleagues. Hugenberg's resignation from the cabinet (which many had initially thought he would dominate), on 26 June, was inevitable after embarrassing the German government through his behaviour at the World Economic Conference in London earlier in the month. Without consulting Hitler, the cabinet, or Foreign Minister von Neurath, Hugenberg had sent a memorandum to the Economic Committee of the Conference rejecting free trade, demanding the return of German colonies and land for settlement in the east. His departure from the cabinet signified the end for his party. Far from functioning as the 'real' leader of Germany, as many had imagined he would do, and far from ensuring with his conservative colleagues in the cabinet that Hitler would be 'boxed in', Hugenberg had rapidly become yesterday's man. Few regretted it. Playing with fire, Hugenberg, along with his party, the DNVP, had been consumed by it.

The Catholic parties held out a little longer. But their position was undermined by the negotiations, led by Papen, for a Reich Concordat with the Holy See, in which the Vatican accepted a ban on the political activities of the clergy in Germany. This meant in effect that, in the attempt to defend the position of the Catholic Church in Germany, political Catholicism had been sacrificed. By that stage, in any case, the Zentrum had been losing its members at an alarming rate, many of them anxious to accommodate themselves to the new times. Catholic bishops had taken over from the Zentrum leaders as the main spokesmen for the Church in dealings with the regime, and were more concerned to preserve the Church's institutions, organizations, and schools than to sustain the weakened position of the Catholic political parties. Intimidation and pressure did the rest. The arrest of 2,000 functionaries in late June by Himmler's Bavarian Political Police concentrated minds and brought the swift reading of the last rites for the BVP on 4 July. A day later, the Zentrum, the last-remaining political party outside the NSDAP, dissolved itself. Little over a week later, the 'Law against the New Construction of Parties' left the NSDAP as the only legal political party in Germany.

VII

What was happening at the centre of politics was happening also at the grass-roots – not just in political life, but in every organizational form of social activity. Intimidation of those posing any obstacle and opportunism of those now seeking the first opportunity to jump on the bandwagon proved an irresistible combination. In countless small towns and villages, Nazis took over local government. Teachers and civil servants were particularly prominent in the rush to join the party. So swollen did the NSDAP's membership rolls become with the mass influx of those anxious to cast in their lot with the new regime – the 'March Fallen' (*Märzgefallene*) as the 'Old Fighters' cynically dubbed them – that on 1 May a bar was imposed on further entrants. Two and a half million Germans had by now joined the party, 1.6 million of them since Hitler had become Chancellor. Opportunism intermingled with genuine idealism.

Much the same applied also to the broad cultural sphere. Goebbels took up with great energy and enthusiasm his task of ensuring that the press, radio, film production, theatre, music, the visual arts, literature, and all other forms of cultural activity were reorganized. But the most striking feature of the 'coordination' of culture was the alacrity and eagerness with which intellectuals, writers, artists, performers, and publicists actively collaborated in moves which not only impoverished and straitjacketed German culture for the next twelve years, but banned and outlawed some of its most glittering exponents.

The hopes long cherished of the coming great leader eradicated the critical faculties of many intellectuals, blinding them to the magnitude of the assault on freedom of thought as well as action that they often welcomed. Many of the neo-conservative intellectuals whose ideas had helped pave the way for the Third Reich were soon to be massively disillusioned. Hitler turned out for them in practice to be not the mystic leader they had longed for in their dreams. But they had helped prepare the ground for the Führer cult that was taken up in its myriad form by so many others.

Hardly a protest was raised at the purges of university professors under the new civil service law in April 1933 as many of Germany's most distinguished academics were dismissed and forced into exile. The

Prussian Academy of Arts had by then already undertaken its own 'cleansing', demanding loyalty to the regime from all choosing to remain within its hallowed membership.

The symbolic moment of capitulation of German intellectuals to the 'new spirit' of 1933 came with the burning on 10 May of the books of authors unacceptable to the regime. University faculties and senates collaborated. Their members, with few exceptions, attended the bonfires. The poet Heinrich Heine (1797–1856), whose works were among those consumed by the flames, had written: 'Where books are burnt, in the end people are also burnt.'

VIII

Scarcely any of the transformation of Germany during the spring and summer of 1933 had followed direct orders from the Reich Chancellery. Hitler had rarely been personally involved. But he was the main beneficiary. During these months popular adulation of the new Chancellor had reached untold levels. The Führer cult was established, not now just within the party, but throughout state and society, as the very basis of the new Germany. Hitler's standing and power, at home and increasingly abroad, were thereby immeasurably boosted.

Already in spring 1933, the personality cult surrounding Hitler was burgeoning, and developing extraordinary manifestations. 'Poems' – usually unctuous doggerel verse, sometimes with a pseudo-religious tone – were composed in his honour. 'Hitler-Oaks' and 'Hitler-Lindens', trees whose ancient pagan symbolism gave them special significance to völkisch nationalists and nordic cultists, were planted in towns and villages all over Germany. Towns and cities rushed to confer honorary citizenship on the new Chancellor. Streets and squares were named after him.

The levels of hero-worship had never been witnessed before in Germany. Not even the Bismarck cult in the last years of the founder of the Reich had come remotely near matching it. Hitler's forty-fourth birthday on 20 April 1933 saw an extraordinary outpouring of adulation as the entire country glutted itself with festivities in honour of the 'Leader of the New Germany'. However well orchestrated the propaganda, it was able to tap popular sentiments and quasi-religious levels of devotion that could not simply be manufactured. Hitler was on the way to becoming no longer the party leader, but the symbol of national unity.

And it became more and more difficult for bystanders who were less than fanatical worshippers of the new god to avoid at least an outward sign of acquiescence in the boundless adoration. The most banal expression of acquiescence, the 'Heil Hitler' greeting, now rapidly spread. For civil servants, it was made compulsory a day before Hitler's party was established as the only one permissible in Germany. Those unable to raise the right arm through physical disability were ordered to raise their left arm. The 'German Greeting' – 'Heil Hitler!' – was the outward sign that the country had been turned into a 'Führer state'.

What of the man at the centre of this astonishing idolization? Putzi Hanfstaengl, by now head of the Foreign Press Section of the Propaganda Ministry, though not part of the 'inner circle', still saw Hitler at that time frequently and at close quarters. He later commented how difficult it was to gain access to Hitler, even at this early period of his Chancellorship. Hitler had taken his long-standing Bavarian entourage – the 'Chauffeureska' as Hanfstaengl called it – into the Reich Chancellery with him. His adjutants and chauffeur, Brückner, Schaub, Schreck (successor to Emil Maurice, sacked after his flirtation with Geli Raubal), and his court photographer Heinrich Hoffmann were omnipresent, often hindering contact, frequently interfering in a conversation with some form of distraction, invariably listening, later backing Hitler's own impressions and prejudices. Even Foreign Minister Neurath and Reichsbank President Schacht found it difficult to gain Hitler's attention for more than a minute or two without some intervention from one or other member of the 'Chauffeureska'. Only Göring and Himmler, according to Hanfstaengl, could invariably reckon with a brief private audience on request with Hitler, though Goebbels, at least, should be added to Hanfstaengl's short-list. Hitler's unpredictability and lack of any form of routine did not help. As had always been the case, he tended to be late in bed – often after relaxing by watching a film (one of his favourites was *King Kong*) in his private cinema. Sometimes he scarcely appeared during the mornings, except to hear reports from Hans Heinrich Lammers, the head of the Reich Chancellery, and to look over the press with Goebbels's right-hand man in the Propaganda Ministry, Walther Funk. The high-point of the day was lunch. The chef in the Reich Chancellery, who had been brought from the Brown House in

Munich, had a difficult time in preparing a meal ordered for one o'clock but often served as much as two hours later, when Hitler finally appeared. Otto Dietrich, the press chief, took to eating in any case beforehand in the Kaiserhof, turning up at 1.30 p.m. prepared for all eventualities. Hitler's table guests changed daily but were invariably trusty party comrades. Even during the first months, conservative ministers were seldom present. Given the company, it was obvious that Hitler would hardly, if ever, find himself contradicted. Any sort of remark, however, could prompt a lengthy tirade – usually resembling his earlier propaganda attacks on political opponents or recollections of battles fought and won.

It would have been impossible for Hitler to avoid the effects of the fawning sycophancy which surrounded him daily, sifting the type of information that reached him, and cocooning him from the outside world. His sense of reality was by this very process distorted. His contact with those who saw things in a fundamentally different light was restricted in the main to stage-managed interviews with dignatories, diplomats, or foreign journalists. The German people were little more than a faceless, adoring mass, his only direct relationship to them in now relatively infrequent speeches and radio addresses. But the popular adulation he received was like a drug to him. His own self-confidence was already soaring. Casual disparaging comments about Bismarck indicated that he now plainly saw the founder of the Reich as his inferior. What would turn into a fatal sense of infallibility was more than embryonically present.

How much of the adulation of Hitler that spread so rapidly throughout society in 1933 was genuine, how much contrived or opportunistic, is impossible to know. The result was in any case much the same. The near-deification of Hitler gave the Chancellor a status that left all other cabinet ministers and all other party bosses in the shade. Possibilities of questioning, let alone opposing, measures which Hitler was known to favour were becoming as good as non-existent. Hitler's authority now opened doors to radical action previously closed, lifted constraints, and removed barriers on measures that before 30 January 1933 had seemed barely conceivable. Without direct transmission of orders, initiatives imagined to be in tune with Hitler's aims could be undertaken – and have good chances of success.

One such case was the 'sterilization law' – the 'Law for the Prevention of Hereditarily Diseased Offspring' – approved by the cabinet on 14 July 1933. Hitler had nothing directly to do with the preparation of the law (which was portrayed as having benefits for the immediate family as well as for society in general). But it was prepared in the knowledge that it accorded with his expressed sentiments. And when it came before the cabinet, it did meet with his outright approval in the face of the objections of Vice-Chancellor Papen, concerned about Catholic feeling regarding the law. Papen's plea for sterilization only with the willing consent of the person concerned was simply brushed aside by the Chancellor.

Though from a Nazi point of view a modest beginning in racial engineering, the consequences of the law were far from minor: some 400,000 victims would be compulsorily sterilized under the provisions of the Act before the end of the Third Reich.

If Papen was hinting at the cabinet meeting that the Catholic Church might cause difficulties over the sterilization law, he knew better than anyone that this was unlikely to be the case. Less than a week before, he had initialled on behalf of the Reich Goverment the Reich Concordat with the Vatican which he himself had done so much to bring about. The Concordat would be signed among great pomp and circumstance in Rome on 20 July. Despite the continuing molestation of Catholic clergy and other outrages committed by Nazi radicals against the Church and its organizations, the Vatican had been keen to reach agreement with the new government. Even serious continued harassment once the Concordat had been signed did not deter the Vatican from agreeing to its ratification on 10 September. Hitler himself had laid great store on a Concordat from the beginning of his Chancellorship, primarily with a view to eliminating any role for 'political Catholicism' in Germany. At the very same cabinet meeting at which the sterilization law was approved, he underlined the triumph which the Concordat marked for his regime. Only a short time earlier, he remarked, he would not have thought it possible 'that the Church would be ready to commit the bishops to this state. That this had happened, was without doubt an unreserved recognition of the present regime.' Indeed, it was an unqualified triumph for Hitler. The German episcopacy poured out effusive statements of thanks and congratulations.

Surprisingly, the Protestant Church turned out to be less easy to handle in the first months of Hitler's Chancellorship. Though nominally supported by some two-thirds of the population, it was divided into twenty-eight separate regional Churches, with different doctrinal emphases. Perhaps Hitler's scant regard led him to underestimate the minefield of intermingled religion and politics that he entered when he brought his influence to bear in support of attempts to create a unified Reich Church. His own interest, as always in such matters, was purely opportunistic. Hitler's choice – on whose advice is unclear – as prospective Reich Bishop fell on Ludwig Müller, a fifty-year-old former naval chaplain with no obvious qualifications for the position except a high regard for his own importance and an ardent admiration for the Reich Chancellor and his Movement. Hitler told Müller he wanted speedy unification, without any trouble, and ending with a Church accepting Nazi leadership.

Müller turned out, however, to be a disastrous choice. At the election of the Reich Bishop on 26 May by leaders of the Evangelical Church, he gained the support of the nazified wing, the 'German Christians', but was rejected by all other sides. Nazi propaganda supported the German Christians. Hitler himself publicly backed Müller and on the day before the election broadcast his support for the forces within the Church behind the new policies of the state.

The German Christians swept to a convincing victory on 23 July. But it turned out to be a pyrrhic one. By September, Martin Niemöller, the pastor of Dahlem, a well-to-do suburb of Berlin, had received some 2,000 replies to his circular inviting pastors to join him in setting up a 'Pastors' Emergency League', upholding the traditional allegiance to the Holy Scripture and Confessions of the Reformation. It was the beginning of what would eventually turn into the 'Confessing Church', which would develop for some pastors into the vehicle for opposition not just to the Church policy of the state, but to the state itself.

Ludwig Müller was finally elected Reich Bishop on 27 September. But by then, Nazi backing for the German Christians – Müller's chief prop of support – was already on the wane. Hitler was by now keen to distance himself from the German Christians, whose activities were increasingly seen as counter-productive, and to detach himself from the internal Church conflict. A German Christian rally, attended by 20,000 people, in the Sportpalast in Berlin in mid-November caused such scandal following an outrageous speech attacking the Old Testament and the theology of the 'Rabbi Paul', and preaching the need for depictions of a more 'heroic' Jesus, that Hitler felt compelled to complete his dissociation from Church matters. The '*Gleichschaltung*' experiment had proved a failure. It was time to abandon it. Hitler promptly lost whatever interest he had had in the Protestant Church. He would in future on more than one occasion again be forced to intervene. But the Church conflict was for him no more than an irritation.

IX

By autumn 1933, the discord in the Protestant Church was in any case a mere side-show in Hitler's eyes. Of immeasurably greater moment was Germany's international position. In a dramatic move on 14 October, Hitler took Germany out of the disarmament talks at Geneva, and out of the League of Nations. Overnight, international relations were set on a new footing. The Stresemann era of foreign policy was definitively at an end. The 'diplomatic revolution' in Europe had begun.

Hitler had played only a limited role in foreign policy during the first months of the Third Reich. The new, ambitious revisionist course – aimed at reversion to the borders of 1914, re-acquisition of former colonies (and winning of some new ones), incorporation of Austria, and German dominance in eastern and south-eastern Europe – was worked out by foreign ministry professionals and put forward to the cabinet as early as March 1933. By the end of April, Germany's delegate to the Geneva disarmament talks, Rudolf Nadolny, was already speaking in private about intentions of building a large army of 600,000 men. If Britain and France were to agree to only a far smaller army of 300,000 while minimally reducing their own armed forces, or if they agreed to disarm substantially but refused to allow any German rearmament, Nadolny held out the prospect of Germany walking out of the disarmament negotiations, and perhaps of the League of Nations itself. Meanwhile, the new, hawkish Reichswehr Minister, Blomberg, was impatient to break with Geneva without delay, and to proceed unilaterally to as rapid a rearmament programme as possible. Hitler's own line at this time was a far more cautious one. He entertained real fears of intervention while German defences were so weak.

The talks at Geneva remained deadlocked. A variety of plans were advanced by the British, French, and Italians offering Germany some concessions beyond the provisions of Versailles, but retaining clear supremacy in armaments for the western powers. None had any prospect of acceptance in Germany, though Hitler was prepared to follow a tactically more moderate line than that pressed by Neurath and Blomberg. In contrast to the army's impatience for immediate – but unobtainable – equality of armaments, Hitler, the shrewder tactician, was prepared to play the waiting game. At this point, he could only hope that the evident differences between Britain and France on the disarmament question would play into his hands. Eventually, they would do so. Though both major western powers were anxious at the prospect of a rearming Germany, worried by some of the aggressive tones coming from Berlin, and concerned at the Nazi wave of terror activity in Austria, there were significant divisions between them. These meant there was no real prospect of the military intervention that Hitler so feared. Britain was prepared to be more amenable than the French. The hope was that through minor concessions, German rearmament could effectively be retarded. But the British felt tugged along by the French hard line, while fearing that it would force Germany out of the League of Nations.

It was, however, Britain that took the lead, on 28 April, supported by France, in presenting Germany with only the minimal concession of the right to a 200,000-man army, but demanding a ban on all paramilitary organizations. Blomberg and Neurath responded angrily in public. Hitler, worried about the threat of sanctions by the western powers, and Polish sabre-rattling in the east, bowed to superior might. He told the cabinet that the question of rearmament would not be solved around the conference table. A new method was needed. There was no possibility at the present time of rearmament 'by normal methods'. The unity of the German people in the disarmament question had to be shown 'to the world'. He picked up a suggestion put to cabinet by Foreign Minister von Neurath of a speech to the Reichstag, which would then find acclamation as government policy.

Hitler seemed to speak, in his address to the Reichstag on 17 May, in the diction of a statesman interested in securing the peace and well-being of his own country, and of the whole of Europe. 'We respect the national rights also of other peoples,' he stated, and 'wish from the innermost heart to live with them in peace and friendship.' His demands for equal treatment for Germany in the question of disarmament could sound nothing but justified to German ears, and outside Germany, too.

Germany was prepared to renounce weapons of aggression, if other countries would do the same, he declared. Any attempt to force a disarmament settlement on Germany could only be dictated by the intention of driving the country from the disarmament negotiations, he claimed. 'As a continually defamed people, it would be hard for us to stay within the League of Nations,' ran his scarcely veiled threat. It was a clever piece of rhetoric. He sounded the voice of reason, putting his adversaries in the western democracies on a propaganda defensive.

The stalemated Geneva talks were postponed until June, then until October. During this period there were no concrete plans for Germany to break with the League of Nations. Even later that month, neither Hitler nor his Foreign Minister Neurath were reckoning with an early withdrawal. As late as 4 October, Hitler appears to have been thinking of further negotiations. But on that very day news arrived of a more unyielding British stance on German rearmament, toughened to back the French, and taking no account of demands for equality. That afternoon, Blomberg sought an audience with Hitler in the Reich Chancellery. Neurath later acknowledged that he, too, had advised Hitler at the end of September that there was nothing more to be gained in Geneva. Hitler recognized that the time was now ripe to leave the League in circumstances which looked as if Germany was the wronged party. The propaganda advantage, especially at home where he could be certain of massive popular support, was too good a chance to miss.

The cabinet was finally informed on 13 October. With a sure eye as always on the propaganda value of plebiscitary acclaim, Hitler told his ministers that Germany's position would be strengthened by the dissolution of the Reichstag, the setting of new elections, and 'requiring the German people to identify with the peace policy of the Reich government through a plebiscite'.

The following day, the Geneva Conference received official notification of the German withdrawal. The consequences were far-reaching. The disarmament talks now lost their meaning. The League of Nations, which Japan had already left earlier in the year, was fatally weakened. In the decision to leave the League the timing and propaganda exploitation were vintage Hitler. But Blomberg, especially, and Neurath had been pressing for withdrawal long before Hitler became convinced that the moment had arrived for Germany to gain maximum advantage. Hitler had not least been able to benefit from the shaky basis of European diplomacy at the outset of his Chancellorship. The world economic crisis had undermined the 'fulfilment policy' on which Stresemann's strategy, and the basis of European security, had been built. The European diplomatic order was, therefore, already no more stable than a house of cards when Hitler took up office. The German withdrawal from the League of Nations was the first card to be removed from the house. The others would soon come tumbling down.

On the evening of 14 October, in an astutely constructed broadcast sure of a positive resonance among the millions of listeners throughout the country, Hitler announced the dissolution of the Reichstag. New elections, set for 12 November, now provided the opportunity to have a purely National Socialist Reichstag, free of the remnants of the dissolved parties. Even though only one party was contesting the elections, Hitler flew once more throughout Germany holding election addresses. The propaganda campaign directed its energies almost entirely to accomplishing a show of loyalty to Hitler personally – now regularly referred to even in the still existent non-Nazi press as simply 'the Führer'. Electoral manipulation was still not as refined as it was to become in the 1936 and 1938 plebiscites. But it was far from absent. Various forms of chicanery were commonplace. Secrecy at the ballot-box was far from guaranteed. And pressure to conform was obvious. Even so, the official result – 95.1 per cent in the plebiscite, 92.1 per cent in the 'Reichstag election' – marked a genuine triumph for Hitler. Abroad as well as at home, even allowing for manipulation and lack of freedom, it had to be concluded that the vast majority of the German people backed him. His stature as a national leader above party interest was massively enhanced.

Hitler's conquest of Germany was still, however, incomplete. Behind the euphoria of the plebiscite result, a long-standing problem was now threatening to endanger the regime itself: the problem of the SA.

11

Securing Total Power

I

Hitler's unruly party army, the SA, had outlived its purpose. That had been to win power. Everything had been predicated on the attainment of that single goal. What would follow the winning of power, what would be the purpose and function of the SA in the new state, what benefits would flow for ordinary stormtroopers, had never been clarified. Now, months after the 'seizure of power', the SA's 'politics of hooliganism' were a force for disruption in the state. And particularly in the military ambitions of its leader, Ernst Röhm, the SA was an increasingly destabilizing factor, above all in relations with the Reichswehr. But its elimination, or disempowering, was no simple matter. It was a huge organization, far bigger than the party itself. It contained many of the most ardent 'old fighters' (in a literal sense) in the Movement. And it had been the backbone of the violent activism which had forced the pace of the Nazi revolution since Hitler had become Chancellor. Röhm's ambitions, as we have seen in earlier chapters, had never been identical with those of Hitler. A large paramilitary organization that had never accepted its subordination to the political wing of the party had caused tensions, and occasional rebellion, since the 1920s. But, whatever the crises, Hitler had always managed to retain the SA's loyalty. To challenge the SA's leadership risked losing that loyalty. It could not be done easily or approached lightly.

The problem of the SA was inextricably bound up with the other threat to the consolidation of Hitler's power. Reich President Hindenburg was old and frail. The issue of the succession would loom within the foreseeable future. Hindenburg, the symbol of 'old' Germany, and 'old' Prussia, was the figurehead behind which stood still powerful forces with somewhat ambivalent loyalties towards the new state. Most important among them was the army, of which as Head of State Hindenburg was supreme commander. The Reichswehr leadership was intensely and increasingly alarmed by the military pretensions of the SA. Failure on Hitler's part to solve the problem of the SA could conceivably lead to army leaders favouring an alternative as Head of State on Hindenburg's death – perhaps resulting in a restoration of the monarchy, and a *de facto* military dictatorship. Such a development would have met with favour among sections, not just of the military old guard, but of some national-conservative groups, which had favoured an authoritarian, anti-democratic form of state but had become appalled by the Hitler regime. The office of the Vice-Chancellor, Papen, gradually emerged as the focal point of hopes of blunting the edge of the Nazi revolution. Since Papen continued to enjoy the favour of the Reich President, such 'reactionaries', though small in number, could not be discounted in power-political terms. And since at the same time there were growing worries among business leaders about serious and mounting economic problems, the threat to the consolidation of Hitler's power – and with that of the regime itself – was a real one.

Ernst Röhm's SA had been the spearhead of the Nazi revolution in the first months of 1933. The explosion of elemental violence had needed no commands from above. The SA had long been kept on a leash, told to wait for the day of reckoning. Now it could scarcely be contained. Orgies of hate-filled revenge against political enemies and horrifically brutal assaults on Jews were daily occurrences. A large proportion of the estimated 100,000 persons taken into custody in these turbulent months were held in makeshift SA prisons and camps. Some hundred of these were set up in the Berlin area alone. Many victims were bestially tortured. The minimal figure of some 500–600 murdered in what the Nazis themselves proclaimed as a bloodless and legal revolution can largely be placed on the account of the SA. The first Gestapo chief, Rudolf Diels, described after the war the conditions in one of the SA's Berlin prisons: 'The "interrogations" had begun and ended with a beating. A dozen fellows had laid into their victims at intervals of some hours with iron bars, rubber coshes, and whips. Smashed teeth and broken bones bore witness to the tortures. As we entered, these living skeletons with festering wounds lay in rows on the rotting straw . . .'

As long as the terror was levelled in the main at Communists, Socialists, and Jews, it was in any case not likely to be widely unpopular, and could be played down as 'excesses' of the 'national uprising'. But already by the summer, the number of incidents mounted in which overbearing and loutish behaviour by SA men caused widespread public offence even in pro-Nazi circles. By this time, complaints were pouring in from industry, commerce, and local government offices about disturbances and intolerable actions by stormtroopers. The Foreign Office added its own protest at incidents where foreign diplomats had been insulted or even manhandled. The SA was threatening to become completely uncontrollable. Steps had to be taken. Reich President Hindenburg himself requested Hitler to restore order.

The need for Hitler to act became especially urgent after Röhm had openly stated the SA's aim of continuing the 'German Revolution' in the teeth of attempts by conservatives, reactionaries, and opportunist fellow-travellers to undermine and tame it. Röhm was clearly signalling to the new rulers of Germany that for him the revolution was only just starting; and that he would demand a leading role for himself and the mighty organization he headed – by now some 4½ million strong.

Forced now for the first time to choose between the demands of the party's paramilitary wing and the 'big battalions' pressing for order, Hitler summoned the Reich Governors to a meeting in the Reich Chancellery on 6 July. 'The revolution is not a permanent condition,' he announced; 'it must not turn into a lasting situation. It is necessary to divert the the river of revolution that has broken free into the secure bed of evolution.' Other Nazi leaders – Frick, Göring, Goebbels, and Heß – took up the message in the weeks that followed. There was an unmistakable change of course.

Röhm's ambitions were, however, undaunted. They amounted to little less than the creation of an 'SA state', with extensive powers in the police, in military matters, and in the civil administration. It was not just a matter of Röhm's own power ambitions. Within the gigantic army of Brownshirts, expectations of the wondrous shangri-la to follow the day when National Socialism took power had been hugely disappointed. Though they had poured out their bile on their political enemies, the offices, financial rewards, and power they had naïvely believed would flow their way remained elusive. Talk of a 'second revolution', however little it was grounded in any clear programme of social change, was, therefore, bound to find strong resonance among rank-and-file stormtroopers.

Ernst Röhm had, then, no difficulty in expanding his popularity among SA men through his continued dark threats in early 1934 about further revolution which would accomplish what the 'national uprising' had failed to bring about. He remained publicly loyal to Hitler. Privately, he was highly critical of Hitler's policy towards the Reichswehr and his dependency on Blomberg and Reichenau. And he did nothing to deter the growth of a personality cult elevating his leadership of the SA. At the Reich Party Rally of Victory in 1933, he had been the most prominent party leader after Hitler, clearly featuring as the Führer's right-hand man. By early 1934, Hitler had been largely forced from the pages of the SA's newspaper, *SA-Mann*, by the expanding Röhm-cult.

At least in public, the loyalty was reciprocated. Hitler wavered, as he would continue to do during the first months of 1934, between Röhm's SA and the Reichswehr. He could not bring himself to discipline, let alone dismiss, Röhm. The political damage and loss of face and popularity involved made such a move risky. But the realities of power compelled him to side with the Reichswehr leadership. This became fully clear only at the end of February.

By 2 February 1934, at a meeting of his Gauleiter, Hitler was again criticizing the SA in all but name. Only 'idiots' thought the revolution was not over; there were those in the Movement who only understood 'revolution' as meaning 'a permanent condition of chaos'.

The previous day, Röhm had sent Blomberg a memorandum on relations between the army and SA. What he appeared to be demanding – no copy of the actual memorandum has survived – was no less than the concession of national defence as the domain of the SA, and a reduction of the function of the armed forces to the provision of trained men for the SA. So crass were the demands that it seems highly likely that Blomberg deliberately falsified or misconstrued them when addressing a meeting of army District Commanders on 2 February in Berlin. They were predictably horrified. Now Hitler had to decide, stated Blomberg. The army lobbied him. In a conscious attempt to win his support against the SA, Blomberg, without any pressure from the Nazi leadership, introduced the NSDAP's emblem into the army and accepted the 'Aryan Paragraph' for the officer corps, leading to the prompt dismissal of some seventy members of the armed forces. Röhm, too, sought to win his support. But, faced with having to choose between the Reichswehr, with Hindenburg's backing, or his party army, Hitler could now only decide one way.

By 27 February the army leaders had worked out their 'guidelines for cooperation with the SA', which formed the basis for Hitler's speech the next day and had, therefore, certainly been agreed with him. At the meeting in the Reichswehr Ministry on 28 February, attended by Reichswehr, SA, and SS leaders, Hitler rejected outright Röhm's plans for an SA-militia. The SA was to confine its activities to political, not military, matters. A militia, such as Röhm was suggesting, was not suitable even for minimal national defence. He was determined to build up a well-trained 'people's army' in the Reichswehr, equipped with the most modern weapons, which must be prepared for all eventualities on defence within five years and suitable for attack after eight years. He demanded of the SA that they obey his orders. For the transitional period before the planned Wehrmacht was set up, he approved Blomberg's suggestion to deploy the SA for tasks of border protection and pre-military training. But 'the Wehrmacht must be the sole bearer of weapons of the nation'.

Röhm and Blomberg had to sign and shake hands on the 'agreement'. Hitler departed. Champagne followed. But the atmosphere was anything but cordial. When the officers had left, Röhm was overheard to remark: 'What the ridiculous corporal declared doesn't apply to us. Hitler has no loyalty and has at least to be sent on leave. If not with, then we'll manage the thing without Hitler.' The person taking note of these treasonable remarks was SA-Obergruppenführer Viktor Lutze, who reported what had gone on to Hitler. 'We'll have to let the thing ripen' was all he gleaned as reply. But the show of loyalty was noted. When he needed a new SA chief after the events of 30 June, Lutze was Hitler's man.

II

From the beginning of 1934, Hitler seems to have recognized that he would be faced with no choice but to cut Röhm down to size. How to tackle him was, however, unclear. Hitler deferred the problem. He simply awaited developments. The Reichswehr leadership, too, was biding its time, expecting a gradual escalation, but looking then to a final showdown. Relations between the army and the SA continued to fester. But Hitler did, it seems, order the monitoring of SA activities. According to the later account of Gestapo chief Rudolf Diels, it was in

January 1934 that Hitler requested him and Göring to collect material on the excesses of the SA. From the end of February onwards, the Reichswehr leadership started assembling its own intelligence on SA activities, which was passed to Hitler. Once Himmler and Heydrich had taken over the Prussian Gestapo in April, the build-up of a dossier on the SA was evidently intensified. Röhm's foreign contacts were noted, as well as those with figures at home known to be cool towards the regime, such as former Chancellor Schleicher.

By this time, Röhm had incited an ensemble of powerful enemies, who would eventually coagulate into an unholy alliance against the SA. Göring was so keen to be rid of the SA's alternative power-base in Prussia – which he himself had done much to establish, starting when he made the SA auxiliary police in February 1933 – that he was even prepared by 20 April to concede control over the Prussian Gestapo to Heinrich Himmler, thus paving the way for the creation of a centralized police-state in the hands of the SS. Himmler himself, and even more so his cold and dangerous henchman Reinhard Heydrich, recognized that their ambitions to construct such an empire – the key edifice of power and control in the Third Reich – rested on the élite SS breaking with its superior body, the SA, and eliminating the power-base held by Röhm. In the party, the head of the organization, installed in April 1933 with the grand title of Deputy Führer, Rudolf Heß, and the increasingly powerful figure behind the scenes Martin Bormann, were more than aware of the contempt in which the Political Organization was held by Röhm's men and the threat of the SA actually replacing the party, or making it redundant. For the army, as already noted, Röhm's aim to subordinate the Reichswehr to the interests of a people's militia was anathema. Intensified military exercises, expansive parades, and, not least, reports of extensive weapon collections in the hands of the SA, did little to calm the nerves.

At the centre of this web of countervailing interests and intrigue, united only in the anxiety to be rid of the menace of the SA, Hitler's sharp instinct for the realities of power by now must have made it plain that he had to break with Röhm.

In April it became known that Hindenburg was seriously ill. Hitler and Blomberg had already been told that the end was not far off. At the beginning of June, the Reich President retired to his estate at Neudeck in East Prussia. The most important prop of the conservatives was now far from the centre of the action. And the succession issue was imminent. Moreover, to remove the obstacle which the SA was providing to recommencing talks about rearmament with the western powers, Hitler had, at the end of May, ordered the SA to stop military exercises, and, in the last talks he had with Röhm, a few days later, had sent the stormtroopers on leave for a month.

This defusing of the situation, together with Hindenburg's absence, made the situation more difficult, rather than easier, for the conservatives. But Papen used a speech on 17 June at the University of Marburg to deliver a passionate warning against the dangers of a 'second revolution' and a heated broadside against the 'selfishness, lack of character, insincerity, lack of chivalry, and arrogance' featuring under the guise of the German revolution. He even criticized the creation of a 'false personality cult'. 'Great men are not made by propaganda, but grow out of their actions,' he declared. 'No nation can live in a continuous state of revolution,' he went on. 'Permanent dynamism permits no solid foundations to be laid. Germany cannot live in a continuous state of unrest, to which no one sees an end.' The speech met with roars of applause within the hall. Outside, Goebbels moved swiftly to have it banned, though not before copies of the speech had been run off and circulated, both within Germany and to the foreign press. Word of it quickly went round. Never again in the Third Reich was such striking criticism at the heart of the regime to come from such a prominent figure. But if Papen and his friends were hoping to prompt action by the army, supported by the President, to 'tame' Hitler, they were disappointed. As it was, the Marburg speech served as the decisive trigger to the brutal action taken at the end of the month.

Hitler's own mood towards the 'reactionaries' was darkening visibly. Without specifying any names, his speech at Gera at the Party Rally of the Thuringian Gau on 17 June, the same day as Papen's speech, gave a plain indication of his fury at the activities of the Papen circle. He castigated them as 'dwarves', alluding, it seems, to Papen himself as a 'tiny worm'. Then came the threat: 'If they should at any time attempt, even in a small way, to move from their criticism to a new act of perjury, they can be sure that what confronts them today is not the cowardly and corrupt bourgeoisie of 1918 but the fist of the entire people. It is the fist of the nation that is clenched and will smash down anyone who dares to undertake even the slightest attempt at sabotage.' Such a mood prefigured the murder of some prominent members of the conservative 'reaction' on 30 June. In fact, in the immediate aftermath of the Papen speech, a strike against the 'reactionaries' seemed more likely than a showdown with the SA.

At the imposition of the ban on publishing his speech, Papen went to see Hitler. He said Goebbels's action left him no alternative but to resign. He intended to inform the Reich President of this unless the ban were lifted and Hitler declared himself ready to follow the policies outlined in the speech. Hitler reacted cleverly – in wholly different manner from his tirades in the presence of his party members. He acknowledged that Goebbels was in the wrong in his action, and that he would order the ban to be lifted. He also attacked the insubordination of the SA and stated that they would have to be dealt with. He asked Papen, however, to delay his resignation until he could accompany him to visit the President for a joint interview to discuss the entire situation. Papen conceded – and the moment was lost.

Hitler wasted no time. He arranged an audience alone with Hindenburg on 21 June. On the way up the steps to Hindenburg's residence, Schloß Neudeck, he was met by Blomberg, who had been summoned by the President in the furore following Papen's speech. Blomberg told him bluntly that it was urgently necessary to take measures to ensure internal peace in Germany. If the Reich Government was incapable of relieving the current state of tension, the President would declare martial law and hand over control to the army. Hitler realized that there could be no further prevarication. He had to act. There was no alternative but to placate the army – behind which stood the President. And that meant destroying the power of the SA without delay.

What Hitler had in mind at this stage is unclear. He seems to have spoken about deposing Röhm, or having him arrested. By now, however, Heydrich's SD – the part of the labyrinthine SS organization responsible for internal surveillance – and the Gestapo were working overtime to concoct alarmist reports of an imminent SA putsch. SS and SD leaders were summoned to Berlin around 25 June to be instructed by Himmler and Heydrich about the measures to be taken in the event of an SA revolt, expected any time. For all their unruliness, the SA had never contemplated such a move. The leadership remained loyal to Hitler. But now, the readiness to believe that Röhm was planning a takeover was readily embraced by all the SA's powerful enemies. The Reichswehr, during May and June becoming increasingly suspicious about the ambitions of the SA leadership, made weapons and transport available to the SS (whose small size and – at this time – confinement to largely policing work posed no threat to the military). An SA putsch was now thought likely in summer or autumn. The entire Reichswehr leadership were prepared for imminent action against Röhm. The psychological state for a strike against the SA was rapidly forming. Alarm bells were set ringing loudly on 26 June through what seemed to be an order by Röhm for arming the SA in preparation for an attack on the Reichswehr. The 'order', in fact a near-certain fake (though by whom was never established), had mysteriously found its way into the office of the Abwehr chief, Captain Conrad Patzig. Lutze was present when Blomberg and Reichenau presented Hitler the following day with the 'evidence'. Hitler had already hinted to Blomberg two days earlier that he would summon SA leaders to a conference at Bad Wiessee on the Tegernsee, some fifty miles south-east of Munich, where Röhm was residing, and have them arrested. This decision seems to have been confirmed at the meeting with Blomberg and Reichenau on 27 June. The same day, SS-Obergruppenführer Sepp Dietrich, commander of Hitler's house-guards, the Leibstandarte-SS Adolf Hitler, arranged with the Reichswehr to pick up the arms needed for a 'secret and very important commission of the Führer'.

III

The timing of the 'action' seems to have been finally determined on the evening of 28 June, while Hitler, together with Göring and Lutze, was in Essen for the wedding of Gauleiter Terboven. During the wedding reception, Hitler had received a message from Himmler, informing him that Oskar von Hindenburg had agreed to arrange for his father to receive Papen, probably on 30 June. It marked a final attempt to win the Reich President's approval for moves to constrain the power not only of Röhm and the SA, but of Hitler himself. Hitler left the wedding reception straight away and raced back to his hotel. There, according to Lutze, he decided there was no time to lose: he had to strike.

Röhm's adjutant was ordered by telephone to ensure that all SA leaders attended a meeting with Hitler in Bad Wiessee on the late morning of 30 June. In the meantime, the army had been put on alert. Göring flew back to Berlin to take charge of matters there, ready at a word to move not only against the SA, but also the Papen group.

Rumours of unrest in the SA were passed to Hitler, whose mood was becoming blacker by the minute. The telephone rang. The 'rebels', it was reported, were ready to strike in Berlin. There was, in fact, no putsch attempt at all. But groups of SA men in different parts of Germany, aware of the stories circulating of an impending strike against the SA, or the deposition of Röhm, were going on the rampage. Sepp Dietrich was ordered to leave for Munich immediately. Soon after midnight, he phoned Hitler from Munich and was given further orders to pick up two companies of the Leibstandarte and be in Bad Wiessee by eleven in the morning. Around 2 a.m. Hitler left to fly to Munich, accompanied by his adjutants Brückner, Schaub, and Schreck, along with Goebbels, Lutze, and Press Chief Dietrich. The first glimmers of dawn were breaking through as he arrived. He was met by Gauleiter Adolf Wagner and two Reichswehr officers, who told him that the Munich SA, shouting abuse at the Führer, had attempted an armed demonstration in the city. Though a serious disturbance, it was, in fact, merely the biggest of the protest actions of despairing stormtroopers, when as many as 3,000 armed SA men had rampaged through Munich in the early hours, denouncing the 'treachery' against the SA, shouting: 'The Führer is against us, the Reichswehr is against us; SA out on the streets.' However, Hitler had not heard of the Munich disturbances before he arrived there in the early hours of the morning. Now, in blind rage at what he interpreted as the betrayal by Röhm – 'the blackest day of my life', he was heard to say – he decided not to wait till the following morning, but to act immediately.

He and his entourage raced to the Bavarian Ministry of the Interior. The local SA leaders Obergruppenführer Schneidhuber and Gruppenführer Schmid were peremptorily summoned. Hitler's fury was still rising as he awaited them. By now he had worked himself into a near-hysterical state of mind, reminiscent of the night of the Reichstag fire. Accepting no explanations, he ripped their rank badges from their shoulders, shouting 'You are under arrest and will be shot.' Bewildered and frightened, they were taken off to Stadelheim prison.

Hitler, without waiting for Dietrich's SS men to arrive, now demanded to be taken immediately to Bad Wiessee. It was just after 6.30 a.m. as the three cars pulled up outside the Hotel Hanselbauer in the resort on the Tegernsee, where Röhm and other SA leaders were still sleeping off an evening's drinking. Hitler, followed by members of his entourage and a number of policemen, stormed up to Röhm's room and, pistol in hand, denounced him as a traitor (which the astonished Chief of Staff vehemently denied) and declared him under arrest. Edmund Heines, the Breslau SA leader, was found in a nearby room in bed with a young man – a scene that Goebbels's propaganda later made much of to heap moral opprobrium on the SA. Other arrests of Röhm's staff followed.

Hitler and his entourage then travelled back to the Brown House. At midday he spoke to party and SA leaders gathered in the 'Senators' Hall'. The atmosphere was murderous. Hitler was beside himself, in a frenzy of rage, spittle dribbling from his mouth as he began to speak. He spoke of the 'worst treachery in world history'. Röhm, he claimed, had received 12 million Marks in bribes from France to have him arrested and killed, to deliver Germany to its enemies. The SA chief and his co-conspirators, Hitler railed, would be punished as examples. He would have them all shot. One after the other, the Nazi leaders demanded the extermination of the SA 'traitors'. Heß pleaded that the task of shooting Röhm fall to him.

Back in his own room, Hitler gave the order for the immediate shooting of six of the SA men held in Stadelheim, marking crosses against their names in a list provided by the prison administration. They were promptly taken out and shot by Dietrich's men. Not even a peremptory trial was held. The men were simply told before being shot: 'You have been condemned to death by the Führer! Heil Hitler!'

Röhm's name was not among the initial six marked by Hitler for instant execution. One witness later claimed to have overheard Hitler saying that Röhm had been spared because of his many earlier services to the Movement. A similar remark was noted by Alfred Rosenberg in his diary. 'Hitler did not want to have Röhm shot,' he wrote. 'He stood at one time at my side before the People's Court,' Hitler had said to the head of the Nazi publishing empire, Max Amann.

The loss of face at having to murder his right-hand man on account of his alleged rebellion was most likely the chief reason for Hitler's reluctance to order Röhm's death. For the moment, at any rate, he hesitated about having Röhm killed. In Berlin, meanwhile, there was no hesitation. Immediately on return from Bad Wiessee, Goebbels had telephoned Göring with the password 'Kolibri' ('Humming Bird'), which set in motion the murder-squads in the capital city and the rest of the country. Herbert von Bose, Papen's press secretary, was brutally shot down by a Gestapo hit-squad after the Vice-Chancellery had been stormed by SS men. Edgar Jung, an intellectual on the conservative Right and speech-writer for Papen, in 'protective custody' since 25 June, was also murdered, found dead in a ditch near Oranienburg on 1 July. Papen's staff were arrested. The Vice-Chancellor himself, whose murder would have proved a diplomatic embarrassment, was placed under house-arrest. The killing was extended to others who had nothing to do with the leadership of the SA. Old scores were settled. Gregor Strasser was taken to Gestapo headquarters and shot in one of the cells. General Schleicher and his wife were shot dead in their own home. Also among the victims was Major-General von Bredow, one of Schleicher's right-hand men. In Munich, Hitler's old adversary Ritter von Kahr was dragged away by SS men and later found hacked to death near Dachau. In all, there were twenty-two victims in and around Munich, mostly killed through 'local initiative'. The blood-lust had developed its own momentum.

Hitler arrived back in Berlin around ten o'clock on the evening of 30 June, tired, drawn, and unshaven, to be met by Göring, Himmler, and a guard of honour. He hesitated until late the following morning about the fate of the former SA Chief of Staff. He was, it seems, put under pressure by Himmler and Göring to have Röhm liquidated. In the early afternoon of Sunday 1 July, during a garden party at the Reich Chancellery for cabinet members and their wives, Hitler finally agreed. Even now, however, he was keen that Röhm take his own life rather than be 'executed'. Theodor Eicke, Commandant of Dachau Concentration Camp, was ordered to go to Stadelheim and offer Röhm the chance to recognize the enormity of his actions by killing himself. If not, he was to be shot. Along with his deputy, SS-Sturmbannführer Michael Lippert, and a third SS man from the camp, Eicke drove to Stadelheim. Röhm was left with a pistol. After ten minutes, no shot had been heard, and the pistol was untouched on the small table near the door of the cell, where it had been left. Eicke and Lippert returned to the cell, each with pistol drawn, signalled to Röhm, standing and bare-chested, and trying to speak, that they would wait no longer, took careful aim, and shot him dead. Hitler's published announcement was terse: 'The former Chief of Staff Röhm was given the opportunity to draw the consequences of his treacherous behaviour. He did not do so and was thereupon shot.'

On 2 July, Hitler formally announced the end of the 'cleansing action'. Some estimates put the total number killed at 150–200 persons.

With the SA still in a state of shock and uncertainty, the purge of its mass membership began under the new leader, the Hitler loyalist Viktor Lutze. Within a year, the SA had been reduced in size by over 40 per cent. Many subordinate leaders were dismissed in disciplinary hearings. The structures built up by Röhm as the foundation of his power within the organization were meanwhile systematically dismantled. The SA was turned into little more than a military sports and training body. For anyone still harbouring alternative ideas, the ruthlessness shown by Hitler had left its own unmistakable message.

IV

Outside Germany, there was horror at the butchery, even more so at the gangster methods used by the state's leaders. Within Germany, it was a different matter. Public expressions of gratitude to Hitler were not long in coming. Already on 1 July, Reichswehr Minister Blomberg, in a statement to the armed forces, praised the 'soldierly determination and exemplary courage' shown by the Führer in attacking and crushing 'the traitors and mutineers'. The gratitude of the armed forces, he added, would be marked by 'devotion and loyalty'. The following day, the Reich President sent Hitler a telegram expressing his own 'deep-felt gratitude' for the 'resolute intervention' and 'courageous personal involvement' which had 'rescued the German people from a serious danger'. Much later, when they were both in prison in Nuremberg, Papen asked Göring whether the President had ever seen the congratulatory telegram sent in his name. Göring replied that Otto Meissner, Hindenburg's State Secretary, had asked him, half-jokingly, whether he had been 'satisfied with the text'.

Hitler himself gave a lengthy account of the 'plot' by Röhm to a meeting of ministers on the morning of 3 July. Anticipating any allegations about the lawlessness of his actions, he likened his actions to those of the captain of a ship putting down a mutiny, where immediate action to smash a revolt was necessary, and a formal trial was impossible. He asked the cabinet to accept the draft Law for the Emergency Defence of the State that he was laying before them. In a single, brief paragraph, the law read: 'The measures taken on 30 June and 1 and 2 July for the suppression of high treasonable and state treasonable attacks are, as emergency defence of the state, legal.' The Reich Minister of Justice, the conservative Franz Gürtner, declared that the draft did not create new law, but simply confirmed existing law. Reichswehr Minister Blomberg thanked the Chancellor in the name of the cabinet for his 'resolute and courageous action through which he had protected the German people from civil war'. With this statement of suppliance by the head of the armed forces, and the acceptance by the head of the judicial system of the legality of acts of brute violence, the law acknowledging Hitler's right to commit murder in the interest of the state was unanimously accepted. The law was signed by Hitler, Frick, and Gürtner.

The account to the cabinet was in essence the basis of the justification which Hitler offered in his lengthy speech to the Reichstag on 13 July. If not one of his best rhetorical performances, it was certainly one of the most remarkable, and most effective, he was ever to deliver. The atmosphere was tense. Thirteen members of the Reichstag had been among those murdered; friends and former comrades-in-arms of the SA leaders were among those present. The presence of armed SS men flanking the rostrum and at various points of the hall was an indication of Hitler's wariness, even among the serried ranks of party members. After he had offered a lengthy, fabricated account of the 'revolt' and the part allegedly played in the conspiracy by General Schleicher, Major-General Bredow, and Gregor Strasser, he came to the most extraordinary sections of the speech. In these, the head of the German government openly accepted full responsibility for what amounted to mass murder. Hitler turned defence into attack. 'Mutinies are broken according to eternal, iron laws. If I am reproached with not turning to the law-courts for sentence, I can only say: in this hour, I was responsible for the fate of the German nation and thereby the supreme judge of the German people ... I gave the order to shoot those most guilty of this treason, and I further gave the order to burn out down to the raw flesh the ulcers of our internal well-poisoning and the poisoning from abroad.' The cheering was tumultuous. Not just among the Nazi Reichstag members, but in the country at large, Hitler's ruthless substitution of the rule of law by murder in the name of *raison d'état* was applauded. It matched exactly what Nazi parlance dubbed the 'healthy sentiments of the people'.

The public was ignorant of the plots, intrigues, and power-games taking place behind the scenes. What people saw for the most part was the welcome removal of a scourge. Once the SA had done its job in crushing the Left, the bullying and strutting arrogance, open acts of violence, daily disturbances, and constant unruliness of the stormtroopers were a massive affront to the sense of order, not just among the middle classes. Instead of being shocked by Hitler's resort to shooting without trial, most people – accepting, too, the official versions of the planned putsch – acclaimed the swift and resolute actions of their Leader.

There was great admiration for what was seen to be Hitler's protection of the 'little man' against the outrageous abuses of power of the over-mighty SA leadership. Even more so, the emphasis that Hitler had placed in his speech on the immorality and corruption of the SA leaders left a big mark on public responses. The twelve points laid down by Hitler in his order to the new Chief of Staff, Viktor Lutze, on 30 June had focused heavily on the need to eradicate homosexuality, debauchery, drunkenness, and high living from the SA. Hitler had explicitly pointed to the misuse of large amounts of money for banquets and limousines. The homosexuality of Röhm, Heines, and others among the SA leaders, known to Hitler and other Nazi leaders for years, was highlighted as particularly shocking in Goebbels's propaganda. Above all, Hitler was seen as the restorer of order. That murder on the orders of the head of government was the basis of the 'restoration of order' passed people by, was ignored, or – most generally – met with their approval. There were wide expectations that Hitler would extend the purge to the rest of the party – an indication of the distance that had already developed between Hitler's own massive popularity and the sullied image of the party's 'little Hitlers', the power-crazed functionaries found in towns and villages throughout the land.

There was no show of disapproval of Hitler's state murders from any quarter. Both Churches remained silent, even though the Catholic Action leader, Erich Klausener, had been among the victims. Two generals had also been murdered. Though a few of their fellow officers momentarily thought there should be an investigation, most were too busy clinking their champagne glasses in celebration at the destruction of the SA. As for any sign that the legal profession might distance itself from acts of blatant illegality, the foremost legal theorist in the country, Carl Schmitt, published an article directly relating to Hitler's speech on 13 July. Its title was: 'The Führer Protects the Law'.

The smashing of the SA removed the one organization that was seriously destabilizing the regime and directly threatening Hitler's own position. The army leadership could celebrate the demise of their rival, and the fact that Hitler had backed their power in the state. The army's triumph was, however, a hollow one. Its complicity in the events of 30 June 1934 bound it more closely to Hitler. But in so doing, it opened the door fully to the crucial extension of Hitler's power following Hindenburg's death. The generals might have thought Hitler was their man after 30 June. The reality was different. The next few years would show that the 'Röhm affair' was a vital stage on the way to the army becoming Hitler's tool, not his master.

The other major beneficiary was the SS. 'With regard to the great services of the SS, especially in connection with the events of the 30th of June,' Hitler removed its subordination to the SA. From 20 July 1934 onwards, it was responsible to him alone. Instead of any dependence on the huge and unreliable SA, with its own power pretensions, Hitler had elevated the smaller, élite praetorian guard, its loyalty unquestioned, its leaders already in almost total command of the police. The most crucial ideological weapon in the armoury of Hitler's state was forged.

Not least, the crushing of the SA leadership showed what Hitler wanted it to show: that those opposing the regime had to reckon with losing their heads. All would-be opponents could now be absolutely clear that Hitler would stop at nothing to hold on to power, that he would not hesitate to use the utmost brutality to smash those in his way.

V

An early intimation that a head of government who had had his own immediate predecessor as Chancellor, General von Schleicher, murdered might also not shy away from involvement in violence abroad was provided by the assassination of the Austrian Chancellor Engelbert Dolfuss in a failed putsch attempt undertaken by Austrian SS men on 25 July while Hitler was attending the Bayreuth Festival. Hitler's own role, and the extent to which he had detailed information of the putsch plans, is less than wholly clear. The initiative for the coup attempt clearly came from local Nazis. However, it seems that Hitler was aware of it, and gave his approval. The putsch attempt was rapidly put down. Under Kurt Schuschnigg, successor to the murdered Dollfuss, the Austrian authoritarian regime, treading its tightrope between the predatory powers of Germany and Italy, continued in existence – for the present.

The international embarrassment for Hitler was enormous, the damage to relations with Italy considerable. For a time, it even looked as if Italian intervention was likely. Papen found Hitler in a near-hysterical state, denouncing the idiocy of the Austrian Nazis for landing him in such a mess. Every attempt was made by the German government, however unconvincingly, to dissociate itself from the coup. The headquarters of the Austrian NSDAP in Munich were closed down. A new policy of restraint in Austria was imposed. But at least one consequence of the ill-fated affair pleased Hitler. He found the answer to what to do with Papen – who had 'just been in our way since the Röhm business', as Göring reportedly put it. He made him the new German ambassador in Vienna.

In Neudeck, meanwhile, Hindenburg was dying. His condition had been worsening during the previous weeks. On 1 August, Hitler told the cabinet that the doctors were giving Hindenburg less than twenty-four hours to live. The following morning, the Reich President was dead.

So close to the goal of total power, Hitler had left nothing to chance. The Enabling Act had explicitly stipulated that the rights of the Reich President would be left untouched. But on 1 August, while Hindenburg was still alive, Hitler had all his ministers put their names to a law determining that, on Hindenburg's death, the office of the Reich President would be combined with that of the Reich Chancellor. The reason subsequently given was that the title 'Reich President' was uniquely bound up with the 'greatness' of the deceased. Hitler wished from now on, in a ruling to apply 'for all time', to be addressed as 'Führer and Reich Chancellor'. The change in his powers was to be put to the German people for confirmation in a 'free plebiscite', scheduled for 19 August.

Among the signatories to the 'Law on the Head of State of the German Reich' of 1 August 1934 had been Reichswehr Minister Blomberg. The law meant that, on Hindenburg's death, Hitler would automatically become supreme commander of the armed forces. The possibility of the army appealing over the head of the government to the Reich President as supreme commander thereby disappeared. This caused no concern to the Reichswehr leadership. Blomberg and Reichenau were, in any case, determined to go further. They were keen to exploit the moment to bind Hitler, as they imagined, more closely to the armed forces. The fateful step they took, however, had precisely the opposite effect. As Blomberg later made clear, it was without any request by Hitler, and without consulting him, that he and Reichenau hastily devised the oath of unconditional loyalty to the person of the Führer, taken by every officer and soldier in the armed forces in ceremonies throughout the land on 2 August, almost before Hindenburg's corpse had gone cold. The oath meant that the distinction between loyalty to the state and loyalty to Hitler had been eradicated. Opposition was made more difficult. For those later hesitant about joining the conspiracy against Hitler, the oath would also provide an excuse. Far from creating a dependence of Hitler on the army, the oath, stemming from ill-conceived ambitions of the Reichswehr leadership, marked the symbolic moment when the army chained itself to the Führer.

'Today Hitler is the Whole of Germany,' ran a headline on 4 August. The funeral of the Reich President, held with great pomp and circumstance at the Tannenberg Memorial in East Prussia, the scene of his great victory in the First World War, saw Hindenburg, who had represented the only countervailing source of loyalty, 'enter Valhalla', as Hitler put it. Hindenburg had wanted to be buried at Neudeck. Ever alert to propaganda opportunities, Hitler insisted on his burial in the Tannenberg Memorial. On 19 August, the silent coup of the first days of the month duly gained its ritual plebiscitary confirmation. According to the official figures, 89.9 per cent of the voters supported Hitler's constitutionally now unlimited powers as head of state, head of government, leader of the party, and supreme commander of the armed forces. The result, disappointing though it was to the Nazi leadership, and less impressive as a show of support than might perhaps have been imagined when all account is taken of the obvious pressures and manipulation, nevertheless reflected the fact that Hitler had the backing, much of it fervently enthusiastic, of the great majority of the German people.

In the few weeks embracing the Röhm affair and the death of Hindenburg, Hitler had removed all remaining threats to his position with an ease which even in the spring and early summer of 1934 could have been barely imagined. He was now institutionally unchallengeable, backed by the 'big battalions', adored by much of the population. He had secured total power. The Führer state was established. Germany had bound itself to the dictatorship it had created.

After the crisis-ridden summer, Hitler was, by September, once again in his element on the huge propaganda stage of the Nuremberg Rally. In contrast even to the previous year's rally, this was consciously created as a vehicle of the Führer cult. Hitler now towered above his Movement, which had assembled to pay him homage. The film which the talented and glamorous director Leni Riefenstahl made of the rally subsequently played to packed houses throughout Germany, and made its own significant contribution to the glorification of Hitler. The title of the film, devised by Hitler himself, was *Triumph of the Will*. In reality, his triumph owed only a little to will. It owed far more to those who had much to gain – or thought they had – by placing the German state at Hitler's disposal.

12

Working Towards the Führer

I

Everyone with opportunity to observe it knows that the Führer can only with great difficulty order from above everything that he intends to carry out sooner or later. On the contrary, until now everyone has best worked in his place in the new Germany if, so to speak, he works towards the Führer.

This was the central idea of a speech made by Werner Willikens, State Secretary in the Prussian Agriculture Ministry, at a meeting of representatives from Länder agriculture ministries held in Berlin on 21 February 1934. Willikens continued:

Very often, and in many places, it has been the case that individuals, already in previous years, have waited for commands and orders. Unfortunately, that will probably also be so in future. Rather, however, it is the duty of every single person to attempt, in the spirit of the Führer, to work towards him. Anyone making mistakes will come to notice it soon enough. But the one who works correctly towards the Führer along his lines and towards his aim will in future as previously have the finest reward of one day suddenly attaining the legal confirmation of his work.

These comments, made in a routine speech, hold a key to how the Third Reich operated. Between Hindenburg's death at the beginning of August 1934 and the Blomberg–Fritsch crisis in late January and early February 1938, the Führer state took shape. These were the 'normal' years of the Third Reich that lived in the memories of many contemporaries as the 'good' years (though they were scarcely that for the already growing numbers of victims of Nazism). But they were also years in which the 'cumulative radicalization' so characteristic of the Nazi regime began to gather pace. One feature of this process was the fragmentation of government as Hitler's form of personalized rule distorted the machinery of administration and called into being a panoply of overlapping and competing agencies dependent in differing ways upon the 'will of the Führer'. At the same time, the racial and expansionist goals at the heart of Hitler's own *Weltanschauung* began in these years gradually to come more sharply into focus, though by no means always as a direct consequence of Hitler's own actions. Not least, these were the years in which Hitler's prestige and power, institutionally unchallengeable after the summer of 1934, expanded to the point where it was absolute.

These three tendencies – erosion of collective government, emergence of clearer ideological goals, and Führer absolutism – were closely interrelated. Hitler's personal actions, particularly in the realm of foreign policy, were certainly vital to the development. But the decisive component was that unwittingly singled out in his speech by Werner Willikens. Hitler's personalized form of rule invited radical initiatives from below and offered such initiatives backing, so long as they were in line with his broadly defined goals. This promoted ferocious competition at all levels of the regime, among competing agencies, and among individuals within those agencies. In the Darwinist jungle of the Third Reich, the way to power and advancement was through anticipating the 'Führer will', and, without waiting for directives, taking initiatives to promote what were presumed to be Hitler's aims and wishes. For party functionaries and ideologues and for SS 'technocrats of power', 'working towards the Führer' could have a literal meaning. But, metaphorically, ordinary citizens denouncing neighbours to the Gestapo, often turning personal animosity or resentment to their advantage through political slur, businessmen happy to exploit anti-Jewish legislation to rid themselves of competitors, and the many others whose daily forms of minor cooperation with the regime took place at the cost of others, were – whatever their motives – indirectly 'working towards the Führer'. They were as a consequence helping drive on an unstoppable radicalization which saw the gradual emergence in concrete shape of policy objectives embodied in the 'mission' of the Führer.

Through 'working towards the Führer', initiatives were taken, pressures created, legislation instigated – all in ways which fell into line with what were taken to be Hitler's aims, and without the Dictator necessarily having to dictate. The result was continuing radicalization of policy in a direction which brought Hitler's own ideological imperatives more plainly into view as practicable policy options. The disintegration of the formal machinery of government and the accompanying ideological radicalization resulted then directly and inexorably from the specific form of personalized rule under Hitler. Conversely, both decisively shaped the process by which Hitler's personalized power was able to free itself from all institutional constraints and become absolute.

Those close to Hitler later claimed that they detected a change in him after Hindenburg's death. According to Press Chief Otto Dietrich, the years 1935 and 1936, with Hitler 'now as absolute ruler on the lookout for new deeds', were 'the most significant' in his development 'from domestic reformer and social leader of the people to the later foreign-policy desperado and gambler in international politics'. 'In these years,' Dietrich went on, 'a certain change also made itself noticeable in Hitler's personal conduct and behaviour. He became increasingly unwilling to receive visitors on political matters if they had not been ordered by him to attend. Equally, he knew how to distance himself inwardly from his entourage. While, before the takeover of power, they had the possibility of putting forward their differing political opinion, he now as head of state and person of standing kept strictly out of all unrequested political discussion . . . Hitler began to hate objections to his views and doubts on their infallibility . . . He wanted to speak, but not to listen. He wanted to be the hammer, not the anvil.'

Hitler's increasing withdrawal from domestic politics once the period of consolidation of power had come to an end in August 1934 was, as Dietrich's remarks suggest, not simply a matter of character and choice. It also directly mirrored his position as Leader, whose prestige and image could not allow him to be politically embarrassed or sullied by association with unpopular policy choices. Hitler represented, and as the regime's central integrating mechanism *had* to represent, the image of national unity. He could not be seen to be involved in internal, day-to-day political conflict. Beyond that, his growing aloofness reflected, too, the effective transformation of domestic politics into propaganda and indoctrination. Choice and debate about options – the essence of politics – had by now been removed from the public arena (even if, of course, bitter disputes and conflicts continued behind the scenes). 'Politics' within a 'coordinated' Germany now amounted to what Hitler had since the early 1920s regarded as its sole aim: the 'nationalization of the masses' in preparation for the great and inevitable struggle against external enemies. But this goal, the creation of a strong, united, and impregnable 'national community', was so all-embracing, so universal in its impact, that it amounted to little more than an extremely powerful emotional incitement to formulate policy initiatives in every sphere of the regime's activity, affecting all walks of life. What his form of leadership, linked to the broad 'directions for action' which he embodied – national revival, 'removal' of Jews, racial 'improvement', and restoration of Germany's power and standing in the world – did was to unleash an unending dynamic in all avenues of policy-making. As Willikens had remarked, the greatest chances of success (and best opportunities for personal aggrandizement), occurred where individuals could demonstrate how effectively they were 'working towards the Führer'. But since this frenzy of activity was uncoordinated – and could not be coordinated – because of Hitler's need to avoid being openly drawn into disputes, it inexorably led to endemic conflict (within the general understanding of following the 'Führer's will'). And this in turn merely reinforced the impossibility of Hitler's personal involvement in resolving the conflict. Hitler was, therefore, at one and the same time the absolutely indispensable fulcrum of the entire regime, and yet largely detached from any formal machinery of government. The result, inevitably, was a high level of governmental and administrative disorder.

Hitler's personal temperament, his unbureaucratic style of operating, his Darwinistic inclination to side with the stronger, and the aloofness necessitated by his role as Führer, all merged together to produce a most extraordinary phenomenon: a highly modern, advanced state without any central coordinating body and with a head of government largely disengaged from the machinery of government. Cabinet meetings (which Hitler had never liked running) now lost significance. There were only twelve gatherings of ministers in 1935. By 1937, this had fallen to a mere six meetings. After 5 February 1938, the cabinet never met again. During the war, Hitler would even ban his ministers getting together occasionally over a glass of beer. In the absence of cabinet discussions which might have determined priorities, a flood of legislation emanating independently from each ministry had to be formulated by a cumbersome and grossly inefficient process whereby drafts were circulated and recirculated among ministers until some agreement was reached. Only at that stage would Hitler, if he approved after its contents were briefly summarized for him, sign the bill (usually scarcely bothering to read it) and turn it into law. Hans Heinrich Lammers, the head of the Reich Chancellery, and sole link between the ministers and the Führer, naturally attained considerable influence over the way legislation (or other business of ministers) was presented to Hitler. Where Lammers decided that the Führer was too busy with other pressing matters of state, legislation that had taken months to prepare could simply be ignored or postponed, sometimes indefinitely. Alternatively, Hitler intervened, sometimes in minutiae, on the basis of some one-sided piece of information he had been fed. The result was an increasing arbitrariness as Hitler's highly personalized style of rule came into inevitable – and ultimately irreconcilable – conflict with bureaucracy's need for regulated norms and clearly-defined procedures. Hitler's ingrained secretiveness, his preference for one-to-one meetings (which he could easily dominate) with his subordinates, and his strong favouritism among ministers and other leaders in party as well as state, were added ingredients that went to undermine formal patterns of government and administration.

Access to Hitler was naturally a key element in the continuing power-struggle within the regime. Ministers who had for some reason fallen out of favour could find it impossible to speak to him. Agriculture Minister Walther Darré, for instance, was in the later 1930s to attempt in vain for over two years to gain an audience with the Führer to discuss the country's seriously worsening agricultural problems. Though they could not hinder the access of 'court favourites' like Goebbels and the highly ambitious young architect, Albert Speer – skilful in pandering to Hitler's obsession with building plans and a rapidly rising star in the Nazi firmament – Hitler's adjutants acquired a good deal of informal power through their control of the portals of the Führer.

Fritz Wiedemann, during the First World War Hitler's immediate superior and in the mid-1930s one of his adjutants, later recalled the extraordinary style of his arbitrary and haphazard form of personal rule. In 1935, commented Wiedemann, Hitler still maintained a relatively orderly routine. Mornings, between about 10.00 a.m. and lunch at 1.00 or 2.00 p.m., were normally taken up with meetings with Lammers, State Secretary Meissner, Funk (from the Propaganda Ministry) and ministers or other significant figures who had pressing business to discuss. In the afternoons, Hitler held discussions with military or foreign-policy advisers, though he preferred to talk to Speer about building plans. Gradually, however, any formal routine crumbled. Hitler reverted to the type of dilettante lifestyle which, in essence, he had enjoyed as a youth in Linz and Vienna. 'Later on,' recalled Wiedemann, 'Hitler appeared as a rule only just before lunch, quickly read the press summaries provided by Reich Press Chief Dr Dietrich, then went to eat. It became, therefore, ever more difficult for Lammers and Meissner to acquire decisions from Hitler which he alone as head of state could take.' When Hitler was at his residence on the Obersalzberg, it was even worse. 'There he invariably left his room only approaching 2.00 p.m. Then it was lunch. The afternoon was mainly taken up with a walk, and in the evenings, straight after the evening meal, films were shown.'

The walks were always downhill, with a car stationed at the bottom to ferry Hitler and his accompaniment back up again. Hitler's detestation of physical exercise and fear of embarrassment through lack of athleticism remained acute. The whole area was cordoned off during the afternoon walk, to keep away the crowds of sightseers eager for a glimpse of the Führer. Instead, the tradition set in of the visitors' 'march-past'. Up to 2,000 people of all ages and from all parts of Germany, whose devotion had persuaded them to follow the steep paths up to the Obersalzberg and often wait hours, marched, at a signal from one of the adjutants, in a silent column past Hitler. For Wiedemann, the adulation had quasi-religious overtones.

Hitler rarely missed his evening film. The adjutants had to see to it that a fresh film was on offer each day. Hitler invariably preferred light entertainment to serious documentaries, and, according to Wiedemann, probably gleaned some of his strong prejudices about the culture of other nations from such films.

In the Reich Chancellery, the company was almost exclusively male – the atmosphere part way between that of a men's club and an officers' mess (with a whiff of the gangsters' den thrown in). On the Obersalzberg, the presence of women (Eva Braun and wives or lady-friends of members of Hitler's entourage) helped to lighten the atmosphere, and political talk was banned as long as they were there. Hitler was courteous, even charming in a somewhat awkwardly stiff and formal fashion, to his guests, especially towards women. He was invariably correct and attentive in dealings with the secretaries, adjutants, and other attendants on his personal staff, who for the most part liked as well as respected him. He could be kind and thoughtful, as well as generous, in his choice of birthday and Christmas presents for his entourage. Even so, whether at the Reich Chancellery or on the Obersalzberg, the constrictions and tedium of living in close proximity to Hitler were considerable. Genuine informality and relaxation were difficult when he was present. Wherever he was, he dominated. In conversation, he would brook no contradiction. Guests at meals were often nervous or hesitant lest a false word incur his displeasure. His adjutants were more concerned late at night lest a guest unwittingly lead on to one of Hitler's favourite topics – notably the First World War, or the navy – where he would launch into yet another endless monologue which they would be forced to sit through until the early hours.

Hitler's unmethodical, even casual, approach to the flood of often serious matters of government brought to his attention was a guarantee of administrative disorder. 'He disliked reading files,' recalled Wiedemann. 'I got decisions out of him, even on very important matters, without him ever asking me for the relevant papers. He took the view that many things sorted themselves out if they were left alone.'

Hitler's lethargy regarding paperwork knew one major exception. When it came to preparing his speeches, which he composed himself, he would withdraw into his room and could work deep into the night several evenings running, occupying three secretaries taking dictation straight into the typewriter before carefully correcting the drafts. The public image was vital. He remained, above all, the propagandist *par excellence*.

Even had Hitler been far more conscientious and less idiosyncratic and haphazard in his style of leadership, he would have found the highly personalized direction of the complex and varied issues of a modern state beyond him. As it was, the doors were opened wide to mismanagement and corruption on a massive scale. Hitler coupled financial incompetence and disinterest with an entirely exploitative and cavalier usage of public funds. Posts were found for 'old fighters'. Vast amounts of money were poured into the construction of imposing representative buildings. Architects and builders were lavishly rewarded. For favoured building or artistic projects, money was no object. Leading figures in the regime could draw upon enormous salaries, enjoy tax relief, and benefit further from gifts, donations, and bribes to accommodate their extravagant tastes in palatial homes, fine trappings, works of art, and other material luxuries – including, of course, the inevitable showy limousines.

Corruption was rife at all levels of the regime. Hitler was happy to indulge the infinite craving for the material trappings of power and success of his underlings, aware that corruption on a massive scale ensured loyalty as the Third Reich developed into a modern variant of a feudal system resting on personal allegiance rewarded by private fiefdoms. He himself, by now a millionaire on the proceeds of sales of *Mein Kampf*, led his publicly acclaimed spartan lifestyle (as regards his food and clothing) in a context of untold luxury. Alongside his magnificent apartments – his official one in Berlin and his private one in Munich – the initially somewhat modest alpine residence, Haus Wachenfeld on the Obersalzberg, was now converted at vast expense into the grandiose Berghof, suitable for state visits of foreign dignitaries. His restless energy demanded that he and his sizeable entourage were almost constantly on the move within Germany. For that, a special train with eleven coaches containing sleeping compartments, a fleet of limousines, and three aeroplanes stood at his disposal.

Even more serious than the way corrupt party despots profited from the bonanza of a seemingly unlimited free-for-all with public funds was the corruption of the political system itself. In the increasing absence of any formal procedures for arriving at political decisions, favoured party bosses with access to Hitler were often able, over lunch or at coffee, to put forward some initiative and manipulate a comment of approval to their own advantage. Hitler's sparse involvement in initiating domestic policy during the mid- and later 1930s and the disintegration of any centralized body for policy formulation meant that there was wide scope for those able to exert pressure for action in areas broadly echoing the aims of nationalization of the masses and exclusion of those deemed not to belong to the 'national community'. The pressure came above all from two sources: the party (both its central office and its provincial bosses, the Gauleiter) and the élite organization, the SS (now merging into the police to become an ideologically driven state security force of immense power). Using Hitler's professed (and unlimited) goals of national rebirth and strength through racial purity to legitimate their demands and actions, they ensured that the dynamic unleashed by the takeover of power would not subside.

Once power had been attained in 1933, the NSDAP, its numbers now rapidly swelling through the intake of hundreds of thousands of opportunists, became in essence a loosely coordinated vehicle of propaganda and social control. After becoming Chancellor, Hitler had taken little interest in the party as an institution. The weak and ineffectual, but devotedly loyal Rudolf Heß was in April made Hitler's deputy in charge of the party. Since Robert Ley was left running the party's organizational matters, Heß's authority was from the outset far from complete. Nor was Heß in a strong position in his dealings with the Gauleiter, most of whom could rely on their long-standing personal bonds with Hitler to uphold their power-base in the provinces. Neither a genuine, hierarchical structure of command at the top of the party, nor a collective body for determining party policy was ever instituted. The 'Reich Leadership' of the party remained a group of individuals who never met as a type of Politburo; Gauleiter conferences only took place at Hitler's own behest, to hear a speech from the Führer, not to discuss policy; while a party senate was never called into existence. The party acquired, therefore, neither a coherent structure nor a systematic policy which it could enforce upon the state administration. Its essential nature – that of a 'Führer party' tied to emotively powerful but loosely-defined general aims embodied in the person of the Führer and held together by the Führer cult – ruled out both. Even so, once Heß was given in 1934 what amounted to veto rights over draft legislation by government ministers and, the following year, over the appointment of higher civil servants, the party had indeed made significant inroads into the purely governmental arena. The possibilities of intervention, however unsystematic, did now increase the party's influence, above all in what it saw as crucial ideological spheres. Race policy and the 'Church struggle' were among the most important of these. In both areas, the party had no difficulty in mobilizing its activists, whose radicalism in turn forced the government into legislative action. In fact, the party leadership often found itself compelled to respond to pressures from below, stirred up by Gauleiter playing their own game, or emanating sometimes from radical activists at local level. Whatever the derivation, in this way, the continuum of radicalization in issues associated with the Führer's aims was sustained.

By the mid-1930s, Hitler paid little attention to the workings of the party. The dualism of party and state was never resolved – and was not resolvable. Hitler himself welcomed the overlaps in competence and lack of clarity. Sensitive as always to any organizational framework which might have constrained his own power, he undermined all attempts at

'Reich reform' by Frick, aimed at producing a more rational authoritarian state structure.

Hitler's approach to the state, as to all power-relations, was purely exploitative and opportunistic. It was for him, as he had expressly stated in *Mein Kampf*, simply a means to an end – the vague notion of 'upholding and advancing a community of physically and mentally similar beings', the 'sustaining of those racial basic elements which, as bestowers of culture, create the beauty and dignity of a higher type of human being'. It followed that he gave no consideration to forms and structures, only to effect. His crude notion was that if a specific sphere of policy could not be best served by a government ministry, weighed down by bureaucracy, then another organization, run as unbureaucratically as possible, should manage it. The new bodies were usually set up as directly responsible to Hitler himself, and straddled party and state without belonging to either. In reality, of course, this process merely erected new, competing, sometimes overlapping bureaucracies and led to unending demarcation disputes. These did not trouble Hitler. But their effect was at one and the same time to undermine still further any coherence of government and administration, and to promote the growing autonomy within the regime of Hitler's own position as Führer.

The most important, and ideologically radical, new plenipotentiary institution, directly dependent on Hitler, was the combined SS-police apparatus which had fully emerged by mid-1936. Already before the 'Röhm-Putsch', Himmler had extended his initial power-base in Bavaria to gain control over the police in one state after another. After the SS had played such a key part in breaking the power of the SA leadership at the end of June, Himmler had been able to push home his advantage until Göring conceded full control over the security police in the largest of the states, Prussia. Attempts by Reich Minister of the Interior Frick and Justice Minister Gürtner to curb autonomous police power, expanding through the unrestricted use of 'protective custody' and control of the growing domain of the concentration camps, also ended in predictable failure. Where legal restrictions on the power of the police were mooted, Himmler could invariably reckon with Hitler's backing. On 17 June, Hitler's decree created a unified Reich police under Himmler's command. The most powerful agency of repression thus merged with the most dynamic ideological force in the Nazi Movement. Himmler's subordination to Frick through the office he had just taken up as Chief of the German Police existed only on paper. As head of the SS, Himmler was personally subordinate only to Hitler himself. With the politicization of conventional 'criminal' actions through the blending of the criminal and political police in the newly-formed 'security police' a week later, the ideological power-house of the Third Reich and executive organ of the 'Führer will' had essentially taken shape.

The instrument had been forged which saw the realization of the Führer's *Weltanschauung* as its central aim. Intensification of radicalism was built into the nature of such a police force which combined ruthlessness and efficiency of persecution with ideological purpose and dynamism. Directions and dictates from Hitler were not needed. The SS and police had individuals and departments more than capable of ensuring that the discrimination kept spiralling. The rise of Adolf Eichmann from an insignificant figure collecting information on Zionism, but located in what would rapidly emerge as a key department – the SD's 'Jewish Desk' in Berlin – to 'manager' of the 'Final Solution' showed how initiative and readiness to grasp opportunities not only brought its rewards in power and aggrandizement to the individual concerned, but also pushed on the process of radicalization precisely in those areas most closely connected with Hitler's own ideological fixations.

In the mid-1930s this process was still in its early stages. But pressures for action from the party in ideological concerns regarded as central to National Socialism, and the instrumentalization of those concerns through the expanding repressive apparatus of the police, meant that there was no sagging ideological momentum once power had been consolidated. And as initiatives formulated at different levels and by different agencies of the regime attempted to accommodate the ideological drive, the 'idea' of National Socialism, located in the person of the Führer, thus gradually became translated from utopian 'vision' into realizable policy objectives.

II

The beginnings of this process were also visible in Germany's foreign relations. Hitler's own greatest contribution to events with such momentous consequences lay in his gambling instinct, his use of bluff, and his sharp antennae for the weak spots of his opponents. He took the key decisions; he alone determined the timing. But little else was Hitler's own work. The broad aims of rearmament and revision of Versailles – though each notion hid a variety of interpretations – united policy-makers and power-groups, whatever the differences in emphasis, in the military and the Foreign Office.

Once Germany's diplomatic isolation was sealed by its withdrawal from the League of Nations, any opportunity of bilateral agreements in eastern Europe which would prevent German ambitions being contained by the multilateral pacts strived for by the French was to be seized. The first indicator of such a move – marking a notable shift in German foreign policy – was the startling ten-year non-aggression pact with Poland, signed on 26 January 1934. Germany's departure from the League of Nations had intensified the mutual interest in an improved relationship. The pact benefited Germany in undermining French influence in eastern Europe (thereby removing the possibility of any combined Franco-Polish military action against Germany). For the Poles, it provided at least the temporary security felt necessary in the light of diminished protection afforded through the League of Nations, weakened by the German withdrawal.

Hitler was prepared to appear generous in his dealings with the Poles. There was a new urgency in negotiations. Neurath and the Foreign Office, initially set for a different course, swiftly trimmed their sails to the new wind. 'As if by orders from the top, a change of front toward us is taking place all along the line. In Hitlerite spheres they talk about the new Polish-German friendship,' noted Józef Lipski, Polish minister to Berlin, on 3 December 1933. In conditions of great secrecy, a ten-year non-aggression treaty was prepared and sprung on an astonished Europe on 26 January 1934. This early shift in German foreign policy plainly bore Hitler's imprint. 'No parliamentary minister between 1920 and 1933 could have gone so far,' noted Ernst von Weizsäcker, at that time German ambassador in Bern.

The rapprochement with Poland meant, inevitably, a new course towards the Soviet Union. Initially, little or nothing had altered the modus vivendi based on mutual advantage, which, despite deteriorating relations during the last years of the Weimar Republic, and despite ideological antipathy, had existed since the treaties of Rapallo in 1922, and Berlin in 1926. From summer onwards, however, contrary to the wishes of the Foreign Office and (despite mounting concern) of its Soviet equivalent though in line with the clamour of the Nazi movement, diplomatic relations worsened significantly. In autumn 1933, Hitler himself ruled out any repair of relations. During 1934, despite the efforts of the German ambassador Rudolf Nadolny and Soviet overtures for better relations, the deterioration continued. Hitler himself blocked any improvement, leading to Nadolny's resignation. The inevitable consequence was to push the Soviet Union closer to France, thus enlarging the spectre of encirclement on which Nazi propaganda so readily played.

In early 1935, the Soviet Union was still little more than a side issue in German foreign policy. Relations with the western powers were the chief concern. The divisions, weakness, and need to carry domestic opinion of the western democracies would soon play into Hitler's hands. In the meantime, a rich propaganda gift was about to fall into Hitler's lap with the return of the Saar territory to Germany through the plebiscite of 13 January 1935. The Versailles Treaty had removed the Saarland from Germany, placing it under League of Nations control for fifteen years, and affording France the right to its resources. After fifteen years it was foreseen that the Saar inhabitants – roughly half a million voters – should decide whether they would prefer to return to Germany, become part of France, or retain the status quo. It was always likely that the majority of the largely German-speaking population, where resentment at the treatment meted out in 1919 still smouldered fiercely, would want to return to Germany. A good deal of work by the German government prepared the ground, and as the plebiscite day approached Goebbels unleashed a massive barrage of propaganda directed at the Saar inhabitants and raising consciousness of the issue at home.

The Saar territory was overwhelmingly Catholic, with a large industrial working-class segment of the population – the two social groups which had proved least enthusiastic about Nazism within Germany itself. In the light of the ferocious repression of the Left and the threatening, if still largely sporadic, persecution of the Catholic Church that had followed the Nazi takeover in Germany, opponents of the Hitler regime in the Saar could still harbour illusions of a substantial anti-Nazi vote. But the Catholic authorities put their weight behind a return to Germany. And many Saar Catholics already looked to Hitler as the leader who would rescue them from Bolshevism. On the Left, the massive erosion of party loyalties had set in long before the plebiscite. For all their propaganda efforts, the message of the dwindling number of Social

Democrat and Communist functionaries fell largely on stony ground. Nazi propaganda had little difficulty in trumpeting the alternative to a return to Germany: continued massive unemployment, economic exploitation by France, and lack of any political voice. Some concerted intimidation, as in the Reich itself during the 'time of struggle', did the rest.

When the votes were counted, just under 91 per cent of the Saar's electorate had freely chosen dictatorship. At least two-thirds of the former supporters of both left-wing parties had supported the return to Germany. Any lingering doubts about whether Hitler had the genuine backing of the German people were dispelled.

Hitler milked his triumph for all that it was worth. At the same time, he was careful to make dove-like noises for public consumption. He hoped, he declared, that as a consequence of the settlement of the Saar issue, 'relations between Germany and France had improved once and for all. Just as we want peace, so we must hope that our great neighbouring people is also willing and ready to seek this peace with us'. His true thoughts were different. The Saar triumph had strengthened his hand. He had to exploit the advantage. Western diplomats awaited his next move. They would not wait long.

Anxious to do nothing to jeopardize the Saar campaign, especial caution had been deployed in rearmament, either on Hitler's orders or those of the Foreign Office. It could, therefore, be expected that the demands of the armed forces leadership for acclerated rearmament would gain new impetus following the Saar triumph. Army leaders were divided about the tempo of expansion, but not about its necessity or the aim of an eventual thirty-six-division peacetime army, the size eventually determined by Hitler in March 1935. They reckoned with moving to a conscript army by summer 1935. Only the timing remained to be determined – on the basis of the foreign-policy situation.

This had become strained again in early 1935. A joint British-French communiqué on 3 February had condemned unilateral rearmament, and advanced proposals for general restrictions of arms levels and an international defence-pact against aggression from the air. After some delay, the German response on 15 February expressed the wish for clarificatory talks with the British government. The British Foreign Secretary Sir John Simon and Lord Privy Seal Anthony Eden were accordingly invited for talks in Berlin on 7 March. Three days before the planned visit, the publication of a British Government *White Book*, announcing increases in military expenditure as a result of the growing insecurity in Europe caused by German rearmament and the bellicose atmosphere being cultivated in the Reich, led to a furious outcry in the German press. Hitler promptly developed a 'diplomatic' cold and postponed Simon's visit.

Three days after the visit should have taken place, on 10 March, Göring announced the existence of a German air-force – an outright breach of the Versailles Treaty. For effect, in comments to diplomats, he almost doubled the numbers of aircraft actually at Germany's disposal at the time. Just prior to this, the French had renewed their military treaty of 1921 with Belgium. And on 15 March the French National Assembly approved the lengthening of the period of military service from one to two years. The moves of the arch-enemy, France, prompted Hitler's reaction. They provided the pretext. Alert as ever to both the political and the propaganda advantages to be gained from the actions of his opponents, he decided to take the step now which in any case would soon have been forthcoming.

On 13 March, Lieutenant-Colonel Hoßbach, Hitler's Wehrmacht adjutant, was ordered to present himself the next morning in the Hotel Vier Jahreszeiten in Munich. When he arrived, Hitler was still in bed. Only shortly before midday was the military adjutant summoned to be told that the Führer had decided to reintroduce conscription in the immediate future – a move which would in the eyes of the entire world graphically demonstrate Germany's newly regained autonomy and cast aside the military restrictions of Versailles. Hitler expounded his reasons for two hours. The advantageous foreign-policy situation, in which other European states were adjusting their military strength, and especially the measures being taken in France, were decisive. Hoßbach was then asked what size the new army should be. Astonishingly, Hitler did not consider directly consulting the Commander-in-Chief of the Army, General Werner Fritsch, or the Chief of the General Staff, Ludwig Beck, on this vital topic. It was expected that Hoßbach would be familiar with the thinking of the military leadership. Subject to approval from War Minister Blomberg and Fritsch, Hoßbach stipulated thirty-six divisions. This matched the final size of the peacetime army that the military leadership had envisaged *as a future goal*. It implied an army of 550,000 men, five-and-a-half times the size of the post-Versailles army, and a third larger than that envisaged by Beck in a memorandum written only nine days earlier. Hitler accepted Hoßbach's figures without demur. What had been meant by the army chiefs as a level to be attained only gradually was now determined as the immediate size.

The more spectacular, the better, was always Hitler's maxim in a propaganda coup. Secrecy both to achieve the greatest surprise and avoid damaging leaks that could provoke dangerous repercussions was another. Hitler had taken his decision without consulting either his military leaders or relevant ministers. It was the first time this had happened in a serious matter of foreign policy, and the first time that Hitler encountered opposition from the heads of the armed forces. Only Hoßbach's pleading on 14 March had persuaded Hitler to inform Blomberg, Fritsch, and selected cabinet ministers of what he had in store two days later. He had initially been unwilling to disclose to them what he intended on the grounds that there might then be a risk to secrecy. The War Minister and armed forces leadership were astonished and appalled that Hitler was prepared to take the step at such a sensitive juncture in foreign policy. It was not that they disagreed with the expansion of the armed forces, or its scale; merely that the timing and way it was done struck them as irresponsible and unnecessarily risky. The Foreign Ministry was more sanguine about the risks involved, reckoning the danger of military intervention to be slight. Britain's reaction would be decisive. And various indicators reaching Berlin pointed to the fact that the British were increasingly inclined to accept German rearmament. While the military leadership recoiled, therefore, civilian members of the cabinet welcomed Hitler's move.

The relative calm of the other members of the cabinet evidently helped to soothe Blomberg's nerves. Fritsch, too, had come round to giving his approval. His objections – remembered by Hitler years later – were by now confined to technical problems arising from the planned speed of rearmament.

Later that afternoon, Saturday 16 March, Hitler, with Neurath at his side, informed foreign ambassadors of his imminent action. Then the dramatic news was announced. Hitler proclaimed the new Wehrmacht of thirty-six divisions, and the introduction of general military service. Special editions of newspapers were rushed out, eulogizing 'the first great measure to liquidate Versailles', the erasing of the shame of defeat, and the restoration of Germany's military standing. Delirious crowds gathered outside the Reich Chancellery cheering Hitler. The German people were completely unprepared for what he had done. Many reacted initially with shock, worried about the consequences abroad and possibility even of a new war. But the mood – at least of the vast majority – rapidly turned to euphoria when it was realized that the western powers would do nothing. It was felt that Germany had the right to rearm, since France had done nothing to *dis*arm. Hitler's prestige soared. People admired his nerve and boldness. He had put the French in their place, and achieved what 'the others' had failed to bring about in fourteen years. 'Enthusiasm on 17 March enormous,' ran one report from oppositional sources. 'The whole of Munich was on its feet. People can be compelled to sing, but not forced to sing with such enthusiasm . . . Hitler has again gained extraordinary ground among the people. He is loved by many.'

Foreign governments were also taken by surprise by Hitler's move. French and Czech diplomacy went into overdrive. In each case, sluggish negotiations for treaties with Moscow were speeded up. In Italy, Mussolini made sabre-rattling noises against Germany, provoking for a time an atmosphere resembling that of 1915, and looked for closer alliance with France. But Great Britain held the key. And Britain's interests overseas in the Empire and in the troubled Far East, alongside a prevalent concern about the threat of Bolshevism, encouraged a more pro-German stance completely at odds with French diplomacy and to Hitler's direct advantage. Without consulting the French, the British government put out on 18 March a flat, formal protest at the German unilateral action, then, in the same protest note and to the astonishment of German diplomats, asked whether the Reich government was still interested in a meeting between Simon and Hitler.

Hitler was confident and self-assured when the postponed visit of Simon and Eden eventually took place in the Reich Chancellery, on 25 March. Paul Schmidt, meeting Hitler for the first time and acting as his interpreter, noted the cordial atmosphere at the beginning of the talks. He had expected the 'raging demagogue' he had heard on the radio, but was instead impressed by the skill and intelligence with which Hitler conducted the negotiations. In the first morning session of almost four hours, Simon and Eden could do no more than pose the occasional question during Hitler's monologues on the menace of Bolshevism. Alongside his repeated attacks on Soviet expansionist intentions, Hitler's main theme was equality of treatment for Germany in armaments levels. He insisted to Simon on parity in air-forces with Britain and France.

Asked about the current strength of the German air-force, Hitler hesitated, then declared: 'We have already attained parity with Great Britain.' Simon and Eden were sceptical, but said nothing. Nor did they when Hitler named a ratio of 35 per cent of English naval strength as the German demand, but their lack of immediate objection gave a hint to their hosts that they were not opposed. The British had shown themselves as pliant, willing to negotiate, insistent on upholding peace, but ready to make concessions at the expense of solidarity with the French. The German stance, on the other hand, had been unyielding, inflexible on all points of substance. The courting of the British appeared to be making headway. The post-war European settlement was visibly crumbling. All Hitler needed to do was to stand firm; all the signs were that the British would move to accommodate him. The seeds of appeasement had been sown.

Though British avowals of international solidarity continued, the much-trumpeted Stresa Front – the outcome of the meeting in Stresa of the leaders of Britain, France, and Italy on 11 April 1935, at which they pledged to uphold the 1925 Pact of Locarno guaranteeing the western borders of the Reich and to support Austria's integrity – existed on paper only. But the isolation arising from Stresa, the League of Nations' condemnation of Germany, and the French pact with the Soviet Union had to be broken. This was the backcloth to Hitler's second 'peace speech' – following that of 17 May 1933 – to the Reichstag on 21 May 1935. 'What else could I wish for other than calm and peace?' he rhetorically asked. 'Germany needs peace, and wants peace.' He was keen to appear reasonable and moderate while reiterating German demands for equal rights in armament. He dismissed any hint of a threat in the armaments programme. He wanted, he stated (as he had done privately to Simon and Eden), no more than parity in air weaponry and a limit of 35 per cent of British naval tonnage. He scorned press suggestions that this would lead to a demand for the possession of colonies. Nor had Germany any wish or capability for naval rivalry with Great Britain. 'The German Reich government recognizes of itself the overwhelming necessity for existence and thereby the justification of dominance at sea to protect the British Empire, just as, on the other hand, we are determined to do everything necessary in protection of our own continental existence and freedom.' The framework of the desired alliance with Britain had been outlined.

The Foreign Offices of both countries were critical of schemes for a naval accord. But the British Admiralty found the 35 per cent limit acceptable, as long as there was no weakening of the British position vis-à-vis the Japanese navy – seen as the greater threat. The British cabinet conceded. Despite the fact that Germany had been condemned for its breach of Versailles as recently as mid-April by the League of Nations, the British, following Hitler's 'peace speech' of 21 May, had taken up German feelers for the naval talks in London, first mooted on Simon's visit to Berlin in March.

Leading the German delegation, when the talks began on 4 June, was Joachim von Ribbentrop. The linguistically able but boundlessly vain, arrogant, and pompous former champagne salesman had joined the party only in 1932. But with the passion of the late convert he had from the start showed fanatical commitment and devotion to Hitler – reminding the interpreter Schmidt, who saw him frequently at close quarters, of the dog on the label of the gramophone company His Master's Voice. In 1934, as newly appointed 'Commissioner for Disarmament Questions', he had been sent by Hitler as a type of roving envoy to Rome, London, and Paris to try to improve relations, though at the time had achieved little. Despite his lack of obvious success, Hitler, distrustful of the career diplomats at the Foreign Office, continued to favour him. On 1 June 1935, he was provided with the grand title of 'Ambassador Extraordinary and Plenipotentiary on Special Mission'. His moment of triumph in London awaited.

The Anglo-German Naval Agreement was finally concluded on 18 June. Germany could now construct a navy of 35 per cent of the British navy, and a submarine fleet the size of that of Britain. Ribbentrop had covered himself with glory. Hitler had gained a major diplomatic triumph – and experienced, he said, the happiest day of his life. For the German people, Hitler seemed to be achieving the unimaginable. The world, meanwhile, looked on in astonishment. Great Britain, party to the condemnation of Germany for breach of treaties, had wholly undermined the Stresa Front, left its allies in the lurch, and assisted Hitler in tearing a further large strip off the Versailles Treaty. Whether peace would be more secure as a result already gave grave cause for doubt.

Within little over three months, European diplomacy was plunged still further into turmoil. Mussolini's invasion of Abyssinia – an atavistic imperialist adventure designed to restore Italy's status as a world power and satisfy national pride and a dictator's ambitions – was launched on 3 October. The invasion was unanimously condemned by the members of the League of Nations. But their slow and half-hearted application of economic sanctions – which left out the key commodity, oil – did little but show up once more the League's ineffectiveness. Divisions were once more exposed between the two western democracies.

Mussolini's action had plunged the League into crisis once more. It had blasted apart the accord reached at Stresa. Europe was on the move. Hitler could await rich pickings.

III

While events on the diplomatic front were turning Hitler's way in the spring and summer of 1935, the new wave of anti-Jewish violence – after a relative lull since the later months of 1933 – that swept across the land between May and September spurred further radicalization in the area of his chief ideological obsession. Heavily preoccupied with foreign policy at this time, Hitler was only sporadically involved in the months before the hastily improvised promulgation of the notorious Nuremberg Laws at the Party Rally in September. 'With regard to the Jews, too,' Hitler commented at a much later date, 'I had for long to remain inactive.' His inactivity was tactical, not temperamental. 'There's no point in artificially creating additional difficulties,' he added. 'The more cleverly you proceed, the better.' There was little need for him to be active. All he had to do was provide backing for the party radicals – or, even less, do nothing to hinder their activism (until it eventually became counter-productive) – then introduce the discriminatory legislation which the agitation had prompted. Knowing that actions to 'remove' the Jews were in line with Hitler's aims and met with his approval largely provided its own momentum.

Chiefly on account of foreign-policy sensitivities and economic precariousness, the regime had during 1934 reined in the violence against Jews which had characterized the early months of Nazi rule. Barbarity had merely subsided – and far from totally. Ferocious discrimination continued unabated. Intimidation was unrelenting. In some areas, like Streicher's Franconia, the economic boycott remained as fierce as ever and the poisonous atmosphere invited brutal actions. Even so, the exodus of Jews fleeing from Germany slowed down markedly; some even came back, thinking the worst over. Then, early in 1935 with the Saar plebiscite out of the way, the brakes on antisemitic action began to be loosened. Written and spoken propaganda stoked the fires of violence, inciting action from party formations – including units of the Hitler Youth, SA, SS, and the small traders' organization, NS-Hago – that scarcely needed encouragement. The Franconian Gauleiter, Julius Streicher, the most rabid and primitive antisemite among the party leaders, was at the forefront. Streicher's own quasi-pornographic newspaper, *Der Stürmer*, which had never ceased dispensing its poison despite frequent brushes even with Nazi authorities, now excelled itself in a new and intensified campaign of filth, centring upon endless stories of 'racial defilement'. Sales quadrupled during 1935, chiefly on account of the support from local party organizations.

The tone was changing at the very top. In March 1934, Heß had banned anti-Jewish propaganda by the NS-Hago, indicating that Hitler's authorization was needed for any boycott. But at the end of April 1935, Wiedemann told Bormann that Hitler did not favour the prohibition, sought by some, of the anti-Jewish notice-boards – 'Jews Not Wanted Here' (or even more threatening versions) – on the roadside, at the entry to villages, and in public places. The notice-boards as a result now spread rapidly. Radicals at the grass-roots gleaned the obvious message from the barrage of propaganda and the speeches of party notables that they were being given the green light to attack the Jews in any way they saw fit.

The party leaders were, in fact, reacting to and channelling pressures emanating from radicals at the grass-roots of the Movement. The continuing serious disaffection within the ranks of the SA, scarcely abated since the 'Röhm affair', was the underlying impetus to the new wave of violence directed at the Jews. Feeling cheated of the brave new world they thought was theirs, alienated and demoralized, the young toughs in the SA needed a new sense of purpose. Attacking Jews provided it. Given a green light from above, they encountered no barrier and, in fact, every encouragement. The feeling among party activists, and especially stormtroopers, summarized in one Gestapo report in spring 1935, was that 'the Jewish problem' had to be 'set in motion by us from below', and 'that the government would then have to follow'.

The instrumental value of the new wave of agitation and violence was made plain in reports from the Rhineland from Gauleiter Grohé of Cologne-Aachen, who thought in March and April 1935 that a new boycott and intensified attack on the Jews would help 'to raise the rather depressed mood among the lower middle classes'. Grohé, an ardent radical in 'the Jewish Question', went on to congratulate himself on the extent to which party activism had been revitalized and the morale of the lower middle class reinvigorated by the new attacks on the Jews.

Despite the aims of the Nazi programme, in the eyes of the Movement's radicals little had been done by early 1935 to eradicate the Jews from German society. There was a good deal of feeling among fanatical antisemites that the state bureaucracy had deflected the party's drive and not produced much by way of legislation to eliminate Jewish influence. The new wave of violence now led, therefore, to vociferous demands for the introduction of discriminatory legislation against the Jews which would go some way towards fulfilling the party's programme. The state bureaucracy also felt under pressure from actions of the Gestapo, leading to retrospective legal sanction for police discriminatory measures, such as the Gestapo's ban, independently declared, in February 1935 on Jews raising the swastika flag.

Attempts to mobilize the apathetic masses behind the violent antisemitic campaign of the party formations backfired. Instead of galvanizing the discontented, the antisemitic wave merely fuelled already prominent criticism of the party. There was little participation from those who did not belong to party formations. Many people ignored exhortations to boycott Jewish shops and stores. And the public displays of violence accompanying the 'boycott movement', as Jews were beaten up by Nazi thugs and their property vandalized, met with wide condemnation. Not much of the criticism was on humanitarian grounds. Economic self-interest played a large part. So did worries that the violence might be extended to attacks on the Churches. The methods rather than the aims were attacked. There were few principled objections to discrimination against Jews. What concerned people above all were the hooliganism, mob violence, distasteful scenes, and disturbances of order.

Accordingly, across the summer the violence became counter-productive, and the authorities felt compelled to take steps to condemn it and restore order. The terror on the streets had done its job for the time being. It had pushed the discrimination still further. The radicalization demanded action from above.

At last, Hitler, silent on the issue throughout the summer, was forced to take a stance. Schacht had warned him in a memorandum as early as 3 May of the economic damage being done by combating the Jews through illegal means. Hitler had reacted at the time only by commenting that everything would turn out all right as matters developed. But now, on 8 August, he ordered a halt to all 'individual actions', which Heß relayed to the party the following day. On 20 August, Reich Minister of the Interior Frick took up Hitler's ban in threatening those continuing to perpetrate such acts with stiff punishment. The stage had now been reached where the state authorities were engaged in the repression of party members seeking to implement what they knew Hitler wanted and what was a central tenet of party doctrine. It was little wonder that the police, increasingly compelled to intervene against party activists engaged in violent outrages against Jews, also wanted an end to the public disturbances. Hitler stood aloof from the fray but uneasily positioned between the radicals and the conservatives. His instincts, as ever, were with the radicals, whose bitter disappointment at what they saw as a betrayal of Nazi principles was evident. But political sense dictated that he should heed the conservatives. Led by Schacht, these wanted a regulation of antisemitic activity through legislation. This in any case fed into growing demands within the party for tough discriminatory measures, especially against 'racial defilement'. Out of the need to reconcile these conflicting positions, the Nuremberg Laws emerged.

Shrill demands for harsh legislation against the Jews had mounted sharply in spring and summer 1935. Frick had appeared in April to offer the prospect of a new, discriminatory law on rights of state citizenship, but nothing had emerged to satisfy those who saw a central feature of the Party Programme still not implemented after two years of Nazi rule. Party organs demanded in June that Jews be excluded from state citizenship and called for the death penalty for Jews renting property to 'aryans', employing them as servants, serving them as doctors or lawyers, or engaging in 'racial defilement'.

The issue of banning intermarriage and outlawing sexual relations between Jews and 'aryans' had by this time gone to the top of the agenda of the demands of the radicals. Racial purity, they claimed, could only be attained through total physical apartheid. Even a single instance of sexual intercourse between a Jew and an 'aryan', announced Streicher, was sufficient to prevent the woman from ever giving birth to a 'pure-blooded aryan' child. 'Defilement' of 'German' girls through predatory Jews, a constant allegation of the vicious *Stürmer* and its imitators, had by now become a central theme of the anti-Jewish agitation.

Streicher spoke in May 1935 of a forthcoming ban on marriages between Jews and Germans. In early August, Goebbels proclaimed that such marriages would be prohibited. Meanwhile, activists were taking matters into their own hands. SA men demonstrated in front of the houses of newly-weds where one partner was Jewish. Even without a law, officials at some registry offices were refusing to perform 'mixed marriages'. Since they were not legally banned, others carried out the ceremony. Still others informed the Gestapo of an intended marriage. The Gestapo itself pressed the Justice Ministry for a speedy regulation of the confused situation. A further impulse arose from the new Defence Law of 21 May 1935, banning marriage with 'persons of non-aryan origin' for members of the newly-formed Wehrmacht. By July, bowing to pressure from within the Movement, Frick had decided to introduce legislation to ban 'mixed marriages'. Some form of draft bill had already been worked upon in the Justice Ministry. The delay in bringing forward legislation largely arose from the question of how to deal with the 'Mischlinge' – those of partial Jewish descent.

On 18 August, in a speech in Königsberg, Schacht had indicated that anti-Jewish legislation in accordance with the Party Programme was 'in preparation' and had to be regarded as a central aim of the government. Schacht summoned state and party leaders two days later to the Ministry of Economics to discuss 'the Jewish Question'. He fiercely attacked the party's violent methods as causing great harm to the economy and rearmament drive, concluding that it was vital to carry out the party's programme, but only through legislation. The meeting ended by agreeing that party and state should combine to bring suggestions to the Reich government 'about desirable measures'.

An account of the meeting prepared for the State Secretary in the Foreign Ministry commented:

In the main, the departmental representatives drew attention to the practical disadvantages for their departmental work, whilst the Party justified the necessity for radical action against the Jews with politico-emotional and abstract ideological considerations . . .

For all the vehemence of his arguments, Schacht had not wanted to, or felt able to, challenge the principle of excluding the Jews. 'Herr Schacht did not draw the logical conclusion,' stated the Foreign Ministry's report, 'and demand a radical change in the party's Jewish programme, nor even in the methods of applying it, for instance a ban on *Der Stürmer*. On the contrary, he kept up the fiction of abiding a hundred per cent by the Jewish programme.' Schacht's meeting had clearly highlighted the differences between party and state, between radicals and pragmatists, between fanatics and conservatives. There was no fundamental disagreement about aims; merely about methods. However, the matter could not be allowed to drag on indefinitely. A resolution had to be found in the near future.

The minutes of the meeting were sent to Hitler, who also discussed the matter with Schacht on 9 September. This was a day before Hitler left to join the hundreds of thousands of the party faithful assembled for the annual ritual in Nuremberg for the 'Reich Party Rally of Freedom' – 'the High Mass of our party', as Goebbels called it. It was not at that point with the intention of proclaiming the anti-Jewish 'citizenship' and 'blood' laws during the Party Rally. A significant part in their emergence was played by the lobbying at Nuremberg of one of the most fanatical proponents of a ban on sexual relations between Germans and Jews, Dr Gerhard Wagner, the Reich Doctors' Leader, who had been advocating a ban on marriages between 'aryans' and Jews since 1933.

Two days into the Party Rally, on 12 September, Wagner announced in a speech that within a short time a 'Law to Protect German Blood' would prevent the further 'bastardization' of the German people. A year later, Wagner claimed that he had no idea, when making his announcement, that the Führer would introduce the Nuremberg Laws within days. Probably Hitler had given Wagner no specific indication of when the 'Blood Law' would be promulgated. But since Wagner had unequivocally announced such a law as imminent, he must have been given an unambiguous sign by Hitler that action would follow in the immediate future. At any rate, late the very next evening, 13 September, Dr Bernhard Lösener, in charge of preparation of legislation on the 'Jewish Question' in the Reich Ministry of the Interior, was, to his surprise, ordered to Nuremberg. He and a colleague, Ministerialrat Franz Albrecht Medicus, arrived in the morning of 14 September to be told by their superiors in the Interior Ministry, State Secretaries Hans Pfundtner and Wilhelm Stuckart, that Hitler had instructed them the previous day to prepare a law to regulate the problems of marriage between 'aryans' and 'non-aryans'. They had immediately begun work on a draft. It seems likely that the urging of Wagner, in Hitler's company for hours at the crucial time and doubtless supported by other Nazi leaders, had been instrumental in the decision to bring in the long-desired law there and then. Wagner was the link between Hitler and those given the task of drafting the law, who were not altogether clear – since they had received no written instructions – on exactly what came from the Doctors' Leader and what came from Hitler himself.

The atmosphere was ripe. The summer of intimidation and violence towards Jews had seen to that. The increasingly shrill demands for action in the 'Jewish Question' formed a menacing backcloth to the highpoint of the party's year as hundreds of thousands of the faithful arrived in Nuremberg, its walls, towers, and houses bedecked by swastika banners, the air full of expectancy at the great spectacle to follow.

Preparations for the notorious laws which would determine the fate of thousands were little short of chaotic. Lösener and Medicus had arrived in Nuremberg on Saturday, 14 September. The specially summoned Reichstag meeting was scheduled for 8 p.m. the following day. There was little time for the already weary civil servants to draft the required legislation. Whatever the prior work on anti-Jewish legislation in the Ministries of the Interior and Justice had been, it had plainly not passed the initial stages. No definition of a Jew had been agreed upon. The party were pressing for inclusion of Mischlinge (those of mixed descent). But the complexities of this were considerable. The work went on at a furious pace. During the course of the day, Lösener was sent more than once to battle his way through the huge crowds to Frick, staying at a villa on the other side of the city and showing little interest in the matter. Hitler, at Wagner's insistence, rejected the first versions Frick brought to him as too mild. Around midnight, Frick returned from Hitler with the order to prepare for him four versions of the Blood Law – varying in the severity of the penalties for offences against the law – and, in addition, to complete the legislative programme, to draft a Reich Citizenship Law. Within half an hour, they had drawn up in the briefest of terms a law distinguishing state subjects from Reich citizens, for which only those of German or related blood were eligible. Though almost devoid of content, the law provided the framework for the mass of subsidiary decrees that in the following years were to push German Jews to the outer fringes of society, prisoners in their own land. At 2.30 a.m. Frick returned with Hitler's approval. The civil servants learnt only when the Reichstag assembled which of the four drafts of the 'Blood Law' Hitler had chosen. Possibly following the intervention of either Neurath or, more likely, Gürtner, he had chosen the mildest. However, he struck out with his own hand the restriction to 'full Jews', adding further to the confusion by ordering this restriction to be included in the version published by the German News Agency. Marriage and extra-marital sexual relations between Jews and Germans were outlawed, and to be punished with stiff penalties. Jews were also barred from employing German women under the age of forty-five as servants.

The Nuremberg Laws, it is plain, had been a compromise adopted by Hitler, counter to his instincts, to defuse the anti-Jewish agitation of the party, which over the summer had become unpopular not merely in wide sections of the population but, because of its harmful economic effects, among conservative sections of the leadership. The compromise did not please party radicals. It was a compromise, even so, which placated those in the party who had been pressing for legislation, especially on 'racial defilement'. And in putting the brakes on agitation and open violence, it had nevertheless taken the discrimination on to new terrain. Disappointment among activists at the retreat from a direct assault on Jews was tempered by the recognition, as one report put it, 'that the Führer had for outward appearances to ban individual actions against the Jews in consideration of foreign policy, but in reality was wholly in agreement that each individual should continue on his own initiative the fight against Jewry in the most rigorous and radical form'.

The dialectic of radicalization in the 'Jewish Question' in 1935 had been along the following lines: pressure from below; green light from above; further violence from below; brakes from above assuaging the radicals through discriminatory legislation. The process had ratcheted up the persecution several notches.

The Nuremberg Laws served their purpose in dampening the wild attacks on the Jews which had punctuated the summer. Most ordinary Germans not among the ranks of the party fanatics had disapproved of the violence, but not of the aims of anti-Jewish policy – the exclusion of Jews from German society, and ultimately their removal from Germany itself. They mainly approved now of the legal framework to separate

Jews and Germans as offering a permanent basis for discrimination without the unseemly violence. Hitler had associated himself with the search for a 'legal' solution. His popularity was little affected.

The thorny question of defining a Jew had still to be tackled. Drafts of the first implementation ordinances under the Reich Citizenship Law, legally defining a Jew, were formulated to try to comply with Hitler's presumed views. But although Hitler intervened on occasion, even on points of minute detail, his sporadic involvement was insufficient to bring the tug-of-war between Heß's office and the Ministry of the Interior to a speedy end. The Ministry wanted to classify as 'Jews' only those with more than two 'non-aryan' grandparents. The party – with Reich Doctors' Leader Wagner applying pressure – insisted on the inclusion of 'quarter-Jews'. Numerous meetings brought no result. Meanwhile, without awaiting a definition, some ministries were already imposing a variety of discriminatory measures on those of 'mixed' background, using different criteria. A decision was urgently necessary. But Hitler would not come down on one side or the other. 'Jewish Question still not decided,' noted Goebbels on 1 October. 'We debate for a long time about it, but the Führer is still wavering.'

By early November, with still no final resolution in sight, Schacht and the Reichsbank Directorate, claiming the uncertainty was damaging the economy and the foreign-exchange rate, joined in the pressure on Hitler to end the dispute. Hitler had no intention of being pinned down to accepting security of rights for Jews under the legislation, as the Reichsbank wanted. The prospect of open confrontation between party representatives and state ministers of the Interior, Economics, and Foreign Affairs, and likely defeat for the party, at a meeting scheduled for 5 November to reach a final decision, made Hitler call off the meeting at short notice. A week later, the First Supplementary Decree to the Reich Citizenship Law finally ended the uncertainty. Wagner got his way on most points. But on the definition of a Jew, the Ministry of the Interior could point to some success. Three-quarter Jews were counted as Jewish. Half-Jews (with two Jewish and two 'aryan' grandparents) were reckoned as Jewish only if practising the Jewish faith, married (since the promulgation of the Nuremberg Laws) to a Jew, the child of a marriage with a Jewish partner, or the illegitimate child of a Jew and 'aryan'. The definition of a Jew had ended with a contradiction. For legislative purposes, it had been impossible to arrive at a biological definition of race dependent on blood types. So it had been necessary to resort to religious belief to determine who was racially a Jew. As a result, it was possible to imagine descendants of 'pure aryan' parents converted to Judaism who would thereby be regarded as racial Jews. It was absurd, but merely highlighted the absurdity of the entire exercise.

The approach of the Winter Olympics in Garmisch-Partenkirchen, then the summer games in Berlin, along with the sensitive foreign-policy situation, meant that the regime was anxious to avoid any repetition of the violence of the summer of 1935. For the next two years, though the wheel of discrimination carried on turning, the 'Jewish Question' was kept away from the forefront of politics. When Wilhelm Gustloff, the leading NSDAP representative in Switzerland, was assassinated by a young Jew in February 1936, the circumstances did not lend themselves to wild retaliation. Frick, in collaboration with Heß, strictly banned 'individual actions'. Hitler restrained his natural instinct, and confined himself to a relatively low-key generalized attack on Jewry at Gustloff's funeral. Germany remained quiet. The absence of violence following Gustloff's murder is as clear a guide as the outrages in the anti-Jewish wave of 1935 to the fact that the regime could control, when it wanted to, the pressures for action within the ranks of the party radicals. In 1935 it had been useful to encourage and respond to such pressures. In 1936 it was opportune to keep them in check.

For Hitler, whatever the tactical considerations, the aim of destroying the Jews – his central political idea since 1919 – remained unaltered. He revealed his approach to a meeting of party District Leaders at the end of April 1937, in immediate juxtaposition to comments on the Jews: 'I don't straight away want violently to demand an opponent to fight. I don't say "fight" because I want to fight. Instead, I say: "I want to destroy you!" And now let skill help me to manoeuvre you so far into the corner that you can't strike any blow. And then you get the stab into the heart.'

In practice, however, as had been the position during the summer of 1935 before the Nuremberg Rally, Hitler needed do little to push forward the radicalization of the 'Jewish Question'. By now, even though still not centrally coordinated, the 'Jewish Question' pervaded all key areas of government; party pressure at headquarters and in the localities for new forms of discrimination was unceasing; civil servants complied with ever tighter constraints under the provisions of the 'Reich Citizenship Law'; the law-courts were engaged in the persecution of Jews under the provisions of the Nuremberg Laws; the police were looking for further ways to hasten the elimination of Jews and speed up their departure from Germany; and the general public, for the most part, passively accepted the discrimination where they did not directly encourage or participate in it. Antisemitism had come by now to suffuse all walks of life. 'The Nazis have indeed brought off a deepening of the gap between the people and the Jews,' ran a report from the illegal socialist opposition for January 1936. 'The feeling that the Jews are another race is today a general one.'

IV

Hitler, by late 1935, was already well on the way to establishing – backed by the untiring efforts of the propaganda machine – his standing as a national leader, transcending purely party interest. He stood for the successes, the achievements of the regime. His popularity soared also among those who were otherwise critical of National Socialism. With the party, it was a different matter. The party could be, and often was, blamed for all the continuing ills of daily life – for the gulf between expectations and reality that had brought widespread disillusionment in the wake of the initial exaggerated hopes of rapid material improvement in the Third Reich.

Not least, the party's image had badly suffered through its attacks on the Christian Churches. The dismal mood in those parts of the country worst affected by the assault on the Churches was only part of a wider drop in the popularity of the regime in the winter of 1935–6. Hitler was aware of the deterioration in the political situation within Germany, and of the material conditions underlying the worsening mood of the population. Anger, especially in the working class, was rising by autumn 1935 as a result of food shortages, rising food-prices, and renewed growth in unemployment.

As the domestic problems deepened, however, the Abyssinian crisis, causing disarray in the League of Nations, presented Hitler with new opportunities to look to foreign-policy success. He was swiftly alert to the potential for breaking out of Germany's international isolation, driving a further deep wedge between the Stresa signatories, and attaining, perhaps, a further revision of Versailles. Given the domestic situation, a foreign-policy triumph would, moreover, be most welcome.

Under the terms of the 1919 peace settlement, the German Reich had been prohibited from erecting fortifications, stationing troops, or undertaking any military preparations on the left bank of the Rhine and within a fifty-kilometre strip on the right bank. The status of the demilitarized Rhineland had subsequently been endorsed by the Locarno Pact of 1925, which Germany had signed. Any unilateral alteration of that status by Germany would amount to a devastating breach of the post-war settlement.

The remilitarization of the Rhineland would have been on the agenda of any German nationalist government. The army viewed it as essential for the rearmament plans it had established in December 1933, and for western defence. The Foreign Ministry presumed the demilitarized status would be ended by negotiation at some point. Hitler had talked confidentially of the abolition of the demilitarized zone as early as 1934. He spoke of it again, in broad terms, in summer 1935. However likely the reoccupation would have been within the next year or two, the seizing of that opportunity, the timing and character of the coup, were Hitler's. They bore his hallmark at all points.

The opportunity was provided by Mussolini. As we have noted, his Abyssinian adventure, provoking the League of Nations' condemnation of an unprovoked attack on a member-state and the imposition of economic sanctions, broke the fragile Stresa Front. Italy, faced with a pessimistic military outlook, sanctions starting to bite, and looking for friends, turned away from France and Britain, towards Germany. The stumbling-block to good relations had since 1933 been the Austrian question. Since the Dollfuss assassination in mid-1934, the climate had been frosty. This now swiftly altered. Mussolini signalled in January 1936 that he had nothing against Austria in effect becoming a satellite of Germany. The path to the 'Axis' immediately opened up. Later the same month he publicly claimed the French and British talk of possible joint military action against Italy in the Mediterranean – not that this was in reality ever likely – had destroyed the balance of Locarno, and could only lead to the collapse of the Locarno system. Hitler took note. Then, in an interview with Ambassador Hassell, Mussolini acknowledged that Italy would offer no support for France and Britain should Hitler decide to take action in response to the ratification of the Franco-Soviet mutual assistance pact, currently before the French Chamber of Deputies, and viewed by Berlin as a breach of Locarno. The message was clear: from Italy's point of view, Germany could re-enter the Rhineland with impunity.

The Abyssinian crisis had also damaged Anglo-French relations, and driven the two democracies further apart. The French government realized that a move to remilitarize the Rhineland was inevitable. Most observers tipped autumn 1936, once the Olympics were out of the way. Few thought Hitler would take great risks over the Rhineland when conventional diplomacy would ultimately succeed. Ministers rejected independent military action against flagrant German violation. In any case, the French military leadership – grossly exaggerating German armed strength – had made it plain that they opposed military retaliation, and that the reaction to any *fait accompli* should be purely political. The truth was: the French had no stomach for a fight over the Rhineland. And Hitler and the German Foreign Office, fed intelligence from Paris, were aware of this. Soundings had also led Hitler and von Neurath to a strong presumption that Britain, too, would refrain from any military action in the event of a coup. They saw Britain as for the time being weakened militarily, preoccupied politically with domestic affairs and with the Abyssinian crisis, unwilling to regard the preservation of the demilitarization of the Rhineland as a vital British interest, and possessing some sympathy for German demands. The chances of success in a swift move to remilitarize the Rhineland were, therefore, high; the likelihood of military retaliation by France or Britain relatively low. That was, of course, as long as the assessment in Berlin of the likely reactions of the European powers was correct. Nothing was certain. Not all Hitler's advisers favoured the risk he was increasingly prepared to take without delay. But Hitler had been proved right in his boldness when leaving the League of Nations in 1933 and reintroducing conscription in 1935. He had gained confidence. His role in the Rhineland crisis was still more assertive, less than ever ready to bow to the caution recommended by the military and diplomats.

Rumours were rife in Berlin at the beginning of February that Hitler was planning to march troops into the Rhineland in the near future. Nothing at that point had been decided. Hitler pondered the matter while he was in Garmisch-Partenkirchen for the opening of the Winter Olympics on 6 February. He invited objections, particularly from the

Foreign Office. During February, he discussed the pros and cons with Neurath, Blomberg, Fritsch, Ribbentrop, Göring, then with Hassell, the ambassador in Rome. A wider circle within the Foreign Office and military leadership were aware of the pending decision. Fritsch and Beck were opposed; Blomberg as usual went along with Hitler. Foreign Minister Neurath also had grave doubts. He thought 'speeding up' the action was not worth the risk. Though it was not likely that Germany would face military retaliation, further international isolation would be the result. Hassell also argued that there was no hurry, since there would be future chances to abolish the demilitarized zone. Both were of the view that Hitler should at least await the ratification of the French-Soviet Pact by the Senate in Paris. This, as an alleged breach of Locarno, was to serve as the pretext. Hitler preferred to strike after ratification by the Chamber of Deputies, without waiting for the Senate. Whatever the caution of the career diplomats, Hitler was, as always, egged on in the most unctuous fashion by the sycophantic Ribbentrop.

Hitler told Hassell that the reoccupation of the Rhineland was 'from a military point of view an absolute necessity'. He had originally had 1937 in mind for such a step. But the favourable international constellation, the advantage of the French-Soviet Pact (given the anti-Soviet feeling in Britain and France) as the occasion, and the fact that the military strength of the other powers, especially of the Russians, was on the increase and would soon alter the military balance, were reasons for acting sooner, not later. He did not believe there would be military retaliation. At worst there might be economic sanctions. At discussions on 19 February, Hassell argued that the change for the better in Italy's fortunes in Abyssinia and the dropping of oil sanctions had lessened the chances of Italian support. Hitler countered by stressing the disadvantages of delay. 'Attack in this case, too,' he characteristically argued – to 'lively assent from Ribbentrop' – 'was the better strategy.'

But he continued to waver. His arguments had failed to convince the diplomats and military leaders. The advice he was receiving favoured caution, not boldness. This was the case as late as the end of February. However determined Hitler was on an early strike, the precise timing still had to be decided. At lunch on 29 February, he had yet to make up his mind.

But the following day, Sunday 1 March, with Munich bathed in beautiful spring-like weather, Hitler turned up at the hotel where

Goebbels was staying in a good mood. The decision had been taken. 'It's another critical moment, but now is the time for action,' wrote Goebbels. 'Fortune favours the brave! He who dares nothing wins nothing.'

The next day, 2 March, Goebbels attended a meeting in the Reich Chancellery at 11 a.m. The heads of the armed forces – Göring, Blomberg, Fritsch, and Raeder – were there. So was Ribbentrop. Hitler told them he had made his decision. The Reichstag would be summoned for Saturday, 7 March. There the proclamation of the remilitarization of the Rhineland would be made. At the same time, he would offer Germany's re-entry into the League of Nations, an air pact, and a non-aggression treaty with France. The acute danger would thereby be reduced, Germany's isolation prevented, and sovereignty once and for all restored. The Reichstag would be dissolved and new elections announced, with foreign-policy slogans. Fritsch had to arrange for the troop transport during Friday night. 'Everything has to happen as quick as lightning.' Troop movements would be camouflaged by making them look like SA and Labour Front exercises. The military leaders had their doubts. Members of the cabinet were informed individually only on the afternoon of the following day, Frick and Heß as late as the evening. By then, invitations to the Reichstag had already gone out – but, to keep up the deception, only to a beer evening. By Wednesday Hitler was working on his Reichstag speech; Goebbels was already preparing the election campaign. Warning voices from the Foreign Ministry could still be registered on the Thursday. By Friday evening Hitler had completed his speech. The cabinet met to be informed for the first time collectively of what was planned. Goebbels announced that the Reichstag would meet at noon the next day. The only item on the agenda was a government declaration. Plans for the election campaign were finalized. Workers in the Propaganda Ministry were not permitted to leave the building overnight to prevent any leaks. 'Success lies in surprise,' noted Goebbels. 'Berlin trembles with tension,' he added next morning.

The Reichstag, too, was tense as Hitler rose, amid enormous applause, to speak. The deputies, all in Nazi uniform, still did not know what to expect. The speech was aimed not just at those present, but at the millions of radio listeners. After a lengthy preamble denouncing Versailles, restating Germany's demands for equality and security, and declaring his peaceful aims, a screaming onslaught on Bolshevism brought wild applause. This took Hitler into his argument that the French-Soviet Pact had invalidated Locarno. He read out the memorandum which von Neurath had given to the ambassadors of the Locarno signatories that morning, stating that the Locarno Treaty had lost its meaning. He paused for a brief moment, then continued: 'Germany regards itself, therefore, as for its part no longer bound by this dissolved pact . . . In the interest of the primitive rights of a people to the security of its borders and safeguarding of its defence capability, the German Reich government has therefore from today restored the full and unrestricted sovereignty of the Reich in the demilitarized zone of the Rhineland.' At this, wrote the American journalist, William Shirer, witnessing the scene, the 600 Reichstag deputies, 'little men with big bodies and bulging necks and cropped hair and pouched bellies and brown uniforms and heavy boots, little men of clay in his fine hands, leap to their feet like automatons, their right arms upstretched in the Nazi salute, and scream "*Heil's*"'. When the tumult eventually subsided, Hitler advanced his 'peace proposals' for Europe: a non-aggression pact with Belgium and France; demilitarization of *both* sides of their joint borders; an air pact; non-aggression treaties, similar to that with Poland, with other eastern neighbours; and Germany's return to the League of Nations. Some thought Hitler was offering too much. They had no need to worry. As Hitler knew, there was not the slightest chance of his 'offer' proving acceptable. He moved to the climax. 'Men, deputies of the German Reichstag! In this historic hour when in the western provinces of the Reich German troops are at this moment moving into their future peace-time garrisons, we all unite in two sacred inner vows.' He was interrupted by a deafening tumult from the assembled deputies. 'They spring, yelling and crying, to their feet,' William Shirer recorded. 'The audience in the galleries does the same, all except a few diplomats and about fifty of us correspondents. Their hands are raised in slavish salute, their faces now contorted with hysteria, their mouths wide open, shouting, shouting, their eyes, burning with fanaticism, glued on the new god, the Messiah. The Messiah plays his role superbly.'

Around 1.00 p.m., just as Hitler was reaching the highpoint of his peroration, German troops approached the Hohenzollern Bridge in Cologne. Two plane-loads of journalists, hand-picked by Goebbels, were there to record the historic moment. Word had quickly got round Cologne that morning. Thousands packed the banks of the Rhine and thronged the streets near the bridge. The soldiers received a delirious reception as they crossed. Women strewed the way with flowers. Catholic priests blessed them. Cardinal Schulte offered praise to Hitler for 'sending back our army'. The 'Church struggle' was temporarily forgotten.

The force to be sent into the demilitarized zone numbered no more than 30,000 regulars, augmented by units of the Landespolizei. A mere 3,000 men were to penetrate deep into the zone. The remainder had taken up positions for the most part behind the eastern bank of the Rhine. The forward troops were to be prepared to withdraw within an hour in the event of likely military confrontation with the French. There was no chance of this. As we have seen, it had been ruled out in advance by French military leaders. French intelligence – counting SA, SS, and other Nazi formations as soldiers – had come up with an extraordinary figure of 295,000 for the German military force in the Rhineland. In reality, one French division would have sufficed to terminate Hitler's adventure. 'Had the French then marched into the Rhineland,' Hitler was reported to have commented more than once at a later date, 'we would have had to withdraw again with our tails between our legs. The military force at our disposal would not have sufficed even for limited resistance.' The forty-eight hours following the entry of the German troops into the Rhineland were, he claimed, the most tense of his life. He was speaking, as usual, for effect.

The risk had, in fact, been only a moderate one. The western democracies had lacked both the will and the unity needed to make intervention likely. But the triumph for Hitler was priceless. Not only had he outwitted the major powers, which had again shown themselves incapable of adjusting to a style of power-politics that did not play by the rules of conventional diplomacy. He had scored a further victory over the conservative forces at home in the military and the Foreign Office. As in March 1935 the caution and timidity in the armed forces' leadership and among the career diplomats had proved misplaced. The Rhineland was the biggest reward yet for boldness. His contempt for the 'professionals' in the army and Foreign Office deepened. His boundless egomania gained another massive boost.

The popular euphoria at the news of the reoccupation of the Rhineland far outstripped even the feelings of national celebration in 1933 or 1935 following previous triumphs. People were beside themselves with delight. The initial widespread fear that Hitler's action would bring war was rapidly dissipated. It was almost impossible not to be caught up in the infectious mood of joy. It extended far beyond firm Nazi supporters. Opposition groups were demoralized. New admiration for Hitler, support for his defiance of the west, attack on Versailles, restoration of sovereignty over German territory, and promises of peace were – sometimes grudgingly – recorded by opponents of the regime.

The 'election' campaign that followed the Rhineland spectacular – new elections had been set for 29 March – was no more than a triumphant procession for Hitler. Ecstatic, adoring crowds greeted him on his passage through Germany. Goebbels outdid himself in the saturation coverage of his propaganda – carried into the most outlying villages by armies of activists trumpeting the Führer's great deeds. The 'election' result – 98.9 per cent 'for the List and therefore for the Führer' – gave Hitler what he wanted: the overwhelming majority of the German people united behind him, massive popular support for his position at home and abroad. Though the official figures owed something to electoral 'irregularities', and a good deal more to fear and intimidation, the overwhelming backing for Hitler – his enormous popularity now further bolstered by the Rhineland coup – could not be gainsaid.

The Rhineland triumph left a significant mark on Hitler. The change that Dietrich, Wiedemann, and others saw in him dated from around this time. From now on he was more than ever a believer in his own infallibility. A sense of his own greatness had been instilled in Hitler by his admirers since the early 1920s. He had readily embraced the aura attached to him. It had offered insatiable nourishment for his already incipient all-consuming egomania. Since then, the internal, and above all the foreign-policy successes, since 1933, accredited by growing millions to the Führer's genius, had immensely magnified the tendency. Hitler swallowed the boundless adulation. He became the foremost believer in his own Führer cult. Hubris – that overweening arrogance which courts disaster – was inevitable. The point where hubris takes over had been reached by 1936.

Germany had been conquered. It was not enough. Expansion beckoned. World peace would soon be threatened. Everything was coming about as he alone had foreseen it, thought Hitler. He had come to regard himself as ordained by Providence. 'I go with the certainty of a sleepwalker along the path laid out for me by Providence,' he told a huge gathering in Munich on 14 March. His mastery over all other power-groups within the regime was by now well-nigh complete, his position unassailable, his popularity immense. Few at this point had the foresight to realize that the path laid out by Providence led into the abyss.

13
Ceaseless Radicalization

I

To shrewd observers, it was clear: Hitler's Rhineland coup had been the catalyst to a major power-shift in Europe; Germany's ascendancy was an unpredictable and highly destabilizing element in the international order; the odds against a new European war in the foreseeable future had markedly shortened.

To the German public, Hitler once more professed himself a man of peace, cleverly insinuating who was to blame for the gathering storm-clouds of war. Speaking to a vast audience in the Berlin Lustgarten (a huge square in the city centre) on 1 May – once an international day of celebration of labouring people, now redubbed the 'National Day of Celebration of the German People' – he posed the rhetorical question: 'I ask myself,' he declared, 'who are then these elements who wish to have no rest, no peace, and no understanding, who must continually agitate and sow mistrust? Who are they actually?' Immediately picking up the implication, the crowd bayed: 'The Jews.' Hitler began again: 'I know ...' and was interrupted by cheering that lasted for several minutes. When at last he was able to continue, he picked up his sentence, though – the desired effect achieved – now in quite different vein: 'I know it is not the millions who would have to take up weapons if the intentions of these agitators were to succeed. Those are not the ones ...'

The summer of 1936 was, however, as Hitler knew only too well, no time to stir up a new antisemitic campaign. In August, the Olympic Games were due to be staged in Berlin. Sport would be turned into a vehicle of nationalist politics and propaganda as never before. Nazi aesthetics of power would never have a wider audience. With the eyes of the world on Berlin, it was an opportunity not to be missed to present the new Germany's best face to its hundreds of thousands of visitors from across the globe. No expense or effort had been spared in this cause. The positive image could not be endangered by putting the 'dark' side of the regime on view. Open anti-Jewish violence, such as had punctuated the previous summer, could not be permitted. With some difficulties, antisemitism was kept under wraps. The antisemitic zealots in the party had temporarily to be reined in. Other objectives were for the time being more important. Hitler could afford to bide his time in dealing with the Jews.

The Olympics were an enormous propaganda success for the Nazi regime. Hitler's Germany was open to viewing for visitors from all over the world. Most of them went away mightily impressed. Away from the glamour of the Olympic Games and out of the public eye, the contrast with the external image of peaceful goodwill was sharp. By this time, the self-induced crisis in the German economy arising from the inability to provide both for guns and butter – to sustain supplies of raw materials both for armaments and for consumption – was reaching its watershed. A decision on the economic direction the country would take could not be deferred much longer.

II

Already by spring 1936, it had become clear that it was no longer possible to reconcile the demands of rapid rearmament and growing domestic consumption. Supplies of raw materials for the armaments industry were sufficient for only two months. Fuel supplies for the armed forces were in a particularly critical state. Economics Minister Hjalmar Schacht was by now thoroughly alarmed at the accelerating tempo of rearmament and its inevitably damaging consequences for the economy. Only a sharp reduction in living standards (impossible without endangering the regime's stability) or a big increase in exports (equally impossible given the regime's priorities, exchange rate difficulties, and the condition of external markets) could in his view provide for an expanding armaments industry. He was adamant, therefore, that it was time to put the brakes on rearmament.

The military had other ideas. The leaders of the armed forces, uninterested in the niceties of economics but fully taken up by the potential of modern advanced weaponry, pressed unabatedly for rapid and massive acceleration of the armaments programme. The army leaders were not acting in response to pressure from Hitler. They had their own agenda. They were at the same time 'working towards the Führer', consciously or unconsciously acting 'along his lines and towards his aim' in the full knowledge that their rearmament ambitions wholly coincided with his political aims, and that they could depend upon his backing against attempts to throttle back on armament expenditure. Reich War Minister Werner von Blomberg, Colonel-General Werner Freiherr von Fritsch, Commander-in-Chief of the Army, and General Ludwig Beck, Chief of the Army General Staff, were thereby paving the way, in providing the necessary armed might, for the later expansionism which would leave them all trailing in Hitler's wake.

Even so, the economic impasse seemed complete. Huge increases in allocation of scarce foreign currency were demanded by both the Ministry of Food and the Ministry of Armaments. The position could not be sustained. Fundamental economic priorities had to be established as a matter of urgency. Autarky and export lobbies could not both be satisfied. Hitler remained for months inactive. He had no patent solution to the problem. The key figure at this point was Göring.

Hoping to keep the party off his back, Schacht helped persuade Hitler to install Göring at the beginning of April as Plenipotentiary for the Securing of the Raw Materials and Foreign Exchange Demands of the Reich. Göring's brief was to overcome the crisis, get rearmament moving again, and force through a policy of autarky in fuel production. But by now Göring was in the driving-seat. Schacht was rapidly becoming yesterday's man. In May, shocked at the new power-base that his own machiavellian manoeuvrings had unwittingly helped to create for Göring, the Economics Minister protested to Hitler. Hitler waved him away. He did not want anything more to do with the matter, he was reported as telling Schacht, and the Economics Minister was advised to take it up with Göring himself. 'It won't go well with Schacht for much longer,' commented Goebbels. 'He doesn't belong in his heart to us.' But Göring, too, he thought would have difficulties with the foreign-exchange and raw-materials issue, pointing out: 'He doesn't understand too much about it.'

It was not necessary that he did. His role was to throw around his considerable weight, force the pace, bring a sense of urgency into play, make things happen. 'He brings the energy. Whether he has the economic know-how and experience as well? Who knows? Anyway, he'll do plenty of bragging,' was Goebbels's assessment.

Göring soon had a team of technical experts assembled under Lieutenant-Colonel Fritz Löb of the Luftwaffe. In the research department of Löb's planning team, run by the chemical firm IG-Farben's director Karl Krauch, solutions were rapidly advanced for maximizing production of synthetic fuels and rapidly attaining self-sufficiency in mineral-oil extraction. By midsummer, Löb's planners had come up with a detailed programme for overcoming the unabated crisis. It envisaged a sharp tilt to a more directed economy with distinct priorities built on an all-out drive both to secure the armaments programme and to improve food provisioning through maximum attainable autarky in specific fields and production of substitute raw materials such as synthetic fuels, rubber, and industrial fats. It was not a war economy; but it was the nearest thing to a war economy in peacetime.

At the end of July, while Hitler was in Bayreuth and Berchtesgaden, Göring had a number of opportunities to discuss with him his plans for the economy. On 30 July he obtained Hitler's agreement to present them with a splash at the coming Reich Party Rally in September.

Hitler had meanwhile become increasingly preoccupied with the looming threat, as he saw it, from Bolshevism, and with the prospect that the mounting international turmoil could lead to war in the nearer rather than more distant future. Whatever tactical opportunism he deployed, and however much he played on the theme for propaganda purposes, there is no doubt that the coming showdown with Bolshevism remained – as it had been since the mid-1920s at the latest – the lodestar of Hitler's thinking on foreign policy. In 1936, this future titanic struggle started to come into sharper focus.

After meeting the Japanese ambassador in Berlin early in June, Hitler repeated his view that deepening conflict was on the way in the Far East, though he now thought that Japan would 'thrash' Russia. At that point, 'this colossus will start to totter. And then our great hour will have arrived. Then we must supply ourselves with land for 100 years,' he told Goebbels. 'Let's hope we're ready then,' the Propaganda Minister added in his diary notes, 'and that the Führer is still alive. So that action will be taken.'

By this time, events in Spain were also focusing Hitler's attention on the threat of Bolshevism. Until then, he had scarcely given a thought to Spain. But on the evening of 25 July, his decision – against the advice of the Foreign Office – to send aid to General Franco committed Germany to involvement in what was rapidly to turn into the Spanish Civil War.

On 17 July army garrisons in Spanish Morocco rose against the elected government. The Commander-in-Chief of the army in Morocco, General Francisco Franco, put himself next morning at the head of the rebellion. But a mutiny of sailors loyal to the Republic denied him the transport facilities he needed to get his army to the mainland, most of which remained in Republican hands. The few planes he was able to lay hands upon did not amount to much in terms of an airlift. In these unpropitious circumstances, Franco turned to Mussolini and Hitler. It took over a week to overcome Mussolini's initial refusal to help the Spanish rebels. Hitler was persuaded within a matter of hours. Ideological and strategic considerations – the likelihood of Bolshevism triumphing on the Iberian peninsula – were uppermost in his mind. But the potential for gaining access to urgently needed raw materials for the rearmament programme – an aspect emphasized by Göring – also appears to have played its part in the decision.

In contrast to the position of the Foreign Ministry, Hitler had convinced himself that the dangers of being sandwiched between two Bolshevik blocs outweighed the risks of German involvement in the Spanish crisis – even if, as seemed likely, it should turn into fully-blown and protracted civil war. War against the Soviet Union – the struggle for Germany's 'living space' – was, in his view, at some point inevitable. The prospect of a Bolshevik Spain was a dangerous complication. He decided to provide Franco with the aid requested. It was an indication both of Hitler's own greatly increased self-confidence and of the weakened position of those who had advised him on international affairs that he took the decision alone. Possibly, knowing the reluctance of the Foreign Office to become involved, and aware that Göring, for all his interest in possible economic gains, shared some of its reservations, Hitler was keen to present doubters with a *fait accompli*.

Only after Hitler had taken the decision were Göring and Blomberg summoned. Göring, despite his hopes of economic gains from intervention, was initially 'horrified' about the risk of international complications through intervention in Spain. But faced with Hitler's usual intransigence, once he had arrived at a decision, Göring was soon won over. Blomberg, his influence – not least after his nervousness over the Rhineland affair – now waning compared with the powerful position he had once held, went along without objection. Ribbentrop, too, when he was told on arrival in Bayreuth that Hitler intended to support Franco, initially warned against involvement in Spain. But Hitler was adamant. He had already ordered aircraft to be put at Franco's disposal. The crucial consideration was ideological: 'If Spain really goes communist, France in her present situation will also be bolshevized in due course, and then Germany is finished. Wedged between the powerful Soviet *bloc* in the East and a strong communist Franco-Spanish *bloc* in the West, we could do hardly anything if Moscow chose to attack us.' Hitler brushed aside Ribbentrop's weak objections – fresh complications with Britain, and the strength of the French bourgeoisie in holding out against Bolshevism – and simply ended the conversation by stating that he had already made his decision.

Despite the warnings he had received that Germany could be sucked into a military quagmire, and however strongly ideological consider-ations weighed with him, Hitler probably intervened only on the assump-tion that German aid would tip the balance quickly and decisively in Franco's favour. Short-term gains, not long-term involvement, were the premiss of Hitler's impulsive decision. Significant military and economic involvement in Spain began only in October.

The ideological impetus behind Hitler's readiness to involve Germany in the Spanish maelstrom – his intensified preoccupation with the threat of Bolshevism – was not a cover for the economic considerations that weighed so heavily with Göring. This is borne out by his private as well as his public utterances. Publicly, as he had told Goebbels the previous day would be the case, in his opening proclamation to the Reich Party Rally in Nuremberg on 9 September, he announced that the 'greatest world danger' of which he had warned for so long – the 'revolutionizing of the continent' through the work of 'Bolshevik wire-pullers' run by 'an international Jewish revolutionary headquarters in Moscow' – was becoming reality. Germany's military rebuilding had been undertaken precisely to prevent what was turning Spain into ruins from taking place in Germany. Out of the public eye, his sentiments were hardly different when he addressed the cabinet for three hours on the foreign-policy situation at the beginning of December. He concentrated on the danger of Bolshevism. Europe was divided into two camps. There was no more going back. He described the tactics of the 'Reds'. Spain had become the decisive issue. France, ruled by Prime Minister Léon Blum – seen as an 'agent of the Soviets', a 'Zionist and world-destroyer' – would be the next victim. The victor in Spain would gain great prestige. The consequences for the rest of Europe, and in particular for Germany and for the remnants of Communism in the country, were major ones. This was the reason, he went on, for German aid in armaments to Spain. 'Germany can only wish that the crisis is deferred until we are ready,' he declared. 'When it comes, seize the opportunity. Get into the pater-noster lift at the right time. But also get out again at the right time. Rearm. Money can play no role.' Only two weeks or so earlier, Goebbels had recorded in his diary: 'After dinner I talked thoroughly with the Führer alone. He is very content with the situation. Rearmament is proceeding. We're sticking in fabulous sums. In 1938 we'll be completely ready. The showdown with Bolshevism is coming. Then we want to be prepared. The army is now completely won over by us. Führer untouch-able . . . Dominance in Europe for us is as good as certain. Just let no chance pass by. Therefore rearm.'

III

The announcement of the Four-Year Plan at the Nuremberg Party Rally in September had by then pushed rearmament policy on to a new plane. Priorities had been established. They meant in practice that balancing consumer and rearmament spending could only be sustained for a limited period of time through a crash programme which maximized autarkic potential to prepare Germany as rapidly as possible for the confrontation which Hitler deemed inevitable and other leading figures in the regime thought probable, if not highly likely, within the following few years. Through the introduction of the Four-Year Plan, Germany was economically pushed in the direction of expansion and war. Economics and ideology were by now thoroughly interwoven. Even so, the decision to move to the Four-Year Plan was ultimately an ideological one. Econ-omic options were still open – even if the policies of the previous three years meant they had already narrowed sharply. Schacht, Goerdeler, and others, backed by important sectors of industry, favoured a retreat from an armaments-led economy to a re-entry into international markets. Against this, the powerful IG-Farben lobby, linked to the Luftwaffe, pressed for maximizing production of synthetic fuels. The stalemate persisted throughout the summer. The economic crisis which had dogged Germany during the previous winter and spring was unresolved. With no end to the dispute in sight, Hitler was pressed in late August to take sides. The preoccupation with Bolshevism, which had weighed heavily with him throughout the summer, was decisive in his own inimitable approach to Germany's economic problems.

The driving-force behind the creation of what came to be known as the Four-Year Plan was not, however, Hitler but Göring. Following their discussions in Berchtesgaden and Bayreuth in July, Hitler had requested reports from Göring on the economic situation, and how the problems were to be overcome. At the beginning of August Göring had in turn demanded memoranda from different branches of the economy to be sent to him as rapidly as possible. The timing was determined by propaganda considerations, not economic criteria: the proximity of the Reich Party Rally in early September was what counted. The complex reports could not be put together as swiftly as Göring had wanted. By the time he travelled to Berchtesgaden at the beginning of the last week in August, he had only a survey from his Raw Materials and Currency staff about the possibilities of synthetic raw-material production within Germany to hand. He had meanwhile been encountering powerful opposition to his economic plans from Schacht, who was voicing feelings in some important sectors of business and industry. Carl Goerdeler, too, Lord Mayor of Leipzig, who had served Hitler as Reich Price Commissioner and would eventually become a leading opponent of the regime, joined in the criticism towards the end of the month. It was in these circumstances that Hitler was persuaded during the last week of August to dictate a lengthy memorandum on the future direction of the economy – one of the extremely rare occasions in the Third Reich (leaving aside formal laws, decrees, and directives) that he put forward his views in writing.

The memorandum fell into two parts. The first, on 'the political situation', was pure Hitler. It was couched exclusively in ideological terms. The 'reasoning' was, as it had been in *Mein Kampf* and the *Second Book*, social-Darwinist and racially determinist. 'Politics are the conduct and course of the historical struggle for life of peoples,' he began. 'The aim of these struggles is the assertion of existence.' The world was moving towards a new conflict, centred upon Bolshevism, 'whose essence and aim . . . is solely the elimination of those strata of mankind which have hitherto provided the leadership and their replacement by world-wide Jewry.' Germany would be the focus of the inevitable showdown with Bolshevism. 'It is not the aim of this memorandum to prophesy the time when the untenable situation in Europe will become an open crisis. I only want, in these lines, to set down my conviction that this crisis cannot and will not fail to arrive,' he asserted. 'A victory of Bolshevism over Germany would lead not to a Versailles Treaty but to the final destruction, indeed to the annihilation, of the German people . . . In face of the necessity of defence against this danger, all other considerations must recede into the background as being completely irrelevant.'

The second part of the memorandum, dealing with 'Germany's economic situation', and offering a 'programme for a final solution of our vital need', bore unmistakable signs of Göring's influence, resting in turn on the raw material programmes drawn up by his planning staff, with significant input by IG Farben. The resemblance to statements on the economy put forward by Göring earlier in the summer suggests that Hitler either had such statements before him when compiling his memorandum, or that his Raw Materials Commissar worked alongside him in preparing the memorandum. The tone was nonetheless classically Hitlerian – down to the threat of a law 'making the whole of Jewry liable for all damage inflicted by individual specimens of this community of criminals upon the German economy', a threat put into practice some two years later.

A temporary solution to the economic problems was to be found in partial autarky. Maximizing domestic production wherever possible would allow for the necessary food imports, which could not be at the cost of rearmament. Fuel, iron, and synthetic-rubber production had to be stepped up. Cost was irrelevant. Objections – and the opposition voiced in the previous weeks – were taken on board and brushed aside. The nation did not live for the economy; rather, 'finance and the economy, economic leaders and theories must all exclusively serve this struggle for self-assertion in which our people are engaged'. The Ministry of Economics had simply to set the national economic tasks; private industry had to fulfil them. If it could not do so, the National Socialist state, Hitler threatened, would 'succeed in carrying out this task on its own'. Though Germany's economic problems, the memorandum asserted, could be temporarily eased through the measures laid down, they could only finally be solved through the extension of 'living space'. It was 'the task of the political leadership one day to solve this problem'. The memorandum closed by advocating a 'Several Years Plan' – the term 'Four-Year Plan' was not mentioned in the document – to maximize self-sufficiency in existing conditions and make it possible to demand economic sacrifices of the German people. In the next four years, the German army had to be made operational, the economy made ready for war.

Hitler's way of argumentation was characteristic. The inflexibility of its ideological premises coupled with the very broadness of its dogmatic generalities made it impossible for critics to contest it outright without rejection of Hitler himself and his 'world-view'. This 'world-view', whatever tactical adjustments had proved necessary, showed again its inner consistency in the central place assigned to the coming showdown with Bolshevism – an issue which, as we have seen, preoccupied Hitler throughout 1936.

Göring got what he wanted out of Hitler's memorandum. Armed with Hitler's backing, he was able to determine his supremacy in the central arena of the armaments economy. Schacht recognized the scale of the defeat he had suffered. Hitler was reluctant to drop him because of the standing he enjoyed abroad. But his star was now waning fast. Alternative policies to that advanced in Hitler's memorandum could now be condemned out of hand.

Hitler – in so far as he had given any consideration at all to organizational matters – had, it appears, simply imagined that Göring would work through only a small bureaucracy and function as an overlord in coordinating economic policy with the relevant ministries, which would retain their specific responsibilities. Instead, Göring rapidly improvised a panoply of 'special commissioners', backed by their own bureaucratic apparatus, for different facets of the Four-Year Plan, often without clear lines of control, not infrequently overlapping or interfering with the duties of the Ministry of Economics, and all of course answerable to Göring himself. It was a recipe for administrative and economic anarchy.

But the momentum created by the Four-Year Plan was immense. All areas of the economy were affected in the following peacetime years. The resulting pressures on the economy as a whole were not sustainable indefinitely. The economic drive created its own dynamic which fed directly into Hitler's ideological imperative. The ambitious technocrats in the offices and sub-organizations of the Four-Year Plan, not least the leaders of the rapidly expanding chemicals giant IG-Farben, were in their own way – whatever their direct motivation – also 'working towards the Führer'. Territorial expansion became necessary for economic as well as for ideological reasons. And racial policy, too, was pushed on to a new plane as the spoils to be gained from a programme of 'aryanization' were eagerly seized upon as easy pickings in an economy starting to overheat under its own, self-manufactured pressures.

When Hitler drew up his memorandum in late August 1936 all this was in the future. He had no clear notion himself of how it would all unfold. Nor was he specially interested in such questions. Propaganda concerned him more immediately than economics in drawing up the memorandum. He needed the new economic programme as the corner-stone of the Party Rally. His big speech there on the economy was closely based, occasionally word for word, on his August memorandum. He now spoke publicly for the first time of a 'new Four-Year Programme' (recalling his initial 'four-year plan' put forward immediately after his appointment as Chancellor in 1933). The designation 'Four-Year Plan' rapidly caught on in the German press. It became officially so called some weeks later, on 18 October, with Hitler's 'Decree for the Imple-mentation of the Four-Year Plan'.

IV

In the foreign-policy arena, the shifts which had begun during the Abys-sinian crisis were hardening across the summer and autumn of 1936. Clearer contours were beginning to emerge. Diplomatic, strategic, economic, and ideological considerations – separable but often closely interwoven – were starting to take Germany into more dangerous, un-charted waters. The possibility of a new European conflagration – how-ever unimaginable and horrifying the prospect seemed to most of the generation that had lived through the last one – increasingly appeared a real one.

The long-desired alliance with Britain, which had seemed a real possi-bility in June 1935 at the signing of the Naval Pact, had remained elusive. It was still a distant dream. The Abyssinian crisis and the reoccupation of the Rhineland, now the Spanish Civil War, had all provided hurdles to a closer relationship despite German efforts to court those they imagined had power and influence in Britain and some British sympathizers in high places. Ribbentrop, appointed in the summer an unwilling Ambassador to London with a mandate from Hitler to bring Britain into an anti-Comintern pact, had since his triumph with the Naval Agreement become increasingly disillusioned about the prospects of a British alliance. Hitler saw the abdication on 11 December 1936 of King Edward VIII, in the face of opposition in Britain to his proposed marriage to a twice-divorced American, Mrs Wallis Simpson, as a victory for those forces hostile to Germany. Ribbentrop had encouraged him in the view that the King was pro-German and anti-Jewish, and that he had been deposed by an anti-German conspiracy linked to Jews, freemasons, and powerful political lobbies. By the end of the year, Hitler had become more lukewarm about a British alliance. Germany, he concluded, had its interests better served by close ties with Italy.

The rapprochement with Italy – slow and tenuous in the first half of 1936 – had by then come to harden into a new alliance of the two fascist-style militaristic dictatorships dominating central and southern Europe. The Abyssinian crisis, as we noted, had turned Italy towards Germany. The repercussions on Austria were not long in the waiting. Deprived *de facto* of its Italian protector, Austria was swept inevitably further into the German slipstream. Encouraged by the Italians as well as put under pressure by the Germans, Austria was ready by 11 July 1936 to sign a wide-ranging agreement with Germany, improving relations, ending restrictions placed upon the German press, and upon economic and cultural activities within Austria. Though recognizing Austrian independence, the agreement in reality turned the Reich's eastern neighbour into an economic and foreign-policy dependency. It was a development which by this time suited both Germany and Italy. And within weeks, the aid provided by the two dictatorships to the nationalist rebels in Spain, and the rapidly deepening commitment to the Spanish Civil War, brought Italy and Germany still closer together.

The diplomatic benefits from closer ties with Italy were reinforced in Hitler's own eyes by the anti-Bolshevik credentials of Mussolini's regime. In September, he made overtures to Mussolini through his envoy Hans Frank, inviting the Duce to visit Berlin the following year – an invitation readily accepted. There was agreement on a common struggle against Communism, rapid recognition of a Franco government in Spain,

German recognition of the annexation of Abyssinia, and Italian 'satisfaction' at the Austro-German agreement.

Hitler was in effusive mood when he welcomed Mussolini's son-in-law, the vain Count Ciano, to Berchtesgaden on 24 October. He described Mussolini as 'the leading statesman in the world, to whom none may even remotely compare himself'. There was no clash of interests between Italy and Germany, he declared. The Mediterranean was 'an Italian sea'. Germany had to have freedom of action towards the East and the Baltic. He was convinced, he said, that England would attack Italy, Germany, or both, given the opportunity and likely chances of success. A common anti-Bolshevik front, including powers in the East, the Far East, and South America, would however act as a deterrent, and probably even prompt Britain to seek an agreement. If Britain continued its offensive policy, seeking time to rearm, Germany and Italy had the advantage both in material and psychological rearmament, he enthused. In three years, Germany would be ready, in four years more than ready; five years would be better still.

In a speech in the cathedral square in Milan a week later, Mussolini spoke of the line between Berlin and Rome as 'an axis round which all those European States which are animated by a desire for collaboration and peace can revolve'. A new term was coined: 'Axis' – whether in a positive or negative sense – caught the imagination. In Italian and German propaganda, it evoked the might and strength of two countries with kindred philosophies joining forces against common enemies. For the western democracies, it raised the spectre of the combined threat to European peace by two expansionist powers under the leadership of dangerous dictators.

The menacing image became global when, within weeks of the formation of the Axis, Hitler entered a further pact with the one power outside Italy he had singled out in his August memorandum as standing firm against Bolshevism: Japan. The driving force behind the pact, from the German side, had from the beginning been Ribbentrop, operating with Hitler's encouragement. The professionals from the German Foreign Office, far more interested in relations with China, found themselves largely excluded, as 'amateurs' from the Dienststelle Ribbentrop (Ribbentrop Bureau) – the agency for foreign affairs founded in 1934, by now with around 160 persons working for it, upon which Hitler was placing increasing reliance – made the running.

The Japanese military leaders saw in a rapprochement with Berlin the chance to weaken German links with China and gain a potential ally against the Soviet Union. On 27 November 1936 Hitler approved what became known as the Anti-Comintern Pact (which Italy joined a year later), under whose main provision – in a secret protocol – neither party would assist the Soviet Union in any way in the event of it attacking either Germany or Japan. The pact was more important for its symbolism than for its actual provisions: the two most militaristic, expansionist powers in the world had found their way to each other. Though the pact was ostensibly defensive, it had hardly enhanced the prospects for peace on either side of the globe.

In his Reichstag speech on 30 January 1937, celebrating the fourth anniversary of his takeover of power, Hitler announced that 'the time of the so-called surprises' was over. Germany wished 'from now on in loyal fashion' as an equal partner to work with other nations to over-come the problems besetting Europe. This pronouncement was soon to prove even more cynical than it had appeared at the time. That further 'surprises' were inevitable – and not long postponed – was not solely owing to Hitler's temperament and psychology. The forces unleashed in four years of Nazi rule – internal and external – were producing their own dynamic. Those in so many different ways who were 'working towards the Führer' were ensuring, directly or indirectly, that Hitler's own ideological obsessions served as the broad guidelines of policy initiatives. The restlessness – and recklessness – ingrained in Hitler's personality reflected the pressures for action emanating in different ways from the varied components of the regime, loosely held together by aims of national assertiveness and racial purity embodied in the figure of the Leader. Internationally, the fragility and chronic instability of the post-war order had been brutally exposed. Within Germany, the chimeric quest for racial purity, backed by a leadership for which this was a central tenet of belief, could, if circumstances demanded, be contained temporarily, but would inevitably soon reassert itself to turn the screw of discrimination ever tighter. The Nazi regime could not stand still. As Hitler himself was to comment before the end of the year, the alternative to expansion – and to the restless energy which was the regime's lifeblood – was what he called 'sterility', bringing in its wake, after a while, 'tensions of a social kind', while failure to act in the near future could bring internal crisis and a 'weakening point of the regime'.

The bold forward move, Hitler's trademark, was intrinsic to Nazism itself.

V

To most observers, both internal and external, after four years in power the Hitler regime looked stable, strong, and successful. Hitler's own position was untouchable. The image of the great statesman and national leader of genius manufactured by propaganda matched the sentiments and expectations of much of the population. The internal rebuilding of the country and the national triumphs in foreign policy, all attributed to his 'genius', had made him the most popular political leader of any nation in Europe. Most ordinary Germans – like most ordinary people anywhere and at most times – looked forward to peace and prosperity. Hitler appeared to have established the basis for these. He had restored authority to government. Law and order had been re-established. Few were concerned if civil liberties had been destroyed in the process. There was work again. The economy was booming. What a contrast this was to the mass unemployment and economic failure of Weimar democracy. Of course, there was still much to do. And many grievances remained. Not least, the conflict with the Churches was the source of great bitterness. But Hitler was largely exempted from blame. The negative features of daily life, most imagined, were not of the Führer's making. They were the fault of his underlings, who frequently kept him in the dark about what was happening.

Above all, even critics had to admit, Hitler had restored German national pride. From its post-war humiliation, Germany had risen to become once more a major power. Defence through strength had proved a successful strategy. He had taken risks. There had been great fear that these would lead to renewed war. But each time he had been proved right. And Germany's position had been inordinately strengthened as a consequence. Even so, there was widespread relief at the indication, in Hitler's speech of 30 January 1937, that the period of 'surprises' was over. Hitler's comment was seized upon throughout the land as a sign that consolidation and stability would now be the priorities. The illusion would not last long. The year 1937 was to prove the calm before the storm.

Not only ordinary people were taken in by Hitler. Even for those within Germany known to be critical of the regime, Hitler could in a face-to-face meeting create a positive impression. He was good at attuning to the sensitivities of his conversation partner, could be charming, and often appeared reasonable and accommodating. As always, he was a skilled dissembler. On a one-to-one basis, he could pull the wool over the eyes even of hardened critics. After a three-hour meeting with him at the Berghof in early November 1936, the influential Catholic Archbishop of Munich-Freising, Cardinal Faulhaber – a man of sharp acumen, who had often courageously criticized the Nazi attacks on the Catholic Church – went away convinced that Hitler was deeply religious. 'The Reich Chancellor undoubtedly lives in belief in God,' he noted in a confidential report. 'He recognizes Christianity as the builder of western culture.'

Few, even of those who were daily in his company – the regular entourage of adjutants and secretaries – and those with frequent, privileged access, could claim to 'know' Hitler, to get close to the human being inside the shell of the Führer figure. Hitler himself was keen to maintain the distance. 'The masses need an idol,' he was later to say. He played the role not just to the masses, but even to his closest entourage. Despite the torrents of words he poured out in public, and the lengthy monologues he inflicted upon those in his circle, he was by temperament a very private, even secretive, individual. A deeply ingrained sense of distrust and cynicism meant he was unwilling and unable to confide in others. Behind the public figure known to millions, the personality was a closed one. Genuine personal relations were few. Most even of those who had been in his immediate company for years were kept at arm's length. He used the familiar '*Du*' form with a mere handful of people. Even when his boyhood friend August Kubizek met him again the following year, following the Anschluß, Hitler used the formal '*Sie*' mode of address. The conventional mode of addressing Hitler, which had set in after 1933, 'Mein Führer', emphasized the formality of relations. The authority of his position depended upon the preservation of the nimbus attached to him, as he well realized. This in turn demanded the distance of the individual even from those in his immediate *familia*. The 'mystery' of Hitler's personality had important functional, as well as temperamental, causes. Respect for his authority was more important to him than personal warmth.

Hitler's dealings with his personal staff were formal, correct, polite, and courteous. He usually passed a pleasant word or two with his secretaries when any engagements in the late morning were over, and often took tea with them in the afternoons and at night. He enjoyed the joking and songs (accompanied on the accordion) of his chef and *Hausintendant* or major-domo Arthur Kannenberg. He could show sympathy and understanding, as when his new Luftwaffe adjutant, Nicolaus von Below, had – to his embarrassment – to ask to leave for his honeymoon immediately on joining Hitler's service. He sent Christa Schroeder, one of his secretaries, presents when she was ill and visited her in hospital. He enjoyed giving presents to his staff on their birthdays and at Christmas, and paid personal attention to selecting appropriate gifts.

But genuine warmth and affection were missing. The shows of kindness and attentiveness were superficial. Hitler's staff, like most other human beings, were of interest to him only as long as they were useful. However lengthy and loyal their service, if their usefulness was at an end they would be dispensed with. His staff, for their part, admired 'the Boss' as they called him. They respected, at times feared, him. His authority was unquestioned and absolute. Their loyalty to him was equally beyond question. But whether they genuinely liked him as a person is doubtful. There was a certain stiffness about the atmosphere whenever Hitler was present. It was difficult to relax in his company. He was demanding of his staff, who had to work long hours and fit into his eccentric work habits. His secretaries were often on duty in the mornings, but had to be prepared to take dictation of lengthy speeches late at night or into the early hours. Patronizingly complimentary to them on some occasions, on others he would scarcely notice their existence. In his own eyes, more even than in the eyes of those around him, he was the only person that mattered. His wishes, his feelings, his interests alone counted. He could be lenient of misdemeanours when he was unaffected. But where he felt a sense of affront, or that he had been let down, he could be harsh in his treatment of those around him. He was brusque and insulting to the lady-friend, of whom he disapproved, of his Chief Adjutant Wilhelm Brückner, a massive figure, veteran of the SA in the party's early days, and participant in the Beerhall Putsch of 1923. A few years later he was peremptorily to dismiss Brückner, despite his lengthy and dutiful service, following a minor dispute. On another occasion he dismissed his valet Karl Krause, who had served him for several years, again for a trivial matter. Even his jovial hospitality manager, Arthur Kannenberg, who generally enjoyed something of the freedom of a court jester, had to tread carefully. Always anxious at the prospect of any embarrassment that would make him look foolish and damage his standing, Hitler threatened him with punishment if his staff committed any mistakes at receptions.

Hitler strongly disliked any change in the personnel of his immediate entourage. He liked to see the same faces around him. He wanted those about him whom he was used to, and who were used to him. For one whose lifestyle had always been in many respects so 'bohemian', he was remarkably fixed in his routines, inflexible in his habits, and highly reluctant to make alterations to his personal staff.

In 1937 he had four personal adjutants: SA-Gruppenführer Wilhelm Brückner (the chief adjutant); Julius Schaub (formerly the head of his bodyguard, a putsch veteran who had been in prison in Landsberg with Hitler and in his close attendance ever since, looking after his confidential papers, carrying money for the 'Chief's' use, acting as his personal secretary, general factotum, and 'notebook'); Fritz Wiedemann (who had been Hitler's direct superior in the war); and Albert Bormann (the brother of Martin, with whom, however, he was not on speaking terms). Three military adjutants – Colonel Friedrich Hoßbach for the army, Captain Karl-Jesko Otto von Puttkamer for the navy, and Captain Nicolaus von Below for the Luftwaffe – were responsible for Hitler's links with the leaders of the armed forces. Secretaries, valets (one of whom had to be on call at all moments of the day), his pilot Hans Baur, his chauffeur Erich Kempka, the head of the SS-Leibstandarte Adolf Hitler and long-standing Hitler trustee Sepp Dietrich, the leaders of the bodyguard and criminal police attachments, and the doctors who, at different times, attended upon him all formed part of the additional personal staff.

By 1937, Hitler's day followed a fairly regular pattern, at least when he was in Berlin. Late in the morning, he received a knock from his valet, Karl Krause, who would leave newspapers and any important messages outside his room. While Hitler took them in to read, Krause ran his bath and laid out his clothes. Always concerned to avoid being seen naked, Hitler insisted upon dressing himself, without help from his valet. Only towards midday did he emerge from his private suite of rooms (or 'Führer apartment') – a lounge, library, bedroom, and bathroom, together with a small room reserved for Eva Braun – in the renovated Reich Chancellery. He gave any necessary instructions to, or received information from, his military adjutants, was given a press summary by Otto Dietrich, and was told by Hans Heinrich Lammers, head of the Reich Chancellery, of his various engagements. Meetings and discussions, usually carried out while Hitler walked backwards and forwards with his discussion partner in the 'Wintergarten' (or conservatory) looking out on the garden, generally filled the next couple of hours – sometimes longer – so that lunch was frequently delayed.

The spacious and light dining-room had a large round table with a dozen chairs in the centre and four smaller tables, each with six chairs, around it. Hitler sat at the large table with his back to the window, facing a picture by Kaulbach, *Entry of the Sun Goddess*. Some of the guests – among them Goebbels, Göring, and Speer – were regulars. Others were newcomers or were seldom invited. The talk was often of world affairs. But Hitler would tailor the discussion to those present. He was careful in what he said. He consciously set out to impress his opinion on his guests, perhaps at times to gauge their reaction. Sometimes he dominated the 'conversation' with a monologue. At other times, he was content to listen while Goebbels sparred with another guest, or a more general discussion unfolded. Sometimes the table talk was interesting. New guests could find the occasion exciting and Hitler's comments a 'revelation'. Frau Below, the wife of the new Luftwaffe-Adjutant, found the atmosphere, and Hitler's company, at first exhilarating and was greatly impressed by his knowledge of history and art. But for the household staff who had heard it all many times, the midday meal was often a tedious affair.

After lunch there were usually further meetings in the Music Salon with ambassadors, generals, Reich Ministers, foreign dignitaries, or personal acquaintances such as the Wagners or Bruckmanns. Such meetings seldom lasted longer than an hour, and were arranged around tea. Thereafter, Hitler withdrew to his own rooms for a rest, or went for a stroll round the park attached to the Reich Chancellery. He spent no time at all during the day at his massive desk, other than hurriedly to attach his signature to laws, letters of appointment, or other formal documents placed before him. Beyond his major speeches, letters to foreign heads of state, and the occasional formal note of thanks or condolence, he dictated little or nothing to his secretaries. Apart from his temperamental aversion to bureaucracy, he was anxious to avoid committing himself on paper. The consequence was that his adjutants and personal staff often had the task of passing on in written form directives which were unclear, ill thought-out, or spontaneous reactions. The scope for confusion, distortion, and misunderstanding was enormous. What Hitler had originally intended or stated was, by the time it had passed through various hands, often open to different interpretation and impossible to reconstruct with certainty.

The evening meal, around 8 p.m., followed the same pattern as lunch, but there were usually fewer present and talk focused more on Hitler's favourite topics, such as art and history. During the meal, Hitler would be presented by one of the servants (most of whom were drawn from his bodyguard, the Leibstandarte) with a list of films, including those from abroad and German films still unreleased, which Goebbels had provided. (Hitler was delighted at his Christmas present from Goebbels in 1937: thirty feature films of the previous four years, and eighteen Mickey Mouse cartoons.) After the meal, the film chosen for the evening would be shown in the Music Salon. Any members of the household staff and the chauffeurs of any guests present could watch. Hitler's secretaries were, however, not present at the meals in the Reich Chancellery, though they were included in the more relaxed atmosphere at the Berghof. The evening ended with conversation stretching usually to about 2 a.m. before Hitler retired.

In this world within the Reich Chancellery, with its fixed routines and formalities, where he was surrounded by his regular staff and otherwise met for the most part official visitors or guests who were mainly in awe of him, Hitler was cocooned within the role and image of the Führer which had elevated him to demi-god status. Few could behave naturally in his presence. The rough 'old fighters' of the party's early days now came less frequently. Those attending the meals in the Reich Chancellery had for the most part only known him since the nimbus of the 'great leader' had become attached to him. The result only reinforced Hitler's self-belief that he was a 'man of destiny', treading his path 'with the certainty of a sleepwalker'. At the same time, he was ever more cut off from real human contact, isolated in his realm of increasing megalomania. Aways glad to get away from Berlin, it was only while staying with the Wagners during the annual Bayreuth Festival and at his alpine retreat 'on the mountain' above Berchtesgaden that Hitler relaxed some-what. But even at the Berghof, rituals were preserved. Hitler dominated the entire existence of his guests there too. Real informality was as good as impossible in his presence. And Hitler, for all the large numbers of people in attendance on him and paying court to him, remained impoverished when it came to real contact, cut off from any meaningful personal relationship through the shallowness of his emotions and his profoundly egocentric, exploitative attitude towards all other human beings.

It is impossible to be sure of what, if any, emotional satisfaction Hitler gained from his relationship with Eva Braun (whom he had first met in 1929 when, then aged seventeen, she worked in the office of his photographer, Heinrich Hoffmann). It could not have been much. For prestige reasons, he kept her away from the public eye. On the rare occasions she was in Berlin, she was closeted in her little room in the 'Führer Apartment' while Hitler attended official functions or was otherwise engaged. Even in his close circle she was not permitted to be present for meals if any important guests were there. She did not accom-pany Hitler on his numerous journeys, and had to stay for the most part either in his flat in Munich or at the Berghof, the only place where she could emerge as one of the extended 'family'. Even there, however, she was hidden away during receptions for important guests. Hitler often treated her abysmally when she was present, frequently humiliating her in front of others. The contrast with the olde-worlde charm – kissing hands, linking arms, cupping elbows – that he habitually showed to-wards pretty women in his presence merely rubbed salt in the wounds.

Probably the closest that Hitler came to friendship was in his relations with Joseph Goebbels and, increasingly, with his court architect and new favourite, Albert Speer, whom in January 1937 he made responsible for the rebuilding of Berlin. Hitler frequently sought out their company, liked their presence, was fond of their wives and families, and could feel at ease with them. The Goebbels home was a frequent refuge in Berlin. Lengthy talks with Speer about the rebuilding of the capital city amounted to the nearest thing Hitler had to a hobby, a welcome respite from his otherwise total involvement in politics. At least in Goebbels's case there were elements of a father-son relationship. A rare flicker of human concern could be glimpsed when Hitler asked Goebbels to stay for an extra day in Nuremberg after the rally in September 1937, since (according to the Propaganda Minister) he did not like him flying at night. Hitler was the dominant figure – the father-figure. But he may have seen something of himself in each of his two protégés – the brilliant progagandist in Goebbels, the gifted architect in Speer.

In the case of Speer, the fascination for architecture provided an obvious bond. Both had a liking for neo-classical buildings on a monumental scale. Hitler was impressed by Speer's taste in architecture, his energy, and his organizational skill. He had rapidly come to see him as the architect who could put his own grandiose building schemes, envisaged as the representation of Teutonic might and glory that would last for centuries, into practice. But other architects, some better than Speer, were available. The attractiveness of Speer to Hitler went beyond the building mania that linked them closely to each other. Nothing homo-erotic was involved – at least not consciously. But Hitler perhaps found in the handsome, burningly ambitious, talented, and successful architect an unconsciously idealized self-image. What is plain is that both Goebbels and Speer worshipped Hitler. Goebbels's adoration of the father-figure Hitler was undiminished since the mid-1920s. 'He is a fabulous man' was merely one of his effusions of sentiment in 1937 about the figure who was the centre-point of his universe. For Speer, as he himself later recognized, his love of Hitler transcended the power-ambitions that his protector and role-model was able to satisfy – even if it originally arose out of them and could never be completely separated from them.

In earlier years, Hitler had invariably spoken of his own 'mission' as the mere beginning of Germany's passage to world domination. The whole process would take generations to complete. But, flushed with scarcely imaginable triumphs since 1933 and falling ever more victim to the myth of his own greatness, he became increasingly impatient to see his 'mission' fulfilled in his lifetime.

Partly, this was incipient megalomania. He spoke on numerous occasions in 1937 about building plans of staggering monumentality. At midnight on his birthday, he, Goebbels, and Speer stood in front of plans for rebuilding Berlin, fantasizing about a glorious future. 'The Führer won't speak of money. Build, build! It will somehow be paid for!' Goebbels has him saying. 'Frederick the Great didn't ask about money when he built Sanssouci.'

In part, too, it was prompted by Hitler's growing preoccupation with his own mortality and impatience to achieve what he could in his lifetime. Before the mid-1930s, his health had generally been good – astonishingly so given his lack of exercise, poor diet (even before his cranky vegetarianism following the death in 1931 of his niece, Geli Raubal), and high expenditure of nervous energy. However, he already suffered from chronic stomach pains which, at times of stress, became acute spasms. A patent medicine he took – an old trench remedy with a base in gun-cleaning oil – turned out to be mildly poisonous, causing headaches, double vision, dizziness, and ringing in the ears. He had been worried in 1935 that a polyp in his throat (eventually removed in the May of that year) was cancerous. It turned out to be harmless. During 1936, a year of almost continual tension, the stomach cramps were frequently severe, and Hitler also developed eczema on both legs, which had to be covered in bandages. At Christmas 1936, he asked Dr Theodor Morell, a physician who had successfully treated his photographer Heinrich Hoffmann, to try to cure him. Morell gave him vitamins and a new patent remedy for intestinal problems. Goebbels mentioned in June, and again in August 1937, that Hitler was unwell. But by September, Morell's treatment had apparently made a difference. At any rate, Hitler was impressed. He felt fit again, his weight was back to normal, and his eczema had vanished. His belief in Morell would last down to the bunker in 1945. From late 1937 onwards, his increasing hypochondria made him ever more reliant on Morell's pills, drugs, and injections. And the fear of cancer (which had caused his mother's death) never left him. At the end of October, he told a meeting of propaganda leaders that both his parents had died young, and that he probably did not have long to live. 'It was necessary, therefore, to solve the problems that had to be solved (living space) as soon as possible, so that this could still take place in his lifetime. Later generations would no longer be able to accomplish it. Only his person was in the position to bring it about.'

Hitler was seldom out of the public eye in 1937. No opportunity was missed to drive home to the German public an apparently endless array of scarcely credible 'achievements' at home and the glories of his major 'triumphs' in foreign policy. Flushed with success and certain of the adulation of the masses, he wanted to be seen. The bonds between the Führer and the people – the cement of the regime, and dependent upon recurring success and achievement – were thereby reinforced. And for Hitler the ecstasy of his mass audiences provided each time a new injection of the drug to feed his egomania. As always, the effect of his speeches depended heavily upon the atmosphere in which they were held. The content was repetitive and monotonous. The themes were the familiar ones. Past achievements were lauded, grandiose future plans proclaimed, the horrors and menace of Bolshevism emphasized. But there was no conflict between propaganda and ideology. Hitler believed what he was saying.

His lengthy concluding speech at the Reich Party Rally in Nuremberg in early September was an onslaught on 'Jewish Bolshevism'. In passages at times reminiscent of *Mein Kampf*, and in his fiercest public attack on the Jews for many months, he portrayed them as the force behind Bolshevism and its 'general attack on the present-day social order', and spoke of 'the claim of an uncivilized Jewish-Bolshevik international guild of criminals to rule Germany, as an old cultural land of Europe, from Moscow'. This is what the party faithful wanted to hear. But it was far more than window-dressing. Even in private, dictating the speeches to his secretary, when it came to passages on Bolshevism Hitler, red-faced and eyes blazing, would work himself to a frenzy, bellowing at full volume his thunderous denunciations.

VI

Away from the continual propaganda activity revolving around speeches and public appearances, Hitler was largely preoccupied in 1937 with keeping a watchful eye on the changing situation in world affairs and with his gigantic building plans. The continuing conflict with both the Catholic and Protestant Churches, radical though his own instincts were, amounted to a recurrent irritation, especially in the first months of the year, rather than a priority concern (as it was with Goebbels, Rosenberg, and many of the party rank-and-file). With regard to the 'Jewish Question' – to go from the many private discussions with Goebbels which the Propaganda Minister reported in his diary notes – Hitler, unchanged though his views were, showed little active interest and seldom spoke directly on the subject. But however uninvolved he was, the radicalization of the regime continued unabated, forced on in a variety of ways by party activists, ministerial bureaucracy, economic opportunists, and, not least, by an ideologically driven police.

In February 1937 Hitler made it plain to his inner circle that he did not want a 'Church struggle' at this juncture. The time was not ripe for it. He expected 'the great world struggle in a few years' time'. If Germany lost one more war, it would mean the end. The implication was clear: calm should be restored for the time being in relations with the Churches. Instead, the conflict with the Christian Churches intensified. The anti-clericalism and anti-Church sentiments of the grass-roots party activists simply could not be eradicated. The activists could draw on the verbal violence of party leaders towards the Churches for their encouragement. Goebbels's orchestrated attacks on the clergy through the staged 'immorality trials' of Franciscans in 1937 – following usually trumped up or grossly exaggerated allegations of sexual impropriety in the religious orders – provided further ammunition. And, in turn, however much Hitler on some occasions claimed to want a respite in the conflict, his own inflammatory comments gave his immediate underlings all the licence they needed to turn up the heat in the 'Church struggle', confident that they were 'working towards the Führer'.

Hitler's impatience with the Churches prompted frequent outbursts of hostility. In early 1937, he was declaring that 'Christianity was ripe for destruction', and that the Churches must yield to the 'primacy of the state', railing against any compromise with 'the most horrible institution imaginable'. In April, Goebbels reported with satisfaction that the Führer was becoming more radical in the 'Church Question', and had approved the start of the 'immorality trials' against clergy. Goebbels noted Hitler's verbal attacks on the clergy and his satisfaction with the propaganda campaign on several subsequent occasions over the following few weeks. But Hitler was happy to leave the Propaganda Minister and others to make the running. If Goebbels's diary entries are a guide, Hitler's interest and direct involvement in the 'Church struggle' declined during the second half of the year. Other matters were by now occupying his attention.

The 'Jewish Question' does not appear to have figured prominently among them. Goebbels, who saw Hitler almost on a daily basis at this time and who noted the topics of many private conversations they had together, recorded no more than a couple of instances where the 'Jewish Question' was discussed. Anti-Jewish policy, as we have seen, had gathered pace since 1933 without frequent or coherent central direction. It was no different in 1937. Hitler's views remained unchanged since his first statement on the 'Jewish Question' back in September 1919. He gave a clear indication to a gathering of some 800 District Leaders of the party in April 1937 of his tactical caution but ideological consistency in the 'Jewish Question'. Though he made plain to his enemies that he wanted to destroy them, the struggle had to be conducted cleverly, and over a period of time, he told his avid listeners. Skill would help him manoeuvre them into a corner. Then would come the blow to the heart.

But for the most part, he was content to remain for the time inactive in the 'Jewish Question'. His tacit approval was all that was required. And no more was needed than his tirade against 'Jewish Bolshevism' at the Party Rally in September to act as a green light inviting the new antisemitic wave – even fiercer than that of 1935 – that was to unfold throughout 1938.

After two relatively quiet years, discrimination against the Jews again intensified. Increasingly radical steps were initiated to eliminate them from the economy, and from more and more spheres of social activity. The SD had in fact since the start of the year been advocating renewed pressure on the Jews to force them out of the economy and speed up their emigration from Germany. The manufacture of a 'popular mood hostile to Jews' and the deployment of illegal 'excesses' – mob violence, which was seen as particularly effective – were recommended. By autumn, the climate was becoming more hostile than ever for the Jewish population. Schacht's loss of influence, and finally his departure from the Economics Ministry on 27 November, now removed an obstacle to the 'aryanization' of the economy. Pressure to fulfil this aspect of the Party's Programme mounted. Göring, by this time in effect in charge of the economy, was more than ready to push forward the 'aryanization'. The upswing of the economy made big business, losing the uncertainties of the first years of Nazi rule, willing partners, eager to profit from the takeover of Jewish firms at knock-down prices. By April 1938 more than 60 per cent of Jewish firms had been liquidated or 'aryanized'. From late 1937 onwards, individual Jews also faced an expanding array of discriminatory measures, initiated without central coordination by a variety of ministries and offices – all in their way 'working towards the Führer' – which tightened immeasurably the screw of persecution. Hitler's own contribution, as usual, had largely consisted of setting the tone and providing the sanction and legitimation for the actions of others.

In world affairs, events beyond Hitler's control were causing him to speculate on the timing and circumstances in which the great showdown would occur. By the end of 1937, the signs were that radicalization was gathering pace not just in anti-Jewish policy (and, largely instigated by the Gestapo, in the persecution and repression of other ethnic and social minorities), but also in foreign policy.

Hitler had begun the year by expressing his hope to those at his lunch table that he still had six years to prepare for the coming showdown. 'But, if a very favourable chance comes along,' commented Goebbels, 'he also doesn't want to miss it.' Hitler stressed Russian strength and warned against underestimating the British because of their weak political leadership. He saw opportunities of winning allies in eastern Europe (particularly Poland) and the Balkans as a consequence of Russia's drive for world revolution. Hitler's remarks followed a long briefing by Blomberg earlier that morning in the War Ministry about the rapid expansion of rearmament and the Wehrmacht's preparations for 'Case X' – taken to be Germany, together with its fascist allies against Russia, Czechoslovakia, and Lithuania. The question of German occupation was evidently raised. Hitler, Goebbels, and Blomberg discussed the installation of senior Gauleiter as Civilian Commissars. Hitler was satisfied with what he had heard.

A foretaste of what might be expected from the German leadership in war followed the dropping of two 'red bombs' on the battleship *Deutschland*, stationed off Ibiza, by a Spanish Republican plane on the evening of 29 May, killing twenty-three and injuring over seventy sailors. Admiral Raeder, Commander-in-Chief of the Navy, was dispatched by Blomberg to Munich to bear the brunt of Hitler's fury. Hitler's immediate reaction, 'fuming with rage', as Goebbels put it, was to bomb Valencia in reprisal. But after a hastily arranged conference with Blomberg, Raeder, Göring, and von Neurath, he ordered instead the cruiser *Admiral Scheer* to fire on the southern Spanish harbour town of Almería. Hitler, seething but nervous at the outcome, paced up and down his room in the Reich Chancellery until three o'clock in the morning. The shelling of Almería for an hour left twenty-one civilians dead, fifty-three injured, and destroyed thirty-nine houses. Hitler was satisfied. He had seen it as a prestige question. Prestige had now been restored.

He had by this time lost faith in Spain becoming a genuinely fascist country. He saw Franco as a Spanish variant of General Seeckt (the former 'strong man' in the German army in the 1920s) – a military man without any mass movement behind him. Despite his worries about Spain, however, he had no regrets about ordering German intervention, and pointed to the many advantages which Germany had drawn from its involvement. Goebbels's diary notes reflect Hitler's wider perceptions of world affairs during the latter half of 1937, and his watchful eye on opportunities for German expansion. The radicalization in foreign policy which brought the Anschluß with Austria and then the Sudeten crisis in Czechoslovakia in 1938 were foreshadowed in Hitler's musings on future developments during these months.

The arch-enemy, the Soviet Union, was in Hitler's eyes weakened both by its internal turmoils and by Japanese triumphs in the war against China. He was puzzled by the Stalinist purges. 'Stalin is probably sick in the brain,' Goebbels reported him as saying. 'His bloody regime can otherwise not be explained. But Russia knows nothing other than Bolshevism. That's the danger we have to smash down some day.' A few months later, he was repeating the view that Stalin and his followers were mad. 'Must be exterminated' was his sinister conclusion. He was anticipating that the opportunity might arise following a Japanese victory over China. Once China was smashed, he guessed, Tokyo would turn its attention to Moscow. 'That is then our great hour,' he predicted.

Hitler's belief in an alliance with Britain had by now almost evaporated. His attitude towards Britain had come to resemble that of a lover spurned. Contemptuous of the British government, he also saw Britain greatly weakened as a world power. Egged on by Ribbentrop, by now aggressively anti-British, his hopes rested on his new friend Mussolini.

Nothing was spared in the preparations for a huge extravaganza with all conceivable pomp and circumstance to make the maximum impact on the Duce during his state visit to Germany between 25 and 29 September. Mussolini took home with him an image of German power and might – together with a growing sense that Italy's role in the Axis was destined to be that of junior partner. Hitler was also overjoyed at the outcome. There had been agreement on cooperation in Spain, and on attitudes towards the war in the Far East. Hitler was certain that Italian friendship was assured, since Italy had in any case little alternative. Only the Austrian question, on which Mussolini would not be drawn, remained open. 'Well, wait and see,' commented Goebbels.

From remarks recorded by Goebbels, it is clear that Hitler was already by summer 1937 beginning to turn his eyes towards Austria and Czecho-slovakia, though as yet there was no indication of when and how Germany might move against either state. Nor were ideological or military-strategic motives, however important for Hitler himself, the only ones influencing notions of expansion in central Europe. Continuing economic difficulties, especially in fulfilling the Wehrmacht's demands for raw materials, had been the main stimulus to increased German pressure on Austria since the successful visit by Göring to Italy in January. Gold and foreign-currency reserves, labour supplies, and important raw materials were among the lure of a German takeover of the Alpine Republic. Not surprisingly, therefore, the office of the Four-Year Plan was at the forefront of demands for an Anschluß as soon as possible. The economic significance of the Austrian question was further underlined by Hitler's appointment in July 1937 of Wilhelm Keppler, who had served before 1933 as an important link with business leaders, to coordinate party affairs regarding Vienna. Further concessions to follow on those of the 1936 agreement – including the ending of censorship on *Mein Kampf* – were forced on the Austrian government in July. 'Perhaps we're again coming a step further,' mused Goebbels. 'In Austria, the Führer will some time make a *tabula rasa*,' the Propaganda Minister noted, after a conversation with Hitler at the beginning of August. 'Let's hope we can all still experience it,' he went on. 'He'll go for it then. This state is not a state at all. Its people belong to us and will come to us. The Führer's entry into Vienna will one day be his proudest triumph.' At the end of the Nuremberg Rally, a few weeks later, Hitler told Goebbels that the issue of Austria would sometime be resolved 'with force'. Before the end of the year, Papen was unfolding to Hitler plans to topple the Austrian Chancellor Schuschnigg. Göring and Keppler were by then both convinced that Hitler would tackle the question of Austria during the spring or summer of 1938.

In the case of Czechoslovakia, too, Hitler's intentions were unmistakable to Goebbels. 'Czechia is not a state, either,' he noted in his diary in August. 'It will one day be overrun.' The refusal by Czech authorities to allow children from the Sudeten area to go for holidays to Germany was used by Goebbels as the pretext to launch the beginning of a vitriolic press campaign against the Czechs. Göring had by this time been stressing to the British Ambassador, Nevile Henderson, Germany's rights to Austria and the Sudetenland (in due course also to revision of the Polish border). To a long-standing British acquaintance, the former air attaché in Berlin, Group-Captain Christie, he went farther: Germany must have not simply the Sudetenland, but the whole of Bohemia and Moravia, Göring asserted. By mid-October, following the demands of Konrad Henlein, the Sudeten German leader, for autonomy, Goebbels was predicting that Czechoslovakia would in the future 'have nothing to laugh about'.

On 5 November 1937 the Propaganda Minister lunched, as usual, with Hitler. The general situation was discussed. The Czech question was to be toned down for the time being because Germany was still not in a position to take any action. The issue of colonies was also to be taken more slowly, so as not to awaken false expectations among the population. In the run-up to Christmas, the heat had, too, to be turned down on the 'Church struggle'. The long-running saga of Schacht was nearing its dénouement. Schacht had to go, it was agreed. But the Führer wanted to wait until after the party's ritual putsch commemoration on 9 November before taking any action. In the afternoon, Goebbels went home to continue work. The Führer, he noted, had 'General Staff talks'.

VII

In the gloom of late afternoon, the chiefs of the army, Luftwaffe, and navy, together with War Minister Blomberg, made their way to the Reich Chancellery for a meeting, as they thought, to establish the allocation of steel supplies to the armed forces. The reason for the meeting dated back to late October, when Admiral Raeder, increasingly concerned about Göring's allocation of steel and the preferential treatment of the Luftwaffe, had posed an ultimatum to Blomberg indicating that no expansion of the navy was possible without additional steel supplies. Raeder was unwilling to make concessions. He thought an immediate decision by the Führer was necessary. With the dispute among the branches of the armed forces simmering and the prospect of the arms drive stagnating, Blomberg pressed Hitler for clarification. Eventually, Hitler agreed to the meeting. Blomberg, not Hitler, sent out the invitations to discuss 'the armaments situation and raw materials demands' to the chiefs of the three armed forces' branches. The military leaders had a surprise when they reached the Reich Chancellery at 4 p.m. to find present, alongside Hitler and his military adjutant, Colonel Hoßbach, also the Foreign Minister von Neurath. Another surprise was waiting for them when, instead of dealing with the issue of raw materials allocation (which was discussed relatively briefly only towards the end of the lengthy meeting), Hitler, speaking from prepared notes, launched into a monologue lasting over two hours on Germany's need to expand by use of force within the following few years.

He began by emphasizing the importance of what he had to say. He wanted, he said, to explain his thinking on foreign policy. In the event of his death, what he had to say ought to be viewed as his 'testamentary legacy'. No arrangements had been made for minutes to be taken, but Hoßbach, sitting opposite Hitler at the table, decided that what he was about to hear might be of some moment and started to scribble notes in his diary. He was sure his mentor, the increasingly critical General Beck, would be interested.

Hitler launched into a familiar theme: the need to expand German 'living space'. Without this expansion, 'sterility', leading to social disorder, would set in – an argument reflecting Hitler's premiss that permanent mobilization and ever new goals, foreign and domestic, were necessary to ensure the popular support of the regime. In characteristic vein, he raised alternatives to expansion of 'living space', only to dismiss them. Only limited autarky could be achieved. Food supplies could not be ensured by this route. Dependence on the world economy could never bring economic security, and would leave Germany weak and exposed. 'Living space', he asserted, meant territory for agricultural production in Europe, not acquisition of overseas colonies. Britain and France, both implacably hostile, stood in Germany's way. But Britain and its Empire were weakened. And France faced internal difficulties. His conclusion to the first part of his address was that Germany's problem could only be solved by the use of force, which was always accompanied by risks. Only the questions 'when?' and 'how?' remained to be answered.

He went on to outline three scenarios. Typically, he first argued that time was not on Germany's side, that it would be imperative to act by 1943–5 at the latest. The relative strength in armaments would decrease. Other powers would be prepared for a German offensive. Alluding to the problems of 1935–6, he raised the prospect of economic difficulties producing a new food crisis without the foreign exchange to master it – a potential 'weakening-point of the regime'. Declining birth-rates, falling living standards, and the ageing of the Movement and its leaders were added points to underline what he declared was his 'unalterable determination to solve the German problem of space by 1943–5 at the latest'.

In the other two scenarios, Hitler outlined circumstances in which it would be necessary to strike before 1943–5: if France became so enveloped by internal strife, or embroiled in war with another power, that it was incapable of military action against Germany. In either case the moment would have arrived to attack Czechoslovakia. A war of France and Britain against Italy he saw as a distinct possibility arising from the protracted conflict in Spain (whose prolongation was in Germany's interest). In such an eventuality, Germany must be prepared to take advantage of the circumstances to attack the Czechs and Austria without delay – even as early as 1938. The first objective in any war involving Germany would be to overthrow Czechoslovakia and Austria simultaneously to protect the eastern flank for any possible military operation in the west. Hitler conjectured that Britain, and probably France as well, had already written off Czechoslovakia. Problems within the Empire – Hitler had in mind here primarily the growing pressure for independence in India – and reluctance to become embroiled in a long European war would, he thought, prove decisive in deterring Britain from involvement in a war against Germany. France was unlikely to act without British support. Italy would not object to the elimination of Czechoslovakia. Its attitude towards Austria could not at the moment be determined. It would depend on whether Mussolini were still alive – another implied argument for avoiding delay. Poland would be too concerned about Russia to attack Germany. Russia would be preoccupied with the threat from Japan. The incorporation of Austria and Czechoslovakia would improve the security of Germany's borders, freeing up forces for other uses, and would allow the creation of a further twelve divisions. Assuming the expulsion of 3 million from the two countries, their annexation would mean the acquisition of foodstuffs for 5 to 6 million people. Hitler ended by stating that when the moment arrived the attack upon the Czechs would have to be carried out 'lightning fast'.

Hitler's comments to his armed forces' commanders were in line with what he had been saying for weeks to Goebbels and other party leaders. He wanted to use the occasion of the meeting about raw materials allocation to impress similar arguments upon his military leaders. The meeting on 5 November was the first time that the Commanders-in-Chief of the Wehrmacht had been explicitly told of Hitler's thoughts on the likely timing and circumstances of German expansion into Austria and Czechoslovakia.

Hitler was under no illusion at the negative response to his comments. Blomberg, Fritsch, and Neurath in particular were alarmed at what they heard. It was not the aim of expansion that concerned them. There was no disagreement here with Hitler. His familiar racial interpretation of *Lebensraum* had a different emphasis, but accorded well enough with military-strategic interests in German supremacy in central Europe, and with Göring's aims of economic dominance in south-eastern Europe. Nor did talk of the annexation of Austria and destruction of Czechoslovakia worry them. That both would happen at some point was by late 1937 largely taken for granted. Even General Beck's sharp criticism of Hitler's statement, when he read an account some days later, did not dispute 'the expediency of clearing up the case of Czechia (perhaps also Austria) if the opportunity presents itself'.

What did shock them was the prospect of the early use of force, and with that the grave danger that Germany would be plunged into war with Britain and France. Hitler, they thought, was taking foolhardy risks. They raised objections. Neurath saw an expansion of the Mediterranean conflict, in the way Hitler had conceived it, as highly unlikely. The generals pointed to deficiencies in Hitler's military analysis. On no account must Germany find itself at war with Britain and France was the essence of their remarks. Even Göring, though he kept quiet until the discussion moved on to armaments matters, still favoured trying to reach agreement with Britain. Only Raeder, who had wanted the meeting in the first place, seemed unperturbed. If his later testimony is to be believed, he did not take Hitler's remarks seriously, other than as a vehicle to spur on the army to speed up its armaments. Possible future conflict with Britain was, for Raeder, an inevitable component of planning for naval expansion. But an imminent conflict in the present state of Germany's armaments was, in his view, such 'complete madness' that it could not be envisaged as a serious proposition.

Others were less relaxed. Fritsch had to be reassured by Hitler at the end of the meeting that there was no immediate danger of war, and no need to cancel his planned leave. General Beck, shown a copy of Hoßbach's record of the meeting, found Hitler's remarks 'crushing'. What appalled him was the irresponsibility and dilettantism with which

Hitler was prepared to run the risk of involving Germany in a catastrophic war with the western powers. Neurath, who had arranged with Beck and Fritsch that he would speak to Hitler, had the opportunity to do so in mid-January 1938. Hitler's policies, he warned, meant war. Many of his plans could be attained by more peaceful methods, if somewhat more slowly. Hitler replied that he had no more time.

Blomberg's own doubts expressed at the November meeting were, as usual, short-lived. The pliant War Minister was soon conveying Hitler's wishes to the upper echelons of the Wehrmacht. Within weeks, without Hitler having to give any express order, Chief of Defence Staff Colonel Alfred Jodl, recognizing what was needed, had devised a significant alteration to the previous mobilization plans against Czechoslovakia, aimed at preventing Czech intervention in the event of a war against France. The new directive included the sentence: 'Once Germany has attained its full war preparedness in all spheres, the military basis will have been created to conduct an offensive war against Czechoslovakia and thereby also to carry the German space problem to a triumphant conclusion, even if one or other great power intervenes against us.'

Externally as well as internally, the Third Reich was entering a new, more radical phase. The drift of Hitler's thinking was plain from the November meeting, and from his comments earlier in the autumn. Nothing had been decided, no plans laid, no programme established. It was still 'wait and see'. But Hitler's hand became further strengthened at the end of January and beginning of February 1938 by a chance set of events – a personal scandal involving the War Minister Werner von Blomberg.

VIII

Blomberg was not popular in the top leadership of the army. He was seen as too much Hitler's man and too little the army's. When his personal life led to professional trouble in late January 1938, he had no friends to count upon.

On a September morning in 1937, walking in the Tiergarten, the Field-Marshal, widowed with five grown-up children, met the woman who would change his life and, unwittingly, usher in the biggest internal crisis in the Third Reich since the Röhm affair in the summer of 1934. Blomberg, a lonely and empty individual, rapidly became totally besotted with his new lady-friend, Fräulein Margarethe Gruhn, thirty-five years younger than he was, and from a crassly different social background. Within weeks he had asked her to marry him. He needed the consent of Hitler, as supreme commander of the Wehrmacht. He hinted that his fiancée was a typist, a simple 'girl from the people', and that he was concerned about the response of the officer class to his marriage to someone below his status. Hitler immediately offered to be a witness to the marriage to emphasize his rejection of such outmoded class snobbery, and recommended Göring as the second witness. The wedding was prepared in great secrecy. Even Blomberg's adjutant knew nothing of it until the previous afternoon. The ceremony, attended only by Blomberg's five children and the bride's mother, apart from the wedding couple and the witnesses, Hitler and Göring, took place in the War Ministry on 12 January. There were no celebrations. The simplest note of the wedding was published in the newspapers.

Blomberg had good reason for wanting to keep his bride out of the public eye. She had a past. Around Christmas 1931, then aged eighteen, she had posed for a number of pornographic photos which had come into the hands of the police. The following year the police officially registered her as a prostitute. In 1934 she had again come to the attention of the police, accused of stealing from a client. Now, within days of the wedding, Berlin prostitutes started talking about 'one of them' rising so far up the social ladder that she had married the War Minister. An anonymous phone-call tipped off the head of the army, Colonel-General Fritsch. The Gestapo had by this time also picked up the rumours. The Berlin Police Chief, Wolf Heinrich Graf von Helldorf, was put in the picture and, aware of the political sensitivity of what he saw on the card registering Fräulein Gruhn as a prostitute, immediately took the matter to Blomberg's closest colleague, Head of the Wehrmacht Office, General Wilhelm Keitel, to ascertain that the woman with the police record was indeed identical with the wife of the War Minister. Keitel, who had seen Fräulein Gruhn on only one occasion, heavily veiled at the funeral of Blomberg's mother, could not help Helldorf, but referred him to Göring, who had been a witness at the wedding. Göring established the identity on 21 January. Three days later, Göring stood nervously in the foyer of the Reich Chancellery, a brown file in his hand, awaiting the return of Hitler from a stay in Bavaria.

Hitler was stunned at the news that awaited him. Prudery and racial prejudice went hand in hand when he heard that the indecent photos of Blomberg's bride had been taken by a Jew of Czech origin, with whom she was cohabiting at the time. Scurrilous rumours had it that Hitler took a bath seven times the next day to rid himself of the taint of having kissed the hand of Frau Blomberg. What concerned him above all, however, was the blow to prestige which would follow; that, as a witness at the wedding, he would appear a laughing-stock in the eyes of the world. All night long, as he later recounted, he lay awake, worrying how to avoid a loss of face. The next day, as his adjutant Fritz Wiedemann recalled, he paced up and down his room, his hands behind his back, shaking his head and muttering, ' "If a German Field-Marshal marries a whore, anything in the world is possible." ' Goebbels and Göring tried to cheer him up over lunch. That morning, Hitler had spoken for the first time to his military adjutant Colonel Hoßbach about the matter. He praised Blomberg's achievements. But the Field-Marshal had caused him great embarrassment through not telling him the truth about his bride and involving him as a witness at the wedding. He expressed his sadness at having to lose such a loyal colleague. But because of his wife's past, Blomberg had to go as War Minister. 'Blomberg can't be saved,' noted Goebbels. 'Only the pistol remains for a man of honour . . . The Führer as marriage witness. It's unthinkable. The worst crisis of the regime since the Röhm affair . . . The Führer looks like a corpse.'

Presuming that Blomberg was ignorant of his wife's shady past, and hoping to hush the matter up and prevent a public scandal, Göring hurried to persuade the Field-Marshal to have his marriage immediately annulled. To the astonishment and disgust of Göring and of Hitler, Blomberg refused. On the morning of 27 January, Hitler had his last audience with Blomberg. It began in heated fashion, but became calmer, and ended with Hitler offering Blomberg the prospect of rejoining him, all forgotten, if Germany should be involved in war. A day later, Blomberg was gone – over the border to Italy to begin a year's exile, sweetened by a 50,000 Mark 'golden handshake' and his full pension as a Field-Marshal.

The crisis for Hitler had meanwhile deepened. On the very evening, 24 January, that he was recoiling from the shock of the news about his War Minister, and in a bleak mood, he remembered the whiff of a potential scandal two years earlier concerning the head of the army, Colonel-General von Fritsch. Himmler had presented him at the time, in the summer of 1936, with a file raising suspicions that Fritsch had been blackmailed by a Berlin rent-boy by the name of Otto Schmidt on account of alleged homosexual practices in late 1933. Hitler had refused to believe the allegations, had rejected out of hand any investigation, said he never wanted to hear any more of the matter, and ordered the file destroyed. Now, he told Himmler that he wanted the file reconstructed as a matter of urgency. The reconstruction posed no difficulties since, counter to Hitler's express orders to destroy it, Reinhard Heydrich, head of the Security Police, had had the file put in a safe. Within hours, by 2.15 a.m. in the early morning of 25 January, the file was on Hitler's desk.

Hitler had not summoned the file as part of a well-thought-out strategy to be rid of Fritsch as well as Blomberg. In fact, he was apparently still thinking of Fritsch on the morning of 26 January, a day after he had seen the 'reconstructed' file, as Blomberg's possible successor as War Minister. In the light of the shock he had just received, and his immediate loss of confidence in his leading officers, Hitler now wanted assurance that no further scandals were likely to be forthcoming. But just as the Blomberg case was unexpected, so were developments in the Fritsch case to unfold in an unpredictable fashion. Without the Blomberg affair, Hitler is said subsequently to have told his army adjutant Major Gerhard Engel, the Fritsch case would never have come up again. The second crisis arose from the first.

On the morning of 25 January, in his state of depression over Blomberg, Hitler gave the thin file on Fritsch to Hoßbach with instructions for absolute secrecy. Hoßbach was horrified at the implications for the Wehrmacht of a second scandal. He thought Fritsch, whom he greatly admired, would easily clear up the matter – or would know what to do. Either way, the honour of the army would be preserved. In this frame of mind, he disobeyed Hitler's express order and informed Fritsch about the file. It was a fateful step.

Fritsch, when Hoßbach broke the news of the file on the evening of 25 January, reacted with anger and disgust at the allegations, declaring them a pack of lies. Hoßbach reported back to Hitler. The Dictator showed no sign of anger at the act of disobedience. In fact, he seemed relieved, commenting that since everything was in order, Fritsch could become War Minister. However, Hitler added that Hoßbach had done him a great disservice in destroying the element of secrecy. In fact, Hoßbach had unwittingly done Fritsch an even greater disservice.

When he heard from Hoßbach what was afoot, Fritsch not unnaturally brooded for hours about the allegations. They must have something to do, he thought, with the member of the Hitler Youth with whom he had lunched, usually alone, in 1933–4, in a willingness to comply with the request of the Winter Aid Campaign to provide free meals for the needy. He presumed that malicious tongues had manufactured an illicit relationship out of harmless acts of charity. Thinking he could clear up a misunderstanding, he sought out Hoßbach the following day, 26 January. All he did, however, was raise the private doubts of Hitler's military adjutant. Hoßbach did not think to indicate to Fritsch that to mention the Hitler Youth story might not be tactically the best way to convince Hitler of his innocence.

During the afternoon, Hitler conferred with Himmler, Reich Justice Minister Gürtner, and Göring (who saw Fritsch as his rival for Blomberg's post as War Minister). There was a general air of mistrust. By early evening, Hitler was still wavering. Göring pressed him to come to a decision. Hoßbach chose the moment to suggest that Hitler speak directly about the matter to Fritsch. After some hesitation, Hitler agreed. In the meantime, four Gestapo officers had been sent to the Börgermoor internment camp in the Emsland to fetch Otto Schmidt to Berlin. In Hitler's private library in the Reich Chancellery that evening a remarkable scene ensued: the head of the army, in civilian clothing, was confronted by his accuser, an internee of proven ill-repute, in the presence of his supreme commander and head of state, and the Prussian Minister President Göring.

Hitler looked despondent to Fritsch. But he came straight to the point. He wanted, he said, simply the truth. If Fritsch acknowledged his guilt, he was prepared to have the matter hushed up and send him well away from Germany. He had contemplated the possibility of Fritsch perhaps serving as military adviser to Chiang Kai-shek. Fritsch vehemently professed his innocence. He then made the mistake of telling Hitler about the harmless episode of the Hitler Youth boy. It had precisely the opposite effect to that hoped for by Fritsch. Hitler's suspicions rose immediately. He now gave Fritsch the file. While he was reading it, Fritsch's alleged blackmailer was brought in. Otto Schmidt, who had proved a reliable witness in a number of other cases where he had blackmailed individuals, insisted that he recognized Fritsch as the man in question. Fritsch repeated several times, in a cool and collected manner, that he had never seen the man in his life before and gave Hitler his word of honour that he had nothing to do with the entire affair. Hitler had expected, so he told his generals a few days later, that Fritsch would have thrown the file at his feet. His subdued behaviour did not impress Hitler as an impassioned display of injured innocence. Fritsch for his part found it difficult to believe that Hitler and Göring retained their suspicions and simply ignored the word of honour of a high-ranking German officer. The reality, as Goebbels, recognized, was that Hitler had by now lost faith in Fritsch.

The Gestapo's interrogation of Fritsch on the morning of 27 January, when he again faced his tormentor Schmidt, was inconclusive. Schmidt remained adamant in his accusations, Fritsch indignantly vehement in his denial of any involvement. The level of detail in the accuser's story seemed telling. But as Fritsch pointed out, though to no avail, the detail was erroneous. The alleged meeting with Fritsch was said to have taken place in November 1933. Schmidt claimed to have remembered it as if it had been the previous day. Yet he had Fritsch smoking (which he had not done since 1925), wearing a fur coat (such as he had never possessed), and – Schmidt was repeatedly pressed on this point – announcing himself as 'General of the Artillery von Fritsch', a rank he had attained only on 1 February 1934. The inconsistency in evidence was not picked up or acted upon. It remained a matter of word against word.

Meanwhile, Hitler had given the Fritsch file to Justice Minister Franz Gürtner, and asked for his views. Goebbels had little confidence in the outcome. 'Gürtner has now still to write a legal report,' he wrote. 'But what use is all that. The porcelain is smashed.' Gürtner's report, delivered before the end of the month, was damning. Upturning conventional legal notions, Gürtner stated that Fritsch had not proved his innocence and regarded the issue of the Hitler Youth boy as damaging to his case. But Gürtner insisted upon a legal trial for Fritsch in front of a military court. The military leadership backed the demand. Even if reluctantly, in the case of so prominent a person as the head of the army Hitler had little choice but to concede.

The double scandal of Blomberg and Fritsch had left the Nazi leadership with a major public-relations problem. How was it all to be explained to the people? How was a serious blow to prestige and standing to be avoided? On Thursday 27 January, Hitler, looking pale and grey, decided to cancel his big speech to the Reichstag on the anniversary of the 'seizure of power'. The meeting of the Reich cabinet was also cancelled.

Goebbels suggested that a way out of the political crisis would be for Hitler himself to take over the whole of the Wehrmacht, with the different sections of the armed forces turned into separate ministries. 'And then comes the most difficult question,' he added: 'how to put it to the people. The wildest rumours are circulating. The Führer is at the end of his tether. None of us has slept since Monday.'

Goebbels's suggestion – if indeed it originally came from him – for restructuring the Wehrmacht leadership entirely was at least in part taken up. It offered a neat way out of a choice of successor for Blomberg. Göring's self-evident ambitions for this post were never seriously entertained by Hitler. Blomberg, Keitel, and Wiedemann all spoke out in Göring's favour. Göring himself would have been prepared to give up his control of the Four-Year Plan in return for the War Ministry. Hitler was, however, dismissive of his military abilities. He was not even competent, Hitler scoffed, in running the Luftwaffe, let alone the whole of the armed forces. For the army and the navy, the appointment of Göring (who had in his regular military career never had a rank higher than that of captain) would have been insulting. More than that, it would have amounted for Hitler to a heavy concentration of military command in the hands of one man. Heinrich Himmler also cherished ambitions – though always wholly unrealistic ones for a police chief who headed a small rival military force to that of the army in what would develop into the Waffen-SS, who had not served in the First World War, and who, in the later disparaging comment of one general, scarcely knew how to drive a fire-engine. Hitler told his generals on 5 February that rumours of Himmler taking over had been 'insane twaddle'. A third ambitious hopeful, General Walter von Reichenau, was seen as far too close to the party and too untraditionalist to be acceptable to the army.

In fact, already on 27 January, picking up a suggestion made by Blomberg at his farewell audience, Hitler had decided to take over the Wehrmacht leadership himself, appointing no successor to the War Ministry. Within hours, he was initiating General Keitel (scarcely known to him to this point, but recommended by Blomberg) in his – that is to say, initially Blomberg's – ideas for a new organizational structure for the Wehrmacht. Keitel, he said, would be his sole adviser in questions relating to the Wehrmacht. With one move, this shifted the internal balance of power within the armed forces from the traditionalist leadership and general staff of the army (as the largest sector) to the office of the Wehrmacht, representing the combined forces, and directly dependent upon and pliant towards Hitler. In a statement for army leaders on 7 February, explaining the changes that had taken place, it was claimed that Hitler's takeover of the Wehrmacht command 'was already intended in his programme, but for a later date'. In reality, it was a rapidly taken decision providing a way out of an embarrassing crisis.

His removal for days a matter of little more than timing, Fritsch was asked by Hitler on 3 February for his resignation. By then, an increasingly urgent answer – given the rumours now circulating – to the presentational problem of how to explain the departure of the two most senior military leaders had been found: 'In order to put a smoke-screen round the whole business, a big reshuffle will take place,' noted Goebbels. In a two-hour discussion, alone with Goebbels in his private rooms, Hitler went over the whole affair – how disillusioned he had been by Blomberg, whom he had trusted blindly; how he disbelieved Fritsch despite his denials – 'these sort of people always do that'; how he would take over the Wehrmacht himself with the branches of the armed forces as ministries; and the personnel changes he intended to make, particularly the replacement of Neurath by Ribbentrop at the Foreign Office. 'Führer wants to deflect the spotlight from the Wehrmacht, make Europe hold its breath,' recorded Colonel Jodl in his diary. The Austrian Chancellor Schuschnigg, he added ominously, should be 'trembling'.

Within four days the reshuffle was in place. Twelve generals (apart from Blomberg and Fritsch) were removed, six from the Luftwaffe; fifty-one other posts (a third in the Luftwaffe) were also refilled. Fritsch's post was given to Walther von Brauchitsch – a compromise candidate suggested by Blomberg and Keitel to keep out Reichenau. The navy was left alone. Raeder had, according to Goebbels's report of Hitler's views, 'behaved splendidly during the entire crisis and everything is in order in the navy'. Göring was given a Field-Marshal's baton as consolation prize for missing the War Ministry. Major changes were also undertaken in the diplomatic service. Neurath, having to make way for his arch-rival Ribbentrop, was 'elevated' to a pseudo-position as head of a 'privy council' of ministers which was never to meet. The key ambassadorial posts in Rome, Tokyo, London, and Vienna were given new occupants. Schacht's replacement by Funk at the Ministry of Economics was also announced as part of the general reshuffle.

Blomberg and Fritsch were said to have retired 'on health grounds'. Blomberg would survive the war, still praising the 'genius' of the Führer but dismayed that Hitler had not called upon his services once more, and would die, shunned to the last by his former army comrades, in prison in Nuremberg in March 1946. Fritsch's innocence – the victim of mistaken identity – would be established by a military court in Berlin on 18 March 1938. Though his name had been cleared, he did not gain the rehabilitation he hoped for. Deeply depressed and embittered, but still claiming to be 'a good National Socialist', he volunteered for his old artillery regiment in the Polish campaign and would fall fatally wounded on the outskirts of Warsaw on 22 September 1939.

A communiqué on the sweeping changes – said to be in the interest of the 'strongest concentration of all political, military, and economic forces in the hand of the supreme leader' – was broadcast on the evening of 4 February. The sensational news covered page after page of the following day's newspapers. Great surprise, worries about the likelihood of war, and a flurry of the wildest rumours – including an attack on Hitler's life, mass shootings and arrests, attempts to depose Hitler and Göring and proclaim a military dictatorship, war-plans opposed by the dismissed generals – were common reactions over the next days. The real reasons were kept dark. 'Praise God the people know nothing of it all and would not believe it,' Goebbels reported Hitler as saying. 'Therefore greatest discretion.' Hitler's way to handle it was to emphasize the concentration of forces under his leadership and 'let nothing be noticed'.

The following afternoon, 5 February, a pallid and drawn-looking Hitler addressed his generals. He described what had happened, cited from the police reports, and read out sections of Gürtner's damning assessment on Fritsch. The assembled officers were benumbed. No objections were raised. Hitler's explanations appeared convincing. No one doubted that he could have acted differently. At a crucial moment, the undermining of the moral codex of the officer corps by its leading representatives had weakened the authority of the military leadership and in so doing had considerably strengthened Hitler's position.

Though the crisis was unforeseen, not manufactured, the Blomberg–Fritsch affair engendered a key shift in the relations between Hitler and the most powerful non-Nazi élite, the army. At precisely the moment when Hitler's adventurism was starting to cause shivers of alarm, the army had demonstrated its weakness and without a murmur of protest swallowed his outright dominance even in the immediate domain of the Wehrmacht. Hitler recognized the weakness, was increasingly con- temptuous of the officer corps, and saw himself more and more in the role not only of head of state, but of great military leader.

The outcome of the Blomberg–Fritsch affair amounted to the third stepping-stone – after the Reichstag fire and the 'Röhm-Putsch' – cement- ing Hitler's absolute power and, quite especially, his dominance over the army. With the military emasculated and the hawkish Ribbentrop at the Foreign Office, Hitler's personal drive for the most rapid expansion possible – blending with the expansionist dynamic coming from the economy and the arms race – was unshackled from the forces which could have counselled caution. In the months that followed, the radical dynamic that had been building up through 1937 would take foreign and domestic developments into new terrain. The threat of war would loom ever closer. Racial persecution would again intensify. Hitler's ideological 'vision' was starting to become reality. The momentum which Hitler had done so much to force along, but which was driven too by forces beyond his personality, was carrying him along with it. 'Vision' was beginning to overcome cold, political calculation. The danger-zone was being entered.

14

The Drive for Expansion

I

Since his boyhood days in Linz, Hitler had seen the future of Austria's German-speaking population lying in its incorporation in the German Reich. Like many in his part of Austria, he had favoured the ideas of Georg Schönerer, the Pan-Germanist leader, rejecting the Habsburg monarchy and looking to union with the Wilhelmine Reich in Germany. Defeat in the First World War had then brought the dismembering of the sprawling, multi-ethnic empire of the Habsburgs. The new Austria, the creation of the victorious powers at the Treaty of St Germain in September 1919, was no more than a mere remnant of the former empire. The small alpine republic now had only 7 million citizens (compared with 54 million in the empire), 2 million of them in Vienna itself. It was wracked by daunting social and economic problems, and deep political fissures, accompanied by smouldering resentment about its loss of territory and revised borders. The new Austria was, however, almost entirely German-speaking. The idea of union (or Anschluß) with Germany now became far more appealing and was overwhelmingly supported in plebiscites in the early 1920s. Hitler's rise to power in Germany changed this. It accentuated the already acute divisions between socialists, pan-Germans, and Catholic-conservatives (with their own Austrian-nationalist brand of fascism). Only for the pan-Germans, by now entirely sucked into the Austrian Nazi Movement, was an Anschluß with Hitler's Germany an attractive proposition. But, despite the ban on the Nazi Party in Austria following the German-inspired assassination of the Austrian Chancellor Engelbert Dollfuß in July 1934, the increasing might of the Third Reich and the growing exposure of Austria to German dominance as Italy's protection waned in the wake of the Abyssinian conflict kept the Anschluß hopes alive among one sizeable part of the Austrian population.

For Hitler's regime in Germany, meanwhile, the prospects of attaining the union with Austria implicit in the first point of the Nazi Party Programme of 1920, demanding 'the merger of all Germans ... in a Greater Germany', had become much rosier in the changed diplomatic circumstances following Italy's embroilment in Abyssinia and the triumphant remilitarization of the Rhineland. Hitler had written on the very first page of *Mein Kampf*: 'German-Austria must return to the great German mother-country, and not because of any economic considerations. No, and again no: even if such a union were unimportant from an economic point of view; yes, even if it were harmful, it must nevertheless take place. One blood demands one Reich.' Ideological impulses were, however, far from alone in driving on the quest to bring Austria under German sway. Whatever his emphasis in *Mein Kampf*, by the late 1930s Austria's geographical position, straddling strategically vital stretches of central Europe, and the significant material resources that would accrue to Germany's economy, hard-pressed in the push to rearm as swiftly as possible under the Four-Year Plan, were the key determinants in forcing the pace of policy towards the Reich's eastern neighbour.

On a number of occasions during the second half of 1937, Hitler had spoken in imprecise but menacing terms about moving against Austria. In September he had sounded out Mussolini about a likely Italian reaction, but received inconsequential, if not discouraging, replies. Then the visit to Germany in mid-November by Lord Halifax, Lord Privy Seal and President of the Council in the British Government, close to the recently appointed British Prime Minister Neville Chamberlain and soon to become his Foreign Secretary, had confirmed in Hitler's mind that Britain would do nothing in the event of German action against Austria.

Hitler was by this time ready to end Austria's independence within the foreseeable future. The Austro-German treaty of 11 July 1936 together with improved relations with Italy had inevitably brought greater German pressure on Austria. Only increasingly fragile reliance on Italy and recognizably unrealistic hopes placed in the western powers could hinder the relentless squeeze on Austria's exposed position in central Europe. Papen, now ambassador in Vienna, and Foreign Minister Neurath exerted their own influence where possible, the former largely through direct links with Hitler, the latter through official Foreign Office channels; the growing numbers of Austrian Nazis unfolded a ceaseless clamour of agitation; the bosses of the Four-Year Plan and leaders of the ferrous industries cast envious eyes on Austria's iron-ore deposits and other sources of scarce raw materials; above all, it was Hermann Göring, at this time close to the pinnacle of his power, who, far more than Hitler, throughout 1937 made the running and pushed hardest for an early and radical solution to 'the Austrian question'.

Göring was not simply operating as Hitler's agent in matters relating to 'the Austrian question'. His approach differed in emphasis in significant respects. As with Hitler, anti-Bolshevism was central to his thinking. But Göring's broad notions of foreign policy, which he pushed to a great extent on his own initiative in the mid-1930s, drew more on traditional pan-German concepts of nationalist power-politics to attain hegemony in Europe than on the racial dogmatism central to Hitler's ideology. Return of colonies (never a crucial issue for Hitler), the alliance with Britain (which he continued to strive for long after Hitler's ardour had cooled), and an emphasis on domination in south-eastern Europe to ensure German raw-material supplies from a huge economic sphere of exploitation (*Großraumwirtschaft*, a notion that differed from Hitler's racially determined emphasis on *Lebensraum*), were the basic props of his programme to ensure Germany's hegemony. Within this framework, Austria's geography and raw materials gave it both strategically and economically a pivotal position.

Göring was increasingly determined, now as supremo of the Four-Year Plan, in the face of Germany's mounting problems of securing raw-material supplies, to press for what he called the 'union' or 'merger' of Austria and Germany – even, if necessary, at the expense of the alliance with Italy on which Hitler placed such store. By the beginning of 1938, the noose had tightened around Austria's neck. Göring was pushing hard for currency union. But with Austria stalling for time, and Italy's reactions uncertain, immediate results through diplomatic channels seemed unlikely. An Anschluß resulting from German intervention through force in the imminent future appeared improbable.

At this unpromising juncture, the idea emerged of a meeting between Hitler and the Austrian Chancellor Schuschnigg. According to Papen's later account, he had suggested such a meeting to the Austrian Chancellor in December. He had then put the same suggestion to Neurath and Hitler. He repeated the suggestion to Guido Schmidt, state secretary in the Austrian Foreign Ministry, on 7 January, indicating Hitler's readiness to have a meeting towards the end of the month. Schuschnigg agreed the date. Hitler had then had the meeting postponed because of the Blomberg–Fritsch crisis. It was eventually rearranged for 12 February.

The Austrians had meanwhile uncovered documents embarrassing to the German government, revealing the plans of the Austrian NSDAP for serious disturbances (including, as a provocation, the murder of Papen by Austrian Nazis disguised as members of the Fatherland Front) aimed at bringing down Schuschnigg. At the same time, Schuschnigg was trying to win over Arthur Seyß-Inquart – an Austrian lawyer and Nazi sympathizer who had kept his distance from the rowdier elements within the NSDAP – to incorporate the Nazis in a united patriotic Right in Austria which would appease Berlin but preserve Austrian independence. Seyß was, however, in Hitler's pocket, betraying to Berlin exactly what Schuschnigg was prepared to concede. The terms forced upon Schuschnigg by Hitler at the meeting on 12 February were in essence an expanded version of those which the Austrian Chancellor himself had put to Seyß and were already fully known in Berlin prior to the meeting. The main difference was nevertheless a significant one: that Seyß be made Minister of the Interior, and that his powers should be extended to include control of the police.

At 11 a.m. on 12 February, Papen met the Austrian Chancellor, in the company of Guido Schmidt and an adjutant, on the German-Austrian border at Salzburg, where they had spent the night. The Austrian visitors were not enamoured at hearing that three German generals would be among the party awaiting them at the Berghof. Nicolaus von Below, Hitler's Luftwaffe adjutant, had been told to make sure Keitel was present, and in addition one or two generals of particularly 'martial' demeanour. Below's recommendation of the commanding generals of army and Luftwaffe in Munich, Walter von Reichenau (one of the most thoroughly nazified generals) and Hugo Sperrle (who the previous year had commanded the Legion Condor, the squadrons sent to aid the nationalists in Spain), had met with Hitler's enthusiastic approval. Keitel had arrived that morning from Berlin, along with Ribbentrop. The two generals had travelled from Munich. They were told by Hitler that their presence was purely intended to intimidate Schuschnigg by the implied threat of military force.

Hitler, tense and keyed up, received Schuschnigg on the steps of his alpine retreat with due politeness. However, as soon as they entered the great hall, with its breathtaking view over the mountains, his mood abruptly changed. When Schuschnigg remarked on the beauty of the panorama, Hitler snapped: 'Yes, here my ideas mature. But we haven't come together to talk about the beautiful view and the weather.'

Hitler took Schuschnigg into his study while Papen, Schmidt, Ribbentrop, and the others remained outside. Once inside he launched into a ferocious attack, lasting till lunchtime, on Austria's long history of 'treason' against the German people. 'And this I tell you, Herr Schuschnigg,' he reportedly threatened. 'I am firmly determined to make an end of all this ... I have a historic mission, and this I will fulfil because Providence has destined me to do so ... You don't believe you can hold me up for half an hour, do you? Who knows? Perhaps I'll appear sometime overnight in Vienna; like a spring storm. Then you'll see something.'

Meanwhile, Ribbentrop had presented Guido Schmidt with Hitler's ultimatum: an end to all restrictions on National Socialist activity in Austria, an amnesty for those Nazis arrested, the appointment of Seyß-Inquart to the Ministry of the Interior with control over the security forces, another Nazi sympathizer, Edmund Glaise-Horstenau (a former military archivist and historian), to be made War Minister, and steps to begin the integration of the Austrian economic system with that of Germany. The demands were to be implemented by 15 February – timing determined by Hitler's major speech on foreign policy, set for 20 February.

Hitler threatened to march into Austria if his demands were not met in full. Schuschnigg refused to buckle to the threats. Only the Austrian President, he declared, could make cabinet appointments and grant an amnesty. He could not guarantee that such action would be taken. As Schuschnigg was retreating for further discussions with Schmidt, Hitler's bellow for Keitel to come immediately could be heard throughout the house. When the general, arriving at the double in Hitler's study, asked what was required of him, he was told: 'Nothing. Sit down.' After ten minutes of inconsequential chat, he was told to go.

But the impact of the charade was not lost on Schuschnigg. The threat of military invasion seemed very real. Eventually, Papen brokered a number of alterations in the German demands and, under pressure, the Austrians finally accepted the chief difficulty, the appointment of Seyß-Inquart. Hitler told Schuschnigg: 'For the first time in my life I have made up my mind to reconsider a final decision.' With a heavy heart, Schuschnigg signed.

Two weeks later, when laying down directives for the restless Austrian NSDAP, which had threatened to upset developments through its own wild schemes for disturbances, Hitler emphasized that he wanted to proceed along 'the evolutionary way whether or not the possibility of success could be envisaged at present. The protocol signed by Schuschnigg,' he went on, 'was so far-reaching that if implemented in full the Austrian Question would automatically be solved. A solution through force was something he did not now want if it could in any way be avoided, since for us the foreign-policy danger is diminishing from year to year and the military strength becoming year by year greater.' Hitler's approach was at this time still in line with Göring's evolutionary policy. He plainly reckoned that the tightening of the thumb-screws on Schuschnigg at the February meeting had done the trick. Austria was no more than a German satellite. Extinction of the last remnants of independence would follow as a matter of course. Force was not necessary.

In line with the 'Trojan horse' policy of eroding Austrian independence from the inside, following the Berchtesgaden meeting Hitler had complied with demands from Seyß-Inquart – matching earlier representations by Schuschnigg himself – to depose Captain Josef Leopold, the leader of the unruly Austrian National Socialists, and his associates. Even so, the meeting at the Berghof and Hitler's speech on 20 February, his first broadcast in full on Austrian radio – stating that 'in the long run' it was 'unbearable' for Germans to look on the separation of 10 million fellow Germans by borders imposed through peace treaties – had given the Austrian Nazis a new wind. Disturbances mounted, especially in the province of Styria, in the south-east of the country, where resentment at the loss of territory to the new state of Yugoslavia after the First World War had helped fuel the radicalism that had turned the region into a hotbed of Austrian Nazism. The situation was by now highly volatile, the Nazis barely controllable by Austrian state forces. Schuschnigg's own emotional appeals to Austrian patriotism and independence had merely exacerbated the tension within the country and further irritated Hitler. At the same time, Schuschnigg, evidently impressed by Hitler's threats to use force and anxious to avoid anything that might occasion this, was reassuring Britain, France, and Italy that he had the situation in hand rather than rousing foreign sympathy at German strong-arm tactics. The resignation as Foreign Secretary on 21 February of Anthony Eden, despised by the German leadership, and his replacement by Lord Halifax was meanwhile seen in Berlin as a further indication of British appeasement.

The same tone came across in comments of Sir Nevile Henderson, the British Ambassador in Berlin, when he met Hitler on 3 March. Hitler, in a vile mood, was unyielding. If Britain opposed a just settlement in Austria, where Schuschnigg had the support of only 15 per cent of the population, Germany would have to fight, he declared. And if he intervened, he would do so like lightning. His aim was nevertheless 'that the just interests of the German Austrians should be secured and an end made to oppression by a process of peaceful evolution'. However inadequately the undermining of the Austrian state from within through a combination of infiltration and agitation, backed by German bullying, could be described as 'peaceful evolution', pressure-tactics, not armed takeover, still formed the preferred solution to the Austrian Question.

Such notions were thrown overboard by Schuschnigg's wholly un-expected decision, announced on the morning of 9 March, to hold a referendum on Austrian autonomy four days later. The Nazis themselves had been pressing for years for a plebiscite on Anschluß, confident that they would gain massive support for an issue backed by large numbers of Austrians since 1919. But Schuschnigg's referendum, asking voters to back 'a free and German, independent and social, Christian and united Austria; for freedom and work, and for the equality of all who declare for race and fatherland', was couched in a way that could scarcely fail to bring the desired result. It would be a direct rebuff to union with Germany. German plans were immediately thrown into disarray. Hitler's own prestige was at stake. The moves that followed, culminating in the German march into Austria and the Anschluß, were all now improvised at breakneck speed.

The German government was completely taken aback by Schusch-nigg's gamble. Hitler was at first incredulous. But his astonish-ment rapidly gave way to mounting fury at what he saw as a betrayal of the Berchtesgaden agreement. When Goebbels was suddenly sum-moned to Hitler's presence, Göring was already there. He was told of

Schuschnigg's move – 'an extremely dirty trick' to 'dupe' the Reich through 'a stupid and idiotic plebiscite'. The trio were still unsure how to act. They considered replying either by Nazi abstention from the plebiscite (which would have undermined its legitimacy), or by sending 1,000 aeroplanes to drop leaflets over Austria 'and then actively intervening'. For the time being, the German press was instructed to publish nothing at all about Austria.

By late at night, perhaps egged on by Göring, Hitler was warming up. Goebbels was again called in. Glaise-Horstenau, on a visit in southern Germany when suddenly summoned to Berlin by Göring, was also present. 'The Führer drastically outlines for him his plans,' Goebbels recorded. 'Glaise recoils from the consequences.' But Hitler, who went on to discuss the situation alone with Goebbels until 5 a.m., was now 'in full swing' and showing 'a wonderful fighting mood'. 'He believes the hour has arrived,' noted Goebbels. He wanted to sleep on it. But he was sure that Italy and England would do nothing. Action from France was possible, but not likely. 'Risk not so great as at the time of the occupation of the Rhineland' was the conclusion.

Just how unprepared the German leadership had been was shown by the fact that the Foreign Minister, Ribbentrop, was in London, Reichenau had to be recalled from Cairo, and General Erhard Milch (Göring's right-hand man in the Luftwaffe) was summoned from holiday in Switzerland. Göring himself was scheduled to preside over the military court to hear the Fritsch case, meeting for the first time on 10 March. The hearing was abruptly adjourned when a courier brought a message demanding Göring's presence in the Reich Chancellery. Goebbels had also been called there, arriving to find Hitler deep in thought, bent over maps. Plans were discussed for transporting 4,000 Austrian Nazis who had been exiled to Bavaria, together with a further 7,000 paramilitary reservists.

The Wehrmacht leadership was taken completely by surprise through Hitler's demand for plans for military intervention. Keitel, abruptly ordered to the Reich Chancellery on the morning of 10 March, spinelessly suggested calling in Brauchitsch and Beck, knowing full well that no plans existed, but wishing to avoid having to tell this to Hitler. Brauchitsch was not in Berlin. Beck despairingly told Keitel: 'We have prepared nothing, nothing has happened, nothing.' But his objections were dismissed out of hand by Hitler. He was sent away to report within hours on which army units would be ready to march on the morning of the 12th.

Around midnight Goebbels was once more called to see Hitler. 'The die is cast,' he noted. 'On Saturday march in. Push straight to Vienna. Big aeroplane action. The Führer is going himself to Austria. Göring and I are to stay in Berlin. In a week Austria will be ours.' He discussed the propaganda arrangements with Hitler, then returned to his Ministry to work on them until 4 a.m. No one was now allowed to leave the Ministry till the 'action' began. The activity was feverish. 'Again a great time. With a great historical task ... It's wonderful,' he wrote.

Prominent in Hitler's mind that morning of 11 March was Mussolini's likely reaction. Around midday, he sent a handwritten letter, via his emissary Prince Philipp of Hesse, telling the Duce that as a 'son of this [Austrian] soil' he could no longer stand back but felt compelled to intervene to restore order in his homeland, assuring Mussolini of his undiminished sympathy, and stressed that nothing would alter his agreement to uphold the Brenner border. But whatever the Duce's reaction, Hitler had by then already put out his directive for 'Case Otto', expressing his intention, should other measures – the demands put by Seyß-Inquart to Schuschnigg – fail, of marching into Austria. The action, under his command, was to take place 'without use of force in the form of a peaceful entry welcomed by the people'.

Hitler had put the first ultimatum around 10 a.m., demanding that Schuschnigg call off the referendum for two weeks to allow a plebiscite similar to that in the Saarland in 1935 to be arranged. Schuschnigg was to resign as Chancellor to make way for Seyß-Inquart. All restrictions on the National Socialists were to be lifted. When Schuschnigg, around 2.45 p.m., accepted the postponement of the plebiscite but rejected the demand to resign, Göring acted on his own initiative in repeating the ultimatum for the Chancellor's resignation and replacement by Seyß. Looking harassed and tense, Seyß put the ultimatum to the Austrian cabinet, remarking that he was no more than 'a girl telephone switchboard operator'. At this point, the military preparations in Germany were continuing, 'but march in still uncertain', recorded Goebbels. Plans were discussed for making Hitler Federal President, to be acclaimed by popular vote, 'and then bit by bit to complete the Anschluß'. In the immediate future, the 'coordination' of Austria, not the complete Anschluß, was what was envisaged.

Then news came through that only part of the second ultimatum had been accepted. Schuschnigg's desperate plea for British help had solicited a telegram from Lord Halifax, baldly stating: 'His Majesty's Government are unable to guarantee protection.' About 3.30 p.m. Schuschnigg resigned. But President Wilhelm Miklas was refusing to appoint Seyß-Inquart as Chancellor. A further ultimatum was sent to Vienna, expiring at 7.30 p.m. By now Göring was in full swing. Returning to the Reich Chancellery in the early evening, Nicolaus von Below found him 'in his element', constantly on the phone to Vienna, the complete 'master of the situation'. Just before eight o'clock that evening, Schuschnigg made an emotional speech on the radio, describing the ultimatum. Austria, he said, had yielded to force. To spare bloodshed, the troops would offer no resistance.

By now, Nazi mobs were rampaging through Austrian cities, occupying provincial government buildings. Local Nazi leaders were hoping for *Gleichschaltung* through a seizure of power from within to forestall an invasion from Germany. Göring pressed Seyß-Inquart to send a prearranged telegram, dictated from Berlin, asking the German government for help to 'restore order' in the Austrian cities, 'so that we have legitimation', as Goebbels frankly admitted. At 8.48 p.m. Seyß was still refusing to send the telegram. Göring replied that the telegram need not be sent; all Seyß needed do was to say 'agreed'. Eventually, the telegram was sent at 9.10 p.m. It was irrelevant. Twenty-five minutes earlier, persuaded by Göring that he would lose face by not acting after putting the ultimatum, Hitler had already given the Wehrmacht the order to march. Brauchitsch had left the Reich Chancellery, the invasion order in his pocket, depressed and worried about the response abroad. Just before 10.30 p.m. Hitler heard the news he had been impatiently awaiting: Mussolini was prepared to accept German intervention. 'Please tell Mussolini I will never forget him for it, never, never, never, come what may,' a hugely relieved Hitler gushed over the telephone to Philipp of Hesse. 'If he should ever need any help or be in any danger, he can be sure that do or die I shall stick by him, come what may, even if the whole world rises against him,' he added, carried away by his elation.

At midnight, President Miklas gave in. Seyß-Inquart was appointed Federal Chancellor. All German demands had now been met. But the invasion went ahead. As the American journalist William Shirer, observing the scenes in Vienna, cynically commented: with the invasion Hitler broke the terms of his own ultimatum. The 'friendly visit' of German troops began at 5.30 a.m.

Later that morning, Hitler, accompanied by Keitel, landed in Munich, en route for his triumphal entry into Austria, leaving Göring to serve as his deputy in the Reich. By midday, the cavalcade of grey Mercedes, with open tops despite the freezing weather, had reached Mühldorf am Inn, close to the Austrian border. General Fedor von Bock, Commander-in-Chief of the newly formed 8th Army, hastily put together in two days out of troop units in Bavaria, could tell Hitler that the German troops had been received with flowers and jubilation since crossing the border two hours earlier. Hitler listened to the report of reactions abroad by Reich Press Chief Otto Dietrich. He did not expect either military or political complications, and gave the order to drive on to Linz.

Back in Berlin, Frick was drafting a set of laws to accommodate the German takeover in Austria. A full Anschluß – the complete incorporation of Austria, marking its disappearance as a country – was still not envisaged; at any rate, not in the immediate future. Elections were prescribed for 10 April, with Austria 'under Germany's protection'. Hitler was to be Federal President, determining the constitution. 'We can then push along the development as we want,' commented Goebbels. Hitler himself had not hinted at an Anschluß in his proclamation, read out at midday by Goebbels on German and Austrian radio, stating only that there would be a 'true plebiscite' on Austria's future and fate within a short time.

Shortly before 4 p.m., Hitler crossed the Austrian border over the narrow bridge at his birthplace, Braunau am Inn. The church-bells were ringing. Tens of thousands of people, in ecstasies of joy, lined the streets of the small town. But Hitler did not linger. Propaganda value, not sentiment, had dictated his visit. Braunau played its brief symbolic part. That sufficed. The cavalcade passed on its triumphal journey to Linz.

Progress was much slower than expected because of the jubilant crowds packing the roadsides. It was in darkness, four hours later, that Hitler eventually reached the Upper Austrian capital. His bodyguards pushed a way through the crowd so that he could go the last few yards to the town hall on foot. Peals of bells rang out; the rapturous crowd was screaming 'Heil'; Seyß-Inquart could hardly make himself heard in his introductory remarks. Hitler looked deeply moved. Tears ran down his cheeks. In his speech on the balcony of the Linz town hall, he told the masses, constantly interrupting him with their wild cheering, that Providence must have singled him out to return his homeland to the German Reich. They were witnesses that he had now fulfilled his mission.

Once more, plans were rapidly altered. He had meant to go straight on to Vienna. But he decided to stay in Linz throughout the next day, Sunday the 13th, and enter Vienna on the Monday. The extraordinary reception had made a huge impact on him. He was told that foreign newspapers were already speaking of the 'Anschluß' of Austria to Germany as a fait accompli. It was in this atmosphere that the idea rapidly took shape of annexing Austria immediately.

In an excited mood, Hitler was heard to say that he wanted no half-measures. Stuckart, from the Reich Ministry of the Interior, was hurriedly summoned to Linz to draft legislation. In an interview he gave to the British journalist Ward Price, Hitler hinted that Austria would become a German province 'like Bavaria or Saxony'. He evidently pondered the matter further during the night. The next day, 13 March, the Anschluß, not intended before the previous evening, was completed. Hitler's visit to Leonding, where he laid flowers on his parents' grave and returned to the house where the family had lived, meeting some acquaintances he had not seen for thirty years, perhaps reinforced the belief, stimulated the previous evening by his reception in Linz, that Providence had predestined him to reunite his homeland with the Reich.

Stuckart had meanwhile arrived overnight and was drafting the 'Law for the Reunion of Austria with the German Reich', put together in all haste through much toing and froing between Stuckart in Linz and Keppler in Vienna. Around 5 p.m. the Austrian Ministerial Council – a body by now bearing scant resemblance to the cabinet under Schuschnigg – unanimously accepted Stuckart's draft with one or two minor reformulations. The meeting lasted a mere five minutes and ended with the members of the Council rising to their feet to give the 'German Greeting'. The Austrian President, Wilhelm Miklas, laid down his office about the same time, refusing to sign the reunion law and handing his powers over to Seyß-Inquart. That evening, Seyß-Inquart and Keppler drove to Linz to confirm that the law had been accepted. Hitler signed the law before the evening was out. Austria had become a German province.

Immediately, the Austrian army was sworn in to Hitler. In a surprise move, Gauleiter Josef Bürckel, a trusted 'old fighter' of the Movement but with no connections with Austria, was brought in from the Saar to reorganize the NSDAP. Hitler was well aware of the need to bring the party in Austria fully into line as quickly as possible, and not to leave it in the hands of the turbulent, ill-disciplined, and unpredictable Austrian leadership.

In mid-morning on 14 March, Hitler left Linz for Vienna. Cheering crowds greeted the cavalcade of limousines – thirteen police cars accompanied Hitler's Mercedes – all the way to the capital, where he arrived, again delayed, in the late afternoon. On the orders of Cardinal Innitzer, Archbishop of Vienna, all the Catholic churches in the city pealed their bells in Hitler's honour and flew swastika banners from their steeples – an extraordinary gesture given the 'Church struggle' which had raged in the Reich itself over the previous years. Hitler had to appear repeatedly on the balcony of the Hotel Imperial in response to the crowd's continual shouts of 'We want to see our Führer.'

The next day, 15 March, in beautiful spring weather, Hitler addressed a vast, delirious crowd, estimated at a quarter of a million people, in Vienna's Heldenplatz. The Viennese Nazi Party had been impatiently expecting him to come to the capital for three days. They had had time to ensure the preparations were complete. Work-places were ordered to be closed; many factories and offices had marched their employees as a group to hear the historic speech; schools had not been open since the Saturday; Hitler Youth and girls from the Bund Deutscher Mädel were bussed in from all parts of Austria; party formations had turned out in force. But for all the organization, the wild enthusiasm of the immense crowd was undeniable – and infectious. Those less enthusiastic had already been cowed into submission by the open brutality of the Nazi hordes, exploiting their triumph since the weekend to inflict fearful beatings or to rob and plunder at will, and by the first waves of mass arrests (already numbering between 10,000 and 20,000 in the early days) orchestrated by Himmler and Heydrich, who had arrived in Vienna on 12 March.

Ominous in Hitler's speech was his reference to the 'new mission' of the 'Eastern Marches (*Ostmark*) of the German People' (as the once independent country of Austria was now to be known) as the 'bulwark' against the 'storms of the east'. He ended, to tumultuous cheering lasting for minutes, by declaring 'before history the entry of my homeland into the German Reich'.

In the early evening, Hitler left Vienna and flew to Munich, before returning next day to Berlin to another 'hero's welcome'. Two days later, on 18 March, a hastily summoned Reichstag heard his account of the events leading up to what he described as the 'fulfilment of the supreme historical commission'. He then dissolved the Reichstag and set new elections for 10 April. On 25 March, in Königsberg, he began what was to prove his last 'election' campaign, holding six out of fourteen major speeches in the former Austria. In both parts of the extended Reich, the propaganda machine once more went into overdrive. Newspapers were prohibited from using the word '*ja*' in any context other than in connection with the plebiscite. When the results were announced on 10 April, 99.08 per cent in the 'Old Reich', and 99.75 per cent in 'Austria' voted 'yes' to the Anschluß and to the 'list of the Führer'. Goebbels's Propaganda Ministry congratulated itself. 'Such an almost 100 per cent election result is at the same time a badge of honour for all election propagandists,' it concluded.

From Hitler's perspective, it was a near-perfect result. Whatever the undoubted manipulative methods, ballot-rigging, and pressure to conform which helped produce it, genuine support for Hitler's action had unquestionably been massive. Once again, a foreign-policy triumph had strengthened his hand at home and abroad. For the mass of the German people, Hitler once more seemed a statesman of extraordinary virtuoso talents. For the leaders of the western democracies, anxieties about the mounting instability of central Europe were further magnified.

The Austrian adventure was over. Hitler's attentions were already moving elsewhere. Within days of returning from Vienna, he was poring over maps together with Goebbels. 'Czechia comes first now,' the Propaganda Minister recorded. '. . . And drastically, at the next opportunity . . . The Führer is wonderful . . . A true genius. Now he sits for hours over the map and broods. Moving, when he says he wants to experience the great German Reich of the Teutons himself.'

The Anschluß was a watershed for Hitler, and for the Third Reich. The intoxication of the crowds made him feel like a god. The rapid improvisation of the Anschluß there and then proved once more – so it seemed to him – that he could do anything he wanted. His instincts were, it seemed, always right. The western 'powers' were feeble. The doubters and sceptics at home were, as always, revealed as weak and wrong. There was no one to stand in his way.

Hitler had, with the Anschluß, created 'Greater Germany', now incorporating his homeland. He was impatient for more. The Anschluß suggested to him that the Great Germanic Reich, embracing all Germans and dominating the Continent of Europe, did not have to be a long-term project, as he had once imagined. He could create it himself. But it had to be soon. The incorporation of Austria had seriously weakened the defences of Czechoslovakia – the Slav state he had detested since its foundation, and one allied with the Bolshevik arch-enemy and with France. The next step to German dominance on the European continent beckoned.

The Anschluß did not just set the roller-coaster of foreign expansion moving. It gave massive impetus to the assault on 'internal enemies'. The repression was ferocious – worse even than it had been in Germany following the Nazi takeover in 1933. Supporters of the fallen regime, but especially Socialists, Communists, and Jews – rounded up under the aegis of the rising star in the SD's 'Jewish Department', Adolf Eichmann – were taken in their thousands into 'protective custody'.

Many other Jews were manhandled, beaten, and tortured in horrific ordeals by Nazi thugs, looting and rampaging. Jewish shops were plundered at will. Individual Jews were robbed on the open streets of their money, jewellery, and fur coats. Groups of Jews, men and women, young and old, were dragged from offices, shops, or homes and forced to scrub the pavements in 'cleaning squads', their tormentors standing over them and, watched by crowds of onlookers screaming, 'Work for the Jews at last,' kicking them, drenching them with cold, dirty water, and subjecting them to every conceivable form of merciless humiliation.

Thousands tried to flee. Masses packed the railway stations, trying to get out to Prague. They had the few possessions they could carry with them ransacked by the squads of men with swastika armbands who had assembled at the stations, 'confiscating' property at will, entering compartments on the trains and dragging out arbitrarily selected victims for further mishandling and internment. Those who left on the 11.15 p.m. night express thought they had escaped. But they were turned back at the Czech border. Their ordeal was only just beginning. Others tried to flee by road. Soon, the roads to the Czech border were jammed. They became littered with abandoned cars as their occupants, realizing that the Czech authorities were turning back refugees at the borders, headed into the woods to try to cross the frontier illegally on foot.

For many, there was only one way out. Suicide among the Viennese Jewish community became commonplace in these terrible days.

The quest to root out 'enemies of the people', which in Germany had subsided in the mid-1930s and had begun to gather new pace in 1937, was revitalized through the new 'opportunities' that had opened up in Austria. The radicalized campaign would very quickly be reimported to the 'Old Reich', both in the new and horrifying wave of antisemitism in the summer of 1938, and – behind the scenes but ultimately even more sinister – in the rapid expansion of the SS's involvement in looking for solutions to the 'Jewish Question'.

After the tremors of the Blomberg–Fritsch affair, Hitler's internal position was now stronger than ever. The vast majority of officers were, as regards the Anschluß, of one mind with the people: they could only approve and – if sometimes begrudgingly – admire Hitler's latest triumph. Among the mass of the population, 'the German miracle' brought about by Hitler released what was described as 'an elemental frenzy of enthusiasm' – once it was clear that the western powers would again stand by and do nothing, and that 'our Führer has pulled it off without bloodshed'. It would be the last time that the German people – now with the addition of their cousins to the east whose rapid disillusionment soon dissipated the wild euphoria with which many of them had greeted Hitler – would feel the threat of war lifted so rapidly from them through a foreign-policy coup completed within days and presented as a fait accompli. The next crisis, over the Sudetenland, would drag over months and have them in near-panic over the likelihood of war. And if Hitler had had his way, there would have been war.

II

Down to the Anschluß, the major triumphs in foreign policy had been in line with the revisionist and nationalist expectations of all powerful interests in the Reich, and quite especially those of the army. The methods – on which the army, the Foreign Office, and others often looked askance – were Hitlerian. The timing had been determined by Hitler. The decisions to act were his alone. But in each case there had been powerful backing, as well as some hesitancy, among his advisers. And in each case, he was reflecting diverse currents of revisionist expression. The immense popularity of his triumphs in all sections of the political élite and among the masses of the population testified to the underlying consensus behind the revisionism. The earlier crises had also all been of brief duration. The tension had in each case been short-lived, the success rapidly attained. And in each case, the popular jubilation was in part an expression of relief that the western powers had not intervened, that the threat of another war – something which sent shivers of horror down the spines of most ordinary people – had been averted. The resulting popularity and prestige that accrued to Hitler drew heavily upon his 'triumphs without bloodshed'. The weakness and divisions of the western powers had in each case been the platform for Hitler's bloodless coups.

For the first time, in the summer of 1938, Hitler's foreign policy went beyond revisionism and national integration, even if the western powers did not grasp this. Whatever his public veneer of concern about the treatment of the Sudeten Germans, there was no doubt at all to the ruling groups in Germany aware of Hitler's thinking that he was aiming not just at the incorporation of the Sudetenland in the German Reich, but at destroying the state of Czechoslovakia itself. By the end of May this aim, and the timing envisaged to accomplish it, had been outlined to the army leadership. It meant war – certainly against Czechoslovakia, and probably (so it seemed to others), despite Hitler's presumption of the contrary, against the western powers. Hitler, it became unmistakably plain, actually wanted war.

The sheer recklessness of courting disaster by the wholly unnecessary (in their view) risk of war at this time against the western powers – which they thought Germany in its current state of preparation could not win – appalled and horrified a number of those who knew what Hitler had in mind.

It was not the prospect of destroying Czechoslovakia that alienated them. To German nationalist eyes, Czechoslovakia could only be seen as a major irritant occupying a strategically crucial area. Coloured in addition by anti-Slav prejudice, there was little love lost for a democracy, hostile to the Reich, whose destruction would bring major advantages for Germany's military and economic dominance of central Europe. The army had already planned in 1937 for the possibility of a pre-emptive strike against Czechoslovakia – 'Case Green' – to counter the possibility of the Czechs joining in from the east if their allies, the French, attacked the Reich from the west. As the prospect of a war with the French, something taken extremely seriously in the mid-1930s, had receded, 'Case Green' had been amended a month after the 'Hoßbach meeting' of 5 November 1937 to take account of likely circumstances in which the Wehrmacht could invade Czechoslovakia to solve the problem of 'living space'.

In economic terms, too, the fall of Czechoslovakia offered an enticing prospect. Göring, his staff directing the Four-Year Plan, and the leaders of the arms industry, were for their part casting greedy eyes on the raw materials and armaments plants of Czechoslovakia. The economic pressures for expansion accorded fully with the power-political aims of the regime's leadership. Those who had argued for an alternative economic strategy, most of all of course Schacht, had by now lost their influence. Göring was the dominant figure. And in Göring's dreams of German dominion in south-eastern Europe, the acquisition of Czechoslovakia was plainly pivotal.

But neither military strategy nor economic necessity compelled a Czech crisis in 1938. And even Göring, keen as he was to see the end of the Czech state, was anxious, as were others in the upper echelons of the regime, to avoid what seemed that almost certain consequence of any move against Czechoslovakia: war against the western powers.

It was the vision of national disaster that led for the first time to the tentative emergence of significant strands of opposition to what was regarded as Hitler's madness. In the army leadership (still smarting from the Fritsch scandal), in the Foreign Office, and in other high places, the germs of resistance were planted among those certain that Germany was being driven headlong into catastrophe. In the military, the leading opponents of Hitler's high-risk policy emerged as General Beck, who resigned as Chief of Staff in the summer, and Admiral Wilhelm Canaris, head of the Abwehr (military intelligence). In the Foreign Office, the State Secretary Ernst von Weizsäcker was at the forefront of those in opposition to the policy supported avidly by his immediate superior, Foreign Minister von Ribbentrop. Among civilians with inside knowledge of what was going on, Carl Goerdeler, the former Reich Price Commissar, used his extensive foreign contacts to warn about Hitler's aims.

Nor was there any popular pressure for a foreign adventure, let alone

one which was thought likely to bring war with the western powers. Among ordinary people, excluded from the deliberations in high places which kept Europe on the thinnest of tightropes between war and peace in September, the long-drawn-out crisis over Czechoslovakia, lasting throughout the late spring and summer, unlike earlier crises allowed time for the anxieties about war to gather momentum. The acute tension produced what was described as a 'real war psychosis'. No love was lost on the Czechs. And the relentless propaganda about their alleged persecution of the German minority was not without impact. There were indeed some feelings of real gung-ho aggression, though these were largely confined to gullible younger Germans, who had not lived through the World War. The overwhelming sentiment was a fervent desire that war should be avoided and peace preserved. For the first time there was a hint of lack of confidence in Hitler's policy. Most looked to him to preserve peace, not take Germany into a new war. But this time, both to the leading actors in the drama and to the millions looking on anxiously, war looked a more likely outcome than peace.

Among those with power and influence, the most forthright supporter of war to destroy Czechoslovakia was the new Foreign Minister, Joachim von Ribbentrop, an entirely different entity from the displaced conservative, von Neurath. Ribbentrop was more than keen to stamp his imprint on the Foreign Office – and to make up for the embarrassment he had sustained when, largely at Göring's doing, he had been sidelined in London and allowed to play no part in the Austrian triumph that his arch-rival in foreign policy had been instrumental in orchestrating. He provided Hitler with his main backing in these months. His hatred of Britain – the country which had spurned and ridiculed him – as well as his fawning devotion to the Führer made him the most hawkish of the hawks, a warmonger second only to Hitler himself. When he was not directly spurring on Hitler, he was doing his utmost to shore up the conviction that, when it came to it, Britain would not fight, that any war would be a localized one.

For all Ribbentrop's influence, however, there could be no doubt that the crisis that brought Europe to the very brink of war in the summer of 1938 was instigated and directed by Hitler himself. And unlike the rapid improvisation and breakneck speed which had characterized previous crises, this one was consciously devised to escalate over a period of months.

Until 1938, Hitler's moves in foreign policy had been bold, but not reckless. He had shown shrewd awareness of the weakness of his opponents, a sure instinct for exploiting divisions and uncertainty. His sense of timing had been excellent, his combination of bluff and blackmail effective, his manipulation of propaganda to back his coups masterly. He had gone further and faster than anyone could have expected in revising the terms of Versailles and upturning the post-war diplomatic settlement. From the point of view of the western powers, his methods were, to say the least, unconventional diplomacy – raw, brutal, unpalatable; but his aims were recognizably in accord with traditional German nationalist clamour. Down to and including the Anschluß, Hitler had proved a consummate nationalist politician. During the Sudeten crisis, some sympathy for demands to incorporate the German-speaking areas in the Reich – for another Anschluß of sorts – still existed among those ready to swallow Goebbels's propaganda about the maltreatment of the Sudeten Germans by the Czechs, or at any rate prepared to accept that a further nationality problem was in need of resolution. It took the crisis and its outcome to expose the realization that Hitler would stop at nothing.

The spring of 1938 marked the phase in which Hitler's obsession with accomplishing his 'mission' in his own lifetime started to overtake cold political calculation. The sense of his own infallibility, massively boosted by the triumph of the Anschluß, underscored his increased reliance on his own will, matched by his diminished readiness to listen to countervailing counsel. That he had invariably been proved right in his assessment of the weakness of the western powers in the past, usually in the teeth of the caution of his advisers in the army and Foreign Office, convinced him that his current evaluation was unerringly correct. He felt the western powers would do nothing to defend Czechoslovakia. At the same time, this strengthened his conviction that the Reich's position relative to the western powers could only worsen as their inevitable build-up of arms began to catch up with that of Germany. To remain inactive – a recurring element in the way he thought – was, he asserted, not an option: it would merely play into the hands of his enemies. Therefore, he characteristically reasoned: act without delay to retain the initiative.

The time was ripe in his view to strike against Czechoslovakia. Until Czechoslovakia was eliminated – this was the key strategic element in

Hitler's idea – Germany would be incapable of taking action either in the east or in the west. He had moved from a position of a foreign policy supported by Great Britain to one where he was prepared to act without Britain, and, if need be, against Britain. Despite the forebodings of others, war against Czechoslovakia in his view carried few risks. And if the western powers, contrary to expectation, were foolish enough to become involved, Germany would defeat them.

More important even than why Hitler was in such a hurry to destroy Czechoslovakia is why he was by this time in a position to override or ignore weighty objections and to determine that Germany should be taken to the very brink of general European war. Decisive in this was the process, which we have followed, of the expansion of his power, relative to other agencies of power in the regime, to the point where, by spring 1938, it had freed itself from all institutional constraints and had established unchallenged supremacy over all sections of the 'power cartel'. The five years of Hitler's highly personalized form of rule had eroded all semblance of collective involvement in policy-making. This fragmentation at one and the same time rendered the organization of any opposition within the power-élite almost impossible – not to speak of any attached dangers to life and liberty – and inordinately strengthened Hitler's own power. The scope for more cautious counsel to apply the brakes had sharply diminished. The constant Hobbesian 'war of all against all', the competing power fiefdoms that characterized the National Socialist regime, took place at the level below Hitler, enhancing his extraordinary position as the fount of all authority and dividing both individual and sectional interests of the different power entities (the Movement, the state bureaucracy, the army, big business, the police, and the sub-branches of each). Hitler was, therefore, as the sole linchpin, able internally to deal, as in foreign policy, through bilateral relations – offering his support here, denying it there, remaining the sole arbiter, even when he preferred (or felt compelled) to let matters ride and let his subordinates battle it out among themselves. It was less a planned strategy of 'divide and rule' than an inevitable consequence of Führer authority. Without any coordinating bodies to unify policy, each sectional interest in the Third Reich could thrive only with the legitimacy of the Führer's backing. Each one inevitably, therefore, 'worked towards the Führer' in order to gain or sustain that backing, ensuring thereby that his power grew still further and that his own ideological obsessions were promoted.

The inexorable disintegration of coherent structures of rule was therefore not only a product of the all-pervasive Führer cult reflecting and embellishing Hitler's absolute supremacy, but at the same time underpinned the myth of the all-seeing, all-knowing infallible Leader, elevating it to the very principle of government itself. Moreover, as we have witnessed throughout, Hitler had in the process swallowed the Führer cult himself, hook, line, and sinker. He was the most ardent believer in his own infallibility and destiny. It was not a good premiss for rational decision-making.

The compliance of all sections of the regime in the growth of the Führer cult, the exemption made for Hitler himself even by vehement internal critics of the party or Gestapo, and the full awareness of the immense popularity of the 'great Leader', all contributed to making it extraordinarily difficult by summer 1938 – the first time that deep anxieties about the course of his leadership surfaced – now to contemplate withdrawing support, let alone take oppositional action of any kind.

In any case, the extent of opposition to plans for an assault on Czechoslovakia should not be exaggerated. From within the regime, only the army had the potential to block Hitler. The Blomberg–Fritsch affair had certainly left a legacy of anger, distaste, and distrust among the army leadership. But this was directed less at Hitler personally, than at the leadership of the SS and police.

Following the changes of February 1938, the army's own position, in relation to Hitler, had weakened. In the process, the army leadership had been transformed into an adjunct of Hitler's power rather than the 'state within the state' which it had effectively been since Bismarck's era. By the summer of 1938, whatever the anxieties about the risk of war with the western powers, the leadership of the armed forces was divided within itself. Hitler could depend upon unquestioning support from Keitel and Jodl in the High Command of the Wehrmacht. Brauchitsch could be relied upon to keep the army in line, whatever the reservations of some of the generals. Raeder was, as always, fully behind Hitler and already preparing the navy for eventual war with Britain. The head of the Luftwaffe, Göring, fearful of such a war and seeing it as the negation of his own conception of German expansionist policy, nevertheless bowed axiomatically to the Führer's superior authority at all points where his approach started to diverge from Hitler's own. When Beck felt compelled to resign as Chief of Staff, therefore, he stirred no broad protest within the army, let alone in the other branches of the Wehrmacht. Instead, he isolated himself and henceforth formed his links with equally isolated and disaffected individuals within the armed forces, the Foreign Office, and other state ministries who began to contemplate ways of removing Hitler. They were well aware that they were swimming against a strong tide. Whatever doubts and worries there might be, they knew that the consensus behind Hitler within the power-élites was unbroken. They were conscious, too, that from the masses, despite mounting anxieties about war, Hitler could still summon immense reserves of fanatical support. The prospects of successful resistance were, therefore, not good.

It was scarcely surprising, then, that there would be overwhelming compliance and no challenge to Hitler's leadership, or to his dangerous policy, as the crisis unfolded throughout the summer. Despite reservations, all sections of the regime's power-élite had by this point come to bind themselves to Hitler – whether to flourish or perish.

III

The international constellation also played completely into Hitler's hands. Czechoslovakia, despite its formal treaties with France and the Soviet Union, was exposed and friendless. France's vacillation during the summer reflected a desperation to avoid having to fulfil its treaty obligations to Czechoslovakia through military involvement for which there was neither the will nor the preparation. The French were fearful of Czechoslovakia coming under German control. But they were even more fearful of becoming embroiled in a war to defend the Czechs. The Soviet Union, in any case preoccupied with its internal upheavals, could only help the defence of Czechoslovakia if its troops were permitted to cross Polish or Romanian soil – a prospect which could be ruled out. Poland and Hungary both looked greedily to the possibility of their own revisionist gains at the expense of a dismembered Czechoslovakia. Italy, having conceded to the rapidly emerging senior partner in the Axis over the key issue of Austria, had no obvious interest in propping up

Czechoslovakia. Great Britain, preoccupied with global commitments and problems in different parts of its Empire, and aware of its military unreadiness for an increasingly likely conflict with Germany, was anxious at all costs to avoid prematurely being drawn into a war over a nationality problem in a central European country to which it was bound by no treaty obligations. The British knew the French were not prepared to help the Czechs. The government were still giving Hitler the benefit of the doubt, ready to believe that designs on Sudeten territory did not amount to 'international power lust' or mean that he was envisaging a future attack on France and Britain. Beyond this, it was accepted in London that the Czechs were indeed oppressing the Sudeten German minority. Pressure on the Czechs to comply with Hitler's demands was an inevitable response – and one backed by the French.

On top of its increasingly hopeless international position, Czechoslovakia's internal fragility also greatly assisted Hitler. Not just the clamour of the Sudeten Germans, but the designs of the Slovaks for their own autonomy placed the Czech government in an impossible situation. Undermined from without and within, the only new democracy surviving from the post-war settlement was about to be deserted by its 'friends' and devoured by its enemies.

Within two weeks of the Anschluß, in discussions in Berlin with the Sudeten German leader Konrad Henlein, Hitler was indicating that the Czech question would be solved 'before long'. He also prescribed the general strategy of stipulating demands which the Prague government could not meet – vital to prevent the Czechoslovakian government at any stage falling in line with British pressure to accommodate the Sudeten Germans. Henlein wasted no time in putting forward his demands, amounting to autonomy for Sudeten Germans, on 24 April at the Congress of the Sudeten German Party at Karlsbad (Karlovy Vary). One demand to be kept up Henlein's sleeve, which Hitler was certain from his knowledge of the Austria-Hungarian multinational state could never be accepted, was for German regiments within the Czechoslovakian army. In Germany itself, the strategy was to turn up the volume of propaganda at the alleged oppression of the Sudeten Germans by the Czechs. If necessary, incidents to fuel the agitation could be manufactured. Militarily, Hitler was hoping to prevent British intervention, and was certain the French would not act alone. A key deterrent, in his view, was the building of a 400-mile concrete fortification (planned to include 'dragon's teeth' anti-tank devices and gun emplacements, with over 11,000 bunkers and reinforced dug-outs) along Germany's western border – the 'Westwall' – to provide a significant obstruction to any French invasion. The direct interest which Hitler took in the Westwall and the urgency in completing the fortifications were directly related to the question of timing in any blow aimed at the Czechs. At this stage, in late March and April 1938, Hitler evidently had no precise time-scale in mind for the destruction of Czechoslovakia.

This was still the case when Hitler instructed Keitel, on 21 April, to draw up plans for military action against Czechoslovakia. Hitler indicated that he did not intend to attack Czechoslovakia in the near future unless circumstances within the country or fortuitous international developments offered an opportunity. This would then have to be seized so rapidly – military action would have to prove decisive within four days – that the western powers would realize the pointlessness of intervention. Keitel and Jodl were in no hurry to work out the operational plan which, when eventually presented to Hitler in draft on 20 May, still represented what Keitel had taken to be Hitler's intentions a month earlier. 'It is not my intention to smash Czechoslovakia by military action within the immediate future,' the draft began.

In the interim, Hitler had reacted angrily to a memorandum composed on 5 May by army Chief of Staff General Beck, emphasizing Germany's military incapacity to win a long war, and warning of the dangers of British intervention in the event of military action against Czechoslovakia that year. Hitler was even more scathing when Göring reported to him how little progress had been made on the Westwall (where construction work had been under the direction of Army Group Command 2, headed by General Wilhelm Adam). He accused the General Staff of sabotaging his plans, removed the army's construction chiefs, and put Fritz Todt – his civil engineering expert who, since 1933, had masterminded the building of the motorways – in charge. It was an example of Hitler's increasingly high-handed way of dealing with the army leadership. Hitler still recalled what he saw as the army's obstructionism as late as 1942.

The question of Mussolini's attitude towards German action over Czechoslovakia had been high on Hitler's agenda during his state visit to Italy at the beginning of May. Hitler had done much to dispel any initial coolness towards the visit with his speech in Rome on the evening of 7 May in which he enthused over the natural 'alpine border' providing a 'clear separation of the living spaces of the two nations'. This public renunciation of any claim on the South Tyrol was no more than Hitler had been stating since the mid-1920s. But, coming so soon after the Anschluß, it was important in assuaging the Italians, not least since Hitler was anxious to sound them out over Czechoslovakia. The soundings were, from Hitler's point of view, the most successful part of the visit. He took Mussolini's remarks as encouragement to proceed against the Czechs. State Secretary von Weizsäcker noted that Italy intended to stay neutral in any war between Germany and Czechoslovakia. Diplomatically, Hitler had achieved what he wanted from the visit. At this point the 'Weekend Crisis' intervened.

Reports reaching the French and British embassies and the Prague government on 19–20 May of German troop movements near the Czech border were treated seriously, given the shrill German anti-Czech propaganda and the tension in the Sudetenland on account of the imminent local elections there. The Czechoslovakian government responded to what they took to be a threat of imminent invasion by partially mobilizing their military reserves – close on 180,000 men. Tension rose still further when two Sudeten Germans were killed in an incident involving the Czech police. Meanwhile, Keitel's explicit reassurance to the British Ambassador Henderson that the movements were no more than routine spring manoeuvres, which had been given to the press, had led to a furious tirade by Ribbentrop, incensed that Henderson had not gone through proper diplomatic channels in publishing the information, and threatening that Germany would fight as it had done in 1914 should war break out.

This had the effect of stirring genuine alarm in the British Ambassador, worried that he had been misled by Keitel, and that a German invasion of Czechoslovakia was imminent. On the afternoon of Saturday, 21 May, Henderson was instructed by the British Foreign Secretary Lord Halifax to inform Ribbentrop that the French were bound to intervene in the event of an attack on Czechoslovakia, and that the Germans should not depend upon the British standing by. Ribbentrop's hysterical reply was scarcely reassuring: 'If France were really so crazy as to attack us, it would lead to perhaps the greatest defeat in French history, and if Britain were to join her, then once again we should have to fight to the death.' By the Sunday, 22 May, however, British reconnaissance on the borders had revealed nothing untoward. It had been a false alarm.

The crisis blew over as quickly as it had started. But Hitler was affronted by the loss of German prestige. Keitel later recalled Hitler stating that he was not prepared to tolerate 'such a provocation' by the Czechs, and demanding the fastest possible preparations for a strike. It was not as a result of the crisis that Hitler resolved to crush Czechoslovakia before the year was out. But the crisis accelerated matters. The blow to pride reinforced his determination to act as soon as possible. Delay was ruled out.

After days of brooding over the issue at the Berghof, pondering the advice of his military leaders that Germany was ill-equipped for an early strike against the Czechs, Hitler returned to Berlin and summoned a meeting of his top generals, together with leading figures from the Foreign Ministry, for 28 May. He told his generals bluntly: 'I am utterly determined that Czechoslovakia should disappear from the map.' He claimed Germany was stronger than in 1914. He pointed to the train of successes since 1933. But there was no such thing as a lasting state of contentment. Life was a constant struggle. And Germany needed living space in Europe, and in colonial possessions. The current generation had to solve the problem. France and Britain would remain hostile to an expansion of German power. Czechoslovakia was Germany's most dangerous enemy in the event of conflict with the West. Therefore it was necessary to eliminate Czechoslovakia. He gave the incomplete state of Czech fortifications, the underdeveloped British and French armaments programmes, and the advantageous international situation as reasons for early action. The western fortifications were to be drastically speeded up. These would provide the framework for a 'lightning march into Czechoslovakia'.

Two days later, the revised 'Case Green' was ready. Its basic lines were unchanged from those drawn up earlier in the month by Keitel and Jodl. But the preamble now ran: 'It is my unalterable decision to smash Czechoslovakia by military action in the foreseeable future.' Keitel's covering note laid down that preparations must be complete by 1 October at the latest. From that date on, Hitler was determined to 'exploit every favourable political opportunity' to accomplish his aim. It was a decision for war – if need be, even against the western powers.

Chief of Staff Beck responded with two memoranda of 29 May and

3 June, highly critical both of Hitler's political assumptions with regard to Britain and France, and of the operational directives for 'Case Green'. The 'cardinal point' (as he put it) of disagreement was about the prospect of a war against France and Britain which, Beck was certain, Germany would lose. What only gradually became clear to Beck was how far he had isolated himself even in the army's own high command. In particular, the head of the army, Brauchitsch, though sharing some of Beck's reservations, would undertake nothing which might appear to challenge or criticize Hitler's plans. The distance between Brauchitsch and Beck became more marked. Increasingly, the head of the army looked to Beck's deputy, General Franz Halder.

Beck's own position, and the force of his operational arguments, weakened notably in mid-June when the results of war games demonstrated, in contrast to his grim prognostications, that Czechoslovakia would in all probability be overrun within eleven days, with the consequence that troops could rapidly be sent to fight on the western front. Increasingly despairing and isolated, Beck went so far in summer as to advocate collective resignation of the military leadership to force Hitler to give way, to be followed by a purge of the 'radicals' responsible for the high-risk international adventurism. 'The soldierly duty [of the highest leaders of the Wehrmacht],' he wrote on 16 July 1938, 'has a limit at the point where their knowledge, conscience, and responsibility prohibits the execution of an order. If their advice and warnings in such a situation are not listened to, they have the right and duty to the people and to history to resign from their posts. If they all act with a united will, the deployment of military action is impossible. They will thereby have saved their Fatherland from the worst, from destruction . . . Extraordinary times demand extraordinary actions.'

It proved impossible to win over Brauchitsch to the idea of any generals' ultimatum to Hitler, even though the army Commander-in-Chief accepted much of Beck's military analysis and shared his fears of western intervention. At a meeting of top generals summoned for 4 August, Brauchitsch did not deliver the speech which Beck had prepared for him. Instead, distancing himself from the Chief of the General Staff, he had Beck read out his own memorandum of 16 July, with its highly pessimistic assessment of eventualities following an invasion of Czechoslovakia. Most of those present agreed that Germany could not win a war against the western powers. But Reichenau, speaking 'from his personal knowledge of the Führer', warned against individual generals approaching Hitler with such an argument; it would have the reverse effect to that which they wanted. And General Ernst Busch questioned whether it was the business of soldiers to intervene in political matters. As Brauchitsch recognized, those present opposed the risk of a war over Czechoslovakia. He himself commented that a new world war would bring the end of German culture. But there was no agreement on what practical consequences should follow. Colonel-General Gerd von Rundstedt, one of the most senior and respected officers, was unwilling to provoke a new crisis between Hitler and the army through challenging him on his war-risk policy. Lieutenant-General Erich von Manstein, Commander of the 18th Infantry Division, who would later distinguish himself as a military tactician of unusual calibre, advised Beck to rid himself of the burden of responsibility – a matter for the political leadership – and play a full part in securing success against Czechoslovakia.

Brauchitsch, spineless though he was, was plainly not alone in his unwillingness to face Hitler with an ultimatum. The reality was that there was no collective support for a frontal challenge. Brauchitsch contented himself with passing on Beck's memorandum to Hitler via one of his adjutants. When Hitler heard what had taken place at the meeting, he was incandescent. Brauchitsch was summoned to the Berghof and subjected to such a ferocious high-decibel verbal assault that those sitting on the terrace below the open windows of Hitler's room felt embarrassed enough to move inside.

Hitler responded by summoning – an unorthodox step – not the top military leadership, but a selective group of the second tier of senior officers, those who might be expecting rapid promotion in the event of a military conflict, to the Berghof for a meeting on 10 August. He was evidently hoping to gain influence over his staff chiefs through their subordinates. But he was disappointed. His harangue, lasting several hours, left his audience – which was fully acquainted with the content of Beck's July memorandum – still unconvinced. The crisis of confidence between Hitler and the army general staff had reached serious levels. At the same time, the assembled officers were divided among themselves, with some of them increasingly critical of Beck.

The Chief of the General Staff made a last attempt to persuade Brauchitsch to take a firm stance against Hitler. It was whistling in the wind. On 18 August, Beck finally tendered the resignation he had already prepared a month earlier. Even then, he missed a last trick. He accepted Hitler's request – 'for foreign-policy reasons' – not to publicize his resignation. A final opportunity to turn the unease running through the army, and through the German people, into an open challenge to the political leadership of the Reich – and when Beck knew that only Ribbentrop, and perhaps Himmler, fully backed Hitler – was lost. Beck's path into fundamental resistance was a courageous one. But in summer 1938 he gradually became, at least as regards political strategy, an isolated figure in the military leadership. As he himself saw it several months later: 'I warned – and in the end I was alone.' Ironically, he had been more responsible than any other individual for supplying Hitler with the military might which the Dictator could not wait to use.

Hitler was by this time, therefore, assured of the compliance of the military, even if they were reluctant rather than enthusiastic in their backing for war against the Czechs, and even if relations were tense and distrustful. And as long as the generals fell into line, his own position was secure, his policy unchallengeable.

As it transpired, his reading of international politics turned out to be closer to the mark than that of Beck and the generals. In the guessing- and second-guessing political poker-game that ran through the summer, the western powers were anxious to avoid war at all costs, while the east European neighbours of Czechoslovakia were keen to profit from any war but unwilling to take risks. By midsummer, Ribbentrop regarded the die as cast. He told Weizsäcker 'that the Führer was firmly resolved to settle the Czech affair by force of arms'. Mid-October was the latest possible date because of flying conditions. 'The other powers would definitely not do anything about it and if they did we would take them on as well and win.'

Hitler himself spent much of the summer at the Berghof. Despite the Sudeten crisis, his daily routine differed little from previous years: he got up late, went for walks, watched films, and relaxed in the company of his regular entourage and favoured visitors like Albert Speer. Whether on the basis of newspaper reports, or through information fed to him by those able to gain access, he intervened – sometimes quirkily – in an array of minutiae: punishment for traffic offences, altering the base of a statue, considerations of whether all cigarettes should be made nicotine-free, or the type of holes to be put into flagpoles. He also interfered directly in the course of justice, ordering the death penalty for the perpetrator of a series of highway robberies, and the speediest possible conviction for the alleged serial killer of a number of women.

But the Czechoslovakian crisis was never far away. Hitler was preoccupied with the operational planning for 'Green'. His confidence in his generals dwindled as his anger at their scepticism towards his plans mounted. He also involved himself in the smallest detail of the building of the Westwall – a key component in his plans to overrun the Czechs without French intervention and the bluff to discourage Germany's western neighbours from even attempting to cross the Rhine. He was still expecting the fortifications to be complete by the autumn – by the onset of frost, as he told Goebbels – at which point he reckoned Germany would be unassailable from the west. But the sluggish progress made by the army made him furious. When General Adam claimed that the extra 12,000 bunkers he had ordered were an impossibility, Hitler flew into a rage, declaring that for Todt the word 'impossible' did not exist. He felt driven to dictate a lengthy memorandum, drawing on his own wartime experiences, laying down his notions of the nature of the fortifications to be erected, down to sleeping, eating, drinking, and lavatory arrangements in the bunkers – since new recruits in their first battle often suffered from diarrhoea, he claimed to recall. The Westwall had priority over all other major building projects. By the end of August, 148,000 workers and 50,000 army sappers were stationed at the fortifications. Autobahn and housing construction had been temporarily halted to make use of the workers.

By this time, the end of August, the crisis was beginning to move towards its climacteric phase. When Goebbels saw him on the Obersalzberg on the last day of August, Hitler was in a determined and optimistic mood: he did not think Britain would intervene. 'He knows what he wants and goes straight towards his goal,' remarked Goebbels. By now, Goebbels too knew that the planned time for action was October.

Ordinary people were, of course, wholly unaware of the planned aggression. The weeks of anti-Czech propaganda, often near-hysterical in tone, had shaped the impression that the issue was about the despicable persecution of the German minority, not the military destruction of Czechoslovakia. But whether or not the Sudeten Germans came 'home into the Reich' was, for the overwhelming majority of the population, less important than avoiding the war which Hitler was determined to have. 'The war psychosis is growing,' noted Goebbels. 'A gloomy mood lies over the land. Everyone awaits what is coming.' Reports on popular opinion compiled by the SD and other agencies uniformly registered similar sentiments. 'There exists in the broadest sections of the population,' ran one report in early September, 'the earnest concern that in the long or short run a war will put an end to the economic prosperity and have a terrible end for Germany.'

IV

During August, the British had indirectly exerted pressure on the Czechs to comply with Sudeten German demands through the mission of Lord Runciman, aimed at playing for time, mediating between the Sudeten German Party and the Prague government, and solving the Sudeten question within the framework of the continued existence of the state of Czechoslovakia. By the end of the month, the British government had learnt from their contacts with oppositional sources in Germany that Hitler intended to attack Czechoslovakia within weeks. The crucial moment, they imagined, would probably follow Hitler's speech to the Reich Party Rally in Nuremberg in mid-September. On 30 August, in an emergency meeting, the British cabinet declined to offer a formal warning to Hitler of likely British intervention in the event of German aggression. Instead, it was decided to apply further pressure on the Czechs, who were effectively given an ultimatum: accept Henlein's programme to give virtual autonomy for the Sudeten Germans within the Czechoslovakian state, as laid down in his Karlsbad speech in April, or be doomed. On 5 September, President Eduard Beneš, faced with such an unenviable choice, bowed to the pressure.

This in fact left Henlein and the Sudeten German leadership in a predicament: entirely against expectations, their demands had been met almost in their entirety. With that, Hitler's pretext for war was undermined. Desperate for an excuse to break off negotiations with the Czechs, the Sudeten Germans grasped at an incident in which the Czech police manhandled three local Germans accused of spying and smuggling weapons. It was enough to keep matters on the boil until Hitler's big speech on 12 September.

Increasingly worried though the Sudeten German leaders themselves were about the prospect of war, Henlein's party was simply dancing to

Hitler's tune. Hitler had told Henlein's right-hand man, Karl Hermann Frank, as early as 26 August to instigate provocative 'incidents'. He followed it up with instructions to carry out the 'incidents' on 4 September. He had left Frank in no doubt at all of his intentions. 'Führer is determined on war,' Frank had reported. Hitler had verbally lashed Beneš, saying he wanted him taken alive and would himself string him up. Three days later, on 29 August, it was known, from what was emanating from Hitler's entourage, that Czech compliance, under British pressure, to the Karlsbad demands would no longer be sufficient. 'So the Führer wants war,' was the conclusion drawn by Helmuth Groscurth, head of Department II of the Abwehr.

When he met Henlein at the Berghof on 2 September, however, Hitler was giving little away. He implied to the Sudeten leader that he would act that month, though specified no date. Knowing that Hitler had a military solution in mind, Henlein nevertheless told his British contact, Frank Ashton-Gwatkin, Runciman's assistant, that the Führer favoured a peaceful settlement – information which further nourished appeasement ambitions. The reality was very different: at a military conference at the Berghof on the day after his meeting with Henlein, Hitler determined details of 'Case Green', the attack on Czechoslovakia, ready to be launched on 1 October.

Hitler was by this stage impervious to the alarm signals being registered in diplomatic circles. When Admiral Canaris returned from Italy with reports that the Italians were urgently advising against war, and would not participate themselves, Hitler took them simply as a reflection of the divisions between the general staff and the Duce, similar to those he was experiencing with the army in Germany. He remained adamant that Britain was bluffing, playing for time, insufficiently armed, and would stay neutral. Warnings about the poor state of the German navy met with the same response. The present time, with the harvest secured, he continued to argue, was the most favourable for military action. By December, it would be too late. He was equally dismissive about warning noises from France. When the German Ambassador in Paris, Johannes von Welczek, reported his strong impression that France would reluctantly be obliged to honour the obligation to the Czechs, Hitler simply pushed the report to one side, saying it did not interest him. Hearing of this, Lord Halifax pointed it out to the British cabinet as evidence that 'Herr Hitler was possibly or even probably mad.'

With German propaganda reaching fever-pitch, Hitler delivered his long-awaited and much feared tirade against the Czechs at the final assembly of the Party Congress on 12 September. Venomous though the attacks on the Czechs were, with an unmistakable threat if 'self-determination' were not granted, Hitler fell short of demanding the handing over of the Sudetenland, or a plebiscite to determine the issue. In Germany there was an air of impending war and great tension. The anxious Czechs thought war and peace hung in the balance that day. But in Hitler's timetable, it was still over two weeks too early.

Even so, Hitler's speech triggered a wave of disturbances in the Sudeten region. These incidents, and the near-panic which had gripped the French government, persuaded Neville Chamberlain that, if the German offensive expected for late September were to be avoided, face-to-face talks with Hitler – an idea worked out already in late August – were necessary. On the evening of 14 September, the sensational news broke in Germany: Chamberlain had requested a meeting with Hitler, who had invited him to the Obersalzberg for midday on the following day.

Early on the morning of 15 September, the sixty-nine-year-old British Prime Minister – a prim, reserved, austere figure – took off from Croydon airport in a twin-engined Lockheed, hoping, as he said, to secure peace. He was cheered by the Munich crowds as he was driven in an open car from the airport to the station to be taken in Hitler's special train to Berchtesgaden. It was raining, the sky dark and threatening, by the time Chamberlain reached the Berghof.

After some desultory small-talk, Hitler retreated with the British Prime Minister to his study. Ribbentrop, to his intense irritation, was left out of the discussions. Only the interpreter Paul Schmidt was present. For three hours Hitler and Chamberlain talked as the peace of Europe hung in the balance. Hitler paraded the German grievances, with occasional outbursts against Beneš. Chamberlain listened expressionless as the storm outside swelled to match the menacing atmosphere inside the alpine retreat. He said he was prepared to consider any solution to accommodate German interests, as long as force was ruled out. Hitler heatedly retorted: 'Who is speaking of force? Herr Beneš is using force against my countrymen in the Sudetenland. Herr Beneš, and not I, mobilized in May. I won't accept it any longer. I'll settle this question myself in the near future one way or another.' 'If I've understood you correctly,' Chamberlain angrily replied, 'then you're determined in any event to proceed against Czechoslovakia. If that is your intention, why have you had me coming to Berchtesgaden at all? Under these circumstances it's best if I leave straight away. Apparently, it's all pointless.' It was an effective counter-thrust to the bluster. Hitler, to Schmidt's astonishment, retreated. 'If you recognize the principle of self-determination for the treatment of the Sudeten question, then we can discuss how to put the principle into practice,' he stated. Chamberlain said he would have to consult his cabinet colleagues. But when he declared his readiness thereafter to meet Hitler again, the mood lifted. Chamberlain won Hitler's agreement to undertake no military action in the meantime. With that, the meeting was over.

Immediately after the meeting, Hitler told Ribbentrop and Weizsäcker what had happened, rubbing his hands with pleasure at the outcome. He claimed he had manoeuvred Chamberlain into a corner. His 'brutally announced intention, even at the risk of a general European war, of solving the Czech question' – he had not spoken of the 'Sudeten question' – along with his concession that Germany's territorial claims in Europe would then be satisfied, had, he asserted, forced Chamberlain to cede the Sudetenland. Hitler had, he went on, been unable to reject the proposal of a plebiscite. If the Czechs were to refuse one, 'the way would be clear for the German invasion'. If Czechoslovakia yielded on the Sudetenland, the rest of the country would be taken over later, perhaps the following spring. In any event, there would have to be a war, and during his own lifetime.

Hitler was clearly satisfied with the way the talks had gone. He spoke to his immediate circle at the Berghof the next day about the discussions. As the night before, it appeared that he might now after all be prepared to consider a diplomatic solution – at least for the immediate future. Chamberlain's visit had impressed him and, in a way, unsettled him. Dealing at first hand with a democratic leader who had to return to consult with the members of his government, and was answerable to parliament, left a tinge of uncertainty. He was, he said, still basically intending to march on Prague. But for the first time there were signs of wavering. He was starting to look for a possible retreat. Only very unwillingly, he hinted, if it proved unavoidable in the light of the general European situation, would he go along with the British proposal. Beyond that, things could be settled with the Czechs without the British being involved. Czechoslovakia was in any case, he added, difficult to rule, given its ethnic mix and the claims of the other minorities – Poles, Hungarians, and especially the Slovaks. There was, Hitler's immediate circle felt, now a glimmer of hope that war would be avoided.

Chamberlain reported to the British cabinet his belief that he had dissuaded Hitler from an immediate march into Czechoslovakia and that the German dictator's aims were 'strictly limited'. If self-determination for the Sudeten Germans were to be granted, he thought, it would mark the end of German claims on Czechoslovakia. The extent to which Chamberlain had allowed himself to be deluded by the person-ality and assurances of Germany's dictator is apparent in the private evaluation he offered one of his sisters, Ida, on returning to England: 'In spite of the harshness and ruthlessness I thought I saw in his face, I got the impression that here was a man who could be relied upon when he had given his word.'

The next days were spent applying pressure to the Czechs to acquiesce in their own dismemberment. Preferably avoiding a plebiscite, the joint approach to Prague of the British and French was to compel the Czechs to make territorial concessions in return for an international guarantee against unprovoked aggression. On 21 September, the Czechs yielded. Chamberlain's second meeting with Hitler had meanwhile been arranged for 22 September. Hitler, too, was by now feeling the tension. He relaxed by watching entertainment films. He did not want to see anything more serious. His options remained open. As his comments following Cham-berlain's visit had shown, he was now evidently moving away from the all-out high-risk military destruction of Czechoslovakia in a single blow, on which he had insisted, despite much internal opposition, throughout the summer. Instead, there were pointers that he was now moving in the direction of the territorial solution not unlike the one which would eventually form the basis of the Munich Agreement. He did not think he would get the Sudetenland without a fight from the Czechs, though he imagined the western powers would leave Beneš to his fate. So he reckoned with limited military confrontation to secure the Sudetenland as a first stage. The destruction of the rest of Czechoslovakia would then follow, perhaps immediately, but at any rate within a short time.

On 19 September he showed Goebbels the map that would represent his demands to Chamberlain at their next meeting. The idea was to force acceptance of as broad a demarcation line as possible. The territory to be conceded was to be vacated by the Czechs and occupied by German troops within eight days. Military preparations, as Goebbels was now informed, would not be ready before then. If there was any dispute, a plebiscite by Christmas would be demanded. Should Chamberlain demand further negotiations, the Führer would feel no longer bound by any agreements and would have freedom of action. 'The Führer will show Chamberlain his map, and then – end, basta! Only in that way can this problem be solved,' commented Goebbels.

V

On the afternoon of 22 September, Hitler and Chamberlain met again, this time in the plush Hotel Dreesen in Bad Godesberg, with its fine outlook on the Rhine. Chamberlain had flown from England that morning, and was accommodated on the opposite bank of the river at the Petersberg Hotel.

Their meeting began with a shock for Chamberlain. He initially reported how the demands raised at Berchtesgaden had been met. He mentioned the proposed British-French guarantee of the new borders of Czechoslovakia, and the desired German non-aggression pact with the Czechs. He sat back in his chair, a self-satisfied look on his face. He was astounded when Hitler retorted: 'I'm sorry, Herr Chamberlain, that I can no longer go into these things. After the development of the last days, this solution no longer applies.' Chamberlain sat bolt upright, angry and astonished. Hitler claimed he could not sign a non-aggression pact with Czechoslovakia until the demands of Poland and Hungary were met. He had some criticisms of the proposed treaties. Above all, the envisaged time-scale was too long. Working himself up into a frenzy about Beneš and the alleged terroristic repression of the Sudeten Germans, he demanded the occupation of the Sudeten territory immediately. Chamberlain pointed out that this was a completely new demand, going far beyond the terms outlined at Berchtesgaden. He returned, depressed and angry, to his hotel on the other bank of the Rhine.

Chamberlain did not appear for the prearranged meeting the next morning. Instead, he sent a letter to Hitler stating that it was impossible for him to approve a plan which would be seen by public opinion in Britain, France, and the rest of the world as deviating from the previously agreed principles. Nor had he any doubts, he wrote, that the Czechs would mobilize their armed forces to resist any entry of German troops into the Sudetenland. Hitler and Ribbentrop hastily deliberated. Then Hitler dictated a lengthy reply – amounting to little more than his verbal statements the previous day and insisting on the immediate transfer of the Sudeten territory to end 'Czech tyranny' and uphold 'the dignity of a great power'. The interpreter Schmidt was designated to translate the four- to five-page letter, and take it by hand to Chamberlain. The British Prime Minister received it calmly. His own response was given to Ribbentrop within two hours or so. He offered to take the new demands to the Czechs, said he would have to return to England to prepare for this, and requested a memorandum from the German government which, it was agreed, would be delivered later that evening by Hitler.

It was almost eleven o'clock when Chamberlain returned to the Hotel Dreesen. The drama of the late-night meeting was enhanced by the presence of advisers on both sides, fully aware of the peace of Europe hanging by a thread, as Schmidt began to translate Hitler's memorandum. It demanded the complete withdrawal of the Czech army from the territory drawn on a map, to be ceded to Germany by 28 September. Hitler had spoken to Goebbels on 21 September of demands for eight days for Czech withdrawal and German occupation. He was now, late on the evening of 23 September, demanding the beginning of withdrawal in little over two days and completion in four. Chamberlain raised his hands in despair. 'That's an ultimatum,' he protested. 'With great disappointment and deep regret I must register, Herr Reich Chancellor,' he remarked, 'that you have not supported in the slightest my efforts to maintain peace.'

At this tense point, news arrived that Beneš had announced the general mobilization of the Czech armed forces. For some moments no one spoke. War now seemed inevitable. Then Hitler, in little more than a whisper, told Chamberlain that despite this provocation he would hold to his word and undertake nothing against Czechoslovakia – at least as long as the British Prime Minister remained on German soil. As a special concession, he would agree to 1 October as the date for Czech withdrawal from the Sudeten territory. It was the date he had set weeks earlier as the moment for the attack on Czechoslovakia. He altered the date by hand in the memorandum, adding that the borders would look very different if he were to proceed with force against Czechoslovakia. Chamberlain agreed to take the revised memorandum to the Czechs. After the drama, the meeting ended in relative harmony. Chamberlain flew back, disappointed but not despairing, next morning to London to report to his cabinet.

While Chamberlain was meeting his cabinet, on Sunday, 25 September, Hitler was strolling through the gardens of the Reich Chancellery on a warm, early autumn afternoon, with Goebbels, talking at length about his next moves. 'He doesn't believe that Benesch [Beneš] will yield,' noted the Propaganda Minister the following day in his diary. 'But then a terrible judgement will strike him. On 27–28 September our military build-up will be ready. The Führer then has 5 days' room for manoeuvre. He already established these dates on 28 May. And things have turned out just as he predicted. The Führer is a divinatory genius. But first comes our mobilization. This will proceed so lightning-fast that the world will experience a miracle. In 8–10 days all that will be ready. If we attack the Czechs from our borders, the Führer reckons it will take 2–3 weeks. But if we attack them after our entry, he thinks it will be finished in 8 days. The radical solution is the best. Otherwise, we'll never be rid of the thing.' This somewhat garbled account appears to indicate that Hitler was at this juncture contemplating a two-stage invasion of Czechoslovakia: first the Sudeten area, then at a later, and unspecified, point, the rest of the country. This matches the notion reported by Weizsäcker after the first meeting with Chamberlain. Hitler was not bluffing, therefore, in his plans to take the Sudetenland by force on 1 October if it was not conceded beforehand. But he had retreated from the intention, which had existed since the spring, of the destruction of the whole of Czechoslovakia by a single military operation at the beginning of October.

The mood in London was, meanwhile, changing. Following his experience in Godesberg, Chamberlain was moving towards a harder line, and the British cabinet with him. After talks with the French, it was decided that the Czechs would not be pressed into accepting the new terms. Sir Horace Wilson, Chamberlain's closest adviser, was to go as the Prime Minister's envoy to Berlin to recommend a supervised territorial transfer and at the same time warn Hitler that in the event of German military action against Czechoslovakia France would honour its alliance commitments and Britain would support France.

On the late afternoon of 26 September, Wilson, accompanied by Sir Nevile Henderson and Ivone Kirkpatrick, first secretary in the British Embassy, were received by Hitler in his study in the Reich Chancellery. That evening Hitler was to deliver a ferocious attack on Czechoslovakia in the Sportpalast. Wilson had not chosen a good moment to expect rational deliberation of the letter from Chamberlain that he presented to the German dictator. Hitler listened, plainly agitated, to the translation of the letter, informing him that the Czechs had rejected the terms he had laid down at Godesberg. Part-way through he exploded with anger, jumping to his feet, shouting: 'There's no point at all in somehow negotiating any further.' He made for the door, as if ending the meeting forthwith with his visitors left in his own study. But he pulled himself together and returned to his seat while the rest of the letter was translated. As soon as it was over, there was another frenzied outburst. The interpreter, Paul Schmidt, later commented that he had never before seen Hitler so incandescent. Wilson's attempts to discuss the issues rationally and his cool warning of the implications of German military action merely provoked him further. 'If France and England want to strike,' he ranted, 'let them go ahead. I don't give a damn.' He gave the Czechs till 2 p.m. on Wednesday, 28 September, to accept the terms of the Godesberg Memorandum and German occupation of the Sudetenland by 1 October. Otherwise Germany would take it by force. He recommended a visit to the Sportpalast that evening to Wilson, so that he would sense the mood in Germany for himself.

The ears of the world were on Hitler's speech to the tense audience of around 20,000 or so packed into the cavernous Sportpalast. The large number of diplomats and journalists present were glued to every word. The American journalist William Shirer, sitting in the balcony directly above the German Chancellor, thought Hitler 'in the worst state of excitement I've ever seen him in'. His speech – 'a psychological masterpiece' in Goebbels's judgement – was perfectly tuned to the whipped-up anti-Czech mood of the party faithful. He was soon into full swing, launching into endless tirades against Beneš and the Czechoslovakian state. He had assured the British Prime Minister, he stated, that he had no further territorial demands in Europe once the Sudeten problem was solved. The decision for war or peace rested with Beneš: 'He will either accept this offer and finally give freedom to the Germans, or we will take this freedom ourselves!' he threatened. 'We are determined. Herr Beneš may now choose,' he concluded.

The masses in the hall, who had interrupted almost every sentence with their fanatical applause, shouted, cheered, and chanted for minutes when he had ended: 'Führer command, we will follow!' Hitler had worked himself into an almost orgasmic frenzy by the end of his speech. When Goebbels, closing the meeting, pledged the loyalty of all the German people to him and declared that 'a November 1918 will never be repeated', Hitler, according to Shirer, 'looked up to him, a wild, eager expression in his eyes . . . leaped to his feet and with a fanatical fire in his eyes . . . brought his right hand, after a grand sweep, pounding down on the table and yelled . . . "Ja". Then he slumped into his chair exhausted.'

Hitler was in no mood for compromise when Sir Horace Wilson returned next morning to the Reich Chancellery with another letter from Chamberlain guaranteeing, should Germany refrain from force, the implementation of the Czech withdrawal from the Sudeten territory. When Wilson asked whether he should take any message back to London, Hitler replied that the Czechs had the option only of accepting or rejecting the German memorandum. In the event of rejection, he shouted, repeating himself two or three times, 'I will smash the Czechs.' Wilson, a tall figure, then drew himself to his full height and slowly but emphatically delivered a further message from Chamberlain: 'If, in pursuit of her Treaty obligations, France became actively engaged in hostilities against Germany, the United Kingdom would feel obliged to support her.' Enraged, Hitler barked back: 'If France and England strike, let them do so. It's a matter of complete indifference to me. I am prepared for every eventuality. I can only take note of the position. It is Tuesday today, and by next Monday we shall all be at war.' The meeting ended at that point. As Schmidt recalled, it was impossible to talk rationally with Hitler that morning.

Still, Wilson's warnings were not lost on Hitler. In calmer mood, he had Weizsäcker draft him a letter to Chamberlain, asking him to persuade the Czechs to see reason and assuring him that he had no further interest in Czechoslovakia once the Sudeten Germans had been incorporated into the Reich.

Late that afternoon a motorized division began its ominous parade through Wilhelmstraße past the government buildings. For three hours,

Hitler stood at his window as it rumbled past. According to the recollections of his Luftwaffe adjutant Nicolaus von Below, he had ordered the display not to test the martial spirit of the Berlin people, but to impress foreign diplomats and journalists with German military might and readiness for war. If that was the aim, the attempt misfired. The American journalist William Shirer reported on the sullen response of the Berliners – ducking into doorways, refusing to look on, ignoring the military display – as 'the most striking demonstration against war I've ever seen'. Hitler was reportedly disappointed and angry at the lack of enthusiasm shown by Berliners. The contrast with the reactions of the hand-picked audience in the Sportpalast was vivid. It was a glimpse of the mood throughout the country. Whatever the feelings about the Sudeten Germans, only a small fanaticized minority thought them worth a war against the western powers.

But if Hitler was disappointed that the mood of the people did not resemble that of August 1914, his determination to press ahead with military action on 1 October, if the Czechs did not yield, was unshaken, as he made clear that evening to Ribbentrop and Weizsäcker. Ribbentrop was by now, however, practically the only hawkish influence on Hitler. From all other sides, pressures were mounting for him to pull back from the brink.

For Hitler, to retreat from an 'unalterable decision' was tantamount to a loss of face. Even so, for those used to dealing at close quarters with him, the unthinkable happened. The following morning of 28 September, hours before the expiry of the ultimatum to Czechoslovakia, he changed his mind and conceded to the demands for a negotiated settlement. 'One can't grasp this change. Führer has given in, and fundamentally,' noted Helmuth Groscurth.

The decisive intervention was Mussolini's. Feelers for such a move had been put out by an increasingly anxious Göring a fortnight or so earlier. Göring had also tried, through Henderson, to interest the British in the notion of a conference of the major powers to settle the Sudeten question by negotiation. Before Mussolini's critical move, the British and French had also applied maximum pressure. Chamberlain had replied to Hitler's letter, emphasizing his incredulity that the German Chancellor was prepared to risk a world war perhaps bringing the end of civilization 'for the sake of a few days' delay in settling this long-standing problem'. His letter contained proposals, agreed with the French, to press the

Czechs into immediate cession of the Sudeten territory, the transfer to be guaranteed by Britain and to begin on 1 October. An International Boundary Commission would work out the details of the territorial settlement. The British Prime Minister indicated that he was prepared to come to Berlin immediately, together with the representatives of France and Italy, to discuss the whole issue. Chamberlain also wrote to Mussolini, urging agreement with his proposal 'which will keep all our peoples out of war'.

The French, too, had been active. The ambassador in Berlin, André François-Poncet, had been instructed at 4 a.m. to put proposals similar to Chamberlain's before Hitler. His request early next morning for an audience with Hitler was not welcomed by Ribbentrop, still spoiling for war. But after intercession by Göring, prompted by Henderson, Hitler agreed to see the French Ambassador at 11.15 a.m.

François-Poncet, when eventually his audience was granted, warned Hitler that he would not be able to localize a military conflict with Czechoslovakia, but would set Europe in flames. Since he could attain almost all his demands without war, the risk seemed senseless. At that point, around 11.40 a.m., the discussion was interrupted by a message that the Italian ambassador Bernardo Attolico wished to see Hitler immediately on a matter of great urgency. Hitler left the room with his interpreter, Schmidt. The tall, stooping, red-faced ambassador lost no time in coming to the point. He breathlessly announced to Hitler that the British government had let Mussolini know that it would welcome his mediation in the Sudeten question. The areas of disagreement were small. The Duce supported Germany, the ambassador went on, but was 'of the opinion that the acceptance of the English proposal would be advantageous' and appealed for a postponement of the planned mobilization. After a moment's pause, Hitler replied: 'Tell the Duce I accept his proposal.' It was shortly before noon. Hitler now had his way of climbing down without losing face. 'We have no jumping-off point for war,' commented Goebbels. 'You can't carry out a world war on account of modalities.'

When the British Ambassador Henderson entered at 12.15 p.m. with Chamberlain's letter, Hitler told him that at the request of his 'great friend and ally, Signor Mussolini', he had postponed mobilization for twenty-four hours. The climax of war-fever had passed. During Henderson's hour-long audience, Attolico interrupted once more to tell Hitler that Mussolini had agreed to the British proposals for a meeting of the four major powers. When the dramatic news reached Chamberlain, towards the end of a speech about the crisis he was making to a packed and tense House of Commons, which was expecting an announcement meaning war, the house erupted. 'We stood on our benches, waved our order papers, shouted until we were hoarse – a scene of indescribable enthusiasm,' recorded one Member of Parliament. 'Peace must now be saved.'

War was averted – at least for the present. 'The heavens are beginning to lighten somewhat,' wrote Goebbels. 'We probably still have the possibility of taking the Sudeten German territory peacefully. The major solution still remains open, and we will further rearm for future eventualities.'

Already early the next afternoon, Hitler, Mussolini, Chamberlain, and Édouard Daladier, the small, quiet, dapper premier of France, together with Ribbentrop, Weizsäcker, Ciano, Wilson, and Alexis Léger, State Secretary in the French Foreign Office, took their seats around a table in the newly constructed Führerbau amid the complex of party buildings centred around the Brown House – the large and imposing party headquarters – in Munich. There they proceeded to carve up Czechoslovakia.

The four heads of government began by stating their relative positions on the Sudeten issue. They all – Hitler, too – spoke against a solution by force. The discussions focused upon the written proposal to settle the Sudeten question, by now translated into all four languages, that Mussolini had delivered the previous day (though the text had actually been sketched out by Göring, then formalized in the German Foreign Office under Weizsäcker's eye with some input by Neurath but avoiding any involvement by Ribbentrop, before being handed to the Italian ambassador). It provided the basis for what would become known as the notorious Munich Agreement. The circle of those involved in discussions had now widened to include Göring and the Ambassadors of Italy, France, and Great Britain (Attolico, François-Poncet, and Henderson), as well as legal advisers, secretaries, and adjutants. But it was now mainly a matter of legal technicalities and complex points of detail. The main work was done. That evening, Hitler invited the participants to a festive dinner. Chamberlain and Daladier found their excuses. After the dirty work had been done, they had little taste for celebration.

The deliberations had lasted in all for some thirteen hours. But, sensational though the four-power summit meeting was for the outside world, the real decision had already been taken around midday on 28 September, when Hitler had agreed to Mussolini's proposal for a negotiated settlement. Eventually, around 2.30 a.m. on the morning of 30 September, the draft agreement was signed. These terms were in effect those of the Godesberg Memorandum, modified by the final Anglo-French proposals, and with dates entered for a progressive German occupation, to be completed within ten days. 'We have then essentially achieved everything that we wanted according to the small plan,' commented Goebbels. 'The big plan is for the moment, given the prevailing circumstances, not yet realizable.'

Hitler looked pale, tired, and out of sorts when Chamberlain visited him in his apartment in Prinzregentenplatz to present him with a joint declaration of Germany's and Britain's determination never to go to war with one another again. Chamberlain had suggested the private meeting during a lull in proceedings the previous day. Hitler had, the British Prime Minister remarked, 'jumped at the idea'. Chamberlain regarded the meeting as 'a very friendly and pleasant talk'. 'At the end,' he went on, 'I pulled out the declaration which I had prepared beforehand and asked if he would sign it.' After a moment's hesitation, Hitler – with some reluctance it seemed to the interpreter Paul Schmidt – appended his signature. For him, the document was meaningless. And for him Munich was no great cause for celebration. He felt cheated of the greater triumph which he was certain would have come from the limited war with the Czechs – his aim all summer. But when the next crisis duly came, he was even more confident that he knew his adversaries: 'Our enemies are small worms,' he would tell his generals in August 1939. 'I saw them in Munich.'

Hitler was scornful, too, of his generals after Munich. Their opposition to his plans had infuriated him all summer. How he would have reacted had he been aware that no less a person than his new Chief of Staff, General Halder, had been involved in plans for a *coup d'état* in the event of war over Czechoslovakia can be left to the imagination. Whether the schemes of the ill-coordinated groups involved in the nascent conspiracy would actually have come to anything is an open question. But with the Munich Agreement, the chance was irredeemably gone. Chamberlain returned home to a hero's welcome. But for German opponents of the Nazi regime, who had hoped to used Hitler's military adventurism as the weapon of his own deposition and destruction, Chamberlain was anything but the hero of the hour. 'Chamberlain saved Hitler,' was how they bitterly regarded the appeasement diplomacy of the western powers.

Hitler's own popularity and prestige reached new heights after Munich. He returned to another triumphant welcome in Berlin. But he was well aware that the elemental tide of euphoria reflected the relief that peace had been preserved. The 'home-coming' of the Sudeten Germans was of only secondary importance. He was being fêted not as the 'first soldier of the Reich', but as the saviour of the peace he had not wanted. At the critical hour, the German people, in his eyes, had lacked enthusiasm for war. The spirit of 1914 had been missing. Psychological rearmament had still to take place. A few weeks later, addressing a select audience of several hundred German journalists and editors, he gave a remarkably frank indication of his feelings: 'Circumstances have compelled me to speak for decades almost solely of peace,' he declared. 'It is natural that such a . . . peace propaganda also has its dubious side. It can only too easily lead to the view establishing itself in the minds of many people that the present regime is identical with the determination and will to preserve peace under all circumstances. That would not only lead to a wrong assessment of the aims of this system, but would also above all lead to the German nation, instead of being forearmed in the face of events, being filled with a spirit which, as defeatism, in the long run would take away and must take away the successes of the present regime.' It was necessary, therefore, to transform the psychology of the German people, to make them see that some things could only be attained through force, and to represent foreign-policy issues in such a way that 'the inner voice of the people itself slowly begins to cry out for the use of force'.

The speech is revealing. Popular backing for war had to be manufactured, since war and expansion were irrevocably bound up with the survival of the regime. Successes, unending triumphs, were indispensable for the regime, and for Hitler's own popularity and prestige on which, ultimately, the regime depended. Only through expansion – itself impossible without war – could Germany, and the National Socialist regime, survive. This was Hitler's thinking. The gamble for expansion was inescapable. It was not a matter of personal choice.

The legacy of Munich was fatally to weaken those who might even now have constrained Hitler. Any potential limits – external and internal – on his freedom of action instead disappeared. Hitler's drive to war was unabated. And next time he was determined he would not be blocked by last-minute diplomatic manoeuvres of the western powers, whose weakness he had seen with his own eyes at Munich.

15

Marks of a Genocidal Mentality

I

The ideological dynamic of the Nazi regime was by no means solely a matter of Hitler's personalized *Weltanschauung*. In fact, Hitler's ideological aims had so far played only a subordinate role in his expansionist policy, and would not figure prominently in the Polish crisis during the summer of 1939. The party and its numerous sub-organizations were, of course, important in sustaining the pressure for ever-new discriminatory measures against ideological target-groups. But little in the way of coherent planning could be expected from the central party office, under the charge of Rudolf Heß, Hitler's deputy in party affairs. The key agency was not the party, but the SS.

The interest in expansion was self-evident. Buoyed by their successes in Austria and the Sudetenland, Himmler, Heydrich, and the top echelons of the SS were keen to extend – naturally, under Hitler's aegis – their own empire. Already in August 1938, a decree by Hitler met Himmler's wish to develop an armed wing of the SS. It provided in effect a fourth branch of the armed forces – far smaller than the others, but envisaged as a body of ideologically motivated 'political soldiers' standing at the Führer's 'exclusive disposal'. It was little wonder that Himmler had been one of the hawks during the Sudeten crisis, aligning himself with Ribbentrop, and encouraging Hitler's aggression. The leaders of the SS were now looking to territorial gains to provide them with opportunities for ideological experimentation on the way to the fulfilment of the vision of a racially purified Greater German Reich under the heel of the chosen caste of the SS élite. In a world after Hitler, with 'final victory' achieved, the SS were determined to be the masters of Germany and Europe.

They saw their mission as the ruthless eradication of Germany's ideological enemies, who, in Himmler's strange vision, were numerous and menacing. He told top SS leaders in early November 1938: 'We must be clear that in the next ten years we will certainly encounter unheard of critical conflicts. It is not only the struggle of the nations, which in this case are put forward by the opposing side merely as a front, but it is the ideological struggle of the entire Jewry, freemasonry, Marxism, and churches of the world. These forces – of which I presume the Jews to be the driving spirit, the origin of all the negatives – are clear that if Germany and Italy are not annihilated, they will be annihilated. That is a simple conclusion. In Germany the Jew cannot hold out. This is a question of years. We will drive them out more and more with an unprecedented ruthlessness . . .'

The speech was held a day before Germany exploded in an orgy of elemental violence against its Jewish minority in the notorious pogrom of 9–10 November 1938, cynically dubbed in popular parlance, on account of the millions of fragments of broken glass littering the pavements of Berlin outside wrecked Jewish shops, 'Reich Crystal Night' (*Reichskristallnacht*). This night of horror, a retreat in a modern state to the savagery associated with bygone ages, laid bare to the world the barbarism of the Nazi regime. Within Germany, it brought immediate draconian measures to exclude Jews from the economy, accompanied by a restructuring of anti-Jewish policy, placing it now directly under the control of the SS, whose leaders linked war, expansion, and eradication of Jewry.

Such a linkage was not only reinforced in the eyes of the SS in the aftermath of 'Crystal Night'. For Hitler, too, the connection between the war he knew was coming and the destruction of Europe's Jews was now beginning to take concrete shape. Since the 1920s he had not deviated from the view that German salvation could only come through a titanic struggle for supremacy in Europe, and for eventual world power, against mighty enemies backed by the mightiest enemy of all, perhaps more powerful even than the Third Reich itself: international Jewry. It was a colossal gamble. But for Hitler it was a gamble that could not be avoided. And for him, the fate of the Jews was inextricably bound up with that gamble.

The nationwide pogrom carried out by rampaging Nazi mobs on the night of 9–10 November was the culmination of a third wave of anti-semitic violence – worse even than those of 1933 and 1935 – that had begun in the spring of 1938 and run on as the domestic accompaniment to the foreign-political crisis throughout the summer and autumn. Part of the background to the summer of violence was the open terror on the streets of Vienna in March, and the 'success' that Eichmann had scored in forcing the emigration of the Viennese Jews. Nazi leaders in cities of the 'old Reich', particularly Berlin, took note. The chance to be rid of 'their' Jews seemed to open up. A second strand in the background was the 'aryanization' drive to hound Jews out of German economic life. At the beginning of 1933 there had been some 50,000 Jewish businesses in Germany. By July 1938, there were only 9,000 left. The big push to exclude the Jews came between spring and autumn 1938. The 1,690 businesses in Jewish hands in Munich in February 1938, for instance, had fallen to only 666 (two-thirds of them owned by foreign citizens) by October. The 'aryanization' drive not only closed businesses, or saw them bought out for a pittance by new 'aryan' owners. It also brought a new flood of legislative measures imposing a variety of discriminatory restrictions and occupational bans – such as on Jewish doctors and lawyers – even to the extent of preventing Jews from trying to eke out a living as pedlars. It was a short step from legislation to pinpoint remaining Jewish businesses to identifying Jewish persons. A decree of 17 August had made it compulsory for male Jews to add the forename 'Israel', females the forename 'Sara', to their existing names and, on pain of imprisonment, to use those names in all official matters. On 5 October, they were compelled to have a 'J' stamped in their passports. A few days later, Göring declared that 'the Jewish Question must now be tackled with all means available, for they [the Jews] must get out of the economy'.

Alongside the legislation, inevitably, went the violence. Scores of localized attacks on Jewish property and on individual Jews, usually carried out by members of party formations, punctuated the summer months. Far more than had been the case in the earlier antisemitic waves, attention of party activists increasingly focused on synagogues and Jewish cemeteries, which were repeatedly vandalized. As an indicator of their mood, and an 'ordered' foretaste of what would follow across the land during 'Crystal Night', the main synagogue in Munich was demolished on 9 June, the first in Germany to be destroyed by the Nazis. During a visit to the city a few days earlier, Hitler had taken objection to its proximity to the Deutsches Künstlerhaus ('House of German

Artists'). The official reason given was that the building was a hindrance to traffic.

Hitler saw it as important that he should not be publicly associated with the anti-Jewish campaign as it gathered momentum during 1938. No discussion by the press of the 'Jewish Question' was, for example, permitted in connection with his visits to different parts of Germany in that year. Preserving his image, both at home and – especially in the light of the developing Czech crisis – abroad, through avoiding personal association with distasteful actions towards the Jews appears to have been the motive. Hence, he insisted in September 1938, at the height of the Sudeten crisis, that his signing of the fifth implementation ordinance under the Reich Citizenship Law, to oust Jewish lawyers, should not be publicized at that stage in order to prevent any possible deterioration of Germany's image – clearly meaning his own image – at such a tense moment.

In fact, he had to do little or nothing to stir the escalating campaign against the Jews. Others made the running, took the initiative, pressed for action – always, of course, on the assumption that this was in line with Nazism's great mission. It was a classic case of 'working towards the Führer' – taking for granted (usually on grounds of self-interest) that he approved of measures aimed at the 'removal' of the Jews, measures seen as plainly furthering his long-term goals. Party activists in the Movement's various formations needed no encouragement to unleash further attacks on Jews and their property. 'Aryans' in business, from the smallest to the largest, looked to every opportunity to profit at the expense of their Jewish counterparts. Hundreds of Jewish businesses – including long-established private banks such as Warburg and Bleichröder – were now forced, often through gangster-like extortion, to sell out for a fraction of their value to 'aryan' buyers. Big business gained most. Giant concerns like Mannesmann, Krupp, Thyssen, Flick, and IG-Farben, and leading banks such as the Deutsche Bank and the Dresdner Bank, were the major beneficiaries, while a variety of business consortia, corrupt party functionaries, and untold numbers of small commercial enterprises grabbed what they could. 'Aryan' pillars of the establishment like doctors and lawyers were equally welcoming of the economic advantages that could come their way with the expulsion of Jews from the medical and legal professions. University professors turned their skills, without prompting, to defining alleged negative characteristics of the Jewish character and pyschology. And all the time, civil servants worked like beavers to hone the legislation that turned Jews into outcasts and pariahs, their lives into torment and misery. The police, particularly the Gestapo – helped as always by eager citizens anxious to denounce Jews or those seen as 'friends of Jews' – served as a proactive enforcement agency, deploying their 'rational' methods of arrest and internment in concentration camps rather than the crude violence of the party hotheads, though with the same objective. Not least, the SD – beginning life as the party's own intelligence organization, but developing into the crucial surveillance and ideological planning agency within the rapidly expanding SS – was advancing on its way to adopting the pivotal role in the shaping of anti-Jewish policy.

Each group, agency, or individual involved in pushing forward the radicalization of anti-Jewish discrimination had vested interests and a specific agenda. Uniting them all and giving justification to them was the vision of racial purification and, in particular, of a 'Jew-free' Germany embodied in the person of the Führer. Hitler's role was, therefore, crucial, even if at times indirect. His broad sanction was needed. But for the most part little more was required.

There is no doubt that Hitler fully approved of and backed the new drive against the Jews, even if he took care to remain out of the limelight. One of the main agitators for radical action against the Jews, Joseph Goebbels, had no difficulty in April 1938 – in the immediate wake of the savage persecution of the Jews in Vienna – in persuading Hitler to support his plans to 'clean up' Berlin, the seat of his own Gau. Hitler's only stipulation was that nothing should be undertaken before his meetings with Mussolini in early May. A successful outcome of his talks with the Duce was of great importance to him, particularly in the context of his unfolding plans regarding Czechoslovakia. Possible diplomatic repercussions provoked by intensified persecution of Jews in Germany's capital were to be avoided. Goebbels had already discussed his own aims on the 'Jewish Question' with Berlin's Police Chief Wolf Heinrich Graf von Helldorf before he broached the matter with Hitler. 'Then we put it to the Führer. He agrees, but only after his trip to Italy. Jewish establishments will be combed out. Jews will then get a swimming-pool, a few cinemas, and restaurants allocated to them. Otherwise entry forbidden. We'll remove the character of a Jew-paradise from Berlin. Jewish businesses will be marked as such. At any rate, we're now proceeding more radically. The Führer wants gradually to push them all out. Negotiate with Poland and Romania. Madagascar would be the most suitable for them.'

The 'Madagascar solution' had been touted among radical antisemites for decades. Reference to it at this juncture seems to signify that Hitler was moving away from any assumption that emigration would remove the 'Jewish problem' in favour of a solution based upon territorial resettlement. He was conceivably influenced in this by Heydrich, reporting the views of the 'experts' on Jewish policy in the SD. The relative lack of success in 'persuading' Jews to emigrate – little short of three-quarters of the Jewish population recorded in 1933 still lived in Germany, despite the persecution, as late as October 1938 – together with the mounting obstacles to Jewish immigration created by other countries had compelled the SD to revise its views on future anti-Jewish policy. By the end of 1937 the idea of favouring a Jewish state in Palestine, which Eichmann had developed, partly through secret dealings with Zionist contacts, had cooled markedly. Eichmann's own visit to Palestine, arranged with his Zionist go-between, had been an unmitigated failure. And, more importantly, the German Foreign Office was resolutely hostile to the notion of a Jewish state in Palestine. However, emigration remained the objective.

Hitler, too, favoured Palestine as a targeted territory. In early 1938, he reaffirmed the policy, arrived at almost a year earlier, aimed at promoting with all means available the emigration of Jews to any country willing to take them, though looking to Palestine in the first instance. But he was alert to the perceived dangers of creating a Jewish state to threaten Germany at some future date. In any case, other notions were being mooted. Already in 1937 there had been suggestions in the SD of deporting Jews to barren, unwelcoming parts of the world, scarcely capable of sustaining human life and certainly, in the SD's view, incompatible with a renewed flourishing of Jewry and revitalized potential of 'world conspiracy'. In addition to Palestine, Ecuador, Colombia, and Venezuela had been mentioned as possibilities. Nothing came of such ideas at the time. But the suggestions were little different in essence from the old notion, later to be revamped, of Madagascar as an inhospitable territory fit to accommodate Jews until, it was implied, they eventually died out. The notion of Jewish resettlement, already aired in the SD, was itself latently genocidal.

Whatever line of policy was favoured, the 'final goal' (as Hitler's comments to Goebbels indicated) remained indistinct, and as such compatible with all attempts to further the 'removal' of the Jews. This eventual 'removal' was conceived as taking a good number of years to complete. Even following 'Crystal Night', Heydrich was still envisaging an 'emigration action' lasting from eight to ten years. Hitler himself had already inferred to Goebbels towards the end of July 1938 that 'the Jews must be removed from Germany in ten years'. In the meantime, he added, they were to be retained as 'surety'.

Goebbels, meanwhile, was impatient to make headway with the 'racial cleansing' of Berlin. 'A start has to be made somewhere,' he remarked. He thought the removal of Jews from the economy and cultural life of the city could be accomplished within a few months. The programme devised by mid-May for him by Helldorf, and given his approval, put forward a variety of discriminatory measures – including special identity cards for Jews, branding of Jewish shops, bans on Jews using public parks, and special train compartments for Jews – most of which, following the November Pogrom, came to be generally implemented. Helldorf also envisaged the construction of a ghetto in Berlin to be financed by the richer Jews.

Even if this last aim remained unfulfilled, the poisonous atmosphere stirred by Goebbels's agitation – with Hitler's tacit approval – had rapid results. Already on 27 May, a 1,000-strong mob roamed parts of Berlin, smashing windows of shops belonging to Jews, and prompting the police, anxious not to lose the initiative in anti-Jewish policy, to take the owners into 'protective custody'. When in mid-June Jewish stores on the Kurfürstendamm, the prime shopping street in the west of the city, were smeared with antisemitic slogans by party activists, and plundering of some shops took place, concern for Germany's image abroad dictated a halt to the public violence. Hitler intervened directly from Berchtesgaden, following which Goebbels ruefully banned all illegal actions. However, Berlin had set the tone. Similar 'actions', initiated by the local party organizations, were carried out in Frankfurt, Magdeburg, and other towns and cities. The lack of any explicit general ban from above on 'individual actions', as had been imposed in 1935, was taken by party activists in countless localities as a green light to step up their own campaigns. The touchpaper had been lit to the summer and autumn of violence. As the tension in the Czech crisis mounted, local antisemitic initiatives in various regions saw to it that the 'Jewish Question' became a powder-keg, waiting for the spark. The radical tide surged forward. The atmosphere had become menacing in the extreme for the Jews.

Even so, from the perspective of the regime's leadership, how to get the Jews out of the economy and force them to leave Germany still appeared to be questions without obvious answers. As early as January 1937, Eichmann had suggested, in a lengthy internal memorandum, that pogroms were the most effective way of accelerating the sluggish emigration. Like an answer to a prayer, the shooting of the German Third Legation Secretary Ernst vom Rath in Paris by a seventeen-year-old Polish Jew, Herschel Grynszpan, on the morning of 7 November 1938 opened up an opportunity not to be missed. It was an opportunity eagerly seized upon by Goebbels. He had no difficulty in winning Hitler's full backing.

II

Grynszpan had meant to kill the Ambassador. Vom Rath just happened to be the first official he saw. The shooting was an act of despair and revenge for his own miserable existence and for the deportation of his family at the end of October from Hanover – simply deposited, along with a further 18,000 Polish Jews, over the borders with Poland. Two and a half years earlier, when the Jewish medical student David Frankfurter had killed the Nazi leader in Switzerland Wilhelm Gustloff, in Davos, circumstances had demanded that the lid be kept firmly on any wild response by party fanatics in Germany. In the threatening climate of autumn 1938, the situation could scarcely have been more different. Now, the Nazi hordes were to be positively encouraged to turn their wrath on the Jews. The death of vom Rath – he succumbed to his wounds on the afternoon of 9 November – happened, moreover, to coincide with the fifteenth anniversary of Hitler's attempted putsch of 1923. All over Germany, party members were meeting to celebrate one of the legendary events of the 'time of struggle'. The annual commemoration marked a high point in the Nazi calendar. In Munich, as usual, the party bigwigs were gathering.

On the morning following the fateful shooting, the Nazi press, under Goebbels's orchestration, had been awash with vicious attacks on the Jews, guaranteed to incite violence. Sure enough, that evening, 8 November, pogroms – involving the burning of synagogues, destruction of Jewish property, plundering of goods, and maltreatment of individual Jews – were instigated in a number of parts of the country through the agitation of local party leaders without any directives from on high. Usually, the local leaders involved were radical antisemites in areas, such as Hessen, with lengthy traditions of antisemitism. Goebbels noted the disturbances with satisfaction in his diary: 'In Hessen big antisemitic demonstrations. The synagogues are burnt down. If only the anger of the people could now be let loose!' The following day, he referred to the 'demonstrations', burning of synagogues, and demolition of shops in Kassel and Dessau. During the afternoon, news of vom Rath's death came through. 'Now that's done it,' remarked Goebbels.

The party's 'old guard' were meeting that evening in the Old Town Hall in Munich. Hitler, too, was present. On the way there, with Goebbels, he had been told of disturbances against Jews in Munich, but favoured the police taking a lenient line. He could scarcely have avoided being well aware of the anti-Jewish actions in Hessen and elsewhere, as well as the incitements of the press. It was impossible to ignore the fact that, among party radicals, antisemitic tension was running high. But Hitler had given no indication, despite vom Rath's perilous condition at the time and the menacing antisemitic climate, of any intended action when he had spoken to the 'old guard' of the party in his traditional speech at the Bürgerbräukeller the previous evening. By the time the party leaders gathered for the reception on the 9th, Hitler was aware of vom Rath's death. With his own doctor, Karl Brandt, dispatched to the bedside, Hitler had doubtless been kept well informed of the Legation Secretary's deteriorating condition and had heard of his demise at the latest by seven o'clock that evening – in all probability by telephone some hours earlier. According to his Luftwaffe adjutant, Nicolaus von Below, he had already been given the news – which he had received without overt reaction – that afternoon while he was engaged in discussions on military matters in his Munich apartment.

Goebbels and Hitler were seen to confer in agitated fashion during the reception, though their conversation could not be overheard. Hitler left shortly afterwards, earlier than usual and without his customary exchanges with those present, to return to his Munich apartment. Around 10 p.m. Goebbels delivered a brief but highly inflammatory speech, reporting the death of vom Rath, pointing out that there had already been 'retaliatory' action against the Jews in Kurhessen and Magdeburg-Anhalt. He made it abundantly plain without explicitly saying so that the party should organize and carry out 'demonstrations' against the Jews throughout the country, though make it appear that they were expressions of spontaneous popular anger.

Goebbels's diary entry leaves no doubt of the content of his discussion with Hitler. 'I go to the party reception in the Old Town Hall. Huge amount going on. I explain the matter to the Führer. He decides: let the demonstrations continue. Pull back the police. The Jews should for once get to feel the anger of the people. That's right. I immediately give corresponding directives to police and party. Then I speak for a short time in that vein to the party leadership. Storms of applause. All tear straight off to the telephone. Now the people will act.'

Goebbels certainly did his best to make sure 'the people' acted. He put out detailed instructions of what had and had not to be done. He fired up the mood where there was hesitancy. Immediately after he had spoken, the Stoßtrupp Hitler, an 'assault squad' whose traditions reached back to the heady days of pre-putsch beerhouse brawls and bore the Führer's name, was launched to wreak havoc on the streets of Munich. Almost immediately they demolished the old synagogue in Herzog-Rudolf-Straße, left standing after the main synagogue had been destroyed in the summer. Adolf Wagner, Gauleiter of Munich and Upper Bavaria (who as Bavarian Minister of Interior was supposedly responsible for order in the province), himself no moderate in 'the Jewish Question', got cold feet. But Goebbels pushed him into line. The 'capital city of the Movement' of all places was not going to be spared what was happening already all over Germany. Goebbels then gave direct telephone instructions to Berlin to demolish the synagogue in Fasanenstraße, off the Kurfürstendamm.

The top leadership of the police and SS, also gathered in Munich but not present when Goebbels had given his speech, learnt of the 'action' only once it had started. Heydrich, at the time in the Hotel Vier Jahreszeiten, was informed by the Munich Gestapo Office around 11.20 p.m., after the first orders had already gone out to the party and SA. He immediately sought Himmler's directives on how the police should respond. The Reichsführer-SS was contacted in Hitler's Munich apartment. He asked what orders Hitler had for him. Hitler replied – most likely at Himmler's prompting – that he wanted the SS to keep out of the 'action'. Disorder and uncontrolled violence and destruction were not the SS's style. Himmler and Heydrich preferred the 'rational', systematic approach to the 'Jewish Question'. Soon after midnight orders went out that any SS men participating in the 'demonstrations' were to do so only in civilian clothing. At 1.20 a.m. Heydrich telexed all police chiefs instructing the police not to obstruct the destruction of the synagogues and to arrest as many male Jews, especially wealthy ones, as available prison accommodation could take. The figure of 20–30,000 Jews had already been mentioned in a Gestapo directive sent out before midnight.

Meanwhile, across the Reich, party activists – especially SA men – were suddenly summoned by their local leaders and told to burn down synagogues or were turned loose on other Jewish property. Many of those involved had been celebrating at their own commemoration of the Beerhall Putsch, and some were the worse for wear from drink. The 'action' was usually improvised on the spot.

At midnight, at the Feldherrnhalle in Munich where the attempted putsch in 1923 had met its end, Goebbels had witnessed the swearing-in of the SS to Hitler. The Propaganda Minister was ready to return to his hotel when he saw the sky red from the fire of the burning synagogue in Herzog-Rudolf-Straße. Back he went to Gau headquarters. Instructions were given out that the fire-brigade should extinguish only what was necessary to protect nearby buildings. Otherwise they were to let the synagogue burn down. 'The Stoßtrupp is doing dreadful damage,' he commented. Reports came in to him of seventy-five synagogues on fire throughout the Reich, fifteen of them in Berlin. He had evidently by this time heard of the Gestapo directive. 'The Führer has ordered,' he noted, 'that 20–30,000 Jews are immediately to be arrested.' In fact, it had been a Gestapo order with no reference in it to a directive of the Führer. Clearly, however, though he had instigated the pogrom, Goebbels took it that the key decisions came from Hitler. Goebbels went with Julius Schaub, Hitler's general factotum, into the Artists' Club to wait for further news. Schaub was in fine form. 'His old Stoßtrupp past has been revived,' commented Goebbels. He went back to his hotel. He could hear the noise of shattering glass from smashed shop windows. 'Bravo, bravo,' he wrote. After a few hours' snatched sleep, he added: 'The dear Jews will think about it in future before they shoot down

German diplomats like that. And that was the meaning of the exercise.'

All morning new reports of the destruction poured in. Goebbels assessed the situation with Hitler. In the light of the mounting criticism of the 'action', also – though naturally not for humanitarian reasons – from within the top ranks of the Nazi leadership, the decision was taken to halt it. Goebbels prepared a decree to end the destruction, cynically commenting that if it were allowed to continue there was the danger 'that the mob would start to appear'. He reported to Hitler, who was, Goebbels claimed, 'in agreement with everything. His opinions are very radical and aggressive.' 'With minor alterations, the Führer approves my edict on the end of the actions . . . The Führer wants to move to very severe measures against the Jews. They must get their businesses in order themselves. Insurance will pay them nothing. Then the Führer wants gradually to expropriate the Jewish businesses.'

By that time, the night of horror for Germany's Jews had brought the demolition of around 100 synagogues, the burning of several hundred others, the destruction of at least 8,000 Jews' shops and vandalizing of countless apartments. The pavements of the big cities were strewn with shards of glass from the display windows of Jewish-owned stores; merchandise, if not looted, had been hurled on to the streets. Private apartments were wrecked, furniture demolished, mirrors and pictures smashed, clothing shredded, treasured possessions wantonly trashed. The material damage was estimated soon afterwards by Heydrich at several hundred million Marks.

The human misery of the victims was incalculable. Beatings and bestial maltreatment, even of women, children, and the elderly, were commonplace. A hundred or so Jews were murdered. It was little wonder that suicide was commonplace that terrible night. Many more succumbed to brutalities in the weeks following the pogrom in the concentration camps of Dachau, Buchenwald, and Sachsenhausen, where the 30,000 male Jews rounded up by the police had been sent as a means of forcing their emigration.

The scale and nature of the savagery, and the apparent aim of maximizing degradation and humiliation, reflected the success of propaganda in demonizing the figure of the Jew – certainly within the organizations of the party itself – and massively enhanced the process, under way since Hitler's takeover of power, of dehumanizing Jews and excluding them from German society, a vital step on the way to genocide.

The propaganda line of a spontaneous expression of anger by the people was, however, believed by no one. 'The public knows to the last man,' the party's own court later admitted, 'that political actions like that of 9 November are organized and carried out by the party, whether this is admitted or not. If all the synagogues burn down in a single night, that has somehow to be organized, and can only be organized by the party.'

Ordinary citizens, affected by the climate of hatred and propaganda appealing to base instincts, motivated too by sheer material envy and greed, nevertheless followed the party's lead in many places and joined in the destruction and looting of Jewish property. Sometimes individuals regarded as the pillars of their communities were involved. At the same time, there is no doubt that many ordinary people were appalled at what met them when they emerged on the morning of 10 November. A mixture of motives operated. Some, certainly, felt human revulsion at the behaviour of the Nazi hordes and sympathy for the Jews, even to the extent of offering them material help and comfort. Not all motives for the condemnation were as noble. Often, it was the shame inflicted by 'hooligans' on Germany's standing as a 'nation of culture' which rankled. Most commonly of all, there was enormous resentment at the unrestrained destruction of material goods at a time when people were told that every little that was saved contributed to the efforts of the Four-Year Plan.

III

By the morning of 10 November, anger was also rising among leading Nazis responsible for the economy about the material damage which had taken place. Walther Funk, who had replaced Schacht as Economics Minister early in the year, complained directly to Goebbels, but was told, to placate him, that Hitler would soon give Göring an order to exclude the Jews from the economy. Göring himself, who had been in a sleeping-compartment of a train heading from Munich to Berlin as the night of violence had unfolded, was furious when he found out what had happened. His own credibility as economics supremo was at stake. He had exhorted the people, so he told Hitler, to collect discarded toothpaste tubes, rusty nails, and every bit of cast-out material. And now, valuable property had been recklessly destroyed.

When they met at lunchtime on 10 November in his favourite Munich restaurant, the Osteria Bavaria, Hitler made plain to Goebbels his intention to introduce draconian economic measures against the Jews. They were dictated by the perverted notion that the Jews themselves would have to foot the bill for the destruction of their own property by the Nazis. The victims, in other words, were guilty of their own persecution. They would have to repair the damage without any contributions from German insurance firms and would be expropriated. Whether, as Göring later claimed, Goebbels was the initiator of the suggestion to impose a fine of 1,000 million Marks on the Jews is uncertain. More probably Göring, with his direct interest as head of the Four-Year Plan in maximizing the economic exploitation of the Jews, had himself come up with the idea in telephone conversations with Hitler, and perhaps also with Goebbels, that afternoon. Possibly, the idea was Hitler's own, though Goebbels does not refer to it when speaking of his wish for 'very tough measures' at their lunchtime meeting. At any rate, the suggestion was bound to meet with Hitler's favour. He had, after all, in his 'Memorandum on the Four-Year Plan' in 1936, already stated, in connection with accelerating the economic preparations for war, his intention to make the Jews responsible for any damage to the German economy. With the measures decided upon, Hitler decreed 'that now the economic solution should also be carried out', and 'ordered by and large what had to happen'.

This was effectively achieved in the meeting, attended by over 100 persons, which Göring called for 12 November in the Air Ministry. Göring began by stating that the meeting was of fundamental importance. He had received a letter from Bormann, on behalf of the Führer, desiring a coordinated solution to the 'Jewish Question'. The Führer had informed him, in addition, by telephone the previous day that the decisive steps were now to be centrally synchronized. In essence, he went on, the problem was an economic one. It was there that the issue had to be resolved. He castigated the method of 'demonstrations', which damaged the German economy. Then he concentrated on ways of confiscating Jewish businesses and maximizing the possible gain to the Reich from the Jewish misery. Goebbels raised the need for numerous measures of social discrimination against the Jews, which he had been pressing for in Berlin for months: exclusion from cinemas, theatres, parks, beaches and bathing resorts, 'German' schools, and railway compartments used by 'aryans'. Heydrich suggested a distinctive badge to be worn by Jews, which led on to discussion of whether ghettos would be appropriate. In the event, the idea of establishing ghettos was not taken up (though Jews would be forced to leave 'aryan' tenement blocks and be banned from certain parts of the cities, so compelling them in effect to congregate together); and the suggestion of badges was rejected by Hitler himself soon afterwards (presumably to avoid possible recurrence of the pogrom-style violence which had provoked criticism even among the regime's leaders). They would not be introduced in the Reich itself until September 1941.

But 'Crystal Night' had nevertheless spawned completely new openings for radical measures. This was most evident in the economic sphere, to which the meeting returned. Insurance companies were told that they would have to cover the losses, if their foreign business was not to suffer. But the payments would be made to the Reich, not, of course, to the Jews. Towards the end of the lengthy meeting, Göring announced, to the approval of the assembled company, the 'atonement fine' that was to be imposed on the Jews. Later that day, he issued decrees, imposing the billion-Mark fine, excluding Jews from the economy by 1 January 1939, and stipulating that Jews were responsible for paying for the damage to their own property. 'At any rate now a tabula rasa is being made,' commented Goebbels with satisfaction. 'The radical view has triumphed.'

Indeed, the November Pogrom had in the most barbaric way imaginable cleared a pathway through the impasse into which Nazi anti-Jewish policy had manoeuvred itself by 1938. Emigration had been reduced to little more than a trickle, especially since the Evian Conference, where, on the initiative of President Franklin D. Roosevelt, delegates from thirty-two countries had assembled in the French resort, deliberated from 6 to 14 July, then confirmed the unwillingness of the international community to increase immigration quotas for Jews. Moves to remove the Jews from the economy were still proceeding far too slowly to satisfy party fanatics. And anti-Jewish policy had suffered from complete lack of coordination. Hitler himself had been little involved. Goebbels, a driving-force in pressing for tougher measures against the Jews since the spring, had recognized the opportunity that vom Rath's assassination gave him. He sniffed the climate, and knew conditions were ripe. In a personal sense, too, the shooting of vom Rath was timely. Goebbels's marital difficulties and relationship with the Czech film actress Lida Baarova had threatened to lower his standing with Hitler. Now was a chance, by 'working towards the Führer' in such a key area, to win back favour.

One consequence of the night of violence was that the Jews were now desperate to leave Germany. Some 80,000 fled, in the most traumatic circumstances, between the end of 1938 and the beginning of the war. By whatever desperate means, tens of thousands of Jews were able to escape the clutches of the Nazis and flee across neighbouring borders, to Britain, the USA, Latin America, Palestine (despite British prohibitions), and to the distant refuge with the most lenient policy of all: Japanese-occupied Shanghai.

The Nazis' aim of forcing the Jews out had been massively boosted. Beyond that, the problem of their slow-moving elimination from the economy had been tackled. Whatever his criticism of Goebbels, Göring had wasted no time in ensuring that the chance was now taken fully to 'aryanize' the economy, and to profit from 'Reichskristallnacht'. When he spoke, a week later, of the 'very critical state of the Reich finances', he was able to add: 'Aid first of all through the billion imposed on the Jews and through the profits to the Reich from the aryanization of Jewish concerns'. Others, too, in the Nazi leadership seized the chance to push through a flood of new discriminatory measures, intensifying the hopelessness of Jewish existence in Germany. Radicalization fed on radicalization.

The radicalization encountered no opposition of any weight. Ordinary people who expressed their anger, sorrow, distaste, or shame at what had happened were powerless. Those who might have articulated such feelings, such as the leaders of the Christian Churches, among whose precepts was 'love thy neighbour as thyself', kept quiet. Neither major denomination, Protestant or Catholic, raised an official protest or even backing for those courageous individual pastors and priests who did speak out. Within the regime's leadership, those, like Schacht, who had used economic or otherwise tactical objections to try to combat what they saw as counter-productive, wild 'excesses' of the radical antisemites in the party, were now politically impotent. In any case, such economic arguments lost all force with 'Crystal Night'. The leaders of the armed forces, scandalized though some of them were at the 'cultural disgrace' of what had happened, made no public protest. Beyond that, the deep antisemitism running through the armed forces meant that no opposition worth mentioning to Nazi radicalism could be expected from that quarter. Characteristic of the mentality was a letter which the revered Colonel-General von Fritsch wrote, almost a year after his dismissal and only a month after the November Pogrom. Fritsch was reportedly outraged by 'Crystal Night'. But, as with so many, it was the method not the aim that appalled him. He mentioned in his letter that after the previous war he had concluded that Germany had to succeed in three battles in order to become great again. Hitler had won the battle against the working class. The other two battles, against Catholic Ultramontanism, and against the Jews, still continued. 'And the struggle against the Jews is the hardest,' he noted. 'It is to be hoped that the difficulty of this struggle is apparent everywhere.'

'Crystal Night' marked the final fling within Germany of 'pogrom antisemitism'. Willing though he was to make use of the method, Hitler had emphasized as early as 1919 that it could provide no solution to the 'Jewish Question'. The massive material damage caused, the public relations disaster reflected in the almost universal condemnation in the international press, and to a lesser extent the criticism levelled at the 'excesses' (though not at the draconian anti-Jewish legislation that followed them) by broad sections of the German population ensured that the ploy of open violence had had its day. Its place was taken by something which turned out to be even more sinister: the handing-over of practical responsibility for a coordinated anti-Jewish policy to the 'rational' antisemites in the SS. On 24 January 1939, Göring established – based on the model which had functioned effectively in Vienna – a Central Office for Jewish Emigration under the aegis of the Chief of the Security Police, Reinhard Heydrich. The policy was still forced emigration, now transformed into an all-out, accelerated drive to expel the Jews from Germany. But the transfer of overall responsibility to the SS nevertheless began a new phase of anti-Jewish policy. For the victims, it marked a decisive step on the way that was to end in the gas-chambers of the extermination camps.

I V

The open brutality of the November Pogrom, the round-up and incarceration of some 30,000 Jews that followed it, and the draconian measures to force Jews out of the economy had, Goebbels's diary entries make plain, all been explicitly approved by Hitler even if the initiatives had come from others, above all from the Propaganda Minister himself.

To those who saw him late on the evening of 9 November, Hitler had appeared to be shocked and angry at the reports reaching him of what was happening. Himmler, highly critical of Goebbels, was given the impression that Hitler was surprised by what he was hearing when Himmler's chief adjutant Karl Wolff informed them of the burning of the Munich synagogue just before 11.30 that evening. Nicolaus von Below, Hitler's Luftwaffe adjutant, who saw him immediately on his return to his apartment from the 'Old Town Hall', was convinced that there was no dissembling in his apparent anger and condemnation of the destruction. Speer was told by a seemingly regretful and somewhat embarrassed Hitler that he had not wanted the 'excesses'. Speer thought Goebbels had probably pushed him into it. Rosenberg, a few weeks after the events, was convinced that Goebbels, whom he utterly detested, had 'on the basis of a general decree of the Führer ordered the action as it were in his name'. Military leaders, equally ready to pin the blame on 'that swine Goebbels', heard from Hitler that the 'action' had taken place without his knowledge and that one of his Gauleiter had run out of control.

Was Hitler genuinely taken aback by the scale of the 'action', for which he had himself given the green light that very evening? The agitated discussion with Goebbels in the Old Town Hall, like many other instances of blanket verbal authorization given in the unstructured and non-formalized style of reaching decisions in the Third Reich, probably left precise intentions open to interpretation. And certainly, in the course of the night, the welter of criticism from Göring, Himmler, and other leading Nazis made it evident that the 'action' had got out of hand, become counter-productive, and had to be stopped – mainly on account of the material damage it had caused.

But when he consented to Goebbels's suggestion to 'let the demonstrations continue', Hitler knew full well from the accounts from Hessen what the 'demonstrations' amounted to. It took no imagination at all to foresee what would happen if active encouragement were given for a free-for-all against the Jews throughout the Reich. If Hitler had not intended the 'demonstrations' he had approved to take such a course, what, exactly, had he intended? Even on the way to the Old Town Hall, it seems, he had rejected tough police action against anti-Jewish vandals in Munich. The traditional Stoßtrupp Hitler, bearing his own name, had been unleashed on Jewish property in Munich as soon as Goebbels had finished speaking. One of his closest underlings, Julius Schaub, had been in the thick of things with Goebbels, behaving like the Stoßtrupp fighter of old. During the days that followed, Hitler took care to remain equivocal. He did not praise Goebbels, or what had happened. But nor did he openly, even to his close circle, let alone in public, condemn him outright or categorically dissociate himself from the unpopular Propaganda Minister. Goebbels had the feeling that his own policy against the Jews met with Hitler's full approval.

None of this has the ring of actions being taken against Hitler's will, or in opposition to his intentions. Rather, it seems to point, as Speer presumed, to Hitler's embarrassment when it became clear to him that the action he had approved was meeting with little but condemnation even in the highest circles of the regime. If Goebbels himself could feign anger at the burning of synagogues whose destruction he had himself directly incited, and even ordered, Hitler was certainly capable of such cynicism. What anger Hitler harboured was purely at an 'action' that threatened to engulf him in the unpopularity he had failed to predict. Disbelieving that the Führer could have been responsible, his subordinate leaders were all happy to be deceived. They preferred the easier target of Goebbels, who had played the more visible role. From that night on, it was as if Hitler wanted to draw a veil over the whole business. At his speech in Munich to press representatives on the following evening, 10 November, he made not the slightest mention of the onslaught against the Jews. Even in his 'inner circle', he never referred to 'Reichskristallnacht' during the rest of his days. But although he had publicly distanced himself from what had taken place, Hitler had in fact favoured the most extreme steps at every juncture.

The signs are that 'Crystal Night' had a profound impact upon Hitler. For at least two decades, probably longer, he had harboured feelings which fused fear and loathing into a pathological view of Jews as the incarnation of evil threatening German survival. Alongside the pragmatic reasons why Hitler agreed with Goebbels that the time was opportune to unleash the fury of the Nazi Movement against Jews ran the deeply embedded ideological urge to destroy what he saw as Germany's most implacable enemy, responsible in his mind for the war and its most tragic and damaging consequence for the Reich, the November Revolution. This demonization of the Jew and fear of the 'Jewish world conspiracy' was part of a world-view that saw the random and despairing act of Herschel Grynszpan as part of a plot to destroy the mighty German Reich. Hitler had by that time spent months at the epicentre of an international crisis that had brought Europe to the very brink of a new war. In the context of continuing crisis in foreign policy, with the prospect of international conflict never far away, 'Crystal Night' seems to have reinvoked – certainly to have re-emphasized – the presumed links, present in his warped outlook since 1918–19 and fully expounded in *Mein Kampf*, between the power of the Jews and war.

He had commented in the last chapter of *Mein Kampf* that 'the sacrifice of millions at the front' would not have been necessary if 'twelve or fifteen thousand of these Hebrew corrupters of the people had been held under poison gas'. Such rhetoric, appalling though the sentiments were, was not an indication that Hitler already had the 'Final Solution' in mind. But the implicit genocidal link between war and the killing of Jews was there. Göring's remarks at the end of the meeting on 12 November had been an ominous pointer in the same direction: 'If the German Reich comes into foreign-political conflict in the foreseeable future, it can be taken for granted that we in Germany will think in the first instance of bringing about a great showdown with the Jews.'

With war approaching again, the question of the threat of the Jews in a future conflict was evidently present in Hitler's mind. The idea of using the Jews as hostages, part of Hitler's mentality, but also advanced in the SS's organ *Das Schwarze Korps* in October and November 1938, is testimony to the linkage between war and idea of a 'world conspiracy'. 'The Jews living in Germany and Italy are the hostages which fate has placed in our hand so that we can defend ourselves effectively against the attacks of world Jewry,' commented *Das Schwarze Korps* on 27 October 1938, under the headline 'Eye for an Eye, Tooth for a Tooth'. 'Those Jews in Germany are a part of world Jewry,' the same newspaper threatened on 3 November, still days before the nationwide pogrom was unleashed. 'They are also responsible for whatever world Jewry undertakes against Germany, and – they are liable for the damages which world Jewry inflicts and will inflict on us.' The Jews were to be treated as members of a warring power and interned to prevent their engagement for the interests of world Jewry. Hitler had up to this date never attempted to deploy the 'hostage' tactic as a weapon of his foreign policy. Perhaps promptings from the SS leadership now reawakened 'hostage' notions in his mind. Whether or not this was the case, the potential deployment of German Jews as pawns to blackmail the western powers into accepting further German expansion was possibly the reason why, when stating that it was his 'unshakeable will' to solve 'the Jewish problem' in the near future, and at a time when official policy was to press for emigration with all means possible, he showed no interest in the plans advanced by South African Defence and Economics Minister Oswald Pirow, whom he met at the Berghof on 24 November, for international cooperation in the emigration of German Jews. The same motive was probably also behind the horrific threat he made to the Czechoslovakian Foreign Minister Franzíšek Chvalkovský on 21 January 1939. 'The Jews here will be annihilated,' he declared. 'The Jews had not brought about 9 November 1918 for nothing. This day will be avenged.'

Again, rhetoric should not be mistaken for a plan or programme. Hitler was scarcely likely to have revealed plans to exterminate the Jews which, when they did eventually emerge in 1941, were accorded top secrecy, in a comment to a foreign diplomat. Moreover, 'annihilation' (*Vernichtung*) was one of Hitler's favourite words. He tended to reach for it when trying to impress his threats upon his audience, large or small. He would speak more than once the following summer, for instance, of his intention to 'annihilate' the Poles. Horrific though their treatment was after 1939, no genocidal programme followed.

But the language, even so, was not meaningless. The germ of a possible genocidal outcome, however vaguely conceived, was taking shape. Destruction and annihilation, not just emigration, of the Jews was in the air. Already on 24 November *Das Schwarze Korps,* portraying the Jews as sinking ever more to the status of pauperized parasites and criminals, had concluded: 'In the stage of such a development we would therefore be faced with the hard necessity of eradicating the Jewish underworld just as we are accustomed in our ordered state to eradicate criminals: with fire and sword! The result would be the actual and final end of Jewry in Germany, its complete annihilation.' This was not a preview of Auschwitz and Treblinka. But without such a mentality, Auschwitz and Treblinka would not have been possible.

In his speech to the Reichstag on 30 January 1939, the sixth anniversary of his takeover of power, Hitler revealed publicly his implicitly genocidal association of the destruction of the Jews with the advent of another war. As always, he had an eye on the propaganda impact. But his words were more than propaganda. They gave an insight into the pathology of his mind, into the genocidal intent that was beginning to take hold. He had no idea how the war would bring about the destruction of the Jews. But, somehow, he was certain that this would indeed be the outcome of a new conflagration. 'I have very often in my lifetime been a prophet,' he declared, 'and was mostly derided. In the time of my struggle for power it was in the first instance the Jewish people who received only with laughter my prophecies that I would some time take over the leadership of the state and of the entire people in Germany and then, among other things, also bring the Jewish problem to its solution. I believe that this once hollow laughter of Jewry in Germany has meanwhile already stuck in the throat. I want today to be a prophet again: if international finance Jewry inside and outside Europe should succeed in plunging the nations once more into a world war, the result will be not the bolshevization of the earth and thereby the victory of Jewry, but the annihilation of the Jewish race in Europe!' It was a 'prophecy' that Hitler would return to on numerous occasions in the years 1941 and 1942, when the annihilation of the Jews was no longer terrible rhetoric, but terrible reality.

16

Going for Broke

I

After Munich things started to move fast. With the dismembered state of Czechoslovakia now friendless and, with its border fortifications lost, exposed, and at Germany's mercy, the completion of the plans made in 1938 for its liquidation was only a matter of time. As we saw, that had been Hitler's view even before he acceded to the Munich Agreement.

Beyond the rump of Czechoslovakia, German attention was immediately turned on Poland. There was no plan at this stage for invasion and conquest. The aim – soon proving illusory – was to bind Poland to Germany against Russia (thereby also blocking any possibility of an alliance with the French). At the same time, the intention was to reach agreement over Danzig and the Corridor (the land which Germany had been forced to cede to Poland in the Versailles Treaty of 1919, giving the Poles access to the sea but leaving East Prussia detached from the remainder of the Reich). Already by late October, Ribbentrop was proposing to settle all differences between Germany and Poland by an agreement for the return of Danzig together with railway and road passage through the Corridor – not in itself a novel idea – in return for a free port for Poland in the Danzig area and an extension of the non-aggression treaty to twenty-five years with a joint guarantee of frontiers.

The proposal met with a predictably stony response from the Polish government. The obduracy of the Poles, especially over Danzig, rapidly brought the first signs of Hitler's own impatience, and an early indication of preparations to take Danzig by force. Hitler was nevertheless at this point more interested in a negotiated settlement with the Poles. Misleadingly informed by Ribbentrop of Polish readiness in principle to

62. British Royalty at the Berghof. Hitler meets the Duke and Duchess of Windsor on 22 October 1937, during the visit to Germany of the ex-King Edward VIII and his wife, the former Mrs Wallis Simpson.

63. Field-Marshal Werner von Blomberg in 1937. He was to be dismissed from office as War Minister the following January on account of a scandal concerning his wife.

64. Colonel-General Werner Freiherr von Fritsch, Commander-in-Chief of the Army until his dismissal, in the wake of the Blomberg scandal, at the beginning of February 1938 on trumped-up charges of homosexuality.

65. Hitler addresses the exultant masses in Vienna's Heldenplatz on 15 March 1938, following the Anschluß.

66. (*facing page, above*) The Axis: flanked by Mussolini and King Victor-Emmanuel III, Hitler views a parade of troops in Rome during his visit to Italy in May 1938.

67. (*facing page, below*) Hitler is cheered by crowds of admirers in Florence.

68. Part of the exhibition 'The Eternal Jew', which opened in Munich on 8 November 1937 and ran until 31 January 1938, purporting to show the 'typical external features' of Jews and to demonstrate their supposedly Asiatic characteristics. The exhibition drew 412,300 visitors in all – over 5,000 per day. It helped to promote the sharp growth of antisemitic violence in Munich and elsewhere in Germany during 1938.

69. (*below*) 'Jews in Berlin', from the exhibition 'The Eternal Jew', which opened in the Reich capital on 12 November 1938. This was two days after Goebbels had unleashed a nation-wide orgy of violence in which Jewish property was destroyed throughout Germany, leading to mass arrests of Jews and their exclusion from business and commerce.

70. (*left*) The synagogue in Fasanenstraße, Berlin, burns after Nazi stormstroopers set it on fire during the pogrom of 9–10 November 1938.

71. (*right*) The Jewish Community building in Kassel on the morning after the pogrom. Beds, papers, and furniture, thrown out by the Nazi perpetrators, lie on the street. Onlookers and police watch as two people attempt to clear up.

72. Passers-by – some smiling, some looking in apparent bewilderment – outside a demolished and looted Jewish shop in Berlin. The amount of glass smashed by Nazi mobs gave rise to the sarcastic appellation 'Reichskristallnacht'.

73. (*left*) A model family? Reich Propaganda Minister Joseph Goebbels, his wife Magda, and their children Helga, Hilde, and baby Helmut, posing for the camera in 1936.

74. (*below*) Goebbels, broadcasting to the Germans on the eve of Hitler's fiftieth birthday, 20 April 1939. The Propaganda Minister's marriage had been under severe strain during the previous months on account of his affair with the Czech actress Lida Baarova, but for prestige reasons Hitler had insisted that Goebbels and his wife did not separate.

75. An unusual photograph, taken about 1938, of Eva Braun, Hitler's companion since 1932 – a relationship kept secret from the German public until 1945.

76. (*top*) With Hitler looking on, General Wilhelm Keitel, chief of the High Command of the Wehrmacht, greets the British Prime Minister, Neville Chamberlain, at the Berghof on 15 September 1938, during the Sudeten crisis.

77. German troops crossing the Charles Bridge in Prague in March 1939, a few days after Hitler had forced the Czech government to agree to the imposition of a German Protectorate over the country.

78. (*top*) Hitler's imposing 'study' in the Reich Chancellery, used more to impress visitors than for work.

79. Pomp and Circumstance: Hermann Göring addresses Hitler during a ceremonial occasion – probably on Hitler's birthday, 20 April 1939 – in the New Reich Chancellery, designed by Albert Speer and completed in early 1939.

80. (*top*) 'The Führer's birthday': Hitler is amused, on his forty-ninth birthday, 20 April 1938, when Ferdinand Porsche presents him with a model of the Volkswagen, pointing out that the engine is in the boot. None of the 336,000 Germans who ordered and paid for a car partly or in full ever took delivery of a Volkswagen. The vehicles were produced during the war exclusively for military purposes.

81. (*centre*) 'The Führer's birthday': Heinrich Himmler, head of the SS, gives Hitler his present – a valuable equestrian portrait of Frederick the Great by Adolf von Menzel – on the Führer's fiftieth birthday, 20 April 1939, watched by Sepp Dietrich (*centre*), commander of the SS-Leibstandarte Adolf Hitler, and (*extreme right*) Karl Wolff, chief of Himmler's personal staff.

82. (*bottom*) Hitler, in evening dress, walks with Winifred Wagner past cheering crowds during the last Bayreuth Festival before the war, in July 1939.

83. Molotov signs the Non-Aggression Pact of the Soviet Union with Germany in the early hours of 24 August 1939, watched by (*left to right*) Red Army Chief of Staff Marshal Boris S. Shaposhnikov, adjutant to Ribbentrop Richard Schulze, a smug-looking German Foreign Minister Joachim von Ribbentrop, and Joseph Stalin.

84. Hitler in his temporary field-headquarters during the Polish campaign, together with his Wehrmacht adjutants, (*from left to right*) Captain Nicolaus von Below (Luftwaffe), Captain Gerhard Engel (Army), and Colonel Rudolf Schmundt (chief adjutant). Martin Bormann is on Hitler's left.

85. (*top*) Hitler reviewing troops in Warsaw on 5 October 1939 at the conclusion
of the victory over Poland.

86. Hitler during his address to the Party's 'Old Guard' in the Bürgerbräukeller in
Munich on 8 November 1939. Only minutes after he had left the building, a time-bomb
placed by a Swabian joiner, Georg Elser, exploded close to where he had been speaking,
killing eight and injuring more than sixty of those present.

87. (*left*) Arthur Greiser, the fanatical Reich Governor and Gauleiter of Reichsgau Wartheland, the annexed part of western Poland, at the celebration for the 'liberation' of the area on 2 October 1939.

88. (*right*) Albert Forster, Gauleiter of Danzig-West Prussia, a rival to Greiser in the brutal attempt to 'germanize' the annexed parts of Poland.

89. (*left and right*) An ecstatic Hitler at his headquarters 'Wolfsschlucht' (Wolf's Gorge), near Brûly-de-Pesche in Belgium, on hearing the news on 17 June 1940 that France had requested an armistice. Walther Hewel, Ribbentrop's liaison at Führer Headquarters, is on Hitler's right.

90. (*top*) Hitler visiting emplacements on the Maginot Line in Alsace, during his short stay at his headquarters 'Tannenberg', near Freudenstadt in the Black Forest, on 30 June 1940.

91. Hitler in Freudenstadt on 5 July 1940, the last day he was based at 'Tannenberg'.

92. (*overleaf*) An immense crowd gathered on Wilhelmplatz in Berlin on 6 July 1940, wildly cheering the conquering hero on Hitler's return from the triumph over France. Göring is beside Hitler on the balcony of the Reich Chancellery.

move to a new settlement of the Danzig question and the Corridor, he emphasized German-Polish friendship during his speech to the Reichstag on 30 January 1939. Some army leaders, a few days earlier, had been more belligerent. In contrast to their overriding fears of western intervention during the Sudeten crisis, a number of generals now argued that Britain and France would remain inactive – a direct reflection of the weakness of the western powers fully revealed at Munich – and that negotiations with the Poles should be abandoned in favour of military measures. A war against Poland, they claimed, would be popular among the troops and among the German people.

Ribbentrop, aided by Göring, played – for strategic reasons – the moderate on this occasion. For him, the main enemy was not Poland, but Britain. He countered that, through a premature attack in 1939 on Poland and Russia, Germany would become isolated, would forfeit its armaments advantage, and would most likely be forced by western strength to give up any territorial gains made. Instead, Germany needed to act together with Italy and Japan, retaining Polish neutrality until France had been dealt with and Britain at least isolated and denied all power on the Continent, if not militarily defeated. War by Germany and Italy to defeat France and leave Britain isolated had been the basis of the military directives laid down by Keitel, in line with Hitler's instructions, in November 1938. The priority which Hitler accorded in January 1939 to the navy's Z-Plan, for building a big battle-fleet directed squarely at British naval power, indicates that he was looking at this stage to an eventual showdown with the western powers as the prime military objective. The construction at the same time of an 'East Wall' – limited defensive fortifications for the event of possible conflict with Poland over Danzig – is a further pointer in that direction. Russia, and the eradication of Bolshevism, could wait. But neither Hitler nor anyone in his entourage expected war with Britain and France to come about in the way that it would do that autumn.

In the late autumn and winter of 1938–9, differing views about foreign-policy aims and methods existed within the German leadership. Long-term military preparations were directed towards eventual confrontation with the West, but it was well recognized that the armed forces were years away from being ready for any conflict with Britain and France. As in 1938, military leaders' prime fear was confrontation being forced on Germany too soon through impetuous actions and an over-risky foreign policy. Göring and Ribbentrop were advocating diametrically opposed policies towards Britain. Göring's hopes still rested on an expansive policy in south-eastern Europe, backed for the foreseeable future by an understanding with Britain. Ribbentrop, by now violently anti-British, was pinning his hopes on smoothing the problems on Germany's eastern front and tightening the alliance with Italy and Japan to prepare the ground for a move against Britain as soon as was feasible. But at this stage, Göring's star was temporarily on the wane and Ribbentrop's usually clumsy diplomacy was meeting in most instances with little success. Hitler's thoughts, whether or not influenced by Ribbentrop's reasoning, were broadly consonant with those of his Foreign Minister. The coming showdown with Bolshevism, though certainly not displaced in Hitler's own mind as the decisive struggle to be faced at some point in the future, had by now moved again into the shadows. But he was, as usual, content to keep his options open and await developments.

The one certainty was that developments *would* occur, thus providing the opportunity for German expansion. For there was no agency of power or influence in the Third Reich advocating drawing a line under the territorial gains already made. All power-groups were looking to further expansion – with or without war.

Military, strategic, and power-political arguments for expansion were underpinned by economic considerations. By late 1938, the pressures of the forced rearmament programme were making themselves acutely felt. The policy of 'rearm, whatever the cost' was now plainly showing itself to be sustainable only in the short term. Further expansion was necessary if the tensions built into the overheated armaments-driven economy were not to reach explosion point. By 1938–9, it was absolutely evident that further expansion could not be postponed indefinitely if the economic impasses were to be surmounted.

In early January 1939, the Reichsbank Directorate sent Hitler a submission, supported by eight signatories, demanding financial restraint to avoid the 'threatening danger of inflation'. Hitler's reaction was: 'That is mutiny!' Twelve days later, Schacht was sacked as President of the Reichsbank. But the Cassandra voices were not exaggerating. Nor would the problem go away by sacking Schacht. The insatiable demand for raw materials at the same time that consumer demand in the wake of the armaments boom was rising had left public finances in a desolate state.

Beyond the crisis in public finances, the labour shortage which had been growing rapidly since 1937 was by this time posing a real threat both to agriculture and to industry. The only remedy for the foreseeable future was the use of 'foreign labourers' that war and expansion would bring. The mounting economic problems confirmed for Hitler his diagnosis that Germany's position could never be strengthened without territorial conquest.

II

Hitler's regrets over the Munich Agreement and feeling that a chance had been lost to occupy the whole of Czechoslovakia at one fell swoop had grown rather than diminished during the last months of 1938. His impatience to act had mounted accordingly. He was determined not to be hemmed in by the western powers. He was more than ever convinced that they would not have fought for Czechoslovakia, and that they would and could do nothing to prevent Germany extending its dominance in central and eastern Europe. On the other hand, as he had indicated to Goebbels in October, he was certain that Britain would not concede German hegemony in Europe without a fight at some time. The setback which Munich had been in his eyes confirmed his view that war against the West was coming, probably sooner than he had once envisaged, and that there was no time to lose if Germany were to retain its advantage.

Already on 21 October 1938, only three weeks after the Munich settlement, Hitler had given the Wehrmacht a new directive to prepare for the 'liquidation of remainder of the Czech state'. Why was Hitler so insistent on this? Politically it was not necessary. Indeed, the German leadership cannot fail to have recognized that an invasion of Czechoslovakia, tearing up the Munich Agreement and breaking solemn promises given only such a short time earlier, would inevitably have the most serious international repercussions.

Part of the answer is doubtless to be found in Hitler's own personality and psychology. His Austrian background and dislike of Czechs since his youth was probably one element. Yet after occupation, the persecution of the Czechs was by no means as harsh as that subsequently meted out to the conquered Poles. And, following his victorious entry into Prague, Hitler showed remarkably little interest in the Czechs.

More important, certainly, was the feeling that he had been 'cheated' out of his triumph, his 'unalterable wish' altered by western politicians. 'That fellow Chamberlain has spoiled my entry into Prague,' he was overheard saying on his return to Berlin after the agreement at Munich the previous autumn. And yet, Goebbels's diary entries show that Hitler had decided *before* Munich that he would temporarily concede to the western powers, but gobble up the rest of Czechoslovakia in due course, and that the acquisition of the Sudetenland would make that second stage easier. Though a rationalization of the position Hitler had been manoeuvred into, it indicates the acceptance by that date of a two-stage plan to acquire the whole of Czechoslovakia, and does not highlight vengeance as a motive.

There were other reasons for occupying the rump of Czechoslovakia that went beyond Hitler's personal motivation. Economic considerations were of obvious importance. However pliant the Czechs were prepared to be, the fact remained that even after the transfer of October 1938, which brought major raw material deposits to the Reich, immense resources remained in Czecho-Slovakia (as the country, the meaningful hyphen inserted, was now officially called) and outside direct German control. The vast bulk of the industrial wealth and resources of the country lay in the old Czech heartlands of Bohemia and Moravia, not in the largely agricultural Slovakia. An estimated four-fifths of engineering, machine-tool construction, and electrical industries remained in the hands of the Czechs. Textiles, chemicals, and the glass industry were other significant industries that beckoned the Germans. Not least, the Skoda works produced locomotives and machinery as well as arms. Czecho-Slovakia also possessed large quantities of gold and foreign currency that could certainly help relieve some of the shortages of the Four-Year Plan. And a vast amount of equipment could be taken over and redeployed to the advantage of the German army. The Czech arsenal was easily the greatest among the smaller countries of central Europe. The Czech machine-guns, field-guns, and anti-aircraft guns were thought to be better than the German equivalents. They would all be taken over by the Reich, as well as the heavy guns built at the Skoda factories. It was subsequently estimated that enough arms had fallen into Hitler's possession to equip a further twenty divisions.

But of even greater importance than direct economic gain and exploitation was the military-strategic position of what remained of Czecho-Slovakia. As long as the Czechs retained some autonomy, and possession of extensive military equipment and industrial resources, potential difficulties from that quarter could not be ruled out in the event of German involvement in hostilities. More important still: possession of the rectangular, mountain-rimmed territories of Bohemia and Moravia on the south-eastern edge of the Reich offered a recognizable platform for further eastward expansion and military domination. The road to the Balkans was now open. Germany's position against Poland was strengthened. And in the event of conflict in the west, the defences in the east were consolidated.

As late as December 1938, there was no indication that Hitler was preparing an imminent strike against the Czechs. There were hints, however, that the next moves in foreign policy would not be long delayed. Hitler told Ernst Neumann, the German leader in Memel (a seaport on the Baltic with a largely German population, which had been removed from Germany by the Versailles Treaty), on 17 December that annexation of Memelland would take place in the following March or April, and that he wanted no crisis in the area before then. On 13 February, Hitler let it be known to a few associates that he intended to take action against the Czechs in mid-March. German propaganda was adjusted accordingly. The French had already gleaned intelligence in early February that German action against Prague would take place in about six weeks.

Hitler's meeting at the Berghof with the Polish Foreign Minister and strong man in the government, Józef Beck, on 5 January had proved, from the German point of view, disappointing. Hitler had tried to appear accommodating in laying down the need for Danzig to return to Germany, and for access routes across the Corridor to East Prussia. Beck implied that public opinion in Poland would prevent any concessions on Danzig. When Ribbentrop returned empty-handed from his visit to Warsaw on 26 January, indicating that the Poles were not to be moved, Hitler's approach to Poland changed markedly.

From friendly overtures, the policy moved to pressure. Poland was to be excluded from any share in the spoils from the destruction of the Czech state. And turning Slovakia into a German puppet-state would intensify the threat to Poland's southern border. Once the demolition of

Czecho-Slovakia had taken place, therefore, the Germans hoped and expected the Poles to prove more cooperative. The failure of negotiations with the Poles had probably accelerated the decision to destroy the Czech state.

Around this time, according to Goebbels, Hitler spoke practically of nothing else but foreign policy. 'He's always pondering new plans,' Goebbels noted. 'A Napoleonic nature!' The Propaganda Minister had already guessed what was in store when Hitler told him at the end of January he was going 'to the mountain' – to the Obersalzberg – to think about his next steps in foreign policy. 'Perhaps Czechia is up for it again. The problem is after all only half solved,' he wrote.

III

By the beginning of March, in the light of mounting Slovakian nationalist clamour (abetted by Germany) for full independence from Prague, the break-up of what was left of the state of Czecho-Slovakia looked to close observers of the scene to be a matter of time. When the Prague government deposed the Slovakian cabinet, sent police in to occupy government offices in Bratislava, and placed the former Prime Minister, Father Jozef Tiso, under house arrest, Hitler spotted his moment. On 10 March, he told Goebbels, Ribbentrop, and Keitel that he had decided to march in, smash the rump Czech state, and occupy Prague. The invasion was to take place five days later. 'Our borders must stretch to the Carpathians,' noted Goebbels. 'The Führer shouts for joy. This game is dead certain.'

On 12 March orders were given to the army and Luftwaffe to be ready to enter Czecho-Slovakia at 6 a.m. on the 15th, but before then not to approach within ten kilometres of the border. German mobilization was by that stage so obvious that it seemed impossible that the Czechs were unaware of what was happening. The propaganda campaign against the Czechs had meanwhile been sharply stepped up. That evening, Tiso had been visited by German officials and invited to Berlin. The next day he met Hitler. He was told the historic hour of the Slovaks had arrived. If they did nothing, they would be swallowed up by Hungary. Tiso got the message. By the following noon, 14 March, back in Bratislava, he had the Slovak Assembly proclaim independence. The desired request for 'protection' was, however, only forthcoming a day later, after German warships on the Danube had trained their sights on the Slovakian government offices.

Goebbels listened again to Hitler unfolding his plans. The entire 'action' would be over within eight days. The Germans would already be in Prague within a day, their planes within two hours. No bloodshed was expected. 'Then the Führer wants to fit in a lengthy period of political calm,' wrote Goebbels, adding that he did not believe it, however enticing the prospect. A period of calm, he thought, was necessary. 'Gradually, the nerves aren't coping.'

On the morning of 14 March, the anticipated request came from Prague, seeking an audience of the Czech State President Dr Emil Hácha with Hitler. Hácha, a small, shy, somewhat unworldly, and also rather sickly man, in office since the previous November, arrived in Berlin during the course of the evening, after a five-hour train journey. Hitler kept him nervously waiting until midnight to increase the pressure upon him – 'the old tested methods of political tactics', as Goebbels put it. It was around 1 a.m. when, his face red from nervousness and anxiety, the Czech President was eventually ushered into the intimidating surroundings of Hitler's grandiose 'study' in the New Reich Chancellery. A sizeable gathering, including Ribbentrop, the head of his personal staff Walther Hewel, Keitel, Weizsäcker, State Secretary Otto Meissner, Press Chief Otto Dietrich, and interpreter Paul Schmidt, were present. Göring, summoned back from holiday, was also there.

Hitler was at his most intimidating. He launched into a violent tirade against the Czechs and the 'spirit of Beneš' which, he claimed, still lived on. It was necessary in order to safeguard the Reich, he continued, to impose a protectorate over the remainder of Czecho-Slovakia. Hácha and Chvalkovský, the Czech Foreign Minister, who had accompanied the President to Berlin, sat stony-faced and motionless. The entry of German troops was 'irreversible', ranted Hitler. Keitel would confirm that they were already marching towards the Czech border, and would cross it at 6 a.m. Hácha said he wanted no bloodshed, and asked Hitler to halt the military build-up. Hitler refused: it was impossible; the troops were already mobilized. Göring intervened to add that his Luftwaffe would be over Prague by dawn, and it was in Hácha's hands whether bombs fell on the beautiful city. At the threat, the Czech President fainted. He was revived by an injection from Hitler's personal physician, Dr Morell.

Meanwhile, Prague could not be reached by telephone. Eventually, contact was made. The browbeaten President went immediately to the telephone and, on a crackly line, passed on his orders that Czech troops were not to open fire on the invading Germans. Just before 4 a.m., Hácha signed the declaration, placing the fate of his people in the hands of the Leader of the German Reich.

Overjoyed, Hitler went in to see his two secretaries, Christa Schroeder and Gerda Daranowski, who had been on duty that night. 'So, children,' he burst out, pointing to his cheeks, 'each of you give me a kiss there and there . . . This is the happiest day of my life. What has been striven for in vain for centuries, I have been fortunate enough to bring about. I have achieved the union of Czechia with the Reich. Hácha has signed the agreement. I will go down as the greatest German in history.'

Two hours after Hácha had signed, the German army crossed the Czech borders and marched, on schedule, on Prague. By 9.00 a.m. the forward units entered the Czech capital, making slow progress on ice-bound roads, through mist and snow, the wintry weather providing an appropriate backcloth to the end of central Europe's last, betrayed, democracy. The Czech troops, as ordered, remained in their barracks and handed over their weapons.

Hitler left Berlin at midday, travelling in his special train as far as Leipa, some sixty miles north of Prague, where he arrived during the afternoon. A fleet of Mercedes was waiting to take him and his entourage the remainder of the journey to Prague. It was snowing heavily, but he stood for much of the way, his arm outstretched to salute the unending columns of German soldiers they overtook. Unlike his triumphal entries into Austria and the Sudetenland, only a thin smattering of the population watched sullenly and helplessly from the side of the road. A few dared to greet with clenched fists as Hitler's car passed by. But the streets were almost deserted by the time he arrived in Prague in the early evening and drove up to the Hradschin Castle, the ancient residence of the Kings of Bohemia. When the people of Prague awoke next morning, they saw Hitler's standard fluttering on the castle. Twenty-four hours later he was gone. For the Czechs, six long years of subjugation had begun.

Hitler returned to Berlin, via Vienna, on 19 March, to the inevitable, and by now customary, triumphator's reception. Despite the freezing temperatures, huge numbers turned out to welcome the hero. When Hitler descended from his train at the Görlitzer Bahnhof, Göring, tears in his eyes, greeted him with an address embarrassing even by the prevailing standards of sycophancy. Thousands cheered wildly as Hitler was driven to the Reich Chancellery. The experienced hand of Dr Goebbels had organized another massive spectacular. Searchlights formed a 'tunnel of light' along Unter den Linden. A brilliant display of fireworks followed. Hitler then appeared on the balcony of the Reich Chancellery, waving to the ecstatic crowd of his adoring subjects below.

The real response among the German people to the rape of Czecho-Slovakia was, however, more mixed – in any event less euphoric – than that of the cheering multitudes, many of them galvanized by party activists, in Berlin. This time there had been no 'home-coming' of ethnic Germans into the Reich. The vague notion that Bohemia and Moravia had belonged to the 'German living space' for a thousand years left most people cold – certainly most north Germans who had traditionally had little or no connection with the Czech lands. For many, as one report from a Nazi District Leader put it, whatever the joy in the Führer's 'great deeds' and the trust placed in him, 'the needs and cares of daily life are so great that the mood is very quickly gloomy again'. There was a good deal of indifference, scepticism, and criticism, together with worries that war was a big step closer. 'Was that necessary?' many people asked. They remembered Hitler's precise words following the Munich Agreement, that the Sudetenland had been his 'last territorial demand'.

Hitler had been contemptuous of the western powers before the taking of Prague. He correctly judged that once more they would protest, but do nothing. However, everything points to the conclusion that he miscalculated the response of Britain and France *after* the invasion of Czecho-Slovakia. The initial reaction in London was one of shock and dismay at the cynical demolition of the Munich Agreement, despite the warnings the British government had received. Appeasement policy lay shattered in the ruins of the Czecho-Slovakian state. Hitler had broken his promise that he had no further territorial demands to make. And the conquest of Czecho-Slovakia had destroyed the fiction that Hitler's policies were aimed at the uniting of German peoples in a single state. Hitler, it was now abundantly clear – a recognition at last and very late in the day – could not be trusted. He would stop at nothing.

Chamberlain's speech in Birmingham on 17 March hinted at a new policy. 'Is this the last attack upon a small State, or is it to be followed by others?' he asked. 'Is this, in fact, a step in the direction of an attempt to dominate the world by force?' British public opinion was in no doubt. Hitler had united a country deeply divided over Munich. On all sides people were saying that war with Germany was both inevitable and necessary. Recruitment for the armed forces increased almost overnight. It was now clear both to the man in the street and to the government: Hitler had to be tackled.

The following day, 18 March, amid rumours circulating that Germany was threatening Romania, the British cabinet endorsed the Prime Minister's recommendation of a fundamental change in policy. No reliance could any longer be placed on the assurances of the Nazi leaders, Chamberlain stated. The old policy of trying to come to terms with the dictatorships on the assumption that they had limited aims was no longer possible. The policy had shifted from trying to appease Hitler to attempting to deter him. In any new aggression, Germany would be faced at the outset with the choice of pulling back or going to war. The Prime Minister had little doubt as to where trouble might next flare up. 'He thought that Poland was very likely the key to the situation . . . The time had now come for those who were threatened by German aggression (whether immediately or ultimately) to get together. We should enquire how far Poland was prepared to go along these lines.' The British Guarantee to Poland and the genesis of the summer crisis which, this time, would end in war were foreshadowed in Chamberlain's remarks.

Similar reactions were registered in Paris. Daladier let Chamberlain know that the French would speed up rearmament and resist any further aggression. The Americans were told that Daladier was determined to go to war should the Germans act against Danzig or Poland. Even strong advocates of appeasement were now saying enough was enough: there would not be another Munich.

IV

Before the Polish crisis unfolded, Hitler had one other triumph to register – though compared with what had gone before, it was a minor one. The incorporation of Memelland in the German Reich was now to prove the last annexation without bloodshed. After its removal from Germany in 1919, the Memel district, with a mainly German population but a sizeable Lithuanian minority, had been placed under French adminis-tration. The Lithuanians had marched in, forcing the withdrawal of the French occupying force there in January 1923. The following year, under international agreement, the Memel had gained a level of independence, but remained in effect a German enclave under Lithuanian tutelage.

Politically, the return of the territory to Germany was of no great significance. Even symbolically, it was of relatively little importance. Few ordinary Germans took more than a passing interest in the incorpor-ation of such a remote fleck of territory into the Reich. But the acquisi-tion of a port on the Baltic, with the possibility that Lithuania, too, might be turned into a German satellite, had strategic relevance. Alongside the subordination to German influence of Slovakia on the southern borders of Poland, it gave a further edge to German pressure on the Poles.

On 20 March, Ribbentrop subjected the Lithuanian Foreign Minister, Joseph Urbšys, to the usual bullying tactics. Kowno would be bombed, he threatened, if Germany's demand for the immediate return of the Memel were not met. Urbšys returned the next day, 21 March, to Kowno. The Lithuanians were in no mood for a fight. A Lithuanian delegation was sent to Berlin to arrange the details. 'If you apply a bit of pressure, things happen,' noted Goebbels, with satisfaction.

Hitler left Berlin the following afternoon, 22 March, for Swinemünde, where, along with Raeder, he boarded the cruiser *Deutschland*. Late that evening, Ribbentrop and Urbšys agreed terms for the formal transfer of the Memel district to Germany. Hitler's decree was signed the next morning, 23 March. He was back in Berlin by noon next day. This time, he dispensed with the hero's return. Triumphal entries to Berlin could not be allowed to become so frequent that they were routine.

Wasting no time, Ribbentrop had pushed Ambassador Lipski on 21 March to arrange a visit to Berlin by Beck. He indicated that Hitler was losing patience, and that the German press was straining at the leash to be turned loose on the Poles. He repeated the requests about Danzig and the Corridor. In return, Poland might be tempted by the exploitation of Slovakia and the Ukraine.

But the Poles were not prepared to act according to the script. Beck, noting Chamberlain's Birmingham speech, secretly put out feelers to London for a bilateral agreement with Britain. Meanwhile, the Poles mobilized their troops. On 25 March, Hitler still indicated that he did not want to solve the Danzig question by force to avoid driving the Poles into the arms of the British. He had remarked to Goebbels the previous evening that he hoped the Poles would respond to pressure, 'but we must bite into the sour apple and guarantee Poland's borders'.

However, just after noon on 26 March, instead of the desired visit by Beck, Lipski simply presented Ribbentrop with a memorandum representing the Polish Foreign Minister's views. It flatly rejected the German proposals, reminding Ribbentrop for good measure of Hitler's verbal assurance in his speech on 20 February 1938 that Poland's rights and interests would be respected. Ribbentrop lost his temper. Going beyond his mandate from Hitler, he told Lipski that any Polish action against Danzig (of which there was no indication) would be treated as aggression against the Reich. The bullying attempt was lost on Lipski. He replied that any furtherance of German plans directed at the return of Danzig to the Reich meant war with Poland.

By 27 March, meanwhile, Chamberlain, warned that a German strike against Poland might be imminent, was telling the British cabinet he was prepared to offer a unilateral commitment to Poland, aimed at stiffening Polish resolve and deterring Hitler. The policy that had been developing since the march into Prague found its expression in Chamberlain's statement to the House of Commons on 31 March 1939: 'In the event of any action which clearly threatened Polish independence, and which the Polish Government accordingly considered it vital to resist with their national forces, His Majesty's Government would feel themselves bound at once to lend the Polish Government all support in their power.'

This was followed, at the end of Beck's visit to London on 4–6 April, by Chamberlain's announcement to the House of Commons that Britain and Poland had agreed to sign a mutual assistance pact in the event of an attack 'by a European power'.

On hearing of the British Guarantee of 31 March, Hitler fell into a rage. He thumped his fist on the marble-topped table of his study in the Reich Chancellery. 'I'll brew them a devil's potion,' he fumed.

Exactly what he had wanted to avoid had happened. He had expected the pressure on the Poles to work as easily as it had done in the case of the Czechs and the Slovaks. He had presumed the Poles would in due course see sense and yield Danzig and concede the extra-territorial routes through the Corridor. He had taken it for granted that Poland would then become a German satellite – an ally in any later attack on the Soviet Union. He had been determined to keep Poland out of Britain's clutches.

All of this was now upturned. Danzig would have to be taken by force. He had been thwarted by the British and spurned by the Poles. He would teach them a lesson.

Or so he thought. In reality, Hitler's over-confidence, impatience, and misreading of the impact of German aggression against Czecho-Slovakia had produced a fateful miscalculation.

At the end of March Hitler had indicated to Brauchitsch, head of the army, that he would use force against Poland if diplomacy failed. Immediately, the branches of the armed forces began preparing drafts of their own operational plans. These were presented to Hitler in the huge 'Führer type' that he could read without glasses. He added a preamble on political aims. By 3 April the directive for 'Case White' (*Fall Weiß*) was ready. It was issued eight days later. Its first section, written by Hitler himself, began: 'German relations with Poland continue to be based on the principles of avoiding any disturbances. Should Poland, however, change her policy towards Germany, which so far has been based on the same principles as our own, and adopt a threatening attitude towards Germany, a final settlement might become necessary in spite of the Treaty in force with Poland. The aim then will be to destroy Polish military strength, and create in the East a situation which satisfies the requirements of national defence. The Free State of Danzig will be proclaimed a part of the Reich territory by the outbreak of hostilities at the latest. The political leaders consider it their task in this case to isolate Poland if possible, that is to say, to limit the war to Poland only.' The Wehrmacht had to be ready to carry out 'Case White' at any time after 1 September 1939.

Army commanders had been divided over the merits of attacking Czecho-Slovakia only a few months earlier. Now, there was no sign of hesitation. The aims of the coming campaign to destroy Poland were outlined within a fortnight or so by Chief of the General Staff Halder to generals and General Staff officers. Oppositional hopes of staging a coup against Hitler the previous autumn, as the Sudeten crisis was reaching its denouement, had centred upon Halder. At the time, he had indeed been prepared to see Hitler assassinated. It was the same Halder who now evidently relished the prospect of easy and rapid victory over the Poles and envisaged subsequent conflict with the Soviet Union or the western powers. Halder told senior officers that 'thanks to the outstanding, I might say, instinctively sure policy of the Führer', the military situation in central Europe had changed fundamentally. As a consequence, the position of Poland had also significantly altered. Halder said he was certain he was speaking for many in his audience in commenting that with the ending of 'friendly relations' with Poland 'a stone has fallen from the heart'. Poland was now to be ranked among Germany's enemies. The rest of Halder's address dealt with the need to destroy Poland 'in record speed'. The British guarantee would not prevent this happening. He was contemptuous of the capabilities of the Polish army. It formed 'no serious opponent'. He outlined in some detail the course the German attack would take, acknowledging cooperation with the SS and the occupation of the country by the paramilitary formations of the party. The aim, he repeated, was to ensure 'that Poland as rapidly as possible was not only defeated, but liquidated', whether France and Britain should intervene in the West (which on balance he deemed unlikely) or not. The attack had to be 'crushing'. He concluded by looking beyond the Polish conflict: 'We must be finished with Poland within three weeks, if possible already in a fortnight. Then it will depend on the Russians whether the eastern front becomes Europe's fate or not. In any case, a victorious army, filled with the spirit of gigantic victories attained, will be ready either to confront Bolshevism or . . . to be hurled against the West . . .'

On Poland, there was no divergence between Hitler and his Chief of the General Staff. Both wanted to smash Poland at breakneck speed, preferably in an isolated campaign but, if necessary, even with western intervention (though both thought this more improbable than probable). And both looked beyond Poland to a widening of the conflict, eastwards or westwards, at some point. Hitler could be satisfied. He need expect no problems this time from his army leaders.

The contours for the summer crisis of 1939 had been drawn. It would end not with the desired limited conflict to destroy Poland, but with the major European powers locked in another continental war. This was in the first instance a consequence of Hitler's miscalculation that spring. But, as Halder's address to the generals indicated, it had not been Hitler's miscalculation alone.

V

Following one extraordinary triumph upon another, Hitler's self-belief had by this time been magnified into full-blown megalomania. Even among his private guests at the Berghof, he frequently compared himself with Napoleon, Bismarck, and other great historical figures. The rebuilding programmes that constantly preoccupied him were envisaged as his own lasting monument – a testament of greatness like the buildings of the pharaohs or Caesars. He felt he was walking with destiny. In the summer of 1939, such a mentality would drive Germany towards European war.

Hitler made public the abrupt shift in policy towards Poland and Great Britain in his big Reichstag speech of 28 April 1939. The speech, lasting two hours and twenty minutes, had been occasioned by a message sent by President Roosevelt a fortnight earlier. Prompted by the invasion of Czecho-Slovakia, the President had appealed to Hitler to give an assurance that he would desist from any attack for the next twenty-five years on thirty named countries – mainly European, but also including Iraq, Arabia, Syria, Palestine, Egypt, and Iran. Were such an assurance to be given, the United States, declared Roosevelt, would play its part in working for disarmament and equal access to raw materials on world markets. Hitler was incensed by Roosevelt's telegram. That it had been published in Washington before even being received in Berlin was taken as a slight. Hitler also thought it arrogant in tone. And the naming of the thirty countries allowed Hitler to claim that inquiries had been conducted in each, and that none felt threatened by Germany. Some, such as Syria, however, had been, he alleged, unable to reply, since they were deprived of freedom and under the military control of democratic states, while the Republic of Ireland, he asserted, feared aggression from Britain, not from Germany. Roosevelt's raising of the disarmament issue (out of which Hitler had made such capital a few years earlier) handed him a further propaganda gift. With heavy sarcasm, he tore into Roosevelt, 'answering' his claims in twenty-one points, each cheered to the rafters by the assembled members of the Reichstag, roaring with laughter as he poured scorn on the President.

Many German listeners to the broadcast thought it one of the best speeches he had made. William Shirer, the American journalist in Berlin, was inclined to agree: 'Hitler was a superb actor today,' he wrote. The performance was largely for internal consumption. The outside world – at least those countries that felt they had accommodated Hitler for too long – was less impressed.

Preceding the vaudeville, Hitler had chosen the occasion to denounce the Non-Aggression Pact with Poland and the Naval Agreement with Britain. He blamed the renunciation of the naval pact on Britain's 'encirclement policy'. In reality, he was complying with the interests of the German navy, which felt its construction plans restricted by the agreement and had been pressing for some time for Hitler to denounce it. The intransigence of the Poles over Danzig and the Corridor, their mobilization in March, and the alignment with Britain against Germany were given as reasons for the ending of the Polish pact.

Since the end of March, which had brought the British guarantee for Poland, followed soon afterwards by the announcement that there was to be a British-Polish mutual assistance treaty, Hitler had given up on the Poles. The military directives of early April were recognition of this. The Poles, he acknowledged, were not going to concede to German demands without a fight. So they would have their fight. And they would be smashed. Only the timing and conditions remained to be determined.

At a meeting in his study in the New Reich Chancellery on 23 May, Hitler outlined his thinking on Poland and on wider strategic issues to a small group of top military leaders. He held out the prospect not only of an attack on Poland, but also made clear that the more far-reaching aim was to prepare for an inevitable showdown with Britain. Unlike the meeting on 5 November 1937 that Hoßbach had recorded, there is no indication that the military commanders were caused serious disquiet by what they heard. Hitler made his intentions brutally clear. 'It is not Danzig that is at stake. For us it is a matter of expanding our living space in the East and making food supplies secure and also solving the problem of the Baltic States.' It was necessary, he declared, 'to attack Poland at the first suitable opportunity. We cannot expect a repetition of Czechia. There will be war. Our task is to isolate Poland. Success in isolating her will be decisive.' He reserved to himself, therefore, the timing of any strike. Simultaneous conflict with the West had to be avoided. Should it, however, come to that – Hitler revealed here his priorities – 'then the fight must be primarily against England and France'. The war would be an all-out one: 'We must then burn our boats and it will no longer be a question of right or wrong but of to be or not to be for 80 million people.' A war of ten to fifteen years had to be reckoned with. 'The aim is always to bring England to its knees,' he stated. To the relief of those present, who took it as an indication of when he envisaged the conflict with the West taking place, he stipulated that the rearmament programmes were to be targeted at 1943–4 – the same time-scale he had given in November 1937. But no one doubted that Hitler intended to attack Poland that very year.

VI

Throughout the spring and summer frenzied diplomatic efforts were made to try to isolate Poland and deter the western powers from becoming involved in what was intended as a localized conflict. On 22 May, Italy and Germany had signed the so-called 'Pact of Steel', meant to warn Britain and France off backing Poland. Ribbentrop had duped the Italians into signing the bilateral military pact on the understanding that the Führer wanted peace for five years and expected the Poles to settle peacefully once they realized that support from the West would not be forthcoming.

In the attempt to secure the assistance or benevolent neutrality of a number of smaller European countries and prevent them being drawn into the Anglo-French orbit, the German government had mixed success. In the west, Belgian neutrality – whatever Hitler's plans to ignore it when it suited him – was shored up to keep the Western powers from immediate proximity to Germany's industrial heartlands. Every effort had been made in preceding years to promote trading links with the neutral countries of Scandinavia to sustain, above all, the vital imports of iron ore from Sweden. In the Baltic, Latvia and Estonia agreed non-aggression pacts. In central Europe, diplomatic efforts had more patchy results. Hungary, Yugoslavia, and Turkey were unwilling to align themselves closely with Berlin. But persistent pressure had turned Romania into an economic satellite, sealed by treaty in late March 1939, more or less assuring Germany of crucial access to Romanian oil and wheat in the event of hostilities.

The big question-mark concerned the Soviet Union. The regime's anti-christ it might be. But it held the key to the destruction of Poland.

If the USSR could be prevented from linking hands with the West in the tripartite pact that Britain and France were half-heartedly working towards; better still, if the unthinkable – a pact between the Soviet Union and the Reich itself – could be brought about: then Poland would be totally isolated, at Germany's mercy, the Anglo-French guarantees worthless, and Britain – the main opponent – hugely weakened. Such thoughts began to gestate in the mind of Hitler's Foreign Minister in the spring of 1939. In the weeks that followed, it was Ribbentrop on the German side, rather than a hesitant Hitler, who took the initiative in seeking to explore all hints that the Russians might be interested in a rapprochement – hints that had been forthcoming since March.

Within the Soviet leadership, the entrenched belief that the West wanted to encourage German aggression in the east (that is, against the USSR), the recognition that following Munich collective security was dead, the need to head off any aggressive intent from the Japanese in the east, and above all the desperate need to buy time to secure defences for the onslaught thought certain to come at some time, pushed – if for a considerable time only tentatively – in the same direction.

Stalin's speech to the Communist Party Congress on 10 March, attacking the appeasement policy of the West as encouragement of German aggression against the Soviet Union, and declaring his unwillingness to 'pull the chestnuts out of the fire' for the benefit of capitalist powers, had been taken by Ribbentrop as a hint that an opportunity might be opening up. By mid-April the Soviet Ambassador was remarking to Weizsäcker that ideological differences should not hinder better relations. Then, Gustav Hilger, a long-serving diplomat in the German Embassy in Moscow, was brought to the Berghof to explain that the dismissal, on 3 May, of the Soviet Foreign Minister Maxim Litvinov (who had been associated with retaining close ties with the West, partly through a spell as Soviet Ambassador to the USA, and was moreover a Jew), and his replacement by Vyacheslav Molotov, Stalin's right-hand man, had to be seen as a sign that the Soviet dictator was looking for an agreement with Germany.

Around the same time, Ribbentrop heard from the German Ambassador in Moscow, Count Friedrich Werner von der Schulenburg, that the Soviet Union was interested in a rapprochement with Germany. He scented a coup which would dramatically turn the tables on Britain, the country which had dared to spurn him – a coup that would also win him glory and favour in the Führer's eyes, and his place in history as the architect of Germany's triumph. Hitler for his part thought that Russian economic difficulties and the chance spotted by 'the wily fox' Stalin to remove any threat from Poland to the Soviet western borders were at the back of any opening towards Germany. His own interests were to isolate Poland and deter Britain.

Ribbentrop was now able to persuade Hitler to agree to the Soviet requests for resumption of trade negotiations with Moscow, which had been broken off the previous February. Molotov told Schulenburg, however, that a 'political basis' would have to be found before talks could be resumed. He left unclear what he had in mind. Deep suspicions on both sides led to relations cooling again throughout June. Molotov continued to stonewall and keep his options open. Desultory economic discussions were just kept alive. But at the end of June, Hitler, irritated by the difficulties raised by the Soviets in the trade discussions, ordered the ending of all talks. This time the Soviets took the initiative. Within three weeks they were letting it be known that trade talks could be resumed, and that the prospects for an economic agreement were favourable. This was the signal Berlin had been waiting for. Schulenburg in Moscow was ordered to 'pick up the threads again'.

On 26 June, Ribbentrop's Russian expert in the Foreign Ministry's Trade Department, Karl Schnurre, indicated to the Soviet Chargé d'Affaires Georgi Astakhov and trade representative Evgeny Babarin that the trade agreement could be accompanied by a political understanding between Germany and the Soviet Union, taking into account their mutual territorial interests. The response was encouraging. Molotov was non-committal and somewhat negative when he met Schulenburg on 3 August. But two days later, Astakhov was letting Ribbentrop know that the Soviet government was seriously interested in the 'improvement of mutual relations', and willing to contemplate political negotiations.

Towards the end of July, Hitler, Ribbentrop, and Weizsäcker had devised the basis of an agreement with the Soviet Union involving the partition of Poland and the Baltic states. Hints about such an arrangement were dropped to Molotov during his meeting with Schulenburg on 3 August. Stalin was in no rush. He had learned what the Germans were up to, and the broad timing of the intended action against the Poles. But for Hitler there was not a moment to lose. The attack on Poland could not be delayed. Autumn rains, he told Count Ciano in mid-August, would turn the roads into a morass and Poland into 'one vast swamp . . . completely unsuitable for any military operations'. The strike had to come by the end of the month.

VII

Remarkably, for the best part of three months during this summer of high drama, with Europe teetering on the brink of war, Hitler was almost entirely absent from the seat of government in Berlin. Much of the time, as always, when not at his alpine eyrie above Berchtesgaden, he was travelling around Germany. Early in June he visited the construction site of the Volkswagen factory at Fallersleben, where he had laid the foundation stone a year or so earlier. From there it was on to Vienna, to the 'Reich Theatre Week', where he saw the premiere of Richard Strauß's *Friedenstag*, regaling his adjutants with stories of his visits to the opera and theatre there thirty years earlier, and lecturing them on the splendours of Viennese architecture. Before leaving, he visited the grave of his niece, Geli Raubal. He flew on to Linz, where he criticized new worker flats because they lacked the balconies he deemed essential in every apartment. From there he was driven to Berchtesgaden via Lambach, Hafeld, and Fischlham – some of the places associated with his childhood and where he had first attended school.

At the beginning of July, he was in Rechlin in Mecklenburg, inspecting new aircraft prototypes, including the He 176, the first rocket-propelled plane, with a speed of almost 1,000 kilometres an hour. Then in the middle of the month he attended an extraordinary four-day spectacular in Munich, the 'Rally of German Art 1939', culminating in a huge parade with massive floats and extravagant costumes of bygone ages to illustrate 2,000 years of German cultural achievement. Less than a week later he paid his regular visit to the Bayreuth festival. At Haus Wahnfried, in the annexe that the Wagner family had set aside specially for his use, Hitler felt relaxed. There he was 'Uncle Wolf', as he had been known by the Wagners since his early days in politics. While in Bayreuth, looking self-conscious in his white dinner-jacket, he attended performances of *Der fliegende Holländer*, *Tristan und Isolde*, *Die Walküre*, and *Götterdämmerung*, greeting the crowds as usual from the window on the first floor.

There was also a second reunion (following their meeting the previous year in Linz) with his boyhood friend August Kubizek. They spoke of the old days in Linz and Vienna, going to Wagner operas together. Kubizek sheepishly asked Hitler to sign dozens of autographs to take back for his acquaintances. Hitler obliged. The overawed Kubizek, the archetypal local-government officer of a sleepy small town, carefully blotted every signature. They went out for a while, reminiscing in the gathering dusk by Wagner's grave. Then Hitler took Kubizek on a tour of Haus Wahnfried. Kubizek reminded his former friend of the *Rienzi* episode in Linz all those years ago. (Wagner's early opera, based on the story of a fourteenth-century 'tribune of the people' in Rome, had so excited Hitler that late at night, after the performance, he had hauled his friend up the Freinberg, a hill on the edge of Linz, and regaled him about the meaning of what they had seen.) Hitler recounted the tale to Winifried Wagner, ending by saying, with a great deal more pathos than truth: 'That's when it began.' Hitler probably believed his own myth. Kubizek certainly did. Emotional and impressionable as he always had been, and now a well-established victim of the Führer cult, he departed with tears in his eyes. Shortly afterwards, he heard the crowds cheering as Hitler left.

Hitler spent most of August at the Berghof. Other than when he had important visitors to see, daily life there retained its usual patterns. Magda Goebbels told Ciano of her boredom. 'It is always Hitler who talks!' he recalled her saying. 'He can be Führer as much as he likes, but he always repeats himself and bores his guests.'

If less so than in Berlin, strict formalities were still observed. The atmosphere was stuffy, especially in Hitler's presence. Only Eva Braun's sister, Gretl, lightened it somewhat, even smoking (which was much frowned upon), flirting with the orderlies, and determined to have fun whatever dampening effect the Führer might have on things. What little humour otherwise surfaced was often in dubious taste in the male-dominated household, where the women in attendance, including Eva Braun, served mainly as decoration. But in general, the tone was one of extreme politeness, with much kissing of hands, and expressions of 'Gnädige Frau'. Despite Nazi mockery of the bourgeoisie, life at the Berghof was imbued with the intensely bourgeois manners and fashions of the *arriviste* Dictator.

Hitler's lengthy absence from Berlin, while European peace hung by a thread, illustrates how far the disintegration of anything resembling a conventional central government had gone. Few ministers were permitted to see him. Even the usual privileged few had dwindled in number. Goebbels was still out of favour following his affair with Lida Baarova. Göring had not recovered the ground he had lost since Munich. Speer enjoyed the special status of the protégé. He spent much of the summer at Berchtesgaden. But most of the time he was indulging Hitler's passion for architecture, not discussing details of foreign policy. Hitler's 'advisers' on the only issue of real consequence, the question of war and peace, were now largely confined to Ribbentrop, even more hawkish, if anything, than he had been the previous summer, and the military leaders. On the crucial matters of foreign policy, Ribbentrop – when not represented through the head of his personal staff, Walther Hewel, far more liked by the dictator and everyone else than the preening Foreign Minister himself – largely had the field to himself. The second man at the Foreign Ministry, Weizsäcker, left to mind the shop while his boss absented himself from Berlin, claimed not to have seen Hitler, even from a distance, between May and the middle of August. What the Dictator was up to on the Obersalzberg was difficult to fathom in Berlin, Weizsäcker added.

The personalization of government in the hands of one man – amounting in this case to concentration of power to determine over war or peace – was as good as complete.

VIII

Danzig, allegedly the issue dragging Europe towards war, was in reality no more than a pawn in the German game being played from Berchtesgaden. Gauleiter Albert Forster – a thirty-seven-year-old former Franconian bank clerk who had learnt some of his early political lessons under Julius Streicher and had been leader of the NSDAP in Danzig since 1930 – had received detailed instructions from Hitler on a number of occasions throughout the summer on how to keep tension simmering without allowing it to boil over. As had been the case in the Sudetenland the previous year, it was important not to force the issue too soon. Local issues had to chime exactly with the timing determined by Hitler. Incidents were to be manufactured to display to the population in the

Reich, and to the world outside, the alleged injustices perpetrated by the Poles against the Germans in Danzig. Instances of mistreatment – most of them contrived, some genuine – of the German minority in other parts of Poland, too, provided regular fodder for an orchestrated propaganda campaign which, again analogous to that against the Czechs in 1938, had been screaming its banner headlines about the iniquities of the Poles since May.

The propaganda certainly had its effect. The fear of war with the western powers, while still widespread among the German population, was – at least until August – nowhere near as acute as it had been during the Sudeten crisis. People reasoned, with some justification (and backed up by the German press), that despite the guarantees for Poland, the West was hardly likely to fight for Danzig when it had given in over the Sudetenland. Many thought that Hitler had always pulled it off without bloodshed before, and would do so again. Fears of war were nevertheless pervasive. The more general feeling was probably better summed up in the report from a small town in Upper Franconia at the end of July 1939: 'The answer to the question of how the problem "Danzig and the Corridor" is to be solved is still the same among the general public: incorporation in the Reich? Yes. Through war? No.'

But the anxiety about a general war over Danzig did not mean that there was reluctance to see military action against Poland undertaken – as long as the West could be kept out of it. Inciting hatred of the Poles through propaganda was pushing at an open door. 'The mood of the people can be much more quickly whipped up against the Poles than against any other neighbouring people,' commented the exiled Social Democratic organization, the Sopade. Many thought 'it would serve the Poles right if they get it in the neck'. Above all, no one, it was claimed, whatever their political standpoint, wanted a Polish Danzig; the conviction that Danzig was German was universal.

The issue which the Danzig Nazis exploited to heighten the tension was the supervision of the Customs Office by Polish customs inspectors. When the customs inspectors were informed on 4 August – in what turned out to be an initiative of an over-zealous German official – that they would not be allowed to carry out their duties and responded with a threat to close the port to foodstuffs, the local crisis threatened to boil over, and too soon. The Germans reluctantly backed down – as the international press noted. Forster was summoned to Berchtesgaden on

7 August and returned to announce that the Führer had reached the limits of his patience with the Poles, who were probably acting under pressure from London and Paris.

This allegation was transmitted by Forster to Carl Burckhardt, the League of Nations High Commissioner in Danzig. Overlooking no possibility of trying to keep the West out of his war with Poland, Hitler was ready to use the representative of the detested League of Nations as his intermediary. On 10 August, Burckhardt was summoned to the telephone to be told by Gauleiter Forster that Hitler wanted to see him on the Obersalzberg at 4 p.m. next day and was sending his personal plane ready for departure early the following morning. Following a flight in which he was regaled by a euphoric Albert Forster with tales of beerhall fights with Communists during the 'time of struggle', Burckhardt landed in Salzburg and, after a quick snack, was driven up the spiralling road beyond the Berghof itself and up to the 'Eagle's Nest', the recently built spectacular 'Tea House' in the dizzy heights of the mountain peaks.

Hitler was not fond of the 'Eagle's Nest' and seldom went up there. He complained that the air was too thin at that height, and bad for his blood pressure. He worried about an accident on the roads Bormann had had constructed up the sheer mountainside, and about a failure of the lift that had to carry its passengers from the huge, marble-faced hall cut inside the rock to the summit of the mountain, more than 150 feet above. But this was an important visit. Hitler wanted to impress Burckhardt with the dramatic view over the mountain tops, invoking the image of distant majesty, of the Dictator of Germany as lord of all he surveyed.

He played every register in driving home to Burckhardt – and through him to the western powers – the modesty and reasonableness of his claims on Poland and the futility of western support. Almost speechless with rage, he denounced press suggestions that he had lost his nerve and been forced to give way over the issue of the Polish customs officers. His voice rising until he was shouting, he screamed his response to Polish ultimata: if the smallest incident should take place, he would smash the Poles without warning so that not a trace of Poland remained. If that meant general war, then so be it. Germany had to live from its own resources. That was the only issue; the rest nonsense. He accused Britain and France of interference in the reasonable proposals he had made to the Poles. Now the Poles had taken up a position that blocked any agreement once and for all. His generals, hesitant the previous year, were this time raring to be let loose against the Poles.

Burckhardt, as intended, rapidly passed on to the British and French governments the gist of his talks with Hitler. They drew no conclusions from the report other than to urge restraint on the Poles.

While Hitler and Burckhardt were meeting at the 'Eagle's Nest' on the Kehlstein, another meeting was taking place only a few miles away, in Ribbentrop's newly acquired splendrous residence overlooking the lake in Fuschl, not far from Salzburg. Count Ciano, resplendent in uniform, was learning from the German Foreign Minister that the Italians had been deceived for months about Hitler's intentions. The atmosphere was icy. Ribbentrop told Ciano that the 'merciless destruction of Poland by Germany' was inevitable. The conflict would not become a general one. Were Britain and France to intervene, they would be doomed to defeat. But his information 'and above all his *psychological knowledge*' of Britain, he insisted, made him rule out any intervention. Ciano found him unreasoning and obstinate: 'The decision to fight is implacable. He [Ribbentrop] rejects any solution which might give satisfaction to Germany and avoid the struggle.'

The impression was reinforced when Ciano visited the Berghof next day. Hitler was convinced that the conflict would be localized, that Britain and France, whatever noises they were making, would not go to war. It would be necessary one day to fight the western democracies. But he thought it 'out of the question that this struggle can begin now'. Ciano noted: 'He has decided to strike, and strike he will.'

Important news came through for Hitler at the very time that he was underlining to the disenchanted Ciano his determination to attack Poland no later than the end of August: the Russians were prepared to begin talks in Moscow, including the position of Poland. A beaming Ribbentrop took the telephone call at the Berghof. Hitler was summoned from the meeting with Ciano, and rejoined it in high spirits to report the breakthrough. The way was now open.

A flurry of diplomatic activity – Ribbentrop pressing with maximum urgency for the earliest possible agreement, Molotov cannily prevaricating until it was evident that Soviet interest in the Anglo-French mission was dead – unfolded during the following days. The text of a trade treaty, under which German manufactured goods worth 200 million Reich Marks would be exchanged each year for an equivalent amount of Soviet raw materials, was agreed. Finally, on the evening of 19 August, the chattering teleprinter gave Hitler and Ribbentrop, waiting anxiously at the Berghof, the news they wanted: Stalin was willing to sign a non-aggression pact without delay.

Only the proposed date of Ribbentrop's visit – 26 August – posed serious problems. It was the date Hitler had set for the invasion of Poland. Hitler could not wait that long. On 20 August, he decided to intervene personally. He telegraphed a message to Stalin, via the German Embassy in Moscow, requesting the reception of Ribbentrop, armed with full powers to sign a pact, on the 22nd or 23rd. Hitler's intervention made a difference. But once more Stalin and Molotov made Hitler sweat it out. The tension at the Berghof was almost unbearable. It was more than twenty-four hours later, on the evening of 21 August, before the message came through. Stalin had agreed. Ribbentrop was expected in Moscow in two days' time, on 23 August. Hitler slapped himself on the knee in delight. Champagne all round was ordered – though Hitler did not touch any. 'That will really land them in the soup,' he declared, referring to the western powers.

'We're on top again. Now we can sleep more easily,' recorded a delighted Goebbels. 'The question of Bolshevism is for the moment of secondary importance,' he later added, saying that was the Führer's view, too. 'We're in need and eat then like the devil eats flies.' Abroad, Goebbels remarked, the announcement of the imminent non-aggression pact was 'the great world sensation'. But the response was not that which Hitler and Ribbentrop had hoped for. The Poles' fatalistic reaction was that the pact would change nothing. In Paris, where the news of the Soviet-German pact hit especially hard, the French Foreign Minister Georges Bonnet, fearing a German-Soviet entente against Poland, pondered whether it was now better to press the Poles into compromise with Hitler in order to win time for France to prepare its defences. But eventually, after dithering for two days, the French government agreed that France would remain true to its obligations. The British cabinet, meeting on the afternoon of 22 August, was unmoved by the dramatic news, even if MPs were asking searching questions about the failure of British intelligence. The Foreign Secretary coolly, if absurdly, dismissed the pact as perhaps of not very great importance. Instructions went out to embassies that Britain's obligations to Poland remained unaltered. Sir Nevile Henderson's suggestion of a personal letter from the Prime

Minister to Hitler, warning him of Britain's determination to stick by Poland, was taken up.

Meanwhile, in excellent mood on account of his latest triumph, Hitler prepared, on the morning of 22 August, to address all the armed forces' leaders on his plans for Poland. The meeting, at the Berghof, had been arranged before the news from Moscow had come through. Hitler's aim was to convince the generals of the need to attack Poland without delay. The diplomatic coup, by now in the public domain, can only have boosted his self-confidence. It certainly weakened any potential criticism from his audience.

Around fifty officers had assembled in the Great Hall of the Berghof by the time that Hitler began his address at noon. 'It was clear to me that a conflict with Poland had to come sooner or later,' began Hitler. 'I had already made this decision in the spring, but I thought that I would first turn against the West in a few years, and only after that against the East.' Circumstances had caused him to change his thinking, he went on. He pointed in the first instance to his own importance to the situation. Making no concessions to false modesty, he claimed: 'Essentially all depends on me, on my existence, because of my political talents. Furthermore, the fact that probably no one will ever again have the confidence of the whole German people as I have. There will probably never again in the future be a man with more authority than I have. My existence is therefore a factor of great value. But I can be eliminated at any time by a criminal or a lunatic.' He also emphasized the personal role of Mussolini and Franco, whereas Britain and France lacked any 'outstanding personality'. He briefly alluded to Germany's economic difficulties as a further argument for not delaying action. 'It is easy for us to make decisions. We have nothing to lose; we have everything to gain. Because of our restrictions our economic situation is such that we can only hold out for a few more years. Göring can confirm this. We have no other choice. We must act.' He reviewed the constellation of international forces, concluding: 'All these favourable circumstances will no longer prevail in two or three years' time. No one knows how much longer I shall live. Therefore, better a conflict now.'

The high probability was that the West would not intervene, he went on. There was a risk, but the risk had to be taken. 'We are faced,' he stated with his usual apocalyptic dualism, 'with the harsh alternatives of striking or of certain annihilation sooner or later.' He compared the relative arms strength of Germany and the western powers. He concluded that Britain was in no position to help Poland. Nor was there any interest in Britain in a long war. The West had vested its hopes in enmity between Germany and Russia. 'The enemy did not reckon with my great strength of purpose,' he boasted. He had seen only puny figures in Munich. The pact with Russia would be signed within two days. 'Now Poland is in the position in which I want her.' There need be no fear of a blockade. The East would provide the necessary grain, cattle, coal, lead, and zinc. His only fear, Hitler said, in obvious allusion to Munich, was 'that at the last moment some swine or other will yet submit to me a plan for mediation'. He would provide a propaganda pretext for beginning the war, however implausible. He ended by summarizing his philosophy: 'The victor will not be asked afterwards whether he told the truth or not. When starting and waging a war it is not right that matters, but victory. Close your hearts to pity. Act brutally. Eighty million people must obtain what is their right. Their existence must be made secure. The stronger man is right.'

If the generals were not enthused by what Hitler had to say, they posed no objections. The mood was largely fatalistic, resigned. The disastrous collapse in the army's power since the first weeks of 1938 could not have been more apparent. Its still lamented former head, Werner von Fritsch, had remarked to Ulrich von Hassell some months earlier: 'This man – Hitler – is Germany's fate for good or evil. If it's now into the abyss, he'll drag us all with him. There's nothing to be done.' It was an indication of the capitulation of the Wehrmacht leadership to Hitler's will. Hitler's own comments after the meeting indicated that, on the eve of war, he had little confidence in and much contempt for his generals.

Towards the end of his speech, Hitler had broken off momentarily to wish his Foreign Minister success in Moscow. Ribbentrop left at that point to fly to Berlin. In mid-evening, he then flew in Hitler's private Condor to Königsberg and, after a restless and nervous night preparing notes for the negotiations, from there, next morning, on to the Russian capital. Within two hours of landing, Ribbentrop was in the Kremlin. Attended by Schulenburg (the German Ambassador in Moscow), he was taken to a long room where, to his surprise, not just Molotov, but Stalin himself, awaited him. Ribbentrop began by stating Germany's wish for new relations on a lasting basis with the Soviet Union. Stalin replied that, though the two countries had 'poured buckets of filth' over each other for years, there was no obstacle to ending the quarrel. Discussion quickly moved to delineation of spheres of influence. Stalin staked the USSR's claim to Finland, much of the territory of the Baltic states, and Bessarabia. Ribbentrop predictably brought up Poland, and the need for a demarcation line between the Soviet Union and Germany. This – to run along the rivers Vistula, San, and Bug – was swiftly agreed. Progress towards concluding a non-aggression pact was rapid. The territorial changes to accompany it, carving up eastern Europe between Germany and the Soviet Union, were contained in a secret protocol. The only delay occurred when Stalin's claims to the Latvian ports of Libau (Liepaja) and Windau (Ventspils) held up matters for a while. Ribbentrop felt he had to consult.

Nervously waiting at the Berghof, Hitler had by then already had the Moscow embassy telephoned to inquire about progress at the talks. He paced impatiently up and down on the terrace as the sky silhouetted the Unterberg in striking colours of turquoise, then violet, then fiery red. Below remarked that it pointed to a bloody war. If so, replied Hitler, the sooner the better. The more time passed, the bloodier the war would be.

Within minutes there was a call from Moscow. Ribbentrop assured Hitler that the talks were going well, but asked about the Latvian ports. Inside half an hour Hitler had consulted a map and telephoned his reply: 'Yes, agreed.' The last obstacle was removed. Back at the Kremlin in late evening there was a celebratory supper. Vodka and Crimean sparkling wine lubricated the already effervescent mood of mutual self-congratulation. Among the toasts was one proposed by Stalin to Hitler. The texts of the Pact and Protocol had been drawn up in the meantime. Though dated 23 August, they were finally signed by Ribbentrop and Molotov well after midnight. Hitler and Goebbels had been half-watching a film, still too nervous about what was happening in Moscow to enjoy it. Finally, around 1 a.m., Ribbentrop telephoned again: complete success. Hitler congratulated him. 'That will hit like a bombshell,' he remarked.

Relief as well as satisfaction was reflected in Hitler's warm welcome for Ribbentrop on the latter's return next day to Berlin. While his Foreign Minister had been in Moscow, Hitler had begun to think that Britain might after all fight. Now, he was confident that prospect had been ruled out.

IX

While Ribbentrop had been on his way to Moscow, Sir Nevile Henderson, the British Ambassador in Berlin, was flying to Berchtesgaden to deliver the letter composed by the Prime Minister, Neville Chamberlain, following the cabinet meeting on 22 August. In his letter, Chamberlain emphasized his conviction 'that war between our two peoples would be the greatest calamity that could occur'. But he left Hitler in no doubt about the British position. A German-Soviet agreement would not alter Great Britain's obligation to Poland. Britain was, however, ready, if a peaceful atmosphere could be created, to discuss all problems affecting relations with Germany. And Britain was anxious for Poland and Germany to cease their polemics and incitement in order to allow direct discussions between the two countries on the reciprocal treatment of minorities.

Accompanied by Weizsäcker and Hewel, Henderson arrived at the Berghof at 1 p.m. on 23 August. Hitler was at his most aggressive. 'He made no long speeches but his language was violent and exaggerated both as regards England and Poland,' Henderson reported. The German Chancellor launched into a series of wild tirades about British support of the Czechs the previous year, and now of the Poles, and how he had wanted only friendship with Britain. He claimed Britain's 'blank cheque' to Poland ruled out negotiations. He was recriminatory, threatening, and totally unyielding. He finally agreed to reply to Chamberlain within two hours.

On return to Salzburg, Henderson was rapidly recalled to the Berghof. This time the meeting was shorter – under half an hour. Hitler was now calmer, but adamant that he would attack Poland if another German were to be maltreated there. War would be all Britain's fault. 'England' (as he invariably called Britain) 'was determined to destroy and exterminate Germany,' he went on. He was now fifty years old. He preferred war at this point than in five or ten years' time. Henderson countered that talk of extermination was absurd. Hitler replied that England was fighting for lesser races, whereas he was fighting only for Germany. This time the Germans would fight to the last man. It would have been different in 1914 had he been Chancellor then. His repeated offers of friendship to Britain had been contemptuously rejected. He had come to the conclusion that England and Germany could never agree. England had now forced him into the pact with Russia. Henderson stated that war seemed inevitable if Hitler maintained his direct action against Poland. Hitler ended by declaring that only a complete change of British policy towards Germany could convince him of the desire for good relations. The written reply to Chamberlain that he handed to Henderson was couched in much the same vein. It contained the threat – clear in implication if not expression – to order general mobilization, were Britain and France to mobilize their own forces.

Hitler's tirades were, as so often, theatricals. They were a play-acted attempt to break the British Guarantee to Poland by a calculated demonstration of verbal brutality. As soon as Henderson had left, Hitler slapped his thigh – his usual expression of self-congratulation – and exclaimed to Weizsäcker: 'Chamberlain won't survive this discussion. His cabinet will fall this evening.'

Chamberlain's government was still there next day. Hitler's belief in his own powers had outstripped realistic assessment. His commment revealed how out of touch he was with the mood of the British government, now fully backed by public opinion, by this time. He was puzzled, therefore, the following day by the low-key response in Britain to the Soviet Pact, and irritated by the speeches made in Parliament by Chamberlain and Halifax reasserting Britain's resolve to uphold its obligations to Poland. Within twenty-four hours Ribbentrop had persuaded him, since wielding the big stick had produced little effect, to dangle the carrot.

At 12.45 p.m. on 25 August, Henderson was informed that Hitler wished to see him at 1.30 p.m. in the Reich Chancellery. The meeting lasted over an hour. Ribbentrop and the interpreter Paul Schmidt were also present. Hitler was far calmer than he had been in Berchtesgaden. He criticized Chamberlain's speech. But he was prepared to make Britain, he said, 'a large comprehensive offer' and pledge himself to maintain the continued existence of the British Empire once the Polish problem had been solved as a matter of urgency. Hitler was so anxious that his 'offer' be immediately and seriously considered that he suggested that Henderson fly to London, and put a plane at his disposal. Henderson left next morning.

The 'offer' to Britain was, in fact, no more than a ruse, another – and by now increasingly desperate – attempt to detach Britain from support for Poland, and prevent the intended localized war from becoming a general European war. How honest Hitler's 'offer' was can be judged from the fact that at the very time that Henderson was talking in the Reich Chancellery, final preparations were being made for the start of 'Case White' next morning, Saturday, 26 August, at 4.30 a.m.

Already on 12 August, Hitler had set the likely date of the 26th for the invasion of Poland. Goebbels learnt on the morning of the 25th that the mobilization was due to take place that afternoon. At midday, Hitler then gave him propaganda instructions, emphasizing that Germany had been given no choice but to fight against the Poles, and preparing the people for a war, if necessary lasting 'months and years'. Telephone communications between Berlin and London and Paris were cut off for several hours that afternoon. The Tannenberg celebrations and Party Rally were abruptly cancelled. Airports were closed from 26 August. Food rationing was introduced as from 27 August. By midday on the 25th, however, even while Hitler was giving propaganda directives to Goebbels, Keitel's office was telephoning Halder to find out what was the latest time for the march-order, since there might have to be a postponement. The answer was given: no later than 3 p.m. The final order was delayed at 1.30 p.m. because Henderson was at that time in the Reich Chancellery. It was then further held back in the hope that Mussolini would have replied to Hitler's communication of earlier that morning. Under pressure from the military timetable, but anxious for news from Rome, Hitler put the attack on hold for an hour. Finally, without receiving Mussolini's answer, but able to wait no longer, Hitler gave the order at 3.02 p.m. Directives for mobilization were passed to the various troop commanders during the afternoon. Then, amazingly, within five hours the order was cancelled. To a great deal of muttering from army leaders about incompetence, the complex machinery of invasion was halted just in time.

Mussolini's reply had arrived at 5.45 p.m. At 7.30 p.m. Brauchitsch telephoned Halder to rescind the invasion order. A shaken Hitler had changed his mind.

On 24 August Hitler had prepared a lengthy letter for Mussolini, justifying the alliance with the Soviet Union, and indicating that a strike against Poland was imminent. The letter was delivered by the German Ambassador in Rome on the morning of the 25th. Mussolini's answer gave the over-confident Hitler an enormous shock. The Duce did not beat about the bush: Italy was in no position to offer military assistance at the present time. Hitler icily dismissed Attolico, the Italian Ambassador. 'The Italians are behaving just like they did in 1914,' Paul Schmidt heard Hitler remark. 'That alters the entire situation,' judged Goebbels. 'The Führer ponders and contemplates. That's a serious blow for him.' For an hour, the Reich Chancellery rang with comments of disgust at the Axis partner. The word 'treachery' was on many lips. Brauchitsch was hurriedly summoned. When he arrived, around seven that evening, he told Hitler there was still time to halt the attack, and recommended doing so to gain time for the Dictator's 'political game'. Hitler immediately took up the suggestion. At 7.45 p.m. a frantic order was dispatched to Halder to halt the start of hostilities. Keitel emerged from Hitler's room to tell an adjutant: 'The march-order must be rescinded immediately.'

Another piece of bad news arrived for Hitler at much the same time. Minutes before the news from Rome had arrived, Hitler had heard from the French Ambassador, Robert Coulondre, that the French, too, were determined to stick by their obligations to Poland. This in itself was not critical. Hitler was confident that the French could be kept out of the war, if London did not enter. Then Ribbentrop arrived to tell him that the military alliance between Great Britain and Poland agreed on 6 April had been signed late that afternoon. This had happened after Hitler had made his 'offer' to Henderson. Having just signed the alliance, it must have been plain even to Hitler that Britain was unlikely to break it the very next day. Yesterday's hero, Ribbentrop, now found himself all at once out of favour and, in the midst of a foreign-policy crisis on which peace hinged, was not in evidence for over two days. Hitler turned again to the Foreign Minister's great rival, Göring.

Immediately, Göring inquired whether the cancellation of the invasion was permanent. 'No. I will have to see whether we can eliminate England's intervention,' was the reply. When Göring's personal emissary, his Swedish friend, the industrialist Birger Dahlerus, already in London to belabour Lord Halifax with similar vague offers of German good intent that Henderson would shortly bring via the official route, eventually managed, with much difficulty, to place a telephone call to Berlin, he was asked to report back to the Field-Marshal the following evening.

The mood in the Reich Chancellery had not been improved by the message from Daladier on 26 August underlining France's solidarity with Poland. Things at the hub of the German government seemed chaotic. No one had a clear idea of what was going on. Hewel, head of Ribbentrop's personal staff, though with different views from those of his boss, warned Hitler not to underestimate the British. He was a better judge of that than his Minister, he asserted. Hitler angrily broke off the discussion. Brauchitsch thought Hitler did not know what he should do.

Dahlerus certainly found him in a highly agitated state when he was taken towards midnight to the Reich Chancellery. He had brought with him a letter from Lord Halifax, indicating in non-committal terms that negotiations were possible if force were not used against Poland. It added in reality nothing to that which Chamberlain had already stated in his letter of 22 August. It made an impact on Göring, but Hitler did not even look at the letter before launching into a lengthy diatribe, working himself into a nervous frenzy, marching up and down the room, his eyes staring, his voice at one moment indistinct, hurling out facts and figures about the strength of the German armed forces, the next moment shouting as if addressing a party meeting, threatening to annihilate his enemies, giving Dahlerus the impression of someone 'completely abnormal'. Eventually, Hitler calmed down enough to list the points of the offer which he wanted Dahlerus to take to London. Germany wanted a pact or alliance with Britain, would guarantee the Polish borders, and defend the British Empire (even against Italy, Göring added). Britain was to help Germany acquire Danzig and the Corridor, and have Germany's colonies returned. Guarantees were to be provided for the German minority in Poland. Hitler had altered the stakes in a bid to break British backing for Poland. In contrast to the 'offer' made to Henderson, the alliance with Britain now appeared to be available *before* any settlement with Poland.

Dahlerus took the message to London next morning, 27 August. The response was cool and sceptical. Dahlerus was sent back to report that Britain was willing to reach an agreement with Germany, but would not break its guarantee to Poland. Following direct negotiations between Germany and Poland on borders and minorities, the results would require international guarantee. Colonies could be returned in due course, but not under threat of war. The offer to defend the British Empire was rejected. Astonishingly, to Dahlerus, back in Berlin late that evening, Hitler accepted the terms, as long as the Poles had been immediately instructed to contact Germany and begin negotiations.

Halifax made sure this was done. In Warsaw, Beck agreed to begin negotiations. Meanwhile, the German mobilization, which had never been cancelled along with the invasion, rolled on. Before Henderson arrived back in Berlin to bring the official British response, Brauchitsch informed Halder that Hitler had provisionally fixed the new date for the attack as 1 September.

Henderson handed Hitler a translation of the British reply to his 'offer' of 25 August at 10.30 p.m. that evening, the 28th. Ribbentrop and Schmidt were there. Hitler and Henderson spoke for over an hour. For once, Hitler neither interrupted, nor harangued Henderson. He was, according to the British Ambassador, polite, reasonable, and not angered by what he read. The 'friendly atmosphere' noted by Henderson was so only in relative terms. Hitler still spoke of annihilating Poland. The British reply did not in substance extend beyond the informal answer that Dahlerus had conveyed (and had been composed after Hitler's response to that initiative was known). The British government insisted upon a prior settlement of the differences between Germany and Poland. Britain had already gained assurances of Poland's willingness to negotiate. Depending upon the outcome of any settlement and how it was reached, Britain was prepared to work towards a lasting understanding with Germany. But the obligation to Poland would be honoured. Hitler promised a written reply the next day.

At 7.15 p.m. on the evening of 29 August, Henderson, sporting as usual a dark red carnation in the buttonhole of his pin-striped suit, passed down the darkened Wilhelmstraße – Berlin was undergoing experimental blackouts – through a silent, but not hostile, crowd of 300–400 Berliners, to be received at the Reich Chancellery as on the previous night with a roll of drums and guard of honour. Otto Meissner, whose role as head of the so-called Presidential Chancellery was largely representational, and Wilhelm Brückner, the chief adjutant, escorted him to Hitler. Ribbentrop was also present. Hitler was in a less amenable mood than on the previous evening. He gave Henderson his reply. He had again raised the price – exactly as Henlein had been ordered to do in the Sudetenland the previous year, so that it was impossible to meet it. Hitler now demanded the arrival of a Polish emissary with full powers by the following day, Wednesday, 30 August. Even the pliant Henderson, protesting at the impossible time-limit for the arrival of the Polish emissary, said it sounded like an ultimatum. Hitler replied that his generals were pressing him for a decision. They were unwilling to lose any more time because of the onset of the rainy season in Poland. Henderson told Hitler that any attempt to use force against Poland would inevitably result in conflict with Britain.

When Henderson had left, the Italian Ambassador Attolico was ushered in. He had come to tell Hitler that Mussolini was prepared to intercede with Britain if required. The last thing Hitler wanted, as he had made clear to his generals at the meeting on 22 August, was a last-minute intercession to bring about a new Munich – least of all from the partner who had just announced that he could not stand by the pact so recently signed. Hitler coldly told Attolico that direct negotiations with Britain were in hand and that he had already declared his readiness to accept a Polish negotiator.

Hitler had been displeased at Henderson's response to his reply to the British government. He now called in Göring to send Dahlerus once more on the unofficial route to let the British know the gist of the 'generous' terms he was proposing to offer the Poles – return of Danzig to Germany, and a plebiscite on the Corridor (with Germany to be given a 'corridor through the Corridor' if the result went Poland's way). By 5 a.m. on 30 August, Dahlerus was again heading for London in a German military plane. An hour earlier Henderson had already conveyed Lord Halifax's unsurprising response, that the German request for the Polish emissary to appear that very day was unreasonable.

During the day, while talking of peace Hitler prepared for war. In the morning he instructed Albert Forster, a week earlier declared Head of State in Danzig, on the action to be taken in the Free City at the out-break of hostilities. Later, he signed the decree to establish a Ministerial Council for the Defence of the Reich with wide powers to promulgate decrees. Chaired by Göring, its other members were Heß as Deputy Leader of the Party, Frick as plenipotentiary for Reich administration, Funk as plenipotentiary for the economy, Lammers, the head of the Reich Chancellery, and Keitel, chief of the High Command of the Wehr-macht. It had the appearance of a 'war cabinet' to administer the Reich while Hitler preoccupied himself with military matters. In reality, the fragmentation of Reich government had gone too far for that. Hitler's own interest in preventing any centralized body operating as a possible check on his own power was to mean that the Ministerial Council was destined not to bring even a limited resurrection of collective government.

Hitler spent much of the day working on his 'proposals' to be put to the Polish negotiator who, predictably, never arrived. From the outset it had not been a serious suggestion. But when Henderson returned to the Reich Chancellery at midnight to present the British reply to Hitler's communication of the previous evening, he encountered Ribbentrop in a highly nervous state and in a vile temper. Diplomatic niceties were scarcely preserved. After Ribbentrop had read out Hitler's 'proposals' at breakneck speed, so that Henderson was unable to note them down, he refused – on Hitler's express orders – to let the British Ambassador read the document, then hurled it on the table stating that it was now out of date, since no Polish emissary had arrived in Berlin by midnight. In retrospect, Henderson thought that Ribbentrop 'was wilfully throwing away the last chance of a peaceful solution'.

There had, in fact, been no 'last chance'. No Polish emissary had been expected. Ribbentrop was concerned precisely *not* to hand over terms which the British might have passed to the Poles, who might have been prepared to discuss them. Hitler had needed his 'generous suggestion over the regulation of the Danzig and Corridor Question', as Schmidt later heard him say, as 'an alibi, especially for the German people, to show them that I have done everything to preserve peace'.

The army had been told on 30 August to make all preparations for attack on 1 September at 4.30 a.m. If negotiations in London required a postponement, notification would be given before 3 p.m. next day. 'Armed intervention by Western powers now said to be unavoidable,' noted Halder. 'In spite of this, Führer has decided to strike.'

When informed that Ribbentrop had arrived at the Reich Chancellery, Hitler told him he had given the order, and that 'things were rolling'. Ribbentrop wished him luck. 'It looks as if the die is finally cast,' wrote Goebbels.

After making his decision, Hitler cut himself off from external contact. He refused to see the Polish Ambassador, Jozef Lipski, later in the afternoon. Ribbentrop did see him a little later. But hearing that the Ambassador carried no plenipotentiary powers to negotiate, he immediately terminated the interview. Lipski returned to find telephone lines to Warsaw had been cut off.

At 9 p.m. the German radio broadcast Hitler's 'sixteen-point proposal' which Ribbentrop had so crassly presented to Henderson at midnight. By 10.30 p.m. the first reports were coming in of a number of serious border incidents, including an armed 'Polish' assault on the German radio station at Gleiwitz in Upper Silesia. These had been planned for weeks by Heydrich's office, using SS men dressed in Polish uniforms to carry out the attacks. To increase the semblance of authenticity, a number of concentration-camp inmates killed by lethal injections and carried to the sites provided the bodies required.

Throughout Germany, people went about their daily business as normal. But the normality was deceptive. All minds now were fixed on the likelihood of war. A brief war, with scarcely any losses, and confined to Poland, was one thing. But war with the West, which so many with memories of the Great War of 1914–18 had dreaded for years, now seemed almost certain. There was now no mood like that of August 1914, no 'hurrah-patriotism'. The faces of the people told of their anxiety, fears, worries, and resigned acceptance of what they were being faced with. 'Everybody against the war,' wrote the American correspondent William Shirer on 31 August. 'How can a country go into a major war with a population so dead against it?' he asked. 'Trust in the Führer will now probably be subjected to its hardest acid test,' ran a report from the Upper Franconian district of Ebermannstadt. 'The overwhelming proportion of people's comrades expects from him the prevention of the war, if otherwise impossible even at the cost of Danzig and the Corridor.'

How accurate such a report was as a reflection of public opinion cannot be ascertained. The question is in any case irrelevant. Ordinary citizens, whatever their fears, were powerless to affect the course of events. While many of them were fitfully sleeping in the hope that even now, at the eleventh hour and beyond, some miracle would preserve peace, the first shots were fired and bombs dropped near Dirschau at 4.30 a.m. And just over quarter of an hour later in Danzig harbour the elderly German battleship *Schleswig-Holstein*, now a sea-cadet training-ship, focused its heavy guns on the fortified Polish munitions depot on the Westerplatte and opened fire.

By late afternoon the army leadership reported: 'Our troops have crossed the frontier everywhere and are sweeping on toward their objectives of the day, checked only slightly by the Polish forces thrown against them.' In Danzig itself, the purported objective of the conflict between Germany and Poland, border posts and public buildings manned by Poles had been attacked at dawn. The League of Nations High Commissioner had been forced to leave, and the swastika banner raised over his building. Gauleiter Albert Forster proclaimed Danzig's reincorporation in the Reich. In the turmoil of the first day of hostilities, probably few people in Germany took much notice.

On a grey, overcast morning Shirer had found the few people on the streets apathetic. There were not many cheers from those thinly lining the pavements when Hitler drove to the Reichstag shortly before 10 a.m. A hundred or so deputies had been called up to serve in the army. But Göring saw to it that there were no empty spaces when Hitler spoke. The vacancies were simply filled by drafting in party functionaries. Hitler, now wearing Wehrmacht uniform, was on less than top form. He sounded strained. There was less cheering than usual. After a lengthy justification of the alleged need for Germany's military action, he declared: 'Poland has now last night for the first time fired on our territory through regular soldiers. Since 5.45 a.m.' – he meant 4.45 a.m. – 'the fire has been returned. And from now on bomb will be met with bomb.'

Hitler had still not given up hope that the British could be kept out of the conflict. On his return from the Reichstag he had Göring summon Dahlerus to make a last attempt. But he wanted no outside intercession, no repeat of Munich. Mussolini, under the influence of Ciano and Attolico, and unhappy at Italy's humiliation at being unable to offer military support, had been trying for some days to arrange a peace conference. He was now desperate, fearing attack on Italy from Britain and France, to stop the war spreading. Before seeing Dahlerus, Hitler sent the Duce a telegram explicitly stating that he did not want his mediation. Then Dahlerus arrived. He found Hitler in a nervous state. The odour from his mouth was so strong that Dahlerus was tempted to move back a step or two. Hitler was at his most implacable. He was determined to break Polish resistance 'and to annihilate the Polish people', he told Dahlerus. In the next breath he added that he was prepared for further negotiations if the British wanted them. Again the threat followed, in ever more hysterical tones. It was in British interests to avoid a fight with him. But if Britain chose to fight, she would pay dearly. He would fight for one, two, ten years if necessary.

Dahlerus's reports of such hysteria could cut no ice in London. Nor did an official approach on the evening of 2 September, inviting Sir Horace Wilson to Berlin for talks with Hitler and Ribbentrop. Wilson replied straightforwardly that German troops had first to be withdrawn from Polish territory. Otherwise Britain would fight. This was only to repeat the message which the British Ambassador had already passed to Ribbentrop the previous evening. No reply to that message was received. At 9 a.m. on 3 September, Henderson handed the British ultimatum to the interpreter Paul Schmidt, in place of Ribbentrop, who had been unwilling to meet the British Ambassador. Unless assurances were forthcoming by 11 a.m. that Germany was prepared to end its military action and withdraw from Polish soil, the ultimatum read, 'a state of war will exist between the two countries as from that hour'. No such assurances were forthcoming. 'Consequently,' Chamberlain broadcast to the British people and immediately afterwards repeated in the House of Commons, 'this country is at war with Germany.' The French declaration of war followed that afternoon at 5 p.m.

Hitler had led Germany into the general European war he had wanted to avoid for several more years. Military 'insiders' thought the army, 2.3 million strong, through the rapidity of the rearmament programme, was less prepared for a major war than it had been in 1914. Hitler was fighting the war allied with the Soviet Union, the ideological arch-enemy. And he was at war with Great Britain, the would-be 'friend' he had for years tried to woo. Despite all warnings, his plans – at every turn backed by his warmongering Foreign Minister – had been predicated upon his assumption that Britain would not enter the war, though he had shown himself undeterred even by that eventuality. It was little wonder that, if Paul Schmidt's account is to be believed, when Hitler received the British ultimatum on the morning of 3 September, he angrily turned to Ribbentrop and asked: 'What now?'

X

'Responsibility for this terrible catastrophe lies on the shoulders of one man,' Chamberlain had told the House of Commons on 1 September, 'the German Chancellor, who has not hesitated to plunge the world into misery in order to serve his own senseless ambitions.' It was an understandable over-simplification. Such a personalized view necessarily left out the sins of omission and commission by others – including the British government and its French allies – which had assisted in enabling Hitler to accumulate such a unique basis of power that his actions could determine the fate of Europe.

Internationally, Hitler's combination of bullying and blackmail could not have worked but for the fragility of the post-war European settlement. The Treaty of Versailles had given Hitler the basis for his rising demands, accelerating drastically in 1938–9. It had provided the platform for ethnic unrest that Hitler could easily exploit in the cauldron of central and eastern Europe. Not least, it had left an uneasy guilt-complex in the West, especially in Britain. Hitler might rant and exaggerate; his methods might be repellent; but was there not some truth in what he was claiming? The western governments, backed by their war-weary populations, anxious more than all else to do everything possible to avoid a new conflagration, their traditional diplomacy no match for unprecedented techniques of lying and threatening, thought so, and went out of their way to placate Hitler. By the time the western powers fully realized what they were up against, they were no longer in any position to bring the 'mad dog' to heel.

Within Germany, the fracturing of any semblance of collective government over the previous six years left Hitler in the position where he determined alone. No one doubted – the suffocating effect of years of the expanding Führer cult had seen to that – that he had the right to decide, and that his decisions were to be implemented. In the critical days, he saw a good deal of Ribbentrop, Göring, Goebbels, Himmler, and Bormann. Other leading figures in the party, government ministers, even court favourites like Speer, had little or no contact with him. He was naturally also in constant touch with the Wehrmacht leadership. But while Goebbels, for instance, only learnt at second hand about military plans, leaders of the armed forces often had less than full information, or were belatedly told, about diplomatic developments. The cabinet, of course, never met. Remarkable for a complex modern state, there was no government beyond Hitler and whichever individuals he chose to confer with at a particular time. Hitler was the only link of the component parts of the regime. Only in his presence could the key steps be taken. But those admitted to his presence, apart from his usual entourage of secretaries, adjutants, and the like, were for the most part officers needing operational guidelines or those like Ribbentrop or Goebbels who thought like he did and were dependent on him. Internal government of the Reich had become Führer autocracy.

For those in proximity to Hitler, the personalized decision-making meant anything but consistency, clarity, and rationality. On the contrary:

it brought bewildering improvisation, rapid changes of course, uncertainty. Hitler was living off his nerves. That conveyed itself to others around him. External pressures of the course he had embarked upon met Hitler's personal psychology at this point. At the age of fifty, men frequently ruminate on the ambitions they had, and how the time to fulfil them is running out. For Hitler, a man with an extraordinary ego and ambitions to go down in history as the greatest German of all time, and a hypochondriac already prepossessed with his own approaching death, the sense of ageing, of youthful vigour disappearing, of no time to lose was hugely magnified.

Hitler had felt time closing in on him, under pressure to act lest the conditions became more disadvantageous. He had thought of war against the West around 1943–5, against the Soviet Union – though no time-scale was ever given – at some point after that. He had never thought of avoiding war. On the contrary: reliving the lost first great war made him predicate everything on victory in the second great war to come. Germany's future, he had never doubted and had said so on innumerable occasions, could only be determined through war. In the dualistic way in which he always thought, victory would ensure survival, defeat would mean total eradication – the end of the German people. War was for Hitler inevitable. Only the timing and the direction were at issue. And there was no time to wait. Starting from his own strange premisses, given Germany's strained resources and the rapid strides forward in rearmament by Britain and France, there was a certain contorted logic in what he said. Time was running out on the options for Hitler's war.

This strong driving-force in Hitler's mentality was compounded by other strands of his extraordinary psychological make-up. The years of spectacular successes – all attributed by Hitler to the 'triumph of the will' – and the undiluted adulation and sycophancy that surrounded him at every turn, the Führer cult on which the 'system' was built, had by now completely erased in him what little sense of his own limitations had been present. This led him to a calamitous over-estimation of his own abilities, coupled with an extreme denigration of those – particularly in the military – who argued more rationally for greater caution. It went hand in hand with an equally disastrous refusal to contemplate compromise, let alone retreat, as other than a sign of weakness. The experience of the war and its traumatic outcome had doubtless cemented this characteristic. It was certainly there in his early political career, for instance at the time of the attempted putsch in Munich in 1923. But it must have had deeper roots. Psychologists might have answers. At any rate the behaviour trait, increasingly dangerous as Hitler's power expanded to threaten the peace of Europe, was redolent of the spoilt child turned into the would-be macho-man. His inability to comprehend the unwillingness of the British government to yield to his threats produced tantrums of frustrated rage. The certainty that he would get his way through bullying turned into blind fury whenever his bluff was called. The purchase he placed on his own image and standing was narcissistic in the extreme. The number of times he recalled the Czech mobilization of May 1938, then the Polish mobilization of March 1939, as a slight on his prestige was telling. A heightened thirst for revenge was the lasting consequence. Then the rescinding of the order to attack Poland on 26 August, much criticized as a sign of incompetence by the military, he took as a defeat in the eyes of his generals, feeling his prestige threatened. The result was increased impatience to remedy this by a new order at the earliest possible moment, from which there would be no retreat.

Not just external circumstances, but also his personal psyche, pushed him forwards, compelled the risk. Hitler's reply on 29 August, when Göring suggested it was not necessary to 'go for broke', was, therefore, absolutely in character: 'In my life I've always gone for broke.' There was, for him, no other choice.

17
Licensing Barbarism

I

Hitler's 'mission' since he entered politics had been to undo the stain of defeat and humiliation in 1918 by destroying Germany's enemies – internal and external – and restoring national greatness. This 'mission', he had plainly stated on many occasions during the 1920s, could only be accomplished through 'the sword'. It meant war for supremacy. The risk could not be avoided. 'Germany will either be a world power, or there will be no Germany,' he had written in *Mein Kampf*. Nothing had changed over the years in his fanatical belief in this 'mission'.

In war Nazism came into its own. The Nazi Movement had been born out of a lost war. As with Hitler personally, the experience of that war and erasing the stain of that defeat were at its heart. 'National renewal' and preparation for another war to establish the dominance in Europe which the first great war had failed to attain drove it forwards. The new war now brought the circumstances and opportunities for the dramatic radicalization of Nazism's ideological crusade. Long-term goals seemed almost overnight to become attainable policy objectives. Persecution which had targeted usually disliked social minorities was now directed at an entire conquered and subjugated people. The Jews, a tiny proportion of the German population, were not only far more numerous in Poland, but were despised by many within their native land and were now the lowest of the low in the eyes of the brutal occupiers of the country.

As before the war, Hitler set the tone for the escalating barbarism, approved of it, and sanctioned it. But his own actions provide an inadequate explanation of such escalation. The accelerated disintegration of any semblance of collective government, the undermining of legality by an ever-encroaching and ever-expanding police executive, and the power-ambitions of an increasingly autonomous SS leadership all played important parts. These processes had developed between 1933 and 1939 in the Reich itself. They were now, once the occupation of Poland opened up new vistas, to acquire a new momentum altogether. The planners and organizers, theoreticians of domination, and technocrats of power in the SS leadership saw Poland as an experimental playground. They were granted a *tabula rasa* to undertake more or less what they wanted. The Führer's 'vision' served as the legitimation they needed. Party leaders put in to run the civilian administration of the parts of Poland annexed to the Reich, backed by thrusting and 'inventive' civil servants, also saw themselves as 'working towards the Führer' in their efforts to bring about the speediest possible 'Germanization' of their territories. And the occupying army – officers and rank-and-file – imbued with deep-seated anti-Polish prejudice, also needed little encouragement in the ruthlessness with which the conquered Poles were subjugated.

The ideological radicalization which took place in Poland in the eighteen months following the German invasion was an essential precursor to the plans which would unfold in spring 1941 as preparation for the war which Hitler knew at some time he would fight: the war against Bolshevik Russia.

Towards nine o'clock on the evening of 3 September, Hitler had boarded his special armoured train in Berlin's Stettiner Bahnhof and left for the front. For much of the following three weeks, the train – standing initially in Pomerania (Hinterpommern), then later in Upper Silesia – formed the first wartime 'Führer Headquarters'. Among Hitler's accompaniment were two personal adjutants, for the most part Wilhelm Brückner and Julius Schaub, two secretaries (Christa Schroeder and Gerda Daranowski), two manservants, his doctor, Karl Brandt (or sometimes his deputy, Hans-Karl von Hasselbach), and his four military adjutants (Rudolf Schmundt, Karl-Jesko von Puttkamer, Gerhard Engel, and Nicolaus von Below). Behind Hitler's carriage, the first on the train, containing his spacious 'living room', sleeping compartment, and bathroom, together with compartments for his adjutants, was the command carriage that held communications equipment and a conference room for meetings with military leaders. In the next carriage Martin Bormann had his quarters. On the day of the invasion of Poland, he had informed

Lammers that he would 'continue permanently to belong to the Führer's entourage'. From now on, he was never far from Hitler's side – echoing the Führer's wishes, and constantly reminding him of the need to keep up the ideological drive of the regime.

The Polish troops, ill-equipped for modern warfare, were from the outset no match for the invaders. Within the first two days, most aerodromes and almost the whole of the Polish air force were wiped out. The Polish defences were rapidly overrun, the army swiftly in disarray. Already on 5 September Chief of Staff Halder noted: 'Enemy practically defeated.' By the second week of fighting, German forces had advanced to the outskirts of Warsaw. Hitler seldom intervened in the military command. But he took the keenest interest in the progress of the war. He would leave his train most mornings by car to view a different part of the front line. His secretaries, left behind to spend boring days in the airless railway carriage parked in the glare of the blazing sun, tried to dissuade him from touring the battle scenes standing in his car, as he did in Germany. But Hitler was in his element. He was invigorated by war.

On 19 September, Hitler entered Danzig to indescribable scenes of jubilation. He took up accommodation for the next week in the Casino-Hotel at the adjacent resort of Zoppot. From there, on the 22nd and again on the 25th, he flew to the outskirts of Warsaw to view the devastation wrought on the city of a million souls by the bombing and shelling he had ordered. By 27 September, when the military commander of Warsaw eventually surrendered the city, he was back in Berlin, returning quietly with no prearranged hero's reception. Poland no longer existed. An estimated 700,000 Polish soldiers were taken prisoners of war. Around 70,000 were killed in action, and a further 133,000 wounded. German fatalities numbered about 11,000, with 30,000 wounded, and a further 3,400 missing.

Territorial and political plans for Poland were improvised and amended as events unfolded in September and October 1939. On 7 September he had been ready to negotiate with the Poles, recognizing a rump Polish state (with territorial concessions to Germany and breaking of ties with Britain and France), together with an independent western Ukraine. Five days later he still favoured a quasi-autonomous Polish rump state with which he could negotiate a peace in the east, and thought of limiting territorial demands to Upper Silesia and the Corridor if the West stayed out. Another option advanced by Ribbentrop was a division between Germany and Russia, and the creation, out of the rump of Poland, of an autonomous Galician and Polish Ukraine – a proposal unlikely to commend itself to Moscow. The belated Soviet occupation of eastern Poland on 17 September in any case promptly ruled out this possibility. Hitler still left open the final shape of Poland in his Danzig speech on 19 September. During the next days, Stalin made plain his opposition to the existence of a Polish rump state. His initial preference for the demarcation line along the line of the Pissia, Narev, Vistula, and San rivers was then replaced by the proposal to exchange central Polish territories within the Soviet zone between the Vistula and Bug rivers for Lithuania. Once Hitler had accepted this proposal – the basis of the German-Soviet Treaty of Friendship signed on 28 September 1939 – the question of whether or not there would be a Polish rump state was in Berlin's hands alone.

Hitler was still contemplating the possibility of some form of Polish political entity at the end of the month. He held out the prospect of recreating a truncated Polish state – though expressly ruling out any recreation of the Poland of the Versailles settlement – for the last time in his Reichstag speech of 6 October, as part of his 'peace offer' to the West. But by then the provisional arrangements set up to administer occupied Poland had in effect already eliminated what remained of such a prospect. Even before the formality of Chamberlain's rejection of the 'peace offer' on 12 October, they had created their own dynamic militating towards a rump Polish territory – the 'General Government', as it came to be known – alongside the substantial parts of the former Polish state to be incorporated in the Reich itself.

By 26 October, through a series of decrees characterized by extraordinary haste and improvisation, Hitler brought the military administration of occupied Poland to an end, replacing it by civilian rule in the hands of tried and tested 'Old Fighters' of the Movement. Albert Forster, Gauleiter of Danzig, was made head of the new Reichsgau of Danzig-West Prussia. Arthur Greiser, former President of the Danzig Senate, was put in charge of the largest annexed area, Reichsgau Posen (or 'Reichsgau Wartheland', as it was soon to be renamed, though generally known simply as the 'Warthegau'). Hans Frank, the party's legal chief, was appointed General Governor in the rump Polish territory. Other former Polish territory was added to the existing Gaue of East Prussia and Silesia. In each of the incorporated territories, most of all in the Wartheland, the boundaries fixed during the course of October enclosed sizeable areas which had never been part of the former Prussian provinces. The borders of the Reich were thereby extended some 150–200 kilometres to the east. Only in the Danzig area were ethnic Germans in the majority. Elsewhere in the incorporated territories the proportion of Germans in the population seldom reached much over 10 per cent.

It was imperialist conquest, not revisionism. The treatment of the people of the newly conquered territory was unprecedented, its modern forms of barbarism evoking, though in even more terrible fashion, the worst barbaric subjugations of bygone centuries. What was once Poland amounted in the primitive view of its new overlords to no more than a colonial territory in eastern Europe, its resources to be plundered at will, its people regarded – with the help of modern race theories overlaying old prejudice – as inferior human beings to be treated as brutally as thought fit.

II

The terror unleashed from the first days of the invasion of Poland left the violence, persecution, and discrimination that had taken place in the Reich itself since 1933 – dreadful though that had been – completely in the shade. The orgy of atrocities was unleashed from above, exploiting in the initial stages the ethnic antagonism which Nazi agitation and propaganda had done much to incite. The radical, planned programme of 'ethnic cleansing' that followed was authorized by Hitler himself. But its instigation – everything points to this – almost certainly came from the SS leadership. The SS had readily recognized the opportunities there to be grasped from expansion. New possibilities for extending the tentacles of the police state had opened up with the Anschluß. Einsatzgruppen (task forces) of the Security Police had been used there for the first time. They had been deployed again in the Sudeten territory, then the rest of Czecho-Slovakia, where there was even greater scope for the SS's attack on 'enemies of the state'. The way was paved for the massive escalation of uncontrolled brutality in Poland. Once more, five (later six) Einsatzgruppen were sent into action. They interpreted most liberally their brief to shoot 'hostages' in recrimination for any show of hostility, or 'insurgents' – seen as anyone giving the slightest indication of active opposition to the occupying forces. The need to sustain good relations with the Wehrmacht initially restricted the extent and arbitrariness of the shootings. It probably also at first constrained the 'action' aimed at liquidating the Polish nobility, clergy, and intelligentsia. This 'action' nevertheless claimed ultimately an estimated 60,000 victims. Plainly, with the occupation of Poland, the barbarities of the Einsatzgruppen had moved on to a new plane. The platform was established for what was subsequently to take place in the attack on the Soviet Union in 1941.

There was no shortage of eager helpers among the ethnic Germans in the former Polish territories. The explosion of violence recalled, in hugely magnified fashion, the wild and barbarous treatment of 'enemies of the state' in Germany in spring 1933. But now, after six years of cumulative onslaught on every tenet of humane and civilized behaviour, and persistent indoctrination with chauvinistic hatred, the penned-in aggression could be let loose externally on a downtrodden and despised enemy.

Some of the worst German atrocities in the weeks following the invasion were perpetrated by the Volksdeutscher Selbstschutz (Ethnic German Self-Protection), a civilian militia established on Hitler's directions in the first days of September and within little more than a week coming under the control of the SS. Himmler's adjutant, Ludolf von Alvensleben, took over its organization, and later led the Selbstschutz in West Prussia, where the extent of its brutality stood out even in the horrific catalogue of misdeeds of the organization's other branches. Especially in West Prussia, where ethnic conflict had been at its fiercest, the Selbstschutz carried out untold numbers of 'executions' of Polish civilians. The Selbstschutz was eventually wound up – in West Prussia in November, and elsewhere by early 1940 – but only because its uncontrolled atrocities were becoming counter-productive on account of the resulting conflicts with the army and German civil authorities in the occupied areas.

The rampaging actions of the Selbstschutz were only one element of the programme of radical 'ethnic struggle' designed by the SS leadership for the 'new order' in Poland. More systematic 'ethnic cleansing' operations, involving widespread liquidation of targeted groups, were mainly in the hands of the Security Police Einsatzgruppen, following in the wake of the military advance. Already at the end of the first week of the invasion, Heydrich was reported to be enraged – as, apparently, was Hitler too – at the legalities of the military courts, despite 200 executions a day. He was demanding shooting or hanging without trial. 'The nobility, clerics, and Jews must be done away with,' were his reported words. He repeated the same sentiments, referring to a general 'ground cleansing', to Halder's Quartermaster-General Eduard Wagner some days later. Reports of atrocities were not long in arriving. By 10–11 September accounts were coming in of an SS massacre of Jews herded into a church, and of an SS shooting of large numbers of Jews. On 12 September Admiral Canaris, chief of the Abwehr, told Keitel that he had heard 'that extensive shootings were planned in Poland and that especially the nobility and clergy were to be exterminated'. Keitel replied 'that this matter had already been decided by the Führer'. Chief of Staff Halder was already by then heard to have said that 'it was the intention of the Führer and of Göring to annihilate and exterminate the Polish people', and that 'the rest could not even be hinted at in writing'.

What it amounted to – an all-out 'ethnic cleansing' programme – was explained by Heydrich to the commanders of the Einsatzgruppen on 21 September. The thinking was that the former German provinces would become German Gaue. Another Gau with a 'foreign-speaking population' would be established, with its capital in Cracow. An 'eastern wall' would surround the German provinces, with the 'foreign-speaking Gau' forming a type of 'no man's land' in front of it. The Reichsführer-SS was to be appointed Settlement Commissar for the East (an appointment of vital importance, giving Himmler immense, practically unrestricted powers in the east, confirmed by secret edict of Hitler on 7 October). 'The deportation of Jews into the foreign-speaking Gau, expulsion over the demarcation-line has been approved by the Führer,' Heydrich went on. The process was to be spread over a year. As regards 'the solution of the Polish problem', the 3 per cent at most of the Polish leadership in the occupied territories 'had to be rendered harmless' and put in concentration camps. The Einsatzgruppen were to draw up lists of significant leaders, and of various professional and middle-class groups (including teachers and priests) who were to be deported to the designated 'dumping-ground' of the General Government. The 'primitive Poles' were to be used as migrant workers and gradually deported to the 'foreign-speaking Gau'. Jews in rural areas were to be removed, and placed in towns. Jews were systematically to be transported by goods-train from German areas. Heydrich also envisaged the deportation to Poland of the Reich's Jews, and of 30,000 gypsies.

Hitler spoke little over a week later to Rosenberg of the Germanization and deportation programme to be carried out in Poland. The three weeks spent in Poland during the campaign had confirmed his ingrained racial prejudices. 'The Poles,' Rosenberg recalled him saying: 'a thin Germanic layer, below that dreadful material. The Jews, the most horrible thing imaginable. The towns covered in dirt. He has learnt a lot in these weeks. Above all: if Poland had ruled for a few decades over the old parts of the Reich, everything would be lice-ridden and decayed. A clear, masterful hand was now needed to rule here.' Hitler then referred, along similar lines to Heydrich's address to his Einsatzgruppen chiefs, to his plans for the conquered Polish territories. 'He wanted to divide the now established territory into three strips: 1. between the Vistula and the Bug: the entire Jewry (also from the Reich) along with all somehow unreliable elements. On the Vistula an invincible Eastern Wall – even stronger than in the West. 2. Along the previous border a broad belt of Germanization and colonization. Here there would be a great task for the entire people: to create a German granary, strong peasantry, to resettle there good Germans from all over the world. 3. Between, a Polish "form of state". Whether after decades the settlement belt could be pushed forward will have to be left to the future.'

A few days later, Hitler spoke to Goebbels in similar vein. 'The Führer's judgement on the Poles is annihilatory,' Goebbels recorded. 'More animals than human beings . . . The filth of the Poles is unimaginable.' Hitler wanted no assimilation. 'They should be pushed into their reduced state' – meaning the General Government – 'and left entirely among themselves.' If Henry the Lion – the mighty twelfth-century Duke of Saxony and Bavaria, who had resettled peasants on lands in northern and eastern Germany – had conquered the east, the result, given the scope of power available at the time, would have been a 'slavified' German mongrel-race, Hitler went on. 'It's all the better as it is. Now at least we know the laws of race and can act accordingly.'

Hitler hinted in his Reichstag speech of 6 October, though in the vaguest terms for public consumption, at 'cleansing work' and massive ethnic resettlement as preparation for the 'new order of ethnographical relations' in former Poland. Only in confidential dealings with those in the regime's leadership who needed to know – a characteristic technique of his rule not to spread information beyond essential limits – did Hitler speak frankly, as he had done to Rosenberg and Goebbels, about what was intended. At a meeting on 17 October in the Reich Chancellery attended by Keitel, Frank, Himmler, Heß, Bormann, Lammers, Frick, and the State Secretary in the Reich Ministry of the Interior, Stuckart, Hitler outlined the draconian policy for Poland. The military should be happy to be freed from administrative responsibility. The General Government was not to become part of the Reich. It was not the task of the administration there to run it like a model province or to establish a sound economic and financial basis. The Polish intelligentsia were to be deprived of any chance to develop into a ruling class. The standard of living was to remain low: 'We only want to get labour supplies from there.' The administration there was to be given a free hand, independent of Berlin ministries. 'We don't want to do anything there that we do in the Reich,' was ominously noted. Carrying out the work there would involve 'a hard ethnic struggle that will not permit any legal restrictions. The methods will not be compatible with our normal principles.' Rule over the area would 'allow us to purify the Reich area too of Jews and Polacks'. Cooperation of the General Government with the new Gaue of Posen and West Prussia was to take place only for resettlement purposes (through Himmler's new role as head of the programme for the ethnic reordering of Poland). 'Cleverness and hardness in this ethnic struggle,' Hitler ended, with usual recourse to national needs as justification, 'must save us from again having to enter the fields of slaughter on account of this land.' 'The devil's work,' he called it.

Hitler's approval for what Heydrich had set in motion cannot be doubted. Referring back several months later to the chequered relations of the SS and police in Poland with the army leadership, Heydrich pointed out that the work of the Einsatzgruppen in Poland was 'in accordance with the special order of the Führer'. The 'political activity' carried out in Poland by the Reichsführer-SS, which had caused conflict with some of the army leadership, had followed 'the directives of the Führer as well as the General Field-Marshal'. He added 'that the directives according to which the police deployment took place were extraordinarily radical (e.g. orders of liquidation for numerous sectors of the Polish leadership, going into thousands)'. Since the order was not passed on to army leaders, they had presumed that the police and SS were acting arbitrarily.

Indeed, the army commanders on the ground in Poland had been given no explicit instructions about any mandate from Hitler for the murderous 'ethnic cleansing' policy of the SS and Security Police, though Brauchitsch, like Keitel, was well aware of what was intended. This was in itself characteristic of how the regime functioned, and of Hitler's keenness – through keeping full knowledge to the smallest circle possible, and speaking for the most part even there in generalities, however draconian – to cloud his own responsibility. The army's hands were far from unsullied by the atrocities in Poland. Brauchitsch's proclamation to the Poles on 1 September had told them that the Wehrmacht did not regard the population as its enemy, and that all agreements on human rights would be upheld. But already in the first weeks of September numerous army reports recounted plundering, 'arbitrary shootings', 'maltreatment of the unarmed, rapes', 'burning of synagogues', and massacres of Jews by soldiers of the Wehrmacht. The army leaders – even the most pro-Nazi among them – nevertheless regarded such repellent actions as serious lapses of discipline, not part of a consistent racially motivated policy of unremitting 'cleansing' to be furthered with all means possible, and sought to punish those involved through the military courts. (In fact, most were amnestied by Hitler through a decree on 4 October justifying German actions as retaliation 'out of bitterness for the atrocities committed by the Poles'.) The commanders on the ground in Poland, harsh though their own military rule was, did not see the atrocities which they acknowledged among their own troops – in their view regrettable, if inevitable, side-effects of the military conquest of a bitter enemy and perceived 'inferior' people – as part of an exterminatory programme of 'ethnic struggle'. Their approach, draconian though their treatment of the Poles was, differed strikingly from the thinking of Hitler, Himmler, and Heydrich.

Gradually, in the second half of September the unease among army commanders in Poland at the savagery of the SS's actions turned to unmistakable criticism. Awareness of this fed complaints from the Nazi leadership about the 'lack of understanding' in the army of what was required in the 'ethnic struggle'. Hitler told Goebbels on 13 October that the military in Poland were 'too soft and yielding' and would be replaced as soon as possible by civil administration. 'Only force is effective with the Poles,' he added. 'Asia begins in Poland.' On 17 October, in a step notably contributing to the extension of the SS's autonomy, Hitler removed the SS and police from military jurisdiction.

The most forthright – and courageous – denunciations of the continuing horrendous outrages of the SS were made in written reports to Brauchitsch by Colonel-General Johannes Blaskowitz, following the ending of military administration the commander of the army in Poland. His reports condemned the 'criminal atrocities, maltreatment, and plundering carried out by the SS, police, and administration', castigating the 'animal and pathological instincts' of the SS which had brought the slaughter of tens of thousands of Jews and Poles. Blaskowitz feared 'immeasurable brutalization and moral debasement' if the SS were not brought under control – something, he said, which was increasingly impossible within Poland 'since they can well believe themselves officially authorized and justified in committing any act of cruelty'. General Wilhelm Ulex, Commander-in-Chief of the southern section of the front, reported in similar vein.

The weak-kneed response of army Commander-in-Chief von Brauchitsch – in effect an apologia for the barbaric 'ethnic cleansing' policy authorized by Hitler – was fateful. It compromised the position of the army, and pointed the way to the accommodation between army and SS about the genocidal actions to be taken in the Soviet Union in 1941. Brauchitsch spoke of 'regrettable mistakes' in the 'difficult solution' of the 'ethnic-political tasks'. After lengthy discussions with the Reichsführer-SS, he was confident that the future would bring a change. Criticism endangering the 'unity and fighting power of the troops' had to be prohibited. 'The solution of ethnic-political tasks, necessary for securing German living space and ordered by the Führer, had necessarily to lead to otherwise unusual, harsh measures against the Polish population of the occupied area,' he stated. 'The necessarily accelerated execution of these tasks, caused by the imminently decisive struggle of the German people, naturally brought about a further intensification of these measures.' Doubtless anticipating the inevitable explosion at the inadequacies of the army, Brauchitsch did not even deliver Blaskowitz's reports in person to Hitler, but passed on at least the first report on 18 November 1939 via Hitler's army adjutant Gerhard Engel. The expected ferocious denunciation of the 'childish attitudes' in the army leadership inevitably followed. 'You can't wage war with Salvation Army methods,' Hitler raged.

The inquiries Himmler had set in train following the army complaints predictably concluded that it was a matter only of 'trivialities'. But the Reichsführer-SS was angered by the attacks. In March 1940 he eventually sought an opportunity to address the leaders of the army. He accepted responsibility for what had happened, though played down the reports, attributing the accounts of serious atrocities to rumour. According to the memory of one participant, General Weichs, he added that 'he was prepared, in matters that seemed perhaps incomprehensible, to take on responsibility before the people and the world, since the person of the Führer could not be connected with these things'. Another participant, with more cause than most to take a keen interest in Himmler's comments, General Ulex, recalled the Reichsführer-SS saying: 'I do nothing that the Führer does not know about.'

With the sanctioning of the liquidation programme at the core of the barbaric 'ethnic cleansing' drive in Poland, Hitler – and the regime he headed – had crossed the Rubicon. This was no longer a display of outright brutality at home that shocked – as had the massacre of the SA leadership in 1934, or even more so the November Pogrom against the Jews in 1938 – precisely because the structures and traditions of legality in the Reich, whatever the inroads made into them, had not been totally undermined. In what had once been Poland, the violence was unconstrained, systematic, and on a scale never witnessed within the Reich itself. Law, however draconian, counted for nothing. The police were given a free hand. Even the incorporated areas were treated for policing terms as outside the Reich. What was taking place in the conquered territories fell, to be sure, still far short of the all-out genocide that was to emerge during the Russian campaign in the summer of 1941. But it had near-genocidal traits. It was the training-ground for what was to follow.

Hitler's remarks to Rosenberg and Goebbels illustrated how his own impressions of the Poles provided for him the self-justification for the drastic methods he had approved. He had unquestionably been strengthened in these attitudes by Himmler and Heydrich. Goebbels, too, played to Hitler's prejudices in ventilating his own. In mid-October Goebbels told him of the preliminary work carried out on what was to become the nauseating antisemitic 'documentary' film *Der ewige Jude* (The Eternal Jew). Hitler listened with great interest. What Goebbels said to Hitler might be implied from his own reactions when he viewed the first pictures from what he called the 'ghetto film'. The appearance of the degraded and downtrodden Jews, crushed under the Nazi yoke, had come to resemble the caricature that Goebbels's own propaganda had produced. 'Descriptions so terrible and brutal in detail that your blood clots in your veins,' he commented. 'You shrink back at the sight of such brutishness. This Jewry must be annihilated.' A fortnight or so later Goebbels showed Hitler the horrible ritual-slaughter scenes from the film, and reported on his own impressions – already pointing plainly in a genocidal direction – gleaned during his visit to the Lodz ghetto: 'It's indescribable. Those are no longer human beings. They are animals. So it's not a humanitarian but a surgical task. Otherwise Europe will perish through the Jewish disease.'

In a most literal sense, Goebbels, Himmler, Heydrich, and other leading Nazis were 'working towards the Führer', whose authority allowed the realization of their own fantasies. The same was true of countless lesser figures in the racial experiment under way in the occupied territories. Academics – historians at the forefront – excelled themselves in justifying German hegemony in the east. Racial 'experts' in the party set to work to construct the 'scientific' basis for the inferiority of the Poles. Armies of planners, moved to the east, started to let their imagination run riot in devising megalomaniac schemes for ethnic resettlement and social restructuring. Hitler had to do no more than provide the general licence for barbarism. There was no shortage of ready hands to put it into practice.

This began with the heads of the civil administration in occupied Poland. Forster in Danzig-West Prussia, Greiser in the Warthegau, and Frank in the General Government were trusted 'Old Fighters', hand-picked for the task by Hitler. They knew what was expected of them. Regular and precise directives were not necessary.

The combined headship of state and party in the incorporated area, following the structure used in the 'Ostmark' and Sudetenland, provided far greater influence for the party than was the case in the 'Old Reich'. Hitler's attitude towards policy in the incorporated territories was typical. He placed great value on giving his Gauleiter the 'necessary freedom of action' to carry out their difficult tasks. He stressed 'that he only demanded a report from the Gauleiter after ten years that their area was German, that is purely German. He would not ask about the methods they had used to make the area German, and it was immaterial to him if sometime in the future it were established that the methods to win this territory were not pretty or open to legal objection.' The inevitable consequence of this broad mandate – though it was alleged that it ran counter to Hitler's intention - was competition between Greiser and his arch-rival Forster to be the first to announce that his Gau was fully Germanized. Greiser and Forster went about meeting this aim in different ways. While, to Himmler's intense irritation, Forster swept as many Poles in his area as possible into the third group of the *Deutsche Volksliste* (German Ethnic List), giving them German citizenship on approval (constantly subject, that is, to revocation), Greiser pushed fanatically and ruthlessly for complete *apartheid* – the maximum separation of the two ethnic groups. While Forster frequently clashed with Himmler, Greiser gave full support to the policies of the Reichsführer-SS, and worked in the closest cooperation with the Higher SS-and-Police Chief in the Warthegau, Wilhelm Koppe.

The Warthegau turned years of indescribable torment for the subjugated people into the nearest approximation to a vision of the 'New Order' in the east. The vast deportation and resettlement programmes, the ruthless eradication of Polish cultural influence, the mass-closing of Catholic churches and arrests or murder of clergy, the eviction of Poles from their property, and the scarcely believable levels of discrimination against the majority Polish population – always accompanied by the threat of summary execution – were carried out under the aegis of Greiser and Koppe with little need to involve Hitler. Not least, the vicious drive by the same pairing to rid their Germanized area of the lowest of the low – the Jewish minority in the Warthegau – was to form a vital link in the chain that would lead by late 1941 to the 'Final Solution'.

The rapidity with which the geographical divisions and administrative structure for the occupied territories of former Poland had been improvised, the free hand given to party bosses, the widespread autonomy which the police had obtained, and the complete absence of legal constraint, had created a power free-for-all in the 'wild east'. But where conflict among the occupying authorities was most endemic, as in the General Government, the greatest concentration of power was plainly revealed to lie in the hands of the Security Police, represented by the Higher SS-and-Police Chief, backed by Himmler and Heydrich. Himmler's 'Black Order', under the Reichsführer's extended powers as Reich Commissar for the Consolidation of Germandom, and mandated by Hitler to 'cleanse' the east, had come into its own in the new occupied territories.

III

Meanwhile, within the Reich itself the beginning of the war had also marked a vital step in the descent into modern barbarism. Here, too, Hitler now authorized mass murder.

Parallel to the murders in occupied Poland, it was an irreversible advance in the direction of genocide. The programme – euphemistically called the 'euthanasia action' – to kill the mentally ill and others incurably sick that he launched in autumn 1939 was to provide a gangway to the vaster extermination programme to come. And, like the destruction of European Jewry, it was evidently linked in his own mind with the war that, he was certain, would bring the fulfilment of his ideological 'mission'.

It was some time in October that Hitler had one of his secretaries type, on his own headed notepaper and backdated to 1 September 1939 – the day that the war had begun – the single sentence: 'Reichsleiter Bouhler and Dr med. Brandt are commissioned with the responsibility of extending the authority of specified doctors so that, after critical assessment of their condition, those adjudged incurably ill can be granted mercy-death.' He took a pen and signed his name below this lapidary, open-ended death-sentence.

By this time, the killing of mental patients, already authorized verbally by Hitler, was well under way. It suited neither Hitler's style nor his instinct to transmit lethal orders in writing. The reason he did so on this one and only occasion was because of the difficulties, in a land where the writ of law was still presumed to run, already being encountered by those attempting, without any obvious authority, to build an organization in conditions of secrecy to implement a murderous mandate. Even then, knowledge of Hitler's written authorization was confined to as few persons as possible. It was ten months later, on 27 August 1940, before even the Reich Minister of Justice, Franz Gürtner, faced with growing criticism of the illegality of what was inevitably leaking more and more into the open, was shown a facsimile of it.

Indeed, there was no basis of legality for what was taking place. Hitler explicitly refused to have a 'euthanasia' law, rejecting the prospect of a cumbersome bureaucracy and legal constraints. Even according to the legal theories of the time, Hitler's mandate could not be regarded as a formal Führer decree and did not, therefore, possess the character of law. But an order from the Führer, whatever its legal status, was nonetheless seen as binding. That applied also to Reich Justice Minister Gürtner. Once he had seen with his own eyes that Hitler's will stood behind the liquidation of the mentally sick, and that it was not the work of party underlings operating without authority, he gave up his attempts on legal grounds to block or regulate the killings. To a courageous district judge, Lothar Kreyssig, who had written frank protest letters to him about the crass illegality of the action, and on being shown Hitler's authorization had exclaimed that even on the basis of positive legal theory wrong could not be turned into right, Gürtner gave a simple reply: 'If you cannot recognize the will of the Führer as a source of law, as a basis of law, then you cannot remain a judge.' Kreyssig's notice of retirement followed soon afterwards.

The exchange between Gürtner and Kreyssig shows how far the acceptance of 'Führer power' had undermined the essence of law. The genesis of the 'euthanasia action' that Hitler authorized in writing in October 1939 provides, beyond that, a classic example of the way 'working towards the Führer' converted an ideological goal into realizable policy.

Hitler was indispensable to the process. His well-aired views from the 1920s on 'euthanasia' served after 1933 as an encouragement to those, most notably represented in the National Socialist Doctors' League but by no means confined to fanatical Nazis, anxious to act on the 'problem' of what they described as the 'ballast' of society.

The notion of the 'destruction of life not worth living' had already been the subject of much public debate. Doctors had, however, overwhelmingly rejected euthanasia during the Weimar era. Hitler's takeover of power changed the climate – and opened up new possibilities to the medical profession. Some leading psychiatrists were more than ready to exploit them. Hitler's presumed intentions provided guidelines for their endeavours, even if the time was still not deemed right to introduce the programme they wanted. Above all, Hitler's role was decisive in 1938–9 in providing approval for every step that extended into the full 'euthanasia' programme from the autumn of 1939 onwards. Without that approval, it is plain, and without the ideological drive that he embodied, there would have been no 'euthanasia action'.

But the mentality which led to the killing of the mentally sick was no creation of Hitler. Building on foundations firmly laid, especially in the wake of the catastrophic public funding cuts during the Depression years, the erection of the dictatorship had provided licence to the medical and psychiatric professions after 1933 to think the unthinkable. Minority views, constrained even in a failing democracy, could now become mainstream. The process gathered pace. By 1939, doctors and nurses attached to the asylums were aware of what was required. So was the medical bureaucracy which oiled the wheels of the killing machinery. The climate of opinion among the general public was by this time also not unfavourable. Though there were strong feelings against euthanasia, particularly among those attached to the Churches, others were in favour – notably, it seems, in the case of mentally ill or disabled children – or at least passively prepared to accept it.

Finally, but not least, the point at which, coinciding with the outbreak of war, a secret programme of mass murder could be implemented would have been unimaginable without the progressive erosion of legality and disintegration of formal structures of government that had taken place since 1933.

Hitler had given a strong indication of his own thoughts on how to deal with the incurably ill in *Mein Kampf*, where he advocated their sterilization. When he spoke at the Nuremberg Party Rally in 1929 about how the weakest in society should be handled, the economic argument used by the eugenics lobby in the medical profession and others weighed less heavily than questions of 'racial hygiene' and the 'future maintenance of our ethnic strength, indeed of our ethnic nationhood altogether'. 'If Germany were to have a million children a year,' he declared, 'and do away with 700,000–800,000 of the weakest of them, the result would finally be perhaps even a rise in strength.' This implied racial engineering through mass murder, justified through social-Darwinist ideology, not 'euthanasia' in the conventional sense as the voluntary release from terminal illness.

According to the comments of his doctor, Karl Brandt, in his post-war trial, Hitler was known to favour involuntary euthanasia at the latest from 1933 onwards. His position was indicated in his reply in 1935 to the Reich Doctors' Leader Gerhard Wagner. Evidently, Wagner was pressing for radical measures to bring about the 'destruction of life not worth living'. Hitler reportedly told him that he would 'take up and carry out the questions of euthanasia' in the event of a war. He was 'of the opinion that such a problem could be more smoothly and easily carried out in war', and that resistance, as was to be expected from the Churches, would then have less of an impact than in peacetime. He intended, therefore, 'in the event of a war radically to solve the problem of the mental asylums'.

For the next three years, Hitler had little involvement with the 'euthanasia' issue. Others were more active. Evidently encouraged by Hitler's remarks that he did intend, once the opportunity presented itself through the war for which the regime was preparing, to introduce a 'euthanasia programme', Reich Doctors' Leader Wagner pushed forward discussions on how the population should be prepared for such action. Calculations were published on the cost of upkeep of the mentally sick and hereditarily ill, instilling the impression of what could be done for the good of the people with vast resouces now being 'wasted' on 'useless' lives. Cameras were sent into the asylums to produce scenes to horrify the German public and convince them of the need to eliminate those portrayed as the dregs of society for the good of the whole population. The National Socialist Racial and Political Office produced five silent films of this kind between 1935 and 1937.

Meanwhile, the 'Chancellery of the Führer of the NSDAP', the agency which would come to run the 'euthanasia action' from 1939 onwards, was doing all it could to expand its own power-base in the political jungle of the Third Reich. Despite its impressive name, the Führer Chancellery had little actual power. Hitler had set it up at the end of 1934 to deal with correspondence from party members directed to himself as head of the NSDAP. It was officially meant to serve as the agency to keep the Führer in direct touch with the concerns of his people. Much of the correspondence was a matter of trivial complaints, petty grievances, and minor personal squabbles of party members. But a vast number of letters to Hitler did pour in after 1933 – around quarter of a million a year in the later 1930s. And, to preserve the fiction of the Führer listening to the cares of his people, many of them needed attention.

Hitler put the Führer Chancellery under the control of Philipp Bouhler – a member of the Party's *Reichsleitung* (Reich Leadership) since 1933, a quiet, bureaucratic type but intensely loyal and deferential, and ideologically fanatical. Exploiting his direct connections with Hitler, the vagueness of his remit, and the randomness of the business that came the way of the organization he headed, he was now able to expand his own little empire. Of the various departments, the most important was

Department (*Amt*) II (from 1939 Main Department – *Hauptamt*) headed by Bouhler's deputy, Viktor Brack. This Department itself covered a wide range of heterogeneous business but, in its section 'IIb', under Hans Hefelmann, was responsible for handling petitions relating to the Reich Ministry of the Interior, including sensitive issues touching on the competence of the health department of the Ministry. Brack, five years younger than Bouhler, was, if anything, even more ambitious than his boss, and was ideologically attuned to what was wanted. He was ready to grasp an opportunity when he saw one.

This came some time in the first months of 1939. Around that time the father of a severely handicapped child – born blind, with no left forearm and a deformed leg – in Pomßen, near Leipzig, sent in a petition to Hitler, asking for the child to be released through mercy-killing. The petition arrived in Hefelmann's office in the Führer Chancellery. Hefelmann did not consider involving either the Reich Ministry of the Interior or the Reich Ministry of Justice. He thought it should be taken to Hitler himself, to see how the Führer thought it should be handled. This was probably in May or June 1939. Hitler sent his doctor, Karl Brandt, to the University of Leipzig Children's Clinic, to consult the child's doctors with the mandate, if the position was as the father had described it, to authorize the doctors in his name to carry out euthanasia. This was done towards the end of July 1939. Soon after Brandt's return, he was verbally empowered by Hitler, as was Bouhler, to take similar action should other cases arise. (The case of the child from Pomßen was evidently not an isolated instance around this time.) Whether Hitler took this step unprompted, or whether it followed a suggestion from Brandt or the ambitious Bouhler is not known. But between February and May 1939 Hefelmann, on Brandt's instructions, carried out discussions with doctors known to be sympathetic and eventually set up a camouflaged organization that was given the title 'Reich Committee for the Scientific Registration of Serious Hereditary and Congenital Suffering'. Between 5,000 and 8,000 children are estimated to have been put to death, mostly with injections of the barbiturate luminal, under its aegis.

In July Hitler told Lammers, Bormann, and Dr Leonardo Conti (recently appointed Reich Health Leader and State Secretary for Health in the Reich Ministry of the Interior) that he favoured mercy-killing for seriously ill mental patients. Better use of hospitals, doctors, and nursing staff could be made in war, he stated. Conti was commissioned to investigate the feasibility of such a programme. By then, war was looming. Hitler's own comments showed that he continued to see a 'euthanasia programme' in the context of war. By that time, too, Hitler had probably received the evaluation commissioned around the start of the year by Brack from Dr Joseph Mayer, Professor of Moral Theology at the University of Paderborn. Hitler had been uneasy about the likely reaction of the Churches in the event of the introduction of a 'euthanasia programme'. He imagined both the Catholic and Protestant Churches would outrightly oppose it. Mayer, who in 1927 had published a tract in favour of the legal sterilization of the mentally sick, was now asked to assess the attitude of the Catholic Church. He sided with the right of the state to take the lives of the mentally ill. Though this was against orthodox Catholic teaching, Mayer left the impression that unequivocal opposition from the Churches was not to be expected. This was the conclusion which Hitler apparently drew, following further discreet inquiry. The biggest internal obstacle to such a programme appeared to be surmountable. The programme could go ahead.

The organization, set up to deal with the 'euthanasia' of children, was to hand. Brack had heard indirectly of Hitler's instructions to Conti at the July meeting. Spotting his chance, but needing to act without delay, if control were not to be lost to Conti and the Reich Ministry of the Interior, he had Hefelmann draw up a short statistical memorandum on the asylums and took it to Bouhler. The head of the Führer Chancellery had little difficulty in persuading Hitler to extend the authorization he had earlier granted to himself and Brandt to deal with the children's 'euthanasia'. It was in August 1939 that Hitler told Bouhler that he wanted the strictest secrecy maintained, and 'a completely unbureaucratic solution of this problem'. The Reich Ministry of the Interior should be kept out of it as far as possible.

Shortly after this, a sizeable number of doctors were summoned to a meeting in the Reich Chancellery to seek their views on such a programme. They were overwhelmingly in favour and ready to cooperate. They suggested that around 60,000 patients might be 'eligible'. The number involved meant there was a serious problem about maintaining secrecy. Once more, camouflaged organizations were needed. Three were set up to distribute questionnaires to the asylums (the Reich Association of Asylums), handle personnel and finance matters (Community

Foundation for the Care of Asylums), and organize transport (Community Patients' Transport). They were based, under Brack's direction, in an unpretentious villa in Berlin-Charlottenburg, Tiergartenstraße 4, from which the entire 'euthanasia action' drew its code-name 'T4'. Apart from Bouhler, Brandt, and Brack the organization comprised 114 persons.

Plainly, the construction of such an organization and the implementation of its gruesome task needed more than simply the verbal authorization that had sufficed for the children's 'euthanasia' up to then. This is what prompted Hitler's almost casual written authorization some weeks later, backdated (as we noted) to 1 September. This formless empowering, and the way the Führer Chancellery had been able, without the ministries of state even being informed, to expropriate control over a programme calculated to bring the deaths of tens of thousands in an action lacking any basis in law, is the clearest indication of how far internal structures of government had been deformed and superseded by executive agencies devoted to implementing what they saw as the will of the Führer. The cloak-and-dagger secrecy – some leading figures, including Brack, even worked with false names – highlighted the illegality of what was taking place. The regime had taken the step into outright criminality.

The medical staff of the asylums selected their own patients for inclusion in the 'euthanasia action'. They, too, were 'working towards the Führer', whether or not this was their overt motivation. Patients included had their names marked with a red cross. Those to be spared had a blue 'minus' sign against their names. The killing, mostly by carbon monoxide gas administered by doctors under no compulsion to participate, was carried out in selected asylums, the most notorious of which were Grafeneck, Hadamar, Bernburg, Brandenburg, Hartheim, and Sonnenstein.

Alongside the T4 'action', the Gauleiter of Pomerania, Franz Schwede-Coburg, rapidly alerted to the new possibilities, worked closely with the SS in October 1939 to 'clear' the asylums near the coastal towns of Stralsund, Swinemünde, and Stettin to make space for ethnic Germans from the Baltic region (and for an SS barracks at Stralsund). Patients were removed from the asylums, transported to Neustadt, not far from Danzig, and shot by squads of SS men. Gauleiter Erich Koch was quick to follow suit, arranging to pay for the costs of 'evacuating' 1,558 patients from asylums in his Gau of East Prussia, liquidated by an SS squad provided by Wilhelm Koppe, newly-appointed Police Chief in Reichsgau Posen. This was the 'Sonderkommando Lange', which was soon put to use deploying prototype mobile gas-vans to kill the mentally sick in this part of annexed Poland. By mid-1940, these regional 'actions' had claimed the lives of an estimated 10,000 victims.

By the time 'Aktion-T4' was halted – as secretly as it had begun – in August 1941, the target-figure laid down by the doctors in the late summer had been surpassed. In the T4 'action' alone by this date, between 70,000 and 90,000 patients are reckoned to have fallen victim to Hitler's 'euthanasia programme'. Since the killings were neither confined to the T4 'action', nor ended with the halt to that 'action' in 1941, the total number of victims of Nazism's drive to liquidate the mentally ill may have been close on double that number.

IV

Was there the will to halt the already advanced rupture of civilization and descent into modern barbarism that had so swiftly broken new ground since the start of the war? And even if there were the will, could anything be done?

Given Hitler's outright dominance and unassailable position within the regime, significant change could by this time, autumn 1939, be brought about only through his deposition or assassination. This basic truth had been finally grasped the previous summer, during the Sudeten crisis, by those individuals in high-ranking places in the military, Foreign Ministry, and elsewhere close to the levers of power who had tentatively felt their way towards radical opposition to the regime. For long, even some of these individuals had tended to exempt Hitler from the criticism they levelled at others, especially Himmler, Heydrich, and the Gestapo. But by now they were aware that without change at the very top, there would be no change at all. This realization started to forge tighter links between the disparate individuals and groups concerned. Colonel Hans Oster, Chief of Staff at the Abwehr, backed by his boss, the enigmatic Admiral Canaris, was the driving-force in making the Abwehr the centre of an oppositional network, building on the contacts made and relationships forged the previous summer. Oster placed his most trusted associate, implacably opposed to Hitler, Lieutenant-Colonel Helmuth Groscurth, as liaison with Chief of Staff Halder at the headquarters of the Army High Command in Zossen, just south of Berlin. He encouraged Weizsäcker to appoint, as the Foreign Office's liaison at army head-quarters, another opponent of the regime, Rittmeister (Cavalry Major) Hasso von Etzdorf. This was probably done on the initiative of Erich Kordt, head of the Ministerial Bureau who continued, under Weiz-säcker's protection, to make the Foreign Office a further centre of oppositional contacts, placing sympathizers (including his brother, Theo) in embassies abroad. Oster also appointed to his own staff an individual who would play an energetic role in extending and deepening oppositional contacts while officially gathering foreign intelligence: the able and well-connected lawyer Hans Dohnanyi, for some years a close associate of Reich Justice Minister Gürtner, and who had helped clear former Commander-in-Chief of the Army Fritsch of the trumped-up charges of homosexual relations that had been laid against him. Dohnanyi would regularly drive Oster during autumn 1939 – dismal weeks for those opposed to Hitler – to see the man whom practically all who hoped to see an early end to the Nazi regime regarded as the patron of the oppositional groups, former Chief of the General Staff, Ludwig Beck. Gradually, something beginning to resemble a fundamental, con-spiratorial resistance movement among, necessarily, existing or former 'servants' of the regime was in the process of emerging. The dilemma for those individuals, mostly national-conservative in inclination, pat-riots all, in contemplating the unseating of the head of state was great, and even more acute now that Germany was at war.

The autumn of 1939 would provide a crucial testing-time for the national-conservative resistance. In the end, they would resign them-selves to failure. At the centre of their concern was not in the first instance the bestiality in Poland (though the detailed reports of the abominations there certainly served to cement oppositional feeling and the sense of urgency, both for moral reasons and out of a sense of national shame, at the need to be rid of Hitler and his henchmen who were responsible for such criminal acts). Nor was it the 'euthanasia action'. Of the mass murder in the asylums they had not for months any real inkling. At any rate, it was not voiced as a matter of prime concern. The key issue for them, as it had been for two years or so, was the certainty that Hitler was leading Germany to catastrophe through engaging in war with the Western powers. Preventing a calamitous attack on France and Britain, and ending the war, was vital. This issue came to a head in the autumn of 1939, when Hitler was determined to press on with an early attack on the West. But even before he pulled back – because of poor weather conditions – from such a risky venture in the autumn and winter, then went on the following spring to gain unimaginable military successes in the western campaign, the fragility, weakness, and divisions of the nascent resistance had been fully laid bare. No attempt to remove Hitler had been made.

Hitler could by late 1939 be brought down in only one of two ways: a *coup d'état* from above, meaning a strike from within the regime's leadership from those with access to power and military might; or, something which the Dictator never ruled out, an assassination attempt from below, by a maverick individual operating entirely alone, outside any of the known – by now tiny, fragmented, and utterly powerless – left-wing underground resistance groups which could so easily be infiltrated by the Gestapo. While generals and leading civil servants pondered whether they *might* act, but lacked the will and determination to do so, one man with no access to the corridors of power, no political links, and no hard-and-fast ideology, a Swabian joiner by the name of Georg Elser, *did* act. In early November 1939 Elser would come closer to destroying Hitler than anyone until July 1944. Only luck would save the Dictator on this occasion. And Elser's motives, built on the naïvety of elemental feeling rather than arising from the tortured consciences of the better-read and more knowledgeable, would mirror not the interests of those in high places but, without doubt, concerns of countless ordinary Germans at the time. We will return to them shortly.

For Hitler, the swift and comprehensive demolition of Poland did not signal a victory to sit upon and await developments. Certainly, he hoped that the West, having now witnessed the might of the Wehrmacht in action, would – from his point of view – see sense, and come to terms with Germany. The peace feelers that he put out in September and October were couched in this vein. As Weizsäcker – reckoning the chances of peace to be no higher than 20 per cent – put it early in October, summarizing what he understood as Hitler's desired outcome, in the somewhat unlikely event that London might agree to a settlement at the expense of Poland, Germany 'would be spared the awkward decision on how England could be militarily forced down'. As it was,

Hitler, though his overtures were serious enough, had few expectations that Britain would show interest in a settlement, particularly once the British cabinet had announced that it was preparing for a war that would last at least three years. He was sure that the western powers would try to hold out as long as possible, until their armaments programmes were complete. That would mark a danger-point for Germany. Though – a view not shared by his generals – he held the French military in some contempt, he had a high esteem of British resilience and fighting-power. And behind the British, there was always the threat (which at this time he did not rate highly) that in due course the Americans would intervene. So there was no time to lose. On the very day after his return to Berlin, with the shells still raining down on Warsaw, Hitler told his military leaders to prepare for an attack on the West that very autumn.

'Militarily,' he declared, 'time, especially in the psychological and material sense, works against us.' It was, therefore, 'essential that immediate plans for an attack against France be prepared'. The rainy season would arrive within a few weeks. The air-force would be better in spring. 'But we cannot wait,' he insisted. If a settlement with Chamberlain were not possible, he would 'smash the enemy until he collapses'. The defeat of France, it was plainly inferred, would force Britain to terms. The goal was 'to bring England to its knees; to destroy France'. His favoured time for carrying out the attack was the end of October. The Commanders-in-Chief – even Göring – were taken aback. But none protested. Hitler casually threw his notes into the fire when he had finished speaking.

Two days later, Hitler told Rosenberg that he would propose a major peace conference (together with an armistice and demobilization) to regulate all matters rationally. Rosenberg asked whether he intended to prosecute the war in the West. 'Naturally,' replied Hitler. The Maginot Line, Rosenberg recorded him saying, was no longer a deterrent. If the English did not want peace, he would attack them with all means available 'and annihilate them' – again, his favourite phrase.

Hitler's speech to the Reichstag on 6 October indeed held out, as he had indicated to Rosenberg, the prospect of a conference of the leading nations to settle Europe's problems of peace and security. But a starting-point was that the division of Poland between Germany and the Soviet Union was to remain. There would be no recreation of the Poland of the Versailles settlement. It would be peace on Hitler's terms, with no concessions on what he had won. He painted a lurid picture of death and destruction if the western powers should decline his 'offer'. He blamed the warmongering on 'a certain Jewish-international capitalism and journalism', implying in particular Churchill and his supporters. If Churchill's view should prevail, he concluded, then Germany would fight. Riding one of his main hobby-horses, he added: 'A November 1918 will never be repeated in German history.' The speech amounted to an olive-branch clenched in a mailed fist.

Hitler's 'offer' was dismissed by Chamberlain in a speech in the House of Commons six days later. It was what Hitler had expected. He had not waited. On the very day of his Reichstag speech, he stressed to Brauchitsch and Halder that a decisive move in the north-west was necessary to prevent a French advance that autumn through Belgium, threatening the Ruhr. Two days later Brauchitsch was informed that Hitler had provisionally set 25 November as the date of attack. On 9 October, Hitler completed a lengthy memorandum that he had worked on for two nights, outlining and justifying his plans for an attack on the West. He had specifically prepared it because of his awareness of opposition to the idea in the army leadership. Again, he emphasized that time was of the essence. The attack could not begin soon enough. The aim was the complete military defeat of the western powers. He read out the memorandum at a meeting with his military leaders on 10 October. Its contents were embodied in 'Directive No.6 for the Conduct of War' issued later that day (though dated 9 October), stating Hitler's determination 'without letting much time pass by' to take offensive action.

When Hitler heard on 12 October of Chamberlain's rejection of his 'peace offer', he lost no time in announcing, even without waiting for the full text of Chamberlain's speech, that Britain had spurned the hand of peace and that, consequently, the war continued. On 16 October Hitler told Brauchitsch he had given up hope of coming to an agreement with the West. 'The British,' he said, 'will be ready to talk only after defeats. We must get at them as quickly as possible.' He reckoned with a date between 15 and 20 November. Within a matter of days, Hitler had brought this date forward and now fixed 'Case Yellow', as the attack on the West had been code-named, for 12 November.

Speaking to his generals, Hitler confined himself largely to military objectives. To his trusted circle, and to party leaders, he was more expressive. Goebbels found him high in confidence on 11 October. Germany's defeat in the last war, he stated, was solely attributable to treachery. This time traitors would not be spared. He responded to Chamberlain's dismissal of his 'peace offer' by stating that he was glad that he could now 'go for England'. He had given up almost all hope of peace. 'The English will have to learn the hard way,' he stated.

He was in similar mood when he addressed the Reichs- and Gauleiter in a two-hour speech on 21 October. He reckoned war with the West was unavoidable. There was no other choice. But at its end would be 'the great and all-embracing German people's Reich'. He would, Hitler told his party leaders, unleash his major assault on the West – and on England itself – within a fortnight or so. He would use all methods available, including attacks on cities. After defeating England and France he would again turn to the East. Then – an allusion to the Holy Roman Empire of the Middle Ages – he would create a Germany as of old, incorporating Belgium and Switzerland. Hitler was evidently still thinking along such lines when he told Goebbels a few days later he had earmarked Burgundy for the resettlement of the South Tyroleans. 'He's already distributing French provinces,' noted the Propaganda Minister. 'He hurries far ahead of all steps of development. Just like every genius.'

On 6 November Goebbels was again listening to Hitler's views on the war. 'The strike against the western powers will not have to wait much longer,' he recorded. 'Perhaps,' added Goebbels, 'the Führer will succeed sooner than we all think in annulling the Peace of Westphalia. With that his historic life will be crowned.' Goebbels thought the decision to go ahead was imminent.

All the signs are that the pressure for an early strike against the West came directly from Hitler, without initiation or prompting from other quarters. That it received the support of Goebbels and the party leadership was axiomatic. Within the military, it was a different matter. Hitler could reckon with the backing – or at least lack of objection – of Raeder, Commander-in-Chief of the Navy. And whatever his private anxieties, Göring would never deviate in public from Hitler's line. But, as Hitler recognized, the decision to attack the West already in the autumn set him once more on a collision course with the army leadership, spearheaded by Brauchitsch and Halder. On 14 October, primed by Weizsäcker about Hitler's reaction to Chamberlain's speech rejecting his 'peace offer', the head of the army and his Chief of Staff met to discuss the consequences. Halder noted three possibilities: attack, wait, 'fundamental changes'. None offered prospects of decisive success, least of all the last one 'since it is essentially negative and tends to render us vulnerable'. The qualifying remarks were made by Brauchitsch. The weak, ultra-cautious, and tradition-bound Commander-in-Chief of the Army could not look beyond conventional attempts to dissuade Hitler from what he thought was a disastrous course of action. But he was evidently responding to a suggestion floated by Halder, following his discussions with Weizsäcker the previous day, to have Hitler arrested at the moment of the order for attack on the West. The cryptic third possibility signified then no less than the extraordinary fact that in the early stages of a major war the two highest representatives of the army were airing the possibility of a form of *coup d'état* involving the removal of Hitler as head of state.

The differences between the two army leaders were nonetheless wide. And nothing flowed from the discussion in the direction of an embryonic plan to unseat Hitler. Brauchitsch attempted, within the bounds of orthodoxy, to have favoured generals such as Reichenau and Rundstedt try to influence Hitler to change his mind – a fruitless enterprise. Halder went further. By early November he was, if anything, still more convinced that direct action against Hitler was necessary to prevent the imminent catastrophe. In this, his views were coming to correspond with the small numbers of radical opponents of the regime in the Foreign Ministry and in the Abwehr who were now actively contemplating measures to remove Hitler.

In the last weeks of October various notions of deposing Hitler – often unrealistic or scarcely thought through – were furtively pondered by the tiny, disparate, only loosely connected, oppositional groups. Goerdeler and his main contacts – Hassell (the former Ambassador to Rome), Beck, and Johannes Popitz (former State Secretary in the Reich Finance Ministry) – were one such cluster, weighing up for a time whether a transitional government headed by Göring (whose reluctance to engage in war with Britain was known to them) might be an option. This cluster, through Beck, forged loose links with the group based in the Abwehr – Oster, Dohnanyi, Hans-Bernd Gisevius (one-time Gestapo officer but by now radically opposed to Hitler), and Groscurth. The latter grouping worked out a plan of action for a coup, involving the arrest of Hitler (perhaps declaring him mentally ill), along with Himmler,

Heydrich, Ribbentrop, Göring, Goebbels, and other leading Nazis. Encouraged by their chief, Admiral Canaris, and driven on by Oster, the Abwehr group attempted, though with little success, to gain backing for their ideas from selected officers at General Staff headquarters in Zossen. Their ambivalence about Halder meant that they did not approach him directly. Moreover, they knew nothing of the thoughts he had aired to Brauchitsch on 14 October. A third set of individuals sharing the view that Hitler had to be removed and war with the West prevented centred on Weizsäcker in the Foreign Ministry, and was chiefly represented by Erich Kordt, who was able to utilize his position as head of Ribbentrop's Ministerial Bureau to foster contacts at home and abroad. As we noted, this grouping had contact to the Abwehr group and to known sympathizers in the General Staff – mainly staff officers, though at this point not Halder himself – through Weizsäcker's army liaison, Legation Secretary Hasso von Etzdorf.

Halder himself (and his most immediate friend and subordinate General Otto von Stülpnagel) came round to the idea of a putsch by the end of the month, after Hitler had confirmed his intention of a strike on 12 November. Halder sent Stülpnagel to take surreptitious soundings among selected generals about their likely response to a coup. The findings were not encouraging. While army-group commanders such as Bock and Rundstedt were opposed to an offensive against the West, they rejected the idea of a putsch, partly on the grounds that they were themselves unsure whether they would retain the backing of their subordinate officers. In addition, Halder established to his own satisfaction, based on a 'sample' of public opinion drawn from the father of his chauffeur and a few others, that the German people supported Hitler and were not ready for a putsch. Halder's hesitancy reflected his own deep uncertainty about the moral as well as security aspect of a strike against the head of state and supreme commander of the armed forces. Others took a bolder stance. But, though loosely bonded through parallel thoughts of getting rid of Hitler, the different oppositional clusters had no coherent, unified, and agreed plan for action. Nor, while now accepting Halder's readiness to act, was there full confidence in the determination of the Chief of Staff, on whom practically everything depended, to see it through.

This was the position around noon on 5 November when Brauchitsch nervously made his way through the corridors of the Reich Chancellery to confront Hitler directly about the decision to attack the West. If the attack were to go ahead on schedule on 12 November, the order to make operational preparations had to be confirmed to the Commander-in-Chief of the Army by 1 p.m. on the 5th. Among the oppositional groups, the hope was that Brauchitsch could finally be persuaded to go along with a putsch if Hitler, as was to be expected, held firm to his decision for an attack. Halder waited in the ante-room while Brauchitsch and Hitler conferred together. Keitel joined them some while later. The meeting was a fiasco. It lasted no longer than twenty minutes. Brauchitsch hesitantly began to tell Hitler that preparations were not sufficiently advanced for an offensive against the West which, therefore, had every chance of proving catastrophic. He went on to back up his argument by pointing out that the infantry had shown morale and technical weaknesses in the attack on Poland, and that the discipline of officers and men had often been lacking. The Front showed similar symptoms to those of 1917–18, he claimed. This was a bad mistake by Brauchitsch. It diverted from the main issue, and, as Brauchitsch could have anticipated, it provoked Hitler into a furious outburst. He wanted concrete evidence, he fumed, and demanded to know how many death-sentences had been carried out. He did not believe Brauchitsch, and would fly the next night to the front to see for himself. Then he dismissed Brauchitsch's main point. The army was unprepared, he asserted, because it did not want to fight. The weather would still be bad in the spring – and furthermore bad for the enemy too. He knew the 'spirit of Zossen', he raged, and would destroy it. Almost shaking with anger, Hitler marched out of the room, slamming the door, leaving the head of the army speechless, trembling, face as white as chalk, and broken.

'Any sober discussion of these things is impossible with him,' Halder commented, in something of an understatement. But for Halder the impact of the meeting went further. Talk of destroying the 'spirit of Zossen' suggested to the Chief of Staff that Hitler knew of the plot to unseat him. The Gestapo could turn up in Zossen any time. Halder returned in panic to his headquarters and ordered the destruction of all papers relating to the conspiracy. Next day he told Groscurth that the attack in the west would be carried out. There was nothing to be done. 'Very depressing impression,' recorded Groscurth.

Hitler had given the order for the offensive at 1.30 p.m. on 5 November, soon after his interview with Brauchitsch. Two days later the attack was postponed because of poor weather. But the chance to strike against Hitler had been lost. The circumstances would not be as favourable for several years. The order for the attack, meant to be the moment to undertake the proposed coup, had come and gone. Brauchitsch, badly shaken by his audience with Hitler, had indicated that he would do nothing, though would not try to hinder a putsch. Canaris, approached by Halder, was disgusted at the suggestion that he should instigate Hitler's assassination. Other than this suggestion that someone else might take over responsibility for the dirty work, Halder now did little. The moment had passed. He gradually pulled back from the opposition's plans. In the end, he lacked the will, determination, and courage to act. The Abwehr group did not give up. But they acknowledged diminishing prospects of success. Oster's soundings with Generals Witzleben, Leeb, Bock, and Rundstedt produced mixed results. The truth was that the army was divided. Some generals opposed Hitler. But there were more who backed him. And below the high command, there were junior officers, let alone the rank-and-file, whose reactions to any attempt to stop Hitler dead in his tracks were uncertain. Throughout the conflict with the army leadership, Hitler continued to hold the whip-hand. And he had not yielded in the slightest. Despite repeated postponements because of bad weather – twenty-nine in all – he had not cancelled his offensive against the West. Divisions, distrust, fragmentation, but above all a lack of resolve had prevented the oppositional groups – especially the key figures in the military – from acting.

The plotters in the Abwehr, Foreign Ministry, and General Staff headquarters were as astonished as all other Germans when they heard of an attack on Hitler's life that had taken place in the Bürgerbräukeller on the evening of 8 November 1939. They thought it might have come from someone within their own ranks, or been carried out by dissident Nazis, or some other set of opponents – Communists, clerics, or 'reactionaries' – and that Hitler had been tipped off in time. In fact, Hitler, sitting in the compartment of his special train and discussing with Goebbels how the showdown with the clergy would have to await the end of the war, was wholly unaware of what had happened until his journey to Berlin was interrupted at Nuremberg with the news. His first reaction was that the report must be wrong. According to Goebbels, he thought it was a 'hoax'. The official version was soon put out that the British Secret Service was behind the assassination attempt, and that the perpetrator was 'a creature' of Otto Strasser. The capture next day of the British agents Major R. H. Stevens and Captain S. Payne Best on the Dutch border was used by propaganda to underpin this far-fetched interpretation.

The truth was less elaborate – but all the more stunning. The attempt had been carried out by a single person, an ordinary German, a man from the working class, acting without the help or knowledge of anyone else. Where generals had hesitated, he had tried to blow up Hitler to save Germany and Europe from even greater disaster.

His name was Georg Elser. He was a joiner from Königsbronn in Württemberg, thirty-six years old, a loner with few friends. Before 1933 he had supported the KPD in elections, but because in his view it stood for improving the lot of the working classes, not on account of an ideological programme. After 1933 he said he had observed the deterioration in the living-standard of the working class, and restrictions on its freedom. He noticed the anger among workers at the regime. He took part in discussions with workmates about poor conditions, and shared their views. He also shared their anxieties about the coming war which they all expected in the autumn of 1938. After the Munich Agreement he remained convinced, he said, 'that Germany would make further demands of other countries and annex other countries and that therefore a war would be unavoidable'. Prompted by no one, he began to be obsessed by ways of improving the condition of workers and preventing war. He concluded that only the 'elimination' of the regime's leadership – by which he meant Hitler, Göring, and Goebbels – would bring this about. The idea would not leave him. In autumn 1938 he decided that he himself would see it was done.

He read in the newspapers that the next gathering of party leaders would be in the Bürgerbräukeller in early November and travelled to Munich to assess the possibilities for what he had in mind. The security problems were not great. (Security for the events was left to the party, not to the police.) He worked out that the best method would be to place a time-bomb in the pillar behind the dais where Hitler would stand. During the next months he stole explosives from the armaments factory where he was currently working, and designed the mechanism for his time-bomb. At the beginning of August he returned to Munich. Between then and early November he hid over thirty times during the night in the Bürgerbräukeller, working on hollowing out a cavity in the selected pillar and leaving by a side-door early next morning. The bomb was in place, and set, by 6 November. Elser was leaving nothing to chance. He returned on the night of 7 November to make sure it was functioning properly. He pressed his ear to the side of the pillar, and heard the ticking. Nothing had gone wrong. Next morning he left Munich for Konstanz, en route – as he thought – to Switzerland, and safety.

That evening, as always on 8 November, the 'Old Guard' of the party assembled. Hitler's annual address usually lasted from about 8.30 p.m. until about ten o'clock. It had already been announced that, in the circumstances of the war, this year's meeting would begin earlier and that the two-day commemoration of the putsch would be shortened. Hitler began his speech soon after his arrival in the Bürgerbräukeller, at 8.10 p.m., and finished at 9.07 p.m. Escorted by a good number of party big-wigs, he left immediately for the station to take the 9.31 p.m. train back to Berlin.

At twenty past nine the pillar immediately behind the dais where Hitler had stood minutes earlier, and part of the roof directly above, were ripped apart by Elser's bomb. Eight persons were killed in the blast, a further sixty-three injured, sixteen of them seriously. Hitler had been gone no more than ten minutes when the bomb went off.

He attributed his salvation to the work of 'Providence' – a sign that he was to fulfil the task destiny had laid out for him. In its headline on 10 November, the *Völkischer Beobachter* called it 'the miraculous salvation of the Führer'. There was, in fact, nothing providential or miraculous about it. It was pure luck. Hitler's reasons for returning without delay to Berlin were genuine enough. The decision to attack the West had been temporarily postponed on 7 November, with a final decision set for the 9th. Hitler had to be back in the Reich Chancellery by then. It was more important than reminiscing about old times with party stalwarts in the Bürgerbräukeller. Elser could have known nothing about the reasons for the curtailment of Hitler's quick trip to Munich. It was mere chance that the Swabian joiner did not succeed where the generals had failed even to mount an attempt.

Elser himself was already under arrest at the customs post near Konstanz when the bomb went off. He had been picked up trying to cross the Swiss border illegally. It seemed a routine arrest. Only some hours after the explosion did the border officials begin to realize that the contents of Georg Elser's pockets, including a postcard of the Bürger-bräukeller, linked him with the assassination attempt on Hitler. On 14 November, Elser confessed. A few days later he gave a full account of his actions, and the motives behind them. He was interned in Sachsenhausen concentration camp, and treated, remarkably, as a privileged prisoner. Probably Hitler, who continued to believe that Elser was the front-man of an international conspiracy, intended a post-war show-trial to incriminate the British Secret Service. At the end of 1944 or in early 1945 Elser was brought to Dachau. There was to be no show-trial. With the war as good as lost, Elser had no more value to the regime. Shortly before the Americans liberated Dachau, he was taken out and killed.

In his anxieties about the war, Elser spoke for many. He was on far less sure ground with his attribution of blame for the war to the Nazi leadership. The signs are that propaganda had been successful in persuading most ordinary Germans that the western powers were to blame for the prolongation of a war which Hitler had done all he could to avoid. Whatever criticisms – and they were many and bitter – that people had of the party and the regime, Hitler still retained his massive popularity. Few would have applauded a successful assassination attempt. Vast numbers would have been appalled. The chances of a backlash, and a new 'stab-in-the-back' legend, would have been great. People were saying that if the attempt had been successful it would have resulted in internal confusion, benefit to Germany's enemies, loss of the war, worse misery than was caused by Versailles, and the upturning of everything achieved since 1933.

Hitler's hold over Germany was as strong as ever. The failure of those in positions of power to move against him and the repercussions of Elser's bomb-attack demonstrated that his authority was unchallengeable from within the regime's élites and that he was still immensely popular with the masses. He played on this latter point when he addressed a gathering of around 200 commanding generals and other senior Wehrmacht officers in the Reich Chancellery at noon on 23 November.

Hitler's speech was remarkable for its frankness. In the light of the conflict with the army leadership in the previous weeks, its aim was to convince the generals of the need to attack the West without delay. After his usual *tour d'horizon* he reached the characteristic conclusion: 'Everything is determined by the fact that the moment is favourable now; in six months it might not be so any more.' He turned to his own role. 'As the last factor I must in all modesty describe my own person: irreplaceable. Neither a military man nor a civilian could replace me . . . I shall strike and not capitulate. The fate of the Reich depends only on me.' Internal conditions also favoured an early strike, he went on. Revolution from within was impossible. And behind the army stood the strongest armaments industry in the world. Hitler said he was now gambling all he had achieved on victory. At stake was who was to dominate Europe in the future. His decision was unalterable, Hitler went on. 'I shall attack France and England at the most favourable and earliest moment. Breach of the neutrality of Belgium and Holland is of no importance. No one will question that when we have won . . .' His final point was the psychological readiness of the German people. With an eye on the possible deterioration of the backing he had from the German people, he now told the military: 'I want to annihilate the enemy. Behind me stands the German people, whose morale can only grow worse.'

Hitler had been right in his speech: no revolution could be expected from within. Heydrich's police-state ruled that out. But it was not only a matter of repression. Alongside the ruthlessness of the regime towards internal opponents stood the widespread basic consensus reaching across most of society behind much of what the regime had undertaken and, in particular, what were taken to be the remarkable achievements of Hitler himself. Elser's bomb had merely brought a renewed demonstration of his popularity. Meanwhile, the internal opposition was resigned to being unable to act. The navy and Luftwaffe were behind Hitler. The army leadership would, whatever its reservations, fulfil its duty. The division of the generals, coupled with their pronounced sense of duty even when they held a course of action to be disastrous, was Hitler's strength.

Nothing could stop the western offensive. Hitler was by now obsessed with 'beating England'. It was purely a matter of when, not if, the attack on the West would take place. After further short-term postponements, on 16 January 1940 Hitler finally put it off until the spring.

The war was set to continue, and to widen. Also set to escalate was the barbarism that was an intrinsic part of it. At home the killings in the asylums were mounting into a full-scale programme of mass murder. In Poland, the grandiose resettlement schemes presided over by Himmler and Heydrich were seeing the brutal uprooting and deportation of tens of thousands of Poles and Jews into the 'dumping-ground' of the General

Government. Not least, the centre-point of the 'racial cleansing' mania, the 'removal' of the Jews, was farther from solution than ever now that over 2 million Polish Jews had fallen into the hands of the Nazis. In December Goebbels reported to Hitler on his recent visit to Poland. The Führer, he recorded, listened carefully to his account and agreed with his views on the 'Jewish and Polish question'. 'The Jewish danger must be banished from us. But in a few generations it will reappear. There's no panacea.'

Evidently, no 'complete solution' to the 'Jewish problem' was yet in sight. The constant quest to find such a 'panacea' by Nazi underlings working directly or indirectly 'towards the Führer' would nevertheless ensure that, in the conquered and subjugated territories of the east, a 'solution' would gradually begin to emerge before long.

18

Zenith of Power

I

Hitler had placed the Reich in a quandary. The war could not be ended. That was now a decision out of Germany's control, unless Britain could be forced to the conference table or militarily defeated. But neither militarily, as the chiefs of the armed forces made plain, nor economically, as every indicator demonstrated, was Germany equipped at this stage to fight the long war with which, it was known, the British were already reckoning. The Wehrmacht had entered into hostilities in autumn 1939 with no well-laid plans for a major war, and no strategy at all for an offensive in the West. Nothing at all had been clearly thought through. The Luftwaffe was the best equipped of the three branches of the armed forces. But even here, the armaments programme had been targeted at 1942, not 1939. The navy's operational planning was based upon a fleet that could not be ready before 1943. In fact, the 1939 Z-Plan – halted at the start of the war – would leave Germany with severe limitations at sea until 1946. And within the confines of that plan, the building of U-boats necessary for an economic blockade of Britain was deliberately neglected by Hitler in favour of the interests of the army. However, the army itself lacked even sufficient munitions following the brief Polish campaign (in which some 50 per cent of the tanks and motorized units deployed were no longer serviceable) to contemplate an immediate continuation of the war in the West.

Hitler had to gamble everything on the defeat of France. If Britain could be kept from gaining a foothold on the Continent until this were achieved, Hitler was certain that the British would have to sue for peace. Getting Britain out of the war through isolation after a German defeat of France was Hitler's only overall war-strategy as the abnormally icy winter of 1940 gradually gave way to spring. Ranged against Germany at some point, Hitler was aware, would be the might of the USA. Currently still dominated by isolationism, and likely to be preoccupied by the forthcoming presidential elections in the autumn, early involvement in a European conflict could be discounted. But as long as Britain stayed in the war, the participation – at the very least through benevolent neutrality – of the USA, with its immense economic power, could not be ruled out. And that was a factor that was out of Germany's reach. It was all the more reason, objectively as well as simply in Hitler's manic obsession with time, to eliminate Britain from the war without delay.

The East was at this point at the back of Hitler's mind – though not out of it. In his memorandum the previous October he had already remarked that Soviet neutrality could be reckoned with at present, but that no treaty or agreement could guarantee it in the future. 'In eight months, a year, let alone a few years this could all be different,' he had said. 'If all treaties concluded were held to,' he told Goebbels, 'mankind would no longer exist today.' Hitler presumed that the Russians would break the non-aggression pact when it suited them to do so. For the time being they were militarily weak – a condition enhanced by Stalin's inexplicable purges; they were preoccupied with their own affairs in the Baltic, especially the troublesome Finnish war; and they posed, therefore, no danger from the East. They could be dealt with at a later stage. Their current disposition provided still further evidence for Hitler that his attack on the West, and the elimination of Britain from the war, could not wait.

It became clear in early 1940 that, before the western offensive could be launched, it was imperative to secure control over Scandinavia and the northern sea passages. A key consideration was the safeguarding of supplies of Swedish iron-ore, vital for the German war-economy, which were mainly shipped through the port of Narvik in the north of Norway. Hitler had acknowledged to Raeder as early as 1934 how essential it would be for the navy to guarantee the iron-ore imports in the event of war. But he had shown no actual strategic interest in Scandinavia until the first months of 1940. Alongside the need to secure the supplies of ore went, in Hitler's mind, the aim of keeping Britain off the European continent. The navy itself had developed no operational plans for Scandinavia before the outbreak of war. But as the prospect of war with Britain began to take concrete shape in the later 1930s, naval planners started to weigh up the need for bases on the Norwegian coast.

Once war had started, the navy leadership, not Hitler, took the initiative in pressing for the occupation of Denmark and Norway. In October, and again in early December 1939, Raeder, elevated the previous April to the rank of Grand-Admiral, stressed to Hitler the importance to the war-economy of occupying Norway. Increasingly worried by the possibility of being pre-empted by British occupation (under the pretext of assisting the Finns in the war against the Soviet Union), Raeder continued to lobby Hitler for early action. Hitler became seriously alerted to the danger of Allied intervention in Norway after the *Altmark*, carrying around 300 Allied merchant seamen captured in the south Atlantic, had been raided on 16 February in Norwegian waters by a boarding-party from the British destroyer *Cossack*, and the prisoners freed. Now the matter became urgent for him. On 1 March Hitler put out the directive for 'Weserübung' ('Weser Exercise'). Two days later, he underlined the urgency of action in Norway. He wanted an acceleration of preparations, and ordered 'Weser Exercise' to be carried out a few days before the western offensive. As fears of a British occupation mounted throughout March, Raeder finally persuaded Hitler, towards the end of the month, to agree to set a precise date for the operation. When he spoke to his commanders on 1 April, Hitler closely followed Raeder's lines of argument. The next day, the date for the operation was fixed as 9 April. Within forty-eight hours it was learnt that British action was imminent. On 8 April British warships mined the waters around Narvik. The race for Norway was on.

The Allied mine-laying gave Germany the pretext it had been waiting for. Hitler called Goebbels, and explained to him what was afoot while they walked alone in the grounds of the Reich Chancellery in the lovely spring sunshine. Everything was prepared. No worthwhile resistance was to be expected. He was uninterested in America's reaction. Material assistance from the USA would not be forthcoming for eight months or so, manpower not for about one and a half years. 'And we must come to victory in this year. Otherwise the material supremacy of the opposing side would be too great. Also, a long war would be psychologically difficult to bear,' Hitler conceded. He gave Goebbels an insight into his aims for the conquest of the north. 'First we will keep quiet for a short time once we have both countries' – Denmark and Norway – 'and then

England will be plastered. Now we possess a basis for attack.' He was prepared to leave the Kings of Denmark and Norway untouched, as long as they did not create trouble. 'But we will never again give up both countries.'

Landings by air and sea took place in Denmark in the early morning of 9 April. The Danes swiftly decided to offer no resistance. The Norwegian operation went less smoothly. Narvik and Trondheim were taken. But the sinking of the *Blücher*, by a single shell from an ancient coastal battery that landed in the ammunition hold of the new cruiser as it passed through the narrows near Oscarsborg, forced the accompanying ships to turn back and delayed the occupation of Oslo for the few hours that allowed the Norwegian royal family and government to leave the capital. Despite sturdy resistance by the Norwegians and relatively high naval losses at the hands of the British fleet, air superiority, following the swift capture of the airfields, rapidly helped provide the German forces with sufficient control to compel the evacuation of the British, French, and Polish troops who had landed in central Norway by the beginning of May. The Allies eventually took Narvik later in the month, after a protracted struggle, only to be pulled out again by Churchill in early June on account of the mounting danger to Britain from the German offensive in the west. The last Norwegian forces capitulated on the tenth.

'Weser Exercise' had proved a success. But it had been at a cost. Much of the surface-fleet of the German navy had been put out of action for the rest of 1940. Running the occupied parts of Scandinavia from now on sucked in on a more or less permanent basis around 300,000 men, many of them engaged in holding down a Norwegian population bitterly resentful at a German administration that was aided and abetted by Vidkun Quisling's collaborationist movement. And there was a further consequence which would turn out to be to Germany's disadvantage and have major significance for the British war-effort. Indirectly, the British failure led to the end of the Chamberlain government and brought into power the person who would prove himself Hitler's most defiant and unrelenting foe: Winston Churchill.

The eventual success of 'Weser Exercise' concealed to all but the armed forces' leadership Hitler's serious deficiencies as a military commander. The lack of coordination between the branches of the armed forces; the flawed communications between the OKW (Oberkommando der Wehrmacht – High Command of the Armed Forces) and the heads of the navy and, especially, army and Luftwaffe (leading to the need for alterations to directives already signed and issued); Hitler's own reluctance, in larger briefing meetings, to oppose either Raeder or Göring, though advocating a tough line in private; and his constant interference in the minutiae of operations control: all provided for serious complications in the execution of 'Weser Exercise'. On this occasion, the crisis soon passed. Hitler could bask in the glory of another triumph. But when the victories ran out, the flaws in his style of military leadership would prove a lasting weakness.

For now, however, he could turn his full energies to the long-awaited western offensive.

The repeated postponements of 'Case Yellow' (as the western offensive had come to be called) provided not just the opportunity to build up the army after the Polish campaign but also time to rethink operational plans. In Poland, Hitler had kept out of involvement in military operations. Now, in the preparation of the western offensive, he intervened directly for the first time. It set the pattern for the future. Already in the autumn he was uneasy about the directives coming from the Army High Command. Some of the top commanders were equally unconvinced. The plans seemed too conventional. They were what the enemy would expect. Even after modifications they remained less than satisfactory. They envisaged the decisive thrust coming from the north, either side of Liège. Hitler wanted something more daring, something which would retain the crucial element of surprise. His own ideas were still embryonic. They favoured a main line of attack further south – though the Army High Command thought this too risky since it involved attacking across the difficult wooded terrain of the Ardennes, with obvious problems for tank operations. Hitler did not know for some weeks that similar ideas were being more thoroughly worked out by Lieutenant-General Erich von Manstein, chief of staff of Army Group A. Manstein was among those generals concerned at the unimaginative strategy of the Army High Command. Discussions with Heinz Guderian, the general with greatest expertise in tank warfare, led him to conclude that the Ardennes posed no insuperable barrier to a panzer thrust. General von Rundstedt, Manstein's immediate superior, also supported the bolder plan. However, Manstein was unable to persuade Army High Command to adopt his plan. Brauchitsch was adamantly opposed to any alteration to the established strategy and not even prepared to discuss Manstein's plan. Halder at least agreed to take all operational proposals into account in a series of war games. These eventually, by February, were to make him more amenable to the Manstein plan. In January, however, Brauchitsch still refused to take Manstein's operational draft to Hitler, and had the persistent general moved to a new command post in Stettin. Hitler had, even so, been made aware of the basic lines of Manstein's plan in the second half of December. The postponement until spring of 'Yellow' that followed in January then gave him the opportunity to state that he wanted to give the operation a new basis, and above all to ensure absolute secrecy and the element of surprise.

In mid-February the operational plan for 'Yellow' was still not definitively agreed. Hitler was said to have described the existing planning of the Army High Command as the 'ideas of a military cadet'. But nothing had as yet taken their place. At this point, Hitler's Wehrmacht adjutant Rudolf Schmundt took the initiative and arranged for a meeting with Manstein on 17 February. By this time, Jodl had been informed that Hitler favoured a thrust of the motorized units on the southern flank, towards Sedan, where the enemy would least expect them. The army leadership, taking these wishes of Hitler on board and also bearing in mind the outcome of the war games, had already adjusted its strategic thinking when, on 18 February, Hitler spoke of the favourable impression he had gained of Manstein's plan the day before. The die was now cast. By chance, the basic thoughts of the amateur had coincided with the brilliantly unorthodox planning of the professional strategist. Further refined by the OKH (Oberkommando des Heeres – High Command of the Army), the Manstein plan gave Hitler what he wanted: a surprise assault in the most unexpected area which, though not without risk, had the boldness of genius. The famous 'sickle cut' – though the designation was not a contemporary one – was incorporated in the new directive of 24 February. While the Allied forces countered the expected German attack through Belgium, armoured units of Army Group A would rapidly drive through the Ardennes and into the lowlands of northern France towards the coast, scything through Allied forces and pushing them into the path of Army Group B, advancing from the north.

'The Führer presses for action as rapidly as possible,' commented Goebbels in mid-April. 'We can't and won't wait for long.' The attack was finally set for 10 May. Hitler was confident. To those who saw him at close quarters, he appeared calm and optimistic, as if the doubts of previous months had passed, and he was now letting events take their course. He thought that France would capitulate after around six weeks, and that England would then pull out of a war which, to continue, would mean losing its Empire – something wholly unimaginable. The balance of military forces was roughly even. What Hitler had not been fully informed about was the critical state of Germany's raw-material reserves: enough rubber for six months, enough fuel for only four months. Booty from the western campaign would prove crucial in securing the material base for continuing the war.

The level of secrecy maintained even in Hitler's closest entourage in the days leading up to the offensive was profound. When his special armoured train, code-named *Amerika*, pulled out of a small, secluded station on the outskirts of Berlin on the evening of 9 May, his press chief, Otto Dietrich, thought he was en route to visit shipworks in Hamburg, and Hitler's secretaries thought they were setting out for Denmark and Norway to visit the troops. After midnight, the train quietly switched in the vicinity of Hanover from the northbound tracks and turned westward. Even then, the destination was not disclosed. But by now there was no longer any doubt of the purpose of the journey. Hitler was in excellent spirits throughout. Dawn was breaking when they got down from the train at a little station in the Eifel, near Euskirchen. Cars were waiting to drive the company through hilly, woody countryside to their new temporary home: the Führer Headquarters near Münstereifel that had been given the name Felsennest (Rock Eyrie). The accommodation was cramped and simple. Apart from Hitler himself, only Keitel, Schaub, and a manservant had rooms in the first bunker. Jodl, Dr Brandt, Schmundt, Below, Puttkamer, and Keitel's adjutant were in a second. The rest had to be accommodated in the nearby village. The woods around were filled with the springtime twittering of birds. But as his staff gathered in front of Hitler's bunker the peaceful sounds of the countryside in spring were broken by the distant rumble of shell-fire. Hitler pointed to the west. 'Gentlemen, the offensive against the western powers has just started,' he declared.

II

That offensive proceeded with a breathtaking pace that stunned the world. Even Hitler and his military leaders scarcely dared hope for such a scale of early successes. On the northern flank, the Dutch surrender followed within five days, the Queen and government fleeing to exile in England. Before that, the terror-bombing of Rotterdam's old town had brought death and devastation from the skies. It was the trademark of the new type of warfare. Warsaw civilians had suffered it first; the people of British cities would soon come to dread it; and, later in the war, German citizens themselves would be exposed to its full horror. Belgian neutrality, for the second time in under thirty years, was breached along with that of the Dutch. On 28 May the Belgian army would surrender unconditionally, leaving King Leopold in effect a prisoner with the government in exile. Meanwhile, the 'sickle cut' plan was proving a brilliant and decisive success. Aided by the strategic and operational ineptitude of the French military command, German armoured units were able to sweep through the Ardennes, through Luxemburg and southern Belgium into northern France, breaking the thin line of French defence, and crossing the Meuse already on 13 May. Within ten days of the launching of the offensive, by the night of 20–21 May, the advance had covered 150 miles and reached the Channel coast. The 'sickle cut' had worked. The Allied forces had been cut in two; vast numbers were now squeezed between the coast and the oncoming German divisions. On 26 May the War Office in London bowed to what had become increasingly inevitable, and ordered the evacuation of the British Expeditionary Force, the bulk of it by then fighting a desperate rearguard action just east of Dunkirk, the last remaining Channel port in Allied hands. The next days would see almost 340,000 British and French soldiers – the vast proportion of the Allied troops still in combat in north-west France – carried to safety across the Channel in an improvised armada of small boats while the Luftwaffe pounded the harbour and beaches of the port.

The evacuation had been greatly helped by Hitler's decision, at 11.42 a.m. on 24 May, to halt the German advance with the spearhead a mere fifteen miles or so from Dunkirk. Post-war suggestions that Hitler was deliberately allowing the British troops to get away as an act of generosity to encourage Britain to come to the peace table with its armies intact are far-fetched. Hitler himself was alleged to have told his entourage a fortnight or so later that 'the army is the backbone of England and the Empire. If we smash the invasion corps, the Empire is doomed. Since we neither want to nor can inherit it, we must leave it the chance. My generals haven't grasped that.' Such sentiments, if they were indeed expressed in those terms, were no more than a self-justification for a military mistake. For the decision not to move on Dunkirk was taken for military reasons, and on military advice. According to his Luftwaffe adjutant, Nicolaus von Below, 'the English army had no significance for him' at Dunkirk.

Hitler had flown that morning, 24 May, to Charleville, around 125 miles east of the Channel, to visit the headquarters of Colonel-General Gerd von Rundstedt, commander of Army Group A, which had made the remarkable advance in the 'sickle movement' along the southern flank. When Hitler arrived at half-past eleven, Rundstedt gave him a report on the situation. The suggestion to hold back the motorized units came not from Hitler, but from Rundstedt, one of his most trusted generals. Hitler agreed, adding that the tanks had to be conserved for the coming operations in the south and that a further advance would restrict the scope for action of the Luftwaffe. Hitler was keen to press on with the attack to the south without the delay that he thought would come about if they took a few days dealing with the surrounded Allied troops in Dunkirk. When Brauchitsch arrived next morning, the 25th, wanting to advance the tanks on to the plains, Hitler opposed him, arguing that the numerous canals criss-crossing Flanders made it an unsuitable terrain for tanks. But he left the decision to Rundstedt, who rejected the suggestion because of the need to have the tanks recover for the operations to come in the south. Halder, as well as Brauchitsch, was dismayed. They would have to come to terms with a supreme commander of the Wehrmacht who intervened in the direction of operations. But there was no magnanimity in the decision to hold back the tanks. Hitler wanted to strike Britain a knock-out blow to force her to accept peace terms. He had no interest in allowing the British troops to escape captivity or destruction. He had been persuaded by Göring to let the Luftwaffe finish off the encircled enemy. He thought few of the British would escape.

In fact, the Luftwaffe could not deliver on Göring's promises. Despite its claims of success, bad weather and the Royal Air Force contrived to prevent the easy pickings Göring had imagined. Dunkirk did nothing to enhance the Luftwaffe's prestige. Within two days, Hitler realized that the halt order had been an error. On 26 May, he reversed his decision and finally ordered the advance on Dunkirk to prevent further evacuations. Few of the encircled troops had got away by then. But the delay of forty-eight hours proved vital in enabling the British to orchestrate the extraordinary retreat – a masterpiece of improvisation accompanied by much good luck – over the next days.

In military terms Dunkirk seemed, as one stunning success followed another, of secondary importance to Germany. It amounted in reality to a massive defeat for Britain. But that the troops were brought back under such conditions to fight again another day was converted by the new British Prime Minister Churchill (who had come into office on the very day that the western offensive had begun), and by popular myth, into a symbol of the British fighting spirit – the archetypal triumph in adversity. As such, the great setback at Dunkirk provided a boost to British morale at one of the lowest points in the nation's long history. In another way, too, Dunkirk was fateful. If the British Expeditionary Force had been lost, it is almost inconceivable that Churchill would have survived the growing pressure from those powerful forces within Britain that were ready to seek terms with Hitler.

Towards the end of the first week in June, Hitler moved his head-quarters to Brûly-de-Pesche, in southern Belgium, near the border with France. The second stage of the German offensive was beginning. The French lines were rapidly overwhelmed. While the French had more guns and tanks than the Germans, they were hopelessly outmatched in air-power. Not just that: French weaponry and tactics were outdated, not attuned to the demands of modern, mechanized warfare. And, just as important, the French military leadership conveyed their sense of defeatism to the rank-and-file. Discipline collapsed along with morale. Taking their lead from their fighting men, civilians fled from the big cities in their thousands. Some looked to astrology. The faithful placed their trust in prayer and the intercession of St Geneviève. Neither would be enough.

On 14 June German troops penetrated the Maginot Line south of Saarbrücken. That same day, less than five weeks since the launch of the western offensive, their comrades entered Paris. A generation earlier, the fathers and uncles of these soldiers had fought for four years and not reached Paris. Now, the German troops had achieved it in little over four weeks. The disparity in casualty figures mirrored the magnitude of the victory. Allied losses were reckoned at 90,000 dead, 200,000 wounded, and 1.9 million captured or missing. German dead numbered almost 30,000, total casualties just under 165,000.

It was no wonder that Hitler felt on top of the world, slapping his thigh for joy – his usual expression of exultation – and laughing in relief, when he was brought the news at Brûly-de-Pesche on 17 June that Marshal Pétain's new French government had sued for peace. The end of the war seemed imminent. England would now surely give in. Total victory, Hitler imagined, was within his grasp.

Mussolini had brought Italy into the war a week earlier, hoping to cash in on the action just before it was all over, in time to win rich pickings and bask in the glory of a cheap victory. Hitler took no pleasure in greeting his new companion-in-arms when he flew to Munich to meet him on 18 June to discuss the French armistice request. He wanted lenient terms for the French, and swiftly dispelled Mussolini's hopes of getting his hands on part of the French fleet. Hitler was anxious to avoid the French navy going over to the British – something which Churchill had already tried to engineer. 'From all that he says it is clear that he wants to act quickly to end it,' recorded Ciano. 'Hitler is now the gambler who has made a big scoop and would like to get up from the table risking nothing more.'

Having won his great victory without any help from the Italians, Hitler was determined that the embarrassed and disappointed Mussolini, now forced to swallow his role as junior partner in the Axis, should not participate in the armistice negotiations with the French. Already on 20 May, when German tanks had reached the French coast, Hitler had specified that the peace negotiations with France, at which the return of former German territory would be demanded, would take place in the Forest of Compiègne, where the armistice of 1918 had taken place. He now gave orders to retrieve Marshal Foch's railway carriage, pre-served as a museum piece, in which the German generals had signed the ceasefire, and have it brought to the forest clearing. That defeat, and its consequences, had permanently seared Hitler's consciousness. It would now be erased by repaying the humiliation. At quarter past three on the afternoon of 21 June, Hitler, accompanied by Göring,

Raeder, Brauchitsch, Keitel, Ribbentrop, and Heß, viewed the memorial recording the victory over the 'criminal arrogance of the German Reich', then took his place in the carriage, greeting in silence the French delegation. For ten minutes, he listened, again without a word, though, as he later recounted, gripped by the feeling of revenge for the humiliation of November 1918. Keitel read out the preamble to the armistice terms. Hitler then left to return to his headquarters. The symbolic purging of the old debt was completed. 'The disgrace is now extinguished. It's a feeling of being born again,' reported Goebbels after Hitler had told him of the dramatic events late that night on the telephone.

France was to be divided – the north and western seaboard under German occupation, the centre and south to be left as a puppet state, headed by Pétain, with its seat of government at Vichy. Following the signing of the Italian-French armistice on 24 June, all fighting was declared to have ceased at 1.35 a.m. next morning. Hitler proclaimed the end of the war in the west and the 'most glorious victory of all time'. He ordered bells to be rung in the Reich for a week, and flags to be flown for ten days. As the moment for the official conclusion of hostilities drew near, Hitler, sitting at the wooden table in his field headquarters, ordered the lights put out and the windows opened in order to hear, in the darkness, the trumpeter outside mark the historic moment.

He spent part of the next days sightseeing. Max Amann (head of the party's publishing concerns) and Ernst Schmidt, two comrades from the First World War, joined his regular entourage for a nostalgic tour of the battlefields in Flanders, revisiting the places where they had been stationed. Then, on 28 June, before most Parisians were awake, Hitler paid his one and only visit to the occupied French capital. It lasted no more than three hours. Accompanied by the architects Hermann Giesler and Albert Speer, and his favourite sculptor Arno Breker, Hitler landed at Le Bourget airport at, for him, the extraordinarily early hour of half-past five in the morning. The whistle-stop sightseeing tour began at l'Opéra. Hitler was thrilled by its beauty. The tourists moved on. They drove past La Madeleine, whose classical form impressed Hitler, up the Champs Elysées, stopped at the Tomb of the Unknown Soldier below the Arc de Triomphe, viewed the Eiffel Tower, and looked in silence on the tomb of Napoleon in Les Invalides. Hitler admired the dimensions of the Panthéon, but found its interior (as he later recalled) 'a terrible disappointment', and seemed indifferent to the medieval wonders of Paris, like the Sainte Chapelle. The tour ended, curiously, at the nineteenth-century testament to Catholic piety, the church of Sacré-Coeur. With a last look over the city from the heights of Montmartre, Hitler was gone. By mid-morning he was back in his field headquarters. Seeing Paris, he told Speer, had been the dream of his life. But to Goebbels, he said he had found a lot of Paris very disappointing. He had considered destroying it. However, he remarked, according to Speer, 'when we're finished in Berlin, Paris will only be a shadow. Why should we destroy it?'

The reception awaiting Hitler in Berlin when his train pulled into the Anhalter-Bahnhof at three o'clock on 6 July surpassed even the homecomings after the great pre-war triumphs like the Anschluß. Many in the crowds had been standing for six hours as the dull morning gave way to the brilliant sunshine of the afternoon. The streets were strewn with flowers all the way from the station to the Reich Chancellery. Hundreds of thousands cheered themselves hoarse. Hitler, lauded by Keitel as 'the greatest warlord of all time', was called out time after time on to the balcony to soak up the wild adulation of the masses. 'If an increase in feeling for Adolf Hitler was still possible, it has become reality with the day of the return to Berlin,' commented one report from the provinces. In the face of such 'greatness', ran another, 'all pettiness and grumbling are silenced'. Even opponents of the regime found it hard to resist the victory mood. Workers in the armaments factories pressed to be allowed to join the army. People thought final victory was around the corner. Only Britain stood in the way. For perhaps the only time during the Third Reich there was genuine war-fever among the population. Incited by incessant propaganda, hatred of Britain was now widespread. People were thirsting to see the high-and-mighty long-standing rival finally brought to its knees. But mingling with the aggression were still feelings of fear and anxiety. Whether triumphalist, or fearful, the wish to bring the war to a speedy end was almost universal.

Hitler had meanwhile changed his mind about delivering his Reichstag speech on the Monday. On 3 July British ships had sunk a number of French warships moored at the naval base of Mers-el-Kébir, near Oran, in French Algeria, killing 1,250 French sailors in the process. Churchill's move, a show of British determination, was to prevent the battle-fleet of his former allies falling into Hitler's hands. For Hitler, this brought a new situation. He wanted to await developments. He was uncertain whether he ought to go ahead and appeal to England. 'He is still not ready for the final blow,' remarked Goebbels. 'He wants to think over his speech again in peace and for that reason go to the Obersalzberg.' If London should refuse the last offer, then Britain would be 'immediately following dealt an annihilatory blow. The English apparently have no idea what then awaits them.'

While he was at the Berghof, Hitler had talks with his military leaders about a possible invasion of Britain, should his 'peace offer' be rejected. Raeder had advised Hitler in June that a naval landing could only take place once the Luftwaffe had secured air superiority over southern England. He repeated this precondition when he met Hitler on 11 July on the Obersalzberg, advocating 'concentrated bombing' to begin forthwith. But naval ambitions went far beyond a presumed British surrender, thus obviating the need for what Raeder, as well as Hitler, saw as the risky venture of invading Britain. Germany would need a big navy to defend its colonial empire, in particular against the looming threat of the United States. Taking the opportunity to push the interests of the navy, Raeder held out, therefore, the prospect of building up a great battleship fleet to combat any potential Anglo-American naval alliance. The next day Jodl outlined for Hitler initial thoughts on operational plans for a landing. On Saturday, 13 July, it was Halder's turn to travel to the Berghof to report on operational plans. But a landing was to be a last resort. 'The Führer is greatly puzzled by Britain's persisting unwillingness to make peace,' Halder noted. 'He sees the answer (as we do) in Britain's hope on Russia and therefore counts on having to compel her by main force to agree to peace.'

On 16 July Hitler signed 'Directive No. 16 for Preparations of a Landing Operation against England'. The preamble ran: 'Since England, in spite of its militarily hopeless situation, still gives no recognizable signs of readiness to come to terms, I have determined to prepare a landing operation against England and, if need be, to carry it out. The aim of this operation is to exclude the English motherland as a basis for the continuation of the war against Germany, and, if it should be necessary, to occupy it completely.' Operational plans followed. But the qualifications in the preamble – 'if need be', 'if necessary' – indicated Hitler's half-heartedness.

This conveyed itself to his army leaders. Rundstedt, Commander-in-Chief in the West, simply did not take 'Sealion' seriously – a feeling endorsed by Göring's report of Hitler telling him privately that he did not intend to carry out the operation. He never even bothered to attend the amphibious landing exercises. To him and all who studied them, given the strength of the British navy, the logistic difficulties seemed insuperable.

If the British would only see sense, thought Hitler, it would be far more desirable than an invasion. After signing the directive, he fixed his Reichstag speech for the evening of Friday, 19 July.

The Reichstag had a military appearance that evening. Six seats, of deputies who had fallen in the western campaign, had laurel wreaths placed on them. In the front row were the gold-braided top brass of the military, their chests heaving with medals and decorations, many preening themselves on their new promotions to Field-Marshals and Colonel-Generals. (Hitler had a cynical view about promoting his military leaders. Through acts of generosity, as in ancient times, they would be bound all the more, whatever their political views, to their oaths of loyalty, and to him as the bestower of such gifts. He intended their salaries to be tax-free, and would not be miserly with donations of landed estates once the war was finally won. This altered nothing of his view that the army leadership – Brauchitsch and Halder in particular – had been found seriously wanting once more, and that his own judgement had again been proved right in the western campaign.)

The point of his speech, as he told Goebbels earlier that day, was to make Britain a brief but imprecise offer, indicating that it was the last word, and leaving the choice to London. A large part of the speech, which lasted no less than two and a quarter hours, was spent describing the course of the war, praising the military achievements of the commanders, and listing their promotions. As he came to the names of the twelve generals who were to be made Field-Marshals, Hitler saluted each of them. From their places in the balcony, they stood to attention and returned the salute. Special mention was made of Göring, now elevated to Reich Marshal. Göring was like a child with a new toy when Hitler gave him the accompanying insignia. Hitler then emphasized the strength of Germany's position. Only in the last few minutes of his speech did he reach the point that everyone was waiting for: his 'appeal to reason, also in England'. The 'appeal' came and went – in those words, and little besides. There was the usual accusation levelled at Churchill as the warmonger. There was the threat that Britain, and the British Empire, would be destroyed. There was a hypocritical expression of regret for the victims of continued war. And there was the victor's 'appeal to reason'. That was all. It was little wonder that the reaction, even among those around Hitler, was one of disappointment – especially when the British categorical rejection of the 'offer' was announced within the hour.

Hitler had misjudged the mood in Britain. And his speech had not been tuned to offer anything that might tempt the opponents of Churchill, who could have formed a peace-lobby. He was evidently still hoping for a diplomatic solution when he met the Commanders-in-Chief of the Wehrmacht on 21 July. 'Crossing of Channel appears very hazardous to the Führer. On that account, invasion is to be undertaken only if no other way is left to bring terms with Britain,' Halder reported. 'Britain's position is hopeless. The war is won by us,' Hitler stated.

But Britain still put her hopes in America, and in Russia. There was the possibility, said Hitler, referring to rumours of crisis in London, that a cabinet including Lloyd George, Chamberlain, and Halifax might come to power and seek peace-terms. But, failing that, Britain would have to be reduced by an air-offensive combined with intensified sub-marine warfare to the state, by mid-September, when an invasion could be carried out. Hitler would decide within days, after hearing Raeder's report in mid-week on naval operational logistics, whether the invasion would be carried out by autumn. Otherwise, it would be before the following May. The final decision on the intensity of submarine and air attacks would be left until the beginning of August. There was the possibility that the invasion might begin as early as 25 August.

Hitler turned finally to the issue which had already started to bother him: the position of Russia. Stalin, he pointed out, had his own agenda. He was flirting with Britain to keep her in the war, tie down Germany, and exploit the situation to undertake his own expansionist policy. There were no indications of any Russian aggression towards Germany. 'But,' went on Hitler, 'our attention must be turned to tackling the Russian problem and prepare planning.' It would take four to six weeks to assemble the German military force. Its object would be 'to crush the Russian army or at least take as much Russian territory as is necessary to bar enemy air raids on Berlin and Silesian industries'. He also men-tioned the need to protect the Romanian oil-fields. Eighty to 100 div-isions would be required. He contemplated attacking Russia that very autumn. Compared with what had been achieved in the west, Hitler had remarked to Jodl and Keitel already at the time of the French capitulation, 'a campaign against Russia would be child's play'.

It was an astonishing prospect that Hitler held out to his army leaders. He was, of course, not yet committing himself to anything. But the two-front war which had always been anathema was now being actively entertained. Paradoxically, having advocated since the 1920s a showdown with the Soviet Union to destroy Bolshevism and win *Lebensraum*, Hitler had now come back to the idea of a war against Russia for strategic reasons: to force his erstwhile would-be friend, Britain, now stubbornly holding out against the odds, to terms. The ideological aim of smashing Bolshevism, though apparently invoked by Hitler as part of his reasoning, was at this point secondary to the strategic need to get Britain out of the war. It was a sign of the difficulties that Hitler had manoeuvred himself into. Britain would not play his game. But the military lesson he kept saying she would have to be taught, and which the German public now awaited, would be, he knew, a hazardous affair. So he was now moving to a step he – and most of his generals did not disagree – thought less dangerous: an attack on the Soviet Union.

In fact, the army command, worried about the build-up of Soviet troops in southern Russia in connection with Stalin's increasing pressure on the Balkan states, had already, in mid-June, added a further nine motorized divisions to the fifteen divisions previously designated for transfer to the east. And on 3 July Halder, without any orders from Hitler but following indications evidently passed on to him by Weizsäcker, in the Foreign Office, showed himself ready to anticipate the change in direction, to 'work towards the Führer', when he deemed it appropriate to have the possibilities of a campaign against the Soviet Union tested. The Chief of Staff, ahead of Hitler at this point, raised with his operational planners 'the requirements of a military intervention which will compel Russia to recognize Germany's dominant position in Europe'.

Hitler was still avoiding a final decision on Britain. But it was with the impression that Lord Halifax's official spurning of his 'peace offer' in a broadcast speech on the evening of 22 July amounted to 'England's final rejection' that he left, for what was to prove the last time, for Bayreuth, to see next day a performance of *Götterdämmerung*. 'The die is cast,' wrote Goebbels. 'We're tuning press and radio to a fight.' In fact, the die had not been finally cast. Hitler remained unsure how to proceed.

He had long since convinced himself of what German propaganda was trumpeting. It was he who wanted peace. Churchill, backed by the 'Jewish plutocracy', was the warmonger – the obstacle to the triumph. While in Bayreuth, Hitler saw the friend of his youth days, August Kubizek, for the last time. Hitler told Kubizek, as gullible as ever, that the war had hindered all his great plans for rebuilding Germany. 'I did not become Chancellor of the Great German Reich in order to wage war,' he said. Kubizek believed him. Probably Hitler believed himself.

He went from Bayreuth to the Obersalzberg. While he was there, the army leadership learnt from Raeder that the navy could not be ready for operations against England before 15 September. The earliest date for an invasion, depending on the moon and tides, was the 26th of that month. If that date proved impossible, the invasion would have to be put off until the following May. Brauchitsch doubted that the navy could provide the basis for an invasion in the autumn. (In fact, the navy had concluded that it was highly inadvisable to attempt to invade at any point that year, and was extremely sceptical about the prospects of an invasion at all.) Halder agreed with Brauchitsch in eliminating the notion of an operation during bad weather. But they foresaw disadvantages, military and political, in a postponement to the following year. They considered possibilities of weakening Britain's overseas position through attacks on Gibraltar, Haifa, and Suez, support for the Italians in Egypt, and inciting the Russians to move on the Persian Gulf. An attack on Russia was rejected in favour of the maintenance of friendly relations.

Hitler, meantime, had been privately consulting Jodl. On 29 July he asked the Chief of the Wehrmacht Directional Staff about deploying the army in the east, and whether it might be possible to attack and defeat Russia that very autumn. Jodl totally ruled it out on practical grounds. In that case, Hitler said, absolute confidence was needed. Feasibility studies were to be undertaken, but knowledge confined to only a few staff officers. Remarkably, in fact, the Wehrmacht had not waited for Hitler's order. 'The army,' Jodl was later to remark, 'had already learnt of the Führer's intentions at the stage when these were still being weighed up. An operational plan was therefore drawn up even before the order for this was given.' And already in July, as he later put it 'on his own initiative', Major-General Bernhard von Loßberg, from the National Defence Department, headed by Major-General Walter Warlimont, had begun work on an 'operational study for a Russian campaign'. The draft plan was at this stage merely intended to be held in readiness for the point at which it might be needed. Hitler's discussion with Jodl indicated that this point had arrived.

Loßberg, two other members of Warlimont's staff, and Warlimont himself, were sitting in the restaurant car of the special train *Atlas*, in the station at Bad Reichenhall, when Jodl came down from the Berghof to report on his discussion with Hitler. According to Warlimont, the consternation at what they heard – meaning the dreaded war on two fronts – gave rise to an hour of bitter argument. Jodl countered by stating Hitler's opinion that it was better to have the inevitable war against Bolshevism now, with German power at its height, than later; and that by autumn 1941 victory in the east would have brought the Luftwaffe to its peak for deployment against Britain. Whatever the objections – it is impossible to know whether Warlimont was exaggerating them in his post-war account – the feasibility studies under the code-name '*Aufbau-Ost*' ('Build-Up in the East') were now undertaken with a greater sense of urgency.

Two days later, on 31 July, Hitler met his military leaders at the Berghof. Raeder repeated the conclusion his naval planners had reached that the earliest date for an invasion of Britain could be no sooner than 15 September, and favoured postponing it until the following May. Hitler wanted to keep his options open. Things would become difficult with the passing of time. Air attacks should begin straight away. They would determine Germany's relative strength. 'If results of air warfare are unsatisfactory, invasion preparations will be stopped. If we have the impression that the English are crushed and that effects will soon begin to tell, we shall proceed to the attack,' he stated. He remained sceptical about an invasion. The risks were high; so, however, was the prize, he added. But he was already thinking of the next step. What if no invasion took place? He returned to the hopes Britain placed in the USA and in Russia. If Russia were to be eliminated, then America, too, would be lost for Britain because of the increase in Japan's power in the Far East. Russia was 'the factor on which Britain is relying the most'. The British had been 'completely down'. Now they had revived. Russia had been shaken by events in the west. The British were clutching on, hoping for a change in the situation during the next few months.

He moved to his momentous conclusion: remove Russia from the equation. Halder's notes retained Hitler's emphasis. '*With Russia smashed, Britain's last hope would be shattered.* Germany then will be master of Europe and the Balkans. *Decision: Russia's destruction must therefore be made a part of this struggle. Spring 1941. The sooner Russia is crushed the better.* Attack achieves its purpose only if Russian state can be shattered to its roots with one blow. Holding part of the country alone will not do. Standing still for the following winter would be perilous. So it is better to wait a little longer, but with the resolute determination to eliminate Russia . . . If we start in May 1941, we would have five months to finish the job.'

Unlike the anxious reactions on the occasions in 1938 and 1939 when the generals had feared war with Britain, there is no indication that they were horror-struck at what they heard. The fateful underestimation of the Russian military potential was something Hitler shared with his commanders. Intelligence on the Soviet army was poor. But the underestimation was not solely the result of poor intelligence. Airs of disdain for Slavs mingled easily with contempt for what Bolshevism had managed to achieve. Contact with Soviet generals in the partition of Poland had not impressed the Germans. The dismal showing of the Red Army in Finland (where the inadequately equipped Finns had inflicted unexpected and heavy losses on the Soviets in the early stages of the 'Winter War' of 1939–40) had done nothing to improve its image in their eyes. Not least, there was the apparent madness which had prompted Stalin to destroy his own officer corps. Whereas an attack on the British Isles remained a perilous undertaking, an assault on the Soviet Union raised no great alarm. A true 'lightning war' could be expected here.

The day after the meeting on the Berghof, Hitler signed Directive No. 17, intensifying the air-war and sea-war against Britain as the basis for her 'final subjugation'. He explicitly – underscoring the sentence in the Directive – reserved for himself a decision on the use of terror-bombing. The offensive was set to begin four days later, but was postponed until the 8th. It was again postponed on account of the weather conditions until the 13th. From then on, the German fighters sought to sweep the Royal Air Force from the skies. Wave after wave of attacks on the airfields of southern England was launched. Spitfires, Hurricanes and Messerschmitts wheeled, arched, dived, and strafed each other in the dramatic and heroic dogfights on which Britain's survival at this point depended. The early optimistic results announced in Berlin soon proved highly misleading. The task was beyond the Luftwaffe. At first by the skin of their teeth the young British pilots held out, then gradually won the ascendancy. Despite Hitler's orders that he alone was to decide on terror-bombing, 100 planes of the Luftwaffe, acting, it seems, under a loosely worded directive from Göring issued on 2 August, had attacked London's East End on the night of 24 August. As retaliation, the RAF carried out the first British bombing raids on Berlin the following night.

Hitler regarded the bombing of Berlin as a disgrace. As usual, his reaction was to threaten massive retaliation. 'We'll wipe out their cities! We'll put an end to the work of these night pirates,' he fumed at a speech in the Sportpalast on 4 September. He spoke with Göring about undertaking the revenge. From 7 September the nightly bombing of London began. It was the turn of the citizens of Britain's capital to experience night after night the terror from the skies. The shift to terror-bombing marked a move away from the idea of the landing which Hitler had never whole-heartedly favoured. Persuaded by Göring, he now thought for a while that Britain could be bombed to the conference-table without German troops having to undertake the perilous landing. But, dreadful though the 'Blitz' was, the Luftwaffe was simply not powerful enough to bomb Britain to submission.

Between 10 and 13 September there were signs that Hitler had gone utterly cold on the idea of a landing. On 14 September he then told his commanders that the conditions for 'Operation Sealion' – the operational plan to attack Great Britain – had not been attained.

Meanwhile, the dogfights over southern England and the Channel coast intensified during the first fortnight in September, reaching a climacteric on Sunday the 15th. The Wehrmacht admitted 182 planes lost in that fortnight, forty-three on the 15th alone. The horrors of the 'Blitz' would continue for months to be inflicted upon British cities – among the worst devastation the bombing of Coventry on the night of 14 November, as the German onslaught switched to the industrial belt of the Midlands to strike at more manageable targets than London. But the 'Battle of Britain' was over. Hitler had never been convinced that the German air-offensive would successfully lay the basis for the invasion of which he was in any case so sceptical. On 17 September he ordered the indefinite postponement – though, for psychological reasons, not the cancellation – of 'Operation Sealion'.

The peace-overtures had failed. The battle for the skies had failed. Meanwhile, on 3 September the grant of fifty destroyers to Britain by the USA – a deal which Roosevelt had eventually pushed through, initially against much opposition from the isolationists – was, despite the limited use of the elderly warships, the plainest indication to date that Britain might in the foreseeable future be able to reckon with the still dormant military might of the USA. It was increasingly urgent to get Britain out of the war. Hitler's options were, in autumn 1940, still not closed off. There was the possibility of forcing Britain to come to terms through a strategy of attacks on her Mediterranean and Near Eastern strongholds. But once that option also faded Hitler was left with only one possibility: the one that was in his view not only strategically indispensable but embodied one of his most long-standing ideological obsessions. This point would not finally be reached until December 1940. By then it would be time to prepare for the crusade against Bolshevism.

III

In 1940, Hitler was at the zenith of his power. But he did not have enough power to bring the war to the conclusion he wanted. And, within Germany, he was powerless to prevent the governance of the Reich from slipping increasingly out of control. The tendencies already plainly evident before the war – unresolved Party-State dualism, unclear or overlapping spheres of competence, proliferation of ad hoc establishment of improvised 'special authorities' in specific policy areas, administrative anarchy – were now sharply magnified. It was not that Hitler was a 'weak dictator'. His power was recognized and acknowledged on all fronts. Nothing of significance was undertaken in contradiction to his known wishes. His popular support was immense. Opponents were demoralized and without hope. There was no conceivable challenge that could be mounted. The slippage from control did not mean a decline in Hitler's authority. But it did mean that the very nature of that authority had built into it the erosion and undermining of regular patterns of government and, at the same time, the inability to keep in view all aspects of rule of an increasingly expanding and complex Reich. Even someone more able, energetic, and industrious when it came to administration than Hitler could not have done it. And during the first months of the war, as we have seen, Hitler was for lengthy stretches away from

Berlin and overwhelmingly preoccupied with military events. It was impossible for him to stay completely in touch with and be competently involved in the running of the Reich. But in the absence of any organ of collective government to replace the cabinet, which had not met since February 1938, or any genuine delegation of powers (which Hitler constantly shied away from, seeing it as a potentially dangerous dilution of his authority), the disintegration of anything resembling a coherent 'system' of administration inevitably accelerated. Far from diminishing Hitler's power, the continued erosion of any semblance of collective government actually enhanced it. Since, however, this disintegration went hand in hand – part cause, part effect – with the Darwinian struggle carried out through recourse to Hitler's ideological goals, the radicalization entailed in the process of 'working towards the Führer' equally inevitably accelerated.

The ideological drive of National Socialism was inextricable from the endemic conflict within the regime. Without this ideological drive, embodied in Hitler's 'mission' (as perceived by his more fanatical followers), the break-up of government into the near-anarchy of competing fiefdoms and internecine rivalries is inexplicable. But internal radicalization went beyond Hitler's personal involvement. 'Working towards' his 'vision' was the key to success in the internal war of the regime.

However bitter the rivalries, all those involved could have recourse to the 'wishes of the Führer', and claim they were working towards the fulfilment of his 'vision'. At stake were not aims, but methods – and, above all, realms of power. The very nature of the loose mandate given to Hitler's paladins, the scope they were given to build and extend their own empires, and the unclarity of the divisions of competence, guaranteed continued struggle and institutional anarchy. At the same time, it ensured the unfolding of ceaseless energy to drive on the ideological radicalization. Governmental disorder and 'cumulative radicalization' were two sides of the same coin.

Radicalization of the National Socialist 'programme', vague as it was, could not possibly subside. The ways different power-groups and important individuals in positions of influence interpreted the ideological imperative represented by Hitler saw to it that the dream of the new society to be created through war, struggle, conquest, and racial purification was kept in full view. At the grass-roots level, banal – though for the individuals concerned certainly not unimportant – material considerations like the chronic housing shortage, the growing scarcity and increasing cost of consumer goods, or an acute shortage of farm labourers could produce resentments easily channelled towards disparaged minorities and fuelled by petty greed at the prospect of acquiring goods or property belonging to Jews. The flames of such social antagonisms were fanned by the hate-filled messages of propaganda. The mentalities that were fostered offered an open door to the fanaticism of the believers. The internal competition built into the regime ensured that the radical drive was not only sustained, but intensified as fresh opportunities were provided by the war. And as victory seemed imminent, new breathtaking vistas for rooting out racial enemies, displacing inferior populations, and building the 'brave new world' opened up.

With scarcely any direct involvement by Hitler, racial policy unfolded its own dynamic. Within the Reich, pressures to rid Germany of its Jews once and for all increased. In the asylums, the killing of the mentally sick inmates was in full swing. And the security mania of the nation at war, threatened by enemies on all sides and within, coupled with the heightened demands for national unity, encouraged the search for new 'outsider' target groups. 'Foreign workers', especially those from Poland, were in the front line of the intensified persecution.

However, the real crucible was Poland. Here, racial megalomania had carte blanche. But it was precisely the absence of any systematic planning in the free-for-all of unlimited power that produced the unforeseen logistical problems and administrative cul-de-sacs of 'ethnic cleansing' which in turn evoked ever more radical, genocidal approaches.

Those who enjoyed positions of power and influence saw the occupation of Poland as an opportunity to 'solve the Jewish Question' – despite the fact that now more Jews than ever had fallen within the clutches of the Third Reich. For the SS, entirely new perspectives had emerged. Among party leaders, all the Gauleiter wanted to be rid of 'their' Jews and now saw possibilities of doing so. These were starting points. At the same time, for those ruling the parts of former Poland which had been incorporated into the Reich, the expulsion of the Jews from their territories was only part of the wider aim of Germanization, to be achieved as rapidly as possible. This meant also tackling the 'Polish Question', removing thousands of Poles to make room for ethnic Germans from the Baltic and other areas, classifying the 'better elements' as German, and reducing the rest to uneducated helots available to serve the German masters. 'Ethnic cleansing' to produce the required Germanization through resettlement was intrinsically connected with the radicalization of thinking on the 'Jewish Question'.

Beginning only days after the German invasion of Poland, Security Police and party leaders in Prague, Vienna, and Kattowitz – seizing on the notions expounded by Heydrich of a 'Jewish reservation' to be set up east of Cracow – saw the chance of deporting the Jews from their areas. Eichmann's own initiative and ambition appear to have triggered the hopes of immediate expulsion of the Jews. Between 18 and 26 October he organized the transport of several thousands of Jews from Vienna, Kattowitz, and Moravia to the Nisko district, south of Lublin. Gypsies from Vienna were also included in the deportation. At the same time, the resettlement of the Baltic Germans began. Within days of the Nisko transports beginning, the lack of provision for the deported Jews in Poland, creating chaotic circumstances following their arrival, led to their abrupt halt. But it was a foretaste of the greater deportations to come.

At the end of the month, in his new capacity as Reich Commissar for the Consolidation of Germandom, Himmler ordered all Jews to be cleared out of the incorporated territories. The deportation of around 550,000 Jews was envisaged. On top of that came several hundred thousand of the 'especially hostile Polish population', making a figure of about a million persons in all. From the largest of the areas designated for deportations and the resettlement of ethnic Germans, the Warthegau, it proved impossible to match the numbers initially charted for deportation, or the speed at which their removal had been foreseen. Even so, 128,011 Poles and Jews were forcibly deported under horrifying conditions by spring 1940. Sadistic SS men would arrive at night, clear entire tenement blocks, and load up the inhabitants – subjected to every form of bestial humiliation – on to open lorries, despite the intense cold, to be taken to holding camps, from where they were herded into unheated and massively overcrowded cattle-trucks and sent south, without possessions and often without food or water. Deaths were frequent on the journeys. Those who survived often suffered from frostbite or other legacies of their terrible ordeal. The deportees were sent to the General Government, seen in the annexed territories as a type of dumping-ground for undesirables. But the Governor General, Hans Frank, was no keener on having Jews in his area than were the Gauleiter of the incorporated regions. He envisaged them rotting in a reservation, but outside his own territory. In November 1939 Frank had plainly laid down the intentions for his own province. It was a pleasure, he stated, finally to be able physically to tackle the Jewish race: 'The more who die, the better ... The Jews should see that we have arrived. We want to have a half to three-quarters of all Jews put east of the Vistula. We'll suppress these Jews everywhere we can. The whole business is at stake here. The Jews out of the Reich, Vienna, from everywhere. We've no use for Jews in the Reich.'

Around the same time as Frank was voicing such sentiments, the Reich Governor of the Wartheland, Arthur Greiser, speaking of encountering in Lodz 'figures who can scarcely be credited with the designation "person"', was letting it be known that the 'Jewish Question' was as good as solved. However, by early 1940, his hopes (and those of Wilhelm Koppe, police chief of the Warthegau) of the quick expulsion of the Jews into the General Government were already proving vain ones. Hans Frank and his subordinates were starting to raise objections at the numbers of Jews they were being forced to take in, without any clear planning for what was to become of them, and with their own hopes of sending them on further to a reservation – an idea meanwhile abandoned – now vanished. Frank was able to win the support of Göring, whose own interest was in preventing the loss of manpower useful for the war effort. Göring's strong criticism of the 'wild resettlement' at a meeting on 12 February ran counter to Himmler's demands for room for hundreds of thousands of ethnic Germans, already moved from their original homes. The very next day, Jews from Stettin were deported to the Lublin area to make way for Baltic Germans 'with sea-faring jobs'. The police chief of the Lublin district, Odilo Globocnik, suggested that if the Jews coming to the General Government could not feed themselves, or be fed by other Jews, they should be left to starve. On 24 March, at Frank's bidding, Göring felt compelled to ban all 'evacuation' into the General Government 'until further notice'. Greiser was told that his request to deport the Warthegau's Jews would have to be deferred until August. From 1 May 1940 the huge ghetto at Lodz, containing 163,177 persons, initially established only as a temporary measure until the Warthegau's Jews could be pushed over the border into the General Government, was sealed off from the rest of the city. Mortalities from disease and starvation started to rocket during the summer. At a meeting in Cracow on 31 July, Greiser was told by Frank in no uncertain terms of Himmler's assurance, under instructions by Hitler, that no more Jews were to be deported to the General Government. And on 6 November 1940 Frank informed Greiser by telegram that there were to be no further deportations into the General Government before the end of the war. Himmler was aware of this. Any transports would be turned back. The solution which to Greiser had seemed so close to hand a year earlier was indefinitely blocked.

As one door closed, another opened – or, for a brief moment, appeared to open. At the meeting in Cracow at the end of July, Greiser mentioned a new possibility that had emerged. He had heard personally from Himmler, he reported, 'that the intention now exists to shove the Jews overseas into specific areas'. He wanted early clarification.

Resettling Jews on the island of Madagascar, a French colony off the African coast, had for decades been vaguely mooted in antisemitic circles, not just in Germany, as a potential solution to the 'Jewish Question'. With the prospect looming larger in the spring of 1940 of regaining colonial territories in the near future (and acquiring some which had not previously belonged to Germany), Madagascar now began to be evoked as a distinct policy option. It seems to have been Himmler, perhaps testing the waters, who at this point first broached in the highest circles the idea of deporting the Jews to an African colony, though he did not refer specifically to Madagascar. In the middle of May, after a visit to Poland, the Reichsführer-SS produced a six-page memorandum (which Hitler read and approved) entitled 'Some Thoughts on the Treatment of the Alien Population in the East', detailing brutal plans for racial selection in Poland. Only in one brief passage did Himmler mention what he envisaged would happen to the Jews. 'The term "Jew",' he wrote, 'I hope to see completely extinguished through the possibility of a large-scale emigration of all Jews to Africa or to some other colony.'

Sensing what was in the wind, the newly appointed, highly ambitious head of the Foreign Ministry's 'Jewish Desk', Franz Rademacher, prepared a lengthy internal memorandum on 3 June putting forward, as a war aim, three options: removing all Jews from Europe; deporting western European Jews, for example, to Madagascar while leaving eastern Jews in the Lublin district as hostages to keep America paralysed in its fight against Germany (presuming the influence of American Jewry would in these circumstances deter the USA from entering the war); or establishing a Jewish national home in Palestine – a solution he did not favour. This was the first time that Madagascar had been explicitly mentioned in a policy document as a possible 'solution to the Jewish Question'. It was a product of Rademacher's initiative, rather than a result of instructions from above. With the backing of Ribbentrop (who had probably himself gained the approval of Hitler and Himmler), Rademacher set to work to put detail on his proposal to resettle all Europe's Jews on the island of Madagascar, seeing them as under German mandate but Jewish administration. Heydrich, presumably alerted by Himmler at the first opportunity, was, however, not prepared to concede control over such a vital issue to the Foreign Ministry. On 24 June he made plain to Ribbentrop that responsibility for handling the 'Jewish Question' was his, under the commission given to him by Göring in January 1939. Emigration was no longer the answer. 'A territorial final solution will therefore be necessary.' He sought inclusion in all discussions 'which concern themselves with the final solution of the Jewish question' – the first time, it seems, the precise words 'final solution' were used, and at this point plainly in the context of territorial resettlement. By mid-August Eichmann and his right-hand man Theo Dannecker had devised in some detail plans to put 4 million Jews on Madagascar. The SD's plan envisaged no semblance of Jewish autonomous administration. The Jews would exist under strict SS control.

Soon after Rademacher had submitted his original proposal, in early June, the Madagascar idea had evidently been taken to Hitler, presumably by Ribbentrop. The Foreign Minister told Ciano later in the month 'that it is the Führer's intention to create a free Jewish state in Madagascar to which he will compulsorily send the many millions of Jews who live on the territory of the old Reich as well as on the territories recently conquered'. In the middle of August, reporting on a conversation with Hitler, Goebbels still noted: 'We want later to transport the Jews to Madagascar.'

Already by this time, however, the Madagascar plan had had its brief heyday. Putting it into effect would have depended not only on forcing the French to hand over their colony – a relatively simple matter – but on attaining control over the seas through the defeat of the British navy. With the continuation of the war the plan fell by the end of the year into abeyance and was never resurrected. But through the summer, for three months or so, the idea was taken seriously by all the top Nazi leadership, including Hitler himself.

Hitler's rapid endorsement of such an ill-thought-out and impracticable scheme reflected his superficial involvement in anti-Jewish policy during 1940. His main interests that year were plainly elsewhere, in the direction of war strategy. For the time being at least, the 'Jewish Question' was a secondary matter for him. However, the broad mandate to 'solve the Jewish Question' associated with his 'mission', coupled with the blockages in doing so in occupied Poland, sufficed. Others were more active than Hitler himself. To Goebbels, Hitler gave merely the assurance that the Jews were earmarked to leave Berlin, without approving any immediate action. Some had more luck with their demands. As in the east, the Gauleiter given responsibilities in the newly occupied areas in the west were keen to exploit their position to get rid of the Jews from their Gaue. In July Robert Wagner, Gauleiter of Baden and now in charge of Alsace, and Josef Bürckel, Gauleiter of the Saar-Palatinate and Chief of the Civil Administration in Lorraine, both pressed Hitler to allow the expulsion *westwards* into Vichy France of the Jews from their domains. Hitler gave his approval. Some 3,000 Jews were deported that month from Alsace into the unoccupied zone of France. In October, following a further meeting with the two Gauleiter, a total of 6,504 Jews were sent to France in nine trainloads, without any prior consultation with the French authorities, who appeared to have in mind their further deportation to Madagascar as soon as the sea-passage was secure.

Above all, the running in radicalizing anti-Jewish policy was made by the SS and Security Police leadership. While Hitler at this time paid relatively little attention to the 'Jewish Question' when not faced with a particular issue that one of his underlings had raised, Himmler and Heydrich were heavily engaged in planning the 'new order', especially in eastern Europe. Hitler's decision, taken under the impact of the failure to end the war in the west, to prepare for the invasion of the Soviet Union opened up new prospects again in the east for a 'solution' to the 'Jewish Question'. Once more, policy in the General Government was reversed. Hans Frank, who had been expecting in the summer to have the Jews from his area shipped to Madagascar, was now told that they had to stay. Emigration from the General Government was banned. The brutal forced-labour conditions and ghettoization were already highly attritional. Jews were in practice often being worked to death. An overtly genocidal mentality was already evident. Heydrich suggested starting an epidemic in the newly sealed Warsaw ghetto in autumn 1940 in order to exterminate the Jews there through such means. It was into an area in which this mentality prevailed that Frank, so Hitler told him in December, had to be prepared to take more Jews.

With Hitler playing little active role, but providing blanket approval, conditions and mentalities had been created in the occupied territories of former Poland in which full-scale genocide was only one step away.

IV

Before Hitler signed the directive in December 1940 to prepare what would rapidly be shaped into a 'war of annihilation' against the Soviet Union, there was a hiatus in which the immediate future direction of the war remained uncertain. Hitler was ready, during this phase that stretched from September to December 1940, to explore different possibilities of prising Britain out of the conflict before the Americans could enter it. Out of the failure of the 'peripheral strategy', a term hinted at by Jodl at the end of July, which at no stage gained Hitler's full enthusiasm, the hardening of the intention to invade the Soviet Union, first mooted in July, emerged until, on 18 December, it was embodied in a war directive.

With the invasion of Russia in the autumn of 1940, as initially proposed by Hitler, excluded on practical grounds by Jodl, other ways of retaining the strategic initiative had to be sought. Hitler was open to a number of suggestions. Ribbentrop was able to resurrect the idea he had promoted before the war, of an anti-British bloc of Germany, Italy, Japan, and the Soviet Union. The new situation in the wake of the German victories in western Europe now also opened the prospect of extending the anti-British front through gaining the active cooperation of Spain and Vichy France in the Mediterranean zone, together with a number of satellite states in south-eastern Europe. For Japan, the overrunning of the Netherlands and defeat of France, together with the serious weakening of Britain, offered an open invitation to imperialist expansion in south-eastern Asia. The Dutch East Indies and French Indo-China offered irresistible temptation, with the lure of the British possessions – including Singapore, British Borneo, Burma, and beyond that India itself – as an eventual further prize. Japan's interests in expanding to the south made her willing now to ease the long-standing tensions in relations with the Soviet Union. At the same time, Japan was keen to improve relations with Germany, soured since the Hitler–Stalin Pact, in order to have a free hand in south-eastern Asia. Hitler at this time opposed any formal alliance with Japan. Only in late summer, persuaded that Britain would not accept his 'offer', and concerned that America could soon enter the war (a step appearing closer since the news of the destroyer deal with Britain), did Hitler reverse this position. The negotiations that began in late August led to the signing of the Tripartite Pact on 27 September 1940, under which Germany, Italy, and Japan agreed to assist each other in the event of one of the signatories being attacked by an external power not involved in the European or Sino-Japanese conflicts – meaning, of course, the United States.

Raeder, too, was able to take advantage of Hitler's uncertainty in the late summer and autumn of 1940. In September the Commander-in-Chief of the navy put forward two memoranda strongly advocating a strategy directed at destroying Britain's strength in the Mediterranean and Near East. Hitler was not discouraging to Raeder's ambitious proposal – aimed squarely against Great Britain – to seize control (with Spanish assistance) of Gibraltar and the Suez Canal, before pushing through Palestine and Syria to the Turkish border. With Turkey 'in our power', as Raeder put it, the threat of the Soviet Union would be diminished. It would be 'questionable whether then moving against the Russians from the north would still be necessary', he concluded.

Hitler did not demur. He remarked that after the conclusion of the alliance with Japan he wanted to carry out talks with Mussolini and perhaps with Franco before deciding whether it was more advantageous to work with France or Spain.

Franco had opportunistically looked to join the Axis in mid-June, counting on spoils in a war about to be won (as it seemed). He wanted Gibraltar, French Morocco, and Oran, the former Spanish province currently in French Algeria. There was at the time every reason for Hitler to avoid acting on proposals that could have jeopardized the armistice. In September, a diplomatic balancing-act to ensure support for the Mediterranean strategy of France, Spain, and Italy now appeared desirable and timely. Ribbentrop and Ramón Serrano Suñer, Franco's brother-in-law and personal emissary, soon to be the Spanish Foreign Minister, met in Berlin on 16 September. But all that was forthcoming was an offer by Franco to meet Hitler on the Spanish border in October.

Before that, on 4 October, Hitler met Mussolini at the Brenner. Ribbentrop, feeling unwell and uncharacteristically quiet, and Ciano were also present. Hitler raised the question of Spanish intervention, outlining Franco's demands. Mussolini agreed on the stance to be taken towards Spain, reaffirming Italian demands of France to cede Nice, Corsica, Tunis, and Djibouti – claims in effect placed in cold storage at the armistice. Ciano drew the conclusions from the meeting that the proposed landing in Britain would not take place, that the aim was now to win over France to the anti-British coalition, since Britain was proving more difficult to defeat than anticipated, and that the Mediterranean sector had, to Italy's advantage, won greater significance.

The meeting had been cordial. But eight days later Mussolini's patience was stretched once more when he heard, without prior warning, that a German military commission had been dispatched to Bucharest and that the Germans were taking over the defence of the Romanian oil-fields. Mussolini's retaliation was to order the invasion of Greece for the end of the month, to present Hitler this time with a fait accompli. Hitler had warned against such a venture on numerous occasions.

On 20 October Hitler, accompanied by Ribbentrop, set out in his Special Train for southern France, bound first of all for a meeting, two days later, with Pierre Laval, Pétain's deputy and foreign minister in the Vichy regime. This proved encouraging. Laval, full of unctuous humility, opened up the prospect of close French collaboration with Germany, hoping for France's reward through retention of its African possessions and release from heavy reparations – both at the expense of Great Brtain – once a peace-settlement could be concluded. Hitler did not seek firm details. Leaving no doubt that some African possessions would fall to Germany after the war, he was content to offer the inducement that the ease of terms for France would depend on the extent of French cooperation and the rapidity with which the defeat of Britain could be attained.

Hitler's train travelled on to Hendaye, on the Spanish border, for the meeting with the Caudillo on the 23rd. From Hitler's point of view, the meeting was purely exploratory. The next day, as arranged with Laval, he would be talking with Pétain in the same vein. The repulsing by Vichy forces of a British–Gaullist landing at Dakar, the French West African port, a month earlier, and attempt to seize West Africa encouraged the already existing inclination of Hitler and Ribbentrop towards France over Spain if the respective interests of the two could not be reconciled. Hitler knew that his military chiefs were opposed to attempts to bring Spain into the war, and that Weizsäcker had also strongly advised that there was 'no practical worth' in Spain joining the Axis. From Franco's angle, the aim was not to keep Spain out of the war but to make maximum gains from her entry. In effect, Hitler had little or nothing to offer Franco, who wanted a great deal. The contours were set for the difficult meeting to follow.

It took place in the salon of Hitler's train. Franco – little, fat, swarthy in complexion, his droning sing-song voice reminiscent, it was later said, of that of an Islamic prayer-caller – said Spain would gladly fight on the side of Germany during the current war, though the economic difficulties of the country ruled this out. Unmistakably and disappointingly to Spanish ears, however, Hitler spent much of his rambling address dampening down any hopes Franco might have had of major territorial gains at minimal cost. It became ever plainer that he had little concrete to offer Spain. He proposed an alliance, with Spanish entry into the war in January 1941, to be rewarded by Gibraltar. But it was evident that none of the colonial territory in North Africa, coveted by Franco, was earmarked for Spain in Hitler's thinking. The Spanish dictator said nothing for a while. Then he unfolded his list of exorbitant demands of foodstuffs and armaments. At one point, Hitler's irritation was so great that he got up from the table, stating that there was no point in continuing. But he calmed down and carried on. The talks produced, however, no more than an empty agreement, leaving the Spanish to decide when, if ever, they would join the Axis. Hitler was heard to mutter, as he left the meeting: 'There's nothing to be done with this chap.' At Florence a few days later, Hitler told Mussolini that he 'would prefer to have three or four teeth taken out' than go through another nine hours' discussion with Franco.

The discussions with Pétain and Laval in Montoire on 24 October were no more fruitful. Hitler sought France's cooperation in the 'community' of countries he was in the process of organizing against Britain. The aged leader of Vichy France was non-committal. He could confirm the principle of French collaboration with Germany, which Laval had agreed at his meeting with Hitler two days earlier, but could not enter into detail and needed to consult his government before undertaking a binding arrangement. Hitler had offered Pétain nothing specific. He had in return received no precise assurances of active French support, either in the fight against Britain or in steps to regain the territory lost in French Equatorial Africa to the 'Free French' of de Gaulle, allied with Britain. The outcome was therefore inconsequential.

It was not surprising that Hitler and Ribbentrop travelled back to Germany with a sense of disappointment at the hesitancy of the French. It was a slow journey, during which Hitler, dispirited and convinced that his initial instincts had been right, told Keitel and Jodl that he wanted to move against Russia during the summer of 1941.

On crossing the German border Hitler received news that did nothing to improve his mood. He was informed that the Italians were about to invade Greece. He was furious at the stupidity of such a military action to take place in the autumn rains and winter snows of the Balkan hills.

However, during the meeting of the two dictators and their foreign ministers in Florence on 28 October – essentially a report on the negotiations with Franco and Pétain – Hitler contained his feelings about the Italian Greek adventure, and the meeting passed in harmony. Hitler spoke of the mutual distrust between himself and Stalin. However, he said, Molotov would shortly be coming to Berlin. It was his intention, he added, to steer Russian energies towards India. This remarkable idea was Ribbentrop's – part of his scheme to establish spheres of influence for Germany, Italy, Japan, and Russia (the powers forming his intended European–Asiatic Bloc to 'stretch from Japan to Spain'). It was an idea with a very short lifetime.

Briefing his military leaders in early November on his negotiations with Franco and Pétain, Hitler had referred to Russia as 'the entire problem of Europe' and said 'everything must be done to be ready for the great showdown'. But the meeting with his top brass showed that decisions on the prosecution of the war, whether it should be in the east or the west, were still open. Hitler had seemed to his army adjutant Major Engel, attending the meeting, 'visibly depressed', conveying the 'impression that at the moment he does not know how things should proceed'. Molotov's visit in all probability finally convinced Hitler that the only way forward left to him was the one which he had, since the summer, come to favour on strategic grounds, and to which he was in any case ideologically inclined: an attack on the Soviet Union.

Relations with the Soviet Union were already deteriorating seriously by the time Molotov had been invited to Berlin. Soviet designs on parts of Romania (which had been forced earlier in the summer to cede Bessarabia and northern Bukovina) and on Finland (effectively a Soviet satellite following defeat in the recent war) had prompted direct German involvement in these areas. Anxious about the Ploesti oil-fields, Hitler had agreed in September to Marshal Antonescu's request to send a German military mission comprising a number of armoured divisions and air-force units to Romania, on the face of it to reorganize the Romanian army. Russian protests that the German guarantees of Romania's frontiers violated the 1939 pact were dismissed. In late November Romania came fully within the German orbit when she joined the Tripartite Pact. The German stance on Finland had altered at the end of July – the time that an attack on the Soviet Union had first been mooted. Arms deliveries were made and agreements allowing German troops passage to Norway were signed, again despite Soviet protests. Meanwhile, the number of German divisions on the eastern front had been increased to counter the military build-up along the southern borders of the Soviet Union.

Undaunted by the growing difficulties in German–Soviet relations, Ribbentrop impressed upon the more sceptical Hitler the opportunities to build the anti-British continental bloc through including the Soviet Union, too, in the Tripartite Pact. Hitler indicated that he was prepared to see what came of the idea. But on the very day that talks with Molotov began, he put out a directive that, irrespective of the outcome, 'all already orally ordered preparations for the east [were] to be continued'.

The invitation to Molotov had been sent on 13 October – before the fruitless soundings of Franco and Pétain were made. On the morning of 12 November Molotov and his entourage arrived in Berlin. Weizsäcker thought the shabbily dressed Russians looked like extras in a gangster film. The hammer and sickle on Soviet flags fluttering alongside swastika banners provided an extraordinary spectacle in the Reich's capital. But the Internationale was not played, apparently to avoid the possibility of Berliners, still familiar with the words, joining in. The negotiations, in Ribbentrop's study in the lavishly redesigned old Reich President's Palace, went badly from the start. Molotov, cold eyes alert behind a wire pince-nez, an occasional icy smile flitting across his chess-player's face, reminded Paul Schmidt – there to keep a written record of the discussions – of his old mathematics teacher. His pointed, precise remarks and questions posed a stark contrast to Ribbentrop's pompous, long-winded statements. He let Ribbentrop's initial comments, that Britain was already defeated, pass without comment. And he made little response to the German Foreign Minister's strong hints in the opening exchanges that the Soviet Union should direct her territorial interests towards the Persian Gulf, the Middle East, and India (plainly indicated, but not mentioned by name). But when Hitler joined the talks for the afternoon session, and provided his usual grand sweep of strategic interests, Molotov unleashed a hail of precise questions about Finland, the Balkans, the Tripartite Pact, and the proposed spheres of influence in Asia, catching the German leader off guard. Hitler was visibly discomfited, and sought a convenient adjournment.

Molotov had not finished. He began the next day where he had left off the previous afternoon. He did not respond to Hitler's suggestion to look to the south, and to the spoils of the British Empire. He was more interested, he said, in matters of obvious European significance. He pressed Hitler on German interests in Finland, which he saw as contravening the 1939 Pact, and on the border guarantee given to Romania and the military mission sent there. Molotov asked how Germany would react were the Soviet Union to act in the same way towards Bulgaria. Hitler could only reply, unconvincingly, that he would have to consult Mussolini. Molotov indicated Soviet interest in Turkey, giving security in the Dardanelles and an outlet to the Aegean.

Symbolizing the fiasco of the two-day negotiations, the closing banquet in the Soviet Embassy ended in disarray under the wail of air-raid sirens. In his private bunker, Ribbentrop – showing once more his unerring instinct for clumsiness – pulled a draft agreement from his pocket and made one last vain attempt to persuade Molotov to concur in a four-power division of a large proportion of the globe. Molotov coldly reasserted Soviet interest in the Balkans and the Baltic, not the Indian Ocean. The questions that interested the Soviet Union, went on Molotov, somewhat more expansively than during the actual negotiations, were not only Turkey and Bulgaria, and the fate of Romania and Hungary, but also Axis intentions in Yugoslavia, Greece, and Poland. The Soviet government also wanted to know about the German stance on Swedish neutrality. Then there was the question of outlets to the Baltic. Later in the month, Molotov told the German Ambassador in Moscow, Graf von der Schulenburg, that Soviet terms for agreeing to a four-power pact included the withdrawal of German troops from Finland, recognition of Bulgaria as within the Russian sphere of influence, the granting of bases in Turkey, acceptance of Soviet expansion towards the Persian Gulf, and the cession by Japan of southern Sakhalin.

Molotov listed these terms on 26 November. Hitler did not need to wait so long. He viewed the talks in Berlin, he had told his army adjutant Major Engel before Molotov came to the Reich capital, as a test of whether Germany and the Soviet Union would stand 'back to back or breast to breast'. The results of the 'test' were now plain, in Hitler's eyes. The two-day negotiations with Molotov had sufficed to show that irreconcilable territorial interests of Germany and the Soviet Union meant inevitable clashes in the near future. Hitler told Engel that he had in any case expected nothing from Molotov's visit. 'The talks had shown where the Russian plans were heading. M[olotov] had let the cat out of the bag. He (F[ührer]) was really relieved. It would not even remain a marriage of convenience. Letting the Russians into Europe meant the end of central Europe. The Balkans and Finland were also dangerous flanks.'

Hitler's conviction, hardening since the summer, was confirmed: the strike against the Soviet Union had to take place in 1941. Some time in the autumn, probably following Molotov's visit, he sent his adjutants to search out a suitable location for field headquarters in the east. They recommended a spot in East Prussia, near Rastenburg, and he gave Todt orders to begin construction and have the headquarters completed by April. On 3 December he congratulated Field-Marshal Fedor von Bock on his sixtieth birthday and told him that the 'Eastern Question is becoming acute'. He spoke of rumoured links between Russia and America, and Russia and England. To await developments was dangerous. But if the Russians were eliminated from the equation, British hopes of defeating Germany on the continent would vanish, and Japanese freedom from worries about a Soviet attack from the rear meant American intervention would be made more difficult.

Two days later, on 5 December, he reviewed the objectives of the planned attack on the Soviet Union with Brauchitsch and Halder. Soviet ambitions in the Balkans, he declared, were a source of potential problems for the Axis. 'The decision concerning hegemony in Europe will come in the battle against Russia,' he added. 'The Russian is inferior. The army lacks leadership.' The German advantage in terms of leadership, *matériel*, and troops would be at its greatest in the spring. 'When the Russian army is battered once,' continued Hitler, in his crass underestimation of Soviet forces, 'the final disaster is unavoidable.' The aim of the campaign, he stated, was the 'crushing of Russian manpower'. The key strikes were to be on the northern and southern flanks. Moscow, he commented, was 'of no great importance'. Preparations for the campaign were to be advanced in full force. The operation was expected to take place at the end of May. Halder reported Hitler's thoughts to a meeting of military leaders on 13 December. The campaign, he told them, would involve the launching of 130–140 divisions against the Soviet Union by spring 1941. There was no indication that Brauchitsch, Halder, or their subordinate commanders raised objections to Hitler's analysis. On 17 December Hitler summarized his strategy for Jodl by emphasizing 'that we must solve all continental European problems in 1941 since the USA would be in a position to intervene from 1942 onwards'.

The following day, 18 December 1940, Hitler's war directive No. 21 began: 'The German Wehrmacht must be prepared, also before the ending of the war against England, *to crush Soviet Russia in a rapid campaign.*'

The operation had been code-named 'Otto' by the General Staff. It had been referred to as 'Fritz' by the Wehrmacht operational staff, and the draft directive No. 21 laid before Jodl on 12 December had carried that name. When Jodl presented it to him five days later, Hitler changed the code-name to the more imperious 'Barbarossa' – an allusion to the mighty twelfth-century emperor, ruler of Germany's first Reich, who had dominated central Europe and led a crusade against the Infidel. Hitler was now ready to plan his own crusade, against Bolshevism.

On 8–9 January 1941 Hitler held discussions at the Berghof with his military leaders. On the reasons for deciding to attack the Soviet Union, he reiterated arguments he had been deploying since the previous summer. Partly, the argument rested on an understanding of Soviet intentions, sharpened since Molotov's visit. Stalin was shrewd, said Hitler, and would increasingly exploit Germany's difficulties. But the crux of his case was, as ever, the need to pull away what he saw as a vital prop to British interests. 'The possibility of a Russian intervention in the war was sustaining the English,' he went on. 'They would only give up the contest if this last continental hope were demolished.' He did not think 'the English were crazy. If they saw no further chance of winning the war, they would stop fighting, since losing it would mean they no longer had the power to hold together the Empire. Were they able to hold out, could put together forty to fifty divisions, and the USA and Russia were to help them, a very difficult situation for Germany would arise. That must not happen. Up to now he had acted on the principle of always smashing the most important enemy positions to advance a step. Therefore Russia must now be smashed. Either the British would then give in, or Germany would continue the fight against Britain in most favourable circumstances.' 'The smashing of Russia,' added Hitler, 'would also allow Japan to turn with all its might against the USA', hindering American intervention. He pointed to further advantages for Germany. The army in the east could be substantially reduced in size, allowing greater deployment of the armaments industry for the navy and Luftwaffe. 'Germany would then be unassailable. The gigantic territory of Russia contained immeasurable riches. Germany had to dominate it economically and politically, though not annex it. It would then preside over all possibilities of waging the struggle against continents in future. It could then not be defeated by anyone. If the operation were carried through,' Hitler concluded, 'Europe would hold its breath.' If the generals listening had any reservations, they did not voice them.

During 1940 the twin obsessions of Hitler – 'removing the Jews', and *Lebensraum* – had come gradually into sharp focus. Now, in the first half of 1941, the practical preparations for the showdown that Hitler had always wanted could be made. In these months the twin obsessions would merge into each other. The decisive steps into genocidal war were about to be taken.

19

Designing a 'War of Annihilation'

I

Between January and March 1941 the operational plans for 'Barbarossa' were put in place and approved by Hitler. Outwardly confident, he was inwardly less certain. On the very day that the directive for the attack on the Soviet Union was issued to the commanders-in-chief of the Wehrmacht, 18 December 1940, Major Engel had told Brauchitsch (who was still unclear whether Hitler was bluffing about invading the USSR) that the Führer was unsure how things would go. He was distrustful of his own military leaders, uncertain about the strength of the Russians, and disappointed in the intransigence of the British. Hitler's lack of confidence in the operational planning of the army leadership was not fully assuaged in the first months of 1941. His intervention in the planning stage brought early friction with Halder, and led by mid-March to amendments of some significance in the detailed directives for the invasion.

Already by the beginning of February, Hitler had been made aware of doubts – at any rate a mood less than enthusiastic – among some of the army leaders about the prospects of success in the coming campaign. General Thomas had presented to the Army High Command a devastating overview of deficiencies in supplies. Halder had noted in his diary on 28 January the gist of his discussion with Brauchitsch early that afternoon about 'Barbarossa': 'The "purpose" is not clear. We do not hit the British that way. Our economic potential will not be substantially improved. Risk in the west must not be underestimated. It is possible that Italy might collapse after the loss of her colonies, and we get a southern front in Spain, Italy, and Greece. If we are then tied up in Russia, a bad situation will be made worse.' Misgivings were voiced by the three army group commanders, Field-Marshals von Leeb, von Bock, and von Rundstedt, when they lunched with Brauchitsch and Halder on 31 January. Brauchitsch, as usual, was reluctant to voice any concern to Hitler. Bock, however, tentatively did so on 1 February. He thought the German army 'would defeat the Russians if they stood and fought'. But he doubted whether it would be possible to force them to accept peace-terms. Hitler was dismissive. The loss of Leningrad, Moscow, and the Ukraine would compel the Russians to give up the fight. If not, the Germans would press on beyond Moscow to Ekaterinburg. War production, Hitler went on, was equal to any demands. There was an abundance of *matériel*. The economy was thriving. The armed forces had more manpower than was available at the start of the war. Bock did not feel it even worth suggesting that it was still possible to back away from the conflict. 'I will fight,' Hitler stated. 'I am convinced that our attack will sweep over them like a hailstorm.'

Halder pulled his punches at a conference with Hitler on 3 February. He brought up supply difficulties, but pointed to methods by which they could be overcome, and played down the risks that he had been emphasizing only days earlier. The army leaders accepted the priority Hitler gave to the capture of Leningrad and the Baltic coast over Moscow. But they neglected to work out in sufficient detail the consequences of such a strategy. Hitler was informed of the numerical superiority of the Russian troops and tanks. But he thought little of their quality. Everything depended upon rapid victories in the first days, and the securing of the Baltic and the southern flank as far as Rostov. Moscow, as he had repeatedly stressed, could wait. According to Below, Brauchitsch and Halder 'accepted Hitler's directives to wage war against Russia without a single word of objection or opposition'.

In the days that followed the meeting, General Thomas produced further bleak prognoses of the economic situation. Fuel for vehicles sufficed for two months, aircraft fuel till autumn, rubber production until the end of March. Thomas asked Keitel to pass on his report to Hitler. Keitel told him that the Führer would not permit himself to be influenced by economic difficulties. Probably, the report never even reached Hitler. In any case, if Thomas was trying through presentation of dire economic realities to deter Hitler, his method was guaranteed to backfire. A further report demonstrated that if quick victories were attained, and the Caucasus oil-fields acquired, Germany could gain

75 per cent of the materials feeding the Soviet war industry. Such a prognosis could only serve as encouragement to Hitler and to other Nazi leaders.

Hitler remained worried about a number of aspects of the OKH's planning. He was concerned that the army leadership was underestimating the dangers from Soviet strikes at the German flanks from the Pripet Marsh, and called in February for a detailed study to allow him to draw his own conclusions. In mid-March, he contradicted the General Staff's conclusions, asserting – rightly, as things turned out – that the Pripet Marsh was no hindrance to army movement. He also thought the existing plan would leave the German forces overstretched, and too dependent upon what he regarded as the dubious strength of the Romanian, Hungarian, and Slovak divisions – the last of these dismissed merely on the grounds that they were Slavs – on the southern front. He ordered, therefore, the alteration from a two-pronged advance of Army Group South to a single thrust towards Kiev and down the Dnieper. Finally, he repeated his insistence that the crucial objective had to be to secure Leningrad and the Baltic, not push on to Moscow, which, at a meeting with his military leaders on 17 March, he declared was 'completely immaterial'. At this conference, these alterations to the original operational plan were accepted by Brauchitsch and Halder without demur. With that, the military framework for the invasion was in all its essentials finalized.

While the preparations for the great offensive were taking shape, however, Hitler was preoccupied with the dangerous situation that Mussolini's ill-conceived invasion of Greece the previous October had produced in the Balkans, and with remedying the consequence of Italian military incompetence in North Africa.

In all, during the calamitous month of January, the fighting in Libya had seen some 130,000 Italians captured by the British. The likelihood of a complete rout for the Italians in North Africa had to be faced. By 6 February, Hitler was briefing the general he had selected to stop the British advance and hold Tripolitania for the Axis. This was Erwin Rommel, who, with a combination of tactical brilliance and bluff, would throughout the second half of 1941 and most of 1942 turn the tables on the British and keep them at bay in North Africa.

Hitler's hopes of a vital strategic gain in the Mediterranean – notably affecting the situation in North Africa – by the acquisition of Gibraltar were, however, to be dashed again by the obstinacy of General Franco. Already at the end of January, Hitler had been informed by Jodl that 'Operation Felix' – the planned assault on Gibraltar – would have to be shelved, since the earliest it could now take place would be in mid-April. The troops and weapons would by then be needed for 'Barbarossa', at that time scheduled for a possible start only a month later. Hitler still hoped that Mussolini, at his meeting on 12 February with Franco, might persuade the Caudillo to enter the war. The day before the meeting, Hitler sent Franco a personal letter, exhorting him to join forces with the Axis powers and to recognize 'that in such difficult times not so much wise foresight as a bold heart can rescue the nations'. Franco was unimpressed. He repeated Spanish demands on Morocco, as well as Gibraltar. And he put forward in addition, as a price for Spain's entering the war at some indeterminate date, such extortionate demands for grain supplies – saying the 100,000 tons already promised by the Germans were sufficient for only twenty days – that there was no possibility they would be met. Spain, as before, had to be left out of the equation.

I I

Hitler confirmed the 'dreadful conditions' in Spain which Goebbels reported to him the day after his big speech in the Sportpalast on 30 January 1941, to mark the eighth anniversary of his appointment as Chancellor. The Propaganda Minister found Hitler in high spirits, confident that Germany held the strategic initiative, convinced of victory, revitalized as always by the wild enthusiasm – like a drug to him – of the vast crowd of raucous admirers packed into the Sportpalast. 'I've seldom seen him like this in recent times,' Goebbels remarked. 'The Führer always impresses me afresh,' he added. 'He is a true Leader, an inexhaustible giver of strength.'

In his speech, Hitler had concentrated almost exclusively on attacking Britain. He did not devote a single syllable to Russia. But for the first time since the beginning of the war, he reiterated his threat 'that, if the rest of the world should be plunged into a general war through Jewry, the whole of Jewry will have played out its role in Europe!' 'They can still laugh today about it,' he added, menacingly, 'just like they used to laugh at my prophecies. The coming months and years will prove that here, too, I've seen things correctly.' Hitler had made this threat, in similar tones, in his Reichstag speech of 30 January 1939. In repeating it now, he claimed to recall making his 'prophecy' in his speech to the Reichstag at the outbreak of war. But, in fact, he had not mentioned the Jews in his Reichstag speech on 1 September, the day of the invasion of Poland. He would make the same mistake in dating on several other occasions in the following two years. It was an indication, subconscious or more probably intentional, that he directly associated the war with the destruction of the Jews.

Why did he repeat the threat at this juncture? There was no obvious contextual need for it. He had referred earlier in the speech to 'a certain Jewish-international capitalist clique', but otherwise had not played the antisemitic tune. But within the few weeks immediately prior to his speech, Hitler had had the fate of the Jews on his mind, commissioning Heydrich at this point with the task of developing a new plan, replacing the defunct Madagascar scheme, to deport the Jews from the German sphere of domination. Perhaps Hitler had harboured his 'prophecy' in the recesses of his mind since he had originally made it. Perhaps one of his underlings had reminded him of it. But, most probably, it was the inclusion of the extract from his speech in the propaganda film *Der ewige Jude*, which had gone on public release in November 1940, that had stirred Hitler's memory of his earlier comment. Whatever had done so, the repeat of the 'prophecy' at this point was ominous. Though he was uncertain precisely *how* the war would bring about the destruction of European Jewry, he was sure that this would be the outcome. And this was only a matter of months before the war against the arch-enemy of 'Jewish-Bolshevism' was to be launched. The idea of the war to destroy the Jews once and for all was beginning to take concrete shape in Hitler's mind.

According to the account – post-war recollections, resting partly on earlier, lost notes in diary form – of his army adjutant Gerhard Engel, Hitler discussed the 'Jewish Question' soon after his speech, on 2 February, with a group of his intimates. Keitel, Bormann, Ley, Speer, and Ribbentrop's right-hand man and liaison officer Walther Hewel were present. Ley brought up the topic of the Jews. This was the trigger for Hitler to expound at length on his thoughts. He envisaged the war accelerating a solution. But it also created additional difficulties. Originally, it had lain within his reach 'to break the Jewish power at most in Germany'. He had thought at one time, he said, with the assistance of the British of deporting the half a million German Jews to Palestine or Egypt. But that idea had been blocked by diplomatic objections. Now it had to be the aim 'to exclude Jewish influence in the entire area of power of the Axis'. In some countries, like Poland and Slovakia, the Germans themselves could bring that about. In France, it had become more complicated following the armistice, and was especially important there. He spoke of approaching France and demanding the island of Madagascar to accommodate Jewish resettlement. When an evidently incredulous Bormann – aware, no doubt, that the Madagascar Plan had by now been long since shelved by the Foreign Ministry and, more importantly, by the Reich Security Head Office – asked how this could be done during the war, Hitler replied vaguely that he would like to make the whole 'Strength through Joy' fleet (ships belonging to the German Labour Front's leisure programme) available for the task, but feared its exposure to enemy submarines. Then, in somewhat contradictory fashion, he added: 'He was now thinking about something else, not exactly more friendly.'

This cryptic comment was a hint that the defeat of the Soviet Union, anticipated to take only a few months, would open up the prospect of wholesale deportation of the Jews to the newly conquered lands in the east – and forced labour under barbarous conditions in the Pripet marshlands (stretching towards White Russia in what were formerly eastern parts of Poland) and in the frozen, arctic wastes in the north of the Soviet Union. Such ideas were being given their first airing around this time by Himmler, Heydrich, and Eichmann. They would not have hesitated in putting their ideas to Hitler. The thinking was now moving way beyond what had been contemplated under the Madagascar Plan, inhumane though that itself had been. In such an inhospitable climate as that now envisaged, the fate of the Jews would be sealed. Within a few years most of them would starve, freeze, or be worked to death. The idea of a comprehensive territorial solution to the 'Jewish problem' had by now become effectively synonymous with genocide.

Hitler had been under continued pressure from Nazi leaders to deport the Jews from their own territories, with, now as before, the General Government seen as the favoured 'dumping-ground'. Among the most persistent was the Gauleiter of Vienna, and former Hitler Youth Leader, Baldur von Schirach, who had been pressing hard since the previous summer to relieve the chronic housing problems of Vienna by 'evacuating' the city's 60,000 Jews to the General Government. Hitler had finally agreed to this in December 1940. The plans were fully prepared by the beginning of February 1941. Fresh from his visit to Vienna in March, on the third anniversary of the Anschluß, Hitler discussed with Hans Frank and Goebbels the imminent removal of the Jews from Vienna. Goebbels, anxious to be rid of the Jews from Berlin, was placated with an indication that the Reich capital would be next. 'Later, they must sometime get out of Europe altogether,' the Propaganda Minister added.

Despite the problems which had arisen in 1940 about the transfer of Jews and Poles into the General Government, Heydrich (partly under pressure from the Wehrmacht, which needed land for troop exercises) had approved in January 1941 a new plan to expel 771,000 Poles together with the 60,000 Jews from Vienna (bowing to the demands for deportation from Schirach, backed by Hitler) into Hans Frank's domain to make room for the settlement of ethnic Germans. A major driving-force behind the urgency of the ambitious new resettlement programme was the need to accommodate (and incorporate in the work-force) ethnic Germans who had been brought to Poland from Lithuania, Bessarabia, Bukovina and elsewhere in eastern Europe and since then miserably housed in transit camps. Frank's subordinates were dismayed at having to cope with a massive new influx of 'undesirables'. In the event, however, inevitable logistical complications of the new plan soon revealed it as a grandiose exercise in inhumane lunacy. By mid-March the programme had ground to a halt. Only around 25,000 people had been deported into the General Government. And only some 5,000, mainly elderly, Jews had been removed from Vienna. There was still no prospect, within the confines of the territory currently under German control, of attaining either the comprehensive resettlement programme that Himmler was striving for, or, within that programme, solving what seemed to be becoming a more and more intractable problem: removing the Jews.

From comments made by Eichmann's associate Theodor Dannecker, and, subsequently, by Eichmann himself, it was around the turn of the year 1940–41 that Heydrich gained approval from Hitler for his proposal for the 'final evacuation' of German Jews to a 'territory still to be determined'. On 21 January Dannecker noted: 'In accordance with the will of the Führer, the Jewish question within the part of Europe ruled or controlled by Germany is after the war to be subjected to a final solution.' To this end, Heydrich had obtained from Hitler, via Himmler and Göring, the 'commission to put forward a final solution project'. Plainly, at this stage, this was still envisaged as a territorial solution – a replacement for the aborted Madagascar Plan. Eichmann had in mind a figure of around 5.8 million persons.

Two months later, Eichmann told representatives of the Propaganda Ministry that Heydrich 'had been commissioned with the final evacuation of the Jews' and had put forward a proposal to that effect some eight to ten weeks earlier. The proposal had, however, not been accepted 'because the General Government was not in a position at that time to absorb a single Jew or a Pole'. When, on 17 March, Hans Frank visited Berlin to speak privately with Hitler about the General Government – presumably raising the difficulties he was encountering with Heydrich's new deportation scheme – he was reassured, in what amounted to a reversal of previous policy, that the General Government would be the first territory to be made free of Jews. But only three days after this meeting, Eichmann was still talking of Heydrich presiding over the 'final evacuation of the Jews' *into* the General Government. Evidently (at least that was the line that Eichmann was holding to), Heydrich still at this point had his sights set on the General Government as offering the *temporary* basis for a territorial solution. Frank was refusing to contemplate this. And Hitler had now opened up to him the prospect of his territory being the first to be rid of its Jews. Perhaps this was said simply to placate Frank. But in the light of the ideas already taking shape for a comprehensive new territorial solution in the lands, soon to be conquered (it was presumed), of the Soviet Union, it was almost certainly a further indicator that Hitler was now envisaging a new option for a radical solution to the 'Jewish problem' once the war was over by mass deportation to the east.

Heydrich and his boss Himmler were certainly anxious to press home the opportunity to expand their own power-base on a grand scale by exploiting the new potential about to open up in the east. Himmler had lost no time in acquainting himself with Hitler's thinking and, no doubt, taking the chance to advance his own suggestions. On the very evening of the signing of the military directive for 'Operation Barbarossa' on 18 December, he had made his way to the Reich Chancellery for a meeting with Hitler. No record of what was discussed survives. But it is hard to imagine that Himmler did not raise the issue of new tasks for the SS which would be necessary in the coming showdown with 'Jewish-Bolshevism'. It was a matter of no more at this point than obtaining Hitler's broad authority for plans still to be worked out.

Himmler and Heydrich were to be kept busy over the next weeks in plotting their new empire. Himmler informed a select group of SS leaders in January that there would have to be a reduction of some 30 million in the Slav population in the East. The Reich Security Head Office commissioned the same month preparations for extensive police action. By early February Heydrich had already carried out preliminary negotiations with Brauchitsch about using units of the Security Police alongside the army for 'special tasks'. No major difficulties were envisaged.

III

What such 'special tasks' might imply became increasingly clear to a wider circle of those initiated into the thinking for 'Barbarossa' during February and March. On 26 February General Georg Thomas, the Wehrmacht's economics expert, learned from Göring that an early objective during the occupation of the Soviet Union was 'quickly to finish off the Bolshevik leaders'. A week later, on 3 March, Jodl's comments on the draft of operational directions for 'Barbarossa' which had been routinely sent to him made this explicit: 'all Bolshevist leaders or commissars must be liquidated forthwith'. Jodl had altered the draft somewhat before showing it to Hitler. He now summarized Hitler's directions for the 'final version'. These made plain that 'the forthcoming campaign is more than just an armed conflict; it will lead, too, to a showdown between two different ideologies . . . The socialist ideal can no longer be wiped out in the Russia of today. From the internal point of view the formation of new states and governments must inevitably be based on this principle. The Jewish-Bolshevik intelligentsia, as the "oppressor" of the people up to now, must be eliminated.' The task involved, the directions went on, was 'so difficult that it cannot be entrusted to the army'. Jodl had the draft retyped in double-spacing to allow Hitler to make further alterations. When the redrafted version was finally signed by Keitel on 13 March, it specified that 'the Reichsführer-SS has been given by the Führer certain special tasks within the operations zone of the army', though there was now no direct mention of the liquidation of the 'Bolshevik-Jewish intelligentsia' or the 'Bolshevik leaders and commissars'.

Even so, the troops were to be directly instructed about the need to deal mercilessly with the political commissars and Jews they encountered. When he met Göring on 26 March, to deal with a number of issues related to the activities of the police in the eastern campaign, Heydrich was told that the army ought to have a three- to four-page set of directions 'about the danger of the GPU-Organization, the political commissars, Jews etc., so that they would know whom in practice they had to put up against the wall'. Göring went on to emphasize to Heydrich that the powers of the Wehrmacht would be limited in the east, and that Himmler would be left a great deal of independent authority. Heydrich laid before Göring his draft proposals for the 'solution of the Jewish Question', which the Reich Marshal approved with minor amendments. These evidently foresaw the territorial solution, which had been conceived around the turn of the year, and already approved by Himmler and Hitler, of deportation of all the European Jews into the wastelands of the Soviet Union, where they would perish.

During the first three months of 1941, then, the ideological objectives of the attack on the Soviet Union had come sharply into prominence, and had largely been clarified. In the context of the imminent showdown, the barbarism was now adopting forms and dimensions never previously encountered, even in the experimental training-ground of occupied Poland.

In the fateful advance into the regime's planned murderous policy in the Soviet Union, the army leaders were complicitous. On 17 March, Halder noted comments made that day by Hitler: 'The intelligentsia put in by Stalin must be exterminated. The controlling machinery of the Russian Empire must be smashed. In Great Russia force must be used in its most brutal form.' Hitler said nothing here of any wider policy of 'ethnic cleansing'. But the army leadership had two years earlier accepted the policy of annihilating the Polish ruling-class. Given the depth of its prevalent anti-Bolshevism, it would have no difficulty in accepting the need for the liquidation of the Bolshevik intelligentsia. By 26 March, a secret army order laid down, if in bland terms, the basis of the agreement with the Security Police authorizing 'executive measures affecting the civilian population'. The following day, the Commander-in-Chief of the army, Field-Marshal von Brauchitsch, announced to his commanders of the eastern army: 'The troops must be clear that the struggle will be carried out from race to race, and proceed with necessary severity.'

The army was, therefore, already in good measure supportive of the strategic aim and the ideological objective of ruthlessly uprooting and destroying the 'Jewish-Bolshevik' base of the Soviet regime when, on 30 March, in a speech in the Reich Chancellery to over 200 senior officers, Hitler stated with unmistakable clarity his views on the coming war with the Bolshevik arch-foe, and what he expected of his army. This was not the time for talk of strategy and tactics. It was to outline to generals in whom he still had little confidence the nature of the conflict that they were entering. According to Halder's notes, he was forthright: 'Clash of two ideologies. Crushing denunciation of Bolshevism, identified with a social criminality. Communism is an enormous danger for our future. We must forget the concept of comradeship between soldiers. A Communist is no comrade before or after the battle. This is a war of annihilation. If we do not grasp this, we shall still beat the enemy, but thirty years later we shall again have to fight the Communist foe. We do not wage war to preserve the enemy.' He went on to stipulate the 'extermination of the Bolshevist commissars and of the Communist intelligentsia'. 'We must fight against the poison of disintegration,' he continued. 'This is no job for military courts. The individual troop commanders must know the issues at stake. They must be the leaders in this fight ... Commissars and GPU men,' he declared, 'are criminals and must be dealt with as such.' The war would be very different from that in the west. 'In the east, harshness today means lenience in the future.' Commanders had to overcome any personal scruples.

General Warlimont, who was present, recalled 'that none of those present availed themselves of the opportunity even to mention the demands made by Hitler during the morning'. When serving as a witness in a trial sixteen years after the end of the war, Warlimont, explaining the silence of the generals, declared that some had been persuaded by Hitler that Soviet Commissars were not soldiers but 'criminal villains'. Others – himself included – had, he claimed, followed the officers' traditional view that as head of state and supreme commander of the Wehrmacht Hitler 'could do nothing unlawful'.

The day after Hitler's speech to the generals, 31 March 1941, the order was given to prepare, in accordance with the intended conduct of the coming campaign, as he had outlined it, guidelines for the 'treatment of political representatives'. Exactly how this order was given, and by whom, is unclear. Halder presumed, when questioned after the war, that it came from Keitel: 'When one has seen how, dozens of times, Hitler's most casual observation would bring the over-zealous Field-Marshal running to the telephone to let loose all hell, one can easily imagine how a random remark of the dictator would worry Keitel into believing that it was his duty on this occasion to give factual expression to the will of the Führer even before the beginning of hostilities. Then he or one of his subordinates would have telephoned OKH and asked how matters stood. If OKH had in fact been asked such a question, they would naturally have regarded it as a prod in the rear and would have got moving at once.' Whether there had been a direct command by Hitler, or whether – as Halder presumed – Keitel had once more been 'working towards the Führer', the guidelines initiated at the end of March found their way by 12 May into a formal edict. For the first time, they laid down in writing explicit orders for the liquidation of functionaries of the Soviet system. The reasoning given was that 'political representatives and leaders (commissars)' represented a danger since they 'had clearly proved through their previous subversive and seditious work that they reject all European culture, civilization, constitution, and order. They are therefore to be eliminated.'

This formed part of a set of orders for the conduct of the war in the east (following from the framework for the war which Hitler had defined in his speech of 30 March) that were given out by the High Commands of the Army and Wehrmacht in May and June. Their inspiration was Hitler. That is beyond question. But they were put into operative form by leading officers (and their legal advisers), all avidly striving to implement his wishes.

The first draft of Hitler's decree of 13 May 1941, the so-called 'Barbarossa-Decree', defining the application of military law in the arena of Operation Barbarossa, was formulated by the legal branch of the Wehrmacht High Command. The order removed punishable acts committed by enemy civilians from the jurisdiction of military courts. Guerrilla fighters were to be peremptorily shot. Collective reprisals against whole village communities were ordered in cases where individual perpetrators could not be rapidly identified. Actions by members of the Wehrmacht against civilians would not be automatically subject to disciplinary measures, even if normally coming under the heading of a crime.

The 'Commissar Order' itself, dated 6 June, followed on directly from this earlier order. Its formulation was instigated by the Army High Command. The 'Instructions on the Treatment of Political Commissars' began: 'In the struggle against Bolshevism, we must not assume that the enemy's conduct will be based on principles of humanity or of international law. In particular, hate-inspired, cruel, and inhumane treatment of prisoners can be expected on the part of *all grades of political commissars*, who are the real leaders of resistance . . . To show consideration to these elements during this struggle, or to act in accordance with international rules of war, is wrong and endangers both our own security and the rapid pacification of conquered territory . . . Political commissars have initiated barbaric, Asiatic methods of warfare. Consequently, they will be dealt with *immediately* and with maximum severity. As a matter of principle, they will be shot at once, whether captured *during operations or otherwise showing resistance.*'

This did not reflect the imposition of Hitler's will on a reluctant army. In part, the army leadership's rapid compliance in translating Hitler's ideological imperatives into operative decrees was in order to demonstrate its political reliability and avoid losing ground to the SS, as had happened during the Polish campaign. But the grounds for the eager compliance went further than this. In the descent into barbarity the experience in Poland had been a vital element. Eighteen months' involvement in the brutal subjugation of the Poles – even if the worst atrocities were perpetrated by the SS, the sense of disgust at these had been considerable, and a few generals had been bold enough to protest about them – had helped prepare the ground for the readiness to collaborate in the premeditated barbarism of an altogether different order built into Operation Barbarossa.

As the full barbarity of the Commissar Order became more widely known to officers in the weeks immediately prior to the campaign, there were, here too, honourable exceptions. Leading officers from Army Group B (to become Army Group Centre), General Hans von Salmuth and Lieutenant-Colonel Henning von Tresckow (later a driving-force in plans to kill Hitler), for example, let it be known confidentially that they would look for ways of persuading their divisional commanders to ignore the order. Tresckow commented: 'If international law is to be broken, then the Russians, not we, should do it first.' As the remark indicates, that the Commissar Order was a breach of international law was plainly recognized. Field-Marshal Fedor von Bock, Commander of Army Group Centre, rejected the shooting of partisans and civilian suspects as incompatible with army discipline, and used this as a reason to ignore the implementation of the Commissar Order.

But, as Warlimont's post-war comments acknowledged, at least part of the officer corps believed Hitler was right that the Soviet Commissars were 'criminals' and should not be treated as 'soldiers' in the way that the enemy on the western front had been treated. Colonel-General Georg von Küchler, Commander of the 18th Army, for instance, told his divisional commanders on 25 April that peace in Europe could only be attained for any length of time through Germany presiding over territory that secured its food-supply, and that of other states. Without a show-down with the Soviet Union, this was unimaginable. In terms scarcely different from those of Hitler himself, he went on: 'A deep chasm separates us ideologically and racially from Russia. Russia is from the very extent of land it occupies an Asiatic state . . . The aim has to be, to annihilate the European Russia, to dissolve the Russian European state . . . The political commissars and GPU people are criminals. These are the people who tyrannize the population . . . They are to be put on the spot before a field court and sentenced on the basis of the testimony of the inhabitants . . . This will save us German blood and we will advance faster.' Even more categorical was the operational order for Panzer Group 4, issued by Colonel-General Erich Hoepner (who three years later would be executed for his part in the plot to kill Hitler) on 2 May – still before the formulation of the Commissar Order: 'The war against the Soviet Union is a fundamental sector of the struggle for existence of the German people. It is the old struggle of the Germanic people against Slavdom, the defence of European culture against Moscovite-Asiatic inundation, the repulse of Jewish Bolshevism. This struggle has to have as its aim the smashing of present-day Russia and must consequently be carried out with unprecedented severity. Every military action must in conception and execution be led by the iron will mercilessly and totally to annihilate the enemy. In particular, there is to be no sparing the upholders of the current Russian-Bolshevik system.'

The complicity of Küchler, Hoepner, and numerous other generals was built into the way they had been brought up and educated, into the way they thought. The ideological overlap with the Nazi leadership was considerable, and is undeniable. There was support for the creation of an eastern empire. Contempt for Slavs was deeply ingrained. The hatred of Bolshevism was rife throughout the officer corps. Antisemitism – though seldom of the outrightly Hitlerian variety – was also widespread. Together, they blended as the ideological yeast whose fermentation now easily converted the generals into accessories to mass murder in the forthcoming eastern campaign.

IV

In the last week of March, three days before he defined the character of 'Operation Barbarossa' to his generals, Hitler received some highly unwelcome news with consequences for the planning of the eastern campaign. He was told of the military coup in Belgrade that had toppled the government of Prime Minister Cvetkovic and overthrown the regent, Prince Paul, in favour of his nephew, the seventeen-year-old King Peter II. Only two days earlier, in a lavish ceremony on the morning of 25 March in Hitler's presence in the palatial surrounds of Schloß Belvedere in Vienna, Cvetkovic had signed Yugoslavia's adherence to the Tripartite Pact, finally – following much pressure – committing his country to the side of the Axis. Hitler regarded this as 'of extreme importance in connection with the future German military operations in Greece'. Such an operation would have been risky, he told Ciano, if Yugoslavia's stance had been questionable, with the lengthy communications line only some twenty kilometres from the Yugoslav border inside Bulgarian territory. He was much relieved, therefore, although, he noted, 'internal relations in Yugoslavia could despite everything develop in more complicated fashion'. Whatever his forebodings, Keitel found him a few hours after the signing visibly relieved, 'happy that no more unpleasant surprises were to be expected in the Balkans'. It took less than forty-eight hours to shatter this optimism. The fabric of the Balkan strategy, carefully knitted together over several months, had been torn apart.

This strategy had aimed at binding the Balkan states, already closely interlinked economically with the Reich, ever more tightly to Germany. Keeping the area out of the war would have enabled Germany to gain maximum economic benefit to serve its military interests elsewhere. The initial thrust was anti-British, but since Molotov's visit to Berlin German policy in the Balkans had developed an increasingly anti-Soviet tendency.

Mussolini's reckless invasion of Greece the previous October had then brought a major revision of objectives. The threat posed by British military intervention in Greece could not be overlooked. The Soviet Union could not be attacked as long as danger from the south was so self-evident. By 12 November Hitler had issued Directive No. 18, ordering the army to make preparations to occupy from Bulgaria the Greek mainland north of the Aegean should it become necessary, to enable the Luftwaffe to attack any British air-bases threatening the Romanian oil-fields. Neither the Luftwaffe nor navy leadership were satisfied with this, and pressed for the occupation of the whole of Greece and the Peloponnese. By the end of November, the Wehrmacht operational staff agreed. Hitler's Directive No. 20 of 13 December 1940 for 'Operation Marita' still spoke of the occupation of the Aegean north coast, but now held out the possibility of occupying the whole of the Greek mainland, 'should this be necessary'. The intention was to have most of the troops engaged available 'for new deployment' as quickly as possible.

With the directive for 'Barbarossa' following a few days later, it was obvious what 'new deployment' meant. The timing was tight. Hitler had told Ciano in November that Germany could not intervene in the Balkans before the spring. 'Barbarossa' was scheduled to begin in May. When unusually bad weather delayed the complex preparations for 'Marita', the timing problems became more acute. And once Hitler finally decided in March that the operation had to drive the British from the entire Greek mainland and occupy it, the campaign had to be both longer and more extensive than originally anticipated. It was this which caused Hitler, in opposition to the strongly expressed views of the Army High Command, to reduce the size of the force initially earmarked for the southern flank in 'Barbarossa'.

In the intervening months, strenuous efforts had been made on the diplomatic front to secure the allegiance of strategically vital states. Hungary, Romania, and Slovakia had joined the Tripartite Pact in November 1940. Bulgaria, actively courted by Hitler since the previous autumn, finally committed itself to the Axis on 1 March. The last piece in the jigsaw was the hardest to fit in: Yugoslavia. Its geographical position alone made it vital to the success of an attack on Greece. Here, too, therefore, beginning in November, every attempt was made to bring about a formal commitment to the Tripartite Pact. The promise of the Aegean port of Salonika offered some temptation. The threat of German occupation – the stick, as always, alongside the carrot – provided for further concentration of minds. But it was plain that, among the people of Yugoslavia, allegiance to the Axis would not be a popular step. Hitler and Ribbentrop put Prince Paul under heavy pressure when he visited Berlin on 4 March. Despite the fear of internal unrest, which the Regent emphasized, Prince Paul's visit paved the way for the eventual signing of the Tripartite Pact on 25 March. But within hours of the signing, high-ranking Serbian officers, who had long resented Croat influence in the government, staged their coup.

Hitler was given the news on the morning of the 27th. He was outraged. He summoned Keitel and Jodl straight away. He would never accept this, he shouted, waving the telegram from Belgrade. He had been betrayed in the most disgraceful fashion and would smash Yugoslavia whatever the new government promised. There was still just about time to settle the Balkan issue. But there was now great urgency. Halder had also been peremptorily summoned from Zossen. Hitler asked him forthwith how long he needed to prepare an attack on Yugoslavia. Halder provided on the spot the rudiments of an invasion plan, which he had devised in the car on the way from Zossen.

By one o'clock, Hitler was addressing a sizeable gathering of officers from the army and Luftwaffe. 'Führer is determined,' ran the report of the Wehrmacht Operations Staff, '. . . to make all preparations to smash Yugoslavia militarily and as a state-form.' Speed was of the essence. He ordered preparations to begin immediately. The army and Luftwaffe were to indicate their intended tactics by the evening.

The plans for the invasion of Greece and the build-up to 'Barbarossa' were fully revised at breakneck speed to allow for the preliminary assault on Yugoslavia. The operation was eventually scheduled to begin in the early hours of 6 April.

The Yugoslav crisis had caused Hitler's meeting with the hawkish Japanese Foreign Minister, Yosuke Matsuoka, to be put back a few hours. It also necessitated Ribbentrop being called away from the preliminary talks with his Japanese counterpart to attend Hitler's briefing. Matsuoka's visit to Berlin was accompanied by enormous pomp and circumstance. Every effort was made to impress the important guest. As usual on state visits, cheering crowds had been organized – this time waving the little Japanese paper flags that had been handed out in their thousands. The diminutive Matsuoka, invariably dwarfed by lanky SS men around him, occasionally acknowledged the crowd's applause with a wave of his top-hat.

Hitler placed great store on the visit. His hope – encouraged by Raeder and Ribbentrop – was to persuade the Japanese to attack Singapore without delay. With 'Barbarossa' imminent, this would tie up the British in the Far East. The loss of Singapore would be a catastrophic blow for the still undefeated Britain. This in turn, it was thought in Berlin, would serve to keep America out of the war. And any possible rapprochement between Japan and the USA, worrying signs of which were mounting, would be ended at one fell swoop. Hitler sought no military assistance from Japan in the forthcoming war against the Soviet Union. In fact, he was not prepared to divulge anything of 'Barbarossa' – though in his talks with Matsuoka earlier that morning Ribbentrop had indicated a deterioration in Soviet-German relations and strongly hinted at the possibility that Hitler might attack the Soviet Union at some point.

Hitler deployed his full rhetorical repertoire. But he was sorely disappointed at Matsuoka's reply. An attack on Singapore was, the Japanese Foreign Minister declared, merely a matter of time, and in his opinion could not come soon enough. But he did not rule Japan, and his views had not so far prevailed against weighty opposition. 'At the present moment,' he stated, 'he could not under these circumstances enter on behalf of his Japanese Empire into any commitment to act.'

It was clear: Hitler had to reckon without any Japanese military intervention for the foreseeable future. When Matsuoka returned briefly to Berlin in early April to report on his meeting with Mussolini, Hitler was prepared to give him every encouragement. He acceded to the request for technical assistance in submarine construction. He then made an unsolicited offer. Should Japan 'get into' conflict with the United States, Germany would immediately 'draw the consequences'. America would seek to pick off her enemies one by one. 'Therefore Germany would,' Hitler said, 'intervene immediately in case of a conflict Japan-America, for the strength of the three Pact powers was their common action. Their weakness would be in letting themselves be defeated singly.' It was the thinking that would take Germany into war against the United

States later in the year following the Japanese attack on Pearl Harbor. Meanwhile, the Soviet-Japanese neutrality pact which Matsuoka negotiated with Stalin on his way back through Moscow – ensuring that Japan would not be dragged into a conflict between Germany and the Soviet Union, and securing her northern flank in the event of expansion in south-east Asia – came as an unpleasant surprise to Hitler.

While Matsuoka was in Berlin, preparations for 'Marita' were already furiously taking shape. Within little over a week they were ready. 'Operation Marita' began at 5.20 a.m. on Sunday morning, 6 April. Shortly afterwards, Goebbels read out on the radio the proclamation Hitler had dictated. By then, hundreds of Luftwaffe bombers were turning Belgrade into a heap of smoking ruins. Hitler justified the action to the German people as retaliation against a 'Serbian criminal clique' in Belgrade which, in the pay of the British Secret Service, was attempting, as in 1914, to spread the war in the Balkans.

With the campaign in its early stages, Hitler left Berlin on the evening of 10 April, en route for his improvised field headquarters. These were located in his Special Train *Amerika*, stationed at the entrance to a tunnel beneath the Alps on a single-track section of the line from Vienna to Graz, in a wooded area near Mönichkirchen. The Wehrmacht Operational Staff, apart from Hitler's closest advisers, were accommodated in a nearby inn.

Hitler remained in his secluded, heavily guarded field headquarters for a fortnight. He was visited there by King Boris of Bulgaria, Admiral Horthy, the regent of Hungary, and Count Ciano – vultures gathering at the corpse of Yugoslavia. His fifty-second birthday on 20 April was bizarrely celebrated with a concert in front of the Special Train, after Göring had eulogized the Führer's genius as a military commander, and Hitler had shaken the hand of each of his armed forces' chiefs. While there Hitler heard the news of the capitulation of both Yugoslavia and Greece.

After overcoming some early tenacious resistance, the dual campaign against Yugoslavia and Greece had made unexpectedly rapid progress. In fact, German operational planning had grossly overestimated the weak enemy forces. Of the twenty-nine German divisions engaged in the Balkans, only ten were in action for more than six days. On 10 April Zagreb was reached, and an independent Croatian state proclaimed, resting on the slaughterous anti-Serb Ustasha Movement. Two days later

Belgrade was reached. On 17 April the Yugoslav army surrendered unconditionally. Around 344,000 men entered German captivity. Losses on the victors' side were a mere 151 dead with 392 wounded and fifteen missing.

In contrast to the punitive attack on Yugoslavia, Hitler's interest in the conquest of Greece was purely strategic. He forbade the bombing of Athens, and regretted having to fight against the Greeks. If the British had not intervened there (sending troops in early March to assist the Greek struggle against Mussolini's forces), he would never have had to hasten to the help of the Italians, he told Goebbels. Meanwhile, the German 12th Army had rapidly advanced over Yugoslav territory on Salonika, which fell on 9 April. The bulk of the Greek forces capitulated on 21 April. A brief diplomatic farce followed. The blow to Mussolini's prestige demanded that the surrender to the Germans, which had in fact already taken place, be accompanied by a surrender to the Italians. To avoid alienating Mussolini, Hitler was forced to comply. The agreement signed by General List was disowned. Jodl was sent to Salonika with a new armistice. This time the Italians were party to it. This was finally signed, amid Greek protests, on 23 April. Greeks taken prisoner numbered 218,000, British 12,000, against 100 dead and 3,500 wounded or missing on the German side. In a minor 'Dunkirk', the British managed to evacuate 50,000 men – around four-fifths of its Expeditionary Force, which had to leave behind or destroy its heavy equipment. The whole campaign had been completed in under a month.

A follow-up operation to take Crete by landing parachutists was, while he was in Mönichkirchen, somewhat unenthusiastically conceded by Hitler under pressure from Göring, himself being pushed by the commander of the parachutist division, General Kurt Student. By the end of May, this too had proved successful. But it had been hazardous. And the German losses of 2,071 dead, 2,594 wounded, and 1,888 missing from a deployment of around 22,000 men were far higher than in the entire Balkan campaign. 'Operation Mercury' – the attack on Crete – convinced Hitler that mass paratroop landings had had their day. He did not contemplate using them in the assault the following year on Malta. Potentially, the occupation of Crete offered the prospect of intensified assault on the British position in the Middle East. Naval High Command tried to persuade Hitler of this. But his eyes were now turned only in one direction: towards the East.

On 28 April, Hitler had arrived back in Berlin – for the last time the warlord returning in triumph from a lightning victory achieved at minimal cost. Though people in Germany responded in more muted fashion than they had done to the remarkable victories in the west, the Balkan campaign appeared to prove once again that their Leader was a military strategist of genius. His popularity was undiminished. But there were clouds on the horizon. People in their vast majority wanted, as they had done all along, peace: victorious peace, of course, but above all, peace. Their ears pricked up when Hitler spoke of 'a hard year of struggle ahead of us' and, in his triumphant report to the Reichstag on the Balkan campaign on 4 May, of providing even better weapons for German soldiers 'next year'. Their worries were magnified by disturbing rumours of a deterioration in relations with the Soviet Union and of troops assembling on the eastern borders of the Reich.

What the mass of the people had, of course, no inkling of was that Hitler had already put out the directive for the invasion of the Soviet Union almost five months earlier. That directive, of 18 December, had laid down that preparations requiring longer than eight weeks should be completed by 15 May. But it had not stipulated a date for the actual attack. In his speech to military leaders on 27 March, immediately following news of the Yugoslav coup, Hitler had spoken of a delay of up to four weeks as a consequence of the need to take action in the Balkans. Back in Berlin after his stay in Mönichkirchen, he lost no time – assured by Halder of transport availability to take the troops to the east – in arranging a new date for the start of 'Barbarossa' with Jodl: 22 June.

Towards the end of the war, casting round for scapegoats, Hitler looked back on the fateful delay as decisive in the failure of the Russian campaign. 'If we had attacked Russia already from 15 May onwards,' he claimed, '. . . we would have been in a position to conclude the eastern campaign before the onset of winter.' This was simplistic in the extreme – as well as exaggerating the inroads made by the Balkan campaign on the timing of 'Barbarossa'. Weather conditions in an unusually wet spring in central Europe would almost certainly have ruled out a major attack before June – perhaps even mid-June. Moreover, the major wear and tear on the German divisions engaged on the Balkan campaign came less from the belated inclusion of Yugoslavia than from the invasion of Greece – planned over many months in conjunction with the planning for 'Barbarossa'. What did disadvantage the opening of 'Barbarossa' was the need for the redeployment at breakneck speed of divisions that had pushed on as far as southern Greece and now, without recovery time, had rapidly to be transported to their eastern positions. In addition, the damage caused to tanks by rutted and pot-holed roads in the Balkan hills required a huge effort to equip them again for the eastern campaign, and probably contributed to the high rate of mechanical failure during the invasion of Russia. Probably the most serious effect of the Balkan campaign on planning for 'Barbarossa' was the reduction of German forces on the southern flank, to the south of the Pripet marshes. But we have already seen that Hitler took the decision to that effect on 17 March, before the coup in Yugoslavia.

The weaknesses of the plan to invade the Soviet Union could not be laid at the door of the Italians, for their failure in Greece, or the Yugo-slavs, for what Hitler saw as their treachery. The calamity, as it emerged, of 'Barbarossa' was located squarely in the nature of German war aims and ambitions. These were by no means solely a product of Hitler's ideological obsessiveness, megalomania, and indomitable willpower. Certainly, he had provided the driving-force. But he had met no resist-ance to speak of in the higher echelons of the regime. The army, in particular, had fully supported him in the turn to the east. And if Hitler's underestimation of Soviet military power was crass, it was an underestimation shared with his military leaders, who had lost none of their confidence that the war in the Soviet Union would be over long before winter.

V

Meanwhile, Hitler was once more forced by events outside his control, this time close to home, to divert his attention from 'Barbarossa'.

When he stepped down from the rostrum at the end of his speech to Reichstag deputies on 4 May, he took his place, as usual, next to the Deputy Leader of the party, his most slavishly subservient follower, Rudolf Heß. Only a few days later, while Hitler was on the Obersalzberg, the astonishing news came through that his Deputy had taken a Messer-schmitt 110 from Augsburg, flown off on his own en route for Britain, and disappeared. The news struck the Berghof like a bombshell. The first wish was that he was dead. 'It's to be hoped he's crashed into the sea,' Hitler was heard to say. Then came the announcement from London – by then not unexpected – that Heß had landed in Scotland and been taken captive. With the Russian campaign looming, Hitler was now faced with a domestic crisis.

On the afternoon of Saturday, 10 May, Heß had said goodbye to his wife, Ilse, and young son, Wolf Rüdiger, saying he would be back by Monday evening. From Munich he had travelled in his Mercedes to the Messerschmitt works in Augsburg. There, he changed into a fur-lined flying suit and Luftwaffe captain's jacket. (His alias on his mission was to be Hauptmann Alfred Horn.) Shortly before 6 p.m. on a clear, sunlit evening, his Messerschmitt 110 taxied on to the runway and took off. Shortly after 11 p.m., after navigating himself through Germany, across the North Sea, and over the Scottish Lowlands, Heß wriggled out of the cockpit, abandoning his plane not far from Glasgow, and parachuted – something he had never practised – to the ground, injuring his leg as he left the plane.

Air defence had picked up the flight path, and observers had seen the plane's occupant bale out before it exploded in flames. A local Scottish farmhand, Donald McLean, was, however, first on the scene. He quickly established that the parachutist, struggling to get out of his harness, was unarmed. Asked whether he was British or German, Heß replied that he was German; his name was Hauptmann Alfred Horn, and he had an important message to give to the Duke of Hamilton. When Hamilton was informed in the early hours that a captured German pilot was demanding to speak to him, there was no reference to Heß, and the name of Hauptmann Alfred Horn meant nothing to the Duke. Puzzled, and very tired, Hamilton made arrangements to interview the mysterious airman next day, and went to bed.

The Duke, a wing-commander in the RAF, did eventually arrive from his base to talk to the German captive by mid-morning on 11 May. 'Hauptmann Horn' admitted that his true name was Rudolf Heß. The discussion was inconsequential, but convinced Hamilton that he was indeed face to face with Heß. By the evening he had flown south, summoned to report to Churchill at Ditchley Park in Oxfordshire, frequently used by the British Prime Minister as a weekend headquarters. By the following day, Monday 12 May, the professionals from the Foreign Office were involved. It was decided to send Ivone Kirkpatrick, from 1933 to 1938 First Secretary at the British Embassy in Berlin and a strong opponent of Appeasement, to interrogate Heß. Kirkpatrick and Hamilton left to fly to Scotland in the early evening. It was after midnight by the time they arrived at Buchanan Castle, near Loch Lomond, to confront the prisoner.

The first Hitler knew of Heß's disappearance was in the late morning of Sunday, 11 May, when Karl-Heinz Pintsch, one of the Deputy Führer's adjutants, turned up at the Berghof. He was carrying an envelope containing a letter which Heß had given him shortly before taking off, entrusting him to deliver it personally to Hitler. With some difficulty, Pintsch managed to make plain to Hitler's adjutants that it was a matter of the utmost urgency, and that he had to speak personally to the Führer. When Hitler read Heß's letter, the colour drained from his face. Albert Speer, busying himself with architectural sketches at the time, suddenly heard an 'almost animal-like scream'. Then Hitler bellowed, 'Bormann immediately! Where is Bormann?!'

In his letter, Heß had outlined his motives for flying to meet the Duke of Hamilton, and aspects of a plan for peace between Germany and Britain to be put before 'Barbarossa' was launched. He claimed he had made three previous attempts to reach Scotland, but had been forced to abort them because of mechanical problems with the aircraft. His aim was to bring about, through his own person, the realization of Hitler's long-standing idea of friendship with Britain which the Führer himself, despite all efforts, had not succeeded in achieving. If the Führer were not in agreement, then he could have him declared insane.

Göring – residing at the time in his castle at Veldenstein near Nuremberg – was telephoned straight away. Hitler was in no mood for small-talk. 'Göring, get here immediately,' he barked into the telephone. 'Something dreadful has happened.' Ribbentrop was also summoned. Hitler, meanwhile, had ordered Pintsch, the hapless bearer of ill tidings, and Heß's other adjutant, Alfred Leitgen, arrested, and spent his time marching up and down the hall in a rage. The mood in the Berghof was one of high tension and speculation. Amid the turmoil, Hitler was clear-sighted enough to act quickly to rule out any possible power-vacuum in the party leadership arising from Heß's defection. Next day, 12 May, he issued a terse edict stipulating that the former Office of the Deputy Leader would now be termed the Party Chancellery, and be subordinated to him personally. It would be led, as before, by Party Comrade Martin Bormann.

Hitler persuaded himself – taking his lead from what Heß himself in his letter had suggested – that the Deputy Führer was indeed suffering from mental delusion, and insisted on making his 'madness' the centre-point of the extremely awkward communiqué which had to be put out to the German people. There was still no word of Heß's whereabouts when the communiqué was broadcast at 8 p.m. that evening. The communiqué mentioned the letter which had been left behind, showing 'in its confusion unfortunately the traces of a mental derangement', giving rise to fears that he had been the 'victim of hallucinations'. 'Under these circumstances,' the communiqué ended, it had to be presumed that 'Party Comrade Heß had somewhere on his journey crashed, that is, met with an accident.'

Goebbels, overlooked in the first round of Hitler's consultations, had by then also been summoned to the Obersalzberg. 'The Führer is completely crushed,' the Propaganda Minister noted in his diary. 'What a spectacle for the world: a mentally-deranged second man after the Führer.' Meanwhile, early on 13 May, the BBC in London had brought the official announcement that Heß indeed found himself in British captivity.

The first German communiqué composed by Hitler the previous day would plainly no longer suffice. The new communiqué of 13 May acknowledged Heß's flight to Scotland, and capture. It held open the possibility that he had been entrapped by the British Secret Service. Affected by delusions, he had undertaken the action of an idealist without any notion of the consequences. His action, the communiqué ended, would alter nothing in the struggle against Britain.

The two communiqués, forced ultimately to concede that the Deputy Führer had flown to the enemy, and attributing the action to his mental state, bore all the hallmarks of a hasty and ill-judged attempt to play down the enormity of the scandal. Remarkably, Hitler had not turned to Goebbels for propaganda advice on how to present the débâcle, but had relied instead at first on Otto Dietrich, the press chief. Goebbels was highly critical from the outset about the 'mental illness' explanation. A real difficulty had to be faced: how to explain that a man recognized for many years as mentally unbalanced had been left in such an important position in the running of the Reich. 'It's rightly asked how such an idiot could be the second man after the Führer,' Goebbels remarked.

Goebbels felt the blow to prestige so deeply that he wanted to avoid being seen in public. 'It's like an awful dream,' he remarked. 'The Party will have to chew on it for a long time.' Hitler himself was occasionally caught in the line of fire of popular criticism. But, generally, much sympathy was voiced for the Führer who now had this, on top of all his other worries, to contend with. As ever, it was presumed that, while he was working tirelessly on behalf of the nation, he was kept in the dark, let down, or betrayed by some of his most trusted chieftains.

This key element of the 'Führer myth' was one that Hitler himself played to when, on 13 May, he addressed a rapidly arranged meeting of the Reichsleiter and Gauleiter at the Berghof. There was an air of tension when Göring and Bormann, both grim-faced, entered the hall before Hitler made his appearance. Bormann read out Heß's final letter to Hitler. The feeling of shock and anger among those listening was palpable. Then Hitler came into the room. Much as in the last great crisis within the party leadership, in December 1932, he played masterfully on the theme of loyalty and betrayal. Heß had betrayed him, he stated. He appealed to the loyalty of his most trusted 'old fighters'. He declared that Heß had acted without his knowledge, was mentally ill, and had put the Reich in an impossible position with regard to its Axis partners. He had sent Ribbentrop to Rome to placate the Duce. He stressed once more Heß's long-standing odd behaviour (his dealings with astrologists and the like). He castigated the former Deputy Führer's opposition to his own orders in continuing to practise flying. A few days before Heß's defection, he went on, the Deputy Führer had come to see him and asked him pointedly whether he still stood to the programme of cooperation with England that he had laid out in *Mein Kampf*. Hitler said he had, of course, reaffirmed this position.

When he had finished speaking, Hitler leaned against the big table near the window. According to one account, he was 'in tears and looked ten years older'. 'I have never seen the Führer so deeply shocked,' Hans Frank told a gathering of his subordinates in the General Government a few days later. As he stood near the window, gradually all the sixty or seventy persons present rose from their chairs and gathered round him in a semi-circle. No one spoke a word. Then Göring provided an effusive statement of the devotion of all present. The intense anger was reserved only for Heß. The 'core' following had once more rallied around their Leader, as in the 'time of struggle', at a moment of crisis. The regime had suffered a massive jolt; but the party leadership, its backbone, was still holding together.

All who saw Hitler in the days after the news of Heß's defection broke registered his profound shock, dismay, and anger at what he saw as betrayal. This has sometimes been interpreted, as it was also by a number of contemporaries, as clever acting on Hitler's part, concealing a plot which only he and Heß knew about. Hitler was indeed capable, as we have noted on more than one occasion, of putting on a theatrical performance. But if this was acting, it was of Hollywood-Oscar calibre.

That the Deputy Führer had been captured in Britain was something that shook the regime to its foundations. As Goebbels sarcastically pointed out, it never appears to have occurred to Heß that this could be the outcome of his 'mission'. It is hard to imagine that it would not have crossed Hitler's mind, had he been engaged in a plot. But it would have been entirely out of character for Hitler to have involved himself in such a hare-brained scheme. His own acute sensitivity towards any potential threat to his own prestige, towards being made to look foolish in the eyes of his people and the outside world, would itself have been sufficient to have ruled out the notion of sending Heß on a one-man peace-mission to Britain. Moreover, there was every reason, from his own point of view, *not* to have become involved and to have most categorically prohibited what Heß had in mind.

The chances of the Heß flight succeeding were so remote that Hitler would not conceivably have entertained the prospect. And had he done so, it is hard to believe that he would have settled on Heß as his emissary. Heß had not been party to the planning of 'Barbarossa'. He had been little in Hitler's presence over the previous months. His competence was confined strictly to party matters. He had no experience in foreign affairs. And he had never been entrusted previously with any delicate diplomatic negotiations.

In any case, Hitler's motive for contemplating a secret mission such as Heß attempted to carry out would be difficult to grasp. For months Hitler had been single-mindedly preparing to attack and destroy the Soviet Union precisely in order to force Britain out of the war. He and his generals were confident that the Soviet Union would be comprehensively defeated by the autumn. The timetable for the attack left no room for manoeuvre. The last thing Hitler wanted was any hold-up through diplomatic complications arising from the intercession by Heß a few weeks before the invasion was to be launched. Had 'Barbarossa' not taken place before the end of June, it would have had to be postponed to the following year. For Hitler, this would have been unthinkable. He was well aware that there were those in the British establishment who would still prefer to sue for peace. He expected them to do so *after*, not *before*, 'Barbarossa'.

Rudolf Heß at no time, whether during his interrogations after landing in Scotland, in discussions with his fellow-captives while awaiting trial in Nuremberg, or during his long internment in Spandau, implicated Hitler. His story never wavered from the one he gave to Ivone Kirkpatrick at his first interrogation on 13 May 1941. 'He had come here,' so Kirkpatrick summed up in his report, 'without the knowledge of Hitler in order to convince responsible persons that since England could not win the war, the wisest course was to make peace now.'

Heß's British interlocutors rapidly reached the conclusion that he had nothing to offer which went beyond Hitler's public statements, notably his 'peace appeal' before the Reichstag on 19 July 1940. Kirkpatrick concluded his report: 'Heß does not seem . . . to be in the near counsels of the German government as regards operations; and he is not likely to possess more secret information than he could glean in the course of conversations with Hitler and others.' If, in the light of this, Heß was following out orders from Hitler himself, he would have had to be as supreme an actor – and to have continued to be so for the next four decades – as was, reputedly, the Leader he so revered. But, then, to what end? He said nothing that Hitler had not publicly on a number of occasions stated himself. He brought no new negotiating position. It was as if he presumed that the mere fact of the Deputy Führer voluntarily – through an act involving personal courage – putting himself in the hands of the enemy was enough to have made the British government see the good will of the Führer, the earnest intentions behind his aim of cooperation with Britain against Bolshevism, and the need to overthrow the Churchill 'war-faction' and settle amicably. The naïvety of such thinking points heavily in the direction of an attempt inspired by no one but the idealistic, other-worldly, and muddle-headed Heß.

His own motives were not more mysterious or profound than they appeared. Heß had seen over a number of years, but especially since the war had begun, his access to Hitler strongly reduced. His nominal subordinate, Martin Bormann, had in effect been usurping his position, always in the Führer's company, always able to put in a word here or there, always able to translate his wishes into action. A spectacular action to accomplish what the Führer had been striving for over many years would transform his status overnight, turning 'Fräulein Anna', as he was disparagingly dubbed by some in the party, into a national hero.

Heß had remained highly influenced by Karl Haushofer – his former teacher and the leading exponent of geopolitical theories which had influenced the formation of Hitler's ideas of *Lebensraum* – and his son Albrecht (who later became closely involved with resistance groups). Their views had reinforced his belief that everything must be done to prevent the undermining of the 'mission' that Hitler had laid out almost two decades earlier: the attack on Bolshevism *together with*, not in opposition to, Great Britain. Albrecht Haushofer had made several attempts to contact the Duke of Hamilton, whom he had met in Berlin in 1936, but had received no replies to his letters. Hamilton himself strenuously denied, with justification it seems, receiving the letters, and also denied Heß's claim to have met him at the Berlin Olympics in 1936.

By August 1940, when he began to plan his own intervention, Heß was deeply disappointed in the British response to the 'peace-terms' that Hitler had offered. He was aware, too, that Hitler was by this time thinking of attacking the Soviet Union even before Britain was willing to 'see sense' and agree to terms. The original strategy lay thus in tatters. Heß saw his role as that of the Führer's most faithful paladin, now destined to restore through his personal intervention the opportunity to save Europe from Bolshevism – a unique chance wantonly cast away by Churchill's 'warmongering' clique which had taken over the British government. Heß acted without Hitler's knowledge, but in deep (if confused) belief that he was carrying out his wishes.

VI

By the middle of May, after a week preoccupied by the Heß affair, Hitler could begin to turn his attention back to 'Barbarossa'. But the end of what had been a troubled month brought further gloom to the Berghof with the news on 27 May of the loss of the powerful battleship *Bismarck*, sunk in the Atlantic after a fierce clash with British warships and planes. Some 2,300 sailors went down with the ship. Hitler did not brood on the human loss. His fury was directed at the naval leadership for unnecessarily exposing the vessel to enemy attack – a huge risk, he had thought, for potentially little gain.

Meanwhile, the ideological preparations for 'Barbarossa' were now rapidly taking concrete shape. Hitler needed to do nothing more in this regard. He had laid down the guidelines in March. It was during May that Heydrich assembled the four Einsatzgruppen ('task groups') which would accompany the army into the Soviet Union. Each of the Einsatzgruppen comprised between 600 and 1,000 men (drawn largely from varying branches of the police organization, augmented by the Waffen-SS) and was divided into four or five Einsatzkommandos ('task forces') or Sonderkommandos ('special forces'). The middle-ranking commanders for the most part had an educated background. Highly qualified academics, civil servants, lawyers, a Protestant pastor, and even an opera singer, were among them. The top leadership was drawn almost exclusively from the Security Police and SD. Like the leaders of the Reich Security Head Office, they were in the main well-educated men, of the generation, just too young to have fought in the First World War, that had sucked in *völkisch* ideals in German universities during the 1920s. During the second half of May, the 3,000 or so men selected for the Einsatzgruppen gathered in Pretzsch, north-east of Leipzig, where the Border Police School served as their base for the ideological training that would last until the launch of 'Barbarossa'. Heydrich addressed them on a number of occasions. He avoided narrow precision in describing their target-groups when they entered the Soviet Union. But his meaning was, nevertheless, plain. He mentioned that Jewry was the source of Bolshevism in the East and had to be eradicated in accordance with the Führer's aims. And he told them that Communist functionaries and activists, Jews, Gypsies, saboteurs, and agents endangered the security of the troops and were to be executed forthwith. By 22 June the genocidal whirlwind was ready to blow.

'Operation Barbarossa rolls on further,' recorded Goebbels in his diary on 31 May. 'Now the first big wave of camouflage goes into action. The entire state and military apparatus is being mobilized. Only a few people are informed about the true background.' Apart from Goebbels and Ribbentrop, ministers of government departments were kept in the dark. Goebbels's own ministry had to play up the theme of invasion of Britain. Fourteen army divisions were to be moved westwards to give some semblance of reality to the charade.

As part of the subterfuge that action was to be expected *in the West* while preparations for 'Barbarossa' were moving into top gear, Hitler hurriedly arranged another meeting with Mussolini on the Brenner Pass for 2 June. It was little wonder that the Duce could not understand the reason for the hastily devised talks. Hitler's closest Axis partner was unwittingly playing his part in an elaborate game of bluff.

Hitler did not mention a word of 'Barbarossa' to his Italian friends. The published communiqué simply stated that the Führer and Duce had held friendly discussions lasting several hours on the political situation. The deception had been successful. When he met the Japanese Ambassador Oshima the day after his talks with Mussolini, Hitler dropped a broad hint – which was correctly understood – that conflict with the Soviet Union in the near future was unavoidable. But the only foreign statesman to whom he was prepared to divulge more than hints was the Romanian leader Marshal Antonescu, when Hitler met him in Munich on 12 June. Antonescu had to be put broadly in the picture. After all, Hitler was relying on Romanian troops for support on the southern flank. Antonescu was more than happy to comply. He volunteered his forces without Hitler having to ask. When 22 June arrived, he would proclaim to his people a 'holy war' against the Soviet Union. The bait of recovering Bessarabia and North Bukovina, together with the acquisition of parts of the Ukraine, was sufficiently tempting to the Romanian dictator.

On 14 June Hitler held his last major military conference before the start of 'Barbarossa'. The generals arrived at staggered times at the Reich Chancellery to allay suspicion that something major was afoot. Hitler went over the reasons for attacking Russia. Once again, he avowed his confidence that the collapse of the Soviet Union would induce Britain to come to terms. He emphasized that the war was a war against Bolshevism. The Russians would fight hard and put up tough resistance. Heavy air-raids had to be expected. But the Luftwaffe would attain quick successes and smooth the advance of the land forces. The worst of the fighting would be over in about six weeks. But every soldier had to know what he was fighting for: the destruction of Bolshevism. If the war were to be lost, then Europe would be bolshevized. Most of the generals had concerns about opening up the two-front war, the avoidance of which had been a premiss of military planning. But they did not voice any objections. Brauchitsch and Halder did not speak a word.

Two days later Hitler summoned Goebbels to the Reich Chancellery – he was told to enter through a back door in order not to raise suspicions – to explain the situation. The attack on the Soviet Union would be the most massive history had ever seen, he stated. There would be no repeat of Napoleon (a comment perhaps betraying precisely those subconscious fears of history indeed repeating itself). The Russians had around 180–200 divisions, about as many as the Germans, he said, though there was no comparison in quality. And the fact that they were massed on the Reich borders was a great advantage. 'They would be smoothly rolled up.' Hitler thought 'the action' would take about four months. Goebbels estimated even less time would be needed: 'Bolshevism will collapse like a house of cards,' he thought.

On 21 June Hitler dictated the proclamation to the German people to be read out the next day. He was by this time looking over-tired, and was in a highly nervous state, pacing up and down, apprehensive, involving himself in the minutiae of propaganda such as the fanfares that were to be played over the radio to announce German victories. Goebbels was called to see him in the evening. They discussed the proclamation, to which Goebbels added a few suggestions. They marched up and down his rooms for three hours. They tried out the new fanfares for an hour. Hitler gradually relaxed somewhat. 'The Führer is freed from a nightmare the closer the decision comes,' noted Goebbels. 'It's always so with him.' Once more Goebbels returned to the inner necessity of the coming conflict, of which Hitler had convinced himself: 'There is nothing for it than to attack,' he wrote, summing up Hitler's thoughts. 'This cancerous growth has to be burned out. Stalin will fall.' Since July the previous year, Hitler indicated, he had worked on the preparations for what was about to take place. Now the moment had arrived. Everything had been done which could have been done. 'The fortune of war must now decide.' At 2.30 a.m., Hitler finally decided it was time to snatch a few hours' sleep. 'Barbarossa' was due to begin within the next hour.

Goebbels was too nervous to follow his example. At 5.30 a.m., just over two hours after the German guns had opened fire on all borders, the new fanfares sounded over German radios. Goebbels read out Hitler's proclamation. It amounted to a lengthy pseudo-historical justification for German preventive action. The Jewish-Bolshevik rulers in Moscow had sought for two decades to destroy not only Germany, but the whole of Europe. Hitler had been forced, he claimed, through British encirclement policy to take the bitter step of entering the 1939 Pact. But since then the Soviet threat had magnified. At present there were 160 Russian divisions massed on the German borders. 'The hour has now therefore arrived,' Hitler declared, 'to counter this conspiracy of the Jewish-Anglo-Saxon warmongers and the equally Jewish rulers of the Bolshevik headquarters in Moscow.' A slightly amended proclamation went out to the soldiers swarming over the border and marching into Russia.

On 21 June, Hitler had at last composed a letter to his chief ally, Benito Mussolini, belatedly explaining and justifying his reasons for attacking the Soviet Union. Hitler ended his letter with sentences which, as with his comments to Goebbels, give insight into his mentality on the eve of the titanic contest: 'In conclusion, let me say one more thing, Duce. Since I struggled through to this decision, I again feel spiritually free. The partnership with the Soviet Union, in spite of the complete sincerity of the efforts to bring about a final conciliation, was nevertheless often very irksome to me, for in some way or other it seemed to me to be a break with my whole origin, my concepts, and my former obligations. I am happy now to be relieved of these mental agonies.'

The most destructive and barbaric war in the history of mankind was beginning. It was the war that Hitler had wanted since the 1920s – the war against Bolshevism. It was the showdown. He had come to it by a roundabout route. But, finally, Hitler's war was there: a reality.

20

Showdown

I

At dawn on 22 June over 3 million German troops advanced over the borders and into Soviet territory. By a quirk of history, as Goebbels noted somewhat uneasily, it was exactly the same date on which Napoleon's Grand Army had marched on Russia 129 years earlier. The modern invaders deployed over 3,600 tanks, 600,000 motorized vehicles (including armoured cars), 7,000 artillery pieces, and 2,500 aircraft. Not all their transport was mechanized; as in Napoleon's day, they also made use of horses – 625,000 of them. Facing the invading armies, arrayed on the western frontiers of the USSR, were nearly 3 million Soviet soldiers, backed by a number of tanks now estimated to have been as many as 14–15,000 (almost 2,000 of them the most modern designs), over 34,000 artillery pieces, and 8–9,000 fighter-planes. The scale of the titanic clash now beginning, which would chiefly determine the outcome of the Second World War and, beyond that, the shape of Europe for nearly half a century, almost defies the imagination.

Despite the numerical advantage in weaponry of the defending Soviet armies, the early stages of the attack appeared to endorse all the optimism of Hitler and his General Staff about the inferiority of their Bolshevik enemies and the speed with which complete victory could be attained. The three-pronged attack led by Field-Marshals Wilhelm Ritter von Leeb in the north, Fedor von Bock in the centre, and Gerd von Rundstedt in the south initially made astonishing advances. By the end of the first week of July Lithuania and Latvia were in German hands. Leeb's advance in the north, with Leningrad as the target, had reached as far as Ostrov. Army Group Centre had pushed even farther. Much of White Russia had been taken. Minsk was encircled. Bock's advancing armies already had the city of Smolensk in their sights. Further south, by mid-July Rundstedt's troops had captured Zitomir and Berdicev.

The Soviet calamity was immense – and avoidable. Even as the German tanks were rolling forwards, Stalin still thought Hitler was bluffing, that he would not dare attack the Soviet Union until he had finished with Britain. He had anticipated some German territorial demands but was confident that, if necessary, negotiations could stave off an attack in 1941 at least. Stalin's bungling interference and military incompetence had combined with the fear and servility of his generals and the limitations of the inflexible Soviet strategic concept to rule out undertaking the necessary precautions to create defensive dispositions and fight a rearguard action. Instead, whole armies were left in exposed positions, easy prey for the pincer movements of the rapidly advancing panzer armies. In a whole series of huge encirclements, the Red Army suffered staggering losses of men and equipment. By the autumn, some 3 million soldiers had trudged in long, dismal columns into German captivity. A high proportion would suffer terrible inhumanity in the hands of their captors, and not return. Roughly the same number had by then been wounded or killed. The barbaric character of the conflict, evident from its first day, had been determined, as we have seen, by the German plans for a 'war of annihilation' that had taken shape since March. Soviet captives were not treated as soldierly comrades, Geneva conventions were regarded as non-applicable, political commissars – a category interpreted in the widest sense – were peremptorily shot, the civilian population subjected to the cruellest reprisals. Atrocities were not confined to the actions of the Wehrmacht. On the Soviet side, Stalin recovered sufficiently from his trauma at the invasion to proclaim that the conflict was no ordinary war, but a 'great patriotic war' against the invaders. It was necessary, he declared, to form partisan groups to organize 'merciless battle'. Mutual fear of capture fed rapidly and directly into the spiralling barbarization on the eastern front. But it did not cause the barbarization in the first place. The driving-force was the Nazi ideological drive to extirpate 'Jewish-Bolshevism'.

Already on the first day of the invasion reports began reaching Berlin of up to 1,000 Soviet planes destroyed and Brest-Litowsk taken by the advancing trooops. 'We'll soon pull it off,' wrote Goebbels in his diary. He immediately added: 'We must soon pull it off. Among the people there's a somewhat depressed mood. The people want peace . . . Every new theatre of war causes concern and worry.'

The main author of the most deadly clash of the century, which in almost four years of its duration would produce an unimaginable harvest of sorrow for families throughout central and eastern Europe and a level of destruction never experienced in human history, left Berlin around midday on 23 June. Hitler was setting out with his entourage for his new field headquarters in East Prussia. The presumption was, as it had been in earlier campaigns, that he would be there a few weeks, make a tour of newly conquered areas, then return to Berlin. This was only one of his miscalculations. The 'Wolf's Lair' (*Wolfsschanze*) was to be his home in the main for the next three and a half years. He would finally leave it a broken man in a broken country.

The Wolf's Lair – another play on Hitler's favourite pseudonym from the 1920s, when he liked to call himself 'Wolf' (allegedly the meaning of 'Adolf', and implying strength) – was hidden away in the gloomy Masurian woods, about eight kilometres from the small town of Rastenburg. Hitler and his accompaniment arrived there late in the evening of 23 June. The new surroundings were not greatly welcoming. The centre-point consisted of ten bunkers, erected over the winter, camouflaged and in parts protected against air-raids by two metres thickness of concrete. Hitler's bunker was at the northern end of the complex. All its windows faced north so that he could avoid the sun streaming in. There were rooms big enough for military conferences in Hitler's and Keitel's bunkers, and a barracks with a dining-hall for around twenty people. Another complex – known as HQ Area 2 – a little distance away, surrounded by barbed wire and hardly visible from the road, housed the Wehrmacht Operations Staff under Warlimont. The army headquarters, where Brauchitsch and Halder were based, were situated a few kilometres to the north-east. Göring – designated by Hitler on 29 June to be his successor in the event of his death – and the Luftwaffe staff stayed in their special trains.

Hitler's part of the Führer Headquarters, known as 'Security Zone One', swiftly developed its own daily rhythm. The central event was the 'situation briefing' at noon in the bunker shared by Keitel and Jodl. This frequently ran on as long as two hours. Brauchitsch, Halder, and Colonel Adolf Heusinger, chief of the army's Operations Department, attended once or twice a week. The briefing was followed by a lengthy lunch, beginning in these days for the most part punctually at 2 p.m., Hitler confining himself as always strictly to a non-meat diet. Any audiences that he had on non-military matters were arranged for the afternoons. Around 5 p.m. he would call in his secretaries for coffee. A special word of praise was bestowed on the one who could eat most cakes. The second military briefing, given by Jodl, followed at 6 p.m. The evening meal took place at 7.30 p.m., often lasting two hours. Afterwards there were films. The final part of the routine was the gathering of secretaries, adjutants, and guests for tea, to the accompaniment of Hitler's late-night monologues. Those who could snatched a nap some time during the afternoon so they could keep their eyes open in the early hours. Sometimes, it was daylight by the time the nocturnal discussions came to an end.

Hitler always sat in the same place at meals, with his back to the window, flanked by Press Chief Dietrich and Jodl, with Keitel, Bormann, and General Karl Heinrich Bodenschatz, Göring's liaison officer, opposite him. Generals, staff officers, adjutants, Hitler's doctors, and any guests visiting the Führer Headquarters made up the rest of the complement. The atmosphere was good in these early days, and not too formal. The mood at this time was still generally optimistic. Life in the FHQ had not yet reached the stage where it could be described by Jodl as half-way 'between a monastery and a concentration camp'.

Two of Hitler's secretaries, Christa Schroeder and Gerda Daranowski, had also accompanied him to his field headquarters. They had as good as nothing to do. Sleeping, eating, drinking, and chatting filled up most of their day. Much of their energy was spent trying to swat away a constant plague of midges. Hitler complained that his advisers who had picked the spot had chosen 'the most swampy, midge-infested, and climatically unfavourable area for him', and joked that he would have to send in the Luftwaffe on the midge-hunt. But 'the chief' was generally in a good mood during the first part of the Russian campaign.

As in Berlin or at the Berghof, a word during meals on one of Hitler's favourite topics could easily trigger an hour-long monologue. In these early days, he usually faced a big map of the Soviet Union pinned to the wall. At the drop of a hat, he would launch into yet another harangue about the danger that Bolshevism signified for Europe, and how to wait another year would have been too late. On one occasion, his secretaries heard Hitler, as he stood in front of a big map of Europe, point to the

Russian capital and say: 'In four weeks we'll be in Moscow. Moscow will be razed to the ground.' Everything had gone much better than could have been imagined, he remarked. They had been lucky that the Russians had placed their troops on the borders and not pulled the German armies deep into their country, which would have caused difficulties with supplies. Two-thirds of the Bolshevik armed forces and five-sixths of the tanks and aircraft were destroyed or severely damaged, he told Goebbels, on the Propaganda Minister's first visit to Führer Headquarters on 8 July. After assessing the military situation in detail with his Wehrmacht advisers, Goebbels noted, the Führer's conclusion was 'that the war in the East was in the main already won'. There could be no notion of peace terms with the Kremlin. (He would think differently about this only a month later.) Bolshevism would be wiped out and Russia broken up into its component parts, deprived of any intellectual, political, or economic centre. Japan would attack the Soviet Union from the east in a matter of weeks. He foresaw England's fall 'with a sleepwalker's certainty'.

News came in of 3,500 aircraft and over 1,000 Soviet tanks destroyed. But there was other news of fanatical fighting by Soviet soldiers who feared the worst if they surrendered. Hitler was to tell the Japanese Ambassador Oshima on 14 July that 'our enemies are not human beings any more, they are beasts'. It was, then, doubtless echoing her 'chief' and the general atmosphere in FHQ, when Christa Schroeder remarked to a friend that 'from all previous experience it can be said to be a fight against wild animals'.

Hitler had permitted no Wehrmacht reports during the very first days of the campaign. But Sunday, 29 June – a week after the attack had started – was, as Goebbels described it, 'the day of the special announcements'. Twelve of them altogether, each introduced by the 'Russian Fanfare' based on Liszt's 'Les Préludes', were broadcast, beginning at 11 a.m. that morning. Dominance in the air had been attained, the reports proclaimed. Grodno, Brest-Litowsk, Vilna, Kowno, and Dünaburg were in German hands. Two Soviet armies were encircled at Bialystok. Minsk had been taken. The Russians had lost, it was announced, 2,233 tanks and 4,107 aircraft. Enormous quantities of *matériel* had been captured. Vast numbers of prisoners had been taken. But the popular reception in Germany was less enthusiastic than had been hoped. People rapidly tired of the special announcements, one after the other, and were sceptical about the propaganda. Instead of being excited, their senses were dulled. Goebbels was furious at the OKW's presentation, and vowed that it would never be repeated.

The invasion of the Soviet Union was presented to the German public as a preventive war. This had been undertaken by the Führer, so Goebbels's directives to the press ran, to head off at the last minute the threat to the Reich and the entire western culture through the treachery of 'Jewish-Bolshevism'. At any moment the Bolsheviks had been planning to strike against the Reich and to overrun and destroy Europe. Only the Führer's bold action had prevented this. More extraordinary than this propaganda lie is the fact that Hitler and Goebbels had convinced themselves of its truth. Fully aware of its falseness, they had to play out a fiction even among themselves to justify the unprovoked decision to attack and utterly destroy the Soviet Union.

By the end of June the German encirclements at Bialystok and Minsk had produced the astonishing toll of 324,000 Red Army prisoners, 3,300 tanks, and 1,800 artillery pieces captured or destroyed. Little over a fortnight later the end of the battle for Smolensk doubled these figures. Already by the second day of the campaign, German estimates put numbers of aircraft shot down or destroyed on the ground at 2,500. When Göring expressed doubts at the figures they were checked and found to be 2–300 below the actual total. After a month of fighting, the figure for aircraft destroyed had reached 7,564. By early July it was estimated that eighty-nine out of 164 Soviet divisions had been entirely or partially destroyed, and that only nine out of twenty-nine tank divisions of the Red Army were still fit for combat.

The scale of underestimation of Soviet fighting potential would soon come as a severe shock. But in early July it was hardly surprising if the feeling in the German military leadership was that 'Barbarossa' was on course for complete victory, that the campaign would be over, as predicted, before the winter. On 3 July Halder summed up his verdict in words which would come to haunt him: 'It is thus probably no overstatement to say that the Russian campaign has been won in the space of two weeks.' He did at least have the foresight to acknowledge that this did not mean that it was over: 'The sheer geographical vastness of the country and the stubbornness of the resistance, which is carried on with all means, will claim our efforts for many more weeks to come.'

II

The territorial gains brought about by the spectacular successes of the Wehrmacht in the first phase of 'Barbarossa' gave Hitler command over a greater extent of the European continent than any ruler since Napoleon. His rambling, discursive outpourings, in his lunchtime or late-night monologues to his regular retinue, were the purest expression of unbounded, megalomaniac power and breathtaking inhumanity. They were the face of the future in the vast new eastern empire, as he saw it.

'The beauty of the Crimea,' he rhapsodized late at night on 5 July 1941, would be made accessible to Germans through a motorway. It would be their version of the Italian or French riviera. Every German, after the war, he remarked, had to have the chance with his 'People's Car' (*Volkswagen*) personally to see the conquered territories, since he would have 'to be ready if need be to fight for them'. The mistake of the pre-war era of limiting the colonial idea to the property of a few capitalists or companies could not be repeated. Roads would be more important in the future than the railways for passenger transport. Only through travel by road could a country be known, he asserted.

He was asked whether it would be enough to stretch the conquests to the Urals. 'Initially', that would suffice, he replied. But Bolshevism had to be exterminated, and it would be necessary to carry out expeditions from there to eradicate any new centres that might develop. 'St Petersburg' – as he called Leningrad – 'was as a city incomparably more beautiful than Moscow'. But its fate, he decided, was to be identical to that of the capital. 'An example was to be made here, and the city will disappear completely from the earth.' It was to be sealed off, bombarded, and starved out. He imagined, too, that little would ultimately be left of Kiev. He saw the destruction of Soviet cities as the basis for lasting German power in the conquered territories. No military power was to be tolerated within 300 kilometres east of the Urals. 'The border between Europe and Asia,' he stated, 'is not the Urals but the place where the settlements of Germanic types of people stop and pure Slavdom begins. It is our task to push this border as far as possible to the east, and if necessary beyond the Urals.'

Hitler thought the Russian people fit for nothing but hard work under coercion. Their natural and desired condition was one of general disorganization. 'The Ukrainians,' he remarked on another occasion, 'were every bit as idle, disorganized, and nihilistically asiatic as the Greater Russians.' To speak of any sort of work ethic was pointless. All they understood was 'the whip'. He admired Stalin's brutality. The Soviet dictator, he thought, was 'one of the greatest living human beings since, if only through the harshest compulsion, he had succeeded in welding a state out of this Slavic rabbit-family'. He described 'the sly Caucasian' as 'one of the most extraordinary figures of world history', who scarcely ever left his office but could rule from there through a subservient bureaucracy.

Hitler's model for domination and exploitation remained the British Empire. His inspiration for the future rule of his master-race was the Raj. He voiced his admiration on many occasions for the way such a small country as Great Britain had been able to establish its rule throughout the world in a huge colonial empire. British rule in India in particular showed what Germany could do in Russia. It must be possible to control the eastern territory with quarter of a million men, he stated. With that number the British ruled 400 million Indians. Russia would always be dominated by German rulers. They must see to it that the masses were educated to do no more than read road signs, though a reasonable living standard for them was in the German interest. The south of the Ukraine, in particular the Crimea, would be settled by German farmer-soldiers. He would have no worries at all about deporting the existing population somewhere or other to make room for them. The vision was of a latter-day feudal type of settlement: there would be a standing army of 1½–2 million men, providing some 30–40,000 every year for use when their twelve-year service was completed. If they were sons of farmers, they would be given a farmstead, fully equipped, by the Reich in return for their twelve years of military service. They would also be provided with weapons. The only condition was that they must marry country- not town-girls. German peasants would live in beautiful settlements, linked by good roads to the nearest town. Beyond this would be 'the other world', where the Russians lived under German subjugation. Should there be a revolution, 'all we need to do is drop a few bombs on their cities and the business will be over'. After ten years, he foresaw, there would be a German élite, to be counted on when there were new tasks to be undertaken. 'A new type of man will come to the fore, real master-types, who of course can't be used in the west: viceroys.' German administrators would be housed in splendid buildings; the governors would live in 'palaces'.

His musings on the prospect of a German equivalent of India continued on three successive days and nights from 8–11 August. India had given the English pride. The vast spaces had obliged them to rule millions with only a few men. 'What India was for England, the eastern territory will be for us,' he declared.

For Hitler, India was the heart of an Empire that had brought Britain not only power, but prosperity. Ruthless economic exploitation had always been central to his dream of the German empire in the east. Now, it seemed, that dream would soon become reality. 'The Ukraine and then the Volga basin will one day be the granaries of Europe,' he foresaw. 'And we'll also provide Europe with iron. If Sweden won't supply it one of these days, good, then we'll take it from the east. Belgian industry can exchange its products – cheap consumer wares – for corn from these areas. From Thuringia and the Harz mountains, for example, we can remove our poor working-class families to give them big stretches of land.' 'We'll be an exporter of corn for all in Europe who need it,' he went on, a month later. 'In the Crimea we will have citrus fruits, rubber plants (with 40,000 hectares we'll make ourselves independent), and cotton. The Pripet marches will give us reeds. We will deliver to the Ukrainians head-scarves, glass chains as jewellery, and whatever else colonial peoples like. We Germans – that's the main thing – must form a closed community like a fortress. The lowest stable-lad must be superior to any of the natives . . .'

Autarky, in Hitler's thinking, was the basis of security. And the conquest of the East, as he had repeatedly stated in the mid-1920s, would now offer Germany that security. 'The struggle for hegemony in the world will be decided for Europe through the occupation of the Russian space,' he told his entourage in mid-September. 'This makes Europe the firmest place in the world against the threat of blockade.' He returned to the theme a few days later. 'As soon as I recognize a raw material as important for the war, I put every effort into making us independent in it. Iron, coal, oil, corn, livestock, wood – we must have them at our disposal . . . Today I can say: Europe is self-sufficient, as long as we just prevent another mammoth state existing which could utilize European civilization to mobilize Asia against us.' He compared, as he had frequently done many years earlier, the benefits of autarky with the international market economy and the mistakes, as he saw them, made by Britain and America through their dependence upon exports and overseas markets, bringing cut-throat competition, corresponding high tariffs and production costs, and unemployment. Britain had increased unemployment and impoverished its working class by the error of industrializing India, he continued. Germany was not tied to exports, and this had meant that it was the only country without unemployment. 'The country that we are now opening up is for us only a raw-material source and marketing area, not a field for industrial production . . . We won't need any more to look for an active market in the Far East. Here is our market. We simply need to secure it. We'll deliver cotton goods, cooking-pots, all simple articles for satisfying the demand for the necessities of life. We won't be able to produce anything like so much as can be marketed here. I see there great possibilities for the build-up of a strong Reich, a true world-power . . . For the next few hundred years we will have a field of activity without equal.'

Hitler was blunt about his justification for conquering this territory: might was right. A culturally superior people, deprived of 'living space', needed no further justification. It was for him, as always, a matter of the 'laws of nature'. 'If I harm the Russians now, then for the reason that they would otherwise harm me,' he declared. 'The dear God, once again, makes it like that. He suddenly casts the masses of humanity on to the earth and each one has to look after himself and how he gets through. One person takes something away from the other. And at the end you can only say that the stronger wins. That is after all the most sensible order of things.'

There would be no end of the struggle in the east, that was clear, even after a German victory. Hitler spoke of building an 'Eastern Wall' along the Urals as a barrier against sudden inroads from the 'dangerous human reservoir' in Asia. It would be no conventional fortification, but a live wall built of the soldier-farmers who would form the new eastern settlers. 'A permanent border struggle in the east will produce a solid stock and prevent us from sinking back into the softness of a state system based purely on Europe.' War was for Hitler the essence of human activity. 'What meeting a man means for a girl,' he declared, 'war meant for him.' He referred back frequently in these weeks to his own experiences in the First World War, probably the most formative of his life. Looking at the newsreel of the 'Battle of Kiev', he was completely gripped by 'a heroic epic such as there had never previously been'. 'I'm immensely happy to have experienced the war in this way,' he added. If he could wish the German people one thing, he remarked on another occasion, it would be to have a war every fifteen to twenty years. If reproached for the loss of 200,000 lives, he would reply that he had enlarged the German nation by 2½ million, and felt justified in demanding the sacrifice of the lives of a tenth. 'Life is horrible. Coming into being, existing, and passing away, there's always a killing. Everything that is born must later die. Whether it's through illness, accident, or war, that remains the same.'

Hitler's notions of a social 'new order' have to be placed in this setting of conquest, ruthless exploitation, the right of the powerful, racial dominance, and more or less permanent war in a world where life was cheap and readily expendable. His ideas often had their roots in the resentment that still smouldered at the way his own 'talents' had been left unrecognized or the disadvantages of his own social status compared with the privileges of the high-born and well-to-do. Thus he advocated free education, funded by the state, for all talented youngsters. Workers would have annual holidays and could expect once or twice in their lives to go on a sea-cruise. He criticizd the distinctions between different classes of passengers on such cruise ships. And he approved of the introduction of the same food for both officers and men in the army. Hitler might appear to have been promoting ideas of a modern, mobile, classless society, abolishing privilege and resting solely upon achievement. But the central tenet remained race, to which all else was subordinated. Thus, in the east, he said, all Germans would travel in the upholstered first- or second-class railway carriages – to separate them from the native population. It was a social vision which could have obvious attractions for many members of the would-be master-race. The image was of a cornucopia of wealth flowing into the Reich from the east. The Reich would be linked to the new frontiers by motorways cutting through the endless steppes and the enormous Russian spaces. Prosperity and power would be secured through the new breed of supermen who lorded it over the downtrodden Slav masses.

The vision, to those who heard Hitler describe it, appeared excitingly modern: a break with traditional class- and status-bound hierarchies to a society where talent had its reward and there was prosperity for all –

for all Germans, that is. Indeed, elements of Hitler's thinking were un-questionably modern. He looked, for instance, to the benefits of modern technology, envisaging steam-heated greenhouses giving German cities a regular supply of fresh fruit and vegetables all through the winter. He looked, too, to modern transport to open up the east. While the bounty of the east pouring into Germany would be brought by train, the car for Hitler was the vital transport means of the future. But for all its apparent modernity, the social vision was in essence atavistic. The colonial con-quests of the nineteenth century provided its inspiration. What Hitler was offering was a modernized version of old-fashioned imperialist conquest, now translated to the ethnically mixed terrain of eastern Europe where the Slavs would provide the German equivalent of the conquered native populations of India and Africa in the British Empire.

By mid-July, the key steps had been taken to translate the horrendous vision into reality. At an important five-hour meeting in the Führer Headquarters on 16 July attended by Göring, Rosenberg, Lammers, Keitel, and Bormann, Hitler established the basic guidelines of policy and practical arrangements for administering and exploiting the new conquests. Once more, the underlying premiss was the social-Darwinist justification that the strong deserved to inherit the earth. But the sense that what they were doing was morally objectionable nevertheless ran through Hitler's opening comments, as reported by Bormann. 'The motivation of our steps in the eyes of the world must be directed by tactical viewpoints. We must proceed here exactly as in the cases of Norway, Denmark, Holland, and Belgium. In these cases, too, we had said nothing about our intentions and we will sensibly continue not to do this,' Bormann recorded. 'We will then again emphasize that we were compelled to occupy an area to bring order, and to impose security. In the interest of the native population we had to see to providing calm, food, transport etc. etc. Therefore our settlement. It should then not be recognizable that a final settlement is beginning! All necessary measures – shooting, deportation etc. – we will and can do anyway. We don't want to make premature and unnecessary enemies. We will simply act, therefore, as if we wish to carry out a mandate. But it must be clear to us that we will never again leave these territories,' Hitler's blunt statement continued. 'Accordingly, it is a matter of: 1. doing nothing to hinder the final settlement but rather preparing this in secret; 2. emphasizing that we are the liberators . . . Basically, it's a matter of dividing up the giant cake so that we can first rule it, secondly administer it, and thirdly exploit it. The Russians have now given out the order for a partisan war behind our front. This partisan war again has its advantage: it gives us the possibility of exterminating anything opposing us. As a basic principle: the construction of a military power west of the Urals must never again be possible, even if as a consequence we have to wage war for a hundred years.'

Hitler proceeded to make appointments to the key positions in the occupied east. Rosenberg was confirmed next day as head of what appeared on the surface to be the all-powerful Reich Ministry for the Occupied Eastern Territories. But nothing was as it seemed in the Third Reich. Rosenberg's authority, as Hitler's decree made clear, did not touch the respective spheres of competence of the army, Göring's Four-Year Plan organization, and the SS. The big guns, in other words, were outside Rosenberg's control. More than that, Rosenberg's own conception of winning certain nationalities as allies, under German tutelage, against Greater Russia – notions which he and his staff had been working on since the spring – fell foul of Himmler's policy of maximum repression and brutal resettlement and Göring's aims of total economic exploitation. Himmler was within weeks in receipt of plans for deporting in the coming twenty-five years or so over 30 million people into far more inhospitable climes further eastward. Göring was envisaging the starvation in Russia of 20–30 million persons – a prospect advanced even before the German invasion by the Agricultural Group of the Economic Staff for the East. All three – Rosenberg, Himmler, and Göring – could find a common denominator in Hitler's goal of destroying Bolshevism and acquiring 'living space'. But beyond that minimum, Rosenberg's concept – no less ruthless, but more pragmatic – had no chance when opposed to the contrary idea, backed by Hitler's own vision, of absolute rapaciousness and repression.

Opposing Rosenberg's wishes, Hitler had yielded in the conference of 16 July to the suggestion of Göring, backed by Bormann, that the – even by Nazi standards – extraordinarily brutal and independent-minded Erich Koch, Gauleiter of East Prussia, should be made Reich Commissar of the key territory of the Ukraine. Koch, like Hitler, but in contrast to Rosenberg, rejected any idea of a Ukrainian buffer-state. His view was that from the very beginning it was necessary 'to be hard and brutal'. He was held in favour at Führer Headquarters. Everyone there thought he was the most suitable person to carry out the requirements in the Ukraine. It was seen as a compliment when they called him the 'second Stalin'.

In contrast to the tyrant, Koch, who continued to prefer his old East Prussian domain to his new fiefdom, Hinrich Lohse, appointed as Reich Commissar in the Baltic, now renamed the Ostland, made himself a subject of ridicule among the German occupying forces in his own territory with his fanatical and often petty bureaucratization, unleashed in torrents of decrees and directives. For all that, he was weak in the face of the power of the SS, and other competing agencies. Similarly, Wilhelm Kube, appointed at the suggestion of Göring and Rosenberg as Reich Commissar in Belorussia, proved not only corrupt and incompetent on a grandiose scale, but another weak petty dictator in his province, his instructions often ignored by his own subordinates, and forced repeatedly to yield to the superior power of the SS.

The course was set, therefore, for a 'New Order' in the east which belied the very name. Nothing resembled order. Everything resembled the war of all against all, built into the Nazi system in the Reich itself, massively extended in occupied Poland, and now taken to its logical denouement in the conquered lands of the Soviet Union.

III

In fact, despite the extraordinary gains made by the advancing Wehrmacht, July would bring recognition that the operational plan of 'Barbarossa' had failed. And for all the air of confidence that Hitler displayed to his entourage in the Wolf's Lair, these weeks also produced early indications of the tensions and conflicts in military leadership and decision-making that would continue to bedevil the German war effort. Hitler intervened in tactical matters from the outset. As early as 24 June he had told Brauchitsch of his worries that the encirclement at Bialystok was not tight enough. The following day he was expressing concern that Army Groups Centre and South were operating too far in depth. Halder dismissed the worry. 'The old refrain!' he wrote in his diary. 'But that is not going to change anything in our plans.' On 27, 29, and 30 June and again on 2 and 3 July Halder recorded worried queries or interventions by Hitler in tactical deployments of troops. 'What is lacking on top level,' he confided to his diary notes, 'is that confidence in the executive commands which is one of the most essential features of our command organization.'

Halder's irritation at Hitler's interference was understandable. But the errors and misjudgements, even in the first, seemingly so successful, phase of 'Barbarossa', were as much those of the professionals in Army High Command as of the former First World War corporal who now thought he was the greatest warlord of all time.

The mounting conflict with Hitler revolved around the implementation of the 'Barbarossa' strategic plan that had been laid down the previous December. This in turn had emanated from the feasibility studies carried out during the summer by military strategists. Army High Command had favoured making Moscow the key objective. Hitler's own, different, conception was not dissimilar in a number of essentials from the independent strategic study prepared for the Wehrmacht Operational Staff in September 1940, though it differed from this, too, on the crucial question of Moscow.

The emphasis in Hitler's 'Barbarossa Directive' in December, and in all subsequent strategic planning, had been on the thrusts to the north, to take Leningrad and secure the Baltic, and to the south, to seize the Ukraine. Even if unenthusiastically, the Army General Staff had accepted the significant alteration of what it had originally envisaged. According to this amended plan, Army Group Centre was to advance as far as Smolensk before swinging to the north to meet up with Leeb's armies for the assault on Leningrad. The taking of Moscow figured in the agreed plan of 'Barbarossa' only once the occupation of Leningrad and Kronstadt had been completed.

Already on 29 June Hitler was worried that Bock's Army Group Centre, where the advance was especially spectacular, would overreach itself. On 4 July he claimed that he faced the most difficult decision of the campaign: whether to hold to the original 'Barbarossa' plan, amend it to provide for a deep thrust towards the Caucasus (in which Rundstedt would be assisted by some of Army Group Centre's panzer forces), or retain the panzer concentration in the centre and push forward to Moscow. The decision he reached by 8 July was the one wanted by Halder: to press forward the offensive of Army Group Centre with the aim of destroying the mass of the enemy forces west of Moscow. The amended strategy now discarded Army Group Centre's turn towards

Leningrad, built into the original 'Barbarossa' plan. The 'ideal solution', Hitler accepted, would be to leave Leeb's Army Group North to attain its objectives by its own means. However, Hitler was even now by no means reconciled to the priority of capturing Moscow – in his eyes, as he said, 'merely a geographical idea'.

The conflict with Army High Command, supported by Army Group Centre, about concentration on the taking of Moscow as the objective, continued over the next weeks. Hitler pressed, in revised operational form, for priority to be given to the capture of Leningrad, and now included in the south the drive to the industrial area of Kharkhov and into the Caucasus, to be reached before the onset of winter. At the same time, his 'Supplement to Directive No. 33', dated 23 July, indicated that Army Group Centre would destroy the enemy between Smolensk and Moscow by its infantry divisions alone, and would then 'take Moscow into occupation'.

By late July Halder had changed his tune about the certainty and speed of victory. Early in the month he had told Hitler that only forty-six of the known 164 Soviet divisions were still capable of combat. This had been in all probability an over-estimation of the extent of destruction; it was certainly a rash under-estimation of the enemy's ability to replenish its forces. On 23 July he revised the figure to a total of ninety-three divisions. The enemy had been 'decisively weakened', but by no means 'finally smashed', he concluded. As a consequence, since the Soviet reserves of manpower were now seen to be inexhaustible, Halder argued even more forcefully that the aim of further operations had to be the destruction of the areas of armaments production around Moscow.

As the strength of Soviet defences was being revised, the toll on the German army and Luftwaffe also had to be taken into account. Air-crews were showing signs of exhaustion; their planes could not be maintained fast enough. By the end of July only 1,045 aircraft were serviceable. Air-raids on Moscow demanded by Hitler were of little effect because so few planes were available. Most of the seventy-five raids on the Soviet capital carried out over the next months were undertaken by small numbers of bombers, scarcely able to make a pinprick in Soviet armaments production. The infantry were even more in need of rest. They had been marching, and engaged in fierce fighting, for over a month without a break. The original operational plan had foreseen a break for recuperation after twenty days. But the troops had received no rest by the fortieth day, and the first phase of the campaign was not over. By this time, casualties (wounded, missing, and dead) had reached 213,301 officers and men. Moreover, despite miracles worked by Quartermaster-General Eduard Wagner's organization, transport problems on roads often unfit even in midsummer for mechanized transport brought immeasurable problems of maintaining supply-lines of fuel, equipment, and provisions to the rapidly advancing army. Supplies for Army Group Centre required twenty-five goods trains a day. But despite working round the clock to convert the railway lines to a German gauge, only eight to fifteen trains a day were reaching the front line in late July and early August.

It was becoming obvious already by the end of July that the revised 'Barbarossa' operational plan as laid down in Hitler's Supplement to Directive No. 33 could not be carried out before winter descended. Hitler interpreted this as demanding panzer support from Army Group Centre for the assault on Leningrad. Moscow could wait. Halder took the diametrically opposite view. Making Moscow the objective would ensure that the Soviets committed the bulk of their forces to its defence. Taking the city, including its communications system and industries, would split the Soviet Union and render resistance more difficult. The implication was that the capture of the capital would bring about the fall of the Soviet system, and the end of the eastern war. If the attack on Moscow were not pushed through with all speed, the enemy would bring the offensive to a halt before winter, then regroup. The military aim of the war against the Soviet Union would have failed.

Hitler was still adamant that capturing the industrial region of Kharkhov and the Donets Basin and cutting off Soviet oil supplies would undermine resistance more than the fall of Moscow. But he was wavering. At this point, even Jodl and the Wehrmacht Operations Staff had been converted to the need to attack Moscow. Citing the arrival of strong enemy reinforcements facing and flanking Army Group Centre, Hitler now, on 30 July, cancelled the Supplement to Directive No. 33. Halder was momentarily ecstatic. 'This decision frees every thinking soldier of the horrible vision obsessing us these last few days, since the Führer's obstinacy made the final bogging down of the eastern campaign appear imminent.' But when Directive No. 34 was issued the same day it offered Halder little comfort. Army Group Centre was to recuperate for the next attack; in the north the assault on Leningrad was to continue;

and Army Group South was to destroy the enemy forces west of the Dnieper and in the vicinity of Kiev. The real decision – for or against the drive to Moscow – had effectively just been postponed for a while.

In early August Hitler remained wedded to Leningrad as the priority. He reckoned this would be cut off by 20 August, and then troops and aircraft could be redeployed by Army Group Centre. The second priority for Hitler was, as before, 'the south of Russia, especially the Donets region', which formed the 'entire basis of the Russian economy'. Moscow was a clear third on his priority-list. He recognized that in this order of priorities the capital could not be taken before winter. Halder tried unavailingly to get Brauchitsch to obtain a clear decision on whether to put everything into delivering the enemy a fatal blow at Moscow or taking the Ukraine and the Caucasus for economic reasons. He persuaded Jodl to intervene with Hitler to convince him that the objectives of Moscow *and* the Ukraine had to be met.

By now, Halder was realizing the magnitude of the task facing the Wehrmacht. 'The whole situation makes it increasingly plain that we have underestimated the Russian colossus,' he wrote on 11 August. 'At the outset of the war, we reckoned with about 200 enemy divisions. Now we have already counted 360. These divisions indeed are not armed and equipped according to our standards, and their tactical leadership is often poor. But there they are, and if we smash a dozen of them, the Russians simply put up another dozen . . . And so our troops, sprawled over an immense front line, without any depth, are subjected to the incessant attacks of the enemy.'

In his Supplement to Directive No. 34, issued on 12 August, Hitler for the first time stated categorically that once the threats from the flanks were eliminated and the panzer groups were refreshed the attack on the enemy forces massed for the protection of Moscow was to be prosecuted. The aim was 'the removal from the enemy before winter of the entire state, armaments, and communications centre around Moscow', ran the directive. Three days later, however, Hitler intervened once more in the tactical dispositions by ordering panzer forces from the northern flank of Army Group Centre to help Army Group North resist a strong Soviet counter-attack.

His concession, if heavily qualified, on Moscow, then – in effect – rapid negation of the decision, may have been affected by the severe attack of dysentery from which he was suffering in the first half of

August. Despite mounting hypochondria, he had, in fact, over the past years enjoyed remarkably good health – perhaps surprisingly so, given his eating habits and lifestyle. But he had now been laid low at a vital time. Goebbels found him still unwell and 'very irritable', though on the mend, when he visited FHQ on 18 August. The weeks of tension and the unexpected military difficulties of the past month had taken their toll, the Propaganda Minister thought. In fact, electrocardiograms taken at the time indicated that Hitler had rapidly progressive coronary sclerosis. Morell's discussion of the results of the tests could have done little to lift Hitler's mood, or to lessen his hypochondria.

Probably Hitler's ill-health in August, at a time when he was stunned by the recognition of the gross underestimation by German intelligence of the true level of Soviet forces, temporarily weakened his resolve to continue the war in the east. Goebbels was plainly astonished, on his visit to FHQ on 18 August, to hear Hitler entertain thoughts of accepting peace-terms from Stalin and even stating that Bolshevism, without the Red Army, would be no danger to Germany. (Stalin, in fact, appears briefly to have contemplated moves to come to terms, involving large-scale surrender of Soviet territory, in July.) In a pessimistic state of mind about an early and comprehensive victory in the east, Hitler was clutching at straws: perhaps Stalin would sue for peace; maybe Churchill would be brought down; quite suddenly peace might break out. The turnabout could come as quickly as it had done in January 1933, he suggested (and would do so on other occasions down to 1945), when, without prospects at the start of the month, the National Socialists had within a matter of weeks found themselves in power.

Halder's own nerves were by this point also frayed. He now thought the time had come to confront Hitler once and for all with the imperative need to destroy the enemy forces around Moscow. On 18 August Brauchitsch sent Halder's memorandum on to Hitler. It argued that Army Groups North and South would have to attain their objectives from within their own resources, but that the main effort must be the immediate offensive against Moscow, since Army Group Centre would be unable to continue its operations after October on account of weather conditions.

Halder's memorandum had been prepared by Colonel Heusinger, the army's Chief of Operations Department. Two days after its submission, Heusinger discussed the memorandum with Jodl. Hitler's closest military adviser suggested psychological motives behind the Dictator's strategic choices. Heusinger recalled Jodl saying that Hitler had 'an instinctive aversion to treading the same path as Napoleon. Moscow gives him a sinister feeling.' When Heusinger reaffirmed the need to defeat the enemy forces at Moscow, Jodl replied: 'That's what you say. Now I will tell you what the Führer's answer will be: There is at the moment a much better possibility of beating the Russian forces. Their main grouping is now east of Kiev.' Heusinger pressed Jodl to support the memorandum. Jodl finally remarked: 'I will do what I can. But you must admit that the Führer's reasons are well thought out and cannot be pushed aside just like that. We must not try to compel him to do something which goes against his inner convictions. His intuition has generally been right. You can't deny that!' The Führer myth still prevailed – and among those closest to Hitler.

Predictably, Hitler's reply was not long in coming – and was a devastating riposte to Army High Command. On 21 August, Army High Command was told that Hitler rejected its proposals as out of line with his intentions. Instead, he ordered: 'The principal object that must still be achieved before the onset of winter is not the capture of Moscow, but rather, in the South, the occupation of the Crimea and the industrial and coal region of the Donets, together with isolation of the Russian oil regions in the Caucasus and, in the North, the encirclement of Leningrad and junction with the Finns.' The immediate key step was the encirclement and destruction of the exposed Soviet Fifth Army in the region of Kiev through a pincer movement from Army Groups Centre and South. This would open the path for Army Group South to advance south-eastwards towards Rostov and Kharkhov. The capture of the Crimea, Hitler added, was 'of paramount importance for safeguarding our oil supply from Romania'. All means had to be deployed, therefore, to cross the Dnieper quickly to reach the Crimea before the enemy could call up new forces.

Hitler developed his arguments the following day in a 'Study' blaming Army High Command for failing to carry out his operational plan, reaffirming the necessity of shifting the main weight of the attack to the north and south, and relegating Moscow to a secondary target. Brauchitsch was accused of lack of leadership in allowing himself to be swayed by the special interests of the individual army groups. And particularly wounding was the praise, in contrast, handed out to Göring's firm leadership of the Luftwaffe.

In this 'Study' of 22 August, Hitler rehearsed once more the objective of eliminating the Soviet Union as a continental ally of Britain, thereby removing from Britain hope of changing the course of events in Europe. This objective, he claimed, could only be attained through annihilation of Soviet forces and the occupation or destruction of the economic basis for continuing the war, with special emphasis on sources of raw materials. He reasserted the need to concentrate on destroying the Soviet position in the Baltic and on occupying the Ukraine and Black Sea region, which were vital in terms of raw materials for the Soviet war economy. He also underlined the need to protect German oil supplies in Romania. Army High Command was to blame for ignoring his orders to press home the advance on Leningrad. He insisted that the three divisions from Army Group Centre, intended from the beginning of the campaign to assist the numerically weaker Army Group North, should be rapidly supplied, and that the objective of capturing Leningrad would then be met. Once this was done, the motorized units supplied by Army Group Centre could be used to concentrate on their sole remaining objective, the advance on Moscow. In the south, too, there was to be no diversion from original plans. Once the destruction of the Soviet forces east and west of Kiev which threatened the flank of Army Group Centre was accomplished, he argued, the advance on Moscow would be significantly eased. He rejected, therefore, the Army High Command's proposals for the further conduct of operations.

In the privacy of his diary notes, Halder could not contain himself. 'I regard the situation created by the Führer's interference unendurable for the OKH,' he wrote. 'No other but the Führer himself is to blame for the zigzag course caused by his successive orders.' The treatment of Brauchitsch, Halder went on, was 'absolutely outrageous'. Halder had proposed to the Commander-in-Chief that both should offer their resignation. But Brauchitsch had refused such a step 'on the grounds that the resignations would not be accepted and so nothing would be changed'.

Deeply upset, Halder flew next day to Army Group Centre headquarters. The assembled commanders predictably backed his preference for resuming the offensive on Moscow. They were agreed that to move on Kiev would mean a winter campaign. Field-Marshal von Bock suggested that General Heinz Guderian, one of Hitler's favourite commanders, and particularly outspoken at the meeting, should accompany

Halder to Führer Headquarters in an attempt to persuade the dictator to change his mind and agree to Army High Command's plan.

It was getting dark as Halder and Guderian arrived in East Prussia. According to Guderian's later account – naturally aimed at reflecting himself in the best light – Brauchitsch forbade him to raise the question of Moscow. The southern operation had been ordered, the Army Commander-in-Chief declared, so the problem was merely one of how to carry it out. Discussion was pointless. Neither Brauchitsch nor Halder accompanied Guderian when he went in to see Hitler, who was flanked by a large entourage including Keitel, Jodl, and Schmundt. Hitler himself raised the issue of Moscow, according to Guderian, and then, without interruption, let him unfold the arguments for making the advance on the Russian capital the priority. When Guderian had finished, Hitler started. Keeping his temper, he put the alternative case. The raw materials and agricultural base of the Ukraine were vital for the continuation of the war, he stated. The Crimea had to be neutralized to rule out attacks on the Romanian oil-fields. 'My generals know nothing about the economic aspects of war,' Guderian heard him say for the first time. Hitler was adamant. He had already given strict orders for an attack on Kiev as the immediate strategic objective. Action had to be carried out with that in mind. All those present nodded at every sentence that Hitler spoke. The OKW representatives were entirely behind him. Guderian felt isolated. He avoided all further argument. He took the view, so he remarked much later, that since the decision to attack the Ukraine was confirmed, it was now his task to ensure that it was carried out as effectively as possible to ensure victory before the autumn rains.

When he reported to Halder next day, 24 August, the Chief of the Army General Staff fell into a rage at Guderian's complete volte-face on being confronted by Hitler at first hand. Halder's dismay was all the greater since Guderian, whom he had considered as a possible future Army Commander-in-Chief, had been among the most vehement critics of Hitler during the meeting at Army Group Centre Headquarters the previous day. Bock shared Halder's contempt for the way the outspoken and forthright Guderian had caved in under Hitler's pressure. In reality, whatever the opprobrium now heaped on him by his superiors, there had been little prospect of Guderian changing Hitler's mind. At any rate, the die was cast. The great battle for Kiev and mastery of the Ukraine was about to begin.

By the time the 'Battle of Kiev' was over on 25 September – the city of Kiev itself had fallen six days earlier – the Soviet south-west front was totally destroyed. Hitler's insistence on sending Guderian's Panzer Group south to bring about the encirclement had led to an extraordinary victory. An astonishing number of Soviet prisoners – around 665,000 – were taken. The enormous booty captured included 884 tanks and 3,018 artillery pieces. The victory paved the way for Rundstedt to go on to occupy the Ukraine, much of the Crimea, and the Donets Basin, with further huge losses of men and material for the Red Army. In the light of the immense scale of the Soviet losses in the three months since the beginning of 'Barbarossa', the German military leadership now concluded that the thrust to Moscow – given the name 'Operation Typhoon' – could still succeed despite starting so late in the year.

It was scarcely any wonder, basking in the glow of the great victory at Kiev, that Hitler was in ebullient mood when Goebbels spoke alone with him in the Führer Headquarters on 23 September. Hitler's reported comments afford a notable insight into his thinking at this juncture. After bitterly complaining about the difficulties in getting his way with the 'experts' in the General Staff, Hitler expressed the view that the defeats imposed on the Red Army in the Ukraine marked the breakthrough. 'The spell is broken,' Goebbels recorded. Things would now unfold quickly on other parts of the front. New great victories could be expected in the next three to four weeks. By mid-October, the Bolsheviks would be in full retreat. The next thrust was towards Kharkov, which would be reached within days, then to Stalingrad and the Don. Once this industrial area was in German hands, and the Bolsheviks were cut off from their coal supplies and the basis of their armaments production, the war was lost for them.

Leningrad, birthplace of Bolshevism, Hitler repeated, would be destroyed street by street and razed to the ground. Its 5 million population could not be fed. The plough would one day once more pass over the site of the city. Bolshevism began in hunger, blood, and tears. It would end the same way. Asia's entry-gate to Europe would be closed, the Asiatics forced back to where they belonged. A similar fate to Leningrad, he reiterated, might also befall Moscow. The attack on the capital would follow the capture of the industrial basin. The operation to surround the city should be completed by 15 October. And once German troops reached the Caucasus Stalin was lost. Hitler was sure that in such a situation, Japan would not miss the opportunity to make gains in the east of the Soviet Union. What then happened would be up to Stalin. He might capitulate. Or he might seek a 'special peace', which Hitler would naturally take up. With its military power broken, Bolshevism would represent no further danger.

He returned to a familiar theme. With the defeat of Bolshevism, England would have lost its last hope on the Continent. Its final chance of victory would disappear. And the increasing successes by U-boats in the Atlantic which would follow in the next weeks would put further pressure on a Churchill who was betraying signs of nervous strain. Hitler did not rule out Britain removing Churchill in order to seek peace. Hitler's terms would be as they always were: he was prepared to leave the Empire alone, but Britain would have to get out of Europe. The British would probably grant Germany a free hand in the east, but try to retain hegemony in western Europe. That, he would not allow. 'England had always felt itself to be an insular power. It is alien to Europe, or even hostile to Europe. It has no future in Europe.'

All in all, the prospects at this point, in Hitler's eyes, were rosy. One remark indicated, however, that an early end to the conflict was not in sight. Hitler told Goebbels in passing – his assumption would soon prove disastrously misplaced – that all necessary precautions had been made for wintering the troops in the east.

By this time, in fact, Hitler and the Wehrmacht leaders had already arrived at the conclusion that the war in the east would not be over in 1941. The collapse of the Soviet Union, declared an OKW memorandum of 27 August, approved by Hitler, was the next and decisive war aim. But, the memorandum ran, 'if it proves impossible to realize this objective completely during 1941, the continuation of the eastern campaign has top priority for 1942'. The military successes over the summer had been remarkable. But the aim of the quick knock-out blow at the heart of the 'Barbarossa' plan had not been realized. In spite of their vast losses, the Soviet forces had been far from comprehensively destroyed. They continued to be replenished from an apparently limitless reservoir of men and resources, and to fight tooth and nail. German losses were themselves not negligible. Already before the 'Battle of Kiev', casualties numbered almost 400,000, or over 11 per cent of the eastern army. Replacements were becoming more difficult to find. By the end of September, half of the tanks were out of action or in different stages of repair. And by now the autumn rains were already beginning to turn the roads into impassable quagmires. Whatever the successes of the summer, objective grounds for continued optimism had to be strongly qualified. The drive to Moscow that began on 2 October, seeking the decisive victory before the onset of winter, rested on hope more than expectation. It was a desperate last attempt to force the conclusive defeat of the Soviet Union before winter. It amounted to an improvisation marking the failure of the original 'Barbarossa' plan rather than its crowning glory.

Hitler's own responsibility for the difficulties now faced by the German army is evident. Whereas Stalin learnt from the calamities of 1941 and came to leave military matters increasingly to the experts, Hitler's interference in tactical detail as well as grand strategy, arising from his chronic and intensifying distrust of the Army High Command, was, as Halder's difficulties indicated, intensely damaging. The tenacity and stubbornness with which he refused to concede the priority of an attack on Moscow, even when for a while, at the end of July, not just the army leadership but his own closest military adviser, Jodl, had accepted the argument, was quite remarkable. After the glorious victories of 1940, Hitler believed his own military judgement was superior to that of any of his generals. His contempt for Brauchitsch and Halder was reinforced on every occasion that their views on tactics differed from his. Conversely, the weeks of conflict, and the bewildering way in July and August in which directives were arrived at, then amended, undermined the confidence in Hitler not just of the hopelessly supine Brauchitsch and of Halder's Army General Staff, but also of the field commanders.

But the problem was not one-sided. The tension between the conflicting conceptions of the eastern campaign had still been unresolved as far as Halder was concerned when Hitler's Directive No. 21 on 18 December 1940 had indicated Moscow as a secondary rather than primary objective, prefiguring the dispute of the coming summer months. If reluctantly, Army High Command had apparently accepted the alternative strategy which Hitler favoured. Strategic planning of the attack in subsequent months followed from this premiss.

The strategy of first gaining control over the Baltic and cutting off essential Soviet economic heartlands in the south, while at the same time protecting German oil supplies in Romania, before attacking Moscow was not in itself senseless. And the fear that a frontal assault on Moscow would simply drive back instead of enveloping Soviet forces was a real one. Army High Command's preference to deviate from the plan of 'Barbarossa' once the campaign was under way was not a self-evident improvement. The reversion to Halder's originally preferred strategy was tempting because Army Group Centre had advanced faster and more spectacularly than anticipated, and was pressing hard to be allowed to continue and, as it thought, finish the job by taking Moscow. But even more it now followed from the realization that the army's intelligence on Soviet military strength had been woeful. The attack on Moscow, though favoured in the OKH's thinking from an early stage, had in fact come to be a substitute for the 'Barbarossa' plan, which had gone massively awry not simply because of Hitler's interference, but also because of the inadequacy and failures of the army leadership.

Since Hitler had placed the key men, Brauchitsch and Halder, in their posts, he must take a good deal of the blame for their failings. But as Commander-in-Chief of the Army, Brauchitsch was irredeemably weak and ineffectual. His contribution to strategic planning appears to have been minimal. Torn between pressures from his field commanders and bullying from Hitler, he offered a black hole where clear-sighted and determined military leadership was essential. Long before the crisis which would ultimately bring his removal from office, Brauchitsch was a broken reed. The contempt with which Hitler treated him was not without justification.

Halder, partly through his own post-war apologetics and his flirtations (though they came to nothing) with groups opposed to Hitler, has been more generously viewed by posterity. As Chief of the General Staff, responsibility for the planning of army operations was his. The chequered relations with the High Command of the Wehrmacht, in large measure Hitler's own mouthpiece, of course gravely weakened Halder's position. But the Chief of the General Staff failed to highlight difficulties in the original 'Barbarossa' plan. The northward swing of Army Group Centre forces was not fully worked out. The problems that motorized forces would face in the terrain between Leningrad and Moscow were not taken into account. Halder was lukewarm from the outset about the concentration on the Baltic and would have preferred the frontal assault on Moscow. But instead of being settled beforehand, the dispute was left to fester once the campaign was under way.

Moreover, the all-out attack on Moscow that Halder – and

Commander of Army Group Centre von Bock – were urging, would itself have been a highly risky venture. It would then almost certainly have been impossible to eliminate the large Soviet forces on the flanks (as happened in the 'Battle of Kiev'). And the Russians were expecting the attack on the capital. Had the Wehrmacht reached the city, in the absence of a Luftwaffe capable of razing Moscow to the ground (as Hitler wanted), the result would probably have been a preview of what was eventually to happen at Stalingrad.

That the eastern campaign was blown off course already by late summer of 1941 cannot solely, or even mainly, be put down to Hitler's meddling in matters which should have been left to the military professionals. The implication, encountered in some post-war memoirs, that, left to their own devices, the military would have won the war in the east for Germany was both a self-defensive and an arrogant claim. The escalating problems of 'Barbarossa' were ultimately a consequence of the calamitous miscalculation that the Soviet Union would collapse like a pack of cards in the wake of a *Blitzkrieg* resting on some highly optimistic assumptions, gross underestimation of the enemy, and extremely limited resources. This was Hitler's miscalculation. But it was shared by his military planners.

IV

In his lengthy talk with Hitler on 23 September, Goebbels took the opportunity to describe the state of morale within Germany. Hitler, remarked the Propaganda Minister, was well aware of the 'serious psychological test' to which the German people had been subjected over the past weeks. Goebbels pressed Hitler, who had not appeared in public since the start of the Russian campaign and had last spoken to the German people on 4 May, following the victorious Balkan campaign, to come to Berlin to address the nation. Hitler agreed that the time was ripe, and asked Goebbels to prepare a mass meeting to open the Winter Aid campaign at the end of the following week. The date of the speech was fixed for 3 October.

Around 1 p.m. that day, Hitler's train pulled into Berlin. Goebbels was immediately summoned to the Reich Chancellery. He found Hitler looking well and full of optimism. In the privacy of Hitler's room, he was given an overview of the situation at the front. The advance on Moscow, which had begun the previous day, was proceeding beyond expectations. Big successes were being attained. 'The Führer is convinced,' commented Goebbels, 'that if the weather stays moderately favourable the Soviet army will be essentially smashed within a fortnight.'

Cheering crowds, which the party never had any trouble in mobilizing, lined the streets as Hitler was driven in the afternoon to the Sportpalast. A rapturous reception awaited him in the cavernous hall. Goebbels compared it with the mass meetings in the run-up to power. Hitler justified the attack on the Soviet Union as preventive. He said German precautions had been incomplete on only one thing: 'We had no idea how gigantic the preparations of this enemy were against Germany and Europe, and how immense the danger was, how by a hair's breadth we have escaped the annihilation not only of Germany, but of the whole of Europe.' He claimed, at last coming out with the words that his audience were anxious to hear: 'I can say today that this enemy is already broken and will not rise up again.'

Almost every sentence towards the end was interrupted by storms of applause. Hitler, despite the lengthy break, had not lost his touch. The audience in the Sportpalast rose as one in an ecstatic ovation at the end. Hitler was thrilled with his reception. But he was in a hurry to get away. He was driven straight back to the station. By 7 p.m., a mere six hours after he had arrived, he was on his way back to his headquarters in East Prussia.

Goebbels had been with Hitler on the way to the station as the latest news came in from the front. The advance was going even better than expected. Halder purred, soon after its start, that Operation Typhoon was 'making pleasing progress' and pursuing 'an absolutely classical course'. The German army had thrown seventy-eight divisions, comprising almost 2 million men, and nearly 2,000 tanks, supported by a large proportion of the Luftwaffe, against Marshal Timoshenko's forces. Once more, the Wehrmacht seemed invincible. Once more, vast numbers of prisoners – 673,000 of them – fell into German hands, along with immeasurable amounts of booty, this time in the great encirclements of the double battle of Brjansk and Viaz'ma in the first half of October. It was hardly any wonder that the mood in the Führer Headquarters and among the military leadership was buoyant. On the evening of

8 October, Hitler spoke of the decisive turn in the military situation over the previous three days. Werner Koeppen, Rosenberg's liaison at Führer Headquarters, reported to his boss that 'the Russian army can essentially be seen as annihilated'.

Hitler had been in an unusually good mood at the meal table on the evening of 4 October, having just returned from a visit to Army High Command's headquarters to congratulate Brauchitsch on his sixtieth birthday. Not for the first time, he gazed into the future in the 'German East'. Within the next half-century, he foresaw 5 million farms settled there by former soldiers who would hold down the Continent through military force. He placed no value in colonies, he said, and could quickly come to terms with England on that score. Germany needed only a little colonial territory for coffee and tea plantations. Everything else it could produce on the Continent. Cameroon and a part of French Equatorial Africa or the Belgian Congo would suffice for Germany's needs. 'Our Mississippi must be the Volga, not the Niger,' he concluded.

Next evening, after Himmler had regaled those round the dinner table with his impressions of Kiev, and how 80–90 per cent of the impoverished population there could be 'dispensed with', Hitler came round to the subject of German dialects. It started with his dislike of the Saxon accent and spread to a rejection of all German dialects. They made the learning of German for foreigners more difficult. And German now had to be made into the general form of communication in Europe.

Hitler was still in expansive frame of mind when Reich Economics Minister Walther Funk visited him on 13 October. The eastern territories would mean the end of unemployment in Europe, he claimed. He envisaged river links from the Don and the Dnieper between the Black Sea and the Danube, bringing oil and grain to Germany. 'Europe – and not America – will be the land of unlimited possibilities.'

Four days later, the presence of Fritz Todt prompted Hitler to an even more grandiose vision of new roads stretching through the conquered territories. Motorways would now run not just to the Crimea, but to the Caucasus, as well as more northerly areas. German cities would be established as administrative centres on the river-crossings. Three million prisoners-of-war would be available to supply the labour for the next twenty years. German farmsteads would line the roads. 'The monotonous Asiatic-like steppe would soon offer a totally different appearance.' He now spoke of 10 million Germans, as well as settlers from Scandinavia, Holland, Flanders, and even America putting down roots there. The Slav population would 'have to vegetate further in their own dirt away from the big roads'. Knowing how to read the road-signs would be quite sufficient education. Those eating German bread today, he said, did not get worked up about the regaining of the East Elbian granaries with the sword in the twelfth century. 'Here in the east a similar process will repeat itself for a second time as in the conquest of America.' Hitler wished he were ten to fifteen years younger to experience what was going to happen.

But by this time weather conditions alone meant the chances of Hitler's vision ever materializing were sharply diminishing. The weather was already bad. By mid-October, military operations had stalled as heavy rains swept over the front. Units were stranded. The vehicles of Army Group Centre were bogged down on impassable roads. Away from the choked roads, nothing could move. 'The Russians are impeding us far less than the wet and the mud,' commented Field-Marshal Bock. Everywhere, it was a 'struggle with the mud'. On top of that, there were serious shortages of fuel and munitions.

There was also, not before time, concern now about winter provisions for the troops. Hitler directly asked Quartermaster-General Wagner, on a visit to Führer Headquarters, about this on 26 October. Wagner promised that Army Groups North and South would have a half of their necessary provisions by the end of the month, though Army Group Centre, the largest of the three, would only have a third. Supplying the south was especially difficult since the Soviets had destroyed part of the railway track along the Sea of Azov. Even so, when Wagner spoke to Goebbels, he gave the Propaganda Minister the impression that 'everything had been thought of and nothing forgotten'.

In fact, Wagner appears to have become seriously concerned by this vital matter only with the rapid deterioration of the weather in mid-October, while Halder had been aware as early as August that the problem of transport of winter clothing and equipment to the eastern front could only be solved by the defeat of the Red Army before the worst of the weather set in. Brauchitsch was still claiming, when he had lengthy talks with Goebbels on 1 November, that an advance to Stalingrad was possible before the snows arrived and that by the time the troops took up their winter quarters Moscow would be cut off. By now this was wild optimism. Brauchitsch was forced to acknowledge the existing weather problems, the impassable roads, transport difficulties, and the concern about the winter provisioning of the troops. In truth, whatever the unrealism of the Army and Wehrmacht High Commands about what was attainable in their view before the depths of winter, the last two weeks of October had had a highly sobering effect on the front-line commanders and the initial exaggerated hopes of the success of 'Operation Typhoon'. By the end of the month the offensive of Army Group Centre's exhausted troops had ground temporarily to a halt.

The impression which Hitler gave, however, in his traditional speech to the party's old guard, assembled in the Löwenbräukeller in Munich on the late afternoon of 8 November, the anniversary of the 1923 Putsch, was quite different. The speech was intended primarily for domestic consumption. It aimed to boost morale, and to rally round the oldest and most loyal members of Hitler's retinue after the difficult months of summer and autumn. Hitler described the scale of the Soviet losses. 'My Party Comrades,' he declared, 'no army in the world, including the Russian, recovers from those.' 'Never before,' he went on, 'has a giant empire been smashed and struck down in a shorter time than Soviet Russia.' He remarked on enemy claims that the war would last into 1942. 'It can last as long as it wants,' he retorted. 'The last battalion in this field will be a German one.' Despite the triumphalism, it was the strongest hint yet that the war was far from over.

Next day, Hitler was again on his way back to East Prussia, arriving in the Wolf's Lair that evening. In the east, by this time, the snow was falling. Torrential rain had given way to ice and temperatures well below zero Fahrenheit. Even tanks were often unable to cope with ice-covered slopes. For the men, conditions were worsening by the day. There was already an acute shortage of warm clothing to protect them. Severe cases of frostbite were becoming widespread. The combat-strength of the infantry had sunk drastically. Army Group Centre alone had lost by this time approaching 300,000 men, with replacements of little more than half that number available.

It was at this point, on 13 November, that, at a top-level conference of Army Group Centre, in a temperature of –8 degrees Fahrenheit, Guderian's panzer army, as part of the orders for the renewed offensive, was assigned the objective of cutting off Moscow from its eastward communications by taking Gorki, 250 miles to the *east* of the Soviet capital. The astonishing lack of realism in the army's orders derived from the perverse obstinacy with which the General Staff continued to persist in the view that the Red Army was on the point of collapse, and was greatly inferior to the Wehrmacht in fighting-power and leadership. Such views, despite all the evidence to the contrary, still prevailing with Halder (and, indeed, largely shared by the Commander-in-Chief of Army Group Centre, Bock), underlay the memorandum, presented by the General Staff on 7 November, for the second offensive. The hopelessly optimistic goals laid down – the occupation of Maykop (a main source of oil from the Caucasus), Stalingrad, and Gorki were on the wish-list – were the work of Halder and his staff. There was no pressure by Hitler on Halder. In fact, quite the reverse: Halder pressed for acceptance of his operational goals. These corresponded in good measure with goals Hitler had foreseen as attainable only in the following year. Had Hitler been more assertive at this stage in rejecting Halder's proposals, the disasters of the coming weeks might have been avoided. As it was, Hitler's uncertainty, hesitancy, and lack of clarity allowed Army High Command the scope for catastrophic errors of judgement.

The opposition which Halder's plans encountered at the conference on 13 November then resulted in a restriction of the goals to a direct assault on Moscow. This was pushed through in full recognition of the insoluble logistical problems and immense dangers of an advance in near-arctic conditions without any possibility of securing supplies. Even the goal was not clear. The breach of Soviet communications to the east could not possibly be attained. Forward positions in the vicinity of Moscow were utterly exposed. Only the capture of the city itself, bringing – it was presumed – the collapse and capitulation of the Soviet regime and the end of the war, could justify the risk. But with insufficient air-power to bomb the city into submission before the ground-troops arrived, entry into Moscow would have meant street-by-street fighting. With the forces available, and in the prevailing conditions, it is difficult to see how the German army could have proved victorious.

Nevertheless, in mid-November the drive on Moscow recommenced. Hitler was by now distinctly uneasy about the new offensive. On the evening of 25 November he expressed, according to the recollection of his Army Adjutant, Major Gerhard Engel, his 'great concern about the Russian winter and weather'. 'We started a month too late,' he went on, ending, characteristically, by remarking that time was 'his greatest nightmare'.

A few days earlier, Hitler had been more outwardly optimistic in a three-hour conversation with Goebbels. 'If the weather stays favourable, he still wants to make the attempt to encircle Moscow and thereby abandon it to hunger and devastation,' the Propaganda Minister noted. Hitler played down the difficulties; they occurred in every war. 'World history was not made by weather,' he added.

On 29 November, with Hitler once again briefly in Berlin, Goebbels had a further chance to speak with him at length. Hitler appeared full of optimism and confidence, brimming with energy, in excellent health. He professed still to be positive, despite the reversal in Rostov, where General Ewald von Kleist's panzer army had been forced back the previous day after initially taking the city. Hitler now intended to withdraw sufficiently far from the city to allow massive air-raids which would bomb it to oblivion as a 'bloody example'. The Führer had never favoured, wrote Goebbels, taking any of the Soviet major cities. There were no practical advantages in it, and it simply left the problem of feeding the women and children. There was no doubt, Hitler went on, that the enemy had lost most of their great armaments centres. That, he claimed, had been the aim of the war, and had been largely achieved. He hoped to advance further on Moscow. But he acknowledged that a great encirclement was impossible at present. The weather uncertainty meant any attempt to advance a further 200 kilometres to the east, without secure supplies, would be madness. The front-line troops would be cut off and would have to be withdrawn with a great loss of prestige which, at the current time, could not be afforded. So the offensive had to take place on a smaller scale. Hitler still expected Moscow to fall. When it did, there would be little left of it but ruins. In the following year, there would be an expansion of the offensive to the Caucasus to gain possession of Soviet oil supplies – or at least deny them to the Bolsheviks. The Crimea would be turned into a huge German settlement area for the best ethnic types, to be incorporated into the Reich territory as a Gau – named the 'Ostrogoth Gau' as a reminder of the oldest Germanic traditions and the very origins of Germandom. 'What cannot be achieved now, will be achieved in the coming summer,' were Hitler's sentiments, according to Goebbels's notes.

Hitler's show of optimism was put on to delude Goebbels – or himself.

On the very same day that he spoke with the Propaganda Minister, he was told by Walter Rohland – in charge of tank production and just back from a visit to the front – in the presence of Keitel, Jodl, Brauchitsch, and other military leaders, of the superiority of the Soviet panzer production. Rohland also warned, in the light of his own experience gleaned from a trip to the USA in 1930, of the immense armaments potential which would be ranged against Germany should America enter the war. The war would then be lost for Germany. Fritz Todt, one of Hitler's most trusted and gifted ministers, who had arranged the meeting about armaments, followed up Rohland's comments with a statement on German armaments production. Whether in the meeting, or more privately afterwards, Todt added: 'This war can no longer be won militarily.' Hitler listened without interruption, then asked: 'How, then, should I end this war?' Todt replied that the war could only be concluded politically. Hitler retorted: 'I can scarcely still see a way of coming politically to an end.'

As Hitler was returning to East Prussia on the evening of 29 November, the news coming in from the front was not good. Over the next days things were to worsen markedly.

Immediately on his return to the Wolf's Lair, Hitler fell into 'a state of extreme agitation' about the position of Kleist's panzer army, thrown back from Rostov. Kleist wanted to move back to a secure defensive position at the mouth of the Bakhmut River. Hitler forbade this and demanded the retreat be halted further east. Brauchitsch was summoned to Führer Headquarters and subjected to a torrent of abuse. Browbeaten, the Commander-in-Chief, an ill and severely depressed man, passed on the order to the Commander of Army Group South, Field-Marshal von Rundstedt. The reply came from Rundstedt, evidently not realizing that the order had come from Hitler himself, that he could not obey it, and that either the order must be changed or he be relieved of his post. This reply was passed directly to Hitler. In the early hours of the following morning, Rundstedt, one of Hitler's most outstanding and loyal generals, was sacked – the scapegoat for the setback at Rostov – and the command given to Field-Marshal Walter von Reichenau. Later that day, Reichenau telephoned to say the enemy had broken through the line ordered by Hitler and requested permission to retreat to the line Rundstedt had demanded. Hitler concurred.

On 2 December, Hitler flew south to view Kleist's position for himself.

He was put fully in the picture about the reports, which he had not seen, from the Army Group prior to the attack on Rostov. The outcome had been accurately forecast. He exonerated the Army Group and the panzer army from blame. But he did not reinstate Rundstedt. That would have amounted to a public acceptance of his own error.

By that same date, 2 December, German troops, despite the atrocious weather, had advanced almost to Moscow. Reconnaissance troops reached a point only some twelve miles from the city centre. But the offensive had become hopeless. In intense cold – the temperature outside Moscow on 4 December had dropped to –32 degrees Fahrenheit – and without adequate support, Guderian decided on the evening of 5 December to pull back his troops to more secure defensive positions. Hoepner's 4th Panzer Army and Reinhardt's 3rd, some twenty miles north of the Kremlin, were forced to do the same. On 5 December, the same day that the German offensive irredeemably broke down, the Soviet counter-attack began. By the following day, 100 divisions along a 200-mile stretch of the front fell upon the exhausted soldiers of Army Group Centre.

V

Amid the deepening gloom in the Führer Headquarters over events in the east, the best news Hitler could have wished for arrived. Reports came in during the evening of Sunday, 7 December that the Japanese had attacked the American fleet anchored at Pearl Harbor in Hawaii. Early accounts indicated that two battleships and an aircraft carrier had been sunk, and four others and four cruisers severely damaged. The following morning President Roosevelt received the backing of the US Congress to declare war on Japan. Winston Churchill, overjoyed now to have the Americans 'in the same boat' (as Roosevelt had put it to him), had no difficulty in obtaining authorization from the War Cabinet for an immediate British declaration of war.

Hitler thought he had good reason to be delighted. 'We can't lose the war at all,' he exclaimed. 'We now have an ally which has never been conquered in 3,000 years.' This rash assumption was predicated on the view which Hitler had long held: that Japan's intervention would both tie the United States down in the Pacific theatre, and seriously weaken Britain through an assault on its possessions in the Far East.

Relations between Japan and the USA had been sharply deteriorating throughout the autumn. Though kept in the dark about details, the German Ambassador in Tokyo, General Eugen Ott, informed Berlin early in November of his impressions that war between Japan and the USA and Britain was likely. He had also learned that the Japanese administration was about to ask for an assurance that Germany would go to Japan's aid in the event of her becoming engaged in war with the USA.

The Japanese leadership had, in fact, taken the decision on 12 November that, should war with the USA become inevitable, an attempt would be made to reach agreement with Germany on participation in the war against America, and on a commitment to avoid a separate peace. On 21 November Ribbentrop had laid down the Reich's policy to Ott: Berlin regarded it as self-evident that if either country, Germany or Japan, found itself at war with the USA, the other country would not sign a separate peace. Two days later, General Okamoto, the head of the section of the Japanese General Staff dealing with foreign armies, went a stage further. He asked Ambassador Ott whether Germany would regard itself as at war with the USA if Japan were to open hostilities. There is no record of Ribbentrop's replying to Ott's telegram, which arrived on 24 November. But when he met Ambassador Oshima in Berlin on the evening of 28 November, Ribbentrop assured him that Germany would come to Japan's aid if she were to be at war with the USA. And there was no possibility of a separate peace between Germany and the USA under any circumstances. The Führer was determined on this point. Already two days before Ribbentrop met Oshima, Japanese air and naval forces had set out for Hawaii. And on 1 December, the order had been given to attack on the 7th.

Ribbentrop's assurances were fully in line with Hitler's remarks during Matsuoka's visit to Berlin in the spring, that Germany would immediately draw the consequences should Japan get into conflict with the USA. But at this point, before entering any formal agreement with the Japanese, Ribbentrop evidently deemed it necessary to consult Hitler. He told Oshima this on the evening of 1 December. The next day, Hitler flew, as we saw, to visit Army Group South following the setback at Rostov. Bad weather forced him to stay overnight in Poltava on the way back, where he was apparently cut off from communications. He was able to return to his headquarters only on 4 December. Ribbentrop reached him there and gained approval for what amounted to a new tripartite pact – which the German Foreign Minister rapidly agreed with Ciano – stipulating that should war break out between any one of the partners and the USA, the other two states would immediately regard themselves as also at war with America. Already before Pearl Harbor, therefore, Germany had effectively committed itself to war with the USA should Japan – as now seemed inevitable – become involved in hostilities.

The agreement was still unsigned when the Japanese attacked Pearl Harbor. This unprovoked Japanese aggression gave Hitler what he wanted without having already committed himself formally to any action from the German side. However, he was keen to have a revised agreement – completed on 11 December, and now stipulating only an obligation not to conclude an armistice or peace treaty with the USA without mutual consent – for propaganda reasons: to include in his big speech to the Reichstag that afternoon.

As soon as he had heard the news of the Japanese attack, Hitler had telephoned Goebbels, expressing his delight, and ordering the summoning of the Reichstag for Wednesday, 10 December, 'to make the German stance clear'. Goebbels commented: 'We will, on the basis of the Tripartite Pact, probably not avoid a declaration of war on the United States. But that's now not so bad. We're now to a certain extent protected on the flanks. The United States will no longer be so rashly able to provide England with aircraft, weapons, and transport-space, since it can be presumed that they will need all that for their own war with Japan.'

From a propaganda point of view, the Japanese attack at Pearl Harbor was most timely for Hitler. Given the crisis on the eastern front, he had little favourable to include in a progress report to the German people. But now the Japanese attack gave him a positive angle. On 8 December, Ribbentrop told Ambassador Oshima that the Führer was contemplating the best way, from the psychological point of view, of declaring war on the United States. Since he wanted time to prepare carefully such an important speech, Hitler had the assembling of the Reichstag postponed by a day, to 11 December. At least, Goebbels remarked, the time of the speech, three o'clock in the afternoon, though scarcely good for the German public, would allow the Japanese and Americans to hear it.

That Germany *would* declare war on the USA was a matter of course. No agreement with the Japanese compelled it. But Hitler did not hesitate.

A formal declaration might have to wait until the Reichstag could be summoned. But at the earliest opportunity, on the night of 8–9 December, he had already given the order to U-boats to sink American ships. A formal declaration of war was necessary to ensure as far as possible – in accordance with the agreement of 11 December – that Japan would remain in the war. And it was also important, from Hitler's point of view, to retain the initiative, and not let this pass to the United States. Certain, as he had been for many months, that Roosevelt was just looking for the chance to intervene in the European conflict, Hitler thought that his declaration was merely anticipating the inevitable and, in any case, formalizing what was in effect already the situation. Not least, for the German public, it was important to demonstrate that he still controlled events. To await a certain declaration of war from America would, from Hitler's standpoint, have been a sign of weakness. Prestige and propaganda, as always, were never far from the centre of Hitler's considerations. 'A great power doesn't let itself have war declared on it, it declares war itself,' Ribbentrop – doubtless echoing Hitler's sentiments – told Weizsäcker.

Hitler's speech on the afternoon of Thursday, 11 December, was not one of his best. The first half consisted of no more than the lengthy, triumphalist report on the progress of the war which Hitler had intended to provide long before the events of Pearl Harbor. The rest of the speech was largely taken up with a long-drawn-out, sustained attack on Roosevelt. Hitler built up the image of a President, backed by the 'entire satanic insidiousness' of the Jews, set on war and the destruction of Germany. Eventually he came to the climax of his speech: the provocations – up to now unanswered – had finally forced Germany and Italy to act. He read out a version of the statement he had had given to the American Chargé d'Affaires that afternoon, with a formal declaration of war on the USA. He then announced the new agreement, signed that very day, committing Germany, Italy, and Japan to rejecting a unilateral armistice or peace with Britain or the USA.

In Goebbels's view, Hitler's speech had had a 'fantastic' effect on the German people, to whom the declaration of war had come neither as a surprise, nor a shock. In reality, the speech had been able to do little to raise morale, which, given the certain extension of the war into the indefinite future, and now the opening of aggression against a further powerful adversary, had sunk to its lowest point since the conflict began.

Hitler agreed with Goebbels's wishes to prepare the people for un-avoidable setbacks through propaganda more attuned to the realism of the harshness of war and the sacrifices it demanded. Hitler and Goebbels evidently discussed the catastrophic lack of winter clothing for the troops, and the effect this was having on morale. Goebbels was well aware from the bitter criticism in countless soldiers' letters to their loved ones of how bad the impact of the supplies crisis was on morale, both at the front and at home. But Hitler's eyes were already set on the big spring offensive in 1942. And, as always when faced with setbacks, he pointed to the 'struggle for power', and how difficulties had at that time been overcome.

The need to boost morale, in the first instance among those he held responsible for upholding it on the home front, undoubtedly lay behind Hitler's address to his Gauleiter on the afternoon of 12 December.

He began with the consequences of Pearl Harbor. If Japan had not entered the war, he would have at some point had to declare war on the USA. 'Now the East-Asia conflict falls to us like a present in the lap,' Goebbels reported him saying. The psychological significance should not be underrated. Without the conflict between Japan and the USA, a declaration of war on the Americans would have been difficult to accept by the German people. As it was, it was taken as a matter of course. The extension to the conflict also had positive consequences for the U-boat war in the Atlantic. Freed of restraint, he expected the tonnage sunk now to increase greatly – and this would probably be decisive in winning the war.

He turned to the war in the east. Both tone and content were much as they had been with Goebbels in private. He acknowledged that the troops had had for the time being to be pulled back to a defensible line, but, given the supplies problems, saw this as far better than standing some 300 kilometres further east. The troops were now being saved for the coming spring and summer offensive. A new panzer army in preparation within Germany would be ready by then.

It was his firm intention, he declared, in the following year to finish off Soviet Russia at least as far as the Urals. 'Then it would perhaps be possible to reach a point of stabilization in Europe through a sort of half-peace', by which he appeared to mean that Europe would exist as a self-sufficient, heavily armed fortress, leaving the remaining belligerent powers to fight it out in other theatres of war.

He outlined his vision of the future. It was essential after the war was over to undertake a huge social programme embracing workers and farmers. The German people had deserved this. And it would provide – always the political reasoning behind the aim of material improvement – the 'most secure basis of our state system'. The enormous housing programme he had in mind would, he stated openly, be made possible through cheap labour – through depressing wages. The work would be done by the forced labour of the defeated peoples. He pointed out that the prisoners-of-war were now being fully employed in the war economy. This was as it should be, he stated, and had been the case in antiquity, giving rise in the first place to slave labour. German war-debts would doubtless be 200–300 billion Marks. These had to be covered through the work 'in the main of the people who had lost the war'. The cheap labour would allow houses to be built and sold at a substantial profit which would go towards paying off the war-debts within ten to fifteen years.

Hitler put forward once more his vision of the East as Germany's 'future India', which would become within three or four generations 'absolutely German'. There would, he made clear, be no place in this utopia for the Christian Churches. For the time being, he ordered slow progression in the 'Church Question'. 'But it is clear,' noted Goebbels, himself among the most aggressive anti-Church radicals, 'that after the war it has to be generally solved ... There is, namely, an insoluble opposition between the Christian and a Germanic-heroic world-view.'

Pressing engagements in Berlin prevented Hitler from returning that evening, as he had intended, to the Wolf's Lair. When he eventually reached his headquarters again, in the morning of 16 December, it was back to a reality starkly different from the rosy picture he had painted to his Gauleiter. A potentially catastrophic military crisis was unfolding.

VI

Already before Hitler had left for Berlin, Field-Marshal von Bock had outlined the weakness of his Army Group against a concentrated attack, and stated the danger of serious defeat if no reserves were sent. Then, while Hitler was in the Reich capital, as the Soviet counter-offensive penetrated German lines, driving a dangerous wedge between the 2nd and 4th Armies, Guderian reported the desperate position of his troops and a serious 'crisis in confidence' of the field commands. After Schmundt had been sent to Army Group Centre on 14 December to discuss the situation at first hand, Hitler responded immediately, neither awaiting the report from Brauchitsch, who had accompanied Schmundt, nor involving Halder. Colonel-General Friedrich Fromm, Commander of the Reserve Army, was summoned and asked for a report on the divisions that could be sent straight away to the eastern front. Göring and the head of the Wehrmacht transport, Lieutenant-General Rudolf Gercke, were told to arrange the transport. Four and a half divisions of reserves, assembled throughout Germany at breakneck speed, were rushed to the haemorrhaging front. Another nine divisions were drummed up from the western front and the Balkans. On 15 December Jodl passed on to Halder Hitler's order that there must be no retreat where the front could possibly be held. But where the position was untenable, and once preparations for an orderly withdrawal had been made, retreat to a more defensible line was permitted. This matched the recommendations of Bock and of the man who would soon replace him as Commander of Army Group Centre, at this time still commanding the 4th Army, Field-Marshal Günther von Kluge. That evening, Brauchitsch, deeply depressed, told Halder that he saw no way out for the army from its current position. Hitler had by this time long since ceased listening to his broken Army Commander-in-Chief and was dealing directly with his Army Group Commanders.

Bock had, in fact, already recommended to Brauchitsch on 13 December that Hitler should make a decision on whether the Army Group Centre should stand fast and fight its ground, or retreat. In either eventuality, Bock had openly stated, there was the danger that the Army Group would collapse 'in ruins'. Bock advanced no firm recommendation. But he indicated the disadvantages of retreat: the discipline of the troops might give way, and the order to stand-fast at the new line be disobeyed. The implication was plain. The retreat might turn into a rout. Bock's evaluation of the situation, remarkably, had not been passed on to Hitler at the time. He only received it on 16 December, when Bock told Schmundt what he had reported to Brauchitsch three days earlier.

That night, Guderian, who two days earlier had struggled through a blizzard for twenty-two hours to meet Brauchitsch at Roslavl and put his case for a withdrawal, was telephoned on a crackly line by Hitler:

93. Hitler bids farewell to Franco following their talks at Hendaye, on the borders of France and Spain, on 23 October 1940. The smiles concealed the dissatisfaction felt by each of the dictators at the outcome of the talks.

94. Hitler meets the French head of state, Marshal Pétain, at Montoire on 24 October 1940 for talks which produced little tangible result.

95. Ribbentrop talking to Molotov, the Soviet Foreign Minister, at a reception in the Hotel Kaiserhof during the latter's visit to Berlin, 12–14 November 1940. The tough talks with Molotov confirmed to Hitler that he was right to plan for an attack on the Soviet Union in 1941.

96. Hitler and the Japanese Foreign Minister, Matsuoka, in the Reich Chancellery in Berlin on 27 March 1941. Foreign Ministry official and interpreter Dr Paul Schmidt, who compiled the record of the meeting, is on the left. Matsuoka remained non-committal about Japanese intentions. Hitler had earlier that day given directions to his military leaders about the invasion of Yugoslavia.

97. Hitler at his headquarters at Mönichkirchen near Wiener Neustadt in mid-April 1941, during the Balkan campaign, talking to General Alfred Jodl (*left*), head of the Wehrmacht Operations Staff. Nicolaus von Below, his Luftwaffe adjutant, is behind Hitler.

98. A thoughtful Hitler, accompanied by head of the Wehrmacht High Command
Field-Marshal Wilhelm Keitel, travelling by train on 30 June 1941 to the headquarters
of Army High Command in Angerburg, not far from his own new Führer Headquarters
at the Wolf's Lair, near Rastenburg, in East Prussia.

99. An Anti-Bolshevik Poster: 'Europe's Victory is Your Prosperity'. With Britain destroyed, the mailed fist of Nazi Germany smashes Stalin's Bolshevism.

100. Field-Marshal Walther von Brauchitsch (*right*), the weak Commander-in-Chief of the Army between February 1938 and his dismissal in December 1941, in a briefing with General Franz Halder, Chief of the General Staff from 1938 to 1942.

101. Field-Marshal Keitel discussing military matters with Hitler at the Wolf's Lair soon after the invasion of the Soviet Union.

102. Reichsführer-SS and Chief of the German Police Heinrich Himmler (*left*) alongside his right-hand man SS-Obergruppenführer Reinhard Heydrich, head of the Reich Security Head Office. With Hitler's authorization, the steps were taken under their aegis in 1941–2 to implement the 'Final Solution of the Jewish Question'.

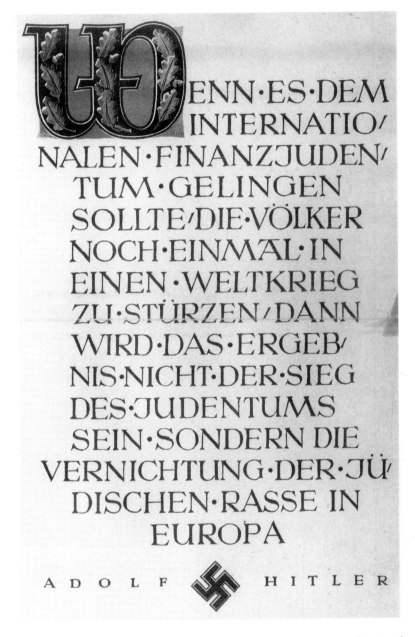

ᴡENN·ES·DEM
INTERNATIO⁄
NALEN·FINANZJUDEN⁄
TUM·GELINGEN
SOLLTE⁄DIE·VÖLKER
NOCH·EINMAL·IN
EINEN·WELTKRIEG
ZU·STÜRZEN⁄DANN
WIRD·DAS·ERGEB⁄
NIS·NICHT·DER·SIEG
DES·JUDENTUMS
SEIN·SONDERN DIE
VERNICHTUNG·DER·JÜ⁄
DISCHEN·RASSE IN
EUROPA

ADOLF HITLER

103. *'Should the international Jewish financiers succeed once again in plunging the nations into a world war, the result will be not the victory of Jews but the annihilation of the Jewish race in Europe' – Adolf Hitler.* The 'prophecy' that Hitler had announced to the Reichstag on 30 January 1939. The poster was produced in September 1941 as a 'Slogan of the week' by the central office of the Nazi Party's Propaganda Department and distributed to party branches throughout the Reich.

104. (*top*) Hitler salutes the coffin of Reinhard Heydrich, who had been assassinated by Czech patriots flown in from Britain, at the state funeral of the Security Police Chief in the Mosaic Salon of the New Reich Chancellery in Berlin on 9 June 1942.

105. (*inset*) Hitler comforts Heydrich's sons at the state funeral. Privately, he was critical of Heydrich's carelessness in regard to his own security. Other Nazi leaders in the photo are, *left to right*: Kurt Daluege (head of the Ordnungspolizei); Bernhard Rust (Reich Minister for Education); Alfred Rosenberg (Reich Minister for the Occupied Eastern Territories); Viktor Lutze (SA Chief of Staff); Baldur von Schirach (Reich Governor and Gauleiter of Vienna); Robert Ley (Nazi Party Organization Leader and head of the German Labour Front); Himmler; Wilhelm Frick (Reich Minister of the Interior); and Göring.

106. (*top*) Hitler addresses 12,000 officers and officer-candidates in the Sportpalast in Berlin on 28 September 1942.

107. Some of the assembled young officers cheering Hitler at the meeting.

108. (*left*) Field-Marshal Fedor von Bock in 1942, as Commander-in-Chief of Army Group South. During the second half of 1941 he had commanded Army Group Centre, which had spearheaded the thrust to Moscow. Though increasingly critical of Hitler's military leadership, he remained a loyalist.

109. (*right*) Field-Marshal Erich von Manstein, possibly Hitler's most gifted military commander. Despite his growing differences with Hitler, he refused to join the conspiracy against him, stating: 'Prussian field-marshals do not mutiny.'

110. (*below*) Hitler speaking on 'Heroes' Memorial Day', 15 March 1942, in the Ehrenhof ('courtyard of honour') of the Armoury on Unter den Linden in Berlin.

111. The Eastern Front, July 1942. Motorized troops drive away from a blazing Russian village they have destroyed.

112. (*left*) Hitler's 'clients': entertaining the heads of satellite states. Hitler greets the Croatian head of state, Dr Ante Pavelic, in the Wolf's Lair on 27 April 1943.

113. (*below*) Hitler on his way to discussions with the Romanian leader, Marshal Antonescu (*centre*), at Führer Headquarters on 11 February 1942. Hitler's interpreter Paul Schmidt is on the left.

114. Hitler greets King Boris III of Bulgaria in the Wolf's Lair on 24 March 1942. Little over a week after a subsequent tense visit, on 15 August 1943, King Boris died suddenly of a heart attack, giving rise to rumours abroad that Hitler had had him poisoned.

115. (*left*) The turn of the Slovakian President, Monsignor Dr Josef Tiso, to visit Hitler on 22 April 1943 at the restored baroque palace of Klessheim, near Salzburg.

116. (*right*) Hitler greets the Finnish leader Marshal Mannerheim at the Wolf's Lair on 27 June 1942. Keitel is in the background.

117. Admiral Horthy, Hungarian head of state, speaks with (*left to right*) Ribbentrop, Keitel, and Martin Bormann during a visit to the Wolf's Lair on 8–10 September 1941. Later visits, as the fortunes of war deteriorated, proved less harmonious than this one.

118. (*top*) The Over-extended Front. By 1942 demands for men and equipment across a vast range of fronts and conditions had generated just the strategic incoherence Hitler had always feared. Norway: A 'Do 24' flying boat is deposited on land by the crane of a salvage vessel, to be towed to a repair hangar.

119. (*centre*) The Over-extended Front. Leningrad: A huge cannon, mounted on a train, fires on the besieged city. The gun weighed 145 tons, had a barrel 16.4 metres long, and had a range of 46.6 kilometres.

120. (*bottom*) The Over-extended Front. Libya: German tanks rolling along the front in Cyrenaica.

121. The Over-extended Front. Bosnia: An expedition to hunt down partisans.

122. An exhausted German soldier on the Eastern Front.

there was to be no withdrawal; the line was to be held; replacements would be sent. Army Group North was told the same day, 16 December, that it had to defend the front to the last man. Army Group South had also to hold the front and would be sent reserves from the Crimea after the imminent fall of Sevastopol. Army Group Centre was informed that extensive withdrawals could not be countenanced because of the wholesale loss of heavy weapons which would ensue. 'With personal commitment of the Commander, subordinate commanders, and officers, the troops were to be compelled to fanatical resistance in their positions without respect for the enemy breaking through on the flanks or rear.'

Hitler's decision that there should be no retreat, conveyed to Brauchitsch and Halder in the night of 16–17 December, was his own. But it seems to have taken Bock's assessment as the justification for the high-risk tactic of no-retreat. His order stated: 'There can be no question of a withdrawal. Only in *some* places has there been deep penetration by the enemy. Setting up rear positions is fantasy. The front is suffering from one thing only: the enemy has more soldiers. It doesn't have more artillery. It's much worse than we are.'

On 13 December, Field-Marshal von Bock had submitted to Brauchitsch his request to be relieved of his command, since, so he claimed, he had not overcome the consequences of his earlier illness. Five days later, Hitler had Brauchitsch inform Bock that the request for leave was granted. Kluge took over the command of Army Group Centre. On 19 December it was the turn – long overdue – of the Commander-in-Chief of the Army, Field-Marshal Walther von Brauchitsch, to depart.

Brauchitsch's sacking had been on the cards for some time. Hitler's military adjutants had been speculating over his replacement since mid-November. His health had for weeks been very poor. He had suffered a serious heart attack in mid-November. At the beginning of December, his health, Halder noted, was 'again giving cause for concern' under the pressure of constant worrying. Hitler spoke of him even in November as 'a totally sick man, at the end of his tether'. Squeezed in the conflict between Hitler and Halder, Brauchitsch's position was indeed unenviable. But his own feebleness had contributed markedly to his misery. Constantly trying to balance demands from his Army Group Commanders and from Halder with the need to please Hitler, his weakness and compliance had left him ever more exposed in the gathering crisis to a Leader who from the start lacked confidence in his army leadership and was determined to intervene in tactical dispositions. It was recognized by those who saw the way Hitler treated him that Brauchitsch was no longer up to the job. Brauchitsch, for his part, was anxious to resign, and tried to do so immediately following the start of the Soviet counter-offensive in the first week of December. He thought of Kluge or Manstein as possible successors.

Hitler disingenuously told Schmundt at the time (and commented along similar lines to his Luftwaffe adjutant, Nicolaus von Below, two days later) that he was clueless about a replacement. Schmundt had for some time favoured Hitler himself taking over as head of the army, to restore confidence, and now put this to him. Hitler said he would think about it. According to Below, it was in the night of 16–17 December that Hitler finally decided to take on the supreme command of the army himself. The names of Manstein and Kesselring were thrown momentarily into the ring. But Hitler did not like Manstein, brilliant commander though he was. And Field-Marshal Albert Kesselring, known as a tough and capable organizer, and an eternal optimist, was earmarked for command of the Luftwaffe in the Mediterranean (and, perhaps, was thought to be too much in Göring's pocket). In any case, Hitler had convinced himself by this time that being in charge of the army was no more than a 'little matter of operational command' that 'anyone can do'. Halder, who, it might have been imagined, would have had most to lose by the change-over, in fact appears to have welcomed it. He seems briefly to have deluded himself that through this move, taking him directly into Hitler's presence in decision-making, he might expand his own influence to matters concerning the entire Wehrmacht. Keitel put an early stop to any such pretensions, ensuring that, as before, Halder's responsibilities were confined to strictly army concerns.

Hitler's takeover of the supreme command of the army was formally announced on 19 December. In one sense, since Brauchitsch had been increasingly bypassed during the deepening crisis, the change was less fundamental than it appeared. But it meant, nevertheless, that Hitler was now taking over direct responsibility for tactics, as well as grand strategy. He was absurdly overloading himself still further. And his takeover of direct command of the army would deprive him, in the eyes of the German public, of scapegoats for future military disasters.

Immediately on the heels of the announcement of Brauchitsch's resignation came an even plainer sign of crisis in the east. On 20 December, Hitler published an appeal to the German people to send warm winter clothing for the troops in the east. Goebbels listed all the items of clothes to be handed in during a lengthy radio broadcast that evening. The population responded with shock and anger – astonished and bitter that the leadership had not made proper provision for basic necessities for their loved ones fighting at the front and exposed to a merciless, polar winter.

Also on the day after Brauchitsch's dismissal, Hitler sent a strongly worded directive to Army Group Centre, reaffirming the order issued four days earlier to hold position and fight to the last man. 'The fanatical will to defend the ground on which the troops are standing,' ran the directive, 'must be injected into the troops with every possible means, even the toughest . . . Talk of Napoleon's retreat is threatening to become reality. Thus, there must only be a withdrawal where there is a prepared position further in the rear.' Where a systematic withdrawal was to take place, Hitler ordered the most brutal scorched-earth policy. 'Every piece of territory which is forced to be left to the enemy must be made unusable for him as far as possible. Every place of habitation must be burnt down and destroyed without consideration for the population, to deprive the enemy of all possibility of shelter.'

One commander more unwilling than most to accept Hitler's 'Halt Order' lying down was the panzer hero Guderian. Through Schmundt, Guderian had a direct line to Hitler. He made use of it to arrange a special meeting at Führer Headquarters where he could put his case for withdrawal openly to Hitler. Guderian had his own way of dealing with military orders which he found unacceptable. With Bock's connivance, he had tacitly ignored or bypassed early orders, usually by acting first and notifying later. But with Bock's replacement by Kluge, that changed. Guderian and Kluge did not get on. Hitler was well informed of Guderian's 'unorthodoxy'. It is perhaps surprising, then, that he was still prepared to grant the tank commander an audience, lasting five hours, on 20 December, and allow him to put his case at length.

All Hitler's military entourage were present. Guderian informed him of the state of the 2nd Panzer Army and 2nd Army, and his intention of retreating. Hitler expressly forbade this. But Guderian was not telling the whole story. The retreat, for which he had presumed to receive authorization from Brauchitsch six days earlier, was already under way.

Hitler was unremitting. He said that the troops should dig in where they stood and hold every square yard of land. Guderian pointed out that the earth was frozen to a depth of five feet. Hitler rejoined that they would then have to blast craters with howitzers, as had been done in Flanders during the First World War. Guderian quietly pointed out that ground conditions in Flanders and Russia in midwinter were scarcely comparable. Hitler insisted on his order. Guderian objected that the loss of life would be enormous; Hitler pointed to the 'sacrifice' of Frederick the Great's men. 'Do you think Frederick the Great's grenadiers were anxious to die?' Hitler retorted. 'They wanted to live, too, but the King was right in asking them to sacrifice themselves. I believe that I, too, am entitled to ask any German soldier to lay down his life.' He thought Guderian was too close to the suffering of his troops, and had too much pity for them. 'You should stand back more,' he suggested. 'Believe me, things appear clearer when examined at longer range.'

Guderian returned to the front empty-handed. Within days, Kluge had requested the tank commander's removal, and on 26 December, Guderian was informed of his dismissal. He was far from the last of the top-line generals to fall from grace during the winter crisis. Within the following three weeks Generals Helmuth Förster, Hans Graf von Sponeck, Erich Hoepner, and Adolf Strauß were sacked, Field-Marshal von Leeb was relieved of his command of Army Group North, and Field-Marshal von Reichenau died of a stroke. Sponeck was sentenced to death – subsequently commuted – for withdrawing his troops from the Kerch peninsula on the Crimean front. Hoepner, also for retreating, was summarily expelled from the army with loss of all his pension rights. By the time that the crisis was overcome, in spring, numerous subordinate commanders had also been replaced.

It was mid-January before Hitler was prepared to concede the tactical withdrawal for which Kluge had been pleading. By the end of the month, the worst was over. The eastern front, at enormous cost, had been stabilized. Hitler claimed full credit for this. It was, in his eyes, once more a 'triumph of the will'. Looking back, a few months later, he blamed the winter crisis on an almost complete failure of leadership in the army. One general had come to him, he said, wanting to retreat. It was plain to him, he went on, that a retreat would have meant 'the fate of Napoleon'. He had ruled out any retreat at all. 'And I pulled it off! That we overcame this winter and are today in the position again to proceed victoriously ... is solely attributable to the bravery of the soldiers at the front and my firm will to hold out, cost what it may.'

Salvation through the Führer's genius was, of course, the line adopted (and believed) by Goebbels and other Nazi leaders. Their public statements combined pure faith and impure propaganda. But despite Halder's outright condemnation – after the war – of Hitler's 'Halt Order', not all military experts were so ready to interpret it as a catastrophic mistake. Kluge's Chief of Staff, General Guenther Blumentritt, for instance, was prepared to acknowledge that the determination to stand fast was both correct and decisive in avoiding a much bigger disaster than actually occurred.

Hitler's early recognition of the dangers of a full-scale collapse of the front, and the utterly ruthless determination with which he resisted demands to retreat, probably did play a part in avoiding a calamity of Napoleonic proportions. But, had he been less inflexible, and paid greater heed to some of the advice coming from his field commanders, the likelihood is that the same end could have been achieved with far smaller loss of life. Moreover, stabilization was finally achieved only after he had relaxed the 'Halt Order' and agreed to a tactical withdrawal to form a new front line.

The strains of the winter crisis had left their mark on Hitler. He was now showing unmistakable signs of physical wear and tear. Goebbels was shocked when he saw him in March. Hitler looked grey, and much aged. He admitted to his Propaganda Minister that he had for some time felt ill and often faint. The winter, he acknowledged, had also affected him psychologically. But he appeared to have withstood the worst. His confidence was, certainly to all outward appearances, undiminished. Hints, given in the autumn, of doubts at the outcome of the war, were no longer heard. Against what had seemed in the depths of the winter crisis almost insuperable odds, Germany was ready by spring to launch another offensive in the east.

The war still had a long way to go. Certainly, the balance of forces at this juncture was by no means one-sided. And the course of events would undergo many vagaries before defeat for Germany appeared inexorable. But the winter of 1941–2 can nevertheless, in retrospect, be seen to be not merely a turning-point, but the beginning of the end. Though it would not become fully plain for some months, Hitler's gamble, on which he had staked nothing less than the future of the nation, had disastrously failed.

21

Fulfilling the 'Prophecy'

I

It was no accident that the war in the east led to genocide. The ideological objective of eradicating 'Jewish-Bolshevism' was central, not peripheral, to what had been deliberately designed as a 'war of annihilation'. It was inseparably bound up with the military campaign. With the murderous onslaught of the Einsatzgruppen, backed by the Wehrmacht, launched in the first days of the invasion, the genocidal character of the conflict was already established. It would rapidly develop into an all-out genocidal programme, the like of which the world had never seen.

Hitler spoke a good deal during the summer and autumn of 1941 to his close entourage in the most brutal terms imaginable, about his ideological aims in crushing the Soviet Union. During the same months, he also spoke on numerous occasions in his monologues in the Führer Headquarters – though invariably in barbaric generalizations – about the Jews. These were the months in which, out of the contradictions and lack of clarity of anti-Jewish policy, a programme to kill all the Jews in Nazi-occupied Europe began to take concrete shape.

In contrast to military affairs, where his repeated interference reflected his constant preoccupation with tactical minutiae and his distrust of the army professionals, Hitler's involvement in ideological matters was less frequent and less direct. He had laid down the guidelines in March 1941. He needed to do little more. Self-combustion would see to it that, once lit, the genocidal fires would rage into a mighty conflagration amid the barbarism of the war to destroy 'Jewish-Bolshevism'. When it came to ideological aims, in contrast to military matters, Hitler had no need to worry that the 'professionals' would let him down. He could rest assured that Himmler and Heydrich, above all, would leave no stone unturned in eliminating the ideological enemy once and for all. And he could be equally certain that they would find willing helpers at all levels among the masters of the new *Imperium* in the east, whether these belonged to the party, the police, or the civilian bureaucracy. Organization, planning, and execution could confidently be left to others. There was no shortage of those keen to 'carry out practical work for our Führer', as one lowly police officer put it. It was sufficient that his authorization for the major steps was provided; and that he could take for granted that, with regard to the 'Jewish Question', his 'prophecy' of 1939 was being fulfilled.

On the eve of 'Barbarossa', Hitler had assured Hans Frank that the Jews would be 'removed' from the General Government 'in the foreseeable future'. Frank's province could therefore be regarded merely as a type of 'transit camp'. Frank registered the pleasure at being able to 'get rid' of the Jews from the General Government, and remarked that Jewry was 'gradually perishing' in Poland. 'The Führer had indeed prophesied that for the Jews,' commented Goebbels. From early in the year the intention had been, as we noted, to deport the Jews from Frank's domain to the east, following the victory over the Soviet Union – expected by the autumn. The Jews from Poland, then from the rest of Europe, would be wiped out in the east within a few years by starvation and being worked to death in the icy wastes of an arctic climate. For those incapable of work, the intended fate, if not spelled out, was not difficult to imagine.

The 5–6 million Jews of the USSR were included in the wholesale resettlement scheme for the racial reordering of eastern Europe, the 'General Plan for the East' which Himmler, two days after the launch of 'Barbarossa', had commissioned his settlement planners to prepare. The Plan envisaged the deportation over the subsequent thirty years of 31 million persons, mainly Slavs, beyond the Urals and into western Siberia. Without doubt, the Jews would have been the first ethnic group to perish in a territorial solution which, for them, was tantamount to their death warrant. What was intended was in itself plainly genocidal. The 'territorial solution' could, therefore, be seen as a type of intended 'final solution'. But shooting or gassing to death all the Jews of Europe – the full-scale industrialized killing programme that evolved over the following months into what would then be a differently defined 'final solution' – was at this stage not in mind.

Reinhard Heydrich had already in March received the green light from Hitler to send the Einsatzgruppen into the Soviet Union in the wake of the Wehrmacht to 'pacify' the conquered areas by eradicating 'subversive elements'. According to a letter which Heydrich sent on 2 July to the four newly appointed Higher SS and Police Leaders for the conquered areas of the Soviet Union, the Einsatzgruppen had been instructed to liquidate, alongside Communist functionaries and an array of 'extremist elements', 'all Jews in the service of the party and state'. Heydrich's verbal briefings must have made clear that the widest interpretation was to be placed on such an instruction.

From the beginning, the killings were far from confined to Jews who were Communist Party or state functionaries. Already on 3 July, for instance, the chief of the Einsatzkommando in Luzk in eastern Poland had some 1,160 Jewish men shot. He said he wanted to put his stamp on the town. In Kowno in Lithuania as many as 2,514 Jews were shot on 6 July. Shootings were carried out by Einsatzkommando 3, based in this area, on twenty days in July. Of the 'executions', totalling 4,400 (according to a meticulous listing), the vast majority were Jews. But the briefings had evidently not been unambiguous. They were capable of being interpreted in different ways. Whereas Einsatzgruppe A, in the Baltic, was almost unconstrained in its killing, Einsatzgruppe B in White Russia initially targeted, in the main, the Jewish 'intelligentsia', while Einsatzgruppe C spoke of working the Jews to death in reclaiming the Pripet Marshes. While some Einsatzkommandos were slaughtering Jews more or less indiscriminately, one killer squad in Chotin on the Dnjestr confined its murderous action in early July to Communist and Jewish 'intellectuals' (apart from doctors).

In the Baltic, the butchery of Einsatzgruppe A was especially ferocious. The first massacre of Jews took place on 24 June, only two days after the beginning of 'Barbarossa', in the small Lithuanian township of Gargzdai, lying just behind the border. Men from the Security Police and a police unit from Memel shot dead 201 Jews that afternoon. By 18 July, the killing squads had claimed 3,300 victims; by August the death-toll had reached between 10,000 and 12,000 mainly male Jews together with Communists.

The killing units were assisted in the early stages by Lithuanian nationalists who were prompted into savage pogroms against the Jews. In Kowno, Jews were clubbed to death one by one by a local enthusiast while crowds of onlookers – women holding their children up to see – clapped and cheered. One eye-witness recalled that around forty-five to fifty Jews were killed in this way within three-quarters of an hour. When the butcher had finished his slaughter, he climbed on to the heap of corpses and played the Lithuanian national anthem on an accordion. German soldiers stood by impassively, some of them taking photographs. The Wehrmacht commander in the area, General-Colonel Ernst Busch, took the view, on hearing reports of the atrocities, that it was a matter of internal Lithuanian disputes, and that he had no authority to intervene. It was seen as exclusively a matter for the security police.

Hitler was keen to keep abreast of the killing operations in the Soviet Union. On 1 August SS-Brigadeführer Heinrich Müller, head of the Gestapo, had passed an enciphered message to the commanders of the four Einsatzgruppen: 'Continual reports from here on the work of the Einsatzgruppen in the east are to be presented to the Führer.'

Goebbels registered his satisfaction, when he received a detailed report in mid-August, at the information that 'vengeance was being wreaked on the Jews in the big towns' of the Baltic, and that they were 'being slain in their masses on the streets by the self-protection organizations'. He connected the killing directly with Hitler's 'prophecy' of January 1939. 'What the Führer prophesied is now taking place,' he wrote, 'that if Jewry succeeded in provoking another war, it would lose its existence.' Three months later, when he visited Vilna, Goebbels spoke again of the 'horrible' 'revenge' of the local population against the Jews, who had been 'shot down in their thousands' and were still being 'executed' by the hundred. The rest had been impressed into ghettos and worked for the benefit of the local economy. The ghetto inhabitants, he commented, were 'vile figures'. He described the Jews as 'the lice of civilized mankind. They had to be somehow eradicated, otherwise they would always again play their torturing and burdensome role. The only way to cope with them is to treat them with the necessary brutality. If you spare them, you'll later be their victim.'

Such were the extreme, pathological expressions of sentiments which, often in scarcely less overtly genocidal form, had a wide currency among the new masters of the eastern territories, and were far from confined to diehard Nazis.

In contrast to the conflicts between the Wehrmacht and the SS following the invasion of Poland, the close cooperation established between

Heydrich and the army leadership in the build-up to 'Barbarossa' enabled the barbarity of the Einsatzgruppen in the eastern campaign to proceed without hindrance, and often in close harmony. The Wehrmacht leadership aligned itself from the start with the ideological aim of combating 'Jewish-Bolshevism'. Cooperation with the SD and Security Police was extensive, and willingly given. Without it, the Einsatzgruppen could not have functioned as they did. 'The relationship to the Wehrmacht is now, as before, wholly untroubled,' ran an Einsatzgruppe report in mid-August. 'Above all, a constantly growing interest in and understanding for the tasks and business of the work of the Security Police can be seen in Wehrmacht circles. This could especially be observed at the executions.'

In an order issued on 12 September 1941, the head of the OKW, Field-Marshal Wilhelm Keitel, declared: 'The struggle against Bolshevism demands ruthless and energetic, rigorous action above all against the Jews, the main carriers of Bolshevism.' Other exhortations from military leaders went still further. A month later, the emphatically pro-Nazi Field-Marshal Walter von Reichenau, Commander-in-Chief of the 6th Army, told his troops: 'The soldier in the eastern sphere is not only a fighter according to the rules of the art of warfare, but also the bearer of a pitiless racial (*völkisch*) ideology and the avenger of all the bestialities which have been inflicted on the German and related ethnic nation. The soldier must therefore have full understanding for the necessity of the severe but just atonement from the Jewish subhumans.' He concluded: 'Only in this way will we fulfil our historic duty of liberating the German people from the Asiatic-Jewish threat once and for all.'

The Commander-in-Chief of the 17th Army, Colonel-General Hermann Hoth, went, if anything, even further than Reichenau. He spoke in an order on the 'Behaviour of German Soldiers in the East', issued on 17 November, of a struggle of 'two inwardly unbridgeable philosophies . . . German feeling of honour and race, centuries-old German soldierly tradition, against asiatic ways of thinking and primitive instincts whipped up by a small number of mainly Jewish intellectuals'. His men should act out of 'belief in a change in the times, in which, on the basis of the superiority of its race and achievements, the leadership of Europe has passed to the German people'. It was a 'mission to rescue European culture from the advance of asiatic barbarism'. He pointed to the way the Red Army had 'bestially murdered' German soldiers. Any sympathy with the native population was wholly misplaced. He stressed the guilt of Jews for circumstances in Germany after the First World War. He saw the extermination of the 'spiritual support of Bolshevism' and 'aid of the partisans' as 'a rule of self-preservation'.

Towards the end of November, the Commander-in-Chief of the 11th Army, Erich von Manstein, in a secret order to his troops, was equally uncompromising. The German people had stood since 22 June, he stated, in a life-and-death struggle against the Bolshevik system, which was not being fought according to traditional European rules of war. The clear implication was that a Soviet regime dominated by Jews was responsible for this. Manstein referred to the Soviet partisan war behind the front lines. Jewry, with 'all the key-points of the political leadership and administration, trade, and crafts' in their hands, formed, he claimed, the 'intermediary between the enemy in the rear and the remainder still fighting of the Red Army and Red Leadership'. From this, he drew his conclusion. 'The Jewish-Bolshevik system must be eradicated once and for all,' he wrote. 'Never again must it enter into our European living space. The German soldier has the task, therefore, not solely of smashing the military means of power of this system. He is also the bearer of a racial idea and avenger of all atrocities perpetrated on him and the German people ... The soldier must show sympathy for the necessity of the hard atonement demanded of Jewry, the spiritual bearer of the Bolshevik terror ...'

Other army commanders increasingly used the spread of partisan warfare as justification for the no-holds-barred treatment of the Jews. Already in the first weeks of 'Barbarossa', Jews were being equated with partisans by some commanders or seen as the major source of their support. But the 'partisan struggle' only began in earnest in the autumn. In the rear area of Army Group Centre, a 'seminar' was organized in September 1941 to allow an exchange of views and experiences between selected officers and leading SS spokesmen on the 'combating of partisans'. The participants took away from their 'orientation course' the plain message to serve as the guideline for future 'pacification' policy: 'Where there's a partisan, there's a Jew, and where there's a Jew, there's a partisan.'

Such voices were influential. There were, however, others. Some commanders insisted on rigorous separation of the Wehrmacht from the actions of the Security Police. One of these, General Karl von Roques, put out an order at the end of July prohibiting any participation by his men in pogroms on the grounds that it was 'unsoldierly' and would seriously damage the standing of the Wehrmacht. However, his order was ineffective. Cases continued to occur in which 'soldiers and also officers had independently undertaken shootings of Jews or participated in them'. In September, he was forced to issue another order, in which he repeated that 'executive measures', especially against Jews, were solely the province of the Higher SS and Police Leader, and any unauthorized shootings by individual soldiers, or participation in 'executive measures' of the SS and police would be treated as disobedience and subjected to disciplinary action.

From letters home from the front, it is plain that many ordinary German soldiers needed little persuasion that the merciless onslaught on the Jews was justified. Subjected for years to incessant indoctrination at school and in the Hitler Youth about the Jews, and inundated since the beginning of 'Barbarossa' with propaganda about horrors of 'Jewish-Bolshevism', on the march into Russia they frequently looked to confirm their prejudices. One soldier, writing home in July, remarked on his shock at 'evidence of Jewish, Bolshevik atrocities, the likes of which I have hardly believed possible', and promised that he and his comrades were taking revenge. Another wrote, also in July: 'Everyone, even the last doubter, knows today that the battle against these subhumans, who've been whipped into a frenzy by the Jews, was not only necessary but came in the nick of time. Our Führer has saved Europe from certain chaos.' Given such a mentality, it was not surprising that many Wehrmacht units were themselves involved in the shooting of Jews and other atrocities from the earliest phase of 'Barbarossa'.

In the early weeks of 'Barbarossa', the 'actions' undertaken by the Einsatzgruppen and their sub-units mainly targeted male Jews. The killing, though horrifying, was on nothing like the scale that it reached from August onwards. One particularly murderous Einsatzkommando in Lithuania, for example, killed *nine* times as many Jews in August and *fourteen* times as many in September as it had done in July. What was regarded as a large-scale 'action' in the first weeks had usually involved the shooting of hundreds of Jews, in rare instances more than 1,000. But by the beginning of October Einsatzkommando 4a, attached to Einsatzgruppe C in the Ukraine, could report with cold precision: 'In retaliation for the arson in Kiev, all Jews were arrested and on 29 and

30.9 a total of 33,771 Jews were executed.' This was the notorious massacre at Babi-Yar, outside Kiev. The Jews – many of them women, children, and old people – had been rounded up in retaliation for a series of explosions in the city, killing some hundreds of German soldiers, a few days earlier, just before Kiev had fallen to the Wehrmacht. They were marched in small groups to the outskirts of the city, forced to undress, then to stand on a mound above the ravine of Babi-Yar. As the repeated salvoes of the killing-squads rang out, the lifeless bodies of the victims fell on to the growing mound of corpses below them.

Women and children – seen as possible 'avengers' of the future – were now, following verbal instructions passed down the line by Himmler, then by the commanders of the various killer squads during August, generally included in the massacres. Thus, Einsatzkommando 3 shot 135 women among 4,239 Jews 'executed' during July, but 26,243 women and 15,112 children in the total of 56,459 Jews murdered during September 1941. Taking the four Einsatzgruppen and their sub-units together, the Jews killed before mid-August numbered around 50,000 – a massive increase on the scale of the murders in Poland, but only a tenth of the estimated half a million who would perish in the next four months.

The huge increase in number of victims demanded different killing techniques. At first, a semblance of martial law and 'execution' by firing-squad was preserved. But after a few weeks, the killers took turns with a sub-machine gun, mowing down their naked victims as they knelt at the edge of a pit.

The actual variation in the scale of the killing operations in the first weeks, and the sharp escalation from around August onwards, strongly suggests that no general mandate to exterminate Soviet Jewry in its entirety had been issued before 'Barbarossa' began. The number of men – around 3,000 in all, the core drawn heavily from the Gestapo, criminal police, regular police (*Ordnungspolizei*), and SD – initially engaged in the Einsatzgruppen actions would, in any case, have been incapable of implementing a full-scale genocidal programme, and could scarcely have been assembled with one in mind. The sharp increase in their numbers through supplementary police battalions began in late July. By the end of the year, there were *eleven* times as many members of the killing units as had been present at the start of 'Barbarossa'.

On 15 August, immediately after witnessing that morning an

'execution' of Jews near Minsk which made him feel sick, Himmler had told his men that he and Hitler would answer to history for the necessary extermination of Jews as 'the carriers of world Bolshevism'. It was during his visits to the killing units in the east that month that Himmler instructed them to widen the slaughter, now to include women and children. Had he received explicit new authorization from Hitler? Or did he presume that the Führer's existing mandate sufficed for the massive extension of the killing operations?

While in FHQ in mid-July, Himmler had received minutes of the important meeting that Hitler had had on the 16th with Göring, Bormann, Lammers, Keitel, and Rosenberg. At the meeting, Hitler had made the telling remarks that the partisan war proclaimed by Stalin provided 'the possibility of exterminating anything opposing us' and that pacification of the conquered territory could best be achieved by shooting dead anyone 'who even looked askance'. A day later, Hitler issued a decree giving Himmler responsibility for security in the newly established civilian regions of German rule in the east. Effectively, this placed the 'Jewish Question' as part of a wider policing remit directly in Himmler's hands.

Within a week, Himmler had increased the 'policing' operations behind the front line in the east by 11,000 men, the start of the far bigger build-up that was to follow. Most probably, catching Hitler's mood at the time, Himmler had pointed out the insufficiency of the forces currently available to him for the 'pacification' of the east, then requested, and been granted, the authority to increase the force to an appropriate level. That the Jews, as had been the case from the beginning of the campaign, were viewed as the prime target group to be extermi- nated – under the pretext of offering the most dangerous opposition to the occupation – would have meant that no specific mandate about their treatment within the general 'pacification' remit was necessary. In dealing with the Jews in the east as he saw fit, Himmler could take it for granted that he was 'working towards the Führer'.

I I

Hitler's own comments about the Jews around this time would certainly have assured Himmler of this. In the twilight hours before dawn on 10 July, Hitler had remarked: ' "I feel like the Robert Koch of politics. He found the bacillus of tuberculosis and through that showed medical scholarship new ways. I discovered the Jews as the bacillus and ferment of all social decomposition. Their ferment. And I have proved one thing: that a state can live without Jews . . ." '

He retained his biological terminology when speaking – with remarkable openness – to the Defence Minister of the newly created, brutally racist state of Croatia, Marshal Sladko Kvaternik, on 22 July. Hitler called Jews 'the scourge of mankind'. 'Jewish commissars' had wielded brutal power in the Baltic, he stated. And now the Lithuanians, Estonians, and Latvians were taking 'bloody revenge' against them. He went on: 'If the Jews had free rein as in the Soviet paradise, they would put the most insane plans into effect. Thus Russia has become a plague-centre for mankind . . . For if only one state tolerates a Jewish family among it, this would provide the core bacillus for a new decomposition. If there were no more Jews in Europe, the unity of the European states would be no longer disturbed. Where the Jews are sent to, whether to Siberia or Madagascar, is immaterial.'

The frame of mind was overtly genocidal. The reference to Madagascar was meaningless. It had been ruled out as an option months earlier. But Siberia, which had in the interim come into favour, would itself have meant genocide of a kind. And, from his comments to Kvaternik, Hitler was plainly contemplating a 'solution to the Jewish Question' not just in the Soviet Union, but throughout the whole of Europe.

No decision for the 'Final Solution' – meaning the physical extermination of the Jews throughout Europe – had yet been taken. But genocide was in the air. In the Warthegau, the biggest of the annexed areas of Poland, the Nazi authorities were still divided in July 1941 about what to do with the Jews whom they had been unable to deport to the General Government. One idea was to concentrate them in one huge camp which could easily be policed, near to the centre of coal production, and gain maximum economic benefit from their ruthless exploitation. But there was the question of what to do about those Jews incapable of working.

A memorandum sent on 16 July 1941 to Eichmann, at Reich Security Head Office, by the head of the SD in Posen, SS-Sturmbannführer Rolf-Heinz Höppner, struck an ominous note. 'There is the danger this winter,' his cynical report to Eichmann read, 'that the Jews can no longer all be fed. It is to be seriously considered whether the most humane solution might not be to finish off those Jews not capable of labour by some sort of fast-working preparation.' Asking for Eichmann's opinion, Höppner concluded: 'The things sound in part fantastic, but would in my view be quite capable of implementation.'

On the last day of the month, Heydrich had Eichmann draft a written authorization from Göring – nominally in charge of anti-Jewish policy since January 1939 – to prepare 'a complete solution of the Jewish question in the German sphere of influence in Europe'. The mandate was framed as a supplement to the task accorded to Heydrich on 24 January 1939, to solve the 'Jewish problem' through 'emigration' and 'evacuation'. Heydrich was now commissioned to produce an over-all plan dealing with the organizational, technical, and material measures necessary. This written mandate was an extension of the verbal one which he had already received from Göring no later than March. It enhanced his authority in dealings with state authorities, and laid down a marker for his control over the 'final solution' once victory in the east – presumed imminent – had been won. There was no need to consult Hitler.

The dragnet was closing on the Jews of Europe. But Heydrich's mandate was not the signal to set up death camps in Poland. The aim at this point was still a territorial solution – to remove the Jews to the east. Within the next few months, recognition that the great gamble of the rapid knockout victory in the east had failed would irrevocably alter that aim.

III

With victory apparently within Germany's grasp, pressures to intensify the discrimination against the Jews and to have them deported from the Reich were building up. The growing privations of the war allowed party activists to turn daily grievances and resentment against the Jews. The SD in Bielefeld reported, for instance, in August 1941 that strong feeling about the 'provocative behaviour of Jews' had brought a ban on Jews attending the weekly markets 'in order to avoid acts of violence'. In addition, there had been general approval, so it was alleged, for an announcement in the local newspapers that Jews would receive no compensation for damage suffered as a result of the war. It was also keenly felt, it was asserted, that Jews should only be served in shops once German customers had had their turn. The threat of resort to self-help and use of force against Jews if nothing was done hung in the air. Ominously, it was nonetheless claimed that these measures would not be enough to satisfy the population. Demands were growing for the introduction of some compulsory mark of identification such as had been worn by Jews in the General Government since the start of the war, in order to prevent Jews from avoiding the restrictions imposed on them.

Evidently, party fanatics were at work – successfully, so it seems – in stirring up opinion against the Jews. The pressure from below was music to the ears of party and police leaders like Goebbels and Heydrich anxious for their own reasons to step up discrimination against the Jews and remove them altogether from Germany as soon as possible. It did not take long for it to be fed through Goebbels to Hitler himself.

An identification mark for Jews was something Hitler had turned down when it had been demanded in the aftermath of 'Crystal Night'. He had not thought it expedient at the time. But he was now to be subjected to renewed pressure to change his mind. By mid-August, Goebbels had convinced himself that the 'Jewish Question' in Berlin had again become 'acute'. He claimed soldiers on leave could not understand how Jews in Berlin could still have 'aryan' servants and big apartments. Jews were undermining morale through comments in queues or on public transport. He thought it necessary, therefore, that they should wear a badge so that they could be immediately recognized.

Three days later a hastily summoned meeting at the Ministry of Propaganda, filled with party hacks, attempted to persuade representatives from other ministries of the need to introduce identification for the Jews. Eichmann, the RSHA (Reich Security Main Office) representative, reported that Heydrich had already put a proposal to this effect to Göring a short while earlier. Göring had sent it back, saying the Führer had to decide. On this, Heydrich had reformulated his proposal, which would be sent to Bormann, for him to speak to Hitler about it. The view from the Propaganda Ministry embroidered upon the remarks Goebbels had entrusted to his diary a few days earlier. The Jews of Berlin, it was alleged, were a 'centre of agitation', occupying much-needed apartments. Among other things, they were responsible, through their hoarding of food, even for the shortage of strawberries in the capital. Soldiers on leave from the east could not comprehend that Jews were still allowed such licence. Most of the Jews were not in employment. These should be 'carted off' to Russia. 'It would be best to kill them altogether.' On the question of 'evacuation of the Jews from the Old Reich', Eichmann commented that Heydrich had put a proposal to the Führer, but that this had been refused, and that the Security Police Chief was now working on an amended proposal for the partial 'evacuation' of Jews from major cities. Given the alleged urgency of the need to protect the mood of the front soldiers, Goebbels, it was announced, intended to seek an audience with the Führer at the earliest opportunity.

This was the purpose of the Propaganda Minister's visit to FHQ on 18 August. He encountered a Hitler recovering from illness, in the middle of a running conflict with his army leaders, in a state of nervous tension, and highly irritable. In this condition, Hitler was doubtless all the more open to radical suggestions. Eventually raising the 'Jewish problem', Goebbels undoubtedly repeated the allegations about Jews damaging morale, especially that of front soldiers. He was pushing at an open door. Hitler must have been reminded of the poor morale which had so disgusted him in Berlin and Munich towards the end of the First World War, for which he (and many others) had blamed the Jews. He granted Goebbels what the Propaganda Minister had come for: permission to force the Jews to wear a badge of identification. According to Goebbels, Hitler expressed his conviction that his Reichstag 'prophecy' – that 'if Jewry succeeded in again provoking a world war, it would end in the destruction of the Jews' – was coming about with a 'certainty to be thought almost uncanny'. The Jews in the east were having to pay the bill, noted Goebbels. Jewry was an alien body among cultural nations. 'At any rate the Jews will not have much cause to laugh in a coming world,' Goebbels reported him as saying.

Next day, Goebbels wrote that he would now become immediately active in the 'Jewish Question', since the Führer had given him permission to introduce a large, yellow Star of David to be worn by every Jew. Once the Jews wore this badge, Goebbels was certain they would rapidly disappear from view in public places. 'If it's for the moment not yet possible to make Berlin into a Jew-free city, the Jews must at least no longer appear in public,' he remarked. 'But beyond that, the Führer has granted me permission to deport the Jews from Berlin to the east as soon as the eastern campaign is over.' Jews, he added, spoiled not just the appearance but the mood of the city. Forcing them to wear a badge would be an improvement. But, he wrote, 'you can only stop it altogether by doing away with them. We have to tackle the problem without any sentimentality.'

On 1 September, a police decree stipulated that all Jews over the age of six had to wear the Star of David. A week later, preparing the population for its introduction, Goebbels ensured that the party Propaganda Department put out a special broadsheet, with massive circulation, in its publication *Wochensprüche* (Weekly Maxims), emblazoned with Hitler's 'prophecy'.

According to SD reports – echoing in the main no doubt hardline feelings in party circles – the introduction of the Yellow Star met with general approval but, in the eyes of some, did not go far enough, and needed to be extended to *Mischlinge* as well as full Jews. Some said the Yellow Star should also be worn on the back. Not all ordinary Germans responded in the same way as the party radicals. There were also numerous indications of distaste and disapproval for the introduction of the Yellow Star, along with sympathy for the victims. It is impossible to be certain which were the more typical responses. Open support for Jews was at any rate dangerous. Goebbels castigated those who felt any sympathy for their plight, threatening them with incarceration in a concentration camp. He turned up his antisemitic invective to an even higher volume. Whatever the level of sympathy, it could carry no weight beside the shrill clamour of the radicals, whose demands – voiced most notably by the Reich Minister of Propaganda – were targeted ever more at removal of the Jews altogether. As Goebbels had recognized, deportation had to wait. But the pressure for it would not let up.

Much of the pressure came from the Security Police. Not surprisingly, the Security Police in the Warthegau, where the Nazi authorities had been trying in vain since autumn 1939 to expel the Jews from the province, were in the front ranks. It must have been towards the end of August that Eichmann asked the SD chief in Posen, SS-Sturmbannführer Rolf-Heinz Höppner – the self-same Höppner who had written to him in July suggesting the possible liquidation of Jews in his area who were incapable of working during the coming winter through a 'fast-working preparation' – for his views on resettlement policy and its administration.

Höppner's fifteen-page memorandum, sent to Eichmann on 3 September, was not concerned solely, or even mainly, with deporting Jews, but the 'Jewish problem' formed nevertheless part of his overview of the potential for extensive resettlement on racial lines. His views corresponded closely with the ideas worked out under the General Plan for the East (*Generalplan Ost*). He envisaged deportations once the war was over 'out of German settlement space' of the 'undesirable sections of the population' from the Great German Reich and of peoples from eastern and south-eastern Europe deemed racially unfit for Germanization. He specifically included 'the ultimate solution of the Jewish Question', not just in Germany but also in all states under German influence, in his suggestions. The areas he had in mind for the vast number of deportees were the 'large spaces in the current Soviet Union'. He added that it would be pure speculation to consider the organization of these territories 'since first the basic decisions have to be taken'. It was essential, however, he stated, that there should be complete clarity from the outset about the fate of the 'undesirables', 'whether the aim is to establish for them permanently a certain form of existence, or whether they should be completely wiped out'.

Höppner, aware of thinking in the upper echelons of the SD, was plainly open to ideas of killing Jews. He himself, after all, had expressed such an idea some weeks earlier. But in early September he was evidently not aware of any decision to exterminate the Jews of Europe. As far as he was concerned, the goal was still their expulsion to the available 'spaces' in the dismantled Soviet Union once the war was over.

IV

Any decision to allow the deportation of the Jews of Europe to the east could only be taken by Hitler. He had rejected Heydrich's proposal to deport them only a few weeks earlier. Without Hitler's approval, Heydrich had been powerless to act. Hitler was even now, in September, unwilling to take this step. He had, of course, presumed that deportations and a final settlement of the 'Jewish Question' would follow upon the victorious end of a war expected to last four or five months. But by this time, Hitler was well aware that this expectation had been an illusion. So practical considerations arose. There was the question of transport. Not enough trains were available to get supplies to the front line. That was more urgent than shipping Jews to the east. And where were the Jews to be sent? The areas currently under German occupation were intended for 'ethnic cleansing', not as a Jewish reservation. Soviet Jews were now being slaughtered there in thousands. But how to deal with an influx of millions more Jews from all over Europe into the area posed problems of an altogether different order. Mass starvation – the fate to which Hitler was prepared to condemn the citizens of Leningrad and Moscow – still required an area to be made available for the Jews to be settled until they starved to death. This had to be in territory intended for the 'export', not 'import', of 'undesirables'. Alternatively, it could only be in the battle-zone itself, or at least in its rear. But this was simply an impracticality; moreover, the Einsatzgruppen had been deployed to wipe out tens of thousands of Jews precisely in such areas; and from Hitler's perspective it would have meant moving the most potent racial enemy to the place where it was most dangerous. So, as long as the war in the east raged, Hitler must have reasoned, the expulsion of the Jews to perish in the barren wastes to be acquired from the Soviet Union simply had to wait.

Suddenly, in mid-September, he changed his mind. There was no overt indication of the reason. But in August, Stalin had ordered the deportation of the Volga Germans – Soviet citizens of German descent who had settled in the eighteenth century along the reaches of the Volga river. At the end of the month the entire population of the region – more than 600,000 people – were forcibly uprooted and deported in cattle-wagons under horrific conditions, allegedly as 'wreckers and spies', to western Siberia and northern Kazakhstan. In all, little short of a million Volga Germans fell victim to the deportations. The news of the savage deportations had become known in Germany in early September. Goebbels had hinted in early September that they could prompt a radical reaction. It was not long in coming. Alfred Rosenberg, the recently appointed Reich Minister for the Occupied Eastern Territories, lost little time in advocating 'the deportation of all the Jews of central Europe' to the east in retaliation. His liaison at Army Headquarters, Otto Bräutigam, was instructed by Rosenberg on 14 September to obtain Hitler's approval for the proposal. Bräutigam eventually succeeded in attracting the interest of Hitler's chief Wehrmacht adjutant, Rudolf Schmundt, who recognized it as 'a very important and urgent matter' which would be of great interest to Hitler.

Revenge and reprisal invariably played a large part in Hitler's motivation. But at first he hesitated. His immediate response was to refer the matter to the Foreign Office. Ribbentrop was initially non-committal. He wanted to discuss it personally with Hitler. Werner Koeppen, Rosenberg's liaison officer at FHQ, noted on 20 September: 'The Führer has so far still made no decision in the question of taking reprisals against the German Jews on account of the treatment of the Volga Germans.' He was said to be contemplating making this move in the event of the United States entering the war. Koeppen's report was, however, already out of date when he submitted it.

Hitler was now, in fact, ready to accept the case that it was urgently necessary to put the long-standing plans for a comprehensive 'solution to the Jewish Question' into action, and that deportation to the east was indeed feasible despite the unfinished war there. Why he was now prepared to bend to such arguments lay partly, no doubt, in his acceptance that an early end to the Russian campaign was not in sight. It was, in fact, precisely the juncture at which he acknowledged that the war in the east would stretch into 1942. Tackling the 'final solution of the Jewish Question', he would have seen, could not wait that long. If victory over Bolshevism had to be delayed, he must have concluded, the time of reckoning with his most powerful adversary, the Jews, should be postponed no longer. They had brought about the war; they would now see his 'prophecy' fulfilled.

It would have been remarkable, when Himmler lunched with Hitler at the Wolf's Lair on 16 September, had the deportation issue not been raised. Almost certainly, the Reichsführer-SS pressed for the Reich's Jews to be deported. The following day, Ribbentrop met Hitler to discuss the Rosenberg proposal. That evening, 17 September, Himmler paid the Foreign Minister a visit. By then, Hitler must have agreed to the suggestions to start deporting German, Austrian, and Czech Jews to the east. Himmler evidently left with the authorization. He gave notification of the decision next day.

On 18 September, Arthur Greiser, Reich Governor and Gauleiter of the Warthegau, received a letter from Himmler. 'The Führer wishes,' ran the missive, 'that the Old Reich and the Protectorate [Bohemia and Moravia] are emptied and freed of Jews from the west to the east as soon as possible.' Himmler told Greiser that it was his intention to deport the Jews first into the Polish territories which had come to the Reich two years earlier, then 'next spring to expel them still further to the east'. With this in mind, he was sending 60,000 Jews to the Lodz ghetto, in Greiser's province, for the winter.

Around the middle of September, then, Hitler had bowed to the pressure to deport the German and Czech Jews to the east, some of them via a temporary stay in Lodz (where the ghetto was already known to be seriously overcrowded). It was the trigger to a crucial new phase in the gradual emergence of a comprehensive programme for genocide.

Hitler's agreement to the deportation of the German Jews was not tantamount to a decision for the 'Final Solution'. It is doubtful whether a single, comprehensive decision of such a kind was ever made. But Hitler's authorization opened the door widely to a whole range of new initiatives from numerous local and regional Nazi leaders who seized on the opportunity now to rid themselves of their own 'Jewish problem', to start killing Jews in their own areas. There was a perceptible quickening of the genocidal tempo over the next few weeks. But there was as yet no coordinated, comprehensive programme of total genocide. This would still take some months to emerge.

V

Within a few days of the decision to deport the Reich Jews, Goebbels was back at FHQ, seizing the opportunity to press once more for the removal of the Jews from Berlin. Before his audience with Hitler, he had the chance to speak with Reinhard Heydrich. Himmler, Neurath, and a number of other leading figures were also in the Wolf's Lair. The occasion for the assembly of notables was Hitler's decision to 'retire' Neurath as Reich Protector in Prague, following intrigues against him by radicals within the Nazi administration in the former Czech capital, able to exploit reports of a mounting incidence of strikes and sabotage. Levels of repression had been relatively constrained under Neurath. But the growing disturbances now prompted Hitler to put in a hard man, Security Police Chief Heydrich – nominally as Deputy Reich Protector

– with a mandate to stamp out with an iron fist all forms of resistance.

Goebbels lost no time in reminding Heydrich of his wish to 'evacuate' the Jews from Berlin as soon as possible. Heydrich evidently told the Propaganda Minister that this would be the case 'as soon as we have reached a clarification of the military question in the east. They [the Jews] should all in the end be transported into the camps established by the Bolsheviks. These camps had been set up by the Jews. What was more fitting, then, than that they should now also be populated by the Jews.'

During his two-hour meeting alone with Hitler, Goebbels had no trouble in eliciting the assurance he wanted, that Berlin would soon be rid of its Jews. 'The Führer is of the opinion,' Goebbels noted down next day, 'that the Jews have eventually to be removed from the whole of Germany. The first cities to be made Jew-free are Berlin, Vienna, and Prague. Berlin is first in the queue, and I have the hope that we'll succeed in the course of this year in transporting a substantial portion of the Berlin Jews away to the east.'

He was in the event to be left less than wholly satisfied. He noted towards the end of October that a beginning had been made with deporting Berlin's Jews. Several thousand had been sent in the first place to Litzmannstadt (as Lodz was now officially called). But he was soon complaining about obstacles to their rapid 'evacuation'. And in November he learnt from Heydrich that the deportations had raised more difficulties than foreseen.

Goebbels kept up the pressure with a hate-filled tirade in *Das Reich* – a 'quality' newspaper reaching over 1½ million homes – on 16 November, entitled 'The Jews are Guilty'. He explicitly cited Hitler's 'prophecy' of the 'annihilation of the Jewish race in Europe', stating: 'We are experiencing right now the fulfilment of this prophecy.' The fate of the Jews, he declared, was 'hard, but more than justified', and any sympathy or regret was entirely misplaced. Goebbels ordered the widest circulation of the article to the troops on the eastern front.

The Propaganda Minister again raised the deportation of Berlin's Jews with Hitler during their three-hour discussion a few days later, on 21 November. Hitler, as usual, was easily able to assuage Goebbels. He told him he agreed with his views on the 'Jewish Question'. He wanted an 'energetic policy' against the Jews – but one which would not 'cause unnecessary difficulties'. The 'evacuation of the Jews' had to take place city by city, and it was still uncertain when Berlin's turn would come. When the time arrived, the 'evacuation' should be concluded as quickly as possible.

Once again, as had repeatedly been the case with Frank in Cracow and Schirach in Vienna, Hitler had raised hopes which encouraged pressure for radical action from his subordinates. That the hopes could be fulfilled less easily than anticipated then simply fanned the flames, encouraging the frantic quest for an ultimate solution to the problem which nothing but the Nazis' own ideological fanaticism had created in the first place.

Both Himmler and Heydrich were still speaking in October of deporting the Jews to the east; Riga, Reval, and Minsk were all mentioned. Plans were set in train for extermination camps in Riga and, it seems, in Mogilew, some 130 miles east of Minsk. Transport difficulties and continued partisan warfare eventually caused their abandonment. But, prompted by the murderous initiatives being undertaken by their minions, who had rapidly realized that they were being shown a green light and lost no time in preparing to set localized genocides in motion, the attention of the SS leaders was starting to switch to Poland, which posed fewer logistical difficulties, as an area in which a 'final solution of the Jewish Question' could take place.

The use of poison gas had already been contemplated before the deportation order was granted. More efficient, less public, and – with characteristic Nazi cynicism – less stressful (for the murderers, that is) ways of killing than mass shootings were required. Gas-vans, already deployed in East Prussia in 1940 to kill 'euthanasia' victims, offered one alternative, though, it soon proved, had their own drawbacks. Other methods, involving stationary killing installations, were considered. At the beginning of September, several hundred Russian prisoners-of-war were gassed in Auschwitz, then a concentration camp mainly for Poles, as an experiment. A large crematorium was then ordered in October from the Erfurt firm of J. A. Topf and Sons. The poison-gas Zyklon-B was used for the first time on the Soviet prisoners; it would by summer 1942 be in regular use for exterminating the Jews of Europe, ferried by the train-load to the huge killing factory of Auschwitz-Birkenau.

Once the decision to deport the Reich Jews to the east had been taken, things began to move rapidly. Heydrich told Gauleiter Alfred Meyer, State Secretary in Rosenberg's Ministry for the Occupied Eastern

Territories, on 4 October that attempts by industry to claim Jews as part of their workforce 'would vitiate the plan of a total evacuation of the Jews from the territories occupied by us'. Later that month, following a visit to Berlin by the Lublin Police Chief, SS-Brigadeführer Odilo Globocnik, evidently aimed at instigating the extermination of the Jews in his district, Polish labourers were commandeered by the SS to construct a camp at Belzec in eastern Poland. Experts on gassing techniques used on patients in the 'euthanasia action' followed a few weeks later, now redeployed in Poland to advise on the gas chambers being erected at Belzec. Initially, the aim was to use Belzec, whose murderous capacity was in the early months relatively small, for the gassing of Jews from the Lublin area who were incapable of work. Only gradually did the liquidation of *all* Polish Jews become clarified as the goal – embodied in what, with the addition of two other camps, Sobibor and Treblinka, in spring 1942, came eventually to be known as 'Aktion Reinhard'.

In the autumn, too, Eichmann was sent to Auschwitz for discussions with Rudolf Höß, the commandant there, about gassing installations. Mass-killing operations at Belzec began in the spring of 1942, in Auschwitz in the summer. They had been preceded by developments in the Warthegau. There, the first of twenty transports in autumn 1941 bringing German Jews to Lodz had arrived on 16 October. The authorities in Lodz had at first objected vehemently to the order in September to take in more Jews. Himmler was implacable. He sharply reprimanded the Government President of Lodz, Friedrich Uebelhoer, himself the bearer of an honorary SS rank. But alongside the reprimand, the Lodz authorities had evidently been assuaged by being told that those Jews incapable of working would soon be liquidated. Mass killings by shooting and gassing (in gas-vans) were already taking place in the autumn weeks. At the same time, Herbert Lange, head of a Special Command which had earlier been deployed at Soldau in East Prussia to gas the inmates of mental asylums, began looking for a suitable location to carry out the systematic extermination of the Jews of the Warthegau. Whether Hitler was consulted on the precise developments or not, his overall approval was almost certainly necessary. By the first week of December 1941, Chelmno, a gas-van station in the south of the Warthegau, had become the first extermination unit to commence operations.

The Warthegau was not the only area scheduled to receive the deportees. Shortly before the killing in Chelmno commenced, the first transports of German Jews had arrived in the Baltic. The initial intention was to send them to Riga, to be placed in a concentration camp outside the city prior to further deportation eastwards. Hitler had approved proposals from the local commander of the Security Police, SS-Sturmbannführer Dr Otto Lange, to set up the concentration camp. Lange had, however, proposed erecting a camp for Latvian Jews. This was turned, in accordance with a 'wish' of the Führer, into the construction of a 'big concentration camp' for Jews from Germany and the Protectorate. Some 25,000 were expected to be interned there, en route, it was said, for an eventual destination 'farther east'. Some Nazi leaders, at least, were well aware by now what deportation to the east meant. When Goebbels, still pressing to have the Jews of Berlin deported as quickly as possible, referred in mid-December to the deportation of Jews from the occupied part of France to the east, he said it was 'in many cases synonymous with the death penalty'.

By the time the first Jews were due to arrive in Riga from the Reich, the building of the camp had scarcely begun. An improvised solution had to be found. Instead of heading for Riga, the trains were diverted to Kowno in Lithuania. Between 25 and 29 November, terrified and exhausted Jews were taken from five trains arriving in Kowno from Berlin, Frankfurt, Munich, Vienna, and Breslau and, without any selection on grounds of ability to work, promptly taken out and shot by members of the locally based Einsatzkommando. The same fate awaited 1,000 German Jews who then did arrive in Riga on 30 November. They were simply taken straight out into the forest and shot, along with some 14,000 Latvian Jews from the Riga ghetto. Himmler had earlier in the month told the police chief in the area, Friedrich Jeckeln, 'that all the Jews in the *Ostland* down to the very last one must be exterminated'.

However certain Jeckeln was of his murderous mandate, other Nazi leaders in the east still had their doubts. Hinrich Lohse, Reich Commissar for the Eastern Region (*Ostland*), and Wilhelm Kube, General Commissar for Belorussia (*Weißruthenien*), were among those who were less sure that Reich Jews were meant to be included in the mass shootings and indiscriminately slaughtered together with the Jews from the east. They now sought urgent clarification from the Reich Ministry for the Occupied Eastern Territories and from Reich Security Head Office. Lohse, pressed by the Wehrmacht to retain Jewish skilled workers, wanted guidance on whether or not economic criteria were relevant in determining whether Jews were to be liquidated. In Minsk, where 12,000 Jews from the local ghetto had been shot by the Security Police to make way for an influx of German Jews, Kube protested that 'people coming from our own cultural sphere' should be treated differently from the 'native brutish hordes'. He wanted to know whether exceptions were to be made for part-Jews (*Mischlinge*), Jews with war decorations, or Jews with 'aryan' partners. Other protests and queries, reflecting both unease and lack of clarity over the intended fate of the Jews from the Reich, reached the Ostministerium and RSHA. These prompted Himmler to intervene on 30 November to try to prohibit the liquidation of the train-load of 1,000 German Jews – many of them elderly, some bearers of the Iron Cross First Class – sent to Riga. His telephone-call came too late. By then the Jews had already been slaughtered by Jeckeln's killing-squads.

The previous day, 29 November, Heydrich had sent out invitations to several State Secretaries and to selected SS representatives to a conference to take place close to the Wannsee, a beautiful lake on the western rim of Berlin, on 9 December. Heydrich wanted to inculcate relevant government ministries in the RSHA's plans to deport to the east all the Jews within Germany's grasp throughout Europe. In addition, he was keen to ensure, in line with the commission he had requested and been granted at the end of July, that his primacy in orchestrating the deportations was recognized by all parties involved. On 8 December, the day before the conference was scheduled to take place, Heydrich had it postponed to 20 January 1942.

The postponement was caused by the dramatic events unfolding in the Pacific and in eastern Europe. The Japanese attack on Pearl Harbor on 7 December would, as Heydrich knew, bring within days a German declaration of war on the USA. With that, the European war would become a world war. Meanwhile, the opening of the first major counter-offensive by the Red Army on 5 December had blocked for the foreseeable future any prospect of mass deportations into Soviet territory. Both developments carried important consequences for the deportation programme. Their impact soon became evident.

Plans to bring about a 'final solution' to the 'Jewish Question' were about to enter a new phase – one more murderous than ever.

VI

Hitler's responsibility for the genocide against the Jews cannot be questioned. Yet for all his public tirades against the Jews, offering the strongest incitement to ever more radical onslaughts of extreme violence, and for all his dark hints that his 'prophecy' was being fulfilled, he was consistently keen to conceal the traces of his involvement in the murder of the Jews. Sensing that the German people were not ready to learn the deadly secret, he was determined – his own general inclination to secrecy was, as always, a marked one – not to speak of it other than in horrific, but imprecise, terms. Even in his inner circle Hitler could never bring himself to speak with outright frankness about the killing of the Jews.

Even so, compared with the first years of the war when he had neither in public nor – to go from Goebbels's diary accounts – in private made much mention of the Jews, Hitler did now, in the months when their fate was being determined, refer to them on numerous occasions. Invariably, whether in public speeches or during comments in his late-night monologues in his East Prussian headquarters, his remarks were confined to generalities – but with menacing allusion to what was happening.

At lunch on 6 October, conversation focused mainly on eliminating Czech resistance following Heydrich's appointment on 27 September as Deputy Reich Protector. Hitler spoke of ways 'to make the Czechs small'. One way was the deportation of the Jews. He was speaking about three weeks after he had agreed to their deportation from the Reich and the Protectorate. His comments reveal at least one of the reasons why he agreed to deport them: he continued to believe in the Jews as dangerous 'fifth-columnists', spreading sedition among the population. It was exactly what he had thought of the role of the Jews in Germany during the First World War. 'All Jews must be removed from the Protectorate,' he declared around the lunch-table, 'and not just into the General Government, but straight away further to the east. This is at present not practical merely because of the great demand of the military for means of transport. Along with the Protectorate's Jews, all the Jews from Berlin and Vienna should disappear at the same time. The Jews are everywhere the pipeline through which all enemy news rushes with the speed of wind into all branches of the population.'

On 21 October, a month after the deportation order, as part of a diatribe comparing 'Jewish Christianity' with 'Jewish Bolshevism', he compared the fall of Rome with latter-day Bolshevization through the Jews. 'If we eradicate this plague,' he concluded, 'we will be carrying out a good deed for mankind, of the significance of which our men out there can have no conception.' Four days later his guests were Himmler (a frequent visitor to the Wolf's Lair during these weeks) and Heydrich. The conversation again revolved mainly around the connections of Jewry and Christianity. Hitler reminded his guests and his regular entourage of his 'prophecy'. 'This criminal race has the two million dead of the World War on its conscience,' he went on, and 'now again hundreds of thousands. Don't anyone tell me we can't send them into the marshes! Who bothers, then, about our people? It's good when the horror precedes us that we are exterminating Jewry.' Though lacking coherence, these notes of Hitler's rantings point to his knowledge of the attempts – eventually given up – in the summer to drown Jewish women by driving them into the Pripet marshes. Hitler's allocation of guilt for the dead of the First World War and the current war to the Jews, and the recourse once more to his 'prophecy', underline his certainty that the destruction of Jewry was imminent. But the consequences flowing from the deportation order of the previous month had still to merge into the full genocidal programme.

On the evening of 5 November, remarks about the 'racial inferiority' of the English lower class led Hitler once more into a monologue about the Jews. As usual, he linked it to the war. This was the 'most idiotic war' that the British had ever begun, he ranted, and would lead in defeat to an outbreak of antisemitism in Britain which would be without parallel. The end of the war, he proclaimed, would bring 'the fall of the Jew'. He then unleashed an extraordinary verbal assault on the lack of ability and creativity of Jews in every walk of life but one: lying and cheating. The Jew's 'entire building will collapse if he is refused a following', he went on. 'I've always said the Jews are the most stupid devils that exist. They don't have a true musician, thinker, no art, nothing, absolutely nothing. They are liars, forgers, deceivers. They've only got anywhere through the simple-mindedness of those around them. If the Jew were not washed by the aryan, he wouldn't be able to see out of his eyes for filth. We can live without the Jews. But they can't live without us.'

The links, as he saw them, between the Jews and the war that they had allegedly inspired, now also, after years in which he had scarcely mentioned the Jews, found a prominent place in his public speeches. But, whatever the rhetorical flourishes, whatever the propaganda motive in appealing to the antisemitic instincts of his hard-core supporters in the party, there cannot be the slightest doubt, on the basis of his private comments, that Hitler believed in what he said.

In his speech to the party's 'Old Guard' on 8 November (a date of especial significance in the Nazi calendar, linking the anniversaries of the putsch and the allegedly Jewish-inspired Revolution of 1918), Hitler pressed home the theme of Jewish guilt for the war. Despite the victories of the previous year, he stated, he had still worried because of his recognition that behind the war stood 'the international Jew'. They had poisoned the peoples through their control of the press, radio, film, and theatre; they had made sure that rearmament and war would benefit their business and financial interests; he had come to know the Jews as the instigators of world conflagration. England, under Jewish influence, had been the driving-force of the 'world-coalition against the German people'. But it had been inevitable that the Soviet Union, 'the greatest servant of Jewry', would one day confront the Reich. Since then it had become plain that the Soviet state was dominated by Jewish commissars. Stalin, too, was no more than 'an instrument in the hand of this almighty Jewry'. Behind him stood 'all those Jews who in thousandfold ramification lead this powerful empire'. This 'insight', Hitler suggested, had weighed heavily upon him, and compelled him to face the danger from the east.

Hitler returned to the alleged 'destructive character' of the Jews when talking again to his usual captive audience in the Wolf's Lair in the small hours of 1–2 December. Again, there was a hint, but no more than that, of what Hitler saw as the natural justice being meted out to the Jews: 'he who destroys life, exposes himself to death. And nothing other than this is happening to them' – to the Jews. The gas-vans of Chelmno would start killing the Jews of the Warthegau in those very days. In Hitler's warped mentality, such killing was natural revenge for the destruction caused by the Jews – above all in the war which he saw as their work. His 'prophecy' motif was evidently never far from his mind in these weeks as the winter crisis was unfolding in the east. It would be at the forefront of his thoughts in the wake of Pearl Harbor. With his declaration of war on the USA on 11 December, Germany was now engaged in a 'world war' – a term used up to then almost exclusively for the devastation of 1914–18. In his Reichstag speech of 30 January 1939, he had 'prophesied' that the destruction of the Jews would be the consequence of a new world war. That war, in his view, had now arrived.

On 12 December, the day after he had announced Germany's declaration of war on the USA, Hitler addressed the Reichsleiter and Gauleiter – an audience of around fifty persons – in his rooms in the Reich Chancellery. Much of his talk ranged over the consequences of Pearl Harbor, the war in the east, and the glorious future awaiting Germany after final victory. He also spoke of the Jews. And once more he evoked his 'prophecy'.

'With regard to the Jewish Question,' Goebbels recorded, summarizing Hitler's comments, 'the Führer is determined to make a clear sweep of it. He prophesied that, if they brought about another world war, they would experience their annihilation. That was no empty talk. The world war is here. The annihilation of Jewry must be the necessary consequence. This question is to be viewed without any sentimentality. We're not here to have sympathy with the Jews, but only sympathy with our German people. If the German people has again now sacrificed around 160,000 dead in the eastern campaign, the originators of this bloody conflict will have to pay for it with their own lives.'

The tone was more menacing and vengeful than ever. The original 'prophecy' had been a warning. Despite the warning, the Jews – in Hitler's view – had unleashed the world war. They would now pay the price.

Hitler still had his 'prophecy' in mind when he spoke privately to Alfred Rosenberg, Reich Minister for the Eastern Territories, on 14 December, two days after his address to the Gauleiter. Referring to the text of a forthcoming speech, on which he wanted Hitler's advice, Rosenberg remarked that his 'standpoint was not to speak of the extermination of Jewry. The Führer approved this stance and said they had burdened us with the war and brought about the destruction so it was no wonder if they would be the first to feel the consequences.'

The party chieftains who had heard Hitler speak on 12 December in the dramatic context of war now against the USA and unfolding crisis on the eastern front understood the message. No order or directive was necessary. They readily grasped that the time of reckoning had come. On 16 December, Hans Frank reported back to leading figures in the administration of the General Government. 'As regards the Jews,' he began, 'I'll tell you quite openly: an end has to be made one way or another.' He referred explicitly to Hitler's 'prophecy' about their destruction in the event of another world war. He repeated Hitler's expression in his address to the Gauleiter that sympathy with the Jews would be wholly misplaced. The war would prove to be only a partial success should the Jews in Europe survive it, Frank went on. 'I will therefore proceed in principle regarding the Jews that they will disappear. They must go,' he declared. He said he was still negotiating about deporting them to the east. He referred to the rescheduled Wannsee Conference in January, where the issue of deportation would be discussed. 'At any event,' he commented, 'a great Jewish migration will commence.' 'But,' he asked, 'what is to happen to the Jews? Do you believe they'll be accommmodated in village settlements in the *Ostland*? They said to us in Berlin: why are you giving us all this trouble? We can't do anything with them in the *Ostland* or in the Reich Commissariat [Ukraine] either. Liquidate them yourselves! . . . We must destroy the Jews wherever we find them and wherever it is possible to do so . . .' A programme for bringing this about was evidently, however, still unknown to Frank. He did not know how it was to happen. 'The Jews are also extraordinarily harmful to us through their gluttony,' he continued. 'We have in the General Government an estimated 2.5 million – perhaps with those closely related to Jews and what goes with it, now 3.5 million Jews. We can't shoot these 3.5 million Jews, we can't poison them, but we must be able to take steps leading somehow to a success in extermination . . .'

The 'Final Solution' was still emerging. The ideology of total annihilation was now taking over from any lingering economic rationale of working the Jews to death. 'Economic considerations should remain fundamentally out of consideration in dealing with the problem' was the answer finally given on 18 December to Lohse's inquiry about using skilled Jewish workers from the Baltic in the armaments industry. On the same day, in a private discussion with Himmler, Hitler confirmed that in the east the partisan war, which had expanded sharply in the autumn, provided a useful framework for destroying the Jews. They were 'to be exterminated as partisans', Himmler noted as the outcome of their discussion. The separate strands of genocide were rapidly being pulled together.

On 20 January 1942, the conference on the 'final solution', postponed from 9 December, eventually took place in a large villa by the Wannsee. Alongside representatives from the Reich ministries of the Interior, Justice, and Eastern Territories, the Foreign Office, from the office of the Four-Year Plan, and from the General Government, sat Gestapo chief SS-Gruppenführer Heinrich Müller, the commanders of the Security Police in the General Government and Latvia, Karl Schoengarth and Otto Lange, together with Adolf Eichmann (the RSHA's deportation expert, who had the task of producing a written record of the meeting).

Heydrich opened the meeting by recapitulating that Göring had given him responsibility – a reference to the mandate of the previous July – for preparing 'the final solution of the European Jewish question'. The meeting aimed to clarify and coordinate organizational arrangements. (Later in the meeting an inconclusive attempt was made to define the status of *Mischlinge* in the framework of deportation plans.) Heydrich surveyed the course of anti-Jewish policy, then declared that 'the evacuation of the Jews to the east has now emerged, with the prior permission of the Führer, as a further possible solution instead of emigration'. He spoke of gathering 'practical experience' in the process for 'the coming final solution of the Jewish question', which would embrace as many as 11 million Jews across Europe (stretching, outside German current territorial control, as far as Britain and Ireland, Switzerland, Spain, Turkey, and French North African colonies). In the gigantic deportation programme, the German-occupied territories would be combed from west to east. The deported Jews would be put to work in large labour gangs. Many – perhaps most – would die in the process. The particularly strong and hardy types who survived would have 'to be dealt with accordingly'.

Heydrich was not orchestrating an existing and finalized programme of mass extermination in death-camps. But the Wannsee Conference was a key stepping-stone on the path to that terrible genocidal finality. A deportation programme aimed at the annihilation of the Jews through forced labour and starvation in occupied Soviet territory following the end of a victorious war had given way to the realization that the Jews would have to be systematically destroyed before the war ended – and that the main locus of their destruction would no longer be the Soviet Union, but the territory of the General Government.

That the General Government should become the first area to implement the 'Final Solution' was directly requested at the conference by its representative, State Secretary Josef Bühler. He wanted the 2½ million Jews in his area – most of them incapable of work, he stressed – 'removed' as quickly as possible. The authorities in the area would do all they could to help expedite the process. Bühler's hopes would be fulfilled over the next months. The regionalized killing in the districts of Lublin and Galicia was extended by spring to the whole of the General Government, as the deportation-trains began to ferry their human cargo to the extermination camps of Belzec, Sobibor, and Treblinka. By this time, a comprehensive programme of systematic annihilation of the Jews embracing the whole of German-occupied Europe was rapidly taking shape. By early June a programme had been constructed for the deportation of Jews from western Europe. The transports from the west began in July. Most left for the largest of the extermination camps by this time in operation, Auschwitz-Birkenau in the annexed territory of Upper Silesia. The 'Final Solution' was under way. The industrialized mass-murder would now continue unabated. By the end of 1942, according to the SS's own calculations, 4 million Jews were already dead.

Hitler had not been involved in the Wannsee Conference. Probably he knew it was taking place; but even this is not certain. There was no need for his involvement. He had signalled yet again in unmistakable terms in December 1941 what the fate of the Jews should be now that Germany was embroiled in another world war. By then, local and regional killing initiatives had already developed their own momentum. Heydrich was more than happy to use Hitler's blanket authorization of deportations to the east now to expand the killing operations into an overall programme of European-wide genocide.

On 30 January 1942, the ninth anniversary of the 'seizure of power', Hitler addressed a packed Sportpalast. As he had been doing privately over the past weeks, he invoked once more – how often he repeated the emphasis in these months is striking – his 'prophecy' of 30 January 1939. As always, he wrongly dated it to the day of the outbreak of war with the attack on Poland. 'We are clear,' he declared, 'that the war can only end either with the extermination of the aryan peoples or the disappearance of Jewry from Europe.' He went on: 'I already stated on 1 September 1939 in the German Reichstag – and I refrain from over-hasty prophecies – that this war will not come to an end as the Jews imagine, with the extermination of the European-aryan peoples, but that the result of this war will be the annihilation of Jewry. For the first time the old Jewish law will now be applied: an eye for an eye, a tooth for a tooth . . . And the hour will come when the most evil world-enemy of all time will have played out its role, at least for a thousand years.'

The message was not lost on his audience. The SD – no doubt picking up comments made above all by avid Nazi supporters – reported that his words had been 'interpreted to mean that the Führer's battle against the Jews would be followed through to the end with merciless consistency, and that very soon the last Jew would disappear from European soil'.

VII

When Goebbels spoke to Hitler in March, the death-mills of Belzec had commenced their grisly operations. As regards the 'Jewish Question', Hitler remained 'pitiless', the Propaganda Minister recorded. 'The Jews must get out of Europe, if need be through use of the most brutal means,' was his view.

A week later, Goebbels left no doubt what 'the most brutal means' implied. 'From the General Government, beginning with Lublin, the Jews are now being deported to the east. A fairly barbaric procedure, not to be described in any greater detail, is being used here, and not much more remains of the Jews themselves. In general, it can probably be established that 60 per cent of them must be liquidated, while only 40 per cent can be put to work . . . A judgement is being carried out on the Jews which is barbaric, but fully deserved. The prophecy which the Führer gave them along the way for bringing about a new world war is beginning to become true in the most terrible fashion. No sentimentality can be allowed to prevail in these things. If we didn't fend them off, the Jews would annihilate us. It's a life-and-death struggle between the aryan race and the Jewish bacillus. No other government and no other regime could produce the strength to solve this question generally. Here, too, the Führer is the unswerving champion and spokesman of a radical solution . . .'

Goebbels himself had played no small part over the years in pushing for a 'radical solution'. He had been one of the most important and high-placed of the party activists pressing Hitler on numerous occasions to take radical action on the 'Jewish Question'. The Security Police had been instrumental in gradually converting an ideological imperative into an extermination plan. Many others, at different levels of the regime, had contributed in greater or lesser measure to the continuing and untrammelled process of radicalization. Complicity was massive, from the Wehrmacht leadership and captains of industry down to party hacks, bureaucratic minions, and ordinary Germans hoping for their own material advantage through the persecution then deportation of a helpless, but unloved, minority which had been deemed to be the implacable enemy of the new 'people's community'.

But Goebbels knew what he was talking about in singling out Hitler's role. This had often been indirect, rather than overt. It had consisted of authorizing more than directing. And the hate-filled tirades, though without equal in their depth of inhumanity, remained at a level of generalities. Nevertheless, there can be no doubt about it: Hitler's role had been decisive and indispensable in the road to the 'Final Solution'. Had he not come to power in 1933 and had a national-conservative government, perhaps a military dictatorship, gained power instead, discriminatory legislation against Jews would in all probability still have been introduced in Germany. But without Hitler, and the unique regime he headed, the creation of a programme to bring about the physical extermination of the Jews of Europe would have been unthinkable.

22

Last Big Throw of the Dice

I

Snow still lay on the ground at the Wolf's Lair. An icy wind gave no respite from the cold. But, at the end of February 1942, there were the first signs that spring was not far away. Hitler could not wait for the awful winter to pass. He felt he had been let down by his military leaders, his logistical planners, his transport organizers; that his army commanders had been faint-hearts, not tough enough when faced with crisis; that his own strength of will and determination had alone staved off catastrophe. The winter crisis had sharpened his sense, never far from the surface, that he had to struggle not just against external enemies, but against those who were inadequate, incapable, or even disloyal, in his own ranks. But the crisis had been surmounted. This in itself was a psychological blow to the enemy, which had also suffered grievously. It was necessary now to attack again as soon as possible; to destroy this mortally weakened enemy in one final great heave. This was how his thoughts ran. In the insomniac nights in his bunker, he was not just wanting to erase the memories of the crisis-ridden cold, dark months. He could hardly wait for the new offensive in the east to start – the push to the Caucasus, Leningrad, and Moscow, which would wrestle back the initiative once more. It would be a colossal gamble. Should it fail, the consequences would be unthinkable.

For those in the Führer Headquarters not preoccupied with military planning, life was dull and monotonous. Hitler's secretaries would go for a daily walk to the next village and back. Otherwise, they whiled away the hours. Chatting, a film in the evenings, and the obligatory gathering each afternoon in the Tea House and late at night again for tea made up the day. 'Since the tea-party always consists of the same people, there is no stimulation from outside, and nobody experiences anything on a personal level,' Christa Schroeder wrote to a friend in February 1942, 'the conversation is often apathetic and tedious, wearying, and irksome. Talk always runs along the same lines.' Hitler's monologues – outlining his expansive vision of the world – were reserved for lunch or the twilight hours. At the afternoon tea-gatherings, politics were never discussed. Anything connected with the war was taboo. There was nothing but small-talk. Those present either had no independent views, or kept them to themselves. Hitler's presence dominated. But it seldom now did much to animate. He was invariably tired, but found it hard to sleep. His insomnia made him reluctant to go to bed. His entourage often wished he would do so. The tedium for those around him seemed at times incessant. Occasionally, it was relieved in the evenings by listening to records – Beethoven symphonies, selections from Wagner, or Hugo Wolf's *Lieder*. Hitler would listen with closed eyes. But he always wanted the same records. His entourage knew the numbers off by heart. He would call out: '*Aida*, last act,' and someone would shout to one of the manservants: 'Number hundred-and-something.'

The war was all that mattered to Hitler. Yet, cocooned in the strange world of the Wolf's Lair, he was increasingly severed from its realities, both at the front and at home. Detachment ruled out all vestiges of humanity. Even towards those in his own entourage who had been with him for many years, there was nothing resembling real affection, let alone friendship; genuine fondness was reserved only for his young Alsatian. Human life and suffering were of no consequence to him. He never visited a field-hospital, nor the homeless after bomb-raids. He saw no massacres, went near no concentration camp, viewed no compound of starving prisoners-of-war. His enemies were in his eyes like vermin to be stamped out. But his profound contempt for human existence extended to his own people. Decisions costing the lives of tens of thousands of his soldiers were made – perhaps it was only thus possible to make them – without consideration for any human plight. The hundreds of thousands of dead and maimed were merely an abstraction, the suffering a necessary and justified sacrifice in the 'heroic struggle' for the survival of the people.

Hitler was by now becoming a remote figure for the German people, a distant warlord. His image had to be refashioned by Goebbels to match the change which the Russian campaign had brought about. The première of the lavish new film *The Great King* in early 1942 allowed Goebbels to stylize Hitler by association as a latter-day Frederick the Great, isolated in his majesty, conducting a heroic struggle for his people against mighty enemies and ultimately overcoming crisis and calamity to emerge triumphant. It was a portrayal which increasingly matched Hitler's self-image during the last years of the war.

But the changed image could do nothing to alter reality: the German people's bonds with Hitler were starting to loosen. And as the war turned inexorably against Germany, Hitler cast around all the more for scapegoats.

An early complication in 1942 arose with the loss of his armaments minister, Dr Fritz Todt, in a fatal air-crash on the morning of 8 February, soon after taking off from the airfield at the Führer Headquarters.

Todt had masterminded the building of the motorways and the Westwall for Hitler. In March 1940 he had been given the task, as a Reich Minister, of coordinating the production of weapons and munitions. Yet a further major office had come his way in July 1941 with the centralization in his hands of control over energy and waterways. In the second half of the year, as the first signs of serious labour shortage in German industry became evident, Todt was commissioned with organizing the mass deployment within Germany of Soviet prisoners-of-war and civilian forced labourers. The accumulation of offices pivotal to the war economy was an indication of Hitler's high esteem for Todt. This was reciprocated. Todt was a convinced National Socialist. But by late 1941, fully aware of the massive armaments potential of the USA and appalled at the logistical incompetence of the Wehrmacht's economic planning during the eastern campaign, he had become deeply pessimistic, certain that the war could not be won.

On the morning of 7 February, Todt had flown to Rastenburg to put to Hitler proposals which had arisen from his meeting a few days earlier with representatives of the armaments industries. The meeting that afternoon was plainly anything but harmonious. In depressed mood, and after a restless night, Todt left next morning to head for Munich in a twin-engined Heinkel 111. Shortly after leaving the runway, the plane turned abruptly, headed to land again, burst into flames, and crashed. The bodies of Todt and four others on board were yanked with long poles from the burning wreckage. An official inquiry ruled out sabotage. But suspicion was never fully allayed. What caused the crash remained a mystery.

Hitler, according to witnesses who saw him at close quarters, was deeply moved by the loss of Todt, whom, it was said, he still greatly admired and needed for the war economy. Even if, as was later often claimed, the breach between him and Todt had become irreparable on account of the Armaments Minister's forcefully expressed conviction that the war could not be won, it is not altogether obvious why Hitler would have been so desperate as to resort to having Todt killed in an arranged air-crash at his own headquarters in circumstances guaranteed to prompt suspicion. Had he been insistent upon dispensing with Todt's services, 'retirement' on ill-health grounds would have offered a simpler solution. The only obvious beneficiary from Todt's demise was the successor Hitler now appointed with remarkable haste: his highly ambitious court architect, Albert Speer. But the only 'evidence' later used to hint at any involvement by Speer was his presence in the Führer Headquarters at the time of the crash and his rejection, a few hours before the planned departure, of an offer of a lift in Todt's aeroplane. Whatever the cause of the crash that killed Todt, it brought Albert Speer, till then in the second rank of Nazi leaders and known only as Hitler's court architect and a personal favourite of the Führer, into the foreground.

Speer's meteoric rise in the 1930s had rested on shrewd exploitation of the would-be architect Hitler's building mania, coupled with his own driving ambition and undoubted organizational talent. Hitler liked Speer. 'He is an artist and has a spirit akin to mine,' he said. 'He is a building-person like me, intelligent, modest, and not an obstinate military-head.' Speer later remarked that he was the nearest Hitler came to having a friend. Now, Speer was in exactly the right place – close to Hitler – when a successor to Todt was needed. Six hours after the Reich Minister's sudden death, Speer was appointed to replace him in all his offices. The appointment came as a surprise to many – including, if we are to take his own version of accounts at face value, Speer himself. But Speer was certainly anticipating succeeding Todt in construction work – and possibly more. At any rate, he lost no time in using Hitler's authority to establish for himself more extensive powers than Todt had ever enjoyed. Speer would soon enough have to battle his way through the jungle of rivalries and intrigues which constituted the governance of the Third Reich. But once Hitler, the day after returning to Berlin for Todt's state funeral on 12 February (at which he himself delivered the oration as his eyes welled with, perhaps crocodile, tears), had publicly backed Speer's supremacy in armaments production in a speech to leaders of the armaments industries, the new minister, still not quite thirty-eight years of age, found that 'I could do within the widest limits practically what I wanted'. Building on the changes his predecessor had initiated, adding his own organizational flair and ruthless drive, and drawing on his favoured standing with Hitler, Speer proved an inspired choice. Over the next two years, despite intensified Allied bombing and the fortunes of war ebbing strongly away from Germany, he presided over a doubling of armaments output.

Hitler was full of confidence when Goebbels had chance to speak at length with him during his stay in Berlin following Todt's funeral. After the travails of the winter, the Dictator had reason to feel as if the corner was turned. During the very days that he was in Berlin the British were suffering two mighty blows to their prestige. Two German battleships, *Gneisenau* and *Scharnhorst*, and the heavy cruiser *Prinz Eugen*, had steamed out of Brest and, under the very noses of the British, passed through the English Channel with minimal damage, heading for safer moorings at Wilhelmshaven and Kiel. Hitler could scarcely contain his delight. At the same time, the news was coming in from the Far East of the imminent fall of Singapore. Most of all, Hitler was content about the prospects in the east. The problems of winter had been overcome, and important lessons learned. 'Troops who can cope with such a winter are unbeatable,' Goebbels noted. Now the great thaw had set in. 'The Führer is planning a few very hard and crushing offensive thrusts, which are already in good measure prepared and will doubtless lead gradually to the smashing of Bolshevism.'

II

On 15 March, Hitler was back again in Berlin. The serious losses over the winter made it essential that he attend the midday ceremony on Heroes' Memorial Day. In his speech, he portrayed the previous months as a struggle above all against the elements in a winter the like of which had not been seen for almost a century and a half. 'But one thing we know today,' he declared. 'The Bolshevik hordes, which were unable to defeat the German soldiers and their allies this winter, will be beaten by us into annihilation this coming summer.'

Many people were too concerned about the rumoured reductions in food rations to pay much attention to the speech. Goebbels was well aware that food supplies had reached a critical point and that it would need a 'work of art' to put across to the people the reasons for the reductions. He acknowledged that the cuts would lead to a 'crisis in the internal mood'. Hitler, in full recognition of the sensitivity of the situation, had summoned the Propaganda Minister to his headquarters to discuss the issue before ration-cuts were announced. Goebbels's view was that the deterioration in morale at home demanded tough measures to counter it. He was determined to take the matter to the Führer, and hoped for the support of Bormann and the party in getting Hitler to intervene to back more radical measures. He felt that, as things were, a radical approach to the law, necessary in total war, was being sabotaged by representatives of the formal legal system. He approved of Bormann's demands for tougher sentences for black-marketeering. And he took it upon himself to press Hitler to change the leadership of the Justice Ministry, which since Gürtner's death the previous year had been run by the State Secretary, Franz Schlegelberger. 'The bourgeois elements still dominate there,' he commented, 'and since the heavens are high and the Führer far away, it's extraordinarily difficult to succeed against these stubborn and listlessly working authorities.' It was in this mood – determined to persuade Hitler to support radical measures, attack privilege, and castigate the state bureaucracy (above all judges and lawyers) – that Goebbels arrived at the Wolf's Lair on the ice-cold morning of 19 March.

He met a Hitler showing clear signs of the strain he had been under during the past months, in a state of mind that left him more than open to Goebbels's radical suggestions. He needed no instruction about the mood in Germany, and the impact the reduction in food rations would have. Lack of transport prevented food being brought from the Ukraine, he complained. The Transport Ministry was blamed for the shortage of locomotives. He was determined to take tough measures. Goebbels then lost no time in berating the 'failure' of the judicial system. Hitler did not demur. Here, too, he was determined to proceed with 'the toughest measures'. Goebbels paraded before Hitler his suggestion for a new comprehensive law to punish offenders against the 'principles of National Socialist leadership of the people'. He wanted the Reich Ministry of Justice placing in new hands, and pressed for Otto Thierack, 'a real National Socialist', an SA-Gruppenführer, and currently President of the notorious People's Court – responsible for dealing with cases of treason and other serious offences against the regime – to take the place left by Gürtner. Five months later, Hitler would make the appointment that Goebbels had wanted, and, in Thierack's hands, the capitulation of the judicial system to the police state would become complete.

For now, Hitler placated Goebbels with a suggestion to prepare the ground for a radical assault on social privilege by recalling the Reichstag and having it bestow upon him 'a special plenipotentiary power' so that 'the evil-doers know that he is covered in every way by the people's community'. Given the powers which Hitler already possessed, the motive was purely populist. An attack on the civil servants and judges, and upon the privileged in society – or, as Hitler put it, 'saboteurs' and 'neglecters of duty in public functions' – could not fail to be popular with the masses. Up to this point, judges could not be dismissed – not even by the Führer. There were limits, too, to his rights of intervention in the military sphere. The case of Colonel-General Erich Hoepner still rankled deeply. Hitler had sacked Hoepner in January and dismissed him from the army in disgrace for retreating in disobedience to his 'Halt Order'. Hoepner had then instituted a law-suit against the Reich over the loss of his pension rights – and won. With Hitler's new powers, this could never happen again. Examples could be set in the military and civilian sector to serve as deterrents to others and 'clear the air'.

'In such a mood,' wrote Goebbels the next day, 'my suggestions for the radicalization of our war-leadership naturally had an absolutely positive effect on the Führer. I only need to touch a topic and I have already got my way. Everything that I put forward individually is accepted piece for piece by the Führer without contradiction.'

The encouragement of Hitler to back the radicalization of the home front continued after Goebbels's return from the Wolf's Lair. Apart from the Propaganda Minister, it came in particular from Bormann and Himmler. On 26 March, the SD reported on a 'crisis of confidence' resulting from the failure of the state to take a tough enough stance against black-marketeers and their corrupt customers among the well-placed and privileged. Himmler, it seems, had directly prompted the report; Bormann made Hitler aware of it. Three days later, Goebbels castigated black-marketeering in *Das Reich*, publicizing two instances of the death-penalty being imposed on profiteers.

It was on this same evening, that of 29 March, that Hitler treated his small audience in the Wolf's Lair to a prolonged diatribe on lawyers and the deficiencies of the legal system, concluding that 'every jurist must be defective by nature, or would become so in time'.

This was only a few days after he had personally intervened in a blind rage with acting Justice Minister Schlegelberger and, when he proved dilatory, with the more eagerly compliant Roland Freisler (later the infamous President of the People's Court as successor to Thierack but at this time Second State Secretary in the Justice Ministry), to insist on the death-penalty for a man named Ewald Schlitt. This was on no more solid basis than the reading of a sensationalized account in a Berlin evening paper of how an Oldenburg court had sentenced Schlitt to only five years in a penitentiary for a horrific physical assault – according to the newspaper account – that had led to the death of his wife in an asylum. The court had been lenient because it took the view that Schlitt had been temporarily deranged. Schlegelberger lacked the courage to present the case fully to Hitler, and to defend the judges at the same time. Instead, he promised to improve the severity of sentencing. Freisler had no compunction in meeting Hitler's wishes. The original sentence was overturned. In a new hearing, Schlitt was duly sentenced to death, and guillotined on 2 April.

Hitler had been so enraged by what he had read on the Schlitt case – which matched all his prejudices about lawyers and fell precisely at the time when the judicial system was being made the scapegoat for the difficulties on the home front – that he had privately threatened, should other 'excessively lenient' sentences be produced, 'to send the Justice Ministry to the devil through a Reichstag law'. As it was, the Schlitt case was brought into service as a pretext to demand from the Reichstag absolute powers over the law itself.

Hitler rang Goebbels on 23 April to tell him that he had now decided to deliver the speech to the Reichstag he had for long had in mind. Goebbels undertook to make the necessary arrangements to summon the Reichstag for 3 p.m. on Sunday, 26 April.

In a shortened lunch just before Hitler's Reichstag speech, a good deal of the talk revolved around the devastation of Rostock in a renewed British raid – the heaviest so far. Much of the housing in the centre of the Baltic harbour-town had been destroyed. But the Heinkel factory had lost only an estimated 10 per cent of its productive capacity. German retaliation to British raids had consisted of attacks on Exeter and Bath. Goebbels favoured the complete devastation of English 'cultural centres'. Hitler, furious at the new attack on Rostock, agreed, according to Goebbels's account. Terror had to be answered with terror. English 'cultural centres', seaside resorts, and 'bourgeois towns' would be razed to the ground. The psychological impact of this – and that was the key thing – would be far greater than that achieved through mostly unsuccessful attempts to hit armaments factories. German bombing would now begin in a big way. He had already given out the directive to prepare a lengthy plan of attack on such lines.

What turned out to be the last ever session of the Great German Reichstag began punctually. Hitler was nervous at the beginning, starting hesitantly, then speaking so fast that parts of his speech were scarcely intelligible. He implied that transport, administration, and justice had been found lacking. There was a side-swipe (without naming names) at Colonel-General Hoepner: 'no one can stand on their well-earned rights', but had to know 'that today there are only duties'. He requested from the Reichstag, therefore, the legal authorization 'to hold each one to fulfilment of his duties' and to dismiss from office without respect to 'acquired rights'. Using the Schlitt case as his example, he launched into a savage attack on the failings of the judiciary. From now on, he said, he would intervene in such cases and dismiss judges 'who visibly fail to recognize the demands of the hour'.

As soon as Hitler had finished speaking, Göring read out the 'Resolution' of the Reichstag, empowering Hitler 'without being bound to existing legal precepts', in his capacity as 'Leader of the Nation, Supreme Commander of the Wehrmacht, Head of Government and supreme occupant of executive power, as supreme law-lord and as Leader of the Party', to remove from office and punish anyone, of whatever status, failing to carry out his duty, without respect to pensionable rights, and without any stipulated formal proceedings.

Naturally, the 'Resolution' was unanimously approved. The last shreds of constitutionality had been torn apart. Hitler now *was* the law.

Many people were surprised that Hitler needed any extension of his powers. They wondered what had gone on that had prompted his scathing attacks on the internal administration. Disappointment was soon registered that no immediate actions appeared to follow his strong words. Lawyers, judges, and civil servants were not unnaturally dismayed by the assault on their professions and standing. What had caused it was in their eyes a mystery. The Führer had evidently, they thought, been crassly misinformed. The consequences were, however, unmistakable. As the head of the judiciary in Dresden pointed out, with the ending of all judicial autonomy Germany had now become a 'true Führer state'.

Hitler's populist instincts had not deserted him. Less elevated sections of the population enthused over his assault on rank and privilege. This had successfully allowed him to divert attention from more fundamental questions about the failures of the previous winter and to provide a much-needed morale-booster through easy attacks on cheap targets.

For the mass of the German people, however, only the prospect of the peace that final victory would bring could sustain morale for any length of time. Many 'despondent souls', ran one party report on the popular mood, were 'struck only by one part of the Führer's speech: where he spoke of the preparations for the winter campaign of 1942–3. The more the homeland has become aware of the cruelty and hardship of the winter struggle in the east, the more the longing for an end to it has increased. But now the end is still not in sight.'

III

Hours after his Reichstag speech, Hitler left for Munich, *en route* to the Berghof and a meeting with Mussolini. He was in expansive mood next lunchtime at his favourite Munich restaurant, the Osteria. He held forth to Hermann Giesler, one of his favoured architects, and his companion-in-arms from the old days of the party's early struggles in Munich Hermann Esser, on his plans for double-decker express trains to run at 200 kilometres an hour on four-metre-wide tracks between Upper Silesia and the Donets Basin. Two days later, at a snow-covered Berghof with Eva Braun acting as hostess, he was regaling his supper guests with complaints about the lack of top Wagnerian tenors in Germany, and the deficiencies of leading conductors Bruno Walter and Hans Knappertsbusch. Walter, a Jew who had become renowned as the director of the Bavarian State Opera and Leipziger Gewandhaus before being forced out by the Nazis in 1933 and emigrating to America, was an 'absolute nonentity', claimed Hitler, who had ruined the orchestra of the Vienna

State Opera to the extent that it was capable only of playing 'beer music'. Although Walter's arch-rival Knappertsbusch, tall, blond, blue-eyed, had the appearance of a model 'aryan' male, listening to him conduct an opera was 'a punishment' to Hitler's mind, as the orchestra drowned out the singing and the conductor performed such gyrations that it was painful to look at him. Only Wilhelm Furtwängler, who had turned the Berlin Philharmonic into such a magnificent orchestra, one of the regime's most important cultural ambassadors, and acknowledged maestro in conducting the Führer's own favourite Beethoven, Brahms, Bruckner, and Wagner, met with his unqualified approval.

Between monologues, he had had 'discussions' with Mussolini in the baroque Klessheim Castle, once a residence of the Prince Bishops of Salzburg, now luxuriously refurbished with furniture and carpets removed from France to make a Nazi guest-house and conference-centre. The atmosphere was cordial. Hitler looked tired to Ciano, and bearing the signs of the strains of the winter. His hair, Ciano noticed, was turning grey. Hitler's primary aim was to convey optimism to Mussolini about the war in the east. Ribbentrop's message to Ciano, in their separate meeting, was no different: the 'genius of the Führer' had mastered the evils of the Russian winter; a coming offensive towards the Caucasus would deprive Russia of fuel, bring the conflict to an end, and force Britain to terms; British hopes from America amounted to 'a colossal bluff'.

The talks continued the next day, now with military leaders present, at the Berghof. How much of a genuine discussion there was is plain from Ciano's description: 'Hitler talks, talks, talks, talks', non-stop for an hour and forty minutes. Mussolini, used himself to dominating all conversation, had to suffer in silence, occasionally casting a surreptitious glance at his watch. Ciano switched off and thought of other things. Keitel yawned and struggled to keep awake. Jodl did not manage it: 'after an epic struggle', he finally fell asleep on a sofa. Mussolini, overawed as always by Hitler, was, apparently, satisfied with the meetings.

A week later, on 8 May, the Wehrmacht began its planned spring offensive. The first targets for Manstein's 11th Army, as laid down in Hitler's directive of 5 April, were the Kerch peninsula and Sevastopol in the Crimea. The directive stipulated the drive on the Caucasus, to capture the oil-fields and occupy the mountain-passes that opened the route to the Persian Gulf, as the main goal of the summer offensive to follow, code-named 'Blue'. The removal of the basis of the Soviet war-economy and the destruction of remaining military forces thought catastrophically weakened over the winter would, it was presumed, bring victory in the east. There, Hitler had reasserted in planning the summer operations, the war would be decided. The key factor was no longer 'living space', but oil. 'If I don't get the oil of Maykop and Grozny,' Hitler admitted, 'then I must finish this war.'

The Wehrmacht and Army High Commands did not contradict the strategic priority. In any case, they had no better alternative to recommend. And the lack of a coordinated command structure meant, as before, competition for Hitler's approval – a military version of 'working towards the Führer'. It was not a matter of Hitler imposing a diktat on his military leaders. Despite his full recognition of the gravity of the German losses over the winter, Halder entirely backed the decision for an all-out offensive to destroy the basis of the Soviet economy. The April directive for 'Blue' bore his clear imprint. And despite the magnitude of their miscalculation the previous year, operational planners, fed by highly flawed intelligence, far from working on the basis of a 'worst-case scenario', backed the optimism about the military and economic weakness of the Soviet Union.

Whatever the presumptions of Soviet losses – on which German intelligence remained woefully weak – the Wehrmacht's own strength, as Halder knew only too well, had been drastically weakened. Over a million of the 3.2 million men who had attacked the Soviet Union on 22 June 1941 were by now dead, captured, or missing. At the end of March, only 5 per cent of army divisions were fully operational. The figures that Halder gave Hitler on 21 April were chilling in the extreme. Some 900,000 men had been lost since the autumn, only 50 per cent replaced (including the call-up of all available twenty-year-olds, and serious inroads into the labour-force at home). Only around 10 per cent of the vehicles lost had been replaced. Losses of weapons were also massive. At the beginning of the spring offensive, the eastern front was short of around 625,000 men. Given such massive shortages, everything was poured into bolstering the southern offensive in the Soviet Union. Of the sixty-eight divisions established on this part of the front, forty-eight had been entirely, and seventeen at least partly, reconstituted.

Poor Soviet intelligence meant the Red Army was again unprepared for the German assault when it came. By 19 May, the Kerch offensive was largely over, with the capture of 150,000 prisoners and a great deal of booty. A heavy Soviet counter on Kharkhov had been, if with difficulty, successfully fended off. By the end of May, the battle at Kharkhov had also resulted in a notable victory, with three Soviet armies destroyed, and over 200,000 men and a huge quantity of booty captured. This was in no small measure owing to Hitler's refusal, fully endorsed by Halder, to allow Field-Marshal Bock, since mid-January Commander of Army Group South, to break off the planned offensive and take up a defensive position.

Hitler had reason to feel pleased with himself when he spoke for two hours behind closed doors in the Reich Chancellery to the Reichsleiter and Gauleiter on the afternoon of 23 May. He had come to Berlin for the funeral of Carl Röver, Gauleiter of Weser-Ems, which had taken place the previous day. After a difficult period, also on the home front, he evidently could not miss the opportunity to bolster the solidarity and loyalty of his long-standing party stalwarts, a vital part of his power-base. And in such company, he was prepared to speak with some candour about his aims.

Hitler emphasized that the war in the east was not comparable with any war in the past. It was not a simple matter of victory or defeat, but of 'triumph or destruction'. He was aware of the enormous capacity of the American armaments programme. But the scale of output claimed by Roosevelt 'could in no way be right'. And he had good information on the scale of Japanese naval construction. He reckoned on serious losses for the American navy when it clashed with the Japanese fleet. He took the view 'that in the past winter we have won the war'. Preparations were now in place to launch the offensive in the south of the Soviet Union to cut off the enemy's oil-supplies. He was determined to finish off the Soviets in the coming summer.

He looked to the future. The Reich would massively extend its land in the east, gaining coal, grain, oil, and above all national security. In the west, too, the Reich would have to be strengthened. The French would 'have to bleed for that'. But there it was a strategic, not an ethnic, question. 'We must solve the ethnic questions in the east.' Once the territory needed for the consolidation of Europe was in German hands, it was his intention to build a gigantic fortification, like the *limes* of Roman times, to separate Asia from Europe. He went on with his vision of a countryside settled by farmer-soldiers, building up a population of

250 millions within seventy or eighty years. Then Germany would be safe against all future threats. It should not be difficult, he claimed, to preserve the ethnic-German character of the conquered territories. 'That would also be the actual meaning of this war. For the serious sacrifice of blood could only be justified through later generations gaining from it the blessing of waving cornfields.' Nice though it would be to acquire a few colonies to provide rubber or coffee, 'our colonial territory is in the east. There are to be found fertile black earth and iron, the bases of our future wealth.' He ended his vision of the future with the vaguest notion of what he understood as a social revolution. The National Socialist Movement, he said, had to make sure that the war did not end in a capitalist victory, but in a victory of the people. A new society would have to be constructed out of the victory, one resting not on money, status, or name, but on courage and test of character. He was confident that victory would be Germany's. Once the 'business in the east' was finished – in the summer, it was to be hoped – 'the war is practically won for us. Then we will be in the position of conducting a large-scale pirate-war against the Anglo-Saxon powers, which in the long run they will not be able to withstand.'

Hitler was in ebullient mood when Goebbels saw him at lunchtime in the Reich Chancellery on 29 May. With the advance to the Caucasus, he told his Propaganda Minister, 'we'll be pressing the Soviet system so to say on its Adam's Apple'. He thought the new Soviet losses at Kerch and Kharkhov were not reparable; Stalin was reaching the end of his resources; there were major difficulties with food-supplies in the Soviet Union; morale there was poor. He had concrete plans for the extension of the Reich borders also in the west. He took it as a matter of course that Belgium, with its ancient Germanic provinces of Flanders and Brabant, would be split into German *Reichsgaue*. So would, whatever the views of Dutch National Socialist leader Anton Mussert, the Netherlands.

Two days earlier, one of Hitler's most important henchmen, Reinhard Heydrich, Chief of the Security Police and since the previous autumn Deputy Protector of Bohemia and Moravia, had been fatally wounded in an assassination attempt carried out by patriotic Czech exiles who had been flown from London – with the aid of the British subversive warfare agency, the Special Operations Executive (SOE) – and para-chuted into the vicinity of Prague. Hitler always favoured brutal reprisals. There could be no doubt that the attack on one of the key representatives of his power would provoke a ferocious response. Over 1,300 Czechs, some 200 of them women, were eventually rounded up by the SS and executed. On 10 June the entire village of Lidice – the name had been found on a Czech SOE agent arrested earlier – would be destroyed, the male inhabitants shot, the women taken to Ravensbrück concentration camp, the children removed.

Hitler's mood was ripe for Goebbels to bring up once more the question of the deportation of Berlin's remaining Jews. The involvement of a number of young Jews (associated with a Communist-linked resistance group led by Herbert Baum) in the arson attempt at the anti-Bolshevik exhibition 'The Soviet Paradise' in Berlin's Lustgarten on 18 May enabled the Propaganda Minister to emphasize the security dangers if the 40,000 or so Jews he reckoned were still in the Reich capital were not deported. He had been doing his best, he had noted a day earlier, to have as many Jews as possible from his domain 'shipped off to the east'. Goebbels now pleaded for 'a more radical Jewish policy' and, he said, 'I push at an open door with the Führer,' who told Speer to find replacements for the Jews in the armaments industry with 'foreign workers' as soon as possible.

Talk moved to the dangers of possible internal revolt in the event of a critical situation in the war. If the danger became acute, Hitler stated, the prisons 'would be emptied through liquidations' to prevent the possibility of the gates being opened to let the 'revolting mob' loose on the people. But in contrast to 1917 there was nothing to fear from the German workers, remarked Hitler. All German workers desired victory. They had most to lose by defeat and would not contemplate stabbing him in the back. 'The Germans take part in subversive movements only when the Jews lure them into it,' Goebbels had Hitler saying. 'Therefore one must liquidate the Jewish danger, cost what it takes.' West-European civilization only provided a façade of assimilation. Back in the ghetto, Jews soon returned to type. But there were elements among them who operated 'with dangerous brutality and thirst for revenge'. 'Therefore,' recorded Goebbels, 'the Führer does not wish at all that the Jews be evacuated to Siberia. There, under the hardest living conditions, they would doubtless again represent a vigorous element. He would most like to see them resettled in Central Africa. There they would live in a climate that would certainly not make them strong and capable of resistance. At any rate, it is the aim of the Führer to make

Western Europe entirely free of Jews. Here they can no longer have any home.'

Did such remarks mean that Hitler was unaware that the 'Final Solution' was under way, that Jews had already been slaughtered in their thousands in Russia and were now being murdered by poison gas in industrialized mass-killing centres already operating in Chelmno, Belzec, Sobibor, and Auschwitz-Birkenau (with Treblinka and Maidanek soon to follow)? That seems inconceivable.

On 9 April 1942, a time when the deportations from western European countries to the gas-chambers of Poland were also getting under way, Hans Frank told his underlings in the General Government that orders for the liquidation of the Jews came 'from higher authority'. Himmler himself was to claim explicitly in an internal, top-secret, letter to SS-Obergruppenführer Gottlob Berger, Chief of the SS Main Office, on 28 July 1942, that he was operating explicitly under Hitler's authority: 'The occupied Eastern territories are being made free of Jews. The Führer has placed the implementation of this very difficult order on my shoulders.'

How much detail Hitler asked for, or was given, cannot be known. According to the post-war testimony of his valet, Heinz Linge, and his personal adjutant, Otto Günsche, extracted by their Soviet captors, Hitler showed a direct interest in the development of gas-chambers and spoke to Himmler about the use of gas-vans. One indication, at the very least, that he was aware of the slaughter of huge numbers of Jews is provided by a report which Himmler had had drawn up for him at the end of 1942 providing statistics on Jews 'executed' in southern Russia on account of alleged connection with 'bandit' activity. Having ordered in mid-December that partisan 'bands' were to be combated 'by the most brutal means', also to be used against women and children, Hitler was presented by Himmler with statistics for southern Russia and the Ukraine on the number of 'bandits' liquidated in the three months of September, October, and November 1942. The figures for those helping the 'bands' or under suspicion of being connected with them listed 363,211 'Jews executed'. The connection with subversive activity was an obvious sham. Others in the same category 'executed' totalled 'only' 14,257.

Four months after this, in April 1943, Himmler would have an abbreviated statistical report on 'the Final Solution of the Jewish Question' sent to Hitler. Aware of the taboo in Hitler's entourge on explicit reference to the mass killing of the Jews, Himmler had the statistical report presented in camouflage-language. The fiction had to be maintained. Himmler ordered the term 'Special Treatment' (itself a euphemism for killing) deleted from the shortened version to be sent to Hitler. His statistician, Dr Richard Korherr, was ordered simply to refer to the 'transport of Jews'. There was reference to Jews being 'sluiced through' unnamed camps. The camouflage-language was there to serve a specific purpose. Hitler would understand what it meant, and recognize the Reichsführer-SS's 'achievement'.

When he spoke at lunchtime on 29 May 1942 to Goebbels and to his other guests at his meal-table about his preference for the 'evacuation' of the Jews to Central Africa, Hitler was sustaining the fiction which had to be upheld even in his 'court circle' that the Jews were being resettled and put to work in the east. Goebbels himself, in his diary entry, went along with the fiction, though he knew only too well what was happening to the Jews in Poland. Hitler had by now internalized his authorization of the killing of the Jews. It was typical of his way of dealing with the 'Final Solution' that he spoke of it either by repeating what he knew had long since ceased to be the case; or by alluding to the removal of Jews from Europe (often in the context of his 'prophecy') at some distant point in the future.

Why was Hitler so anxious to maintain the fiction of resettlement, and uphold the 'terrible secret' even among his inner circle? A partial explanation is doubtless to be found in Hitler's acute personal inclination to extreme secrecy which he translated into a general mode of rule, as laid down in his 'Basic Order' of January 1940, that information should only be available on a 'need-to-know' basis. Knowledge of extermination could provide a propaganda gift to enemies, and perhaps stir up unrest and internal difficulties in the occupied territories, particularly in western Europe. Not least, as regards public opinion in the Reich itself, the Nazi leadership believed that the German people were not ready for the gross inhumanity of the extermination of the Jews. Hitler had agreed with Rosenberg in mid-December 1941, directly following the declaration of war on the USA, that it would be inappropriate to speak of extermination in public. Late in 1942, Bormann was keen to quell rumours circulating about the 'Final Solution' in the east. Himmler would later, speaking to SS leaders, refer to it as 'a never to be written glorious page of our history'. Evidently, it was a secret to be carried to the grave.

In his public statements referring to his 1939 'prophecy', Hitler could now lay claim to his place in 'the glorious page of our history' while still detaching himself from the sordid and horrific realities of mass killing. Beyond that, a further incentive to secrecy was that Hitler wanted no bureaucratic and legal interference. He had experienced this in the 'euthanasia action', necessitating his unique written authorization, and the problems which subsequently arose from it. His tirades about the judicial system and bureaucracy in the spring of 1942 were a further indicator of his sensitivity towards such interference. To avoid any legalistic meddling, Himmler explicitly refused in the summer of 1942 to entertain attempts to define 'a Jew'.

IV

Manstein's difficulties in taking Sevastopol held up the start of 'Operation Blue' – the push to the Caucasus – until the end of June. But at this point, Hitler needed have no doubts that the war was going well. In the Atlantic, the U-boats had met with unprecedented success. In the first six months of 1942, they had sunk almost a third more shipping tonnage than during the whole of 1941, and far fewer U-boats had been lost in the process. And on the evening of 21 June came the stunning news that Rommel had taken Tobruk. Through brilliant tactical manoeuvring during the previous three weeks, Rommel had outwitted the ineffectively led and poorly equipped British 8th Army and was then able to inflict a serious defeat on the Allied cause by seizing the stronghold of Tobruk, on the Libyan coast, capturing 33,000 British and Allied soldiers (many of them South African) and a huge amount of booty. It was a spectacular German victory and a disaster for the British. The doorway to German dominance of Egypt was wide open. All at once there was a glimmering prospect in view of an enormous pincer of Rommel's troops pushing eastwards through Egypt and the Caucasus army sweeping down through the Middle East linking forces to wipe out the British presence in this crucial region. Hitler, overjoyed, immediately promoted Rommel to Field-Marshal. Italian hopes of German support for an invasion of Malta were now finally shelved until later in the year. Hitler backed instead Rommel's plans to advance to the Nile. Within days, German troops were in striking distance of Alexandria.

One dark cloud on an otherwise sunny horizon was, however, the damage being caused to towns in western Germany by British bombing raids. On 30 May, Hitler had said that he did not think much of the RAF's threats of heavy air-raids. Precautions, he claimed, had been taken. The Luftwaffe had so many squadrons stationed in the west that destruction from the air would be doubly repaid. That very night, the city centre of Cologne was devastated by the first 1,000-bomber raid. Hitler was enraged at the failure of the Luftwaffe to defend the Reich, blaming Göring personally for neglecting the construction of sufficient flak installations.

Despite the bombing of Cologne, the military situation put Hitler and his entourage in excellent mood in early June. On the first day of the month Hitler flew to Army Group South's headquarters at Poltava to discuss with Field-Marshal Bock the timing and tactics of the coming offensive. Apart from Manstein, all the commanders were present, as Hitler agreed to Bock's proposal to delay the start of 'Operation Blue' for some days in order to take full advantage of the victory at Kharkhov to destroy Soviet forces in adjacent areas. Hitler informed the commanders that the outcome of 'Blue' would be decisive for the war.

On 4 June, Hitler paid a surprise visit – it had been arranged only the previous day – to Finland. Officially, the visit was to mark the seventy-fifth birthday of the Finnish military hero, Marshal Baron Carl Gustaf von Mannerheim, supreme commander of the Finnish armed forces. The aim was to bolster Finnish solidarity with Germany through underlining for Mannerheim – a veteran of struggles with the Red Army – the immensity of the threat of Bolshevism. The Finns would at the same time be warned about any possible considerations of leaving German 'protection' and putting out feelers to the Soviet Union. In addition, the visit would head off any possible ties of Finland with the western Allies.

The meeting had no concrete results. That was not its aim. For now, Hitler had reassured himself that he had the Finns' continued support. He was well satisfied with the visit. For their part, the Finns maintained their superficially good relations with Germany, while keeping a watchful eye on events. The course of the war over the next six months conveyed its own clear message to them to begin looking for alternative loyalties.

While Hitler was *en route* to Finland, news came through from Prague that Reinhard Heydrich had died of the wounds he had suffered in the attack on 27 May. Back in his headquarters, Hitler put it down to 'stupidity or pure dimwittedness' that 'such an irreplaceable man as Heydrich should expose himself to the danger' of assassins, by driving without adequate bodyguard in an open-top car, and insisted that Nazi leaders comply with proper security precautions. Hitler was in reflective mood at the state funeral in Berlin on 9 June. So soon after the loss of Todt, it seemed to him – and, in fact, was not far from the truth – as if the party and state leadership only assembled for state funerals. He spent time in the evening reminiscing with Goebbels about the early days of the party. 'The Führer is very happy in these memories,' remarked Goebbels. 'He lives from the past, which seems to him like a lost paradise.'

V

'Operation Blue', the great summer offensive in the south, began on 28 June. The offensive, carried out by five armies in two groups against the weakest part of the Soviet front, between Kursk in the north and Taganrog on the Sea of Azov in the south, was able – as Barbarossa had done the previous year – to use the element of surprise to make impressive early gains. Meanwhile, on 1 July, finally, the fall of Sevastopol brought immediate promotion to Field-Marshal for Manstein.

After the initial break through the Russian lines, the rapid advance on Voronezh ended in the capture of the city on 6 July. This brought, however, the first confrontation of the new campaign between Hitler and his generals. Voronezh itself was an unimportant target. But a Soviet counter-attack had tied down two armoured divisions in the city for two days. This slowed the south-eastern advance along the Don and allowed enemy forces to escape. Hitler was enraged that Bock had ignored his instructions that the advance of the panzer divisions was to proceed without any hold-ups to the Volga in order to allow maximum destruction of the Soviet forces. In fact, when he had flown to Bock's headquarters at Poltava on 3 July, Hitler had been far less dogmatic and clear in face-to-face discussion with the field-marshal than he was in the map-room of the Wolf's Lair. But that did not save Bock. Hitler said he was not going to have his plans spoiled by field-marshals as they had been in autumn 1941. Bock was dismissed and replaced by Colonel-General Freiherr Maximilian von Weichs.

To be closer to the southern front, Hitler moved his headquarters on 16 July to a new location, given the name 'Werwolf', near Vinnitsa in the Ukraine. Sixteen planes, their engines already whirring, waited on the runway at the Wolf's Lair that day for Hitler and his entourage to take them on a three-hour flight to their new surrounds. After a car-ride along rutted roads, they finally arrived at the damp, mosquito-infested huts that were to be their homes for the next three and a half months. Even the Wolf's Lair began to seem idyllic. Halder was pleased enough with the layout of the new headquarters. Hitler's secretaries were less happy with their cramped quarters. As at Rastenburg, they had little to do and were bored. For Hitler, the daily routine was unchanged from that in the Wolf's Lair. At meals – his own often consisted of no more than a plate of vegetables with apples to follow – he could still appear open, relaxed, engaged. As always, he monopolized dinner-table topics of conversation on a wide variety of topics that touched on his interests or obsessions. These included the evils of smoking, the construction of a motorway-system throughout the eastern territories, the deficiencies of the legal system, the achievements of Stalin as a latter-day Ghengis Khan, keeping the standard of living low among the subjugated peoples, the need to remove the last Jews from German cities, and the promotion of private initiative rather than a state-controlled economy.

Away from the supper soliloquies, however, tension mounted once more between Hitler and his military leaders. The military advance continued to make ground. But the numbers of Soviet prisoners captured steadily diminished. This was endlessly discussed at FHQ. Hitler's military advisers were worried. They took it that the Soviets were pulling back their forces in preparation for a big counter-offensive, probably on the Volga, in the Stalingrad region. Halder had warned as early as 12 July of concern at the front that the enemy, recognizing German envelopment tactics, was avoiding direct fight and withdrawing to the south. Hitler's view was, however, that the Red Army was close to the end of its tether. He pressed all the more for a speedy advance.

His impulsive, though sometimes unclear or ambiguous, command-style caused constant difficulties for the operational planners. But the essential problem was more far-reaching. Hitler felt compelled by two imperatives: time, and material resources. The offensive had to be completed before the might of Allied resources came fully into play. And possession of the Caucasian oil-fields would, in his view, both be decisive in bringing the war in the east to a successful conclusion, and provide the necessary platform to continue a lengthy war against the Anglo-Saxon powers. If this oil were not gained, Hitler had said, the war would be lost for Germany within three months. Following his own logic, he had, therefore, no choice but to stake everything on the ambitious strike to the Caucasus in a victorious summer offensive. Even if some sceptical voices could be heard, Halder and the professionals in Army High Command had favoured the offensive. But the gap, already opened up the previous summer, between them and the Dictator was rapidly widening. What Hitler saw as the negativity, pessimism, and timidity of Army High Command's traditional approaches drove him into paroxysms of rage. Army planners for their part had cold feet about what increasingly seemed to them a reckless gamble carried out by dilettante methods, more and more likely to end in disaster. But they could not now pull out of the strategy which they had been party to implementing. The German war-effort had set in train its own self-destructive dynamic.

The risk of military disaster was seriously magnified by Hitler's Directive No.45 of 23 July 1942. Thereafter, a calamity was waiting to happen. Unlike the April directive, in which Halder's hand had been visible, this directive rested squarely on a decision by Hitler, which the General Staff had sought to prevent. The directive for the continuation of 'Blue', now renamed 'Operation Braunschweig', began with a worryingly unrealistic claim: 'In a campaign of little more than three weeks, the broad goals set for the southern flank of the eastern front have been essentially achieved. Only weak enemy forces of the Timoshenko armies have succeeded in escaping envelopment and reaching the southern bank of the Don. We have to reckon with their reinforcement from the Caucasus area.'

Earlier in the month, Hitler had divided Army Group South into a northern sector (Army Group B, originally under Field-Marshal von Bock, then, after his sacking, under Colonel-General Freiherr von Weichs) and a southern sector (Army Group A, under Field-Marshal Wilhelm List). The original intention, under his Directive No.41 of 5 April, had been to advance on the Caucasus *following* the encirclement and destruction of Soviet forces in the vicinity of Stalingrad. This was now altered to allow attacks on the Caucasus and Stalingrad (including the taking of the city itself) to proceed *simultaneously*. List's stronger Army Group A was left to destroy enemy forces in the Rostov area, then conquer the whole of the Caucasus region alone. This was to include the eastern coast of the Black Sea, crossing the Kuban and occupying the heights around the oil-fields of Maykop, controlling the almost impenetrable Caucasian mountain passes, and driving south-eastwards to take the oil-rich region around Grozny, then Baku, far to the south on the Caspian Sea. The attack on Stalingrad was left to the weaker Army Group B, which was expected thereafter to press on along the lower Volga to Astrakhan on the Caspian. The strategy was sheer lunacy.

Only the most incautiously optimistic assessment of the weakness of the Soviet forces could have justified the scale of the risk involved. But Hitler took precisely such a view of enemy strength. Moreover, he was as always temperamentally predisposed to a risk-all strategy, with alternatives dismissed out of hand and boats burned to leave no fall-back position. As always, his self-justification could be bolstered by the dogmatic view that there was no alternative. Halder, aware of more realistic appraisals of Soviet strength, and the build-up of forces in the Stalingrad area, but unable to exert any influence upon Hitler, was by now both seriously concerned and frustrated at his own impotence. On 23 July, the day that Hitler issued his Directive No.45, Halder had written in his diary: 'This chronic tendency to underrate enemy capabilities is gradually assuming grotesque proportions and develops into a positive danger. The situation is getting more and more intolerable. There is no room for any serious work. This so-called leadership is characterized by a pathological reacting to the impressions of the moment and a total lack of any understanding of the command machinery and its possibilities.' On 15 August, Halder's notes for his situation report began: 'Overall picture: have we extended the risk too far?' The question was well warranted. But the insight had come rather late in the day.

By mid-August, Army Group A had swept some 350 miles to the south, over the north Caucasian plain. It was now far separated from Army Group B, with a lengthy exposed flank, and formidable logistical problems of ensuring supplies. Its advance slowed markedly in the wooded foothills of the northern Caucasus. Maykop was taken, but the oil-refineries were found in ruins, systematically and expertly destroyed by the retreating Soviet forces. The impetus had been lost. Hitler showed little sense of realism when he spoke privately to Goebbels on 19 August. Operations in the Caucasus, he said, were going extremely well. He wanted to take possession of the oil-wells of Maykop, Grozny, and Baku during the summer, securing Germany's oil supplies and destroying those of the Soviet Union. Once the Soviet border had been reached, the breakthrough into the Near East would follow, occupying Asia Minor and overrunning Iraq, Iran, and Palestine, to cut off Britain's oil supplies. Within two or three days, he wanted to commence the big assault on Stalingrad. He intended to destroy the city completely, leaving no stone on top of another. It was both psychologically and militarily necessary. The forces deployed were reckoned to be sufficient to capture the city within eight days.

The last significant successes of Army Group B, meanwhile, had been in encircling and destroying two Russian armies south-west of Kalac, on the Don due west of Stalingrad, on 8 August. Advancing in punishing heat and hindered through chronic fuel shortage, on 23 August, the 6th Army, under General Friedrich Paulus, succeeded in reaching the Volga, north of Stalingrad. Amid heavy Soviet defences, the advance ground rapidly to a halt. The summer offensive had, as it turned out, run its course in less than two months. As early as 26 August Halder was noting: 'Near Stalingrad, serious tension on account of superior counter-attacks of the enemy. Our divisions are no longer very strong. The command is heavily under nervous strain.' The 6th Army was, however, able to consolidate its position. Over the next weeks, it even gained the advantage. But the nightmare of Stalingrad was only just beginning.

While the southern part of the massively extended front was running out of steam, with the 6th Army now bogged down at Stalingrad and List's Army Group A stalled in the Caucasus, Kluge's Army Group Centre had encountered a damaging setback, suffering horrendous casualties in an ill-fated attempt ordered by Hitler to wipe out Russian forces at Sukhinichi, 150 miles west of Moscow, from where it was hoped to establish the basis for a renewed drive on the capital. Kluge, on a visit to 'Werwolf' on 7 August, had asked Hitler to remove two armoured divisions from the offensive at Sukhinichi to deploy them against a threatening Soviet counter-attack in the Rzhev area. Hitler had refused, insisting that they be retained for the Sukhinichi offensive. Kluge had marched out saying 'You, my Führer, therefore assume responsibility for this.'

And in the north, by the end of August expectations of launching an assault and finally taking the hunger-torn city of Leningrad had been massively dented through the Soviet counter-offensive south of Lake Ladoga. Manstein's 11th Army had been brought up from the southern front to lead the planned final assault on Leningrad in September in the 'Northern Lights' offensive. Instead it found itself engaged in fending off the Soviet strike. There was no possibility of capturing Leningrad and razing it to the ground. The last chance of that had gone. Hitler's outward show of confidence in victory could not altogether conceal his mounting inner anxiety. His temper was on a short fuse. Outbursts of rage became more common. He cast around as always for scapegoats for the rapidly deteriorating military situation in the east. It did not take him long to find them.

Relations with Halder had already reached rock-bottom. On 24 August, the worsening situation at Rzhev had prompted the Chief of the General Staff to urge Hitler to allow a retreat of the 9th Army to a more defensible shorter line. In front of all those assembled at the midday conference, Hitler rounded on Halder. 'You always come here with the same proposal, that of withdrawal,' he raged. 'I demand from the leadership the same toughness as from the front-soldiers.' Halder, deeply insulted, shouted back: 'I have the toughness, my Führer. But out there brave musketeers and lieutenants are falling in thousands and thousands as useless sacrifice in a hopeless situation simply because their commanders are not allowed to make the only reasonable decision and have their hands tied behind their backs.' Hitler stared at Halder. 'What can you, who sat in the same chair in the First World War, too, tell me about the troops, Herr Halder, you, who don't even wear the black insignia of the wounded?' Appalled, and embarrassed, the onlookers dispersed. Hitler tried to smooth Halder's ruffled feathers that evening. But it was plain to all who witnessed the scene that the Chief of Staff's days were numbered.

Even Hitler's military right-hand, the loyal and devoted Jodl, was now made to feel the full impact of his wrath. On 5 September List had asked for Jodl to be sent to Army Group A headquarters at Stalino, north of the Sea of Azov, to discuss the further deployment of the 39th Mountain Corps. The visit took place two days later. From Hitler's point of view, the purpose was to urge List to accelerate the advance on the largely stalled Caucasus front. Hitler's patience at the lack of progress had been extremely thin for some time. But far from bringing back positive news, Jodl returned that evening with a devastating account of conditions. It was no longer possible to force the Soviets back over the mountain passes. The most that could be achieved, with greater mobility and maximum concentration of forces, was a last attempt to reach Grozny and the Caspian Sea. Hitler grew more angry with every sentence. He lashed out at the 'lack of initiative' of the army leadership; and now for the first time attacked Jodl, the messenger bearing bad news. It was the worst crisis in relations between Hitler and his military leaders since the previous August. Hitler was in a towering rage. But Jodl stood his ground. It turned into a shouting-match. Jodl fully backed List's assessment of the position. Hitler exploded. He accused Jodl of betraying his orders, being talked round by List, and taking sides with the Army Group. He had not sent him to the Caucasus, he said, to have him bring back doubts among the troops. Jodl retorted that List was faithfully adhering to the orders Hitler himself had given. Beside himself with rage, Hitler said his words were being twisted. Things would have to be different. He would have to ensure that he could not be deliberately misinterpreted in future. Like a prima donna in a pique, Hitler stormed out, refusing to shake hands (as he invariably had done at the end of their meetings) with Jodl and Keitel. Evidently depressed as well as angry, he said to his Wehrmacht adjutant Schmundt that night, 'I'll be glad when I can take off this detestable uniform and trample on it.' He saw no end to the war in Russia since none of the aims of summer 1942 had been realized. The anxiety about the forthcoming winter was dreadful, he said. 'But on the other hand,' noted Army Adjutant Engel, 'he will retreat nowhere.'

Hitler now shut himself up in his darkened hut during the days. He refused to appear for the communal meals. The military briefings, with as few present as possible, took place in a glacial atmosphere in his own hut, not in the headquarters of the Wehrmacht staff. And he refused to shake hands with anyone. Within forty-eight hours, a group of shorthand typists arrived at FHQ. Hitler had insisted upon a record of all military briefings being taken so that he could not again be misinterpreted.

The day after the confrontation with Jodl, Hitler dismissed List. Demonstrating his distrust of his generals, he himself for the time being took over the command of Army Group A. He was now commander of the armed forces, of one branch of those armed forces, and of one group of that branch. At the same time, Keitel was deputed to tell Halder that he would soon be relieved of his post. Keitel himself and Jodl were also rumoured to be slated for dismissal. Jodl admitted privately that he had been at fault in trying to point out to a dictator where he had gone wrong. This, Jodl said, could only shake his self-confidence – the basis of his personality and actions. Jodl added that whoever his own replacement might be, he could not be more of a staunch National Socialist than he himself was.

In the event, the worsening conditions at Stalingrad and in the Mediterranean prevented the intended replacement of Jodl by Paulus and Keitel by Kesselring. But there was no saving Halder. Hitler complained bitterly to Below that Halder had no comprehension of the difficulties at the front and was devoid of ideas for solutions. He coldly viewed the situation only from maps and had 'completely wrong notions' about the way things were going. Hitler pondered Schmundt's advice to replace Halder by Major-General Kurt Zeitzler, a very different type of character – a small, bald-headed, ambitious, dynamic forty-seven-year-old, firm believer in the Führer, who had been put in by Hitler in April to shake up the army in the west and, as Rundstedt's chief of staff, to build up coastal defences. Göring, too, encouraged Hitler to get rid of Halder.

That point was reached on 24 September. A surprised Zeitzler had by then been summoned to FHQ and told by Hitler of his promotion to full General of the Infantry and of his new responsibilities. After what was to be his last military briefing, Halder was, without ceremony, relieved of his post. His nerves, Hitler told him, were gone, and his own nerves also strained. It was necessary for Halder to go, and for the General Staff to be educated to believe fanatically in 'the idea'. Hitler, Halder noted in his final diary entry, was determined to enforce his will, also in the army.

The traditional General Staff, for long such a powerful force, its Chief now discarded like a spent cartridge, had arrived at its symbolic final point of capitulation to the forces to which it had wedded itself in 1933. Zeitzler began the new regime by demanding from the members of the General Staff belief in the Führer. He himself would soon realize that this alone would not be enough.

VI

The battle for Stalingrad was by now looming. Both sides were aware how critical it would be. The German leadership remained optimistic.

Hitler's plans for the massively over-populated city on the Volga were similar to the annihilatory intentions he had held about Leningrad and Moscow. 'The Führer orders that on entry into the city the entire male population should be done away with,' the Wehrmacht High Command recorded, 'since Stalingrad, with its thoroughly Communist population of a million, is especially dangerous.' Halder noted simply, without additional comment: 'Stalingrad: male population to be destroyed, female to be deported.'

When he visited FHQ on 11 September, Colonel-General von Weichs, Commander of Army Group B, had told Hitler he was confident that the attack on the inner city of Stalingrad could begin almost immediately and be completed within ten days. Indeed, the early signs were that the fall of the city would not be long delayed. But by the second half of September, the contest for Stalingrad had already turned into a battle of scarcely imaginable intensity and ferocity. The fighting was taking place often at point-blank range, street by street, house by house. German and Soviet troops were almost literally at each other's throats. The final taking of what had rapidly become little more than a shell of smoking ruins, it was coming to be realized, could take weeks, even months.

Elsewhere, too, the news was less than encouraging. Rommel's offensive at El Alamein in the direction of the Suez Canal had to be broken off already on 2 September, only three days after it had begun. Rommel remained confident, both publicly and in private, over the next weeks, though he reported on the serious problems with shortages of weapons and equipment when he saw Hitler on 1 October to receive his Field-Marshal's baton. In reality, however, the withdrawal of 2 September would turn out to be the beginning of the end for the Axis in North Africa. Its morale revitalized under a new commander, General Bernard Montgomery, and its lost, out-of-date armour replaced by new Sherman tanks, the 8th Army would by autumn prove more than a match for Rommel's limited forces.

In the Reich itself, the British nightly raids had intensified. Munich,

Bremen, Düsseldorf, and Duisburg were among the cities that now suffered serious destruction. Hitler said he was glad his own apartment in Munich had been badly damaged; he would not have liked it spared – obviously it would not have looked good – if the rest of the city had been attacked. He thought the raid might have a salutary effect in waking up the population of Munich to the realities of the war. Air-raids had another good side, he had told Goebbels in mid-August: the enemy had 'taken work from us' in destroying buildings that would in any case have had to be torn down to allow the improved post-war town planning.

At the end of September, Hitler flew back to Berlin. He had promised Goebbels to use the opening of the Winter Aid campaign to address the nation during the second half of September. Once more, it was important to sustain morale at a vital time.

His Sportpalast speech on 30 September combined a glorification of German military achievements with a sarcastic, mocking attack on Churchill and Roosevelt. This was nothing new, though the hand-picked Sportpalast audience lapped it up. He went on to repeat his prophecy about the Jews – by now a regular weapon in his rhetorical armoury – in the most menacing phrases he had so far used: 'The Jews used to laugh, in Germany too, about my prophecies. I don't know if they're still laughing today, or whether the laughter has already gone out of them. But I, too, can now only offer the assurance: the laughter will go out of them everywhere. And I will also be right in my prophecies.' But the speech was most notable of all for his assurances about the battle for Stalingrad. The metropolis on the Volga, bearing the Soviet leader's name, was being stormed, he declared, and would be taken. 'You can be sure,' he added, 'that nobody will get us away from this place again!'

His public display of optimism was unbounded, even in a more con-fined forum, when he addressed the Reichs- and Gauleiter for almost three hours the following afternoon. 'The capture of Stalingrad,' recorded Goebbels, 'is for him an established fact,' even if it could still take a little time. Surveying the position of his enemies, Hitler came to the remarkable conclusion that 'the war was practically lost for the opposing side, no matter how long it was in a position to carry it on'.

Hitler's absurd optimism at the beginning of October scarcely accorded with the growing anxieties of his military advisers about the situation in Stalingrad. Winter was now no longer far off. Paulus, Weichs, Jodl, and Zeitzler all favoured pulling back from a target which, largely in ruins, had by now lost all significance as a communications and armaments centre, and taking up more secure winter positions. The only alternative was to pour in heavy reinforcements. Hitler's view was that this time winter had been so well prepared for that the soldiers in the east would be living better than most of them had done in peacetime.

On 6 October, after Paulus had reported a temporary halt to the attack because his troops were exhausted, Hitler ordered the 'complete capture' of Stalingrad as the key objective of Army Group B. There might indeed have been something to be said for choosing the protection of even a ruined city to the open, exposed steppes over the winter had the supplies situation been as favourable as Hitler evidently imagined it to be, had the supply lines been secure, and had the threat of a Soviet counter-offensive been less large. However, only insufficient winter provision for the 6th Army had been made. Supply-lines were now over-stretched on an enormously long front, and far from secure on the northern flank. And intelligence was coming in of big concentrations of Soviet troops which might pose real danger to the position of the 6th Army. Withdrawal was the sensible option.

Hitler would not hear of it. At the beginning of October, Zeitzler and Jodl heard him for the first time, in outrightly rejecting their advice about the danger of being bogged down in house-to-house fighting with heavy losses, stress that the capture of the city was necessary not just for operational, but for 'psychological' reasons: to show the world the continued strength of German arms, and to boost the morale of the Axis allies. More than ever contemptuous of generals and military advisers who lacked the necessary strength of will, he refused to countenance any suggestion of withdrawal from Stalingrad. Fear of loss of face had taken over from military reasoning. Hitler's all too public statements in the Sportpalast and then to his Gauleiter had meant that taking Stalingrad had become a matter of prestige. And, though he claimed the fact that the city bore Stalin's name was of no significance, retreat from precisely this city would clearly compound the loss of prestige.

In the meantime, Hitler was starting to acknowledge mounting concern among his military advisers about the build-up of Soviet forces on the northern banks of the Don, the weakest section of the front, where the Wehrmacht was dependent on the resolution of its allied armies – the Romanians, Hungarians, and Italians.

The situation in North Africa was by this time also critical.

Montgomery's 8th Army had begun its big offensive at El Alamein on 23 October. Rommel had quickly been sent back from sick-leave to hold together the defence of the Axis forces and prevent a breakthrough. Hitler's initial confidence that Rommel would hold his ground had rapidly evaporated. Lacking fuel and munitions, and facing a numerically far superior enemy, Rommel was unable to prevent Montgomery's tanks penetrating the German front in the renewed massive onslaught that had begun on 2 November. The following day, Hitler sent a telegram in response to Rommel's depressing account of the position and prospects of his troops. 'In the situation in which you find yourself,' ran his message to Rommel, 'there can be no other thought than to stick it out, not to yield a step, and to throw every weapon and available fighter into the battle.' Everything would be done to send reinforcements. 'It would not be the first time in history that the stronger will triumphed over stronger enemy battalions. But you can show your troops no other way than victory or death.' Rommel had not waited for Hitler's reply. Anticipating what it would be, he had ordered a retreat hours before it arrived. Generals had been peremptorily dismissed for such insubordination during the winter crisis at the beginning of the year. Rommel's standing with the German people – only weeks earlier, he had been fêted as a military hero – was all that now saved him from the same ignominy.

By 7 November, when Hitler travelled to Munich to give his traditional address in the Löwenbräukeller to the marchers in the 1923 Putsch, the news from the Mediterranean had dramatically worsened. *En route* from Berlin to Munich, his special train was halted at a small station in the Thuringian Forest for him to receive a message from the Foreign Office: the Allied armada assembled at Gibraltar, which had for days given rise to speculation about a probable landing in Libya, was disembarking in Algiers and Oran. It would bring the first commitment of American ground-troops to the war in Europe.

Hitler immediately gave orders for the defence of Tunis. But the landing had caught him and his military advisers off-guard. And Oran was out of reach of German bombers, which gave rise to a new torrent of rage at the incompetence of the Luftwaffe's lack of planning. Further down the track, at Bamberg, Ribbentrop joined the train. He pleaded with Hitler to let him put out peace feelers to Stalin via the Soviet Embassy in Stockholm with an offer of far-reaching concessions in the east. Hitler brusquely dismissed the suggestion: a moment of weakness was not the time for negotiations with an enemy. In his speech to the party's 'Old Guard' on the evening of 8 November, Hitler then publicly ruled out any prospect of a negotiated peace. With reference to his earlier 'peace offers', he declared: 'From now on there will be no more offer of peace.'

It was hardly the atmosphere which Hitler would have chosen for a big speech. Not only had he nothing positive to report; the speech had to take place in the midst of a military crisis. But if the party's 'Old Fighters' expected any enlightenment from Hitler on the situation, they were to be disappointed. The usual verbal assaults on Allied leaders and blustering parallels with the internal situation before the 'seizure of power' were all he had to offer. Refusal to compromise, the will to fight, determination to overcome the enemy, the lack of any alternative than complete success, and the certainty of final victory in a war for the very existence of the German people formed the basis of the message. Unlike the Kaiser, who had capitulated in the First World War at 'quarter to twelve', he ended, so he stated, 'in principle always at five past twelve'. And for the fourth and last time in the year, Hitler invoked his 'prophecy' about the Jews.

The speech was not one of Hitler's best. He had been a compelling speaker when he had been able to twist reality in plausible fashion for his audience. But now, he was ignoring unpalatable facts, or turning them on their head. The gap between rhetoric and reality had become too wide. To most Germans, as SD reports were making apparent, Hitler's speeches could no longer have more than a superficial impact. The news of the Allied landing in North Africa cast a deep pall of gloom about mighty forces stacked against Germany in a war whose end seemed even farther away than ever. This came on top of growing unease about Stalingrad. Criticism of the German leadership for embroiling people in such a war was now more commonplace (if necessarily for the most part carefully couched), and often implicitly included Hitler – no longer detached, as he used to be, from the negative side of the regime.

But Hitler's key audience had, primarily, been not the millions glued to their radio-sets, but his oldest party loyalists inside the hall. It was essential to reinforce this backbone of Hitler's personal power, and of the will to hold together the home front. Here, among this audience, Hitler could still tap much of the enthusiasm, commitment, and fanaticism of old. He knew the chords to play. The music was a familiar tune.

But everyone there must have recognized – and in some measure shared – a sense of self-deception in the lyrics.

Hitler's real concern that evening was the reaction of the French to the events in North Africa. He decided upon a meeting in Munich with Laval and Mussolini. By then, news was coming in that the initial resistance was crumbling in French North Africa. The landing had been secured.

By the time Ciano arrived in Munich – Mussolini felt unwell and declined to go – Hitler had heard that General Henri Giraud had put himself at the service of the Allies and been smuggled out of France and transported to North Africa. Commander of the French 7th Army before the debacle of 1940 and imprisoned since that time, Giraud had escaped captivity and fled to unoccupied France earlier in the year. The danger was that he would now provide a figurehead for French resistance in North Africa and a focus of support for the Allies. Suspicion, which soon proved justified, was also mounting by the hour that Admiral Jean François Darlan, too, head of the French armed forces, was preparing to change sides. The Americans had won Darlan over just before the 'Torch' landings with an offer to recognize him as head of the French government. Inevitable conflict with the British, who favoured General Charles de Gaulle (the leader of 'Free France', exiled in London), was to be obviated when a young French monarchist assassinated Darlan just before Christmas.

Hitler had stressed the need to be ready to occupy southern France in his talks with Mussolini at the end of April. When Ciano met Hitler on the evening of 9 November, he had made up his mind. Laval's input would be irrelevant. Hitler would not 'modify his already definite point of view: the total occupation of France, landing in Corsica, a bridgehead in Tunisia'. When he eventually arrived, Laval was treated with scarcely more than contempt. Hitler demanded landing points in Tunisia. Laval tried to wring concessions from Italy. Hitler refused to waste time on such deliberations.

While Laval was in the next room having a smoke, Hitler gave the order to occupy the remainder of France next day – 11 November, and the anniversary of the Armistice of 1918. Laval was to be informed next morning. In a letter to Marshal Pétain and a proclamation to the French people, Hitler justified the occupation through the necessity to defend the coast of southern France and Corsica against Allied invasion from the new base in North Africa. That morning, German troops occupied southern France without military resistance, in accordance with the plans for 'Operation Anton' which had been laid down in May.

At the Berghof for a few days, Hitler's mask of ebullience slipped a little. Below found him deeply worried about the Anglo-American actions. He was also concerned about supplies difficulties in the Mediterranean, which British submarines had intensified. His trust in the Italians had disappeared. He was sure that they were leaking intelligence about the movement of German supply ships to the British. The deficiencies of the Luftwaffe also preoccupied him. As regards the eastern front, he was hoping for 'no new surprises', but feared a large-scale Soviet offensive was imminent.

VII

On 19 November, Zeitzler told Hitler that the Soviet offensive had begun. Immediately, the Soviet forces to the north-west and west of Stalingrad broke through the weak part of the front held by the Romanian 3rd Army. General Ferdinand Heim's 48th Panzer Corps was sent in, but failed to heal the breach. Furious, Hitler dismissed Heim. He later ordered him to be sentenced to death – a sentence not carried out only through the intervention of Schmundt. The next day the Red Army's 'Stalingrad Front' broke through the divisions of the Romanian 4th Army south of the city and met up on 22 November with the Soviet forces that had penetrated from north and west. With that, the 220,000 men of the 6th Army were completely encircled.

Hitler had decided to return to the Wolf's Lair that evening. His train journey back from Berchtesgaden to East Prussia took over twenty hours, owing to repeated lengthy stops to telephone Zeitzler. The new Chief of the General Staff insisted on permission being granted to the 6th Army to fight their way out of Stalingrad. Hitler did not give an inch. Already on 21 November he had sent an order to Paulus: '6th Army to hold, despite danger of temporary encirclement.' On the evening of 22 November, he ordered: 'The army is temporarily encircled by Russian forces. I know the 6th Army and its Commander-in-Chief and know that it will conduct itself bravely in this difficult situation. The 6th Army must know that I am doing everything to help it and to relieve it.' He thought the position could be remedied. Relief could be organized to enable a break-out. But this could not be done overnight. A plan was hastily devised to deploy Colonel-General Hermann Hoth's 4th Panzer Army, south-west of Stalingrad, to prepare an attack to relieve the 6th Army. But it would take about ten days before it could be attempted. In the meantime, Paulus had to hold out, while the troops were supplied by air-lift. It was a major, and highly risky operation. But Göring assured Hitler that it could be done. The Luftwaffe Chief of Staff Hans Jeschonnek did not contradict him. Zeitzler, however, vehemently disagreed. And from within the Luftwaffe itself, Colonel-General Wolfram Freiherr von Richthofen, who normally had Hitler's ear, raised the gravest doubts both on grounds of the weather (with temperatures already plummeting, icy mists, and freezing rain icing up the wings of the planes) and of the numbers of available aircraft. Hitler chose to believe Göring.

Hitler's decision to air-lift supplies to the 6th Army until relief arrived was taken on 23 November. By then he had heard from Paulus that stores of food and equipment were perilously low and certainly insufficient for a defence of the position. Paulus sought permission to attempt to break out. Weichs, Commander-in-Chief of Army Group B, and Chief of the General Staff Zeitzler also fully backed this as the only realistic option. Zeitzler, evidently acting on the basis of a remarkable misunderstanding, actually informed Weichs at 2 a.m. on 24 November that he had 'persuaded the Führer that a break-out was the only possibility of saving the army'. Within four hours the General Staff had to transmit exactly the opposite decision by Hitler: the 6th Army had to stand fast and would be supplied from the air until relief could arrive. The fate of almost quarter of a million men was sealed with this order.

Hitler was not totally isolated in military support for his decision. Field-Marshal von Manstein had arrived that morning, 24 November, at Army Group B headquarters to take command, as ordered by Hitler three days earlier, of a new Army Group Don (which included the trapped 6th Army). The main objective was to shore up the weakened front south and west of Stalingrad, to secure the lines to Army Group A in the Caucasus. He also took command of General Hoth's attempt to relieve the 6th Army. But in contrast to Paulus, Weichs, and Zeitzler, Manstein did not approve an attempt to break out before reinforcements arrived, and took an optimistic view of the chances of an air-lift.

Manstein was one of Hitler's most trusted generals. His assessment can only have strengthened Hitler's own judgement.

By mid-December, Manstein had changed his view diametrically. Richthofen had persuaded him that, in the atrocious weather conditions, an adequate air-lift was impossible. Even if the weather relented, air supplies could not be sustained for any length of time. Manstein now pressed on numerous occasions for a decision to allow the 6th Army to break out. But by then the chances of a break-out had grossly diminished; in fact, once Hoth's relief attempt was held up in heavy fighting some fifty kilometres from Stalingrad and some days later finally forced back, they rapidly became non-existent. On 19 December, Hitler once more rejected all pleas to consider a break-out. Military information in any case now indicated that the 6th Army, greatly weakened and surrounded by mighty Soviet forces, would be able to advance a maximum of thirty kilometres to the south-west – not far enough to meet up with Hoth's relief panzer army. On 21 December, Manstein asked Zeitzler for a final decision on whether the 6th Army should attempt to break out as long as it could still link with the 57th Panzer Corps, or whether the Commander-in-Chief of the Luftwaffe could guarantee air-supplies over a lengthy period of time. Zeitzler cabled back that Göring was confident that the Luftwaffe could supply the 6th Army, though Jeschonnek was by now of a different opinion. Hitler allowed an inquiry of the 6th Army Command about the distance it could expect to advance towards the south if the other fronts could be held. The reply came that there was fuel for twenty kilometres, and that it would be unable to hold position for long. Hoth's army was still fifty-four kilometres away. Still no decision was taken. 'It's as if the Führer is no longer capable [of taking one],' noted the OKW's war-diarist Helmuth Greiner.

6th Army Command itself described the tactic of a mass break-out without relief from the outside – 'Operation Thunderclap' – as 'a catastrophe-solution' ('Katastrophenlösung'). That evening, Hitler dismissed the idea: Paulus only had fuel for a short distance; there was no possibility of breaking out. Two days later, on 23 December, Manstein had to remove units from Hoth's 4th Panzer Army to hold the crumbling left flank of his Army Group. With that, Hoth had to pull back his weakened forces. The attempt to break the siege of Stalingrad had failed. The 6th Army was doomed.

Paulus still sought permission to break out. But by Christmas Eve,

Manstein had given up trying to persuade Hitler to give approval to what by this time could only be seen as a move of sheer desperation, without hope of success. The main priority was now to hold the left flank to prevent an even worse catastrophe. This was essential to enable the retreat of Army Group A from the Caucasus. Zeitzler had put the urgency of this retreat to Hitler on the evening of 27 December. Hitler had reluctantly agreed, then later changed his mind. It was too late. Zeitzler had telephoned through Hitler's initial approval. The retreat from the Caucasus was under way. Stalingrad had become a lesser priority.

Preoccupied though he was with the eastern front, and in particular with the now inevitable catastrophe in Stalingrad, Hitler could not afford to neglect what was happening in North Africa. And he was increasingly worried about the resolve of his Italian allies.

Montgomery had forced Rommel's Afrika Corps into headlong retreat, and would drive the German and Italian army out of Libya altogether during January 1943. Encouraged by Göring, Hitler was now convinced that Rommel had lost his nerve. But at least the 50,000 German and 18,000 Italian troops rushed to Tunis in November and December had seriously held up the Allies, preventing their rapid domination of North Africa and ruling out an early assault on the European continent itself. Even so, Hitler knew the Italians were wobbling. Göring's visit to Rome at the end of November had confirmed that. Their commitment to the war was by now in serious doubt. And when Ciano and Marshal Count Ugo Cavalero, the head of the Italian armed forces, arrived at the Wolf's Lair on 18 December for three days of talks, it was in the immediate wake of the catastrophic collapse of the Italian 8th Army, overwhelmed during the previous two days by the Soviet offensive on the middle stretches of the Don. When Ciano put Mussolini's case for Germany coming to terms with the Soviet Union in order to put maximum effort into defence against the western powers, Hitler was dismissive. Were he to do that, he replied, he would be forced within a short time to fight a reinvigorated Soviet Union once more. The Italian guests were non-committal towards Hitler's exhortations to override all civilian considerations in favour of supplies for North Africa.

For the German people, quite especially for the many German families with loved ones in the 6th Army, Christmas 1942 was a depressing festival. The triumphalist propaganda of September and October, suggesting that victory at Stalingrad was just around the corner, had given way in the weeks following the Soviet counter-offensive to little more than ominous silence. Rumours of the encirclement of the 6th Army – passed on through despairing letters from the soldiers entrapped there – swiftly spread. It soon became evident that the rumours were no less than the truth.

A series of letters from senior officers in the 6th Army, describing their plight in graphic detail, were received by Hitler's Luftwaffe Adjutant, Nicolaus von Below. He showed them to Hitler, reading out key passages. Hitler listened without comment, except once remarking inscrutably that 'the fate of the 6th Army left for all of us a deep duty in the fight for the freedom of the our people'. What he really thought, no one knew.

After Paulus had rejected a call to surrender, the final Soviet attack to destroy the 6th Army began on 10 January. An emissary to the Wolf's Lair, seeking permission for Paulus to have freedom of action to bring an end to the carnage, went unheeded by Hitler. On 15 January, he commissioned Field-Marshal Erhard Milch, the Luftwaffe's armaments supremo and mastermind of all its transportation organization, with flying 300 tons of supplies a day to the besieged army. It was pure fantasy – though partly based on the inaccurate information that Zeitzler complained about on more than one occasion. Snow and ice on the runways in sub-arctic temperatures often prevented take-offs and landings. In any case, on 22 January the last airstrip in the vicinity of Stalingrad was lost. Supplies could now only be dropped from the air. The remaining frozen, half-starved troops, under constant heavy fire, were often unable to salvage them.

By this time, the German people were already being prepared for the worst. After a long period of silence, the Wehrmacht report on 16 January had spoken in ominous terms of a 'heroically courageous defensive struggle against the enemy attacking from all sides'. The press was instructed to speak of 'the great and stirring heroic sacrifice which the troops encircled at Stalingrad are offering the German nation'.

Hitler had bluntly described the plight of the 6th Army to Goebbels on 22 January. There was scarcely a hope of rescuing the troops. It was a 'heroic drama of German history'. News came in as they talked, outlining the rapidly deteriorating situation. Hitler was said by Goebbels to have been 'deeply shaken'. But he did not consider attaching any blame to himself. He complained bitterly about the Luftwaffe, which had not kept its promises about levels of supplies. Schmundt separately told Goebbels that these had been illusory. Göring's staff had given him the optimistic picture they presumed he wanted, and he had passed this on to the Führer. It was a problem that afflicted the entire dictatorship – up to and including Hitler himself. Only positive messages were acceptable. Pessimism (which usually meant realism) was a sign of failure. Distortions of the truth were built into the communications system of the Third Reich at every level – most of all in the top echelons of the regime.

Even more than he felt let down by his own Luftwaffe, Hitler voiced utter contempt for the failure of the German allies to hold the line against the Soviet counter-attack. The Romanians were bad, the Italians worse, and worst of all were the Hungarians. The catastrophe would not have occurred had the entire eastern front been controlled by German units, as he had wanted. The German bakers' and baggage-formations, he fumed, had performed better than the élite Italian, Romanian, and Hungarian divisions. But he did not think the Axis partners were ready to desert. Italy would 'like to dance out of line'; though as long as Mussolini was there, this could be ruled out. The Duce was clever enough to know that it would mean the end of Fascism, and his own end. Romania was essential to Germany for its oil, Hitler said. He had made it plain to the Romanians what would come their way should they attempt anything stupid.

Hitler still hoped – at least that is what he told Goebbels – that parts of the 6th Army could hold out until they could be relieved. In fact, he knew better than anyone that there was not the slightest chance of it. The 6th Army was on its last legs. On 22 January, the very day that Goebbels had had his talks with Hitler at FHQ, Paulus had requested permission to surrender. Hitler rejected it. He then rejected a similar plea from Manstein to allow the 6th Army's surrender. As a point of honour, he stated, there could be no question of capitulation. In the evening, he telegraphed the 6th Army to say that it had made an historic contribution in the greatest struggle in German history. The army was to stand fast 'to the last soldier and the last bullet'.

Since 23 January the 6th Army had been beginning to break up. It was split in two as Soviet troops cutting through from the south and the west of the city joined forces. By 26 January the division of the 6th

Army was complete. One section raised the white flag on the 29th. The same day, Paulus sent Hitler a telegram of congratulations on the tenth anniversary of his take-over of power on the 30th.

The 'celebrations' in Germany for the anniversary of Hitler's day of triumph in January 1933 were in a low key. All bunting was banned. Hitler did not give his usual speech. He remained in his headquarters and left it to Goebbels to read out his proclamation. A single sentence referred to Stalingrad: 'The heroic struggle of our soldiers on the Volga should be a warning for everybody to do the utmost for the struggle for Germany's freedom and the future of our people, and thus in a wider sense for the maintenance of our entire continent.' In Stalingrad itself, the end was approaching. Feelers were put out by the remnants of the 6th Army to the Soviets that very evening, 30 January 1943, for a surrender. Negotiations took place next day. On that day, the announcement was made that Paulus had been promoted to Field-Marshal. He was expected to end the struggle with a hero's death. In the evening, he surrendered. Two days later, on 2 February, the northern sector of the surrounded troops also gave in. The battle of Stalingrad was over. Around 100,000 men from twenty-one German and two Romanian divisions had fallen in battle. A further 113,000 German and Romanian soldiers were taken prisoner. Only a few thousand would survive their captivity.

VIII

Hitler made no mention of the human tragedy when he met his military leaders at the midday conference on 1 February. What concerned him was the prestige lost through Paulus's surrender. He found it impossible to comprehend, and impossible to forgive. 'Here a man can look on while 50–60,000 of his soldiers die and defend themselves bravely to the last. How can he give himself up to the Bolsheviks?' he asked, nearly speechless with anger at what he saw as a betrayal. He could have no respect for an officer who chose captivity to shooting himself. 'How easy it is to do something like that. The pistol – that's simple. What sort of cowardice does it take to pull back from it?' 'No one else is being made field-marshal in this war,' he avowed (though he did not keep to his word). He was certain – it proved an accurate presumption – that, in Soviet hands, Paulus and the other captured generals would within no time be promoting anti-German propaganda. Drawing on horror-stories of tortures in Russian prisons that had circulated in the *völkisch* press since the early 1920s, he said: 'They'll lock them up in the rat-cellar, and two days later they'll have them so softened-up that they'll talk straight away . . . They'll now come into the Lubljanka, and there they'll be eaten by rats. How can someone be so cowardly? I don't understand it. So many people have to die. Then such a man goes and besmirches in the last minute the heroism of so many others. He could release himself from all misery and enter eternity, national immortality, and he prefers to go to Moscow. How can there be a choice? That's crazy.'

For the German people, Paulus's missed chance to gain immortality was scarcely a central concern. Their thoughts, when they heard the dreaded announcement – false to the last – on 3 February that the officers and soldiers of the 6th Army had fought to the final shot and 'died so that Germany might live', were of the human tragedy and the scale of the military disaster. The 'heroic sacrifice' was no consolation to bereft relatives and friends.

The SD reported that the whole nation was 'deeply shaken' by the fate of the 6th Army. There was deep depression, and widespread anger that Stalingrad had not been evacuated or relieved while there was still time. People asked how such optimistic reports had been possible only a short time earlier. They were critical of the underestimation – as in the previous winter – of the Soviet forces. Many now thought the war could not be won, and were anxiously contemplating the consequences of defeat.

Hitler had until Stalingrad been largely exempted from whatever criticisms people had of the regime. That now altered sharply. His responsibility for the debacle was evident. People had expected Hitler to give an explanation in his speech on 30 January. His obvious reluctance to speak to the nation only heightened the criticism. The regime's opponents were encouraged. Graffiti chalked on walls attacking Hitler, 'the Stalingrad Murderer', were a sign that underground resistance was not extinct. Appalled at what had happened, a number of army officers and highly-placed civil servants revived conspiratorial plans largely dormant since 1938–9.

In Munich, a group of students, together with one of their professors, whose idealism and mounting detestation at the criminal inhumanity of the regime had led them the previous year to form the 'White Rose' opposition-group, now openly displayed their attack on Hitler. The medical students Alexander Schmorell and Hans Scholl had formed the initial driving-force, and had soon been joined by Christoph Probst, Sophie Scholl (Hans's sister), Willi Graf, and Kurt Huber, Professor of Philosophy at Munich University, whose critical attitude to the regime had influenced them in lectures and discussions. All the students came from conservative, middle-class backgrounds. All were fired by Christian beliefs and humanistic idealism. The horrors on the eastern front, experienced for a short time at first hand when Graf, Schmorell, and Hans Scholl were called up, converted the lofty idealism into an explicit, political message. 'Fellow Students!' ran their final manifesto (composed by Professor Huber), distributed in Munich University on 18 February. 'The nation is deeply shaken by the destruction of the men of Stalingrad. The genial strategy of the World War [I] corporal has senselessly and irresponsibly driven three hundred and thirty thousand German men to death and ruin. Führer, we thank you!'

It was a highly courageous show of defiance. But it was suicidal. Hans and Sophie Scholl were denounced by a porter at the university (who was subsequently applauded by pro-Nazi students for his action), and quickly arrested by the Gestapo. Christoph Probst was picked up soon afterwards. Their trial before the 'People's Court', presided over by Roland Freisler, took place within four days. The verdict – the death-sentence – was a foregone conclusion. All three were guillotined the same afternoon. Willi Graf, Kurt Huber, and Alexander Schmorell suffered the same fate some months later. Other students on the fringe of the movement were sentenced to long terms of imprisonment.

The regime had been badly stung. But it was not at the point of collapse. It would lash back without scruple and with utter viciousness at the slightest hint of opposition. The level of brutality towards its own population was about to rise sharply as external adversity mounted.

If Hitler felt any personal remorse for Stalingrad or human sympathy for the dead of the 6th Army and their relatives, he did not let it show. Those in his close proximity could detect the signs of nervous strain. He hinted privately at his worry that his health would not stand up to the pressure. His secretaries had to put up with even longer nocturnal monologues as his insomnia developed chronic proportions. The topics were much the same as ever: his youth in Vienna, the 'time of struggle', the history of mankind, the nature of the cosmos. There was no relief from the boredom for his secretaries, who by now knew his outpourings on all topics more or less off by heart. Even the occasional evenings listening to records to break up the tedium had stopped. Hitler, as he had told Goebbels some weeks earlier, now no longer wanted to listen to music. Talking was like a drug for him. He told one of his doctors two years later that he had to talk – about more or less anything other than military issues – to divert him from sleepless nights pondering troop dispositions and seeing in his mind where every division was at Stalingrad. As Below guessed, the bad news from the North African as well as from the eastern front must have led to serious doubts, in the privacy of his own room in the bunker of his headquarters, about whether the war could still be won. But outwardly, even among his entourage at the Wolf's Lair, he had to sustain the façade of invincibility. No crack could be allowed to show. Hitler remained true to his creed of will and strength. A hint of weakness, in his thinking, was a gift to enemies and subversives. A crevice of demoralization would then swiftly widen to a chasm. The military, and above all else the party, leaders must, therefore, never be allowed a glimmer of any wavering in his own resolution.

There was not a trace of demoralization, depression, or uncertainty when he spoke to the Reichs- and Gauleiter for almost two hours at his headquarters on 7 February. He told them at the very beginning of his address that he believed in victory more than ever. Then he described what Goebbels referred to as 'the catastrophe on the eastern front'. Hitler did not look close to home for the failings. While he said he naturally accepted full responsibility for the events of the winter, he left no doubt where in his view the real fault lay. From the beginning of his political career – indeed, from what is known of his earliest remarks on politics – he had cast around for scapegoats. The trait was too embedded in his psyche for him to stray from it now that, for the first time, an unmitigated national disaster had to be explained. Addressing the party leadership, as in his private discussion with Goebbels a fortnight or so earlier, he once more placed the blame for the disaster at Stalingrad squarely on the 'complete failure' of Germany's allies – the Romanians, Italians, and Hungarians – whose fighting powers met with his 'absolute contempt'.

Not just the search for scapegoats, but the feeling of treachery and betrayal was entrenched in Hitler's thinking. Another strand of his explanation for the disaster at Stalingrad was the prospect of imminent French betrayal, forcing him to retain several divisions, especially SS-divisions, in the west when they were desperately needed in the east. But Hitler had the extraordinary capacity, as his Luftwaffe adjutant Below noted, of turning negative into positive, and convincing his audience of this. A landing by the Allies in France would have been far more danger-ous, he claimed, than that which had taken place in North Africa and had been checked through the occupation of Tunis. He saw grounds for optimism, too, in the success of the U-boats, and in Speer's armaments programme enabling better flak defence against air-raids together with full-scale production by the summer of the Tiger tank.

Much of the rest of Hitler's address was on the 'psychology' of war. The crisis was more psychological than material, he declared, and must therefore be overcome by 'psychological means'. It was the party's task to achieve this. The Gauleiter should remember the 'time of struggle'. Radical measures were now needed. Austerity, sacrifice, and the end of any privileges for certain sectors of society were the order of the day. The setbacks but eventual triumph of Frederick the Great – the implied comparison with Hitler's own leadership was plain – were invoked. The setbacks now being faced, solely the fault of Germany's allies, even had their own psychological advantages. Propaganda and the party's agitation could awaken people to the fact that they had stark alterna-tives: becoming master of Europe, or undergoing 'total liquidation and extermination'.

Hitler pointed out one advantage which, he claimed, the Allies pos-sessed: that they were sustained by international Jewry. The consequence, Goebbels reported Hitler as saying, was 'that we have to eliminate Jewry not only from Reich territory but from the whole of Europe'.

Hitler categorically ruled out, as he always had done, any possibility of capitulation. He stated that any collapse of the German Reich was out of the question. But his further remarks betrayed the fact that he was contemplating precisely that. The event of such a collapse 'would represent the ending of his life', he declared. It was plain who, in such an eventuality, the scapegoats would be: the German people themselves. 'Such a collapse could only be caused through the weakness of the people,' Goebbels recorded Hitler as saying. 'But if the German people turned out to be weak, they would deserve nothing else than to be extinguished by a stronger people; then one could have no sympathy for them.' The sentiment would stay with him to the end.

To the party leadership, the backbone of his support, Hitler could speak in this way. The Gauleiter could be rallied by such rhetoric. They were after all fanatics as Hitler himself was. They were part of his 'sworn community'. The responsibility of the party for the radicalization of the 'home front' was music to their ears. In any case, whatever private doubts (if any) they harboured, they had no choice but to stick with Hitler. They had burnt their boats with him. He was the sole guarantor of their power.

The German people were less easily placated than Hitler's immediate viceroys. When he spoke in Berlin to the nation for the first time since Stalingrad, on the occasion (which this year, of all years, he could not possibly avoid) of Heroes' Memorial Day on 21 March 1943, his speech gave rise to greater criticism than any Hitler speech since he had become Chancellor.

The speech was one of Hitler's shortest. Perhaps anxiety about a possible air-raid made Hitler race through it in such a rapid and dreary monotone. The routine assault on Bolshevism and on Jewry as the force behind the 'merciless war' could stir little enthusiasm. Disappointment was profound. Rumours revived about Hitler's poor health – along with others that it had been a substitute who had spoken, while the real Führer was under house-arrest on the Obersalzberg suffering from a mental breakdown after Stalingrad. Extraordinary was the fact that Hitler never even directly mentioned Stalingrad in a ceremony meant to be devoted to the memory of the fallen and at a time when the trauma was undiminished. And his passing reference, at the end of his speech, to a figure of 542,000 German dead in the war was presumed to be far too low and received with rank incredulity.

Hitler, as more and more ordinary citizens now recognized, had closed off all avenues that might have brought compromise peace. The earlier victories were increasingly seen in a different light. There was no end in sight. But it now seemed clear to increasing numbers of ordinary citizens that Hitler had taken them into a war which could only end in destruction, defeat, and disaster. There was still far to go, but what was revealed after Stalingrad would become ever clearer: for the vast majority of Germans, the love affair with Hitler was at an end. Only the bitter process of divorce remained.

23

Beleaguered

I

'The English claim that the German people have lost their trust in the Führer,' Goebbels declared. It was the opening to the fifth of his ten rhetorical questions towards the end of his two-hour speech proclaiming 'total war' on the evening of 18 February 1943. The hand-picked audience in Berlin's Sportpalast rose as one man to denounce such an outrageous allegation. A chorus of voices arose: 'Führer command, we will obey!' The tumult lasted for what seemed an age. Orchestrating the frenzied mood to perfection, the propaganda maestro eventually broke in to ask: 'Is your trust in the Führer greater, more faithful, and more unshakeable than ever? Is your readiness to follow him in all his ways and to do everything necessary to bring the war to a triumphant end absolute and unrestricted?' Fourteen thousand voices hysterically cried out in unison the answer invited by Goebbels in his bid to quell doubters at home and to relay to the outside world the futility of any hope of inner collapse in Germany. Goebbels ended his morale-boosting peroration – which had been interrupted more than 200 times by clapping, cheering, shouts of approbation, or thunderous applause – with the words of Theodor Körner, the patriotic poet from the time of Prussia's struggle against Napoleon: 'Now people, arise – and storm burst forth!' The great hall erupted. Amid the wild cheering the national anthem 'Deutschland, Deutschland über alles' and the party's 'Horst-Wessel-Lied' rang out. The spectacle ended with cries of 'the great German Leader Adolf Hitler, Sieg Heil, Sieg Heil'.

The speech was intended to demonstrate the complete solidarity of people and leader, conveying Germany's utter determination to carry on, and even intensify, the fight until victory was attained. But the solidarity, despite the impression temporarily left by Goebbels's publicity spectacular, was by this time shrinking fast, the belief in Hitler among the mass of the population seriously undermined. What Goebbels did, in fact, was to solicit from his audience 'a kind of plebiscitary "Ja" to self-destruction' in a war which Germany could by now neither win nor end through a negotiated peace.

Goebbels's hopes that the speech would bring him Hitler's authorization to concentrate the direction of 'total war' in his own hands were swiftly dashed. The Propaganda Minister had long pressed for practical measures to radicalize the war effort. Hitler, shored up by Göring, had, however, resisted imposing increased hardship and material sacrifice on the civilian population. He was conscious as ever of the collapse of morale on the home front during the First World War, certain that this had undermined the military effort and paved the way for revolution. Nevertheless, during the Stalingrad crisis he had finally conceded the aim of the complete mobilization of all conceivable labour and resources of the home front, and some initial measures had been introduced.

Goebbels had, however, miscalculated. Direction of the 'total war' effort largely bypassed him. His ambitions to take control of the home front were ignored. Unable to adjudicate in any rational or systematic fashion in the inevitable conflicts arising from overlapping and sometimes contradictory spheres of competence, but careful as always to protect his own power, Hitler never allowed Goebbels the authority the latter craved on the home front. The 'total war' effort juddered on to partial successes in individual areas. But the absence of strong, consistent leadership from the top on the home front produced what Goebbels lamented as 'a complete lack of direction in German domestic policy'.

The results of Goebbels's big speech, therefore, in terms of his own ambitions to take control of the 'total war' effort, were disappointing. Goebbels was soon to learn anew that he remained only one player in the power-games to try to secure the backing of Hitler's unqualified authority. He would also rapidly realize again that although the Dictator's own authority was undiminished, his physical absence, preoccupation with military matters, and sporadic, semi-detached involvement in the day-to-day governance of the Reich meant that he was more than ever exposed to the influence of those in his presence – 'the entire baggage of court-idiots and irresponsible agitators' – incapable of reconciling or overriding the competing interests of his feuding barons. Even had he been willing, therefore, he was completely unable to impose clear strands of authority to combat the already advanced signs of disintegration in government and administration.

For Hitler, the months after Stalingrad intensified the familiar, ingrained character-traits. The façade of often absurd optimism remained largely intact, even among his inner circle. The show of indomitable will continued. The flights of fantasy, detached from reality, took on new dimensions. But the mask slipped from time to time in remarks revealing deep depression and fatalism. It was fleeting recognition of what he already inwardly acknowledged: he had lost the initiative for ever. The recognition invariably brought new torrents of rage, lashing any who might bear the brunt of the blame – most of all, as ever, his military leaders. They were all liars, disloyal, opposed to National Socialism, reactionaries, and lacking in any cultural appreciation, he ranted. He yearned to have nothing more to do with them. Ultimately, he would blame the German people themselves, whom he would see as too weak to survive and unworthy of him in the great struggle. As setback followed setback, so the beleaguered Führer resorted ever more readily to the search for ruthless revenge and retaliation, both on his external enemies – behind whom, as always, he saw the demonic figure of the Jew – and on any within who might dare to show defeatism, let alone 'betray' him. There were no personal influences that might have moderated his fundamental inhumanity. The man who had been idolized by millions was friendless – apart from (as he himself commented) Eva Braun and his dog, Blondi.

The war, and the hatreds Hitler had invested in it, consumed him ever more. Outside the war and his buildings mania, he could rouse little interest. He was by now in many respects an empty, burnt-out shell of an individual. But his resilience and strength of will remained extraordinary. And in the strangely shapeless regime over which he presided, his power was still immense, unrestricted, and uncontested.

As the war that Hitler had unleashed 'came home to the Reich', the Dictator – now rapidly ageing, becoming increasingly a physical wreck, and showing pronounced signs of intense nervous strain – distanced himself ever more from his people. It was as if he could not face them now that there were no more triumphs to report, and he had to take the responsibility for the mounting losses and misery. Even before the Stalingrad calamity, in early November 1942, when his train had by chance stopped directly alongside a troop train returning from the east carrying dejected-looking, battle-weary soldiers, his only reaction had been to ask one of his manservants to pull down the blinds. As Germany's war fortunes plummeted between 1943 and 1945, the former corporal from an earlier great war never sought to experience at first hand the feelings of ordinary soldiers.

The number of big public speeches he delivered constituted a plain indicator of the widening gulf between Führer and people. In 1940 Hitler had given nine big public addresses, in 1941 seven, in 1942 five. In 1943 he gave only two (apart from a radio broadcast on 10 September). The bulk of his time was spent well away from the government ministries in Berlin's Wilhelmstraße – and well away from the German people – at his field headquarters, or at his mountain eyrie above Berchtesgaden. He spent no more than a few days in Berlin during the whole of 1943. For some three months in all he was at the Berghof. During the rest of the time he was cooped up in his headquarters in East Prussia, leaving aside a number of short visits to the Ukraine.

Goebbels lamented in July 1943 the way Hitler had cut himself off from the masses. These, commented the Propaganda Minister, had provided the acclaim on which his unique authority had rested. He had given them the belief and trust that had been the focal point of the regime's support. But now, in Goebbels's eyes, that relationship was seriously endangered – and with it the stability of the regime. He pointed to the large number and critical tone of the letters – half of them anonymous – arriving at the Propaganda Ministry. 'Above all, the question is again and again raised in these letters,' he went on, 'why the Führer never visits the areas which have suffered from air-raids . . . but especially why the Führer does not even speak to the German people to explain the current situation. I regard it as most necessary that the Führer does that, despite his burden through the events in the military sector. One can't neglect the people too long. Ultimately, they are the heart of our war effort. If the people were once to lose their strength of resistance and belief in the German leadership, then the most serious leadership crisis which ever faced us would have been created.'

I I

The move to 'total war', introduced during the Stalingrad crisis, provided the final demonstration that no semblance of collective government and rational decision-making within the Reich was compatible with Hitler's personal rule.

The drive to mobilize all remaining reserves from the home front – what came to be proclaimed as 'total war' – had its roots in the need to plug the huge gap in military manpower left by the high losses suffered by the Wehrmacht during the first months of 'Barbarossa'.

At Christmas 1942, Hitler had given the orders for more radical measures to raise manpower for the front and the armaments industries. Martin Bormann was commissioned to undertake the coordination of the efforts, in collaboration with Head of the Reich Chancellery, Hans-Heinrich Lammers. Goebbels and Fritz Sauckel (Plenipotentiary for Labour Deployment) were immediately informed. The aim was to close down all businesses whose trade was in 'luxury' items or was otherwise not necessary for the war effort, and to redeploy the personnel in the army or in arms production. Women were to be subject to conscription for work. Releasing men for front-service was impossible, it was agreed, unless women could replace them in a variety of forms of work. According to the Propaganda Ministry, the number of women working had dropped by some 147,000 since the start of the war. And of 8.6 million women in employment at the end of 1942, only 968,000 worked in armaments.

In the spring of 1942, Hitler had rejected outright the conscription of women to work in war industries. But by early 1943, the labour situation had worsened to the extent that he was compelled to concede that the conscription of women could no longer be avoided. Even the forced labour of, by this time, approaching 6 million foreign workers and prisoners-of-war could not compensate for the 11 million or so men who had been called up to the Wehrmacht. In an unpublished Führer Decree of 13 January 1943, women between seventeen and fifty years old were ordered to report for deployment in the war effort.

Even before Hitler signed the decree, the wrangling over spheres of competence had begun in earnest. In order to retain a firm grip on the 'total war' measures and prevent the dissipation of centralized control,

Lammers, backed by the leading civil servants in the Reich Chancellery, Leo Killy and Friedrich Wilhelm Kritzinger, suggested to Hitler that all measures should be taken 'under the authority of the Führer', and that a special body be set up to handle them. The idea was to create a type of small 'war cabinet'. Lammers thought the most appropriate arrangement would be for the heads of the three main executive arms of the Führer's authority – the High Command of the Wehrmacht, the Reich Chancellery, and the Party Chancellery – to act in close collaboration, meeting frequently, keeping regular contact with Hitler himself, and standing above the particularist interests of individual ministries. Hitler agreed. He evidently saw no possible threat to his position from such an arrangement. On the contrary: the three persons involved – Keitel, Lammers, and Bormann – could be guaranteed to uphold his own interests at the expense of any possible over-mighty subjects. An indication that this was, indeed, Hitler's thinking was the exclusion of Göring, Goebbels, and Speer from the coordinating body – soon known as the 'Committee of Three' (*Dreierausschuß*).

From the very outset, the Committee was only empowered to issue enabling ordinances in accordance with the general guidelines Hitler had laid down. It was given no autonomy. Hitler reserved, as always, the final decision on anything of significance to himself. The 'Committee of Three' had, in all, eleven formal meetings between January and August 1943, but rapidly ran up against deeply ingrained vested interests both in government ministries and in party regional offices concerned to hold on to their personnel and to their spheres of competence which might have been threatened in any move to centralize and simplify the regime's tangled lines of administration. It had little chance of breaking down the fiefdoms on which Nazi rule rested, and soon revealed that any hopes of bringing order to the Third Reich's endemic administrative chaos were utterly illusory.

Nevertheless, Hitler's mightiest subjects were determined to do everything they could to sabotage a development which they saw as inimical to their own power-positions – and from which they had been excluded. The first notions of a challenge to the role of the 'Committee of Three' were intimated during the reception in Goebbels's residence following his 'total war' speech on 18 February. Nine days later, Walther Funk (Reich Minister of Economics), Robert Ley (head of the huge German Labour Front), and Albert Speer, the powerful armaments minister, met again over cognac and tea in Goebbels's stately apartments – gloomy now that the light-bulbs had been removed to comply with the new 'total war' demands – to see what could be done. Soon afterwards, at the beginning of March, Goebbels travelled from Berlin down to Berchtesgaden to plot with Göring a way of sidelining the Committee. Speer had already sounded him out. In talks lasting five hours at Göring's palatial villa on the Obersalzberg, partly with Speer present, the Reich Marshal, dressed in 'somewhat baroque clothes', was quickly won over.

The Propaganda Minister's plan – actually it had initally been suggested by Speer – was to revive the Ministerial Council for the Defence of the Reich (established under Göring's chairmanship just before the outbreak of war but long fallen into desuetude), and to give it the membership to turn it into an effective body to rule the Reich, leaving Hitler free to concentrate on the direction of military affairs. He reminded Göring of what threatened if the war were lost: 'Above all as regards the Jewish Question, we are in it so deeply that there is no getting out any longer. And that's good. A Movement and a people that have burnt their boats fight, from experience, with fewer constraints than those that still have a chance of retreat.' The party needed revitaliz-ing. And if Göring could now reactivate the Ministerial Council and put it in the hands of Hitler's most loyal followers, argued Goebbels, the Führer would surely be in agreement. They would choose their moment to put the proposition to Hitler. This would, they knew, not be easy.

The problem, however, especially as Goebbels saw it, went beyond the 'Committee of Three': it was a problem of Hitler himself. To rescue the war effort, stronger leadership at home was needed. Goebbels remained utterly loyal to the person he had for years regarded as an almost deified father-figure. But he saw in Hitler's leadership style – his absence from Berlin, his detachment from the people, his almost total preoccupation with military matters, and, above all, his increasing reliance on Bormann for everything concerning domestic matters – a fundamental weakness in the governance of the Reich.

In his diary, Goebbels complained of a 'leadership crisis'. He thought the problems among the subordinate leaders were so grave that the Führer ought to sweep through them with an iron broom. The Führer carried, indeed, a crushing burden through the war. But that was because he would take no decisions to alter the personnel so that he would not need bothering with every trivial matter. Goebbels thought – though he expressed it discreetly – that Hitler was too weak to do anything. 'When a matter is put to him from the most varied sides,' he wrote, 'the Führer is sometimes somewhat vacillating in his decisions. He also doesn't always react correctly to people. A bit of help is needed there.'

When he had spoken privately in his residence to Speer, Funk, and Ley just over a week after his 'total war' speech, he had gone further. According to Speer's later account, Goebbels had said on that occasion: 'We have not only a "leadership crisis", but strictly speaking a "Leader crisis"!' The others agreed with him. 'We are sitting here in Berlin. Hitler does not hear what we have to say about the situation. I can't influence him politically,' Goebbels bemoaned. 'I can't even report to him about the most urgent measures in my area. Everything goes through Bormann. Hitler must be persuaded to come more often to Berlin.' Goebbels added that Hitler had lost his grip on domestic politics, which Bormann controlled by conveying the impression to the Führer that he still held the reins tightly in his grasp. With Bormann given the title, on 12 April, of 'Secretary of the Führer', the sense, acutely felt by Goebbels, that the Party Chancellery chief was 'managing' Hitler was even further enhanced.

Goebbels and Speer might lament that Hitler's hold on domestic affairs had weakened. But when they saw him in early March, intending to put their proposition to him that Göring should head a revamped Ministerial Council for the Defence of the Reich to direct the home front, it was they who proved weak. Speer had flown to Hitler's headquarters, temporarily moved back to Vinnitsa in the Ukraine, on 5 March to pave the way for a visit by Goebbels. The Propaganda Minister arrived in Vinnitsa three days later. Straight away, Speer urged caution. The continued, almost unhindered, bombing raids on German towns had left Hitler in a foul mood towards Göring and the inadequacies of the Luftwaffe. It was hardly a propitious moment to broach the subject of reinstating the Reich Marshal to the central role in the direction of domestic affairs. Goebbels thought nonetheless that they had to make the attempt.

At their first meeting, over lunch, Hitler, looking tired but otherwise well, and more lively than of late, launched as usual into a bitter onslaught on the generals who, he claimed, were cheating him wherever they could do so. He carried on in the same vein during a private four-hour discussion alone with Goebbels that afternoon. He was furious at Göring, and at the entire Luftwaffe leadership with the exception of the Chief of the General Staff Hans Jeschonnek. Characteristically, Hitler thought the best way of preventing German cities being reduced to heaps of rubble was by responding with 'terror from our side'. Despite his insistence to Speer that they had to go ahead with their proposal, Goebbels evidently concluded during his discussion with Hitler that it would be fruitless to do so. 'In view of the general mood,' he noted, 'I regard it as inopportune to put to the Führer the question of Göring's political leadership; it's at present an unsuitable moment. We must defer the business until somewhat later.' Any hope of raising the matter, even obliquely, when Goebbels and Speer sat with Hitler by the fireside until late in the night was dashed when news came in of a heavy air-raid on Nuremberg. Hitler fell into a towering rage about Göring and the Luftwaffe leadership. Speer and Goebbels, calming Hitler only with difficulty, postponed their plans. They were never resurrected.

Goebbels and Speer had failed at the first hurdle. Face to face with Hitler, they felt unable to confront him. Hitler's fury over Göring was enough to veto even the prospect of any rational discussion about restructuring Reich government.

Goebbels was still talking as late as September of finding enough support to block Lammers's attempt (as the Propaganda Minister saw it) to arrogate authority to himself on the back of a Führer decree empowering him to review any disputes between ministers and decide whether they should be taken to Hitler. But by that time, there was scant need of intrigue to stymie the 'Committee of Three'. It had already atrophied into insignificance.

The failed experiment of the 'Committee of Three' showed conclusively that, however weak their structures, all forms of collective government were doomed by the need to protect the arbitrary 'will of the Führer'. But it was increasingly impossible for this 'will' to be exercised in ways conducive to the functioning of a modern state, let alone one operating under the crisis conditions of a major war. As a system of government, Hitler's dictatorship had no future.

III

Matters at home were far from Hitler's primary concern in the spring and summer of 1943. He was, in fact, almost solely preoccupied with the course of the war. The strain of this had left its mark on him. Guderian, back in favour after a long absence, was struck at their first meeting, on 20 February 1943, by the change in Hitler's physical appearance since the last time he had seen him, back in mid-December 1941: 'In the intervening fourteen months he had aged greatly. His manner was less assured than it had been and his speech was hesitant; his left hand trembled.'

When President Roosevelt, at the end of his meeting to discuss war strategy with Churchill and the Combined Chiefs of Staff at Casablanca in French Morocco between 14 and 24 January 1943, had – to the British Prime Minister's surprise – announced at a concluding press conference that the Allies would impose 'unconditional surrender' on their enemies, it had matched Hitler's Valhalla mentality entirely. For him, the demand altered nothing. It merely added further confirmation that his uncompromising stance was right. As he told his party leaders in early February, he felt liberated as a result from any attempts to persuade him to look for a negotiated peace settlement. It had become, as he had always asserted it would, a clear matter of victory or destruction. Few, even of his closest followers, as Goebbels admitted, could still inwardly believe in the former. But compromises were ruled out. The road to destruction was opening up ever more plainly. For Hitler, closing off escape routes had distinct advantages. Fear of destruction was a strong motivator.

Some of Hitler's leading generals, most notably Manstein, had tried to persuade him immediately after Stalingrad that he should, if not give up the command of the army, at least appoint a supremo on the eastern front who had his trust. Hitler was having none of it. After the bitter conflicts over the previous months, he preferred the compliancy of a Keitel to the sharply couched counter-arguments of a Manstein. It meant a further weakening of Germany's military potential.

Manstein's push to retake Kharkhov and reach the Donets by mid-March had been a much-needed success. Over 50,000 Soviet troops had perished. It had suggested yet again to Hitler that Stalin's reserves must be drying up. Immediately, he wanted to go on the offensive. It was important to strike while the Red Army was still smarting from the reversal at Kharkhov. It was also necessary to send a signal to the German population, deeply embittered by Stalingrad, and to the Reich's allies, that any doubts in final victory were wholly misplaced.

At this point, the split in military planning between the army's General Staff, directly responsible for the eastern front, and the operations branch of Wehrmacht High Command (in charge of all other theatres) surfaced once more. The planners in the High Command of the Wehrmacht favoured a defensive ploy on all fronts to allow the gradual build-up and mobilization of resources throughout Europe for a later grand offensive. The Army High Command thought differently. It wanted a limited but early offensive. Chief of the Army General Staff Kurt Zeitzler had devised an operation involving the envelopment and destruction of a large number of Soviet divisions on a big salient west of Kursk, an important rail junction some 300 miles south of Moscow. Five Soviet armies were located within the westward bulge in the front, around 120 miles wide and 90 miles deep, left from the winter campaign of 1942–3. If victorious, the operation would gravely weaken the Soviet offensive potential.

There was no question which strategy would appeal to Hitler. He swiftly supported the army's plan for a decisive strike on a greatly shortened front – about 150 kilometres compared with 2,000 kilometres in the 'Barbarossa' invasion of 1941. The limited scope of the operation reflected the reduction in German ambitions in the east since June 1941. Even so, a tactical victory would have been of great importance. It would, in all likelihood, have eliminated the prospect of any further Soviet offensive in 1943, thereby freeing German troops for redeployment in the increasingly threatening Mediterranean theatre. The order for what was to become 'Operation Citadel', issued on 13 March, foresaw a pincer attack by part of Manstein's Army Group from the south and Kluge's from the north, enveloping the Soviet troops in the bulge. In his confirmation order of 15 April, Hitler declared: 'This attack is of decisive importance. It must be a quick and conclusive success. It must give us the initiative for this spring and summer . . . Every officer, every soldier must be convinced of the decisive importance of this attack. The victory of Kursk must shine like a beacon to the world.' It was to do so. But hardly as Hitler had imagined.

'Citadel' was scheduled to begin in mid-May. As in the previous two years, however, significant delays set in which were damaging to the operation's success. These were not directly of Hitler's making. But they did again reveal the serious problems in the military command-structure and process of decision-making. They arose from disputes about timing among the leading generals involved. On 4 May, Hitler met them in Munich to discuss 'Citadel'. Manstein and Kluge wanted to press ahead as soon as possible. This was the only chance of imposing serious losses on the enemy. Otherwise, they argued, it was better to call off the operation altogether. They were seriously worried about losing the advantage of surprise and about the build-up of Soviet forces should there be any postponement. The heavy defeat at Stalingrad and weakness of the southern flank deterred other generals from wishing to undertake a new large-scale offensive so quickly. Colonel-General Walter Model – known as an especially tough and capable commander, a reputation which had helped make him one of Hitler's favourites, and detailed to lead the 9th Army's assault from the north – recommended a delay until reinforcements were available. He picked up on the belief of Zeitzler, also high in favour with Hitler, that the heavy Tiger tank, just rolling off the production lines, and the new, lighter, Panther would provide Germany with the decisive breakthrough necessary to regaining the initiative. Hitler had great hopes of both tanks. He gave Model his backing.

On 4 May, he postponed 'Citadel' until mid-June. It was then further postponed, eventually getting under way only in early July. Even by that date, fewer Tigers and Panthers were available than had been envisaged. And the Soviets, tipped off by British intelligence and by a source within the Wehrmacht High Command, had built up their defences and were ready and waiting.

Meanwhile, the situation in North Africa was giving grounds for the gravest concern. Some of Hitler's closest military advisers, Jodl among them, had been quietly resigned to the complete loss of North Africa as early as December 1942. Hitler himself had hinted at one point that he was contemplating the evacuation of German troops. But no action had followed. He was much influenced by the views of the Commander-in-Chief South, Field-Marshal Kesselring, one of nature's optimists and, like most in high places in the Third Reich, compelled in any case to exude optimism whatever his true sentiments and however bleak the situation was in reality. Hitler needed optimists to pander to him – yet another form of 'working towards the Führer'. In the military arena, this reinforced the chances of serious strategic blunders.

In March, buoyed by Manstein's success at Kharkhov, Hitler had declared that the holding of Tunis would be decisive for the outcome of the war. It was, therefore, a top priority. With the refusal to contemplate any withdrawal, the next military disaster beckoned. When Below flew south at the end of the month to view the North African front and report back to Hitler, even Kesselring was unable to hide the fact that Tunis could not be held. Colonel-General Hans-Jürgen von Arnim, who had taken over the North African command from the exhausted and dispirited Rommel, was of the same opinion. Kesselring's staff were even more pessimistic: they saw no chance of successfully fending off an Allied crossing from Tunis to Sicily once – which they regarded as a certainty – North Africa had fallen. When Below reported back, Hitler said little. It seemed to his Luftwaffe adjutant that he had already written off North Africa and was inwardly preparing himself for the eventual defection of his Italian partners to the enemy.

In early April, Hitler had spent the best part of four days at the restored baroque palace of Klessheim, near Salzburg, shoring up Musso-lini's battered morale – half urging, half browbeating the Duce to keep up the fight, knowing how weakened he would be through the massive blow soon to descend in North Africa. Worn down by the strain of war and depression, Mussolini, stepping down from his train with assistance, looked a 'broken old man' to Hitler. The Duce also made a subdued impression on interpreter Dr Paul Schmidt as he pleaded forlornly for a compromise peace in the east in order to bolster defences in the west, ruling out the possibility of defeating the USSR. Dismissing such a notion out of hand, Hitler reminded Mussolini of the threat that the fall of Tunis would pose for Fascism in Italy. He left him with the impression 'that there can be no other salvation for him than to achieve victory with us or to die'. He exhorted him to do the utmost to use the Italian navy to provide supplies for the forces there. The remainder of the visit consisted largely of monologues by Hitler – including long digressions about Prussian history – aimed at stiffening Mussolini's resistance. Hitler was subsequently satisfied that this had been achieved.

The talks with Mussolini amounted to one of a series of meetings with his allies that Hitler conducted during April, while staying at the Berghof. King Boris of Bulgaria, Marshal Antonescu of Romania, Admiral Horthy of Hungary, Prime Minister Vidkun Quisling of Norway, President Tiso of Slovakia, 'Poglavnik' (Leader) Ante Pavelic of Croatia, and Prime Minister Pierre Laval from Vichy France all visited the Berghof or Klessheim by the end of the month. In each case, the purpose was to stiffen resolve – partly by cajoling, partly by scarcely veiled threats – and to keep faint-hearts or waverers tied to the Axis cause.

Hitler let Antonescu know that he was aware of tentative approaches made by Romanian ministers to the Allies. He posed, as usual, a stark choice of outright victory or 'complete destruction' in a fight to the end for 'living space' in the east. Part of Hitler's implicit argument, increasingly, in attempting to prevent support from seeping away was to play on complicity in the persecution of the Jews. His own paranoia about the responsibility of the Jews for the war and all its evils easily led into the suggestive threat that boats had been burned, there was no way out, and retribution in the event of a lost war would be terrible. The hint of this was implicit in his disapproval of Antonescu's treatment of the Jews as too mild, declaring that the more radical the measures the better it was when tackling the Jews.

In his meetings with Horthy at Klessheim on 16–17 April, Hitler was more brusque. Horthy was berated for feelers to the enemy secretly put out by prominent Hungarian sources but tapped by German intelligence. He was told that 'Germany and its allies were in the same boat on a stormy sea. It was obvious that in this situation anyone wanting to get off would drown immediately.' As he had done with Antonescu, though in far harsher terms, Hitler criticized what he saw as an over-mild policy towards the Jews. Horthy had mentioned that, despite tough measures, criminality and the black market were still flourishing in Hungary. Hitler replied that the Jews were to blame. Horthy asked what he was expected to do with the Jews. He had taken away their economic livelihood; he could scarcely have them all killed. Ribbentrop intervened at this point to say that the Jews must be 'annihilated' or locked up in concentration camps. There was no other way. Hitler regaled Horthy with statistics aimed at showing the strength of former Jewish influence in Germany. He compared the 'German' city of Nuremberg with the neighbouring 'Jewish' town of Fürth. Wherever Jews had been left to themselves, he said, they had produced only misery and dereliction. They were pure parasites. He put forward Poland as a model. There, things had been 'thoroughly cleaned up'. If Jews did not want to work 'then they would be shot. If they could not work, then they would have to rot.' As so often, he deployed a favourite bacterial simile. 'They would have to be treated like tuberculosis bacilli from which a healthy body could become infected. This would not be cruel if it were considered that even innocent creatures, like hares and deer, had to be killed. Why should the beasts that want to bring us Bolshevism be spared?'

Hitler's emphasis on the Jews as germ-bacilli, and as responsible for the war and the spread of Bolshevism, was of course nothing new. And his deep-seated belief in the demonic power still purportedly in the hands of the Jews as they were being decimated needs no underlining. But this was the first time that he had used the 'Jewish Question' in diplomatic discussions to put heads of state under pressure to introduce more draconian anti-Jewish measures. What prompted this?

He would have been particularly alerted to the 'Jewish Question' in April 1943. The previous month, he had finally agreed to have what was left of Berlin's Jewish community deported. In April, he was sent the breakdown prepared by the SS's statistician Richard Korherr of almost a million and a half Jews 'evacuated' and 'channelled through' Polish camps. From the middle of the month, he was increasingly frustrated by accounts of the battle raging in the Warsaw ghetto, where the Waffen-SS, sent in to raze it to the ground, were encountering desperate and brave resistance from the inhabitants. Not least, only days before his meeting with Horthy, mass graves containing the remains of thousands of Polish officers, murdered in 1940 by the Soviet Security Police, the NKVD, had been discovered in the Katyn Forest, near Smolensk. Hitler immediately gave Goebbels permission to make maximum propaganda capital out of the issue. He also instructed Goebbels to put the 'Jewish Question' at the forefront of propaganda. Goebbels seized upon the Katyn case as an excellent opportunity to do just this.

Hitler's directive to Goebbels to amplify the propaganda treatment of the persecution of the Jews, and his explicit usage of the 'Jewish Question' in his meetings with foreign dignitaries, plainly indicate instrumental motives. He believed, as he always had done, unquestioningly in the propaganda value of antisemitism. He told his Gauleiter in early May that antisemitism, as propagated by the party in earlier years, had once more to become the core message. He held out hopes of its spread in Britain. Antisemitic propaganda had, he said, to begin from the premiss that the Jews were the leaders of Bolshevism and prominent in western plutocracy. The Jews had to get out of Europe. This had constantly to be repeated in the political conflict built into the war. In his meetings with Antonescu and Horthy, Hitler was speaking, as always, for effect. As we have noted, he hoped to bind his wavering Axis partners closer to the Reich through complicity in the persecution of the Jews.

Though satisfied with the outcome of his talks with Antonescu, Hitler felt he had failed to make an impact on Horthy. Horthy had put forward what Hitler described – only from his perspective could they be seen as such – as 'humanitarian counter-arguments'. Hitler naturally dismissed them. As Goebbels summarized it, Hitler said: 'Towards Jewry there can be no talk of humanity. Jewry must be cast down to the ground.'

Earlier in the spring, Ribbentrop, picking up on fears expressed by Axis partners about their future under German domination, had put to Hitler loose notions of a future European federation. How little ice this cut with the Dictator can be seen from his reactions to his April meetings with heads of state and government – particularly the unsatisfactory discussion with Horthy. He drew the conclusion, he told the Gauleiter in early May, that the 'small-state rubbish' should be 'liquidated as soon as possible'. Europe must have a new form – but this could only be under German leadership. 'We live today,' he went on, 'in a world of destroying and being destroyed.' He expressed his certainty 'that the Reich will one day be master of the whole of Europe', paving the way for world domination. He hinted at the alternative. 'The Führer paints a shocking picture for the Reichs- and Gauleiter of the possibilities facing the Reich in the event of a German defeat. Such a defeat must therefore never find a place in our thoughts. We must regard it from the outset as impossible and determine to fight it to the last breath.'

Speaking to Goebbels on 6 May in Berlin, where he had come to attend the state funeral of SA-Chief Viktor Lutze (who had been killed in a car accident), Hitler accepted that the situation in Tunis was 'fairly hopeless'. The inability to get supplies to the troops meant there was no way out. Goebbels summarized the way Hitler was thinking: 'When you think that 150,000 of our best young people are still in Tunis, you rapidly get an idea of the catastrophe threatening us there. It'll be on the scale of Stalingrad, and certainly also produce the harshest criticism among the German people.' But when he spoke the next day to the

Reichs- and Gauleiter, Hitler never mentioned Tunis, making no reference at all to the latest news that Allied troops had penetrated as far as the outskirts of the city and that the harbour was already in British hands.

Axis troops were, in fact, by then giving themselves up in droves. Within a week, on 13 May, almost a quarter of a million of them – the largest number taken so far by the Allies, around half of them German, the remainder Italian – surrendered. Only about 800 managed to escape. North Africa was lost. The catastrophe left the Italian Axis partner reeling. For Mussolini, the writing was on the wall. But for Hitler, too, the defeat was nothing short of calamitous. One short step across the Straits of Sicily by the Allies would mean that the fortress of Europe was breached through its southern underbelly.

In the Atlantic, meanwhile, the battle was in reality lost, even if it took some months for this to become fully apparent. The resignation on 30 January 1943 as Commander-in-Chief of the Navy of Grand-Admiral Raeder, exponent of what Hitler had come to recognize as an outmoded naval strategy based upon a big surface battle fleet, and his replacement by Karl Dönitz, protagonist of the U-boat, had signalled an important shift in priorities. Hitler told his Gauleiter on 7 May that the U-boat was the weapon to cut through the arteries of the enemy. But, in fact, that very month forty-one U-boats carrying 1,336 men had been lost in the Atlantic – the highest losses in any single month during the war – and the number of vessels in operation at any one time had already passed its peak. The deciphering of German codes by British intelligence, using the 'Ultra' decoder, was allowing U-boat signals to be read. It was possible to know with some precision where the U-boats were operating. The use of long-range Liberators, equipped with radar, and able to cover 'the Atlantic Gap' – the 600-mile-wide stretch of the ocean from Greenland to the Azores, previously out of range of aircraft flying from both British and American shores – was a second strand of the mounting Allied success against the U-boat menace. The crucial supplies between North America and Britain, gravely imperilled over the previous two years, could flow with increasing security. Nothing could hinder the Reich's increasing disadvantage against the material might of the western Allies.

Hitler's greatest worry, once Tunis had fallen, was the condition of his longest-standing ally. By the time he heard a report on the situation in Italy in mid-May from Konstantin Alexander Freiherr von Neurath, son of the former Foreign Minister, and one-time Foreign Office liaison to Rommel's Afrika Korps, Hitler was deeply gloomy. He thought the monarchists and aristocracy had sabotaged the war-effort in Italy from the beginning, despite the Duce's personal strength of will. Hitler was sure that the reactionary forces associated with the King, Victor Emmanuel III – whose nominal powers as head of state had nevertheless still left him as the focus of a potential alternative source of loyalty – would triumph over the revolutionary forces of Fascism. A collapse had to be reckoned with. Plans must be made to defend the Mediterranean without Italy. How this was to be done with an offensive imminent in the east and no troops to spare, he did not say.

Hitler had intended around this time to move back to Vinnitsa. But the postponement of 'Citadel', the precarious situation in the Mediterranean, and problems with his own health made him decide suddenly to return from a short stay at the Wolf's Lair to the Obersalzberg. He remained there until the end of June. During his weeks in the Bavarian Alps, the Ruhr district, Germany's industrial heartland, continued to suffer devastation from the skies. In May there had been spectacular attacks on the big dams that supplied the area's water. Had they been sustained, the damage done would have been incalculable. As it was, the dams could be repaired. Since the 'dam-buster' raids, the major cities of Duisburg, Düsseldorf, Bochum, Dortmund, and Wuppertal-Barmen had been laid waste in intensive night bombardment. The inadequacy of the air-defences was all too apparent. Hitler continued to vent his bile on Göring and the Luftwaffe. But his own powerlessness to do anything about it was exposed. Goebbels at least showed his face, touring the bombed-out cities, speaking at a memorial service in his home town of Elberfeld, and at a big rally in Dortmund. Hitler stayed in his alpine idyll. The Propaganda Minister thought a visit by the Führer psychologically important for the population of the Ruhr. Though Goebbels had been impressed by the positive response he had encountered during his staged tour, more realistic impressions of morale provided in SD reports painted a different picture. Anger at the regime's failure to protect them was widespread. The 'Heil Hitler' greeting had almost disappeared. Hostile remarks about the regime, and about Hitler personally, were commonplace.

Hitler promised Goebbels towards the end of June that he would pay an extended visit to the devastated area. It was to take place 'the next week, or the week after that'. Hitler knew only too well that this was out of the question. He had by then scheduled the beginning of 'Citadel' for the first week in July. And he expected the Allied landing off the Italian coast at any time. The human suffering of the Ruhr population had, ultimately, little meaning for him. 'As regrettable as the personal losses are,' he told Goebbels, 'they have unfortunately to be taken on board in the interest of a superior war-effort.'

While on the Obersalzberg, Hitler was chiefly preoccupied with the prospect of an imminent invasion by the Allies in the south, and the approaching 'Citadel' offensive in the east.

He thought that the Allied landing would come in Sardinia. Sicily was in his view secure enough, and could be held. He thought the Italians more likely to give in bit by bit in deals with the enemy than to capitulate outright. His confidence in Mussolini had finally evaporated. It would be different, he thought, were the Duce still young and fit. But he was old and worn out. The royal family could not be trusted an inch. And – he added a characteristic last reflection – the Jews had not been done away with in Italy, whereas in Germany (as Goebbels summarized) 'we can be very glad that we have followed a radical policy. There are no Jews behind us who could inherit from us.'

As the war had turned remorselessly against Germany, the beleaguered Führer had reverted ever more to his obsession with Jewish responsibility for the conflagration. In his Manichean world-view, the fight to the finish between the forces of good and evil – the aryan race and the Jews – was reaching its climax. There could be no relenting in the struggle to wipe out Jewry.

Little over a month earlier, Hitler had talked at length, prompted by Goebbels, about the 'Jewish Question'. The Propaganda Minister thought it one of the most interesting discussions he had ever had with the Führer. Goebbels had being re-reading *The Protocols of the Elders of Zion* – the crude Russian forgery purporting to outline a Jewish conspiracy to rule the world – with an eye on its use in current propaganda. He raised the matter over lunch. Hitler was certain of the 'absolute authenticity' of the *Protocols*. The Jews, he thought, were not working to a fixed programme; they were following, as always, their 'racial instinct'. The Jews were the same all over the world, Goebbels noted him as saying, whether in the ghettos of the east 'or in the bank palaces of the City [of London] or Wall Street', and would instinctively follow the same aims and use the same methods without the need to work them out together. The question could well be posed, he went on (according to Goebbels's summary of his comments), as to why there were Jews at all. It was the same question – again the familiar insect analogy – as why there were Colorado beetles. His most basic belief – life as struggle – provided, as always, his answer. 'Nature is ruled by the law of struggle. There will always be parasitic forms of existence to accelerate the struggle and intensify the process of selection between the strong and the weak . . . In nature, life always works immediately against parasites; in the existence of peoples that is not exclusively the case. From that results the Jewish danger. So there is nothing else open to modern peoples than to exterminate the Jews.'

The Jews would use all means to defend themselves against this 'gradual process of annihilation'. One of its methods was war. It was the same warped vision embodied in Hitler's 'prophecy': Jews unleashing war, but bringing about their own destruction in the process. World Jewry, in Hitler's view, was on the verge of a historic downfall. This would take time. He was presumably alluding to Jews out of German reach, especially in the USA, when he commented that some decades would be needed 'to cast them out of their power. That is our historic mission, which can not be held up, but only accelerated, by the war. World Jewry thinks it is on the verge of a world victory. This world victory will not come. Instead there will be a world downfall. The peoples who have earliest recognized and fought the Jew will instead accede to world domination.'

Four days after this conversation, on 16 May, SS-Brigadeführer Jürgen Stroop telexed the news: 'The Jewish quarter of Warsaw is no more! The grand operation terminated at 20.15 hours when the Warsaw synagogue was blown up . . . The total number of Jews apprehended and destroyed, according to record, is 56,065 . . .' A force of around 3,000 men, the vast majority from the SS, had used a tank, armoured vehicles, heavy machine-guns, and artillery to blow up and set fire to buildings which the Jews were fiercely defending and to combat the courageous resistance put up by the ghetto's inhabitants, armed with little more than pistols, grenades, and Molotov cocktails. Hitler's long-standing readiness to link Jews with subversive or partisan actions made him all the keener to hasten their destruction. After Himmler had discussed the matter with him on 19 June, he noted that 'the Führer declared, after my report, that the evacuation of the Jews, despite the unrest that would thereby still arise in the next 3 to 4 months, was to be radically carried out and had to be seen through'.

Such discussions were always private. Hitler still did not speak of the fate of the Jews, except in the most generalized fashion, even among his inner circle. It was a topic which all in his company knew to avoid. To think of criticizing the treatment of the Jews was, of course, anathema. The only time the issue was raised occurred unexpectedly during the two-day visit to the Berghof in late June of Baldur von Schirach, Gauleiter of Vienna, and his wife, Henriette. The daughter of his photo-grapher Heinrich Hoffmann, Henriette had known Hitler since she was a child. She thought she could speak openly to him. Her husband had, however, fallen from favour somewhat, partly following Hitler's disapproval of the modern paintings on show in an art exhibition which Schirach had staged in Vienna earlier in the year. Henriette told Baldur on the way to Berchtesgaden that she wanted to let Hitler know what she had witnessed recently in Amsterdam, where she had seen a group of Jewish women brutally herded together and deported. An SS man had offered her valuables taken from the Jews at a knock-down price. Her husband told her not to mention it. Hitler's reactions were unpre-dictable. And – a typical response at the time – in any case she could not change anything.

Already during the first day of their visit, 23 June, Schirach had managed to prompt an angry riposte from Hitler with a suggestion that a different policy in the Ukraine might have paid dividends. Next afternoon, Hitler was in an irritable mood during the statutory visit to the Tea House. The atmosphere was icy. It remained tense in the evening when they gathered around the fire in the hall of the Berghof. Henriette was sitting next to Hitler, nervously rubbing her hands, speaking quietly. All at once, Hitler jumped up, marched up and down the room, and fumed: 'That's all I need, you coming to me with this sentimental twaddle. What concern are these Jewish women to you?' The other guests did not know where to look. There was a protracted, embarrassed silence. The logs could be heard crackling in the fireplace.

When Goebbels arrived, he turned the scene to his advantage by playing on Hitler's aversion to Vienna. Hitler rounded on the hapless Schirach, praising the achievements of Berlin – Goebbels's domain, of course – and castigating his Gauleiter's work in Vienna. Beside himself with anger, Hitler said it was a mistake ever to have sent Schirach to Vienna at all, or to have taken the Viennese into the Reich. Schirach offered to resign. 'That's not for you to decide. You are staying where you are,' was Hitler's response. By then it was four in the morning. Bormann let it be known to the Schirachs that it would be best if they left. They did so without saying their goodbyes, and in high disgrace.

The week before the Schirach incident, Hitler had finally decided to press ahead with the 'Citadel' offensive. His misgivings can only have been increased by Guderian's reports that the Panther still had major weaknesses and was not ready for front-line action. And in the middle of the month, he was presented with the OKW's recommendation that 'Citadel' should be cancelled. It was now running so late that there was an increasing chance that it would clash with the expected Allied offensive in the Mediterranean. Jodl, just back from leave, agreed that it was dangerous and foolhardy to commit troops to the east in the interests of, at best, a limited success when the chief danger at that time lay elsewhere. Again, the split between the OKW and army leadership came into play. Zeitzler objected to what he regarded as interference. Guderian suspected that Zeitzler's influence was decisive in persuading Hitler to go ahead. At any rate, Hitler rejected the advice of the Wehrmacht's Operations Staff. The opening of the offensive was scheduled for 3 July, then postponed one last time for two more days.

At the end of June, Hitler returned to the Wolf's Lair for the beginning of 'Citadel'. On 1 July, he addressed his commanders. The decision to go ahead was determined, he stated, by the need to forestall a Soviet offensive later in the year. A military success would also have a salutary effect on Axis partners, and on morale at home. Four days later, the last German offensive in the east was finally launched. It was the beginning of a disastrous month.

IV

Bombardment from Soviet heavy artillery just before the offensive began gave a clear indication that the Red Army had been alerted to the timing of 'Citadel'. At least 2,700 Soviet tanks had been brought in to defend Kursk. They faced a similar number of German tanks. The mightiest tank battle in history raged for over a week. At first both Model and

Manstein made good inroads, if with heavy losses. The Luftwaffe also had initial successes. But Guderian proved correct in his warnings of the deficiencies of the Panther. Most broke down. Few remained in action after a week. Manstein's drive was hindered rather than helped by the tank in which such high hopes had been placed. The ninety Porsche Tigers deployed by Model also revealed major battlefield weaknesses. They had no machine-guns, so were ill-equipped for close-range fighting. They were unable, therefore, to neutralize the enemy. In the middle of the month, the Soviets launched their own offensive against the German bulge around Orel to the north of the 'Citadel' battlefields, effectively to Model's rear. Though Manstein was still advancing, the northern part of the pincer was now endangered.

On 13 July, Hitler summoned Manstein and Kluge, the two Army Group Commanders, to assess the situation. Manstein was for continuing. Kluge stated that Model's army could not carry on. Reluctantly, Hitler brought 'Citadel' to a premature end. The Soviet losses were greater. But 'Citadel' had signally failed in its objectives.

Equally dire events were unfolding in the Mediterranean. Overnight from 9–10 July, reports came in of an armada of ships carrying large Allied assault forces from North Africa to Sicily. A landing had been expected – though in Sardinia, not Sicily. The precise timing caught Hitler unawares. The German troops in Sicily – only two divisions – were too few in number to hold the entire coast. Defence relied heavily upon Italian forces. Allied air superiority was soon all too evident. And alarming news came in of Italian soldiers casting away their weapons and fleeing. Though heavy fighting continued throughout July, within two days it was plain that the Allied landing had been successful. On 19 July, Hitler flew to see Mussolini in Feltre, near Belluno, in northern Italy. It was to prove the last time he set foot on Italian soil.

The visit was aimed at bolstering the Duce's faltering morale and preventing Italy agreeing a separate peace. Hitler's generals thought the visit had been a wasted effort. Hitler himself – convinced still of the power of his own rhetoric – probably thought he had once more succeeded in stirring Mussolini's fighting spirits. He was soon disabused. On the very evening after the Feltre talks, he was shown an intelligence report sent on by Himmler that a *coup d'état* was being planned to replace Mussolini by Marshal Pietro Badoglio.

During the course of Saturday, 24 July, reports started to come in that the Fascist Grand Council had been summoned for the first time since early in the war. The Council's lengthy deliberations culminated in an astonishing vote to request the King to seek a policy more capable of saving Italy from destruction. Later that morning, the King told Mussolini that, since the war appeared lost and army morale was collapsing, Marshal Badoglio would take over his offices as prime minister. As a stunned Duce left the royal chambers, he was bundled into a waiting ambulance and driven off at speed to house-arrest on the Mediterranean island of Ponza.

By the time of the evening military briefing in the Führer Headquarters, the sensational news from Italy had broken, though there was still not complete clarity. Almost the entire session was taken up with the implications. Since Italy had not pulled out of the war, plans to occupy the country in such an event – code-named 'Alarich' – could not be put into operation. But in a highly agitated mood, Hitler demanded immediate action to occupy Rome and depose the new regime. He denounced what had taken place as 'naked treachery', describing Badoglio as 'our grimmest enemy'. He still had belief in Mussolini – so long as he was propped up by German arms. Presuming the Duce still at liberty, he wanted him brought straight away to Germany. He was confident that in that event the situation could still be remedied. He fumed that he would send troops to Rome the next day to arrest the 'rabble' – the entire government, the King, the Crown Prince, Badoglio, the 'whole bunch'. In two or three days there would then be another coup. He had Göring – 'ice-cold in the most serious crises', as he had repeatedly stated at midday, the Reich Marshal's failings as head of the Luftwaffe temporarily forgotten – telephoned and told him to come as quickly as he could to the Wolf's Lair. Rommel was located in Salonika and summoned to present himself without delay. Hitler intended to put him in overall command in Italy. He wanted Himmler contacted. Goebbels, too, was telephoned and told to leave immediately for East Prussia. The situation, Goebbels acknowledged, was 'extraordinarily critical'. Ribbentrop, still not recovered from a chest infection, was ordered up from Fuschl, his residence in the Salzkammergut near Salzburg. Soon after midnight, Hitler met his military leaders for the third time in little over twelve hours, frantically improvising details for the evacuation from Sicily and the planned occupation of Rome, and for the seizure of the members of the new Italian government.

At ten o'clock that morning, 26 July, Hitler met Goebbels and Göring, just arrived in FHQ. Ribbentrop joined them half an hour later. Hitler gave his interpretation of the situation. He presumed that Mussolini had been forced out of power. Whether he was still alive was not known, but he would certainly be unfree. Hitler saw the forces of Italian free-masonry – banned by Mussolini but still at work behind the scenes – behind the plot. Ultimately, he claimed, the coup was directed at Germany since Badoglio would certainly come to an arrangement with the British and Americans to take Italy out of the war. The British would now look for the best moment for a landing in Italy – perhaps in Genoa in order to cut off German troops in the south. Military precautions to anticipate such a move had to be taken.

Hitler explained, too, his intention of transferring a parachute division, currently based in southern France, to Rome as part of the move to occupy the city. The King, Badoglio, and the members of the new government would be arrested and flown to Germany. Once they were in German hands, things would be different. Possibly Roberto Farinacci, the radical Fascist boss of Cremona and former Party Secretary, who had escaped arrest by fleeing to the German Embassy and was now *en route* to FHQ, could be made head of a puppet government if Mussolini himself could not be rescued. Hitler saw the Vatican, too, as deeply implicated in the plot to oust Mussolini. In the military briefing just after midnight he had talked wildly of occupying the Vatican and 'getting out the whole lot of swine'. Goebbels and Ribbentrop dissuaded him from such rash action, certain to have damaging international reper-cussions. Hitler still pressed for rapid action to capture the new Italian government. Rommel, who by then had also arrived in FHQ, opposed the improvised, high-risk, panicky response. He favoured a carefully prepared action; but that would probably take some eight days to put into place. The meeting ended with the way through the crisis still unclear.

The midday military conference was again taken up with the issue of moving troops to Italy to secure above all the north of the country, and with the hastily devised scheme to capture the Badoglio government. Field-Marshal von Kluge, who had flown in from Army Group Centre – desperately trying to hold the Soviet offensive in the Orel bulge, to the north of Kursk – was abruptly told of the implications of the events in Italy for the eastern front. Hitler said he needed the crack Waffen-SS divisions currently assigned to Manstein in the south of the eastern front to be transferred immediately to Italy. That meant Kluge giving up some of his forces to reinforce Manstein's weakened front. Kluge forcefully pointed out, though to no avail, that this would make defence in the Orel region impossible. But the positions on the Dnieper being prepared for an orderly retreat by his troops to be taken up before winter were far from ready. What he was being asked to do, protested Kluge, was to undertake 'an absolutely overhasty evacuation'. 'Even so, Herr Feldmarshall: we are not master here of our own decisions,' rejoined Hitler. Kluge was left with no choice.

Meanwhile, Farinacci had arrived. His description of what had happened and his criticism of Mussolini did not endear him to Hitler. Any idea of using him as the figurehead of a German-controlled regime was discarded. Hitler spoke individually to his leading henchmen before, in need of a rest after a hectic twenty-four hours, retiring to his rooms to eat alone. He returned for a lengthy conference that evening, attended by thirty-five persons. But the matter was taken no further. Within a few days, he was forced to concede that any notion of occupying Rome and sending in a raiding party to take the members of the Badoglio government and the Italian royal family captive was both precipitate and wholly impracticable. The plans were called off. Hitler's attention focused now on discovering the whereabouts of the Duce and bringing him into German hands as soon as possible.

With the Italian crisis still at its height, the disastrous month of July drew to a close amid the heaviest air-raids to date. Between 24 and 30 July, the Royal Air Force's Bomber Command, using the release of aluminium strips to blind German radar, unleashed 'Operation Gomorrha' – a series of devastating raids on Hamburg, outdoing in death and destruction anything previously experienced in the air-war. Waves of incendiaries whipped up horrific fire-storms, turning the city into a raging inferno, consuming everything and everybody in their path. People suffocated in their thousands in cellars or were burnt to cinders on the streets. An estimated 30,000 people lost their lives; over half a million were left homeless; twenty-four hospitals, fifty-eight churches, and 277 schools lay in ruins; over 50 per cent of the city was completely gutted. As usual, Hitler revealed no sense of remorse at any human losses. He was chiefly concerned about the psychological impact. When he was given news that fifty German planes had mined the Humber estuary, he exploded: 'You can't tell the German people in this situation: that's mined; 50 planes have laid mines! That has no effect at all . . . You only break terror through terror! We have to have counter-attacks. Everything else is rubbish.'

Hitler mistook the mood of a people with whom he had lost touch. What they wanted, in their vast majority, was less the retaliation that was Hitler's only thought than proper defence against the terror from the skies and – above all else – an end to the war that was costing them their homes and their lives. But Hitler remained, as he had been throughout the agony of Hamburg, more taken up with events in Italy.

Though he had still rejected any evacuation of Sicily, insistent that the enemy should not set foot on the Italian mainland, Kesselring had taken steps to prepare the ground for what proved a brilliantly planned evacuation on the night of 11–12 August, catching the Allies by surprise and allowing 40,000 German and 62,000 Italian troops, with their equipment, to escape to safety. But as August drew on, suspicions mounted that it would not be long before the Italians defected. And at the end of the month, directives for action in the event of an Italian defection, in the drawer for months and now refashioned under the code-name 'Axis', were issued.

Under the pressure of the events in Italy, Hitler had finally made one overdue move at home. For months, egged on by Goebbels, he had expressed his dissatisfaction with the Reich Minister of the Interior, Wilhelm Frick, whom he contemptuously regarded as 'old and worn-out'. But he could think of no alternative. He continued to defer any decision until the toppling of Mussolini concentrated his mind, persuading him that the time had come to stiffen the grip on the home front and eliminate any prospect of poor morale turning into subversive action. The man he could depend upon to do this was close at hand.

On 20 August he appointed Reichsführer-SS Heinrich Himmler as the new Reich Minister of the Interior. The appointment amounted to Hitler's tacit recognition that his authority at home now rested on police repression, not the adulation of the masses he had once enjoyed.

On 3 September the first British troops crossed the Straits of Messina to Italy, landing at Reggio di Calabria. That same day, the Italians secretly signed their armistice with the Allies which became public knowledge five days later.

On 8 September Hitler had flown for the second time within a fortnight to Army Group South's headquarters at Zaporozhye, on the lower Dnieper north of the Sea of Azov, to confer with Manstein about the increasingly critical situation on the southern flank of the eastern front. It was to be the last time he set foot on territory captured from the Soviet Union. A few days earlier, following Soviet breakthroughs, he had been forced to authorize withdrawal from the Donets Basin – so important for its rich coal deposits – and from the Kuban bridgehead over the Straits of Kerch, the gateway to the Crimea. Now the Red Army had breached the thin seam which had knitted together Kluge's and Manstein's Army Groups and was pouring through the gap. Retreat was the only possible course of action.

Hitler found a tense atmosphere at the Wolf's Lair on his return. What he had long anticipated was reality. British and American newspapers had that morning, 8 September, carried reports that the capitulation of the Italian army was imminent. By the afternoon, the news was hardening. At 6 p.m. that evening the stories were confirmed by the BBC in London. Once again, Nazi leaders were summoned to Führer Headquarters for a crisis-meeting next day. The order had meanwhile been given to set 'Operation Axis' in motion. 'The Führer,' wrote Goebbels, 'is determined to make a *tabula rasa* in Italy.'

The BBC's premature announcement gave the OKW's Operations Staff a head start. Sixteen German divisions had been moved to the Italian mainland by this time. The battle-hardened SS units withdrawn from the eastern front in late July and early August and troops pulled back from Sicily, Corsica, and Sardinia were in position to take control in central Italy. By 10 September, Rome was in German hands. Italian troops were disarmed. Small pockets of resistance were ruthlessly put down; one division that held out until 22 September ended with 6,000 dead. Over 650,000 soldiers entered German captivity. Only the bulk of the small navy and ineffective air-force escaped and were given over to the Allies. Within a few days Italy was occupied by its former Axis partner.

Hours after the Italian capitulation, the Allies had landed in the Gulf of Salerno, thirty miles or so south-east of Naples. The dogged German resistance they encountered for a week before reinforcements enabled them to break out of their threatened beachhead – linking forces with troops from Montgomery's 8th Army advancing northwards from Reggio di Calabria, and entering Naples on 1 October – was an indicator of what was in store for the Allies during the coming months as the Wehrmacht made them fight for every mile of their northward progression.

It was plain to the German leadership, however, that it would be even more difficult, in the new situation, for the armed forces to cope with the mounting pressures on both the eastern and the southern fronts. Goebbels saw the need looming to seek peace with either the Soviet Union or the western Allies. He suggested the time had come to sound out Stalin. Ribbentrop took the same line. He had tentative feelers put out to see whether the Soviet dictator would bite. But Hitler dismissed the idea. If anything, he said, he preferred to look for an arrangement with Britain – conceivably open to one. But, as always, he would not consider negotiating from a position of weakness. In the absence of the decisive military success he needed, which was receding ever more into the far distance, any hope of persuading him to consider an approach other than the remorseless continuation of the struggle was bound to be illusory.

At least Goebbels, backed by Göring, successfully this time pleaded with Hitler to speak to the German people. To the last minute before recording the broadcast, on 10 September, Hitler showed his reluctance. He wanted to delay, to see how things turned out. Goebbels went through the text with him line by line. Eventually, he got the Führer to the microphone. The speech itself – largely confined to unstinting praise for Mussolini, condemnation of Badoglio and his supporters, the claim that the 'treachery' had been foreseen and every necessary step taken, and a call to maintain confidence and sustain the fight – had nothing of substance to offer, other than a hint at coming retaliation for the bombing of German cities. But Goebbels was satisfied. Reports suggested the speech had gone down well, and helped revive morale.

As far as the situation in Italy itself was concerned, Hitler was at this time resigned to losing any hold over the south of the country. His intention was to withdraw to the Apennines, long foreseen by the OKH Operations Staff as the favoured line of defence. However, he worried about the Allies advancing from Italy through the Balkans. By autumn, this concern was to persuade him to change his mind and defend Italy much farther to the south. A consequence was to tie down forces desperately needed elsewhere.

The Wehrmacht's rapid successes in taking hold of Italy so speedily provided some relief. Hitler's spirits then soared temporarily when the stunning news came through on the evening of 12 September that Mussolini, whose whereabouts had been recently discovered, had been freed from his captors in a ski hotel on the highest mountain in the Abruzzi through an extraordinarily daring raid by parachutists and SS-men carried in by glider and led by the Austrian SS-Hauptsturmführer Otto Skorzeny. The euphoria did not last long. Hitler greeted the ex-Duce warmly when Mussolini, no longer the preening dictator but looking haggard and dressed soberly in a dark suit and black overcoat, was brought to Rastenburg on 14 September. But Mussolini, bereft of the trappings of power, was a broken man. The series of private talks they had left Hitler 'extraordinarily disappointed'. Three days later, Mussolini was dispatched to Munich to begin forming his new regime. By the end of September he had set up his reconstituted Fascist 'Repubblica di Salò' in northern Italy, a repressive, brutish police state run by a combination of cruelty, corruption, and thuggery – but operating unmistakably under the auspices of German masters. The one-time bombastic dictator of Italy was now plainly no more than Hitler's tame puppet, and living on borrowed time.

As autumn progressed, the situation on the eastern front predictably worsened. The redeployment of troops to Italy weakened the chances of staving off the Soviet offensive. And the failure to erect the 'eastern wall' of fortifications along the Dnieper during the two years that it had been in German hands now proved costly. The speed of the Soviet advance gave no opportunity to construct any solid defence line. By the end of September the Red Army had been able to cross the Dnieper and establish important bridgeheads on the west banks of the great river. The German bridgehead at Zaporozhye was lost in early October. By then, the Wehrmacht had been pushed back about 150 miles along the southern front. German and Romanian troops were also cut off on the Crimea, which Hitler refused to evacuate, fearing, as of old, the opportunities it would give for air-attacks on Romanian oil-fields, and concerned about the message it would send to Turkey and Bulgaria. By the end of the month, the Red Army had pushed so far over the big bend of the Dnieper in the south that any notion of the Germans holding their intended defensive line was purely fanciful. To the north, the largest Soviet city in German hands, Kiev, was recaptured on 5–6 November. Manstein wanted to make the attempt to retake it. For Hitler, the lower

Dnieper and the Crimea were more important. Control of the lower Dnieper held the key to the protection of the manganese ores of Nikopol, vital for the German steel industry. And should the Red Army again control the Crimea, the Romanian oil-fields would once more be threatened from the air. But, whatever Hitler's thirst for new military successes, the reality was that by the end of 1943, the limitless granaries of the Ukraine and the industrial heartlands of the northern Caucasus, seen by Hitler on so many occasions as vital to the war effort (as well as the source of future German prosperity in the 'New Order'), were irredeemably lost.

V

Not lost, however, was the war against the Jews. By autumn 1943, 'Aktion Reinhard' was terminated: in the region of 1½ million Jews had been killed in the gas-chambers of extermination camps at Belzec, Sobibor, and Treblinka in eastern Poland. The SS leadership were now pressing hard for the extension of the 'Final Solution' to all remaining corners of the Nazi *imperium* – even those where the deportations were likely to have diplomatic repercussions. Among these were Denmark and Italy.

In September, Hitler complied with the request of Werner Best, the Reich Plenipotentiary in Denmark, to have the Danish Jews deported, dismissing Ribbentrop's anxieties about a possible general strike and other civil disobedience. Though these did not materialize, the round-up of Danish Jews was a resounding failure. Several hundred – under ten per cent of the Jewish population – were captured and deported to Theresienstadt. Most escaped. Countless Danish citizens helped the overwhelming majority of their Jewish countrymen – in all 7,900 persons, including a few hundred non-Jewish marital partners – to flee across the Sound to safety in neutral Sweden in the most remarkable rescue action of the war.

In October, Hitler accepted Ribbentrop's recommendation (prompted by the Reich Security Head Office) to have Rome's 8,000 Jews sent 'as hostages' to the Austrian concentration camp at Mauthausen. Again, the 'action' to round up the Jews misfired. Most of the Jewish community were able to avoid capture. Some were hidden by disgusted non-Jewish citizens. Thousands found shelter in Rome's convents and monasteries, or in the Vatican itself. In return, the Papacy was prepared to maintain public silence on the outrage. Despite Hitler's directive, following his Foreign Minister's advice, those Jews captured were not, in fact, sent to Mauthausen. Of the 1,259 Jews who fell into German hands, the majority were taken straight to Auschwitz.

Hitler's compliance with SS demands to speed up and finish off the 'Final Solution' was unquestionably driven by his wish to complete the destruction of those he held responsible for the war. He wanted, now as before, to see the 'prophecy' he had declared in 1939 and repeatedly referred to fulfilled. But, even more so than in the spring when he had encouraged Goebbels to turn up the volume of antisemitic propaganda, there was also the need, with backs to the wall, to hold together his closest followers in a sworn 'community of fate', bonded by their own knowledge of and implication in the extermination of the Jews.

On 4 October, Reichsführer-SS Heinrich Himmler spoke openly and frankly about the killing of the Jews to SS leaders gathered in the town hall in Posen, the capital of the Warthegau. He said he was 'referring to the Jewish evacuation programme, the extermination of the Jewish people'. It was, he went on, 'a glorious page in our history, and one that has never been written and never can be written. For we know how difficult we would have made it for ourselves if, on top of the bombing raids, the burdens and the deprivations of war, we still had Jews today in every town as secret saboteurs, agitators, and troublemakers. We would now probably have reached the 1916–17 stage when the Jews were still part of the body of the German people.' The mentality was identical with Hitler's. 'We had the moral right, we had the duty to our people,' Himmler concluded, 'to destroy this people which wanted to destroy us . . . We do not want in the end, because we have exterminated a bacillus, to become ill through the bacillus and die.' The vocabulary, too, was redolent of Hitler's own. Himmler did not refer to Hitler. There was no need to do so. The key point for the Reichsführer-SS was not to assign responsibility to a single person. The crucial purpose of his speech was to stress their joint responsibility, that they were all in it together.

Two days later, in the same Golden Hall in Posen, Himmler addressed the Reichs- and Gauleiter of the party. The theme was the same one. He gave, as Goebbels recorded, an 'unvarnished and candid picture' of the treatment of the Jews. Himmler declared: 'We faced the question: what should we do with the women and children? I decided here too to find a completely clear solution. I did not regard myself as justified in exterminating the men – that is to say, to kill them or have them killed – and to allow the avengers in the shape of the children to grow up for our sons and grandchildren. The difficult decision had to be taken to have this people disappear from the earth.' Himmler seemed to be indicating that the extension of the killing to women and children had been his initiative. He immediately, however, associated himself and the SS with a 'commission' – 'the most difficult which we have had so far'. The Gauleiter, among them Goebbels who had spoken directly with Hitler on the subject so many times, would have had no difficulty in presuming whose authority lay behind the 'commission'. Again, the purpose of the remarkably frank disclosures on the taboo subject was plain. Himmler marked on a list those who had not attended his speech or noted its contents.

Himmler's speeches, ensuring that his own subordinates and the party leadership were fully in the picture about the extermination of the Jews, had been – there can be no doubt about it – carried out with Hitler's approval. The very next day, after listening to Himmler, the Gauleiter were ordered to attend the Wolf's Lair to hear Hitler himself give an account of the state of the war. That the Führer would speak explicitly on the 'Final Solution' was axiomatically ruled out. But he could now take it for granted that they understood there was no way out. Their knowledge underlined their complicity. 'The entire German people know,' Hitler had told the Reichs- and Gauleiter, 'that it is a matter of whether they exist or do not exist. The bridges have been destroyed behind them. Only the way forward remains.'

When (for the last time, as it turned out) Hitler addressed the party's Old Guard in Munich's Löwenbräukeller on the putsch anniversary, 8 November, he was as defiant as ever. There would be no capitulation, no repeat of 1918, he declared once again – the nightmare of that year indelibly imprinted on his psyche – and no undermining of the front by subversion at home. Any overheard subversive or defeatist remark, it was clear, would cost the person making it his or her head.

By this time – though of course he made no hint of it in his speech – Hitler was anxious about a looming new grave military threat, one which, if not repulsed, would result in Germany's destruction: what he took to be the certainty of an invasion in the west during the coming year. 'The danger in the east remains,' ran his preamble to his Directive No. 51 on 3 November, 'but a greater danger is looming in the west: the Anglo-Saxon landing! ... If the enemy succeeds here in breaking through our defence on a broad front, the consequences within a short time are unforeseeable. Everything suggests that the enemy, at the latest in spring but perhaps even earlier, will move to attack the western front of Europe.'

To his military advisers, on 20 December, he said he was certain that the invasion would take place some time after mid-February or early March. The next months would be spent in preparation for the coming great assault in the west. This, Hitler remarked, would 'decide the war'.

24

Hoping for Miracles

'The year 1944 will make tough and severe demands of all Germans. The course of the war, in all its enormity, will reach its critical point during this year. We are fully confident that we will successfully surmount it.' This, and the prospect of new cities rising resplendently after the war from the bombed-out ruins, was all Hitler had to offer readers of his New Year proclamation in 1944. Fewer than ever of them were able to share his confidence. For the embattled soldiers at the front, Hitler's message was no different. The military crisis of 1943 had been brought about, he told them, by sabotage and treachery by the French in North Africa and the Italians following the overthrow of Mussolini. But the greatest crisis in German history had been triumphantly mastered. However hard the fighting in the east had been, 'Bolshevism has not achieved its goal.' He glanced at the western Allies, and at the future: 'The plutocratic western world can undertake its threatened attempt at a landing where it wants: it will fail!'

Since Germany had been forced on to the defensive, experiencing only setbacks, Hitler had not changed his tune. His stance had become immobilized, fossilized. In his view, the military disasters had been the consequence of betrayal, incompetence, disobedience of orders, and, above all, weakness. He conceded not a single error or misjudgement on his own part. No capitulation; no surrender; no retreat; no repeat of 1918; hold out at all costs, whatever the odds: this was the unchanging message. Alongside this went the belief – unshakeable (apart, perhaps, from his innermost thoughts and bouts of depression during sleepless nights) but an item of blind faith, not resting on reason – that the strength to hold out would eventually lead to a turning of the tide, and to Germany's final victory. In public, he expressed his unfounded optimism through references to the grace of Providence. As he put it to his soldiers on 1 January 1944, after overcoming the defensive period then returning to the attack to impose devastating blows on the enemy, 'Providence will bestow victory on the people that has done most to earn it.' His instinctive belief in reward for the strongest remained intact. 'If, therefore, Providence grants life as the prize to those who have fought and defended the most courageously, then our people will find mercy from the just arbiter who at all times gave victory to the most meritorious.'

However hollow such sentiments sounded to men at the various fronts, suffering untold hardships, enduring hourly danger, often realizing they would never see their loved ones again, they were, for Hitler himself, far from mere cynical propaganda. He had to believe these ideas – and did, certainly down to the summer of 1944, if not longer. The references, in public and private, to 'Providence' and 'Fate' increased as his own control over the course of the war declined. The views on the course of the war which he expressed to his generals, to other Nazi leaders, and to his immediate entourage gave no inkling that his own resolve was wavering, or that he had become in any way resigned to the prospect of defeat. If it was an act, then it was one brilliantly sustained, and remained substantially unchanged whatever the context or personnel involved. 'It is impressive, with what certainty the Führer believes in his mission,' noted Goebbels in his diary in early June 1944. Others who saw Hitler frequently, in close proximity, and were less impressionable than Goebbels, thought the same. Without the inner conviction, Hitler would have been unable to sway those around him, as he continued so often to do, to find new resolve. Without it, he would not have engaged so fanatically in bitter conflicts with his military leaders. Without it, he would have been incapable, not least, of sustaining in himself the capacity to continue, despite increasingly overwhelming odds.

The astonishing optimism did not give way, despite the mounting crises and calamities of the first half of 1944. But the self-deception involved was colossal. Hitler lived increasingly in a world of illusion, clutching as the year wore on ever more desperately at whatever straws he could find. The invasion, when it came, would be repulsed without doubt, he thought. He placed enormous hopes, too, in the devastating effect of the 'wonder-weapons'. When they failed to match expectations, he would remain convinced that the alliance against him was fragile and would soon fall apart, as had occurred in the Seven Years War two centuries earlier following the indomitable defence of one of his heroes, Frederick the Great. Even at the very end of a catastrophic year for Germany, he would not give up hope of this happening. He would still be hoping for miracles.

He had, however, no rational ways out of the inevitable catastrophe to offer those who, in better times, had lavished their adulation upon him. Albert Speer, in a pen-picture drawn immediately after the war, saw Hitler's earlier 'genius' at finding 'elegant' ways out of crises eroded by relentless overwork imposed on him by war's demands, undermining the intuition which had required the more spacious and leisured life-style suited to an artistic temperament. The change in work-patterns – turning himself, against his natural temperament, into an obsessive workaholic, preoccupied by detail, unable to relax, surrounded by an unchanging and uninspiring entourage – had brought in its train, thought Speer, enormous mental strain together with increased inflexi-bility and obstinacy in decisions which had closed off all but the route to disaster.

It was certainly the case that Hitler's entire existence had been con-sumed by the prosecution of the war. The leisured times of the pre-war years were gone. The impatience with detail, detachment from day-to-day issues, preoccupation with grandiose architectural schemes, gener-ous allocation of time for relaxation, listening to music, watching films, indulging in the indolence which had been a characteristic since his youth, had indeed given way to a punishing work-schedule in which Hitler brooded incessantly over the most detailed matters of military tactics, leaving little or no space for anything unconnected with the conduct of war in a routine essentially unchanged day in and day out. Nights with little sleep; rising late in the mornings; lengthy midday and early evening conferences, often extremely stressful, with his military leaders; a strict, spartan diet, and meals often taken alone in his room; no exercise beyond a brief daily walk with his Alsatian bitch, Blondi; the same surrounds, the same entourage; late-night monologues to try to wind down (at the expense of his bored entourage), reminiscing about his youth, the First World War, and the 'good old times' of the Nazi Party's rise to power; then, finally, another attempt to find sleep: such a routine – only marginally more relaxed when he was at the Berghof –

could not but be in the long run harmful to health and was scarcely conducive to calm and considered, rational reflection.

All who saw him pointed out how Hitler had aged during the war. He had once appeared vigorous, full of energy, to those around him. Now, his hair was greying fast, his eyes were bloodshot, he walked with a stoop, he had difficulty controlling a trembling left arm; for a man in his mid-fifties, he looked old. His health had started to suffer notably from 1941 onwards. The increased numbers of pills and injections provided every day by Dr Morell – ninety varieties in all during the war and twenty-eight different pills each day – could not prevent the physical deterioration.

By 1944, Hitler was a sick man – at times during the year extremely unwell. Cardiograms, the first taken in 1941, had revealed a worsening heart condition. And beyond the chronic stomach and intestinal problems that had increasingly come to plague him, Hitler had since 1942 developed symptoms, becoming more pronounced in 1944, which point with some medical certainty to the onset of Parkinson's Syndrome. Most notably, an uncontrollable trembling of the left arm, jerking in his left leg, and a shuffling gait, were unmistakable to those who saw him at close quarters. But although the strains of the last phase of the war took their toll on him, there is no convincing evidence that Hitler's mental capacity was impaired. His rages and violent mood-swings were inbuilt features of his character, their frequency in the final phase of the war a reflection of the stress from the rapidly deteriorating military conditions and his own inability to change them, bringing, as usual, wild lashings at his generals and any others on whom he could lay the blame that properly began at his own door.

In looking to the loss of 'genius' through pressures of overwork inappropriate to Hitler's alleged natural talent for improvisation, Speer was offering a naive and misleading explanation of Germany's fate, ultimately personalizing it in the 'demonic' figure of Hitler. The adoption of such a harmfully over-burdensome style of working was no chance development. It was the direct outcome of an extreme form of personalized rule which had already by the time war began seriously eroded the more formal and regular structures of government and military command that are essential in modern states. The reins of power were entirely held in Hitler's hands. He was still backed by major power bases. None existed – whatever the growing anxieties among the military, some leading industrialists, and a number of senior figures in the state bureaucracy about the road down which he was taking them – that could bypass the Führer. All vital measures, both in military and in domestic affairs, needed his authorization. There were no overriding coordinating bodies – no war cabinet, no politburo. But Hitler, forced entirely on to the defensive in running the war, was now often almost paralysed in his thinking, and often in his actions. And in matters relating to the 'home front', while refusing to concede an inch of his authority he was, as Goebbels interminably bemoaned, nevertheless incapable of more than sporadic, unsystematic interventions or prevaricating inaction.

Far more gifted individuals than Hitler would have been overstretched and incapable of coping with the scale and nature of the administrative problems involved in the conduct of a world war. Hitler's triumphs in foreign policy in the 1930s, then as war leader until 1941, had not arisen from his 'artistic genius' (as Speer saw it), but in the main from his unerring skill in exploiting the weaknesses and divisions of his opponents, and through the timing of actions carried out at breakneck speed. Not 'artistic genius', but the gambler's instinct when playing for high stakes with a good hand against weak opponents had served Hitler well in those earlier times. Those aggressive instincts worked as long as the initiative could be retained. But once the gamble had failed, and he was playing a losing hand in a long-drawn-out match with the odds becoming increasingly more hopeless, the instincts lost their effectiveness. Hitler's individual characteristics now fatefully merged, in conditions of mounting disaster, into the structural weaknesses of the dictatorship. His ever-increasing distrust of those around him, especially his generals, was one side of the coin. The other was his unbounded egomania, which cholerically expressed itself – all the more pronounced as disasters started to accumulate – in the belief that no one else was competent or trustworthy, and that he alone could ensure victory. His takeover of the operational command of the army in the winter crisis of 1941 had been the most obvious manifestation of this disastrous syndrome.

Speer's explanation was even more deficient in ignoring the fact that Germany's catastrophic situation in 1944 was the direct consequence of the steps which Hitler – overwhelmingly supported by the most powerful forces within the country, and widely acclaimed by the masses – had taken in the years when his 'genius' (in Speer's perception) had been less constrained. Not changes in his work-style, but the direct result of a war he – and much of the military leadership – had wanted meant that Hitler could find no 'elegant' solution to the stranglehold increasingly imposed by the mighty coalition which German aggression had called into being. He was left, therefore, with no choice but to face the reality that the war was lost, or to hold fast to illusions.

Ever fewer Germans shared Hitler's undiminished fatalism about the outcome of the war. The Dictator's rhetoric, so powerful in 'sunnier' periods, had lost its ability to sway the masses. Either they believed what he said; or they believed their own eyes and ears – gazing out over devastated cities, reading the ever-longer lists of fallen soldiers in the death-columns of the newspapers, hearing the sombre radio announcements (however they were dressed up) of further Soviet advances, seeing no sign that the fortunes of war were turning. Hitler sensed that he had lost the confidence of his people. The great orator no longer had his audience. With no triumphs to proclaim, he did not even want to speak to the German people any longer. The bonds between the Führer and the people had been a vital basis of the regime in earlier times. But now, the gulf between ruler and ruled had widened to a chasm.

During 1944 Hitler would distance himself from the German people still further than he had done in the previous two years. He was physically detached – cocooned for the most part in his field headquarters in East Prussia or in his mountain idyll in Bavaria – and scarcely now visible, even in newsreels, for ordinary Germans.

On not a single occasion during 1944 did he appear in public to deliver a speech. When, on 24 February, the anniversary of the proclamation of the Party Programme of 1920, he spoke in the Hofbräuhaus in Munich to the closed circle of the party's 'Old Guard', he expressly refused Goebbels's exhortations to have the speech broadcast and no mention was made of the speech in the newspapers. Twice, on 30 January 1944 and early on 21 July, he addressed the nation on the radio. Otherwise the German people did not hear directly from their Leader throughout 1944. Even his traditional address to the 'Old Fighters' of the party on 8 November was read out by Himmler. For the masses, Hitler had become a largely invisible leader. He was out of sight and for most, probably, increasingly out of mind – except as an obstacle to the ending of the war.

The intensified level of repression during the last years of the war, along with the negative unity forged by fear of the victory of Bolshevism, went a long way towards ensuring that the threat of internal revolt, as had happened in 1918, never materialized. But, for all the continuing (and in some ways astonishing) reserves of strength of the Führer cult among outright Nazi supporters, Hitler had become for the overwhelming majority of Germans the chief hindrance to the ending of the war. Ordinary people might prefer, as they were reported to be saying, 'an end with horror' to 'a horror without end'. But they had no obvious way of altering their fate. Only those who moved in the corridors of power had any possibility of removing Hitler. Some groups of officers, through conspiratorial links with certain highly-placed civil servants, were plotting precisely that. After a number of abortive attempts, their strike would come in July 1944. It would prove the last chance the Germans themselves had to put an end to the Nazi regime. The bitter rivalries of the subordinate leaders, the absence of any centralized forum (equivalent to the Fascist Grand Council in Italy) from which an internal coup could be launched, the shapelessness of the structures of Nazi rule yet the indispensability of Hitler's authority to every facet of that rule, and, not least, the fact that the regime's leaders had burnt their boats with the Dictator in the regime's genocide and other untold acts of inhumanity, ruled out any further possibility of overthrow. With that, the regime had only its own collective suicide in an inexorably lost war to contemplate. But like a mortally wounded wild beast at bay, it fought with the ferocity and ruthlessness that came from desperation. And its Leader, losing touch ever more with reality, hoping for miracles, kept tilting at windmills – ready in Wagnerian style in the event of ultimate apocalyptic catastrophe, and in line with his undiluted social-Darwinistic beliefs, to take his people down in flames with him if it proved incapable of producing the victory he had demanded.

II

Readiness for the invasion in the west, certain to come within the next few months, was the overriding preoccupation of Hitler and his military advisers in early 1944. They were sure that the critical phase directly following the invasion would decide the outcome of the war. Hopes were invested in the fortifications swiftly being erected along the Atlantic coast in France, and in the new, powerful weapons of destruction that were under preparation and would help the Wehrmacht to inflict a resounding defeat on the invaders as soon as they set foot on continental soil. Forced back, with Britain reeling under devastating blows from weapons of untold might, against which there was no defence, the western Allies would realize that Germany could not be defeated; the 'unnatural' alliance with the Soviet Union would split apart; and, freed of the danger in the west, the German Reich could devote all its energies, perhaps now even with British and American backing following a separate peace agreement, to the task of repelling and defeating Bolshevism. So ran the optimistic currents of thought in Hitler's headquarters.

Meanwhile, developments on the eastern front – the key theatre of the war – were more than worrying enough to hold Hitler's attention. A new Soviet offensive in the south of the eastern front had begun on 24 December 1943, making rapid advances, and dampening an already dismal Christmas mood in the Führer Headquarters. Hitler spent New Year's Eve closeted in his rooms alone with Bormann. He took part in no festivities. At least in the company of Martin Bormann, his loyal right-hand in all party matters, he was 'among his own'. In his daily military conferences, it was different. The tensions with his generals were palpable. Some loyalists around Hitler, such as Jodl, shared in some measure his optimism. Others were already more sceptical. According to Hitler's Luftwaffe adjutant, Nicolaus von Below, even the initially starry-eyed Chief of the Army General Staff Kurt Zeitzler by now did not believe a word Hitler said. What Hitler really felt about the war, whether he harboured private doubts that conflicted with the optimism he voiced at all times, was even for those regularly in his close company impossible to deduce.

Whatever his innermost thoughts, his outward stance was predictable. Retreat, whatever the tactical necessity or even advantage to be gained from it, was ruled out. When the retreat then inevitably did eventually take place, it was invariably under less favourable conditions than at the time that it had been initially proposed. 'Will' to hold out was, as always, the supreme value for Hitler. What was, in fact, required was greater military skill and tactical flexibility than the Commander-in-Chief of the Army himself could muster. In these circumstances, Hitler's obstinacy and interference in tactical matters posed ever greater difficulties for his field commanders.

Manstein encountered Hitler's inflexibility again when he flew on 4 January 1944 to Führer Headquarters to report on the rapidly deteriorating situation of Army Group South. Soviet forces, centred on the Dnieper bend, had made major advances. These now posed an ominous threat to the survival of the 4th Panzer Army (located in the region between Vinnitsa and Berichev). The breach of this position would open up a massive gap between Army Groups South and Centre, putting therefore the entire southern front in mortal peril. It demanded, in Manstein's view, the urgent transfer of forces northwards to counter the threat. This could only be done by evacuating the Dnieper bend, abandoning Nikopol (with its manganese supplies) and the Crimea, and drastically reducing the front to a length which could more easily be defended. Hitler refused point-blank to countenance such a proposal. Losing the Crimea, he argued, would prompt Turkey's abandonment of neutrality and the defection of Bulgaria and Romania. Reinforcements for the threatened northern wing could not be drawn from Army Group North, since that could well lead to the defection of Finland, loss of the Baltic, and lack of availability of vital Swedish ore. Forces could not be drawn from the west before the invasion had been repelled. 'There were so many disagreements on the enemy side,' Manstein recalled Hitler stating, 'that the coalition was bound to fall apart one day. To gain time was therefore a matter of paramount importance.' Manstein would simply have to hold out until reinforcements were available.

When the military conference was over, Manstein asked to see Hitler privately, in the company only of Zeitzler. Reluctantly (as usual when unsure of what was coming), Hitler agreed. Once the room had emptied, Manstein began. Hitler's demeanour, already cold, soon touched freezing-point. His eyes bored like gimlets into the field-marshal as Manstein stated that enemy superiority alone was not responsible for the plight of the army in the east, but that this was 'also due to the way in which we are led'. Manstein, persevering undaunted despite the intimidating atmosphere, renewed the request he had put on two earlier occasions, that he himself should be appointed overall Commander-in-Chief for the eastern front with full independence of action within overall strategic objectives, in the way that Rundstedt in the west and Kesselring in Italy enjoyed similar authority. This would have meant the effective surrender by Hitler of his powers of command in the eastern theatre. He was having none of it. But his argument backfired. 'Even I cannot get the field-marshals to obey me!' he retorted. 'Do you imagine, for example, that they would obey you any more readily?' Manstein replied that his orders were never disobeyed. At this, Hitler, his anger under control though the insubordination plainly registered, closed the discussion. Manstein had had the last word. But he returned to his headquarters empty-handed.

Not only had he no prospect of appointment as Commander-in-Chief in the eastern theatre; Manstein's outspoken views were by now prompting doubts in Hitler's mind about his suitability in command of Army Group South. Meanwhile, Hitler's orders for Manstein's troops were clear: there was to be no pulling back. Tenacious German defiance in the Dnieper bend and at Nikopol did in fact succeed in holding up the Soviet advance for the time being. But the loss of this territory, and of the Crimea itself, was a foregone conclusion, merely temporarily delayed.

Guderian, another of Hitler's one-time favourite commanders, fared no better than Manstein when he attempted, at a private audience in January, to persuade Hitler to simplify and unify military command by appointing a trusted general to a new position of Chief of the Wehrmacht General Staff. This, aimed at removing the damaging weakness at the heart of the Wehrmacht High Command, would have meant the dismissal of Keitel. Hitler rejected this out of hand. It would also have signified, as Hitler had no difficulty in recognizing, a diminution of his own powers within the military command. Like Manstein, Guderian had met an immovable obstacle. Like Manstein's, his recommendations of tactical retreats fell on stony ground.

The level to which relations between Hitler and his senior generals – among them those who had been his most loyal and trusted commanders – had sunk was revealed by a flashpoint at the lengthy speech Hitler gave to 100 or so of his military leaders on 27 January. After a simple lunch, during which the atmosphere was noticeably cool, Hitler offered little more (following the usual long-winded resort to the lessons of history, emphasis on 'struggle' as a natural law, and description of his own political awakening and build-up of the party) than an exhortation to hold out. For this, indoctrination in the spirit of National Socialism was vital. Of one thing, he told them, they could be certain: 'that there could never be even the slightest thought of capitulation, whatever might happen'. Hitler spoke of his right to demand of his generals not simply loyalty, but fanatical support. Full of pathos, he declared: 'In the last instance, if I should ever be deserted as supreme Leader, I must have as the last defence around me the entire officer corps who must stand with drawn swords rallied round me.' A minor sensation then occurred: Hitler was interrupted – something which had never happened since the beerhalls of Munich – as Field-Marshal von Manstein exclaimed: 'And so it will be, my Führer.' Hitler was visibly taken aback, and lost the thread of what he was saying. He stared icily, uttered 'That's good. If that's the case, we can never lose this war, never, come what may. For the nation will then go into the war with the strength that is necessary. I note that very gladly, Field-Marshal von Manstein!' He quickly recovered, emphasizing the need, even so, for greater advances in the 'education' of the officer corps. In a literal sense, Manstein's words could be seen to be not only harmless, but encouraging. But, as Manstein himself indicated after the war, the implied meaning was more critical of Hitler. The interruption, the field-marshal later recalled, arose from a rush of blood as he sensed that Hitler had impugned the honour of himself and his fellow officers by implying that their loyalty might be in question.

Hitler, for his part, saw in the interruption a reproach for his mistrust of his generals. The meeting with Manstein three weeks earlier still rankled with him, as did a frank letter which the field-marshal had subsequently sent. Within minutes of the interruption, Hitler had summoned Manstein to his presence. With Keitel in attendance, Hitler forbade Manstein to interrupt in future. 'You yourself would not tolerate such behaviour from your own subordinates,' he stated, adding, in a gratuitous insult, that Manstein's letter to him a few days earlier had presumably been to justify himself to posterity in his war diary. Needled at this, Manstein retorted: 'You must excuse me if I use an English expression in this connection, but all I can say to your interpretation of my motives is that I am a gentleman.' On this discordant note, the audience came to a close. Manstein's days were plainly numbered.

At noon three days later, the eleventh anniversary of the takeover of power, Hitler addressed the German people, confining himself to a relatively short radio address from his headquarters. As his voice crackled through the ether from the Wolf's Lair in East Prussia, the wailing sirens in Berlin announced the onset of another massive air-attack on the city. Symbolically – it might seem in retrospect – the Sportpalast, scene of many Nazi triumphs in the 'time of struggle' before

1933, and where so often since then tens of thousands of the party faithful had gathered to hear Hitler's big speeches, was gutted that night in a hail of incendiaries.

Hitler's radio broadcast could offer listeners nothing of what they yearned to hear: when the war would be over, when the devastation from the air would be ended. Instead, what they heard was no more than a rant (along the usual lines, accompanied by the normal savage vocabulary of 'Jewish bacteria') about the threat of Bolshevism. Not a word was said in consolation to those who had lost loved ones at the front, or about the human misery caused by the bomb-raids. Even Goebbels acknowledged that, in bypassing practically all the issues that preoccupied ordinary people, the speech had failed to make an impact. It was a remarkable contrast with earlier years. His propaganda slogans were now falling on deaf ears. Indirectly, judgement on the speech could be read into reported remarks such as the comment of a Berlin worker, that only 'an idiot can tell me the war will be won'.

III

Scepticism both about the capabilities of German air-defence to protect cities against the menace from the skies, and about the potential for launching retaliatory attacks on Britain, was well justified. Göring's earlier popularity had long since evaporated totally among the mass of the public, as his once much-vaunted Luftwaffe had shown itself utterly incapable of preventing the destruction of German towns and cities. Nor did the latest wave of raids, particularly the severe attack on Berlin, do much to improve the Reich Marshal's standing at Führer Head-quarters. It took little to prompt Hitler to withering tirades against Göring's competence as Luftwaffe chief. In particular, Goebbels, who both as Gauleiter of Berlin and with new responsibilities for coordinating measures for civil defence in the air-war possibly had more first-hand experience than any other Nazi leader of the impact of the Allied bombing of German cities, lost no opportunity whenever he met Hitler to vent his spleen on Göring. But however violently he condemned what Goebbels described as 'Göring's total fiasco' in air-defence, Hitler would not consider parting company with one of his longest-serving paladins. Hitler 'could do nothing about Göring because the authority of the

Reich or the party would thereby suffer the greatest damage'. It would remain Hitler's position throughout the year.

A big hope of making a dent in Allied air superiority rested on the production of the jet-fighter, the Me262, which had been commissioned the previous May. Its speed of up to 800 kilometres per hour meant that it was capable of outflying any enemy aircraft. But when the aircraft designer Professor Willy Messerschmitt had told Hitler of its dispro-portionately heavy fuel consumption, it had led by September 1943 to its production priority being removed. This was restored only a vital quarter of a year later, on 7 January 1944, when Speer and Milch were summoned to Hitler's headquarters to be told, on the basis of English press reports, that British testing of jet-planes was almost complete. Hitler now demanded production on the Me262 to be stepped up immediately. But valuable time had been lost. It was plain that the first machines would take months to produce. Whether Hitler was as clearly informed of this as Speer later claimed is questionable.

Hitler's instincts, as always, veered towards attack as the best form of defence. He looked to the chance to launch devastating weapons of destruction against Great Britain, giving the British a taste of their own medicine and forcing the Allies to rethink their strategy in the air-war. Here, too, his illusions about the speed with which the 'wonder-weapons' could be made ready for deployment, and their likely impact on British war strategy, were shored up by the optimistic prognoses of his advisers.

Speer had persuaded Hitler as long ago as October 1942, after wit-nessing trials at Peenemünde earlier in the year, of the destructive poten-tial of a long-range rocket, the A4 (later better known as the V2), able to enter the stratosphere en route to delivering its unstoppable devastation on England. Hitler had immediately ordered their mass-production on a huge scale. It was, he told Speer, 'the decisive weapon of the war', which would lift the burden on Germany when unleashed on the British. Production was to be advanced with all speed – if need be at the expense of tank production. In February 1944, Speer was still indicating to Goebbels that the rocket programme could be ready by the end of April. In the event, it would be September before the rockets were launched.

The alternative project of the Luftwaffe, the 'Kirschkern' programme, which produced what came to be known as the V1 flying-bombs, was more advanced. This, too, went back to 1942. And, like the A4 project, hopes of it were high and expectations of its production-rate optimistic. Production began in January 1944. Tests were highly encouraging. Speer told Goebbels in early February it would be ready at the beginning of April. Milch pictured for Hitler, a month later, total devastation in London in a wave of 1,500 flying-bombs over ten days, beginning on Hitler's birthday, 20 April, with the remainder to be dispatched the following month. Within three weeks of exposure to such bombing, he imagined, Britain would be on its knees. Given the information he was being fed, Hitler's illusions become rather more explicable. Competition, in this case between the army's A4 project and the 'Kirschkern' programme of the Luftwaffe, played its part. And 'working towards the Führer', striving – as the key to retaining power and position – to accomplish what it was known he would favour, to provide the miracle he wanted, and to accommodate his wishes, however unrealistic, still applied. Reluctance to convey bad or depressing news to him was the opposite side of the same coin. Together, the consequence was inbuilt, systemic over-optimism – shoring up unrealizable hopes, inevitably leading to sour disillusionment.

IV

During February, Hitler, perusing the international press summarized for him as usual in the overview provided by his Press Chief Otto Dietrich, had seen a press notice from Stockholm stating that a general staff officer of the army had been designated to shoot him. SS-Standartenführer Johann Rattenhuber, responsible for Hitler's personal safety, was instructed to tighten security at the Wolf's Lair. All visitors were to be carefully screened; not least, briefcases were to be thoroughly searched. Hitler had reservations, however, about drawing security precautions too tightly. In any case, within days the matter lost its urgency since he decided to leave the Wolf's Lair and move to the Berghof. The recent air-raids on Berlin and increasing Allied air-supremacy meant that the prospect of a raid on Führer Headquarters could no longer be ruled out. It was essential, therefore, to strengthen the walls and roofs of the buildings. While workers from the Organisation Todt were carrying out the extensive work, headquarters would be transferred to

Berchtesgaden. On the evening of 22 February, having announced that he would be speaking to the 'Old Guard' in Munich on the 24th at the annual celebration of the announcement of the Party Programme in 1920, he left the Wolf's Lair in his special train and headed south. He would not return from the Berghof until mid-July.

He had been unwell in the middle of the month. His intestinal problems were accompanied by a severe cold. The trembling in his left leg was noticeable. He also complained of blurred vision in his right eye, diagnosed a fortnight later by an ophthalmic specialist as caused by minute blood-vessel haemhorraging. His health problems were by now chronic, and mounting. But he was a good deal better by the time he arrived on 24 February in one of his old haunts, Munich's Hofbräuhaus, to deliver his big speech to a large gathering of fervent loyalists. In this company, Hitler was in his element. His good speaking-form returned. The old certitudes sufficed. He believed, the assembled fanatics heard, more firmly than ever in the victory that toughness in holding out would bring; retaliation was on its way in massive attacks on London; the Allied invasion, when it came, would be swiftly repelled. The Jews of England and America – held as always to blame for the war – could expect what had already happened to the Jews of Germany. It was a crude attack on the prime Nazi ideological target as compensation for the lack of any tangible military success. But it was exactly what this audience wanted to hear. They loved it.

At the beginning of March, Hitler summoned Goebbels to the Berghof. The immediate reason was the prospect of the imminent defection of Finland. In fact, for the time being this proved a false alarm. Finland would eventually secede only six months later. But the meeting with Goebbels on 3 March was, as usual, not confined to a specific issue, and prompted another *tour d'horizon* by Hitler, allowing a glimpse into his thinking at this juncture.

He told Goebbels that, in the light of the Finnish crisis, he was now determined to put an end to the continued 'treachery' in Hungary. It would be dealt with as soon as possible. On the military situation, Hitler exuded confidence. He thought a shortened front in the east could be held. He wanted to turn to the offensive again in the summer. On the invasion to be expected in all probability during the subsequent months, Hitler was 'absolutely certain' of Germany's chances. He outlined the strength of forces to repel it, emphasizing especially the quality of the

SS-divisions that had been sent there. Even in the air, Hitler reckoned Germany would be able to hold its own. It was rare for Goebbels to offer any hint of criticism of Hitler in his diary entries. But on this occasion the optimism seemed unfounded, even to the Propaganda Minister, who noted: 'I wish these prognoses of the Führer were right. We've been so often disappointed recently that you feel some scepticism rising up within you.'

Hitler also expected a great deal from the 'retaliation', which he envisaged being launched in massive style in the second half of April, and from the new fire-power and radar being built into German fighters. He thought the back of the enemy's air-raids would be broken by the following winter, after which Germany could then 'again be active in the attack on England'. Hitler needed little invitation to pour out his bile on his generals. It was easier for Stalin, he commented. He had had shot the sort of generals who were causing problems in Germany. But as regards the 'Jewish question', Germany was benefiting from its radical policy: 'the Jews can do us no more harm.'

Within just over two weeks of Hitler's talk with Goebbels, Hungary had been invaded – the last German invasion of the war. German intelligence had learned that the Hungarians had attempted to make diplomatic overtures both to the western Allies and to the Soviet Union.

From Hitler's point of view, in full concurrence with the opinion of his military leaders, it was high time to act. Thinking he was coming to discuss, in particular, troop withdrawals from the eastern front, the seventy-five-year-old Hungarian head of state, Admiral Horthy, arrived at Klessheim, together with his foreign minister, war minister, and chief of general staff, on the morning of 18 March. He had walked into a trap.

Hitler at the outset accused the Hungarian government of negotiating with the Allies in an attempt to take Hungary out of the war. Holding fast, as ever, to his notion that the Jews were behind the war, and that, consequently, the continued existence of Jews in any country provided, in effect, a fifth-column subverting and endangering the war-effort, Hitler was especially aggressive in accusing Horthy of allowing almost a million Jews to exist without any hindrance, which had to be seen from the German side as a threat to the eastern and Balkan fronts. Consequently, the German leadership, continued Hitler, had justifiable fears of a defection taking place, similar to that which had happened in

Italy. He had, therefore, decided upon the military occupation of Hungary, and demanded Horthy's agreement to this in a signed joint declaration. Horthy refused to sign. The temperature in the meeting rose. Hitler declared that if Horthy did not sign, the occupation would simply take place without his approval. Any armed resistance would be crushed by Croatian, Slovakian, and Romanian as well as German troops. Horthy threatened to resign. Hitler said that in such an event he could not guarantee the safety of the Admiral's family. At this base blackmail, Horthy sprang to his feet, protesting: 'If everything here is already decided, there's no point in staying any longer. I'm leaving immediately,' and stormed out of the room.

While Horthy was demanding to be taken to his special train, and Ribbentrop was berating Döme Sztojay, the Hungarian Ambassador in Berlin, an air-raid alarm sounded. In fact, the 'air-raid' was merely a ruse, complete with smoke-screen covering of the palace at Klessheim and alleged severance of telephone links with Budapest. This elaborate deceit was used to persuade Horthy to put aside thoughts of a premature departure and compel him to enter into renewed talks with Hitler. The browbeating and chicanery, as usual, did the trick. When Horthy returned to his train that evening, it was in the accompaniment of Security Police chief Ernst Kaltenbrunner and Ribbentrop's emissary in Hungary, Edmund Veesenmeyer, endowed with plenipotentiary powers to ensure that German interests were served. And this was only once Horthy had finally agreed to install a puppet regime, with Sztojay as prime minister, ready to do German bidding.

Next day, 19 March 1944, Hungary was in German hands. Not only could extra raw materials and manpower immediately be exploited for the German war effort; but, as Hitler had told Goebbels a fortnight earlier, the 'Jewish question' could now be tackled in Hungary.

With the German takeover in Budapest, Hungary's large and still intact Jewish community – some 750,000 persons – was doomed. The new masters of Hungary did not lose a minute. Eichmann's men entered Budapest with the German troops. Within days, 2,000 Jews had been rounded up. The first deportation – a train with over 3,000 Jewish men, women, and children packed in indescribable conditions into about forty cattle-wagons – left for Auschwitz a month later. By early June, ninety-two trains had carried almost 300,000 Hungarian Jews to their deaths. When Horthy halted the deportations a month later, triggering the events that would lead to his own deposition, 437,402 Hungarian Jews had been sent to the gas-chambers.

V

On the day that German troops entered Hungary, a strange little ceremony took place at the Berghof. The field-marshals, who had been summoned from different parts of the front, witnessed the presentation to Hitler by their senior, Rundstedt, of a declaration of their loyalty, which they had all signed. The signatures had all been collected, on a tour of the front, by Hitler's chief Wehrmacht adjutant, General Schmundt. The idea, characteristically, had come from Goebbels (though this was kept quiet, and not made known to Hitler). It had been prompted by the anti-German subversive propaganda disseminated from Moscow by the captured General Walter von Seydlitz-Kurzbach and other officers who had fallen into Soviet hands at Stalingrad. In reality, the effect of the Seydlitz propaganda was minimal. But these were nervous times for the Nazi leadership. Schmundt's main intention, in any case, was to remove Hitler's distrust towards his generals, and to improve the icy relations which had been so much in evidence at the January meeting interrupted by Manstein. It was, nevertheless, both remarkable in itself and a clear sign that all was not well if, in the midst of such a titanic conflict, the senior military leaders should see fit to produce a signed declaration of loyalty to their supreme commander and head of state. Manstein, the last field-marshal to sign the document, certainly thought so. He felt the declaration to be quite superfluous from a soldier's point of view. Hitler seemed moved by the occasion. It was a rare moment of harmony in his dealings with his generals.

Normality was, however, soon to be resumed. Within a week, Manstein was back at the Berghof. The 1st Panzer Army, under General Hans Valentin Hube, was in imminent danger of encirclement by Soviet troops who had broken through from Tarnopol to the Dniester. Manstein insisted (against Hube's recommendation that his army seek safety by retreating to the south over the Dniester) on a breakthrough to the west, in order to build a new front in Galicia. For this, reinforcements to assist the 1st Panzer Army would be necessary. And for these to be provided from some other part of the front, Hitler's agreement was necessary. Sharp exchanges took place between Manstein and Hitler at the midday military conference. But Hitler refused to concede to Manstein's request, and held the field-marshal personally responsible for the unfavourable position of his Army Group. Further deliberation was adjourned until the evening. Disgusted, Manstein told Schmundt that he wished to resign his command if his orders did not gain Hitler's approval.

When discussion continued at the evening conference, however, Hitler had, astonishingly, changed his mind. Who or what had persuaded him to do so, or whether he had simply brooded on the matter before altering his decision, is unclear. At any rate, he now offered Manstein the reinforcements he wanted, including an SS Panzer Corps to be taken away from the western front. Manstein went away momentarily satisfied. But Hitler resented having concessions wrung from him – particularly after his initial refusal in front of a sizeable audience. And, from Hitler's point of view, Manstein had in previous weeks been both troublesome and ineffectual in command. Hitler's way of dealing with major military setbacks was invariably (apart from his kid-glove treatment of his old political ally, Göring, as Luftwaffe chief despite the disasters in the air-war) to blame the commander and to look for a replacement who would fire the fighting morale of the troops and shore up their will to continue. It was time for a parting of the ways with Manstein, as it was with another senior field-marshal, Kleist, who, two days after Manstein, had also paid a visit to the Berghof, requesting permission for Army Group A on the Black Sea coast to pull back from the Bug to the Dniester.

On 30 March, Manstein and Kleist were picked up in Hitler's Condor aircraft and taken to the Berghof. Zeitzler told Manstein that after his last visit, Göring, Himmler, and probably Keitel had agitated against him. Zeitzler had himself offered to resign, an offer that had been summarily turned down. Schmundt had seen to it that the dismissals of the two field-marshals were carried out with decorum, not with rancour. They were replaced by Walter Model and Ferdinand Schörner, both tough generals and favourites of Hitler, whom he regarded as ideal for rousing the morale of the troops and instilling rigorous National Socialist fighting spirit in them. At the same time, the names of the army groups were altered to Army Group North Ukraine and Army Group South Ukraine. The Ukraine had, in fact, already been lost. The symbolic renaming was part of the aim of reviving morale by implying that it would soon be retaken.

It would rapidly become clear yet again, however, that changes in personnel and nomenclature would not suffice. The new commanders were no more able to stop the relentless Soviet advance than Manstein and Kleist had been. On 2 April, Hitler issued an operational order which began: 'The Russian offensive on the south of the eastern front has passed its high-point. The Russians have used up and split up their forces. The time has come to bring the Russian advance finally to a halt.' It was a vain hope. A crucial component of the new lines drawn up was the provision for the Crimea, to be held at all cost. It was an impossibility. Odessa, the port on the Black Sea which was vital to supply-lines for the Crimea, had been abandoned on 10 April. By early May, the entire Crimea was lost, with Hitler forced to agree in the night of 8–9 May to the evacuation of Sevastopol by sea. The vain struggle to hold on to the Crimea had cost over 60,000 German and Romanian lives. When the Soviet spring offensive came to a halt, the Germans had been pushed back in some sectors by as much as 600 miles inside a year.

Goebbels had suggested to Hitler that he might speak to the German people on 1 May. He had not been well enough to speak on 'Heroes' Memorial Day' on 12 March, when Grand-Admiral Dönitz – one of the few military leaders whom Hitler greatly respected, and evidently a coming man – substituted for him. Hitler told Goebbels (who remarked on his nervous strain, particularly about Hungary, over the past weeks) that he was sleeping only about three hours a night – an exaggeration, but the long-standing problems of insomnia had certainly worsened. He did show some apparent inclination to give a radio address on 1 May, but claimed his health was not up to giving a speech in public. He did not know whether he could manage it.

It was an excuse. When, following his discussion with Goebbels, he gave a fiery pep-talk, unprepared and without notes, to his party leaders, there was no hint of concern about whether he might break down part-way through his speech (in which he declared, among other confidence-boosting claims, that the Soviet advance also had its advantages in bringing home to all nations the seriousness of the threat). But when speaking to the 'Old Guard', he was in trusted company. A speech, in the circumstances, to a mass audience when he was well aware of the slump in mood of the population was a different matter altogether.

Hitler's birthday that year, his fifty-fifth, had the usual trappings and ceremonials. Goebbels had Berlin emblazoned with banners and a new slogan of resounding pathos: 'Our walls broke, but our hearts didn't.' The State Opera house on Unter den Linden was festively decorated for the usual celebration, attended by dignitaries from state, party, and Wehrmacht. Goebbels portrayed Hitler's historic achievements. The Berlin Philharmonia, conducted by Hans Knappertsbusch, played Beethoven's 'Eroica' Symphony. But the mood among the Nazi faithful at such events was contrived. Goebbels was well aware from reports from the regional Propaganda Offices that the popular mood was 'very critical and sceptical', and that 'the depression in the broad masses' had reached 'worrying levels'.

VI

A familiar face, not seen for some months, had returned to the Berghof in mid-April. Since being admitted to the Red Cross hospital at Hohenlychen, sixty miles north of Berlin, for a knee operation (accompanied by severe nervous strain), Albert Speer had been out of circulation. Hitler had seen him briefly in March, while Speer was convalescing for a short time at Klessheim, but the armaments minister had then left for Meran, in South Tyrol, to recover in the company of his family.

An absent minister was an invitation, in the Third Reich, for others thirsting for power to step into the vacuum. Karl Otto Saur, the able head of the technical office in Speer's ministry, had taken the opportunity to exploit Hitler's favour in his boss's absence. When a Fighter Staff had been set up in March – linking Speer's ministry with the Luftwaffe to speed up and coordinate production of air-defence – Hitler placed it, against Speer's express wishes, in the hands of Saur. And when, stung by the near-unhampered bombing of German cities, Hitler discovered that little progress had been made on the building of huge underground bomb-proof bunkers to protect fighter-production against air-raids, Speer's other right-hand man, Xaver Dorsch, head of the central office of the massive construction apparatus, the Organisation Todt, spotted his chance. Dorsch was commissioned by Hitler with the sole responsibility for the building of the six immense bunkers within the Reich – thereby overriding Speer – accompanied by full authority to assure the work had top priority.

Speer had not reached his high position, however, without an ability to take care of his own interests in the ruthless scheming and jockeying for position that went on around Hitler. He was not prepared to accept the undermining of his own authority without a fight. On 19 April, he wrote a long letter to Hitler complaining at the decisions he had taken and demanding the restoration of his own authority over Dorsch. He let it be known that he wished to resign should Hitler not accede to his wishes. Hitler's initial anger at the letter gave way to the more pragmatic consideration that he still needed Speer's organizational talents. He passed a message to Speer, via Erhard Milch, Luftwaffe armaments supremo, that he still held him in high esteem. On 24 April, Speer appeared at the Berghof. Hitler, formally attired, gloves in hand, came out to meet him, accompanying him like some foreign dignitary into the imposing hall. Speer, his vanity touched, was immediately impressed. Hitler went on to flatter Speer. He told him that he needed him to oversee all building works. He was in agreement with whatever Speer thought right in this area. Speer was won over. That evening, he was back in the Berghof 'family', making small-talk with Eva Braun and the others in the late-night session around the fire. Bormann suggested listening to some music. Records of music by Wagner, naturally, and Johann Strauß's *Fledermaus* were put on. Speer felt at home again.

In Speer's absence, and despite the extensive damage from air-raids, Saur had in fact masterminded a remarkable increase in fighter-production – though with a corresponding decline in output of bombers. Delighted as he was with better prospects of air-defence, Hitler's instincts lay, as always, in aggression and regaining the initiative through bombing. The new chief of the Luftwaffe operations staff, Karl Koller, was, therefore, pushing at an open door when he presented Hitler with a report, in early May, pointing out the dangerous decline in production of bombers, and what was needed to sustain German dominance. Hitler promptly told Göring that the low targets for bomber-production were unacceptable. Göring passed the message to the Fighter Staff that there was to be a trebling of bomber-production – alongside the massive increase in fighters to come off the production lines. Eager to please, as always, Göring had told Hitler of rapid progress in the production of the jet, the Me262, of which the Dictator had such high hopes.

The previous autumn, having removed top priority from production of the Me262 because of its heavy fuel-consumption, Hitler had changed his mind. He had been led to believe – possibly it was a misunderstanding – by the designer, Professor Willi Messerschmitt, that the jet, once in service, could be used not as a fighter, but as a bomber to attack Britain and to play a decisive role in repelling the coming invasion, wreaking havoc on the beaches as Allied troops were disembarking. Göring, at least as unrealistic as his Leader in his expectations, promised the jet-bombers would be available by May. At his meeting with Speer and Milch in January, when he demanded accelerated production of the jet, Hitler had stated, to the horror of the Luftwaffe's technical staff, that he wanted to deploy it as a bomber. Arguments to the contrary were of no avail.

Now, on 23 May, in a meeting at the Berghof with Göring, Saur, and Milch about aircraft production, he heard mention of the Me262 as a fighter. He interrupted. He had presumed, he stated, that it was being built as a bomber. It transpired that his instructions of the previous autumn, unrealistic as they were, had been simply ignored. Hitler exploded in fury, ordering the Me262 – despite all technical objections levelled by the experts present – to be built exclusively as a bomber. Göring lost no time in passing the brickbats down the line to the Luft-waffe construction experts. But he had to tell Hitler that the major redesign needed for the plane would now delay production for five months. Whether fuel would by that time be available for it was another matter. Heavy American air-raids on fuel plants in central and eastern Germany on 12 May, to be followed by even more destructive raids at the end of the month, along with Allied attacks, carried out from bases in Italy, on the Romanian oil-refineries near Ploesti, halved German fuel production. Nimbly taking advantage of Göring's latest embarrassment, Speer had no trouble in persuading Hitler to transfer to his ministry full control over aircraft production.

Three days after the wrangle about the Me262, another, larger, gather-ing took place on the Obersalzberg. A sizeable number of generals and other senior officers, who had been participants in ideological training-courses and were ready to return to the front, had been summoned to the Berghof to hear a speech by Hitler – one of several such speeches he gave between autumn 1943 and summer 1944. They assembled on 26 May in the Platterhof, the big hotel adjacent to the Berghof on the site of the far more modest Pension Moritz, where Hitler had stayed in the 1920s. A central passage in the speech touched on the 'Final Solution'. Hitler spoke of the Jews as a 'foreign body' in the German people which, though not all had understood why he had to proceed 'so brutally and ruthlessly', it had been essential to expel.

He came to the key point. 'In removing the Jews,' he went on, 'I eliminated in Germany the possibility of creating some sort of revolutionary core or nucleus. You could naturally say: Yes, but could you not have done it more simply – or not more simply, since everything else would have been more complicated – but more humanely? Gentlemen,' he continued, 'we are in a life-or-death struggle. If our opponents are victorious in this struggle, the German people would be eradicated. Bolshevism would slaughter millions and millions and millions of our intellectuals. Anyone not dying through a shot in the neck would be deported. The children of the upper classes would be taken away and eliminated. This entire bestiality has been organized by the Jews.' He spoke of 40,000 women and children being burnt to death through the incendiaries dropped on Hamburg, adding: 'Don't expect anything else from me except the ruthless upholding of the national interest in the way which, in my view, will have the greatest effect and benefit for the German nation.' At this the officers burst into loud and lasting applause.

He continued: 'Here just as generally, humanity would amount to the greatest cruelty towards one's own people. If I already incur the Jews' hatred, I at least don't want to miss the advantages of such hatred.' Shouts of 'quite right' were heard from his audience. 'The advantage,' he went on, 'is that we possess a cleanly organized entity with which no one can interfere. Look in contrast at other states. We have gained insight into a state which took the opposite route: Hungary. The entire state undermined and corroded, Jews everywhere, even in the highest places Jews and more Jews, and the entire state covered, I have to say, by a seamless web of agents and spies who have desisted from striking only because they feared that a premature strike would draw us in, though they waited for this strike. I have intervened here too, and this problem will now also be solved.' He cited once again his 'prophecy' of 1939, that in the event of another war not the German nation but Jewry itself would be 'eradicated'. The audience vigorously applauded.

Continuing, he underlined 'one sole principle, the maintenance of our race'. What served this principle, he said, was right; what detracted from it, wrong. He concluded, again to storms of applause, by speaking of the 'mission' of the German people in Europe. As always, he posed stark alternatives: defeat in the war would mean 'the end of our people', victory 'the beginning of our domination over Europe'.

VII

Whatever nervousness was felt at the Berghof in the early days of June about an invasion which was as good as certain to take place within the near future, there were few, if any, signs of it on the surface. To Hitler's Luftwaffe adjutant, Nicolaus von Below, it seemed almost like pre-war times on the Obersalzberg. Hitler would take Below's wife on one side when she was invited to lunch and talk about the children or her parents' farm. In the afternoon, he would gather up his hat, his walking-stick, and his cape, and lead the statutory walk to the Tea House for coffee and cakes. In the evenings, around the fire he would find some relaxation in the inconsequential chat of his guests or would hold forth, as ever, on usual themes – great personalities of history, the future shape of Europe, carrying out the work of Providence in combating Jews and Bolsheviks, the influence of the Churches, and, of course, architectural plans, along with the usual reminiscences of earlier years. Even the news, on 3–4 June, that the Allies had taken Rome, with the German troops pulling back to the Apennines, was received calmly. For all its obvious strategic importance, Italy was, for Hitler, little more than a sideshow. He would have little longer to wait for the main event.

Hitler seemed calm, and looked well compared with his condition in recent months, when Goebbels accompanied him to the Tea House on the afternoon of 5 June. Earlier, he had told the Propaganda Minister that the plans for retaliation were now so advanced that he would be ready to unleash 300–400 of the new pilotless flying-bombs on London within a few days. (He had, in fact, given the order for a major air-attack on London, including use of these new weapons, on 16 May.) He repeated how confident he was that the invasion, when it came, would be repulsed. Rommel, he said, was equally confident. On 4 June Rommel, whom Hitler had the previous autumn made responsible for the Atlantic defences, had even left for a few days' leave with his family near Ulm. Other commanding officers in the west were equally unaware of the imminence of the invasion, though reconnaissance had provided telegraph warnings that very day of things stirring on the other side of the Channel. Nothing of this was reported to OKW at Berchtesgaden or, even more astonishingly, to General Friedrich Dollmann's 7th Army directly on the invasion front.

That evening, Hitler and his entourage viewed the latest newsreel. The discussion moved to films and the theatre. Eva Braun joined in with pointed criticism of some productions. 'We sit then around the hearth until two o'clock at night,' wrote Goebbels, 'exchange reminiscences, take pleasure in the many fine days and weeks we have had together. The Führer inquires about this and that. All in all, the mood is like the good old times.' The heavens opened and a thunderstorm broke as Goebbels left the Berghof. It was four hours since the first news had started to trickle in that the invasion would begin that night. Goebbels had been disinclined to believe the tapping into enemy communications. But coming down the Obersalzberg to his quarters in Berchtesgaden, the news was all too plain; 'the decisive day of the war had begun.'

Hitler went to bed not long after Goebbels had left, probably around 3 a.m. When Speer arrived next morning, seven hours later, Hitler had still not been wakened with the news of the invasion. In fact, it seems that the initial scepticism at the High Command of the Wehrmacht that this indeed was the invasion had been finally dispelled only a little while earlier, probably between 8.15 and 9.30 a.m. Influenced by German intelligence reports, Hitler had spoken a good deal in previous weeks that the invasion would begin with a decoy attack to drag German troops away from the actual landing-place. (In fact, Allied deception through the dropping of dummy parachutists and other diversionary tactics did contribute to initial German confusion about the location of the landing.) His adjutants now hesitated to waken him with mistaken information. According to Speer, Hitler – who had earlier correctly envisaged that the landing would be on the Normandy coast – was still suspicious at the lunchtime military conference that it was a diversionary tactic put across by enemy intelligence. Only then did he agree to the already belated demand of the Commander-in-Chief in the West, Field-Marshal von Rundstedt (who had expressed uncertainty in telegrams earlier that morning about whether the landing was merely a decoy), to deploy two panzer divisions held in reserve in the Paris area against the beachhead that was rapidly being established some 120 miles away. The delay was crucial. Had they moved by night, the panzer divisions might have made a difference. Their movements by day were hampered by heavy Allied air-attacks, and they suffered severe losses of men and matériel.

At the first news of the invasion, Hitler had seemed relieved – as if, thought Goebbels, a great burden had fallen from his shoulders. What he had been expecting for months was now reality. It had taken place, he said, exactly where he had predicted it. The poor weather, he added, was on Germany's side. He exuded confidence, declaring that it was now possible to smash the enemy. He was 'absolutely certain' that the Allied troops, for whose quality he had no high regard, would be repulsed. Göring thought the battle as good as won. Ribbentrop was, as always, 'entirely on the Führer's side. He is also more than sure, without, like the Führer, being able to give reasons in detail for it', wryly commented Goebbels – like Jodl, one of the quiet sceptics. There were good grounds for scepticism. In fact, the delay in reaction on the German side had helped to ensure that by then the battle of the beaches was already as good as lost.

The vanguard of the huge Allied armada of almost 3,000 vessels approaching the Normandy coast had disgorged the first of its American troops on to Utah Beach, on the Cotentin peninsula, at 6.30 a.m., meeting no notable resistance. Landings following shortly afterwards at the British and Canadian sites – Gold, Juno, and Sword Beaches – also went better than expected. Only the second American landing at Omaha Beach, encountering a good German infantry division which happened to be in a state of readiness and behind a particularly firm stretch of fortifications, ran into serious difficulties. Troops landing on the exposed beach were simply mown down. The casualty rate was massive. Omaha gave a horrifying taste of what the landings could have faced elsewhere had the German defence been properly prepared and waiting. But even at Omaha, after several torrid hours of terrible bloodletting, almost 35,000 American troops were finally able to push forward and gain a foothold on French soil. By the end of the day, around 156,000 Allied troops had landed, had forged contact with the 13,000 American and British parachutists dropped behind the flanks of the enemy lines several hours before the landings, and been able successfully to establish beachheads – including one sizeable stretch some thirty kilometres long and ten deep.

What appears at times in retrospect to have been almost an inexorable triumph of 'Operation Overlord' could have turned out quite differently. Hitler's initial optimism had not, in fact, been altogether unfounded. He had presumed the Atlantic coast better fortified than was the case. Even so, the advantage ought in the decisive early stages to have lain with the defenders of the coast – as it did at Omaha. But the dilatory action was costly in the extreme. The divisions among the German commanders and lack of agreement on tactics between Rommel (who favoured close proximity of panzer divisions to the coast in the hope of immediately crushing an invading force) and General Leo Geyr von Schweppenburg, commander of Panzer Group West (wanting to hold the armour back until it was plain where it should be concentrated), had been a significant weakness in the German planning for the invasion. Allied strategic decoys, as we noted, also played a part in the early confusion of the German commanders on the invasion night itself. Not least, massive Allied air-superiority – compared with over 10,000 Allied sorties on D-Day, the Luftwaffe could manage to put in the air only eighty fighters based in Normandy – gave the invading forces a huge advantage in the cover provided during the decisive early stages. Once the Allied troops were ashore and had established their beachheads, the key question was whether they could be reinforced better and faster than the Germans. Here, the fire-power from the air came into its own. The Allied planes could at one and the same time seriously hamper the German supply-lines, and help to ensure that reinforcements kept pouring in across the Normandy beaches. By 12 June, the five Allied beachheads had been consolidated into a single front, and the German defenders, if slowly, were being pushed back. Meanwhile, American troops were already striking out across the Cotentin peninsula. The road to the key port of Cherbourg was opening up.

Nazi leaders, for whom early optimism about repelling the invasion had within days evaporated, retained one big hope: the long-awaited 'miracle weapons'. Not only Hitler thought these would bring a change in war-fortunes. More than fifty sites had been set up on the coast in the Pas de Calais from which the V1 flying-bombs – early cruise missiles powered by jet engines and difficult to shoot down – could be fired off in the direction of London. Hitler had reckoned with the devastating effect of a mass attack on the British capital by hundreds of the new weapons being fired simultaneously. The weapon had then been delayed by a series of production problems. Now Hitler pressed for action. But the launch-sites were not ready. Eventually, on 12 June, ten flying-bombs were catapulted off their ramps. Four crashed on take-off; only five reached London, causing minimal damage. In fury, Hitler wanted to cancel production. But three days later, the sensational effect of the successful launch of 244 V1s on London persuaded him to change his mind. He thought the new destructive force would quickly lead to the evacuation of London and disruption of the Allied war effort.

The triumphalist tones of the Wehrmacht report on the launch of the V1, and of a number of newspaper articles, were equally fanciful, filling Goebbels – still anxious to shore up a mood of hold-out-at-all-costs instead of dangerous optimism – with dismay. The impression had been created, noted the Propaganda Minister with consternation, that the war would be over within days. He was anxious to stop such illusions. The euphoria could quickly turn into blaming the government. He ordered the reports to be toned down, and exaggerated expectations to be dampened – persuading Hitler that his own instructions to the press, guaranteed to foster the euphoric mood, should follow the new guidelines.

The continued advance of the Allies, but what seemed the new prospects offered by the V1, prompted Hitler to fly in the evening of 16 June from Berchtesgaden together with Keitel and Jodl and the rest of his staff to the western front to discuss the situation with his regional commanders, Rundstedt and Rommel. He wanted to boost their wavering morale by underlining the strengths of the V1, while at the same time stressing the imperative need to defend the port of Cherbourg. After their four Focke-Wulf Condors had landed in Metz, Hitler and his entourage drove in the early hours of the next morning in an armour-plated car to Margival, north of Soissons, where the old Führer Headquarters built in 1940 had been installed, at great expense, with new communications equipment and massively reinforced. The talks that morning took place in a nearby bomb-proof railway-tunnel.

Hitler, looking pale and tired, sitting hunched on a stool, fiddled nervously with his glasses and played with coloured pencils while addressing his generals, who had to remain standing. Rundstedt reported on the developments of the previous ten days, concluding that it was now impossible to expel the Allies from France. Hitler bitterly laid the blame at the door of the local commanders. Rommel countered by pointing to the hopelessness of the struggle against such massive superior force of the Allies. Hitler turned to the V1 – a weapon, he said, to decide the war and make the English anxious for peace. Impressed by what they had heard, the field-marshals asked for the V1 to be used against Allied beachheads, only to be told by General Erich Heinemann, the commander responsible for the launch of the flying-bomb, that the weapon was not precise enough in its targeting to allow this. Hitler promised them, however, that they would soon have jet-fighters at their disposal to gain control of the skies. As he himself knew, however, these had, in fact, only just gone into production.

After lunch (taken in a bunker because of the danger of air-attacks), Hitler spoke alone with Rommel. The discussion was heated at times. The field-marshal painted a bleak picture of the prospects. The western front could not be held for much longer, he stated, beseeching Hitler to seek a political solution. 'Pay attention to your invasion front, not to the continuation of the war,' was the blunt reply he received. Hitler waited no longer, and flew back to Salzburg that afternoon. At the Berghof that evening, dissatisfied at the day's proceedings, Hitler remarked to his entourage that Rommel had lost his nerve and become a pessimist. 'Only optimists can pull anything off today,' he added.

The following day, 18 June, the Americans reached the western coast of the Cotentin peninsula, effectively cutting off the peninsula and the port of Cherbourg from reinforcements for the Wehrmacht. Eight days later, the German garrison in Cherbourg surrendered. With this port in their possession (even if it took nearly a month to repair German destruction and make use of the harbour), and almost total control of the skies, the Allies had few further worries about their own reinforcements. Advance against tenacious defence was painfully slow. But the invasion had been a success. Any prospect of forcing the Allied troops, arriving in ever greater numbers, back into the sea had long since dissolved. Hitler was furious that the Allies had gained the initiative. He was left now with little more than the hope that the Alliance would split.

When Goebbels saw him for a three-hour private discussion on 21 June, he remained resistant, however, to suggestions that the time had come to take drastic steps, finally, to introduce the 'total war' that the Propaganda Minister had advocated for so long. After lunch, sitting together in the great hall of the Berghof, with its huge window opening out to a breathtaking panorama of the Alps, Goebbels expounded his argument. He expressed his doubts about groundless optimism, 'not to say illusions', about the war. 'Total war' had remained a mere slogan. The crisis had to be recognized before it could be overcome. A thorough reform of the Wehrmacht was urgently necessary. Göring, he had observed (here came the usual attacks on the Reich Marshal), lived in a complete fantasy world. The Propaganda Minister extended his attack to the remainder of the top military leadership. The Führer needed a Scharnhorst and a Gneisenau – the Prussian military heroes who had created the army that repelled Napoleon – not a Keitel and a Fromm (commander of the Reserve Army), he declared. Goebbels promised that he could raise a million soldiers through a rigorous reorganization of the Wehrmacht and draconian measures in the civilian sphere. The people expected and wanted tough measures. Germany was close to being plunged into a crisis which could remove any possibility of taking such measures with any prospect of success. It was necessary to act with realism, wholly detached from any defeatism, and to act now.

Hitler accepted that there were some weaknesses in the organization of the Wehrmacht, and that few of its leaders were National Socialists. But to dispense with them during the war would be a nonsense, since there were no replacements. All in all, Hitler concluded, the time was not ripe for the extraordinary measures the Propaganda Minister wanted. He told Goebbels that the instant he felt the need to resort to 'final measures', he would bestow the appropriate powers on the Propaganda Minister. But 'for the time being he wanted to proceed along the evolutionary, not revolutionary, way'. Goebbels went away empty-handed, leaving what he regarded as one of the most serious meetings he had had with Hitler sorely disappointed.

Goebbels was evidently dubious about Hitler's continued positive gloss on military prospects. He doubted, correctly, the reassurances that it ought to be possible to hold Cherbourg until the two new divisions from the east could arrive; and Hitler's view that a massive panzer attack could then destroy the Allied bridgehead. On the 'wonder-weapons', however, the Führer's expectations seemed realistic enough to the Propaganda Minister. Hitler did not, he thought, over-estimate the impact of the V1 (short for *Vergeltungswaffe-*1 – 'Retaliation Weapon 1'), as Goebbels had now dubbed the flying-bomb. But he hoped to have the

A4 rocket (later renamed the V2) ready for launching by August, and looked to its destructive power to help decide the war. Hitler ruled out once again any prospect of an 'arrangement' with Britain, but was less inclined – so Goebbels inferred – to dismiss the possibility at some point of coming to terms with the Soviet Union. This could not be entertained given the present military situation, though a significant shift in fortunes in the Far East might alter the position. As Goebbels realized, however, this was entering the realm of vague musings.

The following day, 22 June 1944, exactly three years since the beginning of Operation Barbarossa, the Red Army launched its new big offensive in the east. Hitler had predicted that Stalin would not be able to resist the appeal of launching his assault on that day. The main thrust of the massive offensive – the biggest undertaken, deploying almost 2½ million men and over 5,000 tanks, backed by 5,300 planes, and given by Stalin the code-name 'Bagration' after a military hero in the destruction of Napoleon's Grand Army in 1812 – was aimed at the Wehrmacht's Army Group Centre. Based on fatally flawed intelligence relayed to Chief of the General Staff Zeitzler by the head of the eastern military intelligence service, Reinhard Gehlen, German preparations had, in fact, anticipated an offensive on the southern part of the front, where all the reserves and the bulk of the panzer divisions had been concentrated. Army Group Centre had been left with a meagre thirty-eight divisions, comprising only half as many men and a fifth of the number of tanks as the Red Army had, in a section of the front stretching over some 800 miles. Only belatedly, it appears, did the realization dawn, against Zeitzler's continued advice, that the offensive was likely to come against Army Group Centre. But when Field-Marshal Ernst Busch, Commander-in-Chief of Army Group Centre, recommended shortening the front to more defensible limits, Hitler contemptuously asked whether he too was one of those generals 'who always looked to the rear'.

The relatively mild beginnings of the offensive then misled Hitler's military advisers into thinking at first that it was a decoy. However, the initial opening was sufficient to breach the German defences around Vitebsk. Suddenly, the first big wave of tanks swept through the gap. Others rapidly followed. Bombing and heavy artillery attacks accompanied the assault. Busch appealed to Hitler to abandon the 'fortified places' (*Feste Plätze*) in Vitebsk, Orsha, Mogilev, and Bobruisk, which had been established in the spring in a vain attempt to create a set of key defensive strongholds – fortresses to be held come what may under the command of selected tough generals.

Hitler's answer could have been taken as read. The 'fortified places' were to be held at all costs; every square metre of land was to be defended. Busch, one of Hitler's fervent admirers among the generals, accepted the order without demur. He sought to carry it out unquestioningly as a demonstration of his loyalty. The consequences were predictable. The Red Army swept around the strongholds, and the German not Soviet divisions were tied down, then encircled and finally destroyed by the forces following in the wake of the advance troops. The Wehrmacht divisions lost through such a disastrous tactical error would have been vital in defending other parts of the front.

Within two days of the start of the offensive, the 3rd Panzer Army in Vitebsk had been cut off, followed a further two days later by the encirclement of the 9th Army near Bobruisk. By the first days of July, the 4th Army faced the same fate near Minsk. Reinforcements drawn from the southern part of the front could not prevent its destruction. By the time the offensive through the centre slowed by mid-July, the Soviet breakthrough had advanced well over 200 miles, driven a gap 100 miles wide through the front, and was within striking range of Warsaw. Army Group Centre had by that time lost twenty-eight divisions with 350,000 men in a catastrophe even greater than that at Stalingrad. By this time, devastating offensives in the Baltic and in the south were gathering momentum. The next months would bring even worse calamities and, together with the unstoppable advance of the Allies in the west, would usher in the final phase of the war.

VIII

Whatever Hitler's capabilities as a military strategist had been, they had paid dividends only while Germany held the whip-hand and lightning offensives had been possible. Once a defensive strategy had become the only one available, Hitler's inadequacies as supreme German warlord were fully exposed. It was not that he was wholly devoid of tactical knowledge, despite his lack of formal training. Nor was it the case that professionals who knew better were invariably forced into compliance with the lunatic orders of an amateur military bungler. Hitler's tactics were frequently neither inherently absurd, nor did they usually stand in crass contradiction to the military advice he was receiving.

Even so: at points of crisis, the tensions and conflicts invariably surfaced. And by 1944 the individual military crises were accumulating into one almighty, life-or-death crisis for the regime itself. Hitler's political adroitness was by this time long gone. He dismissed out of hand all contemplation of a possible attempt to reach a political solution. Bridges had been burnt (as he had indicated on several occasions); there was no way back. And, since he refused any notion of negotiating from a position other than one of strength, from which all his earlier successes had derived, there was in any case no opportunity to seek a peace settlement. The gambling instinct which had stood Hitler in such good stead down to 1941 had long since lost its effectiveness in what had become a backs-to-the-wall struggle. But the worse the situation became, the more disastrously self-destructive became Hitler's other overriding and irrational instinct – that 'will' alone would triumph over all adversity, even grossly disparate levels of manpower and weaponry. The innate self-destructive tendency which had always been implicit in his characteristic all-or-nothing stance as a politician now conveyed itself, catastrophically, to military leadership.

It was inevitable that seasoned military strategists and battle-hardened generals, schooled in more subtle forms of tactical command, would clash with him – often stridently – when their reading of the options available was so diametrically at variance with those of their supreme commander, and where the orders he emitted seemed to them so plainly militarily suicidal. They were also, however, schooled in obedience to orders of a superior; and Hitler was head of state, head of the armed forces, and since 1941 – disastrously – commander-in-chief (responsible for tactical decisions) of the army. Refusal to obey was not only an act of military insubordination; it was a treasonable act of political resistance.

Few were prepared to go down that route. But loyalty even to the extent of belief in the Führer's mission was no safeguard against dismissal if near-impossible demands were not met. In accordance with his warped logic, where 'will' had not triumphed, however fraught the circumstances, Hitler blamed the weakness or inadequacy of the commander. Another commander with a superior attitude, he presumed, would bring a different result – however objectively unfavourable the actual position. The commander of Army Group Centre, Field-Marshal Busch, a Hitler loyalist, correspondingly paid the price for the 'failure' of Army Group Centre during the onset of the Soviet offensive. He was dismissed by Hitler on 28 June, and replaced by one of his favourite commanders, the tough and energetic newly-promoted Field-Marshal Walter Model (who at the same time retained his command of Army Group North Ukraine) – dubbed by some, given the frequency with which he was charged with tackling a crisis, 'Hitler's fireman'.

Within days, there was a change of command, too, in the west. Reports to the High Command of the Wehrmacht submitted by the Commander-in-Chief, Field-Marshal von Rundstedt, and the Commander of Panzer Group West, General Geyr von Schweppenburg, had drawn a pessimistic picture of the prospects of holding the lines against enemy inroads in France. Jodl played to Hitler's sentiments by noting that this meant the first step towards the evacuation of France. The report had followed similarly realistic assessments of the situation on the western front delivered by Rundstedt and Rommel at the Berghof two days earlier, on 29 June. On 3 July, Rundstedt received a handwritten notice of his dismissal from Hitler. Officially, he had been replaced on grounds of health. The sacking of Geyr and Field-Marshal Hugo Sperrle, who had been responsible for air-defences in the west, also followed. Rundstedt's replacement, Kluge, at that time high in Hitler's esteem, arrived in France, as Guderian later put it, 'still filled with the optimism that prevailed at Supreme Headquarters'. He soon learnt differently.

Another military leader who fell irredeemably from grace at this time was Chief of the Army General Staff Kurt Zeitzler. When appointed as replacement to Halder in September 1942, Zeitzler had impressed Hitler with his drive, energy, and fighting spirit – the type of military leader he wanted. The relationship had palled visibly since the spring of 1944, when Hitler had pinned a major part of the blame for the loss of the Crimea on Zeitzler. By May, Zeitzler was indicating his wish to resign. The Chief of Staff's strong backing at the end of June for withdrawing the threatened Army Group North in the Baltic to a more defensible line, and his pessimism about the situation on the western front, amounted to the last straw. Zeitzler could no longer see the rationale of Hitler's tactics; Hitler was contemptuous of what he saw as the defeatism of

Zeitzler and the General Staff. At the end of his tether following furious rows with Hitler, Zeitzler simply disappeared from the Berghof on 1 July. He had suffered a nervous breakdown. Hitler never spoke to him again. He would have Zeitzler dismissed from the Wehrmacht in January 1945, refusing him the right to wear uniform. Until his replacement, Guderian, was appointed on 21 July, the army was effectively without a Chief of the General Staff.

The Soviet advance had left the Red Army, in the northern sector of the front, poised not far from Vilna in Lithuania. Already, the borders of East Prussia were in their sights. On 9 July, Hitler flew with Keitel, Dönitz, Himmler, and Luftwaffe Chief of Staff General Günther Korten back to his old headquarters near Rastenburg in East Prussia. Field-Marshal Model and General Johannes Frießner, recently appointed as commander of Army Group North in place of General Georg Linde-mann, joined them from the eastern front. The discussions ranged mainly over plans for the urgent creation of a number of new divisions to shore up the eastern front and protect any inroads into East Prussia. Model and Frießner sounded optimistic. Hitler, too, thought his Luftwaffe adjutant, Below, also remained positive about developments on the eastern front. Hitler flew back to the Berghof that afternoon. He had already hinted that, in the light of the situation in the east, he would have to move his headquarters back to East Prussia, even though the fortifications of his accommodation there were still incomplete. Reading between the lines of one or two comments, Below gained the impression, he later wrote, that during what were to prove Hitler's last days at the Berghof, before he left on 14 July for the Wolf's Lair, never to return, he was no longer under any illusions about the outcome of the war. Even so, any hints of pessimism were more than countered by repeated stress on continuing the war, the impact of the new weapons, and ultimate victory. Once more, it was plain to Below that Hitler would never capitulate. There would be no repeat of 1918. Hitler's political 'mission' had been based from the outset on that premiss. The entire Reich would go down in flames first.

Hitler had lived amid the relative tranquillity of the Obersalzberg for almost four months. The regular entourage at the Berghof had dwindled somewhat in that time. And in the days before departure there had been few guests to enliven proceedings. Hitler himself had seemingly become more reserved. On the last evening, perhaps sensing he would not see the Berghof again, he had paused in front of the pictures hanging in the great hall. Then he had kissed the hand of Below's wife and Frau Brandt, the wife of one of his doctors, bidding them farewell. Next morning, 14 July, he flew back to East Prussia, arriving at the Wolf's Lair, now heavily reinforced and scarcely recognizable from its appearance when first set up in 1941. He arrived in the late morning. At one o'clock he was running the military conference there as if he had never been away. He was more stooping in his gait than earlier. But his continued strength of will, despite the massive setbacks, continued to impress the admiring Below.

For others, this strength of will – or obstinate refusal to face reality – was precisely what was preventing an end to the war and dragging Germany to inevitable catastrophe. They were determined to act before it was too late – to save what was left of the Reich, lay the foundations of a future without Hitler, and show the outside world that there was 'another Germany' beyond the forces of Nazism.

25
Luck of the Devil

I

The attempt to kill Hitler on 20 July 1944 had a lengthy prehistory, dating back as far as the Sudeten crisis of 1938. The complex strands of this prehistory contained in no small measure profound manifestations and admixtures of high ethical values and a transcendental sense of moral duty, codes of honour, political idealism, religious convictions, personal courage, remarkable selflessness, deep humanity, and a love of country that was light-years removed from Nazi chauvinism. The prehistory was also replete – how could it have been otherwise in the circumstances? – with disagreements, doubts, mistakes, miscalculations, moral dilemmas, short-sightedness, hesitancy, ideological splits, personal clashes, bungling organization, distrust – and sheer bad luck.

The actions of a lone assassin, the Swabian joiner Georg Elser, who shared none of the hesitancy of those within the power-echelons of the regime, had come within a whisker of sending Hitler into oblivion in the Bürgerbräukeller on the night of 8 November 1939. Good fortune alone had saved Hitler on that occasion. With the left-wing underground resistance groups, though never eliminated, weak, isolated, and devoid of access to the corridors of power, the only hope of toppling Hitler thereafter lay with those who themselves occupied positions of some power or influence in the regime itself.

On the fringes of the conspiracy, the participation in Nazi rule in itself naturally created ambivalence. Breaking oaths of loyalty was no light matter, even for some whose dislike of Hitler was evident. Prussian values were here a double-edged sword: a deep sense of obedience to authority and service to the state clashed with equally profound feelings of duty to God and to country. Whichever triumphed within an individual: whether heavy-hearted acceptance of service to a head of state regarded as legitimately constituted, however detested; or rejection of such allegiance in the interest of what was taken to be the greater good, should the head of state be leading the country to ruin; this was a matter for conscience and judgement. It could, and did, go either way.

Though there were numerous exceptions to a broad generalization, generational differences played some part. The tendency was greater in a younger generation of officers, for example, than in those who had already attained the highest ranks of general or field-marshal, to entertain thoughts of active participation in an attempt to overthrow the head of state. This was implied in a remark by the man who would lead the attempt on Hitler's life in July 1944, Colonel Claus Schenk Graf von Stauffenberg: 'Since the generals have so far managed nothing, the colonels have now to step in.' On the other hand, views on the morality of assassinating the head of state – in the midst of an external struggle of titanic proportions against an enemy whose victory threatened the very existence of a German state – differed fundamentally on moral, not simply generational, grounds. Any attack on the head of state constituted, of course, high treason. But in a war, distinguishing this from treachery against one's own country, from betrayal to the enemy, was chiefly a matter of individual persuasion and the relative weighting of moral values. And only a very few were in a position to accumulate detailed and first-hand experiences of gross inhumanity at the same time as possessing the means to bring about Hitler's removal. Even fewer were prepared to act.

Beyond ethical considerations, there was the existential fear of the awesome consequences – for the families as well as for the individuals themselves – of discovery of any complicity in a plot to remove the head of state and instigate a *coup d'état*. This was certainly enough to deter many who were sympathetic to the aims of the plotters but unwilling to become involved. Nor was it just the constant dangers of discovery and physical risks that acted as a deterrent. There was also the isolation of resistance. To enter into, even to flirt with, the conspiracy against Hitler meant acknowledging an inner distance from friends, colleagues, comrades, entry into a twilight world of immense peril, and of social, ideological, even moral isolation.

Quite apart from the evident necessity, in a terroristic police state, of minimizing risks through maximum secrecy, the conspirators were themselves well aware of their lack of popular support. Even at this juncture, as the military disasters mounted and ultimate catastrophe beckoned, the fanatical backing for Hitler had by no means evaporated and continued, if as a minority taste, to show remarkable resilience and strength. Those still bound up with the dying regime, those who had invested in it, had committed themselves to it, had burnt their boats with it, and were still true believers in the Führer, were likely to stop at nothing, as adversity mounted, in their unbridled retribution for any sign of opposition. But beyond the fanatics, there were many others who – naïvely, or after deep reflection – thought it not merely wrong, but despicable and treacherous, to undermine one's own country in war. Stauffenberg summed up the conspirators' dilemma a few days before he laid a bomb in the Wolf's Lair: 'It is now time that something was done. But the man who has the courage to do something must do it in the knowledge that he will go down in German history as a traitor. If he does not do it, however, he will be a traitor to his own conscience.'

As this implies, the need to avoid a stab-in-the-back legend such as that which had followed the end of the First World War and left such a baleful legacy for the ill-fated Weimar Republic was a constant burden and anxiety for those who had decided – sometimes with a heavy heart – that Germany's future rested on their capacity to remove Hitler, violently or not, from the scene, constitute a new government, and seek peace terms. They worried about the consequences of removing Hitler and seeming to stab the war effort in the back after a major disaster, even when final victory had become no more than a chimera. Rather than controlling the moment for a strike, the conspirators let it rest on external contingencies that, in the nature of things, they could not orchestrate.

When the strike eventually came, with the invasion consolidated in the west and the Red Army pressing towards the borders of the Reich in the east, the conspirators themselves recognized that they had missed the chance to influence the possible outcome of the war through their action. As one of their key driving-forces, Major-General Henning von Tresckow, from late 1943 Chief of Staff of the 2nd Army in the southern section of the eastern front, put it: 'It's not a matter any more of the practical aim, but of showing the world and history that the German resistance movement at risk of life has dared the decisive stroke. Everything else is a matter of indifference alongside that.'

II

All prospects of opposition to Hitler had been dimmed following the astonishing chain of military successes between autumn 1939 and spring 1941. Then, following the promulgation of the notorious Commissar Law, ordering the liquidation of captured Red Army political commissars, it had been Tresckow, Field-Marshal von Bock's first staff officer at Army Group Centre, who had been instrumental in revitalizing thoughts of resistance among a number of front officers – some of them purposely selected on account of their anti-regime stance. Born in 1901, tall, balding, with a serious demeanour, a professional soldier, fervent upholder of Prussian values, cool and reserved but at the same time a striking and forceful personality, disarmingly modest, but with iron determination, Tresckow had been an early admirer of Hitler though had soon turned into an unbending critic of the lawless and inhumane policies of the regime. Those whom Tresckow was able to bring to Army Group Centre included close allies in the emerging conspiracy against Hitler, notably Fabian von Schlabrendorff – six years younger than Tresckow himself, trained in law, who would serve as a liaison between Army Group Centre and other focal points of the conspiracy – and Rudolph-Christoph Freiherr von Gersdorff, born in 1905, a professional soldier, already an arch-critic of Hitler, and now located in a key position in the intelligence section of Army Group Centre. But attempts to persuade Bock, together with the other two group commanders on the eastern front, Rundstedt and Leeb, to confront Hitler and refuse orders failed. Any realistic prospect of opposition from the front disappeared again until late 1942. By then, in the wake of the unfolding Stalingrad crisis and seeing Hitler as responsible for the certain ruin of Germany, Tresckow was ready to assassinate him.

During the course of 1942, a number of focal points of practically dormant opposition within Germany itself – army and civilian – had begun to flicker back to life. The savagery of the warfare on the eastern front and, in the light of the winter crisis of 1941–2, the magnitude of the calamity towards which Hitler was steering Germany, had revitalized the notions, still less than concrete, that something must be done. Ludwig Beck (former Chief of the Army General Staff), Carl Goerdeler (one-time Reich Price Commissar), Johannes Popitz (Prussian Finance Minister), and Ulrich von Hassell (earlier the German Ambassador in Rome) – all connected with the pre-war conspiracy – met up again in Berlin in March 1942, but decided there were as yet few prospects. Even so, it was agreed that Beck would serve as a central point for the embryonic opposition. Meetings were held soon after with Colonel Hans Oster – head of the central office dealing with foreign intelligence in the Abwehr, the driving-force behind the 1938 conspiracy, who had leaked Germany's invasion plans to Holland in 1940 – and Hans von Dohnanyi, a jurist who had also played a significant part in the 1938 plot, and, like Oster, used his position in the foreign section of the Abwehr to develop good contacts to officers with oppositional tendencies. Around the same time, Oster engineered a close link to a new and important recruit to the oppositional groups, General Friedrich Olbricht, head of the General Army Office in Berlin. Olbricht, born in 1888 and a career soldier, was not one to seek the limelight. He epitomized the desk-general, the organizer, the military administrator. But he was unusual in his pro-Weimar attitude before 1933, and, thereafter – driven largely by Christian and patriotic feelings – in his consistent anti-Hitler stance, even amid the jubilation of the foreign-policy triumphs of the 1930s and the victories of the first phase of the war. His role would emerge as the planner of the *coup d'état* that was to follow upon the successful assassination of Hitler.

Already as the Stalingrad crisis deepened towards the end of 1942, Tresckow – later described by the Gestapo as 'without doubt one of the driving-forces and the "evil spirit" of the putschist circles', and allegedly referred to by Stauffenberg as his 'guiding master' – was pressing for the assassination of Hitler without delay. He had become convinced that nothing could be expected of the top military leadership in initiating a coup. 'They would only follow an order,' was his view. He took it upon himself to provide the 'ignition', as the conspirators labelled the assassination of Hitler that would lead to their removal of the Nazi leadership and takeover of the state. Tresckow had already in the summer of 1942 commissioned Gersdorff with the task of obtaining suitable explosives. Olbricht, meanwhile, coordinated the links with the other conspirators in Berlin and laid the groundwork for a coup to take place in March 1943. The plans to occupy important civilian and military positions in Berlin and other major cities were, in essence, along the lines that were to be followed in July 1944.

One obvious problem was how to get close enough to Hitler to carry out an assassination. Hitler's movements were unpredictable. An undependable schedule had in mid-February 1943 vitiated the intention of two officers, General Hubert Lanz and Major-General Hans Speidel, of arresting Hitler on an expected visit to Army Group B headquarters at Poltava. The visit did not materialize. Hitler's personal security had, meanwhile, been tightened considerably. He was invariably surrounded by SS bodyguards, pistols at the ready, and was always driven by his own chauffeur, Erich Kempka, in one of his limousines, which were stationed at different points in the Reich and in the occupied territories. And Schmundt, Hitler's Wehrmacht adjutant, had told Tresckow and Gersdorff that Hitler wore a bullet-proof vest and hat. This helped persuade them that the possibilities of a selected assassin having time to pull out his pistol, aim accurately, and ensure that his shot would kill Hitler were not great.

Nevertheless, preparations were made to shoot Hitler on a visit to Army Group Centre headquarters at Smolensk on 13 March. This plan was abandoned, since there was a distinct possibility of Field-Marshal von Kluge, commander of Army Group Centre, and other senior officers being killed alongside Hitler. Tresckow reverted to the original plan to blow up Hitler. During the meal at which, had the original plans been carried out, Hitler would have been shot, Tresckow asked one of the Führer's entourage, Lieutenant-Colonel Heinz Brandt, travelling in Hitler's plane, to take back a package for him to Colonel Hellmuth Stieff in Army High Command. The package looked like two bottles of cognac. It was, in fact, two parts of a bomb that Tresckow had put together.

Schlabrendorff carried the package to the aerodrome and gave it to Brandt just as he was climbing into Hitler's Condor ready for take-off. Moments before, Schlabrendorff had pressed the fuse capsule to activate the detonator, set for thirty minutes. It could be expected that Hitler would be blown from the skies shortly before the plane reached Minsk. Schlabrendorff returned as quickly as possible to headquarters and informed the Berlin opposition in the Abwehr that the 'ignition' for the coup had been undertaken. But no news came of an explosion. The tension among Tresckow's group was palpable. Hours later, they heard that Hitler had landed safely at Rastenburg. Schlabrendorff gave the code-word through to Berlin that the attempt had failed. Why there had been no explosion was a mystery. Probably the intense cold had prevented the detonation. For the nervous conspirators, ruminations about the likely cause of failure now took second place to the vital need to recover the incriminating package. Next morning, Schlabrendorff flew to Army High Command with two genuine bottles of cognac, retrieved the bomb, retreated to privacy, cautiously opened the packet with a razor-blade, and with great relief defused it. Mixed with relief, the disappointment among the opposition at such a lost chance was intense.

Immediately, however, another opportunity beckoned. Gersdorff had the possibility of attending the 'Heroes' Memorial Day', to take place on 21 March 1943 in Berlin. Gersdorff declared himself ready to sacrifice his own life in order to blow up Hitler during the ceremony. The attempt was to be made while Hitler was visiting an exhibition of captured Soviet war-booty, laid on to fill in the time between the ceremony in the Zeughaus (the old armoury in the centre of Berlin), and the wreath-laying at the cenotaph outside. Gersdorff positioned himself at the entry to the exhibition, in the rooms of the Zeughaus. He raised his right arm to greet Hitler as the dictator came by. At the same moment, with his left hand, he pressed the detonator charge on the bomb. The best fuse he had been able to come up with lasted ten minutes. He expected Hitler to be in the exhibition for half an hour, more than enough time for the bomb to go off. But this year, possibly fearing an Allied air-raid, Hitler raced through the exhibition, scarcely glancing at the material assembled for him, and was outside within two minutes. Gersdorff could follow Hitler no further. He sought out the nearest toilet and deftly defused the bomb.

Once again, astonishing luck had accompanied Hitler. The depressed and shocked mood following Stalingrad had probably also offered the best possible psychological moment for a coup against him. A successful undertaking at that time might, despite the recently announced 'Unconditional Surrender' strategy of the Allies, have stood a chance of splitting them. The removal of the Nazi leadership and offer of capitulation in the west that Tresckow intended would at any rate have placed the western Allies with a quandary about whether to respond to peace-feelers.

Overtures by opposition groups to the western Allies had been systematically rebuffed long before this time. The resistance was regarded by the British war-leadership (and the Americans shared the view) as little more than a hindrance. A successful coup from within could, it was felt, endanger the alliance with the Soviet Union – exactly the strategy which the conspirators were hoping to achieve – and would cause difficulties in establishing the post-war order in Germany. With the war turning remorselessly in their favour, the Allies were less than ever inclined to give much truck to an internal opposition which, it appeared, had claimed much but achieved nothing, and, furthermore, entertained expectations of holding on to some of the territorial gains that Hitler had made.

This was indeed the case, certainly with some of the older members of the national-conservative group aligned to Goerdeler whose break with Hitler had already taken place in the mid-1930s. These despised the barbarism of the Nazi regime. But they were keen to re-establish Germany's status as a major power, and continued to see the Reich dominating central and eastern Europe. Internally, their ideas were essentially (despite differences of emphasis) oligarchic and authoritarian. They favoured a restoration of the monarchy and limited electoral rights in self-governing communities, resting on Christian family values – the embodiment of the true 'national community' which the Nazis had corrupted.

The notions of Goerdeler and his close associates, whose age, mentality, and upbringing inclined them to look back to the pre-1914 Reich for much of their inspiration, found little favour among a group of a younger generation (mainly born during the first decade of the twentieth century) which gained its common identity through outright opposition to Hitler and his regime. The group, whose leaders were mainly of aristocratic descent, came to be known as 'the Kreisau Circle', a term coined by the Gestapo and drawn from the estate in Silesia where the group held a number of its meetings. The estate belonged to one its central figures, Helmuth James Graf von Moltke, born in 1907, trained in law, a great admirer of British traditions, a descendant of the famous Chief of the General Staff of the Prussian army in Bismarck's era. The ideas of the Kreisau Circle for a 'new order' after Hitler dated back in embryo to 1940, when they were first elaborated by Moltke and his close friend and relative Peter Graf Yorck von Wartenburg, three years older, also trained in law, a formative figure in the group, and with good contacts to the military opposition. Both had rejected Nazism and its gross inhumanity from an early stage. By 1942–3 they were drawing to meetings at Kreisau and in Berlin a number of like-minded friends and associates, ranging across social classes and denominational divisions, including the former Oxford Rhodes Scholar and foreign-policy spokesman of the group, Adam von Trott zu Solz, the Social Democrat Carlo Mierendorff, the socialist pedagogical expert Adolf Reichwein, the Jesuit priest Pater Alfred Delp, and the Protestant pastor Eugen Gerstenmaier.

The Kreisau Circle drew heavily for its inspiration on the idealism of the German youth movement, socialist and Christian philosophies, and experiences of the post-war misery and rise of National Socialism. Moltke, Yorck, and their associates – unlike the Goerdeler group – had no desire to hold on to German hegemony on the continent. They looked instead to a future in which national sovereignty (and the nationalist ideologies which underpinned it) would give way to a federal Europe, modelled in part on the United States of America. They were well aware that major territorial concessions would have to be made by Germany, along with some form of reparation for the peoples of Europe who had suffered so grievously under Nazi rule. Their concept of a new form of state rested heavily upon German Christian and social ideals, looking to democratization from below, through self-governing communities working on the basis of social justice, guaranteed by a central state that was little more than an umbrella organization for localized and particularized interests within a federal structure.

Such notions were inevitably utopian. The Kreisau Circle had no arms to back it, and no access to Hitler. It was dependent upon the army for action. Moltke, who opposed assassination, and Yorck, quite especially, pressed on a number of occasions for a coup to unseat Hitler. This still left out of the equation *how* to remove Hitler, and *who* should do it. Rather than utopian visions of a future social and political order, this was the primary issue that continued to preoccupy Tresckow and his fellow officers who had committed themselves to the opposition. The problem became, if anything, more rather than less difficult during the summer and autumn of 1943. Any expectation that Manstein might commit himself to the opposition was wholly dashed in the summer. 'Prussian field-marshals do not mutiny,' was his lapidary response to Gersdorff's probings. Manstein was at least honest and straightforward. Kluge, by contrast, blew hot and cold – offering backing to Tresckow and Gersdorff, then retreating from it. There was nothing to be gained from that quarter, though those in the opposition continued to persist in the delusion that Kluge was ultimately on their side.

There were other setbacks. Beck was meanwhile quite seriously ill. And Fritz-Dietlof Graf von der Schulenburg – a lawyer by training, who after initially sympathizing with National Socialism and holding a number of high administrative positions in the regime, had come to serve as a liaison between the military and civilian opposition – was interrogated on suspicion that he was involved in plans for a coup, though later released. Others, including Dietrich Bonhoeffer, the radically minded evangelical pastor, were also arrested, as the tentacles of the Gestapo threatened to entangle the leading figures in the resistance. Even worse: Hans von Dohnanyi and Hans Oster from the Abwehr were arrested in April, initially for alleged foreign currency irregularities, though this drew suspicion on their involvement in political opposition. The head of the Abwehr, Admiral Canaris, a professional obfuscator, managed for a time to throw sand in the eyes of the Gestapo agents. But as a centre of the resistance, the Abwehr had become untenable. By February 1944, its foreign department, which Oster had controlled, was incorporated into the Reich Security Head Office, and Canaris, dubious figure that he was for the opposition, himself placed under house arrest.

Tresckow, partly while on leave in Berlin, was tireless in attempting to drive on the plans for action against Hitler. But in October 1943, he was stationed at the head of a regiment at the front, away from his previously influential position in Army Group Centre headquarters. At the same time, in any case, Kluge was injured in a car accident and replaced by Field-Marshal Ernst Busch, an outright Hitler-loyalist, so that an assassination attempt from Army Group Centre could now be ruled out. At this point, Olbricht revived notions, previously entertained but never sustained, of carrying out both the strike against Hitler and the subsequent coup, not through the front army, but from the headquarters of the reserve army in Berlin. Finding an assassin, with access to Hitler, had been a major problem. Now, one was close at hand.

Claus Schenk Graf von Stauffenberg came from a Swabian aristocratic family. Born in 1907, the youngest of three brothers, he grew up under the influence of Catholicism – though his family were non-practising – and of the youth movement. He became particularly attracted to the ideas of the poet Stefan George, then held in extraordinary esteem by an impressionable circle of young admirers, strangely captivated by his vague, neo-conservative cultural mysticism which looked away from the sterilities of bourgeois existence towards a new élite of aristocratic aestheticism, godliness, and manliness. Like many young officers, Stauffenberg was initially attracted by aspects of National Socialism – not least its renewed emphasis on the value of strong armed forces and its anti-Versailles foreign policy – but rejected its racial antisemitism and, after the Blomberg–Fritsch crisis of early 1938, was increasingly critical of Hitler and his drive to war. Even so, serving in Poland he was contemptuous of the Polish people, approved of the colonization of the country, and was enthusiastic about the German victory. He was still more jubilant after the stunning successes in the western campaign, and hinted that he had changed his views on Hitler.

The mounting barbarity of the regime nevertheless appalled him. And when he turned irredeemably against Hitler in the late spring of 1942, it was under the influence of incontrovertible eye-witness reports of massacres of Ukrainian Jews by SS men. Hearing the reports, Stauffenberg concluded that Hitler must be removed. Serving in North Africa with the 10th Panzer Division, he was badly wounded in April 1943, losing his right eye, his right hand, and two fingers from his left hand. Soon after his discharge from hospital in August, speaking to Friedrich Olbricht about a new post as chief of staff in the General War Office in Berlin, he was tentatively asked about joining the resistance. There was little doubt what his answer would be. He had already come to the conclusion that the only way to deal with Hitler was to kill him.

By early September, Stauffenberg had been introduced to the leading figures in the opposition. Like Tresckow, he was a man of action, an organizer more than a theoretician. He deliberated with Tresckow in autumn 1943 about the best way to assassinate Hitler and the related but separate issue of organizing the coup to follow. As a means of taking over the state, they came up with the idea of recasting an operational plan, code-named 'Valkyrie', already devised by Olbricht and approved by Hitler, for mobilizing the reserve army within Germany in the event of serious internal unrest. No later than mid-October, Tresckow had produced an elaborate draft. It envisaged a strike to be carried out by the 18th Artillery Division of Army Group Centre, not just against Hitler, but also against Himmler, Göring, and Ribbentrop, to take place at their respective headquarters in East Prussia. The coup was to be unleashed by the declaration that 'treacherous elements from the SS and the party are attempting to exploit the situation to stab the [army] fighting hard on the eastern front in the back, and to seize power for their own purposes', demanding the proclamation of martial law. The aim of 'Valkyrie' had been to protect the regime; it was now transformed into a strategy for removing it.

Unleashing 'Valkyrie' posed two problems, however, once Tresckow's new stationing in mid-October meant that the coup would have to be directed from Berlin, not from Army Group Centre. The first was that, in the changed circumstances, the command had to be issued by the head of the reserve army. This was Colonel-General Friedrich Fromm, born in 1888 into a Protestant family with strong military traditions, a huge man, somewhat reserved in character, with strong beliefs in the army as the guarantor of Germany's status as a world-power. Fromm was no outright Hitler loyalist, but a fence-sitter who remained non-committal in his cautious desire to keep his options open and back whichever came out on top, the regime or the putschists – a policy which would eventually backfire upon him. The other problem was the old one of access to Hitler. Tresckow had concluded that only an assassination attempt in Führer Headquarters could get round the unpredictability of Hitler's schedule and the tight security precautions surrounding him. The difficulty was to find someone prepared to carry out the attempt who had reason to be in Hitler's close proximity in Führer Headquarters.

Stauffenberg, who had brought new dynamism to the sagging momentum of the opposition, wanted a strike against Hitler by mid-November. But who would carry it out? Two officers approached by Stauffenberg declined. The attempt had to be postponed. Meanwhile, Stauffenberg had been introduced to Captain Axel Freiherr von dem Bussche, whose courage in action had won him the Iron Cross, First Class, among other decorations. Witnessing a mass shooting of thousands of Jews in the Ukraine in October 1942 had been a searing experience for Bussche, and opened him to any prospect of doing away with Hitler and his regime. He was prepared to sacrifice his own life by springing on Hitler with a detonated grenade while the Führer was visiting a display of new uniforms.

Bad luck continued to dog the plans. One such uniform display, in December 1943, had to be cancelled when the train carrying the new uniforms was hit in an air-raid and the uniforms destroyed. Before Bussche could be brought back for another attempt, he was badly wounded on the eastern front in January 1944, losing a leg and dropping out of consideration for Stauffenberg's plans.

Lieutenant Ewald Heinrich von Kleist, son of the Prussian landowner, and long-standing critic of Hitler, Ewald von Kleist-Schmenzin, expressed himself willing to take over. Everything was set for Hitler's visit to a uniform display in mid-February. But the display was once again cancelled.

Yet another chance arose when Rittmeister Eberhard von Breitenbuch, aide-de-camp to Field-Marshal Busch (Kluge's successor as Commander-in-Chief of Army Group Centre) and already initiated in plans to eliminate Hitler, had the opportunity to accompany Busch to a military briefing at the Berghof on 11 March 1944. Breitenbuch had declared himself ready to shoot Hitler in the head. His Browning pistol was in his trouser pocket, and ready to fire as soon as he came close to Hitler. But on this occasion, ADCs were not permitted in the briefing. Luck was still on Hitler's side.

Even Stauffenberg began to lose heart – especially once the western Allies had established a firm footing on the soil of France. The Gestapo by now had the scent of the opposition; a number of arrests of leading figures pointed to the intensifying danger. Would it not now be better to await the inevitable defeat? Would even a successful strike against Hitler be anything more than a largely empty gesture? Tresckow gave the answer: it was vital that the coup took place, that the outside world should see that there was a German resistance movement prepared at the cost of its members' lives to topple such an unholy regime.

A last opportunity presented itself. On 1 July 1944, now promoted to colonel, Stauffenberg was appointed Fromm's chief of staff – in effect, his deputy. It provided him with what had been hitherto lacking: access to Hitler at military briefings related to the home army. He no longer needed look for someone to carry out the assassination. He could do it himself.

The difficulty with Stauffenberg taking over the role of assassin was that he would be needed at the same time in Berlin to organize the coup from the headquarters of the reserve army. The double role meant that the chances of failure were thereby enhanced. It was far from ideal. But the risk had to be taken.

On 6 July, Stauffenberg was present, for the first time in his capacity as chief of staff to Fromm, at two hour-long briefings at the Berghof.

He had explosives with him. But, it seems, an appropriate opportunity did not present itself. Whatever the reason, he made no attempt on this occasion. Impatient to act, Stauffenberg resolved to try at his next visit to the Berghof, five days later. But the absence of Himmler, whom the conspirators wanted to eliminate along with Hitler, deterred him. Again, nothing happened. On 15 July, when he was once more at Führer Headquarters (now moved back to the Wolf's Lair in East Prussia), Stauffenberg was determined to act. Once more, nothing happened. Most probably, it seems, he had been unable to set the charge in time for the first of the three briefings that afternoon. While the second short briefing was taking place, he was telephoning Berlin to clarify whether he should in any case go through with the attempt in the absence of Himmler. And during the third briefing, he was himself directly involved in the presentation, which deprived him of all possibility of priming the bomb and carrying out the attack. This time, Olbricht even issued the 'Valkyrie' order. It had to be passed off as a practice alarm-drill. The error could not be repeated. Next time, the issue of the 'Valkyrie' order could not go out ahead of the assassination attempt. It would have to wait for Stauffenberg's confirmation that Hitler was dead. After the bungling of the opportunity on the 15th, the third time that he had taken such a high risk to no avail, Stauffenberg prepared for what he told his fellow conspirators, gathered at his home in Berlin's Wannsee on the evening of 16 July, would be a last attempt. This would take place during his next visit to the Wolf's Lair, in the briefing scheduled for 20 July.

III

After a two-hour flight from Berlin, Stauffenberg and his adjutant, Lieutenant Werner von Haeften, landed at Rastenburg at 10.15 a.m. on 20 July. Stauffenberg was immediately driven the four miles to the Wolf's Lair. Haeften accompanied Major-General Stieff, who had flown in the same plane, to Army High Command, before returning later to Führer Headquarters. By 11.30 a.m. Stauffenberg was in a pre-briefing, directed by Keitel, that lasted three-quarters of an hour. Time was pressing since Hitler's briefing, owing to the arrival of Mussolini that afternoon, was to take place half an hour earlier than usual, at 12.30 p.m.

As soon as the meeting with Keitel was over, Stauffenberg asked where he could freshen up and change his shirt. It was a hot day, and an unremarkable request; but he needed to hurry. Haeften, carrying the briefcase containing the bomb, met him in the corridor. As soon as they were in the toilet, they began hastily to prepare to set the time-fuses in the two explosive devices they had brought with them, and to place the devices, each weighing around a kilogram, in Stauffenberg's briefcase. Stauffenberg set the first charge. The bomb could go off any time after quarter of an hour, given the hot and stuffy conditions, and would explode within half an hour at most. Outside, Keitel was getting impatient. Just then, a telephone call came from General Erich Fellgiebel, head of communications at Wehrmacht High Command and commissioned, in the plot against Hitler, with the vital task of blocking communications to and from Führer Headquarters following an assassination attempt. Keitel's adjutant, Major Ernst John von Freyend, took the call. Fellgiebel wanted to speak to Stauffenberg and requested him to call back. There was no time for that. Freyend sent Sergeant-Major Werner Vogel to tell Stauffenberg of Fellgiebel's message, and to hurry him along. Vogel found Stauffenberg and Haeften busy with some object. On being told to hurry, Stauffenberg brusquely replied that he was on his way. Freyend then shouted that he should come along at once. Vogel waited by the open door. Stauffenberg hastily closed his briefcase. There was no chance of setting the time-fuse for the second device he and Haeften had brought with them. Haeften stuffed this, along with sundry papers, in his own bag. It was a decisive moment. Had the second device, even without the charge being set, been placed in Stauffenberg's bag along with the first, it would have been detonated by the explosion, more than doubling the effect. Almost certainly, in such an event, no one would have survived.

The briefing, taking place as usual in the wooden barrack-hut inside the high fence of the closely guarded inner perimeter of the Wolf's Lair, had already begun when Stauffenberg was ushered in. Hitler, seated in the middle of the long side of the table nearest to the door, facing the windows, was listening to Major-General Adolf Heusinger, chief of operations at General Staff headquarters, describe the rapidly worsening position on the eastern front. Hitler absent-mindedly shook hands with Stauffenberg, when Keitel introduced him, and returned to Heusinger's report. Stauffenberg had requested a place as close as possible to the

Führer. His hearing disability, together with the need to have his papers close to hand when he reported on the creation of a number of new divisions from the reserve army to help block the Soviet breakthrough into Poland and East Prussia, gave him a good excuse. Room was found for him on Hitler's right, towards the end of the table. Freyend, who had carried Stauffenberg's briefcase into the room, placed it under the table, against the outside of the solid right-hand table-leg.

No sooner had he arrived in the room, than Stauffenberg made an excuse to leave it. This attracted no special attention. There was much to-ing and fro-ing during the daily conferences. Attending to important telephone calls or temporarily being summoned away was a regular occurrence. Stauffenberg left his cap and belt behind to suggest that he would be returning. Once outside the room, he asked Freyend to arrange the connection for the call which he still had to make to General Fell-giebel. But as soon as Freyend returned to the briefing, Stauffenberg hung up and hurried back to the Wehrmacht adjutants' building, where he met Haeften and Fellgiebel. Lieutenant Ludolf Gerhard Sander, a communications officer in Fellgiebel's department, was also there. Stauffenberg's absence in the briefing had meanwhile been noted; he had been needed to provide a point of information during Heusinger's presentation. But there was no sinister thought in anyone's mind at this point. At the adjutancy, Stauffenberg and Haeften were anxiously making arrangements for the car that had been organized to rush them to the airfield. At that moment, they heard a deafening explosion from the direction of the barracks. Fellgiebel gave Stauffenberg a startled look. Stauffenberg shrugged his shoulders. Sander seemed unsurprised. Mines around the complex were constantly being detonated by wild animals, he remarked. It was around quarter to one.

Stauffenberg and Haeften left for the airfield in their chauffeured car as expeditiously as could be done without causing suspicion. The alarm had still not been raised when Stauffenberg bluffed his way past the guards on the gate of the inner zone. He had greater difficulty leaving the outer perimeter. The alarm had by then been sounded. He had to telephone an officer, Rittmeister (cavalry captain) Leonhard von Möllendorf, who knew him and was prepared to authorize his passage. Once out, it was full speed along the bending road to the airfield. On the way, Haeften hurled away a package containing the second explo-sive. The car dropped them 100 yards from the waiting plane, and immediately turned back. By 1.15 p.m. they were on their way back to Berlin. They were firmly convinced that Hitler was dead.

Hitler had been bent over the heavy oaken table, propped up on his elbow, chin in his hand, studying air reconnaissance positions on a map, when the bomb went off – with a flash of blue and yellow flame and an ear-splitting explosion. Windows and doors blew out. Clouds of thick smoke billowed up. Flying glass splinters, pieces of wood, and showers of paper and other debris flew in all directions. Parts of the wrecked hut were aflame. For a time there was pandemonium. Twenty-four persons had been in the briefing-hut at the time of the explosion. Some were hurled to the floor or blown across the room. Others had hair or clothes in flames. There were cries of help. Human shapes stumbled around – concussed, part-blinded, eardrums shattered – in the smoke and debris, desperately seeking to get out of the ruins of the hut. The less fortunate lay in the wreckage, some fatally injured. Of those in the barrack-hut, only Keitel and Hitler avoided concussion; and Keitel alone escaped burst eardrums.

Hitler had, remarkably, survived with no more than superficial injuries. After the initial shock of the blast, he established that he was all in one piece and could move. Then he made for the door through the wreckage, beating flames from his trousers and putting out the singed hair on the back of his head as he went. He bumped into Keitel, who embraced him, weeping and crying out: 'My Führer, you are alive, you are alive!' Keitel helped Hitler, his uniform jacket torn, his black trousers and beneath them long white underwear in shreds, out of the building. But he was able to walk without difficulty. He immediately returned to his bunker. Dr Morell was summoned urgently. Hitler had a swollen and painful right arm, which he could barely lift, swellings and abrasions on his left arm, burns and blisters on his hands and legs (which were also full of wood-splinters), and cuts to his forehead. But those, alongside the burst eardrums, were the worst injuries he had suffered. When Linge, his valet, panic-stricken, rushed in, Hitler was composed, and with a grim smile on his face said: 'Linge, someone has tried to kill me.'

Below, Hitler's Luftwaffe adjutant, had been composed enough, despite the shock and the lacerations to his face through glass shards, to rush to the signals hut, where he demanded a block on all communications apart from those from Hitler, Keitel, and Jodl. At the same time, Below had Himmler and Göring summoned to Hitler's bunker. Then he made his way there himself. Hitler was sitting in his study, relief written on his face, ready to show off – with a tinge of pride, it seemed – his shredded clothing. His attention had already turned to the question of who had carried out the assassination attempt. According to Below, he rejected suggestions (which he appears initially to have believed) that the bomb had been planted by Organisation Todt workers who were temporarily at Führer Headquarters to complete the reinforcement of the compound against air-raids. By this time, suspicion had turned indubitably to the missing Stauffenberg. The search for Stauffenberg and investigation into the assassination attempt began around 2 p.m., though it was not at that point realized that this had been the signal for a general uprising against the regime. Hitler's rage at the army leaders he had always distrusted mounted by the minute. He was ready to wreak terrible vengeance on those whom he saw as stabbing the Reich in the back in its hour of crisis.

IV

Stauffenberg was by now well on his way back to Berlin. The conspirators there were anxiously awaiting his return, or news of what had happened to him, hesitating to act, still unsure whether to proceed with 'Operation Valkyrie'. The message that Fellgiebel had managed to get through, even before Stauffenberg had taken off from Rastenburg, was less clear than he thought. It was that something terrible had happened; the Führer was still alive. That was all. There were no details. It was unclear whether the bomb had gone off, whether Stauffenberg had been prevented (as a few days earlier) from carrying out the attack, or whether Stauffenberg had been arrested, whether, in fact, he was even still alive. Further messages seeping through indicated that something had certainly happened in the Wolf's Lair, but that Hitler had survived. Should 'Valkyrie' still go ahead? No contingency plans had been made for carrying out a coup if Hitler were still alive. And without confirmed news of Hitler's death, Fromm, in his position as commander of the reserve army, would certainly not give his approval for the coup. Olbricht concluded that to take any action before hearing definitive news would be to court disaster for all concerned. Vital time was lost. Meanwhile, it had only proved temporarily possible to block communications from the

Wolf's Lair. Soon after 4 p.m. that afternoon, before any coup had been started, the lines were fully open again.

Stauffenberg arrived back in Berlin between 2.45 and 3.15 p.m. There was no car to meet him. His chauffeur was waiting at Rangsdorf aerodrome. But Stauffenberg's plane had flown to Tempelhof (or possibly another Berlin aerodrome – this detail is not fully clear), and he had impatiently to telephone for a car to take him and Haeften to Bendlerstraße. It was a further delay. Stauffenberg did not reach the headquarters of the conspiracy, where tension was at fever-pitch, until 4.30 p.m. Haeften had in the meantime telephoned from the aerodrome to Bendlerstraße. He announced – the first time the conspirators heard the message – that Hitler was dead. Stauffenberg repeated this when he and Haeften arrived in Bendlerstraße. He had stood with General Fellgiebel outside the barrack-hut, he said, and seen with his own eyes first-aid men running to help and emergency vehicles arriving. No one could have survived such an explosion, was his conclusion. However convincing he was for those anxious to believe his message, a key figure, Colonel-General Fromm, knew otherwise. He had spoken to Keitel around 4 p.m. and been told that the Führer had suffered only minor injuries. That apart, Keitel had asked where, in the meantime, Colonel Stauffenberg might be.

Fromm refused outright Olbricht's request that he should sign the orders for 'Valkyrie'. But by the time Olbricht had returned to his room to announce Fromm's refusal, his impatient chief of staff Colonel Mertz von Quirnheim, a friend of Stauffenberg, and long closely involved in the plot, had already begun the action with a cabled message to regional military commanders, beginning with the words: 'The Führer, Adolf Hitler, is dead.' When Fromm tried to have Mertz arrested, Stauffenberg informed him that, on the contrary, it was he, Fromm, who was under arrest.

By now, several of the leading conspirators had been contacted and had begun assembling in the Bendlerstraße. Beck was there, already announcing that he had taken over command in the state; and that Field-Marshal Erwin von Witzleben, former commander-in-chief in France, and long involved in the conspiracy, was new commander-in-chief of the army. Colonel-General Hoepner, Fromm's designated successor in the coup, dismissed by Hitler in disgrace in early 1942 and forbidden to wear a uniform again, arrived around 4.30 p.m. in civilian clothes, carrying a suitcase. It contained his uniform, which he donned once more that evening.

Scenes in the Bendlerstraße were increasingly chaotic. Conspiring to arrange a *coup d'état* in a police state is scarcely a simple matter. But even in the existential circumstances prevailing, much smacked of dilettante organization. Too many loose ends had been left dangling. Too little attention had been paid to small but important details in timing, coordination, and, not least, communications. Nothing had been done about blowing up the communications centre at Führer Head-quarters or otherwise putting it permanently out of action. No steps were taken to gain immediate control of radio stations in Berlin and other cities. No broadcast was made by the putschists. Party and SS leaders were not arrested. The master-propagandist, Goebbels himself, was left at bay. Among the conspirators, too many were involved in issuing and carrying out commands. There was too much uncertainty; and too much hesitation. Everything had been predicated upon killing Hitler. It had simply been taken for granted that if Stauffenberg suc-ceeded in exploding his bomb, Hitler would be dead. Once that premiss was called into question, then disproved, the haphazard lines of a plan for the *coup d'état* swiftly unravelled. What was crucial, in the absence of confirmed news of Hitler's demise, was that there were too many regime-loyalists, and too many waverers, with too much to lose by committing themselves to the side of the conspirators.

Despite Stauffenberg's intense avowals of Hitler's death, the depress-ing news for the conspirators of his survival gathered strength. By mid-evening, it was increasingly obvious to the insurrectionists that their coup had faltered beyond repair.

It rapidly became plain in Führer Headquarters that the assassination attempt was the signal for a military and political insurrection against the regime. By mid-afternoon, Hitler had given command of the reserve army to Himmler. And Keitel had informed army districts that an attempt on the Führer's life had been made, but that he still lived, and on no account were orders from the conspirators to be obeyed. Loyalists could be found even in the Bendlerstraße, the seat of the uprising. The communications officer there, also in receipt of Keitel's order, was by the evening, as the conspirators were becoming more and more desperate, passing on the message that the orders he was having to transmit on their behalf were invalid. Fromm's adjutants were meanwhile able to spread the word in the building that Hitler was still alive, and to collect together a number of officers prepared to challenge the conspirators, whose already limited and hesitant support, inside and outside Bendler-straße, was by now rapidly draining away. Early instances where army units initially supported the coup dwindled once news of Hitler's survival hardened.

This was the case, too, in Paris. The military commander there, General Karl Heinrich von Stülpnagel, and his subordinate officers, had firmly backed the insurrectionists. But the supreme commander in the west, Field-Marshal von Kluge, vacillated as ever. In a vain call from Berlin, Beck failed to persuade him to commit himself to the rising. Once he learnt that the assassination attempt had failed, Kluge countered Stülpnagel's orders to have the entire SS, SD, and Gestapo in Paris arrested, dismissed the general, denounced his actions to Keitel, and later congratulated Hitler on surviving a treacherous attack on his life.

By this time, the events in Berlin had reached their denouement. In the late morning, Goebbels had been hosting a speech about Germany's armaments position, attended by ministers, leading civil servants, and industrialists, given by Speer in the Propaganda Ministry. After he had closed the meeting, Goebbels had taken Walther Funk and Albert Speer back with him into his study to talk about mobilizing remaining re-sources within Germany. While they were talking, he was suddenly called to take an urgent telephone call from Führer Headquarters. Despite the swift block on communications, he had his own hot-line to FHQ, which, evidently, still remained open. The call was from Press Chief Otto Dietrich, who broke the news to Goebbels that there had been an attack on Hitler's life. This was within minutes of the explosion taking place. There were few details at this stage, other than that Hitler was alive. Goebbels, told that Organisation Todt workers had probably been responsible, angrily reproached Speer about the evidently over-casual security precautions that had been taken.

The Propaganda Minister was unusually quiet and pensive over lunch. Somewhat remarkably, in the circumstances, he then retired for his usual afternoon siesta. He was awakened between 2 and 3 p.m. by the head of his press office, Wilfried von Oven, who had just taken a phone-call from an agitated Heinz Lorenz, Dietrich's deputy. Lorenz had dictated a brief text – drafted, he said, by Hitler himself – for immediate radio transmission. Goebbels was little taken with the terse wording, and remarked that urgency in transmitting the news was less important than making sure it was suitably couched for public consumption. He gave instructions to prepare an adequately massaged commentary. At this stage, the Propaganda Minister clearly had no idea of the gravity of the situation, that army officers had been involved, and that an uprising had been unleashed. Believing a breach of security had allowed unreliable OT workers to perpetrate some attack, he had been told that Hitler was alive. More than that he did not know. Even so, his own behaviour after first hearing the news, and then during the afternoon, when he attended to regular business and showed unusual dilatoriness in putting out the broadcast urgently demanded from Führer Headquarters, was odd. Possibly he had decided that any immediate crisis had passed, and that he would await further information before putting out any press communiqué. More probably, he was unsure of developments and wanted to hedge his bets.

Eventually, after this lengthy interval, further news from the Wolf's Lair ended his inaction. He rang Speer and told him to drop everything and rush over to his residence, close to the Brandenburg Gate. There he told Speer he had heard from Führer Headquarters that a full-scale military putsch in the entire Reich was under way. Speer immediately offered Goebbels his support in any attempt to defeat and crush the uprising. Within minutes, Speer noticed armed troops on the streets outside, ringing the building. By this time, it was early evening, around 6.30 p.m. Goebbels took one glance and disappeared into his bedroom, putting a little box of cyanide pills – 'for all eventualities' – into his pocket. The fact that he had been unable to locate Himmler made him worried. Perhaps the Reichsführer-SS had fallen into the hands of the putschists? Perhaps he was even behind the coup? Suspicions were rife. The elimination of such an important figure as Goebbels ought to have been a priority for the conspirators. Amazingly, no one had even thought to cut off his telephone. This, and the fact that the leaders of the uprising had put out no proclamation over the radio, persuaded the Propaganda Minister that all was not lost, even though he heard disquieting reports of troops moving on Berlin.

The guard-battalion surrounding Goebbels's house was under the command of Major Otto Ernst Remer, thirty-two years old at the time, a fanatical Hitler loyalist, who initially believed the fiction constructed by the plotters that they were putting down a rising by disaffected groups in the SS and party against the Führer. When ordered by his superior, the Berlin City Commandant, Major-General Paul von Hase, to take part in sealing off the government quarter, Remer obeyed without demur. He soon became suspicious, however, that what he had first heard was untrue; that he was, in fact, helping suppress not a putsch of party and SS leaders against Hitler, but a military coup against the regime by rebellious officers. As luck had it, Lieutenant Hans Hagen, charged with inspiring Nazi principles among the troops, had that afternoon lectured Remer's battalion on behalf of the Propaganda Ministry. Hagen now used his fortuitous contact to Remer to help undermine the conspiracy against Hitler. He persuaded Goebbels to speak directly to Remer, to convince him of what was really happening, and to win him over. Hagen then sought out Remer, played on the seeds of doubt in his mind about the action in which he was engaged, and talked him into disregarding the orders of his superior, Hase, and going to see Goebbels. At this point, Remer was still unsure whether Goebbels was part of an internal party coup against Hitler. If he made a mistake, it could cost him his head. However, after some hesitation, he agreed to meet the Propaganda Minister.

Goebbels reminded him of his oath to the Führer. Remer expressed his loyalty to Hitler and the party, but remarked that the Führer was dead. 'The Führer is alive!' Goebbels retorted. 'I spoke with him only a few minutes ago.' The uncertain Remer was visibly wavering. Goebbels offered to let Remer speak himself with Hitler. It was around 7 p.m. Within minutes, the call to the Wolf's Lair was made. Hitler asked Remer whether he recognized his voice. Standing rigidly to attention, Remer said he did. 'Do you hear me? So I'm alive! The attempt has failed,' he registered Hitler saying. 'A tiny clique of ambitious officers wanted to do away with me. But now we have the saboteurs of the front. We'll make short shrift of this plague. You are commissioned by me with the task of immediately restoring calm and security in the Reich capital, if necessary by force. You are under my personal command for this purpose until the Reichsführer-SS arrives in the Reich capital!' Remer needed no further persuasion. All Speer, in the room at the time, could hear, was 'Jawohl, my Führer … Jawohl, as you order, my Führer.' Remer was put in charge of security in Berlin to replace Hase. He was to follow all instructions from Goebbels.

Remer arranged for Goebbels to speak to his men. Goebbels addressed the guard-battalion in the garden of his residence around 8.30 p.m., and rapidly won them over. Almost two hours earlier, he had put out a radio communiqué telling listeners of the attack on Hitler, but how the Führer had suffered only minor abrasions, had received Mussolini that afternoon, and was already back at his work. For those still wavering, the news of Hitler's survival was a vital piece of information. Between 8 and 9 p.m. the cordon around the government quarter was lifted. The guard-battalion was by now needed for other duties: rooting out the conspirators in their headquarters in Bendlerstraße. The high-point of the conspiracy had passed. For the plotters, the writing was on the wall.

V

Some were already seeking to extricate themselves even before Goebbels's communiqué broadcast the news of Hitler's survival. By mid-evening, the group of conspirators in the Bendlerblock, the Wehrmacht High Command building in the Bendlerstraße, were as good as all that was left of the uprising. Remer's guard-battalion was surrounding the building. Panzer units loyal to the regime were closing in on Berlin's city centre. Troop commanders were no longer prepared to listen to the plotters' orders. Even in the Bendlerblock itself, senior officers were refusing to take orders from the conspirators, reminding them of the oath they had taken to Hitler which, since the radio had broadcast news of his survival, was still valid.

A group of staff officers, dissatisfied with Olbricht's increasingly lame explanation of what was happening, and, whatever their feelings towards Hitler, not unnaturally anxious in the light of an evidently lost cause to save their own skins, became rebellious. Soon after 9 p.m., arming themselves, they returned to Olbricht's room. While their spokesman, Lieutenant-Colonel Franz Herber, was talking to Olbricht, shots were fired in the corridor, one of which hit Stauffenberg in the shoulder. It was a brief flurry, no more. Herber and his men pressed into Fromm's office, where Colonel-General Hoepner, the conspirators' choice as commander of the reserve army, Mertz, Beck, Haeften, and the injured Stauffenberg also gathered. Herber demanded to speak to Fromm and was told he was still in his apartment (where he had been kept under guard since the afternoon). One of the rebel officers immediately made his way there, was admitted, and told Fromm what had happened. The guard outside Fromm's door had by now vanished. Liberated, Fromm returned to his office to confront the putschists. It was around 10 p.m. when his massive frame appeared in the doorway of his office. He scornfully cast his eye over the utterly dispirited leaders of the insurrection. 'So, gentlemen,' he declared, 'now I'm going to do to you what you did to me this afternoon.'

What the conspirators had done to Fromm had been to lock him in his room and give him sandwiches and wine. Fromm was less naïve. He had his neck to save – or so he thought. He told the putschists they were under arrest and demanded they surrender all weapons. Beck asked to retain his 'for private use'. Fromm ordered him to make use of it immediately. Beck said at that moment he was thinking of earlier days. Fromm urged him to get on with it. Beck put the gun to his head, but succeeded only in grazing himself on the temple. Fromm offered the others a few moments should they wish to write any last words. Hoepner availed himself of the opportunity, sitting at Olbricht's desk; so did Olbricht himself. Beck, meanwhile, reeling from the glancing blow to his head, refused attempts to take the pistol from him, and insisted on being allowed another shot. Even then, he only managed a severe head-wound. With Beck writhing on the floor, Fromm left the room to learn that a unit of the guard-battalion had entered the courtyard of the Bendlerblock. He knew, too, that Himmler, the newly appointed commander of the reserve army, was on his way. There was no time to lose. He returned to his room after five minutes and announced that he had held a court-martial in the name of the Führer. Mertz, Olbricht, Haeften, and 'this colonel whose name I will no longer mention' had been sentenced to death. 'Take a few men and execute this sentence downstairs in the yard at once,' he ordered an officer standing by. Stauffenberg tried to take all responsibility on his own shoulders, stating that the others had been merely carrying out his orders. Fromm said nothing, as the four men were taken to their execution, and Hoepner – initially also earmarked for execution, but spared for the time being following a private discussion with Fromm – was led out into captivity. With a glance at the dying Beck, Fromm commanded one of the officers to finish him off. The former Chief of the General Staff was unceremoniously dragged into the adjacent room and shot dead.

The condemned men were rapidly escorted downstairs into the

courtyard, where a firing-squad of ten men drawn from the guard-battalion was already waiting. To add to the macabre scene, the drivers of the vehicles parked in the courtyard had been ordered to turn their headlights on the little pile of sand near the doorway from which Stauffenberg and his fellow-conspirators emerged. Without ceremony, Olbricht was put on the sand-heap and promptly shot. Next to be brought forward was Stauffenberg. Just as the execution-squad opened fire, Haeften threw himself in front of Stauffenberg, and died first. It was to no avail. Stauffenberg was immediately placed again on the sand-heap. As the shots rang out, he was heard to cry: 'Long live holy Germany.' Seconds later, the execution of the last of the four, Mertz von Quirnheim, followed. Fromm at once had a telegram dispatched, announcing the bloody suppression of the attempted coup and the execution of the ringleaders. Then he gave an impassioned address to those assembled in the courtyard, attributing Hitler's wondrous salvation to the work of Providence. He ended with a three-fold 'Sieg Heil' to the Führer.

While the bodies of the executed men, along with Beck's corpse, which had been dragged downstairs into the yard, were taken off in a lorry to be buried – next day Himmler had them exhumed and cremated – the remaining conspirators in the Bendlerblock were arrested. It was around half an hour after midnight.

Apart from the lingering remnants of the coup in Paris, Prague, and Vienna, and apart from the terrible and inevitable reprisals to follow, the last attempt to topple Hitler and his regime from within was over.

VI

Hours earlier on this eventful 20 July 1944, shortly after arriving back in his bunker following the explosion, Hitler had refused to contemplate cancelling the planned visit of the Duce, scheduled for 2.30 p.m. that afternoon, but delayed half an hour because of the late arrival of Mussolini's train. It was to prove the last of the seventeen meetings of the two dictators. It was certainly the strangest. Outwardly composed, there was little to denote that Hitler had just escaped an attempt on his life. He greeted Mussolini with his left hand, since he had difficulty in raising his injured right arm. He told the shocked Duce what had happened, then led him to the ruined wooden hut where the explosion had taken place. In a macabre scene, amid the devastation, accompanied only by the interpreter, Paul Schmidt, Hitler described to his fellow-dictator where he had stood, right arm leaning on the table as he studied the map, when the bomb went off. He showed him the singed hair at the back of his head. Hitler sat down on an upturned box. Schmidt found a still usable stool amid the debris for Mussolini. For a few moments, neither dictator said a word. Then Hitler, in a quiet voice, said: 'When I go through it all again . . . I conclude from my wondrous salvation, while others present in the room received serious injuries . . . that nothing is going to happen to me.' He was ever more convinced, he added, that it was given to him to lead their common cause to a victorious end.

The same theme, that Providence had saved him, ran through Hitler's address transmitted by all radio stations soon after midnight. Hitler said he was speaking to the German people for two reasons: to let them hear his voice, and know that he was uninjured and well; and to tell them about a crime without parallel in German history. 'A tiny clique of ambitious, unconscionable, and at the same time criminal, stupid officers has forged a plot to eliminate me and at the same time to eradicate with me the staff practically of the German armed forces' leadership.' He likened it to the stab-in-the-back of 1918. But this time, the 'tiny gang of criminal elements' would be 'mercilessly eradicated'. On three separate occasions he referred to his survival as 'a sign of Providence that I must continue my work, and therefore will continue it'.

In fact, as so often in his life, it had not been Providence that had saved him, but luck: the luck of the devil.

26

No Way Out

I

'Now I finally have the swine who have been sabotaging my work for years,' raged Hitler as details of the plot against him started to emerge. 'Now I have proof: the entire General Staff is contaminated.' His long-standing, deep-seated distrust of his army leaders had found its confirmation. It suddenly seemed blindingly obvious to him why his military plans had encountered such setbacks: they had been sabotaged throughout by the treachery of his army officers. 'Now I know why all my great plans in Russia had to fail in recent years,' he ranted. 'It was all treason! But for those traitors, we would have won long ago. Here is my justification before history' (an indication, too, that Hitler was consciously looking to his place in the pantheon of Teutonic heroes). Goebbels, as so often, echoed Hitler's sentiments. 'The generals are not opposed to the Führer because we are experiencing crises at the front,' he entered in his diary. 'Rather, we are experiencing crises at the front because the generals are opposed to the Führer.' Hitler was convinced of an 'inner blood-poisoning'. With leading positions occupied by traitors bent on destroying the Reich, he railed, with key figures such as General Eduard Wagner (responsible as Quartermaster-General for army supplies) and General Erich Fellgiebel (chief of signals operations at Führer Head-quarters) connected to the conspiracy, it was no wonder that German military tactics had been known in advance by the Red Army. It had been 'permanent treachery' all along. It was symptomatic of an under-lying 'crisis in morale'. Action ought to have been taken sooner. It had been known, after all, for one and a half years that there were traitors in the army. But now, an end had to be made. 'These most base creatures to have worn the soldier's uniform in the whole of history, this rabble which has preserved itself from bygone times, must be got rid of and driven out.' Military recovery would follow recovery from the crisis in morale. It would be 'Germany's salvation'.

Vengeance was uppermost in Hitler's mind. There would be no mercy in the task of cleansing the Augean stables. Swift and ruthless action would be taken. He would 'wipe out and eradicate' the lot of them, he raged. 'These criminals' would not be granted an honourable soldier's execution by firing-squad. They would be expelled from the Wehrmacht, brought as civilians before the court, and executed within two hours of sentence. 'They must hang immediately, without any mercy,' he declared. He gave orders to set up a military 'Court of Honour', in which senior generals (including among others Keitel, Rundstedt – who presided – and Guderian) would expel in disgrace those found to have been involved in the plot. Those subsequently sentenced to death by the People's Court, he ordered, were to be hanged in prison clothing as criminals. He spoke favourably of Stalin's purges of his officers. 'The Führer is extraordinarily furious at the generals, especially those of the General Staff,' noted Goebbels after seeing Hitler on 22 July. 'He is absolutely determined to set a bloody example and to eradicate a free-masons' lodge which has been opposed to us all the time and has only awaited the moment to stab us in the back in the most critical hour. The punishment which must now be meted out has to have historic dimensions.'

Hitler had been outraged at Colonel-General Fromm's peremptory action in having Stauffenberg and the other leaders of the attempted coup immediately executed by firing-squad. He gave orders forthwith that other plotters captured should appear before the People's Court. The President of the People's Court, Roland Freisler, a fanatical Nazi who, despite early sympathies with the radical Left, had been ideologi-cally committed to the *völkisch* cause since the early 1920s, saw himself – a classical instance of 'working towards the Führer' – as pronouncing judgement as the 'Führer would judge the case himself'. The People's Court was, for him, expressly a 'political court'. Under his presidency, the number of death sentences delivered by the court had risen from 102 in 1941 to 2,097 in 1944. It was little wonder that he had already gained notoriety as a 'hanging judge'. Recapitulating Hitler's comments at their recent meeting, Goebbels remarked that those implicated in the plot were to be brought before the People's Court 'and sentenced to death'. Freisler, he added, 'would find the right tone to deal with them'. Hitler himself was keen above all that the conspirators should be permitted 'no time for long speeches' during their defence. 'But Freisler will see to that,' he added. 'That's our Vyschinsky' – a reference to Stalin's notorious prosecutor in the show-trials of the 1930s.

It took little encouragement from Goebbels to persuade Hitler that Fromm, Stauffenberg's direct superior officer, had acted so swiftly in an attempt to cover up his own complicity. Fromm had, in fact, already been named by Bormann in a circular to the Gauleiter in mid-evening of 20 July as one of those to be arrested as part of the 'reactionary gang of criminals' behind the conspiracy. Following the suppression of the coup in the Bendlerblock and the swift execution of Stauffenberg, Olbricht, Haeften, and Mertz von Quirnheim, Fromm had made his way to the Propaganda Ministry, wanting to speak on the telephone with Hitler. Instead of connecting him, Goebbels had had Fromm seated in another room while he himself telephoned Führer Headquarters. He soon had the decision he wanted. Goebbels immediately had the former Commander-in-Chief of the Reserve Army placed under armed guard. After months of imprisonment, a mockery of a trial before the People's Court, and a trumped-up conviction on grounds of alleged cowardice – despite the less-than-heroic motive of self-preservation that had dictated his role on centre-stage in the Bendlerblock on 20 July, he was no coward – Fromm would eventually die at the hands of a firing-squad in March 1945.

In the confusion in the Bendlerblock late on the night of 20 July, it had looked for a time as if other executions would follow those of the coup's leaders (together with the assisted suicide of Beck). But the arrival soon after midnight of an SS unit under the command of Sturmbann-führer Otto Skorzeny – the rescuer of Mussolini from captivity the previous summer – along with the appearance at the scene of SD chief Ernst Kaltenbrunner and Major Otto Ernst Remer, newly appointed commander of the Berlin guards battalion and largely responsible for putting down the coup, blocked further summary executions and ended the upheaval. Meanwhile, Himmler himself had flown to Berlin and, in his new temporary capacity as Commander-in-Chief of the Reserve Army, had given orders that no further independent action was to be taken against officers held in suspicion.

Shortly before 4 a.m., Bormann was able to inform the party's provincial chieftains, the Gauleiter, that the putsch was at an end. By then, those arrested in the Bendlerstraße – including Stauffenberg's brother, Berthold, former senior civil-servant and deputy Police President of Berlin Fritz-Dietlof von der Schulenburg, leading member of the Kreisau Circle Peter Graf Yorck von Wartenburg, Protestant pastor Eugen Gerstenmaier, and landholder and officer in the Abwehr Ulrich Wilhelm Graf Schwerin von Schwanenfeld – had been led off to await their fate. Former Colonel-General Erich Hoepner, arrested by Fromm but not executed, and Field-Marshal Erwin von Witzleben, who had left the Bendlerstraße before the collapse of the coup, were also promptly taken into custody, along with a number of others who had been implicated. Prussian Finance Minister Popitz, former Economics Minister Schacht, former Chief of Staff Colonel-General Halder, Major-General Stieff, and, from the Abwehr, Admiral Canaris and Major-General Oster were also swiftly arrested. Major Hans Ulrich von Oertzen, liaison officer for the Berlin Defence District (*Wehrkreis* III), who had given out the first 'Valkyrie' orders, blew himself up with a hand-grenade. Major-General Henning von Tresckow, the early driving-force behind the attempts to assassinate Hitler, killed himself in similar fashion at the front near Ostrov in Poland. General Wagner shot himself. General Fellgiebel refused to do so. 'You stand your ground, you don't do that,' he told his aide-de-camp. Well aware that his arrest was imminent, he spent much of the afternoon, remarkably, at the Wolf's Lair, even congratulated Hitler on his survival, and awaited his inevitable fate.

Those who fell into the clutches of the Gestapo had to reckon with fearsome torture. It was endured for the most part with the idealism, even heroism, which had sustained them throughout their perilous opposition. In the early stages of their investigations, the Gestapo managed to squeeze out remarkably limited information, beyond what they already knew, from those they so grievously maltreated. Even so, as the 'Special Commission, 20 July', set up on the day after the attempted coup, expanded its investigations, the numbers arrested rapidly swelled to 600 persons. Almost all the leading figures in the various branches of the conspiracy were rapidly captured, though Goerdeler held out under cover until 12 August. Reports reached Hitler daily of new names of those implicated. His early belief that it had been no more than a 'tiny clique' of officers which had opposed him had proved mistaken. The conspiracy had tentacles stretching further than he could have imagined.

He was particularly incensed that even Graf Helldorf, Berlin Police President, 'Old Fighter' of the Nazi Movement, and a former SA leader, turned out to have been deeply implicated. As the list lengthened, and the extent of the conspiracy became clear, Hitler's fury and bitter resentment against the conservatives – especially the landed aristocracy – who had never fully accepted him mounted. 'We wiped out the class struggle on the Left, but unfortunately forgot to finish off the class struggle on the Right,' he was heard to remark. But now was the worst possible time to encourage divisiveness within the people; the general showdown with the aristocracy would have to wait till the war was over.

On 7 August, the intended show-trials began at the People's Court in Berlin. The first eight – including Witzleben, Hoepner, Stieff, and Yorck – of what became a regular procession of the accused were each marched by two policemen into a courtroom bedecked with swastikas, holding around 300 selected spectators (including the journalists hand-picked by Goebbels). There they had to endure the ferocious wrath, scathing contempt, and ruthless humiliation heaped on them by the red-robed president of the court, Judge Roland Freisler. Seated beneath a bust of Hitler, Freisler's face reflected in its contortions extremes of hatred and derision. He presided over no more than a base mockery of any semblance of a legal trial, with the death-sentence a certainty from the outset. The accused men bore visible signs of their torment in prison. To degrade them even in physical appearance, they were shabbily dressed, without collars and ties, and were handcuffed until seated in the courtroom. Witzleben was even deprived of braces or a belt, so that he had to hold up his trousers with one hand. The accused were not allowed to express themselves properly or explain their motivation before Freisler cut them short, bawling insults, calling them knaves, traitors, cowardly murderers. The order had been given – probably by Goebbels, though undoubtedly with Hitler's authorization – for the court proceedings to be filmed with a view to showing extracts in the newsreels as well as in a 'documentary' entitled 'Traitors before the People's Court'. So loudly did Freisler shout that the cameramen had to inform him that he was ruining their sound recordings. Nevertheless, the accused managed some moments of courageous defiance. For instance, after the death sentence had predictably been pronounced, General Fellgiebel uttered: 'Then hurry with the hanging, Mr President; otherwise you will hang earlier than we.' And Field-Marshal von Witzleben called out: 'You can hand us over to the hangman. In three months the enraged and tormented people will call you to account, and will drag you alive through the muck of the street.' Such a black farce were the trials that even Reich Justice Minister Otto Georg Thierack, himself a fanatical Nazi who in his ideological ardour had by this time surrendered practically the last vestiges of a completely perverted legal system to the arbitrary police lawlessness of the SS, subsequently complained about Freisler's conduct.

Once the verdicts had been pronounced, the condemned men were taken off, many of them to Plötzensee Prison in Berlin. On Hitler's instructions they were denied any last rites or pastoral care (though this callous order was at least partially bypassed in practice). The normal mode of execution for civilian capital offences in the Third Reich was beheading. But Hitler had reportedly ordered that he wanted those behind the conspiracy of 20 July 1944 'hanged, hung up like meat-carcasses'. In the small, single-storey execution room, with whitewashed walls, divided by a black curtain, hooks, indeed like meat-hooks, had been placed on a rail just below the ceiling. Usually, the only light in the room came from two windows, dimly revealing a frequently used guillotine. Now, however, certainly for the first groups of conspirators being led to their doom, the executions were to be filmed and photo-graphed, and the macabre scene was illuminated with bright lights, like a film studio. On a small table in the corner of the room stood a table with a bottle of cognac – for the executioners, not to steady the nerves of the victims. The condemned men were led in, handcuffed and wearing prison trousers. There were no last words, no comfort from a priest or pastor; nothing but the black humour of the hangman. Eye-witness accounts speak of the steadfastness and dignity of those executed. The hanging was carried out within twenty seconds of the prisoner entering the room. Death was not, however, immediate. Sometimes it came quickly; in other cases, the agony was slow – lasting more than twenty minutes. In an added gratuitous obscenity, some of the condemned men had their trousers pulled down by their executioners before they died. And all the time the camera whirred. The photographs and grisly film were taken to Führer Headquarters. Speer later reported seeing a pile of such photographs lying on Hitler's map-table when he visited the Wolf's Lair on 18 August. SS-men and some civilians, he added, went into a viewing of the executions in the cinema that evening, though they were not joined by any members of the Wehrmacht. Whether

Hitler saw the film of the executions is uncertain; the testimony is contradictory.

Most of the executions connected with the attempted coup of 20 July 1944 followed within the next weeks. Some took place only months later. By the time the blood-letting subsided, the death-toll of those directly implicated numbered around 200. But it was Hitler's last triumph.

The Stauffenberg plot left its lasting mark on him. The injuries he had suffered in the bomb blast had been, as we saw, relatively superficial. As if to emphasize his own indestructibility and his manliness in surmounting pain, he made light of his injuries and even joked about them to his entourage. But they were less trivial than Hitler himself implied. Blood was still seeping through the bandages from the skin wounds almost a fortnight after the bomb-attack. He suffered sharp pain in especially the right ear, and his hearing was impaired. He was treated by Dr Erwin Giesing, an ear, nose, and throat specialist in a nearby hospital, then by Professor Karl von Eicken, who had removed a throat polyp in 1935 and was now flown in from Berlin. But the ruptured eardrums, the worst injury, continued bleeding for days, and took several weeks to heal. He thought for some time that his right ear would never recover. The disturbance to his balance from the inner-ear injuries made his eyes turn to the right and gave him a tendency to lean rightwards when he walked. There was also frequent dizziness and malaise. His blood pressure was too high. He looked aged, ill, and strained. Eleven days after the attack on his life, he told those present at the daily military briefing that he was unfit to speak in public for the time being; he could not stand up for long, feared a sudden attack of dizziness, and was also worried about not walking straight. A few weeks later, Hitler admitted to his doctor, Morell, that the weeks since the bomb-attack had been 'the worst of his life' – adding that he had mastered the difficulties 'with a heroism no German could dream of'. Strangely, the trembling in Hitler's left leg and hands practically disappeared following the blast. Morell attributed it to the nervous shock. By mid-September, however, the tremor had returned. By this time, the heavy daily doses of pills and injections could do nothing to head off the long-term deterioration in Hitler's health. At least as serious were the psychological effects.

His sense of distrust and betrayal now reached paranoid levels. Outward precautions were swiftly taken. Security was at once massively tightened at Führer Headquarters. At military briefings, all personnel were from now on thoroughly searched for weapons and explosives. Hitler's food and medicines were tested for poison. Any presents of foodstuffs, such as chocolates or caviar (which he was fond of), were immediately destroyed. But the outward security measures could do nothing to alter the deep shock that some of his own generals had turned against him. According to Guderian, whom he appointed as successor to Zeitzler as Chief of the Army General Staff within hours of Stauffenberg's bomb exploding, 'he believed no one any more. It had already been difficult enough dealing with him; it now became a torture that grew steadily worse from month to month. He frequently lost all self-control and his language grew increasingly violent. In his intimate circle he now found no restraining influence.'

In 1918, according to his distorted vision of the momentous weeks of defeat and revolution, enemies from within had stabbed in the back those fighting at the front. His entire life in politics had been aimed at reversing that disaster, and in eliminating any possible repetition in a new war. Now, a new variant of such treachery had emerged – led, this time, not by Marxist subversives at home threatening the military effort, but by officers of the Wehrmacht who had come close to undermining the war-effort on the home front. Suspicion had always been deeply embedded in Hitler's nature. But the events of 20 July now transformed the underlying suspicion into the most visceral belief in treachery and betrayal all around him in the army, aimed once more at stabbing in the back a nation engaged in a titanic struggle for its very survival.

Alongside the thirsting for brutal revenge, the failed bomb-plot gave a further mighty boost to Hitler's sense of walking with destiny. With 'Providence' on his side, as he imagined, his survival was to him the guarantee that he would fulfil his historic mission. It intensified the descent into pure messianism. 'These criminals who wanted to do away with me have no idea what would have happened to the German people,' Hitler told his secretaries. 'They don't know the plans of our enemies, who want to annihilate Germany so that it can never arise again. If they think that the western powers are strong enough without Germany to hold Bolshevism in check, they are deceiving themselves. This war must be won by us. Otherwise Europe will be lost to Bolshevism. And I will see to it that no one else can hold me back or eliminate me. I am the only one who knows the danger, and the only one who can prevent it.' Such sentiments were redolent, through a distorting mirror, of the Wagnerian redeemer-figure, a hero who alone could save the holders of the Grail, indeed the world itself, from disaster – a latter-day Parsifal.

But, once more looking to his own place in history, and to the reasons why the path of destiny had led to mounting tragedy for Germany, instead of glorious victory, he found a further reason, beyond the treachery of his generals: the weakness of the people. If Speer can be believed, Hitler gave at this time an intimation that the German people might not deserve him, might have proved weak, have failed its test before history, and thus be condemned to destruction. It was one of the few hints, whether in public or in private, amid the continued outpourings of optimism about the outcome of the war, that Hitler indeed contemplated, even momentarily, the possibility of total defeat.

Whatever the positive gloss he instinctively and insistently placed upon news of the latest setbacks as he continued to play the role of Führer to perfection, he was not devoid of understanding for the significance of the successful landing of the western Allies in Normandy, the dramatic collapse of the eastern front which left the Red Army in striking distance of the borders of the Reich itself, the ceaseless bombing that the Luftwaffe was powerless to prevent, the overwhelming Allied superiority in weaponry and raw materials, and gloomy reports of a mounting, critical fuel shortage. Kluge and Rommel had both urged Hitler to end the war which he could not win. But he continued to dismiss out of hand all talk of suing for peace. The situation was 'not yet ripe for a political solution', he declared. 'To hope for a favourable political moment to do something during a time of severe military defeats is naturally childish and naïve,' he went on, during the military briefing session with his generals on 31 August 1944. 'Such moments can present themselves when you have successes.' But where were the successes likely to materialize? All he could point to was a feeling of certainty that at some point the Allied coalition would break down under the weight of its inner tensions. It was a matter of waiting for that moment, however tough the situation was.

'My task has been,' he continued, 'especially since 1941 under no circumstances to lose my nerve.' He lived, he said, just to carry out this struggle since he knew that it it could only be won through a will of iron. Instead of spreading this iron will, the General Staff officers had undermined it, disseminating nothing but pessimism. But the fight would continue, if necessary even on the Rhine. He once more evoked one of his great heroes of history. 'We will under all circumstances carry on the struggle until, as Frederick the Great said, one of our damned opponents is tired of fighting any longer, and until we get a peace which secures the existence of the German nation for the next fifty or a hundred years and' – he was back at a central obsession – 'which, above all, does not defile our honour a second time, as happened in 1918.' This thought brought him directly to the bomb plot, and to his own survival. 'Fate could have taken a different turn,' he continued, adding with some pathos: 'If my life had been ended, it would have been for me personally, I might say, only a liberation from worries, sleepless nights, and severe nervous strain. In a mere fraction of a second you're freed from all that and have rest and your eternal peace. For the fact that I'm still alive, I nevertheless have to thank Providence.'

They were somewhat rambling thoughts. But they were plain enough in meaning: a negotiated peace could not be considered except from a position of strength (which was in realistic terms unimaginable); the only hope was to hold out until the Allied coalition collapsed (but time, and the crass imbalance of material resources, were scarcely on Germany's side); his historic role, as he saw it, was to eradicate any possibility of a second capitulation on the lines of that of November 1918; he alone stood between Germany and calamity; but suicide would bring release for him (whatever the consequences for the German people) within a split second. In Hitler's extraordinary perspective, his historic task was to continue the fight to the point of utter destruction – and even self-destruction – in order to prevent another 'November 1918' and to erase the memory of that 'disgrace' for the nation. It was a task of infinitely greater honour than negotiating a peace from weakness – something which would bring new shame on himself and the German people. It amounted to scarcely less than a realization that the time for a last stand was approaching, and that no holds would be barred in a struggle likely to end in oblivion, where the only remaining monumental vision was the quest for historical greatness – even if Reich and people should go down in flames in the process.

This meant in turn that there was no way out. The failure of the conspiracy to remove Hitler took away the last opportunity of a negotiated end to the war. The horrors of a war which Germany had inflicted on the rest of Europe were rebounding – if, even now, in far milder form – on to the Reich itself. With internal resistance crushed, and a leadership unable to bring victory, incapable of staving off defeat, and unwilling to attempt to find peace, only total military destruction could bring a release.

For Hitler's countless victims throughout Europe, the human misery had, in fact, still not reached its peak. It would rise in crescendo in the months still to come.

II

The institutional pillars of the regime – the Wehrmacht, the party, ministries of state, and the SS-controlled security apparatus – remained intact in the second half of 1944. And Hitler, the keystone bonding the regime's structure together, was still, paradoxically, indispensable to its survival while – by now even in the eyes of some close to the leadership – at the same time driving Germany inexorably towards perdition. The predictable rallying round Hitler following the July assassination attempt could not for long conceal the fact that the regime's edifice was beginning to crumble as the Nazi empire throughout Europe shrivelled and the increasing certainty of a lost war made even some of those who had gained most from Nazism start looking for possible exit-routes. The aftermath of the bomb-plot saw the regime enter its most radical phase. But it was a radicalism that mirrored an increasingly desperate regime's reaction to internal as well as external crisis.

Hitler's own obvious reaction in the wake of the shock of Stauffen-berg's bomb had been to turn to his firm loyalist base, the party leader-ship, and to his most long-standing and trusted band of paladins. In the backs-to-the-wall atmosphere of the last months, the party was to play a more dominant role than at any time since the 'seizure of power', invoking the overcoming of adversity in the 'time of struggle', attempting to instil the 'fighting spirit of National Socialism' throughout the entire people in the increasingly vain attempt to combat overwhelming Allied arms and material superiority by little more than fanatical will-power.

As had invariably been the case in a crisis, Hitler had lost no time following the attempted coup on 20 July in ensuring the continued loyalty of the Gauleiter, the party's provincial chieftains. Among them were some who had been among his most dependable lieutenants for close on two decades. Collectively, the Gauleiter constituted now, as before, a vital prop of his rule. His provincial viceroys were now, their party positions enhanced through their extensive powers as Reich Defence Commissars, his insurance against any prospect of army-led unrest or possible insurrection in the regions. Increasingly over the next months, as the threads of state administration started to fray and ultimately fell apart, the party chieftains – especially those who acted as Reich Defence Commissars in their regions – were decisive in holding together in the provinces what was left of Nazi rule.

Extended scope for propaganda, mobilization, and tightened control over the population – the overriding tasks of the party as most people looked beyond the end of the regime and looming military defeat into an uncertain future – fell to the Reich Defence Commissars in the last desperate drive to maximize resources for 'total war'. The shortages of available men to be sent to the front, and workers for the armaments industries, had mounted alarmingly throughout the first half of 1944. Hitler's authorization in January to Fritz Sauckel, Plenipotentiary for Labour Deployment, to make up the manpower shortages through forced labour extracted from the occupied territories, while at the same time according Speer protection for the labour employed in his armaments plants in France, had done nothing to resolve the difficulty and merely sharpened the conflict between Sauckel and Speer. Apart from Speer, the SS, the Wehrmacht, and the party had also proved adept at preventing any inroads into their personnel. Bormann had even presided over a 51 per cent increase in the number of 'reserved occupations', exempt from call-up, in the party administration between May 1943 and June 1944.

Meanwhile, the labour shortage had been greatly magnified through the double military disaster in June of the Allied landing in Normandy and the Red Army's devastating offensive on the eastern front. This had prompted Goebbels and Speer to link their efforts to persuade Hitler to agree to a drastic radicalization of the 'home front' to comb out all remaining manpower for the war effort. Both had sent him lengthy memoranda in mid-July, promising huge labour savings to tide over the situation until new weaponry became available and the anti-German coalition broke up. But before the Stauffenberg bomb, Hitler had, as we noted, shown little readiness to comply with their radical demands.

123. Hitler viewing the Wehrmacht parade after laying a wreath at the cenotaph on Unter den Linden on 'Heroes' Memorial Day', 21 March 1943. Behind Hitler (*left to right*) are Göring, Keitel, Commander-in-Chief of the Navy Karl Dönitz, and Himmler. Shortly beforehand, a planned attempt to kill Hitler by opponents from within Army Group Centre had had to be aborted when the dictator's usual timetable on the day was altered without notice.

124. Hitler is saluted by the Party's 'Old Guard' in the Löwenbräukeller in Munich on 8 November 1943, the twentieth anniversary of the Beerhall Putsch. Göring is to Hitler's right. It was to be the last time that Hitler would appear in person at this symbolic ritual, a high point in the Nazi calendar.

125. Martin Bormann, head of the Party Chancellery (following the flight of Rudolf Heß to Scotland in May 1941). From the beginning of the war onwards he was invariably at Hitler's side, and in April 1943 was officially appointed Secretary to the Führer. This proximity, together with his control of the party, gave him great power.

126. Hitler and Goebbels, still capable of raising a smile despite military disasters and mounting domestic problems, photographed during a walk on the Obersalzberg above Berchtesgaden in June 1943.

127. (*left*) The Eastern Front in spring and autumn. A German vehicle bogged down in heavy mud.

128. (*above right*) The Eastern Front in winter. Tanks and armoured vehicles, unusable in the conditions, had to be dug in at strategic points to secure them against Soviet attacks.

129. The Eastern Front in summer. Limitless space. A Waffen-SS unit treks across seemingly unending fields.

130. (*top*) The 'Final Solution'. French Jews being deported in 1942. Frightened faces peer out from behind the barbed-wire covering the slats of the railway-wagon.

131. The 'Final Solution'. Polish Jews forced to dig their own grave, 1942.

132. The 'Final Solution'. Incinerators at Majdanek with skeletons of camp-prisoners
murdered on the approach of the Red Army and liberation of the camp on
27 July 1944.

133. Hitler and Himmler take a wintry walk on the Obersalzberg in March 1944.

134. The 'White Rose' resistance group of Munich students. Christoph Probst (*left*) with Sophie and Hans Scholl in July 1942. On 22 February the following year, they were sentenced to death and beheaded on the same day for distributing leaflets in Munich University, in the wake of the disaster at Stalingrad, condemning the inhumanity of the Nazi regime.

135. (*above left*) The brilliant tank commander Heinz Guderian. Though he clearly recognized that Hitler was leading Germany to catastrophe, he condemned the attempt to assassinate him on 20 July 1944. A day later, Guderian was appointed Chief of the General Staff, retaining the position until his dismissal on 28 March 1945.

136. (*above right*) General Ludwig Beck, who, following his resignation – because of Hitler's insistence on risking war over Czechoslovakia – as Chief of the General Staff in 1938, became a central figure in the conservative resistance, committing suicide on 20 July 1944 after the failure of the bomb-plot.

137. (*right*) Colonel Claus Schenk Graf von Stauffenberg, the driving-force behind the conspiracy to kill Hitler on 20 July 1944, who took upon himself the responsibility both for carrying out the assassination in the Wolf's Lair and for directing the intended coup d'état in Berlin. On its failure, he was arrested and shot by a firing-squad late that night.

138. (*below*) Major-General Henning von Tresckow, one of the most courageous figures in the resistance, the inspiration of several plans, hatched within Army Group Centre, to kill Hitler in 1943. Stauffenberg regarded Tresckow as his mentor. This is one of the last photographs of him, taken in 1944. He committed suicide on 21 July on the Eastern Front on learning of the failure of the bomb-plot.

139. (*left*) Hitler, looking shaken, just after the assassination attempt on 20 July 1944.
140. (*right*) Hitler's trousers, shredded by the bomb-blast.

141. (*facing page, above*) Hitler greets Mussolini at Führer Headquarters – the last time they would meet – some three hours after Stauffenberg's bomb had exploded on 20 July 1944. Hitler had to shake hands with his left hand because his right arm had been slightly injured in the blast.

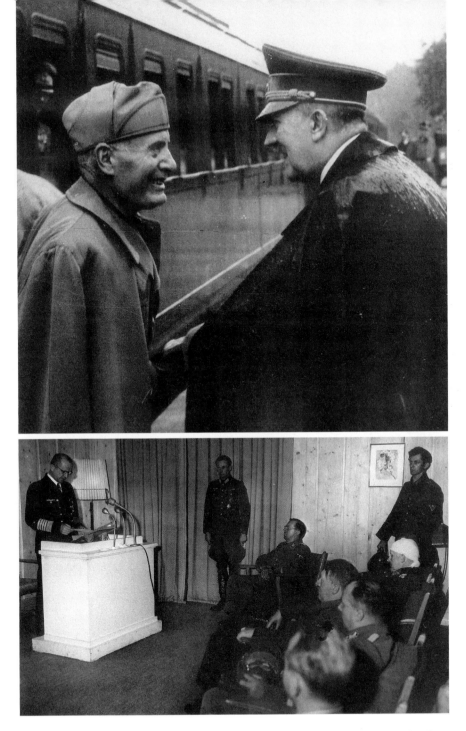

142. Grand-Admiral Dönitz professes the loyalty of the navy in a broadcast shortly after midnight on 21 July 1944, just after Hitler and Göring had spoken to the German people. Listening to Dönitz are Bormann (*left, next to Hitler*) and Jodl (*on Hitler's right, with bandaged head*).

143. An ageing Hitler, pictured at the Berghof in 1944.

144. Wonder-Weapons: a V1 flying-bomb is taken to its launch-pad.

145. (*left*) Wonder-Weapons: a V2 rocket, ready for launch at Cuxhaven.

146. (*right*) Wonder-Weapons: An American soldier stands alongside a Me 262 on the advance into Germany in April 1945. Hitler had for a long time insisted on having the jet-fighter designed as a bomber. When finally deployed as a fighter, it was far too late to be effective.

147. Scraping the barrel. Ill-equipped men of the 'Volkssturm' – the people's militia established by Hitler on 25 September 1944, ordering all able-bodied men between 16 and 60 to take up arms – pictured during a swearing-in ceremony in Berlin in December 1944.

148. The last 'Heroes' Memorial Day', 11 March 1945. Hitler did not appear, leaving it to Göring (flanked by Dönitz on his left, and Keitel on his right) to lay the wreath at the cenotaph on Unter den Linden.

149. Women and children fleeing as the Red Army attacks Danzig in March 1945.

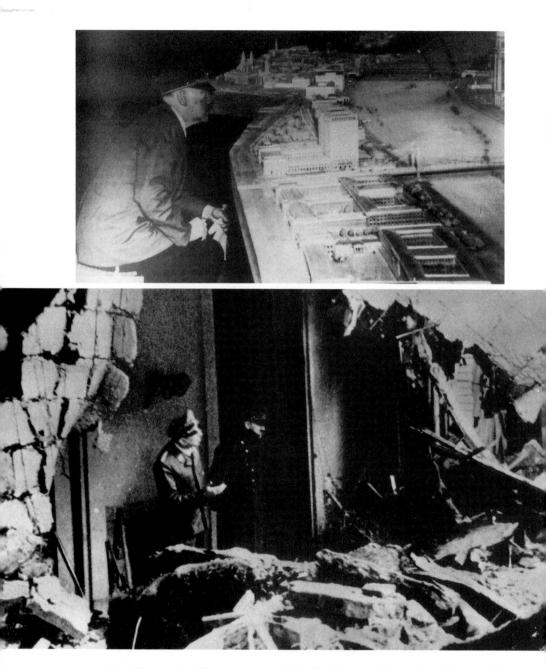

150. (*top*) Fantasy: In February 1945, with the Red Army within striking distance of
Berlin, Hitler ponders the model of the intended postwar rebuilding of his hometown
of Linz, designed for him by his architect Hermann Giesler.

151. Reality: Hitler, with his adjutant Julius Schaub, standing in the ruins of
the Reich Chancellery in Berlin in March 1945, a few weeks before his suicide.

Whatever the accompanying rhetoric, and the undoubted feeling (which Goebbels's own propaganda had helped feed) among the under-privileged that many of the better-off were still able to escape the burdens of war, and were not pulling their weight in the national cause, such demands were bound to be unpopular in many circles, antagonize powerful vested interests, and also convey an impression of desperation. And, as the state administration rushed to point out, the gains might well be less than impressive; only one in twelve of those in the civil service who had not been called up was under forty-three, and more than two-thirds were over fifty-five years old.

Hitler had told his Propaganda Minister as recently as June that the time was not ripe for 'a big appeal to total war in the true meaning of the word', that the crises would be surmounted 'in the usual way', but that he would be ready to introduce 'wholly abnormal measures' should 'more serious crises take place'. Hitler's change of mind, directly follow-ing the failed assassination attempt, in deciding to grant Goebbels the new authority he had coveted, as Reich Plenipotentiary for the Total War Effort, was a tacit admission that the regime was faced with a more fundamental crisis than ever before.

Goebbels's decisive action to put down the uprising on 20 July unques-tionably weighed heavily in his favour when Hitler looked for the man to supervise the radicalization of the home front. And where before he had faced a hesitant Hitler, he was now pushing at an open door in his demands for draconian measures. The decision had in effect already been taken when, at a meeting of ministerial representatives along with some other leading figures in the regime two days after Stauffenberg's assassination attempt, head of the Reich Chancellery Lammers proposed the bestowing of wide-ranging powers on the Propaganda Minister to bring about the reform of the state and public life. Himmler was given extensive complementary powers at the same time to reorganize the Wehrmacht and comb out all remaining manpower. The following day, 23 July, the regime's leaders, now joined by Göring, assembled at the Wolf's Lair, where Hitler himself, heavily leaning on Goebbels's memor-andum of the previous week, confirmed the new role of the Propaganda Minister. Hitler demanded 'something fundamental' if the war were still to be won. Massive reserves were available, he claimed, but had not been deployed. This would now have to be done without respect to person, position, or office. He pointed to the party in the early days, which had achieved 'the greatest historic success' with only a simple administrative apparatus. Goebbels noted with interest the change in Hitler's views since their previous meeting a month or so earlier. The assassination attempt and the events on the eastern front had produced clarity in his decisions, Goebbels noted in his diary. To his own staff, the Propaganda Minister laconically remarked that 'it takes a bomb under his arse to make Hitler see reason'.

Goebbels relished his moment of triumph. He appeared to have finally achieved what he had desired for so long: control over the 'home front' with 'the most extensive plenipotentiary powers . . . that have up to now been granted in the National Socialist Reich', with rights – the decisive factor in his view – to issue directives to ministers and the highest-ranking governmental authorities. To his staff, he spoke of having 'practically full dictatorial powers' within the Reich.

However, nothing was ever quite what it seemed in the Third Reich. The decree itself limited Goebbels's powers in some respects. He could issue directives to the 'highest Reich authorities'. But only they could issue any consequential decrees and ordinances. And these had to be agreed with Lammers, Bormann, and Himmler (in the capacity he had adopted when becoming Interior Minister, as Plenipotentiary for Reich Administration). Any directives related to the party itself had to have Bormann's support (and, behind Bormann, to correspond with Hitler's own wishes). Unresolved objections to Goebbels's directives had to pass to Lammers for Hitler's own final decision. Beyond the wording of the decree itself, Hitler let Goebbels know that those authorities directly responsible to him – those involved in the rebuilding plans for Berlin, Munich, and Linz, his motor-vehicle staff, and the personnel of the Reich Chancellery, Presidential Chancellery, and Party Chancellery – were also excluded from the directives. The Wehrmacht, its recruitment now under Himmler's authority, had been exempt from the outset.

Such restrictions on his powers left Goebbels's enthusiasm for his new task undimmed. The belief that 'will' would overcome all problems was immediately put into action as with his usual forceful energy he unleashed a veritable frenzy of activity in his new role. The staff of fifty that he rapidly assembled from a number of ministries, most prominently from his own Propaganda Ministry, prided themselves on their unbureaucratic methods, swift decision-making, and improvisation. As his main agents in ensuring that directives were implemented in the regions, leaving no stone unturned in the quest to comb out all reserves of untapped labour, Goebbels looked to the party's Gauleiter, bolstering their already extensive powers as Reich Defence Commissars. They could be relied upon, in his view, to reinvoke the spirit of the 'time of struggle', to ensure that bureaucracy did not get in the way of action. (In practice, the cooperation of the Gauleiter was assured as long as no inroads were made into the personnel of their own party offices. Bormann ensured that they were well protected.)

Behind the actionism of the party, Goebbels also needed Hitler's backing. He ensured that this was forthcoming through a constant stream of bulletins on progress (*Führer-Informationen*), printed out on a 'Führer-Machine' – a typewriter with greatly enlarged characters which Hitler's failing eyesight could cope with – recording successes and couching general recommendations (such as simplifying unnecessary bureaucratic paperwork) in such a way that, given Hitler's frame of mind, approval would be as good as automatic, thereby opening up yet further avenues for intervention. Nevertheless, Hitler did not give blanket approval to all measures suggested by Goebbels. He could rely upon Bormann to bring to his attention any proposals which his own still sharp antennae would tell him might have an unnecessarily harmful impact on morale, both at home and quite especially among soldiers at the front.

Goebbels certainly produced a new, extreme austerity drive within Germany in the first weeks in his new office as Total War Plenipoteniary. But a large proportion of the 451,800 men sifted out of the administration and economy were too old for military service. Goebbels was forced, therefore, to turn to fit men in reserved occupations – work thought essential for the war-effort, including skilled employment in armaments factories or food production. Their replacement, where possible, by older, less fit, less experienced, less qualified workers was both administratively complicated and inefficient. And the net addition of women workers numbered only little over quarter of a million. Athough, partly through Goebbels's measures, it proved possible to send around a million men to the front between August and December 1944, German losses in the first three of those months numbered 1,189,000 dead and wounded. Whatever the trumpeting by Goebbels of his achievements as Reich Plenipotentiary for the Total War Effort, the reality was that he was scraping the bottom of the barrel.

And among the most bizarre aspects of the 'total war' drive in the second half of 1944 was the fact that at precisely the time he was combing out the last reserves of manpower, Goebbels – according to film director Veit Harlan – was allowing him, at Hitler's express command, to deploy 187,000 soldiers, withdrawn from active service, as extras for the epic colour film of national heroism, *Kolberg*, depicting the defence of the small Baltic town against Napoleon as a model for the achievements of total war. According to Harlan, Hitler as well as Goebbels was 'convinced that such a film was more useful than a military victory'. Even in the terminal crisis of the regime, propaganda had to come first.

The evocation of heroic defence of the fatherland by the masses against the invading Napoleonic army – the myth enunciated in *Kolberg* – was put to direct use in the most vivid expression of the last-ditch drive to 'total war': the launching by Heinrich Himmler of the Volkssturm, or people's militia, on 18 October 1944, the 131st anniversary of the legendary defeat of Napoleon in the 'Battle of the Peoples' near Leipzig, when a coalition of forces under Blücher's leadership liberated German territory from the troops of the French Emperor once and for all. The Volkssturm was the military embodiment of the party's belief in 'triumph of the will'. It was the party's attempt to militarize the homeland, symbolizing unity through the people's participation in national defence, overcoming the deficiencies in weapons and resources through sheer willpower.

Though Goebbels continued to harbour the belief that he would incorporate in his 'total war' commission the organization of the 'Volkswehr' (People's Defence), as it was initially to be called, leaving the military aspects to the SA, Bormann and Himmler had come to an agreement to divide responsibility between them. Drafts for a decree by Hitler were put forward in early September. He eventually signed the decree on 26 September, though it was dated to the previous day. It spoke of the 'final aim' of the enemy alliance as 'the eradication of the German person'. This enemy must now be repulsed until a peace securing Germany's future could be guaranteed. To attain this end, Hitler's decree went on, in typical parlance, 'we set the total deployment of all Germans against the known total annihilatory will of our Jewish-international enemies'. In each party Gau, the 'German Volkssturm' was to be established, comprising all men capable of bearing weapons between the ages of sixteen and sixty. Training, military organization, and provision of weaponry fell to Himmler as Commander of the Reserve Army. Political and organizational matters were the province of Bormann, acting on Hitler's behalf. Party functionaries were given the task of forming companies and battalions. A total number of 6 million Volkssturm men was envisaged. Each Volkssturm man had to swear an oath that he would be 'unconditionally loyal and obedient to the Führer of the Great German Reich Adolf Hitler', and would 'rather die than abandon the freedom and thereby the social future of my people'.

The men called up had to provide their own clothing, as well as eating and drinking utensils, cooking equipment, a rucksack, and blanket. And since munitions for the front were in short supply, the weaponry for the men of the Volkssturm was predictably miserable. It was little wonder that the Volkssturm was largely unpopular, and widely seen as pointless on the grounds that the war was already lost. Reluctance to serve in the Volkssturm, especially on the eastern front, was well justified. Gauleiter Erich Koch reported severe losses among Volkssturm units in East Prussia already in October. The losses were militarily pointless. They did not hold up the Red Army's advance by a single day. In all, approaching 175,000 citizens who were mainly too old, too young, or too weak to fight lost their lives in the Volkssturm. The futility of the losses was a clear sign that Germany was close to military bankruptcy.

As the autumn of 1944 headed towards what would prove the last winter of the war, the fabric of the regime was still holding together. But the threads were visibly starting to fray. The closing of the ranks which had followed Stauffenberg's assassination attempt had temporarily seen a revitalization of the élan of the party. Hitler had, almost as a reflex, turned inwards to those he trusted. His distance, not just from the army leaders he detested, but also from the organs of state administration, started to extend immeasurably with his increased reliance on a diminishing number of his long-standing paladins. Bormann's position, dependent upon the combination of his role as head of the party organization and, especially, his proximity to Hitler as the Führer's secretary and mouthpiece, guarding the portals and restricting access, was particularly strengthened. He was one of the winners from the changed circumstances after 20 July. Another was Goebbels who, like Bormann, had seized the opportunity to enhance his own position of power as the party increased its hold over practically all walks of life within Germany. Mobilization and control had been the essence of party activity since the beginning. Now, as the regime tottered, it returned to its essence.

Another development, from a most unlikely source, provides in retrospect – at the time it was still well concealed – the clearest indication that the regime was starting to teeter. Among the biggest beneficiaries of the failed coup of 20 July 1944 had been Reichsführer-SS Heinrich Himmler. Hitler had given 'loyal Heinrich', his trusted head of the labyrinthine security organization, overall responsibility for uncovering the background to the conspiracy and for rounding up the plotters. And beyond his other extensive powers, Himmler had now also gained direct entrée into the military sphere as Commander of the Reserve Army, with a remit to undertake a full-scale reorganization. He was soon, as we have seen, also to have control over the people's militia, the Volkssturm. Yet at this very time, Himmler, conceivably now the most powerful individual in Germany after Hitler, was playing a double game, combining every manifestation of utmost loyalty with secret overtures to the West in the forlorn hope of saving not just his skin but his position of power in the event of the British and Americans eventually seeing sense and turning, with the help of his SS, to fend off the threat of Communism. In October, Himmler used an SS intermediary to put to an Italian industrialist with good connections in England a proposal to make twenty-five German divisions in Italy available to the Allies as a defence against Communism in return for a guarantee of the preservation of the Reich's territory and population. Both the British and the Americans rejected the overtures out of hand. In this scenario, Hitler would have been dispensable. But it was pure self-delusion. Himmler was too centrally implicated in the most appalling facets of the Nazi regime to be taken seriously by the Allies as a prospective leader of a post-Hitlerian Germany. For Himmler, too, there was no way out. Without Hitler's backing, his power would evaporate like a breath in the chill morning air. This was as true in late 1944 as at any other time during the Third Reich.

Hitler's authority remained intact. But if they could have found an escape route by removing him or discarding him, there were now those among his closest paladins who would have followed it.

III

Meanwhile, the vice around Hitler's Reich was tightening. Between June and September the Wehrmacht lost on all fronts well over a million men killed, captured, or missing. The losses of tanks, guns, planes, and other armaments were incalculable. The war in the air was by now almost wholly one-sided. Fuel shortages left many German fighters unable to take to the air as the British and American bomber armadas wreaked havoc on German towns and cities with impunity by day as well as by night. The war at sea had also by this time been definitively lost by Germany. The U-boat fleet had never recovered from its losses in the second half of 1943, while Allied convoys could now cross the Atlantic almost unmolested. In the meantime, the territories of the Nazi empire were shrinking markedly by the end of the summer following the advances of the Allies on both western and eastern fronts since June.

On the western front, Germany's military commanders had by then long viewed the continuation of the war as pointless. On replacing Rundstedt in early June, the weak and impressionable Kluge was easily persuaded by Hitler that the western commanders, especially Rommel, had been far too pessimistic in their judgement of the situation. After a two-day visit to the front, however, Kluge had been forced to admit that Rommel was right. In his letter to Hitler of 15 July, Rommel had explicitly stated that, heroically though the troops were fighting, 'the unequal struggle is heading for its end'. He felt, therefore, compelled to ask Hitler, he wrote, 'to draw the consequences from this position without delay'. He let the leaders of the conspiracy against Hitler know that he would be prepared to join them if the demands for an end to the war were dismissed. Germany's most renowned field-marshal was never put to the test. Three days before Stauffenberg's bomb exploded, Rommel was seriously injured when his car skidded from the road after being strafed by an enemy aircraft.

Five days after the assassination attempt on Hitler, 'Operation Cobra', the Allied attack southwards towards Avranches, began with a ferocious 'carpet-bombing' assault by over 2,000 aircraft, dropping 47,000 tons of bombs on an already weakened German panzer division in an area of only six or so square miles. It ended on 30 July with the taking of Avranches and the opening not only of the route to the Brittany coastal ports, but also to the exposed German flank towards the east, and to the heart of France.

The significance of the loss of Avranches was still not fully appreciated when Hitler provided Jodl with his overview of the entire military situation on the evening of 31 July. Hitler was far from unrealistic in his assessment. He was well aware of how threatening the position was on all fronts, and how impossible it was in the current circumstances to combat the overwhelming Allied superiority in men and materials, above all in air-power. His main hope was to buy time. Weapon technology, more planes, and an eventual split in the alliance would open up new opportunities. He had to get some breathing-space in the west, he told his Luftwaffe adjutant, Nicolaus von Below, shortly after his briefing with Jodl. Then, with new panzer divisions and fighter formations, he could launch a major offensive on the western front. In common with many observers, Below had thought it more important to concentrate all forces against the Red Army in the east. Hitler replied that he could attack the Russians at a later point. But this could not be done with the Americans already in the Reich. (He led Below to believe at the same time that he feared the power of the Jews in the USA more than the power of the Bolsheviks.) His strategy was, therefore, to gain time, inflict a major blow on the western Allies, hope for a split in the alliance, and turn on the Russians from a new position of strength.

Hitler thought, so he told Jodl, that the eastern front could be stabilized, as long as additional forces could be mobilized. But a breakthrough by the enemy in the east, whether in East Prussia or Silesia, imperilling the homeland itself and bearing serious psychological consequences, would pose a critical danger. Any destabilization on the eastern front would, he went on, affect the stance of Turkey, Romania, Bulgaria, and Hungary. Preventive measures had to be taken. It was vital to secure Hungary, both for vital raw materials such as bauxite and manganese and for communications lines with south-eastern Europe. Bulgaria was essential to securing a hold on the Balkans and obtaining ore from Greece. He also feared a British landing in the Balkans or on the Dalmatian islands, which Germany was scarcely in a position to ward off and which 'could naturally lead to catastrophic consequences'.

On the Italian front, Hitler saw the greatest advantage in the tying down of significant Allied forces which could otherwise be deployed elsewhere. The withdrawal of German forces into the Apennines would remove tactical mobility, would still not prevent an Allied advance, and would leave only retreat to alpine defence positions as a possibility – thereby freeing up Allied troops for the western front. But as a last resort, he was prepared to give up Italy (and the entire Balkans), pull back German troops to the Alps, and withdraw his main forces for the vital struggle on the western front.

This was for him the decisive theatre of war. The troops would not understand him remaining in East Prussia when valuable western parts of the Reich were threatened, and behind them the Ruhr – Germany's industrial heartland. Preparations would have to be made to move Führer Headquarters to the west. Command would have to be centralized. Kluge, supreme commander in the west, could not be left with the responsibility. So paranoid was Hitler by now about treachery within the army, that he told Jodl it would be necessary in such an event to avoid communicating such a plan to army command in the west – pointing to Stülpnagel's involvement in the plot against him – since it would probably be immediately betrayed to the enemy.

Hitler pointed to what he saw as a decisive issue in the west. 'If we lose France as a war area, we lose the basis of the U-boat war.' (Though the U-boats were ineffective in the second half of 1944, Hitler was persuaded by Dönitz that new, improved submarines would soon be ready, and would be a vital weapon in the war against the western powers.) In addition, essential raw materials – he singled out wolfram (important for steel production) and electro-technical products – would be lost. If it were not so important to the war effort to hold on to France, he said, he would vacate the coastal areas – still vital for U-boat bases at Brest and St Nazaire – and pull back mobile forces to a more defensible line. But he saw no prospect at present of holding such a line with the forces available, wherever the line might be drawn. 'We've got to be clear,' he stated, 'that a change could come about in France only if we succeed – even for a certain time – in gaining air-supremacy.' But he drew the conclusion that, 'however bitter it might be at the moment', everything had to be done to hold back 'for the most extreme case' as a 'last reserve' whatever Luftwaffe divisions could be assembled in the Reich – though that could take weeks – to be deployed wherever it might be possible 'at the last throw of the dice' to bring about a decisive shift in fortunes.

Hitler was desperate to buy time. 'I can't operate myself,' he said, 'but

I can make it colossally difficult for the enemy to operate in the depths of the area.' For this, it was essential to deprive the enemy of access to ports on the French coast, preventing the landing of troops, armaments, and provisions. (At this point only Cherbourg, with a much damaged harbour, was in Allied hands.) Hitler was prepared, as he bluntly stated, 'simply to sacrifice certain troops' to this end. The ports were to be held, he emphasized, 'under all circumstances, with complete disregard for the people there, to make it impossible for the enemy to supply unlimited numbers of men'. Should this not happen, a breakthrough could come quickly. Along with this, in an early glimpse of what would become a 'scorched-earth' policy targeted finally at the Reich itself, all railway installations, including track and locomotives, were to be destroyed, as were bridges. The ports, too, were in the last resort to be destroyed if they could not be held. If the ports could be held for between six and ten weeks in the autumn, precious time would have been gained.

Time was, however, not on Hitler's side. Learning of the gravity of the Allied capture of Avranches, he ordered – picking up on an operational plan that had been put forward by Kluge – an immediate counter-strike westwards from Mortain, initially intended to take place on 2 August, aimed at retaking Avranches and splitting the advancing American forces under General George S. Patton. The counter-offensive, eventually launched on 7 August, proved disastrous. It lasted only a day, could not prevent some of Patton's troops from sweeping down into Brittany (where stiff defence, however, saw the garrison at Brest hold out until 19 September), and ended with the German forces in disarray but narrowly avoiding even worse calamity.

On 15 August Hitler refused Kluge's request to pull back around 100,000 troops threatened with imminent disaster through encirclement near Falaise. When he was unable to reach Kluge that day – the field-marshal had entered the battle-zone itself in the heart of the 'Falaise pocket' and his radio had been put out of action by enemy fire – Hitler, well aware of Kluge's flirtation with the conspiracy against him and of his pessimism about the western front, jumped to the conclusion that he was negotiating a surrender with the western Allies. It was, said Hitler, 'the worst day of his life'. He promptly recalled Field-Marshal Model, one of his most trusted generals, from the eastern front, appointed him to take over from Kluge and dispatched him to western front headquarters. Until Model arrived, Kluge had not even been informed by Hitler that he was about to be dismissed. Hitler's peremptory hand-written note, handed over by Model and ordering Kluge back to Germany, ended with the threateningly ambiguous comment that the field-marshal should contemplate in which direction he wished to go. Model's arrival was unable to alter the plight of the German troops, but under his command – assisted by tactical errors of the Allied ground-forces commander, General Montgomery – it proved possible to squeeze out at the last minute some 50,000 men from the ever-closing 'Falaise pocket' to fight again another day, closer to home. As many again, however, were taken prisoner and a further 10,000 killed.

Kluge must have reckoned with the near certainty that he would be promptly arrested, expelled from the Wehrmacht, and put before the People's Court for his connections with the plotters against Hitler. On the way back to Germany on 19 August, in the vicinity of Metz, he asked his chauffeur to stop the car for a rest. Depressed, worn out, and in despair, he swallowed a cyanide pill.

The day before, he had written a letter to Hitler. The field-marshal, who (as Hitler knew) had had prior knowledge of the bomb-plot, and who had even the year before Stauffenberg's attempt shown sympathy for Tresckow and the oppositional group in Army Group Centre, used his dying words to praise Hitler's leadership. 'My Führer, I have always admired your greatness,' he wrote. 'You have led an honest, an entirely great struggle,' he continued, with reference to the war in the east. 'History will testify to that.' He then appealed to Hitler now to show the necessary greatness to bring to an end a struggle with no prospect of success in order to release the suffering of his people. This dying plea was as far as he would go to distance himself from the Dictator's war leadership. He ended with a final vow of loyalty: 'I depart from you, my Führer, to whom I was inwardly closer than you perhaps imagined, in the consciousness of having carried out my duty to the very limits.'

Hitler's direct reaction to the letter is not known. But Kluge's suicide merely convinced him not only of the field-marshal's implication in the bomb-plot, but also that he had been trying to surrender his forces in the west to the enemy. Hitler found it difficult to comprehend, as he bitterly reflected. He had promoted Kluge twice, given him the highest honours, made him sizeable donations (including a cheque for RM 250,000 tax-free on his sixtieth birthday, and a big supplement to his field-marshal's salary). He was anxious to prevent any news seeping out about Kluge's alleged attempt to capitulate. It could seriously affect morale; it would certainly bring further contempt on the army. He let the generals know about Kluge's suicide. But for public consumption the field-marshal's death – from a heart-attack, it was said – was announced only after his body had lain in the church on his Brandenburg estate for a fortnight. Kluge's funeral was a quiet affair. Hitler had banned all ceremonials.

On the day that Kluge had temporarily been out of contact, 15 August, the Allies undertook 'Operation Dragoon', the landing of troops on the French Mediterranean coast. Quickly capturing Marseilles and Toulon, they pushed northwards, forcing Hitler reluctantly to agree to the withdrawal to the north of almost all his forces in southern France in the attempt to build a cohesive front along the upper Marne and Saône stretching to the Swiss border. The end of the German occupation of France was now in sight. Though it would take several more weeks to complete, the symbolic moment arrived when, prompted by strikes, a popular uprising, and attacks by the French Resistance against the German occupiers, and by the eventual readiness of the German Commander, General Dietrich von Choltitz, to surrender (despite orders from Hitler to reduce Paris to rubble if it could not be held), the Allied Supreme Commander, General Dwight D. Eisenhower, gave a French division the honour of liberating the French capital on 24 August.

By now, the western Allies had over 2 million men on the Continent. Advancing into Belgium, they liberated Brussels on 3 September and next day captured the important port of Antwerp before the harbour installations could be destroyed. Only Cherbourg, of the major Channel ports, had up to this point been in Allied hands, and supplies through that route were seriously hampered by the level of destruction. Antwerp was vital to the assault on Germany. But it was as late as 27 November before the Scheldt estuary was secured and before the approaches to the harbour were fully cleared of mines. In the interim, the Allied drive towards the German borders suffered a major setback with the serious losses suffered, especially by British troops, in ten days of bitter fighting in the combined airborne and land operation – 'Market Garden' – launched on 17 September, to seize the river-crossings at Grave, Nijmegen, and Arnhem. Beyond supply problems, battle fatigue, and replacing the men lost, the Allied advance was stalling because of the stiff German defence, aided by shortened supply-lines, redeployment of the men extricated from the Falaise Pocket, and reinforcements drawn from the east. In the west, it was plain, despite the dramatic Allied successes since D-Day, the war was far from over.

In the east, following the Red Army's big summer offensive, the German network of alliances with Balkan countries started to unravel in August much as Hitler had feared. On 2 August, Turkey announced that it was breaking off relations with Germany. Economically, it meant the loss of chrome supplies. Militarily, it was clear that Turkey would at some point join the Allies. On 20 August, when the Soviets attacked Army Group South Ukraine, Romanian units deserted en masse, many of them joining the enemy and turning on their former allies. Reaching the Danube before the retreating Germans, Romanian troops closed the river-crossing. Sixteen German divisions, exposed to the onslaught of the Red Army, were totally destroyed. It was a military calamity of the first order. Three days later, Antonescu was deposed following a coup in Bucharest. His successor, King Michael, sued for peace. Romania swapped sides, declaring war on Germany – and on Hungary (from which it now intended to regain the territory in Transylvania that it had been compelled to give up in 1940). The Red Army, joined by Romanian units, was now free to sweep across the Danube. The Wehrmacht, meanwhile, had lost 380,000 indispensable troops within a fortnight.

Bulgaria, a country which since 1941 had played a careful diplomatic hand, was by this time hopelessly exposed. Soviet troops crossed its borders on 8 September (the USSR having declared war three days earlier), and on the same day Bulgaria rapidly switched sides and declared war on Germany. The German control over the entire Balkan region now held by the most slender of threads. The collapse of Romania and Bulgaria, followed by rapid Soviet occupation, meant the urgent withdrawal of German troops from Greece was imperative. This began in September. In mid-October British airborne troops were able to occupy Athens. By then, Tito's partisan army was on the verge of entry into Belgrade. German troops were meanwhile engaged in the brutal suppression, finally accomplished by the end of October, of a rising, undertaken in the main by Soviet-inspired indigenous partisans alongside a sizeable minority of the 60,000-strong army, in the puppet state of Slovakia. Most important of all, from Hitler's point of view, in the gathering mayhem in south-eastern Europe, Hungary, his chief ally but long wavering, had immediately following the volte-face in Romania begun urgent soundings for peace with the Soviet Union.

In these same critical weeks, Hitler was also losing a vital ally in northern Europe. The danger signals about Finland's position had been flashing brightly for months. On 2 September, State President Mannerheim informed Hitler that Finland was unable to continue the struggle. Relations were to be broken off immediately. German troops were to leave the country by 15 September. On 19 September, Finland signed an armistice with the Soviet Union.

In these same momentous months, throughout the whole of August and September, the German leadership was also faced with suppressing the dangerous rising in Warsaw, which had begun on 1 August, two days after tanks of the Red Army had pushed into the suburbs of Warsaw on the east of the Vistula and Soviet radio had encouraged the city's inhabitants to rise against their occupiers. The Poles were aware that they could reckon with little help from the western powers. But they were unprepared to be left in the lurch by the Soviet Union. However, the Red Army halted at the Vistula and did not enter the city while Stalin – cynically conscious of containing hopes of Polish independence in a post-war order – neither aided the Poles nor, until it was too late, facilitated attempts by the British and Americans to supply the insurgents with weapons and munitions.

Unaware of Stalin's ploy, the German Chief of Staff Guderian, fearing cooperation between the insurgents and the Red Army, asked Hitler to include Warsaw – still under the aegis of Hans Frank as Governor General – in the military zone of operations and place it thereby under Wehrmacht control. Hitler refused. Instead, he handed over full responsibility for the crushing of the rising to SS chief Himmler, who ordered the total destruction of Warsaw. Men, women, and children were slaughtered in their thousands while Warsaw burned. By the time General Bor-Komorowski, head of the Polish underground army, surrendered on 2 October, the savage repression had left Polish civilian victims numbering around 200,000. German losses amounted to some 26,000 men killed, wounded, or missing. On 11 October, Hans Frank received notification that all raw materials, textiles, and furniture left in Warsaw were to be removed before the smouldering remains of the city were razed to the ground.

IV

As the news from all parts of his empire turned from appalling to disastrous, Hitler fell ill. On 8 September, he complained to Morell, his doctor, of pressure around his right eye. In his notes, Morell indicated blood-pressure. Six days later, he recorded fluctuating blood-pressure 'following great agitation'. Next day, 15 September, Morell noted: 'Complains of dizziness, throbbing head, and return of the tremor to his legs, particularly the left, and hands.' His left ankle was swollen. Again, 'much agitation' was registered by Morell. Hitler's blood-pressure was regularly too high, sometimes worryingly so. It was an indication that he had a cardiac problem, and an electrocardiogram on 24 September did indicate progressive arteriosclerosis (though no acute anginal danger).

During the night before his cardiogram, Hitler's acute stomach spasms returned. They were so bad the following night that he was unable to get up in the morning – an extremely rare occurrence – and seemed unusually apathetic. By 27 September, his skin had a yellowish appearance. By now he was quite ill. The jaundice, accompanied by high temperature and severe stomach cramps, kept him in bed during the following days. It was 2 October before the yellow skin-colouring finally disappeared and Hitler felt well enough to get out of bed, dress himself, and make his way to the first situation briefing since he had fallen ill. He still seemed lifeless, however, to those in his company. By the middle of the month, when he felt himself again, he had lost sixteen pounds in weight.

While Hitler was suffering from jaundice, Dr Giesing, the ear, nose, and throat specialist who had been brought in to treat him after Stauffenberg's bomb had exploded, began to be suspicious about Morell's treatment. He started to wonder whether the little black tablets that Hitler took each day on Morell's prescription, 'Dr Koester's Anti-Gas Pills', were in fact a contributory cause of the Dictator's chronic stomach complaint rather than a satisfactory medicine for it. Whatever his concern for Hitler, Giesing's own ambitions to oust and displace Morell probably played a part in what he did next. He managed to lay hands on a number of the pills, had them analysed, and discovered that they contained strychnine. Giesing dosed himself with the pills and found they had mildly harmful effects – effects he associated with those on Hitler. Giesing made mention of his findings, and his suspicions, to Hitler's other attendant doctors, Dr Karl Brandt and Dr Hans-Karl von Hasselbach, who passed on the sentiments to others in Hitler's entourage. When Hitler found out, he was furious. He announced his complete faith in Morell, and dismissed Brandt and Hasselbach, who had both been with him since the early years of his rule. Giesing, too, was requested to leave Hitler's service. Their replacement was one of Himmler's former staff doctors, SS-Obersturmbannführer Ludwig Stumpfegger.

Morell's diagnoses and methods of treatment were indeed often questionable. Many of the innumerable tablets, medicines, and injections he prescribed for Hitler were of dubious value, often useless, and in some instances even exacerbated the problem (particularly relating to the chronic intestinal disorder). But allegations that Morell was intentionally harming Hitler were misplaced. The fat, unctuous, heavily perspiring Morell was both physically unattractive and, through his privileged access to Hitler, provoked much resentment in the 'court circle'. That he visibly exploited the relationship to his patient to further his own power, influence, and material advantage simply magnified the ill-feeling towards Morell. But, whatever his considerable limitations as a medical practitioner, Morell was certainly doing his best for the Leader he so much admired and to whom he was devoted.

The hypochondriac Hitler was, in turn, dependent upon Morell. He needed to believe, and apparently did believe, that Morell's treatment was the best he could get, and was beneficial. In that way, Morell might indeed have been good for Hitler. At any rate, Morell and his medicines, were neither a major nor even minor part of the explanation of Germany's plight in the autumn of 1944. That Hitler was poisoned by the strychnine and belladonna in the anti-gas pills or other medicaments, drugged on the opiates given him to relieve his intestinal spasms, or dependent upon the cocaine which formed 1 per cent of the ophthalmic drops prescribed by Dr Giesing for conjunctivitis, can be discounted. Probably by now he was indeed dependent upon the noxious cocktail of drugs dispensed by Morell. These included regular stimulants to combat his tiredness and sustain his energy and may well have intensified his violent mood-swings and physical decline. However, his physical problems in autumn 1944, chronic though they were, had largely arisen from lifestyle, diet, lack of exercise, and excessive stress, on top of likely congenital weaknesses (which probably accounted for the cardiac problem as well as Parkinson's Syndrome). Mentally, he was under enormous strain, which magnified his deeply embedded extreme personality traits. His phobias, hypochondria, and hysterical reactions were probable indicators of some form of personality disorder or psychiatric abnormality. An element of paranoia underwrote his entire political 'career', and became even more evident towards the end. But Hitler did not suffer from any of the major psychotic disorders. He was certainly not clinically insane. If there was lunacy in the position Germany found itself in by the autumn of 1944, it was not the purported insanity of one man but that of the high-stakes 'winner-takes-all' gamble for continental dominance and world power which the country's leaders – not just Hitler – backed by much of a gullible population had earlier been prepared to take, and which was now costing the country dearly and revealed as a high-risk policy without an exit-clause.

V

That all ways out were closed off was made plain once again during these weeks. Hints had come from Japan in late August that Stalin might entertain ideas of a peace settlement with Hitler's Germany. Japan was interested in brokering such a peace, since it would leave Germany able to devote its entire war effort to the western Allies, thereby, it was hoped, draining the energies of the USA away from the Pacific. With massive casualties on the Soviet side, the territories lost since 1941 regained, and a presumed interest in Stalin wishing to harness what was left of German industrial potential for a later fight with the West, Tokyo thought prospects for a negotiated peace were not altogether negligible. On 4 September, Oshima, the Japanese Ambassador in Berlin, travelled to East Prussia to put the suggestion to take up feelers with Stalin directly to Hitler. The response was predictable. Germany would soon launch a fresh counter-offensive with new weapons at its disposal. And there were, in any case, no signs that Stalin was entertaining thoughts of peace. Only a block on his advance might make him change his mind, Hitler realistically concluded. He wanted no overtures to be made by the Japanese for the present.

Oshima evidently did not give up. Later in the month, he used the pretext of a discussion with Werner Naumann, State Secretary in the Propaganda Ministry, about the 'total war' effort to bring the suggestion of a separate peace with the Soviet Union to Goebbels's ears. He could be certain that by this route the proposal would again reach Hitler, perhaps with the backing of one who was known to carry influence at Führer Headquarters.

Naumann's report was plainly the first Goebbels had heard of the Japanese suggestion. The Propaganda Minister called the discussion between his State Secretary and the Japanese Ambassador 'quite sensational'. Oshima told Naumann, according to Goebbels's summary, that Germany should make every attempt to reach a 'special peace'. Such an arrangement would be possible, he led Naumann to believe. He was frank about the Japanese interest, forced by its own problems in the war, in giving Germany a free hand in the west. He thought Stalin, a realist, would be open to suggestions if Germany were prepared to accept 'sacrifices', and criticized the inflexibility of German foreign policy. Goebbels noted that Oshima's proposal amounted to a reversal of German war policy, and was aware that the position of the pro-German Japanese Ambassador at home had been seriously weakened as the fortunes of war had turned. But, as Oshima had presumed, Goebbels immediately passed on the information to Bormann and Himmler, for further transmission to Hitler himself.

Goebbels decided that more must be done. But rather than try to put the case verbally to Hitler, he decided to prepare a lengthy memorandum. By midnight on 20 September, after he had worked all afternoon and evening on it, the memorandum was ready. Rehearsing what he had heard from Oshima, he suggested that Stalin's cold realism, knowing that he would sooner or later find himself in conflict with the west, offered an opening, since the Soviet leader would not want either to exhaust his own military strength or allow the German armaments potential to fall into the hands of the western powers. He pointed to Japan's self-interest in brokering a deal. An arrangement with Stalin would provide new prospects in the west, and place the Anglo-Americans in a position where they could not indefinitely continue the war. 'What we would attain,' he stated, 'would not be the victory that we dreamed of in 1941, but it would still be the greatest victory in German history.

The sacrifices that the German people had made in this war would thereby be fully justified.'

Goebbels waited impatiently for Hitler's reactions to his memorandum. Eventually, he learnt that Hitler had read it, but then put it away without comment. A promised audience to discuss it with him never materialized. Hitler's illness intervened. But in any case, there is no indication that Hitler took the slightest notice of his Propaganda Minister's suggestion. His own plans ran along quite different lines. The idea of a western offensive, which he had hatched in mid-August, was taking concrete shape. He was contemplating a final attempt to turn the tide: using the last reserves of troops and weapons for an offensive through the Ardennes in late autumn or winter aimed at inflicting a significant blow on the western Allies by retaking Antwerp (depriving them of their major continental port) and even forcing them 'back into the Atlantic'. 'A single breakthrough on the western front! You will see!' he told Speer. 'That will lead to a collapse and panic among the Americans. We'll drive through in the middle and take Antwerp. With that, they'll have lost their supply harbour. And there'll be a huge encirclement of the entire English army with hundreds of thousands of prisoners. Like it was in Russia!'

The objective was to gain time to develop new weapons. From a new position of strength, he could then turn against the Russians. He was well aware that the 'wonder weapons' were, in their current state of deployment, incapable of bringing any decisive change in war fortunes, or of satisfying the exaggerated hopes that incessant propaganda had raised in them among the German public. When he had first seen the prototypes of the V2, Hitler had envisaged 5,000 of the rockets being directed against Britain in a massive initial onslaught. But when the eventual launch took place on 8 September, it proved possible only to dispatch twenty-five rockets in a period of ten days. They were little more than a pin-prick in the Allied thrust against Nazi Germany. Even so, Hitler expected a great deal from the further deployment of the weapon. By the end of the war, through the brutal exploitation of foreign workers, it had proved possible to aim over 3,000 V2s mainly at London, Antwerp, and Brussels. There was no defence against the missiles. Their terroristic effect was considerable, causing the deaths of 2,724 persons in England and many more in Belgium. Their military effect was, however, negligible.

Meanwhile, the development of the one secret weapon certainly capable of affecting Germany's war fortunes, the atomic bomb, had been worked on since the start of the war (though with only slow progress). The research was given special support by Speer in 1942 but, despite his offer of increased funding, was still nowhere near completion and – though the German nuclear scientists were unaware of it – lagged far behind advances made in the USA. There had seemed no need to force research on such a weapon during the early, triumphant phase of the war. By the time of Speer's meeting with leading atomic scientists, including Otto Hahn and Werner Heisenberg, in mid-1942, a nuclear weapon was – as the Armaments Minister was told – theoretically possible but in practice several years off. Hitler, already aware in a general sense of the feasibility of an atomic bomb in the more distant future, took Speer's report as confirmation that he would never live to see its deployment, that it could play no part in the present war. Consequently, he took no great interest in it. By this time, in any case, the resources needed to deploy it were not simply not available – and were diminishing fast. It is as well that the bomb was not on offer: Hitler would not have hesitated for an instant to drop it on London and Moscow.

A key part of Hitler's strategy was the deployment of large numbers of fighters on the western front to regain the initiative in the air. He had emphasized this in his briefing with Jodl at the end of July. In August, when Speer and Adolf Galland, the flying ace who headed the Luftwaffe's fighter arm, tried to persuade him to use the fighters in the Reich rather than at the western front, he had exploded in such a frenzy of rage that he had ordered a stop to all aircraft production in favour of total concentration on flak. Speer had ignored the outburst of frustration. In September, fighter production reached a record 2,878 aircraft – a two-and-a-half-fold increase over production in January. Hitler had his fighters.

Whether they would have any fuel was another question. Hitler knew that raw materials and fuel had sunk to perilous levels. Speer sent him a memorandum on 5 September pointing out that the loss of chrome from Turkey meant that the entire armaments production would grind to a halt within sixteen or so months, by 1 January 1946. Hitler took the news calmly. It can only have encouraged him in the thought that there was nothing to lose, and that everything had to be staked on the new western offensive. He was also informed by Speer that the fuel situation was so critical that fighter squadrons were being grounded and army movements restricted. To make 17,500 tons of fuel – what had formerly been two-and-a-half days' production – available for the Ardennes Offensive, delivery to other parts of the front had to be seriously curtailed.

Together with Jodl, Hitler pored over maps of the Ardennes while lying on his sick-bed at the end of September. He later told Goebbels that he had spent the weeks of his illness almost exclusively brooding over his revenge. Now he was well again, he could begin to put his intentions into effect. It would be his final gamble. As he knew, it was a long shot. 'If it doesn't succeed,' he told Speer, 'I see no other possibility of bringing the war to a favourable conclusion.' 'But,' he added, 'we'll pull through.'

Before he could fully focus his attention on operational preparations for the coming offensive, a lingering remnant of the July bomb-plot momentarily detained him. Hitler had suspected since early August that Rommel had known about the plot against him. This had been confirmed by the testimony of Lieutenant-Colonel Cäsar von Hofacker, a member of Stülpnagel's staff in Paris implicated in the plot, who had provided a written statement of Rommel's support for the conspiracy. Hitler showed the statement to Keitel and had Rommel summoned to see him. The field-marshal, recuperating from his injuries at home near Ulm, claimed he was not fit to travel. At this, Keitel wrote Rommel a letter, drafted by Hitler, suggesting he report to the Führer if innocent. Otherwise, he would face trial. He should weigh up the consequences and if necessary act on them. Hitler ordered the letter and Hofacker's incriminating statement to be taken to Rommel by General Wilhelm Burgdorf (the replacement for Schmundt, who had died of the injuries he received in the bomb-blast on 20 July, as his chief Wehrmacht adjutant).

Burgdorf, accompanied by his deputy, General Ernst Maisel, drove to Rommel's home at Herrlingen on Saturday, 14 October, and handed over the letter together with Hofacker's statement. Rommel inquired whether Hitler was aware of the statement. He then requested a little time to think matters over. He did not take long. Hitler had given orders to Burgdorf that Rommel should be prevented from shooting himself – the traditional mode of suicide among officers – and should be offered poison so that the death could be attributed to brain damage following the car accident. Mindful of Rommel's popularity among the German public, Hitler offered him a state funeral with all honours. Faced with expulsion from the army, trial before the People's Court, certain execution, and inevitable recriminations for his family, Rommel took the poison.

Hitler was represented by Rundstedt at the state funeral in the town hall at Ulm on 18 October. Rundstedt declared in his eulogy that Rommel's 'heart belonged to the Führer'. Addressing the dead field-marshal, he intoned: 'Our Führer and Supreme Commander sends you through me his thanks and his greetings.' For public consumption, Hitler announced the same day that Rommel had succumbed to his severe wounds following his car-accident. 'With him, one of our best army leaders has passed away ... His name has entered the history of the German people.'

Another, more far-reaching, problem preoccupied Hitler in the middle of October: Hungary's attempt to defect from its alliance with Germany. Hitler had feared (and expected) this eventuality for weeks. The feelers, known to German intelligence, put out both to the western Allies and to the Soviet Union after Romania's defection gave a clear sign of the way things were moving. At the beginning of October, Horthy had sent a delegation to Moscow to begin negotiations to take Hungary out of the war. Tough conditions laid down by Molotov, on behalf of the Allies, for Hungary to change sides, including an immediate declaration of war on Germany, were accepted by Horthy and signed by the Hungarian delegation in Moscow on 11 October. Their implementation had to await the coup being prepared in Budapest against the German forces in Hungary. Pressed by the Soviet Union to act, Horthy informed the German envoy Edmund Veesenmayer on 15 October that Hungary was leaving the German alliance and announced the armistice in a radio broadcast in the early afternoon.

Hitler had not stood idly by while these developments were taking place. Both strategically, and also on account of its economic importance for foodstuffs and fuel supplies, everything had to be done to prevent Hungary going the way of Romania and Bulgaria. For weeks, Hitler had been preparing his own counter-coup in Budapest, aimed at ousting Horthy, replacing him with a puppet government under Ferencz Szalasi – fanatical leader of the radical Hungarian fascist party, the Arrow Cross – and thus ensuring that Hungary did not defect. Already in mid-September Otto Skorzeny, Hitler's leading trouble-shooter (since his daring rescue of Mussolini a year earlier), had been called to the Wolf's Lair and ordered to prepare an operational plan to seize by force the Citadel in Budapest – the fortress which was the residence of Horthy and his entourage – should Hungary betray its alliance with Germany.

Skorzeny immediately began detailed planning of the complex operation. It involved the kidnapping of Horthy's son, Miklós (who, as German intelligence knew, had been working through Yugoslav contacts to promote a separate peace with the Soviet Union) in order to blackmail his father into abandoning intentions to defect. In a daring ambush on the morning of Sunday, 15 October, Skorzeny's men, following a five-minute flurry of shooting with Hungarian bodyguards, carried off the younger Horthy, rolled up in a carpet, bundled him into a waiting lorry, whisked him to an airfield, and put him in a plane bound for Vienna and his eventual destination, Mauthausen concentration camp.

Admiral Horthy was faced with the fact of his son's kidnap when Veesenmayer arrived for their prearranged meeting at noon. Veesenmayer told Horthy that at the first sign of 'treason', his son would be shot. The Regent's response was a combination of furious protestation and near nervous collapse. Neither was, of course, to any avail. But nor could German threats deter him from making his radio announcement two hours later of the separate peace with the Soviet Union. No sooner had he finished speaking than the radio building was seized by Arrow Cross men, who put out a counter-declaration avowing Hungary's continuation of the fight against the Soviet Union on Germany's side. A little later Szalasi announced his takeover of power. That evening, the blackmail on Horthy came into full effect. He was told that if he resigned and formally handed over power to Szalasi, he would be given asylum in Germany, and his son would be freed; if not, the Citadel would be taken by force. Horthy buckled under the extreme pressure. He agreed to step down from office and make way for Szalasi. Skorzeny met little resistance when, accompanied by units of 'Panther' and 'Goliath' tanks, he entered the Citadel early next morning. Two days later, on 18 October, Horthy was on his way to Germany in a special train, accompanied by Skorzeny and a German army escort. He would spend the remainder of the war 'as the Führer's guest', in Schloß Hirschberg, near Weilheim, in Upper Bavaria. Under its new, fanatical fascist leadership, Hungary's fate remained tied to Germany's until the encircled defendants of Budapest gave up the struggle on 11 February 1945. Only a few hundred succeeded in breaking through to German lines. It was the end of Hitler's last remaining ally in south-eastern Europe.

With the failure of Horthy's attempt to take Hungary out of the war, the final torment of the largest Jewish community still under German control began. As we noted earlier, Horthy had halted deportations – mainly to Auschwitz – in July. By that date, 437,402 Jews – more than half of the entire community – had been sent to their deaths. By the time of the deposition of Horthy and takeover of power by Szalasi in mid-October, Himmler was halting the 'Final Solution' and terminating the killings at Auschwitz. But the desperate labour shortage in Germany now led to plans to deploy Hungarian Jews as slave labourers in the underground assembly sites of V2 missiles. Without trains to transport them, they would have to walk. Within days of Szalasi taking over, tens of thousands of Jews – women as well as men – were being rounded up and, by the end of the month, beginning what for so many would turn into death marches as they succumbed to exhaustion, cold, and the torture of both Hungarian and SS guards. So high was the death rate among Jewish women, in fact, that Szalasi, probably concerned for his own skin as the war fortunes continued to worsen for Germany, stopped the treks in mid-November. Subsequent attempts of the SS to remove more Jews by rail were vitiated by lack of transport. Meanwhile, for the 70,000 remaining Budapest Jews, crammed into a ghetto within range of Soviet guns, deprived of all property, terrorized and killed at will by Arrow Cross men, the daily nightmare continued until the surrender of the city in February. It is estimated that the bodies of up to 10,000 Jews were lying unburied in the streets and houses of Budapest by that time.

Meanwhile, on 21 October a delighted Hitler, recovered from his recent illness, was welcoming Skorzeny with outstretched arms as he led him into his dimly-lit bunker at the Wolf's Lair to hear the story of his triumph in Budapest and reward him with promotion to Obersturmbannführer. When Skorzeny stood up to leave, Hitler detained him: 'Don't go, Skorzeny,' he remarked. 'I have perhaps the most important job in your life for you. So far very few people know of the preparations for a secret plan in which you have a great part to play. In December, Germany will start a great offensive, which may well decide her fate.'

He proceeded to give Skorzeny a detailed outline of the military operation which would from now on occupy so much of his time: the
Ardennes Offensive.

VI

Hitler had laid out his demands for an Ardennes offensive on
16 September. Guderian voiced grave misgivings because of the situation
on the eastern front, the theatre for which he was directly responsible.
Jodl warned of air supremacy and the likelihood of parachute landings.
Hitler ignored them. He wanted, he said, 1,500 fighters by 1 November,
when preparations for the offensive must be complete. The launch of
the offensive would take place in bad weather, when enemy aircraft
were badly handicapped. Enemy forces would be split and encircled.
Antwerp would be taken, leaving the enemy without an escape route.

By this time, the enemy was already on German soil in the west. By
mid-September, American soldiers from the 1st US Army had penetrated
the Westwall and reached the outskirts of Aachen, which was finally
taken on 21 October.

A few days earlier, the enemy had also burst into German territory in
the east. On 16 October, the '3rd White Russian Front', led by General
Ivan Tscherniakowski, had broken through into East Prussia as far as
Nemmersdorf, Goldap – the first sizeable town in the province – and
the fringes of Gumbinnen, heading for Königsberg. The roads were full
of refugees fleeing in panic from the oncoming Russians. The Red Army
was within striking reach of Führer Headquarters. For the time being,
Hitler resisted pressure to leave the Wolf's Lair. A move to the Berghof
or to Berlin, he thought, would send the wrong signals to his fighting
men at the front. He gave strict instructions that there should be no talk
of leaving. But the staff was reduced, while Schaub packed all Hitler's
files and possessions, ready to depart at any moment. It proved possible
to delay the moment. Gumbinnen was recaptured – revealing horrifying
scenes of atrocities (including untold cases of women raped and murdered, and houses plundered at will by Soviet troops). The Red Army
was forced on the defensive in East Prussia. Goldap, too, was retaken
by the Wehrmacht a fortnight or so later. The immediate danger was
contained.

When Nicolaus von Below returned to the Wolf's Lair on 24 October, after recuperating for several weeks from the effects of the bomb-blast on 20 July, he found the Dictator heavily involved in preparations for the Ardennes offensive, expected to take place in late November or early December. The big anxiety, as ever, was whether by then the Luftwaffe would be in any position to provide the necessary air cover. The failure of the Luftwaffe, Below was told by naval adjutant Karl-Jesko von Puttkamer, was still the 'number one topic', and there was permanent tension between Hitler and Göring. Though he put the best face on it, Hitler was well aware that air-power was his weakest suit; hence, the constant tirades against Göring. The odds in the coming offensive were far more heavily stacked against him than he was prepared to acknowledge.

Immersed in military matters and facing calamity on all sides, Hitler was in no mood to travel through a war-weary Reich to address the party's Old Guard as usual on 8 November, the anniversary of the putsch in 1923 and the most sacred date in the Nazi calendar. Instead, a pale shadow of the normal event was scheduled to take place for the first time not on the actual anniversary of the putsch, but on the following Sunday, 12 November, in Munich. Its centrepiece was a proclamation by Hitler to be read out by Himmler. As Goebbels pointed out, this had nothing like the effect of hearing Hitler himself, particularly when read out in Himmler's cold diction.

The proclamation itself could only have been a disappointment for those hoping for news of some reversal of war fortunes or – the desire of most people – a hint that the war would soon be over. It offered no more than the old refrain that eventual triumph would come. And Hitler made it clear that as long as he was alive, there would be no capitulation, no end to the fighting. He was, he said, 'unshakeable in his will to give the world to follow a no less praiseworthy example in this struggle than great Germans have given in the past'. It was a veiled hint that what now remained for him to fight for was his place in history. The 'heroic' struggle he envisaged, one of Wagnerian proportions, ruled out any contemplation of capitulation, the shameful act of 1918. The fight to the last, it seemed clear, was destined to drag down to destruction the German people itself with the 'heroic' self-destruction of its warlord.

The warlord's own end was now starting to occupy his mind. Perhaps a renewed bout of illness, now affecting his throat, prompted his depressed mood. It may also have encouraged him to agree with Bormann that the time had indeed finally come to move his headquarters from East Prussia, since it had been established that he needed a minor operation in Berlin to remove a polyp from his vocal cords. On the afternoon of 20 November, Hitler and his entourage boarded his special train bound for Berlin and left the Wolf's Lair for good.

So little was Hitler a real presence for the German people by this time that, as Goebbels had to note, rumours were rife that he was seriously ill, or even dead. Goebbels had the opportunity to speak at length with him at the beginning of December. He found him recovered from his stomach troubles, able to eat and drink normally again. He was also over the operation to his vocal cords, and his voice was back to normal. Hitler told him he had come to Berlin to prepare for the coming attack in the west. Everything was prepared for a major blow to the Allies which would give him not just a military but also a political success. He said he had worked day and night on the plan for the offensive, also during his illness. Goebbels thought Hitler back to his old form.

Hitler outlined the grandiose aim of the offensive. Antwerp would be taken within eight to ten days. The intention was to smash the entire enemy force to the north and south, then turn a massive rocket attack on London. A major success would have a huge impact on morale at home, and affect attitudes towards Germany abroad. Hitler, in Goebbels's judgement, was like a man revived. The prospect of a new offensive, and of regaining the initiative, had evidently worked on him like a drug.

Operational plans for the Ardennes offensive had been devised by the OKW in September and put to Hitler on 9 October. The objective of the operation – the sweep through the Eifel and Ardennes through Belgium to the Channel coast, taking Antwerp – was finalized at this point. The detailed plans of the offensive were outlined by Jodl to senior western commanders on 3 November. Sixteen divisions, eight of them armoured, would form the focal point of the attack. SS-Oberstgruppenführer Sepp Dietrich would lead the 6th SS-Panzer Army; General Hasso von Manteuffel the 5th Panzer Army. Without exception, the assembled military commanders thought the objective – the taking of Antwerp, some 125 miles away – quite unrealistic. The forces available to them were simply inadequate, they argued, especially in winter conditions. At best, they claimed, a more limited objective – recovery of Aachen and the adjacent parts of the Westwall, with perhaps the base being laid for a later westward push – might be attained. Jodl ruled out the objections. He made clear to the commanders that limited gains would not suffice. Hitler had to be in a position, as a result of the offensive, to 'make the western powers ready to negotiate'. On 10 November, Hitler signed the order for the offensive. He acknowledged in the preamble that he was prepared 'to accept the maximum risk in order to proceed with this operation'.

Hitler left Berlin on the evening of 10 December and moved his headquarters to Ziegenberg, not far from Bad Nauheim, close to the western front. Bunkers and barracks had been constructed in a woodland area by the Organization Todt earlier in the war. Rundstedt and his staff were quartered in a stately residence nearby.

In two groups, on the day of his arrival, 11 December, and again the following day, Hitler spoke to his military commanders at the 'Adlerhorst' ('Eagle's Eyrie'), as the new headquarters were called, to brief them on the coming offensive. After a lengthy preamble giving his own account of the background to the war, he outlined his thinking behind the offensive. Psychological considerations, as always, were paramount for Hitler. War could only be endured as long as there was hope of victory. It was necessary, therefore, to destroy this hope through offensive action. A defensive strategy could not achieve this goal. It had to be followed by successful attack. 'I have striven, therefore, from the beginning to conduct the war wherever possible in the offensive,' he stated. 'Wars are finally decided through the recognition by one side or the other that the war as such can no longer be won. To get the enemy to realize this is therefore the most important task.' If forced back on to the defensive, it was all the more important to convince the enemy that victory was not in sight. Hitler came to another unalterable premiss of his conduct of the war. 'It is also important to strengthen these psychological factors in letting no moment pass without making plain to the enemy that whatever he does he can never reckon with capitulation, never, never. That is the decisive point.' He referred, almost inevitably, to the reversal of Frederick the Great's fortunes in the Seven Years War. Here, he had reached another constant in his thinking: the will of the heroic leader, which alone made triumph out of adversity possible when all around him despaired of success.

This brought him to the fragility (he thought) of the coalition he was facing. 'If a few really heavy blows were inflicted,' he argued, 'it could happen any moment that this artificially sustained common front could suddenly collapse with a huge clap of thunder.' The tensions between the Soviet and western Allies had, indeed, become more apparent during the second half of 1944. But Hitler was certainly rational enough to know that his own destruction, and that of the regime he headed, provided sufficient common ground to hold the coalition together until Germany's defeat. He knew, too, that neither the western Allies nor – despite what Oshima had told him – the Soviets would look for peace with Germany while they were militarily so totally in the ascendancy.

As the supreme propagandist of old, he could always summon up absolute conviction when addressing an audience and needing to persuade them that what he was proposing was the only alternative on offer. It had proved his greatest strength since the early 1920s. The hints of pessimism – or greater realism – to Below and others in the weeks before the Ardennes offensive, even though only momentary slips of his guard, suggest, however, that Hitler was well aware of the size of the gamble in the Ardennes. He had to take it because, indeed, from his perspective, there was no alternative way out. If the long-shot were to come off, he reasoned, and a serious defeat were to be inflicted on the western powers while new German weaponry started to come into operation and before the expected Soviet winter offensive could begin, then new options could open up. At any rate, the only alternative to the gamble, as he saw it, was to fight for every inch of German soil in a rearguard struggle certain ultimately to end not just in defeat but in Germany's total destruction – and his own. The gamble had to be taken.

'Operation Autumn Mist' – the Ardennes offensive – began in the early morning of 16 December. All possible reserves had been mustered. Around 200,000 German troops backed by 600 tanks were launched against a front comprising around 80,000 American soldiers with 400 tanks. The weather was perfect for the German attack, with heavy cloud hindering enemy aircraft. The American forces were taken by surprise. Sepp Dietrich's SS-Panzer Army soon encountered strong defence on the north of the front and could make only slow progress. Manteuffel's 5th Panzer Army broke through in the south, however, and pressed forward in a deep cut of some sixty-five miles to within a few miles of the river Meuse, laying siege to the town of Bastogne, an important communications point. But Bastogne held out, tying down three German divisions in the process before eventually being relieved by General Patton's 3rd US Army.

Manteuffel's advance had meanwhile slowed, handicapped by difficult terrain, bad weather, broken bridges, and fuel shortages as well as increasingly stiff American resistance. On 24 December, the weather lifted, exposing the German troops to relentless air attacks by some 5,000 Allied aircraft. Troop movements could now only take place at night. Supply-lines and German airfields were heavily bombed. German fighters suffered serious losses. Once Patton had broken through the German front to relieve Bastogne on 26 December, Manteuffel had to give up any hopes of advancing further. 'Operation Autumn Mist' had failed.

Hitler was still not prepared, however, to bow to the inevitable. As a diversion, he ordered a subsidiary offensive in the north of Alsace ('Operation North Wind'). The aim was to cut off and destroy the American forces in the north-eastern corner of Alsace, enabling Manteuffel to continue the main offensive in the Ardennes. Once more Hitler addressed the commanders of the operation. And once more he laid the stress on the all-or-nothing nature of the struggle for Germany's existence. Again, he ruled out the possibility of Germany fighting indefinitely a defensive war. For strategic and psychological reasons it was essential to return to the offensive, and to seize the initiative. The operation would be decisive, he claimed. Its success would automatically remove the threat to the southern part of the Ardennes offensive, and with that the Wehrmacht would have forced the enemy out of half of the western front. 'Then we'll want to have a further look,' he added.

One slip of the tongue seemed to reveal, however, his realization that the ambitious aim he had placed in the Ardennes offensive could no longer be attained; that he knew he could no longer force the Allies off the Continent; and that, therefore, defensive operations would have to continue in the west as in the east. He spoke at one point of 'the un-shakeable aim' of the operation as producing merely 'in part' a 'cleansing' of the situation in the west. It implied that his speech to the commanders had been little more than the elevation of hope over reason.

'North Wind' began on New Year's Day. It was Hitler's last offensive – and his least effective. German troops were able to advance no more than about twenty kilometres, making a few minor gains and causing Eisenhower to pull back forces in the Strasbourg area for a time. But the offensive was too weak to have much effect. It proved possible to halt it without the Americans having to withdraw troops from the Ardennes. 'North Wind' had proved to be little more than a momentary stiff breeze.

Even more devastating was the death-blow to the Luftwaffe, imparted on 1 January, the same day that 'North Wind' had commenced. It had finally proved possible to launch a German air-offensive – though with disastrous consequences. Around 800 German fighters and bombers engaged in mass attacks on Allied airfields in northern France, Belgium, and Holland. They succeeded in destroying or seriously damaging almost 300 planes, limiting Allied air-power for a week or more. But 277 German planes were also lost. There was no possibility of the Luftwaffe recovering from such losses. It was effectively at an end.

On New Year's Day 1945, German radios broadcast Hitler's traditional address to the German people. It held nothing new for them. Hitler offered them not a sentence on the effect of 'wonder weapons', steps to counter the terror from the skies, or anything specific on military progress on the fronts. Above all, he gave no hint that the end of the war was near. He spoke only of its continuation in 1945 and until a final victory – which by now only dreamers could imagine – was attained. His audience had heard it all many times before: the reaffirmation that 'a 9 November in the German Reich will never repeat itself'; that Germany's enemies, led by 'the Jewish-international world conspiracy', intended to 'eradicate' its people; that Germany's plight had been caused by the weakness of its allies; that the combined effort of front and homeland showed the 'essence of our social community' and an indomitable spirit, incapable of destruction; and that 'the Jewish-international world enemy' would not only fail in its attempt 'to destroy Europe and eradicate its peoples, but would bring about its own destruction'.

Few remained convinced. Many, like some observers in the Stuttgart area, were probably ready to acknowledge that 'the Führer has worked for war from the very beginning'. Far from being the genius of Goebbels's propaganda, such observers remarked, Hitler had 'intentionally unleashed this world conflagration in order to be proclaimed as the great "transformer of mankind"'. It was belated recognition of the catastrophic impact of the leader they had earlier supported, cheered, eulogized. Their backing had helped to put him in the position where his power over the German state was total. By now, in the absence of either the ability or the readiness – especially since the events of 20 July – of those with access to the corridors of power to defy his authority, let alone oust him, this man quite simply held the fate of the German people in his own hands. He had again avowed, as he always had done, his adamant refusal to contemplate capitulation in any event. This meant that the suffering of the German people – and of the countless victims of the regime they had at one time so enthusiastically supported – had to go on. It would cease, it was abundantly clear, only when Hitler himself ceased to exist. And that could only mean Germany's total defeat, ruin, and occupation.

With the petering out of the Ardennes offensive, all hope of repelling the relentless advance from the west was gone. And in the east, the Red Army was waiting for the moment to launch its winter offensive. Hitler was compelled by 3 January to accept that 'continuation of the originally planned operation [in the Ardennes] no longer has any prospect of success'. Five days later came the tacit acknowledgement that his last gamble had been a losing throw of the dice with his approval of the withdrawal of the 6th Panzer Army to the north-west of Bastogne, and next day, his order to pull back his SS panzer divisions from the front. On 14 January, the day before Hitler left his headquarters on the western front to return to Berlin, the High Command of the Wehrmacht acknowledged that 'the initiative in the area of the offensive has passed to the enemy'.

Hitler had stated categorically in his briefings before the Ardennes and Alsace offensives that Germany could not indefinitely sustain a defensive war. By now, he had used up his last precious reserves of man-power, lost untold quantities of weaponry, and exhausted his remaining divisions in an offensive that had cost the lives of about 80,000 German soldiers (at the same time weakening the eastern front and paving the way for the rapid inroads of the Red Army in the coming weeks). He had also seen the remnants of the Luftwaffe devastated to the point of no return; while rapidly dwindling supplies of fuel and other supplies essential for the war effort held out in any case the prospect of continuing the struggle only for a few more months. The logic was plain: the last faint glimmer of hope had been extinguished, the last exit route cut off. Defeat was inevitable. Hitler had not lost touch with reality. He realized this. Below found him one evening after the failure of the offensive in his bunker after air-raid sirens had sounded, deeply depressed. He spoke of taking his own life since the last chance of success had evaporated. He was savage in his criticism of the failure of the Luftwaffe, and of the 'traitors' in the army. According to Below's later recollection, Hitler said: 'I know the war is lost. The superior power is too great. I've been betrayed. Since 20 July everything has come out that I didn't think possible. Precisely those were against me who have profited most from National Socialism. I spoilt them all and decorated them. That's the thanks. I'd like most of all to put a bullet through my head.' But, as so often, Hitler rapidly pulled himself together, saying: 'We'll not capitulate. Never. We can go down. But we'll take a world with us.'

This was what kept him going. It had underpinned his political 'career' since the beginning. There would be no repeat of 1918: no stab-in-the-back; no capitulation. That – and his place in history as a German hero brought down by weakness and betrayal – was all that was left to him.

27

Into the Abyss

I

Hitler was still reeling from the failure of the Ardennes offensive, his last big hope, when all hell broke loose on the eastern front. The Soviet offensive had started. The main thrust, from bridgeheads on the Vistula, south of Warsaw, was aimed at southern Poland, then on to the vital Silesian industrial belt, and the river Oder, the last barrier before Berlin. Marshal Ivan Konev's 1st Ukrainian Front began the attack on 12 January, following a five-hour artillery barrage, from the Baranov bridgehead on the southern Vistula. It was rapidly followed, farther to the north, from the bridgeheads at Polavy and Magnuszev, by an assault from Marshal Georgi Zhukov's 1st Belorussian Front. A secondary thrust, by the 2nd and 3rd Belorussian Fronts, from bridgeheads on the river Narev to the north of Warsaw, aimed at cutting off German troops in East Prussia.

The Red Army's superiority in numbers was overwhelming. In the vital central sector of the 900-kilometre front that stretched from the Carpathians to the Baltic, some 2,200,000 Soviet troops were arrayed against 400,000 on the German side. But at the key bridgeheads on the Vistula, from where the offensive was launched, the imbalance was massive. The German general staff calculated that it was 11 to 1 in infantry, 7 to 1 in tanks, and 20 to 1 in guns in favour of the Red Army. Aware from the reports of General Reinhard Gehlen, head of 'Foreign Armies East' department, of the huge build-up of Soviet forces and of an impending offensive, Guderian had pleaded with Hitler at Christmas, when the Ardennes offensive had already lost impetus, to transfer troops to the east. Hitler had dismissed Gehlen's reports as enemy bluff, 'the greatest imposture since Genghis Khan'. When, on a further visit to

Führer Headquarters at Ziegenberg on New Year's Day 1945 Guderian had wrung the release of four divisions out of Hitler, the Dictator insisted they be sent to Hungary, not to the centre of the eastern front where military intelligence was pointing to the looming peril. On 9 January, Guderian had made a further trip to Ziegenberg to show Hitler diagrams and charts displaying the relative strength of forces in the vulnerable areas on the Vistula. Hitler, in a rage, rejected them as 'completely idiotic', and told Guderian that whoever had compiled them should be shut up in a lunatic asylum. Guderian defended Gehlen and stood his ground. The storm subsided as rapidly as it had blown up. But Hitler nevertheless contemptuously refused the urgent recommendations to evacuate parts of the Vistula and Narev, withdraw to more defensible positions, and transfer forces from the west to shore up these weak points of the front. Guderian remarked, prophetically: 'The Eastern Front is like a house of cards. If the front is broken through at one point, all the rest will collapse.' Hitler's reply was that 'The Eastern Front must help itself and make do with what it's got.' As Guderian later commented, it was an 'ostrich strategy'.

A week later, on 16 January, with the Red Army already making massive advances, Hitler, now back in Berlin, was finally prepared to transfer troops from west to east. But Guderian was outraged to learn that Sepp Dietrich's 6th Panzer Army – brought back from the unsuccessful Ardennes campaign and forming the bulk of the new forces available – was to be sent to Hungary, where Hitler was hoping to force the Russians back across the Danube and relieve Budapest. With German synthetic oil-plants destroyed by air-raids in mid-January, retention of the Hungarian oil-fields and refineries was, for him, the vital consideration. Without them, he argued, the German war effort was doomed anyway. Nor did Guderian have much success in trying to persuade Hitler to evacuate by sea over the Baltic the German troops in grave danger of being cut off in Courland, on the tip of Latvia, for redeployment on the eastern front. Dönitz had been instrumental in persuading Hitler that Courland was a vital coastal area for the new U-boats which, he claimed, were almost ready to be turned against the West. The consequence was that 200,000 desperately needed troops were tied up in Courland until Germany's capitulation in May.

As Guderian had predicted, the Wehrmacht was wholly incapable of blocking the Red Army's advance. By 17 January, the Soviet troops had steamrollered over the troops in their path. The way to the German frontier now lay open before them. Overhead, Soviet planes controlled the skies, strafing and bombing at will. Some German divisions were surrounded; others retreated westward as fast as they could go. Warsaw was evacuated by the remaining German forces on 17 January, driving Hitler into such a paroxysm of rage that, at a critical point of the advance when they were needed for vital military operations, he had several officers from the General Staff who had issued signals connected with the withdrawal from Warsaw arrested and – together with Guderian himself – interrogated for hours by the head of the Reich Security Head Office, Ernst Kaltenbrunner, and chief of the Gestapo, Heinrich Müller.

On 18 January, Soviet troops entered Budapest. The battles in the city would last until mid-February, bitter fighting around Lake Balaton and in other parts of Hungary for several weeks longer. But however much weight Hitler attached to it, the uneven contest could have only one outcome. And Hungary formed little more than a sideshow to the major catastrophe for the Reich unfolding to the north, where Soviet troops encountered little serious opposition as they advanced at great speed through Poland. Lodz was taken. The towns of Kalisz and Posen in the Warthegau were already in their sights. On 20 January, they crossed the German border in the Posen area and in Silesia.

Still further north, German forces were in disarray in the face of Soviet advances into East Prussia. Colonel-General Hans Reinhardt, commander of Army Group Centre which was defending East Prussia, was sacked by a raging Hitler for evacuating coastal positions when Soviet troops broke through on 26 January, cutting off two German armies. General Friedrich Hoßbach, commanding the 4th Army, was also peremptorily dismissed by a furious Hitler for ignoring orders to hold ground – and not consulting his Army Group about his decision – when faced with a hopeless position and in grave danger of encirclement. In a wild temper, Hitler accused both Reinhardt and Hoßbach of treason. But a change of personnel – the capable Austrian Colonel-General Lothar Rendulic in place of Reinhardt, and General Friedrich-Wilhelm Müller for Hoßbach – could do nothing to alter the disastrous German collapse in the face of hopeless odds, in East Prussia as on the rest of the eastern front. This proved equally true in Hitler's replacement on 17 January of Colonel-General Josef Harpe, made the scapegoat for the collapse of the Vistula front, by his favourite, Colonel-General Ferdinand Schörner, and his ill-judged appointment on 25 January of Reichsführer-SS Heinrich Himmler, in the teeth of Guderian's strident objections, to take command of the newly formed and hastily constituted Army Group Vistula, which aimed to stave off the Soviet advance into Pomerania. The hope that 'triumph of the will' and the toughness of one of his most trusted 'hard' men would prevail rapidly proved ill-founded. Himmler, backed by courageous but militarily inexperienced Waffen-SS officers, soon found that combating the might of the Red Army was a far stiffer task than rounding up and persecuting helpless political opponents and 'racial inferiors'. By mid-February, Hitler was forced to concede that Army Group Vistula was inadequately led. After a furious row with Guderian lasting two hours, Hitler suddenly backed down and assigned General Walther Wenck to Himmler's headquarters to take over effective command of the planned limited counter-offensive on the Oder in Pomerania. The Reichsführer-SS's failure as a military commander would finally – and belatedly – be recognized by Hitler in his replacement by Colonel-General Gotthard Heinrici on 20 March. It marked a significant point in the growing estrangement of Hitler and his SS chief.

The catastrophe on the eastern front was by that time well-nigh complete. In the south, fired by the fanatical Nazi leadership of Gauleiter Karl Hanke, Breslau held out under siege until early May. Glogau, to the north-west, also continued to resist. But the defiance was of little military significance. By the end of January, the key industrial region of Silesia was lost to Germany. By 23 January Russian troops had already reached the Oder between Oppeln and Ohlau; five days later, they crossed it at Steinau, south of Breslau. Further north, Posen was encircled and most of the Warthegau lost. Its Gauleiter, Arthur Greiser, one of Hitler's most brutal henchmen, who had imposed a reign of terror on the predominantly Polish population of his fiefdom, had already fled westwards, along with other Nazi leaders from the region, in an attempt – ultimately to prove futile – to save his own skin. His flight, like that of other party representatives, fuelled the anger and contempt of ordinary people at the behaviour of Nazi bigwigs.

By the first days of February, Soviet troops had established a bridge-head over the Oder between Küstrin and Frankfurt an der Oder. Even now, Hitler, waving his fists in a frenzy of rage, refused to listen to

Guderian's entreaties to evacuate forthwith the military outposts in the Balkans, Italy, Norway, and, especially, Courland to free up reserves to defend the capital. All that Guderian could muster was poured into a short-lived German counter-offensive in Pomerania in mid-February. Easily fending this off, the Red Army occupied practically the whole of Pomerania during February and early March. Though the surrounded Königsberg was still holding out, most of East Prussia was by now also in Soviet hands.

The immense Soviet gains of January had by then been consolidated, and even extended. Zhukov's men had advanced almost 300 miles since the middle of January. From the bridgehead on the Oder near Küstrin, Berlin lay open to attack, only forty or so miles away. The last obstacle en route to the capital had been surmounted. But the rapidity of the advance had meant that Soviet supply-lines lagged behind. They needed to be assembled across the wrecked transport routes of a battered Poland. Soviet strategists reckoned, furthermore, that wet spring weather was certain to hamper military manoeuvres. And it was plain that the bloody battles in store to take Berlin would require detailed preparation. The final assault on the capital, they concluded, could wait for the time being.

While this disaster of colossal proportions was unfolding on the eastern front, the Allies in the west were swiftly reasserting themselves after staving off the Ardennes offensive. By early February, some 2 million American, British, Canadian, and French soldiers were ready for the assault on Germany. The attack of the Canadian 1st Army, which began on 8 February south of Nijmegen in the Wesel direction, met stiff opposition and could at first advance only slowly, amid bitter fighting. But in the last week of the month, American troops to the south-west pushed rapidly forwards towards Cologne, reaching the Rhine south of Düsseldorf on 2 March and the outskirts of Cologne three days later. Hitler's dismissal – again – of Field-Marshal Gerd von Rundstedt, Commander-in-Chief in the West, who had tried in vain to persuade him to withdraw his forces behind the Rhine, and replacement on 10 March by Field-Marshal Albert Kesselring, the former tenacious defender of German positions in Italy, made no difference.

Retreating German troops had blown up the Rhine bridges everywhere as they went – except Remagen, between Bonn and Koblenz, which was discovered intact, as the retreating Germans failed to detonate in time the explosives they had laid, and immediately secured by American forces of the 1st US Army under General Courtney H. Hodges on 7 March. With a bridgehead swiftly established, the last natural barrier in the way of the western Allies had been crossed. Within a fortnight, American troops had again crossed the Rhine at Oppenheim, south of Mainz. By then, the banks of the Rhine between Koblenz and Ludwigshafen were under American control. Further north, Montgomery now enjoyed a staged moment of glory as, watched by Churchill and Eisenhower, his troops crossed the Lower Rhine on 23–24 March following a massive air and artillery assault on Wesel. The most serious German resistance had by now been largely overcome. A third of all the German forces arrayed on the western front had been lost since early February – 293,000 men captured, 60,000 killed or wounded. Hitler's insistence on refusing to concede any territory west of the Rhine, rather than retreating to fight from behind the river, as Rundstedt had recommended, had itself contributed significantly to the magnitude and speed of the Allied success.

As German defences were collapsing on both eastern and western fronts and enemy forces prepared to strike at the very heart of the Reich, German cities as well as military installations and fuel plants were being subjected to the most ferocious bombing of the entire war. Pressed by the British Air Chief Marshal Arthur Harris's Bomber Command, the American and British chiefs of staff had agreed by the end of January to exploit the shock of the Soviet offensive by extending the planned air-attacks on strategic targets – mainly oil-plants and transport interchanges – to include the area-bombing and destruction of Berlin, Leipzig, Dresden, and other cities in central and eastern Germany. The aim was to intensify the mounting chaos in the big urban centres in the east of the Reich, as thousands of refugees fled westwards from the path of the Red Army. In addition, the western Allies were keen to demonstrate to Stalin, about to meet Churchill and Roosevelt at Yalta, that they were lending support to the Soviet offensive through their bombing campaign. The result was to magnify massively the terror from the skies as the bombs rained down on near-defenceless citizens. Beyond the forty-three large-scale precision attacks on Magdeburg, Gelsenkirchen, Botrop, Leuna, Ludwigshafen, and other targeted installations that laid waste Germany's fuel production, massive raids directed at civilian centres of population turned German inner-cities into wastelands. Berlin was hit on 3 February by the most damaging raid it had suffered so far during the war, killing 3,000 and injuring a further 2,000 people. Some of its poorer inner-city areas suffered most. Ten days later, on the night of 13–14 February, the beautiful city of Dresden, the glittering cultural capital of Saxony, renowned for its fine china but scarcely a major industrial centre, and now teeming with refugees, was turned into a towering inferno as thousands of incendiaries and explosive bombs were dropped by waves of RAF Lancaster bombers (followed next day by a further massive raid by American B-17s). Up to 40,000 citizens are estimated to have lost their lives in the most ruthless display experienced of Allied air superiority and strength. Other devastated cities included Essen, Dortmund, Mainz, Munich, Nuremberg, and Würzburg. In the last four and a half months of the war, 471,000 tons of bombs were dropped on Germany, double the amount during the entire year of 1943. In March alone, almost three times as many bombs were dispatched as during the whole of the year 1942.

By that time, Germany – militarily and economically – was on its knees. But as long as Hitler lived, there could be no prospect of surrender.

II

The man at the centre of the rapidly imploding system that had unleashed unprecedented horror and misery on the countless victims of the Nazi regime boarded his special train at Ziegenberg, his western headquarters, on the evening of 15 January 1945 and, with his regular entourage of orderlies, secretaries, and adjutants, left for Berlin. His hopes of military success in the west were definitively at an end. Trying to stave off the Soviet offensive in the east was now the urgent priority. His departure had been prompted by Guderian's opposition to his order on 15 January to transfer the powerful Panzer Corps 'Großdeutschland' from East Prussia to the vicinity of Kielce in Poland, where the Red Army was threatening to break through and expose the way forward through the Warthegau. Not only, Guderian pointed out, was the manoeuvre impossible to execute in time to block the Soviet advance; it would at the same time gravely weaken the defences of East Prussia just as the Soviet attack from the Narev was placing that province in the utmost peril. As it was, the 'Großdeutschland' troops sat in railway sidings while the Führer and his Chief of the General Staff argued on the telephone about their deployment. Hitler would not rescind his order. But the dispute helped to persuade him that he needed to direct affairs at closer quarters. It was time to move back to Berlin.

His train, its blinds down, pulled into the capital that night. Triumphant arrivals in Berlin were no more than distant memories. As his car made its way amid the rubble through unlit streets to the Reich Chancellery – now cold and dismal, its pictures, carpets, and tapestries removed to safety in view of the increasing air-raids on Berlin – few inhabitants of the city even knew he had returned; probably still fewer cared. Hitler in any case had no wish to see them. The path to his portals was blocked for all but the few who had the requisite papers and passes to satisfy the intense scrutiny of SS guards armed with machine guns and posted at a series of security checks. Even the Chief of the General Staff had to surrender his weapons and have his briefcase meticulously examined.

Hitler was completely immersed during the next days in the events on the eastern front. Seemingly incapable of acknowledging the objective imbalances in forces and the tactical weaknesses which had left the Vistula front so exposed, he thought he scented betrayal at every point. Frequent rantings about the incompetence or treachery of his generals dragged out the twice-daily military briefings to inordinate length. Guderian reckoned that his trips from General Staff Headquarters at Zossen, south of Berlin, twice a day took up around three hours. A further four to six hours were consumed during the conferences themselves. From the Chief of Staff's point of view, it was time wasted.

The regular clashes between Hitler and his one-time admirer Guderian reflected what were by now wholly and irreconcilably conflicting philosophies with no middle-ground between them. For Hitler, capitulation could not be contemplated, even if the price was the total destruction of Germany. For the Chief of Staff, the destruction of Germany must be prevented, even if the price was capitulation – at any rate, in the west. Guderian – and he was far from alone in this – saw the only hope of preventing the complete destruction of Germany as putting everything into blocking the Soviet onslaught and at the same time opening negotiations for an armistice with the West, however poor the bargaining base. Perhaps the West could be persuaded that it was in its own interests to prevent Russian dominance of a post-war Germany by accepting the surrender of the western parts of the country to enable the Reich to defend its eastern borders.

This was the proposition that Guderian outlined on 23 January to Dr Paul Barandon, the Foreign Ministry's new liaison with the army. It was a faint hope but, as Guderian noted, drowning men clutch at straws. He hoped that Barandon would engineer for him an audience with Ribbentrop, and that the Foreign Minister and he could approach Hitler immediately with a view to ending the war. Barandon arranged the interview. Ribbentrop, when Guderian met him two days later, seemed shocked at the prospect of the Russians at the gates of Berlin within a few weeks. But he declared himself a loyal follower of the Führer, knew the latter's antipathy to any peace feelers, and was unwilling to support Guderian. As Guderian entered the briefing room that evening, he heard Hitler in a loud and agitated voice say: 'So when the Chief of the General Staff goes to see the Foreign Minister and informs him of the situation in the East with the object of securing an armistice in the West, he is doing neither more nor less than committing high treason!' Ribbentrop had, of course, promptly reported to Hitler the content of his talks with Guderian. No action followed. But it was a warning shot across the bows. 'I forbid most decisively generalizations and conclusions about the overall situation,' Speer recalled Hitler ranting. 'That remains my business. Anyone in future claiming to another person that the war is lost will be treated as a traitor to his country with all the consequences for him and his family. I will act without respect for position and standing.' The head of the Security Police, Ernst Kaltenbrunner, from now on sat silently but menacingly in the background during the briefing sessions.

In fact, despite this outburst – and Ribbentrop's refusal to entertain Guderian's suggestion – Hitler was aware in early 1945 of his Foreign Minister's extremely tentative feelers via Stockholm, Bern, and Madrid to the western Allies to end the war with Germany and join the fight against Bolshevism. He knew, too, of Ribbentrop's consideration of an alternative suggestion: approaching the Soviet Union to help crush Britain. Hitler had first opposed any idea of peace feelers. Then he appeared to change his mind. 'Nothing will come of it,' Hitler told Ribbentrop. 'But if you really want, you can try it.' However, not only was there no prospect of either the Soviets or the western Allies showing genuine readiness to enter peace negotiations at this stage; Ribbentrop knew that Hitler had not the slightest wish to pursue them. A premiss of any peace-talks, as Hitler well realized, would have been his own removal. That in itself was sufficient to make him dismiss in fury any idea of negotiations. As the Foreign Minister himself later remarked, Hitler 'regarded any peace feeler as a sign of weakness'. His soundings, so he said, merely 'showed that no serious peace talk was possible' as long as Hitler lived.

This was equally plain to Goebbels. The Propaganda Minister was approached by Göring at the end of January, disconsolate at events in the east and despairing of Germany's military chances. Göring was prepared, he said, to use his Swedish contacts to put out feelers to Britain and sought the help of Goebbels in persuading Hitler that, since any overtures from Ribbentrop (regarded with utter contempt by the Reich Marshal as well as the Propaganda Minister) were doomed to failure, he should try this avenue. Goebbels was not encouraging. Privately, he was unwilling to push the case with Hitler since he ran the risk of losing the Führer's confidence, which, he added pointedly, 'is indeed the entire basis of my work'. In any case, Göring could only act, he noted, with Hitler's approval 'and the Führer won't grant him such approval'. Göring thought Hitler too intransigent, and wondered whether he wanted a political solution at all. He did, replied Goebbels, but 'the Führer does not see such a possibility existing at present'.

Hitler's lingering hopes, as ever, were in a split in the alliance against him. If Britain and the USA wanted to prevent a bolshevization of Europe, he told Goebbels, they would have to turn to Germany for help. The coalition had to break; it was a matter of holding out until the moment arrived. Goebbels privately thought Hitler too optimistic.

Jodl and Göring played to this illusion, however, at the military briefing on 27 January. However gloomy his attitude had been when speaking to Goebbels, in Hitler's presence Göring sang to a different tune. The Soviet advance had unquestionably dashed British plans, he and Jodl reckoned. Göring thought that if things went much further they could expect a telegram from the British saying they were prepared to join forces to prevent a Soviet occupation of Germany. Hitler suggested the National Committee of Free Germany, the 'traitors' organization' based in Moscow and linked with General Seydlitz, from the 6th Army lost at Stalingrad, could come in useful. He had told Ribbentrop, he said, to filter a story to the British that the Soviets had trained up

200,000 Communists under the leadership of German officers, ready to march. The prospect of a Russian-led national government in Germany would be certain to stir up anxiety in Britain, he averred. The British did not enter the war to see 'the East come to the Atlantic', Göring added. Hitler commented: 'English newspapers are already writing bitterly: what's the point of the war?'

He nevertheless saw no opening for overtures to his western enemies, when Goebbels tentatively broached the issue. In discussions with his Propaganda Minister on successive days at the end of January, appearing drained with fatigue, he reflected on the failure of the intended alliance with Britain. This might have been possible, he thought, had Chamberlain remained Prime Minister. But it had been totally vitiated by Churchill, 'the actual father of the war'. On the other hand, he continued to express admiration for Stalin's brutal realism as a revolutionary who knew exactly what he wanted and had learnt his method of atrocities from Genghis Khan. Here, too, Hitler dismissed any prospect of negotiations. 'He wanted,' he declared to Goebbels, 'to prove himself worthy of the great examples from history.' Should he succeed in transforming Germany's fortunes, thought the Propaganda Minister, without a trace of cynicism, he would be not only the man of the century, but of the millennium.

Goebbels continued to find Hitler over-optimistic about the chances of staving off the Soviet advance. Indeed, however pessimistic or fatalistic he was in dark moments, Hitler was as yet far from ready to give up the fight. He spoke of his aims in the forthcoming offensive in Hungary. Once he was again in possession of Hungarian oil, he would pour in additional divisions from Germany to liberate Upper Silesia. The whole operation would take around two months. The air of unreality did not escape Goebbels. It would take a great deal of luck to succeed, he noted.

Goebbels had been 'astonished' that Hitler, after showing such repeated reluctance for two years to speak in public, had so readily taken up a suggestion to broadcast to the nation on 30 January, the twelfth anniversary of the 'seizure of power'. Hitler presumably felt that at such a point of national crisis, with the enemy already deep inside the Reich, not to have spoken on such an important date in the Nazi calendar would have sent out the worst possible signals to the German people. It was imperative that he strengthen the will to fight, most of all on Germany's shrinking borders.

His recorded speech, broadcast at 10 p.m. that evening, amounted to little more than an attempt to stiffen morale, to appeal to fighting spirit, to demand extreme sacrifice in 'the most serious crisis for Europe in many centuries', and to emphasize his own will to fight on and refusal to contemplate anything other than victory. He referred, inevitably, to a 'Jewish-international world conspiracy', to 'Kremlin Jews', the 'spectre of asiatic Bolshevism', and of a 'storm-flood from inner Asia'. But the military disasters of the previous fortnight were not touched upon with a single word. And only a single sentence mentioned 'the horrible fate now taking place in the east, and eradicating people in their tens and hundreds of thousands in villages, in the marches, in the country, and in towns', which would eventually 'be fought off and mastered'. The speech could have appealed to few beyond remaining diehards.

That same day, 30 January, Speer had a memorandum passed to Hitler. It told him that the war economy and armaments production were at an end. Following the loss of Upper Silesia, there was no possibility of meeting the needs of the front in munitions, weapons, and tanks. 'The material superiority of the enemy can, accordingly, no longer be compensated for by the bravery of our soldiers.' Hitler's cold response made plain that he did not take kindly to receiving such reports that smacked of defeatism. He forbade Speer to pass the memorandum to anyone, adding that conclusions from the armaments position were his alone to draw. Short of the miracle for which he was still waiting, it must nevertheless have been obvious to Hitler, as to all those around him, that Germany could last out neither economically nor militarily for much longer.

Speer, long after the events, posed the question why even at this point Hitler was not faced with any joint action from those with regular contact to him to demand an explanation of how he intended to bring the war to an end. (He gave no hint of what might have followed from such an unlikely scenario.) Göring, Himmler, Ribbentrop, and even in some ways Goebbels, had, after all, been among the Nazi leaders who at one time or another had broached the question of peace overtures to the enemy, which Hitler had repeatedly dismissed out of hand. Now the end was near, and Germany was facing not just military defeat but total destruction. 'Surely something must happen,' Speer whispered to Dönitz during a briefing in early February, when further disasters were reported. Dönitz replied coolly that he was there only to represent the navy. The Führer would know what he was doing.

The reply provided at the same time an answer to the question Speer raised many years later. There was no prospect of any united front against Hitler even now, and even among those who saw with crystal clarity the abyss looming before them. The aftermath of the plot against him the previous year had left none of his entourage in the slightest doubt of the ruthlessness with which he would turn on anyone seen as a threat. But the impossibility of any combined front against Hitler did not rest alone, or even primarily, on fear. The innermost structure of the regime had long depended upon the way Hitler could play off his paladins against each other. Their deep divisions and animosities were reconciled only in their unquestioning loyalty and adherence to the Leader, from whom all remaining shreds of power and authority were still drawn. The Führer cult was still far from dead in this inner part of the 'charismatic community'. Keitel, Jodl, and Dönitz, among the highest ranks of the military leaders, were still wholly bound to Hitler, their loyalty unshaken, their admiration undiluted. Göring, his prestige at rock-bottom, had long since lost all energy to undertake anything against Hitler, and certainly lacked the will to do so. The same was true of Ribbentrop, who was in any case devoid of friends within the Nazi hierarchy and held by most in contempt as well as loathing. Goebbels, Labour Front leader Robert Ley, and, not least, the party leader in closest proximity to Hitler, Martin Bormann, were among the most radical supporters of his uncompromising line and remained wholly loyal. Speer, for his part, was – whatever his post-war feelings – one of the least likely to lead a fronde against Hitler, confront him with an ultimatum, or serve as focal point of a combined approach to put pressure on him. The scenario contemplated by Speer long after the events was, therefore, utterly inconceivable. The 'charismatic community' was compelled by its inner logic to follow the Leader on whom it had always depended – even when he was visibly taking it to perdition.

III

The government quarter of Berlin, like much of the rest of the city, was already a dismal and depressing sight even before, in broad daylight on 3 February, a huge American fleet of bombers unleashed a new hail of destruction from the skies in the heaviest raid of the war on the Reich capital. The Old Reich Chancellery, the neo-baroque palace dating back to Bismarck's time, was ruined, now little more than an empty shell. The New Reich Chancellery, designed by Speer, also suffered a number of direct hits. Bormann's headquarters in the Party Chancellery were severely damaged, and other buildings at the hub of the Nazi empire were demolished fully or in part. The whole area was a mass of rubble. Bomb craters pitted the Chancellery garden. For a time there was a complete power-failure, and water was available only from a water-cart standing in front of the Reich Chancellery. But unlike most of the population in the bombed-out districts of Berlin and elsewhere, at least the leaders of the Third Reich could still find alternative shelter and accommodation, however modest by their standards.

His apartments in the Reich Chancellery largely gutted by incendiaries, Hitler now moved underground for much of the time, shuffling down the seemingly unending stone steps, flanked by bare concrete walls, that led to the claustrophobic, labyrinthine subterranean world of the Führer Bunker, a two-storey construction deep below the garden of the Reich Chancellery. The enormous bunker complex had been deepened in 1943 – extending an earlier bunker (originally meant for possible future use as an air-raid shelter) dating from 1936 – and heavily reinforced during Hitler's stay at his western headquarters. The complex was completely self-contained, with its own heating, lighting, and water-pumps run from a diesel generator. Hitler had slept there since returning to Berlin. From now on, it would provide a macabre domicile for the remaining weeks of his life.

The bunker was far removed from the palatial surrounds to which he had been accustomed since 1933. An attempt to retain a degree of splendour at least remained in the corridor leading up to his bunker, which had been converted into a type of waiting-room, laid with a red carpet, and provided with rows of elegant chairs lined against walls hung with paintings brought down from his apartments. From here, a small ante-room gave way to the curtained entrance to his study. This was only around nine by twelve feet in size and seemed oppressive. A door on the right opened on to his bedroom, which had doors leading into a small briefing room, into his bathroom, and a tiny dressing room (and from there into what was to become Eva Braun's bedroom). A writing-desk, a small sofa, a table, and three armchairs were squeezed into the study, making it cramped and uncomfortable. A large portrait of Frederick the Great entirely dominated the room, offering a constant reminder to Hitler of the seeming rewards for holding out when all appeared lost until the tide miraculously turned. 'When bad news threatens to crush my spirit I derive fresh courage from the contemplation of this picture,' Hitler was heard to remark.

At first, even after he had moved his living quarters into the bunker, Hitler continued to spend part of the day in the undamaged wing of the Reich Chancellery. He lunched each day with his secretaries behind closed curtains in a dingy room lit by electric light. Since the operations room in the Old Reich Chancellery building was no longer usable, the afternoon military conferences, usually beginning about 3 p.m. and lasting two to three hours, were at this time held around the map-table in Hitler's imposing study in the New Reich Chancellery, with its polished floor, thick carpet, paintings, leather armchairs and couch, and – remarkably – still intact grey-curtained ceiling-high windows. The circle of participants had by now been widened to include Bormann, Himmler, Kaltenbrunner, and often Ribbentrop. Afterwards, Hitler would usually drink a cup of tea with his secretaries and adjutants before returning to the safety of his underground abode. For the evening meal his entourage trekked through kitchens and corridors, past machine rooms, ventilation shafts, and toilets, through two heavy iron gates, and down to the Führer Bunker. The first time he ventured down to visit Hitler, Goebbels spoke of finding his way through the corridors 'just like in a maze of trenches'. Over the next weeks, Hitler transferred almost all of his activities to the bunker, leaving it only for occasional snatches of fresh air to let Blondi out for a few minutes in the Chancellery garden or to take lunch with his secretaries above ground. From then on, he seldom saw daylight. For him and his 'court', spending almost their entire existence in the confines of the underground headquarters, night and day lost most of their meaning.

Hitler's day usually began around this time with the sound of air-raid sirens in the late morning. Linge was instructed to wake him, if he were not already awake, at noon, sometimes as late as 1 p.m. Often – probably affected by the unholy concoction of pills, potions, and injections he had daily (including stimulants as well as sedatives) – he had slept, so he claimed, for as little as three hours. The air-raids made him anxious. He would immediately dress and shave. The outer appearance of the Führer had to be maintained. He could not face his entourage unshaven and in night clothes even during an air-raid. The afternoons were almost exclusively taken up with lunch and the first of the lengthy twice-daily military briefings. The evening meal, usually not beginning until eight o'clock, sometimes later, frequently dragged out until late in the evening. Hitler sometimes retired for an hour or two, taking a sleep until it was time for the second military briefing. By now, it was usually 1 a.m. By the end of the briefing – invariably stressful in the extreme for all who attended, including Hitler himself – he was ready to slump on the sofa in his room. He was not too tired, however, to hold forth to his secretaries and other members of his close circle, summoned to join him for tea in the middle of the night. He would regale them, as he had done throughout the war, for up to two hours with banalities and monologues about the Church, race problems, the classical world, or the German character. After fondling Blondi and playing for a while with her puppy (which he had named 'Wolf'), he would at last allow his secretaries to retreat and finally retire himself to bed. It was by then, as a rule, according to Linge's planned schedule, around five o'clock in the morning, though in practice often much later.

A piece of pure escapism punctuated at this time Hitler's daily dose of gloom from the fronts: his visits to the model of his home-town Linz, his intended place of retirement, as it was to have been rebuilt at the end of the war, following a glorious German victory. The model had been designed by his architect Hermann Giesler (who had been commissioned by Hitler in autumn 1940 with the rebuilding of Linz), and was set up in February 1945 in the spacious cellar of the New Reich Chancellery. In January 1945, as the failure of the Ardennes offensive became apparent, as the eastern front caved in under the Red Army's assault, and as bombs rained down also on the Danube region in which Linz was situated, Giesler's office was repeatedly telephoned by Hitler's adjutants, and by Bormann. The Führer kept speaking of the model of Linz, they told Giesler; when would it be ready for him to inspect?

Giesler's team worked through the nights to meet Hitler's request. When the model was finally ready for him to see, on 9 February, Hitler was entranced. Bent over the model, he viewed it from all angles, and in different kinds of lighting. He asked for a seat. He checked the proportions of the different buildings. He asked about the details of the bridges. He studied the model for a long time, apparently lost in thought. While Giesler stayed in Berlin, Hitler accompanied him twice daily to view the model, in the afternoon and again during the night. Others in his entourage were taken down to have his building plans explained to them as they pored over the model. Looking down on the model of a city which, he knew, would never be built, Hitler could fall into reverie, revisiting the fantasies of his youth, when he would dream with his friend Kubizek about rebuilding Linz. They were distant days. It was soon back to a far harsher reality.

He spoke with Goebbels early in February about the defence of Berlin. They discussed the possible evacuation of some of the government offices to Thuringia. Hitler told Goebbels, however, that he was determined to stay in Berlin 'and to defend the city'. Hitler was still optimistic that the Oder front could be held. Goebbels was more sceptical. Hitler and Goebbels spoke of the war in the east as a historic struggle to save the 'European cultural world' from latter-day Huns and Mongols. Those would fare best who had burnt their boats and contemplated no compromises. 'At any rate we never entertain even a thought of capitulation,' noted Goebbels. Nevertheless, with Hitler still adamant that the coalition against him would collapse within the year, Goebbels recommended putting out feelers for an opening to the British. He did not embroider upon how this might be achieved. Hitler, as always, claimed the time was not conducive to such a move. Indeed, he feared that the British might turn to more draconian war methods, including the use of poison gas. In such an eventuality, he was determined to have large numbers of the Anglo-American prisoners in German hands shot.

On the evening of 12 February, 'the Big Three' – Roosevelt, Stalin, and Churchill – put out a communiqué from Yalta on the Crimea, where they had been conferring for a week, spending much of the time on the post-war shape of Germany and Europe. The communiqué left the Nazi leadership under no illusions about Allied plans for Germany: the country would be divided and demilitarized, its industry controlled, reparations paid; war criminals would be put on trial; the Nazi Party would be abolished. 'We know now where we are,' commented Goebbels. Hitler was immediately informed. He seemed unimpressed. He needed no further confirmation of his unchanging view that capitulation was pointless. The Allied leaders, he commented, 'want to separate the German people from its leadership. I've always said: there's no question of another capitulation.' After a brief pause, he added: 'History does not repeat itself.'

The following night, the city centre of Dresden was obliterated. Hitler heard the news of the devastation stony-faced, fists clenched. Goebbels, said to have been shaking with fury, immediately demanded the execution of tens of thousands of Allied prisoners-of-war, one for each citizen killed in air-raids. Hitler was taken with the idea. Brutal German treatment of prisoners-of-war would, he was certain, prompt retaliation by the Allies. That would deter German soldiers on the western front from deserting. Guderian recalled Hitler stating: 'The soldiers on the eastern front fight far better. The reason they give in so easily in the west is simply the fault of that stupid Geneva convention which promises them good treatment as prisoners. We must scrap this idiotic convention.' It took the efforts of Jodl, Keitel, Dönitz, and Ribbentrop, viewing such a reaction as counter-productive, to dissuade him from such a drastic step.

A few days later, Hitler summoned the Gauleiter, his most trusted party viceroys, to the Reich Chancellery for what would prove to be a final meeting. The last time they had assembled had been in early August of the previous year, shortly after Stauffenberg's attempt on Hitler's life. The present occasion was the twenty-fifth anniversary of the proclamation of the Party Programme in the Hofbräuhaus in Munich on 24 February 1920.

Hitler had frequently addressed the Gauleiter at moments of crisis during the past years. The real purpose of the present gathering was to rally the core of his support as the regime faced its gravest crisis. He had nothing resembling good news to impart. In the west, the Allies were pressing towards the Rhine. In the east, the counter-offensive launched a few days earlier in Pomerania offered no more than a fleeting ray of light in the deep gloom. Himmler's Army Group Vistula was encountering that very day a renewed assault from the Red Army. The absence of Erich Koch, whose East Prussian Gau was almost completely cut off by the Red Army, and Karl Hanke, besieged in Breslau, was a reminder of the fate of the eastern provinces. And the cluster of Gauleiter pressing Martin Mutschmann, Gauleiter of Saxony, for news about Dresden, or their party comrades from the Rhineland about the failure of the Ardennes offensive and the fighting in the west, told its own tale.

Hitler's appearance, when he entered the hall at 2 p.m. that afternoon, was a shock to many of the Gauleiter, who had not seen him for six months or so. His physical condition had deteriorated sharply even during the space of those six months. He was more haggard, aged, and bent than ever, shuffling in an unsteady gait as if dragging his legs. His left hand and arm trembled uncontrollably. His face was drained of colour; his eyes bloodshot, with bags underneath them; occasionally a drop of saliva trickled from the corner of his mouth.

Bormann had warned the Gauleiter in advance not to raise any criticism. There was, as ever, little likelihood of confrontation. But the sympathy at Hitler's outward appearance did deflect from the initial critical mood. Perhaps playing on this, he gave up at one point an attempt to raise a glass of water to his mouth in a trembling hand, without spilling it, and made reference to his own debilitation. He spoke sitting down at a small table for an hour and a half, his notes spread out in front of him. He began, as so often, with the 'heroic' party history. With present and future so bleak, he had come more and more to take refuge in the 'triumphs' of the past. He looked back now once more to the First World War, his decision to enter politics, and the struggle of National Socialism in the Weimar Republic. He lauded the new spirit created by the party after 1933. But his audience did not want to hear of the distant past. They were anxious to know how, if at all, he would overcome the overwhelming crisis currently sweeping over them. As usual, he dealt only in generalities. He spoke of the approaching decisive hour of the war, which would determine the shape of the coming century. He pointed as usual to the 'new weapons', which would bring about the change in fortune, praising the jets and new U-boats. His main aim was to fire up his sturdiest supporters for a final effort, to stiffen their morale and enthuse them to fight to the end so that they in turn would stir up the people in their region to selfless sacrifice, indomitable defence, and refusal to capitulate. If the German people should lose the war, he declared (in a further demonstration of his unchanged social-Darwinism), then it would indicate that it did not possess the 'internal value' that had been attributed to it, and he would have no sympathy with this people. He tried to persuade the Gauleiter that he alone could judge the course of events correctly. But even in this circle, among the party chieftains who for so many years had been the backbone of his power, few could share his optimism. His ability to motivate his closest supporters by the force of his rhetoric had dissolved.

This was even more the case for the mass of the population, where the words of the greatest demagogue known to history had by this time been drained of all impact, and were generally regarded as little more than empty phrases, bearing the promise of nothing other than further suffering until the war could be ended. The anniversary of the promulgation of the Party Programme had, until 1942, been traditionally the date of a big speech by Hitler in the Festsaal of the Hofbräuhaus in Munich. In 1945, as in 1942 and 1943, Hitler confined himself to a proclamation. Read out by Hermann Esser, one of his Munich cronies from the early days of the party, the proclamation was to prove Hitler's final public statement to the German people.

It amounted to no more than yet a further repeat of the long empty phrases of the old message. National Socialism alone had given the people the toughness to combat the threat to its very existence of an 'unnatural alliance', 'a diabolical pact between democratic capitalism and Jewish Bolshevism'. The atrocities of Bolshevism – 'this Jewish plague' – were now being experienced directly in the eastern parts of the Reich. Only 'extreme fanaticism and resolute steadfastness' could ward off the peril of 'this Jewish-Bolshevik annihilation of peoples and its west European and American pimps'. Weakness would and must perish. It was a 'duty to maintain the freedom of the German nation for the future' and – the unmistakable attempt to shore up fighting spirit through instilling fear – 'not to let German labour be shipped off to Siberia'. Its fanatical hatred for 'the destroyer of mankind' bolstered by the suffering it had endured, National Socialist Germany would continue the fight until 'the historical turning' came about. It would be that year. He ended on a note of pathos. His life had only the value it possessed for the nation. He wanted to share the suffering of the people, and almost regretted that the Berghof had not been bombed, which would have enabled him to share the sense of loss of possessions. (On this, the Allies were ready to oblige a few weeks later.) 'The life left to us,' he declared at the close, 'can serve only one command, that is to make good what the international Jewish criminals and their henchmen have done to our people.'

A poignant commentary was voiced in the routine report of the SD station in Berchtesgaden, where once thousands of 'pilgrims' had poured in to try to catch a glance of the Führer during his stays at the Berghof. 'Among the overwhelming majority of people's comrades,' the report ran, 'the content of the proclamation whistled by like the wind in the empty boughs.'

It was presumably Hitler's sensitivity to his public image that made him refuse Goebbels's request for a press report to shore up morale. He must have been alert to the inevitable derision that would be induced by reports of soldiers – many of them by now no more than boys – cheering him on a brief visit he and a small entourage had paid on 3 March to troops at Wriezen, some forty miles north-east of Berlin, just behind the Oder front. The news from the eastern front had left Hitler in a depressed mood, the shaking left hand more noticeable than ever, when the Propaganda Minister saw him the following evening. In Pomerania, Soviet tanks had broken through and were now outside Kolberg, on the Baltic. (When the town finally had to be evacuated later in the month, Goebbels suppressed the news because of the blatantly contradictory image of the nationalist epic colour-film he had had made on the town's stand against Napoleon, meant to stir modern-day defiance against the Red Army.) Himmler, the commander of Army Group Vistula, responsible for Pomerania's defence, had taken to his sick-bed – suffering, it seems, from nothing worse than a heavy cold on top of overwrought nerves – and retreated to the clinic at Hohenlychen, sixty or so miles north of Berlin, for convalescence. Hitler, as always, blamed the General Staff for the debacle. He was still hopeful of blocking the Red Army's advance; Goebbels had his doubts. Further south, the Czech industrial areas were under dire threat. Without them, Goebbels could not see how minimal armaments demands could any longer be met. Hitler hoped they could hold out, there and in Silesia, and inflict serious reverses on the Red Army with a counter-offensive – to prove the last of the war – beginning on 6 March.

In the west, Hitler was still optimistic about holding the Rhine. In reality, US troops were on the verge of entering Cologne, and only days later would take the bridge at Remagen and secure a foothold across the mighty artery. Goebbels, ready as so often to counter Hitler's instinctive optimism with cautious hints of realism, pointed out that, should the western defences not hold, 'our last political war argument would collapse', since the Anglo-Americans would be able to penetrate to central Germany and would have no interest in any negotiations. The growing crisis in the Alliance remained a straw to clutch at. But Goebbels was aware that Germany might be prostrate before it materialized.

Hitler still thought Stalin more likely than the western powers to show interest in negotiations. Whereas Roosevelt and Churchill would have difficulties with public opinion, Stalin could ignore it in reversing his war-policy overnight. But, as always, Hitler emphasized that the basis of any 'special peace' could only be military success. Pushing the Soviets back and inflicting heavy losses on them would make them more amenable. A new division of Poland, the return of Hungary and Croatia to German sovereignty, and operational freedom against the West would, Hitler hoped, be the prize. Thereafter, his aim, according to Goebbels, was to 'continue the struggle against England with the most brutal energy'. Britain, he thought, turning on the country that had spurned his earlier advances, was the 'eternal trouble-causer in Europe'. Sweeping it out of the Continent for good would bring Germany – at least for a while – some peace. Goebbels reflected that the Soviet atrocities were a handicap for Hitler's way forward. But he noted laconically that Europe had once survived the ravages of the Mongols: 'The storms from the east come and go, and Europe has to cope with them.'

Goebbels remained the fervent devotee of Hitler that he had been for twenty years. Though often frustrated and critical behind his leader's back at what he saw as undue reluctance to take measures necessary to radicalize the home front, and weakness in personnel matters – particularly the repeated unwillingness to dismiss Göring and Ribbentrop (both of whom he saw as bearing undue responsibility for Germany's plight) – Goebbels never ceased to be enthused once more by Hitler after spending time in his company. For Goebbels, Hitler's determination and optimism shone through the 'desolate mood' of the Reich Chancellery. 'If anyone can master the crisis, then he can,' the Propaganda Minister remarked. 'No one else can be found who is anywhere near touching him.'

But, though his personal subordination for the father-figure he had for so long revered remained, even Goebbels was no longer persuaded by Hitler's apparent confidence in turning the tide. He was anticipating the end, looking to the history books. Magda and the children would join him and stay in Berlin, come what may, he told Hitler. If the struggle could not be mastered, then at least it had to be sustained with honour, he wrote. He was gripped by Thomas's Carlyle's biography, glorifying the heroism of Frederick the Great, and presented Hitler with a copy. He read out to him the passages relating the King's reward for his unbending resolution in circumstances of mounting despair during the Seven Years War by the sudden and dramatic upturn in his fortunes.

Hitler's eyes filled with tears. Hitler, too, was looking to his place in history. 'It must be our ambition,' he told Goebbels on 11 March, 'Heroes' Memorial Day', 'also in our times to set an example for later generations to look to in similar crises and pressures, just as we today have to look to the past heroes of history.' The theme ran through his proclamation to the Wehrmacht that day. He declared it his 'unalterable decision . . . to provide the world to come with no worse example than bygone times have left us'. The sentence that followed encapsulated the essence of Hitler's political 'career': 'The year 1918 will therefore not repeat itself.'

IV

To rule this out, no price – even self-destruction – was too high. In his characteristic 'either-or' way of thinking, Hitler had invariably posed total destruction as the alternative to the total victory for which he had striven. Inwardly convinced that his enemies were intent on bringing about that total destruction – the Morgenthau Plan of 1944, envisaging the reduction of a defeated Germany to the status of an agricultural country with a pre-industrial economy had given sustenance to this belief – no measure was for him too radical in the fight for survival. Consistent only with his own warped and peculiar brand of logic, he was prepared to take measures with such far-reaching consequences for the German population that the very survival he claimed to be fighting for was fundamentally threatened. Ultimately, the continued existence of the German people – if it showed itself incapable of defeating its enemies – was less important to him than the refusal to capitulate.

Few, even of his closest acolytes, were ready to follow this self-destructive urge to the letter. Albert Speer was one of those looking to the future after a lost war. Perhaps the ambitious Speer was still hoping to have some part to play in a Germany without Hitler. At any rate, he knew the war was irredeemably lost. And he was looking to save what could be saved of the economic substance of the country. He had no interest in a Germany going down in a maelstrom of destruction to satisfy the irrational and pointless principle of 'heroic' self-sacrifice rather than capitulation. He knew only too well that the preservation of Germany's material substance for a post-Hitler future had long been the aim of the leading industrialists with whom he had worked so closely. He had hindered the implementation of Hitler's orders for the destruction of French industry. And in recent weeks, he had arranged with Colonel-General Heinrici in Upper Silesia, Field-Marshal Model in the Ruhr (now on the verge of being taken by the western Allies), and Colonel-General Guderian for the entire eastern front that factories, mines, railways, roads, bridges, waterworks, gasworks, power-stations, and other installations vital to the German economy should be spared destruction wherever possible.

On 18 March, Speer passed to Below a memorandum he had drafted three days earlier. Below was to choose a favourable moment to hand it to Hitler. The memorandum stated plainly that the final collapse of the German economy would occur within four to eight weeks, after which the war could not be continued. The prime duty of those leading the country must be to do what they could for the civilian population. But detonating bridges, with the consequent major destruction of the transport infrastructure, would signify 'the elimination of all further possibility of existence for the German people'. Speer concluded: 'We have no right, at this stage of the war, to undertake destruction which could affect the existence of the people . . . We have the duty of leaving the people every possibility of establishing a reconstruction in the distant future.'

A strong hint of Hitler's likely response could be gleaned at the military briefing that evening, when the topic arose of evacuation of the local population from the combat zone in the Saar. Despite an almost total lack of transport, Hitler's express order was that the complete evacuation should be undertaken forthwith. Consideration could not be given to the population. A few hours after the briefing ended, just before Speer left for a tour of the threatened areas on the western front, Hitler summoned him. According to Speer's recollection, noted down ten days later, Hitler told him coldly that should the war be lost, the people would also be lost, and that there was no need to take consideration even of its most primitive survival. The German people had proved the weaker in the struggle. Only those who were inferior would remain.

Hitler had promised Speer a written reply to his memorandum. It was not long in coming, and was predictably the opposite of what Speer had recommended. Whatever the cost, in Hitler's view, intact vital installations for industrial production could not be allowed to fall into enemy hands as had happened in Upper Silesia and the Saar. His decree of 19 March, headed 'Destructive Measures on Reich Territory', was consistent with a philosophy by now wholly at odds with Speer's. 'The struggle for the existence of our people,' his decree ran, 'compels the use of all means, also within the territory of the Reich, to weaken the fighting power of our enemy and its further advance. All possibilities of imparting directly or indirectly lasting damage to the striking power of the enemy must be exploited. It is an error to believe that undestroyed or only temporarily disabled transport, communications, industrial, and supplies installations can again be made operational for our own purposes at the recapture of lost territories. The enemy will leave us only scorched earth at its retreat and drop any consideration for the population. I therefore order: 1) All military transport, communications, industrial, and supplies installations as well as material assets within Reich territory, which the enemy can render usable immediately or within the foreseeable future are to be destroyed. 2) Those responsible for the implementation of this destruction are: military command authorities for all military objects, including transport and communications installations, the Gauleiter and Reich Defence Commissars for all industrial and supplies installations and other material assets. The troops are to provide the necessary aid to the Gauleiter and Reich Defence Commissars in the implementation of their task . . .'

The decree was never put into practice. Though, initially, several Gauleiter – prominent among them Gauleiter Friedrich Karl Florian in Düsseldorf – were eager to carry out Hitler's orders to the letter, Speer was eventually successful in persuading them of the futility of the intended action. In any case, the Gauleiter agreed that it was in practice impossible to implement the order. Model was one of the front-line military commanders also prepared to cooperate with Speer in keeping destruction of industrial plant to a minimum. By the end of March, with difficulty, Speer had managed to convince Hitler – aware though he was of the Armaments Minister's effective sabotage of his order – that he should be granted overall responsibility for implementing all measures for destruction. This took the key decisions out of the hands of the Gauleiter, Hitler's key representatives in the regions. It meant, as Hitler knew, that everything possible would be done to avoid the destruction he had ordered.

The non-implementation of the 'scorched earth' order was the first obvious sign that Hitler's authority was beginning to wane, his writ ceasing to run. 'We're giving out orders in Berlin that in practice no longer arrive lower down, let alone can be implemented,' remarked Goebbels at the end of March. 'I see in that the danger of an extraordinary dwindling of authority.'

Hitler continued to see himself as indispensable. 'If anything happens to me, Germany is lost, since I have no successor,' he told his secretaries. 'Heß has gone mad, Göring has squandered the sympathies of the German people, and Himmler is rejected by the party,' was his assessment.

Hitler had been absolutely dismissive of Göring's leadership qualities in 'turbulent times' in speaking to Goebbels in mid-February 1945. As 'leader of the nation', he was 'utterly unimaginable'. Tirades about the Reich Marshal were commonplace. On one occasion, fists clenched, face flushed with anger, he humiliated Göring in front of all present at a military briefing, threatening to reduce him to the ranks and dissolve the Luftwaffe as a separate branch of the armed forces. Göring could only withdraw to the ante-room and swallow a few glasses of brandy. But despite regular exposure to Goebbels's vitriol about the Reich Marshal and impassioned entreaties to dismiss him, Hitler persisted in his view that he had no suitable replacement.

Hitler's attitude towards Himmler had also hardened. His blind fury at the retreat of divisions – including that specially named after him, the Leibstandarte-SS Adolf Hitler – of Sepp Dietrich's 6th Panzer Army in the face of heavy losses and imminent encirclement in bitter fighting on the Danube was directed at Himmler. The Reichsführer-SS was in despair at the breach with Hitler, symbolized in the order he was forced to carry to Dietrich commanding his four Waffen-SS divisions, among them the élite Leibstandarte Adolf Hitler, to remove their armlets in disgrace. With Hitler now feeling betrayed even by his own SS commanders, Himmler's waning star sank steeply through his own evident failings as Commander of Army Group Vistula. Hitler held the Reichsführer-SS personally responsible for the failure to block the Soviet advance through Pomerania. He accused him of having immediately fallen under the influence of the General Staff – a heinous offence in Hitler's eyes – and even of direct disobedience of his orders to build up anti-tank defences in Pomerania. Blaming others as usual, he took the view that Pomerania could have been held if Himmler had followed his orders. He intended, he told Goebbels, to make plain to him at their next meeting that any repetition would lead to an irreparable breach. Whether the rift was further deepened through rumours abroad – in fact, close to the truth – linking Himmler's name with peace soundings is unclear. But there was no doubt that Himmler's standing with Hitler had slumped dramatically. The Reichsführer-SS remained, for his part, both dismayed at the rupture in relations, and cautious in the extreme, aware that even now his authority hinged solely on Hitler's continued favour. But after being relieved of his command of Army Group Vistula on 20 March, Himmler increasingly went his own way.

The circle of those Hitler trusted was diminishing sharply. At the same time, his intolerance of any contradiction of his views had become as good as absolute. The one remaining voice among his generals which had been increasingly outspoken in its criticism was that of Colonel-General Guderian. Where Keitel spoke with so little authority that younger officers scornfully dubbed him the 'Reich Garage Attendant', and Jodl carefully attuned his briefings to Hitler's moods and anticipated his wishes, Guderian was terse, pointed, and frank in his remarks. The conflicts, which had mounted since Christmas in their intensity, were ended abruptly at the end of March with Guderian's dismissal. By that time, the final German offensive near Lake Balaton in Hungary, started on 6 March, had failed and the Soviets were marching on the last remaining oil reserves open to Germany; the Red Army had meanwhile cut off Königsberg in East Prussia, broken through at Oppeln in Upper Silesia, taken Kolberg on the Baltic coast, opened up German defences close to Danzig, and surrounded the SS battalions fiercely defending the strategically important stronghold of Küstrin on the Oder. In the west, outside Guderian's sphere of responsibility, the news was at least as sombre. General Patton's 3rd US Army had taken Darmstadt and reached the river Main; and American tanks had entered the outskirts of Frankfurt. Hitler had not expected the western front to collapse so rapidly. As always, he smelled betrayal. And, characteristically, he was now ready to make Guderian the scapegoat for the dire situation on the eastern front.

Guderian had been expecting a stormy meeting when he arrived at Hitler's bunker on 28 March for the afternoon briefing. He was determined to continue his defence of General Theodor Busse against the accusation that he held responsibility for the failure of his 9th Army to relieve the encircled troops at Küstrin. But Hitler was not prepared to listen. He peremptorily adjourned the meeting, keeping only Keitel and Guderian back. Without demur, the Chief of Staff was told that his health problems demanded he take with immediate effect six weeks' convalescent leave. He was replaced by the more compliant General Hans Krebs.

Reports were by now coming in from Kesselring's headquarters that the western front in the region of Hanau and Frankfurt am Main was showing serious signs of disintegration. White flags were being hoisted; women were embracing American soldiers as they entered; troops, not wanting to fight any longer, were fleeing from any prospect of battle or simply surrendering. Kesselring wanted Hitler to speak without delay to shore up the wavering will to fight. Goebbels agreed. Churchill and Stalin had both spoken to their nations at times of utmost peril. Germany's position was even worse. 'In such a serious situation, the nation cannot remain without an appeal from the highest authority,' Goebbels noted. He telephoned General Burgdorf, Hitler's chief Wehrmacht adjutant, and impressed upon him the need to persuade Hitler to speak to the German people. Next day, walking for an hour among the ruins of the Reich Chancellery garden alongside the bent figure of Hitler, Goebbels tried to exert all his own influence in pleading with him to give a ten- or fifteen-minute radio address. Hitler did not want to speak, however, 'because at present he has nothing positive to offer'. Goebbels did not give up. Hitler finally agreed. But Goebbels's evident scepticism proved justified. A few days later, Hitler again promised to give his speech – but only after he had gained a success in the west. He knew he should speak to the people. But the SD had informed him that his previous speech – his proclamation on 24 February – had been criticized for not saying anything new. And Goebbels acknowledged that, indeed, he had nothing new to offer the people. The Propaganda Minister repeated his hope that Hitler would nevertheless speak to them. 'The people were waiting for at least a slogan,' he urged. But Hitler had by now even run out of propaganda slogans for the people of Germany.

Goebbels remained puzzled – and, behind his admiration, irritated and frustrated – at Hitler's reluctance to take what the Propaganda Minister regarded as vital, radical steps even at this later hour to change Germany's fortunes. In this, he privately reflected, Frederick the Great had been far more ruthless. Hitler, by contrast, accepted the diagnosis of the problem. But no action followed. He took the setbacks and grave dangers, thought Goebbels, too lightly – at least, he pointedly added, in his presence; 'privately, he will certainly think differently.' He was still confident of the split among the Allies he had so long been predicting. 'But it pains me,' Goebbels noted, 'that he is at present not to be moved to do anything to deepen the political crisis in the enemy camp. He doesn't change personnel, either in the Reich government or in the diplomatic service. Göring stays. Ribbentrop stays. All failures – apart from the second rank – are retained, and it would in my view be so necessary to undertake here in particular a change of personnel because this would be of such decisive importance for the morale of our people. I press and press; but I can't convince the Führer of the necessity of these measures that I put forward.' It was, Goebbels pointed out, 'as if he lived in the clouds'.

Not only Hitler held on to a make-believe world. 'One day, the Reich of our dreams will emerge,' wrote Gerda Bormann to her husband. 'Shall we, I wonder, or our children, live to see it?' 'I have every hope that we shall!' jotted Martin, between the lines. 'In some ways, you know, this reminds me of the "Twilight of the Gods" in the Edda,' Gerda's letter continued. 'The monsters are storming the bridge of the Gods . . . the citadel of the Gods crumbles, and all seems lost; and then, suddenly a new citadel rises, more beautiful than ever before . . . We are not the first to engage in mortal combat with the powers of the under-world, and that we feel impelled, and are also able, to do so should give us a conviction of ultimate victory.'

An air of unreality also pervaded, in part, the administrative machines of party and state. Though, certainly, the state bureaucracy – now mostly removed from Berlin – was confronted with the actualities of a lost war in trying to cope with the acute problems of refugees from the east, housing the homeless from bomb-damaged cities, and ensuring that public facilities were kept running, much of what remained of civil administration – massively hampered through repeated breakdowns in postal and rail communications – had little to do with the everyday needs of the population. The sober-minded and long-serving Finance Minister, Lutz Graf Schwerin von Krosigk, for instance, completed at the end of March his plans for tax reform – criticized by Goebbels (as if they were about to be implemented) for their 'unsocial' emphasis on consumer tax, which would affect the mass of the population, rather than income tax. That much of the country was by this time under enemy occupation seemed irrelevant.

Meanwhile, Martin Bormann was still working feverishly on restructuring the party to control the new, peacetime Germany that would emerge from the war. And as the Reich shrank, lines of communication disintegrated, and directives became increasingly overtaken by events, he sent more circulars, decrees, and promulgations than ever – over 400 in the last four months of the war – cascading down to lower functionaries of the party. 'Again a mass of new decrees and orders pour in from Bormann,' noted Goebbels on 4 April. 'Bormann has made a paper chancellery out of the Party Chancellery. Every day he sends out a mountain of letters and files which Gauleiter at present in the midst of the struggle can in practice not even read. In part, it's a matter of completely useless stuff of no value for the practical struggle.' A party bureaucracy in overdrive poured out regulations on provision of bread grain, small-arms training of women and girls, repair of railways and road communications, eking out additional food from wild vegetables, fruit, and mushrooms, and a host of other issues.

Alongside such miscellanea went the constant demands and exhortations to hold out, whatever the cost. Bormann informed party functionaries on 1 April that summary and draconian punishment for desertion awaited 'any scoundrel ... who does not fight to the last breath'. He detailed functionaries to work with Wehrmacht units in stiffening morale in areas close to the front and to set up quasi-guerrilla organizations such as the 'Freikorps Adolf Hitler' (drawn from the party's functionaries) and the 'Werwolf' (to be made up largely of Hitler Youth members) to carry on the fight through partisan activity in the occupied areas of the Reich. German propaganda sought to convey the impression to the Allies that they were endangered by an extensively organized underground resistance-movement. In practice, the 'Werwolf' was of scant military significance, and was mainly a threat, in its arbitrary and vicious retribution, to German citizens revealing any traces of 'defeatism'.

On 15 April Bormann put out a circular to Political Leaders of the Party: 'The Führer expects that you will master every situation in your Gaue, if necessary with lightning speed and extreme brutality . . .' Like more and more of his missives, it existed largely on paper. Correspondence to reality was minimal. It was a classic illustration of the continuing illusory and despairing belief in the triumph of will alone. But even the unconstrained and arbitrary violence of a regime patently in its death-throes could not contain the open manifestations of disintegration. Ever fewer brown party uniforms were to be seen on the streets. And ever more party functionaries were disappearing into the ether as the enemy approached, looking more to self-preservation than to heroic last stands. 'The behaviour of our Gau and District Leaders in the west has led to a strong drop in confidence among the population,' commented Goebbels. 'As a consequence, the Party is fairly played out in the west.'

During early April, the last German troops pulled out of Hungary. Bratislava fell to the Red Army as it advanced on Vienna. To the north, the German troops cut off in Königsberg surrendered the city on 9 April. In the west, Allied troops pushed through Westphalia, taking Münster and Hamm. By 10 April, Essen and Hanover were in American hands. The vice was tightening on the Ruhr, Germany's battered industrial heartland. A sudden shaft of optimism penetrated the dense gloom enveloping Hitler's bunker: the news came through of the death on 12 April, at his winter retreat in Warm Springs, Georgia, of one of his greatest adversaries, and linchpin in the unholy coalition of forces against him, President Roosevelt.

Goebbels rang up, elated, to congratulate Hitler. Two weeks earlier, the Propaganda Minister had been given a file of astrological material, including a horoscope of the Führer. It prophesied an improvement in Germany's military position in the second half of April. Goebbels's sole interest in the material, he said, was for propaganda purposes, to give people something to cling on to. It served this purpose now, for the moment, for Hitler. 'Here, read this!' Hitler, looking revitalized and in an excited voice, instructed Speer. 'Here! You never wanted to believe it. Here! ... Here we have the great miracle that I always foretold. Who's right now? The war is not lost. Read it! Roosevelt is dead!' It seemed to him like the hand of Providence yet again. Goebbels, fresh from his reading of Carlyle's biography of Frederick the Great, reminded Hitler of the death of the Czarina Elisabeth that had brought a sudden change of fortune for the Prussian King in the Seven Years War. The artificial coalition enemies aligned against Germany would now break up. History was repeating itself. Whether Hitler was as convinced as he seemed that the hand of Providence had produced the turning-point of the war is uncertain. One close to him in these days, his Luftwaffe adjutant Nicolaus von Below, thought him more sober at the news than Goebbels – whose cynical eye was, as always, directed at the possible propaganda advantages.

Even for those who saw him at close quarters, it was difficult to be sure of Hitler's true feelings about the war. Field-Marshal Kesselring, who saw Hitler for the last time on 12 April, the day of Roosevelt's death, later recalled: 'He was still optimistic. How far he was play-acting it is hard to decide. Looking back, I am inclined to think that he was literally obsessed with the idea of some miraculous salvation, that he clung to it like a drowning man to a straw.'

Whether genuine or contrived, Hitler's jubilation did not last long. On 13 April, the news was given to him that Vienna had been taken by the Red Army. The following day, American attacks succeeded in splitting German forces defending the Ruhr. Within three days, the fighting in the Ruhr was over. Field-Marshal Model, a long-standing favourite of Hitler, dissolved his encircled Army Group B rather than offer formal capitulation. It made no difference. Around 325,000 German troops and thirty generals gave themselves up to the Americans on 17 April. Model committed suicide four days later in a wooded area south of Duisburg.

On 15 April, in anticipation of a new Soviet offensive – which he thought, probably taken in by Stalin's disinformation directed at the western Allies, would first sweep through Saxony to Prague to head off the Americans before tackling Berlin – Hitler had issued a 'basic order' for the eventuality that the Reich might be split in two. He set up a supreme commander – in effect his military representative – to take full responsibility for the defence of the Reich, should communications be broken, in whichever part he himself was not situated. Grand-Admiral Dönitz was designated for the northern zone, Field-Marshal Kesselring for the south. The implication was that Hitler was keeping the option open of carrying on the fight from the south, in the fastness of the Bavarian Alps.

On the same day, Hitler issued what would turn out to be his last proclamation to the soldiers on the eastern front. It played heavily on the stories of Soviet atrocities. 'For the last time, the Jewish-Bolshevik mortal enemy has set out with its masses on the attack,' it began. 'He is attempting to demolish Germany and to exterminate our people. You soldiers from the East know yourselves in large measure what fate threatens above all German women, girls, and children. While old men and children are murdered, women and girls are denigrated to barrack-whores. The rest are marched off to Siberia.' It went on to alert the troops to the slightest sign of treachery, particularly – the long-standing exaggeration of the influence of the National Committee for a Free Germany, established in Moscow by captured German officers – troops fighting against them in German uniforms receiving Russian pay. Any-one not known to them ordering a retreat was to be captured and 'if need be immediately dispatched, irrespective of rank'. The proclamation had its climax in the slogan: 'Berlin stays German, Vienna will be German again, and Europe will never be Russian.'

It was to no avail. In the early hours of 16 April, a huge artillery barrage announced the launch of the awaited assault from the line of the Oder and Neisse rivers by over a million Soviet troops under Marshal Zhukov and Marshal Konev. The German defenders from the 9th Army and, to its south, the 4th Panzer Army fought tenaciously. The Soviets suffered some significant losses. For a few hours, the front held. But the odds were hopeless. During the afternoon, after renewed heavy artillery bombardment, the German line was broken north of Küstrin on the west bank of the Oder. The gap between the 9th Army and the 4th Panzer Army quickly widened. Soviet infantry poured through, rapidly followed by hundreds of tanks, and over the next two days extended and consolidated their hold in the area south of Frankfurt an der Oder. From then on the Oder front caved in completely. There could now be only one outcome. The Red Army drove on over and past the lingering defences. Berlin was directly in its sights.

General Busse's 9th Army was pushed back towards the south of the city. Hitler had ordered Busse to hold a line which his Army Group Commander, Colonel-General Heinrici, had thought exposed the 9th Army to encirclement. Ignoring Hitler's orders, Heinrici nevertheless commanded withdrawal westwards. By that time, only parts of Busse's army could evade imminent encirclement. Meanwhile, the German General Staff was forced to flee from its headquarters in secure bunkers at Zossen to the Wannsee – its column of retreating vehicles mistaken by German planes for part of a Soviet unit and attacked from the air as they went. To the north, the forces under Colonel-General Heinrici and SS-Obergruppenführer Felix Steiner were the last barrier to the ever more menacing prospect of encirclement of the city as the Red Army pushed through Eberswalde to Oranienburg. By 20 April, Soviet tanks had reached the outskirts of the capital. That afternoon, Berlin was under fire.

The rumble of artillery fire could be plainly heard from the Reich Chancellery. There, with the Red Army on the doorstep, and to the accompaniment of almost non-stop bombing by Allied planes, leading Nazis gathered for what they knew would be the last time – to celebrate Hitler's fifty-sixth birthday, and, in most cases, to say their farewells. It was the start of the last rites for the Third Reich.

28

Extinction

I

The atmosphere in the bunker on 20 April 1945, Hitler's fifty-sixth birthday, was more funereal than celebratory. There was no trace of the pomp and circumstance of earlier years. The gaunt ruins of the Reich Chancellery were themselves a stark reminder, if one was needed, that there was no cause for celebration. Hitler felt this himself. His birthday with the Russians at the gates of Berlin was – everything points to this – an embarrassment to him, and for all those who were obliged to offer him their birthday greetings.

Traditionally, Hitler's personal staff gathered to be the first to offer their congratulations on the stroke of midnight. This year, Hitler, in depressed mood, had already told his valet, Heinz Linge, that he did not want to receive his household; there were no grounds for congratulation. Linge was ordered to pass on the message. Predictably, this Führer order was ignored. Waiting in the ante-room, as midnight approached, to offer their formal congratulations were Chief Wehrmacht Adjutant General Wilhelm Burgdorf, Himmler's liaison SS-Gruppenführer Hermann Fegelein (who had recently married Eva Braun's sister, Gretl), the long-serving factotum Julius Schaub, a member of the 'household' since the mid-1920s, Hitler's adjutants NSKK-Oberführer Alwin-Broder Albrecht and SS-Sturmbannführer Otto Günsche, Ribbentrop's liaison Walther Hewel, and press officer Heinz Lorenz. Hitler, tired and dejected, said Linge should inform them that he had no time to receive them. Only following Fegelein's intercession with his sister-in-law Eva Braun (who had returned to the Reich Chancellery some weeks earlier, announcing she was staying with Hitler, and resisting all attempts to persuade her to leave) did he concede, trudging down the assembled line of his staff to receive their murmured birthday greetings with a limp handshake and a vacant expression. Further muted, almost embarrassed, congratulations followed from the military leaders attending the first briefing of the day. Afterwards, Hitler drank tea in his study with Eva Braun. It was approaching nine o'clock in the morning before he finally went to bed, only to be disturbed almost immediately by General Burgdorf with the news of a Soviet breakthrough and advance towards Cottbus, some sixty miles south-east of Berlin, on the southern part of the front. Hitler took the news standing in his nightshirt at the door of his bedroom, and told Linge he had not slept up to then and to waken him an hour later than normal, at 2 p.m.

After breakfasting, playing with his alsatian puppy for a while, and having Linge administer his cocaine eye-drops, he slowly climbed the steps into the Reich Chancellery park. Waiting with raised arms in the Nazi salute were delegations from the Courland army, from SS units in Berlin, and twenty boys from the Hitler Youth who had distinguished themselves in combat. Was this what Berlin's defence relied upon? one of Hitler's secretaries wondered. Hitler muttered a few words to them, patted one or two on the cheek, and within minutes left them to carry on the fight against Russian tanks.

Bormann, Himmler, Goebbels, Reich Youth Leader Artur Axmann, and Dr Morell were among those in a further line waiting to be received at the door of the Chancellery's Winter Garden. Looking drained and listless, his face ashen, his stoop pronounced, Hitler went through the motions of a brief address. Not surprisingly, he was by now incapable of raising spirits. Lunch with Christa Schroeder and senior secretary Johanna Wolf was a depressing affair. Afterwards, he retraced his steps down into the bowels of the earth for the late afternoon briefing. He would not leave the bunker again alive.

By now, most of the leading figures in the Reich – at least, those in the Berlin vicinity – were assembled. Göring, Dönitz, Keitel, Ribbentrop, Speer, Jodl, Himmler, Kaltenbrunner, the new Chief of Staff General Hans Krebs, and others all presented their greetings. No one spoke of the looming catastrophe. They all swore their undying loyalty. Everyone noticed that Göring had discarded his resplendent silver-grey uniform with gold-braided epaulettes for khaki – 'like an American general', as one participant at the briefing remarked. Hitler passed no comment.

The imminent assault on Berlin dominated the briefing. The news from the southern rim of the city was catastrophic. Göring pointed out that only a single road to the south, through the Bayerischer Wald, was still open; it could be blocked at any moment. His chief of staff, General Karl Koller, added that any later attempt to transfer the High Command of the Wehrmacht by air to new headquarters could be ruled out. Hitler was pressed from all sides to leave at once for Berchtesgaden. He objected that he could not expect his troops to fight the decisive battle for Berlin if he removed himself to safety. Keitel had told Koller before the briefing that Hitler was determined to stay in Berlin. When greeting Hitler, Keitel had murmured words of confidence that he would take urgent decisions before the Reich capital became a battleground. It was a strong hint that Hitler and his entourage should leave for the south while there was still time. Hitler interrupted, saying: 'Keitel, I know what I want. I will fight on in front of, within, or behind Berlin.' Nevertheless, Hitler now seemed indecisive. Increasingly agitated, he declared moments later that he would leave it to fate whether he died in the capital or flew at the last moment to the Obersalzberg.

There was no indecision about Göring. He had sent his wife Emmy and daughter Edda to the safety of the Bavarian mountains more than two months earlier. He had written his will in February. Crate-loads of his looted art treasures from Carinhall, his palatial country residence in the Schorfheide, forty miles north of Berlin, had been shipped south in March. Half a million marks were transferred to his account in Berchtesgaden. By the time he arrived at the Reich Chancellery to pass on his birthday wishes to Hitler, Carinhall was mined with explosives; his own remaining belongings were packed and loaded on to lorries, ready to go on to the Obersalzberg. Göring lost no time at the end of the briefing session in seeking out a private word with Hitler. It was urgent, said the Reich Marshal, that he go to southern Germany to command the Luftwaffe from there. He needed to leave Berlin that very night. Hitler scarcely seemed to notice. He muttered a few words, shook hands absent-mindedly, and the first paladin of the Reich departed, hurriedly and without fanfare. It seemed to Albert Speer, standing a few feet away, to be a parting of ways that symbolized the imminent end of the Third Reich.

It was the first of numerous departures. Most of those who had come to proffer their birthday greetings to Hitler and make avowals of their undying loyalty were waiting nervously for the moment when they could hasten from the doomed city. Convoys of cars were soon heading out of Berlin north, south, and west, on any roads still open. Dönitz left for the north, armed with Hitler's instructions – the implementation of the directive five days earlier on division of command should the Reich be geographically split – to take over the leadership in the north and continue the struggle. It was a sign of Dönitz's high standing with Hitler on account of his uncompromising support for the stance of fighting to the last, and of hopes for a continuation of the U-boat war, that he was given plenipotentiary powers to issue all relevant orders to state and party, as well as to the Wehrmacht in the northern zone. Himmler, Kaltenbrunner, and Ribbentrop soon followed. Speer left later that night in the direction of Hamburg, without any formal farewell.

Hitler, according to Julius Schaub's post-war testimony, was deeply disappointed at the desire of his paladins to leave the bunker in barely concealed haste. He gave no more than a perfunctory nod of valediction to those who, now that his power was as good as ended, were anxious to save what they could of themselves and their possessions. By this time, most of the army top-brass had left. And Bormann had already told the remaining government ministers – Finance Minister Lutz Graf Schwerin-Krosigk, Transport Minister Julius Dorpmüller, Justice Minister Otto Georg Thierack, Minister for the Occupied Eastern Territories (a long redundant post) Alfred Rosenberg, Education Minister Bernhard Rust, and Labour Minister Franz Seldte – together with head of the Presidential Chancellery, the old survivor, Otto Meissner, to make hasty preparations to leave for the south, since the road would soon be blocked. Hitler's naval adjutant, Admiral Karl-Jesko von Puttkamer, was dispatched to the Obersalzberg to destroy important papers there. His two older secretaries, Johanna Wolf and Christa Schroeder, were summoned to his study that evening and told to be ready to leave for the Berghof within the hour. Four days earlier, he had told them in confident tones: 'Berlin will stay German. We must just gain time.' Now, he said, the situation had changed so much in the past four days, that he had to break up his staff.

The scene in the courtyard of the Reich Chancellery was near-chaotic as vehicles were stuffed with bags and suitcases, the rumble of artillery a reminder of how close the Red Army was as the cars hurried through the night, through clouds of smoke billowing from burning buildings, past shadowy ruins and Volkssturm men setting up street barricades, to waiting aeroplanes. During the following three nights, some twenty flights were made from Gatow and Staaken aerodromes in Berlin, taking most of Hitler's staff to Berchtesgaden.

Late in the evening, the remaining adjutants, secretaries, and his young Austrian diet cook, Constanze Manziarly, gathered in his room for a drink with Hitler and Eva Braun. There was no talk here of the war. Hitler's youngest secretary, Traudl Junge, had been shocked to hear him admit for the first time in her presence earlier that day that he no longer believed in victory. *He* might be ready to go under; her own life, she felt, had barely begun. Once Hitler – early for him – had retired to his room, she was glad to join Eva Braun, and other bunker 'inmates', even including Bormann and Morell, in an 'unofficial' party in the old living room on the first floor of Hitler's apartment in the Reich Chancellery. In the ghostly surrounds of a room stripped of almost all its former splendour, with the gramophone scratching out the only record they could find – a smaltzy pre-war hit called 'Red Roses Bring You Happiness' – they laughed, danced, and drank champagne, trying to enjoy an hour or two of escapism, before a nearby explosion sharply jolted them back to reality.

When Hitler was awakened at 9.30 next morning, it was to the news that the centre of Berlin was under artillery fire. He was at first incredulous, immediately demanding information from Karl Koller, Luftwaffe chief of staff, on the position of the Soviet artillery battery. An observation post at Berlin's zoo provided the answer: the battery was no more than eight miles away in the suburb of Marzahn. The dragnet was closing fast. The information scarcely helped to calm Hitler's increasingly volatile moods. As the day wore on, he seemed increasingly like a man at the end of his tether, nerves ragged, under intense strain, close to breaking point. Irrational reactions when a frenzy of almost hysterically barked-out orders proved impossible to implement, or demands for information impossible to supply, point in this direction.

Soon he was on the telephone again to Koller, this time demanding figures of German planes in action in the south of city. Communications failures meant Koller was unable to provide them. Hitler rang once more, this time wanting to know why the jets based near Prague had not been operational the previous day. Koller explained that enemy fighters had attacked the airfields so persistently that the jets had been unable to take off. 'Then we don't need the jets any more. The Luftwaffe is superfluous,' Hitler had replied in fury. 'The entire Luftwaffe leadership should be hanged straight away!'

II

The drowning man clutched at yet another straw. The Soviets had extended their lines so far to the north-east of Berlin that it opened up the chance, thought Hitler and Chief of Staff Krebs, for the Panzer Corps led by SS-Obergruppenführer Felix Steiner to launch a counter-attack with good chances of success. A flurry of telephone calls with more than a hint of near-hysteria assigned a motley variety of remaining units, including naval and Luftwaffe forces untrained in ground warfare and without heavy armour, to Steiner's command. 'Every commander withholding forces has forfeited his life within five hours,' Hitler screamed at Koller. 'The commanders must know that. You yourself guarantee with your head that the last man is deployed.' Any retreat to the west was strictly forbidden to Steiner's forces. Officers unwilling to obey were to be shot immediately. 'On the success of your assignment depends the fate of the German capital,' Hitler told Steiner – adding that the commander's life also hinged on the execution of the order. At the same time, Busse's 9th Army, to the south of Berlin, was ordered to restabilize and reinforce the defensive line from Königswusterhausen to Cottbus. In addition, aided by a northward push of parts of Schörner's Army Group Centre, still doggedly fighting in the vicinity of Elsterwerda, around sixty miles south of Berlin, it was to attack and cut off Konev's tank forces that had broken through to their rear. It was an illusory hope. But Hitler's false optimism was still being pandered to by some of the generals. His mood visibly brightened after hearing upbeat reports from his most recent field-marshal, Schörner (who had been promoted on 5 April), and from General Wenck about the chances of his newly constructed 12th Army attacking American forces on the Elbe.

Colonel-General Heinrici, Commander of Army Group Vistula, was not one of the eternal optimists who played to Hitler's constant need for good news. He warned of encirclement if the 9th Army were not pulled back. He threatened resignation if Hitler persisted in his orders.

But Hitler did persist; and Heinrici did not resign. The general had implied to Speer days earlier that Berlin would be taken without serious resistance. This thinking was anathema to Hitler. He told Jodl on the day his orders to Steiner and to the 9th Army went out: 'I will fight as long as I have a single soldier. When the last soldier deserts me, I will shoot myself.' Late that night, he still exuded confidence in Steiner's attack. When Koller told him of the inadequacies of the Luftwaffe troops he had been compelled to supply to Steiner's forces, Hitler replied: 'You will see. The Russians will suffer the greatest defeat, the bloodiest defeat in their history before the gates of the city of Berlin.'

It was bravado. Two hours earlier, Dr Morell had found him drained and dejected in his study. The doctor and his medications, however little efficacious in an objective sense, had been for years an important psychological prop for Hitler. Now, Morell wanted to give him a harm-less further dose of glucose. Without any forewarning, Hitler reacted in an uncontrollable outburst, accusing Morell of wanting to drug him with morphine. He knew, he said, that the generals wanted to have him drugged so that they could ship him off to Berchtesgaden. 'Do you take me for a madman?' Hitler railed. Threatening to have him shot, he furiously dismissed the quivering doctor.

The storm had been brewing for days. It burst on the afternoon of 22 April, during the briefing that began at 3.30 p.m. Even as the briefing began, Hitler looked haggard, stony-faced, though extremely agitated, as if his thoughts were elsewhere. He twice left the room to go to his private quarters. Then, as dismaying news came through that Soviet troops had broken the inner defence cordon and were within Berlin's northern suburbs, Hitler was finally told – after a frantic series of telephone calls had elicited contradictory information – that Steiner's attack, which he had impatiently awaited all morning, had not taken place after all. At this, he seemed to snap. He ordered everyone out of the briefing room, apart from Keitel, Jodl, Krebs, and Burgdorf. Even for those who had long experience of Hitler's furious outbursts, the tirade which thundered through the bunker for the next half an hour was a shock. One who witnessed it reported that evening: 'Some-thing broke inside me today that I still can't grasp.' Hitler screamed that he had been betrayed by all those he had trusted. He railed at the long-standing treachery of the army. Now, even the SS was lying to him: after Sepp Dietrich's failure in Hungary, Steiner had not attacked.

The troops would not fight, he ranted, the anti-tank defences were down. As Jodl added, he also knew that munitions and fuel would shortly run out.

Hitler slumped into his chair. The storm subsided. His voice fell to practically a whimper. The war was lost, he sobbed. It was the first time any of his small audience had heard him admit it. They were dumbstruck. He had therefore determined to stay in Berlin, he went on, and to lead the defence of the city. He was physically incapable of fighting himself, and ran the risk of falling wounded into the hands of the enemy. So he would at the last moment shoot himself. All prevailed upon him to change his mind. He should leave Berlin forthwith and move his head-quarters to Berchtesgaden. The troops should be withdrawn from the western front and deployed in the east. Hitler replied that everything was falling apart anyway. He could not do that. Göring could do it. Someone objected that no soldier would fight for the Reich Marshal. 'What does it mean: fight!' asked Hitler. 'There's not much more to fight for, and if it's a matter of negotiations the Reich Marshal can do that better than I can.'

At this, Hitler, his face a deathly pallor, left the briefing room and retreated to his own quarters. He sent for his remaining secretaries, Gerda Christian and Traudl Junge, and his dietician, Constanze Manziarly. Eva Braun was also present as he told his staff they should get ready; a plane would take them south in an hour. 'It's all lost,' he said, 'hopelessly lost.' Somewhat to their own surprise, his secretaries found themselves rejecting the offer to leave and telling Hitler that they would stay with him in the bunker. Eva Braun had already told Hitler she was not leaving.

Urgent telephone calls were meanwhile put through from Dönitz and Himmler. Neither could persuade him to change his mind. Ribbentrop arrived. He was not even allowed to see Hitler. Goebbels was also present. Hitler, highly disturbed, had telephoned him around five o'clock, raving about treachery, betrayal, and cowardice. Goebbels hurried as fast as he could to the bunker, and spoke a while alone with Hitler. He was able to calm him down. Goebbels emerged to announce that on the Führer's orders, he, his wife, and his children would be moving into the bunker and living there from now on. For the Propaganda Minister, Hitler's decision was the logical consequence of his consistent stance; he saw it in full pathos as a historic deed which determined the heroic end in Berlin of a latter-day Siegfried, betrayed by all around him.

For hard-headed military men like Karl Koller, the perspective was very different: Hitler was abandoning the German people at the time of their greatest need; he had renounced his responsibility to armed forces, state, and people at the most critical moment; it was dereliction of duty worse than many offences for which draconian retribution had been meted out.

There were indeed serious practical considerations following from Hitler's hysterical behaviour. He had simply said he was staying in Berlin. The others should leave and go where they wanted. He had no further orders for the Wehrmacht. But he was still supreme commander. Who was now to give orders? Berlin was doomed for certain within a few days. So where were Wehrmacht Headquarters to be? How could forces simply be withdrawn from the western front without any armistice negotiations? After fruitless pleading with Hitler, Keitel decided to travel to the headquarters of General Wenck's 12th Army. Hitler had finally agreed to sign an order to Wenck to abandon his previous operational plans – defending against the Americans on the Elbe – and march on Berlin, linking up with the remnants of the 9th Army, still fighting to the south of the city. The aim was to cut off enemy forces to the south-west of the capital, drive forward 'and liberate again the Reich capital where the Führer resides, trusting in his soldiers'. Wenck's army had been hastily put together at the beginning of April. It was inadequately armed; its panzer support was weak; and many of its troops were poorly trained. They were outnumbered by the Soviet troops facing them, and possessed only a quarter of the weaponry. What Wenck was supposed to do in the unlikely event of breaking through to the centre of Berlin – other than bringing out Hitler, if need be by force (as Keitel later put it) – was left entirely unclear.

Hitler, his equilibrium now temporarily restored, was solicitous enough to make sure that Keitel was well fed before he set out on his journey. Jodl was meanwhile to take steps to ensure that part of the High Command of the Wehrmacht was immediately transferred to Berchtesgaden, while the remainder would be moved to the barracks at Krampnitz, near Potsdam. Hitler's overall direction would remain intact, maintained through telephone links to Krampnitz and Berchtesgaden. The regular briefings would continue, though with reduced personnel.

Meanwhile, Hitler had ordered Schaub to burn all the papers and documents in his private safe in the bunker. He was afterwards instructed to do the same in Munich and at the Berghof. After a perfunctory farewell from the master he had served for twenty years, he left Berlin and flew south. The bunker company had by now shrunk. Those left behind consoled themselves with drink. They referred to the bunker as 'the mortuary' and its inmates as 'a show house of living corpses'. Their main topic of conversation was when and how to commit suicide.

Remarkably, Hitler had regained his composure by the next morning. He was still venting anger at troops that seemed to have evaporated into thin air. 'It's so disgraceful,' he fumed. 'When you think about it all, why still live!' But Keitel's news about his meeting with Wenck had provided yet another glimmer of hope. Hitler ordered all available troops, however ill-equipped, to be added to Wenck's army. Dönitz had already been cabled the previous evening to have all available sailors as the most urgent priority, overriding all naval concerns, flown to Berlin to join the 'German battle of fate' in the Reich capital. Telegrams were also dispatched to Himmler, and to Luftwaffe high command to send their remaining reserves to aid the reinforcement of Berlin. 'The enemy knows I'm here,' Hitler added, referring to Goebbels's proclamation to the Berlin people that day, telling them that the Führer would remain in the city to lead its defence. They would concentrate all their efforts on taking the capital as soon as possible. But that, thought Hitler, gave him a chance to lure them into the trap of Wenck's army. Krebs reckoned they still had four days. 'In four days the business has to be decided,' agreed Hitler.

That afternoon, Albert Speer arrived back in the bunker. He had had a tortuous ten-hour journey to cover less than 200 miles from Hamburg. He had quickly given up an attempt to drive along roads choked with refugees desperate to leave Berlin by any route still open, and flew first to the airfield at Rechlin in Mecklenburg, then on to Gatow aerodrome in the west of Berlin. There, he picked up a Fieseler Storch light aircraft, eventually navigating a landing on the East-West Axis approaching the Brandenburg Gate, the wide boulevard on which he had triumphantly paraded six years earlier during Hitler's fiftieth birthday celebrations, now, its lamp-posts removed, converted into a makeshift landing-strip. For weeks, Speer had been working with industrialists and generals to sabotage Hitler's 'scorched earth' orders. Only two days earlier, in

Hamburg, he had recorded an address – never, in the event, broadcast, and probably made with more than one eye on embellishing his own prospects in a world after Hitler – urging an end to the pointless destruction. But despite the growing alienation, Speer could still not break free of Hitler. The emotional bonds remained strong. After his unsung departure on the evening of Hitler's birthday, the former Armaments Minister felt unhappy at ending their special relationship without an appropriate farewell. That was the reason for his wholly unnecessary, extremely hazardous flight back into the cauldron.

On his way to Hitler's room in the bunker, he encountered Bormann. Not anxious to end his own days in the bunker catacombs, the Secretary to the Führer implored Speer to use his influence to persuade Hitler to leave for the south. It was still just possible. In a few more hours it would be too late. Speer gave a non-committal reply. He was then ushered in to see Hitler, who, as Bormann had foreseen, lost no time in asking Speer's opinion whether he should stay in Berlin or fly to Berchtesgaden. Speer did not hesitate. It would be better to end his life as Führer in the Reich capital than in his 'weekend house', he said. Hitler looked tired, apathetic, resigned, burnt out. He had decided to stay in Berlin, he murmured. He had just wanted to hear Speer's opinion. As the previous day, he said he would not fight. There was the danger that he would be captured alive. He was also anxious to avoid his body falling into the hands of his enemy to be displayed as a trophy. So he had given orders to have his body burnt. Eva Braun would die alongside him. 'Believe me, Speer,' he added, 'it will be easy to end my life. A brief moment, and I am freed from everything, released from this miserable existence.'

Minutes later, in the briefing – by now a far smaller affair, over much more quickly, and, because of communications difficulties, often lacking precise, up-to-date intelligence – Hitler, immediately after speaking of his imminent death and cremation, was again trying to exude optimism. Only now did Speer realize how much of an act the role of Führer had always been.

All at once, there was a commotion in the corridor. Bormann hurried in with a telegram for Hitler. It was from Göring. The report of the momentous meeting the previous day, which Koller had personally flown to Berchtesgaden to deliver verbally, had placed the Reich Marshal in a quandary. Koller had helped persuade a hesitant Göring that, through his actions, Hitler had in effect given up the leadership of state and Wehrmacht. As a consequence, the edict of 29 June 1941, nominating Göring as his successor in the event of his incapacity to act, ought to come into force. Göring was still unsure. He could not be certain that Hitler had not changed his mind; and he worried about the influence of his arch-enemy, Bormann. Eventually, Koller suggested sending a telegram. Göring agreed. Koller, advised by Lammers, drafted its careful wording, cautiously stipulating that, had Göring not heard by ten o'clock that evening, he would presume that the terms of the succession law would come into operation, and that he would take over the entire leadership of the Reich. He would take immediate steps, he told Koller, to surrender to the western powers, though not to the Russians.

His telegram to Hitler (with a copy to Below, the Luftwaffe adjutant still in the bunker) gave no inkling of disloyalty. But, as Göring had feared, Bormann was immediately at work to place the worst possible construction upon it. Hitler seemed at first unconcerned, or apathetic. But when Bormann produced another telegram from Göring, summoning Ribbentrop to see him immediately, should he have received no other directive from Hitler or himself by midnight, it was an easy matter to invoke the spectre of treachery once more. Bormann was pushing at an open door. For months, Goebbels (and Bormann himself) had been the most prominent among those urging Hitler to dismiss Göring, portrayed as an incompetent, corrupt, drug-taking sybarite, single-handedly responsible for the debacle of the Luftwaffe and the air-superiority of the Allies, which they saw as so decisive for Germany's plight. Given Hitler's extreme volatility, as the events of the previous day had demonstrated only too plainly, the uncontrolled torrent of rage at Göring's ruination of the Luftwaffe, his corruption, and his morphine addiction was utterly predictable.

Savouring his victory, Bormann swiftly drew up a telegram, stripping Göring of his rights of succession, accusing him of treason, but refraining from further measures if the Reich Marshal resigned all his offices forthwith on health grounds. Göring's agreement was received within half an hour. But that evening, the once most powerful man in the Reich after Hitler was nevertheless put under house-arrest, the Berghof surrounded by SS guards. Hitler's power was fading fast; but it was not yet finally at an end.

Late that night, before leaving the bunker, Speer sat in Eva Braun's room, drinking a bottle of Moët & Chandon and eating cakes and sweets. Eva seemed calm and relaxed. She told Speer that Hitler had wanted to send her back to Munich, but she had refused; she had come to Berlin to end it. At three in the morning, Hitler appeared. Speer felt emotional at saying farewell. He had flown back to the bunker precisely for this purpose. It was, for him, a poignant moment. Hitler proffered a weak handshake. 'You're going then. Good. Good-bye.' That was all.

Another visitor besides Speer had arrived in the bunker unannounced the previous evening: General Helmuth Weidling, commander of the 56th Panzer Corps, attached to the 9th Army fighting to the south-east of Berlin. Communications had been lost with him since the evening of 20 April, and Hitler had ordered him arrested for desertion. Astonishingly, he had made his way back to Berlin, and into the Führer Bunker, to protest his innocence. Hitler was impressed. Next morning, he made Weidling responsible for Berlin's defence, replacing Colonel Ernst Kaether, who had held the post for all of two days.

It was a daunting assignment. Weidling had at his disposal units rapidly patched together, comprising 44,600 soldiers, along with 42,500 Volkssturm men (whose fighting capabilities were severely limited on account both of their age and their miserable equipment), around 2,700 boys from the Hitler Youth, and a few hundred other 'combatants' from the Labour Service and Organisation Todt, assigned to defend the bridges that Wenck's relieving army would have to cross. A further 5,500 sailors had been promised by Dönitz, but were not yet available. Facing them, and closing in on the city by the hour, were some 2½ million combat troops in crack divisions of the Red Army. Weidling knew from the start that his task was an impossible one.

The news from the ever-narrowing fronts around Berlin was meanwhile becoming ever grimmer. By midday on 24 April, Soviet troops from Zhukov's and Konev's armies had met up in the southern suburbs of the city. The encirclement of Busse's 9th Army was complete. Hopes of it fighting its way through to the west to join Wenck's 12th Army – still only in the preparatory stage of its march on the capital – were now illusory. Reports were reaching the Reich Chancellery of bitter street fighting in eastern and southern districts of the capital. Several districts to the north were already in Soviet hands, and the Nauen road, the last main road to the west, was blocked by T34 tanks. Tempelhof aerodrome, close to the city centre, had been bombarded by Soviet artillery since lunchtime. By the evening, Gatow airfield on the banks of the Havel to the west of Berlin had also come under heavy shelling. The East-West Axis, where Albert Speer had landed the previous day, was in practice now Berlin's last remaining thin artery of non-telephonic communication with the outside world.

By dawn next morning, areas close to the city centre had started to come under persistent and intense artillery fire. Around midday, the spearhead of Konev's army, skirting round Berlin to the south, met up with forward units from Zhukov's army, heading round the city to the north, at Ketzin in the west. Berlin was as good as encircled. About the same time, Soviet and American troops were smoking cigarettes together at Torgau, on the Elbe, in central Germany. The Reich was now cut in two.

Symbolically – there was absolutely no military purpose to the operation (other than striking at the possible focus of continued Nazi guerrilla warfare after formal cessation of hostilities from what transpired to be a mythical 'National Redoubt') – Hitler's alpine palace, the Berghof, above Berchtesgaden, had been reduced to smouldering ruins by RAF bombers that morning.

In his ever more isolated and beleaguered underground lair, with communications rapidly worsening, and with operational charts increasingly out of date and almost immediately overtaken by events, Hitler was still sure that he knew best. 'The situation in Berlin looks worse than it is,' he stated, with apparent confidence, on 25 April, having not ventured out of doors for five days. He ordered the city combed for all possible last reserves of manpower to throw into the fray and help prepare the ground from within for the arrival of Wenck. By this time, Wenck had made some advance towards the lakes south of Potsdam. But parts of his army were still engaged in combat with the Americans to the west, on the Elbe north of Wittenberg. And only remnants were by now left of the 9th Army, which was to have joined forces with him. With what he had at his disposal, Wenck had only the remotest chance of reaching Berlin.

But Wenck was now the only hope. Hitler was still looking for one final victory, one last chance to turn the tables on his enemies. Even now, he clung to the belief that the Alliance against him would fall apart if he could deliver a stinging blow to the Red Army. 'I think the moment has come when out of self-preservation-drive the others will confront in any case this hugely swollen proletarian Bolshevik colossus and moloch . . . If I can be successful here and hold the capital, perhaps the hope will grow among the English and Americans that they could maybe still face this whole danger together with a Nazi Germany. And the only man for this is me,' he asserted.

His comments to Goebbels that day were in part still apparently directed at convincing himself that his decision not to go to south Germany and to stay in Berlin was the right one. 'I'd regard it as a thousand times more cowardly to commit suicide on the Obersalzberg than to stand and fall here,' he stated. 'They shouldn't say: "You, as the Führer . . ." I'm only the Führer as long as I can lead. And I can't lead through sitting somewhere on a mountain, but have to have authority over armies that obey. Let me win a victory here, however difficult and tough, then I've a right again to do away with the sluggish elements who are constantly causing an obstruction. Then I'll work with the generals who've proved themselves.'

More than anything, Hitler's words were aimed at his place in history. Even now – egged on, naturally, by Goebbels – he remained the propagandist, looking to image. Whether leading to glorious victory, or sacrificial self-destruction, the last stand in the bunker was necessary for prestige purposes. It never occurred to him to question the continued slaughter of soldiers and civilians to that end. 'Only here can I attain a success,' he told Goebbels, '. . . and even if it's only a moral one, it's at least the possibility of saving face and winning time.' 'Only through a heroic attitude can we survive this hardest of times,' he went on. If he won the 'decisive battle' he would be 'rehabilitated'. It would prove by example that he had been right in dismissing generals for not holding their ground.

And if he were to lose, then he would have perished 'decently', not like some 'inglorious refugee sitting in Berchtesgaden and issuing useless orders from there'. He saw, he said, 'a possibility of repairing history' through gaining a success. 'It's the only chance to restore personal reputation . . . If we leave the world stage in disgrace, we'll have lived for nothing. Whether you continue your life a bit longer or not is completely immaterial. Rather end the struggle in honour than continue in shame and dishonour a few months or years longer.' Goebbels, with

Frederick the Great's exploits at the famous Battle of Leuthen – the Prussian King's epic victory in 1757 over an Austrian army far superior in numbers – tripping once more from his tongue, summed up the 'heroic' alternatives: 'If all goes well, then it's in any case good. If things don't go well and the Führer finds in Berlin an honourable death and Europe were to become bolshevized, then in five years at the latest the Führer would be a legendary personality and National Socialism would have attained mythical status.'

III

Not everyone in the maze of tunnels below the Reich Chancellery was looking to share the 'heroic' end that Hitler and Goebbels were contemplating. 'I don't want to die with that lot down there in the bunker,' thirty-one-year-old Major Bernd von Freytag-Loringhoven, Krebs's tall adjutant, uttered. 'When it comes to the end, I want my head above ground and free.' Even the SS men from Hitler's bodyguard were anxiously asking about Wenck's progress, consoling themselves with drink when off duty, and looking for possible exit-routes from what looked more and more like a certain grave. In the streets above, despite the threat – often carried out – of summary execution by 'flying courts-martial' for 'defeatism', let alone desertion, many elderly Volkssturm men, aware of the utter futility of carrying on such a hopeless unequal fight and looking to avoid a pointless 'hero's' death, sought any opportunity at the approach of Soviet troops to melt away and try to rejoin families taking what refuge they could in cellars and bunkers.

Amid the burning ruins of the great city, living conditions were deteriorating rapidly. Food was running out. The water-supply system had broken down. The old, infirm, wounded, women and children, injured soldiers, refugees, all clung on to life in the cellars, in packed shelters, and in underground stations as hell raged overhead.

As communications increasingly petered out – the lines to Jodl at OKH headquarters went dead for a time in the course of the evening – 'intelligence' of troop movements in the city was gathered for the once-mighty Army High Command in the bunker by using the telephone directory to ring numbers at random. 'Excuse me, madam, have you seen the Russians?' ran the question. 'Yes,' would come a reply, 'half an hour ago two of them were here. They were part of a group of about a dozen tanks at the crossroads.'

Despite the uneven contest, the regular troops, mostly insufficiently trained and badly equipped, often down to their last reserves of ammunition, continued the bitter struggle in Berlin's streets. By the evening of 26 April, Soviet soldiers were close to Alexanderplatz, the very heart of the city. The Reich Chancellery in the government district, under heavy fire all day, was now less than a mile away.

A fresh moment of excitement gripped the inmates of the bunker during the early evening: the unexpected arrival of the wounded Colonel-General of the Luftwaffe Robert Ritter von Greim, and his glamorous female companion, twenty years his junior, the flying-ace and test pilot Hanna Reitsch. Both were fervent, long-standing admirers of Hitler. Greim had been summoned two days earlier to Berlin. He and Reitsch had had to risk an extremely hazardous flight from Munich. Greim's foot had been injured when their Fieseler Storch had been hit by artillery fire on approach to the centre of Berlin, and Reitsch had grabbed the controls and brought the plane down safely on the East-West Axis. They had then requisitioned a car to bring them to the Reich Chancellery. Propped up by Reitsch, the wounded Greim now limped painfully into the bunker. He still did not know why he had come.

Once his foot had been bandaged, Hitler came in to tell him. After railing at Göring's 'betrayal', Hitler informed Greim that he was promoting him to Field-Marshal and appointing him as the new head of the Luftwaffe. It could all have been done by telephone. Instead, Greim had had to risk life and limb to receive the news in person. And, it seemed likely, he and Reitsch were now doomed to end their lives in the bunker. But far from being infuriated or depressed, or both, Greim and Reitsch were exhilarated. They begged to stay in the bunker with Hitler. They were given phials of poison, should the worst happen. But Hitler persuaded Greim that all was not lost. 'Just don't lose faith,' Koller heard Greim say, when he telephoned the bunker. 'It'll all come to a good end. The meeting with the Führer and his vigour have given me extraordinary new strength. It's like the fountain of youth here.' Koller thought it sounded more like a madhouse.

The briefing sessions were by this time much reduced in size and changed in character. Krebs was now the only senior military figure present. Goebbels had joined since taking up residence in the bunker.

Hitler Youth Leader Axmann, General Weidling (responsible for the defence of Berlin), Vice-Admiral Voß (Dönitz's liaison), Colonel Nicolaus von Below (the long-serving Luftwaffe adjutant), and SS-Brigadeführer Wilhelm Mohnke, just appointed by Hitler as commandant of the government quarter of Berlin (which had been dubbed 'The Citadel') were also present.

Discussion at the first meeting on 27 April, in the early hours, centred on the prospects of Wenck breaking through. He had reached the outskirts of Potsdam. But he had only three divisions at his disposal. He desperately needed reinforcements. The chances of Busse's beleaguered 9th Army forcing their way north-westwards to join him were now slim in the extreme. But there were still hopes that troops under Lieutenant-General Rudolf Holste, to the north-west of Berlin, might fight their way south to link up with Wenck. Time was short. Krebs reported heavy street-fighting in the heart of the city. The Soviets had advanced on Alexanderplatz. They would soon have Potsdamer Platz in their sights; and that was where the bunker was situated. 'May God let Wenck come!' intoned Goebbels. 'A dreadful situation crosses my mind,' he added, grimly. 'Wenck is located at Potsdam, and here the Soviets are pressing on Potsdamer Platz!' 'And I'm not in Potsdam, but in Potsdamer Platz,' commented Hitler laconically.

His assessment of the situation was realistic: Wenck's three divisions were not enough. They might suffice to take Potsdam, but they were only infantry divisions, lacking panzer support, and not capable of breaking their way through the Soviet tank units. Voß breathed encouragement. 'Wenck will get here, my Führer! It's only a question of whether he can do it alone.' It was enough for Hitler to lapse into a new reverie. 'You've got to imagine. That'll spread like wildfire through the whole of Berlin when it's known: a German army has broken through in the west and established contact with the Citadel.' The Soviets, he thought, had suffered great losses, were suffering even more in the intense house-to-house fighting, and could only throw more troops into exposed forward positions. The thought sufficed: he had convinced himself that the situation was not wholly bleak. The constant explosions had kept him awake in recent nights. But he would sleep better tonight, he said. He only wanted to be awakened 'if a Russian tank is standing in front of my cabin' so that he had time to do what was necessary.

The second briefing of the day began with Mohnke announcing that the first enemy tanks had managed to penetrate to the Wilhelmplatz, the heart of the government quarter. They had been repulsed – on this occasion – but time was running out. Krebs reckoned the bunker residents had no more than about twenty-four to twenty-six hours; the link-up between the armies of Wenck and Busse had to take place within that time if there was to be any hope. Hitler inwardly knew, however, that this would not happen. He repeatedly bemoaned 'the catastrophic mistake' of the 9th Army, which he blamed for ignoring his orders and trying to penetrate the Soviet lines in the wrong direction. The faint hopes from the remaining forces in the north, those of Holste and Steiner (in whom Hitler had lost all confidence days earlier), were now also – realistically, if not in dreams – largely abandoned.

Despite a desperate plea from Keitel to throw everything into the relief of Berlin, Jodl had diverted the hard-pressed units of Holste and Steiner to fend off Soviet forces to the north of the capital. It was tantamount to giving up on Berlin. Bormann scathingly commented in his diary, in remarks pointedly directed at Reichsführer-SS Himmler's recognized reluctance to deploy Steiner's SS corps to help save Berlin: 'The divisions marching to our relief are held up by Himmler-Jodl! *We* will stand and fall with the Führer: loyal into death. Others believe they have to act "from *higher* insight". They sacrifice the Führer, and their lack of loyalty – shame on them – matches their "feeling of honour".'

Hitler and Goebbels relapsed into reminiscences. They were prompted by Mohnke's remark, entirely without irony: 'We haven't quite brought about what we wanted in 1933, my Führer!' Hitler's explanation – it had scarcely been in his mind at the time – was that he had come to power too early. A year or more later, at Hindenburg's death, would have been the right time. To bring about a complete revolution, the old system needed to have revealed itself as utterly bankrupt. As it was, he had been forced to compromise with Hugenberg, Schleicher – not much of a compromise since the former Reich Chancellor had, in fact, been murdered by Hitler's henchmen at the time of the 'Röhm affair' in 1934 – and other pillars of the old order. By the time of Hindenburg's death, Hitler went on, the determination to rid himself of the conservatives had lessened, and the work of reconstruction was under way. 'Otherwise, thousands would have been eliminated at that time,' he declared. 'It could have happened, if I had come to power through an express will of the people' – presumably meaning a presidential election – 'or through a putsch. You regret it afterwards that you are so good,' he concluded.

This took the discussion inexorably once more back into pathos and an evocation of 'heroism'. He was staying in Berlin, Hitler said, 'so that I have more moral right to act against weakness ... I can't constantly threaten others if I run away myself from the Reich capital at the critical hour ... I've had the right to command in this city. Now I must obey the commands of fate. Even if I could save myself, I won't do it. The captain also goes down with his ship.' Voß, predictably, picked up the metaphor. Pathos and emotion got the better of him, too. 'Here in the Reich Chancellery it's just like the command-bridge of a ship,' he implausibly ruminated. 'One thing here applies to all. We don't want to get away.' (He would, ultimately, like most of the others, nevertheless seek to flee the bunker at the last moment.) 'We belong together. It's only a matter of being an upright community.'

IV

The news trickling in during the day could scarcely have been worse. Wenck's troops, without assistance from the 9th Army (whose encirclement was by now accepted as practically a foregone conclusion), had been pushed back south of Potsdam. There was a 'doomsday' mood in the bunker, alleviated only by copious supplies of alcohol and food from the Reich Chancellery cellars. Hitler told Below he had decided to give Weidling, the Commandant of Berlin, the order to break out. All his staff should go, as well as Bormann and Goebbels. He would stay behind and die in the capital. By evening, amid worsening news, he had changed his mind. An attempt to break out would be useless. He gave Below a poison-capsule, should it come to 'a difficult situation'.

The fate of the encircled 9th Army, with its eleven divisions almost four times as strong as the forces at Wenck's disposal, took Hitler back, like a long-playing record, at the third briefing of the day to what he saw as constant disobedience and disloyalty in the army. Only Schörner, commander of Army Group Centre, was singled out for praise as 'a true warlord'. Dönitz, too, stood in high favour for holding to his promise to send naval units to the defence of Berlin, and to Hitler's personal protection. The faint hope in Wenck was still not totally extinguished. But Hitler was looking to the last stand in the 'Citadel'.

Firm command and reliable troops for the defence of the 'Citadel' were vital. His fear of capture surfaced again. 'I must have the absolute certainty,' he said, following news that enemy tanks had for a short time forced their way into Wilhelmstraße, 'that I will not be dragged out through some crafty trick by a Russian tank.' He saw it as only a question of time before the Soviets brought up heavy artillery to shell the 'Citadel' from close range. 'It's a matter then of a heroic struggle for a last small island,' he commented. 'If the relief doesn't arrive, we have to be clear: it's no bad end to a life to fall in the struggle for the capital of your Reich.'

Not everyone was willing to join a suicide pact. Hermann Fegelein, the swashbuckling, womanizing, cynical opportunist who had risen to high position in the SS through Himmler's favour then sealed his bonds to Hitler's 'court' through marrying Eva Braun's sister, had disappeared from the bunker. His absence was noticed on 27 April. And that evening he was discovered in civilian clothes in his apartment in Charlottenburg, worse the wear from drink, and with a good deal of money in bags packed for departure. He rang Eva Braun to have his sister-in-law intercede. (It seems, in fact, that he may have been more attracted to Eva Braun than he was to her sister; and that he had been in touch with her beforehand from his apartment, attempting to persuade her to leave the bunker before it was too late.) But it was to no avail. He was hauled back into the Reich Chancellery that evening in deep disgrace, stripped of his epaulettes and collar flashes, reduced to the ranks, and kept in an improvised cell until Hitler was ready to see him.

In the early hours of 28 April, despairing calls were made from the bunker to Keitel and Jodl urging all conceivable effort to be made to relieve Berlin as absolute priority. Time was of the essence. There were at most forty-eight hours, it was thought. 'If no help comes within that time, it will be too late,' Krebs told Keitel. 'The Führer passes that on again!!!' From Wenck, there was nothing but silence.

As so often, the bunker inmates thought they smelled the scent of disloyalty and treason. Bormann telegraphed Puttkamer that evening: 'Instead of spurring on the troops who should liberate us with orders and appeals, the men in authority are silent. Loyalty has given way to disloyalty. We remain here. The Reich Chancellery is already a heap of ruins.' In his desk diary, the entry was of high treason and betrayal of the country.

An hour later, the suspicions seemed dramatically confirmed. Heinz Lorenz appeared in the bunker. He had just picked up a message from Reuters, sent by the BBC in London and confirmed in Stockholm. He gave one copy to Bormann, whom he found sitting with Goebbels and Hewel. The other copy he handed to Linge to pass on to Hitler. It confirmed the truth of a disturbing story broadcast in the morning news of Radio Stockholm, relayed to Hitler in mid-afternoon, though initially seeming to lack substance: that the Reichsführer-SS, Heinrich Himmler, had offered to surrender to the western Allies, but that this had been declined. Hitler had at first received the news of Himmler's discussions about capitulation 'with complete contempt'. He had immediately telephoned Admiral Dönitz, who had said he knew nothing of it. Dönitz then in turn contacted Himmler, who categorically denied the report and recommended ignoring it rather than putting out a denial on the radio. But Hitler continued to brood on it. Perhaps he was expecting something of the sort. His distrust of Himmler had grown in recent weeks. The disobedience, as he saw it, of Sepp Dietrich in Hungary and of Felix Steiner in the failure to attempt the relief of Berlin showed, it seemed, that even the SS were now disloyal to him. As the day wore on, so it appeared to Below, Hitler's bitterness towards Himmler mounted.

And now it all fell into place: the earlier story had been correct, and Himmler's denial a lie. More than that: the Reuters report had added that 'Himmler had informed the western Allies that he could implement an unconditional surrender and support it.' It amounted to an implication that the Reichsführer-SS was now de facto head of state, that Hitler had been disempowered. This was a bombshell. This could on no account be tolerated. This was base treason.

Whether Hitler had earlier been aware of Himmler's tentative steps towards the western powers through the intermediacy of Count Folke Bernadotte, Vice-President of the Swedish Red Cross and a close relative of the King of Sweden, is uncertain. The Reichsführer's dealings with Bernadotte had stretched back some two months. SS-Brigadeführer Walter Schellenberg, head of the Foreign Intelligence Service in the Reich Security Main Office, had instigated the meetings and acted as intermediary. Bernadotte's initial aim had been to bargain for the release of prisoners – particularly Scandinavians – from concentration camps. From Himmler's point of view, urged on by Schellenberg, Bernadotte offered a possible opening to the West. As Germany's military situation had drastically deteriorated, Himmler, still hesitant and evidently under great nervous strain, had become more amenable to gestures at humanitarian concessions aimed at showing himself in as good a light as possible. Like most Nazi leaders, he was looking to survive, not throw himself on the funeral pyre in the Berlin *Götterdämmerung*. In March, he had agreed, in contravention of Hitler's wishes, to allow concentration camps to be handed over to the approaching enemy, not destroyed. He had conceded the release of small numbers of Jews and other prisoners, to be sent to Switzerland and Sweden. At his second meeting with Bernadotte at the beginning of April, he had also consented to let Danish and Norwegian women and the sick in camps be taken to Sweden. At the same time, he still regarded the camp prisoners as his 'hostages' – bargaining counters in any negotiations with the West.

Bernadotte had brushed aside Schellenberg's suggestion – almost certainly prompted by Himmler – that he might sound out Eisenhower about the possibility of a surrender in the west. Such a proposition, Bernadotte had pointed out, had to come from the Reichsführer himself. Himmler was, however, in a state of chronic indecision as well as extreme nervous tension. He saw clearly the writing on the wall; the war was irredeemably lost. But he was well aware that Hitler would take Germany down into perdition with him rather than capitulate. Himmler, in common with most Nazi leaders, wanted to save his own skin. And he still hankered after some role in a post-Hitler settlement. As dogmatic as Hitler in the fight against Bolshevism, he harboured the notable illusion that the enemy might overlook his part in monstrous crimes against humanity because of his value to the continuation of the struggle against the mortal enemy not just of Germany, but also of the West. He could not, however, even now free himself from his bonds with Hitler. He still hankered after Hitler's favour, and was distressed at the way he had fallen into discredit after his failure as commander of Army Group Vistula. Not least: now, as before, he feared Hitler.

A third meeting with Bernadotte on 21 April, at which the Reichsführer-SS looked extremely drawn and in a highly nervous state, made no progress on the issue of overtures to the West. Himmler still remained ultra-cautious, unwilling to risk any initiative. Possibly, as Schellenberg later suggested, he had already decided by lunchtime on 22 April that the time had come to act, though this seems doubtful. What certainly convinced him was the news which Fegelein telephoned through to him from the Führer Bunker that day of Hitler's extraordinary fit of pent-up fury and his uncontrolled tirade against treachery on all sides – not least directed at the SS on account of Steiner's failure to launch the ordered counter-offensive – culminating in his announcement that he would stay and die in Berlin. At this, Himmler's indecision evaporated.

On 23 April, Count Bernadotte had agreed, somewhat reluctantly, to Schellenberg's suggestion to meet Himmler for a fourth time that evening. The meeting took place in the Swedish Consulate in Lübeck, eerily lit by candles because of a power cut. 'Hitler is very probably already dead,' Himmler began. At any rate, his end could be no more than a few days away. Before now, his oath of loyalty had prevented him from acting, Himmler went on. But with Hitler dead or on the verge of death, the situation was different. He now had a free hand. There could be no surrender to the Soviet Union. He was, and always would be, the sworn enemy of Bolshevism. He insisted that the struggle against Bolshevism must continue. But he was ready to declare Germany defeated by the western powers, and begged Bernadotte to pass his offer of capitulation to General Eisenhower in order to prevent further senseless destruction. Still by candlelight, Himmler drafted a letter to Sweden's Foreign Minister, to be handed to him by Bernadotte, and passed on to the western Allies.

Himmler, like Göring (if in a different way), had taken the news of Hitler's outburst on 22 April to imply the Führer's effective abdication. Like Göring, Himmler was soon to be disabused of such presumption. His immediate instinct, however, now that his own decision had been clarified, was to build a cabinet, invent (at Schellenberg's suggestion) the name for a new party – the 'Party of National Concentration' – and ponder whether he should bow or shake hands when he met Eisenhower. It apparently never occurred to him that his offer of capitulation might be turned down. But that outcome – as good as certain to all beyond the perimeters of the detached mental world of Nazi leaders at this juncture – was precisely what had happened by the time, during the course of the afternoon of 28 April, the sensational news filtered out that the Reichsführer-SS was willing to capitulate.

For Hitler, this was the last straw. That his 'loyal Heinrich', whose SS had as its motto 'My honour is loyalty', should now stab him in the back: this was the end. It was the betrayal of all betrayals. The bunker reverberated to a final elemental explosion of fury. All his stored-up venom was now poured out on Himmler in a last paroxysm of seething rage. It was, he screamed, 'the most shameful betrayal in human history'.

When the outburst subsided, Hitler retired to his rooms with Goebbels and Bormann for a lengthy discussion. As soon as he reappeared, he sent for the imprisoned Fegelein and subjected him to a fearsome verbal assault. Fegelein's recent disappearance now appeared to have sinister significance: joining the base treachery of the Reichsführer-SS. Hitler's paranoid suspicions were running riot. Possibly Himmler was plotting to assassinate him; or to hand him over to the enemy. And Fegelein was part of the plot. Out of consideration for Eva Braun, Hitler's first, relatively lenient, reaction to Fegelein's desertion had been to have her disgraced brother-in-law assigned to Mohnke's troops for the defence of Berlin. But Günsche and Bormann had persuaded Hitler to hand him over to a court martial instead. One was now hastily improvised. After the merest formalities, Fegelein was summarily sentenced to death, immediately taken out, then shot in the back by an SD man even before he could be put in front of a firing-squad. For some of the bunker inmates, there was a sense of shock that one from within the 'inner circle' was guilty of such 'betrayal', and had been so peremptorily dispatched. For Hitler, it was the closest he could come to revenge on the Reichsführer-SS himself.

V

By now, Soviet troops had forced their way into Potsdamer Platz and streets in the immediate vicinity of the Reich Chancellery. They were no more than a few hundred yards away. A breakdown in communications for most of the day had left the bunker inmates desperate for any news of Wenck's army (which remained, hemmed in, south of Potsdam). In the prevailing climate within the bunker, even the lapdog Keitel and the ever-reliable Jodl were now coming under suspicion of treachery for not bringing about the relief of Berlin.

Soon after midnight, following Fegelein's execution, Hitler commissioned Greim to deploy the Luftwaffe in making every effort to aid Wenck through attacks on Soviet positions blocking his route to Berlin. It was the faintest of faint hopes. He had a second commission for Greim – one, if anything, even more important. Greim was to leave Berlin and fly to Dönitz in Plön to ensure that the traitor, Himmler, was arrested – better still, liquidated forthwith. To this end, an Arado 96 training plane had been ordered to Berlin from Rechlin and, astonishingly, had defied all odds in touching down on the East-West Axis. Protesting their wish to stay with Hitler in the bunker, Greim, on crutches and far from recovered from his injured foot, and his companion Hanna Reitsch nonetheless accepted the commission, were driven in an armoured vehicle to the plane, waiting close to the Brandenburg Gate, managed to take off, and, even more remarkably, to negotiate the heavy Soviet anti-aircraft fire to fly to Rechlin, from where they later flew to Plön. The perilous journey was pointless. The few planes Greim was able to order into the defence of Berlin made not the slightest difference. And by the time he reached Dönitz's headquarters, the Grand Admiral had nothing to gain by having Himmler arrested, let alone shot. Even avoiding death in the bunker was no consolation to Greim and Reitsch. 'It is the greatest sorrow of our lives that we were not permitted to die with the Führer,' they chorused some days later. 'One should kneel in reverence at the altar of the Fatherland and pray.'

After Greim and Reitsch had left, Hitler became calmer. It was time to make preparations. As long as Hitler had had a future, he had ruled out marriage. His life, he had said, was devoted to Germany. There was no room for a wife. It had also been politically inconvenient. No one outside the inner circle was to know of Eva Braun's existence. She had been forced to accept that she was no more than an appendage, there when Hitler wanted her to be, stored well out of sight for the rest of the time. But she had chosen to come to the bunker. And she had refused Hitler's own entreaties to leave. She had committed herself to him once and for all, when others were deserting. The marriage now cost him nothing. He did it simply to please Eva Braun, to give her what she had wanted more than anything at a moment when marrying him was the least enviable fate in the world.

Eva Braun had dropped a hint earlier in the day that this would be her wedding night. Now, following the departure of Greim and Reitsch, not long after midnight on 29 April, in the most macabre surrounds, with the bunker shaking from nearby explosions, Hitler and Eva Braun exchanged married vows in the conference-room in front of one of Goebbels's minor officials, city councillor Walter Wagner, dressed in Nazi uniform with a Volkssturm armband, who had been brought to the bunker in an armoured car to conduct the bizarre ceremony. Goebbels and Bormann were witnesses. The rest of the staff waited outside to congratulate the newly wedded couple. Champagne, sandwiches, and reminiscences – with somewhat forced joviality – of happier days followed.

Just before the wedding ceremony, Hitler had asked his youngest secretary, Traudl Junge, to go with him to the room where his military conferences took place. It had been about 11.30 p.m. when he said that he wanted her to take down some dictation. She was still wondering what this might be at such a late hour when, leaning on the table, he started to dictate his last will and testament.

He began with a brief Private Testament. He referred first to his marriage to Eva Braun, and her decision to come to Berlin and die at his side. He disposed of his possessions to the party – or, should it no longer exist, to the state; he still hoped his collection of paintings would go to a gallery in Linz; and he appointed Martin Bormann as executor to see that relatives and his long-serving staff had some reward for their support.

He came to the more significant part. 'This is my political testament,' he declared. Traudl Junge paused for a moment, expectantly. But she had heard it all before. His last words for posterity were a piece of pure self-justification. The rhetoric is instantly recognizable, redolent of *Mein Kampf* and countless speeches; the central idea of the responsibility of international Jewry for the death, suffering, and destruction in the war remained unchanged, even as he himself now looked death in the face. 'It is untrue that I or anyone else in Germany wanted the war in 1939,' he dictated. 'It was desired and instigated exclusively by those international statesmen who were either of Jewish descent or who worked for Jewish interests . . . Centuries will pass away, but out of the ruins of our towns and cultural monuments the hatred will ever renew itself against those ultimately responsible whom we have to thank for everything: international Jewry and its helpers.' The conspiracy theory continued unabated. He attributed the rejection of his proposal on the eve of the attack on Poland partly to the business interests of 'leading circles in English politics', partly to the 'influence of propaganda organized by international Jewry'.

He came to a key passage – an oblique reference to the 'Final Solution' – relating once more to the fulfilment of the 'prophecy' of 1939: 'I also left no doubt that, if the nations of Europe are again to be regarded as mere blocks of shares of these international money and finance conspirators, then that race, too, which is really guilty of this murderous struggle, will be called to account: Jewry! I further left no one in doubt that this time millions of children of Europe's aryan peoples would not die of hunger, millions of grown men would not suffer death, and hundreds of thousands of women and children not be burnt and bombed to death in the towns, without the real culprit having to atone for his guilt, even if by more humane means.'

Despite all its setbacks, the six-year struggle, he went on, would one day go down in history as 'the most glorious and valiant manifestation of a nation's will to existence'. He himself could not forsake Berlin. The forces there were too small to hold out against the enemy and – the inevitable side-swipe against those deemed to have betrayed him – 'our own resistance is gradually devalued by deluded and characterless subjects'. He would choose death at the appropriate moment.

Again, he gave an indication of his own fear of what he saw as the still dominant power of the Jews: 'I do not wish to fall into the hands of enemies who, for the amusement of their whipped-up masses, will need a spectacle arranged by Jews.'

A renaissance of National Socialism, he avowed, would eventually emerge from the sacrifice of the soldiers and his own death alongside them. He ended with an exhortation to continue the struggle. He begged the heads of the armed forces to instil the spirit of National Socialism in the troops. His long-standing scapegoat, the officer corps of the army, did not even now go unscathed: 'May it at some time be part of the concept of honour of the German officer – as is already the case in our navy – that the surrender of a district or a town is impossible and that above all the leaders have to proceed here with a shining example in most loyal fulfilment of their duty unto death.'

In the second part of his Testament, Hitler went through the charade of nominating a successor government for what was left of the Reich. The tone was vindictive. Göring and Himmler were formally expelled from the party and from all their offices for the damage they had done through negotiating with the enemy 'without my knowledge and against my wishes', for attempting to take power in the state, and for disloyalty to his person. Nor was there any place in the new government for Speer. The new head of state and head of the armed forces was Grand Admiral

Dönitz – less of a surprise than at first sight, given his specially high standing in Hitler's eyes in the closing phase of the war, and in view particularly of the responsibility he had already been given a few days earlier for party and state affairs as well as military matters in the northern part of the country. Significantly, however, Dönitz was not to inherit the title of Führer. Instead, the title of Reich President, dropped in 1934 on Hindenburg's death, was reinvented. Goebbels, who had been pressing for so long for full control over internal affairs, was rewarded for his loyalty by being appointed Chancellor of a Reich that scarcely any longer existed. Bormann, another who had proved his loyalty, was made Party Minister. Goebbels – who, together with Bormann, kept bringing Fräulein Junge the names of further ministers for typing in the list – probably engineered the dismissal at this late point of his old adversary Ribbentrop, and his replacement as Foreign Minister by Arthur Seyß-Inquart. Hitler's favourite general, Schörner, was to be Commander-in-Chief of the Army, while Gauleiter Karl Hanke, still holding out in Breslau, was to take over from Himmler as Reichsführer-SS and Chief of the German Police. The tough Munich Gauleiter, Paul Giesler, was made Interior Minister, with Karl-Otto Saur replacing Speer as Minister for Armaments. The pointless job of Propaganda Minister fell to Goebbels's State Secretary, Werner Naumann. Old survivors included Schwerin-Krosigk (Finance), Funk (Economics), Thierack (Justice), and Herbert Backe (Agriculture). Hitler commissioned them with continuing the task – 'the work of coming centuries' – of building up a National Socialist state. 'Above all,' the Political Testament concluded, 'I charge the leadership of the nation and their subjects with the meticulous observance of the race-laws and the merciless resistance to the universal poisoner of all peoples, international Jewry.'

It was turned 4 a.m. when Goebbels, Bormann, Burgdorf, and Krebs signed the Political Testament, and Nicolaus von Below added his signature to the Private Testament.

Hitler, looking weary, took himself off to rest. He had completed the winding-up order on the Third Reich. Only the final act of self-destruction remained.

For Fräulein Junge, however, the night's secretarial duties were not yet over. Soon after Hitler had retired, Goebbels, in a highly emotional state, white-faced, tears running down his cheeks, appeared in the ante-room, where she was finishing her work. He asked her to draft his own coda to Hitler's will. Hitler, he said, had ordered him to leave Berlin as a member of the new government. But 'if the Führer is dead, my life is meaningless', he told her. Of all the Nazi leaders, Goebbels was the one who for weeks had assessed with some realism the military prospects, had repeatedly evoked the imagery of heroism, looking to his own place in the pantheon of Teutonic heroes, and had accordingly brought his wife and children to the bunker to die alongside their adored Leader in a final act of *Nibelungentreue*. It was, therefore, utterly consistent when he now dictated: 'For the first time in my life, I must categorically refuse to obey an order of the Führer.' His wife and children joined him in this refusal. He would, he continued, lose all self-respect – quite apart from the demands of personal loyalty – were he to 'leave the Führer alone in his hour of greatest need'. Betrayal was in his mind, as in that of his master. 'In the delirium of treachery, which surrounds the Führer in these critical days of the war,' he had Fräulein Junge type, 'there have to be at least a few who stay unconditionally loyal to him even unto death, even if this contradicts a formal, objectively well-founded order which finds expression in his Political Testament.' Consequently, he – together with his wife and children (who, were they old enough to judge, would be in agreement) – were firmly resolved not to leave the Reich capital 'and rather at the Führer's side to end a life which for me personally has no further value if it cannot be used in the service of the Führer and by his side'. It was 5.30 a.m. before this last act in the nocturnal drama closed.

VI

The mood in the bunker now sank to zero-level. Despair was now written on everyone's face. All knew it was only a matter of hours before Hitler killed himself, and wondered what the future held for them after his death. There was much talk of the best methods of committing suicide. Secretaries, adjutants, and any others who wanted them had by now been given the brass-cased ampoules containing prussic acid supplied by Dr Ludwig Stumpfegger, the SS surgeon who had joined the 'court' the previous October. Hitler's paranoia stretched now to doubts about the capsules. He had shown his alsatian bitch Blondi more affection in recent years than any human being, probably including even Eva Braun. Now, as the end approached, he had the poison tested on Blondi. Professor Werner Haase was summoned from his duties in the nearby public air-raid shelter beneath the New Reich Chancellery building nearby. Shortly before the afternoon briefing on 29 April, aided by Hitler's dog-attendant, Sergeant Fritz Tornow, he forced open the dog's jaws and crushed the prussic acid capsule with a pair of pliers. The dog slumped in an instant motionless to the ground. Hitler was not present. However, he entered the room immediately afterwards. He glanced for a few seconds at the dead dog. Then, his face like a mask, he left without saying anything and shut himself in his room.

The bunker community had by this time dwindled still further. Three emissaries – Bormann's adjutant, SS-Standartenführer Wilhelm Zander, Hitler's army adjutant Major Willi Johannmeier, and Acting Press Chief Heinz Lorenz – had left that morning as couriers on a perilous, and fruitless, mission to deliver copies of the Testament to Dönitz, Schörner, and the Nazi Party's headquarters, the 'Brown House' in Munich. By this time, normal telephone communications had finally broken down, though naval and party telegraph wires remained usable, with difficulty, to the end. But dispatch runners brought reports that Soviet troops had brought up their lines to a mere 400–500 metres from the Reich Chancellery. The Berlin Commandant General Weidling informed Hitler that they had begun a concentrated attack on the 'Citadel'; resistance could only be sustained for a short time. Three young officers, Major Bernd von Loringhoven (Krebs's adjutant), his friend Gerhard Boldt (the Chief of Staff's orderly), and Lieutenant-Colonel Rudolf Weiß (General Burgdorf's adjutant), decided to try a last chance to escape from their predestined tomb. They put it to Krebs that they should break out in the attempt to reach Wenck. He agreed; so, following the midday conference, did Hitler. As he shook hands wearily with them, he said: 'Give my regards to Wenck. Tell him to hurry or it will be too late.'

That afternoon, Below too, who had been a member of Hitler's 'household' since 1937, decided to try his luck. He asked if Hitler would permit him to attempt to get through to the west. Hitler readily agreed. Below left late that night, bearing a letter from Hitler to Keitel which, from Below's memory of it (the letter itself was destroyed), repeated his praise for the navy, his attribution of blame for the Luftwaffe's failure exclusively to Göring, and his condemnation of the General Staff

together with the disloyalty and betrayal which had for so long undermined his efforts. He could not believe, he said, that the sacrifices of the
German people had been in vain. The aim had still to be the winning of
territory in the East.

By this time, Hitler had learned that Mussolini had been captured and
executed by Italian partisans. Whether he was told the details – how
Mussolini had been hanged upside down in a square in Milan, together
with his mistress Clara Petacci, and stoned by a mob – is uncertain. If
he did learn the full gory tale, it could have done no more than confirm
his anxiety to take his own life before it was too late, and to prevent his
body from being seized by his enemies. During the late-evening briefing,
General Weidling had told Hitler that the Russians would reach the
Reich Chancellery no later than 1 May. There was little time remaining.

Nevertheless, Hitler undertook one last attempt to ascertain the possibilities of relief, even at this late hour. With nothing heard throughout
the day of Wenck's progress (or lack of it), he cabled five questions to
Jodl in the most recent OKW headquarters in Dobbin at eleven o'clock
that evening, asking in the tersest fashion where Wenck's spearheads
were, when the attack would come, where the 9th Army was, where
Holste's troops were, and when *their* attack might be expected.

Keitel's reply arrived shortly before 3 a.m. on 30 April: Wenck's army
was still engaged south of the Schwielow Lake, outside Potsdam, and
unable to continue its attack on Berlin. The 9th Army was encircled.
The Korps Holste had been forced on to the defensive. Keitel added,
below the report: 'Attacks on Berlin not advanced anywhere.' It was
now plain beyond any equivocation: there would be no relief of the
Reich capital.

Hitler had, in fact, already given up. Before 2 a.m. he had said goodbye
to a gathering of around twenty to twenty-five servants and guards. He
mentioned Himmler's treachery and told them that he had decided to
take his own life rather than be captured by the Russians and put on
show like an exhibit in a museum. He shook hands with each of them,
thanked them for their service, released them from their oath to him,
and hoped they would find their way to the British or Americans rather
than fall into Russian hands. He then went through the same farewell
ceremony with the two doctors, Haase and Schenck, and the nurses and
assistants, who had served in the emergency hospital established below
the New Reich Chancellery.

At dawn, Soviet artillery opened up intensive bombardment of the Reich Chancellery and neighbouring buildings. Hitler inquired soon afterwards of the commandant of the 'Citadel', SS-Brigadeführer Mohnke, how long he could hold out. He was told for one to two days at most. In the last briefing, in the late morning, Berlin's commandant, General Weidling, was even more pessimistic. Munition was fast running out; air-supplies had dried up and any replenishment was out of the question; morale was at rock-bottom; the fighting was now in a very small area of the city. The battle for Berlin would in all probability, he concluded, be over that evening. After a long silence, Hitler, in a tired voice, asked Mohnke's view. The 'Citadel' commandant concurred. Hitler wearily levered himself out of his chair. Weidling pressed him for a decision on whether, in the event of a total ammunitions failure, the remaining troops could attempt to break out. Hitler spoke briefly with Krebs, then gave permission – which he confirmed in writing – for a break-out to be attempted in small numbers. As before, he rejected emphatically a capitulation of the capital.

He sent for Bormann. It was by now around noon. He told him the time had come; he would shoot himself that afternoon. Eva Braun would also commit suicide. Their bodies were to be burnt. He then summoned his personal adjutant, SS-Sturmbannführer Otto Günsche. He did not want to be put on display in some waxworks in Moscow, he said. He commissioned Günsche with making the arrangements for the cremation, and for ensuring that it was carried out according to his instructions. Hitler was calm and collected. Günsche, less calm, immediately rushed to telephone Hitler's chauffeur, Erich Kempka, to obtain as much petrol as was available. He impressed upon him the urgency. The Soviets could reach the Chancellery garden at any time.

Hitler took lunch as usual around 1 p.m. with his secretaries, Traudl Junge and Gerda Christian, and his dietician Fräulein Manziarly. Eva Braun was not present. Hitler was composed, giving no hint that his death was imminent. Some time after the meal had ended, Günsche told the secretaries that Hitler wished to say farewell to them. They joined Martin Bormann, Joseph and Magda Goebbels, General Burgdorf and General Krebs, and others from the 'inner circle' of the bunker community. Looking more stooped than ever, Hitler, dressed as usual in his uniform jacket and black trousers, appeared alongside Eva Braun, who was wearing a blue dress with white trimmings. He held out his hand to each of them, muttered a few words, and, within a few minutes and without further formalities, returned to his study.

Eva Braun went into Magda Goebbels's room with her. Magda, on whom three days earlier Hitler had pinned his own Golden Party Badge – a signal token of esteem for one of his most fervent admirers – was in a tearful state. She was conscious not only that this was the end for the Führer she revered but that within hours she would be taking, as well as her own life, the lives of her six children, still playing happily in the corridors of the bunker. Highly agitated, Magda immediately reappeared, asking Günsche if she could speak to Hitler again. Hitler somewhat begrudgingly agreed and went in to see Magda. It was said that she begged him a last time to leave Berlin. The response was predictable and unemotional. Inside a minute, Hitler had retreated behind the doors of his study for the last time. Eva Braun followed him almost immediately. It was shortly before half-past three.

For the next few minutes, Goebbels, Bormann, Axmann (who had arrived too late to say his own farewell to Hitler) and the remaining members of the bunker community waited. Günsche stood on guard outside Hitler's room. The only noise was the drone of the diesel ventilator. In the upstairs part of the bunker, Traudl Junge chatted with the Goebbels children as they ate their lunch.

After waiting ten minutes or so, still without a sound from Hitler's room, Linge took the initiative. He took Bormann with him and cautiously opened the door. In the cramped study, Hitler and Eva Braun sat alongside each other on the small sofa. Eva Braun was slumped to Hitler's left. A strong whiff of bitter almonds – the distinctive smell of prussic acid – drifted up from her body. Hitler's head drooped lifelessly. Blood dripped from a bullet-hole in his right temple. His 7.65mm. Walther pistol lay by his foot.

Epilogue

I

Hitler was dead. Only the last obsequies remained. They would not detain the inhabitants of the bunker for long. The man who, living, had dominated their existence to the last was now merely a corpse to be disposed of as rapidly as possible. With the Russians at the portals of the Reich Chancellery, the bunker inmates had thoughts other than their dead leader on their minds.

Within minutes of the deaths being established, the bodies of Adolf Hitler and his wife of a day-and-a-half, Eva Braun, were wrapped in the blankets that Heinz Linge, Hitler's valet, had quickly fetched. The corpses were then lifted from the sofa and carried through the bunker, up twenty-five feet or so of stairs, and into the garden of the Reich Chancellery. Linge, helped by three SS guards, brought out the remains of Hitler, head covered by the blanket, his lower legs protruding. Martin Bormann carried Eva Braun's body into the corridor, where Erich Kempka, Hitler's chauffeur, relieved him of his burden. Otto Günsche, Hitler's personal adjutant, and commissioned with overseeing the burning of the bodies, then took over on the stairs and carried Eva Braun up into the garden. He laid the bodies side by side, Eva Braun to Hitler's right, on a piece of flat, open, sandy ground only about three metres from the door down to the bunker. It was impossible to look around for any more suitable spot. Even this location, close to the bunker door, was extremely hazardous, since an unceasing rain of shells from the Soviet barrage continued to bombard the whole area, including the garden itself. General Hans Krebs, Hitler's last Chief of the General Staff, Wilhelm Burgdorf, his Wehrmacht adjutant, Joseph Goebbels, newly appointed Chancellor of what was left of the Reich, and Martin

Bormann, now designated Party Minister, had followed the small cortège and joined the extraordinary funeral party witnessing the macabre scene.

A good store of petrol had been gathered in the bunker in readiness. Kempka had himself provided, at Günsche's request, as much as 200 litres. More was stored in the bunker's machine-room. The petrol was now swiftly poured over the bodies. Nonetheless, as the hail of shells continued, setting the funeral pyre alight with the matches Goebbels supplied proved difficult. Günsche was about to try with a grenade, when Linge managed to find some paper to make a torch. Bormann was finally able to get it burning, and either he or Linge hurled it on to the pyre, immediately retreating to the safety of the doorway. Someone rapidly closed the bunker door, leaving open only a small crevice, through which a ball of fire was seen to erupt around the petrol-soaked bodies. Arms briefly raised in a final 'Heil Hitler' salute, the tiny funeral party hurriedly departed underground, away from the danger of the exploding shells. As the flames consumed the bodies in a suitably infernal setting, the end of the leader whose presence had a mere few years earlier electrified millions was witnessed by not a single one even of his closest followers.

Neither Linge nor Günsche, the two men entrusted by Hitler with the disposal of the bodies, returned to ensure that the task was complete. One of the guards in the Chancellery garden, Hermann Karnau, later testified (though, like a number of the witnesses in the bunker, he gave contradictory versions at different times) that, when he revisited the cremation site, the bodies had been reduced to little more than ashes, which collapsed when he touched them with his foot. Another guard, Erich Mansfeld, recalled that he had viewed the scene together with Karnau around 6 p.m. Karnau had shouted to him that it was all over. When they went across together, they found two charcoaled, shrivelled, unrecognizable bodies. Günsche himself told of commissioning, around half an hour after returning from the cremation, two SS men from the Führer Escort Squad (*Führerbegleitkommando*), Hauptsturmführer Ewald Lindloff and Obersturmführer Hans Reisser, with ensuring that the remains of the bodies were buried. Lindloff later reported that he had carried out the order. The bodies, he said, had been already thoroughly burnt and were in a 'shocking state', torn open – Günsche presumed – in the heavy bombardment of the garden. Reisser's involvement was not needed. Günsche told him, an hour and a half after giving him the order, that Lindloff had already carried it out. It was by this time no later than 6.30 p.m. on 30 April.

There had been little left of Hitler and Eva Braun for Lindloff to dispose of. Their few mortal remains joined those of numerous other unidentifiable bodies (or parts of them), some from the hospital below the New Reich Chancellery, which had rapidly been thrown into bomb-craters in the vicinity of the bunker exit during the previous days. The intense bombardment which continued for a further twenty-four hours or so played its own part in destroying and scattering the human remains strewn around the Chancellery garden.

When the Soviet victors arrived there on 2 May they immediately began a vigorous search for the bodies of Hitler and Eva Braun. Nine days later, they showed the dental technician Fritz Echtmann, who had worked for Hitler's dentist, Dr Johann Hugo Blaschke, since 1938, part of a jaw-bone and two dental bridges. He was able to identify from his records one of the bridges as that of Hitler, the other as Eva Braun's. The lower jaw-bone, too, was Hitler's. These earthly remains of the once all-powerful ruler of Germany were subsequently taken to Moscow and kept in a cigar-box. Part of a skull with a bullet-hole in it, thought to be Hitler's, was discovered in 1946 and also found its way to Moscow. The other presumed remains of Hitler and Eva Braun – what, exactly, the Soviets found is still unclear – were deposited initially in an unmarked grave in a forest far to the west of Berlin, reburied in 1946 in a plot of land in Magdeburg, then finally exhumed and burnt in 1970.

II

The bunker inmates were finally free to think of their own survival. Even while the bodies still burned in the Chancellery garden above, they had forgotten their vows of self-immolation alongside their leader and were agreeing to do what he had always and explicitly ruled out: seek a last-minute arrangement with the Soviet Union. An emissary was sent out under a white flag to try to engineer a meeting of General Krebs (who, as a former military attaché in Moscow, had the advantage of speaking fluent Russian) with Marshal Zhukov. At 10 p.m. that evening, Krebs went over the Soviet lines bearing a letter from Goebbels and Bormann.

It was an anxious night for those incarcerated in the bunker. And when Krebs returned around 6 a.m. next morning it was only to report that the Soviet side insisted upon unconditional surrender and demanded a declaration to that effect by 4 p.m. that afternoon, 1 May.

This was the end. It was time for final preparations – on the sole remaining principle of save what can be saved. At 10.53 a.m., a telegram for Dönitz arrived in Plön: 'Testament in force. I'll come to you as quickly as possible. Until then, in my view, hold back from publication. Bormann.' Earlier that morning, more than nine hours after the grotesque scene in the Chancellery garden, the Grand-Admiral, still believing Hitler was alive, had telegraphed an expression of his continued unconditional loyalty to the bunker. Only now did he realize that Hitler was dead. This was confirmed in a further telegram – the last to leave the bunker – dictated by Goebbels and arriving at Plön at 3.18 p.m. that afternoon. Neither the Wehrmacht nor the German people were as yet aware of Hitler's death. When they were finally told, seven hours later, in a broadcast at 10.26 p.m. that night, it was, typically, with a double distortion of the truth: that Hitler had died that afternoon – it was the previous day – and that his death had taken place in combat 'at his post in the Reich Chancellery, while fighting to his last breath against Bolshevism'. In his proclamation to the Wehrmacht, Dönitz spoke of the Führer's 'heroic death'. The Wehrmacht's report stated that he had fallen 'at the head of the heroic defenders of the Reich capital'. The delay in informing Dönitz had plainly been to allow Bormann and Goebbels the final opportunity of a negotiated surrender to the Red Army without consulting the new head of state. The untruth relayed by Dönitz to the Wehrmacht and German people was to prevent a predictable response by the troops, had they been aware of Hitler's suicide, that the Führer had deserted them at the last. This was, in fact, precisely the message which General Helmuth Weidling, the German commander in Berlin, conveyed to his troops when ordering them, in the early hours of 2 May, to cease fighting. 'On 30.4.45 the Führer took his own life and thereby abandoned those who had sworn him loyalty,' ran the order. 'At the Führer's command you believe that you must still fight for Berlin, although the lack of heavy weaponry and munitions, and the overall situation shows the struggle to be pointless ... In agreement with the High Command of the Soviet troops, I therefore demand you to end the fighting immediately.'

By then, the drama in the bunker was finally over. Most of those still entombed below the Reich Chancellery had spent the afternoon and evening of 1 May planning their break-out. Goebbels was not among them. Along with his wife, Magda, he was now making arrangements for their own suicides – and for taking the lives of their six children. In the early evening, Magda summoned Helmut Gustav Kunz, adjutant to the head doctor in the SS medical administration in the Reich Chancellery, and asked him to give each of the children – Helga, Hilde, Helmut, Holde, Hedda, and Heide, aged between twelve and four – a shot of morphine. It was about 8.40 p.m. when Kunz carried out the request. Once they had fallen into a drugged sleep, Dr Ludwig Stumpfegger, Hitler's own physician at the end, crushed a phial of prussic acid in the mouth of each of the children.

Later that evening, as Wilhelm Mohnke, commandant of the 'Citadel', gave orders for the mass break-out from the bunker, Goebbels instructed his adjutant, Günther Schwägermann, to take care of the burning of his and Magda's bodies. He gave him the silver-framed signed photograph of Hitler that for so many years had stood on his desk as a memento. Then he and his wife, after saying their brief farewells, climbed the stairs to the Chancellery garden, and bit on the prussic acid capsules. An SS orderly fired two shots into the bodies to make sure. Far less petrol was available for the unceremonious cremation than had been saved for burning the bodies of Hitler and Eva Braun. Soviet troops had little difficulty in identifying the corpses when they entered the Chancellery garden next day.

Krebs, Burgdorf, and Franz Schädle, head of Hitler's escort squad, also chose to end their lives in the bunker before the Russians arrived. The rest of the company sought their luck late that evening in the mass escape, undertaken in groups. The underground railway tunnel brought them to Friedrichstraße station, a few hundred yards to the north of the ruined Reich Chancellery. But once on the surface, in the burning hell of Berlin, with shells falling all around, confusion took over. The groups found themselves split up in the chaos. Individuals took what chances they could. A few, including the secretaries Gerda Christian, Traudl Junge, and Else Krüger, managed, remarkably, to make their way through to the west. Most, among them Otto Günsche and Heinz Linge, fell into Soviet hands and years of misery and maltreatment in Moscow prisons. Most of the others were killed seeking a route to safety, or took the last decision left to them. Prominent among the latter were Hitler's constant right hand during the war years, Martin Bormann, and his doctor, Ludwig Stumpfegger. Both had given up their hopes of escape and, rather than fall into Soviet hands, had swallowed poison in the early hours of 2 May 1945 in Berlin's Invalidenstraße.

III

Outside Berlin, the winding-up orders on the Third Reich were meanwhile in the process of being served. However, they were carried out by the new Dönitz regime – based in Flensburg in the north of Schleswig-Holstein – with great reluctance, and only under the evident compulsion of the hopeless military situation. At the end of the First World War, disastrous though the defeat had been, it had proved possible to save the existence of the Reich and the German army. The basis for the hopes of national rebirth had been laid. Dönitz held to the illusion that this much might be achieved a second time. Even at this late hour, he was hoping through the offer of partial capitulation to the west to avoid total and unconditional surrender on all fronts, at the same time sustaining, with western backing, the German Reich to form, alongside the western powers, a common front against Bolshevism. For this, he needed to gain time – also to allow withdrawal to the west of as many as possible of the Wehrmacht troops still engaged in bitter fighting against the Red Army. He was ready to sanction, therefore, the German capitulation in northern Italy on 2 May, which had already been agreed between Himmler's former right-hand man Karl Wolff and OSS chief Allen Dulles on the day before Hitler's suicide. He also reluctantly conceded on 4 May a further partial capitulation involving German troops in north-west Germany, Holland, and Denmark. In the south, where the Americans reached Munich on the day of Hitler's death, Innsbruck on 3 May, and Linz – Hitler's home town – four days later, Kesselring negotiated the surrender of the German divisions in the northern Alps on the 5th and in Austria on 7 May. Dönitz did not, however, include in the partial capitulation the German troops further east, still fighting in Yugoslavia.

The Grand Admiral's hopes of rescuing the remnants of Hitler's Reich were visible in his choice of cabinet. Though he rejected Himmler's overtures for inclusion, and turned his back, too, on Ribbentrop, he retained several members of Hitler's cabinet, among them Albert Speer, while foreign affairs and the direction of the cabinet were placed in the hands of the long-standing finance minister Schwerin von Krosigk, who, it was presumed, would appear unsullied by the worst crimes of Nazism. He made no changes in the High Command of the Wehrmacht. Hitler's mainstays, Keitel and Jodl, were left in post. The Nazi Party was neither banned nor dissolved. Pictures of Hitler still adorned the walls of government offices in Flensburg. One of the few concessions that Dönitz made was the reintroduction of the military salute in the Wehrmacht to replace the 'Heil Hitler' greeting. But military courts continued to hand out death-sentences even as the last rites on the Third Reich were being pronounced.

The tactics employed by Dönitz were at least successful in enabling an estimated 1.8 million German soldiers to avoid Soviet captivity by surrendering to the western Allies – though at a high cost of continuing bloodshed and suffering before the fighting could be finally terminated. While the eastern front had since 1941 been the main theatre of war, under a third of the 10 million or so German prisoners-of-war fell into Soviet hands. But Dönitz's intentions of a one-sided, partial capitulation to win the West at this late stage to the defence against Bolshevism cut little ice with Allied leaders. When his envoy (and successor as Commander-in-Chief of the Navy) Admiral Hans-Georg von Friedeburg journeyed with a delegation to Rheims, Eisenhower's headquarters, hoping to seal an agreement with the western Allies amounting to a capitulation to the West, but not to the Soviet Union, Eisenhower was having none of it. He insisted on a full and unconditional surrender on all fronts. Accordingly, on 6 May, Dönitz sent Jodl to Rheims on seemingly the same mission – to persuade the West to accept German surrender, but to avoid total capitulation – though this time with powers to agree to a complete capitulation (following final authorization from Flensburg) and instructions to gain maximum time – at least four days – in order to bring back the largest German fighting unit still in combat, Army Group Centre, across American lines. Eisenhower remained unmoved. He insisted on the capitulation being signed that very day, 6 May, with effect from midnight on 9 May, and threatened a renewal of air-raids if the agreement were not forthcoming. Jodl was given half an hour to think it over. After difficulties in communication with

Flensburg, Dönitz, faced with no alternative, eventually conceded his authorization in the early hours. At 2.41 a.m. on 7 May, in the presence of representatives of all four of the Allied powers, the capitulation was signed, stipulating a complete ending of all German military engagements by the end of the following day.

The document to which the signatures were appended was, however, a shortened version of the original text of surrender, agreed by all the Allies. It was, in fact, regarded by the OKW leadership as 'not final', and to be replaced by 'a general capitulation treaty' still to be signed. Meanwhile, the order had gone out to bring back as many troops and as speedily as possible to the west for surrender to the British and Americans. At Stalin's insistence, Allied representatives assembled once more, on 9 May, just after midnight, this time at Karlshorst on the outskirts of Berlin, headquarters of Marshal Zhukov, to sign the full document of capitulation. Since the terms agreed at Rheims had already come into effect a few minutes earlier, the document was dated 8 May. Keitel, Friedeburg, and Colonel-General Hans-Jürgen Stumpff (representing the Commander-in-Chief of the Luftwaffe, Ritter von Greim) signed from the German side. Zhukov, the British Air-Marshal Arthur W. Tedder (representing Eisenhower), the French General Jean de Lattre de Tassigny, and the US General Carl Spaatz signed for the Allies.

The last Wehrmacht report, on 9 May 1945, retained a tone of pride, speaking of 'the unique achievement of front and homeland' which would 'in a later, just verdict of history find its final appreciation'. These words, hollow for millions, followed the declaration: 'On command of the Grand Admiral the Wehrmacht has stopped the fight which had become hopeless. The struggle lasting almost six years is accordingly at an end.'

Hitler's war was over. The reckoning was about to begin.

IV

Many of those bearing heaviest responsibility, after Hitler, for the terrible suffering of the previous years and the deep pall of sorrow left behind escaped full retribution. Suicide, Hitler had always said, was easy. Some of his leading henchmen now followed his example. Heinrich Himmler, the embodiment of police terror, captured by the British under false identity and wearing the uniform of a Wehrmacht sergeant, crunched a phial of potassium cyanide in an interrogation centre near Lüneburg on 23 May as soon as his true identity had been established. Robert Ley, the stridently antisemitic head of the German Labour Front, taken by American troops in the mountains of the Tyrol, strangled himself in the lavatory of his prison cell at Nuremberg on 24 October while awaiting trial. Arrested by US forces near Berchtesgaden on 9 May 1945, Hermann Göring, for so long Hitler's designated successor until his abrupt dismissal in the last days of the Third Reich, also committed suicide – cheating the hangman awaiting his presence next day on the late evening of 15 October 1946 after being convicted on all charges, including crimes against humanity, at the International Military Tribunal in Nuremberg.

Others among the regime's leaders, unwilling or unable to end their own lives, suffered the fate imposed upon them by the Tribunal and were hanged at Nuremberg. Convicted for crimes against humanity – in all but one case war crimes, and in some instances conspiracy to commit or actual commission of crimes against peace – the warmongering former Foreign Minister Joachim von Ribbentrop; chief of the High Command of the Wehrmacht Wilhelm Keitel; head of the Operations Department of the Wehrmacht and Hitler's chief military adviser Alfred Jodl; Nazi ideological guru and Reich Minister for the Occupied Eastern Territories Alfred Rosenberg; Reich Minister of the Interior (until his removal from office in 1943) Wilhelm Frick; Hitler's key man in Vienna at the time of the Anschluß and later Reich Commissar in the Netherlands Arthur Seyß-Inquart; Labour Plenipotentiary Fritz Sauckel, who presided over the slave-labour programme; Heydrich's fearsome successor as head of the RSHA Ernst Kaltenbrunner; Governor-General of Poland and leading Nazi lawyer Hans Frank; and the former Gauleiter of Franconia, leading Jew-baiter Julius Streicher were executed on 16 October 1946. Few mourned them.

Albert Speer, the Armaments Minister whose hands were barely less dirty than Sauckel's in the exploitation of forced labour, was one of those fortunate to escape the hangman's noose. Like the last head of state Admiral Dönitz, Economics Minister Walther Funk, Foreign Minister (until his replacement by Ribbentrop in 1938) Konstantin von Neurath, head of the navy Erich Raeder, long-time Hitler Youth leader and Gauleiter of Vienna Baldur von Schirach, and (until his flight to

Scotland in 1941) deputy head of the Nazi Party Rudolf Heß, Speer was given a long prison sentence. Funk, Neurath, and Raeder were released early on health grounds. Dönitz, Speer, and Schirach left prison each after serving the full sentence – in Speer's case to become a celebrity, best-selling author, and pundit on the Third Reich with a belated guilt complex as his trademark. Heß was to commit suicide in 1987, still serving a life-sentence in Spandau prison in Berlin.

Among second-ranking Nazis implicated in the regime's most heinous crimes, the most notorious, the manager of the 'Final Solution' Adolf Eichmann, was to be dramatically abducted from Argentina by Israeli agents, tried in Jerusalem, and hanged in 1962. The commandant of Auschwitz Rudolf Höß, the butcher of the Warsaw ghetto Jürgen Stroop, the terror of the Poles in the Warthegau Gauleiter Arthur Greiser, and his scarcely less fanatical counterpart in Danzig-West Prussia Albert Forster were all hanged at earlier dates after trials in Poland. The Poles proved more humanitarian than their previous tormentors in commuting, on account of his poor health, the death-sentence on the notably (even by Nazi standards) cruel and brutal former Gauleiter of East Prussia Erich Koch to a term of life-imprisonment.

Many implicated in crimes against humanity escaped lightly. Hinrich Lohse, former Reich Commissar in the Baltic, was released in 1951 on grounds of ill-health after serving only three years of a ten-year sentence. He died peacefully in his home town in 1964. Wilhelm Koppe, SS leader in the Warthegau and alongside Greiser the instigator of Chelmno extermination camp, where over 150,000 Jews lost their lives, was able to prosper under a pseudonym as the director of a chocolate factory in Bonn until the 1960s. When discovered and arraigned for his part in mass murder in Poland he was deemed unfit to stand trial, eventually dying in his bed in 1975. Countless others, who in 'working towards the Führer' had exercised positions of great power, often determining life or death (including doctors implicated in the 'euthanasia action') and lining their own pockets at the same time through boundless corruption and ruthless careerism, were able wholly or in part to avoid serious retribution for their actions – in some cases building successful post-war careers for themselves.

Few of those forced to account for their actions under Hitler showed remorse or contrition, let alone guilt. With scant exception, they showed themselves, when called to book, incapable of acknowledging their own contribution to the remorseless slide into barbarism during the Nazi era. Alongside the inevitable lies, distortions, and excuses often went, it seems, a psychological block on recognizing responsibility for their actions. It amounted to a self-deception that mirrored the total collapse of their value-system and the demolition of the idealized image of Hitler to which they had clung for so many years – which, indeed, had usually underpinned or at least given justification for their motivation. They had been content for years to see their power, careers, ambitions, aspirations depend solely on Hitler. Now, it was in a perverse sense logical that their own plight would be attributed solely to what they saw as Hitler's lunacy and criminality. From being the revered leader whose utopian vision they had eagerly followed, Hitler was now the scapegoat who had betrayed their trust and seduced them through the brilliance of his rhetoric into becoming helpless accomplices to his barbaric plans.

Such a psychology applied not merely to many of those most heavily incriminated in the Nazi experiment to determine who should inhabit this planet. Countless ordinary Germans were now prepared to find an explanation for or defence of their own actions (or lack of action) in the alleged seductive powers of Hitler – a leader promising salvation but in the end delivering damnation. Alternatively, they looked to a level of totalitarian terror that had left them with no alternative but to follow orders of which they disapproved. Both responses were wide of the mark.

Hitler's regime, as we have had ample cause to acknowledge, was – certainly for most of its twelve-year duration – no narrowly based tyranny imposing its will upon the hostile masses of the population. And, until the 'running amok' of the last phase of the war, the terror – at least within Germany – had been specifically targeted at defined racial and political enemies, not random and arbitrary, while the level of at least partial consensus in all reaches of society had been extensive. Generalizations about the mentalities and behaviour of millions of Germans in the Nazi era are bound to be of limited application – apart, perhaps, from the generalization that, for the great mass of the population, the figurative colours to look for are less likely to be stark black and white than varying and chequered shades of grey. Even so, it remains the case that, collectively, the inhabitants of a highly modern, sophisticated, pluralistic society which, following a lost war, was experiencing deep-seated national humiliation, economic bankruptcy, acute social, political, and ideological polarization, and a generally perceived complete failure of a discredited political system, had been prepared in increasing numbers to place their trust in the chiliastic vision of a self-professed political saviour. Once, as can now more easily be seen, a series of relatively cheap and easy (though in reality exceedingly dangerous) national triumphs had been achieved, still further vast numbers were prepared to swallow their doubts and to believe in the destiny of their great leader. Moreover, these triumphs, however much they were portrayed by propaganda as attributable to the achievements of one man, had been brought about not only with huge mass acclaim, but also with a very high level of support from almost all of the non-Nazi élite-groups – business, industry, civil service, above all the armed forces – which controlled practically every avenue of power outside the upper echelons of the Nazi Movement itself. Though the consensus was in many respects a shallow one, resting upon differing degrees of backing for the various strands of the overall ideological vision which Hitler embodied, it offered nevertheless until the middle of the war an extremely wide and potent platform of support for Hitler to build upon and exploit.

The rise from the depths of national degradation to the heights of national greatness seemed for so many (as propaganda never ceased to trumpet) to be a near-miracle – a work of redemption brought about by the unique genius of the Führer. Hitler's power was able thereby to draw on strong elements of pseudo-religious belief translated into the mysticism of national salvation and rebirth – emanating in part no doubt from declining institutional religion and from the psychologically needed substitution in some quarters for the quasi-religious associations with the monarchy – which also compensated in some ways for the many negative aspects of everyday life under Nazi rule. Even to the very end there were intelligent individuals prepared to exempt Hitler from knowledge of the atrocities committed in Poland and Russia – and to attach blame instead to Himmler. The Führer cult, accepted not only by millions of believers but pandered to in their own interests by all in positions of authority and influence, even if they were often inwardly critical or sceptical, enabled Hitler's power to shake off all constraints and become absolute. By the time realization dawned that the road to riches was proving the road to ruin, the personalized rule of the leader was out of control. Hitler was by now – though this had not always been so – incapable of being checked by the splintered parts of an increasingly fragmented regime bound together largely by the commitment to the ruler himself and, increasingly, fear of the alternative: Bolshevism. The road to perdition lay open, but – other than the courageous attempts by small groups or individuals which ultimately failed through bad luck even more than through bad planning – there was by now little alternative but to follow this road.

The price to be paid – by the German people, above all by the regime's untold numbers of victims inside and outside Germany – was beyond calculation. The material price was immense. Writing to *The Times* on 12 November 1945, the left-wing British Jewish publisher Victor Gollancz described his impressions in Düsseldorf: 'I am never likely to forget the unspeakable wickedness of which the Nazis were guilty. But when I see the swollen bodies and living skeletons in hospitals here and elsewhere . . . then I think, not of Germans, but of men and women. I am sure I should have the same feelings if I were in Greece or Poland. But I happen to be in Germany, and write of what I see here.' The moral price was, if anything, even more immeasurable. Decades would not fully erase the simple but compelling sentiment painted in huge letters at the scene of Hitler's annual celebration of the 1923 putsch, the Feldherrnhalle in Munich, in May 1945: 'I am ashamed to be a German.' 'Europe has never known such a calamity to her civilization and nobody can say when she will begin to recover from its effects,' was the telling and at the same time prophetic comment of one British newspaper, the *Manchester Guardian*, only three days after the suicide in the bunker. The trauma which was Hitler's lasting legacy was only just beginning.

V

Never in history has such ruination – physical and moral – been associated with the name of one man. That the ruination had far deeper roots and far more profound causes than the aims and actions of this one man has been evident in the preceding chapters. That the previously unprobed depths of inhumanity plumbed by the Nazi regime could draw upon wide-ranging complicity at all levels of society has been equally apparent. But Hitler's name justifiably stands for all time as that of the chief instigator of the most profound collapse of civilization in modern times.

The extreme form of personal rule which an ill-educated beerhall demagogue and racist bigot, a narcissistic, megalomaniac, self-styled national saviour, was allowed to acquire and exercise in a modern, economically advanced, and cultured land known for its philosophers and poets was absolutely decisive in the terrible unfolding of events in those fateful twelve years.

Hitler was the main author of a war leaving over 50 million dead and millions more grieving their lost ones and trying to put their shattered lives together again. Hitler was the chief inspiration of a genocide the like of which the world had never known, rightly to be viewed in coming times as a defining episode of the twentieth century. The Reich whose glory he had sought lay at the end wrecked, its remnants to be divided among the victorious and occupying powers. The arch-enemy, Bolshevism, stood in the Reich capital itself and presided over half of Europe. Even the German people, whose survival he had said was the very reason for his political fight, had proved ultimately dispensable to him.

In the event, the German people he was prepared to see damned alongside him proved capable of surviving even a Hitler. Beyond the repairing of broken lives and broken homes in broken towns and cities, the searing moral imprint of Hitler's era would remain. Gradually, nevertheless, a new society, resting in time, mercifully, on new values, would emerge from the ruins of the old. For in its maelstrom of destruction Hitler's rule had also conclusively demonstrated the utter bankruptcy of the hyper-nationalistic and racist world-power ambitions (and the social and political structures that upheld them) that had prevailed in Germany over the previous half a century and twice taken Europe and the wider world into calamitous war.

The old Germany was gone with Hitler. The Germany which had produced Adolf Hitler, had seen its future in his vision, had so readily served him, and had shared in his hubris, had also to share his nemesis.

Main Published Primary Sources on Hitler

Adolf Hitler: Monologe im Führerhauptquartier 1941–1944. Die Aufzeichnungen Heinrich Heims, ed. Werner Jochmann, Hamburg, 1980 (*Hitler's Table Talk, 1941–1944*, introd. by H. R. Trevor-Roper, London, 1953).

Akten der Partei-Kanzlei, ed. Institut für Zeitgeschichte, 4 vols, Munich, 1983–92.

Akten der Reichskanzlei. Die Regierung Hitler 1933–1938, 4 vols, Boppard/Munich, 1983–99.

Akten zur Deutschen Auswärtigen Politik 1918–1945. (Serie D: 1.9.37–11.12.41; Serie E: 1941–1945).

Baur, Hans, *Ich flog Mächtige der Erde*, Kempten, 1956.

Becker, Josef and Ruth (eds.), *Hitlers Machtergreifung*, 2nd edn, Munich, 1992.

Below, Nicolaus von, *Als Hitlers Adjutant 1937–1945*, Mainz, 1980 (*At Hitler's Side*, London, 2001).

The Bormann Letters: The Private Correspondence between Martin Bormann and his Wife from January 1943 to April 1945, ed. H. R. Trevor-Roper, London, 1954.

Das Buch Hitler. Geheimdossier des NKWD für Josef W. Stalin, zusammengestellt aufgrund der Verhörprotokolle des Persönlichen Adjutanten Hitlers, Otto Günsche, und des Kammerdieners Heinz Linge, Moskau 1948/49, ed. Henrik Eberle and Matthias Uhl, Bergisch-Gladbach, 2005 (*The Hitler Book*, London, 2005).

Burckhardt, Carl J., *Meine Danziger Mission 1937–1939*, Munich, 1962.

Ciano, Galeazzo, *Tagebücher 1937/38*, Hamburg, 1949 (*Ciano's Diary 1937–1943*, London, 2002).

Ciano's Diary 1939–1943, ed. Malcolm Muggeridge, London/Toronto, 1947.

Ciano's Diplomatic Papers, ed. Malcolm Muggeridge, London, 1948.

Coulondre, Robert, *Von Moskau nach Berlin 1936–1939. Erinnerungen des französischen Botschafters*, Bonn, 1950.

Dahlerus, Birger, *Der letzte Versuch. London–Berlin. Sommer 1939*, Munich, 1948.

Das Diensttagebuch des deutschen Generalgouverneurs in Polen 1939–1945, ed. Werner Präg and Wolfgang Jacobmeyer, Stuttgart, 1975.

Der Dienstkalender Heinrich Himmlers 1941/42, ed. Peter Witte et al., Hamburg, 1999.

Deuerlein, Ernst (ed.), *Der Hitler-Putsch. Bayerische Dokumente zum 8./9. November 1923*, Stuttgart, 1962.

Deuerlein, Ernst (ed.), *Der Austieg der NSDAP in Augenzeugenberichten*, Munich, 1974.

Dietrich, Otto, *Zwölf Jahre mit Hitler*, Cologne (n.d., 1955?).

Documents on British Foreign Policy, 1919–1939, 2nd Series, 1929–1938, 3rd Series, 1938–1939, London, 1947–61.

Documents on German Foreign Policy, 1918–1945, Series C (1933–1937), The Third Reich: First Phase; Series D (1937–1945), London, 1957–66.

Dodd, William E. and Martha (eds.), *Ambassador Dodd's Diary, 1933–1938*, London, 1941.

Doenitz, Karl, *Memoirs. Ten Years and Twenty Days*, New York, 1997.

Dollmann, Eugen, *Dolmetscher der Diktatoren*, Bayreuth, 1963.

Domarus, Max (ed.), *Hitler, Reden und Proklamationen 1932–1945*, 2 vols, in 4 parts, Wiesbaden, 1973 (*Hitler: Speeches and Proclamations, 1932–1945*, London, 1990–).

Engel, Gerhard, *Heeresadjutant bei Hitler 1938–1943*, ed. Hildegard von Kotze, Stuttgart, 1974.

François-Poncet, André, *Souvenirs d'une ambassade à Berlin, Septembre 1931–Octobre 1938*, Paris, 1946.

Frank, Hans, *Im Angesicht des Galgens*, Munich/Gräfelfing, 1953.

Fröhlich, Elke (ed.), *Die Tagebücher von Joseph Goebbels. Teil I, Aufzeichnungen 1923–1941*, 14 vols, *Teil II, Diktate 1941–1945*, 15 vols, Munich 1993–2006.

'*Führer-Erlasse*' *1939–1945*, ed. Martin Moll, Stuttgart, 1997.

Galante, Pierre, and Silianoff, Eugen, *Last Witnesses in the Bunker*, London, 1989.

Generaloberst Halder: Kriegstagebuch, ed. Hans-Adolf Jacobsen, 3 vols, Stuttgart, 1962–4 (*The Halder War Diary, 1939–1942*, ed. Charles Burdick and Hans-Adolf Jacobsen, abridged, London, 1988).

Giesler, Hermann, *Ein anderer Hitler. Erlebnisse, Gespräche, Reflexionen*, Leoni am Starnberger See, 1977.

Gisevius, Hans Bernd, *Bis zum bittern Ende*, 2 vols, Zurich, 1946 (*To the Bitter End*, Cambridge, Mass., 1947).

Görlitz, Walter (ed.), *Generalfeldmarschall Keitel. Verbrecher oder Offizier? Erinnerungen, Briefe, Dokumente des Chefs OKW*, Göttingen/Berlin/Frankfurt, 1961.

Haffner, Sebastian, *Geschichte eines Deutschen. Die Erinnerungen 1914–1933*, Stuttgart-Munich, 2000 (*Defying Hitler: A Memoir*, London, 2002).

Hanfstaengl, Ernst, *15 Jahre mit Hitler. Zwischen Weißem und Braunem Haus*, 2nd edn, Munich/Zurich, 1980 (*Hitler. The Missing Years*, London, 1957).

Heinz, Heinz A., *Germany's Hitler*, 2nd edn, London, 1938.

Henderson, Nevile, *Failure of a Mission. Berlin, 1937–1939*, London, 1940.

Hill, Leonidas E. (ed.), *Die Weizsäcker-Papiere 1933–1950*, Frankfurt am Main, 1974.

Hitler, Adolf, *Mein Kampf*, 876–880th reprint, Munich, 1943 (*Mein Kampf*, trans. by Ralph Manheim with an introduction by D. C. Watt, London, 1969).

Hitlers politisches Testament. Die Bormann-Diktate vom Februar und April 1945, Hamburg, 1981 (*The Testament of Adolf Hitler. The Hitler-Bormann Documents, February–April 1945, with an Introduction by H. R. Trevor-Roper*, London, 1961).

Der Hitler-Prozeß 1924. Wortlaut der Hauptverhandlung vor dem Volksgericht München I, ed. Lothar Gruchamm and Reinhard Weber, assisted by Otto Gritschneder, 4 vols, Munich, 1997–9.

Hitler. Reden, Schriften, Anordnungen: February 1925 bis Januar 1933, ed. Institut für Zeitgeschichte, 5 vols (in 12 parts), Munich, 1992–8.

Hitlers Lagebesprechungen – Die Protokollfragmente seiner militärischen Konferenzen 1942–1945, ed. Helmut Heibert, Stuttgart, 1962 (*Hitler and his Generals. Military Conferences 1942–1945*, ed. Helmut Heiber and David M. Glantz, London, 2002).

Hitlers Weisungen für die Kriegführung 1939–1945. Dokumente des Oberkommandos der Wehrmacht, ed. Walther Hubatsch, Munich, 1965 (*Hitler's War Directives*, ed. Hugh Trevor-Roper, London, 1964).

Hoffmann, Heinrich, *Hitler Was My Friend*, London, 1955.

Hoßbach, Friedrich, *Zwischen Wehrmacht und Hitler 1934–1938*, Wolfenbüttel, 1949.

Irving, David (ed.), *The Secret Diaries of Hitler's Doctor*, paperback edn, London, 1990.

Jäckel, Eberhard, and Kuhn, Axel (eds.), *Hitler. Sämtliche Aufzeichnungen 1905–1924*, Stuttgart, 1980.

Jacobsen, Hans-Adolf (ed.), *Dokumente zur Vorgeschichte des Westfeldzuges 1939–1940*, Göttingen, 1956.

Jacobsen, Hans-Adolf (ed.), *Dokumente zum Westfeldzug 1940*, Göttingen, 1960.

Jochmann, Werner (ed.), *Nationalsozialismus und Revolution*, Frankfurt am Main, 1963.

Junge, Traudl, *Bis zur letzten Stunde. Hitler's Sekretärin erzählt ihr Leben*, Munich, 2002 (*Until the Final Hour*, London, 2003).

Kempka, Erich, *Die letzten Tage mit Adolf Hitler*, Preußisch-Oldendorf, 1975.

Kersten, Felix, *The Kersten Memoirs 1940–1945*, London, 1956.

Koller, Karl, *Der letzte Monat. Die Tagebuchaufzeichnungen des ehemaligen chefs des Generalstabes der deutschen Luftwaffe vom 14. April bis 27. Mai 1945*, Mannheim, 1949.

Kordt, Erich, *Nicht aus den Akten . . . Die Wilhelmstraße in Frieden und Krieg. Erlebnisse, Begegnungen und Eindrücke 1928–1945*, Stuttgart, 1950.

Kotze, Hildegart von, and Krausnick, Helmut (eds.), *'Es spricht der Führer'. 7 exemplarische Hitler-Reden*, Gütersloh, 1966.

Krebs, Albert, *Tendenzen und Gestalten der NSDAP*, Stuttgart, 1959.

Kriegstagebuch des Oberkommandos der Wehrmacht (Wehrmachtsführungsstab), ed. Percy Ernst Schramm, 4 vols (in 6 parts), Frankfurt am Main, 1961–5.

Kubizek, August, *Adolf Hitler. Mein Jugendfreund*, 5th edn, Graz, 1989 (*The Young Hitler I Knew*, London, 2006).

Lagevorträge des Oberbefehlshabers der Kriegsmarine vor Hitler 1939–1945, ed. Gerhard Wagner, Munich, 1972 (*Fuehrer Conferences on Naval Affairs 1939–1945*, London, 1990).

Linge, Heinz, 'Kronzeuge Linge. Der Kammerdiener des "Führers" ', *Revue*, Munich, November 1955–March 1956.

Linge, Heinz, *Bis zum Untergang. Als Chef des persönlichen Dienstes bei Hitler*, Munich/Berlin, 1980.

Lipski, Josef, *Diplomat in Berlin 1933–1939*, ed. Waclaw Jedrzejewicz, New York/London, 1968.

Loringhoven, Bernd Freytag von, *In the Bunker with Hitler. The Last Witness Speaks*, London, 2006.

Ludecke (= Lüdecke), Kurt G. W., *I Knew Hitler*, London, 1938.

Maser, Werner, *Hitlers Briefe und Notizen. Sein Weltbild in handschriftlichen Dokumenten*, Düsseldorf, 1973.

Meissner, Otto, *Staatssekretär unter Ebert-Hindenburg-Hitler*, Hamburg, 1950.

The Memoirs of Field-Marshal Kesselring, Greenhill Books edn, London, 1997.

Nazi Conspiracy and Aggression, ed. Office of the United States Chief of Counsel for Prosecution of Axis Criminality, 11 vols, Washington, 1946–8.

Noakes, Jeremy, and Pridham, Geoffrey (eds.), *Nazism 1919–1945: A Documentary Reader*, 4 vols, Exeter, 1983–98.

Orr, Thomas, 'Das war Hitler', *Revue*, Munich Series, Nr 37, 1952 – Nr 8, 1953.

Papen, Franz von, *Memoirs*, London, 1952.

Picker, Henry, *Tischgespräche im Hauptquartier 1941–2*, ed. Percy Ernst Schramm, Stuttgart, 1963.

Raeder, Erich, *Mein Leben von 1935 bis Spandau 1955*, 2 vols, Tübingen, 1957.

Ribbentrop, Joachim von, *Zwischen London und Moskau*, ed. Analies von Ribbentrop, Leoni am Starnberger See, 1953 (*The Ribbentrop Memoirs*, London, 1954).

Röhm, Ernst, *Die Geschichte eines Hochverräters*, 2nd edn, Munich, 1930.

Rosenberg, Alfred, *Letzte Aufzeichnungen. Ideal und Idole der nationalsozialistischen Revolution*, Göttingen, 1948.

Schacht, Hjalmar, *Abrechnung mit Hitler*, Berlin/Frankfurt am Main, 1949 (*Account Settled*, London, 1949).

Schirach, Baldur von, *Ich glaubte an Hitler*, Hamburg, 1967.

Schmidt, Paul, *Statist auf diplomatischer Bühne 1923–1945. Erlebnisse des Chefdolmetschers im Auswärtigen Amt mit den Staatsmänner Europas*, Bonn, 1953.

Schroeder, Christa, *Er war mein Chef. Aus dem Nachlaß der Sekretärin von Adolf Hitler*, Munich/Vienna, 1985.

Schwerin von Krosigk, Lutz Graf, *Es geschah in Deutschland*, Tübingen/Stuttgart, 1951.

Seraphim, Hans-Günther (ed.), *Das politische Tagebuch Alfred Rosenbergs 1934/35 und 1939/40*, Munich, 1964.

Shirer, William, *Berlin Diary, 1934–1941*, paperback edn, London, 1970.

Speer, Albert, *Erinnerungen*, Frankfurt am Main/Berlin, 1969 (*Inside the Third Reich*, London, 1970).

Staatsmänner und Diplomaten bei Hitler. Vertrauliche Aufzeichnungen 1939–1941, ed. Andreas Hillgruber, Frankfurt am Main, 1969.

Staatsmänner und Diplomaten bei Hitler. Vertrauliche Aufzeichnungen 1942–1944, ed. Andreas Hillgruber, Frankfurt am Main, 1970.

Strasser, Otto, *Ministersessel oder Revolution?*, Berlin, 1930.

Strasser, Otto, *Hitler und ich*, Constance, 1948 (*Hitler and I*, Boston, 1940).

Trial of the Major War Criminals before the International Military Tribunal, 42 vols, Nuremberg, 1947–9.

Trials of War Criminals before the Nuernberg Military Tribunals, 12 vols, Nuremberg, 1946–9.

Tyrell, Albrecht (ed.), *Führer befiehl ... Selbstzeugnisse aus der 'Kampfzeit' der NSDAP*, Düsseldorf, 1969.

Wagner, Eduard, *Der Generalquartiermeister. Briefe und Tagebuchaufzeichnungen des Generalquartiermeisters des Heeres General der Artillerie Eduard Wagner*, ed. Elisabeth Wagner, Munich/Vienna, 1963.

Wagner, Otto, *Hitler aus nächster Nähe. Aufzeichnungen eines Vertrauten 1929–1932*, ed. Henry A. Turner, 2nd edn, Kiel, 1987.

Warlimont, Walter, *Inside Hitler's Headquarters, 1939–45*, orig. publ. 1964, Presidio paperback edn, Novato, n.d.

' "... warum dann überhaupt noch leben!" Hitlers Lagebesprechungen am 23., 25. und 27. April 1945', *Der Spiegel*, 10 January 1966, pp.32–46.

Weinberg, Gerhard L. (ed.), *Hitlers Zweites Buch. Ein Dokument aus dem Jahr 1928*, Stuttgart, 1961 (*Hitler's Second Book*, New York, 2003).

Weizsäcker, Ernst von, *Erinnerungen*, Munich, 1950 (*Memoirs*, London, 1951).

Wiedemann, Fritz, *Der Mann, der Feldherr werden wollte*, Velbert/Kettwig, 1964.

Zoller, Albert, *Hitler privat. Erlebnisbericht seiner Geheimsekretärin*, Düsseldorf, 1949.

INDEX

Glaise-Horstenau, Edmund 405, 408
Glasgow 611
Gleichschaltung ('coordination') 282–3,
  291, 297, 410
Gleiwitz 508
Globocnik, Odilo 575, 688
Glogau 891
Gneisenau (battleship) 704
Gneisenau, August Graf Neithardt von 809
Godesberg Memorandum 438–9, 440,
  441, 445
Godin, Reinhart, Freiherr von 59
Goebbels, Joseph:
  adoration of H 171, 173, 181, 379, 592,
    909
  and Allied bombing raids 790, 905
  and Allied invasion 804, 805, 808–10
  and annexation of Memelland (1939) 481
  anti-clericalism 661
  appointed Gauleiter of Berlin 171
  appointed Propaganda Leader of Nazi
    Party 200
  and Ardennes offensive 881
  and assassination attempts on H
    (November 1939) 544–5; (July 1944)
    836–9, 843, 844–5, 847
  and Austrian Question 385–6, 407–8,
    409, 411, 414
  background 167–8
  and Balkan campaign 607
  and ban on intermarriage 343
  and battle for Stalingrad 737, 739, 742
  and Blomberg scandal (1938) 393
  and bombing of the *Deutschland* (1937)
    384
  and Bormann's restructuring for
    peacetime Germany 916–17
  and boycott of Jewish businesses 286
  brings news of death of Roosevelt 918
  and Brüning's resignation 229–30
  Christmas present to H (1937) 377
  and 'Committee of Three' 750–51
  conflict with Churches 381, 382
  construction of 'Westwall' 431
  and Czechoslovakia 386, 420, 431, 445,
    476, 477, 479
  on dangers of H's declining authority 913,
    915–16
  and deal with Schleicher 232–3
  and declaration of war against United
    States 658, 659–60
  and deportations and massacres of Jews
    595, 669, 671, 680–81, 683, 685–7,
    689, 694, 698–9
  diary 168, 361, 364, 381, 385, 456, 457,
    465, 691, 780, 843

  disappointed by H 170, 171
  and disposal of H's body 956–7
  and economic crisis of 1936 360–61
  field-marshals' declaration of loyalty
    (March 1944) 796
  and 'Final Solution' 714–15, 777
  and Frick 771
  and Fritsch scandal (1938) 396, 397, 398,
    399
  in Führer Bunker 902, 923, 929–30, 931,
    936–7, 938, 939, 940–41, 943, 946,
    950, 954, 955
  on generals' opposition to H 843, 844–5
  and 'German Revolution' 303
  and German surrender 958, 959
  H proposes for Ministry for the People's
    Education 232
  and Heß affair (May 1941) 613–14, 615
  his 'Damascus' 170–71, 173
  and H's last Testament 950–51
  on H's negotiations with Hindenburg
    243, 254
  in H's Reich Chancellery entourage 293,
    324, 376
  ideological fanaticism 168
  inferiority complex 168
  and invasion of Hungary (March 1944)
    793–4
  and Italian crisis (July 1943) 768–9
  and 'Jewish Question' 347, 381, 452–5,
    577–8, 679, 694, 698–9, 759–60,
    763–4
  Kolberg (film) 858, 908
  and 'leadership crisis' 748, 751–3
  and Leipzig Reichswehr trial (1930) 207
  marital problems 463, 492
  memorandum to H (September 1944)
    872–3
  and Munich Agreement negotiations
    (1938) 436–7, 438–9, 441, 444, 445
  and Nazi atrocities in Poland 521, 525–6,
    549
  and the 'Night of the Long Knives' 310,
    311–12, 315
  and north German NSDAP 167–9, 170
  and November pogrom (1938) 455–63,
    465–7
  and Nuremberg rallies 344
  and occupation of France 561, 562
  and opening of Western Front 540, 555
  and Operation Barbarossa 618, 620–21,
    622, 623–4, 626, 627
  organizes torchlight procession
    (30 January 1933) 261
  and Papen's Marburg speech (1934)
    307–8